SAINT THOMAS AQUINAS

COMMENTARY ON THE GOSPEL OF MATTHEW, CHAPTERS 1-12

Translated by Jeremy Holmes and Beth Mortensen
Edited by The Aquinas Institute

BIBLICAL COMMENTARIES

Volume 33
Latin/English Edition of the Works of St. Thomas Aquinas

The Aquinas Institute for the Study of Sacred Doctrine
Lander, Wyoming
2013

This printing was funded in part by donations made in memory of:
Marcus Berquist, Rose Johanna Trumbull, John and Mary Deignan,
Thomas and Eleanor Sullivan, and Fr. John T. Feeney and his sister Mary.

The printing was also made possible by a donation from Patricia Lynch,
and by a donation made in honor of Fr. Brian McMaster.

Published with the ecclesiastical approval of
The Most Reverend Paul D. Etienne, DD, STL
Bishop of Cheyenne
Given on July 16, 2013

PUBLISHER'S CATALOGING-IN-PUBLICATION DATA

Thomas Aquinas, Saint, 1225?-1274
    Commentary on the Gospel of Matthew, chapters 1-12 / Saint Thomas Aquinas; edited by The Aquinas Institute;
    translated by Jeremy Holmes, Beth Mortensen
    p. 408 cm.
    ISBN 978-1-62340-015-6

1. Bible. N.T. Matthew--Commentaries--Early works to 1800. I. Title. II. Series

BS2575.T4612 2013
226'.2'07--dc23   2013942416

Notes on the Text

Sacred Scripture

The text of Sacred Scripture presented at the beginning of each lecture is given in Latin, English, and Greek. Since St. Thomas appears to be familiar with more than one translation, quotes from memory, and often enough paraphrases, it has proven difficult to reconstruct the version of Scripture St. Thomas was working with. However, the closest available version of Scripture to St. Thomas's text was found to be the Clementine Vulgate of 1598, and this version of the Vulgate is the one found at the beginning of each lecture. The choice of an English version of Scripture to parallel to the Vulgate was therefore the Douay-Rheims. Both of these versions have been slightly modified to fit the text of St. Thomas. The Greek text is from the Nestle-Aland, *Novum Testamentum Graece*, 27th Revised Edition, edited by Barbara Aland, Kurt Aland, Johannes Karavidopoulos, Carlo M. Martini, and Bruce M. Metzger in cooperation with the Institute for New Testament Textual Research, Münster/Westphalia, © 1993 Deutsche Bibelgesellschaft, Stuttgart. Used with permission. The numbering of Scripture in the lecture headings and the English translation of the commentary is taken from the Nestle-Aland 27th Revised Edition and the RSV, while the numbering St. Thomas uses in the Latin text has been kept intact.

Latin Text of St. Thomas

The Latin text used in this volume is based on the 1951 Marietti edition, with the missing texts of Matthew 5:11-6:8 and 6:14-19 taken from the texts that were found by the Leonine Commission and confirmed to be authentic. Various pieces of the missing texts had been published in the following publications. The Aquinas Institute has gathered its own texts independently of these publications, and has checked its texts against these publications for accuracy.

The text for lectures 3 and 6, as well as the last paragraph of lecture 5 in Chapter 5 and lecture 3 in Chapter 6, was first published in *Opera Omnia ut sunt in Indice Thomistico Additis 61 ex Aliis Medii Aevi Auctoribus, t. 6, codex 087, n. 1 & 2: ex Lectura Super Mattheum*, edited by R. Busa, published by Frommann-Hoolzbog, Stuttgart-Bad Cannstadt. The text for lectures 4 and 5 in Chapter 5, with the exception of the last paragraph of lecture 5, was first published in H.V. Shooner's *La Lectura in Matthaeum de S. Thomas*, found in *Angelicum* 33 (1956). The text for lectures 7 through 12 in Chapter 5 was first published in J.P. Renard's *La Lectura super Matthaeum V, 20-48 de Thomas d'Aquin*, found in *Recherches de Theologie Ancienne et Medievale* 50 (1983). The text of lectures 1 through 2 and 4 through 5 in Chapter 6 was recently printed in *Commentary on the Gospel of Saint Matthew, Appendix: Transcription of Basel Manuscript B.V. 12*, edited by H. Kraml and P.M. Kimball, published by Dolorosa Press (2012).

English Translation of St. Thomas

The English translation used in this volume was prepared by Jeremy Holmes and Beth Mortensen. It has been edited and revised by The Aquinas Institute.

The Aquinas Institute requests your assistance in the continued perfection of these texts.
If you discover any errors, please send a note to us by e-mail: editor@theaquinasinstitute.org.

DEDICATED WITH LOVE TO
OUR LADY OF MT. CARMEL

Contents

Commentary on the Gospel of Matthew, Chapters 1-12

Prologue of St. Jerome

I. *Matthaeus ex Iudaea sicut in ordine primus ponitur, ita Evangelium in Iudaea primus scripsit, cuius vocatio ad Dominum ex publicanis actibus fuit. Duorum in generatione Christi principia praesumens: unius cuius prima circumcisio in carne, alterius cuius secundum cor electio fuit: ex utrisque enim patribus Christus. Sicque quaternario numero triformiter posito, principium a credendi fine in electionis tempus porrigens, et ex electione usque in transmigrationis diem dirigens, atque a transmigrationis die usque in Christum definiens, decursam adventus Domini ostendit generationem, et numero satisfaciens et tempori; ut et se quid esset ostenderet, et Dei in se opus monstrans, etiam in his quorum genus posuit, Christi operantis a principio testimonium non negaret.*

II. *Quarum omnium rerum tempus, ordo, numerus, dispositio, vel ratio quod fidei necessarium est, Deus Christus est, qui factus ex muliere, factus sub lege, natus ex virgine, passus in carne, omnia in cruce fixit, ut triumphans ea in semetipso, resurgens in corpore et Patris nomen in patribus Filio, et Filii nomen Patri restituens in filiis, sine principio, sine fine, ostendens unum se cum Patre esse, quia unus est.*

III. *In quo Evangelio utile est desiderantibus Deum, sic prima vel media vel perfecta cognoscere, ut et vocationem Apostoli, et opus Evangelii, et dilectionem Dei in carne nascentis per universa legentes intelligant, atque id in eo, in quo reprehensi sunt et apprehendere appetunt, recognoscant.*

IV. *Nobis autem in hoc studio argumenti fuit, et fidem factae rei tradere, et operantis Dei intelligendam diligenter esse dispositionem a quaerentibus non tacere.*

I. *Matthew from Judea, just as he is placed first in order, so he first wrote a Gospel in Judea, whose calling to the Lord was from the acts of a publican. He takes up first the origins of two fathers in the generation of Christ: one whose first circumcision was in the flesh, and another whose election was according to the heart; for Christ came from both fathers. And thus, the number fourteen set down triformly, presenting the origin from the faith of believing to the time of election, and setting it in order from the election to the day of the transmigration, and then giving an exact description from the transmigration down to the Christ, he sets forth the hurried generation of the coming of the Lord, giving sufficient attention both to number and to time; both that he might display himself, what he is, and also pointing to the work of God in himself, as well as in those whose race he set forth, that he might not deny the testimony of Christ working from the beginning.*

II. *The time, the order, the number, the arrangement or reason of all these things, what is necessary for faith, that Christ is God, who was made from a woman, made under the law, born of a virgin, suffered in the flesh, fastened all things to the cross, so triumphing over them in himself, rising in the flesh and restoring the name of the Father to the Son in the fathers, and the name of the Son to the Father in the sons, without beginning, without end, showing himself to be one with the Father, because they are one.*

III. *In which Gospel it is useful to those desiring God to understand in this way the first or the middle or the perfect things, so that reading they might understand both the calling of the Apostle and the work of the Gospel and, through all, the love of God born in the flesh, and then reflect on this thing in which they are held back and desire to take hold of.*

IV. *But for us in the pursuit of the preface there has been this: to hand on both the faith of things done, and not to leave unmentioned the arrangement, to be understood diligently by those who are seeking, of the God who is at work.*

Exposition of St. Thomas

1. *Matthaeus ex Iudaea* et cetera. Evangelio Matthaei Hieronymus praemittit prologum, in quo tria facit:

primo enim ipsum auctorem describit;

secundo Evangelii mysteria aperit, ibi *duorum in generatione Christi principia praesumens*;

tertio suam intentionem ostendit, ibi *nobis autem in hoc studio argumenti fuit.*

2. Auctorem vero ipsum describit ex quatuor: primo ex nomine, cum dicit *Matthaeus*; secundo ex origine,

1. *Matthew from Judea.* Jerome places a prologue before the Gospel of Matthew, in which he does three things:

first, he describes the author himself;

second, he opens the mysteries of the Gospel, at *takes up the origins of two in the generation of Christ*;

third, he indicates his own intention, at *for us however in the pursuit of the preface.*

2. He describes the author himself by four things: first by name, when he says *Matthew*; second by origin, when he

cum dicit *ex Iudaea*; tertio ex scribendi ordine, ibi *sicut in ordine primus ponitur*; quarto ex vocatione, ibi, *cuius vocatio ad Dominum*, idest ad Christum et cetera. De hoc Matth. IX, 9 et Luc. V, 27.

Et nota quod Glossa interlinearis, quae dicit: *primus, idest ante quem nullus* etc., videtur velle, quod alii post Matthaeum scripserint in Iudaea, quod non est verum: solus enim Matthaeus scripsit in Iudaea, Marcus in Italia, Lucas in Achaia, Ioannes in Asia.

3. Consequenter ipsius Evangelii mysteria aperit.

Et primo aperit mysteria circa principium Evangelii;

secundo ostendit eadem mysteria requirenda esse et in medio, et in fine, ibi *in quo Evangelio utile est* et cetera.

In principio autem Evangelii duo tanguntur. Primo ponitur quasi quidam titulus, cum dicitur, **liber generationis**; secundo generationis cuiusdam series describitur, cum dicitur, **Abraham genuit Isaac** et cetera.

Primo ergo ponit mysteria tituli, vel quae tanguntur in titulo;

secundo mysteria generationis, ibi *sicque quaterdenario*.

4. In titulo autem dicitur **liber generationis Iesu Christi**; ubi tanguntur duo principia, scilicet David et Abraham. Et hoc quia Abrahae prius datum est praeceptum de circumcisione; ad Rom. IV, 11: *signum accepit circumcisionis, signaculum iustitiae fidei, quae est in praeputio, ut sit ipse pater omnium credentium.* David autem electus est a Domino; I Reg. XIII, 14: *inveni virum secundum cor meum.* Unde propter hoc isti duo tanguntur, ut denotetur quod Christus traxit originem ex circumcisis patribus et electis. Et hoc est, *duorum*, hominum, vel duorum principiorum, idest duo principia, scilicet David et Abraham.

5. Consequenter ponit mysteria, quae tanguntur in genealogia.

Et primo tangit mysteria ipsius Evangelii, vel Evangelistae;

secundo ipsius Christi, ibi *quarum omnium rerum* et cetera.

6. Et est mysterium quod Evangelista genealogiam Christi per tres tesseradecades distinxit: quarum prima est ab Abraham usque ad David; secunda a David usque ad transmigrationem; tertia usque ad Christum; ut ostenderet Christum esse et de circumcisis, et de electis, et de transmigrantibus. Et hoc est *triformiter posito*, idest tripliciter repetito, supra in genealogia, *a credendi fide*, idest ab ipso Abraham, qui fuit primum exemplar credendi, *in electionis tempus porrigens*, idest usque ad ipsum David deducens, *et ab electione*, idest ab ipso David, *in transmigrationis diem dirigens; et a transmigrationis*

says *from Judea*; third by order of writing, at *as he is placed first in order*; fourth by calling, at *whose calling to the Lord*, i.e., to Christ. Concerning this, see Matthew 9:9 and Luke 5:27.

And note that the interlinear Gloss, which says *first, i.e., before whom no one*, seems to want to say that others after Matthew have written in Judea, which is not true. Only Matthew wrote in Judea; Mark wrote in Italy, Luke in Achaia, and John in Asia.

3. Next, he opens the mysteries of the Gospel itself.

And first, he opens the mysteries which concern the beginning of the Gospel;

second, he shows that the same mysteries are to be sought in the middle; and at the end, at *in which Gospel it is useful*.

Now at the beginning of the Gospel two things are touched upon. First, a title is set down, so to speak, when it says, **the book of the generation**; second, the series of a certain generation is described, when it says, **Abraham begot Isaac**.

First, therefore, Jerome sets out the mysteries of the title, or of those things touched upon in the title;

second, the mysteries of the generation, at *and thus, the number fourteen*.

4. Now it says in the title, **the book of the generation of Jesus Christ**. Here two origins are touched upon, namely David and Abraham. And this is because the precept about circumcision was given to Abraham first; second *he received the sign of circumcision, a seal of justice of the faith which he had, being uncircumcised: that he might be a father of all who believe* (Rom 4:11). But David was chosen by the Lord: *the Lord has sought a man according to his own heart* (1 Sam 13:14). For this reason, these two are touched upon in order to point out that Christ took origin from the circumcised fathers and the chosen. And this is the *of two*, i.e., of two men, or of two origins, David and Abraham.

5. Next, he sets out the mysteries which are touched upon in the genealogy.

And first, he touches on the mysteries of the Gospel itself, or of the Evangelist;

second, of Christ, at *of all these things*.

6. And it is a mystery that the Evangelist divides the genealogy of Christ into three fourteens. The first of these is from Abraham to David, the second from David to the transmigration, the third to Christ—that he might show Christ to be from the circumcised and from the chosen and from those who transmigrated. And this is *set down triformly*, i.e., repeated three times in the genealogy. *From the faith of believing*, i.e., from Abraham himself, who was the first model of believing. *To the time of election*, i.e., leading down even to David. *And setting it in order from the election*, i.e., from David himself, *to the day of the transmigration*.

2

die usque in Christum definiens, patet, *decursam*, idest breviter et cursorie tactam, *adventus Domini ostendit generationem, et numero satisfaciens et tempori.* Patet.

7. *Quarum omnium rerum* et cetera. Nota quod in hac generationis serie quatuor tanguntur, *tempus, numerus, ordo et dispositio sive ratio*; quia ab Abraham usque ad David et cetera. Omnia ista nil aliud ostendunt nisi quod *Deus Christus est*: hoc enim intendit secundum dispositionem et rationem allegoricam, quod Christus est Deus. *Quod est fidei necessarium*, scilicet quod *Christus Deus est*, idest in omnibus non est plus de necessitate fidei, nisi quod Christus est Deus.

Qui factus ex muliere et cetera. Nota, et expone, et signa capitula.

Et omnia in cruce fixit, idest peccata, secundum quod de medio tulit, quod adversum nos chirographum erat. Item melius: Christus secundum Deum et hominem qui est omnia, secundum illud, Ioan. XII, 32, *ego si exaltatus fuero a terra, omnia traham ad meipsum*, et Phil. II, 10: *ut in nomine Domini omne genuflectatur caelestium, terrestrium et Infernorum. Ut triumphans ea in semetipso*, quia per trophaeum crucis omnia sibi subiecit, et de quolibet triumphavit.

8. *Et Patris nomen in patribus Filio.* Ad evidentiam autem huius notandum, quod in serie generationis ponuntur quidam patres et quidam filii, sicut patet. Item ponitur ibi quidam pater sine patre, sicut Adam: quidam filius sine filio, sicut Iesus. Item ponuntur quidam qui sunt patres et filii, sicut omnes intermedii. Per hoc autem mystice designatur, quod in Trinitate est Pater et Filius, sicut in hac genealogia sunt quidam patres, quidam filii. Item per hoc quod primus pater non habet patrem in hac serie, nec ultimus filius filium, ostenditur quod isti sunt ab aeterno. Item per hoc quod unus et idem in persona est pater et filius respectu diversorum, tangitur quod isti sunt unum, non quidem in persona, sed natura.

Et hoc est quod dicit *et Patris nomen* restituens *Filio in patribus*, idest quod Filius habeat Patrem; *in patribus*, idest per hoc quod ponuntur ibi quidam patres. *Et nomen restituens Patri*, idest quod Pater habeat Filium, et hoc *in filiis*, idest per hoc quod ponuntur ibi aliqui filii *sine principio et sine fine*: quia pater primus non habet patrem, nec ultimus filius filium. *Ostendens se unum esse cum Patre*, idest unus naturae, *quia unus*, in persona, scilicet Pater et Filius, respectu tamen diversorum, in dicta genealogia.

Nota interlinearem quae dicit: *unus Christus*; quod nihil est dictum.

And from the day of the transmigration. This is clear. *He shows the hurried*, i.e., briefly and cursorily touched upon, *generation of the coming of the Lord, giving sufficient attention both to number and to time.* This is clear.

7. *Of all these things, the time.* Note that in this series of the generation four things are touched upon: *the time, the order, the number, and the arrangement or the reason*, because the time from Abraham to David is touched upon. The reason is the arrangement. All these things show nothing other than that *Christ is God*; for he intends this according to an allegorical arrangement and reason, namely that Christ is God. *What is necessary for faith*, namely that *Christ is God*, i.e., in all things there is nothing of more necessity for faith than that Christ is God.

Who was made from a woman. Note, explain, and indicate the chapters.

And fastened all things to the cross, i.e., all sins, according as he took from the middle, because the handwriting was against us (Col 4:14). Or better: Christ as God and as man, because he is all things: *and I, if I be lifted up from the earth, will draw all things to myself* (John 12:32), and: *that in the name of Jesus every knee should bow, of those that are in heaven, on earth, and under the earth* (Phil 2:10). *So triumphing*, because through the trophy of the cross he subjected all things to himself, and has triumphed over anything at all.

8. *And the name of the Father to the Son in the fathers.* For clarity it should be noted that certain fathers and certain sons are placed in the series of the generation, as is clear. Again, a certain father without a father is placed there, namely Abraham, and a certain son without a son, namely Jesus. Similarly, certain ones who are both fathers and sons are placed there, namely all the ones in between Abraham and Jesus. This indicates mystically that in the Trinity there is a Father and a Son, just as in this genealogy there are certain fathers and certain sons. Similarly, the fact that the first father does not have a father in this series, nor the last son a son, shows that they are eternal. Again, the fact that one and the same person is father and son with respect to different persons, indicates that they are one, not indeed in person, but in nature.

And this is what Jerome means by restoring *the name of the Father to the Son in the fathers*, i.e., that the Son has a Father; *in the fathers*, i.e., through the fact that certain fathers are placed there in the series. *And restoring the name of the Father*, i.e., that the Father has a Son, and this is **in the sons**, i.e., through the fact that certain sons are placed there. *Without beginning and without end*, because the first father does not have a father, nor the last son a son. [*Showing himself to be one with the Father*,] i.e., of one nature, *because they are one*, namely in person, yet with respect to different persons in the aforementioned genealogy.

Note the interlinear Gloss which says, *one Christ*. This should certainly not be said.

9. Consequenter ostendit consimilia mysteria requirenda esse in dicto Evangelio, non solum in principio, sed etiam in medio et fine: et hoc est, *in quo Evangelio*, scilicet Matthaei, *utile est desiderantibus Deum sic*, idest eodem modo sicut diximus, *cognoscere prima*, idest principium, *vel media, vel perfecta*, finem, et consummationem; *ut et vocationem apostoli* et cetera. Scriptum est Phil. III, 12: *sequor autem, si quo modo comprehendam*.

10. *Nobis autem*. Hic ostendit intentionem suam, scilicet quod intendit quod ea quae hic dicuntur, vera sunt in historia, et tamen spiritualiter intelligenda.

Nobis autem fuit hoc, idest haec intentio, *in studio argumenti*, idest prologi.

9. Next, he shows that similar mysteries are to be sought in the aforementioned Gospel, not only at the beginning, but also in the middle and at the end. And this is what Jerome means by, *in which Gospel*, namely the Gospel of Matthew, *it is useful to those desiring God to understand in this way*, i.e., in the same way as we have said, *to understand the first* i.e., the beginning, *or the middle, or the perfect things*, the end and consummation, *so that reading, they might understand*. It is written: *I follow after, if I may by any means apprehend* (Phil 3:12).

10. *But for us*. Here he shows his own intention, namely that he means that those things which are said here are true in history, and nevertheless are to be understood spiritually.

But for us in the pursuit of this preface, i.e., the prologue, *there has been this*, i.e., this intention. And so on—explain as you wish.

CHAPTER 1

Lecture 1

1:1 Liber generationis Iesu Christi, filii David, filii Abraham. [n. 12]

1:1 Βίβλος γενέσεως Ἰησοῦ Χριστοῦ υἱοῦ Δαυὶδ υἱοῦ Ἀβραάμ.

1:1 The book of the generation of Jesus Christ, the son of David, the son of Abraham: [n. 12]

---

11. Inter evangelistas Matthaeus praecipue versatur circa humanitatem Christi: unde secundum Gregorium per hominem significatur in figura quatuor animalium. Per humanitatem autem Christus in mundum introivit, progressus est, et exivit.

Et ideo dividitur totum Evangelium in tres partes.

Primo enim agit Evangelista de Christi humanitatis in mundum ingressu;

secundo de eius processu;

tertio de eius egressu.

Secunda pars incipit cap. III, 1, ibi *in diebus autem illis venit Ioannes Baptista praedicans in deserto Iudaeae.* Tertia, capite XXI, 1 *et cum appropinquassent Ierosolymis et venissent Bethphage ad Montem Oliveti.*

In prima parte duo facit:

primo describitur Christi generatio;

secundo ipsius generationis subditur manifestatio, cap. II, ibi *cum natus esset Iesus in Bethlehem Iudae in diebus Herodis regis.*

In prima parte tria facit:

primo enim quasi titulus totius libri praeponitur, cum dicitur *liber generationis Iesu Christi*;

secundo patrum series texitur, *Abraham genuit Isaac*;

tertio cum dicitur *Christi autem generatio sic erat*, generatio Christi in speciali describitur.

12. Titulus autem qui praemittitur, est iste *liber generationis Iesu Christi*.

Et videtur esse oratio imperfecta. Ponitur enim ibi nominativus sine verbo; sed non est. Matthaeus enim Evangelium Hebraeis conscripsit, et ideo in scribendo morem Iudaeorum servavit. Consuetum est autem apud Hebraeos sic loqui, sicut cum dicitur: *visio Isaiae filii Amos*, subauditur, haec est nec oportet apponere. Ita hic cum dicitur *liber generationis*, subauditur, hic est.

Et hic etiam modus loquendi consuetus est apud nos: si enim velimus aliquem librum intitulare, dicitur

11. Among the evangelists, Matthew is especially concerned with the humanity of Christ; hence according to Gregory he is signified by a man in the figure of the four animals. Now, it is through his humanity that Christ entered, advanced in, and left the world.

And for this reason the whole Gospel is divided into three parts.

For the Evangelist treats first of Christ's entrance into the world through his humanity;

second, of his advance;

third, of his departure.

The second part begins at *and in those days came John the Baptist preaching in the desert of Judea* (Matt 3:1). The third part begins at *and when they drew near to Jerusalem, and had come to Bethphage, unto Mount Olivet* (Matt 21:1).

In the first part he does two things:

first, he describes the generation of Christ;

second, he adds a manifestation of that generation, at *when Jesus therefore was born in Bethlehem of Judah, in the days of King Herod* (Matt 2:1).

In the first part, he does three things:

first, he prefaces a title as it were of the whole book, when he says, *the book of the generation of Jesus Christ*;

second, the series of fathers is put together, *Abraham begot Isaac* (Matt 1:2);

third, when it says *but the generation of Christ was thus*, the generation of Christ is described in particular.

12. Now the title prefaced is this: *the book of the generation of Jesus Christ*.

It seems to be an imperfect sentence, since a nominative is set down there without a verb, but it is not. For Matthew wrote his Gospel for the Hebrews, and so in his writing he followed the custom of the Jews. Now it is customary among the Hebrews to speak this way; for example, when it is said: *the vision of Isaiah the son of Amos* (Isa 1:1), the phrase *this is* is understood, and does not need to be added. So here when it says, *the book of the generation*, *this is* is understood.

And this way of speaking is also customary among us. For if we wish to give a title to some book, it is called

Priscianus Maior vel *Minor*; nec oportet apponere *hic est* vel *incipit*.

13. Item quaeritur, cum parva particula istius libri sit de generatione Christi, quare intitulavit librum suum sic.

Et dicendum, quod Matthaeus, qui scripsit Hebraeis, in scribendo modum Hebraeorum servavit. Consuetum est autem apud Hebraeos libros suos a principio intitulare, sicut dicitur Genesis, quia ibi agitur de generatione; unde Gen. V, 1: *hic est liber generationis Adam.* Et liber Exodi, quia in prima parte agitur de exitu filiorum Israel de Aegypto.

14. Sed quaeritur quare additur **Iesu Christi**.

Et dicendum quod secundum Apostolum, I Corinth. XV, 22, *sicut in Adam omnes moriuntur, ita in Christo omnes vivificabuntur.* Viderat autem Matthaeus librum primum Veteris Testamenti, in quo agitur de generatione, in quo dictum est cap. V, 1, *hic est liber generationis Adam.* Ut ergo Novum Testamentum, in quo agitur de regeneratione et restauratione, ei responderet per oppositum, dicit **liber generationis Iesu Christi**, ut ostenderet quod idem est auctor utriusque.

15. Hic autem quaeritur de hoc quod hic dicitur **liber generationis Iesu Christi**. Contrarium enim habetur Isa. LIII, 8, ubi dicitur, *generationem eius quis enarrabit?*

Sed sensus est, secundum Hieronymum, quod in Christo est duplex generatio. Scilicet divina, quae enarrari non potest: quia etsi aliquo modo dicimus Filium genitum, modum tamen quo gignitur, nec homo, nec angelus potest comprehendere. Alia autem est humana, de qua agit, sed tamen in hac etiam generatione sunt multa difficilia. Et ideo, secundum Remigium, perpauci sunt qui possint eam enarrare.

16. Item quaeritur de hoc quod dicit **generationis**, cum hic plures texantur generationes.

Sed dicendum, quod licet multae enumerentur generationes, omnes tamen introducuntur propter unam, scilicet propter generationem Christi, de qua inferius: **Christi autem generatio sic erat**.

17. Describitur autem ille cuius generatio texitur primo a nomine, cum dicitur **Iesu**; secundo ab officio, cum dicitur **Christi**; tertio ab origine, cum dicitur **filii David, filii Abraham**.

18. Quamvis autem fuerint et alii, qui vocati sunt Iesus, sicut Iesus filius Nave, de quo Eccli. XLVI, 1: *fortis in bello Iesus Nave successor Moysi in prophetis*, et alius circa aedificationem templi, de quo in Zach. III, 1, isti tamen fuerunt Iesus nominales et figurales, inquantum scilicet figurabant istum.

Priscianus the Greater or *Lesser*, nor is it necessary to add *this is* or *here begins*.

13. It is also asked, why did he title his book this way, when a very small portion of this book is about the generation of Christ?

And one should say that Matthew, who wrote to the Hebrews, followed the style of the Hebrews in his writing. Now, the Hebrews customarily title books from their beginnings, as Genesis is called Genesis because it treats there of generation; hence we find, *this is the book of the generation of Adam* (Gen 5:1). And so also the book of Exodus, which in the first part treats of the exodus of the children of Israel out of Egypt.

14. But it is asked why **of Jesus Christ** is added.

One should say that according to the Apostle: *as in Adam all die, so also in Christ all will be made alive* (1 Cor 15:22). Now, Matthew had seen that in the first book of the Old Testament, which treats of generation, it says: *this is the book of the generation of Adam* (Gen 5:1). In order therefore that the New Testament, which treats of regeneration and repair, might correspond to the Old Testament by contrast, he says, **the book of the generation of Jesus Christ**; and to show that the same one is author of both Testaments.

15. But here a question is asked about the fact that it says, **the book of the generation of Jesus Christ**. For this is contrary to Isaiah: *who will declare his generation?* (Isa 53:8).

According to Jerome, the sense of this quotation is that there is a twofold generation in Christ. There is the divine generation, of course, which cannot be recounted; even if in some way we call the Son begotten, neither man nor angel can comprehend the manner in which he is begotten. The other is the human generation, which Matthew considers, yet there are many difficulties in this generation as well. And this is why, according to Remigius, there are very few who could recount it.

16. Again, a question is asked about the fact that he says **of the generation**, when multiple generations are put together here.

One should say that, although many generations are enumerated, still all are included for the sake of one, namely for the sake of the generation of Christ, concerning which it says below, **but the generation of Christ was thus**.

17. Now, he whose generation is put together is described first by name, when it says **Jesus**; second by office, when it says **Christ**; third by origin, when it says, **the son of David, the son of Abraham**.

18. There have been others who were also called Jesus, like Jesus the son of Nave, of whom it is said: *valiant in war was Jesus the son of Nave, who was successor of Moses among the prophets* (Sir 46:1); there was also another around the time of the building of the temple (Zech 3:1). But those men were Jesus in name and figure, namely insofar as they prefigured him.

Ille Iesus introduxit populum Israel in terram promissionis; sed iste Iesus, idest salvator noster, non in terram carnalem, sed introducit nos in caelestem; Hebr. XII, 2: *ipsum enim habemus auctorem, et consummatorem in sanguine eius* et cetera.

Et recte dicitur **Iesu**, quod nomen convenit ei secundum utramque naturam, scilicet divinam et humanam. Secundum quidem humanam in carne sua passus est, et explevit mysterium nostrae redemptionis: et cum passio illa non haberet efficaciam nisi ex virtute divinitatis adiunctae, propter hoc dicitur infra: **vocabitur nomen eius Iesus: ipse enim salvum faciet populum suum a peccatis eorum**.

Sed quaeritur quare dicit **Christi**. Nonne suffecisset **Iesu**? Respondeo, hoc ideo factum esse, quia, ut dictum est, et alii vocati sunt Iesus.

19. Ab officio autem describit eum, cum dicit **Christi**, idest uncti.

Nota autem tres unctiones in veteri lege. Unctus enim est Aaron in sacerdotem, Levit. VIII, 11. Unctus est Saul a Samuele in regem, I Reg. X, 1, et David, I Reg. XVI, 13. *Unctus est et Eliseus in prophetam*, III Reg. c. XIX, 16. Quia ergo Christus fuit verus sacerdos in Psal. CIX, 4: *tu es sacerdos in aeternum secundum ordinem Melchisedech* etc., et rex et propheta, ideo dicitur recte Christus, propter tria officia quae ipse exercuit.

20. Filii David, filii Abraham. Hic est duplex quaestio, scilicet de numero, et de ordine.

Ad primum, quare istos duos nominavit. Propter illam rationem quae in prologo dicta est, quod Abraham propheta fuit. Gen. XX, 7 dixit Dominus ad Abimelech regem Gerarae: *redde uxorem viro suo, quia propheta est*. Item fuit sacerdos, Genes. XV, 9, dum implevit officium sacerdotis, offerendo scilicet hostiam Domino: *sume*, inquit, *mihi vaccam triennem* et cetera. David autem propheta fuit, sicut patet Act. II, 30. Fuit etiam rex, sicut patet II Reg. II, 4. Quia ergo Christus fuit rex, et propheta, et sacerdos; ideo recte dicitur filius istorum. Si enim solum Abraham nominasset, non signaretur quod Christus rex fuisset. Item si solum David, non denotaretur in Christo sacerdotalis dignitas; et ideo utrumque posuit.

Ad secundum dicendum quod, secundum Hieronymum, David praeponitur, et commutatur ordo propter necessitatem texendi genealogiam; si enim primo diceret **filii Abraham**, secundo **filii David**, oporteret secundo repetere Abraham, ut continuaretur ordo genealogiae. Secundum Ambrosium autem dicendum, quod David praeponitur ratione dignitatis; ad David enim facta est repromissio de ipso capite, cum dicitur Ps. CXXXI, 11: *de fructu ventris tui ponam super sedem*

That Jesus led the people of Israel into the land of the promise; but this Jesus, i.e., our Savior, led us not into a fleshly land, but into a heavenly land. *For we have him as the author and finisher in his blood* (Heb 12:2).

And he is rightly called **Jesus**. This name befits him according to either nature, whether the divine or the human. Through the human he suffered in his flesh and completed the mystery of our redemption; but since that suffering would have had no efficacy except by the power of the divinity joined to it, it says below: **you will call his name Jesus. For he will save his people from their sins** (Matt 1:21).

But it is asked why he says, **Christ**. Would not **Jesus** have been enough? I respond that he said this because others were also called Jesus.

19. Moreover he describes him by office when he says, **Christ**, i.e., the anointed.

Note that there were three anointings in the old law. For Aaron was anointed as a priest (Lev 8:11–12). Saul was anointed by Samuel as a king (1 Sam 10:1), and then David (1 Sam 16:13). Eliseus was also anointed as a prophet: *Eliseus the son of Saphat, of Abelmeula, you will anoint to be prophet* (1 Kgs 19:16). Since therefore Christ was a true priest, according to the Psalm: *you are a priest for ever* (Ps 109:4), and a king and a prophet, he is rightly called **Christ**, on account of the three offices which he exercised.

20. The son of David, the son of Abraham. Here there are two questions, namely about number and order.

Regarding the first, the question is why he named these two. Besides the reason given in the prologue, one should say that Abraham was a prophet. The Lord said to Abimelech the king of Gerar, *now therefore restore the man his wife, for he is a prophet* (Gen 20:7). Similarly, he was a priest inasmuch as he exercised the function of a priest, namely by offering a victim to the Lord; *and the Lord answered, and said: take me a cow of three years old* (Gen 15:9). Moreover, David was a prophet (Acts 2:30) and he was also a king (2 Sam 2:4). Since therefore Christ was a king and a prophet and a priest, he is rightly called the son of these men. For had he named only Abraham, it would not have indicated that Christ was a king; while if David alone had been named, it would not have shown the priestly dignity in Christ. This is why he put down both.

As regards the second question, according to Jerome one should say that David is put first and the order changed because he needed to put together the genealogy. For if he had said first **the son of Abraham**, and second **the son of David**, he would have had to repeat Abraham a second time to continue the order of the genealogy. But according to Ambrose, David was named first by reason of dignity. For a promise concerning the head himself was made to David, when it is said: *of the fruit of your womb I will set*

tuam. Sed ad Abraham de membris, scilicet de Ecclesia; unde Genes. XXII, 18: *in semine tuo benedicentur omnes gentes terrae.*

21. Hic notandum, quod multi fuerunt errores de Christo.

Quidam enim erraverunt circa eius divinitatem, sicut Paulus Samosatenus, Photinus, et Sabellius; quidam circa humanitatem; et quidam circa utramque. Alii autem erraverunt circa eius personam.

Circa humanitatem eius primus erravit Manichaeus, qui dixit eum non verum corpus, sed phantasticum accepisse. Contra quod est quod dicit Dominus Luc. ult., 39: *palpate, et videte, quia spiritus carnem et ossa non habet, sicut me videtis habere.* Secundo post eum erravit Valentinus, qui dixit eum corpus caeleste secum attulisse, non de Virgine assumpsisse, sed per eam sicut aquam per canale transisse. Sed contra est quod dicitur Rom. c. I, 3: *qui factus est ei ex semine David secundum carnem.* Tertius error fuit Apollinaris, qui dixit eum tantum accepisse corpus, et non animam, sed loco animae habuisse divinitatem. Sed contra est quod frequenter dicitur: *nunc anima mea turbata est.* Sed propter hoc ipse idem mutavit postea opinionem, et dixit Christum habuisse animam vegetabilem et sensibilem, non tamen rationalem, sed loco eius divinitatem. Sed tunc sequeretur inconveniens, quod Christus non esset plus homo quam unum brutum.

Hos autem errores quasi quadam sorte diviserunt sibi quatuor Evangelistae. Marcus enim et Ioannes principaliter errores illos, qui sunt circa divinitatem, destruxerunt; unde Ioannes in principio statim dixit: *in principio erat Verbum.* Et Marcus exorsus est sic: *initium Evangelii Iesu Christi Filii Dei,* non dixit *filii Abraham.* Matthaeus autem et Lucas illos, qui circa eius humanitatem sunt errores, destruunt in principio.

22. Unde nota quod in hoc quod dicitur **filii David, filii Abraham**, omnes errores qui fuerunt circa Christi humanitatem excluduntur.

Filius enim non dicitur alicuius aliquis, nisi per generationem univocam, quae est secundum convenientiam in specie. Quantumcumque enim aliquid generetur ex homine, nisi participet eamdem specie naturam, numquam dicitur filius, sicut patet de pediculis et huiusmodi. Si igitur Christus est filius David et Abraham, oportet eum habere eamdem naturam ratione eiusdem speciei; non autem haberet eamdem naturam secundum speciem, si non haberet corpus verum et naturale, nec si illud de caelo attulisset; nec etiam si careret anima sensitiva, sive rationali. Unde patet exclusio omnis erroris.

upon your throne (Ps 131:11). But to Abraham a promise was made concerning the members, that is, concerning the Church; hence: *and in your seed will all the nations of the earth be blessed* (Gen 22:18).

21. Here it should be noted that there have been many errors about Christ.

For some have erred about his divinity, as did Paul of Samosata, Photinus, and Sabellius; some have erred about his humanity; and some have erred about both. Others have erred about his person.

The first to err about his humanity was Manichaeus, who said that he took up, not a true body, but the appearance of a body. Contrary to this is what the Lord says: *handle, and see: for a spirit does not have flesh and bones, as you see me to have* (Luke 24:39). Second, after Manichaeus, Valentinus erred, who said that he took for himself a celestial body, and that he did not take it up from the Virgin but rather passed through her like water through a canal. But contrary to this it is said: *who was made to him of the seed of David, according to the flesh* (Rom 1:3). The third error was that of Apollinaris, who said that he took only a body and not a soul, but that he had the divinity in place of a soul. But contrary to this is what is frequently said: *now is my soul troubled.* But because of this saying, Apollinarus himself later changed his position and said that Christ had a vegetative and a sensitive soul, but nonetheless not a rational soul, but rather in its place the divinity. But in this case something unfitting would follow, namely that Christ would be no more a man than one of the brutes.

Now, the four evangelists have divided these errors among themselves by lot, so to speak. For Mark and John have destroyed chiefly those errors which concern the divinity. Hence John says right away at the beginning of his Gospel: *in the beginning was the Word.* And Mark starts this way: *the beginning of the Gospel of Jesus Christ, the Son of God;* he does not say, *the son of Abraham.* But Matthew and Luke at the beginning of their Gospels destroy those errors which concern his humanity.

22. So notice that when it says here, **the son of David, the son of Abraham**, all errors which concern Christ's humanity are excluded.

For one is only called someone's son through a univocal generation, which is according to a sameness in species. For however much a thing may be generated from a man, it will never be called a son unless it shares the same nature in species, as is clear from the case of lice and other such creatures. If therefore Christ is the son of David and of Abraham, he must have the same nature as they do by reason of the same species; moreover, he would not have the same nature according to species if he did not have a true and natural body, nor if he had taken it from heaven, nor if he had lacked a sensitive soul, or a rational soul. Hence the exclusion of every error is clear.

Lecture 2

1:2 Abraham genuit Isaac. Isaac autem genuit Iacob. Iacob autem genuit Iudam, et fratres eius. [n. 24]

1:3 Iudas autem genuit Phares, et Zaram de Thamar. Phares autem genuit Esrom. Esrom autem genuit Aram. [n. 33]

1:4 Aram autem genuit Aminadab. Aminadab autem genuit Naasson. Naasson autem genuit Salmon. [n. 38]

1:5 Salmon autem genuit Booz de Rahab. Booz autem genuit Obed ex Ruth. Obed autem genuit Iesse, Iesse autem genuit David regem. [n. 45]

1:6 Iesse autem genuit David Regem. David autem genuit Salomenem ex ea, quae fuit Uriae, [n. 51]

1:2 Ἀβραὰμ ἐγέννησεν τὸν Ἰσαάκ, Ἰσαὰκ δὲ ἐγέννησεν τὸν Ἰακώβ, Ἰακὼβ δὲ ἐγέννησεν τὸν Ἰούδαν καὶ τοὺς ἀδελφοὺς αὐτοῦ,

1:3 Ἰούδας δὲ ἐγέννησεν τὸν Φάρες καὶ τὸν Ζάρα ἐκ τῆς Θαμάρ, Φάρες δὲ ἐγέννησεν τὸν Ἐσρώμ, Ἐσρὼμ δὲ ἐγέννησεν τὸν Ἀράμ,

1:4 Ἀρὰμ δὲ ἐγέννησεν τὸν Ἀμιναδάβ, Ἀμιναδὰβ δὲ ἐγέννησεν τὸν Ναασσών, Ναασσὼν δὲ ἐγέννησεν τὸν Σαλμών,

1:5 Σαλμὼν δὲ ἐγέννησεν τὸν Βόες ἐκ τῆς Ῥαχάβ, Βόες δὲ ἐγέννησεν τὸν Ἰωβὴδ ἐκ τῆς Ῥούθ, Ἰωβὴδ δὲ ἐγέννησεν τὸν Ἰεσσαί,

1:6 Ἰεσσαὶ δὲ ἐγέννησεν τὸν Δαυὶδ τὸν βασιλέα. Δαυὶδ δὲ ἐγέννησεν τὸν Σολομῶνα ἐκ τῆς τοῦ Οὐρίου,

1:2 Abraham begot Isaac. And Isaac begot Jacob. And Jacob begot Judas and his brethren. [n. 24]

1:3 And Judas begot Phares and Zara of Thamar. And Phares begot Esron. And Esron begot Aram. [n. 33]

1:4 And Aram begot Aminadab. And Aminadab begot Naasson. And Naasson begot Salmon. [n. 38]

1:5 And Salmon begot Booz of Rahab. And Booz begot Obed of Ruth. And Obed begot Jesse. [n. 45]

1:6 And Jesse begot David the King. And David the King begot Solomon, of her that had been the wife of Urias. [n. 51]

---

23. Proposito titulo, hic series genealogiae texitur: et dividitur in partes tres, secundum tres quaterdenarios quibus dicta genealogiae series texitur.

Primus quaterdenarius est ab Abraham usque ad David, qui procedit per patriarchas. Secundus procedit a David usque ad transmigrationem Babylonis, qui procedit per reges. Tertius a transmigratione Babylonis usque ad Christum, qui incipit a ducibus, et procedit per personas privatas.

Secunda, ibi *David autem Rex genuit Salomonem.* Tertia, ibi *et post transmigrationem Babylonis* et cetera.

Prima dividitur in tres. Primo enim ponuntur patres qui fuerunt ante ingressum in Aegyptum; secundo ponuntur illi qui fuerunt in ipso exitu, et terrae promissionis ingressu; tertio illi qui fuerunt post ingressum terrae promissionis.

24. Dicit ergo primo *Abraham genuit Isaac.*

Hic considerandum est, antequam ulterius procedamus, quod duo Evangelistae generationem Christi secundum carnem prosequuntur, scilicet Lucas, et Matthaeus; sed differenter. Et haec differentia attenditur quantum ad quinque. Primo enim differunt quantum ad situm; secundo quantum ad ordinem; tertio quantum ad modum; quarto quantum ad terminum; quinto quantum ad personas numeratas.

23. Having set down the title, here he puts together the series of the genealogy. And it is divided into three parts, according to the three fourteens by which the aforesaid genealogical series is put together.

The first fourteen is from Abraham to David, which proceeds through the patriarchs. The second is from David to the deportation to Babylon, and proceeds through the kings. The third is from the Babylonian deportation to Christ, and, beginning from leaders, it proceeds through private persons.

The second begins at *David the King begot Solomon.* The third, at *and after the transmigration of Babylon* (Matt 1:12).

The first is divided into three parts. For the fathers who lived before the entrance into Egypt are placed first; second are placed those who lived at the time of the exodus and of the entrance into the promised land; third, those who lived after the entrance into the promised land.

24. He says then first, *Abraham begot Isaac.*

Before we proceed further, recall that two of the evangelists trace Christ's generation according to the flesh, namely Luke and Matthew; but each traces it differently. There are differences between them in five respects. For they differ: first, as regards location in the Gospel; second, as regards the order of names; third, as regards the manner of expression; fourth, as regards the point where they end; fifth, as regards the persons enumerated.

25. Primo dico quod differunt quantum ad situm: quia Matthaeus generationem Christi in principio Evangelii incipit texere; Lucas autem non in principio, sed post baptismum.

Et ratio huius est, secundum Augustinum, quoniam Matthaeus generationem Christi carnalem suscepit describendam, et ideo statim in principio debuit eam ponere. Lucas autem maxime intendit commendare in Christo personam sacerdotalem: ad sacerdotem autem pertinet expiatio peccatorum, et ideo post baptismum, in quo fit peccatorum expiatio, convenienter a Luca ponitur Christi generatio.

26. Secundo autem, Lucas et Matthaeus in texendo genealogiam Christi differunt quantum ad ordinem: quia Matthaeus texit Christi generationem incipiendo ab Abraham, et descendendo usque ad Christum, Lucas autem incipit a Christo et ascendendo procedit usque ad Abraham et etiam ultra.

Et ratio est quia, secundum Apostolum, Rom. IV, 25, in Christo fuerunt duo, scilicet humilitas suscipiendi defectus naturae nostrae, et potestas divinitatis et gratiae, per quam nos ab huius defectibus expiavit; Rom. VIII, 3: *misit Deus Filium suum in similitudinem carnis peccati*, propter primum, *et de peccato damnavit peccatum in carne*, propter secundum. Matthaeus ergo, qui intendit generationem Christi carnalem, per quam descendit usque ad infirmitatis nostrae assumptionem, congrue eius generationem descendendo describit. Sed Lucas, qui in ipso commendat sacerdotalem dignitatem, per quam Deo reconciliamur, et ipsi Christo unimur, congrue ascendendo procedit.

27. Tertio differunt quantum ad modum: quia in enarratione genealogiae Matthaeus utitur hoc verbo **genuit**, sed Lucas hoc verbo *fuit*. Et hoc est, quia Matthaeus in tota enarratione sua non ponit nisi patres carnales; sed Lucas ponit multos patres secundum legem, sive per adoptionem. Praeceptum enim fuit in lege quod si aliquis moreretur sine filiis, quod frater eius acciperet sponsam eius, et generaret sibi filios: unde filii illi non erant eius qui generabat, sed per quamdam adoptionem imputabantur priori. Unde Lucas, qui ponit multos filios genitos per adoptionem, non dicit genuit, sed *fuit*; quia quamvis ipsi eos non generassent, eorum tamen per quamdam adoptionem erant. Matthaeus autem, qui ponit solum patres carnales, dicit **genuit**.

Ratio autem huius est quia, sicut dictum est, Matthaeus versatur maxime circa Christi humanitatem. Et quia secundum carnem natus est ex patribus carnalibus, ideo in genealogia Matthaei nullus ponitur, qui non fuerit pater carnalis. Lucas autem commendat maxime in Christo sacerdotalem dignitatem, per quam adoptamur in filios Dei; et ideo non solum carnales, sed etiam legales patres posuit.

25. First, I say that they differ according to location in the Gospel. For Matthew commences putting together the generation of Christ at the beginning of his Gospel; Luke places it, not at the beginning, but after the baptism.

According to Augustine, the reason for this is that Matthew took up the fleshly generation of Christ as the thing to be described, and so he had to put it right at the beginning. Luke however intended most of all to set forward in Christ a priestly person; now the expiation of sins pertains to a priest, and so Luke fittingly places the generation of Christ after a baptism, in which the expiation of sins takes place.

26. Second, Luke and Matthew differ in putting together Christ's genealogy as regards order. For Matthew puts together Christ's generation by beginning with Abraham and descending to Christ, while Luke begins from Christ and, ascending, proceeds to Abraham and beyond.

The reason is that, as the Apostle says (Rom 4:25), there are two things in Christ, namely the humility of accepting the defects of our nature, and the power of the divinity and of grace through which he purified us from such defects; *God sending his own Son, in the likeness of sinful flesh and of sin*, because of the first, and *has condemned sin in the flesh* (Rom 8:3), because of the second. Matthew, therefore, who aims at the fleshly generation of Christ, through which he descended even to the assumption of our weakness, fittingly describes his generation by descending. But Luke, who sets forward his priestly dignity, through which we are reconciled to God and united to Christ himself, fittingly proceeds by ascending.

27. Third, they differ as regards manner. For in recounting the genealogy Matthew uses the verb **begot** while Luke uses the verb *was*. And this is because in his entire account Matthew includes only those who were fathers according to the flesh, while Luke includes many who were fathers according to law, or adoption. For the law commanded that if someone were to die without children, his brother should take his wife and beget children for him; hence those children did not belong to the one who begot them, but rather by a kind of adoption they were imputed to the first man. Hence Luke, who includes more than one son begotten by adoption, does not say begot, but *who was*; because although they had not begotten those men, nevertheless those men were theirs by a kind of adoption. But Matthew, who put down only fathers according to the flesh, says **begot**.

Now the reason for this is that, as was said, Matthew is concerned with Christ's humanity. And since according to the flesh he was born of fathers according to the flesh, Matthew placed none in the genealogy who were not fathers according to the flesh. But Luke emphasizes Christ's priestly dignity, through which we are adopted as sons of God, and so he puts down not only fleshly but also legal fathers.

28. Quarto differunt quantum ad terminum: quia Matthaeus generationem suam incipit ab Abraham, et protendit usque ad Christum; Lucas autem a Christo, non solum usque ad Abraham, sed etiam usque ad Deum.

Cuius ratio potest sumi ex hoc quod Matthaeus scripsit Hebraeis. Hebraei autem maxime gloriabantur de Abraham, Ioan. VIII, 33: *semen Abrahae sumus*, qui fuit primum credendi principium; et ideo Matthaeus ab Abraham incepit. Lucas autem scripsit Graecis, qui nihil de Abraham sciebant nisi per Christum: si enim non fuisset Christus, nihil unquam scivissent de Abraham; et ideo Lucas incepit a Christo, et terminavit non solum in Abraham, sed in Deum.

29. Quinto differunt quantum ad personas enumeratas: quia in tota serie genealogiae Lucae nulla prorsus de muliere fit mentio; in Matthaeo autem aliquae interponuntur mulieres.

Cuius ratio est, secundum Ambrosium, quia Lucas, sicut dictum est, commendat maxime sacerdotalem dignitatem; in sacerdote autem maxima requiritur puritas. Matthaeus autem eius texit generationem carnalem: et ideo ibi ponuntur aliquae mulieres.

30. Notandum tamen quod in tota genealogia Matthaei non ponuntur nisi mulieres peccatrices, vel quae in aliquo fuerant peccato notatae, sicut Thamar, quae fornicata est, Gen. XXXVIII, 24, et Ruth, quae fuit idololatra, quia gentilis, et uxor Uriae, quae fuit adultera, II Reg. XI, 2 ss. Et hoc ad designandum, secundum Hieronymum, quod ille cuius genealogia texitur, intravit propter peccatores redimendos.

Alia ratio tangitur ab Ambrosio, scilicet ut tolleretur confusio Ecclesiae. Si enim Christus ex peccatoribus nasci voluit, non debent infideles irridere, si peccatores ad Ecclesiam veniant.

Alia ratio potest assignari, credo secundum Chrysostomum, ut ostendatur imperfectio legis: et quod Christus venit legem implere. Per hoc enim quod tanguntur quaedam mulieres peccatrices, denotatur quod illi, qui erant maximi in lege, erant peccatores; sicut David et Iudas. Et in hoc designat imperfectionem aliorum. Si enim isti fuerunt peccatores, multo magis et alii; Rom. III, 23: *omnes peccaverunt, et egent gloria Dei*. Et ideo isti ponuntur in generatione Christi, ut designetur, quod ipse legem impleverat.

Nota tamen quod istae mulieres quamvis fuerint omnes peccatrices, non tamen pro tempore illo quo texitur earum genealogia, sed iam erant mundatae per poenitentiam.

31. Dicit ergo ***Abraham genuit Isaac***. Notandum primo, quod hic duo sunt consideranda secundum litteram, sive sensum litteralem. Primo, quod per patres istos

28. Fourth, they differ as regards the ending point. For Matthew begins his generation from Abraham and extends it to Christ; Luke however extends his genealogy from Christ, not only to Abraham, but even to God.

The reason for this can be found in the fact that Matthew wrote to the Hebrews. Now the Hebrews prided themselves chiefly on Abraham. *We are the seed of Abraham* (John 8:33), who was the first beginning of believing. And so Matthew began from Abraham. But Luke wrote to the Greeks, who knew nothing of Abraham except through Christ; for if there had not been Christ, they would never have known anything about Abraham. And so Luke began from Christ, and ended not merely in Abraham, but in God.

29. Fifth, they differ as regards the persons enumerated. For in the whole series of the genealogy Luke mentions absolutely nothing about a woman, but in Matthew some women are interspersed.

According to Ambrose, the reason for this is that Luke, as was said, sets forward most of all the priestly dignity. Now in a priest, purity is required most of all. But Matthew puts together his generation according to the flesh, and for this reason some women are set down there.

30. Yet one should notice that in the entire genealogy of Matthew the only women set down are sinners, or those who were known for some sin, as was Thamar who fornicated (Gen 38), and Ruth who was an idolater because she was a gentile, and the wife of Urias who was an adulteress (2 Sam 11). And according to Jerome, this is to point out that he whose genealogy is put together here entered for the sake of redeeming sinners.

Ambrose touches upon another reason, namely to remove the Church's embarrassment. For if Christ willed to be born of sinners, unbelievers ought not to laugh if sinners come to the Church.

Another reason can be given, I believe according to Chrysostom, namely to show the imperfection of the law, and to show that Christ came to fulfill the law. For the fact that certain sinful women are mentioned points out that those who were greatest in the law were sinners, such as David and Judas. And by this he points out the imperfection of the others; for if those men were sinners, much more the others as well. *All have sinned* (Rom 3:23). And so these are placed in the generation of Christ to indicate that he himself had fulfilled the law.

Yet notice that those women, however much they may all have been sinners, still they were not sinners during the time in which their genealogy was put together, but were already cleansed through penitence.

31. He says then, ***Abraham begot Isaac***. One should note first that there are three things here to be considered: the letter, or the literal sense; second, that the fathers who

positos designatur Christus; secundo, quod etiam ista referuntur, et possunt referri, ad instructionem nostram.

Dicit ergo primo **Abraham genuit Isaac**. Et hoc habetur Genes. XXI. *Isaac autem genuit Iacob*, Genes. XXV.

32. *Iacob autem genuit Iudam et fratres eius*. Hic quaeritur, cum Abraham alium habuerit filium quam Isaac, scilicet Ismael, et similiter Isaac, quare non fit mentio de eis, sicut hic dicitur **Iudam et fratres**.

Item, quare magis exprimitur Iudas ex nomine, quam alii.

Ratio est, quia Iudas et fratres eius sub cultura unius Dei permanserunt: et ideo de eis fit mentio in generatione Christi, non autem *Isaac, et Ismael*, nec *Iacob, et Esau*.

Ad secundum, quod hoc fuit ut impleri ostenderetur in Christo prophetia Iacob, Genes. XLIX, 10: *non auferetur sceptrum de Iuda, et dux de femore eius, donec veniat, qui mittendus est: et ipse erit expectatio gentium*. Manifestum enim est quod de Iuda ortus est Dominus, ut dicitur Hebr. VII, 14; et ideo fit magis mentio de ipso quam de aliis.

33. *Iudas autem genuit Phares* et cetera. Hic quaeritur, cum Dominus non sit natus de Zaram, sed de Phares, quare fit mentio de eo.

Item, quare nominaliter exprimitur. Prius enim dixit **fratres eius**, quare ergo expressit nomen Zaram?

Et dicendum, secundum Ambrosium, quod hoc in mysterio factum est. Ad cuius evidentiam nota historiam, quae habetur Genes. XXXVIII, quod in partu Thamar prior apparuit Zaram, in cuius manu obstetrix ligavit filum coccineum dicens: *iste egredietur prior*, et ideo vocavit nomen eius Zaram: postea *illo retrahente manum egressus est alter*, dicente obstetrice: *quare propter te divisa est maceria?* Zaram autem, qui prior apparuit, significat populum Iudaeorum, in cuius manu obstetrix filum coccineum ligavit, hoc est circumcisionem, quae fiebat cum sanguinis effusione. Sed *illo retrahente manum* etc. *egressus est alter*: quia *caecitas ex parte contigit in Iudaeis*. Sic enim populus gentilis divisus intravit in lucem fidei, egressus de vulva ignorantiae et infidelitatis.

34. Secundo notandum, quod per patres positos in generatione Christi signatur Christus ratione vel nominis, vel facti, vel alicuius alterius, sicut per se patet.

Abraham enim interpretatur 'pater multarum gentium,' et significat Christum, de quo Hebr. c. II, 10: *qui multos filios in gloriam adduxerat*. Item Abraham ex praecepto Domini exivit de terra sua, Gen. XII, 4, et Christus est, qui dixit, Ierem. XII, 17: *reliqui domum meam, dimisi haereditatem meam* et cetera. Similiter Abraham, qui risit dicendo: *nunc risum fecit mihi Dominus*, Gen. XXI, 6,

are set down designate Christ; third, that even they are referred, or can be referred, to our instruction.

He says then first, **Abraham begot Isaac**. And this is found elsewhere in Scripture (Gen 21). **And Isaac begot Jacob** (Gen 25).

32. *Jacob begot Judas and his brethren*. Here it is asked, since Abraham had another son besides Isaac, namely Ishmael, and similarly Isaac had other sons, why does he not mention them the way it says here, ***Judas and his brethren***?

Similarly, why is Judas mentioned by name any more than the others?

The reason is that Judas and his brothers remained under the worship of the one God, and this is why they are mentioned in the generation of Christ. And it does not say, *Isaac and Ishmael*, or *Jacob and Esau*.

As regards the second question, this was to show that the prophecy of Jacob was fulfilled in Christ: *the sceptre will not be taken away from Judah, nor a ruler from his thigh, till he come that is to be sent, and he will be the expectation of nations* (Gen 49:10). *For it is evident that our Lord sprung out of Judah* (Heb 7:14). For this reason he is mentioned rather than the others.

33. *And Judas begot Phares and Zara of Thamar*. Here it is asked, since the Lord was not born of Zara, but of Phares, why he is mentioned.

And why he is described by name? For previously it said, **his brethren**. So why does he mention the name of Zara?

And one should say, according to Ambrose, that this was done in a mystery. To make this clear, notice the history, that in Thamar's labor Zara appeared first (Gen 38). The midwife tied a scarlet thread onto his hand, saying, *this will come forth the first*, and so she called his name Zara. Later, *he drawing back his hand, the other came forth*, and the midwife said, *why is the partition divided for you?* Now Zara, who appeared first, signifies the people of the Jews, onto whose hand the midwife tied a scarlet thread, that is, circumcision, which was accompanied by a flow of blood. *But he drawing back his hand, the other came forth* (2 Cor 1), because *blindness in part has happened in Israel* (Rom 11:25). For in this way the gentile people, separated from God's people, entered into the light of faith. It came forth from the womb of ignorance and unbelief.

34. Second, one should note that Christ is signified by the fathers set down in the generation of Christ by reason either of name, or of deed, or of some other thing, as is self-evident.

Abraham is interpreted 'father of many nations'. He signifies Christ, about whom it is said, *who had brought many children into glory* (Heb 2:10). Again, Abraham left his own land at the Lord's command (Gen 12:4), and it is Christ who said: *I have forsaken my house* (Jer 12:7). Similarly it was Abraham who laughed, saying: *God has made a laughter for me* (Gen 21:6), and it is Christ at whose birth joy was

et Christus est, in cuius nativitate non solum uni persone, sed toti mundo gaudium nuntiatur; Luc. II, 10: *ecce evangelizo vobis gaudium magnum, quod erit omni populo, quia natus est vobis hodie salvator, qui est Christus Dominus.* Similiter per Iacob, et ratione interpretationis, et ratione facti, sicut patet in hoc, quod supposuit lapidem, idest duritiem crucis, capiti suo. Similiter per Iudam, et Phares, qui interpretatur 'divisio': ipse enim dividet oves ab hoedis, infra XXV, 32.

35. Moraliter autem in istis generationibus designatur status nostrae iustificationis, secundum sex quae requiruntur ad iustificationem.

Scilicet fides per Abraham iustificatum ex fidei iustitia; alibi enim ipse principium dicitur fidei; Rom. IV, 11: *ut sit pater omnium credentium per praeputium.* Isaac spes, quia interpretatur 'risus'; Rom. XII, 12: *spe gaudentes.* Iacob caritas, qui duxit duas uxores, Liam, quae interpretatur 'laborans', et Rachel; idest duas vitas, quae sunt in caritate secundum duo praecepta: contemplativa enim delectatur in Deo, activa autem est per quam subvenitur proximo. Iudas, confessio, quae duplex est: fidei, Rom. X, 10: *corde creditur ad iustitiam; ore autem confessio fit ad salutem,* et peccatorum: *confitemini alterutrum peccata vestra,* Iac. V, 16. Ex hoc autem sequitur duplex effectus, scilicet destructio vitiorum, quae per Phares designatur, et origo virtutum, quae significatur per Zaram. Et ista oriuntur de Thamar, quae interpretatur 'amaritudo'; Isa. XXXVIII, 15: *recogitabo tibi omnes annos meos in amaritudine animae meae.*

36. *Phares autem genuit Esron.* Hic ponitur series genealogiae patrum, qui nati sunt in Aegypto, vel in exitu eius. Sicut enim per Phares, qui interpretatur 'divisio,' significatur Christus, infra XXV, 32: ***separabit agnos ab hoedis,*** ita per Esron, qui interpretatur 'sagitta,' vel 'atrium.' Dicitur enim 'sagitta' propter efficaciam praedicationis, qua audientium corda penetravit; Psalm. XLIV, 6: *sagittae tuae acutae, populi sub te cadent in corda inimicorum regis.* 'Atrium' autem propter latitudinem caritatis, qua non solum amicos, sed etiam inimicos dilexit; Rom. V, 10: *cum inimici essemus, reconciliati sumus Deo per mortem Filii eius*; Isa. LIII, 12: *ipse pro transgressoribus rogavit*; et idem Luc. XXIII, 34: *Pater, dimitte illis: non enim sciunt quid faciunt.*

37. *Esron autem genuit aram.* Aram autem interpretatur 'electus,' vel 'excelsus': Isa. XLII, 1: *ecce puer meus, et ipse est excelsus super omnes*; Ephes. I, 21: *ipsum constituit super omnem principatum.*

38. *Aram autem genuit Aminadab,* qui interpretatur 'spontaneus.' Ipse est in cuius persona dicit Psalmista LIII, 8: *voluntarie sacrificabo tibi, et confitebor nomini tuo, quoniam bonum est, domine*; et Isa. LIII, 7: *oblatus est, quia ipse voluit, et non aperuit os suum* etc.,

announced, not to one person only, but to the whole world. *Behold, I bring you good tidings of great joy, that shall be to all the people* (Luke 2:10). Similarly, Christ is signified by Jacob, both because of the interpretation of his name and because of what he did, as is clear in the fact that he placed a stone, i.e., the severity of the cross, beneath his head. Similarly by Judas and Phares, who is interpreted 'division'; for he will divide the sheep from the goats (Matt 25:32).

35. Now the status of our justification is indicated morally in these generations, according to the six things required for justification.

Namely, faith is signifed by Abraham, who was justified by the justice of faith. For elsewhere he is called a beginning of faith for others; *which is in the flesh of our circumcision* (Rom 4:11). Isaac signifies hope, because he is interpreted as 'laughter'; *rejoicing in hope* (Rom 12:12). Love is signified by Jacob, who took two wives, Lia, whose name means 'laboring', and Rachel; two lives, which are lived in love in keeping with the two precepts: the contemplative life, which delights in God, and the active life, through which one's neighbor is helped. Judas signifies confession, which is twofold: the confession of faith: *with the heart, we believe* (Rom 10:10); and the confession of sinners: *confess therefore your sins one to another* (Jas 5:16). Now two effects follow from this, namely the destruction of vice, which is signified by Phares, and the beginning of virtue, which is signified by Zara. And these arise from Thamar, who is interpreted 'bitterness'; *I will recount to you all my years in the bitterness of my soul* (Isa 38:15).

36. *And Phares begot Esron.* Here is set down the series of the genealogy of the fathers who were born in Egypt or in the exodus. For as Christ is signified through Phares, who is interpreted as 'division': ***he will separate them one from another, as the shepherd separates the sheep from the goats*** (Matt 25:32), so he is also signified through Esron, who is interpreted 'arrow', or 'hall'. For he is called 'arrow' on account of the efficacy of his preaching, by which he pierced the hearts of those who heard: *your arrows are sharp* (Ps 44:6). He is called 'hall' on account of the breadth of his charity, by which he loved not only friends, but even enemies: *when we were enemies, we were reconciled to God by the death of his Son* (Rom 5:10); *he has prayed for the transgressors* (Isa 53:12); and: *Father, forgive them: for they know not what they do* (Luke 23:34).

37. *And Esron begot Aram.* Now Aram is interpreted 'elect', or 'exalted'. *Behold my servant, and he is exalted above all* (Isa 42:1); *setting him on his right hand in the heavenly places, above all principality* (Eph 1:21).

38. *And Aram begot Aminadab,* who is interpreted 'spontaneous'. It is in his person that the Psalmist says: *I will freely sacrifice to you, and will give praise, O God, to your name: because it is good* (Ps 53:8); and: *he has borne the sins of many, and has prayed for the transgressors* (Isa 53:12); *I*

Io. VI, 38: *non veni facere voluntatem meam, sed eius qui misit me.*

39. Aminadab autem genuit Naasson, qui interpretatur 'augurium' vel 'serpentinum': quia Christus non solum praesentia, sed etiam praeterita, et futura cognovit; ad Hebr. IV, 13: *omnia nuda et aperta sunt oculis eius.* Item 'serpentinum' propter prudentiam; prudentia enim attribuitur serpenti, infra X, 16: **estote prudentes sicut serpentes**; Iob XII, 16: *ipse novit decipientem et eum qui decipitur.*

40. Nota quod iste Naasson fuit in tempore Moysi, et exivit cum eo de Aegypto, et fuit unus princeps in tribu Iuda in deserto, sicut habetur in Numer. I, 7.

Sed advertendum, quod Exodi XIII, 18, ubi nostra littera habet, *filii Israel ascenderunt armati de Aegypto*, aquila transtulit *instructi*, propter aequivocationem; melior est autem littera Septuaginta: *filii Israel quinta generatione exierunt de Aegypto.*

41. Sed contra. Naasson iste non fuit quintus a Iacob, sed septimus, sicut patet computando Iacob, Iudam etc. usque ad Naasson. Ergo non quinta, sed septima generatione.

Sed dicitur quod non est computandum per tribum Iuda, sed per tribum levi, sub cuius ductu exierunt filii Israel de Aegypto; Ps. LXXVI, 21: *deduxisti sicut oves populum tuum in manu Moysi et Aaron.* Et patet quod tantum sunt quinque generationes. Iacob enim genuit levi, levi autem genuit Caath, Caath genuit Amram, Amram autem genuit Moysen et Aaron, sicut patet Exod. II; et sub Moyse exierunt de Aegypto.

42. Ubi nota quod inter omnes tribus magis multiplicabatur tribus Iuda: et hoc quia ex ea erant reges futuri, qui debebant pugnare. Inter omnes autem minus multiplicabatur tribus Levi: et hoc quia praeordinata erat ad officium divinum, et sacerdotium, ad quod pauciores sufficiebant. Et ideo vult quod etiam computando per tribum Iuda, sit verum quod dicitur Gen. XV, 16: *quinta generatione revertentur huc.* Dicit ergo Hieronymus, illud quod ibi dicitur, intelligendum esse computando per tribum Levi; quod autem hic dicitur, per tribum Iuda. Phares enim ipse cum Iacob et Iuda patre suo intravit in Aegyptum. Et ideo istae generationes non sunt computandae a Iacob, sed a Phares, qui et ipse intravit in Aegyptum. Et patet quod Naasson fuit quintus a Phares. Similiter Levi ipse intravit in Aegyptum cum patre suo Iacob. Et ideo a Levi, et non a Iacob, computandae sunt generationes. Clarum autem est quod Moyses fuit quartus a Levi.

43. Naasson autem genuit Salmon. Salmon interpretatur 'sensibilis': et significat Christum, *in quo sunt omnes thesauri sapientiae et scientiae absconditi.*

came down from heaven, not to do my own will, but the will of him who sent me (John 6:38).

39. And Aminadab begot Naasson, who is interpreted 'omen' or 'serpent-like', because Christ knew not only the present but also the past and the future; *all things are naked and open to his eyes* (Heb 4:13). Similarly, 'serpent-like' because of prudence, for prudence is attributed to the serpent. Below: **be therefore wise as serpents** (Matt 10:16); *with him is strength and wisdom: he knows both the deceiver, and him who is deceived* (Job 12:16).

40. Note that this man Naasson lived in the time of Moses, and came out with him from Egypt, and was one of the princes of the tribe of Judah in the desert (Num 1:7).

But one should be aware that where our texts have, *the children of Israel went up armed out of the land of Egypt* (Exod 13:18), Aquila translated it as *instructed*, owing to an equivocation. But the text of the Septuagint is better: *the children of Israel went up out of Egypt in the fifth generation.*

41. On the contrary: Naasson was not the fifth from Jacob, but the seventh, as is clear by counting up Jacob, Judas, and so on, down to Naasson. Therefore it was not in the fifth, but in the seventh generation.

But it is said that it should not be calculated through the tribe of Judas, but through the tribe of Levi, under whose leadership the children of Israel went up out of Egypt; *you have conducted your people like sheep, by the hand of Moses and Aaron* (Ps 76:21). And it is clear that there were only five generations counting this way: for Jacob begot Levi, and Levi begot Caath, and Caath begot Amram, and Amram begot Moses and Aaron (Exod 6:20). And under Moses they went up from the land of Egypt.

42. Note here that, among all the tribes, the tribe of Judas was multiplying the most, because from that tribe were to come kings, who were supposed to fight. But among them all, the tribe of Levi was multiplying the least, because it was preordained to the divine service and to the priesthood, for which a smaller number sufficed. But Jerome would have it that they went up in the fifth generation even calculating through the tribe of Judas. *In the fifth generation they will return hither* (Gen 15:16). Therefore, Jerome says, what is said there should be understood by calculating through the tribe of Levi, but what is said here should be understood by calculating through the tribe of Judas. For Phares himself entered into Egypt with Jacob and his father Judas. And it is clear that Naasson was the fifth from Phares. Similarly, Levi himself entered into Egypt with his father Jacob. And therefore the generations should be calculated from Levi, and not from Jacob. And it is clear that Moses was the fourth from Levi.

43. And Naasson begot Salmon. Salmon is interpreted 'sensitive'; and he signifies Christ, *in whom all treasures of wisdom and knowledge are hidden* (Col 2:3).

44. Moraliter hic notandum, quod sicut in prima generatione significatur ordo nostrae iustificationis quantum ad statum incipientium; ita in ista secunda generatione, quae similiter continet quinque, significatur profectus proficientium. Primum enim quod sequitur ex quo homo est iustificatus a peccato, est quod ipse habet zelum animarum. Et ideo bene Phares genuit Esron, qui interpretatur 'sagitta,' propter efficaciam praedicationis qua penetrantur corda auditorum; Isa. XLIX, 2: *posuit me quasi sagittam electam.* Et ita adapta alia.

45. *Salmon autem genuit Booz* et cetera. Hic ponuntur patres qui fuerunt nati post ingressum terrae promissionis. Salmon enim fuit genitus in deserto, et intravit cum Iosue in terram promissionis, et accepit uxorem Rahab meretricem, de qua genuit Booz.

Booz interpretatur 'fortis'; Ier. XVI, 19: *Dominus fortitudo mea et robur meum.* Rahab autem interpretatur 'fames,' vel 'latitudo': et significat Ecclesiam, quia ad ipsam pertinet illa beatitudo, Matth. V, 6: **beati qui esuriunt, et sitiunt iustitiam, quoniam ipsi saturabuntur** et cetera. Interpretatur etiam 'latitudo,' quia Ecclesia per totum orbem dilatata est; Isa. LIV, 2: *dilata locum tentorii tui, et pelles tabernaculorum tuorum extende* et cetera. Item interpretatur 'impetus,' quia impetu praedicationis reges et philosophos convertit. Item significat Ecclesiam ratione facti. Rahab filum coccineum misit in fenestram, per quem liberata est a subversione Iericho, Iosue II, 21. Fenestra nostra est os: filum ergo in fenestra est confessio passionis Christi, per quam Ecclesia liberata est a morte. Item ratione coniugii, quia sicut Rahab iuncta est in matrimonio Salmon, qui fuit princeps in tribu Iuda; sic Christus desponsavit sibi Ecclesiam; II Cor. c. XI, 2: *despondi enim vos uni viro virginem castam exhibere Christo.*

46. Sed hic quaeritur, secundum litteram, cum Rahab fuerit meretrix, quomodo tanto principi, qui erat maior inter alios, desponsata est?

Et est dicendum, quod Rahab maximum quid fecit, eo quod contempto populo suo et ritu paterno, cultum Dei Israel elegit. Et ideo quasi pro maximo honore nobilissimo principi data fuit.

47. *Booz autem genuit Obed ex Ruth.* Hoc habetur Ruth ult. cap. Obed interpretatur 'serviens' vel 'servitus': et significat Christum, de quo per prophetam: *servire me fecistis peccatis vestris,* Is. XLIII, 24. Ruth autem significat Ecclesiam de gentibus natam ratione loci: fuit enim Moabitis. Moab interpretatur 'ex patre'; Io. VIII, 44: *vos ex patre diabolo estis*; et iterum ratione coniugii, ut patet in Glossa.

48. Sed quaeritur, quare istae mulieres hic nominantur, cum fuerint peccatrices.

44. Morally, one should note here that as in the first generation the order of our justification as regards the status of the beginner is signified, so in this second generation, which similarly contains five, the progress of the proficient is signified. For the first thing following from the fact that a man is justified from sin is that he has zeal for souls. And therefore well did Phares beget Esron, who is interpreted 'arrow', owing to the efficacy of the preaching by which the hearts of those who hear are pierced; *he . . . has made me as a chosen arrow* (Isa 49:2). And the others fit in the same way.

45. *And Salmon begot Booz.* Here are placed the fathers who were born after the entrance into the land of promise. For Salmon was begotten in the desert, and entered with Josue into the land of promise, and took Rahab the harlot as his wife, from whom he begot Booz.

Booz is interpreted 'strong'; *O Lord, my might, and my strength* (Jer 16:19). Rahab is interpreted as 'hunger' or 'width'; and she signifies the Church, because to her pertains that beatitude: **blessed are they who hunger and thirst** (Matt 5:6). She is also interpreted as 'width', because the Church is spread throughout the whole world; *stretch out the skins of your tabernacles* (Isa 54:2). Similarly, she is interpreted as 'attack', because by the attack of preaching she has converted kings and philosophers. Again, she signifies the Church by reason of deed. Rahab put a scarlet rope in her window, through which she was freed from the sacking of Jericho (Jos 2:21). Our window is the mouth; therefore the rope in the window is the confession of Christ's passion, through which the Church is freed from death. Again by reason of her spouse, because as Rahab was joined in marriage to Salmon, who was a prince of the tribe of Judah, so Christ has espoused the Church to himself; *for I have espoused you to one husband that I may present you as a chaste virgin to Christ* (2 Cor 11:2).

46. But it is asked, according to the letter, since Rahab was a harlot, how was she espoused to so great a prince, who was great among other princes?

And one should say that what Rahab did was most great, because she chose the worship of the God of Israel in contempt of her own people and of the rite of her fathers. And therefore as a most great honor, as it were, she was given to a most noble prince.

47. *And Booz begot Obed of Ruth.* This is found in the last chapter of Ruth. Obed is interpreted 'serving' or 'servant'; and he signifies Christ, of whom it was said through the prophet: *but you have made me to serve with your sins* (Isa 43:24). Moreover, Ruth signifies the Church born from the gentiles by reason of place, for she was a Moabitess. Moab is interpreted 'from father'; *you are of your father the devil* (John 8:44); and again by reason of her spouse, as is clear in the Gloss.

48. But it is asked why these women are named here, since they were sinners.

Hieronymus assignat rationem de Ruth, ut scilicet impleretur vaticinium Isa. XVI, 1: *emitte agnum, domine, dominatorem terrae de Petra deserti*. Petra deserti est, scilicet mali, et significatur Ruth Moabitis. Ambrosius autem assignat rationem dicens: *futurum enim erat ut Ecclesia congregaretur de gentibus infidelibus; et ideo poterat erubescere et confundi, nisi viderent Christum etiam de peccatricibus nasci*. Unde ut tolleretur eorum erubescentia, et confusio, nominandae sunt.

49. Sed quaeritur, Deut. XXIII, 3 dicitur: *Moabitae et Ammonitae non intrabunt Ecclesiam*; cum ergo Ruth fuerit Moabitis, quomodo recepta est in Ecclesiam?

Sed dicendum per Apostolum ad Gal. V, 18, quod *qui spiritu ducuntur, non sunt sub lege*: semper enim in lege magis debet observari intentio legislatoris quam verba legis. Quae enim fuit causa quare prohibuit Dominus ut non intrarent Ecclesiam? Quia scilicet invenit in eis idololatriam, ne scilicet pertraherent Iudaeos ad idololatriam. Unde ista, quae iam erat conversa, non erat idololatra; et ideo non erat subiecta prohibitioni.

50. *Obed autem genuit Iesse*, Ruth ultim. Iesse autem interpretatur 'sacrificium' vel 'incendium'; et significat eum qui obtulit semetipsum hostiam Deo in odorem suavitatis.

Sed quaeritur: cum iste alio nomine vocatus sit *Isai*, sicut patet I Reg. in multis locis, et illud nomen esset solemnius, quare non nominavit eum Evangelista sic?

Et dicendum, quod hoc fuit ut ostenderetur in Christo impletum esse quod dictum est per prophetam Isaiam, XI, 1: *egredietur virga de radice Iesse*.

51. *Iesse autem genuit David Regem*. David interpretatur 'manu fortis' et 'aspectu desiderabilis'; quae omnia competunt Christo, sicut patet. Ipse enim fortis est qui diabolum superavit; Luc. XI, 22: *si autem fortior illo superveniens vicerit eum, universa arma eius auferet, in quibus confidebat, et spolia eius distribuet*. Item ipse *speciosus forma prae filiis hominum*, Psal. XLIV, 3.

52. Sed hic quaeritur: cum plures alii fuerint reges, quare solus iste dicitur rex? Et dicendum quod iste primus rex fuit in tribu Iuda, de qua ortus est Dominus: quamvis enim Saul fuerit rex, ipse tamen fuit de tribu Beniamin. Secunda ratio, quia alii propter meritum ipsius David regnaverunt; Psal. LXXXVIII, 30: *et ponam in saeculum saeculi semen eius, et thronum eius sicut dies caeli*. Tertia ratio, ut ostenderetur impleta prophetia Ier. XXIII, 5: *suscitabo David germen iustum, et regnabit rex, et sapiens erit, et faciet iudicium, et iustitiam in terra*;

Jerome gives a reason for Ruth, namely that the prophesy of Isaiah might be fulfilled: *send forth, O Lord, the lamb, the ruler of the earth, from Petra of the desert* (Isa 16:1). Petra is from the desert, that is from evil, and signifies Ruth the Moabitess. Ambrose also gives a reason, saying: *for it was going to happen that the Church would be gathered together from the unbelieving nations; and so the Church could have blushed and been embarrassed if they had not seen that even Christ was born from sinners*. Hence to remove the blushing and embarrassment, these sinners had to be named.

49. But it is asked: *the Ammonite and the Moabite, even after the tenth generation will not enter into the Church of the Lord for ever* (Deut 23:3); so since Ruth was a Moabitess, how was she received into the Church?

But one should say through the Apostle, that *if you are led by the spirit, you are not under the law* (Gal 5:18); for in a law, the intention of the legislator ought always to be observed more than the words of the law. For what was the reason why the Lord commanded that the Ammonites and Moabites not enter the Church? Clearly, because he found idolatry in them, i.e., lest they drag the Jews into idolatry. Hence this woman, who was already converted, was not an idolater, and so was not subject to the prohibition.

50. *And Obed begot Jesse* (also Ruth 4:22). Now Jesse is interpreted as 'sacrifice' or 'burning'; and he signifies him who offered himself as a victim to God in the odor of sweetness.

But it is asked: since this man is called by another name, *Isai*, as is clear in many places in 1 Samuel, and this name is more solemn, why did the Evangelist not name him this way?

And one should say that this was done to show that the prophecy which was spoken through the prophet Isaiah was fulfilled in Christ: *and there will come forth a rod out of the root of Jesse, and a flower will rise up out of his root* (Isa 11:1).

51. *And Jesse begot David the King*. David is interpreted as 'strong of hand' and 'desirable in appearance'; all of which belongs to Christ, as is clear. For he who overcame the devil is strong; *but if a stronger one than he come upon him, and overcome him; he will take away all his armour in which he trusted, and will distribute his spoils* (Luke 11:22). Similarly, he is *beautiful above the sons of men* (Ps 44:3).

52. But here it is asked: since there were many other kings, why is only this man called a king? And one should say that this man was the first king in the tribe of Judas, from whom the Lord is descended; for although Saul was a king, yet he was of the tribe of Benjamin. A second reason, because it was owing to the merit of David himself that the others reigned; *and I will make his seed to endure for evermore: and his throne as the days of heaven* (Ps 88:30). A third reason, to show that the prophecy of Jeremiah was fulfilled: *I will raise up to David a just branch: and a king will reign, and will be wise, and will execute judgment and

Isa. c. IX, 7: *super solium David, et super regnum eius sedebit* et cetera.

53. Moraliter vero in ista generatione designatur fructus perfectorum, sicut in aliis fructus incipientium, et proficientium.

Primum enim quod requiritur in homine perfecto est quod ipse sit fortis ad aggrediendum adversa, ut scilicet non retardetur propter aliquam difficultatem: et hoc significatur per Booz; interpretatur enim 'fortis'; Isa. XL, 31: *qui sperant in Domino, mutabunt fortitudinem, assument pennas sicut aquilae; current, et non laborabunt, ambulabunt, et non deficient*; Prov. ult., 10: *mulierem fortem quis inveniet?* et cetera. Secundum est humilitas servientis, ut quanto scilicet magnus est, tanto humiliet se in omnibus; et hoc significatur per Obed, qui et ipse interpretatur 'serviens' vel 'servitus'; Luc. c. XXII, 26: *qui maior est vestrum, fiat sicut minister*. Tertium est fervor caritatis, quod significatur per Iesse, qui interpretatur 'incensum' vel 'incendium'; Psal. CXL, 2: *dirigatur oratio mea sicut incensum in conspectu tuo* et cetera. Et ex hoc pervenitur ad regnum, et ad gloriam: quia Iesse genuit David Regem; Apoc. c. V, 10: *fecit nos Deo nostro regnum, et sacerdotes Deo patri suo*; I Petr. II, 9: *vos estis genus electum, regale sacerdotium, gens sancta, populus acquisitionis.*

justice in the earth (Jer 23:5); *he will sit upon the throne of David, and upon his kingdom* (Isa 9:7).

53. But morally, the fruit of those who are perfect is indicated in this generation, as in the others the fruits of the beginners and of the proficients are indicated.

For the first thing which is required in a perfect man is that he be strong in attacking adversities, so that he will not be held back on account of some difficulty; and this is signified through Booz, who is interpreted as 'strong'; *but they that hope in the Lord will renew their strength, they will take wings as eagles, they will run and not be weary, they will walk and not faint* (Isa 40:31); *who will find a valiant woman?* (Prov 31:10). The second thing required is the humility of one who serves, so that to the degree he is great, to that degree he will humble himself in all things; and this is signified through Obed, who is interpreted as 'the one serving' or 'servant'; **he who is the greatest among you will be your servant** (Matt 23:11). The third thing required is fervor of charity, which is signified through Jesse, who is interpreted as 'burnt', or 'burning'; *let my prayer be directed as incense in thy sight* (Ps 140:2). And from this, one comes to the kingdom and to glory, for Jesse begot David the King: *and has made us to our God a kingdom and priests* (Rev 5:10); *but you are a chosen generation, a kingly priesthood, a holy nation, a purchased people* (1 Pet 2:9).

Lecture 3

1:6 Iesse autem genuit David Regem. David autem Rex genuit Salomonem, ex ea quae fuit Uriae. [n. 55]

1:7 Salomon autem genuit Roboam: Roboam autem genuit Abiam. Abias autem genuit Asa. [n. 59]

1:8 Asa autem genuit Iosaphat. Iosaphat autem genuit Ioram. Ioram autem genuit Oziam. [n. 62]

1:9 Ozias autem genuit Ioatham. Ioatham autem genuit Achaz. Achaz autem genuit Ezechiam. [n. 68]

1:10 Ezechias autem genuit Manassen. Manasses autem genuit Amon. Amon autem genuit Iosiam. [n. 71]

1:11 Iosias autem genuit Iechoniam, et fratres eius in transmigratione Babylonis. [n. 74]

1:6 Ἰεσσαὶ δὲ ἐγέννησεν τὸν Δαυὶδ τὸν βασιλέα. Δαυὶδ δὲ ἐγέννησεν τὸν Σολομῶνα ἐκ τῆς τοῦ Οὐρίου,

1:7 Σολομὼν δὲ ἐγέννησεν τὸν Ῥοβοάμ, Ῥοβοὰμ δὲ ἐγέννησεν τὸν Ἀβιά, Ἀβιὰ δὲ ἐγέννησεν τὸν Ἀσάφ,

1:8 Ἀσὰφ δὲ ἐγέννησεν τὸν Ἰωσαφάτ, Ἰωσαφὰτ δὲ ἐγέννησεν τὸν Ἰωράμ, Ἰωρὰμ δὲ ἐγέννησεν τὸν Ὀζίαν,

1:9 Ὀζίας δὲ ἐγέννησεν τὸν Ἰωαθάμ, Ἰωαθὰμ δὲ ἐγέννησεν τὸν Ἀχάζ, Ἀχὰζ δὲ ἐγέννησεν τὸν Ἐζεκίαν,

1:10 Ἐζεκίας δὲ ἐγέννησεν τὸν Μανασσῆ, Μανασσῆς δὲ ἐγέννησεν τὸν Ἀμώς, Ἀμὼς δὲ ἐγέννησεν τὸν Ἰωσίαν,

1:11 Ἰωσίας δὲ ἐγέννησεν τὸν Ἰεχονίαν καὶ τοὺς ἀδελφοὺς αὐτοῦ ἐπὶ τῆς μετοικεσίας Βαβυλῶνος.

1:6 And Jesse begot David the King. And David the King begot Solomon, of her that had been the wife of Urias. [n. 55]

1:7 And Solomon begot Roboam. And Roboam begot Abia. And Abia begot Asa. [n. 59]

1:8 And Asa begot Josaphat. And Josaphat begot Joram. And Joram begot Ozias. [n. 62]

1:9 And Ozias begot Joatham. And Joatham begot Achaz. And Achaz begot Ezechias. [n. 68]

1:10 And Ezechias begot Manasses. And Manesses begot Amon. And Amon begot Josias. [n. 71]

1:11 And Josias begot Jechonias and his brethren in the transmigration of Babylon. [n. 74]

---

54. Posita serie genealogiae patrum, quae cucurrit per patriarchas, hic ponit seriem patrum, quae procedit per reges: et dividitur in duo.

Primo ponuntur reges, qui nati sunt ex Israel sine commixtione seminis alieni; secundo ponuntur reges, qui secuti sunt coniunctionem alienae copulae, ibi *Ioram autem genuit Oziam.*

55. Hic est duplex quaestio. Lucas enim computando generationem Christi ascendit per Nathan; Matthaeus autem descendendo procedit a David ad Christum per Salomonem: unde videtur esse quaedam contrarietas.

Sed dicendum, sicut dictum est, Lucas in genealogia Christi ponit multos patres, qui non fuerunt patres carnalis originis per propagationem, sed secundum legalem adoptionem; Matthaeus autem nullum ponit, qui non fuerit pater carnalis.

Et verum est quod secundum carnem Dominus descendit a David per Salomonem, et non per Nathan; et tamen, secundum Augustinum, non vacat mysterio quod Matthaeus a David per Salomonem descendit ad Christum, Lucas autem a Christo ad David per Nathan ascendit. Matthaeus enim generationem Christi carnalem susceperat describendam, secundum quam Christus usque ad similitudinem carnis peccati descendit: et ideo recte Matthaeus in eius generatione a David per Salomonem descendit, cum cuius matre ipse David peccavit;

54. The series of the genealogy of the fathers which ran through the patriarchs having been set down, here he sets down the series of the fathers which proceeds through the kings. And it is divided into two parts.

First, he sets down the kings who were born from Israel, without mixture of alien seed; second, he sets down the kings who came from a foreign marriage, at *Joram begot Ozias.*

55. Here there is a twofold question. For Luke, working out the generation of Christ, ascends through Nathan; but Matthew, descending, proceeds from David to Christ through Solomon. Hence there seems to be a certain contrariety.

But one should say, as was said before, that Luke places many fathers in Christ's genealogy who were not fathers according to fleshly origin, through propogation, but according to legal adoption; but Matthew set down no one who was not a father according to the flesh.

And it is true that, according to the flesh, the Lord descended from David through Solomon, and not through Nathan; and nevertheless, according to Augustine, it is not an empty mystery that Matthew descends from David to Christ through Solomon, while Luke ascends from Christ to David through Nathan. For Matthew undertook to describe the fleshly generation of Christ, according to which Christ descended even to the likeness of the body of sin (Rom 8:3); and so Matthew rightly descends from David through Solomon in his generation, with whose mother

Lucas autem, qui maxime commendare intendit in Christo sacerdotalem dignitatem, per quam fuit peccatorum expiatio, recte per Nathan ad David ascendit, qui fuit vir sanctus.

Nota tamen quod secundum eumdem Augustinum in libro *Retractationum*, non est intelligendum quod idem fuit Nathan propheta, qui eum reprehendit, et filius quem genuit; sed solum quod fuerunt similes in nomine.

56. Secundo quaeritur quare Bersabee non nominatur ex nomine, sicut Thamar, Rahab et Ruth.

Et dicendum, quod aliae, quamvis per aliquod tempus fuerint peccatrices, tamen postea fuerunt conversae et poenitentes; haec autem turpiter peccavit crimen adulterii et in consensu homicidii: et ideo propter verecundiam subticetur eius nomen.

57. Nota tamen quod in Scriptura recitantur aliquando peccata magnorum, sicut David et aliorum; et hoc, quia diabolus non solum parvos et inferiores, sed etiam magnos prostravit: adversarius enim noster est. Et ideo propter cautelam recitantur, ut qui stat videat ne cadat.

Alia ratio est, ne aliquis putaret eos plusquam homines esse. Si enim aliquis solam in eis perfectionem consideraret, decipi posset per idololatriam; sed cum videt eos per peccatum corruisse, non credit iam aliquid amplius ab homine in eis esse.

58. Nota etiam hoc, secundum Gregorium, quod aliquando factum litterale est malum et significatum est bonum; aliquando vero factum bonum et significatum malum.

Urias enim fuit vir bonus et iustus, nec de aliquo in Scriptura reprehenditur; et tamen significat diabolum. Bersabee autem fuit peccatrix; et tamen rem bonam significat, scilicet Ecclesiam, ut notat Glossa II Reg. XII, et etiam Glossa quae dicitur exponere figuram secundum sensum allegoricum.

Urias enim interpretatur 'lux mea Deus', et significat diabolum, qui lucem divinitatis appetivit; Isa. XIV, 14: *ero similis Altissimo*. Bersabee interpretatur 'puteus septem', vel 'puteus societatis'; et significat Ecclesiam de gentibus, propter septiformem gratiam baptismalem. Hanc sibi desponsaverat primo diabolus; sed David, idest Christus, abstulit eam ab eo, et copulavit sibi, et ipsum diabolum interfecit. Aliter Bersabee significat legem, per cuius vias populus inductus est, qui non vult ingredi in domum per spiritualem intelligentiam, et ideo defert litteras mortis suae, quia *littera occidit*, II Cor. III, 6. Sed David, idest Christus, abstulit a Iudaeis legem, quando docuit eam spiritualiter intelligendam.

59. *Salomon autem genuit Roboam* et cetera. Sicut autem David interpretatur 'manu fortis', vel 'aspectu

David sinned; but Luke, who aimed most of all at the priestly dignity of Christ, through which the expiation of sins came about, rightly ascends to David through Nathan, who was a holy man.

But note that according to the same Augustine in the *Book of Retractions*, one should not understand that Nathan the prophet, who reproached him, and the son whom he bore were the same man, but only that they were alike in name.

56. Second, it is asked why Bethsabee is not named by her name, the way Thamar, Rahab, and Ruth were.

And one should say that the others, although they may have been sinners for some time, still afterwards they were converted and repentant; this one, however, basely sinned in the crime of adultery and in consent to a murder; and so her name is veiled for modesty's sake.

57. Yet notice that in Scripture the sins of the great are sometimes recounted, like those of David and of others; and this is because the devil overthrows not only the small and lesser, but even the great, for he is our adversary. And so they are recounted for caution's sake, that he who stands may watch lest he fall.

Another reason is so that no one will think them to be more than men. For if someone were to contemplate only the perfection in them, he could be deceived through idolatry; but when he sees them fall through sin, then he does not believe that there is anything more than man in them.

58. Note this also, according to Gregory: sometimes a thing done literally is bad and the thing signified is good; while sometimes the thing done is good and the thing signified is bad.

For Urias was a good man and just, nor was he blamed for anything in Scripture; and yet he signifies the devil. Bethsabee was a sinner, and yet she signifies a good thing, namely the Church, as the Gloss notes on 2 Samuel 12, and also the Gloss which is said to explain the figure according to the allegorical sense.

For Urias is interpreted as 'God my light', and signifies the devil, who desired the light of divinity; *I will be like the Most High* (Isa 14:14). Bethsabee is interpreted as 'seven wells', or 'the well of society'; and she signifies the Church, gathered from the gentiles, because of the sevenfold grace of baptism. She first espoused herself to the devil; but David, i.e., Christ, took her away from him, and joined her to himself, and killed the devil. In another way, Bethsabee signifies the law, through whose paths the people were brought in, who did not wish to enter into the house through spiritual understanding, and therefore carried the letter of their own death, because *the letter kills* (2 Cor 3:6). But David, i.e., Christ, took the law away from the Jews, when he taught that it should be understood spiritually.

59. *And Solomon begot Roboam.* Now, as David is interpreted 'strong of hand', or 'desirable in appearance', so

desiderabilis,' ita Salomon 'pacificus': et hoc est rectum, quia ex fortitudine operationis bonae provenit pax conscientiae; Ps. CXVIII, 165: *pax multa diligentibus legem tuam.* Contingit autem quod ex pace conscientiae homo velit alios ad bonum venire.

Unde **Salomon genuit Roboam**, qui interpretatur 'impetus': quia impetu praedicationis movetur, habens pacem conscientiae ad dilatandum nomen Christi; sicut legitur de apostolis, Is. XXVII, 6: *qui ingrediuntur impetu ad Iacob, florebit et germinabit Israel, et implebunt faciem orbis semine.*

Utrumque autem significat Christum, quia ipse est pax. Item ipse Roboam, qui populum impetu praedicationis convertit.

60. Roboam autem genuit Abiam, qui interpretatur 'pater Deus': quia ex hoc quod homo studet ad profectum aliorum spiritualem, vel corporalem per opera misericordiae, efficitur dignus paternitate Dei, ut infra V, 44: **benefacite his qui oderunt vos, ut sitis filii Patris vestri, qui in caelis est** et cetera. Et Luc. VI, 36: *estote misericordes.*

Hoc etiam competit Christo, cui dicitur: *ego ero illi in Patrem, et ipse erit mihi in Filium.*

61. Abias autem genuit Asa, qui interpretatur 'attollens': quia quandoque homo ex hoc quod efficitur pater et superior aliorum, incurrit quamdam negligentiam securitatis; ideo **Abias genuit Asa**, ut scilicet homo sit in continuo profectu, et attollat se semper ad maiora.

Hoc etiam competit Christo, qui dicitur 'attollens,' idest crescens; Luc. II, 40: *puer autem crescebat.* Vel 'attollens,' quia abstulit peccata mundi.

62. Asa autem genuit Iosaphat, qui interpretatur 'iudicans,' quia ex hoc quod semper crescit homo spiritualis, efficitur iudicans; I Cor. II, 15: *spiritualis homo omnia diiudicat.*

Et hoc Christo competit, quia *Pater omne iudicium dedit Filio.*

63. Iosaphat autem genuit Ioram, qui interpretatur 'habitans in excelsis'; quia ille qui iudex constituitur, debet in excelsis habitare; Isa. XXXIII, 16: *iste in excelsis habitabit.* Quomodo autem hoc sit, dicit Apostolus: *nostra conversatio in caelis est.*

Et hoc competit Christo, quia *excelsus super omnes gentes dominus*, Psal. CXII, 4.

64. Ioram autem genuit Oziam. Hic est quaestio litteralis. Nam I Par. III, 11 dicitur quod Ioram genuit Ochoziam. Ochozias autem genuit Ioram. Ioras autem genuit Amasiam, qui et Azarias dicitur. Amasias autem genuit Oziam. In duobus ergo videtur Evangelista

Solomon is interpreted 'peaceful': and this is right, because out of the strength of good works comes peace of conscience; *much peace have they who love your law* (Ps 118:165). Now, it happens that out of peace of conscience a man wishes others to come to the good.

Hence **Solomon begot Roboam**, who is interpreted 'force', because the one who has peace of conscience is moved by the force of preaching to spread the name of Christ; as is written about the apostles: *when they will rush in unto Jacob, Israel will blossom and bud, and they will fill the face of the world with seed* (Isa 27:6).

Moreover, either name signifies Christ, who is himself peace. Similarly, he who converted the people by the force of preaching is himself Roboam.

60. And Roboam begot Abia, who is interpreted 'God the Father'; because by the fact that a man is eager for the spiritual profit of others, or for the corporeal profit of others through works of mercy, he is made worthy of the fatherhood of God, as is said below: **pray for those who persecute and calumniate you: that you may be the children of your Father who is in heaven** (Matt 5:44). And: *be therefore merciful, as your Father also is merciful* (Luke 6:36).

This also belongs to Christ, to whom it is said: *I will be to him a Father, and he will be to me a Son* (Heb 1:5).

61. And Abia begot Asa, who is interpreted 'lifting up'; because sometimes by the fact that a man is made a father and superior to others, he falls into a certain negligence out of security; this is why **Abia begot Asa**, that is, in order that a man may be continually perfected, and lift himself up toward greater things.

This also belongs to Christ, who is called 'one lifting up', i.e., growing; *and the child grew* (Luke 2:40). Or 'one lifting up', because he lifts away the sins of the world.

62. And Asa begot Josaphat, who is interpreted 'one judging', because when a man is always growing spiritually, he is made one who judges; *but the spiritual man judges all things* (1 Cor 2:15).

And this belongs to Christ, because *the Father has given all judgment to the Son* (John 5:22).

63. And Josaphat begot Joram, who is interpreted, 'one dwelling on high', because he who is made a judge ought to dwell on high; *he will dwell on high* (Isa 33:16). And the Apostle says how this should be: *but our conversation is in heaven* (Phil 3:20).

And this belongs to Christ, because he is *high above all nations* (Ps 112:4).

64. And Joram begot Ozias. Here there is a literal question. For it is said that Joram begot Ochozias (1 Chr 3:11). Now Ochozias begot Joas, and Joas begot Amasias, who is also called Azarias. And Amasias begot Ozias. So the Evangelist seems to have been mistaken in two things. First,

in genealogiae serie defecisse. Primo quia Ioram non genuit Oziam, sed Amasiam; secundo, quia omisit tres generationes.

Et dicendum ad primum, quod generare aliquem alium potest intelligi dupliciter, mediate vel immediate: immediate, sicut pater carnalis immediate generat filium; et sic Ioram non genuit Oziam. Alio modo mediate, sicut nos dicimur *filii Adam*; et sic filius potest dici genitus ab avo vel proavo, quia ab ipso per generationem mediatam descendit.

65. Quare autem omisit tres reges, triplex ratio assignatur. Prima a Hieronymo; qui dicit, sicut scriptum est Exod. XX, 5, *Dominus visitat peccata patrum in tertiam et quartam generationem, his qui patrum sceleris efficiuntur imitatores.* Ioram autem duxit uxorem filiam Iezabel, scilicet Athaliam, quae traxit eum ad idololatriam. Ochozias etiam magis quam pater idololatriae deditus fuit. Et similiter Ioras, qui cum scelere idololatriae etiam Zachariam filium Ioiadae occidit: et ideo isti tres quasi indigni excluduntur a generatione Christi.

Chrysostomus aliam assignat rationem. Praecepit enim Dominus IV Reg. IX Iehu filio Nansi, quod ipse extirparet domum Achab, qui diligens fuit in executione praecepti, et tamen a cultura deorum non recessit: adoravit enim vitulos conflatiles. Et quia diligenter perfecit Domini imperium destruendo domum Achab, dictum est ad eum, quod filii eius usque in quartam generationem sederent super thronum domus Israel; unde sicut Iehu meruit regnum Israel usque in tertiam vel quartam generationem, ita per oppositum Ioram, qui commiscuit se feminis gentilibus, et transtulit iniquitatem domus Israel ad domum Iuda, debuit amittere nomen posteritatis in genealogia Christi usque in quartam generationem, facta expiatione peccati.

Augustinus in *Quaest. Novi et Vet. Test.* aliam assignat rationem. Dicit enim, quod quidam fuerunt boni, et bonos invenerunt patres, sicut Isaac et Iacob; quidam mali, et tamen bonos invenerunt patres, sicut Salomon, qui peccator fuit, et tamen David virum iustum et sanctum habuit patrem; quidam nec boni fuerunt, nec bonos patres habuerunt, sicut fuerunt isti tres, ut patet per praedicta. Ioram peccavit, et peccatum eius continuatum fuit usque ad Oziam, qui pene nihil mali fecit, nisi quod incensum adolevit; continuatio autem peccati causa vel ratio est destructionis. Et ideo isti tres qui in peccato idololatriae permanserunt, excluduntur a genealogia Christi.

66. Ratio autem mystice assignatur propter tres quaterdenarios, per quos Matthaeus genealogiam Christi describere intendit. Ozias autem interpretatur 'robustus Domini'; et signat Christum, de quo in Psal. CXVII, 14:

because Joram did not beget Ozias, but rather Amasias did; second, because he omits three generations.

And with regard to the first difficulty, one should say that for someone to beget someone can be understood in two ways, mediately and immediately: immediately, as a fleshly father immediately begets his son; and in this way Joram did not beget Ozias. In another way mediately, as we are called *sons of Adam*; and in this way a son can be said to be begotten by his grandfather or his great grandfather, because he descended from him through an intermediate generation.

65. And as to why he omits three kings, three reasons can be given. First, by Jerome, who says, as it is also written: *the Lord visits the sins of the fathers on the third and the fourth generation, on those who are made imitaters of their fathers' crimes* (Exod 20:5). Now, Joram took as a wife the daughter of Jezabel, namely Athalia, who drew him into idolatry. Ochozias was given to idolatry even more than his father. And likewise with Joas, who along with the crime of idolatry also killed Zacharias the son of Joiada; and for this reason these three are excluded from the Christ's generation, as though unworthy.

Chrysostom gives another reason. For the Lord commanded Jehu the son of Namsi to wipe out the house of Achab (2 Kgs 9); he was diligent in carrying out the command, but still he did not withdraw from the worship of the gods, for he adored molten bulls. And because he diligently performed the command of the Lord by destroying the house of Achab, he was told that his sons would sit on the throne of Israel until the fourth generation; hence as Jehu merited the kingdom of Israel until the third or fourth generation, so in the opposite way Joram, who mixed himself with gentile women, and carried the iniquity of the house of Israel over into the house of Judah, had to lose the name of his posterity in Christ's genealogy until the fourth generation, expiation for the sin having then been made.

Augustine gives another reason in *Questions on the Old and New Testaments*. For he says that some men were good, and had good men as fathers, like Isaac and Jacob; some men were evil, and yet had good men as fathers, like Solomon, who was a sinner, and yet had David as a father, a man just and holy; some men were neither good nor had good men as fathers, as were these three, as is clear from what has been said. Joram sinned, and his sin was continued until Ozias, who did almost nothing bad, except that he burned incense; but the continuation of sin is the cause or reason for destruction. And so these three who persisted in the sin of idolatry are excluded from Christ's genealogy.

66. Moreover, mystically, a reason is given on account of the three fourteens, through which Matthew intended to trace out the genealogy of Christ. Now, Ozias is interpreted 'strong one of the Lord'; and he signifies Christ, of

fortitudo mea, et laus Dominus, factus est mihi in salutem et cetera. Mystice autem **Ioram genuit Oziam**, quia qui in excelso habitant, debent esse fortiter operantes.

67. Nota quod sub hoc Ozia prophetavit Isaias, ut patet Isa. I, 1. Propter enim peccatum principum, et regum, et etiam populi, abstulit Deus prophetiam et doctrinam; unde sub rege bono coepit iterum emanatio prophetiae.

68. *Ozias autem genuit Ioatham*, qui interpretatur 'profectus'; et significat Christum, per quem Ecclesia proficit quotidie. Et sic bene **Ozias genuit Ioatham** quia qui fortiter operantur, sunt in continuo profectu; Psalmi LXXXIII, 8: *ibunt de virtute in virtutem.*

69. *Ioatham autem genuit Achaz*, qui interpretatur 'comprehendens'; quia per continuum profectum virtutum venit homo ad cognitionem Dei; Ps. CXVIII, 104: *a mandatis tuis intellexi, propterea odivi omnem viam iniquitatis*; Ps. LXIII, 10: *annuntiaverunt opera Dei, ostendendo in opere, et facta eius intellexerunt.* Propter quod Paulus ad Philippenses III, 12: *sequor, si quo modo comprehendam, in quo et comprehensus sum a Christo Iesu.* Et hoc competit Christo, qui solus perfecte divinitatem comprehendit; Lc. X, 22: *nemo novit Patrem nisi Filius.*

70. *Achaz autem genuit Ezechiam*, idest 'fortis Dominus': quia talis habet fortitudinem a Domino; II regum XXII, 2: *Dominus fortitudo mea, et robur meum.* Et hoc competit Christo, *qui fortis est in praelio.*

71. *Ezechias autem genuit Manassen*, et interpretatur 'oblivio': quia qui iam perfecte Deum cognoscit, istorum temporalium obliviscitur; Ps. XLIV, 11: *obliviscere populum tuum, et domum patris tui*; Gen. XLI, 51: *oblivisci me fecit dominus Deus omnium laborum meorum.*

Et hoc Christo convenit, de quo dicitur Ez. XVIII, 21: *si impius egerit poenitentiam ab omnibus peccatis suis, quae operatus est, omnium iniquitatum eius, quas operatus est, non recordabor.*

72. *Manasses autem genuit Amon*, idest 'fidelis' et 'nutriens': quia vere est ille fidelis qui contemnit temporalia. Secundum enim Gregorium, fraus est filia avaritiae: et ideo qui temporalia perfecte contemnit, iam non curat de infidelitate. Unde recte **Manasses genuit Amon**. Hoc etiam interpretatur 'nutriens': quia qui temporalia contemnit, debet inde nutrire pauperes per misericordiam; infra XIX, 21: *si vis perfectus esse, vade, et vende omnia quae habes*, ecce contemptus, *et da pauperibus*, ecce nutrimentum.

Hoc autem Christo competit, qui vere fidelis est, Ps. CXLIV, 13: *fidelis Dominus in omnibus verbis suis*, et iterum nutritius, Os. XI, 3: *ego qui nutritius Ephraim*,

whom it is said: *the Lord is my strength and my praise: and he is become my salvation* (Ps 117:14). Further, **Joram begot Ozias** mystically, because he who dwells on high ought to work strongly.

67. Note that Isaiah prophesied under Ozias, as is clear from: *the vision of Isaiah the son of Amos, which he saw concerning Judah and Jerusalem in the days of Ozias, Joathan, Achaz, and Ezechias, kings of Judah* (Isa 1:1). For owing to the sin of the princes, and the kings, and even the people, God took away prophecy and teaching; hence under a good king the flow of prophecy began again.

68. *And Ozias begot Joatham*, who is interpreted 'advance'; and he signifies Christ, through whom the Church makes advances daily. And thus well did **Ozias beget Joatham**, because he who works strongly is continually advancing; *they will go from virtue to virtue* (Ps 83:8).

69. *And Joatham begot Achaz*, who is interpreted as 'one who comprehends'; because through unceasing advance in virtue a man comes to the knowledge of God; *by your commandments I have had understanding: therefore have I hated every way of iniquity* (Ps 118:104); *and they declared the works of God: and understood his doings* (Ps 63:10). On account of which Paul says: *I follow after, if I may by any means apprehend, wherein I am also apprehended by Christ Jesus* (Phil 3:12). And this belongs to Christ, who alone perfectly comprehends the divinity; Matt 11:27, *Neither does any one know the Father, but the Son.*

70. *And Achaz begot Ezechias*, that is, 'strong one of the Lord'; because such a one has strength from the Lord; *the Lord is my rock, and my strength, and my savior* (2 Sam 22:2). And this belongs to Christ, *who is strong in battle* (Ps 23:8).

71. *And Ezechias begot Manasses*, and he is interpreted 'forgetfulness', because he who knows God perfectly is forgetful of temporal things; *forget your people and your father's house* (Ps 44:11); *and he called the name of the first born Manasses, saying, God has made me to forget all my labors, and my father's house* (Gen 41:51).

And this belongs to Christ, of whom it is said: *but if the wicked does penance for all his sins which he has committed . . . I will not remember all his iniquities that he has done* (Ezek 18:21–22).

72. *And Manesses begot Amon*, i.e., 'faithful' and 'nourisher'; because he is truly faithful who despises temporal things. For according to Gregory, fraud is the daughter of avarice, and so he who perfectly despises temporal things no longer wishes to be unfaithful. Hence it is right that **Manesses begot Amon**. He is also interpreted as 'nourisher' because he who despises temporal things ought from there to nourish the poor out of mercy; below: **if you will be perfect, go sell what you have**, behold, the contempt, **and give to the poor**, behold, the nourishment (Matt 19:21).

And this belongs to Christ, who is truly faithful: *the Lord is faithful in all his words* (Ps 144:13), and likewise a nourisher: *and I was like a nourisher to Ephraim, I carried*

portabam eos in brachiis meis, et nescierunt quod curarem eos; infra XXIII, 37: **quoties volui congregare filios tuos quemadmodum gallinae congregant pullos suos sub alas, et noluisti?**

73. **Amon autem genuit Iosiam**, qui interpretatur 'salus Domini', vel 'incensum'; quia ex hoc consequitur homo salutem, quod etiam temporalia obliviscitur et largitur, sive distribuit. Vel 'incensum'.

Hoc competit Christo; Ps. LXXIII, 12: *qui operatus est salutem in medio terrae, et se obtulit sacrificium Deo in odorem suavitatis*, Eph. V, 2.

74. **Iosias autem genuit Iechoniam et fratres eius**, qui interpretatur 'praeparatio Domini', vel 'resurrectio'; et significat Christum, qui praeparavit nobis locum, Ioan. XIV, 2, et qui dicit Ioan. XI, 25: *ego sum resurrectio et vita*, et per hanc venimus ad resurrectionem.

75. Hic autem triplex est quaestio secundum litteram. Primo quaeritur, quomodo dicatur Iosias genuisse Iechoniam; et tamen non ipsum, sed patrem eius Ioakim genuit.

Et ad hoc est duplex responsio. Secundum enim Chrysostomum, cui consentit Augustinus, nomen Ioakim praetermittitur omnino; et hoc quia non per divinam ordinationem regnavit, sed per Pharaonis potentiam, qui ipsum in regno instituit, incarcerato primogenito fratre eius Ioathan, qui regnaverat ante eum. Et ad hoc nota historiam IV Reg. XXII, et II Paral. XXXVI, 1 ss. Habuit etiam Iosias tres filios, Ioathan, Ioakim, qui et Eliacim, et Sedeciam. Si enim, ut dicit Augustinus, illi tres reges removentur de genealogia, quia per idololatriae depravati sunt, quanto magis iste, qui non per Deum, vel prophetam, sed per gentilis hominis positionem institutus est in regno?

Sententia est non verba Hieronymi, ut vult et ei consentit Ambrosius, quod uterque dictus est Ioakim, et ille qui ponitur in fine quaterdenarii, et qui ponitur in principio tertii, et uterque Iechonias et Ioakim idem sunt. Unde notandum, quod Iosias tres habuit filios, Ioakim, qui et Eliacim, Ioathan, et Sedeciam. Mortuo autem Iosia regnavit pro eo Ioathas, medius scilicet filius; quo capto a Pharaone rege Aegypti, et incarcerato, constituit fratrem eius primogenitum Ioakim regem, imponens ei tributum; postea Nabuchodonosor rex Babylonis, superato rege Aegypti, obsedit Ierusalem, et cepit Ioakim, quem sub tributo remisit in Ierusalem. Postea autem cum vellet Ioakim rebellare contra regem Babylonis, confisus de auxilio regis Aegypti, ascendit Nabuchodonosor Ierusalem, et cepit eum, et occidit, et constituit filium eius pro eo Ioachim, quem et Iechoniam nominavit nomine patris; quo facto timens Nabuchodonosor, ne iste memor mortis patris confoederaretur cum rege Aegypti, rediit in Ierusalem, et obsedit eam; et Iechonias, vel Ioakim iste, filius scilicet alterius, de consilio Ieremiae tradidit se

them in my arms: and they knew not that I healed them (Hos 11:3); and below: **how often would I have gathered together your children, as the hen gathers her chickens under her wings, and you would not?** (Matt 23:37).

73. **And Amon begot Josias**, who is interpreted as 'health of the Lord', or 'incense'; because a man obtains health from the fact that that he is forgetful of temporal things and gives or distributes them freely. Or 'incense'.

This belongs to Christ: *he has wrought salvation in the midst of the earth* (Ps 73:12); *and he offered himself as a sacrifice to God in the odor of sweetness* (Eph 5:2).

74. **And Josias begot Jechonias and his brethren**, who is interpreted as 'the preparation of the Lord', or 'the resurrection'; and he signifies Christ, who prepared a place for us (John 14:2), and who said: *I am the resurrection and the life* (John 11:25), and through him we come to the resurrection.

75. Now there are three questions here according to the letter. First, it is asked how Josias is said to have begotten Jechonias; and yet he did not beget Jechonias himself, but rather begot his father Joakim.

And to this there are two responses. For according to Chrysostom, with whom Augustine agrees, the name Joakim is omitted altogether; and this is because he did not reign by divine ordination, but through the power of Pharaoh, who established him in the kingdom, his first-born brother Joathas who reigned before him having been thrown in prison. And note the history about this (2 Kgs 22; 2 Chr 36). Josias also had three sons: Joathas, Joakim, who was also called Eliakim, and Sedecias. For if, as Augustine says, those three kings were removed from the genealogy because they were corrupted by idolotry, how much more this man, who was not established in the kingdom by God, or by a prophet, but was placed there by a gentile man?

This opinion is not what Jerome says, since he would have it, and Ambrose agrees with him, that both are called Joakim, both he who is placed at the end of the fourteen, and he who is placed in the beginning of the third, and that both Jechonias and Joakim are the same. Hence one should note that Josias had three sons: Joakim, who was also called Eliakim, Joathas, and Sedecias. Josias having died, Joathas reigned in his stead, that is, the middle son. When he was captured by Pharaoh the king of Egypt and thrown in prison, Pharaoh established his brother Joakim, the first-born, as king, imposing a tribute on him. Later, Nabuchodonosor the king of Babylon, having defeated the king of Egypt, laid siege to Jerusalem, and captured Joachim, whom he released into Jerusalem under tribute. But later, when Joakim wished to rebel against the king of Babylon, relying on the help of the king of Egypt, Nabuchodonosor went up to Jerusalem and captured and killed him, and established his son Joachim in his stead, whom he named Jechonias as well, with the name of his father. After he had done this, Nabuchodonosor, fearing that he would remember his

regi Nabuchodonosor, et uxorem, et filios; et isti proprie dicuntur transmigrasse in transmigrationem. Nabuchodonosor vero constituit regem eius Sedeciam fratrem patris eius, et ipsum Ioachim duxit in Babylonem; et ille est de quo dicitur post: ***et post transmigrationem***.

76. Sed quare nominatus est Iechonias, cum nomen eius fuerit Ioachim?

Et dicendum, quod istud nomen impositum fuit a propheta, scilicet Ieremia; Ier. XXII, 24: *haec dicit Dominus: si fuerit Iechonias filius Ioakim regis Iuda, annulus in manu dextera mea, inde evellam eum*; et infra: *numquid vas fictile atque contritum vir iste Iechonias?* Et ideo potius nominatur ab Evangelista tali nomine, ut ostendatur Evangelistam concordare cum propheta.

77. Nota etiam quod quamvis idem sit nomen, diversimode tamen scribitur. Primi enim Ioakim nomen scribitur per 'k', et videtur dici *Ioakim*; sed secundi scribitur per ghimel, unde dicitur *Ioachim*: et ideo diversas habent interpretationes. Primum enim interpretatur 'resurrectio'; secundum vero 'praeparatio Domini.'

78. Secundo quaeritur quare dicitur ***Iechoniam et fratres eius***. Multi enim fuerunt de regibus qui fratres habuerunt, sed numquam dicitur, vel fit mentio de fratribus.

Et dicendum, secundum Ambrosium, quod ubicumque fit mentio de fratribus, sicut cum dicitur ***Iudam et fratres eius, et Phares et Zaram de Thamar***, hoc significat quod aequales fuerunt in sanctitate, vel malitia. Isti autem tres omnes sunt mali.

Aliter potest dici, quod ideo quia istorum fratrum quilibet regnavit, sicut patet per ea quae dicta sunt, sic autem non fuit de fratribus aliorum regum.

79. Tertio quaeritur de hoc quod dicitur in transmigratione. Videtur falsum, quia Iosias numquam transmigravit.

Et dicendum hoc accipiendum esse secundum praescientiam divinam, secundum quam ordinatum erat eos quos tunc generabat, transmigrandos esse. Vel dicendum, quod *in transmigratione* idem est ac prope transmigrationem, sive iam imminente.

father's death and make an alliance with the king of Egypt, returned to Jerusalem and besieged her; and Jechonias, or Joachim, namely the son of the other, gave himself up to Nabuchodonosor on the advice of Jeremiah, together with his wife and children; and these are properly said to have transmigrated in the transmigration. But Nabuchodonosor established Sedecias the brother of his father as his king, and led Joachim himself into Babylon; and it is he of whom it is said afterwards: ***and after the transmigration*** (Matt 1:12).

76. But why was he named Jechonias, since his name was Joachim?

And one should say that this name was given by a prophet, namely by Jeremiah; *as I live, says the Lord, if Jechonias the son of Joakim the king of Judah were a ring on my right hand, I would pluck him thence* (Jer 22:24); and below: *is this man Jechonias an earthen and a broken vessel?* (Jer 22:28). And so the Evangelist prefers to name him this way, so that the Evangelist might be seen to be in harmony with the prophet.

77. Notice also that although the name is the same, still it is written in different ways. For the name of the first Joakim is written with a 'k', and seems to be said *Joakim*; but the name of the second is written with a ghimel, and hence is said *Joachim*; and so they have different interpretations. For the first is interpreted as 'the resurrection', the second as 'the preparation of the Lord'.

78. Second, it is asked why it says, ***Jechonias and his brethren***. For there were many of the kings who had brothers, but it never speaks or makes mention of the brothers.

And one should say, according to Ambrose, that wherever mention is made of brothers, as when it says, ***Judas and his brethren***, and ***Phares and Zara of Thamar***, this indicates that they were equal in sanctity or wickedness. Now, these three were wicked.

In another way, one can say that it is because each of these brothers reigned, as is clear from what has been said, but this was not the case with the brothers of the other kings.

79. Third, there is a question concerning what is said about the deportation. It seems to be false, because Josias was never deported.

And one should say that this should be taken according to God's foreknowledge, according to which it had been ordained that those who were begotten at that time should be deported. Or, one should say that ***after the transmigration*** is the same as near the deportation, or with the deportation already drawing near.

Lecture 4

1:12 Et post transmigrationem Babylonis Iechonias genuit Salathihel. Salathihel autem genuit Zorobabel. [n. 80]

1:13 Zorobabel autem genuit Abiud. Abiud autem genuit Eliacim. Eliacim autem genuit Azor. [n. 84]

1:14 Azor autem genuit Sadoch. Sadoch autem genuit Achim. Achim autem genuit Eliud. [n. 85]

1:15 Eliud autem genuit Eleazar. Eleazar autem genuit Mathan. Mathan autem genuit Iacob. [n. 86]

1:16 Iacob autem genuit Ioseph virum Mariae, de qua natus est Iesus, qui vocatur Christus. [n. 92]

1:17 Omnes itaque generationes ab Abraham usque ad David generationes quatuordecim, et a David usque ad transmigrationem Babylonis generationes quatuordecim, et a transmigratione Babylonis usque ad Christum generationes quatuordecim. [n. 98]

1:18 Christi autem generatio sic erat. Cum esset desponsata mater eius Maria Ioseph antequam convenirent, inventa est in utero habens de Spiritu Sancto. [n. 102]

1:19 Ioseph autem vir eius, cum esset iustus, et nollet eam traducere, voluit occulte dimittere eam. [n. 114]

1:20 Haec autem eo cogitante, ecce angelus Domini in somnis apparuit ei dicens: Ioseph fili David noli timere accipere Mariam coniugem tuam; quod enim in ea natum est, de Spiritu Sancto est. [n. 119]

1:21 Pariet autem filium, et vocabis nomen eius Iesum. Ipse enim salvum faciet populum suum a peccatis eorum. [n. 134]

1:12 Μετὰ δὲ τὴν μετοικεσίαν Βαβυλῶνος Ἰεχονίας ἐγέννησεν τὸν Σαλαθιήλ, Σαλαθιὴλ δὲ ἐγέννησεν τὸν Ζοροβαβέλ,

1:13 Ζοροβαβὲλ δὲ ἐγέννησεν τὸν Ἀβιούδ, Ἀβιοὺδ δὲ ἐγέννησεν τὸν Ἐλιακίμ, Ἐλιακὶμ δὲ ἐγέννησεν τὸν Ἀζώρ,

1:14 Ἀζὼρ δὲ ἐγέννησεν τὸν Σαδώκ, Σαδὼκ δὲ ἐγέννησεν τὸν Ἀχίμ, Ἀχὶμ δὲ ἐγέννησεν τὸν Ἐλιούδ,

1:15 Ἐλιοὺδ δὲ ἐγέννησεν τὸν Ἐλεάζαρ, Ἐλεάζαρ δὲ ἐγέννησεν τὸν Ματθάν, Ματθὰν δὲ ἐγέννησεν τὸν Ἰακώβ,

1:16 Ἰακὼβ δὲ ἐγέννησεν τὸν Ἰωσὴφ τὸν ἄνδρα Μαρίας, ἐξ ἧς ἐγεννήθη Ἰησοῦς ὁ λεγόμενος χριστός.

1:17 Πᾶσαι οὖν αἱ γενεαὶ ἀπὸ Ἀβραὰμ ἕως Δαυὶδ γενεαὶ δεκατέσσαρες, καὶ ἀπὸ Δαυὶδ ἕως τῆς μετοικεσίας Βαβυλῶνος γενεαὶ δεκατέσσαρες, καὶ ἀπὸ τῆς μετοικεσίας Βαβυλῶνος ἕως τοῦ Χριστοῦ γενεαὶ δεκατέσσαρες.

1:18 Τοῦ δὲ Ἰησοῦ Χριστοῦ ἡ γένεσις οὕτως ἦν. μνηστευθείσης τῆς μητρὸς αὐτοῦ Μαρίας τῷ Ἰωσήφ, πρὶν ἢ συνελθεῖν αὐτοὺς εὑρέθη ἐν γαστρὶ ἔχουσα ἐκ πνεύματος ἁγίου.

1:19 Ἰωσὴφ δὲ ὁ ἀνὴρ αὐτῆς, δίκαιος ὢν καὶ μὴ θέλων αὐτὴν δειγματίσαι, ἐβουλήθη λάθρᾳ ἀπολῦσαι αὐτήν.

1:20 ταῦτα δὲ αὐτοῦ ἐνθυμηθέντος ἰδοὺ ἄγγελος κυρίου κατ᾽ ὄναρ ἐφάνη αὐτῷ λέγων· Ἰωσὴφ υἱὸς Δαυίδ, μὴ φοβηθῇς παραλαβεῖν Μαρίαν τὴν γυναῖκά σου· τὸ γὰρ ἐν αὐτῇ γεννηθὲν ἐκ πνεύματός ἐστιν ἁγίου.

1:21 τέξεται δὲ υἱόν, καὶ καλέσεις τὸ ὄνομα αὐτοῦ Ἰησοῦν· αὐτὸς γὰρ σώσει τὸν λαὸν αὐτοῦ ἀπὸ τῶν ἁμαρτιῶν αὐτῶν.

1:12 And after the transmigration of Babylon, Jechonias begot Salathiel. And Salathiel begot Zorobabel. [n. 80]

1:13 And Zorobabel begot Abiud. And Abiud begot Eliacim. And Eliacim begot Azor. [n. 84]

1:14 And Azor begot Sadoc. And Sadoc begot Achim. And Achim begot Eliud. [n. 85]

1:15 And Eliud begot Eleazar. And Eleazar begot Mathan. And Mathan begot Jacob. [n. 86]

1:16 And Jacob begot Joseph the husband of Mary, of whom was born Jesus, who is called Christ. [n. 92]

1:17 So all the generations, from Abraham to David, are fourteen generations. And from David to the transmigration of Babylon are fourteen generations: and from the transmigration of Babylon to Christ are fourteen generations. [n. 98]

1:18 But the generation of Christ was thus: when his mother, Mary, was espoused to Joseph, before they came together, she was found with child, of the Holy Spirit. [n. 102]

1:19 Whereupon Joseph her husband, being a just man, and not willing to expose her publicly, wanted to put her away privately. [n. 114]

1:20 But while he thought on these things, behold the angel of the Lord appeared to him in his sleep, saying: Joseph, son of David, do not fear to take unto you Mary your wife, for he who is born in her, is of the Holy Spirit. [n. 119]

1:21 And she will bring forth a son: and you will call his name Jesus. For he will save his people from their sins. [n. 134]

80. Hic ponitur tertius quaterdenarius generationis Christi, qui procedit per personas privatas.

De isto Iechonia, sicut dictum est supra, fuit duplex opinio. Hieronymus enim et Ambrosius volunt quod alter fuerit ille qui ponitur in fine primi quaterdenarii et vocatus est *Ioakim*; alter vero qui dictus est *Ioachim*. Secundum vero Augustinum, ut supra.

Ista enim transmigratio filiorum Israel significat translationem fidei ad gentes; Act. XIII, v. 46: *vobis oportebat primum loqui verbum Dei*. In illa transmigratione facta est quasi quaedam reflexio Iudaeorum ad gentes. Unde quasi quidam constituitur angulus; et ideo Iechonias iste significat Christum, qui factus est lapis angularis, in seipso utrumque copulans populum, Iudaeorum et gentium; Ps. CXVII, v. 22: *lapidem quem reprobaverunt aedificantes, hic factus est in caput anguli*.

81. Sed hic quaeritur, Ier. XXII, 30 dicitur: *scribe virum istum*, Sedeciam, *virum sterilem, qui in diebus suis non prosperabitur; nec enim erit qui sedeat de semine eius super solium David*. Quomodo ergo dicitur Christus descendisse a David per Sedeciam, cum de Christo scripserit sic Is. IX, 2: *super solium David, et super regnum eius sedebit?*

Et dicendum, secundum Ambrosium, quod cum Christus dicitur sedere super solium, intelligitur de regno spirituali, non corporali, nisi inquantum per regnum David corporale significatur spirituale.

82. *Salathiel autem genuit Zorobabel*. Contra: I Paralipom. III, 17 dicitur, quod filii Iechoniae fuerunt Asir, Salathiel, et Melchiram, et Phadaia. Phadaia autem filios habuit Zorobabel, et Semei; de Abiud autem nulla prorsus fit ibi mentio. Ergo videtur, quod male dicit Evangelista, quod Salathiel genuit Zorobabel, et quod Zorobabel genuit Abiud.

Ad hoc tripliciter respondetur in Glossa. Una responsio, quod in libro Paralipomenon multa depravata sunt vitio scriptorum, praecipue de his quae pertinent ad numerum et ad nomina. Unde istis generationibus vitiatis prohibet Apostolus intendere, quae magis quaestionem quam utilitatem inducunt, I Tim. I, 4.

Alia est responsio, quod Salathiel binomius fuit: vocatus est enim Salathiel, et Caphadara; et ideo liber Paralipomenon dicit Zorobabel filium Capha, Evangelista vero filium Salathiel. Nulla est ergo contrarietas.

Tertia est responsio, et verior, quod Salathiel, et Caphadara fuerunt fratres, sicut dicit liber Paralipomenon. Caphadara autem genuit filium quem vocavit eodem nomine, scilicet Zorobabel, et iste genuit Abiud. Dicendum etiam quod liber Paralipomenon narrat genealogiam

80. Here he sets out the third fourteen of Christ's generation, which proceeds through private persons.

As was said above, there are two opinions about this man Jechonias. For Jerome and Ambrose would have it that there is one man who is placed in the end of the first fourteen and is called *Joakim*, and another who is called *Joachim*. According to Augustine, however, see above.

For the transmigration of the sons of Israel signifies the transfer of the faith to the gentiles; *to you it behoved us first to speak the word of God* (Acts 13:46). In the transmigration there happened so to speak a certain return of the Jews to the gentiles. Hence it was established as a certain corner, so to speak; and for this reason, this man Jechonias signifies Christ, who was made the cornerstone, joining in himself both peoples, the Jews and the gentiles; *the stone which the builders rejected; the same is become the head of the corner* (Ps 117:22).

81. But there is a question here: *write this man*, Sedecias, *barren, a man that will not prosper in his days: for there will not be a man of his seed that will sit upon the throne of David* (Jer 22:30). So how is Christ said to have descended from David through Sedecias, since it is written of Christ: *he will sit upon the throne of David, and upon his kingdom?* (Isa 9:2)

And one should say, according to Ambrose, that since Christ is said to sit above the throne, this is understood as concerning a spiritual kingdom, not a corporeal one, except insofar as the spiritual is signified through the corporeal kingdom of David.

82. *And Salathiel begot Zorobabel*. On the contrary: it is said that the sons of Jechonias were Asir, Salathiel, and Melchiram, and Phadaia (1 Chr 3:17). And Phadaia had sons, Zorobabel and Semei; but of Abiud no mention is made at all. So it seems that the Evangelist speaks badly, saying that Salathiel begot Zorobabel, and that Zorobabel begot Abiud.

The Gloss responds to this in three ways. One response is that in the book of Chronicles many things are corrupted by the fault of the scribes, and principally in those things which pertain to numbers and names. Hence the Apostle forbids any attention being given to those corrupted generations, which bring in more questions than usefulness (1 Tim 1:4).

There is another response, that Salathiel had two names; for he was called Salathiel and Caphadara; and hence the book of Chronicles calls Zorobabel the son of Capha, and the Evangelist calls him the son of Salathiel. Therefore there is no contrariety.

There is a third response, and a truer one, that Salathiel and Caphadara were brothers, as is said in the book of Chronicles. Now, Caphadara begot a son whom he named by the same name, i.e., Zorobabel, and this man begot Abiud. It should also be said that the Book of Chronicles tells

ipsius Capha; Evangelista generationem Salathiel, quia de eo erat Christus nasciturus.

83. Notandum autem quod de illis qui fuerunt ab Abiud usque ad Ioseph, nulla fit mentio in libris Sacrae Scripturae, sed ex annalibus Hebraeorum, quos Herodes pro magna parte comburi fecit ut occultaretur ignobilitas sui generis, accepta sunt. Patet littera.

84. Sensum mysticum prosequamur.

Nota ergo quod in hac parte genealogiae ponuntur tres ordines. Primus est ordo doctorum, et continet quatuor generationes.

Ante orationem enim requiritur praeparatio, secundum illud Eccli. XVIII, 23: *ante orationem praepara animam tuam*; et ideo de Iechonia, qui interpretatur 'praeparatio Domini', sequitur Salathiel, qui interpretatur 'petitio mea'; et designant Christum, qui in omnibus *exauditus est pro sua reverentia*, Hebr. V, 7.

Oratio autem debet praecedere doctrinam, secundum illud ad Eph. VI, 19: *orate, ut detur sermo in apertione oris mei*; et ideo Salathiel sequitur Zorobabel, qui interpretatur 'magister Babel', idest 'confusionis'; quia per doctrinam et praedicationem apostolorum revocatae sunt gentes ad Deum verum, et hoc fuit ad confusionem idololatriae; et hoc competit principaliter Christo, qui dicit: *vocatis me, magister, et domine, et bene dicitis*, Io. XIII, v. 13.

Per doctrinam autem, et praedicationem acquirit homo patris dignitatem; unde patres dicuntur eorum qui instruuntur spiritualiter; I Cor. IV, 15: *nam et si decem millia paedagogorum habeatis in Christo, sed non multos patres: in Christo enim Iesu per Evangelium filii sumus*. Et ideo sequitur **Zorobabel autem genuit Abiud**, qui interpretatur 'pater meus iste'; et hoc competit Christo; Ps. LXXXVIII, 27: *ipse invocabit me, pater meus es tu*.

85. *Abiud autem genuit Eliacim*. Hic designatur ordo incipientium, scilicet auditorum.

Primum autem quod fit per praedicationem in auditore, et quod debet praedicator intendere, est quod resurgat a vitiis ad virtutes, secundum illud Eph. V, 4: *surge qui dormis*; et ideo **Abiud genuit Eliacim**, qui interpretatur 'resurrectio'; et competit Christo, qui dicit, Io. XI, 26: *omnis qui credit in me, habet vitam aeternam*.

Non autem resurgens potest pervenire ad statum iustitiae nisi per auxilium Dei: et ideo, postquam resurrexit, indiget homo auxilio Dei, secundum illud Ps. CXX, 2: *auxilium meum a Domino*; et ideo sequitur **Eliacim autem genuit Azor**, qui interpretatur 'adiutus'. Et hoc etiam competit Christo, de quo in Ps. XXVI, 9: *adiutor meus esto, Domine*. Et per hoc auxilium devenitur ad iustitiam: unde **Azor genuit Sadoch**, qui interpretatur 'iustus';

the genealogy of this Capha; the Evangelist tells the generation of Salathiel, because Christ was to be born from him.

83. Now it should be noted that no mention is made in the books of Sacred Scripture of those who were from Abiud to Joseph, but they were taken from the annals of the Hebrews, which for the most part Herod burned to hide the ignobility of his own ancestry. The meaning of the letter is clear here.

84. Let us pursue the mystical sense.

Note then that in this part of the genealogy three orders are placed. The first is the order of teachers, and it contains four generations.

For preparation is required before prayer: *before prayer prepare your soul* (Sir 18:23); and hence from Jechonias, who is interpreted as 'the preparation of the Lord', comes Salathiel, who is interpreted as 'my prayer'; and he indicates Christ, who in all things *was heard because of his reverence* (Heb 5:7).

Now prayer ought to precede teaching: *and pray for me, that speech may be given me, that I may open my mouth with confidence* (Eph 6:19); and so Salathiel is followed by Zorobabel, who is interpreted 'the teacher of Babel', i.e., 'of confusion'; because through the doctrine and preaching of the apostles the nations were called back to the true God, and this was to the confusion of idolatry; and this belongs principally to Christ, who says: *you call me Master, and Lord; and you say well, for so I am* (John 13:13).

Further, through teaching and preaching a man acquires the dignity of a father; hence they are called fathers of those who are spiritually instructed: *for if you have ten thousand instructors in Christ, yet not many fathers. For in Christ Jesus, by the Gospel, we are sons* (1 Cor 4:15). And so there follows **Zorobabel begot Abiud**, who is interpreted as 'my father'; and this belongs to Christ; *he will cry out to me: you are my father* (Ps 88:27).

85. *And Abiud begot Eliacim*. Here the order of beginners, i.e., of listeners, is indicated.

Now the first thing which comes about in the listener through preaching, and that at which the preacher should aim, is that he rise again from vices to virtues: *rise you who sleep* (Eph 5:14); and so **Abiud begot Eliacim**, who is interpreted as 'the resurrection'; and this belongs to Christ, who says, *he who believes in me, has everlasting life* (John 6:47).

Now, the one rising again cannot attain to the state of justice except through the help of God; and therefore, after he has risen, a man needs the help of God: *my help is from the Lord* (Ps 120:2); and so there follows **Eliacim begot Azor**, who is interpreted as 'one helped'. And this also belongs to Christ, of whom it is said: *be my helper . . . O God my Savior* (Ps 26:9). And through this help one comes to justice; hence **Azor begot Sadoc**, who is interpreted as 'the

Rom. III, v. 22: *iustitia Dei per fidem Iesu Christi in omnes, et super omnes qui credunt in eum.*

Consummatio autem iustitiae sive finis, est caritas: finis iustitiae Christus, *finis praecepti est caritas,* I Tim. I, 5. Tantum sunt duo praecepta, scilicet dilectio Dei, et proximi; I Io. c. IV, 21: *et hoc mandatum habemus a Deo, ut qui diligit Deum, diligat et fratrem suum.* Et ideo Sadoch sequitur Achim, et Achim Eliud. Achim interpretatur 'frater meus': unde signat dilectionem proximi; Ps. CXXXII, 1: *ecce quam bonum et quam iucundum habitare fratres in unum.* Hoc competit Christo, qui caro, et frater noster est. Et quia dilectio proximi non potest esse sine dilectione Dei, ideo sequitur **Eliud autem genuit Achim**. Eliud interpretatur 'Deus meus'; Ps. XVII, 2: *diligam te, Domine*: et hoc competit Christo; Ps. XXX, v. 15: *Deus meus es tu.*

86. ***Achim autem genuit Eleazar***. Hic designatur ordo proficientium.

Non potest autem profici sine auxilio divino, unde primum quod requiritur ad proficiendum est auxilium divinum; et ideo Eliud recte sequitur Eleazar, qui interpretatur 'Deus meus adiutor'; Ps. LXXXIII, 6: *beatus vir cuius est auxilium abs te.* Sed quia Deus multis modis potest iuvare ad salutem, ut removendo prohibentia et dando occasiones, potissimum adiutorium est per donum gratiae suae; I Cor. c. XV, 10: *gratia Dei sum id quod sum.* Et ideo Eleazar, idest adiutorium Dei, sequitur Mathan, qui interpretatur 'donum', scilicet gratiae divinae: et hoc competit Christo, qui est etiam donans; Io. III, 16: *sic Deus dilexit mundum, ut Filium suum unigenitum daret*; Eph. IV, 8: *dedit dona hominibus.* Sed quia homo posset tantum confidere de dono gratiae, quod ipse incideret in negligentiam, non cooperando per liberum arbitrium gratiae, ideo sequitur Iacob, qui interpretatur 'luctator'; propter hoc I Cor. XV, 10: *gratia Dei sum id quod sum,* et sequitur: *et gratia eius in me vacua non fuit*; II Cor. VI, 1: *hortamur vos ne in vacuum gratiam Dei recipiatis.* Nunc autem sequitur Ioseph, idest 'augmentum', quia per gratiam, et liberi arbitrii conatum venit homo ad augmentum; Prov. IV, 8: *iustorum semita quasi lux splendens procedit, et crescit usque ad perfectam diem.* Unde **Iacob genuit Ioseph virum Mariae.**

87. Sed hic oritur duplex quaestio. Primo enim quaeritur de contrarietate quae videtur esse inter Lucam et Matthaeum: Lucas enim dicit quod Ioseph *fuit Heli, qui fuit Mathat*; Matthaeus autem dicit quod fuit Iacob: ergo videtur esse contrarietas inter eos.

Sed dicendum est ad hoc, quod duo fuerunt de eadem stirpe, sed non de eadem familia, scilicet Mathan et Mathat. Fuerunt enim de stirpe David; sed unus descendit de stirpe David per Salomonem, scilicet Mathan; alius

just'; *the justice of God, by faith of Jesus Christ, unto all and upon all them that believe in him* (Rom 3:22).

Further, the consummation of justice, or the end, is charity: the end of justice is Christ; *the end of the commandment is charity* (1 Tim 1:5). There are only two commandments, namely the love of God and the love of neighbor; *and this commandment we have from God, that he, who loves God, love also his brother* (1 John 4:21). And therefore Sadoc is followed by Achim, and Achim by Eliud. Achim is interpreted as 'my brother'; hence he signifies love of neighbor; *behold how good and how pleasant it is for brethren to dwell in unity* (Ps 132:1). This belongs to Christ, who is our flesh and our brother. And because love of neighbor cannot be without love of God, there follows **Eliud begot Achim**. Eliud is interpreted as 'my God'; *I will love you, O Lord* (Ps 17:2); and this belongs to Christ: *you are my God* (Ps 30:15).

86. ***Achim begot Eleazar***. Here the order of proficients is indicated.

Now, one cannot advance without the help of God; hence the first thing required for advancing is the help of God; and so Eliud is rightly followed by Eleazar, who is interpreted 'God my helper'; *blessed is the man whose help is from you* (Ps 83:6). But since God can help one toward health in many ways, as by removing obstacles and providing occasions, the most powerful of helps is through the gift of his grace; *but by the grace of God, I am what I am* (1 Cor 15:10). And so Eleazar, i.e., the help of God, is followed by Mathan, who is interpreted as 'gift', namely the gift of divine grace; and this belongs to Christ, who is also one who gives; *for God so loved the world, as to give his only begotten Son* (John 3:16); *he gave gifts to men* (Eph 4:8). But because a man can have so much confidence in the gift of grace that he falls into negligence, by not cooperating with grace through free judgment, there follows Jacob, who is interpreted as 'wrestler'; on account of this it is said: *but by the grace of God, I am what I am,* and then follows, *his grace in me has not been void* (1 Cor 15:10); *and we helping do exhort you, that you receive not the grace of God in vain* (2 Cor 6:1). Further, there now follows Joseph, i.e., 'increase', because a man comes to increase through grace and the effort of the free judgment; *but the path of the just, as a shining light, goes forwards and increases even to perfect day* (Prov 4:18). Hence **Jacob begot Joseph the husband of Mary.**

87. But here there arises a twofold question. For first, there is a question about a seeming contrariety between Luke and Matthew; for Luke says that Joseph *was of Heli, who was of Mathat* (Luke 3:23); but Matthew says that he was of Jacob; so there seems to be a contrariety between them.

But to this it should be said that there were two of the same root, but not of the same family, namely Mathan and Mathat. For they were from the root of David, but one descended from the root of David through Solomon,

per Nathan, scilicet Mathat. Accepit ergo Mathan uxorem Hesta nomine, ex qua genuit Iacob; mortuo autem Mathan, quia lex non prohibebat viduam nubere, nupsit fratri eius Mathat, qui genuit de ea Heli. Unde Iacob et Heli fuerunt fratres de eadem matre, sed non de eodem patre. Accepit autem Heli uxorem, et mortuus est sine liberis; unde Iacob, ut suscitaret semen fratri suo, accepit eamdem uxorem, et genuit Ioseph. Unde Ioseph fuit filius Iacob secundum carnem, sed filius Heli secundum adoptionem. Et ideo Matthaeus, qui ponit in genealogia Christi solum patres carnales, dicit Ioseph filium Iacob; Lucas autem, qui ponit multos qui non fuerunt patres carnales, dicit eum filium Heli. Ratio autem huius diversitatis dicta est superius.

88. Notandum autem quod quando frater accipiebat uxorem fratris, ut suscitaret nomen eius, non est ita intelligendum quod filius ille qui generabatur, vocaretur nomine fratris defuncti: Booz enim qui accepit Ruth, ut suscitaret semen Elimelech, genuit filium, quem non vocavit Elimelech, sed Obed; sed pro tanto dicitur suscitare nomen eius, quia filius ille ei adscribebatur secundum legem: nec est hoc inconveniens, quia, sicut dicitur in *Ecclesiastica historia*, ipsi apostoli et evangelistae fuerunt instructi a proximis parentibus Christi de genealogia Christi, qui eam partim memoria, partim ex dictis libris Paralipom. corde tenebant.

89. Secunda quaestio est: Matthaeus intendit scribere generationem Christi. Cum ergo Christus non fuerit filius Ioseph, sed solum Mariae, ad quid necesse fuit protendere generationem Christi ab Abraham usque ad Ioseph?

Ad quod dicendum, quod consuetum fuit apud Iudaeos, et est usque hodie, accipere uxorem de tribu sua, unde Num. XXXVI, 7 dicitur quod *accipiat uxorem quisque de tribu et cognatione sua*. Et quamvis hoc non necessario observaretur, tamen ex consuetudine observabatur. Unde Ioseph Mariam tamquam sibi propinquissimam duxit uxorem. Et ideo quia erant de eodem genere, per hoc quod ostenditur Ioseph a David descendisse, ostenditur etiam Mariam et Christum de semine David fuisse.

90. Sed unde potest haberi hoc quod Ioseph et Maria fuerint de eadem tribu? Patet ex hoc quod habetur Luc. II, 4, quia cum debuisset fieri descriptio, ascendit ipse Ioseph et Maria in civitatem David, quae est Bethlehem. Unde per hoc quod eam duxit secum, patet quod de eadem erant familia.

91. Sed quaeritur quare per Mariam non ostendit Christi generationem ex David.

Dicendum quod non est consuetum apud Hebraeos, nec etiam gentiles, genealogiam texere per mulieres;

namely Mathan; the other descended through Nathan, namely Mathat. So Mathan took a wife by the name of Hesta, out of whom he begot Jacob; Mathan having died, since the law did not prohibit a widow from marrying, she married his cousin Mathat, who begot Heli from her. Hence Jacob and Heli were brothers from the same mother, but not from the same father. Now, Heli took a wife, and died without children; hence Jacob, that he might raise up seed for his brother, took the same wife, and begot Joseph. Hence Joseph was the son of Jacob according to the flesh, but the son of Heli according to adoption. And so Matthew, who places in the genealogy of Christ only the fathers according to the flesh, says that Joseph was the son of Jacob; but Luke, who places many in the genealogy who were not fathers according to the flesh, says that he was the son of Heli. The reason for this difference was stated above.

88. But it should be noted that when a brother took the wife of his brother to sustain his name, it should not be taken in such a way that the son who was begotten would be called by the name of the dead brother; for Booz who took Ruth, that he might raise up seed for Elimelech, begot a son who was not called Elimelech, but Obed; but he is said to sustain his name to this extent, that the son is attributed to him according to law. Nor is this unfitting, because, as is said in *Church History*, the apostles and evangelists themselves were taught by the immediate parents of Christ about the genealogy of Christ, who held it in their hearts partly by memory, and partly from the aforementioned books of the Chronicles.

89. The second question is this: Matthew intended to write down the generation of Christ. So since Christ was not the son of Joseph, but only of Mary, why was it necessary to trace the generation of Christ from Abraham to Joseph?

To which it should be said that it was the custom among the Jews, and is so even today, to take a wife from one's own tribe, hence it is said that *all men will marry wives of their own tribe and kindred* (Num 36:7). And although this was not observed out of necessity, still it was observed by custom. Hence Joseph took Mary his wife as the one closest to himself. And so, since they were of the same stock, from the fact that Joseph is shown to have descended from David, Mary and Christ are shown to have been of the seed of David as well.

90. But how can it be known that Joseph and Mary were of the same tribe? It is clear from what is said in Luke, because when there was to be an enrollment, Joseph and Mary went up into the city of David, which is Bethlehem (Luke 2:4). Hence by fact that he brought her with him, it is clear that they were of the same family.

91. But it is asked why he did not show the generation of Christ from David through Mary.

It should be said that it is not the custom among the Hebrews, nor even among the gentiles, to put together a

unde Christus, qui venerat pro salute hominum, voluit in hoc imitari, vel observare mores hominum; et sic non per feminas eius genealogia describitur, praecipue cum sine periculo veritatis posset per viros eius genealogia cognosci.

92. *Virum Mariae*. Hieronymus: *cum audieris 'virum,' suspicio non oriatur nuptiarum.*

Contra. Nonne fuit verum matrimonium? Dicendum quod sic, quia ibi fuerunt tria bona matrimonii: proles, ipse Deus; fides, quia nullum adulterium; et sacramentum, quia indivisibilis coniunctio animarum.

Quid ergo dicendum? Hoc intelligitur quantum ad nuptiarum complementum, quod est per carnalem copulam. Ideo autem, ut dicit Augustinus, nominatur *vir* Mariae, ut ostendatur matrimonium esse inter pari voto continentes.

93. Sed quomodo fuit matrimonium? Votum enim impedit matrimonium contrahendum et dirimit contractum. Cum ergo Beata Virgo voverit virginitatem, nullum videtur fuisse matrimonium.

Praeterea. Consensit in carnalem copulam, si fuit matrimonium.

Sed dicendum quod Beata Virgo angebatur inter duo: ex una enim parte angebatur propter maledictum legis, cui subiacebat sterilis; ex alia parte angebatur propter propositum servandae castitatis; et ideo virginitatem proposuit, nisi Dominus aliter ordinaret; unde divinae dispositioni se commisit.

Quod dicitur, quod consensit in carnalem copulam, dicendum quod non; sed in matrimonium directe, in carnalem autem copulam quasi implicite, si Deus voluisset.

94. *De qua natus est Iesus qui vocatur Christus*. Hic duplex error excluditur. Unus qui dicit Christum fuisse filium Ioseph: et hoc excluditur per hoc quod dicitur *de qua*. Si enim fuisset filius Ioseph, dixisset *de quo*, vel saltem *de quibus*.

Alius excluditur error, scilicet Valentini, qui dicit Christum non assumpsisse corpus de Beata Virgine sed de caelo apportasse, et per Beatam Virginem, sicut per canale, transisse. Contra est quod dicitur *de qua*. Si enim ita esset sicut dicit, dixisset Evangelista non *de qua*, sed *per quam*, vel *a qua*, vel *ex qua*, vel aliquid tale. Haec enim praepositio 'de' semper notat consubstantialitatem; non autem haec praepositio 'ex'; unde potest dici: *ex mane fit dies*, et quod arca procedit ex artifice, numquam dicitur, *de artifice*. Unde per hoc quod dicit *de*, denotat quod de corpore B. Virginis formatum est corpus

genealogy through women; hence Christ, who had come for the salvation of man, wished in this to imitate or observe the customs of men; and so his genealogy is not traced through women, especially since his genealogy can be known through men without risk to the truth.

92. *The husband of Mary*. Jerome: *when you hear 'husband', let not a suspicion of nuptials arise.*

On the contrary: was there not a true marriage? One should say so, because the three goods of marriage were present: children, God himself; faith, because neither committed adultery; and the sacrament, because of the indivisible conjoining of souls.

What then should be said? This statement of Jerome's is understood as regarding the completion of marriage, which is bodily union. Now, he is named the ***husband*** of Mary, as Augustine says, that the marriage might be shown to be between those continuing in a mutual vow.

93. But how was there a marriage? For a vow impedes the contracting of matrimony and breaks off the thing contracted. Since therefore the Blessed Virgin vowed virginity, it seems that there would have been no marriage.

Furthermore, if there was a marriage, she consented to a bodily union.

But one should say that the Blessed Virgin was hard pressed between two things: for on the one hand she was pressed by the curse of the law, to which the infertile woman was subject; on the other hand, she was pressed by the plan of serving chastity; and so she planned on virginity, unless the Lord should arrange otherwise; hence she entrusted herself to the divine arrangement.

To what is said, that she consented to a bodily union, one should say that she did not; she consented to marriage directly, but to a bodily union implicitly, so to speak, if God should will it.

94. *Of whom was born Jesus, who is called Christ*. Here two errors are excluded. One, which says that Christ was the son of Joseph; and this is excluded by the fact that it says *de qua*. For if he had been the son of Joseph, it would have said *de quo*, or at least *de quibus*.

The other error is also excluded, namely the error of Valentinus, who said that Christ did not take up a body from the Blessed Virgin, but rather brought a body down from heaven, and passed through the Blessed Virgin as through a canal. Against this is what is said here, ***of whom***. For if it were as he says, the Evangelist would not have said ***of whom***, but *through whom*, or *by whom*, or *out of whom*, or something like this. For this preposition 'of' always specifies consubstantiality; but not this preposition 'out of'; hence one can say, *out of the morning comes the day*, and that the box proceeds out of the builder; but one never says

Christi; Gal. IV, 4: *misit Deus Filium suum factum ex muliere, factum sub lege.*

95. Hic cavendus est error Nestorii, qui duas in Christo personas posuit, et ideo non concedit Deum natum, vel passum; nec alia quae sunt Dei, ut esse ab aeterno, vel creasse stellas, attribuit homini. Unde in quadam sua epistola accipit istam auctoritatem ad confirmationem sui erroris: *de qua natus est Iesus*, non dicit *Deus*, sed *Iesus*: quod est nomen hominis, et **Christus**.

Sed secundum hoc nulla esset unio in Christo, nec Christus diceretur unus.

96. Unde nota, quod in Christo, quia fit unio duarum naturarum in una persona, fit communicatio idiomatum, ut illa quae sunt Dei attribuantur homini, et e converso. Et potest poni exemplum qualecumque de duobus accidentibus in subiecto, sicut pomum dicitur album et saporosum. Et quantum ad saporosum dicitur album, ratione qua pomum est album, et e converso.

97. *Qui vocatur Christus.* Nota. Simpliciter dicitur **Christus** sine additione, ad denotandum quod oleo invisibili unctus est, non materiali, sicut reges, vel prophetae in lege. Ps. XLIV, 8: *unxit te Deus, Deus tuus oleo laetitiae prae consortibus tuis.*

98. *Omnes ergo generationes.* Posita generatione Christi, hic concludit numerum generationum: et dividit eas per tres quaterdenarios.

Primus quaterdenarius est ab Abraham usque ad David inclusive, ut scilicet David numeretur in illo primo quaterdenario; et hoc est **omnes ergo generationes**. Secundus quaterdenarius protenditur a David exclusive, ita scilicet quod ipse David non numeretur, sed incipiatur a Salomone, et terminatur ad transmigrationem Babylonis; et hoc est **et a David usque ad transmigrationem Babylonis**. Tertius incipit a transmigratione Babylonis, et terminatur in Christum, ita quod Christus sit quaterdenarius.

99. Sed quaeritur quare Evangelista ita diligenter et attente distinxit generationem Christi per tres quaterdenarios.

Chrysostomus assignat rationem: quia in istis tribus quaterdenariis semper facta est aliqua mutatio in populo Israel. In primo enim quaterdenario fuerunt sub ducibus; in secundo sub regibus; in tertio sub pontificibus. Et ipse Christus est dux, et rex, et pontifex; Is. XXXIII, 22: *Dominus iudex noster, Dominus legifer noster, Dominus rex noster.* Et de eius sacerdotio dicitur in Ps. CIX, 4: *tu es sacerdos in aeternum secundum ordinem Melchisedech.*

Aliam rationem assignat ipse, ut scilicet ostenderetur necessitas adventus Christi. In primo enim quaterdenario petierunt regem contra voluntatem Dei, et legem

of the builder. Hence by that fact that he says **of**, he specifies that the body of Christ was formed of the body of the Blessed Virgin; *God sent his Son, made of a woman, made under the law* (Gal 4:4).

95. Here one must beware the error of Nestorius, who placed two persons in Christ, and so did not admit that God was born, or suffered; nor did he attribute to a man the other things which belong to God, such as to be eternal, or to have created the stars. Hence in a certain letter of his he takes this Scriptural text as a confirmation of his own error: **of whom was born Jesus**, it does not say *God*, but **Jesus**, which is the name of a man, and **Christ**.

But according to this there would be no union in Christ, nor would Christ be called one.

96. Hence note that in Christ, since there came about a union of two natures in one person, there also came about a communication of idioms, so that those things which belong to God are attributed to a man, and vice versa. And whatever example can be taken from two accidents in one subject: a fruit is called white and tasty; and it is called white with regard to the tasty, for the reason that the fruit is white, and vice versa.

97. *Who is called Christ.* Note: he is called **Christ** simply, with nothing added, to mark that he is anointed with an invisible oil, not with a material oil as were the kings or the prophets in the law. *God, your God, has anointed you with the oil of gladness above your fellows* (Ps 44:8).

98. *So all the generations.* The generation of Christ having been set down, here he concludes the number of the generations; and he divides them into three fourteens.

The first fourteen is from Abraham to David, inclusively, I mean so that David is included in the first fourteen; and so this is **all the generations**. The second fourteen is extended from David exclusively, I mean so that David is not numbered, but rather it begins from Solomon, and ends at the transmigration of Babylon; and this is **and from David to the transmigration of Babylon**. The third begins from the transmigration of Babylon and ends in Christ, so that Christ is the fourteenth.

99. But it is asked why the Evangelist so diligently and attentively distinguished the generation of Christ into three fourteens.

Chrysostom gives a reason: because in these three fourteens some change always happens in the people of Israel. For in the first fourteen they were under leaders; in the second, under the kings; in the third, under the high priests; *for the Lord is our judge, the Lord is our lawgiver, the Lord is our king* (Isa 33:22). And it says about his priesthood: *you are a priest for ever according to the order of Melchisedech* (Ps 109:4).

He gives another reason, namely to show the necessity of the coming of Christ. For in the first fourteen they asked for a king against the will of God, and went against

transgressi sunt. In secundo autem propter peccata sua ducti sunt in captivitatem. Sed in tertio per Christum ab omni culpa, et miseria, et a servitute peccati spirituali liberamur.

Hieronymus tertiam assignat rationem, quia per istos signantur tria tempora, quibus omnium hominum vita ducitur. Per primum enim quaterdenarium signatur tempus ante legem, quia in illo ponuntur aliqui patres qui fuerunt ante legem; per secundum, tempus sub lege, quia omnes illi qui ponuntur sunt sub lege; per tertium autem, tempus gratiae, quia terminatur ad Christum, per quem scilicet *gratia et veritas facta est*, Io. I, 17.

100. Congruit etiam ista distinctio mysterio: quia quaterdenarius est numerus compositum ex quatuor et decem. Per decem ergo Vetus intelligitur Testamentum, quod datum est in decem mandatis. Per quatuor autem, Evangelium, quod in quatuor libris distinguitur. Tres autem quaterdenarii designant fidem Trinitatis. Unde per hoc quod Matthaeus genealogiam in tres quaterdenarios dividit, designatur quod per Novum et Vetus Testamentum in fide Trinitatis pervenitur ad Christum.

101. De numero autem generationum est duplex opinio. Secundum enim Hieronymum, qui dicit quod alius est Iechonias in fine primi quaterdenarii et in principio secundi, sunt quadraginta duae generationes: tot enim faciunt quaterdenarii tres. Sed secundum Augustinum non sunt nisi quadraginta una; et quod Christus sit ille unus.

Et hoc competit mysterio. Quadragenarius enim numerus consurgit ex ductu quatuor in decem, et e converso. Secundum autem Platonicos, quatuor est numerus corporum: corpus enim componitur ex quatuor elementis; decem autem est numerus, qui consurgit ex aggregatione numerorum linealium: unus enim, duo, tres et quatuor faciunt decem. Et quia Matthaeus intendit declarare quomodo Christus linealiter descendit ad nos, ideo per quadraginta generationes venit ad nos Christus. Lucas autem qui intendit in Christo commendare sacerdotalem dignitatem, cui competit expiatio peccatorum infra XVIII, 22: ***non dico tibi usque septies, sed usque septuagies septies*** etc. ponit generationes septuaginta septem; consurgit enim iste numerus ex ductu septem in undecim: septies enim undecim sunt septuaginta septem. Per undecim ergo intelligitur transgressio Decalogi; per septem autem septiformis gratia, per quam fit remissio peccatorum.

Quod autem secundum Hieronymum sunt quadraginta duae generationes, etiam non vacat a mysterio, quia per illas duas intelliguntur duo praecepta caritatis; vel duo Testamenta: Novum et Vetus.

the law. Moreover, in the second fourteen they were led into captivity. But in the third we were liberated from all guilt, and misery, and from the spiritual servitude of sin through Christ.

Jerome gives a third reason, that through these three fourteens are indicated three times in which the life of all men is led. For the time before the law is signified by the first fourteen, because some fathers who were before the law are placed in it; the time under the law is indicated by the second fourteen, because all those who are put there are under the law; and the time of grace is indicated by the third fourteen, because it ends at Christ, through whom *came grace and truth* (John 1:17).

100. This distinction also fits together with a mystery, because fourteen is a number composed out of four and ten. So by ten the Old Testament is understood, which was given in ten commandments. And by four is understood the Gospel, which is distinguished into four books. Moreover, the three fourteens indicate the faith of the Trinity. Hence by the fact that Matthew divides the genealogy into three fourteens, he indicates that through the New and the Old Testament we come to Christ in the faith of the Trinity.

101. Now there are three opinions about the number of the generations. For according to Jerome, who says that the Jechonias at the end of the first fourteen and the Jechonias in the beginning of the second are different, there are forty-two generations; for three fourteens makes that many. But according to Augustine there are only forty-one; and Christ himself is the one.

And this harmonizes with a mystery. For the number forty arises from four led into ten, and vice versa. Now, according to the Platonists, four is the number of the body, for the body is composed of four elements; but ten is the number which arises from the addition of the linear numbers: for one, two, three, and four make ten. And because he intended to explain how Christ descended linearly to us, he came to Christ through forty generations. But Luke, who intended to set forth the priestly dignity, to which pertains the expiation of sins below: ***I do not say to you, till seven times; but till seventy times seven times*** (Matt 18:22), sets down seventy-seven generations; for this number arises from seven led into eleven, for seven elevens are seventy-seven. So through eleven the breaking of the ten commandments is understood, and through seven the sevenfold grace, through which comes the remission of sins.

But that there are forty-two generations according to Jerome does not lack a mystery either, because through those two the two precepts of charity are understood; or the two Testaments, the Old and the New.

102. *Christi autem generatio sic erat*. Posita genealogia Christi in generali, hic describitur generatio eius in speciali: et dividitur in tres partes.

Primo ponit quemdam titulum;

secundo Evangelista describit generationis modum, ibi *cum esset desponsata mater eius Maria Ioseph*:

tertio probat generationis modum, ibi *Ioseph autem vir eius*.

103. Dicit ergo *Christi autem*. Hoc dupliciter legitur. Secundum Chrysostomum enim est quasi quidam prologus dicendorum; sed secundum Remigium est quidam epilogus dictorum. Primo modo legitur sic: ita dictum est de genealogia Christi, quomodo Abraham genuit Isaac etc. per carnalem admixtionem, sed *Christi generatio sic erat*, supple: sicut dicetur in sequentibus. Secundo modo legitur sic, ut sit epilogus praecedentium: ita Abraham etc. usque ad Christum. *Christi autem generatio sic erat*; supple: ut ab Abraham per David et alios protenderetur ad Christum.

104. Consequenter describit generationis modum;

et primo describit personam generantem, cum dicit *cum esset desponsata*;

secundo ipsam Christi generationem, cum dicit *antequam convenirent inventa est in utero habens*;

tertio generationis actorem, *de Spiritu Sancto*.

Personam generantem describit a tribus.

Primo a conditione, cum dicit *desponsata . . . Ioseph*;

secundo a dignitate *mater eius*;

tertio a proprio nomine *Maria*.

105. Dicit ergo *cum esset desponsata mater eius Maria Ioseph*.

Sed hic statim oritur quaestio. Cum Christus voluerit nasci de virgine, quare voluit matrem suam desponsari?

Ratio, secundum Hieronymum, triplex assignatur. Prima est ut credibilius esset testimonium virginitatis eius. Si enim non fuisset desponsata, et diceret se esse virginem, cum esset impraegnata, non videretur ob aliud dicere, nisi ut celaret crimen adulterii. Sed cum desponsata erat, non habebat necesse mentiri. Et ideo magis esset credendum ei; Ps. XCII, 5: *testimonia tua credibilia facta sunt nimis*. Alia ratio est ut haberet praesidium viri, sive cum fugeret in Aegyptum, sive cum inde rediret. Tertia fuit, ut partus eius diabolo celaretur, ne scilicet si ipse sciret, impediret passionem eius, et fructum nostrae redemptionis; I Cor. II, 8: *si enim cognovissent,*

102. *But the generation of Christ was thus*. Having set down the genealogy of Christ in general, here he describes his generation in particular. And it is divided into three parts.

First, he sets down a certain title;

second, the Evangelist describes the manner of the generation, at *when his mother, Mary, was espoused to Joseph*;

third, he confirms the manner of the generation, at *whereupon Joseph her husband*.

103. So he says, *but the generation of Christ was thus*. This is read in two ways. For according to Chrysostom it is as it were a certain prologue to what will be said; but according to Remigius it is a certain epilogue to what was said before. In the first way, it is read thus: this was recounted about the genealogy of Christ, how Abraham begot Isaac through bodily mingling, but *the generation of Christ was thus*, supply: as will be said in what follows. In the second way, it is read so as to be an epilogue to what comes before: Abraham, and in this way until Christ. *Now the generation of Christ was thus*, supply: so as to extend from Abraham through David to Christ.

104. Next, he describes the manner of the generation;

and first he describes the person generating, when he says, *when as his mother Mary was espoused*;

second, he describes the very generation of Christ, when he says, *before they came together, she was found with child*;

third, he describes the author of the generation, *of the Holy Spirit*.

He describes the person generating by three things.

First, by condition, when he says, *espoused to Joseph*;

second, by dignity, *his mother*;

third, by proper name, *Mary*.

105. He says then, *when as his mother Mary was espoused to Joseph*.

But here a question arises at once. Since Christ wished to be born of a virgin, why did he wish his mother to be espoused?

According to Jerome, three reasons are given. The first is so that the testimony of her virginity might be believable. For if she had not been espoused, and had said that she was a virgin while she was pregnant, she would seem to say this for no other reason than to hide the crime of adultery. But since she had been espoused, she had no need to lie. And therefore it would be more worthy of belief from her; *your testimonies are become exceedingly credible* (Ps 92:5). Another reason is so that she would have the protection of a man, both when she fled into Egypt and when she returned from there. The third was so that his birth would be hidden from the devil, lest he should impede Christ's passion

numquam Dominum gloriae crucifixissent; exponitur de daemone, idest non crucifigi permisisset.

106. Sed contra. Diabolus numquid non cognoscit an ista est virgo? Virginitas enim eius erat in carne non corrupta. Ergo diabolus potuit scire eam esse virginem.

Sed dicendum, secundum Ambrosium, qui etiam istam rationem assignat, quod diaboli possunt aliqua subtilitate naturae, quae tamen non possunt nisi divina permissione. Unde diabolus eius virginitatem cognosceret, nisi a diligenti consideratione divinitus fuisset prohibitus.

Secundum Ambrosium assignatur triplex ratio. Prima est propter honorem matris Domini conservandum: maluit Dominus de ortu suo homines dubitare, quam de pudicitia matris. Et ideo voluit eam desponsari, ut tolleretur suspicio adulterii: ipse enim venerat legem adimplere, non solvere; Matth. V, 17: **non veni solvere, sed adimplere**; Ex. XX, 12 dicitur, *honora patrem tuum et matrem tuam*. Alia ratio est, ut virginibus notatis de adulterio auferretur excusatio: si enim mater Domini non fuisset desponsata, et tamen gravida, possent similiter se per eam excusare; Ps. CXL, 4: *non declines cor meum in verba malitiae, ad excusandas excusationes in peccatis*. Tertia ratio, quia Christus Ecclesiam sibi desponsavit, quae virgo est; II Cor. II, 2: *despondi enim vos*. Et ideo de virgine desponsata nasci voluit in signum quod Ecclesiam sibi desponsavit.

107. *Cum ergo esset desponsata*. Sed cui? *Ioseph*.

Secundum Chrysostomum, Ioseph fuit faber lignarius; et signat Christum, qui per lignum crucis omnia restauravit, caelestia et cetera.

108. *Mater eius*, idest Dei. Hic ostenditur eius dignitas: nulli enim creaturae hoc concessum est, nec homini, nec angelo, ut esset pater, aut mater Dei; sed hoc fuit privilegium gratiae singularis, ut non solum hominis, sed Dei mater fieret; et ideo in Apoc. c. XII, 1 dicitur: *mulier amicta sole*, quasi tota repleta divinitate. Quod negavit Nestorius; et hoc quia divinitas non fuit accepta a Virgine. Contra quem Ignatius martyr pulchro exemplo utitur ad ostendendum quod fuit mater Dei. Constat, inquit, quod in generatione hominum communium mulier dicitur mater: et tamen mulier non dat animam rationalem, quae a Deo est, sed ministrat substantiam ad corporis formationem. Sic igitur mulier dicitur mater totius hominis, quia id quod sumptum est de ea, unitur animae rationali. Similiter cum humanitas Christi sumpta sit de Beata Virgine, propter unionem ad divinitatem dicitur Beata Virgo non solum mater hominis, sed

and the fruit of our redemption if he knew; *for if they had known it, they would never have crucified the Lord of glory* (1 Cor 2:8); this is interpreted as concerning the demon, i.e., he would not have permitted Christ to be crucified.

106. On the contrary, did not the devil know whether she was a virgin? For her virginity in her body was not corrupted. So the devil could know that she was a virgin.

But one should say, according to Ambrose, who also gives this reason, that some things are possible to the devil by the subtlety of his nature which nevertheless are only possible by divine permission. Hence the devil would have known her virginity, if he had not been divinely restrained from diligent examination.

According to Ambrose, three reasons are given. The first is for the sake of the honor of the Lord's mother, which had to be preserved; the Lord preferred that men have doubts about his own origin rather than about the chastity of his mother. And so he wished her to be espoused, so that the suspicion of adultery would be taken away, for he came to fulfill the law, not to destroy it; *I am not come to destroy, but to fulfill* (Matt 5:17); *honor your father and your mother* (Exod 20:12). Another reason is so that, once her virginity was recorded, an excuse would be taken away from the adulterer; for if the mother of the Lord had not been espoused, and yet was pregnant, they could in a similar manner excuse themselves through her. *Incline not my heart to evil words; to make excuses in sins* (Ps 140:4). The third reason is because Christ espoused to himself the Church, which is a virgin; *for I have espoused you to one husband that I may present you as a chaste virgin to Christ* (2 Cor 11:2). And so he wished to be born of an espoused virgin as a sign that he espoused the Church to himself.

107. *When his mother, Mary, was espoused*. To whom? *To Joseph.*

According to Chrysostom, Joseph was a craftsman, a carpenter; and he signifies Christ, who through the wood of the cross restored all things, heavenly.

108. *His mother*, i.e., God's mother. Here her dignity is shown, for it is not permitted to any creature, neither man nor angel, that he should be the father or the mother of God, but this was a privilege of singular grace, that she should become the mother not only of a man, but of God; and so it is said, *a woman clothed with the sun* (Rev 12:1), as though entirely filled with divinity. Nestorius denied this, because the divinity was not taken from the Virgin. Against which Ignatius Martyr used a beautiful example to show that she was the mother of God. It is agreed, he said, that in the generation of common men the woman is called the mother; and yet the mother does not give the rational soul, which is from God, but rather supplies the substance for the formation of the body. So in this way the woman is called the mother of the whole man because that which is taken from her is united to the rational soul. Similarly, since the humanity of Christ was taken from the Blessed Virgin,

etiam Dei; quamvis ab ipsa non sumatur divinitas; sicut nec in aliis anima rationalis sumitur a matre.

109. *Maria*, proprium nomen. Interpretatur 'maris stella,' vel 'illuminatrix,' et suo sermone *Domina*: unde in Apoc. XII, 1 describitur luna sub pedibus eius.

110. *Antequam convenirent* et cetera.

Hic obiicit Elvidius: *si antequam convenirent, ergo aliquando convenerunt*. Unde iste negavit virginitatem matris Christi: non ante partum, nec in partu, sed post partum dicit quod fuit cognita a viro.

Et respondet Hieronymus, quod sine dubio hoc quod dicitur **antequam**, semper importat ordinem ad futurum. Sed hoc potest esse dupliciter: vel secundum rationem, vel secundum intellectus acceptionem. Si enim dicatur: *antequam comederem in portu Romae, navigavi ad Africam*, non est intelligendum quod postquam navigaverim ad Africam comederim; sed quia proposueram comedere, et praeventus navigatione non comedi. Ita est hic. Non est ita intelligendum quod postea realiter convenirent, sicut dicit impius ille; sed quia ex hoc ipso quod sibi desponsata erat secundum communem opinionem, licebat eis aliquando convenire, quamvis numquam convenerint.

Remigius aliter exponit, ut intelligatur de solemni celebratione nuptiarum: ante enim erat et fiebat per aliquos dies desponsatio, et interim sponsa non erat sub custodia viri; postea autem fiebat solemnis celebratio nuptiarum, et tunc traducebatur ad domum viri. De his nuptiis loquitur Evangelista hic. Et secundum hoc non habet locum obiectio Elvidii.

Inventa est in utero habens. Nota proprietatem verbi: proprie enim illud 'inventum' dicitur, de quo non sperabatur, nec putabatur; et Ioseph tantam habebat opinionem de pudicitia Mariae, quod praeter aestimationem eius fuit quod invenit eam gravidam.

111. *In utero habens*, supple ab *ipso Ioseph*, qui, sicut dicit Hieronymus, *maritali licentia pene omnia secreta eius rimabatur*. *De Spiritu Sancto*. Hic tangitur Actor conceptionis.

Hoc autem legendum est divisim ab illo praecedenti. Non enim legendum est, aut intelligendum quod Ioseph invenerit eam habentem in utero de Spiritu Sancto; sed solum quod invenit eam gravidam. Et ne oriretur auditoribus interim suspicio adulterii, addidit **de Spiritu Sancto**, idest de virtute Spiritus Sancti, non de substantia, ne filius Spiritus Sancti credatur; Luc. I, 35: *Spiritus Sanctus superveniet in te, et virtus Altissimi obumbravit tibi*.

112. Quamvis autem secundum Augustinum indivisibilia sint opera Trinitatis, et ideo ipsam conceptionem

the Blessed Virgin is called the mother not only of a man, but also of God, on account of the union with the divinity, although the divinity is not taken from her, just as the rational soul is not taken from the mother in others.

109. *Mary*, her proper name. It is interpreted as 'star of the sea', or 'illuminatrix', and by her own words *Lady*; hence in Rev 12:1 a moon is described as under her feet.

110. *Before they came together*.

Here Helvidius objected: *if this was before they came together, then at sometime they came together*. Hence he denied the virginity of Christ's mother; not before the birth, nor during the birth, but after the birth he says that she was known by a man.

And Jerome responds that, without a doubt, this **before** which is said here always brings in an order to the future. But this can be in either of two ways: either according to *ratio*, or according to the intellect's reception. For if it be said, *before I was eating in the port of Rome, I sailed to Africa*, it should not be understood that after I sailed to Africa I ate; but that I had proposed to eat, and being prevented by the sailing I did not eat. And so it is here. It should not be understood in this way, that afterward they really came together, as that impious man says; but that by the very fact that she was espoused to him according to common opinion, it was lawful for them to come together, although they never did come together.

Remigius explains it in another way, so that it is understood of the solemn celebration of nuptials; for beforehand she was and remained for some days espoused, and meanwhile the spouse was not under the man's care; but after the solemn celebration of the nuptials happened, then she was led to the man's home. It is of these nuptials that the Evangelist speaks here. And according to this the objection of Helvidius has no place.

She was found with child. Notice the character of the word: for that is properly called 'found' about which one neither hopes nor supposes; and Joseph had only an opinion about the chastity of Mary, because, contrary to his expectation, it happened that he found her pregnant.

111. *She was found with child*, supply *by Joseph himself*, who, as Jerome says, *with marital freedom was searching out almost all her secrets*. *Of the Holy Spirit*. Here the Author of the conception is touched upon.

Now, this should be read separately from that which comes before. For it should not be read or understood that Joseph found her with child of the Holy Spirit, but only that he found her pregnant. And lest there arise meanwhile in the hearers a suspicion of adultery, he added **of the Holy Spirit**, i.e., of the power of the Holy Spirit, not of the substance, nor should he be thought to be the son of the Holy Spirit; *the Holy Spirit will come upon you, and the power of the Most High will overshadow you* (Luke 1:35).

112. Now, although according to St. Augustine the works of the Trinity are indivisible, and not only the Holy

non solum Spiritus Sanctus, sed etiam Pater et Filius operati sint; tamen per quamdam appropriationem Spiritui Sancto attribuitur. Et hoc tribus rationibus. Prima ratio est, quia Spiritus Sanctus amor est. Hoc autem fuit signum maximi amoris, quod Deus Filium suum incarnari voluerit; Io. III, 16: *sic Deus dilexit mundum, ut Filium suum unigenitum daret.* Secunda, quia Spiritui Sancto attribuitur gratia; I Cor. XII, 4: *divisiones gratiarum sunt, idem autem Spiritus*; et hoc fuit maxima gratia. Tertia ratio assignatur in gestis Nicaeni Concilii, et est, quod in nobis est duplex verbum: verbum cordis et verbum vocis. Verbum cordis est ipsa conceptio intellectus, quae occulta est hominibus, nisi quatenus per vocem exprimitur, sive per verbum vocis. Verbo autem cordis comparatur Verbum aeternum ante incarnationem, quando erat apud Patrem, et nobis absconditum; sed verbo vocis comparatur Verbum incarnatum quod iam nobis apparuit, et manifestum est. Verbum autem cordis non coniungitur voci nisi mediante spiritu; et ideo recte incarnatio Verbi, per quam nobis visibile apparuit, mediante Spiritu Sancto facta est.

113. Nota hic quatuor rationes quare Christus de virgine nasci voluit. Quarum prima fuit, quia peccatum originale contrahitur in prole ex commixtione viri et mulieris: unde si Christus natus fuisset de concubitu coniugali, peccatum originale contraxisset. Hoc autem esset inconveniens, cum ipse ad hoc venisset in mundum ut peccata nostra tolleret: unde peccati contagione infici non debuit.

Secunda, quia Christus praecipuus fuit doctor castitatis; infra XIX, 12: **sunt eunuchi qui se castraverunt propter regnum caelorum.**

Tertia propter puritatem et munditiam. *In malevolam animam non introibit sapientia*, Sap. I, 4. Unde decuit ut venter matris eius nulla corruptione pollueretur.

Quarta propter proprietatem Verbi: quia sicut Verbum sine corruptione cordis emanat a corde, ita Christus de virgine nasci voluit et debuit sine corruptione.

114. *Ioseph autem vir eius cum esset iustus.* Postquam posuit generationis modum, hic confirmat ipsum per testimonium. Cum enim supra dixerit Evangelista, quod mater Iesu inventa est in utero habens, et quod hoc erat de Spiritu Sancto, posset aliquis credere quod Evangelista hoc apposuisset ob gratiam Magistri; ideo hic Evangelista confirmat generationis modum supradictum. Et

primo praenuntiatione prophetica, **hoc autem factum est**;

secundo revelatione angelica, ibi **exurgens autem Ioseph.**

Spirit brought about the conception, but the Father and the Son as well, nevertheless it is attributed to the Holy Spirit by a certain appropriation. And this is for three reasons. The first reason is that the Holy Spirit is love: and this is a sign of the greatest love, that God willed that his own Son should be incarnated; *for God so loved the world, as to give his only begotten Son* (John 3:16). Second, because grace is attributed to the Holy Spirit; *now there are diversities of graces, but the same Spirit* (1 Cor 12:4); and this was the greatest grace. The third reason is given in the acts of the Nicene Council, and is that there are two words in us: that of the heart, and that of the voice. The word of the heart is the very concept of the intellect, which is hidden to men, except insofar as it is expressed through the voice, or through the word of the voice. Now, the word of the heart is compared to the eternal Word before the incarnation, when he was with the Father and hidden to us; but the word of the voice is compared to the incarnate Word which then appeared to us and was manifest. But the word of the heart is not joined to the word of the voice except by the mediation of the spirit; and therefore the incarnation of the Word, through which he appeared visibly to us, is rightly done by the mediation of the Spirit.

113. Note here four reasons why Christ wished to be born of a virgin. The first of the four was that original sin is contracted in a child from the mingling of a man and a woman; hence if Christ had been born of the conjugal act, he would have contracted original sin. But this would be unfitting, since he had come into the world to take away our sins; hence he should not have been infected by the touch of sin.

Second, because Christ was a particular teacher of chastity; below: **there are eunuchs, who have made themselves eunuchs for the kingdom of heaven** (Matt 19:12).

Third, on account of purity and modesty. *For wisdom will not enter into a malicious soul, nor dwell in a body subject to sins* (Wis 1:4). Hence it was proper that the womb of his mother be polluted by no corruption.

Fourth, on account of the special character of the Word; because just as the Word comes forth from the heart without corruption of the heart, so Christ wished to be born of a virgin without corruption of the virgin.

114. **Whereupon Joseph her husband, being a just man.** Having set out the mode of the generation, here he confirms it by testimony. For since the Evangelist had said above that the mother of Jesus was found with child, and that this was of the Holy Spirit, someone could think that the Evangelist had set this to favor his Teacher; so the Evangelist confirms here the manner of generation mentioned before.

And first, by a prophetic foretelling, **now all this was done** (Matt 1:22);

second, by the angelic revelation, at, **and Joseph rising up from sleep** (Matt 1:24).

In prima parte sunt tria.

Primo introducitur persona, cui facta est revelatio;

secundo persona revelans, ibi *haec autem eo cogitante, ecce angelus Domini apparuit*;

tertio ponuntur verba revelationis, ibi *Ioseph fili David*.

115. Persona autem, cui fit revelatio, commendatur ex duobus, scilicet ex hoc quod est iustus, et ideo non mentiretur; secundo ex hoc quod sponsus, sive vir, et ideo crimen in ea non pateretur; Prov. VI, 34: *zelus et furor viri non parcet in die vindictae.*

Dicit ergo ita: *inventa est* a Ioseph *habens in utero*, sed *Ioseph vir eius cum esset iustus, et nollet eam traducere.*

Hic est duplex sanctorum sententia, Ambrosii videlicet, et Augustini.

116. Augustinus enim vult, quod Ioseph, qui non erat praesens, quando facta est Annuntiatio angelica, rediens, et inveniens eam gravidam, habuit suspicionem adulterii.

Sed tunc statim oritur quaestio: quomodo iustus erat, si eam quam suspectam habebat de adulterio, nolebat traducere, idest crimen ipsius propalare? In hoc enim videbatur ei in peccato consentire, et Rom. I, 32 dicitur, quod *non solum qui faciunt, sed etiam qui consentiunt facientibus, digni sunt morte.*

Sed ad hoc est triplex responsio. Prima est secundum Chrysostomum, quod duplex est iustitia: una enim est iustitia, quae est virtus cardinalis, quae dicitur iustitia specialis; alia est iustitia legalis, quae includit omnem virtutem, et pietatem, et clementiam, et huiusmodi. Quando ergo dicitur quod Ioseph iustus erat, intelligendum est de iustitia generali, ut iustitia accipiatur pro pietate. Unde quia iustus erat, idest pius, noluit eam traducere. Alia est responsio Augustini, qui dicit, quod duplex est peccatum, scilicet peccatum occultum et peccatum manifestum: peccatum enim occultum non est publice arguendum, sed aliter est ei remedium adhibendum. Suspicio ergo adulterii, quam habuit Ioseph, erat suspicio peccati occulti, et non manifesti, quia ipse solus sciebat; et iterum si alii scirent eam gravidam, non possent opinari nisi quod de ipso esset; et ideo crimen eius non debuisset propalasse. Tertia vero responsio est Rabani, quod etiam Ioseph iustus fuit et pius: in hoc enim quod pius, non voluit crimen propalare; sed in hoc quod voluit eam dimittere, apparuit iustus: sciebat enim quod *qui tenet adulteram, stultus et insipiens est*, ut dicitur Prov. XVIII, 22.

117. Secundum autem Hieronymum et Origenem non habuit suspicionem adulterii. Noverat enim Ioseph

In the first part, there are three things.

First, the person to whom the revelation was made is introduced;

second, the person revealing is introduced, at, *but while he thought on these things, behold the angel of the Lord appeared to him*;

third, the words of the revelation are set out, at *Joseph, son of David*.

115. Now the person to whom the revelation was made is commended by two things, namely by the fact that he is just, and therefore would not lie; second by the fact that he is the spouse, or husband, and therefore would not suffer a crime in her; *the jealousy and rage of the husband will not spare in the day of revenge* (Prov 6:34).

So he speaks in this way: *she was found* by Joseph, *to be with child*, but *Joseph her husband, being a just man, and not willing to expose her publicly*.

Here there are two opinions of the saints, namely that of Ambrose and that of Augustine.

116. For Augustine would have it that Joseph, who was not present when the angelic announcement was made, returning and finding her pregnant, had a suspicion of adultery.

But then right away a question arises: how was he just, if he did not wish to hand over her whom he suspected of adultery, i.e., to make her crime known? For by this he seemed to consent to her sin, and it is said that *they who do such things, are worthy of death; and not only they that do it, but they also that consent to them that do* (Rom 1:32).

But there are three responses to this. The first is, following Chrysostom, that justice is twofold: for there is one justice which is a cardinal virtue, which is called special justice; another is legal justice, which includes all virtues: piety, and mercy, and such. So when it is said that Joseph was just, this should be understood of justice in general, as justice is taken for piety. Hence since he was just, i.e., pious, he did not wish to hand her over. Another response is that of Augustine, who says that sin is twofold, namely hidden sin and manifest sin; for hidden sin should not be publicly disclosed, but a remedy should be applied to it in some other way. So the suspicion of adultery which Joseph had was a suspicion of a hidden sin, and not of a manifest one, because he alone knew; and again, if others were to know that she was pregnant, they could only suppose that it was from him. And therefore her crime ought not to have been made known. The third response is that of Rabanus, that Joseph was both just and pious, for by the fact that he did not wish to make her crime known, he was pious, but by the fact that he wished to send her away, he appeared just; for he knew that *he who keeps an adulteress, is foolish and wicked* (Prov 18:22).

117. But according to Jerome and Origen, he had no suspicion of adultery. For Joseph knew Mary's chastity;

pudicitiam Mariae; legerat in Scriptura quod *virgo concipiet*, Is. VII, 14 et cap. XI, 1: *egredietur virga de radice Iesse, et flos de radice eius ascendet* etc.; noverat etiam Mariam de David generatione descendisse. Unde facilius credebat hoc in ea impletum esse, quam ipsam fornicatam fuisse. Et ideo indignum reputans se tantae cohabitare sanctitati, voluit occulte dimittere eam, sicut Petrus dixit: *exi a me, domine, quia homo peccator sum*, Luc. V, 8. Unde nolebat eam traducere, idest ad se ducere, et in coniugem accipere, se indignum reputans.

Vel, secundum aliorum sententiam, ignorans finem, ne tamquam reus haberetur si celaret, et secum eam teneret.

118. *Haec autem eo cogitante.* Hic persona revelans introducitur: et tanguntur tria.

Primo enim tangitur tempus;

secundo persona revelans introducitur; *ecce angelus*:

tertio revelationis modus exprimitur, *apparuit in somnis*.

119. Dicit ergo *haec autem eo cogitante*, idest dum ista secum in mente revolveret, *ecce angelus Domini apparuit*.

Nota quod duo commendantur hic de Ioseph, scilicet sapientia et clementia. Sapientia quidem in hoc, quod ipse antequam ageret, deliberavit; Prov. IV, 25: *palpebrae tuae praecedant gressus tuos*: hoc est, nihil facias sine iudicio et deliberatione rationis. Item, clementia sive pietas in hoc quod factum eius non propalavit, vel promulgavit, contra multos qui statim illud quod habent in corde, volunt exterius publicare; Prov. XXV, 28: *sicut urbs patens, et absque murorum ambitu, ita vir, qui non potest in loquendo cohibere spiritum suum.*

Et ideo meruit instrui, sive consolari.

120. Unde sequitur *ecce angelus Domini apparuit*: quasi in promptu sit adiutorium Dei; Ps. IX, 10: *adiutor in opportunitatibus, in tribulatione*; Ps. LIII, 6: *ecce enim Deus adiuvat me, et Dominus susceptor est animae meae.*

Angelus Domini: nihil enim melius potuit excusare, quam ille qui conscius erat virginitatis servatae. Unde ille idem angelus qui missus est ad Mariam, Luc. I, 26, creditur missus ad Ioseph, Ps. XXXIII, 8: *immittet angelus Domini in circuitu timentium eum*, scilicet Mariae, et Ioseph, ut ipsam liberaret ab infamia, et Ioseph in perturbatione non dimitteret.

121. Sed hic quaeritur, quare non a principio facta est Ioseph revelatio, antequam ita perturbaretur.

he had read in the Scriptures that *a virgin will conceive* (Isa 7:14), and, *and there will come forth a rod out of the root of Jesse, and a flower will rise up out of his root* (Isa 11:1); he also knew that Mary was descended from David. Hence he more easily believed that this had been fulfilled in her than that she had fornicated. And therefore, considering himself unworthy to live with such great sanctity, he wished to hide her away, just as Peter said, *depart from me, for I am a sinful man, O Lord* (Luke 5:8). Hence he did not wish to hand her over, i.e., to take her to himself, and receive her in marriage, considering himself unworthy.

Or according to the opinion of others, not knowing the end, lest he be held accountable if he were to conceal it, and keep her with himself.

118. *But while he thought on these things.* Here he introduces the person revealing. And he touches upon three things.

For first, he touches upon the time;

second, the person revealing is introduced, **behold the angel of the Lord**;

third, the mode of the revelation is expressed, **appeared to him in his sleep**.

119. So he says, **but while he thought on these things**, i.e., while he turned these things over in his mind, **behold the angel of the Lord appeared**.

Notice that two things are commended here about Joseph, namely wisdom and mercy. Wisdom indeed in the fact that he deliberated before he acted; *let your eyes look straight on, and let your eyelids go before your steps* (Prov 4:25): this means, do nothing without the judgment and deliberation of reason. Similarly, mercy or piety in the fact that he did not make known or proclaim her deed, as opposed to many men who want to announce immediately that which they have in their heart; *as a city that lies open and is not compassed with walls, so is a man that cannot refrain his own spirit in speaking* (Prov 25:28).

And therefore he deserved to be instructed, or consoled.

120. Hence follows **behold the angel of the Lord appeared**, the help of God being, so to speak, ready at hand; *and the Lord is become . . . a helper in due time in tribulation* (Ps 9:10); *for behold God is my helper: and the Lord is the protector of my soul* (Ps 53:6).

The angel of the Lord, for none could better excuse her than he who was aware of her protected virginity. Hence that same angel who was sent to Mary (Luke 1:26), is believed to have been sent to Joseph; *the angel of the Lord will encamp round about them* (Ps 33:8), namely Mary and Joseph, so as to rescue her from infamy, and so as not to abandon Joseph in turmoil.

121. But here it is asked why a revelation was not made to Joseph from the beginning, before he was disturbed in this way.

Item, quare Maria ei non revelavit Annuntiationem angelicam, quae sibi facta fuerat.

Et dicendum ad primum, quod hoc fecit ut testimonium eius esset credibilius. Sicut enim Dominus Thomam apostolum permisit dubitare de sua resurrectione, ut scilicet dubitans palparet, et palpans crederet, et credendo infidelitatis in nobis vulnus amoveret; sic permisit Dominus Ioseph de pudicitia Mariae dubitare, ut dubitans revelationem angelicam acciperet, et accipiendo firmius crederet.

Ad hoc quod quaeritur secundo, dicendum, quod si Maria ei dixisset, ipse non credidisset.

122. *Apparuit ei in somnis*: ecce modus revelationis.

Nota quod apparere proprie est illius rei, quae de natura sua est invisibilis, tamen in potestate sua est ut videatur: sicut est Deus, vel angelus; illa enim quae de sui natura habent ut videantur, proprie apparere non dicuntur: unde dicitur apparitio divina, vel angelica. Unde proprie loquitur.

123. *Apparuit in somnis*.

Sed hic quaeritur quare in somnis.

Ratio redditur in Glossa, quia Ioseph quodammodo dubitans erat: unde quasi quodammodo dormiebat, et ideo recte in somnis dicitur angelus apparuisse ei.

Alia ratio potest assignari melior, sicut enim dicit Apostolus, I Cor. XIV, 22, *prophetia data est fidelibus, signa autem infidelibus*. Proprie autem revelatio, quae dicitur prophetica, fit in somnis; Num. XII, 6: *si quis fuerit inter vos propheta Domini, in visione apparebo ei, vel per somnium loquar ad illum*: et ideo quia Ioseph iustus erat, et fidelis, ipsi tamquam fideli debuit fieri apparitio, quae competit credentibus, scilicet revelatio quasi prophetica. Quia vero apparitio corporalis est miraculosa, talis apparitio sibi non competebat, cum ipse crederet, et esset fidelis.

124. Sed tunc quaeritur, quare Mariae facta est visibilis apparitio, cum ipsa esset fidelissima.

Et dicendum est, quod mysterium incarnationis a principio revelatum est Virgini Mariae, quando difficilius erat ad credendum; et ideo oportuit quod sibi fieret apparitio visibilis. Ipsi vero Ioseph non est revelatum a principio, sed magis quando iam pro magna parte erat impletum, cum iam videret alvum eius intumescere, unde facilius poterat credere; et ideo sufficiebat sibi apparitio quae fit in somnis.

125. *Ioseph fili David*. Hic revelationis verba ponuntur: et dividitur in tres partes, secundum tria quae facit angelus:

primo enim Mariae et Ioseph prohibet divortium;

Similarly, why did not Mary reveal to him the angelic announcement which had been made to her?

And to the first, one should say that this was done so that his testimony would be more believable. For as the Lord permitted the apostle Thomas to doubt his resurrection, so that he might touch, and touching, believe, and by believing he might remove the wound of unbelief in us; in the same way the Lord permitted Joseph to doubt the chastity of Mary so that, doubting, he might receive the angelic revelation, and by receiving it believe more firmly.

To the second question it should be said that if Mary had spoken to him, he would not have believed her.

122. *Appeared to him in his sleep*: behold, the mode of revelation.

Note that to appear is proper to that which of its own nature is invisible, yet has it within its power that it be seen, as is God, or an angel; for those things which have it of their own nature that they are seen are not properly said to appear. Hence it is called a divine apparition, or an angelic apparition. Hence this is properly spoken.

123. *Appeared to him in his sleep*.

But here it is asked, why in his sleep?

And a reason is given in the Gloss, namely that Joseph was in a certain way doubting; hence he was in a certain way sleeping, so to speak, and therefore rightly is the angel said to have appeared to him in his sleep.

Another and better reason can be given, for as the Apostle says, *tongues are for a sign, not to believers, but to unbelievers; but prophecies not to unbelievers, but to believers* (1 Cor 14:22). Now a revelation, which is called a prophecy, properly happens in sleep; *if there be among you a prophet of the Lord, I will appear to him in a vision, or I will speak to him in a dream* (Num 12:6); and so since Joseph was just and faithful, there should have come to him, as to one who is faithful, an apparition, as befits those who believe; that is, a prophetic revelation, as it were. Since indeed a bodily apparition is miraculous, such an apparition did not befit him, since he believed, and was faithful.

124. But then it is asked why a visible apparition was made to Mary, since she was most faithful.

And one should say that the mystery of the incarnation was revealed to the Virgin Mary in the beginning, when it was most difficult to believe; and so it was necessary that a visible apparition be made to her. However, it was not revealed to Joseph in the beginning, but rather when it was for the most part completed already, since he already saw her womb to have grown big; hence he was more easily able to believe, and so an apparition which came in his sleep was enough for him.

125. *Joseph, son of David*. Here the words of the revelation are set down; and it is divided into three parts, according to the three things which the angel does.

For first, he forbids the separation of Mary and Joseph;

secundo incarnationis aperit mysterium, cum dicit *quod in ea natum est, de Spiritu Sancto est*;

tertio ipsius Ioseph futurum praenuntiat obsequium, quod scilicet puero exhibebat, ibi *pariet autem filium*.

126. Dicit igitur *Ioseph*. Vocat eum ut reddat eum attentum ad audiendum, et ut revocet eum ad seipsum. Hoc commune est in Scriptura, quod scilicet quando praemittitur apparitio, quae est de superius, requirit in auditore quamdam mentis elevationem, et attentionem; Ez. II, 1: *fili hominis, sta super pedes tuos, et loquar tecum*, et infra, *fili hominis, audi quaecumque loquor ad te, et noli esse exasperans*. Hab. II, 1: *super custodiam meam stabo*.

127. *Fili David*. Ideo genus exprimit ut avertat illud quod dicitur Is. VII, 13: *audite, domus David: numquid parum est molestos esse hominibus, quia molesti estis et Deo meo?* et cetera. Signum enim datum fuit non uni personae, sed toti tribui sive domui: unde quia de hoc debebat eum instruere, iubetur in expressione generis sui vaticinium prophetae ad memoriam reducere.

128. *Noli timere*. Omnis apparitio, sive sit boni, vel mali angeli, timorem quemdam incutit: et hoc, quia talis apparitio est inconsueta, et quasi extranea naturae hominis; et ideo ponit hominem quasi extra se. Sed in hoc est differentia, quia apparitio mali angeli terrorem incutit, et in ipso terrore hominem dimittit, ut scilicet hominem quasi extra se positum facilius pertrahat ad peccatum; sed boni angeli apparitio, quamvis terrorem incutiat, tamen statim subditur conclusio, et assecutio consolationis, ut scilicet homo ad se redeat, et quae sibi dicuntur advertat; unde Luc. I, ubi dicitur quod apparuit angelus Zachariae, statim sequitur: *ne timeas*, et similiter in eodem: *ne timeas, Maria*.

129. Unde post apparitionem factam Ioseph statim subditur consolatio. Duplicem habebat iste timorem, scilicet Dei, et etiam peccati, ne scilicet Mariae cohabitando peccaret tamquam conscius peccati, et ideo, *ne timeas*, subditur, scilicet metu peccati, *accipere Mariam coniugem tuam*.

Nota quod *coniux* dicitur, non propter matrimonium, sed propter desponsationem: consuetudo enim est Scripturae et sponsas vocare coniuges, et coniuges sponsas.

130. Sed quaeritur, quomodo iubet eam accipere, cum eam nondum dimisisset.

Et dicendum quod licet eam corporaliter non dimisisset, tamen in animo eam dimiserat: et ideo iubetur

second, he opens the mystery of the incarnation, when he says, *he who is born in her, is of the Holy Spirit*;

third, he foretells the future service of Joseph himself, namely that which he showed to the child, at *she will bring forth a son*.

126. He says then, *Joseph*. He calls him so as to render him attentive for listening, and so as to recall him to himself. This is common in the Scriptures, namely that when an apparition is sent which is from someone higher, he seeks in the hearer a certain elevation of the mind, and attention; *son of man, stand upon your feet, and I will speak to you* (Ezek 2:1). And below that, *but you, O son of man, hear all that I say to you: and do not provoke me*. And: *I will stand upon my watch, and fix my foot upon the tower: and I will watch, to see what will be said to me* (Hab 2:1).

127. *Son of David*. He pronounced the name of the family so that he might ward off that which is said: *hear therefore, O house of David: is it a small thing for you to be grievous to men, that you are grievous to my God also?* (Isa 7:13). For the sign was given not to one person, but to an entire tribe or house; hence because he was supposed to instruct him about this, Joseph is commanded by the pronunciation of his family name to recall to remember the prophet's saying.

128. *Do not fear*. Every apparition, whether it be of a good angel or a bad one, instills a certain fear; and this is because such an apparition is against the custom and outside the nature of man, so to speak, and so it places a man outside of himself, so to speak. But there is this difference, that the apparition of a bad angel instills terror, and leaves a man in that terror, namely to draw the man placed as it were outside of himself more easily to sin; but in the apparition of a good angel, although it instills terror, yet at once an end of the terror is given, and a gain in consolation, namely that the man might be led back into himself, and attend to what is said to him. Hence in Luke, where it says that an angel appeared to Zachary, there follows at once, *do not fear, Zachary*, and likewise in the same chapter, *do not fear, Mary* (Luke 1:13, 30).

129. Hence after the apparition Joseph is given consolation at once. He had a twofold fear, namely of God and also of sin, that is, he feared lest he should sin by living with Mary as if co-aware of sin, and so next is added *fear not*, namely with a dread of sin, *to take unto you Mary your wife*.

Note that *wife* is said, not on account of matrimony, but on account of espousal; for it is the custom of Scripture both to call the espoused married, and the married espoused.

130. But it is asked, how he could command Joseph to take her, since he had not sent her away?

And one should say that although he had not sent her away bodily, nevertheless he had sent her away in his soul;

eam accipere. Vel *ne timeas accipere* quantum ad solemnitatem, et nuptiarum celebrationem.

131. *Quod enim in ea natum est, de Spiritu Sancto est*. Hic aperit incarnationis mysterium.

Et nota quod cum tria ibi fuerint, scilicet ipsa Virgo concipiens, Filius Dei conceptus, et virtus activa Spiritus Sancti; duo bene exprimit angelus, scilicet concipientem, et conceptionis Actorem; sed tertium, ipsum Dei Filium conceptum, non exprimit nisi indefinite: *quod enim*, inquit, *in ea natum est*: et hoc ut denotetur quod ipsum est ineffabile et incomprehensibile, non solum homini, sed etiam ipsis angelis. *Quod enim*, inquit, *in ea natum est*, non dicit, de ea, quia nasci de matre est in lucem prodire: in matre nasci est ipsum concipi, *de Spiritu Sancto est*.

Hoc est ergo testimonium angelicum, quod inducit Evangelista ad probandum quod supra dixerat *inventa est in utero habens de Spiritu Sancto*.

132. Nota quod in conceptione aliarum mulierum, in semine viri est virtus formativa, cuius subiectum est semen, et per hanc virtutem formatur foetus, et vegetatur in corpore mulieris. Hanc autem supplevit virtus Spiritus Sancti. Et ideo aliquando invenitur dictum a sanctis, quod Spiritus Sanctus fuit ibi pro semine, aliquando tamen dicitur quod non fuit ibi semen. Et hoc est, quia in semine viri sunt duo, scilicet ipsa corrupta substantia, quae descendit a corpore viri, et ipsa formativa virtus.

Dicendum ergo, quod Spiritus Sanctus fuit pro semine quantum ad virtutem formativam; sed non fuit ibi pro semine quantum ad corpulentam substantiam, quia non de substantia Spiritus Sancti facta est caro Christi, vel conceptio eius. Et ideo patet, quod Spiritus Sanctus non potest dici pater Christi, quia nec secundum divinam naturam, nec secundum humanam. Secundum divinam naturam quidem, quia quamvis Christus sit eiusdem gloriae cum Spiritu Sancto, Filius tamen secundum divinam naturam nihil accipit a Spiritu Sancto: et ideo non potest dici filius eius; filius enim aliquid accipit a patre. Similiter nec secundum humanam, quia pater et filius debent convenire in substantia; Christus autem, quamvis sit conceptus virtute Spiritus Sancti, non tamen de substantia Spiritus Sancti.

133. Sed contra hoc quod dicitur *de Spiritu Sancto* est, quod Prov. IX, 1 dicitur, quod *Sapientia aedificavit sibi domum*. Ergo videtur quod ipsamet Divina Sapientia, idest Dei Filius, sibi humanam naturam univit, et ita non est facta virtute Spiritus Sancti.

Sed duplex est responsio, secundum Augustinum. Prima, quod verbum illud quod scribitur Prov. IX, 1, intelligitur de Ecclesia, quam Christus in sanguine suo fundavit. Alia est, quod indivisa sunt opera Trinitatis: et

and therefore he is commanded to take her. Or *do not fear* to take her as regards the solemnity and the celebration of nuptials.

131. *For he who is born in her, is of the Holy Spirit*. Here he opens the mystery of the incarnation.

And notice that since three things were there, namely the Virgin conceiving, the Son of God conceived, and the active power of the Holy Spirit, the angel expressed two of them well, namely the one conceiving and the author of the conception; but the third, the Son of God conceived, he only expresses indefinitely: *for he who*, he says, *is born in her*, and this is done to indicate that he is ineffable and incomprehensible, not only to men, but even to the angels. *He who*, he says, *is born in her*, he does not say, *of her*, because to be born of a mother is to advance into the light, while to be born in a mother is to be conceived, *is of the Holy Spirit*.

So this is the angelic testimony which the Evangelist brings in to confirm what he had said, that *she was found with child, of the Holy Spirit*.

132. Note that in the conception of other women, the formative power is in the seed of the man, the subject of which power is the seed, and through this power the fetus is formed and enlivened in the body of the woman. But the Holy Spirit supplied this. And for this reason the saints are sometimes found to say that the Holy Spirit was there instead of seed, while sometimes they say that no seed was there. And this is because there are two things in the seed of a man, namely the corrupted substance which comes down from the body of the man, and the formative power itself.

It should be said therefore that the Holy Spirit was *instead of seed* as regards the formative power; but he was not there *instead of seed* as regards bodily substance, because neither the flesh of Christ nor his conception was made from the substance of the Holy Spirit. And so it is clear that the Holy Spirit cannot be called the father of Christ, because he is a father neither according to the divine nature, nor according to the human. Indeed, not according to the divine nature, because although Christ is of the same glory with the Holy Spirit, yet the Son according to the divine nature takes nothing from the Holy Spirit, and so cannot be called his son, for a son takes something from the father. Likewise not according to the human, because father and son ought to agree in substance; but although Christ was conceived by the power of the Holy Spirit, nevertheless he is not of the substance of the Holy Spirit.

133. But against what is said, *is of the Holy Spirit*, it is said that *Wisdom has built herself a house* (Prov 9:1). So it seems that the Divine Wisdom itself, i.e., the Son of God, united himself to human nature, and thus is not made by the power of the Holy Spirit.

But there are two responses, according to Augustine. First, that what is written in Proverbs 9:1 is understood of the Church, which Christ founded in his own blood. Another is that the works of the Trinity are indivisible, and

ideo illud quod facit Filius, facit etiam Spiritus Sanctus, sed tamen per quamdam appropriationem attribuitur Spiritui Sancto. Et ratio huius dicta fuit superius.

134. *Pariet autem filium*. Hic praenuntiat obsequium, quod exhibebit Ioseph puero iam nato, et facit tria:

primo enim praenuntiat virginis partum;

secundo praemonstrat obsequium ab ipso Ioseph puero exhibendum, cum dicit *et vocabis nomen*;

tertio aperit nomen impositum ipsi puero, cum dicit *Iesum*.

135. Dicit ergo *pariet*. Ita concepit de Spiritu Sancto quidem primo, sed *pariet filium*. Non dicit *tibi*, quia ipse puerum non genuit. Luc. I, 13 dictum est Zachariae: *uxor tua pariet tibi filium*, quia ipsum Zacharias genuit. Vel ideo non dicit, *tibi*, ut ostendatur, quod pro omnibus natus est: non solum tibi, vel ipsi pariet filium, sed toti mundo; Luc. II, 10: *ecce annuntio vobis gaudium magnum, quia natus est vobis hodie Salvator, qui est Christus Dominus in civitate David* et cetera.

136. Sed quia Ioseph posset dicere: *ita concepit ipsa de Spiritu Sancto, et pariet filium, quid ergo ad me? In nullo sum ei necessarius*. Ideo subdit ipsius Ioseph obsequium *vocabis nomen eius*.

Consuetudo erat apud Hebraeos, et est hodie, quod die octavo circumcidebant puerum, et tunc imponebant ei nomen; et hoc factum est per Ioseph: unde in hoc opere minister fuit. Unde dicitur ei *vocabis*; non dicitur *impones*, quia iam est sibi impositum; Is. LXII, 2: *vocabitur tibi nomen novum, quod os Domini nominavit*.

137. *Iesum*, hoc est nomen a Deo impositum. Et reddit causam *ipse enim salvum faciet populum suum*, quem sibi acquisivit sanguine suo, hoc est *populum eius*. Dan. IX, v. 26 dicitur: *non erit populus eius, qui est eum negaturus*; unde est populus Domini per fidem; I Petr. II, 9: *vos estis genus electum, regale sacerdotium, gens sancta, populus acquisitionis*.

A peccatis eorum. In libro Iudic. frequenter dicitur quod talis, vel talis salvavit Israel: sed a quibus? Ab inimicis carnalibus; hic autem a peccatis, remittendo peccata, quod soli Deo competit. Luc. V, 24: *ut autem sciatis, quia Filius hominis habet potestatem in terra dimittendi peccata*.

138. Nota, quod hic confunditur Nestorius, qui dicebat, quod illa, quae Dei sunt, ut esse ab aeterno, esse omnipotens, vel huiusmodi, non conveniunt illi homini. Ecce quod ille idem homo, qui natus est de Virgine, qui vocatur Iesus, *ipse salvum faciet populum suum a peccatis eorum*. Unde cum peccata dimittere non possit nisi

therefore what the Son does, the Holy Spirit does also, and yet this action is attributed to the Holy Spirit by a certain appropriation. And the reason for this was stated above.

134. *She will bring forth a son*. Here he foretells the service which Joseph will show to the child when born, and he does three things:

for first, he foretells the Virgin's labor;

second, he reveals beforehand the service which Joseph himself was to show the child when he says, *and you will call his name*;

third, he discloses the name given to the child, when he says *Jesus*.

135. He says then, *she will bring forth*. Thus indeed she conceived of the Holy Spirit at first, but *she will bring forth*. He does not say *for you*, because Joseph himself did not beget the child. it is said to Zachary: *your wife Elizabeth will bear you a son* (Luke 1:13), because Zachary himself begot him. Or he does not say *for you* to show that he was born for all: she will not bear a son only for you, or for this man, but for the whole world; *behold, I bring you good tidings of great joy, that will be to all the people: for, this day, is born to you a Savior, who is Christ the Lord, in the city of David* (Luke 2:10).

136. But because Joseph could say, *she conceived of the Holy Spirit in this way, and she will bear a son; what then is there for me? I am not necessary to her at all*, he adds Joseph's own service: *you will call his name*.

It was the custom among the Hebrews, and still is today, that they circumcised the child on the eighth day, and at that time gave him a name; and this was done by Joseph. So he was the agent in this work. Hence it is said to him, *you will call*; it is not said, *you will give*, because it is already given to him; *you will be called by a new name, which the mouth of the Lord will name* (Isa 62:2).

137. *Jesus*, this is the name given by God. And he gives the cause: *for he will save his people*; what he will acquire for himself by his own blood is *his people*. *The people that will deny him will not be his* (Dan 9:26); hence it is the people of the Lord through faith. *But you are a chosen generation, a kingly priesthood, a holy nation, a purchased people* (1 Pet 2:9).

From their sins. In the book of Judges it frequently says that such or such a one will save Israel: but from what? From bodily enemies in that case, but here from sins, by the forgiveness of sins, which belongs to God alone. *But that you may know that the Son of man has power on earth to forgive sins* (Luke 5:24).

138. Note that Nestorius is confounded here, who said that those things which are of God, as to be eternal, to be omnipotent, or so on, do not belong to this man. Behold, this same man, who was born of the Virgin, who is called Jesus, *he will save his people from their sins*. Hence, since no once can forgive sins but God alone, it is necessary to

solus Deus, oportet dicere quod iste homo sit Deus, et quod ea, quae Dei sunt, ei verissime conveniunt.

say that this man is God, and that those things which are of God most truly belong to him.

Lecture 5

1:22 Hoc autem totum factum est, ut adimpleretur id quod dictum est a Domino per Prophetam dicentem: [n. 139]

1:23 ecce virgo in utero habebit, et pariet filium, et vocabunt nomen eius Emmanuel quod est interpretatum, nobiscum Deus. [n. 140]

1:22 τοῦτο δὲ ὅλον γέγονεν ἵνα πληρωθῇ τὸ ῥηθὲν ὑπὸ κυρίου διὰ τοῦ προφήτου λέγοντος·

1:23 ἰδοὺ ἡ παρθένος ἐν γαστρὶ ἕξει καὶ τέξεται υἱόν, καὶ καλέσουσιν τὸ ὄνομα αὐτοῦ Ἐμμανουήλ, ὅ ἐστιν μεθερμηνευόμενον μεθ᾽ ἡμῶν ὁ θεός.

1:22 Now all this was done that it might be fulfilled what the Lord spoke by the Prophet, saying: [n. 139]

1:23 behold a virgin will be with child, and bring forth a son, and they will will his name Emmanuel, which being interpreted is, God with us. [n. 140]

---

139. Praemiserat Evangelista, quod mater Dei inventa est in utero habens de Spiritu Sancto, et hoc supra probavit per angelicam revelationem, hic probat per prophetiae praenuntiationem; unde dicit **hoc totum factum est ut adimpleretur quod dictum est a Domino per Prophetam**.

Et sciendum quod ista particula dupliciter potest introduci hic. Chrysostomus enim vult quod totum hoc dixerit angelus et prophetiam introduxerit. Et ratio est, quia ipse, ne quod praenuntiabat videretur novum, subito voluit ostendere quod ab antiquo praenuntiatum erat; Is. XLVIII, 3: *qui fecit iam quod futurum est*, secundum aliam translationem.

Alii dicunt, et credo melius, quod istud, scilicet **hoc totum factum est** etc., sunt verba Evangelistae. Nam ibi terminantur verba angeli: **et ipse salvum faciet** et cetera. Et inducit ea Evangelista propter tria. Primo, ut ostendat quod Vetus Testamentum est de Christo; Act. c. X, 43: *huic omnes prophetae testimonium perhibent, remissionem peccatorum accipere per nomen eius omnes qui credunt in eum*. Secundo ut facilius Christo credant: Io. V, 46: *si crederetis Moysi, crederetis forsitan et mihi: de me enim ille scripsit*. Tertio ad ostendendum conformitatem Veteris et Novi Testamenti; Col. II, 17: *quae sunt umbra futurorum, corpus autem Christi*.

140. Sed ad hoc quod sciatur quid in ista prophetia contineatur, sciendum quod tria annuntiat angelus. Primo enim dixit **quod in ea natum est** etc.; secundo **pariet filium**; tertio **vocabitur nomen eius Iesum**. Ista per ordinem in prophetia continentur. Et primum probat quod dicit **'ecce virgo'**; secundo **'pariet autem'**; tertio **'et vocabitur'**. Ergo de Spiritu Sancto erat, quod per virginitatem concepit. Et hoc, quod dicitur in prophetia, *ecce virgo concipiet*; Is. XXXV, 2: *germinans germinabit, et exultabit laetabunda, et laudans* et cetera. Item **'virgo pariet filium'**, quia in pariendo in nullo laesa est virginitas; Is. XI, 1: *egredietur virga de radice Iesse, et flos de*

139. The Evangelist had set out before that the mother of God was found with child of the Holy Spirit, and above he confirmed this by the angelic revelation. Here he confirms it by the prophet's foretelling it; hence he says, **now all this was done that it might be fulfilled what the Lord spoke by the Prophet**.

And it should be known that this little part can be brought in here in two ways. For Chrysostom would have it that the angel said all this and brought in the prophecy, too. And the reason is that he wished to show that it had been foretold from of old, lest it seem that he was suddenly foretelling something new; *who makes now what is to come* (Isa 48:3), according to another translation.

Others say, and I believe better, that these words, namely **all this was done**, are the Evangelist's words. For the words of the angel are ended at **for he will save his people from their sins** (Matt 1:21). And the Evangelist brings them in for the sake of three things. First, to show that the Old Testament is about Christ; *to him all the prophets give testimony, that by his name all receive remission of sins, who believe in him* (Acts 10:43). Second, so that they might more easily believe Christ; *for if you did believe Moses, you would perhaps believe me also; for he wrote of me* (John 5:46). Third, to show the conformity of the Old and New Testaments; *which are a shadow of things to come, but the body is of Christ* (Col 2:17).

140. But that you may know what is contained in this prophecy, you should know that the angel announced three things. For first he said, **for he who is born in her** (Matt 1:20); second, **she will bring forth a son** (Matt 1:21); third, **and you will call his name Jesus** (Matt 1:21). These things are contained in the prophecy in order. And first he confirms what he says, **'behold a virgin'**; second, **'will be with child'**; third, **'they will call his name'**. Therefore it was of the Holy Spirit that she conceived while still a virgin. And this is what is said in the prophecy: *behold a virgin will conceive* (Isa 7:14); *it will bud forth and blossom, and will rejoice with joy and praise* (Isa 35:2). And similarly the

radice eius ascendet et cetera. Christus quidem flos est. Ergo in nullo laesa est virginitas.

141. Sequitur *'et vocabitur nomen eius Emmanuel.'*

Sed quaeritur, quare non consonat hoc cum verbis angeli, dicendo *et vocabitur Iesus*?

Dicendum, quod ista repromissio facta fuit Iudaeis, qui ex adventu Christi salutem haberent. Et Iesus 'salvator' interpretatur, quod idem est quod *'Emmanuel', nobiscum Deus*.

Est enim Deus nobiscum quatuor modis: per naturae assumptionem, Io. I, 14: *Verbum caro factum est*, per naturae conformitatem, quia in omnibus similis, Phil. II, 7: *in similitudinem hominum factus, et habitu inventus ut homo*, per conversationem corporalem, Bar. III, 38: *post hoc in terris visus est, et cum hominibus conversatus est*, per spiritualem conversationem, infra ult., 20: *ecce ego vobiscum sum omnibus diebus usque ad consummationem saeculi*.

142. Sed quaerendum, circa litteram, cur Evangelista non utitur eisdem verbis cum propheta, sed utitur nomine *Iesu*.

Sed dicendum, quod eodem spiritu loquebatur. Tamen Hieronymus dicit quod ideo Evangelista dixit *habebit*, quia iam de facto loquebatur.

143. Item quaerendum, cur in Isaia dicitur *et vocabitur*, hic autem dicitur *et vocabunt*.

Sed Hieronymus dicit, quod hic dicitur *vocabunt*, quia quod primo angeli vocaverunt annuntiando, Luc. II, 21, postea apostoli vocaverunt praedicando et magnificando. *Ut in nomine Iesu omne genu flectatur* etc., Phil. c. II, 10.

144. *Quod est interpretatum nobiscum Deus*. Sed quaeritur, quis apposuit hanc interpretationem prophetiae *nobiscum Deus*, propheta, an Evangelista? Et videtur quod non Evangelista, quia hac non indiguit, quia scripsit in Hebraeo.

Sed dicendum, uno modo, quia *'Emmanuel'* est nomen compositum, ideo Evangelista illud etiam in Hebraeo interpretatus est. Vel dicendum, quod ille, qui primo transtulit de Hebraeo, interpretatus est.

145. Et notandum, quod in Glossa dicitur quod triplex est species prophetiae, scilicet praedestinationis, praescientiae et comminationis; et differunt.

Prophetia enim dicitur praenuntiatio eorum, quae sunt procul, idest futurorum; sed futurorum quaedam sunt quae solus Deus facit; quaedam vero, etsi Deus facit, tamen fiunt per nos et per alias etiam creaturas;

'virgin will bring forth a son', because her virginity was not harmed in any way by giving birth; *and there will come forth a rod out of the root of Jesse, and a flower will rise up out of his root* (Isa 11:1). Christ is certainly the flower. Therefore in no way is her virginity harmed.

141. There follows *'and they will call his name Emmanuel.'*

But it is asked, why does not this agree with the angel's words, by saying, *and you will call his name Jesus*?

One should say that this promise had been made to the Jews, who would have salvation from Christ's coming. And Jesus is interpreted as 'savior', which is the same as *'Emmanuel', God with us*.

For God is with us in four ways: through the assumption of nature, *and the Word was made flesh* (John 1:14); through the conformity of nature, *and in habit found as a man* (Phil 2:7); through bodily interaction, *afterwards he was seen upon earth, and conversed with men* (Bar 3:38); and through spiritual interaction, *I am with you all days, even to the consummation of the world* (Matt 28:20).

142. But one should ask, concerning the letter, why the Evangelist does not use the same words as the prophet, but rather uses the name *Jesus*.

But one should say that he spoke in the same spirit. Still, Jerome says that the Evangelist said, *will be with child*, because he was speaking of something already accomplished.

143. Similarly, one should ask why it says in Isaiah, *his name will be called* (Isa 7:14), while it says here, *and they will call*.

But Jerome says that it says here, *they will call*, because what the angel first named by announcing (Luke 2:21), the apostles afterwards named by preaching and magnifying. *That in the name of Jesus every knee should bow* (Phil 2:10).

144. *Which is interpreted as, God with us*. But it is asked, who added this interpretation of the prophecy *God with us*, the prophet or the Evangelist? And it seems that it was not the Evangelist, because he did not need this, since he wrote in Hebrew.

But one should say, in one way, that *'Emmanuel'* is a composite name, so the Evangelist interpreted it even in Hebrew. Or one should say that the one who first translated this Gospel from Hebrew interpreted it.

145. And one should note that the Gloss says that there are three species of prophecy: namely that of predestination, that of foreknowledge, and that of threatening; and these differ.

For prophecy names a foretelling of those things which are distant, i.e., in the future; but there are some things in the future which only God does; some things which, although God does them, still they come about through us

quaedam autem sunt quae nullo modo Deus facit, ut mala. Praenuntiatio illorum, quae solus Deus facit vocatur prophetia praedestinationis, sicut conceptus Virginis; unde illud Is. VII, 14: *ecce virgo concipiet*, est prophetia praedestinationis. Sed ea quae fiunt a causis secundis, possunt dupliciter considerari. Primo, secundum quod sunt in praescientia Dei, verbi gratia de Lazaro; si enim aliquis consideret causas naturales, diceret quod numquam surgeret, et verum diceret: cum tamen deberet resuscitari secundum ordinem divinae praescientiae. Ergo quando prophetia est praenuntiatio secundum quod est in praescientia divina, semper impletur; quando autem secundum ordinem causarum inferiorum, non semper, sicut patet Is. XXXVIII, v. 1, quando Isaias ad Ezechiam dixit: *dispone domui tuae, quoniam morieris tu, et non vives* et cetera.

146. Sed numquid prophetia imponit necessitatem praescientiae?

Et dicendum quod non; quia prophetia est quoddam signum divinae praescientiae, quae non imponit necessitatem rebus praescitis, quia considerat futura in sua praesentialitate. Quicquid enim agitur, est Deo praesens, quia eius intuitus se extendit ad omne tempus; si enim video aliquid praesens, non imponit necessitatem meus intuitus, sicut quando aliquem sedere video. Et hoc modo istas prophetias, quae in isto libro inducuntur, intelleximus.

147. Considerandum est enim tres errores fuisse.

Unus Manichaeorum dicentium, quod in toto Veteri Testamento non invenitur prophetia de Christo: et quicquid inductum est in Novo Testamento de Veteri, totum est ex corruptione.

Contra quod Rom. I, 1: *Paulus servus Christi, vocatus apostolus, segregatus in Evangelium Dei, quod ante promiserat per prophetas suos* et cetera. Et quod loquatur de Iudaeorum prophetiis, patet infra c. IX, 5: *quorum patres, ex quibus est Christus secundum carnem* et cetera.

148. Alius fuit Theodori dicentis, quod nihil eorum quae inducuntur de Veteri Testamento, sunt ad litteram de Christo, sed sunt adaptata, sicut quando inducunt illud Virgilii

talia pendebat memorans, fixusque manebat

hoc enim adaptatum est de Christo; et tunc illud **ut adimpleretur**, debet sic exponi, quasi diceret Evangelista: *et hoc potest adaptari*.

Contra quod Lc. ult., 44: *oportet impleri omnia quae scripta sunt in lege Moysi, et prophetis, et Psalmis de me*. Et sciendum quod in Veteri Testamento aliqua sunt quae referuntur ad Christum, et de eo solo dicuntur, sicut illud *ecce virgo in utero concipiet, et pariet filium*, Is. VII, 14; et illud Ps. XXI, 2: *Deus, Deus meus, respice in me, quare me*

and through other creatures as well; further, there are some things which God in no way does, such as evil. The foretelling of those things which only God does is called the prophecy of predestination, such as the conception of the Virgin; hence *behold a virgin will conceive* (Isa 7:14) is a prophecy of predestination. But those things which come about by secondary causes can be considered in two ways. First, according as they are in the foreknowledge of God, e.g., concerning Lazarus; for if someone were to consider the natural causes, he would say that Lazarus would never rise, and he would speak truly; while nevertheless he was to be raised up according to the order of divine foreknowledge. Therefore, when a prophecy foretells according to what is in the divine foreknowledge, it is always fulfilled; but when it foretells according to inferior causes, it is not always fulfilled, as is clear when Isaiah said to Ezechias, *take order with your house, for you will die, and not live* (Isa 38:1).

146. But does not a prophecy of foreknowledge impose necessity?

And one should say that it does not, because a prophecy is a particular sign of God's foreknowledge, which foreknowledge does not impose necessity on the things foreknown, because he considers future things in his own presentiality. For whatever is done is present to God, since his gaze extends to every time; for if I see something present, my gaze does not impose necessity, as when I see someone sitting. And we have understood the prophecies which are brought into this book in this way.

147. For one should consider that there have been three errors.

One is that of the Manichees, who say that no prophecies about Christ are found in the Old Testament; and whatever has been brought into the New Testament from the Old is wholly by corruption.

This is against what is said, *Paul, a servant of Jesus Christ, called to be an apostle, separated unto the Gospel of God, which he had promised before, by his prophets, in the holy Scriptures* (Rom 1:1–2). And what is said about the prophets of the Jews is clear below: *whose are the fathers, and of whom is Christ, according to the flesh* (Rom 9:5).

148. Another error was that of Theodore of Mopsuestia, who says that none of those things which are brought in from the Old Testament are literally about Christ, but are made to fit, as when they bring in that line from Virgil:

he hung remembering such things, and remained pierced

For this is made to fit with Christ. And then **that it might be fulfilled** should be explained in this way, as though the Evangelist had said: *and this can be made to fit*.

But against this: *that all things must needs be fulfilled, which are written in the law of Moses, and in the prophets, and in the Psalms, concerning me* (Luke 24:44). And one should know that in the Old Testament there are certain things which are referred to Christ and are said only of him, as this line, *behold a virgin will conceive, and bear a*

dereliquisti? et cetera. Et si quis alium sensum litteralem poneret, esset haereticus, et haeresis damnata est. Sed quia non solum verba Veteris Testamenti, sed etiam facta significant de Christo, aliquando dicuntur aliqua ad litteram de aliquibus aliis, sed referuntur ad Christum, inquantum illa gerunt figuram Christi, sicut de Salomone dicitur: *et dominabitur a mari usque ad mare* etc.; hoc enim non fuit impletum in eo.

149. Tertius error fuit Iudaeorum.

Sciendum autem, quod Iudaei specialiter obiiciunt contra istam auctoritatem, quia in Hebraeo non habetur *virgo*, sed *alma*, quod idem est quod *adolescentula*. Unde ad litteram non sunt dicta de Christo sed de Emmanuel, vel de quodam filio Isaiae, secundum alios.

Sed contra hos obiicit Hieronymus: et quod de filio Isaiae non potuerit dici, probatur, quia iam erat natus, quando hoc dictum fuit. Item non invenitur aliquis famosus fuisse tempore illo, qui vocaretur Emmanuel. Item non est signum quod iuvencula pariat. Unde dicit Hieronymus, quod *alma* est aequivocum, et significat quandoque aetatem, quandoque absconditam, et tunc significat virginem studiose conservatam; et sic significat hic.

Item obiiciunt Iudaei, quod illud datum fuit ut signum. Is. VII, 3: *venient duo reges contra Achaz* etc., et promisit quod liberarentur ab his dando hoc signum ad Achaz.

Sed dicendum, quod dedit hoc signum non solum ad Achaz, sed etiam ad domum David, quia dicit *audite ergo, domus David*; quasi dicat Propheta: *Dominus adiuvabit te contra istum regem, quia ipse multo maiora faciet, quia non solum ipsius liberatio erit, sed totius mundi.*

150. Sed revertamur ad litteram. **Hoc totum factum est**.

Sed contra. Angelus multa praemiserat, scilicet **quod in ea natum est** etc., **pariet** etc., et iterum, **vocabitur** et cetera. Hoc vero non totum factum erat.

Sed dicendum uno modo, secundum Rabanum, ut **hoc totum factum** etc. referatur ad praeterita facta, quod angelus apparuit Virgini, et dixit illa verba, **hoc totum factum fuit**, ad conservationem Virginis, ut ly **ut** teneatur causaliter. Vel refertur ad ea quae praenuntiaverat; et potest dici **totum factum** propter praedestinationem.

Vel dicendum, quod Evangelista scribebat quando totum factum erat; et ideo refertur ad id. Unde ly **ut** tenetur consecutive, quia non voluit Deus incarnari propter hoc ut impleretur prophetia, quasi Vetus Testamentum dignius sit Novo; sed consecutum est ad prophetiam hoc quod Christus incarnaretur.

son (Isa 7:14); and this one: *O God my God, look upon me: why have you forsaken me?* (Ps 21:2). And if someone were to set down another literal sense, he would be a heretic, and heresy is accursed. But since not only the words of the Old Testament, but even its deeds signify things about Christ, sometimes some things are said literally about others, but are referred to Christ insofar as they bear a figure of Christ, as it is said about Solomon: *and he will rule from sea to sea* (Ps 71:8), for this was not fulfilled in him.

149. The third error is that of the Jews.

One should know that the Jews especially object to this Scriptural text, because in Hebrew there is not *virgin*, but *alma*, which is the same as *young woman*. Hence literally these things are not said of Christ, but of Emmanuel, or of a certain son of Isaiah, according to others.

But Jerome objected against these men, and proved that it could not be said of the son of Isaiah, because he was already born when this was said. Likewise, no famous person who was called Emmanuel is found to have lived at that time. Again, that a girl should conceive is not a sign. Hence Jerome says that *alma* is an equivocal word, and sometimes indicates age, and sometimes a thing hidden, and then it means a virgin zealously guarded; and thus it means here.

Again, the Jews objected that this was given as a sign. *Two kings came out against Achaz* (Isa 7:3), and by giving this sign to Achaz the prophet promised that they would be freed from these kings.

But one should say that he gave this sign not only to Achaz, but also to the house of David, because he says, *hear therefore, O house of David* (Isa 7:13); as though the Prophet had said, *the Lord will help you against this king, because he will do much greater things, since there will be not only the liberation of this man, but of the whole world.*

150. But let us return to the text. **Now all this was done**.

On the contrary, the angel had promised many things, namely **he who is born in her**, **is of the Holy Spirit** (Matt 1:20), and **she will bring forth a son** (Matt 1:21), and again, **you will call his name**. But this had not all been done.

But one should say in one way, according to Rabanus, that the phrase **all this was done**, is referred to the things done before: that the angel appeared to the Virgin, and said these words, **all this was done**, for the safekeeping of the Virgin, according as the **that** is taken causally. Or it is referred to those things which were foretold; and it can be called **all done** because of predestination.

Or one should say that the Evangelist wrote after it was all done, and so it refers to this. Hence the **that** is taken consecutively, because he would not have it that God was incarnated for the sake of fulfilling the prophecy, as though the Old Testament were more worthy than the New; but it followed upon the prophecy that Christ was incarnated.

Lecture 6

1:24 Exsurgens autem Ioseph a somno, fecit sicut praecepit ei angelus Domini, et accepit coniugem suam. [n. 152]

1:25 Et non cognoscebat eam, donec peperit filium suum primogenitum: et vocavit nomen eius Iesum. [n. 155]

1:24 ἐγερθεὶς δὲ ὁ Ἰωσὴφ ἀπὸ τοῦ ὕπνου ἐποίησεν ὡς προσέταξεν αὐτῷ ὁ ἄγγελος κυρίου καὶ παρέλαβεν τὴν γυναῖκα αὐτοῦ,

1:25 καὶ οὐκ ἐγίνωσκεν αὐτὴν ἕως οὗ ἔτεκεν υἱόν· καὶ ἐκάλεσεν τὸ ὄνομα αὐτοῦ Ἰησοῦν.

1:24 And Joseph rising up from sleep, did as the angel of the Lord had commanded him, and took unto him his wife. [n. 152]

1:25 And he did not know her until she brought forth her firstborn son: and he called his name Jesus. [n. 155]

---

151. Supra probavit Evangelista, quod mater Dei de Spiritu Sancto concepit, ex duobus, scilicet ex revelatione angeli, et ex praenuntiatione prophetae, hoc idem intendit ostendere ex obedientia Ioseph, qui non acquievisset verbis angeli, ut Mariam susciperet in sponsam, nisi cognovisset eam impraegnatam de Spiritu Sancto.

Et circa hoc duo facit:

primo ponitur obedientia ipsius sponsi ad angelum;

secundo describitur obedientiae modus, ibi *et accepit*.

152. Et nota quod quia per inobedientiam primi hominis prolapsi sumus in peccatum, Rom. V, 19: *per inobedientiam unius hominis peccatores constituti sunt multi*, ideo in principio reparationis nostrae proponitur obedientia.

Et possumus quatuor notare, quae sunt necessaria ad obedientiam. Primum est ut sit ordinata. Et dico ordinata, quia primo deserenda sunt vitia, et postea obediendum est ad operationem virtutum; Hier. IV, 3: *novate vobis novale, et nolite serere super spinas* et cetera. Et ideo hic dicitur, quod *Ioseph exurgens a somno*, pigritiae scilicet et dubietatis. De hoc somno dicitur Eph. V, 14: *surge qui dormis, et exurge a mortuis*. Secundum vero est, quod debet esse festina: et hoc est quod dicitur Eccli. V, 8: *non differas de die in diem, non tardes converti ad Dominum. Subito enim veniet ira illius*. Et ideo hic dicitur quod statim *fecit sicut praecepit ei*. Glossa: *quisquis a Deo monetur, solvat moras, surgat a somno, faciat quod iubetur*. Tertium vero, quod debet esse perfecta, ut non solum quod iubetur, sed eo modo quo iubetur fiat et quo eis imperatur. Unde hic dicitur *sicut praeceperat*. Glossa: *perfecta obedientia. Col. c. III, 20: filii, obedite parentibus per omnia*. Quartum, quod debet esse discreta, ut obediatur cui obediendum est, et in quo, ut non fiat aliquid contra Deum: unde dicit quod *fecit sicut praecepit ei angelus*, non malus sed Dei. I Io. IV, 1: *nolite omni spiritui*

151. Above, by two things, namely by the revelation of the angel, and by the prophet's foretelling, the Evangelist confirmed that the mother of God conceived of the Holy Spirit; here he aims to show the same thing by Joseph's obedience, who would not have assented to the angel's command that he should take Mary as his wife unless he had known that she was impregnated of the Holy Spirit.

And concerning this he does two things:

first, he sets down her spouse's obedience to the angel;

second, he describes the manner of the obedience, at *and took*.

152. And notice that since we fell into sin through the disobedience of the first man, *for as by the disobedience of one man, many were made sinners* (Rom 5:19), therefore obedience is put forward at the beginning of our renewal.

And we can note four things which are necessary for obedience. The first is that it be set in order. And I say set in order, because first vices should be given up, and afterwards one should obey unto the working of the virtues; *break up anew your fallow ground, and sow not upon thorns* (Jer 4:3). And so it says here that *Joseph rising up from sleep*, namely the sleep of laziness and unbelief. It is said about this sleep: *rise you who sleep, and arise from the dead* (Eph 5:14). The second is that it ought to be prompt; and this is what it is said: *delay not to be converted to the Lord, and defer it not from day to day* (Sir 5:8). And so it says here that he immediately *did as the angel commanded him*. The Gloss: *whoever is taught by the Lord, let him scatter the obstacles, rise from sleep, and do what is commanded*. The third, that it should be perfect, so that not only does what is commanded come about, but it comes about in the way in which it was commanded by the one who ordered these things. Hence it says here, *as the angel of the Lord had commanded*. The Gloss: *perfect obedience. Children, obey your parents in all things* (Col 3:20). The fourth, that it should be discerning, so that he is obeyed who should be obeyed, and in what he should

credere, sed probate spiritus, si ex Deo sint, quoniam multi pseudoprophetae exierunt in mundum et cetera.

153. *Et accepit*. Hic ostenditur in quibus obedivit: et ponuntur tria. Primo obedientia quam exhibuit ad angelum; secundo reverentia quam exhibuit ad matrem; tertio obsequium quod exhibuit Christo nato.

154. Angelus praecepit Ioseph *noli timere accipere Mariam coniugem tuam*. Et fecit Ioseph *sicut praecepit* et cetera. Ubi patet quod invenit mulierem bonam.

Sed numquid non habebat eam in domo? Quare ergo dicit, *exurgens . . . accepit*?

Respondet Chrysostomus: *quia eam non eiecerat a domo, sed a corde*. Vel quia primo ducebatur, sed postea celebrandae sunt nuptiae, et tunc dicitur, et est coniux.

155. Et ne aliquis suspicaretur quod copula carnalis interveniret, subiungit *et non cognoscebat eam*.

Ubi sciendum quod hoc verbum 'cognoscere' dupliciter accipitur in Sacra Scriptura: quandoque pro agnitione, Io. XIV, 7: *et amodo cognoscetis eum et vidistis eum*, aliquando pro carnali copula, sicut Gen. IV, 1: *Adam vero cognovit uxorem suam Evam* etc., scilicet carnaliter.

156. Sed obiicitur, quia non dicitur simpliciter *cognoscebat* etc., sed, *donec peperit filium suum*. Ergo postea cognovit; unde etiam dixit Elvidius: quamvis virgo concepit Christum, tamen postea habuit alios filios ex Ioseph.

Et ideo dicit Hieronymus, quod 'donec' aliquando significat aliquid finitum, et determinatum, sicut dicam *non veniam donec comedo* quia postea significo me venturum; quandoque significat infinite, et indeterminate, verbi gratia I Cor. XV, 25: *oportet et illum regnare, donec ponat omnes inimicos sub pedibus eius*. Numquid postea non regnabit? Immo: sed utitur Scriptura tali modo loquendi quia intendit removere illud quod potest esse dubium. Dubium enim esse poterat utrum regnaret, quando non posuerat inimicos sub pedibus. Item dubium esse poterat, cum Beata Virgo peperisset, an ante partum fuisset cognita a Ioseph, quia primum nulli debebat venire in dubium; scilicet quoniam angeli decantaverunt: *gloria in excelsis Deo, et in terra pax hominibus bonae voluntatis*, Lc. II, 14. Et ideo hoc intendit Evangelista.

Et argumentatur optime Hieronymus contra Elvidium: tu dicis, Elvidi, quod ante non cognovit Ioseph, quia fuit admonitus in somnis ab angelo. Si ergo admonitio in somnis tantum valuit quod non coniungeret se

be obeyed, so that nothing will come about against God; hence he says, *as the angel of the Lord had commanded*, not a bad angel but an angel of God. *Dearly beloved, believe not every spirit, but try the spirits if they be of God: because many false prophets are gone out into the world* (1 John 4:1).

153. *And took*. Here is shown in what things he obeyed. And three things are set down. First, the obedience which he showed to the angel; second, the reverence which he showed to the mother; third, the service which he gave to Christ after birth.

154. The angel commanded Joseph, *do not fear to take unto you Mary your wife* (Matt 1:20). And Joseph *did as the angel of the Lord had commanded*. It is clear here that he found the woman good.

But did he not have her in his house? So why does it say, *rising . . . he took*?

Chrysostom responds: *because he had not thrown her from the house, but from his heart*. Or because she was first betrothed, and afterwards the nuptials were to be celebrated, and at that point she is called, and is, a married person.

155. And lest someone should suspect that a bodily union came in the meanwhile, he adds, *and he did not know her*.

Here one should understand that this word 'to know' is taken in two ways in Sacred Scripture: sometimes for recognition, *and from henceforth you will know him, and you have seen him* (John 14:7); sometimes for bodily union: *and Adam knew Eve his wife* (Gen 4:1), that is, bodily.

156. But it is objected that because it does not say simply *he did not know her* but *until she brought forth her firstborn son*, therefore he knew her afterward; hence Helvidius also said: although a virgin conceived Christ, yet afterwards she had other sons by Joseph.

And so Jerome says that 'until' sometimes indicates something limited and determinate, as I say, *I will not come until I eat*, because I signify that I will come afterwards; sometimes it indicates something unlimited and indeterminate, for example: *he must reign, until he has put all his enemies under his feet* (1 Cor 15:25). Will he not reign afterwards? Yes indeed, but Scripture uses such a way of speaking because it aims to remove that which could be a doubt. For there could be a doubt as to whether he was reigning when his enemies had not been put under his feet. Similarly, since the Blessed Virgin had given birth, there could be a doubt as to whether she had been known by Joseph before the birth, because the first should never come into doubt by anyone; namely because the angels have sung, *glory to God in the highest; and on earth peace to men of good will* (Luke 2:14). And so the Evangelist aimed at this.

And Jerome argued most well against Helvidius: you say, Helvidius, that Joseph did not know her before, because he had been warned in a dream by the angel. If therefore a warning in sleep was so strong that he did not join himself

Mariae, quanto magis angelorum cognitio, pastorum et magorum adoratio?

157. Chrysostomus autem accepit cognitionem pro agnitione intellectuali. ***Non cognoscebat*** scilicet quantae dignitatis esset; sed postquam peperit, cognovit. Alii dicunt quod accipitur pro agnitione sensibili; et sic est satis probabilis horum opinio. Dicunt enim quod Moyses ex locutione Domini habuit tantam claritatem in facie, ut filii Israel non posset intendere in faciem eius, II Cor. III, 7. Ergo si ex consortio Dei hoc habuit Moyses, multo magis haec Beata Virgo, quae portavit eum in utero, habuit tantam claritatem in facie quod Ioseph non cognoscebat eam. Sed prima expositio est magis litteralis.

158. Item dicit Elvidius quod littera dicit, ***donec peperit filium suum primogenitum***. Primum dicitur respectu posterioris. Ergo habuit alios.

Respondet Hieronymus, quod consuetum est in Sacra Scriptura quod primogeniti vocantur illi, quos alii non praecedunt: Ex. XIII, 12 dicitur quod primogeniti Iudaeorum offerrentur Domino. Quaerit Hieronymus: numquid oportebat expectare quod non offerrentur donec nasceretur secundus? Ergo primogeniti dicuntur quos alii non praecedunt; et sic intelligitur hic.

159. Sequitur obsequium. Lc. II, 21, plenius exequitur hoc, sed Matthaeus breviter tangit. Ita enim vult Spiritus Sanctus, quod quae unus dixit, alius taceat.

Vocavit nomen eius Iesum; istud quidem nomen non parum celebre fuit apud antiquos et desideratum; Gen. XLIX, 18: *salutare tuum expectabo, domine*. Et Hab. III, 18: *ego autem in Domino gaudebo, et exultabo in Deo Iesu meo*.

to Mary, how much more the knowledge of the angels, of the shepherds, and of the wise men?

157. But Chrysostom takes knowledge as intellectual recognition. ***He did not know her***, that is, how great her dignity was; but after she bore the child he knew. Others say that it is taken as sensible recognition; and in a certain way the opinion of these men is probable enough. For they say that Moses had such a brightness on his face from the Lord's speech that the children of Israel could not look at his face (2 Cor 3:7). So if Moses had this from close association with God, much more did the Blessed Virgin, who bore him in the womb, have such a brightness on her face that Joseph did not know her. But the first explanation is more literal.

158. Again, Helvidius says that the text says, ***until she brought forth her firstborn son***. The ***firstborn*** is said with respect to what comes after. Therefore she had others.

Jerome responds that it is customary in Sacred Scripture that the one whom others do not precede is called the firstborn; Exodus says that the firstborn of the Jews were offered to the Lord (Exod 13:12). Jerome asks: was it necessary to think that they would not be offered until the second was born? Therefore those whom others do not precede are called the firstborn; and so it is understood here.

159. Then follows the service. Luke follows this up more completely (Luke 2:21), but Matthew touches upon it briefly. For so the Holy Spirit wished it to be, that those things which one has said, the other should touch upon.

He called his name Jesus; this name indeed was more than slightly famous and longed for among the ancients; *I will look for your salvation, O Lord* (Gen 49:18). And, *but I will rejoice in the Lord: and I will joy in God my Jesus* (Hab 3:18).

Chapter 2

Lecture 1

^{2:1} Cum ergo natus esset Iesus in Bethlehem Iudae in diebus Herodis Regis, ecce magi ab oriente venerunt Ierosolymam, [n. 161]

^{2:1} Τοῦ δὲ Ἰησοῦ γεννηθέντος ἐν Βηθλέεμ τῆς Ἰουδαίας ἐν ἡμέραις Ἡρῴδου τοῦ βασιλέως, ἰδοὺ μάγοι ἀπὸ ἀνατολῶν παρεγένοντο εἰς Ἱεροσόλυμα

^{2:1} When Jesus therefore was born in Bethlehem of Judah, in the days of King Herod, behold, there came magi from the east to Jerusalem, [n. 161]

^{2:2} dicentes: ubi est qui natus est rex Iudaeorum? Vidimus enim stellam eius in oriente et venimus adorare eum. [n. 168]

^{2:2} λέγοντες· ποῦ ἐστιν ὁ τεχθεὶς βασιλεὺς τῶν Ἰουδαίων; εἴδομεν γὰρ αὐτοῦ τὸν ἀστέρα ἐν τῇ ἀνατολῇ καὶ ἤλθομεν προσκυνῆσαι αὐτῷ.

^{2:2} saying: where is he who is born king of the Jews? For we have seen his star in the east, and are come to adore him. [n. 168]

---

160. Supra egit Evangelista de Christi generatione, hic intendit manifestare eius nativitatem.

Et primo, testimonio magorum;

secundo, testimonio innocentum, ibi *qui cum recessissent*.

Circa primum tria ponuntur:

primo enim annuntiatur Christi nativitas;

secundo inquiritur locus;

tertio inquiritur persona.

Secundum ibi *audiens autem Herodes*. Tertium ibi *tunc Herodes*.

Circa primum tria facit:

primo enim proponitur Christi nativitas, cui testimonium perhibetur;

secundo inducuntur testes;

tertio ponitur testimonium.

Secundum ibi *ecce magi*. Tertium ibi *ubi est qui natus est?*

161. Circa primum quatuor tanguntur: nativitas, nomen nati, locus et tempus.

Primum ibi *cum ergo natus esset*. Et notandum, quod Lucas plenius exequitur nativitatem, sicut e converso Matthaeus plenius exequitur de adoratione magorum, quam Lucas.

Nomen tangitur ibi *Iesus*. Locus ibi *in Bethlehem Iudae*, non *Iudaeae*, quia Iudaea vocatur tota regio populi Israelitici; sed *Iudae*; ista est terra illa, quae venerat in sortem Iudae. Dicitur *Bethlehem Iudae* ad differentiam alterius Bethlehem, quae est in tribu Zabulon, de qua Iosue IX, 10.

162. Et nota, quod ista tria verba *cum natus esset Iesus in Bethlehem Iudae in diebus Herodis Regis*, congrue ponuntur. Bethlehem enim significat Ecclesiam, in qua natus est Iesus, qui est verus panis, de quo Io. VI, 51: *ego sum panis vivus qui de caelo descendi*. Nulli ergo

160. Above, the Evangelist treated of the generation of Christ; here he intends to make clear his birth.

And first, the witness of the magi;

second, the witness of the innocents, at *and after they had departed* (Matt 2:13).

Concerning the first, he does three things:

for first the birth of Christ is announced;

second, the place is sought;

third, the person is sought.

The second is at *and King Herod hearing this* (Matt 2:3); the third is at *then Herod* (Matt 2:7).

Concerning the first, he does three things:

for first, he sets out Christ's birth, to which testimony is given;

second, he brings in the witnesses;

third, he sets down the testimony.

The second is at *behold, there came magi*. The third is at *where is he who is born?*

161. Concerning the first, he touches on four things: the birth, the name of the one born, the place, and the time.

The first is at *when Jesus therefore was born*. And it should be noted that Luke follows this up more completely, as on the other hand Matthew follows up the adoration of the magi more completely than Luke.

The name is touched upon at *Jesus*. The place, at *in Bethlehem of Judah*, not *of Judea*, because the entire region of the Israelite people is called Judea, but *of Judah*. This is the land which fell to the lot of Judas. It says *Bethlehem of Judah* to distinguish it from another Bethlehem which is in the tribe of Zabulon (Josh 19:10).

162. And notice that these three words, *when Jesus therefore was born in Bethlehem of Judah, in the days of King Herod*, are fittingly set down. For Bethlehem signifies the Church, in which Jesus was born who is the true bread, of whom it is said, *I am the living bread which came down*

provenit salus, nisi sit in domo Domini. In his Salvator natus est Christus; Is. LX, 18: *occupabit salus muros tuos, et portas tuas laudatio* et cetera.

Et addidit **Regis**, ad differentiam alterius Herodis: hic enim fuit, sub quo natus est Christus, Ascalonita; alius autem, qui Ioannem occidit, fuit filius huius Herodis, et non fuit rex.

163. Sed quaeritur quare Scriptura facit mentionem de isto tempore. Et dicendum propter tres rationes. Primo, ut completam ostendat esse prophetiam Iacobi, Gen. penult., 10: *non auferetur sceptrum de Iuda, et dux de femore eius, donec veniat, qui mittendus est, et ipse erit expectatio gentium.* Herodes enim fuit primus alienigena, qui regnavit in Iudaea. Secunda ratio est, quod maior morbus indiget maiori et meliori medico. Populus autem Israel tunc erat in maxima afflictione sub gentili Dominio, et ideo indigebat maximo consolatore: in aliis enim afflictionibus suis mittebantur eis prophetae, sed nunc propter magnitudinem afflictionis mittebatur eis prophetarum Dominus; Ps. XCIII, 19: *secundum multitudinem dolorum meorum in corde meo consolationes tuae laetificaverunt animam meam.*

164. Inde ponuntur testes, ibi *ecce magi*. Et describuntur tripliciter: a professione, a regione, et a loco, ubi testimonium dederunt.

De primo dicit *ecce magi*: qui secundum communem usum loquendi vocantur incantatores; sed lingua Persica vocat magos philosophos et sapientes. Isti quidem venerunt ad Iesum, quia gloriam sapientiae, quam possidebant, recognoverunt a Christo. Et sunt quidem primitiae gentium, quia primo venerunt ad Christum. Et impletur, secundum Augustinum, in istorum adventu illud Isaiae VIII, 4: *antequam sciat puer vocare patrem suum, et matrem suam, auferetur fortitudo Damasci, et spolia Samariae coram rege Assyriorum* etc.; ante enim quam Christus loqueretur, eripuit fortitudinem Damasci, et divitias et spolia Samariae, idest idololatriam. Dimiserunt enim illi idololatriam, et munera obtulerunt.

Item considerandum quod ad Christum venerunt aliqui ex Iudaeis, scilicet pastores; aliqui ex gentibus, scilicet magi: ipse enim Christus est lapis angularis, qui fecit utraque unum.

Et quare magi et pastores? Quia pastores magis simplices, et isti magis peccatores, ad significandum quod Christus utrosque recipit.

Quot autem fuerint illi magi, Evangelista non dicit. Videtur autem, secundum munera, quod fuerunt tres reges, quamvis plures alii in eis repraesentabantur; Is. LX, 3: *ambulabunt gentes in lumine tuo.*

from heaven (John 6:51). Therefore, salvation comes to no one unless he is in the house of the Lord. In these the Savior is born, Christ; *iniquity will no more be heard in your land, wasting nor destruction in your borders, and salvation will possess your walls, and praise your gates* (Isa 60:18).

And he added **King** to distinguish him from another Herod, for this was the one under whom Christ was born, the Ashkelonite; but the other, who killed John, was the son of this Herod, and was not a king.

163. But it is asked why Scripture mentions the time. And one should say, for three reasons. First, to show that Jacob's prophecy is fulfilled: *the sceptre will not be taken away from Judah, nor a ruler from his thigh, till he come that is to be sent, and he will be the expectation of nations* (Gen 49:10). For Herod was the first foreigner who reigned in Judea. The second reason is that a bigger sickness requires a bigger and better medicine. Now, the people of Israel were then in the greatest torment under a gentile lord, and so needed the greatest comforter; for in some of their torments prophets were sent to them, but now, on account of the greatness of the torment, the Lord of prophets was sent to them. *According to the multitude of my sorrows in my heart, your comforts have given joy to my soul* (Ps 93:19).

164. From there, he sets down the witnesses, at **behold, there came magi**. And they are described in three ways: by profession, by region, and by the place where they gave testimony.

And first he says, **behold . . . magi**, who according the common way of speaking are called incantators; but in the Persian language, philosophers and wise men are called magi. Indeed, these men came to Jesus because they had recognized that the glory of the wisdom which they possessed was from Christ. And they are a certain first-fruits of the gentiles, because they first came to Christ. And according to Augustine, the prophecy of Isaiah is fulfilled by their coming: *for before the child know to call his father and his mother, the strength of Damascus, and the spoils of Samaria will be taken away before the king of the Assyrians* (Isa 8:4); for before Christ spoke, he took away the strength of Damascus and the riches and spoils of Samaria, i.e., idolatry. For they had given up idolatry, and brought gifts.

Similarly, one should consider that some came to Christ from the Jews, namely the shepherds, and some from the gentiles, namely the magi; for Christ himself is the stone at the corner, who makes both into one.

And why magi and shepherds? Because the shepherds were more simple, and these magi were more sinful, to indicate that Christ accepts both.

The Evangelist does not say how many magi there were. But it seems, according to the gifts, that there were three kings, however many others were represented among them; *and the gentiles will walk in your light, and kings in the brightness of your rising* (Isa 60:3).

165. De secundo, scilicet de regione, dicit *ab oriente*.

Et notandum quod quidam ab oriente exponunt *a finibus orientis*; sed tunc quomodo in tam paucis diebus venissent? Et respondetur, ut quidam dicunt, quod miraculose venerunt; alii quod dromedarios habuerunt. Chrysostomus tamen dicit, quod stella apparuit eis per duos annos ante nativitatem, et quod tunc se paraverunt, et venerunt Ierosolymam in duobus annis et tredecim diebus.

Aliter autem potest exponi, ut dicatur *ab oriente*, idest a quadam regione quae erat prope Ierusalem a parte Orientali; dicuntur enim isti fuisse de secta Balaam, qui dixit Num. XXIV, 17: *orietur stella ex Iacob*, qui Balaam habitabat iuxta terram promissionis in parte Orientali.

166. Sequitur de loco *Ierosolymam venerunt*. Sed quare venerunt Ierusalem? Duplex est ratio. Una quia erat civitas regia; unde regem Iudaeorum in regia civitate quaerebant; item hoc factum fuit ex divina dispensatione, ut primo testimonium ferretur de Christo in Ierusalem, ut adimpleretur prophetia Is. II, 3: *de Sion exibit lex, et verbum Domini de Ierusalem*.

167. Consequenter ponitur testimonium, ibi *ubi est qui natus est?* In quo tria dicunt:

primo denuntiant regis nativitatem;

secundo afferunt nativitatis signum, ibi *vidimus enim stellam eius*;

tertio profitentur pium propositum, ibi *et venimus adorare*.

168. Dicunt ergo *ubi est?* Considerandum autem quod isti magi sunt primitiae gentium, et praefigurant in se statum nostrum. Isti enim aliquid supponunt, scilicet Christi nativitatem, et aliquid quaerunt, scilicet locum; et quidem nos fide tenemus Christum, sed aliquid quaerimus, scilicet spe: videbimus enim eum facie ad faciem. II Cor. V, 7: *per fidem ambulamus, et non per speciem*.

Sed quaestio est. Cum ipsi audissent regem esse in Ierusalem, quomodo ista dicebant? Omnis enim qui alium regem profitetur in civitate regis, se exponit periculo. Sed certe hoc zelo fidei faciebant. Unde in istis nuntiabatur fides illa intrepida. Infra c. X, 28: *nolite timere eos qui occidunt corpus*.

169. Consequenter proponunt signum huius nativitatis *vidimus*.

Et nota quod in istis verbis fuit occasio duorum errorum. Quidam, sicut Priscillianistae, dixerunt omnes actus hominum fato agi et regi. Et confirmant per hoc, *vidimus enim stellam eius*. Ergo natus est sub aliqua stella. Alius error Manichaeorum, qui reprobant fatum, et per

165. Concerning the second thing, namely the region, he says, *from the east*.

And it should be noted that some explain this as *from the end of the east*; but then how had they come in so few days? And the response is, as some say, that they came miraculously; others, that they had camels. But Chrysostom says that the star appeared to them two years before the birth, and that they prepared themselves at that time, and came to Jerusalem in two years and three days.

However, it can be explained in another way, so as to say *from the east*, i.e., from a certain region which was close by the eastern part of Jerusalem; for they say that these men were of the sect of Balaam, who said: *a star will rise out of Jacob* (Num 24:17). This Balaam lived next to the land of promise in the eastern region.

166. There follows, concerning the place, *to Jerusalem*. But why did they come to Jerusalem? There are two reasons. One, because it was the royal city; hence they were seeking the king of the Jews in the royal city. Again, this was done by divine arrangement, so that the first testimony to Christ might be given in Jerusalem, so that the prophecy might be fulfilled: *the law will come forth from Zion, and the word of the Lord from Jerusalem* (Isa 2:3).

167. Next he sets down the testimony, *where is he who is born*, in which they say three things:

first, they announce the birth of the king;

second, they produce a sign of his birth, at *for we have seen his star*;

third, they declare a pious purpose, at *and are come to adore him*.

168. They say then, *where is he who is born?* Now, one should consider that these magi are the first-fruits of the gentiles, and they prefigure in themselves our state. For they supposed one thing, namely the birth of Christ, and they sought another thing, namely the place; and indeed we hold to the faith of Christ, but we seek something, namely by hope, for we will see him face to face. *We walk by faith, and not by sight* (2 Cor 5:7).

But there is a question. Since they had heard that there was a king in Jerusalem, how did they say those things? For all who profess another king in the city of the king expose themselves to danger. But surely they acted out of the zeal of faith. Hence their fearless faith is announced in these words. Below: *and do not fear those who kill the body* (Matt 10:28).

169. Next they set forth a sign of this birth, *we have seen*.

And notice that there is an occasion for two errors in these words. Some men, such as the Priscilians, said that every human act is performed and guided by fate. And they confirmed their opinion by this text, *for we have seen his star*. Therefore he was born under some star. Another error

consequens istud Evangelium; quia dicebant quod Matthaeus introducit fatum. Sed excluditur error utriusque.

170. Sed antequam procedamus ad expositionem litterae, oportet primo videre quid est fatum, et quomodo sunt haec credenda, et quomodo non.

Nota ergo quod videmus multa in rebus humanis per accidens et casualiter accidere. Contingit autem aliquid casuale et fortuitum esse relatum ad causam inferiorem, quod relatum ad causam superiorem non est fortuitum: sicut si aliquis dominus mittat tres ad quaerendum aliquem, et unus nesciat de alio, si occurrant sibi invicem, est eis casuale; sed si referantur ad intentionem domini, non est casuale.

Sed secundum hoc fuit duplex opinio de fato. Quidam dixerunt quod ista casualia non reducuntur in aliam causam superiorem ordinantem: et isti sustulerunt fatum, et ultra hoc omnem providentiam divinam. Et fuit, secundum Augustinum, haec opinio Tullii. Sed dicimus quod ista casualia reducuntur in causam superiorem ordinantem. Sed cum 'fatum' dicatur a *for, faris*, quasi quoddam pronuntiatum et prolocutum, a qua causa sit ista ordinatio, est differentia. Quidam enim dixerunt quod est ex virtute corporum supercaelestium. Unde dicunt fatum nihil aliud esse quam dispositio siderum.

Alii ista contingentia reducunt in providentiam divinam. Sed primo modo negandum est esse fatum. Actus enim humani non reguntur secundum dispositionem corporum caelestium: quod patet ad praesens, cum multae sint ad hoc rationes efficaces.

Primo, quia impossibile est, quod virtus corporalis agat supra virtutem incorpoream, quia nihil inferius in ordine naturae agit in superiorem naturam. In anima autem sunt quaedam potentiae elevatae supra corpus; quaedam potentiae sunt organis affixae, scilicet potentiae sensitivae et nutritivae: et corpora quidem caelestia, quamvis directe agant supra corpora inferiora, et mutent ea per se, per accidens tamen agunt in potentiis organis affixis. In potentiis autem organis non affixis nullo modo agunt necessitando, sed inclinando tantum. Dicimus enim istum hominem iracundum, idest pronum ad iracundiam, et hoc ex causis caelestibus, sed directe electio ut sic in voluntate est. Unde numquam potest fieri tanta dispositio in corpore humano, quin superabundet iudicium liberi arbitrii. Unde quicumque poneret liberum arbitrium sub corporibus caelestibus, de necessitate poneret sensum ab intellectu non differre.

Secundo, quia per hoc excluditur omnis cultus divinus, quia tunc omnia essent ex necessitate; et sic tunc etiam regimen reipublicae destrueretur, quia nec oporteret consiliari, neque aliquid providere, et huiusmodi.

---

is that of the Manichees, who rejected fate, and as a consequence rejected this Gospel, because they said that Matthew brought in fate. But both errors are excluded.

170. But before we proceed to the explanation of the text, it is necessary to see what fate is, and in what way these things should be believed, and in what way not.

Note then that we see that many things in human affairs happen *per accidens* and accidentally. Now, it happens that some chance and fortuitous thing is related to a lower cause, which is not fortuitous as related to a higher cause; as if some lord sent three servants to search for someone, and one servant did not know the other. If they met one another, it would be by chance, for them; but if one looks to the intention of the lord, it would not be by chance.

But in accord with this there are two opinions about fate. Some said that these chance things are not traced back into some higher ordering cause, and they did away with fate, and beyond this with all divine providence. And this, according to Augustine, was Cicero's opinion. But we say that these chance things are traced back into a higher ordering cause. But since 'fate' is taken from *for, faris* as though a certain pronouncement and speaking out by which the ordering of things is caused, there is a difference amongst those who believe in fate. For some have said that it is by the power of the bodies above the heavens that things are ordered. Hence they say that fate is nothing other than the arrangement of the stars.

Others lead these happenstance things back into divine providence. But one should deny that the first way is fate. For human acts are not guided according to the arrangement of the heavenly bodies; which is clear right away, since there are many things which work for this argument.

First, because it is impossible that a bodily power should act on a non-bodily power, because nothing lower in the order of nature acts on a higher nature. Now, there are certain powers in the soul elevated above the body, while certain powers are attached to an organ, namely the sensitive and nutritive powers. And certainly the heavenly bodies, although they directly act on lower bodies, and change them *per se*, yet they act *per accidens* on the powers attached to organs. But in the powers not attached to organs they in no way act by necessitating, but only by inclining. For we say that this man is angry, i.e., prone to anger, and this is from heavenly causes; but directly, choice as such is in the will. Hence there can never come about such an arrangement in the human body but that the opinion of free judgment is far greater. Hence whoever would put free judgment under the heavenly bodies would of necessity hold that sense and intellect do not differ.

Second, because all divine worship is excluded by this notion of fate, because then all things would be of necessity; and thus even the directing of the republic would be destroyed, because then it would not be necessary either to deliberate, or to provide for anything, and so on.

Tertio, quia nos attribueremus Deo malitias hominum; quod esset ipsum infamare, qui Creator est stellarum.

Patet ergo quod hoc dicere est contra fidem omnino. Et ideo dicit Gregorius: *absit a fidelium cordibus ut fatum aliquid esse dicatur*. Si autem vis vocari fatum divinam providentiam, tunc aliquid est. Sed, sicut dicit Augustinus, quia nihil commune debemus habere cum infidelibus, non hoc nomen ei imponere debemus, unde dicit: *linguam corrigas, sententiam teneas*.

Non ergo potest dici **vidimus stellam**, idest a qua tota vita eius dependeat; quia, secundum Augustinum, tunc stella non sequeretur generatum, quia tunc Christus magis diceretur fatum stellae, quam e converso.

171. Et notandum quod ista stella non fuit de primis causatis: quod patet ex quatuor. Primo ex motu, quia nulla stella movetur de septentrione in meridiem. Regio autem Persarum, unde isti magi veniebant, est posita ad septentrionem. Item, aliae numquam quiescunt; ista autem non continue movebatur. Tertio ex tempore, quia in die nulla lucet; ista autem de die praebebat lucem magis. Quarto ex situ, quia non in firmamento, quod patet, quia isti per eam determinate distinxerunt domum.

Ergo dicendum quod ista specialiter creata fuit ad servitium Christi. Et ideo dicit **vidimus stellam eius**, idest ad obsequium eius factam.

172. Quidam autem dicunt, quod ista stella fuit Spiritus Sanctus, qui, sicut super baptizatum apparuit in specie columbae, ita et nunc in specie stellae. Alii dicunt quod fuit angelus.

Sed dicendum est quod vera stella fuit. Et voluit ostendi sub indicio stellae, primo, quia conveniebat ei. Est enim rex caelorum, et ideo per caeleste indicium voluit manifestari; Ps. XVIII, 1: *caeli enarrant gloriam Dei et opera manuum eius annuntiat firmamentum*; Iudaeis quidem per angelos, per quos legem acceperant; Gal. III, 19: *lex data est per angelos*; gentilibus per stellam, quia per creaturas in cognitionem Dei venerunt; Rom. I, 20: *invisibilia Dei per ea quae facta sunt, intellecta conspiciuntur*.

Secundo, quia congruebat his quibus demonstrabatur, scilicet gentilibus, quorum vocatio promissa fuit Abrahae in similitudinem stellarum; Gen. XV, 5: *suspice caelum, et numera stellas si potes* et cetera. Unde tam in nativitate, quam in passione factum est signum in caelo, quod omnibus gentibus Christum notum fecit.

Item, congruebat omnibus, quia ipse est Salvator omnium.

Third, because we would attribute to God the wickedness of men, which would be to insult him who is the Creator of the stars.

Therefore it is clear that to say this is entirely contrary to the faith. And so Gregory says: *be it gone from the hearts of the faithful that fate is said to be something!* Now, if you wish divine providence to be called fate, then that is something. But, as Augustine says, since we ought not have anything in common with the infidels, we ought not to give this name to it. Hence he says, *correct the tongue, hold the opinion*.

Therefore it cannot be said, **we have seen his star**, i.e., the star from which his whole life depends; for according to Augustine, then the star would not have followed the one generated, since then Christ would be called rather the fate of the star than the other way around.

171. And one should note that this star was not one of the first things caused, which is clear from four things. First, from motion, because no star moves from the north into the south. Now, the region of the Persians, from which these magi came, is set in the north. Likewise, the other stars never rest; but this one did not move constantly. Third, from time, because no star shines in the day, but this one offered light to the magi during the day. Fourth, from position, because it was not positioned in the firmament, as is clear, because the magi clearly picked out the house by means of it.

And so one should say that this star had been specially created for the service of Christ. And therefore it says, **we have seen his star**, i.e., the one made for his service.

172. But certain men say that this star was the Holy Spirit, who, just as he appeared above the baptized Christ in the appearance of a dove, so also now in the appearance of a star. Others say that it was an angel.

But one should say that it was a true star. And he wished to be revealed under the guidance of a star, first, because it befit him. For he is the king of the heavens, and so he wished to be known through heavenly guidance; *the heavens show forth the glory of God, and the firmament declares the work of his hands* (Ps 18:2); indeed, he wished to be known to the Jews through angels, through whom they received the law: *being ordained by angels* (Gal 3:19), and to the gentiles through a star, because they came to the knowledge of God through creatures; *for the invisible things of him, from the creation of the world, are clearly seen, being understood by the things that are made* (Rom 1:20).

Second, because it fit with those to whom he was shown, namely with the gentiles, whose calling was promised to Abraham in the likeness of stars; *look up to heaven and number the stars, if you can* (Gen 15:5). Hence both in the birth and in the passion, there was a sign in heaven which made Christ known to all the gentiles.

Again, it fit with all, because he himself is the Savior of all.

173. Sed dicit *in oriente*, quod exponitur dupliciter. Secundum Rabanum, sic: stella existens in Iudaea apparuit illis gentibus in oriente. Vel: nos vidimus stellam in oriente. Istud melius dicitur. Unde *ecce stella, quam viderant in oriente antecedebat eos.*

Item patet ex hoc quod ista secundum situm erat propinqua terrae, quia aliter non distinxisset locum. Ergo non potuisset videri a tam remota regione.

174. Consequenter ponitur pium propositum *et venimus adorare.*

Hic est duplex quaestio. Dicit enim Augustinus: *numquid isti erant curiosi, quod quandocumque fieret aliquod indicium per aliquam stellam quaererent regem natum?* Hoc enim stultum fuisset.

Sed dicendum quod non praestaverunt obsequium regi terreno, sed caelesti: in quo virtus divina ostenditur affuisse; quia aliter si terrenum regem quaesissent, totam devotionem amisissent, quando vilibus pannis invenerunt involutum.

175. Sed quaerit iterum Augustinus: quomodo ex stella potuerunt scire, quod homo Deus natus esset? Et respondet quod hoc fuit angelo revelante; qui enim ostendit eis stellam, misit angelum qui hoc revelaret. Leo Papa dicit, quod sicut exterius oculi replebantur lumine istius stellae: ita interius radius divinus revelabat. Tertia ratio: quia isti erant de stirpe Balaam, qui dixit: *orietur stella ex Iacob.* Unde habuerunt a prophetia eius. Et ideo videndo tantam claritatem stellae, suspicati sunt, quod rex caelestis natus esset, et ideo quaerebant. Et hoc est *et venimus adorare.* In hoc impletum est illud Ps. LXXI, 11: *et adorabunt eum omnes reges, omnes gentes servient ei.*

173. But he says, *in the east*, which is explained in two ways. According to Rabanus, this way: a star existing in Judah appeared to these gentiles in the east. Or: we have seen the star in the east. This is better said. Hence, *behold the star which they had seen in the east, went before them* (Matt 2:9).

Likewise, it is clear from the fact that this star was positioned near to the earth, since otherwise they would not have distinguished the place of Christ's birth. Therefore it could not have been seen from so remote a region.

174. Next the pious intention is set down, *and are come to adore him.*

Here there are two questions. For Augustine says, *were they not rather odd, since whenever there was some indication by some star they went seeking the king who was born?* For this would have been stupid.

But one should say that did they not give service to an earthly king, but to a heavenly king; in this the divine power is shown to have been present, because otherwise, if they had sought an earthly king, they would have lost all devotion when they found him wrapped in worthless rags.

175. But again Augustine asks: how were they able to know from a star that a man-God had been born? And he responds that this was by the revelation of an angel; for the one who showed them the star sent an angel who revealed this. Pope Leo says that, as the exterior eyes were filled with the light of that star, so the interior divine ray revealed the mystery to them. The third reason: because they were of the stock of Balaam, who said, *a star will rise out of Jacob* (Num 24:17). Hence they had it from his prophecy. And thus, seeing so bright a star, they suspected that the heavenly king had been born, and so they sought him. And this is *and are come to adore him*. In this is fulfilled: *and all kings of the earth will adore him: all nations will serve him* (Ps 71:11).

Lecture 2

2:3 Audiens autem Herodes Rex turbatus est et omnis Ierosolyma cum illo. [n. 177]

2:4 Et congregans omnes principes sacerdotum, et scribas populi, sciscitabatur ab eis, ubi Christus nasceretur. [n. 180]

2:5 At illi dixerunt ei: in Bethlehem Iudae. Sic enim scriptum est per prophetam. [n. 182]

2:6 *Et tu, Bethlehem terra Iuda, nequaquam minima es in principibus Iuda; ex te enim exiet dux, qui regat populum meum Israel.* [n. 184]

2:7 Tunc Herodes clam vocatis magis, diligenter didicit ab eis tempus stellae quae apparuit eis; [n. 186]

2:8 et mittens illos in Bethlehem, dixit: ite, et interrogate diligenter de puero; et cum inveneritis, renuntiate mihi, ut et ego veniens adorem eum. [n. 188]

2:9 Qui, cum audissent regem, abierunt. Et ecce stella, quam viderant in oriente, antecedebat eos, usque dum veniens staret supra ubi erat puer. [n. 190]

2:3 ἀκούσας δὲ ὁ βασιλεὺς Ἡρῴδης ἐταράχθη καὶ πᾶσα Ἱεροσόλυμα μετ᾽ αὐτοῦ,

2:4 καὶ συναγαγὼν πάντας τοὺς ἀρχιερεῖς καὶ γραμματεῖς τοῦ λαοῦ ἐπυνθάνετο παρ᾽ αὐτῶν ποῦ ὁ χριστὸς γεννᾶται.

2:5 οἱ δὲ εἶπαν αὐτῷ· ἐν Βηθλέεμ τῆς Ἰουδαίας· οὕτως γὰρ γέγραπται διὰ τοῦ προφήτου·

2:6 καὶ σὺ Βηθλέεμ, γῆ Ἰούδα, οὐδαμῶς ἐλαχίστη εἶ ἐν τοῖς ἡγεμόσιν Ἰούδα· ἐκ σοῦ γὰρ ἐξελεύσεται ἡγούμενος, ὅστις ποιμανεῖ τὸν λαόν μου τὸν Ἰσραήλ.

2:7 Τότε Ἡρῴδης λάθρα καλέσας τοὺς μάγους ἠκρίβωσεν παρ᾽ αὐτῶν τὸν χρόνον τοῦ φαινομένου ἀστέρος,

2:8 καὶ πέμψας αὐτοὺς εἰς Βηθλέεμ εἶπεν· πορευθέντες ἐξετάσατε ἀκριβῶς περὶ τοῦ παιδίου· ἐπὰν δὲ εὕρητε, ἀπαγγείλατέ μοι, ὅπως κἀγὼ ἐλθὼν προσκυνήσω αὐτῷ.

2:9 οἱ δὲ ἀκούσαντες τοῦ βασιλέως ἐπορεύθησαν καὶ ἰδοὺ ὁ ἀστήρ, ὃν εἶδον ἐν τῇ ἀνατολῇ, προῆγεν αὐτούς, ἕως ἐλθὼν ἐστάθη ἐπάνω οὗ ἦν τὸ παιδίον.

2:3 And King Herod, hearing this, was troubled, and all Jerusalem with him. [n. 177]

2:4 And assembling together all the chief priests and the scribes of the people, he inquired of them where the Christ would be born. [n. 180]

2:5 But they said to him: in Bethlehem of Judah. For so it is written by the prophet: [n. 182]

2:6 *and you, Bethlehem the land of Judah, are not the least among the princes of Judah: for out of you will come forth the captain that will rule my people Israel.* [n. 184]

2:7 Then Herod, privately calling the wise men, learned diligently of them the time of the star which appeared to them; [n. 186]

2:8 and sending them into Bethlehem, said: go and diligently inquire after the child, and when you have found him, bring me word again, that I also may come to adore him. [n. 188]

2:9 Who, having heard the king, went their way. And behold the star which they had seen in the east, went before them, until it came and stood over where the child was. [n. 190]

---

176. Praenuntiata Christi nativitate per magos, hic inquirit de loco nativitatis: et ponuntur tria:

> primo ponitur motivum ad inquirendum;
> secundo imponitur inquisitio;
> tertio inventio veritatis.

Secundum ibi *et congregans.* Tertium ibi *at illi dixerunt ei: in Bethlehem Iudae.*

177. Motivum fuit turbatio Herodis; unde *audiens.* Et signanter vocat Herodem *Regem*, ut ostendat esse alium a rege, quem quaerebant.

Fuit autem triplex causa turbationis. Prima processit ex ambitione, quam habebat circa custodiam regni sui, propterea quia alienigena erat. Sciebat enim vel audiverat illud Danielis II, 44: *in diebus regnorum Israel suscitabit Deus caeli regnum, quod in aeternum non dissipabitur, et regnum eius alteri populo non tradetur* et cetera.

176. The birth of Christ having been foretold by the magi, here he inquires about the place of the birth. And three things are set down:

> first, the motive for inquiring is set down;
> second, the inquiry itself is set down;
> third, the discovery of the truth.

The second is at *and assembling together.* The third is at *but they said to him: in Bethlehem of Judah.*

177. The motive was Herod's agitation; hence, *and King Herod, hearing this, was troubled.* And he called Herod the *King* with meaning, to show that he is other than the king whom they are seeking.

Now, there are three causes of agitation. The first proceeds from ambition, which Herod had with regard the preservation of his kingdom, because he was a foreigner. For he knew or had heard *but in the days of those kingdoms the God of heaven will set up a kingdom that will never be destroyed, and his kingdom will not be delivered up to another*

Sed in hoc decipiebatur, quia regnum illud spirituale erat; Io. XVIII, 36: *regnum meum non est de hoc mundo.* Unde Herodes turbabatur timens amissionem regni sui; sed magis turbabatur Diabolus timens regni sui destructionem totalem; Io. XII, 31: *nunc princeps mundi huius eiicietur foras.* Et nota quod homines, sicut dicit Chrysostomus, in sublimibus constituti ex levi verbo contra se prolato conturbantur; Ps. LXXXVII, 16: *exaltatus autem, humiliatus sum et conturbatus*; humiles autem numquam timent.

Secunda causa processit ex timore Romani Imperii. Statutum enim erat a Romano Imperio quod nullus Deus aut rex diceretur sine eorum consensu; unde timebat. Sed iste timor mundanus erat, qui prohibetur; Is. LI, 12: *quis tu ut timeas ab homine mortali, et filio hominis, qui quasi foenum ita arescet?*

Tertia ex rubore verecundiae. Verecundabatur enim coram populo ut alius rex vocaretur; similis in hoc Sauli, qui dixit: *peccavi, sed nunc honora me coram senioribus populi mei, et coram Israel* et cetera. I Reg. XV, 30.

178. Sed mirum quod sequitur *et omnis Ierosolyma cum illo.* Videbatur enim quod deberent gaudere. Sed sciendum quod triplicem causam turbationis habuerunt. Prima fuit ipsorum iniquitas; iniqui enim erant, quibus semper detestabilis est conversatio iustorum. Prov. XIII, 19: *detestantur stulti eos qui fugiunt mala.* Secunda ut placerent Herodi; Eccli. X, 2: *secundum iudicem populi, sic et ministri eius.* Tertia quia timebant ne Herodes hoc audito amplius desaeviret in gentem Iudaeorum.

179. Mystice autem in hoc significatur quod iste terrenus erat. Gregorius: *rex terrae turbatus est, caeli rege nato, quia nimirum terrena altitudo confunditur, cum caelestis celsitudo aperitur.* Is. XXIV, 23: *erubescet luna, et confundetur sol, cum regnaverit Dominus exercituum in monte Sion, et in Ierusalem.*

Et notandum quod, sicut dicit Augustinus, *quid autem erit tribunal iudicantis, quando superbos reges cuna terrebat infantis? Pertimeant reges ad dexteram Patris sedentem, quem rex impius timuit matris ubera lambentem.*

180. *Et congregans.* Hic ponitur inquisitio. Et, sicut dictum est, Herodes sollicitus erat inquirere, et propter regnum, et propter timorem Romanorum: unde inquisivit veritatem.

Sed ad habendam certitudinem de aliquo tria requiruntur ab inquirentibus: creditur enim multitudini, auctoritati, et litteratis. Unde congregavit multos, et auctoritatem habentes, et sapientes. Et hoc est quod dicit *congregans omnes*, quantum ad primum Sap. VI, 26: *multitudo sapientium sanitas est orbis terrarum.* **Principes**

people, and it will break in pieces, and will consume all these kingdoms, and itself will stand for ever (Dan 2:44). But in this he was deceived, because that was a spiritual kingdom: *my kingdom is not of this world* (John 18:36). Hence Herod was disturbed, fearing the total destruction of his kingdom; *now will the prince of this world be cast out* (John 12:31). And notice that, as Chrysostom says, men established in the highest positions are disturbed by the lightest word brought against them; *I am poor, and in labors from my youth: and being exalted have been humbled and troubled* (Ps 87:16); but the humble never fear.

The second cause proceeds from fear of the Roman Emperor. For it was set up as a law by the Roman Emperor that no one should be called a god or a king without his consent; hence he was afraid. But this fear was worldly, which is forbidden; *who are you, that you should be afraid of a mortal man, and of the son of man, who will wither away like grass?* (Isa 51:12)

Third, from the blush of shame. For he was ashamed before the people that another should be called king; as in Saul's request, who said, *I have sinned: yet honor me now before the ancients of my people, and before Israel* (1 Sam 15:30).

178. But what follows is strange: *and all Jerusalem with him.* For it would seem that they should have rejoiced. But one should know that they had three reasons for being disturbed. First was their iniquity; for they were wicked, to whom the behavior of the just is always detestable. *Fools hate them that flee from evil things* (Prov 13:19). Second, that they might please Herod; *as the judge of the people is himself, so also are his ministers* (Sir 10:2). Third, because they were afraid lest, when he heard it, Herod should vent his rage all the more upon the Jewish nation.

179. But mystically, this signified that he was earthly. Gregory: *the king of earth was disturbed when the king of heaven was born, doubtless because the earthly is thrown in confusion by loftiness, when the height of heaven is opened. And the moon will blush, and the sun will be ashamed, when the Lord of hosts will reign in MountZion, and in Jerusalem* (Isa 24:23).

And it should be noted that, as Augustine says, *now what will be the judgment seat of the one who judges, when the cradle of an infant terrified the haughty kings? Let kings be in dread of the one sitting at the right hand of the Father, whom the impious king feared sucking at his mother's breasts.*

180. *And assembling together.* Here the inquiry is set down. And, as was said, Herod was anxious to inquire, both for the sake of his kingdom, and for fear of the Romans; hence he inquired after the truth.

But to have certainty about something, three things are sought by the one who inquires: for credence is given to the multitude, to authorities, and to the learned. Hence he gathered many together, both those having authority, and the wise. And this is what it says: *assembling together all*, as regards the first, *now the multitude of the wise is the welfare*

sacerdotum, quantum ad secundum; Mal. II, 7: *labia sacerdotum custodiunt scientiam, et legem requirunt ex ore eius*. **Et scribas**, quantum ad tertium: non ad scribendum tantum dicitur, sed ad interpretandum legis Scripturam; per istos quidem volebat investigare veritatem. Eccl. XXXII, 13: *in medio magnatorum loqui non praesumas, et ubi sunt senes non multum loquaris*.

Sciscitabatur ab eis ubi Christus nasceretur. Magi regem vocaverunt, sed ipsi Christum quaerebant: sciebant enim ex conversatione cum Iudaeis regem Iudaeorum legitimum inungi.

181. Sed quaeritur: aut ipse credebat prophetiae, aut non. Si credebat, sciebat quod non poterat impediri quin ipse regnaret; quare ergo interfecit pueros? Si non credebat, quare ergo quaerebat?

Sed dicendum quod non perfecte credebat, quia ambitiosus erat et ambitio hominem caecum reddit.

182. ***At illi dixerunt: in Bethlehem Iudae***. Hic invenitur veritas. Et

primo ponitur veritas;

secundo confirmatur eius prophetia, ibi *'et tu, Bethlehem, terra Iuda.'*

183. Et sciendum quod Christus voluit nasci in Bethlehem propter tria. Primo ad vitandam gloriam. Propter hoc enim elegit duo loca: unum in quo nasci voluit, scilicet Bethlehem; alium in quo passus fuit, scilicet Ierusalem. Et hoc est contra illos qui gloriam quaerunt, qui volunt nasci in sublimibus locis, et nolunt pati in loco honoris. Ioan. VIII, 50: *ego gloriam meam non quaero*.

Secundo ad confirmationem suae doctrinae, et ostentationem suae veritatis. Si enim natus fuisset in aliqua magna civitate, virtus suae doctrinae potuisset adscribi humanae virtuti; II Cor. VIII, 9: *scitis gratiam Domini nostri Iesu Christi*.

Tertio ad ostendendum se esse de genere David; Lc. II, 3: *Ioseph et Maria ibant in Bethlehem ut profiterentur ibi, eo quod essent de domo, et familia David*.

Competit etiam mysterio, quia Bethlehem interpretatur 'domus panis': et Christus est ille *panis vivus, qui de caelo descendit*, Io. VI, 51.

184. Consequenter confirmatur veritas. Unde *'et tu, Bethlehem,'* et cetera.

Ex ista prophetia duo possemus considerare: magi enim aliquid annuntiabant, et aliquid quaerebant. Et ex ista prophetia ostenditur utrumque: quia quantum ad primum dicit *'et tu Bethlehem'*; quantum ad secundum dicit *'ex te enim exiet dux.'*

Et ita confirmatur nativitas Christi duplici testimonio, scilicet stellae et prophetiae, quia in ore duorum vel

of the whole world (Wis 6:26). **The chief priests**, as regards the second; *for the lips of the priest will keep knowledge, and they will seek the law at his mouth* (Mal 2:7). **And the scribes**, as regards the third: they are not called **scribes** only for writing, but for interpreting the writings of the law; indeed, by these he wished to search out the truth. *In the company of great men take not upon you: and when the ancients are present, speak not much* (Sir 32:13).

He inquired of them where the Christ would be born. The magi had called him a king, but they were seeking the Christ himself; for they knew by conversation with the Jews that the legitimate king of the Jews was anointed.

181. But it is asked: either he believed the prophecy, or he did not. If he believed, he knew that he could not stand in the way, but that this one would reign; why then did he kill the children? If he did not believe, then why did he ask?

But one should say that he did not believe perfectly, because he was ambitious, and ambition makes a man blind.

182. But they said to him: in Bethlehem of Judah. Here the truth is found. And

first, the truth is set down;

second, it is confirmed by the prophecy of it, *'and you Bethlehem the land of Judah.'*

183. And one should know that Christ willed to be born in Bethlehem for three reasons. First, to avoid glory. For he chose two places for this reason: the one in which he was born, namely Bethlehem; the other in which he suffered, namely Jerusalem. And this is against those who seek glory, who wish to be born in high places, and do not wish to suffer in a place of honor. *But I seek not my own glory* (John 8:50).

Second, to confirm his teaching, and show his truth. For if he had been born in some great city, the strength of his teaching could be attributed to human strength; *you know the grace of our Lord Jesus Christ* (2 Cor 8:9).

Third, to show that he was of the family of David; *and Joseph also went up from Galilee, out of the city of Nazareth into Judea, to the city of David, which is called Bethlehem* (Luke 2:3).

It also fits with a mystery, because Bethlehem is interpreted as 'house of bread', and Christ is *the living bread which comes down from heaven* (John 6:51).

184. Next, the truth is confirmed. Hence, *'and you Bethlehem.'*

We can take up two things from this prophecy: for the magi announced one thing, and sought another. And both are shown from this prophecy: for as regard the first it says, *'and you Bethlehem'*; as regards the second it says, *'out of you will come forth the captain.'*

And thus the birth of Christ is confirmed by a twofold testimony, namely that of the star and that of the prophecy, because truth is in the mouth of two or three witnesses; *in*

trium testium est veritas; Deut. XIX, 15: *in ore duorum aut trium testium stabit omne verbum.*

Et nota, quod quando erant omnes infideles, data sunt signa corporalium; quando iam erant fideles, data est prophetia; I Cor. XIV, 22: *itaque linguae in signum sunt non fidelibus, sed infidelibus; prophetiae autem non infidelibus, sed fidelibus.*

185. Et sciendum quod Iudaei dupliciter defecerunt in prolatione prophetiae. Quia ibi dicitur *et tu, Bethlehem Ephrata*, et iterum quia non est ibi, *'nequaquam minima es.'*

Et potest assignari duplex ratio quare mutaverunt. Uno modo potest dici, quod hoc fecerunt ex ignorantia. Alio modo potest dici quod isti usi sunt scienter aliis verbis. Et dicunt sententiam. Quia cum Herodes esset alienigena, non intellexisset auctoritatem prophetae, et ideo dixerunt illud quod notum erat Herodi. Unde dicunt: *'terra Iuda'*, et *'nequaquam minima es'*, idest tu non es minima inter millia hominum Iuda; vel *'in principibus Iuda'*, idest inter principales civitates Iuda. *'Ex te enim exiet dux qui regat populum meum Israel.'* De isto duce habetur Dan. IX, 25: *usque ad Christum ducem*; et Ps. XXX, 5: *dux mihi eris*: regit enim populum Israel non solum carnaliter, sed etiam spiritualiter; Rom. XI, 1: *numquid Deus repulit populum suum?* et cetera. Ps. LXXIX, 2: *qui regis Israel, intende, qui deducis velut ovem Ioseph.*

Et nota quod truncant caudam auctoritatis, scilicet *et egressus eius sicut ab initio, a diebus aeternitatis.* Per quod insinuatur quod non debebat esse rex terrenus, sed caelestis; quod si scivisset Herodes, non fuisset impius. Unde fuerunt causa necis illorum. Item ex illa etiam cauda patet esse falsam interpretationem Iudaeorum, qui exponunt de Zorobabel: quia non convenit ei *et egressus eius ab initio a diebus aeternitatis.* Item non in Iudaea, sed in Babylone natus est.

186. Consequenter inquiritur de persona nati, cum dicit **tunc Herodes, clam vocatis magis, diligenter didicit ab eis tempus stellae quae apparuit eis.**

Et primo ponitur inquisitio;
secundo inventio inquisiti, ibi **invenerunt eum** etc.;

tertio veneratio inventi, ibi **et procidentes adoraverunt eum.**

Ad inquirendum personam ex duobus moti sunt: ex persuasione Herodis, et ex ductu stellae. Unde

circa primum ponitur exhortatio;
secundo studium magorum in mutatione stellae, ibi **qui cum audissent regem abierunt.**

---

the mouth of two or three witnesses every word will stand (Deut 19:15).

And notice that when they were all unbelievers, they were given bodily signs; when they were already believers, a prophecy was given; *wherefore tongues are for a sign, not to believers, but to unbelievers; but prophecies not to unbelievers, but to believers* (1 Cor 14:22).

185. And one should know that the Jews failed in bringing forth the prophecy in two ways. Because it says there, *and you, Bethlehem Ephrata* (Mic 5:2), and again because *'are not the least'* is not there.

And two reasons can be given for why they changed it. In one way, one could say that they did this out of ignorance. In another way, one could say that they knowingly used different words. And they speak an opinion. For since Herod was a foreigner, he would not have understood the text of the prophet, and so they said what would be known to Herod. Hence they say, *'land of Judah'*, and *'are not the least'*, i.e., you are not the smallest among the thousands of men of Judah; or *'among the princes of Judah'*, i.e., among principal cities of Judas. *'For out of you will come forth the captain that will rule my people Israel.'* About this captain it is said, *Christ the captain* (Dan 9:25). And in the Psalms, *you will be my captain*; for he rules the people of Israel not only bodily, but even spiritually; *has God cast away his people?* (Rom 11:1). *Give ear, O you who rule Israel: you who lead Joseph like a sheep* (Ps 79:2).

And note that they cut off the end of the text, namely *and his going forth is from the beginning, from the days of eternity.* It is implied in this that he would not be an earthly king, but a heavenly one; which if Herod had known, he would not have been impious. Hence they were the cause of the murder of those babies. Likewise, it is clear from the end part that the Jews' interpretation is false, who expound this verse as about Zorobabel; because *and his going forth is from the beginning, from the days of eternity* (Mic 5:2) does not fit with him. Again, he was not born in Judah, but in Babylon.

186. Next the person born is inquired about, when it says, **then Herod, privately calling the wise men, learned diligently of them the time of the star which appeared to them.**

And first, the inquiry is set down;
second, the discovery of the one sought, at **they found the child** (Matt 2:11);

third, the veneration of the one found, at **and falling down, they adored him** (Matt 2:11).

They were moved to seek the person by two things: by the persuasion of Herod, and by the guidance of the star. Hence,

concerning the first, an exhortation is set down;
second, the zeal of the magi in the changing of the star, at **who, having heard the king, went their way.**

Circa primum tria ponuntur:

primo enim inquirit tempus;

secundo annuntiat locum, ibi *et mittens illos in Bethlehem*;

tertio iniungit officium inquisitionis, ibi *ite, et interrogate diligenter de puero*.

187. Dicit ergo *tunc Herodes*. Ubi considerandum quod Iudaei sciebant locum, sed non tempus. Unde confutantur a Domino, Lc. XIX, 44: *eo quod non cognovisti tempus visitationis tuae*, et Is. I, 3: *cognovit bos possessorem suum, et asinus praesepe Domini sui; Israel autem me non cognovit, et populus meus non intellexit.* Ergo inquiritur tempus. Et dicit Chrysostomus quod per biennium ante apparuit istis stella. Alii autem quod in ipsa die nativitatis.

188. Annuntiat locum, ibi *et mittens*.

189. Iungit officium inquisitionis, ibi *ite, et interrogate* et cetera. Et admonet duo: et ad hoc quod impleant praemittit tertium. Quantum ad primum dicit *ite* et cetera. Et quaerit insidiose ad occidendum, sicut illi quibus dicitur Io. VII, 34: *quaeretis me, et non invenietis.* Quantum ad secundum dicit sic *cum inveneritis renuntiate mihi*. Et hoc propter malum etiam dicebat; Eccli. XIII, 14: *ex multa loquela tentabit te.* Quantum ad tertium dicit *ut et ego veniens adorem eum*; et quidem dolose promittit Dei cultum; Ier. IX, 8: *sagitta vulnerans lingua eorum dolum locuta est*; Ps. XXVII, 3: *qui loquuntur pacem cum proximo suo, mala autem in cordibus eorum.*

Et nota quod cum magi profiterentur regem, iste vocat puerum, quia *ex abundantia cordis os loquitur*.

Nota etiam, quod petit a Iudaeis ubi Christus nasceretur, volens experiri, et tentare utrum gauderent.

190. Consequenter ponitur studium magorum. Duo iniunxerat: quod inquirerent, et reverterentur; sed unum fecerunt magi. Unde *qui cum audissent regem abierunt*. Aliud autem non fecerunt.

Tales quidem debent esse auditores, quod bona addiscant, mala vero relinquant; infra XXIII, 3: *quae dicunt facite, secundum opera eorum nolite facere* et cetera.

Concerning the first, three things are set down:

for first, he inquires about the time;

second, he announces the place, at *and sending them into Bethlehem*;

third, he charges them with the duty of seeking, at *go and diligently inquire after the child*.

187. So he says, *then Herod*. Here it should be considered that the Jews knew the place, but not the time. Hence they were silenced by the Lord, *because you have not known the time of your visitation* (Luke 19:44), and: *the ox knows his owner, and the ass his master's crib: but Israel has not known me, and my people have not understood* (Isa 1:3). So the time is sought. And Chrysostom says that this star appeared for two years. But others say that it appeared on the very day of the birth.

188. He announces the place, at *and sending*.

189. He charges them with the duty of inquiring at *go and diligently inquire*. And he urges them to two things, and so that they would do them, he added a third. As regards the first he says, *go*. And he sought insidiously, for the sake of killing, like those to whom it is said, *you will seek me, and will not find me* (John 7:34). As regards the second, he speaks this way: *when you have found him, bring me word again*. And he said this for the sake of evil as well; *by much talk he will sift you* (Sir 13:14). As regards the third, he says, *that I also may come to adore him*. And indeed deceitfully he promised worship of God; *their tongue is a piercing arrow, it has spoken deceit* (Jer 9:8); *who speak peace with their neighbor, but evils are in their hearts* (Ps 27:3).

And note that while the magi professed a king, this man calls him a child, because *out of the abundance of the heart the mouth speaks* (Matt 12:34).

Note also that he asked the Jews where the Christ would be born, wishing to test and find out whether they would rejoice.

190. Next, the zeal of the magi is set down. Two things had been enjoined: that they should inquire, and that they should return; but the magi did only one. Hence, *who, having heard the king, went their way*. And they did not do the other.

Indeed, listeners should be such that they learn the good things, and truly leave behind the evil things; below, *all things therefore, whatever they will say to you, observe and do, but according to their works do not* (Matt 23:3).

Lecture 3

2:9 Qui, cum audissent regem, abierunt. Et ecce stella, quam viderant in oriente, antecedebat eos, usque dum veniens staret supra ubi erat puer. [n. 191]

2:10 Videntes autem stellam, gavisi sunt gaudio magno valde. [n. 195]

2:11 Et intrantes domum, invenerunt puerum cum Maria matre eius; et procidentes adoraverunt eum, et apertis thesauris suis obtulerunt ei munera, aurum, thus, et myrrham. [n. 196]

2:12 Et responso accepto in somnis ne redirent ad Herodem, per aliam viam reversi sunt in regionem suam. [n. 202]

2:9 οἱ δὲ ἀκούσαντες τοῦ βασιλέως ἐπορεύθησαν καὶ ἰδοὺ ὁ ἀστήρ, ὃν εἶδον ἐν τῇ ἀνατολῇ, προῆγεν αὐτούς, ἕως ἐλθὼν ἐστάθη ἐπάνω οὗ ἦν τὸ παιδίον.

2:10 ἰδόντες δὲ τὸν ἀστέρα ἐχάρησαν χαρὰν μεγάλην σφόδρα.

2:11 καὶ ἐλθόντες εἰς τὴν οἰκίαν εἶδον τὸ παιδίον μετὰ Μαρίας τῆς μητρὸς αὐτοῦ, καὶ πεσόντες προσεκύνησαν αὐτῷ καὶ ἀνοίξαντες τοὺς θησαυροὺς αὐτῶν προσήνεγκαν αὐτῷ δῶρα, χρυσὸν καὶ λίβανον καὶ σμύρναν.

2:12 καὶ χρηματισθέντες κατ' ὄναρ μὴ ἀνακάμψαι πρὸς Ἡρῴδην, δι' ἄλλης ὁδοῦ ἀνεχώρησαν εἰς τὴν χώραν αὐτῶν.

2:9 Who, having heard the king, went their way. And behold the star, which they had seen in the east, went before them, until it came and stood over where the child was. [n. 191]

2:10 And seeing the star they rejoiced with exceedingly great joy. [n. 195]

2:11 And entering into the house, they found the child with Mary his mother, and falling down they adored him; and opening their treasures, they offered him gifts: gold, frankincense, and myrrh. [n. 196]

2:12 And having received an answer in sleep that they should not return to Herod, they went back another way into their country. [n. 202]

---

191. Supra Evangelista posuit unum motivum magorum, scilicet persuasionem Herodis, hic ponit aliud motivum magorum ad inquirendum Christum, scilicet ducatum stellae; et circa hoc duo facit:

primo enim ponit ducatum stellae;

secundo effectum laetitiae huius ducatus, ibi *videntes autem stellam, gavisi sunt gaudio magno valde*.

Et nota, quod stella primum exequitur suo motu, quia directe ducebat magos ad Christum; item manifestat suo statu pueri locum, ibi *usque dum veniens staret supra ubi erat puer*.

192. Unde quantum ad primum dixit *antecedebat eos*.

Ex hoc autem quod dicit *ecce stella, quam viderant in oriente, antecedebat eos*, datur intelligi quod quando magi declinaverunt in Ierusalem, stella disparuit; recedentibus autem ab Herode, apparuit.

Disparuit autem propter tria. Primo propter confusionem Iudaeorum, qui cum instructi essent in lege, ut Christum quaererent, et gentes non essent instructae, tamen gentes quaerunt, et Iudaei contemnunt. Unde impletur illud Is. LV, 5: *gentes quae te non cognoverunt, ad te current*.

Secundo propter magorum instructionem: non enim solum per stellam Dominus voluit se eis manifestare, sed etiam per legem, ut sic adiungeretur cognitioni creaturarum cognitio legis. *In ore duorum vel trium testium stabit omne verbum*, Deut. XIX, 15. Is. VIII, 20: *ad legem magis et ad testimonium*.

191. Above, the Evangelist set down one of the magi's motives, namely Herod's persuasion; here he sets down the magi's other motive for seeking Christ, namely the guidance of the star. And concerning this, he does two things:

for first, he sets down the guidance of the star;

second, the joyful effect of this guidance, at *and seeing the star they rejoiced with exceedingly great joy*.

And note that the star accomplished the first by its own motion, because it led the magi directly to Christ; likewise, it pointed to the child's place by its own location, at *until it came and stood over where the child was*.

192. Hence as regards the first, he said, *went before them*.

And from the fact that it says, *behold the star, which they had seen in the east, went before them*, one is given to understand that when the magi turned aside into Jerusalem, the star disappeared; but when they withdrew from Herod, it appeared.

Now, it disappeared for three reasons. First, for the confounding of the Jews, for while they were instructed in the law so that they might seek Christ, and the gentiles were not instructed, yet the gentiles sought, and the Jews scorned. Hence it is fulfilled that *the nations that did not know you will run to you* (Isa 55:5).

Second, for the instruction of the magi; for the Lord wished to show himself to them not only through a star, but also through the law, so that the knowledge of the law might be joined to the knowledge of creatures. *In the mouth of two or three witnesses every word will stand* (Deut 19:15). *To the law rather, and to the testimony* (Isa 8:20).

Tertio propter instructionem nostram. Et instruimur de duobus, secundum Glossam. Primo quod qui humanum auxilium quaerunt, deseruntur a divino. Illicitum est enim humanum auxilium quaerere, non quaerendo divinum; Is. XXXI, 1: *vae qui descenditis in Aegyptum ad auxilium, in equis sperantes, habentes fiduciam super quadrigis, quia multae sunt, et super equitibus, quia praevalidi nimis, et non sunt confisi super Sanctum Israel et Dominum non requisierunt.* Secundo instruimur quantum ad hoc, quod nos, qui fideles sumus, non debemus quaerere signa, sicut isti, qui *videntes stellam gavisi sunt* etc.; sed debemus esse contenti doctrinis prophetarum, quia signa data sunt infidelibus.

193. In hoc etiam est duplex mysterium. Stella enim significat Christum; Apoc. ult., 16: *ego sum radix David, stella splendida et matutina.* Unde per istam stellam intelligere possumus gratiam Dei, quam amittimus, cum ad Herodem, idest diabolum, accedimus; Eph. V, 8: *eratis aliquando tenebrae, nunc autem lux in Domino.*

Item, cum ab Herode, idest diabolo, recedimus, stellam, idest Christi gratiam, invenimus: simile Ex. XIII, 21, ubi dicitur, quod Dominus praecedebat Israel, quando exivit de Aegypto, in specie ignis et cetera. Hic autem praecedebat in specie stellae.

194. *Usque dum veniens staret supra ubi erat puer.* Duo intelligimus hic. Unum quod ista stella non erat multum alta, quia aliter non discrevissent domum pueri. Aliud quod stella completo officio suo redacta est in suam materiam.

Ubi erat puer. Frequenter puerum vocat, ut scias illum esse de quo dicitur Is. IX, 6: *puer natus est nobis.*

195. Consequenter ponitur effectus ducatus huius quantum ad magos. Unde *videntes autem stellam gavisi sunt* et cetera. Gavisi sunt propter spem, quam recuperaverunt. Timebant enim, quia de longinquis partibus venerunt, amittere quod sperabant; Rom. XII, v. 12: *spe gaudentes.* Item addit *gaudio*; aliqui enim gaudent, et non gaudent, quia laetitia humana non est perfectum gaudium; Prov. XIV, 13: *extrema gaudii luctus occupat.* Verum autem et perfectum gaudium de Deo est; Is. LXI, 10: *gaudens gaudebo in Domino, et exultabit anima mea in Deo meo.* Tertio addit *magno*, quia isti magna iam cognoscebant de Deo, quia Deum incarnatum, et multum misericordem; Is. XII, 6: *exulta et lauda, habitatio Sion, quia magnus in medio tui Sanctus Israel.* Quarto addit *valde*, quia intense gaudebant; recuperaverant enim quod amiserant; Luc. XV, 10: *gaudium erit angelis Dei* et cetera.

196. Consequenter agitur de inventione pueri. Unde *et intrantes domum, invenerunt puerum.* Et tangit tria: *domum*, quae, si quaeratur qualis erat, ostenditur Luc. II, 7. Item si quaeratur qualis puer, in nullo ab aliis

Third, for our instruction. And we are instructed about two things, according to the Gloss. First, that he who seeks human help will be forsaken by the divine. For it is unlawful to seek after human help by not seeking divine; *woe to them that go down to Egypt for help, trusting in horses, and putting their confidence in chariots, because they are many: and in horsemen, because they are very strong: and have not trusted in the Holy One of Israel, and have not sought after the Lord* (Isa 31:1). Second, we are instructed about this, that we who are faithful should not seek signs, as do those who *seeing the star . . . rejoiced*; but we ought to be content with the teaching of the prophets, because signs are given to those who do not believe.

193. There is also a twofold mystery in this. For the star signifies Christ; *I am the root and stock of David, the bright and morning star* (Rev 22:16). Hence by this star we can understand the grace of God, which we lose when we approach Herod, i.e., the devil; *for you were heretofore darkness, but now light in the Lord* (Eph 5:8).

Similarly, when we withdraw from Herod, i.e., from the devil, we find the star, i.e., the grace of Christ; as in Exodus, where it says that the Lord went before Israel in the appearance of fire when they went up out of Egypt (Exod 13:21). And here he went before in the appearance of a star.

194. *Until it came and stood over where the child was.* We understand two things here. One, that this star was not very high, because otherwise they would not have picked out the house of the child. Another, that the star, having fulfilled its duty, was resolved back into its matter.

Where the child was. It calls him a child frequently, so that you may know that it is he of whom it is said: *a child is born to us* (Isa 9:6).

195. Next, the effect of this guidance is set down with regard to the magi. Hence, *and seeing the star they rejoiced. They rejoiced* because of hope, which they had regained. For they were afraid of losing what they hoped for, because they came from a far distant place; *rejoicing in hope* (Rom 12:12). Again he adds *with joy*; for some men rejoice, and yet do not rejoice, because human happiness is not perfect joy; *mourning takes hold of the end of joy* (Prov 14:13). But true and perfect joy is about God; *I will greatly rejoice in the Lord, and my soul will be joyful in my God* (Isa 61:10). Third, he adds *great*, because these men already knew great things about God, namely that God was incarnate, and very merciful; *rejoice, and praise, O habitation of Zion: for great is he that is in the midst of you, the Holy One of Israel* (Isa 12:6). Fourth, he adds *exceedingly*, because they rejoiced intensely, for they had regained what they had lost; *so I say to you, there will be joy before the angels of God upon one sinner doing penance* (Luke 15:10).

196. Next, he treats of the finding of the child. Hence, *and entering into the house, they found the child.* And he touches upon three things: *the house*, which, if it be asked what sort it was, Luke makes it clear (Luke 2:7). Likewise,

differebat, sicut dicunt sancti. Quantum ad apparentiam, non loquebatur, infirmus videbatur, et huiusmodi. Item si quaeratur qualis mater, respondetur, qualis est uxor carpentarii.

Et hoc ideo dico, quia si isti quaesivissent regem terrenum, videndo ista scandalizati fuissent; sed videntes vilia, et considerantes altissima, moti sunt ad admirationem, et adoraverunt eum. Et hoc est *et procidentes adoraverunt eum*.

Sed quare non fit mentio de Ioseph? Dicendum quod divina dispensatione factum est quod non adesset, ne istis qui primitiae gentium erant, daretur suspicio pravae opinionis.

197. Consequenter tangitur reverentia quam exhibuerunt ad puerum, ibi *et procidentes*.

Et fuit triplex: in adorando, offerendo et obediendo.

198. Dicit ergo *et procidentes adoraverunt eum*, tamquam Deum in homine latentem; Ps. LXXI, 9: *coram illo procident Aethiopes*.

199. Item offerendo, reverentiam exhibuerunt; unde *et apertis thesauris suis*. Consuetudo enim erat apud Persas, quod semper cum munere adorabant; et hoc est *et apertis thesauris suis, obtulerunt ei munera, aurum, thus et myrrham*. Ps. LXXI, 10: *reges Tharsis et insulae munera offerent, reges Arabum et Saba dona adducent*. Is. LX, 6: *omnes de Saba venient, aurum et thus deferentes, et laudem Domino annuntiantes*.

200. Mystice considerandum est quod isti non in via, sed tunc primo aperuerunt thesaurum, quando venerunt ad Christum: similiter nos bona nostra in via non debemus manifestare. Unde reprehenditur hoc inf. XXV de virginibus, et XIII, 44 dicitur: *simile est regnum caelorum thesauro abscondito in agro, quem qui invenit homo abscondit, et prae gaudio illius vadit, et vendit universa quae habet et emit agrum illum*.

201. *Obtulerunt ei munera* et cetera. Aliqui assignant rationem istorum munerum litteralem et dicunt isti, quod tria invenerunt: domum sordidam, puerum infirmum, et matrem pauperem. Et ideo obtulerunt aurum ad sustentationem matris, myrrham ad sustentationem membrorum pueri, thus ad tollendum foetorem.

Sed dicendum, quod aliquid mystice hic praetenditur, et potius ista tria ad tria referuntur, quae offerre debemus, sc. fidem, actionem et contemplationem.

Quantum ad fidem dupliciter: primo quantum ad ea, quae in Christo concurrunt. Scilicet regia dignitas; Ier. XXIII, 5: *regnabit rex, et sapiens erit* etc.; et ideo in tributum obtulerunt *aurum*. Sacerdotii magnitudo; et ideo *thus* in sacrificium. Hominis mortalitas; et ideo

if it be asked what sort of child they found, He differed in nothing from other children, as the saints say. As regards appearance, he did not speak, he seemed weak, and so on. Again, if it be asked what sort of mother they found, it is responded, such as is the wife of a carpenter.

And I say this because if these men had come seeking an earthly king, they would have been scandalized by seeing these things; but seeing worthless things, and considering the things most high, they were moved to admiration, and adored him. And this is *and falling down they adored him*.

But why is no mention made of Joseph? One should say that it happened by divine providence that he was not there, lest these men who were the first-fruits of the gentiles be given the suspicion of a misformed opinion.

197. Next, he touches upon the reverence which they showed to the child, at *and falling down*.

And it was threefold: in adoring, in offering, and in obeying.

198. So he says, *and falling down, they adored him*, as God hidden in man; *before him the Ethiopians will fall down* (Ps 71:9).

199. Again, they showed reverence by offering; hence, *and opening their treasures*. For it was customary among the Persians that they always adored with gifts; and this is *and opening their treasures, they offered him gifts: gold, frankincense, and myrrh*. *The kings of Tharsis and the islands will offer presents: the kings of the Arabians and of Saba will bring gifts* (Ps 71:10). *All they from Saba will come, bringing gold and frankincense: and showing forth praise to the Lord* (Isa 60:6).

200. Mystically, one should consider that these men did not open their treasures on the way, but first opened their treasures when they came to Christ; similarly, we should not make our goods seen on the way. Hence this is reproached below, concerning the virgins (Matt 25:1–12), and it is said: *the kingdom of heaven is like a treasure hidden in a field. Which a man, having found it, hides, and out of joy goes, and sells all that he has, and buys that field* (Matt 13:44).

201. *They offered him gifts*. Some give a literal reason for these gifts, and they say that they found three things: a dirty house, a weak child, and the mother a pauper. And so they offered gold for the sustenance of the mother, myrrh for the sustenance of the child's members, and frankincense to take away the smell.

But it should be said that something is set out mystically here, and these three things are referred more to those three things which we ought to offer, namely faith, action, and contemplation.

As regards faith, in two ways: first as regards those things which come together in Christ. Clearly, the royal dignity; *a king will reign, and he will be wise* (Jer 23:5); and so in tribute they offered *gold*. The greatness of the priesthood; and so they offered *frankincense* in sacrifice. The

myrrham. Item quantum ad fidem Trinitatis, quia designantur in nobis personae Trinitatis.

Secundo possunt referri ad actionem nostram. Per aurum enim potest signari sapientia; Prov. II, 4: *si quasi thesauros effoderis illam, tunc intelliges timorem Domini*. Per thus oratio devota; Ps. CXL, 2: *dirigatur, domine, oratio mea, sicut incensum in conspectu tuo* et cetera. Per myrrham mortificatio carnis: Col. III, 5: *mortificate membra, quae sunt super terram*; Cant. V, 5: *manus meae distillaverunt myrrham*.

Quantum autem ad contemplationem, per ista tria possunt significari vel tres sensus Sacrae Scripturae, scilicet litteralis, sub quo comprehenditur allegoricus, anagogicus et moralis; vel tres partes philosophiae, scilicet moralis, logica et naturalis: omnibus enim his debemus uti ad servitium Dei.

202. Consequenter ponitur quomodo reverentiam exhibuerunt in obediendo. Unde *et responso accepto in somnis, ne redirent ad Herodem, per aliam viam reversi sunt in regionem suam*.

Sed quomodo responsum acceperunt qui non interrogaverunt?

Sed dicendum quod Dominus respondet aliquando interrogationi mentali, et isti intus quaerebant quid placeret Deo de reversione; Ex. XIV, 15: *quid clamas ad me?*

203. Sed numquid sunt revelationes immediate a Deo? Dionysius probat quod non, nisi mediantibus angelis. Quare ergo non nominat angelum?

Sed dicendum, quod quandoque Scriptura facit mentionem de Deo, et non de angelo, hoc fit per quamdam excellentiam illius manifestationis; Gal. III, 19: *lex ordinata per angelum in manu mediatoris*; Act. VII, 37: *hic est Moyses, qui dixit filiis Israel: prophetam suscitabit vobis Deus de fratribus vestris, tamquam me ipsum audietis* et cetera. Unde quod dicit Glossa, quod hoc fuit immediate per Deum, refertur ad modum loquendi Scripturae.

204. *Per aliam viam reversi sunt in regionem suam*. In hoc ostenditur quod ad regionem nostram paradisum, a qua per peccatum expulsi sumus, per obedientiam pervenimus. Prov. IV, 27: *vias quae a dextris sunt novit Dominus; perversae vero sunt quae sunt a sinistris*.

Chrysostomus hic dicit, quod isti reversi egerunt sanctam vitam, et postea facti sunt coadiutores s. Thomae Apostoli; tamen nihil de eis invenitur scriptum in Sacra Scriptura post recessum eorum.

mortality of a man; and so they offered *myrrh*. Similarly, as regards the faith of the Trinity, because the persons of the Trinity are indicated in us.

Second, they can be referred to our action. For wisdom can be indicated through gold; *if you . . . will dig for her as for a treasure: then you will understand the fear of the Lord* (Prov 2:4). Through frankincense, devoted prayer; *let my prayer be directed as incense in thy sight; the lifting up of my hands, as evening sacrifice* (Ps 140:2). Through myrrh, the mortification of the body: *mortify therefore your members which are upon the earth* (Col 3:5); *my hands dropped with myrrh* (Song 5:5).

And as regards contemplation, by these three can be signified the three senses of Sacred Scripture, namely the literal sense, under which are comprehended the allegorical, the anagogical, and the moral; or the three parts of philosophy, namely moral, logic, and natural; for we ought to use all these for the service of God.

202. Next is set down how they showed reverence in obeying. Hence, *and having received an answer in sleep that they should not return to Herod, they went back another way into their country*.

But how did they who did not ask a question receive an answer?

But it should be said that the Lord sometimes responds to a mental question, and these men were asking interiorly what would please God concerning the return; *why do you cry to me?* (Exod 14:15).

203. But are revelations immediately from God? Dionysius proves that they are only through the mediation of angels. So why does he not name the angel?

But one should say that whenever Scripture mentions God and not an angel, this is because of a certain excellence of that manifestation; the law was *ordained by angels in the hand of a mediator* (Gal 3:19); *this is that Moses who said to the children of Israel: a prophet will God raise up to you of your own brethren, as myself: him will you hear* (Acts 7:37). Hence what the Gloss says, that this was immediately from God, is referred to Scripture's manner of speaking.

204. *They went back another way into their country*. This shows that we come to our country, paradise, from which we were expelled by sin, through obedience. *For the Lord knows the ways that are on the right hand: but those are perverse which are on the left hand* (Prov 4:27).

Chrysostom says here that these men, having returned, led holy lives, and later were made co-helpers of St. Thomas the Apostle; yet nothing is found written in the Sacred Scriptures after their return.

Lecture 4

2:13 Qui cum recessissent, ecce angelus Domini apparuit in somnis Ioseph, dicens: surge et accipe puerum, et matrem eius et fuge in Aegyptum, et esto ibi usque dum dicam tibi: futurum est enim ut Herodes quaerat puerum ad perdendum eum. [n. 206]

2:13 Ἀναχωρησάντων δὲ αὐτῶν ἰδοὺ ἄγγελος κυρίου φαίνεται κατ᾽ ὄναρ τῷ Ἰωσὴφ λέγων· ἐγερθεὶς παράλαβε τὸ παιδίον καὶ τὴν μητέρα αὐτοῦ καὶ φεῦγε εἰς Αἴγυπτον καὶ ἴσθι ἐκεῖ ἕως ἂν εἴπω σοι· μέλλει γὰρ Ἡρῴδης ζητεῖν τὸ παιδίον τοῦ ἀπολέσαι αὐτό.

2:13 And after they had departed, behold an angel of the Lord appeared in sleep to Joseph, saying: arise, and take the child and his mother, and fly into Egypt: and be there until I tell you. For it will come to pass that Herod will seek the child to destroy him. [n. 206]

2:14 Qui consurgens accepit puerum, et matrem eius nocte, et secessit in Aegyptum; [n. 213]

2:14 ὁ δὲ ἐγερθεὶς παρέλαβεν τὸ παιδίον καὶ τὴν μητέρα αὐτοῦ νυκτὸς καὶ ἀνεχώρησεν εἰς Αἴγυπτον,

2:14 Who arose, and took the child and his mother by night, and retired into Egypt; [n. 213]

2:15 et erat ibi usque ad obitum Herodis, ut adimpleretur quod dictum est a Domino per prophetam dicentem: ex Aegypto vocavi Filium meum. [n. 213]

2:15 καὶ ἦν ἐκεῖ ἕως τῆς τελευτῆς Ἡρῴδου· ἵνα πληρωθῇ τὸ ῥηθὲν ὑπὸ κυρίου διὰ τοῦ προφήτου λέγοντος· ἐξ Αἰγύπτου ἐκάλεσα τὸν υἱόν μου.

2:15 and he was there until the death of Herod, that it might be fulfilled which the Lord spoke by the prophet, saying: out of Egypt have I called my Son. [n. 213]

2:16 Tunc Herodes videns quoniam inlusus esset a Magis, iratus est valde, et mittens occidit omnes pueros, qui erant in Bethlehem, et in omnibus finibus eius, a bimatu et infra, secundum tempus, quod exquisierat a magis. [n. 217]

2:16 Τότε Ἡρῴδης ἰδὼν ὅτι ἐνεπαίχθη ὑπὸ τῶν μάγων ἐθυμώθη λίαν, καὶ ἀποστείλας ἀνεῖλεν πάντας τοὺς παῖδας τοὺς ἐν Βηθλέεμ καὶ ἐν πᾶσι τοῖς ὁρίοις αὐτῆς ἀπὸ διετοῦς καὶ κατωτέρω, κατὰ τὸν χρόνον ὃν ἠκρίβωσεν παρὰ τῶν μάγων.

2:16 Then Herod perceiving that he was deluded by the magi, was exceedingly angry; and, sending, killed all the male children that were in Bethlehem, and in all the borders thereof, from two years old and under, according to the time which he had diligently inquired of the magi. [n. 217]

2:17 Tunc adimpletum est, quod dictum est per Ieremiam prophetam dicentem: [n. 225]

2:17 τότε ἐπληρώθη τὸ ῥηθὲν διὰ Ἰερεμίου τοῦ προφήτου λέγοντος·

2:17 Then was fulfilled that which was spoken by Jeremiah the prophet, saying: [n. 225]

2:18 vox in Rama audita est, ploratus, et ululatus multus, Rachel plorans filios suos, et noluit consolari, quia non sunt. [n. 228]

2:18 φωνὴ ἐν Ῥαμὰ ἠκούσθη, κλαυθμὸς καὶ ὀδυρμὸς πολύς· Ῥαχὴλ κλαίουσα τὰ τέκνα αὐτῆς, καὶ οὐκ ἤθελεν παρακληθῆναι, ὅτι οὐκ εἰσίν.

2:18 a voice in Rama was heard, lamentation and great mourning; Rachel bewailing her children, and would not be comforted, because they are not. [n. 228]

2:19 Defuncto autem Herode, ecce angelus Domini apparuit in somnis Ioseph in Aegypto, [n. 232]

2:19 Τελευτήσαντος δὲ τοῦ Ἡρῴδου ἰδοὺ ἄγγελος κυρίου φαίνεται κατ᾽ ὄναρ τῷ Ἰωσὴφ ἐν Αἰγύπτῳ

2:19 But when Herod was dead, behold an angel of the Lord appeared in sleep to Joseph in Egypt, [n. 232]

2:20 dicens: surge et accipe puerum, et matrem eius, et vade in terram Israel: defuncti sunt enim, qui quaerebant animam pueri. [n. 234]

2:20 λέγων· ἐγερθεὶς παράλαβε τὸ παιδίον καὶ τὴν μητέρα αὐτοῦ καὶ πορεύου εἰς γῆν Ἰσραήλ· τεθνήκασιν γὰρ οἱ ζητοῦντες τὴν ψυχὴν τοῦ παιδίου.

2:20 saying: arise, and take the child and his mother, and go into the land of Israel. For they are dead who sought the soul of the child. [n. 234]

2:21 Qui consurgens accepit puerum, et matrem eius, et venit in terram Israel. [n. 236]

2:21 ὁ δὲ ἐγερθεὶς παρέλαβεν τὸ παιδίον καὶ τὴν μητέρα αὐτοῦ καὶ εἰσῆλθεν εἰς γῆν Ἰσραήλ.

2:21 Who arose, and took the child and his mother, and came into the land of Israel. [n. 236]

2:22 Audiens autem quod Archelaus regnaret in Iudaea pro Herode patre suo, timuit illo ire: et admonitus in somnis, secessit in partes Galilaeae. [n. 238]

2:23 Et veniens habitavit in civitate, quae vocatur Nazareth, ut adimpleretur quod dictum est per prophetam: quoniam Nazaraeus vocabitur. [n. 239]

2:22 Ἀκούσας δὲ ὅτι Ἀρχέλαος βασιλεύει τῆς Ἰουδαίας ἀντὶ τοῦ πατρὸς αὐτοῦ Ἡρῴδου ἐφοβήθη ἐκεῖ ἀπελθεῖν· χρηματισθεὶς δὲ κατ᾽ ὄναρ ἀνεχώρησεν εἰς τὰ μέρη τῆς Γαλιλαίας,

2:23 καὶ ἐλθὼν κατῴκησεν εἰς πόλιν λεγομένην Ναζαρέτ· ὅπως πληρωθῇ τὸ ῥηθὲν διὰ τῶν προφητῶν ὅτι Ναζωραῖος κληθήσεται.

2:22 But hearing that Archelaus reigned in Judea in place of Herod his father, he was afraid to go there: and being warned in sleep retired into the quarters of Galilee. [n. 238]

2:23 And coming he dwelt in a city called Nazareth: that it might be fulfilled which was said by prophets: that he will be called a Nazarene. [n. 239]

---

205. Supra habitum est quomodo nascenti Christo magi testimonium perhibuerunt, nunc autem agitur quomodo innocentes testimonium perhibent, non loquendo sed moriendo.

Et circa hoc tria facit Evangelista.

Primo enim ponitur occultatio Christi;

secundo interfectio puerorum, ibi *tunc Herodes*;

tertio ponitur reditus ipsius Christi, ibi *defuncto Herode*.

Circa primum tria facit.

Primo enim ponitur admonitio angeli;

secundo ostenditur obedientia Ioseph;

tertio impletio prophetiae.

Secundum ibi *ut adimpleretur*.

Circa primum tria tanguntur.

Primo ponitur tempus apparitionis;

secundo describitur ipsa apparitio et modus apparitionis ibi *ecce angelus*;

tertio ponitur ipsa admonitio facta per angelum, ibi *surge et accipe puerum*.

206. Tempus describitur ibi *qui cum recessissent*. Et intelligendum quod non statim post recessum magorum facta est ista apparitio, quia totum quod dicitur Luc. II, 6, debet interponi, scilicet de purificatione: *postquam impleti sunt dies* et cetera. Non enim Herodes statim cogitavit de interfectione puerorum. Unde cum dicit *qui cum recessissent*, debet interponi tota historia purificationis.

207. Consequenter ponitur ipsa apparitio; unde *ecce angelus apparuit in somnis* et cetera.

In somnis dicitur apparere, quia tunc homines ab actibus exterioribus cessant, et talibus fit revelatio per angelos; Ps. IV, 9: *in pace in idipsum dormiam, et requiescam*; Prov. III, 24: *quiesces, et suavis erit somnus tuus*.

208. In ista admonitione tria ponuntur. Primo enim persuadet angelus fugere; secundo determinat moram; tertio assignat causam.

Dicit ergo *surge*.

205. It was recounted above how the magi bore testimony to Christ at his birth; but now the Evangelist treats of how the innocents bore testimony, not by speaking, but by dying.

And concerning this he does three things:

first, the hiding of Christ is set down;

second, the killing of the children, at *then Herod*;

third, the return of Christ is set down, at *but when Herod was dead*.

Concerning the first, he does three things:

first, the angel's warning is set down;

second, Joseph's obedience is shown;

third, the fulfillment of the prophecy.

The second is at *that it might be fulfilled*.

Concerning the first, three things are touched upon:

first, the time of the apparition is set down;

second, the apparition itself and the mode of the apparition is set down, at *behold, an angel*;

third, the warning itself, given through the angel, is set down at *arise, and take the child*.

206. The time is described at *and after they had departed*. And one should understand that this apparition was not immediately after the departure of the magi, because the whole of what is said in Luke (Luke 2:6) and following should be placed in between, namely about the purification: *and after the days of her purification . . . were accomplished* (Luke 2:22). For Herod did not at once contemplate killing the children. Hence when he says, *and after they had departed*, one ought to put in here the whole history of the purification.

207. Next, the apparition itself is set down; hence, *behold, an angel of the Lord appeared in sleep*.

It is said to appear *in sleep*, because at that time men rest from exterior actions, and to such ones comes a revelation through angels; *in peace in the same I will sleep, and I will rest* (Ps 4:9); *if you sleep, you will not fear: you will rest, and your sleep will be sweet* (Prov 3:24).

208. Three things are included in this warning: first, the angel persuades him to flee; second, he specifies the length of time; third, he gives the reason.

He says then, *arise*.

Et nota, quod, sicut dicit Hilarius, Beata Virgo ante nativitatem ab Angelo nominatur *coniux*, supra I, 5, sed post nativitatem non. Et hoc propter duo. Primo ad commendationem Virginis; sicut enim virgo concepit, ita virgo peperit. Secundo propter dignitatem eius: erat enim mater Dei, qua dignitate nulla maior, et denominatio fit a digniori.

Item quod, sicut dicit Chrysostomus, puer non venerat propter matrem, sed potius e converso; et ideo dicit *accipe puerum, et matrem eius* et cetera.

209. Sed quare *fuge in Aegyptum*? Nonne dicit Ps. XVIII, 15: *Dominus adiutor meus, et redemptor meus?*

Sed sciendum quod propter tria fugit. Primo ad manifestandam suam humanitatem; sicut enim divinitas in stella apparuit, ita humanitas in fuga. Phil. II, 7: *in similitudinem hominum factus.* Secundo propter exemplum; illud enim exemplo ostendit, quod verbo docuit. Infra X, 23: *cum autem persequentur vos in civitate ista, fugite in aliam.* Tertio propter mysterium: sicut enim voluit mori, ut nos a morte revocaret, ita voluit fugere, ut fugientes a facie sua propter peccatum revocaret. Ps. CXXXVIII, 7: *quo ibo a spiritu tuo?*

210. *Et esto ibi.* Sed quare potius in Aegyptum, quam alibi in aliam regionem?

Dicendum propter duas rationes. Prima est, quia proprium est Dei, ut memor sit misericordiae in ira, Hab. III, 8. Dominus enim iratus fuit contra Aegyptios persequentes filios Israel, quia filii Israel erant primogenitus Dei. Et ideo datum est ei, ut obsequeretur unigenito; Is. XIX, 1: *ecce Dominus ascendet super nubem levem, et ingredietur Aegyptum* etc.; ibid. IX, 2: *populus qui ambulabat in tenebris, vidit lucem magnam: habitantibus in regione umbrae mortis lux orta est eis;* Io. I, 14: *vidimus gloriam eius, gloriam quasi unigeniti a Patre, plenum gratiae, et veritatis.*

Secunda, quia ipse induxerat tenebras in Aegypto, ideo voluit eam primo illuminare; et ideo bene ibi fugit; Is. IX, 2: *populus qui ambulabat in tenebris, vidit lucem magnam; habitantibus in regione umbrae mortis lux orta est eis.*

211. Nota quod quando aliquis vult fugere peccatum, primo debet excutere pigritiam; Eph. V, 14: *surge qui dormis, et exurge a mortuis, et illuminabit te Christus.* Secundo debet accipere fiduciam a matre, et Filio, scilicet Christo; Eccli. XXIV, 25: *in me omnis spes vitae et virtutis.* Tertio debet fugere a peccato adiutus auxilio matris et pueri; Ps. LIV, 8: *ecce elongavi fugiens, et mansi in solitudine.*

And notice, as Hilary says, that the Blessed Virgin is called *wife* before the birth, above (Matt 1:5), but not afterwards. And this is for two reasons. First, to commend the Virgin, for just as she conceived as a virgin, so she gave birth as a virgin. Second, on account of her dignity: for she was the mother of God, than which no dignity is greater, and a name is given from what is more dignified.

Notice likewise that, as Chrysostom says, the child had not come for the sake of the mother, but rather the other way around; and so he says, *take the child and his mother.*

209. But why *fly into Egypt*? Does not the Psalm say, *O Lord, my helper, and my redeemer* (Ps 18:15)?

But one should know that he fled for the sake of three things. First, to manifest his humanity; for as the divinity was apparent in the star, so the humanity was apparent in the flight. *Being made in the likeness of men* (Phil 2:7). Second, for the sake of example; for he showed by example what he taught by word. Below, *and when they persecute you in this city, flee into another* (Matt 10:23). Third, owing to a mystery: for just as he wished to die, so that he might call us back from death, so also he wished to flee, so that he might call back those fleeing from his face on account of sin. *Where will I go from your spirit? Or where will I flee from your face?* (Ps 138:7).

210. *And be there.* But why in Egypt, rather than in some other region?

One should say, for two reasons. The first is that it is proper to God that in wrath he is mindful of mercy (Hab 3:8). For the Lord was angry with the Egyptians, who were persecuting the children of Israel, because the children of Israel were God's first-born. And so it is given to Egypt that it should aid the first-born; *behold the Lord will ascend upon a swift cloud, and will enter into Egypt, and the idols of Egypt will be moved at his presence, and the heart of Egypt will melt in the midst thereof* (Isa 19:1). *The people that walked in darkness, have seen a great light: to them that dwelt in the region of the shadow of death, light is risen* (Isa 9:2); *we saw his glory, the glory as it were of the only begotten of the Father, full of grace and truth* (John 1:14).

Second, because he himself had brought darkness into Egypt, so he wished to illuminate it first; and therefore well did he flee there; *the people that walked in darkness, have seen a great light: to them that dwelt in the region of the shadow of death, light is risen* (Isa 9:2).

211. Notice that when someone wishes to flee from sin, he ought first to cast off sloth; *rise you who sleep, and arise from the dead: and Christ will enlighten you* (Eph 5:14). Second, he ought to receive confidence from the mother, and from the Son, namely Christ; *in me is all grace of the way and of the truth, in me is all hope of life and of virtue* (Sir 24:25). Third, he ought to flee from sin, aided by the help of the mother and the child; *lo, I have gone far off flying away; and I abode in the wilderness* (Ps 54:8).

212. Subdit causam huius fugae *futurum est enim, ut Herodes quaerat puerum ad perdendum eum*. Deceptus fuit Herodes, quia voluit perdere qui venerat regnum suum communicare; Lc. XXII, 29: *et ego dispono vobis, sicut disposuit mihi Pater meus regnum*. Secundo, quia eum qui non gloriam mundanam quaerebat; Hebr. XII, 2: *qui proposito sibi gaudio, sustinuit crucem*.

213. *Qui consurgens*. Hic ponitur executio mandati angelici, et ponit eam quantum ad fugam, et quantum ad moram.

Unde *qui consurgens accepit puerum et matrem eius*. Et fit mentio de tempore, unde dicit *nocte*, propter timorem et tribulationem, secundum illud Is. XXVI, 9: *anima mea desideravit te in nocte*, idest in tribulatione; in tribulationibus enim recurrendum est ad Deum: Os. VI, 1: *in tribulatione sua mane consurgent ad me*. *Qui consurgens*. Tunc adimpletum est illud Is. XIX, 1: *ecce Dominus ascendet super nubem levem, et ingredietur Aegyptum*; quod ad litteram impletum est.

Et erat ibi. Dicitur quod septem annos fuit ibi, et habitavit in civitate Heliopoli.

Quantum autem ad mysterium, per Ioseph signantur praedicatores, hoc est apostoli, qui ponuntur ad expellendas tenebras per doctrinam, qui recedentes a Iudaeis conversi sunt ad gentes; Act. XIII, 16: *vobis oportebat primum loqui verbum Dei; sed quoniam repellitis illud, et indignos vos iudicatis aeternae vitae, ecce convertimur ad gentes*.

214. *Et esto ibi usque dum dicam tibi*, idest usquequo finiatur infidelitas Iudaeorum. Rom. II, 25: *caecitas ex parte contigit in Israel*.

215. Consequenter adhibet testimonium prophetiae; unde dicit *ut adimpleretur quod dictum est a Domino per prophetam*. Istud est, secundum translationem Hieronymi, Osee c. XI, 1. In translatione autem Septuaginta non est ita, sed *ex Aegypto vocavi filium eius*.

216. Videtur hic esse quaestio: quia non videtur hoc facere ad propositum, quia praemittitur ibi, *puer Israel* etc., et sic loqui videtur de vocatione Israel de Aegypto.

Sed dicendum quod in omnibus auctoritatibus, quae in Evangeliis vel in epistolis ponuntur de Christo, quaedam distinctio notanda est; quia quaedam dicuntur specialiter de Christo sicut illud Is. LIII, 7: *tamquam ovis ad occisionem ducetur*; quaedam autem dicuntur de quibusdam secundum quod duxerunt figuram Christi. Et sic est ista auctoritas: isti enim non fuerunt filii Israel, nisi inquantum similitudinem gesserunt veri Filii unigeniti. Et hoc est: '*ex Aegypto vocavi Filium meum*', scilicet specialem.

212. He adds next the reason for this flight, *for it will come to pass that Herod will seek the child to destroy him*. Herod had been deceived, because he wanted to destroy the one who had come to share his kingdom; *and I dispose to you, as my Father has disposed to me, a kingdom* (Luke 22:29). Second, because he wished to destroy him who did not seek earthly glory; *who having joy set before him, endured the cross* (Heb 12:2).

213. *Who arose*. Here is set down the execution of the angel's command, and he sets it down as regards the flight, and as regards the length of time.

Hence, *who arose, and took the child and his mother*. And he mentions the time: *by night*, because of fear and tribulation, in accord with: *my soul has desired you in the night* (Isa 26:9), i.e., in tribulation, for in tribulations one should run back to God. *In their affliction they will rise early to me: come, and let us return to the Lord* (Hos 6:1). Then was it fulfilled, *behold the Lord will ascend upon a swift cloud, and will enter into Egypt* (Isa 19:1), which was fulfilled to the letter.

And he was there. It is said that he was there for seven years, and lived in the city of Heliopolis.

And with regard to a mystery, by Joseph are indicated the preachers, i.e., the apostles, who are established as preachers to expel darkness by teaching. Withdrawing from the Jews, they turned to the gentiles; *to you it behoved us first to speak the word of God: but because you reject it, and judge yourselves unworthy of eternal life, behold we turn to the gentiles* (Acts 13:46).

214. *And be there until I tell you*, i.e., until whenever the infidelity of the Jews is finished. *Blindness in part has happened in Israel* (Rom 11:25).

215. Next, he brings in the testimony of the prophet. Hence he says, *that it might be fulfilled which the Lord spoke by the prophet*. This is, according to the translation of Jerome. But in the Septuagint translation it is not this way, but, *out of Egypt I have called his son* (Hos 11:1).

216. There seems to be a question here, because this does not seem to work to the purpose, because just before in the text of the prophecy it says, *because Israel was a child, and I loved him: and I called my son out of Egypt*, and so it seems to speak about the calling of Israel from Egypt.

But one should say that in all the Scriptural texts which are set down in the Gospels and in the epistles about Christ, a certain distinction should be noted; because some speak specially of Christ, as: *he will be led as a sheep to the slaughter* (Isa 53:7); but others speak of certain things according as they introduced a figure of Christ. And such is this text: for those men were only children of Israel insofar as they bore a likeness of the true only-begotten Son. And this is, *'out of Egypt have I called my Son'*, namely the particular Son.

217. *Tunc Herodes*. Hic agitur de interfectione puerorum; et

circa hoc duo facit.

Primo ponitur occasio interfectionis;

secundo ponitur interfectio; ibi *et mittens occidit omnes pueros*;

tertio inducuntur prophetiae, ibi *tunc impletum est*.

218. Occasio fuit ira Herodis: unde *tunc Herodes iratus est*. Iac. I, 20: *ira viri iustitiam Dei non operatur*. Et notandum quod quando aliquis rex amissionem regni suspicatur, cito irascitur et accenditur.

Videns quoniam illusus esset a magis, iratus est valde. Et dicitur *iratus valde* propter duo: quia quando aliquis irascitur, de modica occasione fortiter accenditur. Unde quia in suspicione erat amissionis regni, et illusus fuit a magis, *iratus est valde*. Eccli. XI, 34: *a scintilla una augetur ignis*.

219. *Et mittens*. In ira ista fuit crudelitas quantum ad tria: quantum ad locum, quantum ad multitudinem et quantum ad tempus.

Quantum ad multitudinem, ut unum quaereret, omnes occidit. Unde dicitur *et mittens occidit omnes pueros*. Et nota quod dicit Augustinus quod *iste numquam profuisset tantum obsequio, quantum profuit odio*.

Sed quaeritur, cum non habuerint liberum arbitrium, quomodo dicti sunt mori pro Christo.

Sed, sicut dicitur Io. III, 17, *non misit Deus Filium suum in mundum, ut iudicet mundum, sed ut salvetur mundus per ipsum*. Numquam enim Deus permisisset eos occidi, nisi fuisset eis utile. Unde dicit Augustinus quod idem est dubitare utrum profuerit illis ista occisio, quod est dubitare utrum pueris prosit baptismus: passi sunt enim ut martyres et Christum moriendo confessi sunt, quamvis non loquendo. Apoc. VI, 9: *vidi subtus altare animus interfectorum propter verbum Dei*.

220. Secunda crudelitas est, quia occidit *in omnibus finibus*, timebat enim ne fugeret, scilicet ad aliquam civitatem. Et contigit ei sicut bestiae vulneratae, quae non attendit quem vulnerare debeat; Prov. XXVIII, v. 15: *leo rugiens, et ursus esuriens, princeps impius super populum pauperem*.

221. Tertia quantum ad tempus. Unde *a bimatu*, idest duorum annorum.

Et nota quod Augustinus dicit quod illo anno, quo Christus natus est, innocentes sunt occisi.

222. Sed quare dicit *a bimatu et infra*? Dicunt quidam quod stella apparuit per duos annos ante; unde

217. *Then Herod*. Here he treats of the killing of the children; and

concerning this he does two things:

first, the occasion of the killing is set down;

second, the killing is set down, at *and, sending, killed all the male children*;

third, the prophecies are introduced, at *then was fulfilled*.

218. The occasion was Herod's wrath; hence, *then Herod . . . was exceedingly angry*. *For the anger of man works not the justice of God* (Jas 1:20). And one should note that when some king suspects the loss of his kingdom, he is quickly angered and aroused.

Perceiving that he was deluded by the magi, was exceedingly angry. And it says *exceedingly angry* for two reasons: because when someone is angered, he is strongly aroused by a small pretext. Hence because he suspected the loss of the kingdom, and was deluded by the magi, he *was exceedingly angry*. *Of one spark comes a great fire* (Sir 11:34).

219. *And sending*. There was in this anger a cruelty as regards three things: as regards place, as regards multitude, and as regards time.

As regards multitude, he killed all to seek one. Hence it says, *sending, killed all the male children*. And note that Augustine says, *this man never gained as much service as he did hate*.

But it is asked, since they did not have free judgment, how are they said to die for Christ?

But, as it is said, *God did not send the Son into the world to judge the world, but to save the world through himself* (John 3:17). For God would never have permitted them to be killed, unless it were useful to them. Hence Augustine says that it is the same to doubt whether that killing profited them as to doubt whether children profit by baptism. For they suffered as martyrs, and confessed Christ by dying, although not by speaking. *I saw under the altar the souls of them that were slain for the word of God* (Rev 6:9).

220. The second cruelty is that he killed the male children *in all the borders thereof*, for he feared lest Christ should flee to some city. And Herod was affected like a wounded beast, which pays no attention to whom it should wound; *as a roaring lion, and a hungry bear, so is a wicked prince over the poor people* (Prov 28:15).

221. The third cruelty, as regards time. Hence, *from two years old and under*, i.e., of two years.

And note that Augustine says that the innocents were killed in the very year that Christ was born.

222. But why does he say *from two years old and under*? Some say that the star appeared for two years before

Herodes dubitabat utrum a tempore stellae natus fuisset. Et ideo dicit *secundum tempus quod exquisierat a magis*.

Alii autem dicunt quod isti non sunt occisi eodem anno, sed post duos annos.

223. Sed quare tantum distulit? Triplex ratio redditur a diversis. Una est, quia a principio putabat quod magi fuissent decepti et quod nihil invenissent, sed postquam audivit multa verba de Christo a Zacharia et Simeone et Anna, tunc motus fuit ad quaerendum. Alii dicunt quod hoc fecit ex cautela: timebat enim ne puerum, quem quaerebat, parentes occultassent. Unde primo voluit eos assecurare. Alii quod occupatione impeditus, quia misit post magos usque ad Tharsum Ciliciae et fecit incendi naves eorum. Item fuit occupatus, quia citatus fuit Romae accusatus a filiis. Et sic post reversionem incepit saevire.

224. Et dicit *et infra* etc., quia cogitavit illum esse tantae potentiae, quod posset commutare faciem suam.

Per istam occisionem significatur occisio martyrum, quia pueri per humilitatem et innocentiam, infra XIX, 14: *sinite parvulos, et nolite eos prohibere ad me venire*; item infra XVIII, 3: *nisi conversi fueritis, et efficiamini sicut parvuli, non intrabitis in regnum caelorum*.

In Bethlehem, et in omnibus finibus eius; quia per totum mundum occiduntur, Act. I, v. 8: *eritis mihi testes*, scilicet moriendo. Duo anni sunt duplex caritas, Dei et proximi, quia *fides sine operibus mortua est*, Iac. c. II, 20.

Et nota quod nato Christo, statim persecutio saevit, quia statim quando quis convertitur ad Christum, incipit tentari. Eccli. II, v. 1: *Fili, accedens ad servitutem Dei, sta in iustitia et in timore, et praepara animam tuam ad tentationem*.

225. *Tunc impletum est quod dictum est per Ieremiam Prophetam*. Posita occisione puerorum, hic more suo Evangelista prophetiam annuntiantem ponit, quae est Ier. c. XXXI, 15: *'vox in Rama audita est, lamentationis, luctus et fletus, Rachel plorantis filios suos, et nolentis consolari super eis, quia non sunt.'*

Et notandum quod, sicut dicit Hieronymus, ubicumque per apostolos et evangelistas introducitur aliqua auctoritas Veteris Testamenti, non oportet introducere verbum ex verbo semper, sed sicut dedit eis Spiritus Sanctus, aliquando sensum ex sensu in usu nostro. Ita habemus Ier. XXXI, 15: *vox in excelsis audita est lamentationis, luctus et fletus, Rachel plorantis filios suos, et nolentis consolari super eis, quia non sunt. Et sensus idem est.*

Christ's birth; hence Herod was unsure whether he had been born since the time of the star. And so he says, *according to the time which he had diligently inquired of the magi*.

But others say that these children were not killed in the same year, but after two years.

223. But why did he delay so long? Three reasons are given, by various people. One is that he thought at first that the magi had been deceived, and that they would have found nothing; but afterwards he heard many things about Christ from Zachary and Simeon and Anna, and then he was moved to seek him. Others say that he did this out of caution; for he feared lest the parents should have hidden the child whom he sought. Hence he wanted to make sure of them first. Others say that he was held back by another affair, because he sent after the magi as far as Tharsus of Cilicia and burned their ships. Likewise, he was occupied with another affair because he was summoned to Rome, having been accused by his children. And so after his return he began to rage.

224. And it says, *and under*, because he thought him to be so powerful that he could change his face.

This killing points to the killing of martyrs, because martyrs are children through humility and innocence, below, *suffer the little children, and do not forbid them to come to me* (Matt 19:14); likewise below, *unless you be converted, and become as little children, you will not enter into the kingdom of heaven* (Matt 18:3).

In Bethlehem, and in all the borders thereof; because they are killed throughout the entire world; *you will be witnesses unto me*, namely by dying (Acts 1:8). The two years are the two-fold love, of God and of neighbor, because *faith without works is dead* (Jas 2:26).

And notice that when Christ is born, persecution rages at once, because when someone is converted to Christ, he begins to be tempted at once. *Son, when you come to the service of God, stand in justice and in fear, and prepare your soul for temptation* (Sir 2:1).

225. *Then was fulfilled that which was spoken by Jeremiah the Prophet*. Having set down the killing of the infants, here, as is his custom, the Evangelist places a prophecy foretelling it, which is: *'a voice in Rama was heard, lamentation and great mourning; Rachel bewailing her children, and would not be comforted, because they are not'* (Jer 31:15).

And one should note that, as Jerome says, wherever the apostles or evangelists bring in some text of the Old Testament, it is not always necessary that they bring it in word for word, but as the Holy Spirit gave it to them, sometimes *the sense of the sense*, in our usage. Thus we have: *a voice was heard on high of lamentation, of mourning, and weeping, of Rachel weeping for her children, and refusing to be comforted for them, because they are not* (Jer 31:15). And the sense is the same.

226. Et considerandum quod, quantum ad hanc auctoritatem pertinet, ista est una de illis quae introducuntur in Evangelio, quae tamen sensum litteralem habet, qui est figura eius, quod fuit in Novo Testamento.

Unde ad intellectum eius consideranda est quaedam historia, quae legitur Iudicum XIX ubi dicitur quod propter peccatum commissum circa uxorem Levitae fere tota tribus Beniamin extincta est; et dicitur quod ibi fuit maximus planctus, ita quod fuit auditus de Gabaa usque in Rama longe a Bethlehem per duodecim miliaria. Hoc dicitur *Rachel plorare*, quia mater fuit Beniamin; et est locutio figurativa, scilicet ad exprimendum magnitudinem doloris. Sed haec est prophetia de praeterito.

227. Alio modo est de futuro dupliciter. Quia uno modo potest referri ad captivitatem Israel, qui quando in captivitatem ducebantur, dicuntur in via iuxta Bethlehem plorasse; et tunc dicitur Rachel plorasse, quia sepulta erat ibi, Gen. XXXV, 19. Et dicitur hoc eodem modo loquendi quo locus dicitur plorare mala quae in loco accidunt. Vult ergo dicere propheta quod sicut maximus dolor et luctus fuit, quando extincta est tribus Beniamin, ita futurus est maximus alius tempore captivitatis.

228. Tertio modo exponitur sic. Evangelista assumit factum de occisione innocentum et exaggerat istum dolorem quadrupliciter. Ex diffusione doloris, ex multitudine doloris, ex materia, et inconsolabilitate.

Dicit ergo: *'vox in Rama.'* Quaedam civitas est in tribu Beniamin, Iosue XVIII, 25, et potest accipi pro civitate Liae. Hic autem accipitur pro 'excelso'; et potest dupliciter exponi. Primo sic: *'vox'*, in excelso prolata, *'audita est'*, quia vox quae in loco alto est, longe lateque diffunditur; Is. XL, 9: *supra montem excelsum ascende tu qui evangelizas Sion, exalta in fortitudine vocem tuam.* Vel *'audita est'* in excelso, idest in caelo apud Deum; Eccli. XXXV, 21: *oratio humiliantis se nubes penetrabit, et donec propinquet, non consolabitur, et non discedet donec Altissimus aspiciat.* Et iterum: *nonne lacrimae viduae ad maxillam descendunt, et exclamatio eius super deducentes eas?*

229. *'Ploratus'*: hoc potest referri ad fletum infantium occisorum. *'Et ululatus multus'*; hoc ad matrum ploratus. Vel utrumque ad pueros: *'ploratus'* inquantum elevabantur a militibus, *'ululatus'* inquantum iugulabantur. Maior est dolor matrum, quam filiorum. Item matrum erat dolor assiduus, puerorum fuit brevis: propter quod dicit Zach. XII, 10: *plangent eum quasi super*

226. And one should consider that, as far as pertains to this Scriptural text, this is one of those prophecies which are introduced in the Gospel which nevertheless have a literal sense which is a figure of that which happened in the New Testament.

Hence to understand it one must consider a certain historical account, where it says that because of the sin committed concerning the wife of a Levite, the whole tribe of Benjamin was savagely destroyed (Jusg 19); and it says that there was a most great wailing, so that it was heard from Gabaa even to Rama, about twelve miles distant from Bethlehem. This is called *Rachel weeping*, because Rachel was the mother of Benjamin; and it is a figurative speech, namely to express the magnitude of the sorrow. But this is a prophecy of bygone events.

227. It is also about the future, in two ways. For in one way it can be referred to the captivity of the Israelites, who are said to have wailed on the road next to Bethlehem when they were being led into captivity; and then Rachel is said to have wailed, because she was buried there (Gen 35:19). And this is said in the same way as a place is said to wail over the evils which happen in the place. So the prophet would have it that, just as there was the greatest sorrow and mourning when the tribe of Benjamin was destroyed, so there will come another greatest sorrow at the time of the captivity.

228. In a third way, it is explained thus. The Evangelist takes up the deed of the killing of the innocents and magnifies the sorrow in four ways. From the spreading out of sorrow, from the multitude of sorrows, from the matter, and from the inconsolability.

He says then, *a voice in Rama.* Rama is a certain city in the tribe of Benjamin (Jos 18:25), and can be taken as the city of Lia. Moreover, this is taken as 'high', and can be explained in two ways. First, in this way: *a voice*, sounded forth *on high*, *was heard*, because a voice which is in a high place is spread out far and wide; *get up upon a high mountain, you who bring good tidings to Zion: lift up your voice with strength* (Isa 40:9). Or it *was heard* on high, i.e., in heaven with God; *the prayer of him that humbles himself, will pierce the clouds: and till it come near he will not be comforted: and he will not depart till the Most High behold* (Sir 35:21). And again, *do not the widow's tears run down the cheek, and her cry against him that caused them to fall?* (Sir 35:18).

229. *'Lamentation.'* This can be referred to the crying of the infants who were killed. *'And great mourning'*; this can be referred to the mothers' wailing. Or both can be referred to the children: *'lamentation'* insofar as they were lifted up by the soldiers, *'mourning'* insofar as they had their throats slit. The mothers' sorrow is greater than the children's. Likewise, the mothers' was an enduring sorrow, while the

unigenitum, et dolebunt super eum, ut doleri solet in morte primogeniti.

230. Item ex materia doloris, quia de morte filiorum. Unde *'Rachel plorat.'*

Sed obiicitur, quia Bethlehem non erat in tribu Beniamin, sed in tribu Iuda, qui fuit filius Liae.

Et solvitur tripliciter. Primo, quia Rachel sepulta fuit iuxta Bethlehem, Gen. XXXV, 19. Et ita ploravit pueros eo modo, quo aliquis locus dicitur plorare; Ier. II, 12: *obstupescite, caeli, super hoc, et portae eius, desolamini vehementer, dicit Dominus.*

Vel aliter. Supra habitum est quod Herodes occidit pueros **in Bethlehem, et in omnibus finibus eius** et cetera. Bethlehem autem erat in confinio duarum tribuum, scilicet Iudae et Beniamin; unde de pueris Beniamin occisi sunt: et sic cessat obiectio, sicut exponit Hieronymus.

Augustinus autem aliter exponit et dicit quod consuetudo est quod quando alicui aliqua prospera succedunt, ille, quando adversitates veniunt, magis dolet. Lia et Rachel sorores fuerunt, et isti qui occisi sunt fuerunt de filiis Liae. Et sic corporaliter occisi sunt, ne aeternaliter punirentur, ut in facto Gabaa. Dicitur ergo plorare videns filios suos occidi et damnari.

Vel per Rachel Ecclesia signatur, quia interpretatur *videns Deum*, et Ecclesia per fidem videt: quae plorat filios suos occisos, non quia occisi sunt, sed quia per ipsos poterat alios acquirere. Vel non plorat propter occisos, sed propter occidentes.

231. Sequitur de inconsolabilitate doloris: *'et noluit.'* Et exponitur illud multipliciter. Primo ut referatur ad populum, qui tunc erat. Consolatio enim debetur quamdiu speratur aliquod remedium; sed quando non speratur, non est consolatio, sicut patet in infirmo desperato; et ideo dicit, ut referatur ad opinionem matrum, *'quia non sunt'*, quia scilicet non apparent; Gen. XXXVII, 30: *puer non comparet.* Vel *'noluit consolari, quia non sunt'*, idest ac si non essent: consolatio enim non debetur nisi de malis. Unde secundum hoc refertur ad opinionem Ecclesiae, quae habet eos tamquam regnarent; unde, sicut de regnantibus, gaudet de eis, I Thess. IV, v. 12: *nolumus vos ignorare de dormientibus, ut non contristemini, sicut et ceteri qui spem non habent* vel *'noluit consolari'* de praesenti, sed expectat consolationem in futuro; infra V, 5: **beati qui lugent, quoniam ipsi consolabuntur.**

children's was brief; on account of which it is said, *they will mourn for him as one mourns for an only son, and they will grieve over him, as the manner is to grieve for the death of the firstborn* (Zech 12:10).

230. Again, from the matter of the sorrow, because it was over the death of children. Hence, *'Rachel bewailing.'*

But it is objected that Bethlehem was not in the tribe of Benjamin, but in the tribe of Judas, who was the son of Lia.

And this is resolved in three ways. First, because Rachel was buried next to Bethlehem (Gen 35:19). And thus she lamented the children in the same way that a place is said to lament; *be astonished, O heavens, at this, and gates thereof, be very desolate, says the Lord* (Jer 2:12).

Or in another way. It was said above that Herod killed the children **in Bethlehem, and in all the borders thereof**. Now, Bethlehem was on the common boundary of two tribes, namely of Judas and of Benjamin; hence some of the children of Benjamin were killed; and thus the objection rests, as Jerome explains it.

But Augustine explains it another way, and says that it is customary that when good fortunes follow someone, then adversities come, he sorrows all the more. Lia and Rachel were sisters, and those who were killed were of the sons of Lia. And thus they were killed bodily lest they be punished eternally, as happened in Gabaa. So she is said to lament, seeing that her own children were killed and damned.

Or, the Church is indicated by Rachel, because she is interpreted as *seeing God*, and the Church sees through faith. She laments her slain children, not because they are slain, but because through them she could have acquired others. Or she does not weep on account of the ones killed, but on account of the killers.

231. There follows, concerning the sorrow's inconsolability, *'and she would not.'* And this is explained in many ways. First, as it is referred to the people who lived at that time. For there should be consolation as long as some remedy is hoped for, but when no remedy is hoped for, there is no consolation, as is clear in the case of sick people who have despaired. And for this reason he says it is referred to the mothers' thought *'because they are not'*, namely because they are gone; *the boy does not appear* (Gen 37:30). Or, *'and would not be comforted, because they are not'*, i.e., as if they were not; for consolation should only be over evils. Hence according to this explanation it is referred to the thought of the Church, who sees them as reigning; hence she rejoices over them as over one who reigns, *and we will not have you ignorant, brethren, concerning them that are asleep, that you be not sorrowful, even as others who have no hope* (1 Thess 4:12). Or, she *'would not be comforted'* about the present, but she expects consolation in the future; below, **blessed are they who mourn: for they will be comforted** (Matt 5:5).

232. Consequenter agitur de revocatione Christi; unde *defuncto Herode, ecce angelus Domini apparuit in somnis Ioseph*.

Et primo ponitur apparitio angeli;

secundo mandatum angeli;

tertio executio mandati angeli.

233. Circa primum tria ponuntur. Primo describitur tempus; secundo persona; tertio modus apparitionis.

Dicit ergo *defuncto Herode*: non ille qui fuit in morte Christi, quia ille fuit filius istius. *Ecce angelus apparuit*.

Notandum quod omnis turbatio Ecclesiae secundum mysterium terminatur per mortem persecutorum quia *in perditione impii erit laudatio* Prov. XI, 10. Item nota quod infidelitate Iudaeorum terminata, Christus redibit ad eos. Rom. XI, 26: *et tunc omnis Israel salvus fiet*.

Ecce . . . apparuit. Notandum quod talis est ordo angelorum et hominum, ut divinae illuminationes non fiant nobis nisi per angelos; ad Hebr. I, 14: *omnes sunt administratorii spiritus in ministerium missi propter eos qui haereditatem capiunt salutis*. Unde etiam Christus secundum quod homo, voluit per angelos nuntiari.

Modus, ibi *in somnis Ioseph in Aegypto*.

234. Mandatum, ibi *surge, et accipe puerum*. Non dicit *filium*, non *coniugem*, sed *puerum*, ut designetur dignitas pueri, et integritas matris. In hoc significatur, quod Ioseph non fuit ei datus ad carnalem copulam, sed ad ministerium et custodiam.

235. Consequenter assignat causam *defuncti sunt enim qui quaerebant animam pueri*.

Sed quaeritur, quare dicit *sunt*. Non enim nisi Herodes mortuus erat.

Hoc solvitur dupliciter. Primo quia iste tot mala fecerat, quod Iudaei gaudebant de morte eius: qui praesentiens mandavit adhuc vivens sorori suae, quod nobiliores de Iudaeis interficeret in morte sua; et isti quaesierant animam pueri cum Herode; et hoc est *defuncti sunt enim qui quaerebant animam pueri*. Vel aliter. Mos est Sacrae Scripturae ponere plurale pro singulari: unde *mortui sunt*, idest mortuus est et cetera.

Unde in hoc quod dicit *qui quaerebant animam pueri*, destruitur error Apollinaris, qui dixit, quod divinitas erat in Christo loco animae.

236. Ponitur executio huius mandati *qui consurgens, accepit puerum et matrem eius*; et circa hoc duo facit:

primo ostendit quomodo reversus est in terram Israel;

secundo quam partem vitavit;

232. Next he treats of how Christ was called back; hence, *but when Herod was dead, behold an angel of the Lord appeared in sleep to Joseph in Egypt*.

And first, he sets down the apparition of the angel;

second, the angel's command;

third, the execution of the angel's command.

233. Concerning the first, three things are set down. First, the time is described; second, the person; third, the manner of the apparition.

He says then, *but when Herod was dead*; not the man who was involved in Christ's death, for that man was the son of this one. *Behold, an angel of the Lord appeared*.

One should note that every disturbance of the Church, according to a mystery, is ended by the death of the persecutor, because *when the wicked perish there will be praise* (Prov 11:10). Similarly, note that when the Jews' infidelity was ended, Christ returned to them. *And so all Israel should be saved* (Rom 11:26).

Behold, an angel of the Lord appeared. One should note that the order of angels and men is such that divine enlightenments only come to us through angels; *are they not all ministering spirits, sent to minister for them, who will receive the inheritance of salvation?* (Heb 1:14). Hence even Christ, as a man, wished to be announced by angels.

The manner is at *in sleep to Joseph in Egypt*.

234. The command is at *arise, and take the child*. He does not say *son*, not *spouse*, but *child*, so as to indicate the dignity of the child, and the integrity of the mother. This points out that Joseph had not been given to her for bodily union, but for service and protection.

235. Next he gives the reason: *for they are dead that sought the soul of the child*.

But it is asked why he says, *they*. For none but Herod had died.

This is resolved in two ways. First, because that man had done so many evil things that the Jews rejoiced over his death; having foreseen this, he ordered his sister who was still alive to kill the more noble of the Jews when he died; and these Jews had been seeking the child's soul along with Herod. And this is *for they are dead that sought the soul of the child*. Or in another way: it is the custom of Sacred Scripture to put the plural in place of the singular. Hence *they are dead*, i.e., he is dead.

Hence when he says, *they are dead that sought the soul of the child*, the error of Apollinaris is destroyed, who said that the divinity was in Christ in place of a soul.

236. The execution of this command is set down, *who arose, and took the child and his mother*; and concerning this he does three things:

first, he shows how he returned to the land of Israel;

second, what region he avoided;

tertio qua parte declinavit, ibi *et admonitus in somnis secessit in partes Galilaeae*.

237. Dicit ergo *qui consurgens*. Notandum, quod angelus non dixit *vade in terram Iuda*, vel *in Ierusalem*, sed universaliter *in terram Israel*, sub qua etiam Galilaea potest comprehendi. Unde potest dici, quod Ioseph intravit fines terrae, quam habitabat Iudas.

238. Consequenter ponitur quam partem vitavit, ibi *audiens autem quod Archelaus regnaret in Iudaea*.

Et notanda est hic historia Herodis. Iste Herodes habuit sex filios, et ante mortem suam occidit Alexandrum et Aristobolum; in morte autem sua mandavit ut occideretur Antipater. Unde tres remanserunt, inter quos Archelaus primogenitus fuit, et usurpavit sibi regnum; sed tandem accusatus a Iudaeis apud Caesarem Augustum, ablatum fuit ei regnum et divisum fuit in quatuor partes, et duas habuit Archelaus, duas alias alii diviserunt sibi, ita quod unam tetrarchiam habuit Herodes, aliam Philippus, sicut habetur Lc. III, v. 1. Iste Archelaus missus est in exilium post novem annos regni sui.

239. *Et admonitus in somnis*. Dixerat primo angelus, quod iret ad terram Israel; sed quia Ioseph nondum intellexerat, ideo angelus, qui prius indeterminate revelaverat, nunc determinat. Et hoc est *et admonitus . . . secessit in partes Galilaeae*.

Sed contra. Sicut Archelaus in Iudaea, ita Herodes in Galilaea regnabat. Sed dicendum, quod hoc fuit statim post mortem Herodis, quando Archelaus tenebat totum, quia postmodum facta est divisio.

Sed tunc etiam quaeritur, quare non timuit Archelaum.

Dicendum, quod in Ierusalem erat sedes regni; unde ibi quasi semper morabatur.

Sed quaeritur, quare Luc. II, 41 dicitur quod singulis annis ducebant puerum in Ierusalem.

Et solvit Augustinus, quod secure ducebant per turbam magnam, quae tunc ascendebat; sed periculum fuisset si ibi diu moratus fuisset.

Item quaeritur, quare innuit Evangelista quod quasi per accidens venit Ioseph in Nazareth, sed Lc. II, 39 dicitur quod in Nazareth habuit proprium domicilium.

Sed dicendum, quod angelus dixerat ei, quod iret in terram Israel, quae stricte accepta non continebat Galilaeam, nec Nazareth: et sic intellexit Ioseph; et ideo non proponebat ire in Nazareth.

240. *Ut adimpleretur quod dictum est per prophetam: quoniam Nazaraeus vocabitur*. Hoc non invenitur scriptum, sed potest dici, quod ex multis locis colligitur. Nazarenus igitur interpretatur 'sanctus': et quia Christus

third, into what region he turned aside, at *being warned in sleep retired into the quarters of Galilee*.

237. It says then, *who arose*. One should notice that the angel did not say, *go into the land of Judas*, or *into Jerusalem*, but generally *into the land of Israel*, which can include even Galilee. Hence it can be said that Joseph entered the boundaries of the land in which Judas dwelled.

238. Next he sets down which region he avoided, at *but hearing that Archelaus reigned in Judea*.

And the history of Herod should be noted here. This man Herod had six sons, and before his death he killed Alexander and Aristobolus; when he died, he ordered that Antipater should be killed. Hence three remained, among whom Archelaus was the first-born, and seized the kingdom for himself; but in the end, accused before Caesar Augustus by the Jews, the kingdom was taken away from him and divided into four parts, and Archelaus had two, and the others divided the other parts amongst themselves, so that Herod had one tetrarchy and Philip the other (Luke 3:1). This man Archelaus was sent into exile in the ninth year of his reign.

239. *And being warned in sleep*. The first angel had said that he should go to the land of Israel; but because Joseph did not yet understand, the angel who had revealed vaguely before now specifies. And this is, *being warned in sleep retired into the quarters of Galilee*.

On the contrary. As Archelaus reigned in Judea, so Herod the younger reigned in Galilee. But one should say that this was immediately after the death of Herod the elder, when Archelaus held the entire kingdom, because the division was made later.

But even then one may ask, why did he not fear Archelaus?

One should say that the king's seat was in Jerusalem; hence he stayed there almost all the time.

But it is asked why Luke says that every year they were taking the child into Jerusalem (Luke 2:41).

And Augustine resolves this, saying that they took him safely through the great crowd which went up at that time, but there would have been danger if they had remained there a long while.

Again it is asked why the Evangelist implied that Joseph came into Nazareth as though by accident, while Luke says that he had his own home in Nazareth (Luke 2:39).

But one should say that the angel had told him that he should go into the land of Israel, which taken strictly did not contain Galilee or Nazareth; and this is how Joseph understood it. And this is why he did not intend to go into Nazareth.

240. *That it might be fulfilled which was said by prophets: that he will be called a Nazarene*. This is not found written anywhere, but one can say that it is gathered from many places. For Nazarene is interpreted as 'holy'; and

dicitur sanctus; Dan. IX, 24: *donec ungatur sanctus*; ideo signanter dicitur **per prophetam**. Vel potest dici, quod per Nazarenum interpretatur 'floridus'; et hoc habetur Is. XI, 1: *egredietur virga de radice Iesse, et flos de radice eius ascendet* etc.; et convenit cum eo, quod dicitur Cant. II, 1: *ego flos campi et lilium convallium*.

since Christ is called holy, *and the saint of saints may be anointed* (Dan 9:24), then it was with significance that he said **by prophets**. Or one can say that Nazarene is interpreted as 'blooming', and this is found in Isaiah: *and there will come forth a rod out of the root of Jesse, and a flower will rise up out of his root* (Isa 11:1). And what it said in Song of Songs fits with him, *I am the flower of the field, and the lily of the valleys* (Song 2:1).

CHAPTER 3

Lecture 1

3:1 In diebus autem illis venit Ioannes Baptista praedicans in deserto Iudaeae, [n. 242]

3:2 et dicens poenitentiam agite, appropinquavit enim regnum caelorum. [n. 247]

3:3 hic est enim de quo dictum est per Isaiam prophetam dicentem: *vox clamantis in deserto, parate viam Domini, rectas facite semitas eius.* [n. 251]

3:4 Ipse autem Ioannes habebat vestimentum de pilis camelorum et zonam pelliceam circa lumbos suos; esca autem eius erat locustae et mel silvestre. [n. 256]

3:5 Tunc exibat ad eum Ierosolyma, et omnis Iudaea, et omnis regio circa Iordanem. [n. 257]

3:6 Et baptizabantur ab eo in Iordane confitentes peccata sua. [n. 259]

3:7 Videns autem multos Pharisaeorum et Sadducaeorum, venientes ad baptismum suum, dixit eis: progenies viperarum, quis demonstravit vobis fugere a ventura ira? [n. 261]

3:8 Facite ergo fructum dignum poenitentiae. [n. 266]

3:9 Et ne velitis dicere intra vos: Patrem habemus Abraham. Dico enim vobis, quoniam potest est Deus de lapidibus istis suscitare filios Abrahae. [n. 267]

3:10 Iam enim securis ad radicem arborum posita est. Omnis ergo arbor, quae non facit fructum bonum, excidetur, et in ignem mittetur. [n. 270]

3:1 Ἐν δὲ ταῖς ἡμέραις ἐκείναις παραγίνεται Ἰωάννης ὁ βαπτιστὴς κηρύσσων ἐν τῇ ἐρήμῳ τῆς Ἰουδαίας

3:2 [καὶ] λέγων· μετανοεῖτε· ἤγγικεν γὰρ ἡ βασιλεία τῶν οὐρανῶν.

3:3 οὗτος γάρ ἐστιν ὁ ῥηθεὶς διὰ Ἠσαΐου τοῦ προφήτου λέγοντος· φωνὴ βοῶντος ἐν τῇ ἐρήμῳ· ἑτοιμάσατε τὴν ὁδὸν κυρίου, εὐθείας ποιεῖτε τὰς τρίβους αὐτοῦ.

3:4 αὐτὸς δὲ ὁ Ἰωάννης εἶχεν τὸ ἔνδυμα αὐτοῦ ἀπὸ τριχῶν καμήλου καὶ ζώνην δερματίνην περὶ τὴν ὀσφὺν αὐτοῦ, ἡ δὲ τροφὴ ἦν αὐτοῦ ἀκρίδες καὶ μέλι ἄγριον.

3:5 Τότε ἐξεπορεύετο πρὸς αὐτὸν Ἱεροσόλυμα καὶ πᾶσα ἡ Ἰουδαία καὶ πᾶσα ἡ περίχωρος τοῦ Ἰορδάνου,

3:6 καὶ ἐβαπτίζοντο ἐν τῷ Ἰορδάνῃ ποταμῷ ὑπ᾽ αὐτοῦ ἐξομολογούμενοι τὰς ἁμαρτίας αὐτῶν.

3:7 Ἰδὼν δὲ πολλοὺς τῶν Φαρισαίων καὶ Σαδδουκαίων ἐρχομένους ἐπὶ τὸ βάπτισμα αὐτοῦ εἶπεν αὐτοῖς· γεννήματα ἐχιδνῶν, τίς ὑπέδειξεν ὑμῖν φυγεῖν ἀπὸ τῆς μελλούσης ὀργῆς;

3:8 ποιήσατε οὖν καρπὸν ἄξιον τῆς μετανοίας

3:9 καὶ μὴ δόξητε λέγειν ἐν ἑαυτοῖς· πατέρα ἔχομεν τὸν Ἀβραάμ. λέγω γὰρ ὑμῖν ὅτι δύναται ὁ θεὸς ἐκ τῶν λίθων τούτων ἐγεῖραι τέκνα τῷ Ἀβραάμ.

3:10 ἤδη δὲ ἡ ἀξίνη πρὸς τὴν ῥίζαν τῶν δένδρων κεῖται· πᾶν οὖν δένδρον μὴ ποιοῦν καρπὸν καλὸν ἐκκόπτεται καὶ εἰς πῦρ βάλλεται.

3:1 And in those days came John the Baptist preaching in the desert of Judea. [n. 242]

3:2 And saying: do penance: for the kingdom of heaven is at hand. [n. 247]

3:3 For this is he that was spoken of by Isaiah the prophet, saying: *a voice of one crying in the desert, prepare you all the way of the Lord, make straight his paths.* [n. 251]

3:4 And the same John had his garment of camels' hair, and a leather girdle about his loins: and his meat was locusts and wild honey. [n. 256]

3:5 Then went out to him Jerusalem and all Judea, and all the country about Jordan: [n. 257]

3:6 And were baptized by him in the Jordan, confessing their sins. [n. 259]

3:7 And seeing many of the Pharisees and Sadducees coming to his baptism, he said to them: you brood of vipers, who has showed you to flee from the wrath to come? [n. 261]

3:8 Bring forth therefore fruit worthy of penance. [n. 266]

3:9 And do not think to say within yourselves, we have Abraham for our father. For I tell you that God is able of these stones to raise up children to Abraham. [n. 267]

3:10 For now the axe is laid to the root of the trees. Every tree therefore that does not yield good fruit, will be cut down, and cast into the fire. [n. 270]

3:11 Ego quidem baptizo vos in aqua in poenitentiam; qui autem post me venturus est, fortior me est, cuius non sum dignus calceamenta portare: ipse vos baptizabit in Spiritu Sancto, et igni. [n. 274]

3:12 Cuius ventilabrum in manu sua, et permundabit aream suam, et congregabit triticum in horreum suum, paleas autem comburet igni inextinguibili. [n. 284]

3:11 Ἐγὼ μὲν ὑμᾶς βαπτίζω ἐν ὕδατι εἰς μετάνοιαν, ὁ δὲ ὀπίσω μου ἐρχόμενος ἰσχυρότερός μού ἐστιν, οὗ οὐκ εἰμὶ ἱκανὸς τὰ ὑποδήματα βαστάσαι· αὐτὸς ὑμᾶς βαπτίσει ἐν πνεύματι ἁγίῳ καὶ πυρί·

3:12 οὗ τὸ πτύον ἐν τῇ χειρὶ αὐτοῦ καὶ διακαθαριεῖ τὴν ἅλωνα αὐτοῦ καὶ συνάξει τὸν σῖτον αὐτοῦ εἰς τὴν ἀποθήκην, τὸ δὲ ἄχυρον κατακαύσει πυρὶ ἀσβέστῳ.

3:11 I indeed baptize you in the water unto penance, but he who will come after me, is mightier than I, whose shoes I am not worthy to bear; he will baptize you in the Holy Spirit and fire. [n. 274]

3:12 Whose fan is in his hand, and he will thoroughly cleanse his floor and gather his wheat into the barn; but the chaff he will burn with unquenchable fire. [n. 284]

---

241. Supra egit Evangelista de ingressu Christi in mundum; nunc autem agit de eius processu, qui quidem est attendendus secundum processum suae doctrinae: ad hoc enim venit, Io. XVIII, 37.

Circa doctrinam autem duo considerantur.

Primo enim ponitur praeparatio ad doctrinam; secundo ponitur ipsa doctrina cap. V.

Ad doctorem autem Evangelicae doctrinae duo requiruntur. Primo ut sit velatus sacris mysteriis; secundo ut probatus sit virtutibus: et sic duo praemittuntur ante doctrinam, scilicet baptismus eius, et tentatio cap. IV.

Circa primum duo facit.

Primo introducitur Ioannis Baptismus, ibi *exibat ad eum Ierosolyma*;

secundo instructio baptizatorum, ibi *videns autem multos*.

Invitantur autem dupliciter a Ioanne, scilicet verbo et exemplo. Secundum ibi *ipse autem Ioannes habebat vestimentum de pilis camelorum* et cetera.

Circa doctrinam Ioannis tria facit, sive tanguntur.

Primo persona doctoris introducitur; secundo ponitur doctrina; tertio confirmatio.

Secundum ibi *poenitentiam agite*; tertium ibi *hic est enim de quo dictum est*.

242. Circa personam quinque ponuntur, scilicet tempus, persona, officium, studium, et locus.

Primum ibi *in diebus illis* et cetera. Et notandum quod tempus praedicationis Lucas describit per principes reipublicae et Iudaeorum. Illud ergo quod dicit Lucas, exprimitur hic, cum dicit *in diebus illis*. Nec debet hoc referri ad dies, de quibus facta est mentio, scilicet ad tempus infantiae Christi; non enim est intelligendum hoc fuisse in diebus illis, in quibus Christus reversus est de Aegypto. Sed hoc sic ponitur, quia Christus habitavit

241. Above, the Evangelist treated of the Christ's entrance into the world; but now he treats of his progress, which indeed ought to be dealt with according to the progress of his teaching, because for this he came (John 18:37).

And concerning his teaching, two things are considered:

first, he sets down the preparation for the teaching;
second, he sets down the teaching itself (Matt 5).

Further, two things are required in a teacher of the Gospel teaching: first, that he be veiled by sacred mysteries; second, that he be proven in virtue. And so two things are placed before the teaching, namely his baptism and temptation (Matt 4).

Concerning the first, he does two things:

first, he introduces John the Baptist, at *then went out to him Jerusalem*;

second, the Baptizer's instruction, at *and seeing many*.

Now, they are attracted by John in two ways, namely by word and by example. The second is at *and the same John had his garment of camels' hair*.

Concerning John's teaching he does or touches upon three things:

first, he introduces the person of the teacher; second, he sets down the teaching; third, a confirmation;

the second is at *do penance*; the third is at *for this is he that was spoken of*.

242. Concerning the person, he sets down five things, namely the time, the person, the office, the zeal, and the place.

The first is at *and in those days*. And one should note that Luke describes the time of his preaching by the princes of the republic and of the Jews (Luke 3:1–2). So what Luke says is expressed here, when he says, *and in those days*. Nor should this be referred to the days which were mentioned before, namely to the time of Christ's infancy; for this should not be understood to have happened in the days when Christ returned from Egypt. But this is set down in

continue in Nazareth; Luc. II, 40: *puer autem crescebat, et confortabatur plenus sapientia, et gratia Dei erat in illo.*

243. Secundo ponitur persona, ibi **venit Ioannes**; *venit*, idest apparuit, qui primo occultus erat. Hic est de quo Io. I, 7: *hic venit in testimonium, ut testimonium perhiberet de lumine.*

Sed quare Christus voluit eius testimonium, cum haberet testimonium operum?

Dicendum quod propter tria. Primo propter nos qui ducimur in cognitionem spiritualium per ea quae sunt similia nobis; Io. I, 7: *hic venit ut testimonium perhiberet de lumine. Et quare? Ut omnes crederent per illum.* Secundo propter malitiam Iudaeorum, quia non solum Christus sibi testimonium perhibet, secundum quod ipsi dicebant, Io. VIII, 13: *tu de teipso testimonium perhibes,* sed etiam alius; Io. V, 33: *vos misistis ad Ioannem, et testimonium perhibuit veritati.* Tertio ad ostendendum aequalitatem Christi ad Patrem, quia sicut Pater praenuntios habuit, scilicet prophetas, ita Christus; Luc. I, 76: *tu, puer, propheta Altissimi vocaberis: praeibis enim ante faciem Domini parare vias eius.*

244. Tertio ponitur officium baptizandi. Hoc fuit speciale eius officium, quia primus baptizavit, et fuit eius baptismus praeparatorius ad baptismum Christi: quia si Christus novum ritum adiunxisset, statim potuissent homines scandalizari. Et ideo praevenit Ioannes ut praepararet homines ad baptismum; Io. I, 31: *ut manifestetur in Israel.*

245. Quarto ponitur studium, quia venit, ut diligenter praedicaret. Et hoc est **praedicans** baptismum. Christus quidem baptizaturus ista adiunxit, Matth. ult., 19: *ite, docete omnes gentes, baptizantes eos in nomine Patris, et Filii, et Spiritus Sancti.* Ioannes autem in utroque praeparavit viam.

Et notandum quod Ioannes in trigesimo anno hoc fecit, in qua aetate David etiam factus est rex, et Ioseph gubernacula regni Aegypti suscepit, Gen. XLI, 46. Per quod datur intelligi, quod ad nullum officium debet aliquis assumi ante perfectam aetatem.

246. Quinto ponitur locus **in deserto**. Praedicavit autem in deserto propter quatuor. Primo ut quietius audirent: in civitate enim multi curiosi impedientes convenissent, sed in deserto non nisi studiosi ibant; Eccle. XII, 11: *verba sapientium sicut stimuli, et quasi clavi in altum defixi, quae per magistrorum consilium data sunt a pastore uno.* Secundo quia congruebat suae praedicationi; quia ipse poenitentiam praedicabat. Talis autem debet esse locus poenitentiae, vel corporaliter, vel mentaliter; Ps. LIV, 8: *ecce elongavi fugiens, et mansi in solitudine.* Tertio ad designandam conditionem Ecclesiae, quae per desertum significatur: datur enim intelligi, quod non est in synagoga praedicatio salutis, sed in Ecclesia; Is. LIV, 1: *laetare, sterilis, quae non paris; decanta laudem, et, hinni,*

this way because Christ dwelled in Nazareth without interruption; *and the child grew, and waxed strong, full of wisdom; and the grace of God was in him* (Luke 2:40).

243. Second, the person is set down, at **came John the Baptist**; *came*, i.e., he appeared who was hidden at first. It is he of whom it is said, *this man came for a witness, to give testimony of the light* (John 1:7).

But why did Christ want his testimony, when he had the testimony of works?

One should say, for three reasons. First, for our sake, for we are brought to spiritual knowledge through those things which are like us; *this man came for a witness, to give testimony of the light*, and why? *That all men might believe through him* (John 1:7). Second, owing to the malice of the Jews, because not only did Christ bear testimony to himself, as they said, *you give testimony of yourself* (John 8:13), but another bore testimony as well. *You sent to John, and he gave testimony to the truth* (John 5:33). Third, to show Christ's equality with the Father, because as the Father had heralds, namely the prophets, so also Christ; *and you, child, will be called the prophet of the Highest: for you will go before the face of the Lord to prepare his ways* (Luke 1:76).

244. Third, the office of baptizing is set down. This was his special office, because he baptized first; and his baptism was preparatory to the baptism of Christ, because if Christ had suddenly added a new ritual, men might have been scandalized. And so John came beforehand, to prepare men for baptism; *that he may be made manifest in Israel* (John 1:31).

245. Fourth, the zeal is set down, because he came to preach diligently. And this is **preaching** a baptism. Indeed Christ, the one about to be baptized, added those things: *going therefore, teach all nations; baptizing them in the name of the Father, and of the Son, and of the Holy Spirit* (Matt 28:19). But John prepared the way in both.

And one should note that John did this in his thirtieth year, at which age also David was made king, and Joseph took the helm of the kingdom of Egypt. By which one is given to understand that no one should be taken up for an office before the perfect age.

246. Fifth, the place is set down, **in the desert**. Now, he preached in the desert for four reasons. First, so that they might hear more quietly; for in the city many curious men come together, getting in the way, but only the eager go into the desert; *the words of the wise are as goads, and as nails deeply fastened in, which by the counsel of masters are given from one shepherd* (Eccl 12:11). Second, because it fit with his preaching, since he preached penance. Now, a place of penance ought to be that way, either bodily or mentally; *lo, I have gone far off flying away; and I abode in the wilderness* (Ps 54:8). Third, to point to the Church's condition, which is signified by the desert: for one is given to understand that the preaching of salvation happens not in the synagogue, but in the Church; *give praise, O you barren, that bears not:*

quae non pariebas, quoniam multi filii desertae, magis quam eius quae habebat virum, dicit Dominus. Quarto ad designandam conditionem Iudaeae, quae iam derelinquebatur a Deo; inf. XXIII, 38: *ecce relinquetur vobis domus vestra deserta.*

247. Sequitur *poenitentiam agite* et cetera. Ioannes annuntiat quamdam novam vitam, sicut dicit Augustinus in libro *de Poenitentia*: *nullus qui suae voluntatis arbiter constituitur, potest novam vitam inchoare, nisi poeniteat veteris vitae.* Quaere in Glossa. Et ideo

primo monet ad poenitentiam;

secundo annuntiat salutem, ibi *appropinquabit enim regnum caelorum.*

248. Item *poenitentiam agite*, per quam est remissio peccatorum. Chrysostomus: *nato Filio Dei, Deus misit praeconem in mundum.*

Et notandum quod aliud est poenitentiam agere et poenitere. Ille poenitet qui peccata deflet, et flenda non committit. Et sciendum, quod totum refertur ad propositum mentis, ut scilicet dicatur et flenda non committit, idest, proponit non committere: hoc enim requirit poenitentia. Poenitentiam autem agere est satisfacere pro peccatis; Luc. III, 8: *facite fructus dignos poenitentiae.*

249. Et fit hic quaestio. Cum omnia peccata dimittantur in baptismo, quare Ioannes praenuntians baptismum Christi, incepit a poenitentia?

Et respondetur in Glossa, quod triplex est poenitentia, scilicet ante baptismum, quia oportet ut doleat de peccatis quando accedit; secunda post baptismum, de mortalibus; tertia, de venialibus. Hic agitur de poenitentia quae est post baptismum; unde Petrus dixit Act. II, 38: *poenitentiam agite*, scilicet ut sitis parati ad salutem consequendam.

250. *Appropinquabit.* Et nota quod numquam in Scriptura Veteris Testamenti invenitur promissum regnum caelorum; sed primo Ioannes nuntiat, quod pertinet ad dignitatem eius.

Regnum autem caelorum in Scriptura quatuor modis accipitur. Quandoque enim dicitur ipse Christus habitans in nobis per gratiam; Luc. XVII, 21: *regnum Dei intra vos est.* Et dicitur regnum caelorum, quia per inhabitantem gratiam inchoatur nobis via caelestis regni. Secundo, Sacra Scriptura; infra XXI, 43: *auferetur a vobis regnum Dei*, idest Sacra Scriptura. Et dicitur regnum, quia lex eius ducit ad regnum. Tertio, dicitur praesens Ecclesia militans; infra XIII, 47: *simile est regnum caelorum sagenae missae in mare, et ex omni genere piscium congreganti* et cetera. Et dicitur regnum caelorum, quia ad modum caelestis Ecclesiae est institutum. Quarto dicitur regnum caelorum caelestis curia; infra VIII, 11: *venient ab oriente, et occidente, et recumbent cum Abraham, et Isaac, et Iacob in regno caelorum.* Ante

sing forth praise, and make a joyful noise, you who did not travail with child: for many are the children of the desolate, more than of her that has a husband, says the Lord (Isa 54:1). Fourth, to indicate the condition of the Jews, who were already abandoned by God; below, **behold, your house will be left to you, desolate** (Matt 23:38).

247. There follows **do penance**. John announces a certain new life, as Augustine says in the book *On Penance*: *no one who is established as the judge of his own will can begin a new life, unless he repents of the old life.* Look in the Gloss. And so

first, he advises them to penance;

second, he announces salvation, at **for the kingdom of heaven is at hand**.

248. Again, **do penance**, through which comes the remission of sins. Chrysostom: *the Son of God having been born, God sent a herald into the world.*

And one should note that to do penance and to repent are different. That man repents who *weeps bitterly over sins, and does not commit deeds worthy of tears*; and one should know that the whole thing is referred to the intention in his mind, namely that he be dedicated, and not commit deeds worthy of tears, i.e., intend not to commit such deeds; for penance requires this. But to do penance is to satisfy for sins; *bring forth therefore fruits worthy of penance* (Luke 3:8).

249. And here there is a question. Since all sins are remitted in baptism, why did John, foretelling the baptism of Christ, begin from penance?

And the Gloss responds that penance is threefold, namely: before baptism, because it is necessary that he should sorrow over sins when he approaches; second, after baptism, over mortal sins; third, over venial sins. Here he treats of the penance which is before baptism; whence Peter said: *do penance* (Acts 2:38), namely that you may be prepared for the salvation which is to follow.

250. *Is at hand.* And notice that the promise of the kingdom of heaven is never found in the Old Testament Scriptures; but John is the first to announce it, which pertains to his dignity.

Now, the kingdom of heaven is taken in four ways in the Scriptures. For sometimes Christ himself dwelling in us through grace is called the kingdom of heaven; *for lo, the kingdom of God is within you* (Luke 17:21). And he is called the kingdom of heaven because the road of the heavenly kingdom is begun by grace dwelling in us. Second, the Sacred Scriptures are called the kingdom of God; below, **the kingdom of God will be taken from you** (Matt 21:43), i.e., the Sacred Scriptures. And this is called a kingdom because its law leads to a kingdom. Third, the present Church militant is called the kingdom of heaven; below, **again the kingdom of heaven is like to a net cast into the sea, and gathering together of all kind of fishes** (Matt 13:47). And it is called the kingdom of heaven because it is established after the manner of the heavenly Church. Fourth, the heavenly

tempus autem Ioannis non fiebat mentio, nisi de regno Iebusaeorum, Ex. III, 8, sed modo promittitur regnum caelorum suae Ecclesiae.

251. Consequenter ponitur confirmatio huius praedicationis *hic est de quo dictum est per Isaiam prophetam* et cetera. Et, sicut dicit Augustinus, istud potest dupliciter exponi. Primo quod hoc, scilicet *hic est de quo scriptum est*, sint verba Evangelistae; et tunc sensus est planior. Secundo, illud introducitur a Matthaeo, velut sint verba Ioannis poenitentiam agentis. Unde *hic est*, idest ego sum; et loquitur de se sicut de alio, sicut Ioan. I loquitur de alio sicut de se. Sed non est vis cuius sint verba, quia sensum eumdem habent.

Hic est, ergo, de quo scriptum est, Is. XL, 3: *'vox clamantis in deserto: parate viam Domini, rectas facite in solitudine semitas Dei nostri.'* Tria ponuntur, per quae confirmantur tria praedicta.

Primo praenuntiatur locus praedicationis Ioannis, quia *'vox clamantis in deserto'*;

secundo adventus regni caelorum; unde *'parate viam.'*

Tertio poenitentiam, ibi *'rectas facite semitas eius.'*

252. Dicit ergo *'vox clamantis in deserto.'* Et dicit *'vox'* propter tria. Primo quia, sicut dicit Gregorius, vox verbum praecedit; et Ioannes Christum. Luc. I, 17: *ipse praecedet ante illum in spiritu et virtute Eliae.* Secundo, quia per vocem verbum cognoscitur; vox enim verbum deducit in cognitionem, ita Ioannes Christum; Io. I, 31: *ut manifestetur in Israel, propterea veni ego in aqua baptizans.* Tertio, quia vox sine verbo non facit animi certitudinem; I Cor. XIV, 8: *si incertam vocem det tuba, quis parabit se ad bellum?* Et revelatio divinorum mysteriorum non facta est per Ioannem, nisi inquantum annuntiavit Christum, sed per Christum Verbum; Io. I, 18: *unigenitus qui est in sinu Patris ipse enarravit.*

253. Igitur *'vox clamantis'*; et potest intelligi dupliciter. Primo Christi clamantis, qui in Ioanne loquebatur; II ad Cor. XIII, 3: *an experimentum quaeritis eius qui in me loquitur Christus?* Ita etiam clamavit in omnibus prophetis. Unde semper dicitur: *factum est Verbum Domini ad Ieremiam,* vel *Isaiam* et cetera. Et tamen nullus est dictus *vox*, quia non immediate praecesserunt Christum; Mal. III, 1: *ecce ego mitto angelum meum qui praeparabit viam ante faciem meam. Et statim veniet ad templum sanctum suum dominator quem vos quaeritis, et angelus testamenti quem vos vultis.*

court is called the kingdom of heaven; below, *and I say to you that many will come from the east and the west, and will sit down with Abraham, and Isaac, and Jacob in the kingdom of heaven* (Matt 8:11). Now, before the time of John no mention was made except of the kingdom of the Jebusites (Exod 3:8), and only now is the kingdom of heaven promised to his Church.

251. Next, a confirmation of this statement is set down. *For this is he that was spoken of by Isaiah the prophet.* And, as Augustine says, this can be explained in two ways. First, that this, namely *this is he that* was written of, are the words of the Evangelist; and then the sense is more clear. Second, that this is brought in by Matthew, but as the words of John, who was doing penance. Hence *this is*, i.e., I am; and he speaks of himself as though of another, just as in John he speaks about another just as about himself (John 1). But it does not make much difference whose words they are, because the sense is the same.

This is he, therefore, that was written of, *'a voice of one crying in the desert, prepare you all the way of the Lord, make straight his paths'* (Isa 40:3). Three things are set down, through which the aforementioned three things are confirmed.

First, the place of John's preaching is foretold: *'a voice of one crying in the desert'*;

second, the coming of the kingdom of heaven; hence, *'prepare you all the way'*;

third, penance, at *'make straight his paths.'*

252. He says then, *'a voice of one crying in the desert.'* And he says *'a voice'* for three reasons. First because, as Gregory says, a voice precedes a word; and John precedes Christ. *And he will go before him in the spirit and power of Elias* (Luke 1:17). Second, because a word is known through a voice; for a voice draws a word down to knowledge, and in this way John drew Christ; *that he may be made manifest in Israel, therefore am I come baptizing with water* (John 1:31). Third, because a voice without a word does not bring about certitude of mind *for if the trumpet give an uncertain sound, who will prepare himself to the battle?* (1 Cor 14:8), and the revelation of divine things is not made through John except insofar as he announces Christ, but through Christ, the Word; *the only begotten Son who is in the bosom of the Father, he has declared him* (John 1:18).

253. Therefore, *'a voice of one crying'*; and it can be understood in two ways. First, the voice of Christ crying, who was speaking in John; *do you seek a proof of Christ who speaks in me?* (2 Cor 13:3). And in this way he cried out in all the prophets. Hence it is always said: the Word of the Lord came to Jeremiah, or to Isaiah. And yet none had been called a *voice* because they did not immediately precede Christ; *behold I send my angel, and he will prepare the way before my face. And presently the Lord, whom you seek, and the angel of the testament, whom you desire, will come to his temple* (Mal 3:1).

Vel *'vox clamantis'*, idest Ioannes clamans.

Sciendum quod clamor fit ad surdos, et tales erant Iudaei; Is. XLII, 18: *surdi, audite, et caeci, intuemini ad videndum. Quis caecus, nisi servus meus, et quis surdus, nisi ad quem nuntios meos misi?* Secundo ex indignatione; Ps. CV, 40: *iratus est furore Dominus in populum suum, et abominatus est haereditatem suam.* Tertio ad distantes: et isti elongati a Deo.

254. *'Parate viam Domini.'* Et videtur magis fuisse consonum quod dixisset *parate viam vestram ad suscipiendum Dominum.*

Et sciendum quod nos adeo eramus infirmi, quod non poteramus accedere ad Dominum, nisi ipse veniret ad nos. Et ideo supra dixit Ioannes **appropinquabit enim regnum caelorum**: et hoc est *'parate.'*

Sed quae est ista *'via'*? Fides quae est per auditum; Eph. III, 17: *habitare Christum per fidem in cordibus vestris.* Gregorius: *via fidei devotus auditus est;* Amos IV, 12: *praepara te in occursum Dei tui, Israel.*

255. *'Rectas facite.'* Fides est communis, est una; sed dirigit in diversis operibus. Et ideo *'rectas facite.'* Tunc autem sunt rectae istae viae operum, quando non discordant a lege divina, quae est regula actuum humanorum, sicut secundum voluntatem figuli est regula bonitatis in vasis fictilibus, ut haberi potest Ier. XVIII, 4.

Vel hoc, scilicet *'parate'*, pertinet ad caritatem, quae est de necessitate salutis; Is. c. XXX, 21: *haec est via, ambulate in ea, et non declinetis neque ad dexteram, neque ad sinistram.* Ergo *'via'* intelligitur totum illud quod pertinet ad communem salutem; I Cor. c. XII, 31: *adhuc excellentiorem vobis viam demonstro.*

Semitae vero sunt observationes consiliorum: quae semitae dicuntur esse *'rectae'*, quia non propter inanem gloriam debent fieri; infra VI, 1: **non faciatis iustitiam coram hominibus, ut videamini ab eis**; et Prov. III, 17: *viae eius, viae pulchrae, et omnes semitae eius pacificae.*

256. Consequenter ostenditur, quomodo Ioannes testimonium perhibuit Christo in vita, ibi **ipse autem Ioannes**.

Sed quis perhibuit testimonium de Ioanne, qui perhibebat testimonium Christo? Et dicendum quod vita sua: quia, sicut dicit Chrysostomus, nullus idoneus testis alterius est, nisi sit testis suus, et hoc bona vita; Eccli. c. XIX, 27: *amictus corporis, et risus dentium, et ingressus hominis enuntiant de illo.*

Unde hic describitur austeritas eius in vita, et cibo: et hoc est **ipse autem erat indutus pilis camelorum** et cetera. Alii de lana, Ioannes de pilis: reputabat enim vestimentum de lana mollitiem, quae non convenit praedicatori.

Or, *'a voice of one crying'*, i.e., of John crying out.

One should know that a cry is made to the hard of hearing, and such were the Jews; *hear, you deaf, and, you blind, behold that you may see. Who is blind, but my servant? or deaf, but he to whom I have sent my messengers?* (Isa 42:18–19). Second, out of indignation; *and the Lord was exceedingly angry with his people: and he abhorred his inheritance* (Ps 105:40). Third, to those standing far away: and they were far away from God.

254. *'Prepare you all the way of the Lord.'* And it seems that it would have been more harmonious had he said, *prepare your way for receiving the Lord.*

And one should know that we were so weak that we would not have been able to approach the Lord unless he came to us. And this is why John said above, **the kingdom of heaven is at hand**; and this is, *'prepare.'*

But what is this *'way'*? The faith which is through hearing; *that Christ may dwell by faith in your hearts* (Eph 3:17). Gregory: *the way of faith is consecrated by hearing; be prepared to meet your God, O Israel* (Amos 4:12).

255. *'Make straight his paths.'* The faith is common, is one; but it gives direction in different works. And hence, *'make straight.'* Now, the ways of works are straight when they are not opposed to the divine law, which is the rule of human actions, as a potter is the rule of goodness in earthen vases (Jer 18:4).

Or, *'prepare'*, pertains to charity, which is necessary for salvation; *this is the way, walk you in it: and go not aside neither to the right hand, nor to the left* (Isa 30:21). Therefore, *'the way'* is understood as the whole of that which pertains to common salvation; *and I show unto you yet a more excellent way* (1 Cor 12:31).

Indeed, the paths are the keeping of the counsels, which paths are said to be *'straight'* because they should not be kept for the sake of empty glory; below, **take heed that you do not your justice before men, to be seen by them** (Matt 6:1); and: *her ways are beautiful ways, and all her paths are peaceable* (Prov 3:17).

256. Next is shown the way in which John bore witness to Christ in his life, at **and the same John**.

But who bore witness to John, who was bearing witness to Christ? And one should say that his own life bore him witness: because, as Chrysostom says, no one is a suitable witness for another unless he is his own witness by a good life; *the attire of the body, and the laughter of the teeth, and the gait of the man, show what he is* (Sir 19:27).

Hence his austerity in life and food is described here; and this is **and the same John had his garment of camels' hair**. Others with wool, John with hairs; for he considered clothing made of wool to be a softness which does not befit a preacher.

Item *zona pellicea*. Illud dupliciter exponitur. Hieronymus dicit, quod tunc temporis Iudaei habebant cingulum de lana, sed Ioannes reputans ad mollitiem, accipit de pellibus imitans Eliam, sicut dicitur IV Reg. I, 8. Rabanus exponit sic, et dicit quod Ioannes accipiebat pelles crudas, non paratas, et utebatur eis, ut refraenaret libidinem: et hoc est *et zonam*. Sed sive sic, sive sic exponatur, in utroque tamen austeritas vitae intelligitur.

Cibus autem eius locustae et mel silvestre. Hic cibus non paratus, sed quem natura ministrabat; et sunt locustae animalia quaedam apta ad comedendum.

Et mel silvestre. Hoc dupliciter potest intelligi. Proprie enim mel silvestre dicitur illud, quod non reconditur in alveis artificiose factis, sed invenitur in silvis in aliquibus arboribus. Alii dicunt quod est canna mellis, et quoddam quod invenitur intus in cannis valde dulce; tamen in omnibus his nihil aliud habetur, nisi quod simplicibus erat contentus; I Tim. VI, 8: *habentes alimenta, et quibus tegamur, his contenti sumus*.

257. Consequenter agitur de Baptismo: unde dicitur *tunc exibant*: et tangit tria. Primo quomodo visitabatur a turbis; secundo quomodo turbae baptizabantur; et tertio quomodo confitebantur peccata sua.

258. Et quantum ad primum sciendum, quod tria sunt quae invitabant homines ad exeundum ad Ioannem. Primo nova praedicatio. Numquam audiverant fieri mentionem de regno caelorum, et ideo mirabantur; Iob c. XXXVIII, 33: *numquid nosti ordinem caeli, et pones rationem eius in terra?* Ioannes primo docuit quod ratio regni caelorum non esset ponenda in terra. Secundo propter vitam. Unde dicit *tunc exibant*, videntes scilicet vitam ipsius; Iac. II, 18: *ostende mihi fidem tuam sine operibus, et ego ostendam tibi ex operibus fidem meam* et cetera. Tertio, quia Iudaea privata erat instructione prophetarum. Ps. LXXIII, 9: *signa nostra non vidimus, iam non est propheta*.

259. Et ideo exibant a Iudaea ad videndum; et hoc est *tunc exibant . . . et baptizabantur ab eo in Iordane*.

Sed quare in Iordane? Quia in Iordane primo fuit praefiguratus baptismus. IV Reg. c. II, 8–11, ubi dicitur de Eliseo quod transivit per Iordanem, et Elias raptus est in caelum. Item ibi fuit mundatus Naaman leprosus, qui significat mundatum a peccatis in baptismo. Item quia ipsa interpretatio convenit baptismo; interpretatur enim 'descensus'; et significat humilitatem, quam homo debet habere in Baptismo; I Petr. II, 2: *quasi modo geniti infantes, rationabile, et sine dolo, lac concupiscite*.

260. Tertium ponitur ibi *confitentes peccata sua*. Causa quare confessio est inducta, supra est ostensa, quia de necessitate salutis; Iac. V, 16: *confitemini alterutrum peccata vestra*. Et dicit Glossa, quod ideo inducta est, ut homo habeat erubescentiam. Sed sciendum quod

Similarly, *a leather girdle*. This is explained in two ways. Jerome says that at that time the Jews had a girdle of wool, but John considered this softness, and took his from skins, imitating Elias (2 Kgs 1:8). Rabanus expounds it this way, saying that John took crude, unprepared skins and used them, that he might restrain himself from lust; and this is a *girdle*. But whether it is explained in this way or in that way, still in either case the austerity of his life is understood.

And his meat was locusts and wild honey. This food was not prepared, but what nature supplied; and locusts are certain animals apt for eating.

And wild honey. This can be understood in two ways. For that is properly called wild honey which is not put away in artificially made tubs, but is found in the woods in some tree. Others say that it is reed honey, and one man says that it is found inside reeds, very sweet; yet nothing else is contained in all these explanations except that he was content with simple things; *but having food, and wherewith to be covered, with these we are content* (1 Tim 6:8).

257. Next he treats of the baptism; hence it says, *then went out*. And he touches upon three things: first, how he was visited by the crowds; second, how the crowds were baptized; and third, how they were confessing their sins.

258. And as regards the first, one should know that there were three things which drew men to go out to John. First, the new preaching. They had never heard mention of the kingdom of God, and so they marveled; *do you know the order of heaven, and can you set down the reason of it on the earth?* (Job 38:33). John was the first to teach that the notion of the kingdom of heaven is not to be set down on earth. Second, on account of his life. Hence he says, *then went out to him Jerusalem and all Judea*, namely seeing his life; *show me your faith without works; and I will show you, by works, my faith* (Jas 2:18). Third, because Judea was deprived of the instruction of the prophets. *Our signs we have not seen, there is now no prophet* (Ps 73:9).

259. And so they went out from Judea to see; and this is *then went out to him . . . and were baptized by him in the Jordan*.

But why in the Jordan? Because baptism was first prefigured in the Jordan. It is said about Eliseus that he went across through the Jordan, and Elias was taken up into heaven (2 Kgs 2:8–11). Similarly, Naaman the leper was cleansed there, who signifies the one cleansed from sins in baptisms. Again, because its very meaning fits with baptism; for it is interpreted as 'descent', and it signifies humility, which a man ought to have in baptism. *As newborn babes, desire the rational milk without guile* (1 Pet 2:2).

260. Third, he sets down here *confessing their sins*. The reason why confession is introduced was shown above, namely that it is necessary for salvation; *confess therefore your sins one to another* (Jas 5:16). And the Gloss says that confession is introduced that a man might have shame. But

erubescentia est causa concomitans, sed principalis est propter virtutem clavium: nullus enim posset ligare, vel solvere, nisi sciret quid ligandum, vel solvendum esset. Unde sicut nullus potest amovere necessitatem clavium, ita nullus posset amovere confessionem vocalem.

Sed quaeritur, an accedens ad baptismum confiteri teneatur. Videtur quod non indigeat virtute clavium, cum omnia dimittantur peccata in baptismo.

Sed dicendum, quod tenetur saltem in generali; et hoc facit quando abrenuntiat satanae, et omnibus pompis eius: in hoc enim profitetur se esse satanae obligatum.

261. *Videns autem multos.* Ostenso quod multi a Ioanne baptizabantur, hic agit de instructione eorum.

Et circa hoc duo facit:

primo ponuntur qui sunt qui instruantur;

secundo ponitur eorum instructio, ibi *quis demonstravit vobis fugere a ventura ira?*

262. Dicit ergo *videns autem multos Pharisaeorum et Sadducaeorum.* Sciendum quod apud Iudaeos sunt aliquae sectae, inter quas istae duae erant praecipuae. Pharisaei enim dicebantur quasi a communi vita divisi, propter suas observantias. Isti in multis bene dicebant, tamen deficiebant, quia, ut dicitur, omnia provenire ex necessitate ponebant. Alii, scilicet Sadducaei, dicebantur iusti propter quasdam speciales observantias legis; qui non recipiebant prophetas, nec dicebant animas post corruptionem corporis resuscitari, nec spiritum esse.

Utrique autem ex ipso nomine notabantur, quia 'Phares' divisionem significat, quae opponitur caritati. Et hi omnino erant divisi ab aliis, quasi haberent superabundantem Spiritum Sanctum: hoc enim bonum esset. Alii etiam, scilicet Sadducaei, sibi iustitiam usurpabant; contra quos Rom. X, 3: *ignorantes enim iustitiam Dei, et suam quaerentes statuere, iustitiae Dei non sunt subiecti.* Et tamen quamvis magis iusti apparerent, tamquam ad magistrum, ad Ioannem veniebant; Is. XLIX, 7: *reges videbunt, et consurgent principes, et adorabunt propter Dominum, quia fidelis est, et Sanctum Israel, qui elegit te.*

263. Isti ergo hic convenienter instruuntur. Unde *quis demonstravit vobis fugere a ventura ira?*

Et notandum quod instructio debet variari secundum conditiones auditorum. Simplicibus enim sufficit ea quae ad salutem pertinent breviter loqui; sed sapientibus debent singula explicari; quod innuit Apostolus I Cor. III, v. 1: *non potui vobis loqui tamquam spiritualibus sed quasi carnalibus.* Ita fecit Ioannes: breviter turbas admonuit de poenitentia, et annuntiavit regnum

one should know that shame is a concomitant reason, but the principle reason is because of the power of the key: for no one could bind or loose unless he knew what was to be bound or loosed. Hence just as no one can take away the necessity of the key, so no one can take away vocal confession.

But it is asked whether the one who approaches baptism is bound to confess. It seems that he does not need the power of the key, since everything is forgiven in baptism.

But one should say that one is bound to confess at least in general; and this takes place when one renounces satan and all his pomps, for in this we admit that we are bound to satan.

261. *And seeing many.* Having shown that many were baptized by John, here he treats of their instruction.

And concerning this he does two things:

first is set down who they are who are instructed;

second, their instruction is set down, at *who has showed you to flee from the wrath to come?*

262. It says then, *and seeing many of the Pharisees and Sadducees.* One should know that there were some sects among the Jews, among which there were chiefly these two. For the Pharisees were so called as though separated from the common life, because of their observances. They spoke well in many things, and yet they failed, because, as is said, they held that all things proceed from necessity. The others, namely the Sadducees, were called the just ones owing to certain special observances of the law. They did not accept the prophets, nor did they say that souls are awakened again after the corruption of the body, nor that souls are spirits.

Moreover, both were marked off by the very name, because 'Phares' signifies division, which is opposed to charity. And these were in every way divided from the others, as though they had a superabounding Holy Spirit; for this would be a good thing. The others also, namely the Sadducees, seized justice for themselves; against whom, *for they, not knowing the justice of God, and seeking to establish their own, have not submitted themselves to the justice of God* (Rom 10:3). And yet although they appeared more just, as though teachers, they were coming to John; *kings will see, and princes will rise up, and adore for the Lord's sake, because he is faithful, and for the Holy One of Israel, who has chosen you* (Isa 49:7).

263. Therefore these men are fittingly instructed here. Hence, *who has showed you to flee from the wrath to come?*

And one should note that instruction should be varied according to the condition of the listeners. For to the simple it is enough to speak briefly those things which pertain to salvation; but to the wise the individual points should be explained; which the Apostle implies, *and I, brethren, could not speak to you as unto spiritual, but as unto carnal* (1 Cor 3:1). John did so: he briefly warned the crowds about

caelorum. Ista duo hic explicat per singula Pharisaeis. Unde

primo exhortatur ad poenitentiam;

secundo nuntiat de appropinquatione regni caelorum, ibi *ego quidem baptizo vos* et cetera.

Circa primum duo facit:

primo ponit inductivum ad poenitentiam;

secundo removet ea quae possent a poenitentia retrahere, ibi *et ne velitis dicere intra vos: patrem habemus Abraham*.

Circa primum duo facit:

primo ponit inductionem ad poenitentiam;

secundo ponit perfectae poenitentiae modum, ibi *facite ergo fructum dignum poenitentiae*.

Duo autem sunt quae inducunt ad poenitentiam: recognitio proprii peccati; Is. LVIII, v. 1: *annuntia populo meo scelera eorum*: secundo timor divini iudicii. Ista duo annuntiat Ioannes.

264. Unde dicit *progenies viperarum*.

Et notandum, quod in Sacra Scriptura dicitur filius alicuius ad imitationem; Ez. XVI, v. 45: *pater vester Amorrhaeus*; Io. VIII, 44: *vos ex patre diabolo estis, et desideria patris vestri vultis facere*. Isti similes erant viperis; et ideo dicit *progenies viperarum*. Et sunt similes in tribus, secundum Chrysostomum. Natura enim illius est, quando mordet aliquem, recurrere ad aquam; et si invenit non moritur, alias moritur. Unde Ioannes perpendens intentionem eorum, quare veniebant ad aquam baptismi, dixit *progenies viperarum*. Sed quomodo venenati veniebant ad baptismum? Quia Ioannes promittebat remissionem peccatorum, unde faciebat intrare aquam deponentem pravam intentionem, ideo dicit *agite poenitentiam . . . et baptizabantur ab eo*.

Secunda proprietas est quod nascendo occidit parentes; unde dicitur quasi *vi pariens*, et isti similiter. Infra XXIII, 31: *quem prophetarum non occidistis?*

Tertia ratio est, quia est pulchra exterius, interius habens venenum: isti etiam pulchri sunt exterius quadam simulata iustitia, interius habentes peccata; infra XXIII, 27: *vae vobis quia similes estis sepulcris dealbatis, quae foris apparent hominibus speciosa, intus vero plena sunt ossibus mortuorum et omni spurcitia*; et secundum hoc *progenies viperarum* sonat in malum.

Ambrosius exponit aliter, et dicit, quod prudentia serpentibus adscribitur; inf. X, 16: *estote prudentes sicut serpentes*. Unde Ioannes, commendans eos de prudentia, quia veniebant ad baptismum, dicit *progenies viperarum*.

penance, and announced the kingdom of heaven. Here, he explains these two things to the Pharisees point by point.

Hence, first, he exhorts them to penance;

second, he speaks about the approach of the kingdom of heaven, at *I indeed baptize you*.

Concerning the first, he does two things:

first, he sets out incentives to penance;

second, he removes those things which could draw them back from penance, at *and do not think to say within yourselves, we have Abraham for our father*.

Concerning the first, he does two things:

first, he sets out the incentive to penance;

second, he sets out the manner of perfect penance, at *bring forth therefore fruit worthy of penance*.

Now, there are two things which move one to penance: first, the recognition of one's own sin; *show my people their wicked doings* (Isa 58:1); second, the fear of divine judgment. John announces these two things.

264. Hence he says, *you brood of vipers*.

And one should notice that in Sacred Scripture one is called a son of someone for imitation; *your father an Amorrhite* (Ezek 16:45); *you are of your father the devil, and the desires of your father you will do* (John 8:44). These men were similar to vipers, and so he says, *you brood of vipers*. And they are similar in three ways, according to Chrysostom. For it is the nature of the viper to run back to water when it kills someone, and if it finds water it does not die; otherwise it dies. Hence John, considering their intention, why they were coming to the water of baptism, said, *you brood of vipers*. But how were the venomous ones coming to baptism? Because John was promising the remission of sins, hence he made them enter the water, laying aside their corrupt intention, and this is why he says, *do penance . . . and were baptized by him*.

The second property of the viper is that it kills its parents by being born; hence it is said as though *giving birth by force*, and these men were similar. Below, *which of the prophets have not your fathers persecuted?* (Acts 7:52) [*you are the sons of those who killed the prophets.* (Matt 23:31).]

The third reason is that the viper is exteriorly beautiful, but has poison within. These men were also exteriorly beautiful by a certain pretended justice, but had sins within; below, *woe to you scribes and Pharisees, hypocrites; because you are like whitened sepulchres, which outwardly appear beautiful to men, but within are full of dead men's bones, and of all filthiness* (Matt 23:27); and according to this the *brood of vipers* stands for evil.

Ambrose explains this in another way, and says that prudence is attributed to serpents; below, *be you therefore wise as serpents and simple as doves* (Matt 10:16). Hence John, commending these men for prudence, because they were coming to baptism, says, *you brood of vipers*.

265. Primum ergo quod inducit ad poenitentiam est recognitio proprii peccati; secundum est timor divini iudicii; Prov. XV, 27: *per timorem Domini declinat omnis a malo*; Iob XIX, 29: *scitote esse iudicium*. Et hoc est, quod dicit **quis demonstravit vobis fugere a ventura ira?**

Et sciendum quod Ambrosius et Chrysostomus exponunt de praeteritis, Rabanus de futuris; unde dicit **quis demonstrabit?**

Et secundum Ambrosium sic: **progenies** etc., quasi diceret: *quis demonstravit, ut recederetis a malo?* Quasi dicat: *nullus, nisi Deus*. Ps. LXXXIV, 8: *ostende nobis, domine, misericordiam tuam, et salutare tuum da nobis.* Secundum Chrysostomum, sic: **progenies viperarum**, quia retinent voluntatem peccati, **quis demonstravit vobis fugere**, sicut vos vultis? Non, quia dixit Isaias I, 16: *lavamini, et mundi estote, auferte malum cogitationum vestrarum ab oculis meis.* Non, quia dixit David, Ps. l, 4: *amplius lava me, domine, ab iniquitate mea, et a peccato meo munda me*; et post: *sacrificium Deo spiritus contribulatus, cor contritum et humiliatum, Deus, non despicies.*

Rabanus de futuro sic, quasi diceret: *bonum est quod agatis poenitentiam*, quia aliter **quis demonstrabit?** Ps. CXXXVIII, 7: *quo ibo a spiritu tuo, et quo a facie tua fugiam?*

Ira de Deo non accipitur pro affectu mentis, sed pro effectu: unde eius ira est ultio.

266. Praemissis his duobus ducentibus ad poenitentiam, consequenter concludit Evangelista **facite ergo fructum dignum poenitentiae.** In arbore fructus sunt post flores, et si flores non sequantur fructus, arbor illa nihil valet. Flos enim quidam poenitentiae apparet in contritione, sed fructus est in executione. Eccli. XXIV, 23: *flores mei fructus honoris et honestatis.*

Et notandum quod alius est fructus iustitiae, et alius poenitentiae: plus enim requiritur a poenitente, quam ab eo, qui non peccat. Est autem triplex fructus dignus poenitentiae. Primus est ut puniat in se, quod commisit, et hoc iudicio sacerdotis. Ier. XXXI, v. 19: *postquam convertisti me, egi poenitentiam, et postquam ostendisti mihi, percussi femur meum*: idest carnem meam afflixi. Secundus est ut fugiat peccata, et occasiones peccati, unde dicitur, quod satisfacere est causas peccatorum excidere. Eccli. XXI, 1: *fili, peccasti? Ne adiicias iterum: sed et de pristinis deprecare, ut tibi dimittantur et cetera. Quasi a facie colubri fuge peccatum*, Eccli. c. XXI, 2. Tertius est, ut tantum studeat ad bene agendum, quantum studuit ad peccandum. Rom. VI, 19: *humanum dico propter infirmitatem carnis nostrae. Sicut enim exhibuistis membra vestra servire immunditiae et iniquitati ad iniquitatem, ita nunc exhibete membra vestra servire iustitiae in sanctificationem.*

265. So the first thing which incites one to penance is the recognition of one's own sin; the second is the fear of divine judgment; *by the fear of the Lord every one declines from evil* (Prov 15:27); *know you that there is judgment* (Job 19:29). And this is what he says, **who has showed you to flee from the wrath to come?**

And one should know that Ambrose and Chrysostom explain this as about the past, Rabanus as about the future; hence he says, **who will show you?**

And according to Augustine, thus: **brood**, as though to say: *who has shown you, so that you withdraw from evil?* As though to say: *no one but God. Show us, O Lord, your mercy; and grant us your salvation* (Ps 84:8). According to Chrysostom, thus: **brood of vipers**, because they retain the will for sin, **who has showed you to flee** as you wish to? No, because Isaiah said: *wash yourselves, be clean, take away the evil of your devices from my eyes* (Isa 1:16). No, because David said: *wash me yet more from my iniquity, and cleanse me from my sin*, and afterward, *a sacrifice to God is an afflicted spirit: a contrite and humbled heart, O God, you will not despise* (Ps 1:4).

Rabanus explains it as about the future this way, as though he said: *it is good that you do penance*, because otherwise **who will show you?** *Where will I go from thy spirit? Or where will I flee from your face?* (Ps 138:7).

Wrath as it concerns God is not taken for an affection of the mind, but for an effect: hence his wrath is retribution.

266. These two incentives to penance having been premised, next the Evangelist concludes, **bring forth therefore fruit worthy of penance.** In a tree, the fruits come after the flowers, and if the fruits do not follow the flowers, that tree is of no use. For a certain flower of penance appears in contrition, but the fruit is in the carrying out of the penance. *My flowers are the fruit of honor and riches* (Sir 24:23).

And one should note that the fruit of justice is one thing, and the fruit of penance another; for more is required from the one repenting than from the one who does not sin. Moreover, there are three fruits worthy of penance. The first is that he punish in himself what he has committed, and this by the judgment of a priest. *For after you converted me, I did penance: and after you showed unto me, I struck my thigh* (Jer 31:19); i.e., I afflicted my body. The second is that he should flee from sin, and from the occasions of sin, hence it is said that to satisfy is to cut out the causes of sin. *My son, have you sinned? Do so no more: but for your former sins also pray that they may be forgiven you. Flee from sins as from the face of a serpent* (Sir 21:1–2). The third is that he should be as eager to do good as he was eager to sin. *I speak an human thing, because of the infirmity of your flesh. For as you have yielded your members to serve uncleanness and iniquity, unto iniquity; so now yield your members to serve justice, unto sanctification* (Rom 6:19).

267. Consequenter excludit impedimentum poenitentiae, cum dicit *et ne velitis dicere intra vos: patrem habemus Abraham*. Duplex impedimentum est poenitentiae. Praesumptuositas de se, et desperatio de divino iudicio.

Primo removet primum;

secundo secundum, ibi *iam enim securis ad radicem arborum posita est*.

Circa primum duo facit:

primo excludit impedimentum;

secundo assignat rationem, ibi *dico enim vobis*.

268. Dicit ergo *et ne velitis dicere intra vos: patrem habemus Abraham*. Isti secundum carnem erant de genere Abrahae: unde poterant credere, quod quantumcumque peccarent, Deus misereretur eis propter Abraham; Ex. XXXII, 11: *cur, domine, irascitur furor tuus?* Et post: *recordare Abraham, Isaac, et Iacob servorum tuorum* et cetera. Et ideo excludit hoc Ioannes: *et ne velitis dicere*. Et est modus loquendi; quasi diceret, *non dicatis hoc, quia non valebit vobis*. Rom. IX, 8: *non qui filii sunt carnis, hi filii Dei; sed qui filii sunt promissionis, aestimantur in semine* et cetera. Isti enim multum gloriabantur de Abraham, sed Dominus dicit Io. VIII, 39: *si filii Abrahae estis, opera Abrahae facite*. Contra tales dicit Chrysostomus: *quid prodest ei quem mores deturpant, generatio clara?* Et est etiam hoc in spiritualibus.

269. Consequenter assignat rationem *dico enim vobis*, magis est enim magnum imitari patrem, quam nasci ex eo, *potens est Deus de lapidibus istis suscitare filios Abrahae*. Legitur Iosue IV quod quando populus Israel transivit Iordanem siccis pedibus, in memoriam miraculi, mandavit Iosue, quod extraherentur duodecim lapides ex fundo fluminis, et ponerentur extra, et duodecim de lapidibus exterioribus ponerentur intus. Ioannes autem in illo loco baptizans, eos ostendit.

Potest autem intelligi dupliciter. Ad litteram primo: hoc enim est primum fidei fundamentum, credere omnipotentiam Dei; Iob c. XLII, 2: *scio quia potes, et nulla te latet cogitatio*. Vel possumus intelligere per lapides gentiles, qui dicuntur lapides propter duo: primum quia lapides adorant; secundo propter duritiem. Et licet lapides sint duri, tamen diu conservant impressionem: et licet etiam aedificium ex eis factum tarde fiat, tamen forte est, et durabile. Unde gentiles quamvis fuerint duri ad recipiendum fidem Christi, tamen tenuerunt fortiter. Hoc significatur Ez. XI, 19: *auferam a vobis cor lapideum de carne vestra, et dabo vobis cor carneum, et spiritum meum ponam in medio vestri*.

267. Next, he removes an impediment to penance, when he says, *and do not think to say within yourselves, we have Abraham for our father*. There are two impediments to penance, presumptuousness about oneself, and despair of God's judgment.

First, he removes the first;

second, the second, at *for now the axe is laid to the root of the trees*.

Concerning the first, he does two things:

first, he removes the impediment;

second, he gives the reason, at *for I tell you*.

268. He says then, *and do not think to say within yourselves, we have Abraham for our father*. These were of the race of Abraham according to the flesh, hence they might believe that, however much they sinned, God would have mercy on them for the sake of Abraham; *why, O Lord, is your indignation enkindled against your people?* (Exod 32:11). And later, *remember Abraham, Isaac, and Israel, your servants*. And so John excludes this: *and do not think to say*. And this is the manner of speaking; as though to say: *do not say this, because it will be no use to you*. As, *Not they that are the children of the flesh, are the children of God; but they, that are the children of the promise, are accounted for the seed* (Rom 9:8). For these men were glorying in Abraham, but the Lord says, *if you are the children of Abraham, do the works of Abraham* (John 8:39). Against such men Chrysostom says, *what use is a famous lineage to a man whom behavior makes ugly?* And this is also true in spiritual things.

269. Next, he gives the reason, *for I tell you*, for it is more to imitate a great father than to be born from him, *God is able of these stones to raise up children to Abraham*. It is said that when the people of Israel went across the Jordan with dry feet, Joshua commanded that twelve stones be taken from the bottom of the river and set up beside it, and twelve of the stones outside the river be placed within it, in memory of the miracle (Jos 4). And John, baptizing in that same place, points to these stones.

Now, this can be understood in two ways. First, to the letter: for this is the first foundation of faith, to believe in the omnipotence of God; *I know that you can do all things, and no thought is hid from you* (Job 42:2). Or we can understand by the stones the gentiles, who are called stones for two reasons: first, because they adore stones; second, because of their hardness. And although stones are hard, yet they retain an impression for a long time; and although a building made out of them is also made about slowly, yet it is strong, and durable. Hence the gentiles, although they were hardened as regards receiving the faith of Christ, yet they held it strongly. This is indicated by: *and I will give them one heart, and will put a new spirit in their bowels: and I will take away the stony heart out of their flesh, and will give them a heart of flesh* (Ezek 11:19).

Secundum autem Hieronymum in verbis istis videtur reducere ad memoriam prophetiam Is. LI, 2: *attendite ad Abraham patrem vestrum, et ad Saram quae peperit vos* et cetera. Nominat enim petram Abraham propter impotentiam generandi, et Saram propter sterilitatem; quasi dicat: *Deus, qui fecit potentem Abraham, et foecundam Saram* **potens est de lapidibus istis suscitare filios Abrahae.**

270. *Iam enim securis ad radicem arborum posita est.* Possent enim dicere: nec credimus quod aliqua ira superveniat nobis; et ideo hoc removet dicens **iam enim.** Unde

primo ponit iudicium;

secundo ponit sententiam iudicii.

271. Dicit ergo **iam enim** et cetera. Dupliciter enim aliqui poenitere nolunt: ex desperatione iudicii, quia non credunt iudicium esse; Eccli. V, 1: *ne dixeris: est mihi sufficiens vita*; Iob XIX, 29: *fugite a facie gladii, quoniam ultor iniquitatum gladius est, et scitote esse iudicium.* Aliqui autem ex mora; II Petr. III, 9: *non tardat Deus promissionem suam, sicut quidam aestimant, sed patienter agit propter nos, nolens aliquos perire, sed omnes ad poenitentiam reverti.* Sed utramque Ioannes excludit. Primo primam, cum dicit **iam enim securis**; secundo secundam, cum dicit **posita est**; quasi dicat, *non tardabit.*

272. Et tripliciter intelligitur hoc. Chrysostomus dicit, quod per securim intelligitur districtio divini iudicii, quae quandoque per securim, quandoque per arcum, et gladium designatur; Ps. VII, 13: *nisi conversi fueritis, gladium suum vibrabit, arcum suum tetendit, et paravit illum.*

Hieronymus: per securim praedicatio Evangelii intelligitur, quia sicut per doctrinam Evangelii aliqui ducti sunt ad vitam, ita contemptores ad mortem. Ier. XXIII, 29: *nonne verba mea sicut ignis, et quasi malleus conterens petram?* Lc. II, 34: *ecce positus est hic in ruinam, et resurrectionem multorum in Israel, et in signum cui contradicetur* et cetera. **Iam enim securis ad radicem arborum posita est**; quasi dicat: *in promptu est, ut veniat.*

Secundum Gregorium per securim Redemptor noster intelligitur, qui velut ex manubrio et ferro, ex humanitate et divinitate constat; cuius humanitas, quia patienter expectat, quasi tenetur: divinitas, quasi ferrum incidit. **Securis** ergo **ad radicem ponitur**, quia iudicium fit per Deum et hominem.

273. Et dicit **ad radicem** propter duo, quia in radice fit praecisio universalis, eius etiam quod est in ramis. Item quia quod a radice exciditur, non germinat: quasi diceret: *universalis erit extirpatio malorum.*

But according to Jerome, one seems in these words to be led to recall the prophecy, *look unto Abraham your father, and to Sarah who bore you: for I called him alone, and blessed him, and multiplied him* (Isa 51:2). For he calls Abraham a rock on account of his inability to generate, and Sarah on account of her sterility; as though to say, *God, who made Abraham able to generate, and Sarah fertile,* **is able to raise up children to Abraham from these stones.**

270. *For now the axe is laid to the root of the trees.* For they could say: we do not believe that any wrath will come upon us; and so he removes this, saying, **for now.**

Hence, first, he sets out the judgment;

second, he sets out the sentence of the judgment.

271. He says then, **for now.** For people can be unwilling to repent in two ways: out of a despair of the judgment, because they do not believe that there is a judgment; *I have enough to live on* (Sir 5:1); *flee then from the face of the sword, for the sword is the revenger of iniquities: and know that there is judgment* (Job 19:29). But some, out of delay; *the Lord delays not his promise, as some imagine, but deals patiently for your sake, not willing that any should perish, but that all should return to penance* (2 Pet 3:9). But John excludes both. First, he excludes the first one, when he says, **for now the axe**; second, he excludes the second one when he says, **is laid**, as though to say, *it will not delay.*

272. And this is understood in three ways. Chrysostom says that by the axe is understood the strictness of the divine judgment, which sometimes is indicated through an axe, sometimes through a bow, and sometimes through a sword; *except you will be converted, he will brandish his sword: he has bent his bow and made it ready* (Ps 7:13).

Jerome: by the axe is understood the preaching of the Gospel, because as some are led to life by the teaching of the Gospel, so those who scorn are led to death. *Are not my words as a fire, says the Lord: and as a hammer that breaks the rock in pieces?* (Jer 23:29). *Behold this child is set for the fall, and for the resurrection of many in Israel, and for a sign which will be contradicted* (Luke 2:34). **For now the axe is laid to the root of the trees**, as though to say, *it is in readiness to come.*

According to Gregory, by the axe is understood our Redeemer, who is put together out of humanity and divinity as though out of a handle and iron; whose humanity, because it patiently awaits, is held, so to speak; and whose divinity cuts like iron. Therefore, **the axe is laid to the root**, because judgment comes through God and man.

273. And he says, **is laid to the root**, for two reasons. Because a universal cutting off of even what is in the branches happens at the root. Likewise, because what is cut off from the root does not sprout; as though to say, *the uprooting of the evil will be universal.*

Sequitur ergo, et ponit primo universalitatem dicens **omnis arbor**; quasi dicat: *tam Iudaeus quam gentilis*; Rom. II, 11: *non est acceptatio personarum apud Deum.* Item culpam, quia non facit fructum, propter solam enim omissionem fit punitio; infra XXV, v. 42: **esurivi, et non dedistis mihi manducare.** Tertio ponit duplicem poenam: scilicet temporalem, **excidetur**, scilicet ex hac vita; Lc. XIII, 7: *ecce tres anni sunt, ex quo venio quaerens fructum in ficulnea hac, et non invenio: succide ergo illam*, et post: *ut quid terram occupat?* Et hoc est **excidetur**, cum prosperitate terrena. Item ponit poenam aeternam, unde dicitur **in ignem mittetur**; Is. ult., 24: *vermis eorum non morietur, et ignis eorum non extinguetur.* Et inf. XXV, 41: **ite, maledicti, in ignem aeternum.**

274. Ego quidem baptizo. Supra Ioannes exhortatus fuit ad poenitentiam explendam, modo intendit facere quod frequenter dixerat, scilicet annuntiare regnum caelorum: et circa hoc duo facit.

Primo ponitur praeparatio ad regnum;

secundo agitur de praenuntiatione regni, ibi **qui autem post me venturus est**.

275. Regnum illud Christus est, de quo Lc. XVII, 21: *regnum Dei intra vos est.* Praeparatio quidem est baptismus; unde **ego quidem**, quod mirabile est vobis, **baptizo**, in aqua sola, scilicet quia sum purus homo. Unde non poterat nisi corpus lavare, nec poterat dare Spiritum Sanctum, cum nondum esset solutum pretium pro peccato; Hebr. IX, v. 22: *non enim fit remissio sine sanguine.* Item Spiritus Sanctus nondum descenderat, nec Christus tactu suae carnis aquam sanctificaverat.

Quare ergo baptizabat? Propter tria. Primo, ut praeveniret Christum, baptizando; Lc. I, 76: *praeibis ante faciem Domini parare vias eius.* Secundo, ut congregatis hominibus haberet opportunitatem praedicandi de Christo; Io. I, 31: *ut manifestaretur in Israel, propterea veni ego in aqua baptizans.* Tertio, ut ad baptismum Christi praepararet. Unde consuetudo est in Ecclesia, ut prius catechumeni fiant qui baptizari debent, scilicet ut fiat quaedam praeparatio, et accipiant quoddam signaculum, per quod idonei reputantur: et hoc est quod dicit, **ego baptizo**, ut scilicet sciatis vos aptos esse, qui a Christo baptizari intenditis.

276. Nota, quod Magister in IV *Sent.* dicit, quod baptizati a Ioanne non baptizabantur a Christo, nisi illi qui ponebant spem suam in Ioanne. Sed hoc falsum est; unde dicit **ipse vos baptizabit**.

Item nota, quod Augustinus movet quaestionem. Si post baptismum Ioannis rebaptizabantur, quare non rebaptizabantur post baptismum haereticorum?

It follows therefore, and first he sets down the universality, saying, **every tree**, as though to say: *both Jews and gentiles; for there is no respect of persons with God* (Rom 2:11). Likewise the guilt, because it does not bring forth fruit, for punishment only happens because of an omission; below, **for I was hungry, and you gave me nothing to eat** (Matt 25:42). Third, he sets out two punishments, and first a temporal one, **will be cut down**, that is, in this life; *behold, for these three years I come seeking fruit on this fig tree, and I find none* (Luke 13:7). Cut it done therefore, and later, *why cumbers it the ground?* And this is, **will be cut down**, with earthly prosperity. Next, he sets down an eternal punishment, hence it says, **and cast into the fire**; *their worm will not die, and their fire will not be quenched: and they will be a loathsome sight to all flesh* (Isa 66:24). And below, **depart from me, you cursed, into everlasting fire** (Matt 25:41).

274. I indeed baptize. Above, John exhorted them to the penance which should be accomplished; and now he aims to do what he had said frequently, namely to announce the kingdom of heaven. And concerning this he does two things:

first, he sets down the preparation for the kingdom;

second, he treats of the foretelling of the kingdom, at **he who will come after me**.

275. That kingdom is Christ, of whom it is said, *for lo, the kingdom of God is within you* (Luke 17:21). Certainly, the preparation is baptism; hence **I indeed**, what is marvelous to you, **baptize** in water alone, namely because I am simply a man. Hence he could wash nothing but the body, nor could he give the Holy Spirit, since the price for sin was not yet paid; *without the shedding of blood there is no remission of sins* (Heb 9:22). Again, the Holy Spirit had not yet descended, nor had Christ sanctified the water by the touch of his body.

So why did he baptize? For three reasons. First, so that he might come before Christ, by baptizing; *you will go before the face of the Lord to prepare his ways* (Luke 1:76). Second that, having gathered men together, he might have an opportunity to preach about Christ; *that he may be made manifest in Israel, therefore am I come baptizing with water* (John 1:31). Third, to prepare for the baptism of Christ. It is customary in the Church that those who are to be baptized should first become catechumens, namely, that there should be a certain preparation, and they should receive a certain sign, through which they are reputed fit. And this is what he says, **I baptize**, namely that you who intend to be baptized by Christ may know yourselves to be ready.

276. Note that the Teacher says in chapter four of *The Sentences* that those baptized by John were not baptized by Christ, except for those who put their hope in John. But this is false; hence he says **he will baptize you**.

Again, note that Augustine raises a question. If they will be rebaptized after the baptism of John, why are men not rebaptized after the baptism of heretics?

Dicendum, quod Ioannes baptizabat in persona sua; haeretici in persona Christi; unde baptismus Christi iudicandus est.

277. Consequenter agitur de regno. Et
primo ostendit dignitatem ipsius;
secundo officium eius, ibi *ipse vos baptizabit*.

278. Dicit ergo *qui post me venit*, nascendo, baptizando, praedicando, moriendo, ad Inferos descendendo. Sed hic de duobus tantum loquitur, videlicet de praedicatione et baptismo; unde dicit *qui post me venit*, ad baptizandum et docendum; Lc. I, 17: *ipse praecedet ante illum in spiritu et virtute Eliae*. *Fortior me est*, et fortior eius baptismus; I Reg. II, 2: *non est sanctus ut est Deus*; Iob IX, 19: *si fortitudo quaeritur, robustissimus est*. Et ne sic credatur quod sit comparatio inter eos, dicit *cuius non sum dignus calceamenta portare*; quasi dicat: *incomparabiliter me dignior est*, ut exponit Chrysostomus, *ita ut ei officium non debeam exhibere*.

Sed sciendum quod in aliis tribus Evangeliis non est sic: quia illic dicitur *solvere*, hic *portare*. Unde dicit Augustinus quod Ioannes voluit tantum suam humilitatem, et Christi excellentiam ostendere, et tunc idem significatur in omnibus. Unde dicit, quod hoc fuit per Spiritus Sancti inspirationem, quod in talibus evangelistae dissonent in verbis, ut documentum accipiamus, quod non mentimur, si eumdem sensum cum aliis loquimur, quamvis non eadem verba dicamus. Si vero mysticum aliquid significare voluit, tunc differentia est in verbis Matthaei et aliorum: et possunt in corrigia calceamenti duo significari, quia per calceamentum humanitatem; Ps. LIX, 10: *in Idumaeam extendam calceamentum meum*. Corrigia est unio, qua humanitas ligata est divinitati. Et quia non reputabat se sufficientem ad explicandum mysterium unionis, ideo dicit *cuius non sum dignus calceamenta portare*. Vel mos erat apud Iudaeos, Deut. XXV, 9, quod si quis nollet accipere uxorem fratris sui, deberet solvere corrigiam ab illo, qui uxorem accipiebat. Sponsa Christi Ecclesia est. Tunc ergo Ioannes reputabat se indignum esse accipere sponsam Christi.

279. Vel aliter secundum Hilarium. Calceamentum portant quippe nuntiatores humanitatis Christi per mundum; quod fuit reservatum apostolis; Is. LII, 7: *quam pulchri super montes pedes annuntiantis et praedicantis pacem, annuntiantis bonum, praedicantis salutem*. Ergo Ioannes dicit se non esse dignum portare calceamentum quod apostolis erat reservatum: maius enim officium est evangelizare, quam baptizare; I Cor. I, 17: *non misit me Christus baptizare, sed evangelizare*.

One should say that John baptized in his own person, but heretics baptize in the person of Christ; hence it should be judged to be the baptism of Christ.

277. Next he treats of the kingdom. And
first he shows its dignity;
second, its office, at **he will baptize you**.

278. He says then, **he who will come after me**, in being born, baptizing, preaching, dying, descending into hell. But here he speaks of two things only, namely of preaching and baptism; hence he says, **he who will come after me** to baptize and to teach; *and he will go before him in the spirit and power of Elias* (Luke 1:17). **Is mightier than I**, and his baptism is mightier; *there is none holy as the Lord is* (1 Sam 2:2); *if strength be demanded, he is most strong* (Job 9:19). And lest someone should believe that there is a comparison between them, he says, **whose shoes I am not worthy to bear**; as though to say, *he is incomparably more deserving than I am*, as Chrysostom explains it, *such that I ought not even to show him service*.

But one should know that it is not this way in the other three Gospels, because in those places it says *to loose*, while here it says **to bear**. Hence Augustine says that John wished to show his own humility and Christ's excellence to this degree, and then the same thing is indicated in all the Gospels. Hence he says that it came about through the inspiration of the Holy Spirit that in such matters the evangelists do not harmonize in words, so that we might accept the teaching; for we do not lie if we speak with the same sense as others do, even if we do not speak with the same words. If indeed he wished to signify some mystery, then there is a difference between Matthew and the others: and two things can be signified by the lace of a shoe, because the shoes signify humanity; *into Edom will I stretch out my shoe* (Ps 59:10). The lace is the union by which humanity is bound to the divinity. And because he did not consider himself sufficient to explain the mystery of the union, he said, **whose shoes I am not worthy to bear**. Or, it was the custom among the Jews (Deut 25:9) that if someone did not wish to accept the wife of his brother, he would have his lace untied by the man who accepted the wife. The spouse of Christ is the Church. So then John considered himself unworthy to accept the spouse of Christ.

279. Or in another way, following Hilary. Obviously, those carry a shoe who announce Christ's humanity throughout the world, which was reserved for the apostles. *How beautiful upon the mountains are the feet of him that brings good tidings, and that preaches peace: of him that shows forth good, that preaches salvation* (Isa 52:7). So John says that he is not worthy to bear the shoe which was reserved for the apostles; for to preach the Gospel is a greater office than to baptize; *for Christ sent me not to baptize, but to preach the Gospel* (1 Cor 1:17).

Numquid ergo maiores apostoli Ioanne? Non merito, sed officio Novi Testamenti. Et secundum hunc sensum dicitur infra XI, 11: *qui minor est in regno caelorum, maior est illo*.

280. Vel aliter secundum Chrysostomum. Pedes sunt apostoli, et alii eius famuli, inter quos Ioannes erat. Calceamentum est infirmitas eorum: quia sicut decor pedum non cognoscitur quamdiu teguntur calceamento, ita decor apostolorum; II Cor. XII, 9: *libenter gloriabor in infirmitatibus meis, ut inhabitet in me virtus Christi. Cuius non sum dignus calceamenta portare*: quia nec ipse, nec apostoli se dignos reputant, ut sint ministri Evangelii Christi; II Cor. III, 4: *fiduciam talem habemus per Christum ad Deum: non quod sufficientes simus cogitare aliquid a nobis quasi ex nobis, sed sufficientia nostra ex Deo est*.

Si ergo diversa significat secundum mysterium, quid horum dixit Ioannes?

Dicendum, secundum Augustinum, quod si verba Ioannis ad diversa referuntur, sic utrumque dixit. Vel quod Ioannes turbis praedicans quandoque dixit illud, quandoque aliud.

281. Consequenter agit de officio Christi. Et

primo de officio baptizandi;

secundo de officio iudicandi, ibi *cuius ventilabrum in manu sua*.

282. Dicit ergo *ipse vos baptizabit in Spiritu Sancto et igni*. Multi libri habent *et ignis*. Sed loquuntur more Graecorum, qui carent ablativo. Et dicit *Spiritu Sancto et igni*: in quo datur intelligi quod baptismus Christi habet amplius quam baptismus Ioannis, quia addit super illud, quia Christus in aqua et Spiritu; Io. III, 5: *nisi quis renatus fuerit ex aqua et Spiritu Sancto, non potest introire in regnum Dei*.

Sed nota quod, cum dicit *baptizabit vos in Spiritu Sancto*, insinuat habendam esse affluentiam Spiritus Sancti, quam habentes totaliter abluuntur; Act. I, 5: *vos autem baptizabimini Spiritu Sancto*. Insinuat etiam facilem immutationem.

283. *Et igni*. Istud multipliciter exponitur. Hieronymus dicit, quod idem designatur per Spiritum Sanctum et ignem; Lc. XII, v. 49: *ignem veni mittere in terram, et quid volo nisi ut accendatur?* Idest Spiritum Sanctum. Et ideo etiam in igne apparuit; Act. II, v. 3: *et apparuerunt illis dispartitae linguae tamquam ignis*.

Secundum Chrysostomum per ignem significatur praesens tribulatio, quae purgat peccata; Eccli. XXVII, 6: *vasa figuli probat fornax, et homines iustos tentatio tribulationis*. Sed sciendum, quod dicit, istud baptisma esse necessarium, quia baptismus Spiritus Sancti continet mentem, ne vincatur a tentationibus, sed non totaliter tollit germina carnis: et ideo necessaria est tribulatio,

So were the apostles greater than John? Not by merit, but by having an office of the New Testament. And in this sense, it says below, *yet he that is the lesser in the kingdom of heaven is greater than he* (Matt 11:11).

280. Or in another way, according to Chrysostom. The feet are the apostles and others of his slaves, among whom was John. The shoe is their weakness; because as the feet's beauty is not known so long as they are covered by the shoe, so it is with the beauty of the apostles; *gladly therefore will I glory in my infirmities, that the power of Christ may dwell in me* (2 Cor 12:9). *Whose shoes I am not worthy to bear*; because neither he himself nor the apostles considered themselves worthy to be the ministers of the Gospel of Christ; *and such confidence we have, through Christ, towards God. Not that we are sufficient to think any thing of ourselves, as of ourselves: but our sufficiency is from God* (2 Cor 3:4–5).

So if the Gospels signify different things according to mystery, which of these did John say?

One should say, following Augustine, that if John's words are referred to different things, in this way he said both. Or that John, preaching to the crowds, sometimes said this thing, sometimes another.

281. Next he treats of the office of Christ. And

first, of the office of baptizing;

second, of the office of judging, at *whose fan is in his hand*.

282. He says then, *he will baptize you in the Holy Spirit and fire*. Many books have *and of fire*, but they speak in the fashion of the Greeks, who lack an ablative. And he says, *Holy Spirit and fire*, in which one is given to understand that the baptism of Christ has more than the baptism of John, because it adds something beyond it, for Christ baptizes in water and the Spirit; *amen, amen I say to you, unless a man be born again of water and the Holy Spirit, he cannot enter into the kingdom of God* (John 3:5).

But note that when he says, *he will baptize you in the Holy Spirit*, he implies that the abundance of the Holy Spirit will be had, which completely cleanses the ones who have it; *you will be baptized with the Holy Spirit* (Acts 1:5). He also implies an easy transformation.

283. *And fire*. This is explained in many ways. Jerome says that the same thing is indicated by the Holy Spirit and by fire; *I am come to cast fire on the earth; and what will I, but that it be kindled?* (Luke 12:49), i.e., the Holy Spirit. And so also he appeared in fire; *and there appeared to them parted tongues as it were of fire* (Acts 2:3).

According to Chrysostom, by fire is signified the present affliction, which purges sins; *the furnace tries the potter's vessels, and the trial of affliction just men* (Sir 27:6). But one should know that he says that this baptism is necessary, because the baptism of the Holy Spirit restrains the mind, lest it be overcome by temptation, but it does not entirely take away the buds of the flesh; and so affliction is necessary,

quia caro tunc attrita non germinabit concupiscentiam. Necessarius ergo est ignis qui reficiat carnem. Vel per ignem intelligitur purgatio futura in purgatorio; I Cor. III, 13: *quale sit opus, ignis probabit.*

Hilarius autem exponit de igne inferni, et dicit quod duo intendit in hoc quod dicit, **ipse vos baptizabit Spiritu Sancto et igni**, salutem scilicet quam efficit in praesenti et in futuro. In futuro purgabit per ignem inferni, inquantum attrahet malos; et hoc consonat ei quod sequitur, **paleas autem comburet igni inextinguibili.**

284. Consequenter agitur de iudiciaria potestate **cuius ventilabrum in manu eius**. Et primo tangitur iudiciaria potestas; secundo iudicii effectus; tertio iudicii modus.

Dicit ergo **cuius ventilabrum**, et utitur similitudine. Area dicitur Ecclesia; fruges, fideles, qui congregabuntur per angelos; Lc. c. X, 2: *rogate Dominum messis, ut mittat operarios in messem suam*; Io. IV, 34 *qui misit me ut perficiam opus eius*. Ventilabrum, iudiciaria potestas Christi, quae discernet triticum a paleis; Io. V, 22: *Pater omne iudicium dedit Filio*; Act. X, 42: *ipse est qui constitutus est a Deo iudex vivorum et mortuorum.*

285. **Permundabit**, idest perfecte mundabit. Primo per tribulationes quae sunt quasi quidam ventus, qui si non est, paleae sunt cum tritico: ita etiam quamdiu sunt in Ecclesia, non discernuntur boni a malis; et sicut per minorem ventum paleae tenues expelluntur, et per fortem grossae, ita in Ecclesia, si crescat tribulatio, etiam qui firmi videntur, cadunt; Lc. VIII, 13: *ad tempus credunt, et in tempore tentationis recedunt*. Secundo per sententias praelatorum, quando scilicet excommunicantur; I ad Cor. V, 13: *auferte malum ex vobisipsis*. Tertio in die iudicii, quando segregabuntur boni a malis; infra XXV, 32. **congregabit in horreum suum**, scilicet paradisi, **triticum**, idest electos; Ps. CV, 47: *salvos nos fac, domine Deus noster, et congrega nos de nationibus*. **Paleas autem comburet.**

286. Et nota quod differentia est inter paleas et zizania: aliud enim est semen palearum et zizaniorum, quia palearum est idem semen cum tritico. Unde per zizania possumus intelligere schismaticos, qui non communicant nobiscum in sacramentis; per paleas, fideles, licet malos. Sed utrique igni comburentur. *Igni inextinguibili*; Is. ultim., 24: *ignis eorum non extinguetur.*

Et dicit **inextinguibili**, ad differentiam ignis purgatorii. De hoc igne infra XXV, 41: **ite, maledicti, in ignem aeternum** et cetera.

because the flesh then hardened does not bud forth into concupiscence. Hence the fire which repairs the flesh is necessary. Or, by fire is understood the purgation to come in purgatory; *the fire will try every man's work, of what sort it is* (1 Cor 3:13).

However, Hilary explains this as about the fire of hell, and says that he intends two things in what he says here, **he will baptize you in the Holy Spirit and fire**, namely the salvation which he will bring about in the present and in the future. In the future he will purge by the fire of hell, insofar as he draws the evil; and this harmonizes with what follows, **but the chaff he will burn with unquenchable fire.**

284. Next, he treats of the judiciary power, **whose fan is in his hand**. And first, he touches upon the judiciary power; second, the effect of the judgment; third, the manner of the judgment.

He says then **whose fan**, and he uses a likeness. The floor is the Church; the fruits are the faithful, who will be gathered together by the angels; *pray therefore the Lord of the harvest, that he send laborers into his harvest* (Luke 10:2); *of him who sent me, that I may perfect his work* (John 4:34). The fan is Christ's judiciary power, which separates the wheat from the chaff; *for neither does the Father judge any man, but has given all judgment to the Son* (John 5:22); *it is he who was appointed by God, to be judge of the living and of the dead* (Acts 10:42).

285. **He will thoroughly cleanse**, i.e., he will cleanse perfectly. First, through the afflictions which are as it were a certain wind, without which the chaff is with the wheat. Thus also as long as they are in the Church, the good are not distinguished from the bad; and just as by a small wind the fine chaff is driven out, and by a strong wind the coarse chaff is driven out, so in the Church, if affliction increases, even those who seem strong fall; *they believe for a while, and in time of temptation, they fall away* (Luke 8:13). Second, by the decisions of prelates, namely when they excommunicate; *put away the evil one from among yourselves* (1 Cor 5:3). Third, in the day of judgment, when the good will be separated from the evil; below, **and gather his wheat** i.e., the elect, **into the barn** (Matt 3:12), i.e., paradise; *save us, O Lord, our God: and gather us from among nations* (Ps 105:47). **But the chaff he will burn.**

286. And notice that there is a difference between chaff and weeds; for the seed of chaff is one thing and the seed of weeds another, because chaff is of the same seed as wheat. Hence by weeds we can understand schismatics, who do not join with us in the sacraments; by chaff we can understand those who are faithful, although evil. But both will be burned by fire. **With unquenchable fire**; *and their fire will not be quenched* (Isa 66:24).

And he says, **unquenchable**, to distinguish it from the fire of purgatory. Concerning this fire, it says below, **depart from me, you cursed, into everlasting fire** (Matt 25:41).

Lecture 2

3:13 Tunc venit Iesus a Galilaea in Iordanem ad Ioannem, ut baptizaretur ab eo; [n. 288]

3:14 Ioannes autem prohibebat eum dicens: ego a te debeo baptizari, et tu venis ad me? [n. 292]

3:15 Respondens autem Iesus dixit ei: sine modo. Sic enim decet nos implere omnem iustitiam. Tunc dimisit eum. [n. 293]

3:16 Baptizatus autem Iesus, confestim ascendit de aqua: et ecce aperti sunt ei caeli, et vidit Spiritum Dei descendentem sicut columbam, et venientem super se. [n. 296]

3:17 Et ecce vox de caelo dicens: hic est Filius meus dilectus, in quo mihi conplacui. [n. 302]

3:13 Τότε παραγίνεται ὁ Ἰησοῦς ἀπὸ τῆς Γαλιλαίας ἐπὶ τὸν Ἰορδάνην πρὸς τὸν Ἰωάννην τοῦ βαπτισθῆναι ὑπ᾽ αὐτοῦ.

3:14 ὁ δὲ Ἰωάννης διεκώλυεν αὐτὸν λέγων· ἐγὼ χρείαν ἔχω ὑπὸ σοῦ βαπτισθῆναι, καὶ σὺ ἔρχῃ πρός με;

3:15 ἀποκριθεὶς δὲ ὁ Ἰησοῦς εἶπεν πρὸς αὐτόν· ἄφες ἄρτι, οὕτως γὰρ πρέπον ἐστὶν ἡμῖν πληρῶσαι πᾶσαν δικαιοσύνην. τότε ἀφίησιν αὐτόν.

3:16 βαπτισθεὶς δὲ ὁ Ἰησοῦς εὐθὺς ἀνέβη ἀπὸ τοῦ ὕδατος· καὶ ἰδοὺ ἠνεῴχθησαν [αὐτῷ] οἱ οὐρανοί, καὶ εἶδεν [τὸ] πνεῦμα [τοῦ] θεοῦ καταβαῖνον ὡσεὶ περιστερὰν [καὶ] ἐρχόμενον ἐπ᾽ αὐτόν·

3:17 καὶ ἰδοὺ φωνὴ ἐκ τῶν οὐρανῶν λέγουσα· οὗτός ἐστιν ὁ υἱός μου ὁ ἀγαπητός, ἐν ᾧ εὐδόκησα.

3:13 Then Jesus came from Galilee to the Jordan, unto John, to be baptized by him. [n. 288]

3:14 But John prevented him, saying: I ought to be baptized by you, and you come to me? [n. 292]

3:15 And Jesus answering, said to him: suffer it to be so now. For so it becomes us to fulfill all justice. Then he allowed him. [n. 293]

3:16 And Jesus being baptized, immediately came out of the water: and behold, the heavens were opened to him: and he saw the Spirit of God descending as a dove, and coming upon him. [n. 296]

3:17 And behold a voice from heaven, saying: this is my beloved Son, in whom I am well pleased. [n. 302]

---

287. Supra introduxit Evangelista Ioannem baptizantem, nunc introducit Christum ad baptismum Ioannis venientem:

et circa hoc duo facit.

Primo ponit ea quae praecesserunt baptismum;

secundo consequentia ad baptismum, ibi **baptizatus autem Iesus**.

Circa primum ponuntur quatuor.

Primo mira Christi humilitas;

secundo humilitatis admiratio;

tertio Christi satisfactio admirationi;

quarto Ioannes satisfactioni consentit.

Secundum ibi **Ioannes autem prohibebat eum**; tertium ibi **respondens autem Iesus**; quartum ibi **tunc dimisit eum**.

Circa primum quatuor ponuntur: tempus, personae, loca et officium.

288. Tempus, cum dicit **tunc**, scilicet Ioanne lumen suum habente. Sicut enim sol oritur adhuc apparente lucifero, ita Christus Ioanne praedicante et baptizante, Lc. III, 21. Iob XXXVIII, 32: *numquid producis Luciferum in tempore suo, et vesperum super fines terrae consurgere facis?* Vel **tunc** quando Christus fuit in trigesimo anno, Lc. III, 23, ut daret intelligi quod officium praedicationis, et praelationis non debet aliquis sumere ante perfectam aetatem. Vel **tunc** quando secundum cursum aliorum multa peccata poterat perpetrasse. Unde noluit statim baptizari, sed multo tempore legem servavit,

287. Above, the Evangelist introduced John the Baptist; now he introduces Christ, coming to the baptism of John.

And concerning this, he does two things:

first, he sets down those things preceding the baptism;

second, those things following the baptism, at **and Jesus, being baptized**.

Concerning the first, he sets down four things:

first, the marvelous humility of Christ;

second, the astonishment at this humility;

third, Christ's satisfaction of this astonishment;

fourth, John agrees to the satisfaction.

The second is at **but John prevented him**; the third at **and Jesus, answering**; the fourth at **then he allowed him**.

Concerning the first, he sets down four things: the time, the people, the place, and the office.

288. The time, when he says, **then**, namely when John had his own light. For as the sun shines while the morning star is still visible, so Christ comes while John is preaching and baptizing (Luke 3:21). *Can you bring forth the day star in its time, and make the evening star to rise upon the children of the earth?* (Job 38:32). Or, **then**, when Christ was in his thirtieth year (Luke 3:23), that one may be given to understand that one ought not to take up the office of preaching and of leadership before the perfect age. Or, **then**, when, if he had followed the course of life which others do, he could have committed many sins. Hence he did not wish to

quasi constitutus sub lege, et ut Iudaei non haberent causam scandali, quia non venit solvere legem, infra V, 17. Sed posset alicui videri, quod ideo Christus terminasset legem, quia non potuisset legem implere; et ideo voluit diu observare; et ideo non ita cito baptizatus est.

289. Ponuntur personae, cum dicitur **venit Iesus ad Ioannem**, Dominus ad servum, Creator ad creaturam; infra XI, 29: **discite a me, quia mitis sum et humilis corde.**

290. Loca **a Galilaea.** Ista mystice conveniunt baptizatis, quia Galilaea significat 'transmigrationem': oportet enim baptizatos transmigrare de vitiis ad virtutes; I Petr. II, v. 1: *deponentes omnem malitiam, et omnem dolum, et simulationes, et invidias, et omnes detractiones.*

Item, **in Iordanem.** Iordanis interpretatur 'descensus', et significat humilitatem, quae debet esse in baptizando ad gratiam percipiendam; Iacob. IV, 6: *humilibus autem dat gratiam.*

291. Ponitur officium **ut baptizaretur.** Deus voluit baptizari a Ioanne quatuor rationibus. Primo ut baptismum Ioannis conservaretur, quia illi aliqui detrahebant, infra XXI, v. 24. Secundo, ut suo tactu totam consecraret aquam; et ideo baptismus dicitur fieri de fontibus Salvatoris; Is. XII, 3: *haurietis aquas in gaudio de fontibus salvatoris.* Tertio, ut demonstraret in se veram conditionem hominis, quia sicut fuit in similitudinem carnis peccati, Rom. VIII, 3, ita voluit mundari quasi peccator. Quarto, ut aliis imponeret necessitatem baptizandi: prius enim voluit servare quae imposuit; Act. I, 1: *coepit Iesus facere et docere*, contra illos de quibus infra XXIII, 4: **alligant onera gravia et importabilia, et imponunt in humeros hominum: digito autem suo nolunt ea tangere.**

292. Consequenter ponitur admiratio.

Et nota tria. Primo enim Ioannes recusat honorem sibi oblatum; secundo confitetur suam humilitatem; tertio suam infirmitatem. Secundum ibi **Ioannes autem prohibebat eum**; Eccli. VII, 4: *noli quaerere ab homine ducatum, neque a rege cathedram honoris.* Tertium ibi **ego a te debeo baptizari.**

Cognoscebat enim quod interius baptizaret; et ideo dicit **baptizari** idest ab originali peccato mundari: ita dicit Glossa.

Sed contra, quia erat sanctificatus in utero. Sed dicendum quod ante adventum Christi aliqui quodammodo mundati sunt quantum ad infectionem personae per circumcisionem, et huiusmodi; sed quantum ad culpam et infectionem totius naturae nullus mundatus fuit ante passionem Christi.

be baptized at once, but observed the law for a long time, as though constituted under the law, and so that the Jews would not have a cause for scandal; for he did not come to destroy the law (Matt 5:17). But it could seem to someone that Christ had ended the law, because he had not been able to fulfill the law, and so he willed to observe it for a long time; and this is why he was not baptized so quickly.

289. The persons are set down when he says, **then Jesus came . . . unto John**, the Lord to the servant, the Creator to the creature; below, **learn from me, because I am meek, and humble of heart** (Matt 11:29).

290. The place, **from Galilee.** This fits mystically with having been baptized, because Galilee signifies 'transmigration': for it is necessary that those who are baptized transmigrate from vices to virtues; *wherefore laying away all malice, and all guile, and dissimulations, and envies, and all detractions* (1 Pet 2:1).

Likewise, **to the Jordan.** The Jordan is interpreted as 'descent', and signifies humility, which the baptized should have in order to obtain grace. *And gives grace to the humble* (Jas 4:6).

291. The office is set down at **to be baptized.** God willed to be baptized by John for four reasons. First, so that the baptism of John might be preserved, since there were other men detracting from it (Matt 21:24). Second, so that by his touch he might consecrate all the water; and this is why baptism is said to be carried from the fount of the Savior; *you will draw waters with joy out of the savior's fountains* (Isa 12:3). Third, that he might point out that he bore the true condition of a man in himself, because as he was made in the likeness of the body of sin (Rom 8:3), so he wished to be cleansed as though a sinner. Fourth, so that he might impose upon others the necessity of baptizing; for he wished first to observe what he imposed; *Jesus began to do and to teach* (Acts 1:1), contrary to those of whom it is said below, **for they bind heavy and insupportable burdens, and lay them on men's shoulders; but with a finger of their own they will not move them** (Matt 23:4).

292. Next is set down the astonishment.

And note three things: first, John refused the honor offered to him; second, he confessed his own humility; third, his own weakness. The second is at **but John prevented him**; *seek not of the Lord a pre-eminence, nor of the king the seat of honor* (Sir 7:4). The third is at **I ought to be baptized by you.**

For he knew that he would baptize interiorly; and this is why he says, **to be baptized**, i.e., to be cleansed from original sin. So says the Gloss.

But against this is the fact that he was sanctified in the womb. But one should say that before Christ's coming some were in a certain way cleansed, as regards personal infection, through circumcision and suchlike; but as regards the guilt and infection of the whole nature no one was cleansed before the passion of Christ.

Et tu venis ad me? Ps. CXXXVIII, 6: *mirabilis facta est scientia tua ex me, confortata est, et non potero ad eam.*

293. Consequenter ponitur Christi satisfactio. Nota quod Ioannes unum fecerat, quia *prohibebat*; et duo dixerat: *ego a te debeo baptizari, et tu venis ad me?* Et tamen Christus ad unum non respondit, ad hoc scilicet *ego a te*; sed respondit ad hoc quod prohibebat: unde *sine modo*.

Et dicit *modo*, quia, secundum Chrysostomum, Ioannes postmodum baptizatus est a Christo, non solum baptismo flaminis, sed etiam aquae. Vel *sine modo*, hoc dicit, quia postmodum baptizatus est Ioannes baptismo Spiritus Sancti. Vel *sine modo*, ut baptizer baptismo aquae, quia alio baptismo habeo baptizari, scilicet baptismo passionis; Lc. XII, v. 50: *baptismo habeo baptizari, et quomodo coarctor usque dum perficiatur?* Et isto etiam Ioannes baptizatus est a Christo, inquantum mortuus est pro iustitia, quod idem est quod mori pro Christo. Vel *sine modo*, quando gero formam servilem, implere me humilitatis officium: quia quando apparebo gloriosus, tunc baptizabo te baptismo gloriae.

294. Consequenter respondet Christus admirationi, et dicit *sic enim decet nos implere omnem iustitiam.* Quod exponitur tripliciter. Primo *sic decet nos implere omnem iustitiam*, scilicet per baptismum: futurum enim erat, quod Christus impleret omnem iustitiam, et legis, et naturae; sed voluit per istam viam implere, quia sine baptismo non impletur; Io. III, 3: *nisi quis natus fuerit denuo, non potest videre regnum Dei* et cetera.

Remigius sic exponit: *sic enim decet nos implere omnem iustitiam.* Decet me dare exemplum huius sacramenti, in quo datur plenitudo omnis iustitiae, quia datur plenitudo gratiae et aliarum virtutum; Ps. LXIV, 10: *flumen Dei repletum est aquis*, scilicet gratiarum.

Vel sic: *sic enim decet* etc., idest, decet me habere perfectam humilitatem. Primus gradus est non praeferre se pari, et subiicere se maiori, quod quidem est necessitatis. Secundum cum subiicit se aequali. Perfecta autem, quando praelatus se subiicit inferiori: et hoc est *sic enim decet* etc., idest perfectam humilitatem implere.

295. Sed cum esset inter eos talis altercatio, Christus vicit. Unde *tunc dimisit eum* etc., hoc est permisit ut ab eo baptizaretur. Glossa: vera est humilitas quam non deserit obedientia: pertinaciter enim resistere, superbiae est. I Reg. XV, 23: *quasi scelus idololatriae nolle*

And you come to me? Your knowledge is become wonderful to me: it is high, and I cannot reach it (Ps 138:6).

293. Next, Christ's satisfaction is set down. Notice that John had done one thing, because he **prevented him**; and he had said two things: **I ought to be baptized by you, and you come to me?** And yet Christ did not respond to the first of those, namely to **I ought to be baptized by you**, but rather he responded to the fact that he prevented him; hence, **suffer it to be so now**.

And he says, **now**, because, according to Chrysostom, John was baptized by Christ afterwards, not only with the baptism of wind, but also of water. Or **now**, he says, because afterwards John was baptized with the baptism of the Holy Spirit. Or **now**, so that I may be baptized with the baptism of water, because I have to be baptized with another baptism, namely the baptism of the passion; *and I have a baptism wherewith I am to be baptized: and how am I straitened until it be accomplished?* (Luke 12:50). And John also was baptized by Christ with this baptism, insofar as he died for justice, which is the same as to die for Christ. Or, **now**, while I bear the form of a slave, fulfill in me the office of humility; because when I will appear in glory, then I will baptize you with the baptism of glory.

294. Next, Christ responds to this astonishment, and says, **for so it becomes us to fulfill all justice**, which can be explained in three ways. First, **so it becomes us to fulfill all justice**, namely by baptism; for it was going to happen that Christ would fulfill all justice, both of law and of nature; but he wished to fulfill all justice by this path, because without baptism justice is not fulfilled; *amen, amen I say to thee, unless a man be born again, he cannot see the kingdom of God* (John 3:3).

Remigius explains it this way: **for so it becometh us to fulfill all justice**. It becomes me to give an example of this sacrament, in which the plenitude of all justice is given, because the plenitude of grace and of the other virtues is given in this sacrament; *the river of God is filled with water* (Ps 64:10), that is, with grace.

Or in this way: **for so it becomes us**, that is, it becomes me to have perfect humility. The first step of humility is not to put oneself above one's equal, and to subject oneself to one's superior, which indeed is necessary. The second step is when one subjects oneself to one's equal. But perfect humility is when the one who is superior subjects himself to his inferior; and this is **for so it becomes us**, that is, to fulfill perfect humility.

295. But although there was a dispute between them, Christ won. Hence, **then he allowed him**, that is, John permitted that he should be baptized by him. The Gloss: that humility is true which does not lack obedience; for stubbornly to resist is arrogance. *It is . . . like the crime of*

acquiescere: sic enim laudantur Ieremias et Moyses qui finaliter consenserunt.

296. Consequenter cum dicit *baptizatus autem Iesus confestim ascendit de aqua*, ponuntur quatuor consequentia ad Baptismum. Et sciendum, quod sicut Christus in suo Baptismo dedit exemplum baptizandi aliis, ita in consequentibus Baptismum dedit intelligere quae nos consequamur. Sunt autem quatuor consequentia, scilicet ascensus Christi, aperitio caeli, apparitio Spiritus Sancti, et protestatio Patris.

297. Primum ibi *baptizatus autem Iesus confestim ascendit de aqua*. Et ad litteram hoc dicit, quia fluvius habebat alveos altos. In hoc tamen significatur, quod illi qui baptizantur ascendunt per bona opera. Et dicit *statim*, quia immediate baptizati in Christo induunt Christum; Gal. III, 27: *quicumque enim in Christo baptizati estis, Christum induistis*. Item adipiscuntur haereditatem caelestem; I Petr. I, 3: *regeneravit nos in spem vivam per resurrectionem in haereditatem incorruptibilem*: et hoc est *et aperti sunt caeli*. Hoc non est intelligendum corporaliter, sed imaginaria visione.

298. *Et aperti sunt ei caeli*. Et significat hoc quod humano generi clausum erat caelum per peccatum; Gen. III, 24: *et collocavit ante paradisum voluptatis Cherubim, et flammeum gladium atque versatilem ad custodiendam viam ligni vitae*. Dicitur quod posuit Seraphim, sed apertum est per Christum.

Sed quaeritur, quare aperti sunt ei caeli, cum semper fuerint ei aperti?

Et dicendum, secundum Chrysostomum, quod Evangelista loquitur secundum communem modum locutionis, quia merito baptismi eius aperti sunt nobis: sicut rex amico suo petenti pro alio gratiam, dicit: concedo hoc vobis.

Et sciendum quod tria sunt hominum genera, qui statim ad caelum evolant post mortem: baptizati, ut hic; martyres, unde Act. c. VII, 56: *ecce video caelos apertos, et Filium hominis stantem a dextris virtutis Dei*, et qui peregerunt poenitentiam, Act. X, 19 dicitur quod Petro oranti apertum est caelum.

299. Consequenter ponitur apparitio Spiritus Sancti; unde *et vidit Spiritum Dei descendentem sicut columbam, et venientem super se*. Hoc est quod competit baptizatis, qui accipiunt Spiritum Sanctum in se; Io. III, v. 6: *quod natum est ex Spiritu, spiritus est*, idest spiritualis est. *Et vidit*, non imaginaria visione, alias ipse solus vidisset, *spiritum Dei*, idest columbam.

Et sciendum, quod nihil corporale dicitur de Deo secundum substantiam suam, sed vel per imaginariam

idolatry, to refuse to obey (1 Sam 15:23), for thus Jeremiah and Moses are praised, who finally consented.

296. Next, when he says, *and Jesus being baptized, immediately came out of the water*, he sets down four things following upon the baptism. And one should know that just as Christ in his baptism gave an example of baptizing others, so in the things which followed he let it be understood that we should pursue baptism. Now, there are four things which follow, namely Christ's coming out, the opening of heaven, the appearance of the Holy Spirit, and the testimony of the Father.

297. The first is at *and Jesus being baptized, immediately came out of the water*. And, literally, he says this because the river had deep hollows. Yet by this is signified that those who are baptized ascend through good works. And he says *immediately* because those baptized in Christ immediately put on Christ; *for as many of you as have been baptized in Christ, have put on Christ* (Gal 3:27). Likewise, they gain a heavenly inheritance; *who according to his great mercy has regenerated us unto a lively hope, by the resurrection of Jesus Christ from the dead, unto an inheritance incorruptible* (1 Pet 1:3–4); and this is *and behold, the heavens were opened*. This is not to be understood in a bodily way, but as a vision of the imagination.

298. *And behold, the heavens were opened*. And this signifies that heaven was closed to the human race by sin; *he cast out Adam; and placed before the paradise of pleasure Cherubims, and a flaming sword, turning every way, to keep the way of the tree of life* (Gen 3:24). It says that he placed a Seraphim, but it was opened by Christ.

But it is asked, why were the heavens opened, since they were always open to him?

And one should say, according to Chrysostom, that the Evangelist speaks according to the common manner of speech, because by the merit of his baptism the heavens were opened to us; just as a king says to a friend who begs a favor on behalf of another, I grant this to you.

And one should know that there three kinds of men who fly up to heaven immediately after death: the baptized, as here; martyrs, *behold, I see the heavens opened, and the Son of man standing on the right hand of God* (Acts 7:55); and those who carry through with penitence to the end; it is said that the heaven was opened to Peter while he prayed (Acts 10:19).

299. Next, the appearance of the Holy Spirit is set down; hence, *and he saw the Spirit of God descending as a dove, and coming upon him*. This is what belongs to the baptized, who receives the Holy Spirit into himself; *that which is born of the Spirit, is spirit* (John 3:6), i.e., is spiritual. *And he saw*, not by a vision of the imagination, otherwise only he would have seen it, *the Spirit of God*, i.e., the dove.

And one should know that nothing bodily is said of God according to his own substance, but either by a vision

visionem, Is. VI, 1: *vidi Dominum sedentem super solium excelsum et elevatum* etc., vel per significationem, I cor c. X, 4: *petra autem erat Christus*, vel per assumptionem in unitatem personae, Io. I, 14: *Verbum caro factum est.* Nullo autem istorum modorum Spiritus Sanctus dicitur columba. Quod non per imaginariam visionem, patet, quia communiter ab omnibus visa est. Non per significationem, quia non primo extiterat. Non per assumptionem in unitatem personae. Et ideo est quartus modus, qui est quando de novo formatur aliqua species ad repraesentationem divinorum effectuum, sicut in Ex. III, 2 apparuit Dominus in igne et rubo; et in legislatione, in fulgure et in tonitruo, Ex. XIX, 16. Unde columba fuit ad repraesentandam influentiam Spiritus Sancti: et hoc est *et vidit Spiritum Dei descendentem.*

300. Apparuit autem in specie columbae propter quatuor. Primo propter caritatem; columba enim est animal amorosum. Chrysostomus: *alia dona habet etiam servus diaboli in simulatione, quae habet servus Dei in veritate: solam caritatem Sancti Spiritus non potest immundus spiritus imitari.* Cant. V, 2: *aperi mihi, soror mea, amica mea, columba mea, immaculata mea.* Secundo propter innocentiam et simplicitatem; infra X, 16: *estote prudentes sicut serpentes, et simplices sicut columbae.* Tertio quia habet gemitum pro cantu; et homo sanctificatus per Spiritum Sanctum debet gemere pro peccatis; Nahum II, 7: *et ancillae eius minabantur, gementes ut columbae.* Quarto propter foecunditatem. Unde etiam praecipiebatur in lege, ut offerrent columbam: et hoc convenit baptizatis, quia, sicut dicit Io. III, 6: *quod natum est ex Spiritu, spiritus est.*

Descendentem sicut columbam. Semper emanatio donorum divinorum a Deo in quacumque creatura est per descensum, quia creatura non potest recipere nisi per descensum in illam; Iac. I, 17: *omne datum optimum, et omne donum perfectum desursum est, descendens a Patre luminum.*

301. *Et venientem super se.* Nota. Missio visibilis semper est signum missionis invisibilis: et significat aut gratiam de novo acceptam, aut augmentum gratiae: sicut in apostolis, quando in linguis apparuit Spiritus Sanctus, significavit augmentum gratiae. Item missio talis vel significat gratiam tunc factam, aut prius factam. In Christo autem non significavit novum effectum, quia ab instanti conceptionis suae fuit plenus gratia et veritate; sed gratia quae fuit ante super se, fuit inquantum homo, non inquantum Deus.

302. Consequenter cum dicit *et ecce vox de caelo dicens*, ponitur protestatio Patris *hic est Filius meus.*

Nota quod baptismus non solum facit spirituales, sed etiam filios Dei; Io. I, 12: *dedit eis potestatem filios Dei fieri.*

of the imagination, *I saw the Lord sitting upon a throne high and elevated* (Isa 6:1), or by signification, *and the rock was Christ* (1 Cor 10:4), or by assumption into the unity of person, *the Word was made flesh* (John 1:14). But the Holy Spirit is called a dove in none of those ways. That it was not by a vision of the imagination is clear, because the vision was seen commonly by all. It was not by signification, because he had not been visible at first. It was not by an assumption into the unity of person. And therefore it was in a fourth way, which is when some appearance is newly formed for the representation of divine effects, as when the Lord appeared in fire and bramble (Exod 3:2); and in legislation, in lightnings, and thunder (Exod 19:16). Hence the dove was to represent the inflowing of the Holy Spirit; and this is *and he saw the Spirit of God descending.*

300. Moreover, he appeared in the form of a dove for four reasons. First, owing to its charity; for the dove is an amorous animal. Chrysostom: *the servant of the devil also has in pretense all the other gifts which the servant of God has in truth; only the love of the Holy Spirit the unclean spirit cannot imitate.* As: *open to me, my sister, my love, my dove, my undefiled* (Song 5:2). Second, owing to its innocence and simplicity; below, *be therefore wise as serpents and simple as doves* (Matt 10:16). Third, because the dove has a groan for a song; and the man sanctified by the Holy Spirit should groan because of sins; *her bondwomen were led away mourning as doves, murmuring in their hearts* (Nah 2:7). Fourth, owing to its fertility. Hence also it was commanded in the law that they offer a dove; and this pertains to the baptized, because *that which is born of the Spirit, is spirit* (John 3:6).

Descending as a dove. The flowing out of divine gifts from God into any creature whatsoever is always through a descent; because the creature cannot receive them except through a descent into that creature; *every best gift, and every perfect gift, is from above, coming down from the Father of lights* (Jas 1:17).

301. *And coming upon him.* Note: a visible sending is always the sign of an invisible sending, and it signifies either a newly received grace or the increase of grace; just as in the apostles, when the Holy Spirit appeared in tongues, it signified the increase of grace. Likewise, such a sending signifies either a grace then made, or a grace made before. Now, in Christ it did not signify a new effect, because he was full of grace and truth from the moment of his conception; but rather the grace which was upon him before was insofar as he was man, not insofar as he was God.

302. Next, when he says, *and behold a voice from heaven, saying*, the testimony of the Father is set down: *this is my beloved Son.*

Note that baptism not only makes men spiritual, but even makes them sons of God; *he gave them power to be made the sons of God* (John 1:12).

Et sciendum quod ista vox quasi exprimit illud, quod columba significavit. **Dilectus**, non sicut aliae creaturae, Sap. II, 13, sed tamquam Filius naturalis; Io. V, 20: *Pater diligit Filium, et omnia demonstrat ei quae ipse facit, et maiora his demonstrabit ei opera, ut vos miremini.* Hoc etiam significat Ps. II, 7: *Dominus dixit ad me: Filius meus es tu, ego hodie genui te.*

Sed quia sancti etiam diliguntur ab eo, addit **Filius**, per quod distinguit Filium, secundum unum intellectum, ab aliis. **In quo mihi complacui.** In quocumque enim relucet bonum alicuius, in illo aliquid complacet sibimet, sicut artifex sibi complacet in pulchro artificio suo, et sicut si homo videat suam pulchram imaginem in speculo. Bonitas divina est in qualibet creatura particulari; sed numquam tota perfecta nisi in Filio et Spiritu Sancto; et ideo totum non complacet sibi nisi in Filio, qui tantum habet de bonitate quantum Pater: et hoc est **in quo**, idest, ego complaceo mihi in ipso; Io. III, 35: *Pater diligit Filium, et omnia dedit in manu eius.*

303. Sed nota quod contrarietas quaedam videtur esse inter istum Evangelistam, et alios, quia Marcus I, 11 et Lucas III, 22 dicunt, *tu es Filius meus dilectus*; Matthaeus vero, **est Filius meus dilectus**, et: *in te.* Sed eadem est sententia, quia quod dicitur *tu es*, hoc directe videbatur dici ad Christum; sed dicebat propter alios, quia Christus certus erat de dilectione Patris. Et ideo Matthaeus expressit intentionem dicentis, et dicit **hic est** et cetera. Unde demonstrat quasi aliis dictum esse; ita dixit Augustinus.

304. Item quaeritur, quare Matthaeus et Marcus dicunt **in quo mihi**, Lucas vero, *in te.* Augustinus dicit quod Pater in Filio complacet sibi, et hominibus. Propter hoc ergo quod dicitur **in quo**, significat quod complaceat sibi in hominibus. Unde complaceat aliis mihi, idest ad honorem meum, quia aliqui videntes Filium, glorificaverunt Patrem. Vel secundum utrumque sensum: **in quo mihi complacui**, idest placitum meum fuit implere salutem hominum: et hoc est in te, idest per te.

305. Et nota quod in isto baptismo non solum repraesentatur finis et fructus, sed etiam forma baptismi, quae est, **in nomine Patris, et Filii, et Spiritus Sancti**, infra. Filius enim fuit in carne, Pater in voce, Spiritus Sanctus in columbae specie.

Et nota quod hoc quod seorsum fuit, non pertinet ad divisionem operationis personae de Trinitate, cum, sicut est communis essentia, ita operatio; sed hoc dicitur propter appropriationem quamdam, quia tota Trinitas illud et columbam creavit, et carnem creavit; sed referuntur ista ad diversas personas.

And one should know that this voice expressed, as it were, that which the dove signified. **Beloved**, not like other creatures (Wis 2:13), but as a natural Son; *for the Father loves the Son, and shows him all things which he himself does: and greater works than these will he show him, that you may wonder* (John 5:20). A Psalm also indicates this: *the Lord has said to me: you are my Son, this day have I begotten you* (John 5:20).

But since the saints are also loved by him, he adds **Son**, by which he distinguishes the Son, according to one understanding, from others. **In whom I am well pleased.** For in whatever someone's goodness shines out, something in it pleases him, just as a builder pleases himself by his own beautiful work of art, and just as when a man sees his own beautiful image in a mirror. The divine goodness is in each particular creature, but the perfect whole is never present except in the Son and the Holy Spirit; and therefore the whole does not please him except in the Son, who has just as much goodness as the Father; and this is **in whom**, i.e., I please myself well in him; *the Father loves the Son: and he has given all things into his hand* (John 3:35).

303. But note that there seems to be a certain contrariety between this Evangelist and the others, because Mark and Luke say, *you are my beloved Son* (Mark 1:11: Luke 3:22); but Matthew, **this is my beloved Son**, and they say, *in you*. But the thought is the same, because when it says, *you are*, this seems to be said directly to Christ; but he spoke for the sake of the others, because Christ was certain of the Father's love. And so Matthew expresses the intention of the one speaking, and says, **this is**. Hence he represents it as though said to the others; so Augustine said.

304. Similarly, it is asked why Matthew and Mark say, **in whom**, but Luke says, *in you*. Augustine says that in the Son the Father pleases both himself and men. So because of this, **in whom** indicates that he pleases himself in men. Hence let him please others for me, i.e., to my honor, because those seeing the Son have glorified the Father. Or according to either sense: **in whom I am well pleased**, i.e., it pleased me to complete the salvation of men; and this is in you i.e., through you.

305. And note that in this baptism not only the end and fruit is represented, but also the form of baptism, which is **in the name of the Father, and of the Son, and of the Holy Spirit** (Matt 28:19). For the Son was there in the flesh, the Father in the voice, and the Holy Spirit in the form of a dove.

And note that the fact that these manifestations were formed separately does not regard the division of one person's operation from the rest of the Trinity, since, as the essence is common, so is the operation; but this is said because of a certain appropriation, for the whole Trinity both created the dove and the flesh; but these things are referred back to different persons.

CHAPTER 4

Lecture 1

⁴:¹ Tunc Iesus ductus est in desertum a Spiritu, ut tentaretur a diabolo: [n. 307]

⁴:² et cum ieiunasset quadraginta diebus et quadraginta noctibus, postea esuriit. [n. 312]

⁴:³ Et accedens tentator dixit ei: si Filius Dei es, dic ut lapides isti panes fiant. [n. 316]

⁴:⁴ Qui respondens dixit: scriptum est: *non in solo pane vivet homo, sed in omni verbo quod procedit de ore Dei.* [n. 319]

⁴:⁵ Tunc assumpsit eum diabolus in sanctam civitatem, et statuit eum supra pinnaculum templi, [n. 321]

⁴:⁶ et dixit ei: si Filius Dei es, mitte te deorsum; scriptum est enim: *quia angelis suis mandavit de te, et in manibus tollent te, ne forte offendas ad lapidem pedem tuum.* [n. 329]

⁴:⁷ Ait illi Iesus rursum: scriptum est: *non tentabis Dominum Deum tuum.* [n. 333]

⁴:⁸ Iterum assumpsit eum diabolus in montem excelsum valde, et ostendit ei omnia regna mundi, et gloriam eorum, [n. 334]

⁴:⁹ et dixit ei: haec tibi omnia dabo, si cadens adoraveris me. [n. 338]

⁴:¹⁰ Tunc dixit ei Iesus: vade, satana; scriptum est enim: *Dominum Deum tuum adorabis, et illi soli serviens.* [n. 340]

⁴:¹¹ Tunc reliquit eum diabolus; et ecce angeli accesserunt, et ministrabant ei. [n. 345]

⁴:¹ Τότε ὁ Ἰησοῦς ἀνήχθη εἰς τὴν ἔρημον ὑπὸ τοῦ πνεύματος πειρασθῆναι ὑπὸ τοῦ διαβόλου.

⁴:² καὶ νηστεύσας ἡμέρας τεσσεράκοντα καὶ νύκτας τεσσεράκοντα, ὕστερον ἐπείνασεν.

⁴:³ καὶ προσελθὼν ὁ πειράζων εἶπεν αὐτῷ· εἰ υἱὸς εἶ τοῦ θεοῦ, εἰπὲ ἵνα οἱ λίθοι οὗτοι ἄρτοι γένωνται.

⁴:⁴ ὁ δὲ ἀποκριθεὶς εἶπεν· γέγραπται· οὐκ ἐπ᾽ ἄρτῳ μόνῳ ζήσεται ὁ ἄνθρωπος, ἀλλ᾽ ἐπὶ παντὶ ῥήματι ἐκπορευομένῳ διὰ στόματος θεοῦ.

⁴:⁵ Τότε παραλαμβάνει αὐτὸν ὁ διάβολος εἰς τὴν ἁγίαν πόλιν καὶ ἔστησεν αὐτὸν ἐπὶ τὸ πτερύγιον τοῦ ἱεροῦ

⁴:⁶ καὶ λέγει αὐτῷ· εἰ υἱὸς εἶ τοῦ θεοῦ, βάλε σεαυτὸν κάτω· γέγραπται γὰρ ὅτι τοῖς ἀγγέλοις αὐτοῦ ἐντελεῖται περὶ σοῦ καὶ ἐπὶ χειρῶν ἀροῦσίν σε, μήποτε προσκόψῃς πρὸς λίθον τὸν πόδα σου.

⁴:⁷ ἔφη αὐτῷ ὁ Ἰησοῦς· πάλιν γέγραπται· οὐκ ἐκπειράσεις κύριον τὸν θεόν σου.

⁴:⁸ Πάλιν παραλαμβάνει αὐτὸν ὁ διάβολος εἰς ὄρος ὑψηλὸν λίαν καὶ δείκνυσιν αὐτῷ πάσας τὰς βασιλείας τοῦ κόσμου καὶ τὴν δόξαν αὐτῶν

⁴:⁹ καὶ εἶπεν αὐτῷ· ταῦτά σοι πάντα δώσω, ἐὰν πεσὼν προσκυνήσῃς μοι.

⁴:¹⁰ τότε λέγει αὐτῷ ὁ Ἰησοῦς· ὕπαγε, σατανᾶ· γέγραπται γάρ· κύριον τὸν θεόν σου προσκυνήσεις καὶ αὐτῷ μόνῳ λατρεύσεις.

⁴:¹¹ Τότε ἀφίησιν αὐτὸν ὁ διάβολος, καὶ ἰδοὺ ἄγγελοι προσῆλθον καὶ διηκόνουν αὐτῷ.

⁴:¹ Then Jesus was led by the Spirit into the desert, to be tempted by the devil. [n. 307]

⁴:² And when he had fasted forty days and forty nights, afterwards he was hungry. [n. 312]

⁴:³ And the tempter coming said to him: if you are the Son of God, command that these stones become bread. [n. 316]

⁴:⁴ Who answered and said: it is written, *not in bread alone does man live, but in every word that proceeds from the mouth of God.* [n. 319]

⁴:⁵ Then the devil took him up into the holy city, and set him upon the pinnacle of the temple, [n. 321]

⁴:⁶ and said to him: if you are the Son of God, cast yourself down, for it is written: *that he has given his angels charge over you, and in their hands will they bear you up, lest perhaps you offend your foot against a stone.* [n. 329]

⁴:⁷ Jesus said to him: it is written again: *you shall not tempt the Lord your God.* [n. 333]

⁴:⁸ Again the devil took him up onto a very high mountain, and showed him all the kingdoms of the world, and the glory of them, [n. 334]

⁴:⁹ and said to him: all these will I give you, if falling down you will adore me. [n. 338]

⁴:¹⁰ Then Jesus said to him: begone, satan: for it is written, *the Lord your God shall you adore, and him only shall you serve.* [n. 340]

⁴:¹¹ Then the devil left him; and behold angels came and ministered to him. [n. 345]

306. Supra ostensum est, quod Christus se praeparavit ad doctrinam, baptismum accipiendo; nunc autem tentationem superando.

Circa hoc duo facit:

primo ponitur victoria, quam de tentatione habuit;

secundo, quomodo discipulos ad doctrinam audiendam vocavit, ibi *ambulans autem Iesus iuxta Mare Galilaeae*.

Circa primum tria facit:

primo praemittit quaedam praeambula de tentatione;

secundo ponitur tentationis insultus, ibi *et accedens tentator dixit*;

tertio victoria, ibi *tunc reliquit eum diabolus*.

Ponuntur autem tria praeambula, scilicet locus, ieiunium et famis experientia.

Quantum ad primum quatuor tanguntur: tempus et locus, ductor et finis huius ducatus.

307. Tempus *tunc*, quando scilicet iam declarabatur voce paterna quod esset Filius Dei. In quo dat intelligi, quia illis tentatio imminet, qui efficiuntur filii Dei per baptismum; Eccli. II, 1: *Fili, accedens ad servitutem Dei sta in iustitia et timore, et praepara animam tuam ad tentationem*.

Istud desertum erat inter Ierusalem et Iericho, ubi multi occidebantur, de quo Lc. X, v. 30: *homo quidam descendit ab Ierusalem in Iericho, et incidit in latrones, qui etiam despoliaverunt eum, et plagis impositis abierunt, semivivo relicto*.

308. Et nota quinque rationes, quare quis post acceptam spiritualem gratiam tentatur. Prima ut accipiat experimentum suae iustitiae; Eccli. XXXIV, 9: *qui non est tentatus, qualia scit?* Secundo ad reprimendam superbiam; II Cor. XII, 7: *ne magnitudo revelationum extollat me, datus est mihi stimulus carnis meae, angelus satanae qui me colaphizet* et cetera. Tertio ad confundendum diabolum, ut sciat quanta sit virtus Christi, ut superare non possit. Huius exemplum habetur Iob I, 8: *numquid considerasti servum meum Iob?* et cetera. Quarto, ut fortior reddatur, sicut milites fortes redduntur per experientiam; Iudic. III: *quare voluit dimittere hostes cum filiis Israel?* Quinto, ut suam dignitatem cognoscat: quia quando diabolus aggreditur aliquem, hoc cedit ad honorem, quia diabolus sanctos aggreditur; Iob XL, 10: *cibus eius foenum . . . et habet fiduciam quod influat Iordanis in os eius*.

309. Sequitur de loco *tunc ductus est Iesus in desertum*. Hoc convenit praecedentibus et subsequentibus: quia conveniens fuit quod post baptismum desertum intraret. Hoc significatur in populo Israelitico, qui post transitum Maris Rubri, qui fuit figura baptismi,

306. Above, it was shown that Christ prepared himself for teaching by receiving baptism; and now, by overcoming temptation.

Concerning this, he does two things:

first, the victory which he won over temptation is set down;

second, how he called disciples to hear the teaching, at *and Jesus walking by the Sea of Galilee* (Matt 4:18).

Concerning the first, he does three things:

first he puts forth a certain preface about temptation;

second is set down an assult of temptation, at *and the temptor coming to him said*.

third is the victory, at *there the devil left him*.

Moreover, three preambles are set down, namely the place, the fast, and the experience of hunger.

As regards the first, four things are touched upon: the time and place, the one leading, and the goal of this leading.

307. The time was *then*, namely when it had already been declared by the paternal voice that he was the Son of God. In which one is given to understand that this temptation threatens those who have been made sons of God through baptism; *son, when you come to the service of God, stand in justice and in fear, and prepare your soul for temptation* (Sir 2:1).

That desert was between Jerusalem and Jericho, where many were being killed, concerning which see: *a certain man went down from Jerusalem to Jericho, and fell among robbers, who also stripped him, and having wounded him went away, leaving him half dead* (Luke 10:30).

308. And note five reasons why someone is tempted after receiving spiritual grace. First, so that he may receive experience of his justice; *what does he know, who has not been tried?* (Sir 34:9). Second, to prevent arrogance; *and lest the greatness of the revelations should exalt me, there was given me a sting of my flesh, an angel of satan, to buffet me* (2 Cor 12:7). Third, to confound the devil, so that he may know how great is the strength of Christ, so great that he is not able to overcome it. An example of this is given: *have you considered my servant Job?* (Job 1:8). Fourth, so that he may be made stronger, just as a soldier is made strong by experience; *that afterwards their children might learn to fight with their enemies, and to be trained up to war* (Judg 3:1). Fifth, so that he may know his own dignity; because when the devil attacks someone, it results in honor, since the devil attacks those who are holy; *he eats grass . . . and he trusts that the Jordan may run into his mouth* (Job 40:10, 18).

309. There follows about the place, *then Jesus was led by the Spirit into the desert*. This fits both with what came before and with what follows, because it was fitting that he should go into the desert after baptism. This is signified in the Israelite people, who after the crossing of the Red

in terram promissionis venit per desertum et solitudinem: ita baptizati vitam solitariam et quietam debent
quaerere, corpore mundum derelinquendo, vel mente;
Osee II, v. 14: *ducam eam in solitudinem, et loquar ad
cor eius.* Ps. LIV, 8: *ecce elongavi fugiens, et mansi in solitudine.*

Conveniens enim erat ut exiret in desertum, quasi
ad singulare certamen cum diabolo. Chrysostomus: *ille
in desertum vadit, qui exit extra fines, idest voluntatem,
carnis et mundi, ubi non est locus tentationis. Quomodo
enim de libidine tentatur, qui tota die est cum uxore?* Sed
qui non exeunt a voluntate carnis et mundi, non sunt
filii Dei, sed filii diaboli, qui etiam uxorem propriam habentes, appetunt alienam; sed filii Dei habentes Spiritum
Sanctum ducuntur in desertum, ut tententur cum Christo, de quo sequitur:

310. ductus est *a Spiritu*, intellige *Sancto.*

Sed ille qui ducit, maior est eo qui ducitur. Ergo Spiritus Sanctus maior Christo.

Respondendum: si referatur ad Iesum secundum
quod est Filius Dei, sic est aequalis Spiritui Sancto. Et
aliquis potest alium ducere, vel imperio, et sic est maior:
vel exhortatione, et sic est par; Io. I, 40 s., Andreas duxit
Petrum ad Iesum; et sic ductus est Iesus. Hilarius refert
ad Christum, secundum quod homo: scilicet Spiritus
Sanctus hominem quem repleverat, exponit tentationi.

Homines enim tunc ducuntur a Spiritu Sancto, quando caritate moventur, sic quod non motu proprio moventur, sed alieno, quia sequuntur impetum caritatis;
II Cor. V, 14: *caritas Dei urget nos.* Et sic filii Dei aguntur
a Spiritu Sancto, ut tempus huius vitae, quae plena est
tentationibus Iob VII, 1: *tentatio est vita hominis super
terram,* transeant cum victoria per Christi virtutem.

311. Ipse enim tentari voluit, ut sicut morte sua vicit
nostram, sic tentatione sua superet omnes tentationes
nostras; Hebr. IV, v. 15: *non habemus pontificem, qui non
possit compati infirmitatibus nostris; tentatum autem per
omnia pro similitudine absque peccato.*

Gregorius dicit, quod est triplex tentationis gradus,
scilicet per suggestionem, delectationem et consensum.
Prima ab extrinseco est, et potest esse sine peccato; secunda est ab intrinseco, in qua incipit esse peccatum;
quae quidem perficitur per consensum. Primus gradus
potuit esse in Christo, non alii.

Et nota quod diabolus non fuisset ausus accedere ad
tentandum Christum, nisi prius Christus accessisset ad
eum.

312. Consequenter ponitur secundum praeambulum, scilicet ieiunium *et cum ieiunasset* etc., quod

Sea, which was a figure of baptism, came into the land of
promise through the desert and the wilderness. The baptized should seek solitude and quiet in this way, leaving the
world behind either in body or in mind; *behold I will allure
her, and will lead her into the wilderness: and I will speak to
her heart* (Hos 2:14). *Lo, I have gone far off flying away; and
I abode in the wilderness* (Ps 54:8).

For it was fitting that he should go out into the desert,
as though to a one-on-one combat with the devil. Chrysostom: *that man goes into the desert who escapes beyond the
boundaries, i.e., the will, of the body and of the world, where
there is no place for temptation. For how is he tempted by
lust, who is with a wife the whole day?* But those who do not
escape from the will of the flesh and the world are not sons
of God, but sons of the devil, who even when they have
their own wife desire another; but the sons of God, having
the Holy Spirit, are led into the desert, that they may be
tempted with Christ, about whom there follows:

310. *led by the Spirit*, understand the word *Holy.*

But he who leads is greater than he who is led. Therefore
the Holy Spirit is greater than Christ.

One should respond: if this be referred to Jesus insofar
as he is the Son of God, in this way he is equal with the Holy
Spirit. And someone can lead another either by command,
and in this way he is greater, or by exhortation, and in this
way he is equal; Andrew led Peter to Jesus (John 1:40). And
in this way Jesus was led. Hilary refers this to Christ insofar
as he is a man; that is, the Holy Spirit exposed to temptation
the man whom he had filled.

For men are led by the Holy Spirit when they are moved
by charity, because in this way they are not moved by their
own proper motion, but by another, because they follow
the impulse of charity; *for the charity of Christ presses us*
(2 Cor 5:14). And in this way the sons of God are led by the
Holy Spirit, so that they may cross through the time of this
life, which is full of temptation, *the life of man upon earth is
a warfare* (Job 7:1), with victory by the strength of Christ.

311. He himself willed to be tempted, so that just as he
conquered our death by his own, so he might overcome
all our temptations by his temptation; *for we do not have
a high priest who cannot have compassion on our infirmities: but one tempted in all things like as we are, without sin*
(Heb 4:15).

Gregory says that there are three steps of temptation,
namely suggestion, delight, and consent. The first is from
the outside, and can be present without sin; the second is
from the inside, in which there begins to be sin; which indeed is perfected by consent. The first step could be present
in Christ, but not the others.

And note that the devil would not have dared to approach to tempt Christ, unless Christ had first approached
him.

312. Next, the second preamble is set down, namely the
fast, *and when he had fasted*, which fits both with the past

convenit et praeteritis, et futuris: praeteritis, quia convenienter aliquis post baptismum ieiunat, cum post baptismum non sit otio vacandum, sed exercendum in bonis operibus; Gal. V, 13: *vos autem, fratres, in libertate vocati estis*; libertas autem vera non est committenda carnali vitae.

Item futuris competebat, ut is ieiunaret quem diabolus erat tentaturus, quia **hoc genus daemoniorum non eiicitur nisi per orationem et ieiunium**, inf. XVII, 20.

Quadraginta diebus. Ad litteram hoc intelligendum est. Et addit **et noctibus**, ne crederent aliqui quod comedere liceret in nocte, sicut Saraceni faciunt.

313. Et sciendum quod hic numerus praefiguratur in Veteri Testamento in Moyse et Elia, Ex. XXIV, 18, et III Reg. XIX, 8. Et latet in hoc mysterium, quia numerus huiusmodi consurgit ex denario ducto per quaternarium. Denarius significat legem, quia in decem praeceptis tota lex continetur. Quaternarius significat compositionem carnis, quia caro composita est ex quatuor elementis. Quia igitur nos per suggestionem carnis transgredimur legem divinam, iustum est ut carnem nostram affligamus diebus quadraginta.

Secundum autem Gregorium hic numerus est ad ieiunandum ab Ecclesia institutus, quod per hoc decimas solvimus totius anni: a prima enim dominica usque ad Pascha sunt triginta sex dies ieiunabiles, qui sunt decima pars ipsius anni, sex diebus exceptis. Et ideo ab antiquo a quibusdam addita fuit dies media, qui ieiunabant usque ad mediam noctem Sabbati sancti.

314. Tertium additur, quia **postea esuriit**. Non legitur hoc de Moyse et Elia, qui homines erant; sed Christus esurire voluit, ut suam humanitatem demonstraret; quia aliter diabolus ausus non fuisset accedere ad tentandum eum; Phil. II, 7: *in similitudinem hominum factus, et habitu inventus ut homo*.

315. Consequenter insultus tentationis ponitur; et est triplex.

Primus de gula;

secundus de inani gloria;

tertius de ambitione.

Secundum ibi **tunc assumpsit eum diabolus in sanctam civitatem**. Tertium ibi **iterum assumpsit eum diabolus in montem excelsum valde**.

Circa primum duo facit.

Primo ponit insultum diaboli;

secundo quomodo Christus respondit, ibi **qui respondens** et cetera.

316. **Et accedens tentator dixit**. Hoc enim poterat effici, ut ipse ad Iesum accederet in aliqua forma corporea.

Et est triplex tentatio, quia Deus tentat ut instruat; Gen. XXII, 1: *tentavit Deus Abraham*. Quandoque homo ut addiscat, sicut regina Saba tentavit Salomonem,

and with the future: the past, because one fittingly fasts after baptism, since there is no leisure to be idle after baptism, but one should practice good works; *for you, brethren, have been called unto liberty* (Gal 5:13), but there is no true liberty in pursuing a carnal life.

Likewise, it fits with the future that he who was about to be tempted by the devil should hunger, because **this kind is not cast out except by prayer and fasting** (Matt 17:20).

Forty days. This should be understood literally. And he adds **and forty nights** lest someone should think that he was allowed to eat at night, as the Saracens do.

313. And one should know that this number is prefigured in the Old Testament in Moses and Elias (Exod 24:18: 1 Kgs 19:8). And a mystery is hidden in this, because such a number arises from ten multiplied by four. The ten signifies the law, because the whole law is contained in ten precepts. The four signifies the composition of the body, because the body is composed out of four elements. Since therefore we transgress the divine law at the suggestion of the body, it is just that we afflict our body for forty days.

Further, according to Gregory, this number is set up by the Church for fasting, because this way we spend a tenth part of the whole year: for from the first Sunday to Easter there are thirty-six fasting days, which are a tenth part of the year, six days being excluded. And for this reason the middle days were added by certain men in ancient times, who fasted until the midnight of the holy Sabbath.

314. Third, it adds that **afterwards he was hungry**. This is not written about Moses and Elias, who were men; but Christ desired to hunger, to demonstrate his humanity, because otherwise the devil would not have dared to approach to tempt him. *Being made in the likeness of men, and in habit found as a man* (Phil 2:7).

315. Next, the attack of temptation is set down; and it is threefold.

First, concerning gluttony;

second, concerning vainglory;

third, concerning ambition;

He treats the second at, **then the devil took him up into the holy city**. And the third at, **again the devil took him up onto a very high mountain**.

Concerning the first, he does two things:

first, he shows the attack of the devil;

second, how Christ responded, at **who answered**.

316. **And the tempter coming said**. For he was able to bring it about that he should approach Jesus in some bodily form.

And there are three temptations, for God tempts in order to instruct; *God tempted Abraham* (Gen 22:1). Sometimes a man tempts in order to learn, as the queen of Saba

III Reg. X, 1, ubi de ea dicitur, *sed et regina Saba, audita fama Salomonis, venit tentare eum in aenigmatibus.* Diabolus tentat ut decipiat; I Thess. c. III, 5: *ne forte tentaverit vos is qui tentat.* Quicumque vult tentare de scientia, primo de communibus tentat. Communia autem totius generis humani vitia sunt vitia carnis; et praecipue gula. Item qui vult obsidere castrum, incipit a debiliori parte; homo autem habet duas partes, carnalem et spiritualem. Diabolus ex parte debiliori semper tentat: unde primo de vitiis carnalibus tentat, sicut patet in primo parente, quem primo tentavit de gula.

317. Sed notanda est mira astutia in tentando: ***si Filius Dei es***: ita enim directe de uno tentavit, quod ex obliquo de altero. Unde in primo homine suadebat quod comederet de ligno, quod ad peccatum carnale, scilicet gulae, directe pertinebat; sed latenter inducebat ad superbiam et avaritiam, quae sunt peccata spiritualia; unde dixit, *et eritis sicut dii* Gen. III, 5. Ita in Christo: audierat enim quod Christus venturus esset in mundum, et hic videbatur esse Filius Dei; sed in dubitationem venerat, utrum hic esset ille de quo erat prophetatum, quia nihil inveniebat in eo; Io. XIV, 30: *venit princeps mundi huius, et in me non habet quicquam.* Unde suggerebat quod homini esurienti delectabile est. Item induxit ad appetendum ea quae sunt Dei; et hoc est ***si Filius Dei es, dic ut lapides isti panes fiant.*** Eccle. VIII, 4: *sermo illius potestate plenus est*; et Ps. XXXII, 6: *verbo Domini caeli firmati sunt, et spiritu oris eius omnis virtus eorum.* Ergo potest eius verbo lapis mutari. Ergo volebat inclinare ad hoc, quod si faceret, sciret esse Filium Dei, si non, inducebat ad arrogantiam.

318. Et notandum quod multi homines sunt qui consentiunt peccatis carnalibus, aestimantes, quod non debeant amittere statum spiritualem. Sed si in hoc quod tentatur consentiens homo, non amitteret spiritualitatem, levis esset tentatio. Ita persuadere voluit mulieri diabolus, et Christo, promittens spiritualia.

319. ***Qui respondens dixit: scriptum est: 'non in solo pane vivit homo'.*** In ista responsione dat tria documenta, quae facienda sunt tentato.

Primum ut recurrat ad Scripturae medicinam; Ps. CXVIII, 11: *in corde meo abscondi eloquia tua, ut non peccem tibi* et cetera. Unde dixit, ***scriptum est.***

Secundum documentum ut homo nihil faciat ad arbitrium diaboli. Vegetius: *nihil umquam sapiens dux debet facere ad arbitrium sui hostis, etiam si bonum videatur.* Et

tested Solomon, where it says of her, *and the queen of Saba, having heard of the fame of Solomon in the name of the Lord, came to try him with hard questions* (1 Kgs 10:1). The devil tempts in order to deceive; *lest perhaps he that tempts should have tempted you, and our labor should be made vain* (1 Thess 3:5). Whoever wants to test something concerning science, first tests about the most general things. Now, the most common vices of the whole human race are the vices of the body, and principally gluttony. Again, he who wishes to besiege a castle begins at the weakest part; now a man has two parts, the bodily and the spiritual. The devil always tempts from the weaker part, and hence he tempts first concerning the bodily vices, as is evident in the first parent, whom he first tempted concerning gluttony.

317. But one should note his marvelous cunning in tempting: ***if you are the Son of God***; for he tempted so directly concerning one thing, because he was tempting indirectly concerning another. Hence in the case of the first man he suggested that he eat of the tree, which pertained to a bodily sin directly; but he secretly led him on to arrogance and greed, which are spiritual sins. Hence he said, *you will be as gods* (Gen 3:5). Thus in the case of Christ, he had heard that the Christ was to come into the world, and this man seemed to be the Son of God; but he had come in a state of uncertainty, wondering whether this man was he of whom it had been prophesied, because he found nothing in him; *for the prince of this world comes, and in me he has not any thing* (John 14:30). Hence he suggested that which is delightful to a hungry man, and likewise he led him on to desire the things of God; and this is ***if you are the Son of God, command that these stones become bread.*** *His word is full of power* (Eccl 8:4); and: *by the word of the Lord the heavens were established; and all the power of them by the spirit of his mouth* (Ps 32:6). So he was able to change a stone by his word. Therefore he wished to incline him toward this deed, which if he had done, he would have known him to be the Son of God; if not, he was leading him toward arrogance.

318. And one should note that there are many men who consent to bodily sins, reckoning that they should not lose the spiritual state. But if a man were not to lose spirituality by the fact that he is tempted and consents, the temptation would be a trivial one. Thus the devil wished to persuade the woman, and Christ, promising spiritual things.

319. ***Who answered and said: it is written, 'not in bread alone does man live'.*** Three lessons are given in this reply, which the one tempted should follow.

First, that one should turn back to the medicine of Scripture; *your words have I hidden in my heart, that I may not sin against you* (Ps 118:11). Hence he said, ***it is written.***

The second lesson is that a man should do nothing according to the judgment of the devil. Vegetius: *the wise king should never do anything according to the judgment of his enemy, even if it seems good.* And therefore the Lord, while

ideo Dominus cum posset sine peccato lapides in panem commutare, noluit, quia ille suggerebat.

Tertium est, quod non debet facere sine utilitate, ad ostentationem suae virtutis, quia hoc est vanitas.

320. *Qui respondens dixit: scriptum est: 'non in solo pane vivit homo.'*

Notandum, quod diabolus ad duo nitebatur: primo ducere in affectum carnalium, item praesumptionis. Christus autem contra utrumque primo vitat iactantiam; quasi dicat, *tu vocas Filium Dei, ego nomino hominem;* unde *'non in solo pane vivit homo.'* Item trahit diabolus in affectum carnalium: *dic ut lapides isti panes fiant;* hic trahit se in affectum spiritualium: *'sed in omni verbo quod procedit de ore Dei.'* Quasi dicat, non tantum vita corporalis affectanda est, quantum vita spiritualis, quae conservatur per cibum spiritualem, *'sed in omni verbo quod procedit de ore Dei.'* Io. VI, 69: *Domine, ad quem ibimus? Verba vitae aeternae habes;* Ps. CXVIII, 93: *in aeternum non obliviscar iustificationes tuas, quia in ipsis vivificasti me.*

Et dicit *'in omni verbo'*, quia tota spiritualis doctrina est a Deo, sive ab homine, sive a Deo dicatur. Et iterum *'de ore'*: quia praedicator os Dei; Ier. XV, 19: *si separaveris pretiosum a vili, quasi os meum eris.*

Vel aliter. *'Non in solo'*, idest, non vivit solum homo per panem, sed etiam verbo, idest imperio Dei potest conservari sine aliquo cibo.

321. *Tunc assumpsit eum diabolus in sanctam civitatem.* Posita prima tentatione, de qua diabolus victus fuit, nunc ponitur secunda, scilicet de inani gloria. Et ordo congruus est, quod postquam diabolus se vinctum videret vitio carnali, tentaret de inani gloria, vel superbia: quia *superbia bonis operibus insidiatur, ut pereant,* Augustinus in *Regula.*

Circa istam ergo tentationem tria facit.

Primo ponitur locus tentationis;

secundo insultus, sive conatus tentationis, ibi *si Filius Dei es, mitte te deorsum:*

tertio resistentia Christi, ibi *ait ei Iesus.*

322. Sed sciendum, quod Lucas posuit tertiam tentationem, hic e converso; sed non est vis, secundum Augustinum: quia omnia quae narrantur hic, et in Luca narrantur; nec ponitur in Luca, vel hic quae fuit prima, vel secunda. Rabanus vero dicit quod Lucas attendit ad ordinem historiae; et ideo sic ordinavit, secundum quod factum est. Matthaeus vero naturam tentationis secutus est, quia post tentationem de gula, et de inani gloria, sequitur tentatio de ambitione: ita enim fuit tentatus Adam, quia primo de gula; unde Gen. II, 17: *in quacumque die comederis ex eo, morte morieris;* secundo de

he was able to change the stones into bread without sin, did not want to, because the devil suggested it.

The third is that one should not perform useless work just to show his own strength, because this is vanity.

320. *Who answered and said: it is written, 'not in bread alone does man live.'*

One should notice that the devil presses for two things: first, to lead him into a desire for fleshly things, and likewise into presumption. Against both, however, Christ first avoids boasting: as though to say, *you call me the Son of God; I call myself a man;* hence, *'not in bread alone does man live.'* Likewise, the devil drew him toward a desire for fleshly things: **command that these stones become bread.** Here he draws himself to a desire for spiritual things: *'but in every word that proceeds from the mouth of God.'* As though to say: the bodily life is not so much to be desired as the spiritual life, which is preserved by spiritual food, *'but in every word that proceeds from the mouth of God.' Lord, to whom will we go? You have the words of eternal life* (John 6:69); *your justifications I will never forget: for by them you have given me life* (Ps 118:93).

And he says, *'in every word'*, because all spiritual teaching is from God, whether it is spoken by man or by God. And again, *'from the mouth'*, because the preacher is the mouth of God; *and if you will separate the precious from the vile, you will be as my mouth* (Jer 15:19).

Or in another way: *'not in bread alone'*, i.e., man does not live only by bread, but also by the word, i.e., the command of God can preserve one without any food.

321. *Then the devil took him up into the holy city.* The first temptation having been set down, now the second is set down, namely concerning vainglory. And the order is fitting, because after the devil saw himself defeated in bodily vice, he tempted concerning vainglory, or pride, because *pride lies in ambush for good works, that they may be destroyed,* as Augustine says in his *Regula.*

Concerning this temptation, then, he does three things:

first, the place of the temptation is set down;

second, the attack or attempt of temptation, at *if you are the Son of God, cast yourself down;*

third, the Christ's resistance, at *Jesus said to him.*

322. But one should know that Luke sets down the third temptation here the other way around; but there is no force to this objection, according to Augustine, because everything told here is also told in Luke, nor is it set down here or in Luke which one happened first or second. Rabanus indeed says that Luke attends to the order of history, and so he set this down in order in which it happened. Matthew however followed the nature of the temptation, because after the temptation concerning gluttony, and concerning vainglory, there follows the temptation concerning ambition. For Adam was tempted in this way: first, concerning gluttony, hence: *for in whatever day you will eat of it, thou*

gloria: *eritis sicut dii*; tertio de avaritia, sive ambitione, *scientes bonum et malum*.

323. Sed quare dicit **tunc assumpsit**? Hoc enim nomen **assumptio** vim importat.

Et respondet Hieronymus, quod hoc dicit Evangelista secundum opinionem diaboli, quia quod Christus sustinuit ex virtute, diabolus accepit quasi faceret sua potentia.

324. Dicit **sanctam**, vel quia ibi agebantur sancta, temporalia scilicet sacrificia, et huiusmodi. Vel dicit propter sanctitatem patrum eorum qui ibi fuerunt. Unde ex antiqua consuetudine vocat **sanctam**, licet cessaverit; Is. I, 21: *quomodo facta est meretrix civitas fidelis, plena iudicii?* Sed post dicit, *vocaberis civitas iusti, urbs fidelis* et cetera.

325. Sed sciendum quod Mc. I, 13 dicitur, quod *erat in deserto quadraginta diebus et quadraginta noctibus, et tentabatur a satana.* Ex quo videtur quod omnes tentationes fuerint in deserto. Ergo non videtur verum esse quod dicitur **tunc assumpsit eum diabolus**.

Et est hic duplex responsio. Quidam dicunt, quod omnes tentationes fuerunt in deserto, et quod fuerunt secundum imaginariam visionem, scilicet quod Christus ita imaginabatur, ipso etiam permittente. Alii dicunt, quod fuerunt secundum visionem corporalem: et quod diabolus apparuit ei in specie corporali. Hoc videtur innui, quia dicit, quod **assumpsit eum in sanctam civitatem**. Quidam dicunt quod hoc ideo ad desertum pertinet, quia Ierusalem deserta erat a Deo.

Sed dicendum melius, quod illud, quod dicitur Mc. I, 13 non est intelligendum, quod omnes tentationes fuerint in deserto, nec etiam ipse hoc dicit; sed quod tentabatur a satana. Et ideo sciendum, quod prima tentatio fuit in deserto; aliae duae extra desertum.

326. Sed quaeritur quomodo assumpsit. Dicunt quod deportavit eum supra se. Alii, et melius, quod exhortando induxit ad hoc quod iret; et Christus ex dispositione suae sapientiae ivit in Ierusalem.

327. ***Et statuit eum super pinnaculum templi*** et cetera. Sciendum quod legitur III Reg. c. VI, quod Salomon fecit tria tabulata in templo cum tecto plano, et quaedam pinnacula iuxta templum, per quae poterant homines ascendere: et de hoc dicitur hic ***et statuit eum super pinnaculum templi***. Utrum autem accesserit in primum, vel secundum, vel tertium, hic non dicitur; sed certum est, quod aliquod ascendit.

328. Sed numquid homines non videbant quando diabolus Christum portabat?

Dicendum, secundum illos qui dicunt quod eum portabat, quod Christus sua virtute faciebat, quod videri

will die the death (Gen 2:17); second, concerning glory, *you will be as Gods* (Gen 3:5); third, concerning greed, or ambition, *knowing good and evil.*

323. But why does it say, **then the devil took him up**? For this word **took** implies force.

And Jerome responds that the Evangelist says this according to the devil's opinion, because what Christ put up with out of virtue, the devil took as though he had done by his own power.

324. He says, **the holy city**, either because holy things were done there, namely the temporal sacrifices, and suchlike, or he says it because of the holiness of the fathers of those who were there. Hence he calls it **holy** by an ancient custom, although it ceased to be so; *how is the faithful city, that was full of judgment, become a harlot?* (Isa 1:21). But later it says, *after this you will be called the city of the just, a faithful city* (Isa 1:26).

325. But one should know that it is said: *he was in the desert forty days and forty nights, and was being tempted by satan* (Mark 1:13), on the basis of which it seems that all the temptations happened in the desert. Therefore what is said here does not seem to be true, **then the devil took him up**.

And there are two responses to this. Some say that all the temptations happened in the desert, and that they happened according to a vision of the imagination, namely that Christ was imagining it to be so, he himself permitting it. Others say that they happened according to a bodily vision, and that the devil appeared to him in a bodily form. This seems to be implied, because it says that **the devil took him up into the holy city**. Some say that this related to the desert, because Jerusalem was deserted by God.

But one should say better that what is said in Mark is not to be understood such that all the temptations happened in the desert, nor does he even say that, but that he was tempted by satan (Mark 1:13). And so one should know that the first temptation was in the desert, the other two outside the desert.

326. But it is asked how he was taken up. They say that he carried him upon himself. Others say, and better, that he induced him to go by exhortation; and Christ went into Jerusalem by the arrangement of his own wisdom.

327. **And set him upon the pinnacle of the temple.** One should know that it is written that Solomon made the temple with three stories and a flat roof, and a certain pinnacle next to the temple through which men could go up (1 Kgs 6). And it says here about this pinnacle, **and set him upon the pinnacle of the temple**. Now, whether he went into the first, or the second, or the third, is not said here; but it is certain that he went up something.

328. But would not men have seen when the devil carried Christ?

It should be said, according to those who say that he carried him, that Christ made it happen by his own power

non posset. Vel dicendum quod diabolus in figura hominis erat; et consuetudo erat quod homines sic ascenderent.

329. *Et dixit ei: si Filius Dei es, mitte te deorsum.* Semper diabolus duabus sagittis percutit: ex una parte enim inducit inanem gloriam, ex alia parte homicidium; et hoc est *si Filius Dei es* et cetera.

Sed certe ista consequentia Christo non convenit, quia ei competit ascendere; Io. III, v. 13: *nemo ascendit in caelum, nisi qui descendit de caelo, Filius hominis, qui est in caelo* et cetera. Et dicit *mitte*, quia eius intentio est semper praecipitare, sicut ipse praecipitatus est; Apoc. XII, 4: *cauda draconis trahebat tertiam partem stellarum caeli, et misit eam in terram.*

Notat etiam diabolus infirmitatem suam, quia nullus nisi volens ab eo vincitur; unde dicit *mitte*, non praecipitat; Is. XLI, 23: *incurvare ut transeamus.*

330. Sed quare *supra pinnaculum*? Glossa: *quia in illo loco docebant.* Unde significat quod diabolus magnos de inani gloria tentat. Contra quod Apostolus I Thess. c. II, 6: *nec quaerentes ab hominibus gloriam, neque a vobis, neque ab aliis.* Et dicit *mitte te deorsum* etc., quia homines qui quaerunt gloriam, oportet quod intantum persuadeant ut ostendant Dei filiationem in multis humilem; et ideo dicit Tullius in libro *de Officiis: cavenda est gloriae cupiditas: eripit enim animi libertatem, pro qua magnanimis viris omnis debet esse contentio.*

331. Consequenter inducit auctoritatem *scriptum est*: et utitur ista, non ut doceat, sed ut decipiat; et hoc sumitur argumentum, quod sicut ipse transfigurat se in angelum lucis, ita et sui ministri, qui utuntur auctoritate Sacrae Scripturae ad simplices decipiendum; II Petr. ult., 16: *indocti et instabiles depravant Scripturas ad suam ipsorum perditionem.* Unde hoc praefigurabat diabolus in se sicut in capite. '*Quia angelis suis mandavit de te.*'

332. Nota quod tribus modis depravat quis auctoritatem Sacrae Scripturae: aliquando sicut cum dicitur de uno, et exponitur de alio: sicut si dicitur de uno iusto, et exponitur de Christo; verbi gratia: *qui potuit transgredi, et non est transgressus*, Eccli. XXXI, v. 10. Item Io. XIV, 28 *Pater maior me est*, hoc dicitur de Christo, secundum quod homo. Unde si exponatur de eo secundum quod Filius Dei, depravatur auctoritas. Ita diabolus hic dicit '*angelis*', quia Ps. XC dicit hoc de membro Christi, qui indiget custodia angelorum, quod patet, quia subdit '*ne forte offendas*': hoc enim non potest dici de Christo, quia non poterat offendere occasione alicuius peccati.

329. *And said to him: if you are the Son of God, cast yourself down.* The devil always strikes with two arrows: for on the one hand he leads him to vainglory, on the other hand to homicide; and this is *if you are the Son of God, cast yourself down.*

But certainly this sequence of actions did not fit with Christ, because it befit Christ to ascend; *and no man has ascended into heaven, but he that descended from heaven, the Son of man who is in heaven* (John 3:13). And he says, *cast*, because his intention is always to throw down, just as he himself was thrown down; *and his tail drew the third part of the stars of heaven, and cast them to the earth* (Rev 12:4).

The devil also knew his own weakness, because no one but the willing is conquered by him; hence he says, *cast*, not *fall*; *bow down, that we may go over* (Isa 51:23).

330. But why *upon the pinnacle*? The Gloss: *because they were teaching in that place.* Hence it signifies that the devil tempts the great concerning vainglory. Against which the Apostle says, *nor sought we glory of men, neither of you, nor of others* (1 Thess 2:6). And he says, *cast yourself down*, because men who seek glory must, to that degree, convince others that they display the sonship of God as humble in many things; and for this reason Cicero says in the book *On Offices: the desire of glory should be avoided, for it steals away that liberty of soul for which every struggle of the great souled man should be.*

331. Next, the devil brings in a Scriptural text, *for it is written.* And he uses this text not to teach, but to deceive; and this argument is taken up, because just as he transforms himself into an angel of light, so also do his servants, who use the authority of Sacred Scripture to deceive the simple; *which the unlearned and unstable wrest, as they do also the other Scriptures, to their own destruction* (2 Pet 3:16). Hence the devil prefigures this in himself, as in the head. '*That he has given his angels charge over you.*'

332. Note that someone may twist the authority of Sacred Scripture in three ways. Sometimes as when it speaks about one thing, and is explained as about another, like if it speaks about one just man, and is explained as about Christ; e.g., *he that could have transgressed, and has not transgressed: and could do evil things, and has not done them* (Sir 31:10). Likewise, *the Father is greater than I* (John 14:28), this is said of Christ according as he is a man. Hence if it is explained of him according as he is the Son of God, the Scriptural text is twisted. The devil speaks here of the '*angels*' in this way, because the Psalm says this about the members of Christ (Ps 90), who need the protection of the angels, which is clear, because it adds below, '*lest perhaps you offend*'; for this cannot be said of Christ, because he could not have given offense by occasion of some sin.

that he could not be seen. Or it should be said that the devil was in the figure of a man, and it was normal that men should go up in this way.

Secundo modo depravat, quando inducit quis auctoritatem ad aliquid, ad quod non est auctoritas; sicut illud Prov. XXV, 21 et Rom. XII, 20: *si esurierit inimicus tuus, ciba illum* et cetera. Si enim aliquid facit alicui ut ille puniatur a Deo, hoc facit contra sensum auctoritatis. Ita diabolus, quia Scriptura intendit quod homo iustus ita per angelos custoditur, quod in periculo non incidat; Ps. IX, v. 10: *adiutor in opportunitatibus in tribulatione* et cetera. Diabolus autem exponit quod homo periculo se ingerat, quod est Deum tentare.

Tertio modo quando illud quod est pro se, de auctoritate accipit, et aliud quod est contra se dimittit, quod est mos haeretici: ita fecit hic diabolus quia dimisit illud quod subditur, quod erat contra eum, scilicet: *super aspidem et basiliscum ambulabis, et conculcabis leonem et draconem.* Unde factus est exemplar omnium Scripturas depravantium.

333. *Ait illi Dominus.* Non violentia, sed sapientia se defendit; Sap. VII, 30: *sapientiam non vincit malitia.* Et ideo contra auctoritatem ponit auctoritatem quae exponit praemissam; quasi dicat, *tu dicis ut proiiciam me, ut videam an Deus eripiat me; sed hoc prohibetur in Scriptura;* unde *non tentabis Dominum Deum tuum,* Deut. VI, 16.

Vel aliter, tu tentas, et tentando contra auctoritatem facis; non debet autem uti auctoritate Sacrae Scripturae, qui contra auctoritatem facit. Et Scriptura dicit *'non tentabis'* et cetera. Sed tu tentas Dominum Deum tuum, qui sum ego; Io. XIII, 13: *vos vocatis me, Magister et Domine, et bene dicitis, sum etenim* et cetera. Tamen prima est magis litteralis.

334. Consequenter ponitur tertia tentatio, scilicet de ambitione, vel de avaritia; unde *tunc assumpsit.* Et

ponitur insultus tentationis;

secundo resistentia Christi, ibi *tunc dicit ei Iesus: vade, satana.*

Tentat autem diabolus dupliciter, facto et verbo; unde *haec omnia tibi dabo* et cetera.

In facto duo consideranda sunt. Quia

primo assumpsit in montem;

secundo ostendit omnia regna mundi.

335. Dicit ergo *tunc assumpsit.* De assumptione dictum est supra; sed hoc, scilicet *in montem,* potest dupliciter exponi. Rabanus dicit, quod iste mons erat in deserto, quia secundum eum omnes tentationes in deserto fuerunt. Dicitur autem *excelsus* in comparatione ad aliquos qui in circuitu erant.

The second way a Scriptural text is twisted is when someone brings in a text to something for which it is not a text; like Proverbs and: *but if your enemy be hungry, give him to eat; if he thirst, give him to drink* (Prov 25:21: Rom 12:20). For if someone does this to someone so that he will be punished by God, he does this contrary to the sense of the text. The devil did exactly this, because the Scriptures meant that the just man is protected by the angels in such a way that he does not fall into danger; *a helper in due time in tribulation* (Ps 9:10). But the devil expounds it that a man should throw himself into danger, which is to tempt God.

The third way is when someone accepts from the Scriptural text what is in his favor, and dismisses that which is contrary to him, which is the custom of heretics. Thus the devil does here, because he dismissed that which is added below, which was against him, namely, *you will walk upon the asp and the basilisk: and you will trample under foot the lion and the dragon* (Ps 90:13). Hence he is made the exemplar of all twisting of the Scriptures.

333. *Jesus said to him.* He defends himself, not by violence, but by wisdom; *no evil can overcome wisdom* (Wis 7:30). And so he sets against this Scriptural text a second Scriptural text which explains the one before; as though to say, *you say that I should throw myself down, that I may see whether God will save me; but this is prohibited in the Scriptures.* Hence, *you shall not tempt the Lord your God* (Deut 6:16).

Or in another way, you tempt, and by tempting you act against the Scriptural text; but he who acts against the Scriptural text should not use the authority of Sacred Scripture. And Scripture says, *'you shall not tempt.'* But you tempt the Lord your God, whom I am; *you call me Master, and Lord; and you say well, for so I am* (John 13:13). Yet the first is more literal.

334. Next, the third temptation is set down, namely concerning ambition, or concerning greed; hence, *again the devil took him up.* And

the attack of the temptation is set down;

second, Christ's resistance, at *then Jesus said to him: begone, satan.*

Now, the devil tempts in two ways, by deed and by word; hence, *all these will I give you.*

In the deed, there are two things to be considered, because

first, he takes him up onto the mountain;

second, he shows him all the kingdoms of the world.

335. He says then, *again the devil took him up.* The taking up was discussed above; but this, namely *onto a very high mountain,* can be explained in two ways. Rabanus says that this mountain was in the desert, because according to him all the temptations happened in the desert. It is called *high* in comparison to the others which were in the area.

Chrysostomus autem dicit, quod duxit eum ad maiorem montem de mundo; et hoc videtur littera sonare, cum dicitur *excelsum valde*. In hoc autem significatur, quod diabolus semper ad superbiam erigit, sicut et ipse superbus est; Ier. XIII, 16: *antequam offendant pedes vestri ad montes caliginosos*. Unde etiam dicitur *mons*; Ier. I, 15: *ecce ego convocabo omnes cognationes regnorum aquilonis, ait Dominus*.

336. *Et ostendit ei omnia regna mundi*.

Sciendum quod regnum mundi dupliciter accipitur. Primo spiritualiter: et sic diabolus dicitur regnare in eo; Io. XII, 31: *nunc princeps mundi huius eiicietur foras*. Secundo ad litteram dicitur regnum mundi, secundum quod unus regnat super alium.

Hoc autem quod hic dicitur, videtur quibusdam quod dicatur de regno diaboli; unde *ostendit omnia regna mundi*, scilicet super quae regnabat, *et gloriam eorum* etc., quia quando perfecte regnat super homines, facit eos etiam gloriari; Prov. II, 14: *laetantur cum male fecerint, et exultant in rebus pessimis*; Ps. LI, 3: *quid gloriaris in malitia?* Et hic est ultimus gradus peccati.

Alii exponunt de regno carnali.

337. Sed tunc quaeritur, quomodo potuit ostendere omnia regna mundi.

Remigius dicit, quod miraculose: quia omnia regna in ictu oculi ostendit, sicut etiam de Beato Benedicto legitur, quod ostensus est ei totus mundus in uno intuitu.

Sed sciendum quod istae duae non videntur bonae expositiones, quia non oporteret dicere, quod *assumpsit in montem excelsum valde*: quia totum hoc potuisset fieri in valle. Unde dicit Chrysostomus aliter: *ostendit ei*, non quod ostenderit ei singula regna, sed ad quam partem singulum regnum esset; et non solum hoc, sed *ostendit gloriam eorum*, hoc est expressit ei temporalem gloriam mundi; Osee IV, 7: *gloriam eorum in ignominiam commutabo*; Phil. III, 19: *gloria in confusione ipsorum qui terrena sapiunt*.

338. *Et dixit ei: haec omnia tibi dabo*. In istis verbis duo facit: unum promittit, et aliud expetit: et in promissione est mendax, in expetitione superbus.

Diabolus in primis exploravit si esset Filius Dei; modo credens iam deprehendisse quod non esset, dicit *haec omnia tibi dabo* etc.; ubi mendax est quia haec non erant in potestate sua; Prov. VIII, 15: *per me principes regnant, et potentes decernunt iustitiam*. Daniel IV, 14: *donec cognoscant viventes, quoniam dominatur excelsus in regno hominum, et cuicumque voluerit dabit illud*; alias non dixisset *haec omnia tibi dabo*; nullus enim malus

But Chrysostom says that he led him to the highest mountain in the world; and this seems to correspond with the text, since it says *very high*. Moreover, in this is signified that the devil always rouses one to pride, just as he himself is proud; *give glory to the Lord your God, before it is dark, and before your feet stumble upon the dark mountains* (Jer 13:16). Hence it also says *mountain*; *for behold I will call together all the families of the kingdoms of the north: says the Lord* (Jer 1:15).

336. *And showed him all the kingdoms of the world*.

One should know that the kingdom of the world is taken in two ways. First, spiritually; and thus the devil is said to reign in it. *Now is the judgment of the world: now will the prince of this world be cast out* (John 12:31). Second, the kingdom of the world is said literally, according as one man reigns over another.

To some, what is said here seems to be said about the kingdom of the devil; hence, *and showed him all the kingdoms of the world*, namely over which he was reigning, *and the glory of them*, because when he reigns perfectly over men, he makes them to glory as well. *Who are glad when they have done evil, and rejoice in most wicked things* (Prov 2:14); *why do you glory in malice, you who are mighty in iniquity?* (Ps 51:3). And this is the last step of sin.

Others explain this as about a bodily kingdom.

337. But then it is asked how he could show him all the kingdoms of the world.

Remigius says that it was miraculous, because he showed all the kingdoms in a sweep of the eye, just as it is written about Blessed Benedict, that the whole world was shown to him in one glance.

But one should know that these two do not seem to be good explanations, because then it would not be necessary to say that *the devil took him up into a very high mountain*; because all this could have happened in a valley. Hence Chrysostom says otherwise: *showed him*, not that he showed him the particular kingdoms, but at what part a particular kingdom would be; and not only this, but he showed *the glory of them*, i.e., he expressed to him the temporal glory of the world. *I will change their glory into shame* (Hos 4:7); *whose glory is in their shame; who mind earthly things* (Phil 3:19).

338. *And said to him: all these will I give you, if falling down you will adore me*. He does two things in these words: he promises one thing, and asks for another: in the promise is a lie; in the request, pride.

In the first temptation, the devil had investigated whether he was the Son of God; and believing he had discovered that he was not, he says, *all these will I give you*; here is the lie, because these were not in his power. *By me kings reign, and lawgivers decree just things* (Prov 8:15). *Till the living know that the Most High rules in the kingdom of men; and he will give it to whomever it will please him* (Dan 4:14); otherwise he would not have said, *all these will I give you*,

regnat nisi permissione divina; Iob c. XXXIV, 30: *qui regnare facit hominem hypocritam propter peccata populi.*

Expetiit aliud; unde *si cadens adoraveris me.*

339. Nota tria. Primo quod diabolus semper in id quod in principio appetiit, perseverat; Is. XIV, 13: *in caelum conscendam, super astra Dei exaltabo solium meum, sedebo in monte testamenti in lateribus aquilonis, ascendam super altitudinem nubium, similis ero Altissimo.* Et propterea inducit ad idololatriam homines, volens usurpare sibi quod Dei est.

Item nota quod nullus adorat diabolum nisi cadat, sicut et ipse cecidit; Dan. III, 7: *cadentes adoraverunt statuam auream.* Et ideo dicit *si cadens adoraveris me.*

Tertio, nota hic esse avaritiam. Unde promittit regnum, in quo intelligitur abundantia divitiarum, et excellentia honorum. Et petit quod cadat: quia ambitiosi semper humiliant se ultra debitum. Unde Ambrosius: *habet ambitio domesticum periculum: curvatur obsequio, ut honori donetur: et dum vult esse sublimis, fit deiecta.*

340. Consequenter ponitur deprehensio hostis; unde *tunc dicit ei Iesus:* et circa hoc duo facit.

Primo cohibet tentationem;

secundo inducit auctoritatem, ibi *scriptum est* et cetera.

341. Dicit ergo *tunc dicit ei Iesus.*

Nota quod Christus audierat multas iniurias, sed non curavit. Sed hoc *si cadens adoraveris me,* non sustinuit: quia primae cedebant in iniuriam sui, sed hoc ad iniuriam Dei. Unde Chrysostomus: *iniuria propria toleranda est: iniuriam Dei dissimulare nimis est impium.* Et ideo dicit *vade, satana.* III Reg. XIX, 10: *zelo zelatus sum pro Domino Deo exercituum: quia dereliquerunt pactum suum filii Israel*; Ps. LXVIII, 10: *zelus domus tuae comedit me.*

Item quod non est in potestate diaboli, ut tentet quantum vult, sed quantum Deus permittit; unde dicit *vade*; quasi dicat: *nolo quod amplius tentes:* I Cor. X, 13: *fidelis Deus qui non patietur vos tentari supra id quod potestis, sed faciet etiam cum tentatione proventum, ut possitis sustinere*; Iob XXXVIII, v. 11: *hucusque venies, et non procedes amplius, et hic confringes tumentes fluctus tuos.*

342. Et notandum quod Dominus quasi similia verba dixit Petro infr. XVI, 23. Sed ibi dixit *retro.* Unde alia est sententia hic et ibi: quia satan interpretatur 'adversarius.' Voluit ergo Dominus, quod Petrus iret post eum, qui volebat impedire passionem; sed hic dicit *vade* tantum;

for no evil man reigns except by divine permission. *Who makes a man that is a hypocrite to reign for the sins of the people?* (Job 34:30).

He asks for another thing. Hence, *if falling down you will adore me.*

339. Notice three things. First, that the devil persists in that which he desired at the beginning; *I will ascend into heaven, I will exalt my throne above the stars of God, I will sit in the mountain of the covenant, in the sides of the north. I will ascend above the height of the clouds, I will be like the Most High* (Isa 14:13–14). And on account of this he leads men to idolatry, wishing to seize what is God's for himself.

Likewise, notice that no one adores the devil unless he falls, just as he himself fell; *all the nations, tribes, and languages fell down and adored the golden statue* (Dan 3:7). And this is why he says, *if falling down you will adore me.*

Third, notice that this is greed. Hence he promises a kingdom, in which is understood the abundance of riches, and superiority of honor. And he asks that he fall, because the ambitious always humble themselves further than is due. Hence Ambrose: *ambition has a native danger; it is bent down to service, it may be given to honor, and when it wishes to be lofty, it becomes abject.*

340. Next, the seizing of the enemy is set down; hence, *then Jesus said to him.* And concerning this he does two things:

first, he represses the temptation;

second, he brings in an authority, at *for it is written.*

341. It says then, *Jesus said to him.*

Notice that Christ had listened to many insults, but was not troubled. But this, *if falling down you will adore me,* he did not put up with, because the former things were insulting to himself, but this was insulting to God. Hence Chrysostom: *one's own injury should be tolerated; to ignore the insult of God is greatly impious.* And therefore he says, *begone, satan. With zeal have I been zealous for the Lord God of hosts: for the children of Israel have forsaken your covenant* (1 Kgs 19:10); *for the zeal of your house has eaten me up* (Ps 68:10).

Similarly, notice that it is not in the power of the devil to tempt as much as he wishes, but only so much as God permits; hence he says, *begone,* as though to say, *I do not wish you to tempt any more. God is faithful, who will not suffer you to be tempted above that which you are able: but will make also with temptation issue, that you may be able to bear it* (1 Cor 10:13); *here you will come, and will go no further, and here you will break your swelling waves* (Job 38:11).

342. And one should note that the Lord said similar words, as it were, to Peter (Matt 16:23). But there he said, *go behind me.* Hence the thought there and here is different; because satan is interpreted as 'adversary'. Therefore the Lord willed that Peter, who wished to impede the passion,

quia diabolus eum sequi non potest; et ideo dicit *vade*, scilicet ad infernum; inf. XXV, 41: *ite, maledicti, in ignem aeternum, qui paratus est diabolo et angelis eius*.

343. *Scriptum est*; Deut. VI, 16. Et inducit frequenter tales auctoritates ex Deuteronomio, ut significet doctrinam Novi Testamenti per Deuteronomium significari.

Quod insequitur '*Dominum Deum*', hoc dupliciter inferri potest; quasi dicat, *tu diabole, dicis quod cadens adorem te; sed lex dicit* '*Dominum Deum tuum adorabis.*' Unde potest induci ad hoc quod purus homo non debet adorari. Vel accipiendum est quod loquatur de se tamquam de Deo, '*Dominum Deum tuum adorabis*' etc., *quasi dicat, magis debes adorare me, quam e converso*: quia *scriptum est* et cetera.

Prima tamen est magis litteralis.

344. Et nota, quod duo dicit, scilicet '*adorabis*', et '*servies*': et est inter ista differentia. Homo enim dupliciter se habere debet ad Deum, quia debet ei subiectus esse; et debet se in eum erigere sicut in ultimum finem.

Quantum ad primum debemus ei omnem obedientiam; Act. V, 29: *obedire oportet Deo magis quam hominibus*. Tunc enim sumus ei subiecti, quando omnem eius voluntatem facimus.

In Deum autem erigimur dupliciter: quia aliquando trahimus nos ad ipsum; Ps. XXXIII, v. 6: *accedite ad eum, et illuminamini, et facies vestrae non confundentur*; aliquando alios ad ipsum trahimus; I Cor. III, 9: *Dei enim sumus coadiutores*. Utrumque istorum demonstramus sensibiliter: quia dum prostrationes facimus, admonemus nos quod debemus esse subiecti Deo; et ideo dicit, *Dominum Deum*; Ps. LXXI, 11: *omnes gentes servient ei*. Item in hoc quod offerimus sacrificia et laudes, significamus hoc quod mentem nostram debemus elevare in ipsum: et ad hoc pertinet servitus; et hoc est *et illi soli servies*.

Et est duplex servitus; quaedam quae debetur soli Deo; et ista in Graeco dicitur 'latria': et haec est duplex. Quaedam enim est adoratio quae soli Deo debetur, quae est ut ei prae omnibus serviatur; alia servitus est ut in ipsum tendamus sicut in ultimum finem, aliqua enim est adoratio vel servitus quae solum subiectorum est, sicut quando superioribus serviunt inferiores; Rom. XIII, 1: *omnis anima potestatibus sublimioribus subiecta sit*. Sed non debet illi obedire super omnia, quia numquam contra Deum. Similiter nulla creatura est quae debeat haberi sicut finis ultimus; Ps. CXLV, 3: *nolite confidere in principibus, in filiis hominum, in quibus non est salus*. Ier. XVII, 5: *maledictus homo qui confidit in homine*. Est etiam servitus secunda, quae debetur praelatis; quae in Graeco vocatur 'dulia'.

should go behind him; but here he says only, **begone**, because the devil cannot follow him. And therefore he says, **begone**, namely to hell; **depart from me, you cursed, into everlasting fire which was prepared for the devil and his angels** (Matt 25:41).

343. **It is written** (Deut 6:16). He frequently brings in such texts from Deuteronomy, to indicate that the teaching of the New Testament is signified by Deuteronomy.

That which follows, '**the Lord your God**', can be brought in two ways. First, as though to say, *you devil, you say that falling down I should adore you, but the law says '**you shall adore the Lord your God**.' Hence it can be brought in for this conclusion, that a mere man ought not be adored. Or, it should be taken such that he speaks of himself as though of God, '**the Lord your God shall you adore**', as though to say, *you ought rather to adore me, than the other way around*, because **it is written**.

Yet the first is more literal.

344. And note that he says two things, namely '**shall you adore**', and '**shall you serve**', and there is a difference between these. For a man should relate himself to God in two ways, because he should be subject to him, and should raise himself to him as to the last end.

As regards the first, we owe him every obedience; *we ought to obey God, rather than men* (Acts 5:29). For we are subject to him when we do his every will.

Moreover, we are raised to God in two ways, because sometimes we draw ourselves toward him; *come to him and be enlightened: and your faces will not be confounded* (Ps 33:6); sometimes we draw others toward him; *for we are God's coadjutors* (1 Cor 3:9). We point to either of these ways sensibly, because when we bow down, we remind ourselves that we should be subject to God; and so he says, **the Lord your God**; *all nations will serve him* (Ps 71:11). Likewise, by the fact that we offer sacrifices and praise, we indicate that we should raise our mind to him; and servitude pertains to this, and this is **him only will you serve**.

And there are two servitudes. There is a certain servitude which is due to God alone, and this is called 'latria' in Greek; and this is twofold. For a certain 'latria' is the adoration which is owed to God alone, which is that he be served above all; another servitude is that we should tend toward him as unto the last end, for there is an adoration or servitude which is only of subjects, as when inferiors serve superiors; *let every soul be subject to higher powers* (Rom 13:1). But one ought not to obey man above all, because one ought never to obey him contrary to God. Likewise, there is no creature which one ought to hold as a last end; *put not your trust in princes: in the children of men, in whom there is no salvation* (Ps 145:2–3). *Cursed be the man that trusts in man* (Jer 17:5). There is also a second servitude, which is owed to superiors, which is called 'dulia' in Greek.

345. Consequenter ponitur victoria Christi, et insinuatur in duobus. In recessu diaboli *tunc reliquit eum diabolus*. Iac. IV, 7: *resistite diabolo et fugiet a vobis*.

Et sicut consuetudo erat apud antiquos, quod quando aliqui victoriam habebant, venerabantur; ita hic celebratur triumphus Christi ab angelis. Unde *et ecce angeli accesserunt, et ministrabant ei*. Non dicit *descenderunt*: quia semper cum eo erant, etsi ad horam recesserunt de eius voluntate, ad hoc ut diabolus locum tentandi haberet: exhibebant enim ministerium in exterioribus, scilicet in miraculis, et aliis corporalibus quae fiunt mediantibus angelis, in interioribus enim non indigebat.

In hoc significatur quod homines qui vincunt diabolum, merentur ministerium angelorum; Lc. XVI, 22: *factum est ut moreretur mendicus, et portaretur ab angelis in sinum Abrahae*.

Et sciendum quod diabolus reliquit Christum usque ad tempus: quia post usus est Iudaeis tamquam membris suis ad eum impugnandum et cetera.

345. Next, Christ's victory is set down, and it is implied in two things. In the devil's retreat, *then the devil left him*. *Resist the devil, and he will fly from you* (Jas 4:7).

And just as it was customary among the ancients that when someone had a victory, he was revered, so here Christ's triumph is celebrated by the angels. Hence, *and behold angels came and ministered to him*. It does not say *descended*, because they were always with him, even if they had withdrawn for a time by his will, so that the devil might have a place for tempting. For they ministered to him in exterior things, namely in miracles, and other corporeal things which come about by the mediation of angels, for he needed nothing in interior things.

In this it is indicated that men who conquer the devil merit the service of angels; *and it came to pass, that the beggar died, and was carried by the angels into Abraham's bosom* (Luke 16:22).

And one should know that the devil left Christ only for a time, because afterwards he used the Jews as though his own members, to attack him.

Lecture 2

4:12 Cum autem audisset Iesus quod Ioannes traditus esset, secessit in Galilaeam, [n. 347]

4:13 et relicta civitate Nazareth, venit, et habitavit in civitate Capharnaum maritima, in finibus Zabulon et Nephtalim: [n. 354]

4:14 ut adimpleretur quod dictum est per Isaiam Prophetam: [n. 355]

4:15 *terra Zabulon, et terra Nephtalim: via maris trans Iordanem, Galilaea gentium:* [n. 356]

4:16 *populus qui ambulabat in tenebris, vidit lucem magnam: et sedentibus in regione umbrae mortis lux orta est eis.* [n. 357]

4:17 Exinde coepit Iesus praedicare et dicere: poenitentiam agite: appropinquabit enim regnum caelorum. [n. 360]

4:18 Ambulans autem Iesus iuxta Mare Galilaeae vidit duos fratres, Simonem qui vocatur Petrus, et Andream fratrem eius mittentes rete in mare: erant enim piscatores. [n. 363]

4:19 Et ait illis: venite post me: et faciam vos fieri piscatores hominum. [n. 370]

4:20 At illi relictis retibus et navi secuti sunt eum. [n. 371]

4:21 Et procedens inde vidit alios duos fratres, Iacobum Zebedaei, et Ioannem fratrem eius in navi cum Zebedaeo patre eorum, reficientes retia sua: et vocavit eos. [n. 374]

4:22 Illi autem statim relictis retibus, et patre, secuti sunt eum. [n. 380]

4:12 Ἀκούσας δὲ ὅτι Ἰωάννης παρεδόθη ἀνεχώρησεν εἰς τὴν Γαλιλαίαν.

4:13 καὶ καταλιπὼν τὴν Ναζαρὰ ἐλθὼν κατῴκησεν εἰς Καφαρναοὺμ τὴν παραθαλασσίαν ἐν ὁρίοις Ζαβουλὼν καὶ Νεφθαλίμ·

4:14 ἵνα πληρωθῇ τὸ ῥηθὲν διὰ Ἠσαΐου τοῦ προφήτου λέγοντος·

4:15 γῆ Ζαβουλὼν καὶ γῆ Νεφθαλίμ, ὁδὸν θαλάσσης, πέραν τοῦ Ἰορδάνου, Γαλιλαία τῶν ἐθνῶν,

4:16 ὁ λαὸς ὁ καθήμενος ἐν σκότει φῶς εἶδεν μέγα, καὶ τοῖς καθημένοις ἐν χώρᾳ καὶ σκιᾷ θανάτου φῶς ἀνέτειλεν αὐτοῖς.

4:17 Ἀπὸ τότε ἤρξατο ὁ Ἰησοῦς κηρύσσειν καὶ λέγειν· μετανοεῖτε· ἤγγικεν γὰρ ἡ βασιλεία τῶν οὐρανῶν.

4:18 Περιπατῶν δὲ παρὰ τὴν θάλασσαν τῆς Γαλιλαίας εἶδεν δύο ἀδελφούς, Σίμωνα τὸν λεγόμενον Πέτρον καὶ Ἀνδρέαν τὸν ἀδελφὸν αὐτοῦ, βάλλοντας ἀμφίβληστρον εἰς τὴν θάλασσαν· ἦσαν γὰρ ἁλιεῖς.

4:19 καὶ λέγει αὐτοῖς· δεῦτε ὀπίσω μου, καὶ ποιήσω ὑμᾶς ἁλιεῖς ἀνθρώπων.

4:20 οἱ δὲ εὐθέως ἀφέντες τὰ δίκτυα ἠκολούθησαν αὐτῷ.

4:21 καὶ προβὰς ἐκεῖθεν εἶδεν ἄλλους δύο ἀδελφούς, Ἰάκωβον τὸν τοῦ Ζεβεδαίου καὶ Ἰωάννην τὸν ἀδελφὸν αὐτοῦ, ἐν τῷ πλοίῳ μετὰ Ζεβεδαίου τοῦ πατρὸς αὐτῶν καταρτίζοντας τὰ δίκτυα αὐτῶν, καὶ ἐκάλεσεν αὐτούς.

4:22 οἱ δὲ εὐθέως ἀφέντες τὸ πλοῖον καὶ τὸν πατέρα αὐτῶν ἠκολούθησαν αὐτῷ.

4:12 And when Jesus had heard that John was delivered up, he retired into Galilee: [n. 347]

4:13 and leaving the city Nazareth, he came and dwelt in Capernaum on the sea coast, in the borders of Zabulon and Nephthalim; [n. 354]

4:14 that it might be fulfilled what was said by Isaiah the Prophet: [n. 355]

4:15 *land of Zabulon and land of Nephthalim, the way of the sea beyond the Jordan, Galilee of the gentiles*: [n. 356]

4:16 *the people who walked in darkness, have seen great light: and to them who sat in the region of the shadow of death, light has sprung up.* [n. 357]

4:17 From that time Jesus began to preach, and to say: do penance, for the kingdom of heaven is at hand. [n. 360]

4:18 And Jesus walking by the Sea of Galilee, saw two brothers, Simon who is called Peter, and Andrew his brother, casting a net into the sea: for they were fishermen. [n. 363]

4:19 And he said to them: come after me, and I will make you fishers of men. [n. 370]

4:20 And immediately leaving their nets, they followed him. [n. 371]

4:21 And going on from there, he saw two other brothers, James the son of Zebedee, and John his brother, in a ship with Zebedee their father, mending their nets: and he called them. [n. 374]

4:22 And they immediately left their nets and father, and followed him. [n. 380]

---

346. Supra Evangelista ostendit quomodo Christus examinatus est, et approbatus, scilicet vincendo diabolum, hic ostendit quomodo Christus docere incepit: et circa hoc tria facit.

346. Above, the Evangelist showed how Christ was examined and approved, namely by overcoming the devil; here he shows how Christ began to teach. And concerning this he does three things:

Primo enim describitur locus in quo praedicat;

secundo ostendit quomodo ministros suae praedicationis elegit, ibi *ambulans autem Iesus iuxta mare Galilaeae, vidit duos fratres*;

tertio quomodo turbam ad audiendum induxit, ibi *et circuibat Iesus totam Galilaeam*.

Circa primum describit tempus, locum et modum praedicandi;

secundum ibi *secessit in Galilaeam* etc.; tertium ibi *et exinde coepit Iesus praedicare*.

347. Tempus istud publicae praedicationis Christi fuit post incarcerationem Ioannis; unde dicit *cum autem audisset Iesus quod Ioannes traditus esset*, a Deo scilicet, quia ipso permittente.

348. Et notandum hoc pro intellectu Evangeliorum, quod hic videtur quaedam contrarietas esse inter Ioannem et alios tres: quia illi dicunt quod Christus descendit in Capharnaum post incarcerationem Ioannis; Ioannes vero dicit quod descendit in Capharnaum ante incarcerationem Ioannis: quae tamen in Galilaea erat.

Respondetur, quod Ioannes qui ultimus fuit, supplevit ea quae ab aliis praetermissa sunt.

Sed quare praetermiserunt? Dicendum, quod licet Christus aliqua fecerit primis duobus annis, pauca tamen fecerat respectu eorum quae facta sunt ultimo anno. Ergo dicendum quod Ioannes loquitur de his quae fecit primo et secundo, et aliqua de tertio: isti vero, quae facta sunt ultimo anno.

349. Item quaeritur quot annis Christus praedicavit.

Quidam dicunt, quod duobus annis et dimidio, ut dimidius computetur ab epiphania usque ad Pascha, licet non sit completus: Ioannes enim non fecit mentionem nisi de triplici Pascha, quia post baptismum dicit quod ivit in Ierusalem, Io. II, 13. Postea facit mentionem de Pascha, quando factum fuit miraculum de quinque panibus, et post unus annus fuit usque ad passionem.

Sed ista opinio non videtur vera pro tanto, quia non concordat opinioni Ecclesiae: tenet enim Ecclesia, quod tria miracula sint facta in die epiphaniae, scilicet de adoratione magorum, de baptismo et de conversione aquae in vinum. Oportet ergo dicere quod a baptismo usque ad conversionem aquae in vinum fuerit annus unus. Unde videtur quod Christus tribus annis praedicavit, quia usque ad miraculum de vino fuit unus annus: et inde ad Pascha fuit medius alius: a purificatione alius usque ad passionem: ita enim sentit Ecclesia.

Et secundum hoc dicendum quod Ioannes parum dicit de primo anno; de secundo vero dicit aliquid, scilicet

for first, the place in which he preached is described;

second, he shows how he chose the servants of his preaching, at *and Jesus walking by the sea of Galilee, saw two brothers*;

third, how he brought the crowd to hear, at *and Jesus went about all Galilee* (Matt 4:23).

Concerning the first, he describes the time, the place, and the manner of preaching.

The second is at *he retired into Galilee*; the third, at *from that time Jesus began to preach*.

347. This time of Christ's public preaching was after the imprisonment of John; hence he says, *and when Jesus had heard that John was delivered up*, namely by God, because he permitted it.

348. And one should note this for the understanding of the Gospels, that there is a seeming contrariety here between John and the other three evangelists, because the other three say that Christ came down into Capernaum after the imprisonment of John, but it is said that he came down into Capernaum before the imprisonment of John (John 2:12); which nevertheless was in Galilee.

One should respond that John, who was last, supplied those things which were left out by the others.

But why did they leave this out? One should say that, although Christ did some things in the first two years, yet they were few in comparison with those things which were done in the last year. So one should say that John speaks of those things which he did in the first and second years, and some things from the third; but these other Gospels speak of those things which were done in the last year.

349. Likewise, it is asked how many years Christ preached.

Some say that he preached for two and a half years, as from epiphany to Passover is reckoned as half a year, although it is not completed; for John does not make mention except of three Passovers, for after the baptism he says that he went into Jerusalem (John 2:13). Afterwards he mentions the Passover when he worked the miracle of the five loaves, and after that there was one year until the passion.

But this opinion does not seem true to this extent, that it does not accord with the opinion of the Church. For the Church holds that three miracles were worked on the day of epiphany, namely the adoration of the magi, the baptism, and the changing of water into wine. Therefore, it must be said that from the baptism to the conversion of water into wine was one year. Hence it seems that Christ preached for three years, because it was one year to the miracle of the wine; and from there to the Passover was another; from the purification to the passion was another; so thinks the Church.

And according to this, one should say that John says very little about the first year; he says something about the second, to be sure, namely how he came down into

quomodo descendit Capharnaum: et de quaestione quae fuit de purificatione inter ipsum Christum et Iudaeos.

350. Sciendum etiam quod Ioannes circa Pascha occisus fuit: quia legitur Io. VI, v. 4, quod quando factum fuit miraculum de quinque panibus, quod Pascha proximum erat; et Matth. XIV, 13 dicitur quod Christus, audita morte Ioannis, secessit in Galilaeam. Patet ergo quod Ioannes decollatus fuit circa Pascha: et Christus publice praedicationem non tenuit, nisi per unum annum.

351. Deinde agitur de loco, cum dicitur **secessit in Galilaeam.** Et

primo agitur de loco provinciae;
secundo de civitate.

352. Dicit ergo **secessit**; ista secessio non est prima de qua Ioannes dicit, sed post unum vel duos annos hoc fuit, quia hanc tacent evangelistae.

Secessit autem propter duo. Primo ut differret tempus passionis suae; Io. VII, 6: *tempus meum nondum advenit.* Secundo propter exemplum nostrum, ut scilicet persecutiones fugeremus; Io. XV, 20: *si me persecuti sunt, et vos persequentur.*

Sed mystice declarat quod praedicatio Christi transitura erat ad gentes: quia Iudaei persequebantur gratiam Dei; Act. XIII, 46: *vobis oportebat primum loqui verbum Dei: sed quoniam repulistis illud, et indignos vos iudicatis aeternae vitae, ecce convertimur ad gentes.*

353. Veniens autem in Galilaeam venit primo in Nazareth, sicut dicit Lucas IV, v. 18 ss., et ibi intravit in synagogam, et docuit *Spiritus Domini super me.* Et inde duxerunt eum Iudaei ad supercilium montis, et voluerunt eum praecipitare, et post Christus fugit, et venit in Capharnaum, et ibi statim curavit daemoniacum, de quo Mc. I, 23. Sed hoc Matthaeus omittit.

354. Nazareth autem interpretatur 'flos.' Per hoc intelliguntur doctores legis, qui non veniunt ad maturitatem. Capharnaum enim interpretatur 'villa pulcherrima,' et significat Ecclesiam; Cant. VI, 3: *pulchra es, amica mea*, et cetera. Capharnaum est maritima ad litteram, quia iuxta lacum quemdam dulcem. Iudaei enim omnem congregationem aquarum appellant mare: et mystice, quia Ecclesia posita est iuxta tribulationes mundi.

In finibus Zabulon et Nephtalim. Galilaea enim divisa erat, et una pars erat in tribu Zabulon et Nephtalim. Inde enim electi sunt principes Ecclesiae, scilicet apostoli.

355. *Ut adimpleretur quod dictum est per Isaiam prophetam.* Nota quod hic non dicitur sicut Is. IX, 1; sed ponitur sensus tantum. Isaias sic: *primo tempore alleviata est terra Zabulon et terra Nephtalim: et novissimo aggravata est via maris trans Iordanem Galilaeae gentium:*

Capernaum, and about the question between Christ and the Jews about purification.

350. One should also know that John was killed around the time of the Passover; because it is said that the Passover was near when the miracle of the five loaves was worked (John 6:4); and it is said that Christ, having heard about the death of John, withdrew into Galilee (Matt 14:13). It is clear then that John had been beheaded around the Passover, and Christ had preached publicly for only one year.

351. Next he treats of the place, when he says, **he retired into Galilee.** And

first, the location of the province is treated;
second, of the city.

352. He says then, **he retired**; this withdrawal is not the first, which John speaks about (John 2:12); but this happened after one or two years, because the evangelists are silent about this.

Now, he withdrew for two reasons. First, so that he might put off the time of his passion; *my time is not yet come* (John 7:6). Second, for the sake of our example, namely that we might flee from persecutions; *if they have persecuted me, they will also persecute you* (John 15:20).

But mystically, he indicates that Christ's preaching was going to pass over to the gentiles, because the Jews were persecuting the grace of God; *to you it behoved us first to speak the word of God: but because you reject it, and judge yourselves unworthy of eternal life, behold we turn to the gentiles* (Acts 13:46).

353. And coming into Galilee, he came first into Nazareth (Luke 4:18), and there he went into the synagogue, and taught, *the Spirit of the Lord is upon me* (Luke 4:18: Isa 61:1). And from there the Jews led him to the edge of a cliff, and wanted to throw him down; and afterwards Christ fled, and came into Capernaum, and there he immediately cured a demon-possessed man (Mark 1:23). But Matthew omits this.

354. Now, Nazareth is interpreted as 'flower'. By this the teachers of the law are understood, who did not come to maturity. For Capernaum is interpreted as 'most beautiful village', and signifies the Church; *you are beautiful, O my love* (Song 6:3). Capernaum is literally by the sea, because it was next to a certain pleasant lake. For the Jews called every gathering of waters a sea; and mystically, because the Church is set next to the afflictions of the world.

In the borders of Zabulon and Nephthalim. For Galilee was divided, and one part was in the tribe of Zabulon and Nephthali. For the princes of the Church were chosen from there, namely the apostles.

355. *That it might be fulfilled what was said by Isaiah the prophet.* Notice that this is not said exactly as it is in Isaiah, but the sense only is set down. Isaiah speaks thus: *at the first time the land of Zabulon, and the land of Nephtali was lightened: and at the last the way of the sea beyond the Jordan*

populus qui ambulabat in tenebris vidit lucem magnam et cetera.

Et exponitur tripliciter secundum Hieronymum. Primo sic. *Primo tempore alleviata est* per praedicationem Christi a peccatis, et *novissimo via*, quae iuxta mare Galilaeae, *aggravata est* onere peccatorum, quia post praedicationem Christi persecuti sunt apostolos. Vel aliter. *Primo tempore.* Tangit historiam: quia Rex Assyriorum Teglatphalassar, qui primo venit super terram Iudaeorum, primo duxit in captivitatem illas tribus. Et hoc est *primo tempore alleviata est*: quia tunc peccatores fuerunt primo in captivitatem ducti. *Et novissimo* etc., quia postea totus populus ductus fuit in captivitatem.

Sed quid ad propositum? Dicendum quod ubi primo incepit persecutio, ibi prius Dominus voluit dare consolationem.

Vel aliter. *Primo tempore*, idest tempore praedicationis Christi, *alleviata* etc., idest onere peccatorum exonerata per praedicationem Christi, *et novissimo aggravata est*, idest condensata Christi praedicatio, et multiplicata per Paulum qui ibi praedicavit.

356. Evangelista enim non ponit nisi sensum in constructione: *'terra Zabulon, et terra Nephtalim, via maris trans Iordanem'*, idest iuxta mare. Et dicit *'terra'*, idest populus, ut omnes sint nominati. Et dicit *'Galilaea gentium'*, quia Galilaea dividitur in duas partes: una gentium, alia Iudaeorum: et tunc divisa erat secundum quod dicitur III Reg. c. IX, 11, quia Salomon propter ligna quae Rex Tyri misit ad eum in aedificationem templi, dedit ei viginti oppida: qui cum esset gentilis posuit gentiles ad habitandum; et ideo dicitur *'Galilaea gentium'* et erat in tribu Nephtalim; licet alia in tribu Iuda.

Alia littera: *'trans Iordanem Galilaeae'*, idest in comparatione ad Galilaeam. Sed prima expositio melior est.

357. *'Populus qui ambulabat in tenebris, vidit lucem magnam.'* Duo dicit *'qui ambulabat'*, et *'qui sedebat'*; qui enim est in tenebris a principio quae non sunt multum condensae, nec stupefit ab eis, vadit, maxime quando sperat invenire lucem: et dum stupefactus est a tenebris, stat.

Ista est differentia inter Iudaeos et gentiles: quia Iudaei quamvis essent in tenebris, non tamen totaliter oppressi erant ab eis, quia non omnes colebant idola, sed sperabant Christum venturum, et ideo ambulabant; Is. l, 10: *quis ambulavit in tenebris, et non est lumen ei? Speret in nomine Domini* et cetera. Gentiles vero non expectabant; et ideo non erat spes de luce. Et iterum oppressi erant tenebris, quia idola colebant, quia secundum Ps. LXXV, 2, *notus in Iudaea Deus*, et ideo stabant. Et

of the Galilee of the gentiles was heavily loaded. The people that walked in darkness, have seen a great light (Isa 9:1–2).

And this is explained in three ways, according to Jerome. First, thus. *The first time* it was *lightened* from sins by Christ's preaching, and *at the last the way*, which is next to the sea of Galilee, was *heavily loaded* with the burden of sin, because after Christ's preaching they persecuted the apostles. Or in another way: *at the first time.* He touches upon the history, because the King of the Assyrians, Teglatphalassar, who first came over the land of the Jews, first led those tribes into captivity. And this is *at the first time the land . . . was lightened* because then the sinners were first led into captivity. *And at the last*, because afterward the whole people was led into captivity.

But how is this relevant? One should say that, where persecution first began, there the Lord willed first to give consolation.

Or in another way. *At the first time*, i.e., in the time of Christ's preaching, *the land . . . was lightened*, i.e., they were freed from the burden of sins by Christ's preaching, *and at the last the way . . . was heavily loaded*, i.e., the preaching of Christ was gathered together, and multiplied by Paul, who preached there.

356. For the Evangelist sets down only the sense in the arrangement: *'land of Zabulon and land of Nephthalim, the way of the sea beyond the Jordan'*, i.e., next to the sea. And he says, *'land'*, i.e., people, so that all might be named. And he says, *'Galilee of the gentiles'*, because Galilee is divided into two parts, one of the gentiles, the other of the Jews; and it had been divided at that time (1 Kgs 9:11), because Solomon, on account of the wood which the King of Tyre sent to him for the building of the temple, gave to him twenty cities. Since he was a gentile, he placed gentiles there to live; and therefore it is called *'Galilee of the gentiles'*, and was in the tribe of Nephtali; although the other was in the tribe of Judas.

Other texts: *'beyond the Jordan of Galilee'*, i.e., in comparison to Galilee. But the first explanation is better.

357. *'The people who walked in darkness, have seen a great light.'* He says two things: *'who walked'*, and *'who sat.'* For he who from the beginning is in a darkness which is not thick, and so he is not stupefied by it, goes forward, and most of all when he hopes to find light; and when he is stupefied by the darkness, he stands still.

This is the difference between the Jews and the gentiles, because although the Jews were in darkness, yet they were not entirely oppressed by it, because not all of them worshiped idols, but they hoped in the Christ to come, and therefore they walked; *who is there among you . . . who has walked in darkness, and has no light? let him hope in the name of the Lord, and lean upon his God* (Isa 50:10). But the gentiles were not expecting the Christ, and so there was no hope of light. And again, they were oppressed by

hoc est quod dicitur *'populus qui sedebat in tenebris, vidit lucem magnam.'* Lux Iudaeorum non magna, II Pet. I, 19: *habemus propheticum sermonem, cui bene facitis attendentes sicut lucernae lucenti in caliginoso loco, sed ista magna sicut solis lux;* Mal. IV, 2: *vobis autem timentibus nomen Domini orietur Sol iustitiae.*

358. *'Et sedentibus'*, idest gentibus, *'in regione umbrae mortis.'* Mors est damnatio in inferno; Ps. XLVIII, 15: *mors depascet eos.* *'Umbra mortis'* est similitudo futurae damnationis, quae est in peccatoribus. Magna autem poena eorum qui in inferno sunt, est separatio a Deo. Et quia peccatores iam separati sunt a Deo, ideo similitudinem habent futurae damnationis, sicut et iusti similitudinem habent futurae beatitudinis; II Cor. III, 18: *nos autem gloriam Domini speculantes in eamdem imaginem transformamur a claritate in claritatem.*

359. Et nota quod gentibus *'lux orta est'*, quia ipsi non iverunt ad lucem, sed lux venit ad eos; Io. III, 19: *lux venit in mundum.* *'Orta est eis.'* Et illa terra est in confinio Iudaeorum et gentium, ut ostenderet quod utrosque vocavit; Is. XLIX, 6: *parum est ut sis mihi servus ad suscitandas tribus Iacob, et faeces Israel convertendas.* Et post: *dedi te in lucem gentium, ut sis salus mea usque ad extremum terrae.*

360. *Exinde coepit Iesus praedicare.* Posito loco ubi Christus primo praedicare incepit, hic ponitur modus praedicandi. *Exinde*, scilicet post superationem gulae, inanis gloriae et ambitionis, sive avaritiae, *coepit praedicare*: tales enim convenienter praedicare possunt. Et sic impletur illud Act. I, 1: *coepit Iesus facere et docere.*

Vel *exinde*, idest post incarcerationem Ioannis, incepit publice praedicare: prius enim occulte et quibusdam, Io. I, 38 ss., scilicet Petro, Andreae, Philippo et Natanaeli, sed hic publice. Noluit autem primo praedicare publice, ut daret locum praedicationi Ioannis: aliter nihil valuisset, sicut lumen stellarum offuscatur per lumen solis. Significatur autem per hoc quod cessantibus figuris legis, incepit praedicatio Christi; I Cor. XIII, 10: *cum venerit quod perfectum est, evacuabitur quod ex parte est.* Per Ioannem enim significatur lex; infra XI, 13: *lex et prophetae usque ad Ioannem.*

Poenitentiam agite. Notandum quod eadem verba dicit hic Christus, quae Ioannes, propter duo. Primo enim admonet nos de humilitate, ut scilicet nullus dedignetur verba ab aliis dicta praedicare, cum ipse fons ecclesiasticae scientiae eadem praedicaverit. Secundo quia Ioannes est vox; ipse vero Verbum. Idem autem

the darkness, because they worshiped idols, since: *in Judea God is known* (Isa 50:10), and so they stood still. And this is what is said, *'the people who sat in darkness, have seen a great light.'* The light of the Jews was not great, *and we have the more firm prophetical word: to which you do well to attend, as to a light that shines in a dark place, until the day dawn, and the day star arise in your hearts* (2 Pet 1:19). *But unto you who fear my name, the Sun of justice will arise* (Mal 4:2).

358. *'And to them who sat'*, i.e., the gentiles, *'in the region of the shadow of death.'* *'Death'* is damnation in hell; *they are laid in hell like sheep: death will feed upon them* (Ps 48:15). The *'shadow of death'* is the likeness of future damnation which is in sinners. Now, the great punishment of those who are in hell is separation from God. And because sinners are already separated from God, they have a likeness of future damnation, as the just also have a likeness of future beatitude; *but we all beholding the glory of the Lord with open face, are transformed into the same image from glory to glory, as by the Spirit of the Lord* (2 Cor 3:18).

359. And notice that *'light has sprung up'* to the gentiles, because they had not come to the light, but the light came to them; *the light is come into the world* (John 3:19). *'Light has sprung up.'* And this land is on the border of the Jews and the gentiles, to show that he called both; *it is a small thing that you should be my servant to raise up the tribes of Jacob, and to convert the dregs of Israel. Behold, I have given you to be the light of the gentiles, that you may be my salvation even to the farthest part of the earth* (Isa 49:6).

360. *From that time Jesus began to preach.* The place having been set down where Christ first began to preach, here the manner of preaching is set down. *From that time*, namely after defeating gluttony, vainglory, and ambition or greed, he *began to preach*; for such men can fittingly preach. And in this way is fulfilled, *Jesus began to do and to teach* (Acts 1:1).

Or, *from that time*, i.e., after the imprisonment of John, he began to preach publicly, for at first he preached in a hidden way and to certain men (John 1:38), namely to Peter, Andrew, Philip, and Nathaniel; but here, publicly. Now, at first he did not wish to preach publicly, so as to give place to John's preaching; otherwise it would have done no good, just as the light of a star is obscured by the light of the sun. Moreover, by this it is signified that, the figures of the law having ceased, Christ's preaching began; *but when that which is perfect is come, that which is in part will be done away* (1 Cor 13:10). For John signifies the law; *for all the prophets and the law prophesied until John* (Matt 11:13).

Do penance. One should notice that Christ says here the same words as John, for two reasons. First, he reminds us of humility, namely so that no one would scornfully refuse to preach words said by another, since the very fount of ecclesiastical wisdom preached the same words as John. Second, because John is the voice, but he is the Word. Now,

significatur per verbum et vocem, nisi quia verbum est expressivum vocis.

Circa hoc autem duo facit: unum admonet; aliud promittit.

Primum ibi *poenitentiam agite*; secundum ibi *appropinquabit enim regnum caelorum*.

361. Sed quare non admonuit de iustitia in principio suae praedicationis, sed ad poenitentiam?

Dicendum quod causa fuit, quia prius admonuit de iustitia per legem naturae, et Scripturae, sed transgressi erant; Is. XXIV, 5: *transgressi sunt leges, mutaverunt ius, dissipaverunt foedus sempiternum*. In hoc enim dat intelligere quod omnes peccatores invenit; I Tim. I, 15: *Christus Iesus venit in hunc mundum peccatores salvos facere*; Rom. III, v. 23: *omnes enim peccaverunt, et egent gloria Dei*. Et hoc est *poenitentiam agite*.

362. Promittit autem aliud; unde *appropinquabit enim regnum caelorum*. Ista promissio in duobus differt a promissione Veteris Testamenti; quia ibi temporalia, hic caelestia, et aeterna; Is. I, 19: *si me audieritis, bona terrae comedetis*. Item ibi regnum Chananaeorum et Iebusaeorum; hic regnum caelorum; unde *appropinquabit*, in vos, *regnum caelorum*. Et ideo doctrina Christi dicitur Novum Testamentum: quia facta est ibi nova pactio inter nos et Deum de regno caelorum; Ier. XXXI, 31: *feriam domui Israel et domui Iuda foedus novum*. Secundo quia vetus lex simul cum promissione habebat comminationem; Is. I, 19: *si volueritis, et audieritis me, bona terrae comedetis: quod si nolueritis, et me ad iracundiam provocaveritis, gladius devorabit vos*. Et Deut. XXVIII idem habetur: ubi multae benedictiones promittuntur his qui legem servaverint, et multas comminatur Moyses maledictiones transgressoribus legis. Et hoc ideo est, quia vetus erat lex timoris, nova vero amoris. Augustinus: *brevis differentia, timor et amor*. Hebr. XII, 18: *non enim accessistis ad tractabilem et accessibilem ignem, et turbinem, et caliginem, et procellam, et tubae sonum, et vocem verborum, quam qui audierunt excusaverunt se, ne eis fieret verbum*. Et ideo dicit *appropinquabit regnum caelorum*, scilicet beatitudo aeterna. Et dicit *appropinquabit*, quia ille qui dabat, ad nos descendit, quia nos non poteramus ascendere ad Deum.

363. *Ambulans autem* et cetera. Postquam incepit praedicare, voluit suae praedicationis habere ministros: unde hic advocat ad se eos: et circa hoc duo facit, secundum quod duo paria ministrorum advocat. Quia primo Petrum et Andream; secundo Iacobum et Ioannem.

Circa primum quatuor facit:

the same thing is signified by the word and the voice, because the word is expressive of the voice.

And concerning this he does two things: he urges one thing; he promises another.

The first is at *do penance*; the second is at *for the kingdom of heaven is at hand*.

361. But why did he not give advice about justice at the beginning of his preaching, but to penance?

One should say that the reason was that he first gave advice about justice through the law of nature and the Scriptures, but they had transgressed; *they have transgressed the laws, they have changed the ordinance, they have broken the everlasting covenant* (Isa 24:5). For in this he gives one to understand that he found all men sinners; *Christ Jesus came into this world to save sinners* (1 Tim 1:15); *for all have sinned, and do need the glory of God* (Rom 3:23). And this is *do penance*.

362. He promises another thing; hence, *for the kingdom of heaven is at hand*. This promise differs from the promise of the Old Testament in two ways, because there temporal things were promised, here heavenly and eternal things; *if you are willing, and will hearken to me, you will eat the good things of the land* (Isa 1:19). Similarly, there the kingdom of the Chanaanites and Jebusites was promised, here the kingdom of heaven; hence, *for the kingdom of heaven is at hand* in you. And so Christ's teaching is called the New Testament, because a new agreement was made there between us and God concerning the kingdom of heaven; *I will make a new covenant with the house of Israel, and with the house of Judah* (Jer 31:31). Second, because the old law had a threat along with the promise; *if you are willing, and will hearken to me, you will eat the good things of the land. But if you will not, and will provoke me to wrath: the sword will devour you* (Isa 1:19). And Deuteronomy says the same thing, where many blessings are promised to those who serve the law, and Moses threatens many curses on the transgressors of the law (Deut 28). And this is because the old was a law of fear, but the new a law of love. Augustine: *the difference briefly: fear and love*. As: *for you are not come to a mountain that might be touched, and a burning fire, and a whirlwind, and darkness, and storm, and the sound of a trumpet, and the voice of words, which they that heard excused themselves, that the word might not be spoken to them* (Heb 12:18–19). And so he says, *the kingdom of heaven is at hand*, namely eternal beatitude. And he says, *is at hand*, because the one who was giving descended to us, since we were not able to ascend to God.

363. *And Jesus walking*. After he began to preach, he wished to have servants of his preaching; so here he calls them to himself. And concerning this he does two things, according as he calls two pairs of servants: first he calls Peter and Andrew; second, James and John.

Concerning the first, he does four things:

primo enim describitur locus vocationis;

secundo ponitur conditio vocatorum, ibi *erant enim piscatores*;

tertio vocatio, ibi *et ait illis*;

quarto ipsorum obedientia perfecta, ibi *at illi continuo relictis retibus secuti sunt eum*.

364. Dicit ergo *ambulans iuxta mare Galilaeae*. Locus congruus: quia, sicut dicit Glossa, piscatores vocaturus, ambulat iuxta mare.

Quantum autem ad mysterium, sciendum, quod stare Dei significat aeternitatem et immobilitatem; ipsius ambulare, temporalem nativitatem. Per hoc ergo quod ambulans discipulos vocavit, significatur quod per mysterium suae incarnationis nos ad se traxit; Ps. VII, 7: *exsurge, domine, in praecepto quod mandasti*, idest disposuisti implendum, *et synagoga populorum circumdabit te*.

Et dicit *Galilaeae*, per quod intelligitur turbulentia huius mundi; Is. LVII, 20: *cor impii quasi mare fervens, quod quiescere non potest, et redundant fluctus eius in conculcationem et lutum*. Christus similitudinem habuit peccatoris; Rom. VIII, 3: *misit Deus Filium suum in similitudinem carnis peccati* et cetera.

365. Consequenter vocatorum describitur conditio.

Et primo quantum ad numerum; secundo quantum ad nomina; tertio quantum ad actum; quarto quantum ad officium.

366. Dicit ergo *vidit duos*, non oculo corporis tantum, sed etiam mentis: visus enim eius est respectus misericordiae; unde Ex. III, 7: *videns vidi afflictionem populi mei, qui est in Aegypto* et cetera.

Et nota quod idem significatur per *duos*, et *fratres*: utrumque enim ad caritatem pertinet, quae consistit in dilectione Dei et proximi. Et ideo binos elegit, et binos ad praedicandum misit: et voluit significari per hoc caritas spiritualis, quia caritas firmatur magis, quando in natura fundatur; Ps. CXXXII, v. 1: *ecce quam bonum et quam iucundum habitare fratres in unum*.

367. *Simonem qui vocatur Petrus*, nunc scilicet, sed non tunc: quia Christus postea imposuit ei hoc nomen, sed primo promisit; Io. I, 42: *tu vocaberis Cephas*, sed imposuit Matth. XVI, 18: *tu es Petrus. Et Andream*.

Ista nomina debet habere quilibet praedicator. Simon enim interpretatur 'obediens'; Petrus 'agnoscens'; Andreas 'fortitudo'. Et praedicator debet esse obediens, ut alios possit ad hoc invitare, Prov. XXI, 28: *vir obediens loquetur victorias*: agnoscens, ut alios sciat instruere: I Cor. XIV, 19: *volo quinque verba sensu meo loqui, ut alios instruam*, fortis, ut non terreatur comminationibus; Ier. c. I, 18: *dedi te hodie in civitatem munitam, et in columnam ferream, et in murum aereum*; Ez. III, 8: *dedi faciem tuam valentiorem faciebus eorum, et frontem tuam*

first, the place of the calling is described;

second, the condition of those called is set down, at *for they were fishermen*;

third, the calling, at *and he said to them*;

fourth, their perfect obedience, at *and they immediately leaving their nets, they followed him*.

364. He says then, *walking by the sea of Galilee*. A fitting place, because, as the Gloss says, about to call fishermen, he walked by the sea.

Moreover, as regards the mystery, one should know that God's standing signifies eternity and immobility; his walking, the temporal birth. Therefore, the fact that he called his disciples while walking signifies that he drew us to himself by the mystery of his incarnation; *and arise, O Lord my God, in the precept which you have commanded*, i.e., which you have arranged to be fulfilled, *and a congregation of people will surround you* (Ps 7:7–8).

And he says, *of Galilee*, by which is understood the turbulence of this world; *but the wicked are like the raging sea, which cannot rest, and the waves thereof cast up dirt and mire* (Isa 57:20). Christ has the likeness of a sinner; *God sending his own Son, in the likeness of sinful flesh and of sin* (Rom 8:3).

365. Next, the condition of the ones called is described.

And first, as regards number; second, as regards name; third, as regards acts; fourth, as regards office.

366. It says then that he *saw two*, not only with the eye of the body, but also with that of the mind; for his vision is a refuge of mercy; hence, *I have seen the affliction of my people in Egypt* (Exod 3:7).

And note that the same thing is signified by *two* and *brothers*, for both pertain to charity, which consists in the love of God and of neighbor. And this is why he chose pairs, and sent pairs for preaching; and he wished to signify spiritual charity by this, for charity is made more firm when it is founded on nature; *behold how good and how pleasant it is for brethren to dwell in unity* (Ps 132:1).

367. *Simon who is called Peter*, that is, now, but not then, because Christ gave this name to him afterwards, but at first promised it; *you will be called Cephas* (John 1:42), but he gave it in Matthew: *you are Peter* (Matt 16:18). *And Andrew.*

Any preacher ought to have these names. For Simon is interpreted as 'obedient'; Peter, as 'discerning'; Andrew, as 'courage'. And the preacher should be obedient, so he can invite others to this; *an obedient man will speak of victory* (Prov 21:28). Discerning, so that he may instruct others; *I had rather speak five words with my understanding, that I may instruct others also* (1 Cor 14:19). Courageous, so that he may not be frightened by threats; *for behold I have made you this day a fortified city, and a pillar of iron, and a wall of brass* (Jer 1:18); *behold I have made your face stronger than*

duriorem frontibus eorum, ut adamantem, et ut silicem dedi faciem tuam.

368. Sequitur *mittentes rete in mare*.

Quaerit Chrysostomus quare Dominus captavit istam horam. Et dicit, ut daretur exemplum quod numquam debemus omittere servitium Dei propter occupationes. Vel ideo, quia per hunc actum praefigurabatur actus futurorum praedicatorum, quia per verba praedicantium quasi per retia trahuntur homines.

369. Ponitur officium *erant enim piscatores*. Et sciendum quod inter omnes homines, piscatores sunt simpliciores; et Dominus de simplicissimo statu voluit habere homines, et illos eligere, ut non imputaretur sapientiae humanae id quod factum fuit per eos; I Cor. I, 26: *videte vocationem nostram, fratres, quia non multi sapientes secundum carnem, non multi potentes, non multi nobiles; sed quae stulta sunt mundi eligit Deus, ut confundat sapientes*. Et ideo non elegit Augustinum, aut Cyprianum oratorem, sed Petrum piscatorem: et de piscatore lucratus est et imperatorem, et oratorem.

370. *Et ait*. Hic ponitur vocatio, circa quam tria consideranda sunt. Primo enim invitat; secundo ducatum promittit; tertio praemium.

Dicit ergo *venite*. Hoc ex sola liberalitate divina est, ut ad se trahat; Eccli. XXIV, 26: *transite ad me omnes qui concupiscitis me, et a generationibus meis adimplemini*; infra c. XI, 28: *venite ad me omnes qui laboratis et onerati estis, et ego reficiam vos*. *Post me*, quasi dicat: ego vado, et vos venite *post me*, quia ego ero dux vester; Prov. IV, 11: *viam sapientiae monstrabo tibi, et ducam te per semitas aequitatis; quas cum ingressus fueris, non arctabuntur gressus tui, et currens non habebis offendiculum*; Ps. CXXXVIII, 17: *mihi autem nimis honorificati sunt amici tui, Deus, nimis confortatus est principatus eorum*. *Faciam*, quasi, commutabo vestrum officium in maius. De istis dicitur Ier. XVI, 16: *ecce ego mittam piscatores multos, dicit Dominus, et piscabuntur eos* et cetera.

Et dicit *faciam*, quia frustra laborat praedicatio exterius, nisi adsit interius gratia Redemptoris: non enim virtute sua trahebant homines, sed operatione Christi. Et ideo dicit *faciam*. Ista quidem est maxima dignitas; unde Dionysius: nihil dignius in officio hominum quam Dei cooperatorem fieri. Dignitas enim sola in sua claritate consistit. Ad illam autem dignitatem magis appropinquant qui sic illuminantur quod alia illuminent. Quamquam vero illuminent homines qui sequuntur Christum, et quantum ad iustitiam magna faciunt, sed tamen asserunt dignitatem Christi quantum ad unum tantum; vita autem praedicatorum quantum ad duo;

their faces: and your forehead harder than their foreheads. I have made your face like an adamant and like flint: fear them not, neither be dismayed at their presence (Ezek 3:8).

368. There follows, *casting a net into the sea*.

Chysostom asks why the Lord seized upon this hour. And he says, in order to give example that we ought never to omit the service of God on account of occupations. Or for this reason, because by this act was prefigured the future act of preaching, since men are drawn by the words of preaching as though by nets.

369. The office is set down, *for they were fishermen*. And one should know that among all men, fishermen are the most simple; and the Lord wished to have men from the most simple state in life, and chose these so that what was done through them would not be attributed to human wisdom; *for see your vocation, brethren, that there are not many wise according to the flesh, not many mighty, not many noble: but the foolish things of the world has God chosen, that he may confound the wise (1 Cor 1:26–27).* And therefore he did not choose an Augustine, or a Cyprian the orator, but Peter the fisherman; and from a fisherman he gained both a commander and an orator.

370. *And he said to them.* Here the calling is set down, concerning which three things are to be considered: first, he invites; second, he promises guidance; third, a reward.

He says then, *come*. This is only out of the divine generosity, that he draws them to himself; *come over to me, all you who desire me, and be filled with my fruits (Sir 24:26); come to me, all you who labor, and are burdened, and I will refresh you (Matt 11:28). After me*, as though to say, I am going, and you come *after me*, because I will be your leader; *I will show you the way of wisdom, I will lead you by the paths of equity: which when you have entered, your steps will not be straitened, and when you run, you will not meet a stumblingblock (Prov 4:11–12); but to me your friends, O God, are made exceedingly honorable: their principality is exceedingly strengthened (Ps 138:17). I will make*, as though, I will change your office into a greater one. It is said of these, *behold I will send many fishers, says the Lord, and they will fish them (Jer 16:16).*

And he says, *I will make*, because preaching labors exteriorly in vain, unless there is present the interior grace of the Redeemer; for they did not draw men by their own power, but by the working of Christ. And therefore he says, *I will make*. Indeed, this is the greatest dignity; hence Dionysius: *there is nothing more dignified among human offices than to become a co-worker of God.* For dignity consists only in his brightness. Moreover, those approach more to that dignity who are so illumined that they illumine others. Although indeed those who follow Christ illuminate men, and are made great with regard to justice, nevertheless they obtain the dignity of Christ regarding one thing only; the

Dan. XII, 3: *qui ad iustitiam erudiunt multos, fulgebunt quasi stellae in perpetuas aeternitates.*

371. Ponitur eorum obedientia *at illi, relictis retibus et navi, secuti sunt eum.* Et ostendit obedientiam eorum quantum ad tria.

Primo quantum ad promptitudinem, quia non distulerunt: unde *at illi.* Contra illos de quibus Eccli. V, 8: *ne differas de die in diem*; Gal. I, 15: *cum autem placuit ei qui me segregavit ex utero matris meae, et vocavit per gratiam suam, ut revelaret Filium suum in me, ut evangelizarem illum in gentibus, continuo non acquievi carni et sanguini.* Is. l, 5: *Dominus aperuit mihi aurem, ego autem non contradico, retrorsum non abii.*

372. Secundo quantum ad expeditionem, quia reliquerunt; quia non pensandus est census, sed affectus; quia omnia dimittit qui quicquid habere potest, dimittit.

Sed quae necessitas relinquendi omnia? Chrysostomus: *nullus potest possidere divitias, et perfecte ad regnum caelorum venire; sunt enim impedimentum virtutis, diminuunt enim sollicitudinem aeternorum, propter quod non perfecte potest homo inhaerere divinis.* Et ideo dimittenda sunt; I Cor. c. IX, 25: *omnis qui in agone contendit, ab omnibus se abstinet* et cetera.

373. Tertio quantum ad executionem, quia secuti sunt eum: non est enim nimis magnum dimittere omnia, sed perfectio consistit in sequela ipsius, quae est per caritatem; I Cor. XIII, 3: *si distribuero in cibos pauperum omnes facultates meas, et si tradidero corpus meum ita ut ardeam, caritatem autem non habuero, nihil mihi prodest.* Non enim consistit per se in exterioribus perfectio, scilicet paupertate, virginitate, et huiusmodi, nisi quia ista sunt instrumenta ad caritatem; et ideo dicit *et secuti sunt eum.*

374. Consequenter agitur de alia vocatione: *et procedens inde vidit alios duos fratres, Iacobum Zebedaei et Ioannem fratrem eius.* Et

primo describuntur vocati;

secundo ponitur vocatio, ibi *et vocavit* etc.;

tertio obedientiam vocatorum, ibi *illi autem, relictis retibus et patre, secuti sunt eum.*

Vocati quadrupliciter describuntur. Quantum ad numerum, nomina, pietatem, et paupertatem.

375. Dicit ergo *et procedens inde vidit alios duos fratres.* Nota quod a principio vocavit fratres: et quamvis multos alios vocavit, tamen de istis specialiter fit mentio, quia praecipui erant, et quia binos vocavit eos; lex enim nova in caritate fundatur; unde et in Veteri Testamento duos fratres vocavit, Aaron et Moysen, quia etiam

life of the preachers is made great regarding two things. They who are learned will shine as the brightness of the firmament: and they who instruct many to justice, as stars for all eternity (Dan 12:3).

371. Their obedience is set down at *and immediately leaving their nets, they followed him.* And he shows their obedience with regard to three things.

First, with regard to promptitude, because they did not put it off; hence, *and immediately*, contrary to those of whom it is said: *defer it not from day to day* (Sir 5:8); *but when it pleased him, who separated me from my mother's womb, and called me by his grace, to reveal his Son in me, that I might preach him among the gentiles, immediately I condescended not to flesh and blood* (Gal 1:15–16). *The Lord has opened my ear, and I do not resist; I have not gone back* (Isa 50:5)

372. Second, regarding readiness, because they left everything behind, since wealth is not to be considered, but disposition; because he leaves all things who leaves whatever he can have.

But what is the necessity for leaving all things? Chrysostom: *no one can possess riches, and come perfectly to the kingdom of heaven; for they are an impediment to virtue, for they lessen the concern for eternal things, on account of which a man cannot perfectly inherit divine things.* And therefore they should be left; *and every one that strives for the mastery, refrains himself from all things* (1 Cor 9:25).

373. Third, as regards execution, because they followed him: for it is not exceedingly great to leave all things, but perfection consists in following him, which is accomplished by charity. *And if I should distribute all my goods to feed the poor, and if I should deliver my body to be burned, and have not charity, it profits me nothing* (1 Cor 13:3). For perfection does not consist *per se* in exterior things, that is, poverty, virginity, and suchlike, unless because these things are instruments for charity; and this is why it says, *they followed him.*

374. Next, he treats of the other calling: *and going on from there, he saw two other brothers, James the son of Zebedee, and John his brother.* And

first, the ones called are described;

second, the calling is set down, at *and he called them*;

third, the obedience of the ones called, at *and they immediately left their nets and father, and followed him.*

The ones called are described in four ways: as regards number, names, piety, and poverty.

375. It says then, *and going on from there, he saw two other brothers.* Note that from the beginning he called brothers; and although he called many others, nevertheless special mention is made of these, because they were first, and because he called them in pairs. For the new law is founded on charity; hence in the Old Testament he called two brothers, Aaron and Moses, because the command

ibi dabatur mandatum de caritate. Et quia perfectior est nova, ideo in principio vocatur duplex numerus fratrum.

376. *Iacobum Zebedaei, et Ioannem fratrem eius*.

Per istos quatuor designatur doctrina quatuor Evangeliorum, vel quatuor virtutes: quia per Petrum, qui interpretatur 'agnoscens,' virtus prudentiae; per Andream, qui interpretatur 'virilis,' seu 'fortissimus,' virtus fortitudinis; per Iacobum, qui interpretatur 'supplantator,' virtus iustitiae; per Ioannem propter virginitatem, virtus temperantiae.

377. Ponitur pietas, quia erant cum Zebedaeo patre. Chrysostomus: *admiranda est eorum pietas, quia pauperes arte piscatoria panem quaerunt, et tamen senem patrem non derelinquunt.* Eccli. III, 8: *qui timet Deum, honorat parentes.*

378. Paupertas designatur in hoc, quia reficiebant retia sua. Nihilominus per istos qui mittebant retia, signantur illi qui in prima aetate negotiantur in mundo; per istos qui iam miserunt, et reficiebant, significantur illi qui diu negotiati sunt in mundo; et sunt iam per peccatum absorpti, et vocantur ad Christum. Thren. III, 27: *bonum est viro, cum portaverit iugum domini ab adolescentia sua.*

379. *Et vocavit eos*, interius et exterius; ad Rom. VIII, 30: *quos praedestinavit, hos et vocavit.* Vocare interius nihil aliud est quam praebere auxilium humanae menti cum vult convertere nos.

380. Sequitur de obedientia ***illi autem, relictis retibus et patre, secuti sunt eum*.** Nota quod duo superiores navem tantum, isti autem reliquerunt retia, navem et patrem: in quo significatur quod propter Christum debemus omittere omnes terrenas occupationes, quae designantur per rete; II Tim. II, 4: *nemo militans Deo implicat se negotiis saecularibus*; divitias, sive possessiones, quae designantur per navem; infra XIX, 21: ***si vis perfectus esse, vade et vende omnia quae habes, et da pauperibus, et habebis thesaurum in caelo, et veni, sequere me***; affectum carnalem, qui per patrem; Ps. XLIV, 11: *obliviscere populum tuum, et domum patris tui.*

Mystice vero per Zebedaeum significatur mundus, qui interpretatur 'fluxus vehemens.'

381. Sed hic est quaestio: videtur enim quod isti peccaverunt dimittendo patrem senem et pauperem, quia filii tenentur subvenire parentibus. Et generaliter quaeritur utrum alicui liceat dimittere parentes in ultima necessitate, intrando religionem.

Dicendum quod consilium numquam praeiudicat praecepto; sed hoc, scilicet *honora patrem tuum et matrem tuam*, Ex. XX, 12 est praeceptum; et ideo si pater nullo modo possit vivere nisi adiutus a filio, filius non debet intrare religionem. Sed hic casus non erat in Zebedaeo, quia poterat se iuvare, et habebat necessaria.

about charity was given even there. And because the new is more perfect, therefore in the beginning a twofold number of brothers is called.

376. *James the son of Zebedee, and John his brother*.

By these four is indicated the teaching of the four Gospels, or the four virtues; because by Peter, who is interpreted as 'discerning', the virtue of prudence is indicated; by Andrew, who is interpreted 'manly', or 'most courageous', the virtue of fortitude; by James, who is interpreted 'supplanter', the virtue of justice; by John, on account of virginity, the virtue of temperance.

377. Their piety is set down, since they were with Zebedee their father. Chrysostom: *their piety is to be wondered at, because being poor, they sought bread by the art of fishing, and yet did not leave their old father.* As: *he who fears the Lord, honors his parents* (Sir 3:8).

378. Their poverty is indicated by the fact that they were mending their nets. Nonetheless, by those who were casting the nets are signified those who carried on business in the world in the first age; by those who had already cast and were mending, are indicated those who had carried on business in the world for a long time; and they are already engrossed by sin, and are called to Christ. *It is good for a man, when he has borne the yoke from his youth* (Lam 3:27).

379. *And he called them*, interiorly and exteriorly; *and whom he predestined, them he also called* (Rom 8:30). To call interiorly is nothing other than to offer aid to the human mind when he wishes to convert us.

380. There follows, concerning obedience, ***and they immediately left their nets and father, and followed him***. Note that the two above left only a boat, but these left nets, boat, and father; in which is signified that for the sake of Christ we should lay aside all earthly occupations, which are designated by the net: *no man, being a soldier to God, entangles himself with secular businesses* (2 Tim 2:4); riches, or possessions, which are indicated by the boat, ***if you will be perfect, go sell what you have, and give to the poor, and you will have treasure in heaven, and come follow me*** (Matt 19:21); carnal passion, which is indicated by the father, *forget your people and your father's house* (Ps 44:11).

But mystically, by Zebedee, who is interpreted 'violent stream', is signified the world.

381. But there is a question here: for it seems that these men sinned by leaving their father, old and poor, because children are bound to support their parents. And generally, it is asked whether it is permitted for someone to leave parents in their last need, by entering religion.

One should say that a counsel never acts against a precept; but this, namely, *honor your father and your mother* (Exod 20:12), is a precept; and therefore if the father can in no way live unless helped by the child, the child ought not to enter religion. But this was not the case with Zebedee, who was able to help himself, and had the necessary things.

382. Item est quaestio litteralis. Matthaeus enim videtur hic contrarius Ioanni et Lucae: Ioannes enim I, 28 dicit eos vocatos iuxta Iordanem; hic dicit iuxta Mare Galilaeae. Item Lucas V, 10 dicit quod simul vocavit Petrum et Andream, Iacobum et Ioannem, licet de aliis duobus non fiat mentio, quia creditur quod ibi fuerint. Item ibi dicitur quod omnes simul, hic quod seorsum.

Sed sciendum quod trina fuit vocatio apostolorum. Primo enim vocati sunt ad Christi familiaritatem, et illud dicitur Io., I, et hoc in primo anno praedicationis Christi. Nec obstat quod dicitur post: *ascenderunt cum eo discipuli eius in Cana Galilaeae*, quia secundum Augustinum non tunc erant discipuli, sed futuri erant: sicut si dicatur quod Paulus Apostolus natus fuerit in Tharso Ciliciae, cum tunc non esset apostolus. Vel dicendum quod loquitur de aliis discipulis, qui vocantur omnes credentes in Christo. Secundo vocati fuerunt ad discipulatum; et de ista dicitur Lc. cap. V. Tertia vocatio fuit ut totaliter Christo adhaererent: et de ista hic dicitur; quod patet, secundum Augustinum, quia Luc. V, 11 de hoc habetur, *et subductis ad terram navibus*; ergo habebant navim, et curabant de ea, quasi ad eam redituri; hic vero dicit, **at illi, relictis omnibus** et cetera. Et ideo dicendum, quod de ultima sequela loquitur hic.

382. Likewise, there is a literal question. For Matthew here seems contrary to John and Luke; for John says that they were called by the Jordan (John 1:28); here Matthew says by the Sea of Galilee. Similarly, Luke says that he called at the same time Peter and Andrew, James and John, even though he does not mention the other two, for it is believed that they were there (Luke 5:10). Similarly, there it says that all were called at once, here that they were called separately.

But one should know that there were three callings of the apostles. For first they were called to familiarity with Christ, (John 1), and this was in the first year of Christ's preaching. Nor does what is said afterward present an obstacle, that *his disciples went up with him into Cana of Galilee* (cf. John 2:1–2), because according to Augustine they were not disciples at that time, but were going to be; just as if it said that Paul the Apostle was born in Tharsus of Ciliciae, when he was not an apostle at the time. Or one should say that it speaks of the other disciples, which names all those who believed in Christ. Second, they were called to discipleship (Luke 5). The third calling was so that they might cling entirely to Christ; and it speaks here about this; which is clear, according to Augustine, because Luke says, *and having brought their boats to land* (Luke 5:11). Therefore they had boats, and cared for them as though about to return to them; but it says here, **and they immediately left** everything. And therefore one should say that he speaks here of the last following.

Lecture 3

4:23 Et circuibat Iesus totam Galilaeam docens in synagogis eorum, et praedicans Evangelium regni: et sanans omnem languorem et omnem infirmitatem in populo. [n. 384]

4:24 Et abiit opinio eius in totam Syriam, et obtulerunt ei omnes male habentes, variis languoribus et tormentis conprehensos, et qui daemonia habebant, et lunaticos, et paralyticos: et curavit eos. [n. 389]

4:25 Et secutae sunt eum turbae multae de Galilaea, et Decapoli, et de Ierosolymis, et Iudaea et de trans Iordanem. [n. 394]

4:23 Καὶ περιῆγεν ἐν ὅλῃ τῇ Γαλιλαίᾳ διδάσκων ἐν ταῖς συναγωγαῖς αὐτῶν καὶ κηρύσσων τὸ εὐαγγέλιον τῆς βασιλείας καὶ θεραπεύων πᾶσαν νόσον καὶ πᾶσαν μαλακίαν ἐν τῷ λαῷ.

4:24 Καὶ ἀπῆλθεν ἡ ἀκοὴ αὐτοῦ εἰς ὅλην τὴν Συρίαν· καὶ προσήνεγκαν αὐτῷ πάντας τοὺς κακῶς ἔχοντας ποικίλαις νόσοις καὶ βασάνοις συνεχομένους [καὶ] δαιμονιζομένους καὶ σεληνιαζομένους καὶ παραλυτικούς, καὶ ἐθεράπευσεν αὐτούς.

4:25 καὶ ἠκολούθησαν αὐτῷ ὄχλοι πολλοὶ ἀπὸ τῆς Γαλιλαίας καὶ Δεκαπόλεως καὶ Ἱεροσολύμων καὶ Ἰουδαίας καὶ πέραν τοῦ Ἰορδάνου.

4:23 And Jesus went about all Galilee, teaching in their synagogues, and preaching the Gospel of the kingdom: and healing all manner of sickness and every infirmity, among the people. [n. 384]

4:24 And his fame went throughout all Syria, and they presented to him all sick people who were taken with diverse diseases and torments, and such as were possessed by devils, and lunatics, and paralytics, and he cured them. [n. 389]

4:25 And many people followed him from Galilee, and from Decapolis, and from Jerusalem, and from Judea, and from beyond the Jordan. [n. 394]

---

383. Consuetudo est apud reges, quod congregato exercitu procedunt ad bellum: ita Christus, congregato exercitu apostolorum, procedit ad pugnandum contra diabolum per officium praedicationis, ad expellendum eum de mundo. Unde hic agitur de doctrina et praedicatione Christi. Et ponitur

primo Christi praedicatio;

secundo effectus praedicationis, ibi *abiit opinio eius in totam Syriam* et cetera.

Circa primum tria tangit.

Primo sollicitudinem docentis et modum docendi, et propositae doctrinae confirmationem.

384. Et sollicitudo ostenditur in duobus, quia non quaerebat propriam quietem; unde *circuibat*; Rom. XII, 11: *sollicitudine non pigri*. Secundo quia non erat acceptator personarum, terrarum, vel villarum, sed *circuibat totam Galilaeam*, absque differentia; Mc. I, 38: *eamus in proximas civitates, ut et ibi praedicem*; Ps. CII, 22: *in omni loco dominationis eius*.

385. Modus, ibi *in synagogis docens*. Duo dicit *docens et praedicans*; docens quae agenda sunt in praesenti, praedicans de futuris: vel docens ea quae pertinent ad instructionem morum, Is. XLVIII, 17: *ego Dominus docens te utilia*, praedicans futura; Is. LII, 7: *quam pulchri super montem pedes annuntiantis et praedicantis pacem, annuntiantis bonum, praedicantis salutem*. Vel docens naturales iustitias: quaedam enim in theologia traduntur quae naturalis ratio dictat, scilicet iustitia, et huiusmodi: et quantum ad hoc dicit *docens*; quaedam vero

383. It is customary amongst kings that, the army being gathered together, they proceed to war; just so, Christ, with the army of apostles gathered together, proceeds to fighting against the devil by the office of preaching, to expel him from the world. Hence Christ's teaching and preaching is treated of here. And set down is

first, Christ's preaching;

second, the effect of the preaching, at *and his fame went throughout all Syria*.

Concerning the first, he touches upon three things.

First, the concern of the one teaching, and the manner of teaching, and the confirmation of the teaching set forth.

384. And the concern is shown in two things, because he was not seeking his own rest; hence, he *went about*; *in carefulness, not slothful* (Rom 12:11). Second, because he was not an acceptor of persons, whether of region or of village, but he *went about all Galilee*, without difference; *let us go into the neighbouring towns and cities, that I may preach there also* (Mark 1:38); *in every place of his dominion* (Ps 102:22).

385. The manner, at *teaching in their synagogues*. He says two things, *teaching* and *preaching*: teaching what should be done in the present, and foretelling the future; or teaching those things which pertain to the instruction of morals, *I am the Lord your God who teaches you profitable things* (Isa 48:17), foretelling the future, *how beautiful upon the mountains are the feet of him who brings good tidings, and who preaches peace: of him who shows forth good, who preaches salvation* (Isa 52:7). Or teaching natural justice, for certain things are brought forward in theology which natural reason dictates, namely justice and suchlike,

quae excedunt rationem, sicut mysterium Trinitatis, et huiusmodi: et quantum ad hoc dicit *praedicans*.

386. Sed obiicitur de hoc quod dicit Glossa, quod doceret naturales iustitias, ut est castitas, et humilitas, et huiusmodi: naturales enim virtutes non videntur posse dici virtutes, quia virtutes sunt per gratiam.

Et dicendum quod inclinatio et inchoatio est naturalis; sed perfectio, qua gratus homo redditur, est ex gratia, politica, et ex assuetudine.

387. *In synagogis eorum*. Nota duo. Primum quia quaerebat multitudinem, ut praedicatio magis proficeret; Ps. XXXIV, 18: *confitebor tibi in ecclesia magna*. Item quia solum Iudaeis praedicabat; Act. XIII, 46: *vobis primum oportuit praedicari verbum Dei*. *Et praedicans Evangelium regni*: non fabulas et curiosa, sed quae ad Dei regnum pertinebant, et ea quae hominibus proficerent.

388. Consequenter confirmatur praedicatio miraculis; Mc. ult., 20: *illi autem profecti praedicaverunt ubique, Domino cooperante, et sermonem confirmante sequentibus signis*. Unde *sanans*. Languor potest referri ad infirmitates corporales, infirmitas ad infirmitatem animae: non enim minores sunt infirmitates animae quam corporis. Vel per languores graves infirmitates et diuturnas; per infirmitates quamcumque aliam; Ps. CII, 3: *qui sanat omnes infirmitates tuas*; Eccli. X, 12: *brevem languorem praecidit medicus*. Datur intelligi etiam in hoc quod praedicatores debent suam doctrinam confirmare per opera; et si non per miracula, per vitam virtuosam; Rom. XV, 18: *non audeo aliquid loqui eorum quae per me non efficit Christus in obedientiam gentium in verbo et factis, in virtute signorum et prodigiorum, in virtute Spiritus Sancti*.

389. *Et abiit opinio eius in totam Syriam*. Hic ponitur effectus praedicationis: et est triplex, scilicet fama circa exemplum, fiducia quam homines de eo habebant, et devotio qua homines eum sequebantur.

390. Dicit ergo *abiit opinio eius in totam Syriam*. Syria est regio a Capharnaum usque ad mare magnum: unde et in terra gentilium divulgatum est. Hoc etiam pertinet ad praedicatores, ut habeant testimonium bonum; Eccli. XLI, 15: *curam habe de bono nomine*; II Tim. II, 15: *sollicite autem cura teipsum probabilem exhibere Deo operarium inconfusibilem, recte tractantem verbum veritatis*.

Per *Syriam* autem potest intelligi superbia mundi, quia sic interpretatur: et fama Christi per totum mundum diffusa est.

391. Fiducia, ibi *et obtulerunt ei omnes male habentes*; sciebant enim quod sanare poterat; Ier. XVII, 14: *sana me, domine, et sanabor; salvum me fac, et salvus ero*.

and regarding this he says, *teaching*; but certain things are brought forth which exceed reason, such as the mystery of the Trinity and suchlike, and regarding this he says, *preaching*.

386. But there is an objection here about what the Gloss says, that he was teaching natural justice, such as chastity, and humility, and so on: for it does not seem that the natural virtues can be called virtues, since the virtues come through grace.

And one should say that the inclination, and the beginning, is natural; but the perfection, by which a man is rendered pleasing, is by grace, political things, and habituation.

387. *In their synagogues*. Note two things. First, that he sought the multitude, so that the preaching might accomplish more; *I will give thanks to you in a great church* (Ps 34:18). Likewise, that he preached only to the Jews; *to you it behooved us first to speak the word of God* (Acts 13:46). *And preaching the Gospel of the kingdom*: not fables and curious things, but those things which pertained to the kingdom of God, and those which would profit men.

388. Next, the preaching is confirmed by miracles; *but they going forth preached everywhere: the Lord working withal, and confirming the word with signs that followed* (Mark 16:20). Hence, *healing*. Sickness can be referred to bodily infirmity, and infirmities to infirmity of the soul; for the infirmities of the soul are not less than the the infirmities of the body. Or, by sicknesses are meant heavy and long-lasting infirmities, while by infirmities are meant any other. *Who heals all your diseases* (Ps 102:3); *the physician cuts off a short sickness* (Sir 10:12). One is also given to understand in this that preachers should confirm their teaching with works; even if not with miracles, with a virtuous life; *for I dare not to speak of any of those things which Christ works not by me, for the obedience of the gentiles, by word and deed, by the virtue of signs and wonders, in the power of the Holy Spirit* (Rom 15:18–19).

389. *And his fame went throughout all Syria*. Here the effect of the preaching is set down. And it is threefold, namely regarding example, the confidence which men had in him, and the devotion with which men followed him.

390. It says then, *and his fame went throughout all Syria*. Syria is the region from Capernaum to the great sea; hence, he was made well known in the land of the gentiles, too. This also pertains to preachers, that they should have good testimony; *take care of a good name* (Sir 41:15); *carefully study to present yourself approved unto God, a workman that does not need to be ashamed, rightly handling the word of truth* (2 Tim 2:15).

Moreover, by *Syria* can be understood the pride of the world, because it is so interpreted; and the fame of Christ is spread through the whole world.

391. The confidence, at *they presented to him all sick people who were taken with diverse diseases*; for they knew that he could heal. *Heal me, O Lord, and I will be healed:*

Et dicit primo *abiit opinio eius* etc., et post, *obtulerunt ei* etc., quia quando aliquis habet famam de sanctitate, homines facilius detegunt ei conscientiae vulnus. *Variis languoribus et tormentis comprehensos.* Per istas graves infirmitates designantur infirmitates spirituales. Per languores possunt intelligi diuturnae infirmitates, et signatur infirmitas diu perseverans; Eccli. X, 11: *languor prolixior gravat medicum.* Et quia aliqui gravantur infirmitate, aliqui vero acerbitate doloris, hoc significatur cum dicit *et tormentis comprehensos*: et significantur illi qui habent conscientiam gravatam remordentem; Ps. XVII, 5: *circumdederunt me dolores mortis, dolores Inferni circumdederunt me.* *Et qui daemonia habebant*; et hoc est quod dicitur Lc. VI, 1: *et qui vexabantur a spiritibus immundis, curabantur.* Per hoc intelliguntur illi qui colebant idola; Ps. XCV, 5: *omnes dii gentium daemonia*; I Cor. X, 20: *nolo vos socios fieri daemoniorum.*

392. *Lunatici* proprie dicuntur qui patiuntur infirmitatem cuiusdam amentiae in defectu lunae: et tunc arripiuntur a daemonibus. Et diabolus tunc magis affligit propter duas rationes. Unam assignat Hieronymus, et est ut infamet creaturam Dei; et hoc etiam fit in effectibus magicae artis, qua invocantur daemones sub certis constellationibus et daemones veniunt ad hoc ut extollant creaturam, et inducant ad idololatriam.

Secunda ratio est melior, quia diabolus non potest aliquid, nisi per virtutes corporis. Non est autem dubium, quod corpora inferiora immutantur secundum diversas immutationes corporum superiorum. Et ideo tunc diabolus invocatus libenter venit, quando videt superiora corpora operari ad illum effectum pro quo invocatur. In defectu autem lunae, sicut patet, humiditates deficiunt; et ideo defectus lunae facit ad talem infirmitatem, quando terra non abundat humoribus; et ideo diabolus tunc magis vexat: et hoc est *et lunaticos*.

393. Per *istos* possumus intelligere inconstantes Eccli. XXVII, 12: *homo sanctus in sapientia manet sicut sol: nam stultus sicut luna mutatur*, qui habent propositum caste vivendi, sed vincuntur passionibus, secundum illud Rom. VII, 15: *non enim quod volo bonum, hoc facio, sed quod odi malum, illud ago.* *Et paralyticos.* Paralytici proprie dicuntur, qui habent membra resoluta, ita quod non possunt habere officium membrorum. Per istos significantur ignorantes: et isti omnes a Christo curantur; unde *et curavit eos*, scilicet perfecte.

394. Consequenter ponitur tertius effectus, scilicet devotio sequentium; unde *et secutae sunt eum turbae multae*; Ps. VII, 8: *exurge, domine, in praecepto quod mandasti, et synagoga populorum circumdabit te.*

save me, and I will be saved (Jer 17:14). And it says first, ***his fame went throughout***, and after that, ***they presented to him***, because when someone has a reputation for holiness, men more readily expose their wounds to his knowledge. ***With diverse diseases and torments***. By these heavy infirmities are indicated spiritual infirmities. By ***diseases*** can be understood long-lasting infirmities, and enduring infirmity is indicated; *a long sickness is troublesome to the physician* (Sir 10:11). And because some are burdened by infirmity, and others by the bitterness of sorrow, this is indicated when it says, ***and torments***; and those who have a tormenting, burdened conscience are indicated. *The sorrows of death surrounded me: and the torrents of iniquity troubled me* (Ps 17:5). ***And such as were possessed by devils***; and this is what is said in Luke, *and they that were troubled with unclean spirits, were cured* (Luke 6:18). By this is understood those who worshipped idols; *for all the gods of the gentiles are devils* (Ps 95:5); *and I would not that you should be made partakers with devils* (1 Cor 10:20).

392. Those are properly called ***lunatics*** who suffer a certain weakness of insanity in the waning of the moon; and then they are taken up by demons. And the devil afflicts them more at that time for two reasons. Jerome gives one, and it is that he might defame a creature of God; and this also happens in the effects of the magic art, by which demons are called under certain constellations, and demons come for this purpose, that they might exalt the creature, and lead men into idolatry.

The second reason is better: because the devil cannot do anything except through the powers of a body. Now, there is no doubt that lower bodies are changed according to the various changes of the higher bodies. And therefore the devil, called at that time, comes gladly when he sees the higher bodies working toward that effect for which he is called. Moreover, in the waning of the moon, as is clear, fluids are diminished; and so the waning of the moon works toward such infirmity, when the earth is not full of fluids. And this is why the devil vexes more at that time; and this is ***and lunatics***.

393. By ***them*** we can understand the inconstant, *a holy man continues in wisdom as the sun: but a fool is changed as the moon* (Sir 27:12), who have the intention of living chastely, but are overcome by passions, *for I do not that good which I will; but the evil which I hate, that I do* (Rom 7:15). ***And paralytics***. Those are properly called paralytics who have their members loosened such that they are not able to gain control of their members. By these are signified the ignorant; and all these are cured by Christ, hence, ***and he cured them***, that is, perfectly.

394. Next, the third effect is set down, namely the devotion of those who followed; hence, ***and many people followed him***. *And arise, O Lord my God, in the precept which you have commanded: and a congregation of people will surround you* (Ps 7:7–8).

Sciendum autem quod diversimode aliqui sequebantur, quia quidam studio salutis, scilicet spiritualis, scilicet apostoli; unde supra: *relictis omnibus sequuti sunt eum*; et infra XIX, 27: *ecce nos reliquimus omnia, et secuti sumus te*. Quidam studio salutis corporalis; Lc. VI, 17: *turba copiosa plebis ab omni Iudaea, et Ierusalem, et maritima, et Tyri, et Sidonis, qui venerant ut audirent eum, et sanarentur a languoribus suis*. Quidam curiositate tantum videndi miracula; Io. VI, 2: *et sequebantur eum multi, quia videbant signa quae faciebat super his qui infirmabantur*. Alii ad insidiandum, ut Pharisaei et Scribae; Ier. XX, 10: *audivi contumelias multorum, et terrorem in circuitu*.

395. De Galilaea. Provincia est ubi Christus praecipue praedicabat, et interpretatur 'transmigratio.' Per hoc significantur illi qui debent transmigrare de vitiis ad virtutes. *Et Decapoli*. Regio est ubi sunt decem villae; et significantur illi qui student ad observantiam decem mandatorum. *Et de Ierosolymis*. Ierosolyma interpretatur 'visio pacis'; et significat illos qui desiderio pacis ad Christum veniunt; Ps. CXVIII, 165: *pax multa diligentibus nomen tuum*. *Et de Iudaea*. Iudaea interpretatur 'confessio'; et significat illos qui per peccatorum remissionem ad Christum veniunt; Ps. CXIII, v. 2: *facta est Iudaea sanctificatio eius*. *Et de trans Iordanem*; et significantur illi qui per baptismum ad Christum veniunt: in Iordane enim fuit figuratus baptismus.

But one should know that men were following in different ways. For some, that is, the apostles, followed with a zeal for salvation, namely spiritual salvation; hence above: *leaving their nets, they followed him* (Matt 4:20); and, *behold we have left all things, and have followed you* (Matt 19:27). Some followed with a zeal for bodily salvation; *and a very great multitude of people from all Judea and Jerusalem, and the sea coast both of Tyre and Sidon, who had come to hear him, and to be healed of their diseases* (Luke 6:17–18). Some followed only out of curiosity, to see miracles; *and a great multitude followed him, because they saw the miracles which he did on them that were diseased* (John 6:2). Others followed to lie in ambush, such as the Pharisees and scribes; *for I heard the reproaches of many, and terror on every side* (Jer 20:10).

395. From Galilee. This is the province where Christ first began to preach, and it is interpreted as 'transmigration'. This signifies those who should transmigrate from vices to virtues. *And from Decapolis*. This is a region where there are ten villages; and it signifies those who are zealous in observing the ten commandments. *And from Jerusalem*. Jerusalem is interpreted as 'vision of peace'; and it signifies those who come to Christ in the desire for peace; *much peace have those who love your law* (Ps 118:165). *And from Judea*. Judea is interpreted as 'confession', and signifies those who come to Christ through the remission of sins; *made his sanctuary, Israel his dominion* (Ps 113:2). *And from beyond the Jordan*. And this signifies those who come to Christ through baptism, for baptism was prefigured in the Jordan.

Chapter 5

Lecture 1

5:1 Videns autem Iesus turbas, ascendit in montem: et cum sedisset, accesserunt ad eum discipuli eius. [n. 396]

5:2 Et aperiens os suum docebat eos, dicens: [n. 401]

5:1 Ἰδὼν δὲ τοὺς ὄχλους ἀνέβη εἰς τὸ ὄρος, καὶ καθίσαντος αὐτοῦ προσῆλθαν αὐτῷ οἱ μαθηταὶ αὐτοῦ·

5:2 καὶ ἀνοίξας τὸ στόμα αὐτοῦ ἐδίδασκεν αὐτοὺς λέγων·

5:1 And seeing the multitudes, he went up onto a mountain, and when he had sat down, his disciples came to him. [n. 396]

5:2 And opening his mouth, he taught them, saying: [n. 401]

---

396. *Videns autem Iesus turbas.* Hic Dominus suam doctrinam proponit: et dividitur in partes tres.

In prima ponitur doctrina Christi;

in secunda ponitur virtus doctrinae;

in tertia finis ad quem perducit.

Secundum in cap. XIII; tertium in cap. XVII.

Prima dividitur in tres.

In secunda instruuntur ministri doctrinae;

in tertia confunduntur adversarii.

Secunda in cap. X; tertia in capite XI.

Prima dividitur in duas.

In prima proponitur doctrina Christi;

in secunda confirmatur per miracula, in cap. VIII.

Prima in duas.

In prima praemittitur quasi quidam titulus ad doctrinam;

in secunda explicatur ipsa doctrina, ibi *beati pauperes spiritu*.

Circa primum tria facit.

Primo describit locum, ubi doctrina fuit proposita;

secundo auditores doctrinae;

tertio ponit modum docendi.

Secundum ibi *et cum sedisset*; tertium ibi *et aperiens os suum docebat eos*.

397. Dicit ergo, ita dixi quod secuti sunt et cetera. *Videns autem Iesus turbas.* Ista littera duplicem intellectum habere potest. Primo sic. *Ascendit* ad docendum turbas, scilicet non fugiens. Unde Chrysostomus dicit, quod sicut artifex, quando videt praeparatam materiam, delectatur operari, ita sacerdos delectatur praedicare, quando populum videt congregatum; et ideo, *ascendit*; Ps. XXXIV, 18: *confitebor tibi in ecclesia magna.*

396. *And seeing the multitudes.* Here the Lord sets forth his own teaching; and it is divided into three parts.

In the first, Christ's teaching is set forth;

in the second, the power of the teaching;

in the third, the end to which it leads.

The second is in chapter thirteen; the third, in chapter seventeen.

The first is divided into three parts.

In the second, the ministers of the teaching are instructed;

in the third, adversaries are confounded.

The second is in chapter ten; the third, in chapter eleven.

The first is divided into two parts.

In the first, Christ's teaching is set forth;

in the second, it is confirmed by miracles, in chapter eight.

The first, into two parts.

In the first, a certain title is prefaced, as it were, to the teaching;

in the second, the teaching itself is explained, at *blessed are the poor in spirit* (Matt 5:3).

Concerning the first, he does three things.

First, he describes the place where the teaching was set forth;

second, those who heard the teaching;

third, he sets out the manner of teaching.

The second is at *and when he had sat down*; the third, at *and opening his mouth, he taught them*.

397. He says therefore, as I said, that they followed him. *And seeing the multitudes, he went up onto a mountain.* This text can be understood in two ways. First, as follows. *He went up* with the aim of teaching the crowds, that is, not fleeing. Hence Chrysostom says that just as a craftsman, when he sees material prepared, delights in working, so the priest delights in preaching when he sees the people gathered together. And so, *he went up*; *I will give thanks to you in a great assembly* (Ps 34:18).

Vel aliter. *Ascendit*, fugiens scilicet turbas, ut securius discipulos doceret; Eccl. IX, v. 17: *verba sapientium audiuntur in silentio*.

398. Et notandum quod legitur quod Christus habebat tria refugia: quandoque enim fugiebat ad montem, sicut dicitur hic; et Io. VIII, 1: *Iesus autem perrexit in Montem Oliveti*. Aliquando ad navem; Lc. V, 1: *cum turbae multae irruerent in eum . . . ascendens in unam navim, quae erat Simonis . . . sedens docebat*. Tertium in desertum; Mc. VI, 31: *eamus seorsum in desertum*.

Et satis convenienter; in tribus enim homo potest habere refugium ad Deum: in protectione divinae altitudinis, quae per montem significatur; Ps. CXXIV, 1: *qui confidunt in Domino sicut mons Sion*. In societate ecclesiastica, quae per navem designatur; Ps. CXXI, v. 3: *Ierusalem quae aedificatur ut civitas, cuius participatio eius in idipsum*. In solitudine religionis, quae per desertum accipitur, per contemptum temporalium; Osee II, 14: *ducam eam in solitudinem, et loquar ad cor eius*; Ps. LIV, 8: *ecce elongavi fugiens, et mansi in solitudine*.

399. Ascendit autem in montem propter quinque rationes. Prima ad ostensionem suae excellentiae: ipse enim est mons, de quo Ps. LXVII, 16: *mons Dei, mons pinguis*. Secunda ad ostendendum quod doctor huius doctrinae debet ad eminentiam vitae conscendere; Is. XL, 9: *super montem excelsum ascende tu qui evangelizas Sion*. Chrysostomus: *nemo potest in valle consistere, et de caelo loqui* et cetera. Tertia ratio ad ostendendum altitudinem Ecclesiae cui doctrina proponitur; Is. II, 2: *erit mons domus Domini in vertice montium, et elevabitur super colles*. Quarto ad ostendendum perfectionem huius doctrinae, quia perfectissima; Ps. XXXV, 7: *iustitia tua sicut montes Dei*. Quinto ut congrueret ista veteri legislationi, quae data fuit in monte. Exod. XIX et XXIV.

400. Consequenter ponuntur auditores *et cum sedisset, accesserunt ad eum discipuli eius*. Duo possunt notari in sessione eius. Humiliatio; Ps. CXXXVIII, 2: *tu cognovisti sessionem meam*. Quando erat in altitudine divinae maiestatis, non poterat capi eius doctrina; sed tunc coeperunt homines capere, quando se humiliavit. Vel hoc pertinet ad dignitatem magisterii; infra XXIII, 2: *super cathedram Moysi sederunt Scribae et Pharisaei*. Ad studium enim sapientiae requiritur quies. *Accesserunt ad eum discipuli eius* etc., non tantum corpore, sed animo; Ps. XXXIII, 6: *accedite ad eum, et illuminamini*; Deut. XXXIII, 3: *qui appropinquant pedibus eius, accipient de doctrina illius*.

Et nota quod quando Dominus praedicavit turbis, stetit; Lc. VI, 17: *descendens Iesus de monte stetit in loco campestri*; sed hic quando discipulis, sedit. Ex hoc

Or in another way. *He went up*, that is, fleeing from the crowds, so that he might teach the disciples more safely; *the words of the wise are heard in silence* (Eccl 9:17).

398. And one should note that Christ had three places of refuge: for sometimes he fled to a mountain, as is said here and at *Jesus went to the Mount of Olives* (John 8:1). Sometimes, to a boat; *when the multitudes pressed upon him to hear the word of God . . . going into one of the ships that was Simon's . . . he taught, seated* (Luke 5:1–3). Third, into the desert; *come apart into a desert place, and rest a little* (Mark 6:31).

And fittingly enough, for a man can take refuge in God in three ways: in the protection of the divine loftiness, which is signified by the mountain; *they that trust in the Lord will be as Mount Zion* (Ps 125:1). In the ecclesiastical society, which is indicated by the boat; *Jerusalem, which is built as a city, which is compact together* (Ps 122:3). In the solitude of religious life, which is understood by the desert, through the contempt of temporal things; *behold I will allure her, and will lead her into the wilderness: and I will speak to her heart* (Hos 2:14); *lo, I have gone far off flying away; and I abode in the wilderness* (Ps 55:6–7).

399. Moreover, he went up onto the mountain for five reasons. First, to show his excellence: for he himself is the mountain of whom it is said, *the mountain of God is a fat mountain* (Ps 68:15). Second, to show that the teacher of this teaching ought to climb up in the loftiness of his life; *get you up upon a high mountain, you who bring good tidings to Zion* (Isa 40:9). Chrysostom: *no one can linger in a valley who speaks of heaven*. The third reason, to show the loftiness of the Church to whom the teaching is set forth; *and in the last days the mountain of the house of the Lord will be prepared on the top of mountains, and it will be exalted above the hills* (Isa 2:2). Fourth, to show the perfection of this teaching, because it is most perfect; *your justice is as the mountains of God* (Ps 36:6). Fifth, that it might correspond to the old law, which had been given on a mountain (Exod 19, 24).

400. Next, the hearers are set down, *and when he had sat down, his disciples came to him*. One can note two things in his sitting. A humbling; *you have known my sitting down, and my rising up* (Ps 139:2). When he was in the loftiness of divine majesty, his teaching could not be grasped; but when he humbled himself, then men began to understand. Or, this pertains to the dignity of the teacher; *the scribes and the Pharisees have sat on the chair of Moses* (Matt 23:2). For rest is necessary for one who is zealous for wisdom. *His disciples came to him*, not only in body, but in soul; *come to him and be enlightened* (Ps 34:5); *they that approach to his feet, will receive of his doctrine* (Deut 33:3).

And notice that when the Lord preached to the crowds, he stood; *and coming down with them, he stood in a plain place* (Luke 6:17); but here, when he taught the disciples, he

inolevit consuetudo quod turbis praedicatur stando, religiosis sedendo.

401. *Et aperiens os suum docebat eos*. Hic ponitur modus doctrinae.

In hoc quod dicit *aperiens*, significatur quod diu ante tacuerat. Et demonstrat quod magnum et longum erat facturus sermonem, sicut dicit Augustinus. Vel quod magna et profunda dicturus erat; sic enim consueverunt facere homines; Iob III, 1: *post hoc Iob aperuit os suum, et maledixit diei suo*.

Et dicit *suum*: prius enim aperuit ora prophetarum; Sap. X, 21: *sapientia aperuit os mutorum, et linguas infantium fecit disertas*: ipse enim est Sapientia Patris.

402. Sed hic est quaestio: hic enim sermo ponitur quantum ad multa etiam Lc. VI, 20 ss. Sed videtur hic et ibi contrarietas, sicut patet in textu.

Et ponit Augustinus duas solutiones. Una est quod iste est alius sermo ab illo: ipse enim primo ascendit in montem, et fecit hunc sermonem discipulis, et postea descendens invenit turbam congregatam, cui eadem praedicavit, et multa recapitulavit: et de hoc dicitur Lc. VI, 20 ss. Vel aliter dicendum, quod unus mons erat, et habebat planitiem in latere: illam planitiem elevabat monticulus alius. Unde Dominus ascendit in montem, idest in planitiem illius montis. Et primo ascendit superius, et convocavit discipulos, et ibi elegit duodecim apostolos, sicut patet in Luca: et postea descendens invenit turbam congregatam, et venientibus discipulis sedit, et habuit sermonem istum ad turbas et discipulos. Et hoc videtur verius: quia Matthaeus dicit in fine sermonis, quod *mirabantur turbae super doctrina eius*. Tamen quodcumque accipiatur, non est contrarietas.

sat. Out of this grew the custom that one preaches to the crowds standing, and to religious sitting.

401. *And opening his mouth, he taught them*. Here the manner of teaching is set down.

The fact that it says *opening* signifies that he had been silent for a long time before. And it shows that the sermon was going to be great and long, as Augustine says. Or that he was about to say great and profound things; for men often do this; *after this Job opened his mouth, and cursed his day* (Job 3:1).

And it says, *his*, for earlier he had opened the mouths of the prophets; *for wisdom opened the mouth of the dumb, and made the tongues of infants eloquent* (Wis 10:21): for he himself is the Wisdom of the Father.

402. But there is a question here, for this sermon is set down in Luke, for the most part (Luke 6:20–49). But there seems to be a contradiction between this account and that one, as is evident in the text.

And Augustine sets down two solutions. One is that this is a different sermon from that one; for he first went up onto a mountain, and gave this sermon to the disciples, and afterwards, coming down, found the crowd gathered together, to whom he preached the same things and recapitulated many things; and Luke speaks about this. Or otherwise one should say that there was one mountain, and it had a level area on the side; another little mountain raised up that level area. Hence the Lord went up onto a mountain, i.e., onto the level area of this mountain. And first he went up higher, and called together the disciples, and there chose the twelve apostles, as is clear in Luke; and afterwards, coming down, he found the crowd gathered together, and, when the disciples came, he sat, and gave this sermon to the crowd and to the disciples. And this seems more true, because Matthew says at the end of the sermon that *the multitudes hearing it, were in admiration at his doctrine* (Matt 22:33). Yet however it is taken, there is no contradiction.

Lecture 2

5:3 Beati pauperes spiritu, quoniam ipsorum est regnum caelorum. [n. 405]

5:4 Beati mites, quoniam ipsi possidebunt terram. [n. 406]

5:5 Beati qui lugent, quoniam ipsi consolabuntur. [n. 406]

5:6 Beati qui esuriunt et sitiunt iustitiam, quoniam ipsi saturabuntur. [n. 406]

5:7 Beati misericordes, quoniam ipsi misericordiam consequentur. [n. 406]

5:8 Beati mundo corde, quoniam ipsi Deum videbunt. [n. 407]

5:9 Beati pacifici, quoniam filii Dei vocabuntur. [n. 407]

5:10 Beati qui persecutionem patiuntur propter iustitiam, quoniam ipsorum est regnum caelorum. [n. 437]

5:3 Μακάριοι οἱ πτωχοὶ τῷ πνεύματι, ὅτι αὐτῶν ἐστιν ἡ βασιλεία τῶν οὐρανῶν.

5:4 μακάριοι οἱ πενθοῦντες, ὅτι αὐτοὶ παρακληθήσονται.

5:5 μακάριοι οἱ πραεῖς, ὅτι αὐτοὶ κληρονομήσουσιν τὴν γῆν.

5:6 μακάριοι οἱ πεινῶντες καὶ διψῶντες τὴν δικαιοσύνην, ὅτι αὐτοὶ χορτασθήσονται.

5:7 μακάριοι οἱ ἐλεήμονες, ὅτι αὐτοὶ ἐλεηθήσονται.

5:8 μακάριοι οἱ καθαροὶ τῇ καρδίᾳ, ὅτι αὐτοὶ τὸν θεὸν ὄψονται.

5:9 μακάριοι οἱ εἰρηνοποιοί, ὅτι αὐτοὶ υἱοὶ θεοῦ κληθήσονται.

5:10 μακάριοι οἱ δεδιωγμένοι ἕνεκεν δικαιοσύνης, ὅτι αὐτῶν ἐστιν ἡ βασιλεία τῶν οὐρανῶν.

5:3 Blessed are the poor in spirit: for theirs is the kingdom of heaven. [n. 405]

5:4 Blessed are the meek: for they will possess the land. [n. 406]

5:5 Blessed are they who mourn: for they will be comforted. [n. 406]

5:6 Blessed are they who hunger and thirst after justice: for they will have their fill. [n. 406]

5:7 Blessed are the merciful: for they will obtain mercy. [n. 406]

5:8 Blessed are the clean of heart: for they will see God. [n. 407]

5:9 Blessed are the peacemakers: for they will be called children of God. [n. 407]

5:10 Blessed are they who suffer persecution for justice's sake: for theirs is the kingdom of heaven. [n. 437]

---

403. Posuit supra Evangelista quasi brevem titulum doctrinae Christi, nunc ponit ipsam doctrinam, et effectum eius, scilicet admirationem turbarum.

Considerandum autem, quod secundum Augustinum in isto sermone Domini tota perfectio vitae nostrae continetur. Et probat per id quod Dominus subiungit finem ad quem ducit, scilicet repromissionem aliquam. Id autem quod maxime homo desiderat, est beatitudo. Unde Dominus hic tria facit.

Primo praemittit praemium quod consequitur istos qui istam doctrinam accipiunt;

secundo ponit praecepta, ibi **nolite putare quoniam veni solvere legem** etc.;

tertio docet quomodo aliquis potest pervenire ad observandum ea, ibi **petite et accipietis**.

Circa primum duo facit, quia huius doctrinae aliqui sunt observatores tantum, aliqui ministri.

Primo ergo describit beatitudinem observantium;

secundo ministrantium, ibi **beati estis cum maledixerint vobis**.

404. Notandum autem quod hic ponuntur plura de beatitudinibus; sed numquam aliquis in verbis Domini posset ita subtiliter loqui, quod pertingeret ad propositum Domini. Sciendum tamen quod in istis verbis includitur omnis plena beatitudo: omnes enim homines

403. Above, the Evangelist set down a brief title, as it were, of the teaching of Christ; now he sets down the teaching itself, and its effect, namely, the wonder of the crowds.

Now it should be considered that, according to Augustine, the whole perfection of our life is contained in this sermon of the Lord. And he proves it by the fact that the Lord includes the end to which he leads us, that is, a promise. But that which man desires most of all is beatitude. Hence the Lord does three things.

First, he promises a reward, which those who accept this teaching will obtain;

second, he sets down the precepts, at **do not think that I have come to destroy the law** (Matt 5:17);

third, he teaches how someone can succeed in observing them, at **ask, and it will be given to you** (Matt 7:7).

Concerning the first, he does two things, because some are only observers of this teaching, others ministers.

First, therefore, he describes the beatitude of the one who observes the precepts;

second, the beatitude of the ministers, at **blessed are you when they will revile you** (Matt 5:11).

404. Now, one should note that many things are set down here about the beatitudes; but never could anyone speak so skillfully about the Lord's words that he could attain to the Lord's purpose. Yet one should know that all complete happiness is included in these words: for all men

appetunt beatitudinem, sed differunt in iudicando de beatitudine; et ideo quidam istud, quidam illud appetunt.

Invenimus autem quadruplicem opinionem de beatitudine. Quidam enim credunt, quod in exterioribus tantum consistat, scilicet in affluentia istorum temporalium; Ps. CXLIII, v. 15: *beatum dixerunt populum cui haec sunt*. Alii quod perfecta beatitudo consistit in hoc quod homo satisfaciat voluntati suae; unde dicimus: beatus est qui vivit ut vult. Eccle. III, 12: *et cognovi quod non esset melius nisi laetari* et cetera. Alii dicunt quod perfecta beatitudo consistit in virtutibus activae vitae. Alii quod in virtutibus contemplativae vitae, scilicet divinorum et intelligibilium, sicut Aristoteles.

Omnes autem istae opiniones falsae sunt: quamvis non eodem modo. Unde Dominus omnes reprobat.

405. Opinionem illorum qui dixerunt quod consistit in affluentia exteriorum, reprobat: unde dicit **beati pauperes**, scilicet quasi, non beati affluentes.

406. Opinionem vero eorum qui ponebant beatitudinem in satisfactione appetitus, reprobat cum dicit **beati misericordes**.

Sed sciendum quod triplex est appetitus in homine: irascibilis, qui appetit vindictam de inimicis, et hoc reprobat, cum dicit **beati mites**. Concupiscibilis, cuius bonum est gaudere et delectari: hoc reprobat cum dicit **beati qui lugent**. Voluntatis, qui est duplex, secundum quod duo quaerit. Primo quod voluntas nulla superiori lege coerceatur; secundo quod possit restringere alios ut subditos: unde desiderat praeesse, et non subesse. Dominus autem contrarium ostendit quantum ad utrumque. Et quantum ad primum dicit **beati qui esuriunt et sitiunt iustitiam**. Quantum autem ad secundum dicit **beati misericordes**. Ergo et illi qui ponunt beatitudinem in exteriori affluentia, et qui in satisfactione appetitus, errant.

407. Illi autem qui ponunt beatitudinem in actibus activae vitae, scilicet moralibus, errant; sed minus, quia illud est via ad beatitudinem. Unde Dominus non reprobat tamquam malum, sed ostendit ordinatum ad beatitudinem: quia vel ordinantur ad seipsum, sicut temperantia et huiusmodi, et finis eorum est munditia cordis, quia faciunt vincere passiones; vel ordinantur ad alterum, et sic finis eorum est pax, et huiusmodi: *opus enim iustitiae est pax*. Et ideo istae virtutes sunt viae in beatitudinem, et non ipsa beatitudo; et hoc est **beati mundo corde quoniam ipsi Deum videbunt**. Non dicit *vident*, quia hoc esset ipsa beatitudo. Et iterum **beati pacifici**,

desire happiness, but they differ in their judgments about happiness, and for this reason some men desire this, others desire that.

But we find four opinions about happiness. For some believe that it consists only in exterior things, namely in an abundance of temporal things; *they have called the people happy, that have these things* (Ps 144:15). Others, that perfect beatitude consists in the fact that a man fulfills his own will; hence we say, blessed is he who lives as he wants. *And I have known that there was no better thing than to rejoice, and to do well in this life* (Eccl 3:12). Others say that perfect beatitude consists in the virtues of the active life. Others, that it consists in the virtues of the contemplative life, namely of divine and intelligible things, as Aristotle says.

But all these opinions are false, although not in the same way. Hence the Lord condemns all these.

405. He condemns the opinion of those who say that it consists in the abundance of exterior things: hence, he says, **blessed are the poor**, as though to say, the wealthy are not happy.

406. And he condemns the opinion of those who place beatitude in the satisfaction of appetite when he says, **blessed are the merciful**.

But one should know that there are three appetites in man. The irascible, which desires vengeance on enemies, and he condemns this when he says, **blessed are the meek**. The concupiscible, whose good is to rejoice and be delighted; he condemns this when he says, **blessed are they who mourn**. The will, which is twofold, according as it seeks two things: first, that the will be forced by no higher law; second, that it be able to bind others as subjects: hence it desires to command, and not to be under another. But the Lord shows the contrary regarding both. And regarding the first, he says, **blessed are they who hunger and thirst after justice**. Regarding the second, he says, **blessed are the merciful**. Therefore both those who place beatitude in the abundance of exterior things and those who place it in the satisfaction of appetite are wrong.

407. Those, however, who place beatitude in the actions of the active life, namely, in moral acts, are wrong, but less so, because that is the way to beatitude. Hence the Lord does not condemn them as though evil, but shows the ordering to beatitude. Because the virtues of the active life are either ordered to oneself, such as temperance and others of this kind, and their end is cleanness of heart, because they enable one to conquer the passions; or they are ordered to another, and so their end is peace, and of this kind: *the work of justice will be peace* (Isa 32:17). And therefore these virtues are ways to beatitude, and not beatitude itself; and this is **blessed are the clean of heart: for they will see God**. He

non quia pacifici, sed quia in aliud tendunt, **quoniam filii Dei vocabuntur**.

408. Illorum autem opinio qui dicunt quod beatitudo consistit in contemplatione divinorum, reprobat Dominus quantum ad tempus, quia alias vera est, quia ultima felicitas consistit in visione optimi intelligibilis, scilicet Dei: unde dicit **videbunt**.

Et notandum quod, secundum Philosophum, ad hoc quod actus contemplativi faciant beatum, duo requiruntur: unum substantialiter, scilicet quod sit actus altissimi intelligibilis, quod est Deus; aliud formaliter, scilicet amor et delectatio: delectatio enim perficit felicitatem, sicut pulchritudo iuventutem. Et ideo Dominus duo ponit **Deum videbunt** et **filii Dei vocabuntur**: hoc enim pertinet ad unionem amoris; I Io. cap. III, v. 1: *videte qualem caritatem dedit nobis Pater, ut filii Dei nominemur et simus*.

409. Item notandum quod in istis beatitudinibus quaedam ponuntur ut merita, et quaedam ut praemia: et hoc in singulis. **Beati pauperes spiritu**: ecce meritum; **quoniam ipsorum est regnum caelorum**: ecce praemium, et sic in aliis.

410. Et notandum est etiam aliquid circa meritum in communi, et aliquid circa praemium in communi. Circa meritum sciendum, quod Philosophus distinguit duplex genus virtutis: unum communis, quae perficit hominem humano modo; aliud specialis, quam vocat heroicam, quae perficit supra humanum modum. Quando enim fortis timet ubi est timendum, istud est virtus; sed si non timeret, esset vitium. Si autem in nullo timeret confisus Dei auxilio, ista virtus esset supra humanum modum: et istae virtutes vocantur divinae. Isti ergo actus sunt perfecti, et virtus etiam, secundum Philosophum, est operatio perfecta. Ergo ista merita vel sunt actus donorum, vel actus virtutum secundum quod perficiuntur a donis.

411. Item nota quod actus virtutum sunt illi de quibus lex praecipit; merita autem beatitudinis sunt actus virtutum; et ideo omnia quae praecipiuntur et infra continentur, referuntur ad istas beatitudines. Unde sicut Moyses primo proposuit praecepta, et post multa dixit, quae omnia referebantur ad praecepta proposita: ita Christus in doctrina sua, primo praemisit istas beatitudines, ad quas omnia alia reducuntur.

412. Circa primum autem notandum, quod Deus est praemium eorum qui ei serviunt; Thren. III, 24: *pars mea Dominus, dixit anima mea, propterea expectabo eum*; Ps. XV, 5: *Dominus pars haereditatis meae et calicis mei*; Gen. XV, 7: *ego Dominus qui eduxi te de Ur Chaldaeorum, ut darem tibi terram istam, et possideres eam*.

does not say, *they see*, because this would be beatitude itself. And similarly, **blessed are the peacemakers**, not because they make peace, but because they tend toward something else: *for they will be called children of God*.

408. Now, the opinion of those who say that beatitude consists in the contemplation of divine things is condemned by the Lord only as to the timing, for otherwise it is true; because the last happiness does consist in the vision of the best intelligible, namely God; hence he says, **they will see**.

And one should note that, according to the Philosopher, two things are required for the contemplative act to make one happy: one has to do with the substance, namely, that it be the act of the highest intelligible, which is God; the other has to do with form, namely love and delight, for delight perfects happiness just as beauty perfects youth. And therefore the Lord sets down two things, **they will see God** and **they will be called children of God**, for this pertains to the union of love. *Behold what manner of charity the Father has bestowed upon us, that we should be called, and should be the sons of God* (1 John 3:1).

409. Likewise, one should note that in these beatitudes, certain things are set down as merits, and certain things as rewards: and this is clear in each case. **Blessed are the poor in spirit**: here is a merit; **for theirs is the kingdom of heaven**: here is the reward; and so on in the others.

410. And one should note also something about merit in general, and something about reward in general. About merit, one should know that the Philosopher distinguishes two kinds of virtue: one common, which perfects a man in a human manner; the other special, which he calls heroic, which perfects above the human manner. For when a brave man fears where there is something to be feared, that is a virtue; but if he did not fear, it would be a vice. But if he feared nothing, trusting in the help of God, that would be a virtue above the human manner; and these virtues are called divine. Therefore, these acts are perfect, and virtue also is a perfect operation, according to the Philosopher. So these merits are either acts of the gifts, or acts of the virtues according as they are perfected by the gifts.

411. Likewise, note that the acts of the virtues are those about which the law commands; moreover, the merits of the beatitudes are acts of the virtues; and therefore all those things which are commanded and are contained below are referred back to these beatitudes. Hence just as Moses first set down the commandments, and afterwards said many things which were all referred back to the commandments given, so Christ in his teaching first sets forth these beatitudes, to which all the others are reduced.

412. Concerning the first, one should note that God is the reward of those who serve him; *the Lord is my portion, said my soul: therefore will I wait for him* (Lam 3:24); *the Lord is the portion of my inheritance and of my cup* (Ps 16:5); *I am the Lord who brought you out from Ur of the Chaldees, to give you this land, and that you might possess it* (Gen 15:7).

eam. Et sicut Augustinus dicit in II *Confessionum, anima cum recedit a te, bona quaerit extra te.* Homines autem diversa quaerunt; sed quidquid inveniri potest in qualibet vita, totum Dominus repromisit in Deo. Aliqui enim ponunt summum bonum affluentiam divitiarum, per quam possunt pervenire ad maximas dignitates; Dominus promittit regnum quod complectitur utrumque; sed ad hoc regnum dicit perveniri per viam paupertatis, non divitiarum. Unde *beati pauperes.* Alii perveniunt ad istos honores per bella; Dominus autem dicit *beati mites* et cetera. Alii consolationes quaerunt per voluptates; Dominus dicit *beati qui lugent.* Aliqui nolunt subdi; Dominus autem dicit, *beati qui esuriunt et sitiunt iustitiam.* Aliqui volunt vitare malum opprimendo subditos; Dominus dicit *beati misericordes* et cetera. Aliqui ponunt visionem Dei in contemplatione veritatis in via; Dominus autem promittit in patria; unde *beati mundo corde* et cetera.

413. Et notandum quod ista praemia, quae Dominus hic tangit, possunt dupliciter haberi, scilicet perfecte et consummate, et sic in patria tantum: et secundum inchoationem et imperfecte, et sic in via. Unde sancti habent quamdam inchoationem illius beatitudinis. Et quia in hac vita non possunt explicari illa sicut erunt in patria; ideo Augustinus exponit secundum quod sunt in hac vita *beati* ergo *pauperes spiritu*: non spe tantum, sed etiam re. Lc. XVII, v. 21: *regnum Dei intra vos est.*

Unde istis praemissis, accedamus ad litteram.

414. In istis beatitudinibus duo facit Evangelista.
Primo ponuntur ipsae beatitudines;
secundo manifestatio beatitudinum, ibi *beati qui persecutionem patiuntur propter iustitiam; quoniam ipsorum est regnum caelorum*; hoc enim est declarativum omnium beatitudinum.

Virtus autem tria facit: quia removet a malo, operatur et facit operari bonum, et disponit ad optimum.

Primo ergo determinat de primo, ibi *beati pauperes*; de secundo, ibi *beati qui esuriunt*; de tertio, ibi *beati mundo corde*, determinat.

Removet autem virtus a tribus malis: cupiditatis, crudelitatis sive inquietudinis, et voluptatis noxiae.

Primum notatur ibi *beati pauperes*; secundum ibi *beati misericordes*; tertio ibi *beati qui lugent.*

415. Dicit ergo *beati pauperes*, dupliciter legitur.

Primo sic *beati pauperes*, idest humiles, qui se aestimant pauperes: illi enim sunt vere humiles, qui se pauperes aestimant, non solum in exterioribus, sed etiam in

And as Augustine says in Book II of the *Confessions*: *when a soul turns away from you, it seeks goods outside of you.* Now, men seek diverse things; but anything that can be found in any life, the Lord promises in its entirety in God. For some place the highest good in the abundance of riches, through which they can attain the greatest dignity; the Lord promises a kingdom which embraces both, but he says that one must arrive at this kingdom by the way of poverty, not of riches. Hence, *blessed are the poor.* Others arrive at this honor through war; but the Lord says, *blessed are the meek.* Others seek consolations through pleasure; the Lord says, *blessed are they who mourn.* Some are unwilling to be subject to another; but the Lord says, *blessed are they who hunger and thirst after justice.* Some wish to avoid evil by oppressing those subject to them; the Lord says, *blessed are the merciful.* Some place the vision of God in the contemplation of truth in this life; but the Lord promises this vision in the homeland; hence, *blessed are the clean of heart.*

413. And one should notice that these rewards, which the Lord touches upon here, can be had in two ways, namely perfectly and completely, and they are had in this way only in the homeland; or as a beginning and imperfectly, and they are had in this way in this life. Hence the saints have a certain beginning of that beatitude. And because these things cannot be explained in this life as they will be in the homeland, therefore Augustine explains them according as they are in this life; therefore, *blessed are the poor in spirit*: not in hope only, but also in actuality. *For lo, the kingdom of God is within you* (Luke 17:21).

Hence, these things having been prefaced, let us proceed to the text.

414. The Evangelist does two things in these beatitudes.
First, the beatitudes themselves are set down;
second, a manifestation of the beatitudes, at *blessed are they who suffer persecution for justice's sake: for theirs is the kingdom of heaven*; for this expresses all the beatitudes.

Now, virtue does three things: for it removes one from evil, works and makes one to work what is good, and disposes one to what is best.

First, then, he determines about the first, at *blessed are the poor*; about the second, at *blessed are they who hunger*; about the third, at *blessed are the clean of heart.*

Moreover, virtue removes one from three evils: greed, cruelty or disturbance, and harmful pleasure.

The first is noted at *blessed are the poor*; the second, at *blessed are the merciful*; the third, at *blessed are they who mourn.*

415. He says then, *blessed are the poor.* It is read in two ways.

First, in this way: *blessed are the poor*, i.e., the humble, who reckon themselves to be poor; for they are the truly humble who reckon themselves poor, not only in external

interioribus; Ps. XXXIX, 18: *ego autem mendicus sum et pauper*, contra illud Apoc. III, 17: *dicis quia dives sum, et locupletatus, et nullius egeo, et nescis quia tu es miser, et miserabilis, et pauper, et caecus, et nudus* et cetera.

Et tunc hoc quod dicit *spiritu*, potest tripliciter legi. Spiritus enim aliquando dicitur superbia hominis; Is. II, 22: *quiescite ab homine, cuius spiritus in naribus est, quia excelsus reputatus est ipse*; Is. XXV, 4: *spiritus robustorum quasi turbo impellens parietem*. Et dicitur superbia *spiritus* quia sicut per flatum inflantur utres, ita per superbiam homines; Col. II, 18: *inflatus sensu carnis suae*. Ergo **beati pauperes**, scilicet hi, qui parum habent de spiritu superbiae. Vel accipitur *spiritus* pro voluntate hominis. Quidam enim sunt necessitate humiles, et isti non sunt beati, sed qui humilitatem affectant. Tertio accipitur pro Spiritu Sancto; unde **beati pauperes Spiritu**, qui humiles sunt per Spiritum Sanctum. Et istae duae quasi ad idem redeunt. Et dicit **pauperes spiritu**, quia humilitas dat Spiritum Sanctum; Is. LXVI, 2: *ad quem respiciam nisi ad pauperculum, et contritum spiritu, et trementem sermones meos?*

Istis pauperibus repromittitur regnum, in quo intelligitur summa excellentia. Et licet istud retribuatur cuilibet virtuti, specialiter tamen datur humilitati; quia *omnis qui se humiliat exaltabitur*, infra cap. XXIII, 12. Et Prov. XXIX, 23: *humilem spiritum suscipiet gloria*.

416. Vel aliter, secundum Hieronymum. **Pauperes spiritu**, ad litteram, in abdicatione rerum temporalium. Et dicit *spiritu*: quia quidam pauperes necessitate sunt, sed non debetur illis beatitudo, sed illis qui voluntate. Et isti dicuntur dupliciter; quia etsi aliqui divitias habent, tamen non habent eas in corde; Ps. LXI, 11: *divitiae si affluant, nolite cor apponere*. Aliqui nec habent, nec affectant, et istud securius est, quia mens trahitur a spiritualibus ex divitiis: et isti dicuntur proprie **pauperes spiritu**, quia actus donorum, qui sunt supra humanum modum, sunt hominis beati: et quod homo omnes divitias abiiciat, ut nec aliquo etiam modo appetat, hoc est supra humanum modum.

417. Istis autem repromittitur **regnum caelorum**, in quo notatur non solum altitudo honoris, sed affluentia divitiarum; Iac. II, 5: *nonne Deus eligit pauperes in hoc mundo, divites in fide?*

Et nota quod Moyses primo promisit divitias; Deut. XXVIII, 1: *faciet te Dominus Deus tuus excelsiorem cunctis gentibus, quae versantur in terra*; et infra: *benedictus tu in civitate, et benedictus in agro*. Et ideo ut distinguat Dominus legem veterem a nova, primo ponit beatitudinem in contemptu divitiarum temporalium.

things, but even in interior things; *I am a beggar and poor* (Ps 40:17); on the other hand: *I am rich, and made wealthy, and have need of nothing: and know not, that you are wretched, and miserable, and poor, and blind, and naked* (Rev 3:17).

And then what is said, *in spirit*, can be read in three ways. For the pride of a man is sometimes called the spirit; *cease therefore from the man, whose breath is in his nostrils, for he is reputed high* (Isa 2:22); *the spirit of the mighty is like a whirlwind beating against a wall* (Isa 25:4). And pride is called *spirit* because as breath inflates a bag, so pride inflates men: *puffed up by the sense of his flesh* (Col 2:18). Therefore, **blessed are the poor**, namely those who have little of the spirit of pride. Or *spirit* is taken as the will of man. For some are humble by necessity, and these are not blessed, but rather those who put on humility. Third, it is taken as the Holy Spirit; hence, **blessed are the poor in the Spirit**, who are humble through the Holy Spirit. And these two come to the same thing, so to speak. And he says, **the poor in spirit**, because humility gives one the Holy Spirit; *but for whom will I have respect, except him that is poor and little, and of a contrite spirit, and that trembles at my words?* (Isa 66:2).

To these poor ones is promised the kingdom, in which is understood the highest excellence. And although this is bestowed upon any virtue, yet it is especially given to humility; because *he who humbles himself, will be exalted* (Luke 14:11). And, *glory will uphold the humble of spirit* (Prov 29:23).

416. Or in another way, according to Jerome. **Poor in spirit**, literally, in renunciation of temporal things. And he says, **in spirit**, because some are poor by necessity, but beatitude is not due them, but rather to those who are poor by will. And those who are poor by will are so called in two ways, because although some have riches, yet they do not have them in their heart; *if riches abound, set not your heart upon them* (Ps 62:11). Others neither have, nor desire, and this is more secure, because the mind is drawn from spiritual things by riches. And these are properly called **poor in spirit**, because the acts of the gifts, which are above the human manner, are those of the blessed man: and that a man should reject all riches, so that he does not even desire them in some way, this is above the human manner.

417. To these is promised **the kingdom of heaven**, in which is indicated not only loftiness of honor, but the abundance of riches; *has not God chosen the poor in this world, rich in faith, and heirs of the kingdom which God has promised to those who love him?* (Jas 2:5).

And note that Moses first promised riches; *the Lord your God will make you higher than all the nations that are on the earth* (Deut 28:1); and further down, *blessed will you be in the city, and blessed in the field*. And therefore, that the Lord might distinguish the old law from the new, he first places beatitude in the contempt of temporal riches.

418. Item, secundum Augustinum nota, quod ista beatitudo pertinet ad donum timoris: quia timor, maxime filialis, facit habere reverentiam ad Deum; et ex hoc contemnit homo divitias. Ponit Isaias beatitudines descendendo; Is. XI, 1: *egredietur virga de radice Iesse, et flos de radice eius ascendet, et requiescet super eum spiritus Domini, spiritus sapientiae et intellectus, spiritus consilii et fortitudinis, spiritus scientiae et pietatis, et replebit eum spiritus timoris Domini.* Christus e converso a dono timoris, scilicet a paupertate, quia Isaias praenuntiavit adventum Christi ad terram; Christus autem de terra sursum trahebat.

419. *Beati mites*. Haec est secunda beatitudo; sed ne aliquis dicat quod sufficit paupertas ad beatitudinem, ostendit quod non sufficit: immo requiritur mansuetudo, quae temperat circa iras, sicut temperantia circa concupiscentias: ille enim est mitis, qui nec irritatur. Hoc autem poterit fieri per virtutem, ut scilicet non irascaris nisi causa iusta; sed si habeas etiam causam iustam, et non provocaris, hoc est supra humanum modum; et ideo dicit ***beati mites***. Pugna enim est propter abundantiam exteriorum rerum; et ideo numquam esset turbatio, si homo divitias non affectaret; et ideo qui non sunt mites, non sunt pauperes spiritu. Et propterea statim subiungit ***beati mites***.

Et nota, quod hoc in duobus consistit. Primo quod homo non irascatur; secundo, quod si irascatur, iram temperet. Ita dicit Ambrosius: *prudentis est irae motus temperare, nec minor virtus dicitur temperate irasci, quam omnino non irasci est: plurimumque hoc levius, illud fortius existimo* et cetera.

420. Chrysostomus dicit: *inter multas promissiones aeternas ponit unam terrenam.* Unde, ad litteram, ***terram*** istam ***possident*** mites. Multi enim litigant, ut possessiones acquirant, sed frequenter vitam et omnia perdunt; sed frequenter mansueti totum habent; Ps. XXXVI, 11: *mansueti haereditabunt terram.*

Sed melius exponitur, ut referatur ad futurum. Et potest tunc exponi multipliciter. Hilarius sic: ***possidebunt terram***, idest corpus Christi glorificatum, quia erunt conformes in corpore suo illi claritati; Is. XXXIII, v. 17: *videbunt regem in decore suo; oculi eius cernent terram de longe*; Phil. III, 21: *reformabit corpus humilitatis nostrae configuratum corpori claritatis suae.*

Vel aliter. Ista terra modo est mortuorum, quia subiecta est corruptioni, sed liberabitur a corruptione secundum Apostolum, Rom. c. VIII, 21. Ergo ista terra, quando erit clarificata et liberata a servitute corruptionis, vocabitur terra viventium. Vel per ***terram*** intelligitur caelum Empyreum, in quo sunt beati: et vocatur ***terra***, quia sicut se habet terra ad caelum, ita caelum illud

418. Likewise note, following Augustine, that this beatitude pertains to the gift of fear. Because fear, most of all filial fear, makes one have reverence toward God; and out of this a man despises riches. Isaiah sets out the beatitudes in descending order: *and there will come forth a rod out of the root of Jesse, and a flower will rise up out of his root. And the spirit of the Lord will rest upon him: the spirit of wisdom, and of understanding, the spirit of counsel, and of fortitude, the spirit of knowledge, and of piety. And the spirit of the fear of the Lord will fill him* (Isa 11:1–3). Christ sets them out the other way around, from the gift of fear, namely from poverty, because Isaiah foretold the coming of Christ to earth, but Christ drew men up from the earth.

419. *Blessed are the meek*. This is the second beatitude; but lest someone say that poverty is enough for beatitude, he shows that it is not enough: rather gentleness is required, which restrains one with regard to anger, just as temperance restrains one with regard to concupiscence; for he is meek who does not grow angry. Now this could come about by virtue, namely that you are not angered except by a just cause; but if you are not provoked even when you have a just cause, this is above the human manner; and therefore he says, ***blessed are the meek***. For fighting is on account of an abundance of external things; and therefore there would be no disturbance if a man did not desire riches. And therefore those who are not meek are not poor in spirit. And this is why he immediately adds, ***blessed are the meek***.

And note that this consists in two things. First, that a man is not angered; second, that if he is angered, he restrains his anger. Ambrose speaks this way: *it belongs to the prudent man to moderate the motion of anger, nor is it called a lesser virtue to be angry with restraint, than not to be angered at all. I judge the latter much easier, the former much harder.*

420. Chrysostom says: *among many eternal promises, he places one earthly promise.* Hence, literally, the meek ***possess*** that ***land***. For many go to court to acquire possessions, but frequently they lose their life and all their things; but frequently the gentle have it all: *the meek will inherit the land* (Ps 37:11).

But it is better explained as referred to the future. And then it can be explained in many ways. Hilary speaks this way: ***they will possess the land***, i.e., the glorified body of Christ, because they will be conformed to that brilliance in their own body; *his eyes will see the king in his beauty, they will see the land far off* (Isa 33:17); *who will reform the body of our lowness, made like to the body of his glory* (Phil 3:21).

Or in another way. This land is the land of the dead for a while, because it is subjected to corruption, but it will be freed from corruption, according to the Apostle (Rom 8:21). Therefore this land, when it is glorified and freed from the servitude of corruption, will be called the land of the living. Or, by ***the land*** is understood the fiery heaven, where the blessed are; and it is called ***the land***, because just as the land

ad caelum Sanctae Trinitatis. Vel **possidebunt terram**, idest corpus suum glorificatum.

Augustinus exponit metaphorice: et dicit quod per hoc intelligenda est quaedam soliditas sanctorum in cognitione primae veritatis; Ps. XXVI, 13: *credo videre bona Domini in terra viventium.*

421. Ista secunda beatitudo adaptatur dono pietatis: quia illi proprie irascuntur, qui non sunt contenti divina ordinatione.

422. Beati qui lugent et cetera. Positae sunt duae beatitudines, per quas abstrahimur a malo cupiditatis et crudelitatis; hic ponitur tertia, per quam abstrahimur a malo noxiae voluptatis, vel iucunditatis: et hoc est **beati qui lugent**.

In Veteri Testamento terrena promittebat, et terrenam iucunditatem; Ier. XXXI, 12: *confluent ad bona Domini super frumento, vino et oleo* etc.; et post: *laetabitur virgo in choro, iuvenes et senes simul.* Sed per contrarium Dominus ponit beatitudinem in luctu.

Notandum autem quod non quicumque ploratus luctus dici potest; sed ille quo quis mortuum plorat sibi dilectum: Dominus enim per excessum loquitur hic. Sicut supra **beati pauperes**, ita hic de maximo luctu mentionem facit; sicut enim nullam recipiunt consolationem hi qui mortuum plorant, ita Dominus vult vitam nostram in luctu esse; Ier. VI, 26: *luctum unigeniti fac tibi, planctum amarum* et cetera.

Et potest iste luctus tripliciter exponi. Primo pro peccatis non solum propriis, sed etiam alienis: quia si lugemus mortuos carnaliter, multo magis spiritualiter; I Reg. XVI, v. 1: *usquequo tu luges, Saul?* et cetera. Ier. IX, 1: *quis dabit capiti meo aquam, et oculis meis fontem lacrimarum? Et plorabo die ac nocte interfectos filiae populi mei.* Ponitur autem satis congrue ista beatitudo post praemissam. Posset enim quis dicere: sufficit non facere malum: et verum est a principio ante peccatum; sed post commissum peccatum non sufficit nisi satisfacias. Secundo potest accipi de luctu pro incolatu praesentis miseriae; Ps. CXIX, 5: *heu mihi, quia incolatus meus prolongatus est.* Istud est *irriguum superius et inferius*, de quo Ios. XV, 19: *pro peccatis plorate, et pro caelestis patriae incolatu.* Tertio, secundum Augustinum, pro luctu quem habent homines de gaudiis saeculi, quae dimittunt veniendo ad Christum: homines enim aliqui saeculo moriuntur, et saeculum moritur eis; Gal. ult., 14: *per quem mihi mundus crucifixus est, et ego mundo.* Nos autem sicut de mortuis lugemus, ita illi lugent: quia non potest esse quin, in dimittendo, aliquem dolorem sentiant.

is related to heaven, so is that heaven related to the heaven of the Holy Trinity. Or, **they will possess the land**, i.e., their own glorified body.

Augustine explains this metaphorically, and he says that by this one should understand a certain solidity of the saints in the knowledge of the first truth; *I believe I shall see the good things of the Lord in the land of the living* (Ps 27:13).

421. This second beatitude is related to the gift of piety, because those get angry, properly speaking, who are not contented with the divine ordering of things.

422. Blessed are they who mourn. Two beatitudes were mentioned by which we are drawn away from the evils of desire and of cruelty; here a third is set down, by which we are drawn away from the evil of harmful pleasure or enjoyment. And this is **blessed are they who mourn**.

In the Old Testament, he promised earthly things, and earthly enjoyment; *and they will flow together to the good things of the Lord, for the corn, and wine, and oil* (Jer 31:12). Then after that, *then will the virgin rejoice in the dance, the young men and old men together.* But the Lord on the contrary places beatitude in mourning.

But one should notice that not just any lamenting can be called mourning, but that by which someone laments a dead one dear to him; for the Lord speaks here by way of excess. Just as above, **blessed are the poor**, so here he mentions the greatest grief; for just as those who grieve the dead receive no consolation, so the Lord wishes our life to be in mourning; *make mourning as for an only son, a bitter lamentation* (Jer 6:26).

And this mourning can be explained in three ways. First, for sins, not only personal, but another's as well, for if we mourn those who are dead in body, much more those who are dead spiritually; *how long will you mourn for Saul?* (1 Sam 16:1); *who will give water to my head, and a fountain of tears to my eyes? And I will weep day and night for the slain of the daughter of my people* (Jer 9:1). Now this beatitude is set down fittingly enough after the previous one. For someone could say, 'it is enough not to do evil,' and this is true in the beginning, before sin; but after a sin is committed, it is not enough unless you make satisfaction. Second, it can be taken as mourning for our dwelling in present misery; *woe is me, that my sojourning is prolonged!* (Ps 120:5). This is *the watering above and below*, about which, *weep over your sins, and over the sojourning of the heavenly homeland* (Jos 15:19). Third, according to Augustine, for the mourning which men make over the joys of the world, which they abandon by coming to Christ; for some men die to the world, and the world dies to them; *but God forbid that I should glory, save in the cross of our Lord Jesus Christ; by whom the world is crucified to me, and I to the world* (Gal 6:14). Now as we mourn over the dead, so these men mourn, because it cannot be but that they feel some sorrow in abandoning everything.

423. Isti autem triplici luctui triplex consolatio respondet: quia luctui pro peccatis datur remissio peccatorum, quam petebat David dicens Ps. l, 14: *redde mihi laetitiam salutaris tui.* Dilationi caelestis patriae, et incolatui praesentis miseriae respondet consolatio vitae aeternae, de qua Ier. XXXI, v. 13: *convertam luctum vestrum in gaudium, et consolabor eos, et laetificabo a dolore suo*; et Is. ult., 13: *in Ierusalem consolabimini.* Tertio luctui respondet consolatio divini amoris: quando enim aliquis dolet de amissione rei dilectae, consolationem recipit si aliam rem magis dilectam acquirit. Unde homines consolantur, quando pro temporalibus rebus recipiunt spirituales et aeternas, quod est Spiritum Sanctum recipere; quare dicitur Paraclitus Io. XV, 26. Per Spiritum Sanctum enim, qui est amor divinus, homines gaudebunt; Io. XVI, 20: *tristitia vestra convertetur in gaudium.*

424. Et notandum, quod ista beatitudo appropriatur dono scientiae, quia illi lugent qui miserias aliorum cognoscunt: unde de quibusdam talem scientiam non habentibus dicitur Sap. XIV, 22: *in magno viventes inscientiae bello, et tot et tam magna mala pacem appellant*; e converso Eccle. I, 18: *qui addit scientiam, addit et laborem.*

425. Et notandum quod ista praemia ita ordinantur, quod semper secundum addit super primum. Primo enim dixit **beati pauperes, quoniam ipsorum est regnum caelorum**; postea **quoniam ipsi possidebunt terram**: plus enim est possidere, quam habere tantum. Item postea **quoniam ipsi consolabuntur**: plus enim est consolari, quam possidere, aliqui enim possident ista, sed non delectantur in eis.

426. Consequenter positis beatitudinibus, quae pertinent ad remotionem mali, hic ponitur beatitudo quae pertinet ad operationem boni. Est autem duplex bonum nostrum, iustitiae scilicet, et misericordiae. Et ideo duo ponit.

427. Quantum ad primum dicit **beati qui esuriunt et sitiunt iustitiam**. Iustitia tripliciter sumitur, secundum Chrysostomum et Philosophum. Quandoque enim pro omni virtute: et dicitur omnis virtus iustitia legalis, quae praecipit de actibus virtutum. Unde inquantum homo obedit legi, implet opus omnium virtutum. Alio modo secundum quod est specialis virtus, de quatuor cardinalibus, quae opponitur avaritiae, vel iniustitiae, et est circa emptiones, venditiones, conductiones.

Quod ergo dicit hic **qui esuriunt iustitiam**, potest intelligi generaliter, vel specialiter.

Si intelligatur de generali, hoc dicit propter duas rationes. Prima Hieronymi, qui dicit quod non sufficit quod homo iustitiae opus operetur, nisi cum desiderio operetur; Ps. LIII, 8: *voluntarie sacrificabo tibi* et cetera.

423. Moreover, to these three mournings correspond three consolations, because to the mourning for sins corresponds remission of sins, which David begged for, saying, *restore unto me the joy of your salvation* (Ps 51:12). To the delay of the heavenly homeland and the dwelling in present misery corresponds the consolation of eternal life, about which it is said, *I will turn their mourning into joy, and will comfort them, and make them joyful after their sorrow* (Jer 31:13); and, *you will be comforted in Jerusalem* (Isa 66:13). To the third mourning corresponds the consolation of divine love; for when someone sorrows over the loss of a thing loved, he takes consolation if he acquires another thing more loved. Hence men are consoled when instead of temporal things they receive spiritual and eternal things, which is to receive the Holy Spirit; which is why he is called the Comforter (John 15:26). For men rejoice through the Holy Spirit, who is the divine love; *your sorrow will be turned into joy* (John 16:20).

424. And one should note that this beatitude is appropriated to the gift of knowledge, because they mourn who know the misery of others; hence it says about certain men who do not have such knowledge, *they lived in a great war of ignorance, they call so many and so great evils peace* (Wis 14:22); on the other hand, *he that adds knowledge, adds also labor* (Eccl 1:18).

425. And one should notice that this reward is so ordained that the second is always added onto the first. For first he said, **blessed are the poor in spirit: for theirs is the kingdom of heaven**; afterward, **for they will possess the land**: for it is more to possess than merely to have. Likewise, afterward, **for they will be comforted**: for it is more to be consoled than to possess, for some possess things but do not take delight in them.

426. Next, those beatitudes being set down which pertain to the removal of evil, here the beatitude which pertains to the working of good is set down. And our good is twofold, namely the good of justice and the good of mercy. And so he sets out two things.

427. As regards the first, he says, **blessed are they who hunger and thirst after justice**. Justice is taken in three ways, according to Chrysostom and the Philosopher. For sometimes it is taken as every virtue: and every virtue is called legal justice, which commands concerning the acts of the virtues. Hence insofar as a man obeys the law, he fulfills the work of all the virtues. It is taken in another way as a particular virtue, one of the four cardinal virtues, to which is opposed greed, or injustice, and it concerns buying, selling, and renting.

So what he says here, **who hunger after justice**, can be understood generally, or particularly.

If it is understood as about the general meaning of justice, he says this for two reasons. The first is Jerome's, who says that it is not enough that a man should work the work of justice, unless he works with desire; *I will freely sacrifice*

Et alibi, Ps. XLI, 3: *sitivit anima mea ad Deum fontem vivum* et cetera. Amos VIII, 11: *mittam famem in terram istam, non famem panis, neque sitim aquae, sed audiendi verbum Dei*. Ergo est esuries quando cum desiderio operatur quis.

Alia ratio. Iustitia est duplex, perfecta et imperfecta: perfectam in mundo habere non possumus, quia *si dixerimus quia peccatum non habemus, ipsi nos seducimus, et veritas in nobis non est*, I Io. I, 8. Et Is. LXIV, 6: *omnes iustitiae nostrae quasi pannus menstruatae*. Sed hanc habemus in caelo; Is. LX, v. 21: *populus tuus omnes iusti in perpetuum haereditabunt terram*. Sed desiderium iustitiae possumus hic habere: et ideo dicit **beati qui esuriunt et sitiunt iustitiam** et cetera. Et est simile illud quod Pythagoras fecit. Tempore enim Pythagorae illi qui studebant, vocabantur 'sophi', idest sapientes; Pythagoras autem noluit vocari 'sophos', idest sapiens, sed 'philosophus', hoc est sapientiae amator: ita vult Dominus quod sui sint, et vocentur amatores iustitiae.

Si autem intelligatur de iustitia speciali, quae est, quod homo reddat unicuique quod suum est, convenienter dicitur **beati qui esuriunt** etc.; quia esuries et sitis proprie avarorum est, quia numquam satiantur qui aliena iniuste possidere desiderant: unde ista esuries, de qua dicit Dominus, opponitur huic, scilicet avarorum. Et vult Dominus quod ita anhelemus ad istam iustitiam, quod numquam quasi satiemur in vita ista, sicut avarus numquam satiatur. **Beati** ergo **qui esuriunt et sitiunt iustitiam, quoniam ipsi saturabuntur**.

428. Conveniens praemium ponitur **saturabuntur**, et primum in aeterna visione, videbunt enim Deum per essentiam; Ps. XVI, v. 15: *satiabor cum apparuerit gloria tua*: ibi enim nihil restabit ad desiderandum; Ps. CII, 5: *qui replet in bonis desiderium tuum*; Prov. X, 24: *desiderium suum iustis dabitur*.

Secundo in praesenti. Et haec est duplex. Una est in bonis spiritualibus, hoc est in impletione mandatorum Dei; Io. IV, 34: *meus cibus est ut faciam voluntatem eius qui misit me, ut perficiam opus eius*: et de isto exponit Augustinus. Alio modo accipitur de saturitate rerum temporalium. Homines iniusti numquam saturantur, sed homines qui habent terminum suum ipsam iustitiam, ultra non procedunt; Prov. XIII, 25: *iustus comedit, et replet animam suam*.

429. Ista beatitudo secundum Augustinum reducitur ad donum fortitudinis: quia quod homo iuste operetur, hoc pertinet ad fortitudinem. Item superaddit aliquid praemio supra posito, quia saturari est implere totaliter desiderium.

Item nota quod primo dicit **beati qui lugent**: homo enim quando infirmus est, non appetit comedere, sed tunc appetere incipit, quando iam incipit sanari; et ita est

to you (Ps 54:6). And in another place, *my soul has thirsted after the strong living God; when will I come and appear before the face of God?* (Ps 42:2). *I will send forth a famine into the land: not a famine of bread, nor a thirst of water, but of hearing the word of the Lord* (Amos 8:11). Therefore it is a hunger when someone works with desire.

Another reason. Justice is twofold, perfect and imperfect. We cannot have perfect justice in this world, because *if we say that we have no sin, we deceive ourselves, and the truth is not in us* (1 John 1:8). And, *all our justices are as the rag of a menstruous woman* (Isa 64:6). But we have this in heaven; *your people will be all just, they will inherit the land for ever* (Isa 60:21). But we can have a desire for justice here: and therefore, he says, **blessed are they who hunger and thirst after justice**. And what Pythagoras did is similar. For in the time of Pythagoras, those who studied were called 'sophi', i.e., wise men; but Pythagoras did not wish to be called 'sophos', i.e., wise, but 'philosopher', that is, a lover of wisdom; in this way the Lord wills that his own be and be called lovers of justice.

But if it is understood as about particular justice, which is that a man render to each what is his own, then it is fittingly said, **blessed are they who hunger**, because hunger and thirst properly belong to the greedy, since those who desire to possess another's goods unjustly are never satisfied. Hence the hunger about which the Lord speaks is opposed to this one, namely the hunger of the greedy. And the Lord wills that we pant after that justice in this way, because we will never be, as it were, satisfied in this life, just as the greedy man is never satisfied. **Blessed are they who hunger and thirst after justice: for they will have their fill**.

428. A fitting reward is set forth, **they will have their fill**, and it is first in the eternal vision, for they will see God through his essence; *I will be satisfied when your glory will appear* (Ps 17:15). For there nothing remains to be desired; *who satisfies your desire with good things* (Ps 103:5); *to the just their desire will be given* (Prov 10:24).

Second, in the present. And this satisfaction is twofold. One is in spiritual goods, that is in the fulfillment of God's commands; *my meat is to do the will of him that sent me, that I may perfect his work* (John 4:34); and Augustine explains this. In another way, it is taken as concerning a plenitude of temporal things. Unjust men are never filled, but men who have as their end justice itself, do not go beyond it; *the just eats and fills his soul: but the belly of the wicked is never to be filled* (Prov 13:25).

429. According to Augustine, this beatitude is reduced to the gift of fortitude, because it pertains to fortitude that a man works justly. Likewise, he adds something to the reward set out above, because to be filled is to fulfill the desires entirely.

Likewise, note that first he says, **blessed are they who mourn**, for when a man is ill, he does not desire to eat, but he begins to desire when he has just begun to be healed;

in spiritualibus, quod quando homines sunt in peccato, non sentiunt famem spiritualem, sed quando dimittunt peccata, tunc sentiunt; et ideo statim subdit *beati misericordes*: quia iustitia sine misericordia crudelitas est, misericordia sine iustitia mater est dissolutionis. Et ideo oportet quod utrumque coniungatur, secundum illud Prov. III, 3: *misericordia et veritas non te deserant* et cetera. Ps. LXXXIV, 11: *misericordia et veritas obviaverunt sibi* et cetera.

430. *Beati misericordes, quoniam ipsi misericordiam consequentur*. Misericordem esse est habere miserum cor de miseria aliorum: tunc autem habemus misericordiam de miseria aliorum, quando illam reputamus quasi nostram. De nostra autem dolemus, et studemus repellere. Ergo tunc vere misericors es, quando miseriam aliorum studes repellere.

Est autem duplex miseria proximi. Prima in istis rebus temporalibus; et ad istam debemus habere miserum cor; I Io. III, 17: *qui habuerit substantiam huius mundi, et viderit fratrem suum necesse habere, et clauserit viscera sua ab eo, quomodo caritas Dei manet in eo?* Secunda qua homo per peccatum miser efficitur: quia, sicut beatitudo est in operibus virtutum, ita miseria propria in vitiis; Prov. XIV, 34: *miseros facit populos peccatum*. Et ideo quando admonemus corruentes ut redeant, misericordes sumus; infra IX, v. 36: *videns autem Iesus turbas, misericordia motus est*. Isti ergo misericordes beati.

431. Et quare? *Quoniam ipsi misericordiam consequentur*. Et sciendum quod semper dona Dei excedunt merita nostra; Eccli. XXXV, 13: *quoniam Dominus retribuens est, et septies tantum retribuet tibi*. Ergo multo maior est misericordia quam Dominus impendet nobis, quam illa quam impendimus proximo.

Ista misericordia inchoatur in hac vita dupliciter. Primo, quia relaxantur peccata; Ps. CII, 3: *qui propitiatur omnibus iniquitatibus tuis*. Secundo, quia removet defectus temporales, ita quod *solem suum facit oriri*; perficietur tamen in futuro, quando omnis miseria, et culpae, et poenae removebuntur; Ps. XXXV, 6: *Domine, in caelo misericordia tua*. Et hoc est *quoniam ipsi misericordiam consequentur*.

432. Ista beatitudo reducitur ad donum consilii: quia hoc est singulare consilium ut inter pericula huius mundi misericordiam consequamur; I Tim. IV, 8: *pietas ad omnia utilis est*; Dan. IV, 24: *consilium meum regi placeat*.

433. Sic ergo positi sunt actus virtutum, quibus removemur a malo, et operamur bonum. Nunc ponuntur actus quibus disponimur ad optimum; unde *beati mundo corde* et cetera. Ista beatitudo in duobus consistit: in visione Dei et dilectione proximi, unde

and so it is in the spiritual life, for when men are in sin, they do not feel spiritual hunger, but when they abandon sin, then they feel it. And therefore he immediately adds, *blessed are the merciful*, because justice without mercy is cruelty, while mercy without justice is the mother of laxity. And so it is necessary that both be joined together: *let not mercy and truth leave you* (Prov 3:3). *Mercy and truth have met each other: justice and peace have kissed* (Ps 85:10).

430. *Blessed are the merciful: for they will obtain mercy*. To be merciful is to have a miserable heart at the misery of others. Moreover, we have pity on the miseries of others when we think of them as our own. Now, we sorrow for our miseries, and we are eager to drive them away; therefore you are truly merciful when you are eager to drive away the misery of others.

And the misery of one's neighbor is twofold. First, in temporal things, and for this we should have a miserable heart; *he who has the substance of this world, and will see his brother in need, and will shut up his innermost from him: how does the charity of God abide in him?* (1 John 3:17). Second, when a man is made miserable through sin; because, just as there is beatitude in the works of the virtues, so there is a particular misery in vices. *Sin makes nations miserable* (Prov 14:34). And therefore, when we warn those falling so that they may return, we are merciful; *and seeing the multitudes, he had compassion on them* (Matt 9:36). Therefore, these merciful ones are blessed.

431. And why? *For they will obtain mercy*. And one should know that the gifts of God always exceed our merit; *for the Lord makes recompense, and will give you seven times as much* (Sir 35:13). Therefore the mercy which our Lord has on us is much greater than that which we have on our neighbor.

This mercy is begun in this life in two ways. First, because sins are loosed: *who forgives all your iniquities* (Ps 103:3). Second, because he removes temporal defects, such that he *makes his sun to rise* (Matt 5:45); yet it will be perfected in the future, when every misery, both of guilt and of punishment, will be taken away. *O Lord, your mercy is in heaven* (Ps 36:6). And this is *for they will obtain mercy*.

432. This beatitude is reduced to the gift of counsel; because this is a unique counsel, that we should obtain mercy amidst the dangers of this world. *Godliness is profitable to all things* (1 Tim 4:8); *wherefore, O king, let my counsel be acceptable to you* (Dan 4:24).

433. So in this way are set down the acts of the virtues by which we are withdrawn from what is evil and do what is good. Now are set down the acts by which we are disposed to what is best; hence, *blessed are the clean of heart*. This beatitude consists in two things: in the vision of God and in the love of neighbor. Hence,

primo ponit beatitudinem quae pertinet ad visionem Dei;

secundo beatitudinem quae pertinet ad dilectionem proximi, ibi *beati pacifici* et cetera.

434. Dicit ergo *beati mundo corde, quoniam ipsi Deum videbunt.*

Hic primo est quaestio litteralis. Habemus enim quod Deus videri non potest: I Io. IV, v. 12: *Deum nemo vidit unquam.* Et ne aliquis diceret, quod quamvis nullus videat in praesenti, videbit in futuro, removet hoc Apostolus I Tim. ult., 16: *lucem habitat inaccessibilem, quem nullus hominum vidit, sed nec videre potest.*

Sed sciendum quod circa hoc sunt diversae opiniones. Aliqui enim posuerunt quod numquam Deus per essentiam videatur, sed in aliqua refulgentia suae claritatis; sed hoc reprobat Glossa super illud Exod. XXXIII, 20: *non videbit me homo, et vivet,* propter duo. Primo, quia hoc repugnat auctoritati Sacrae Scripturae, I Io. III, 2: *videbimus eum sicuti est.* Item I Cor. XIII, 12: *videmus nunc per speculum in aenigmate, tunc autem facie ad faciem.* Item rationi, quia beatitudo hominis est ultimum bonum hominis, in quo quietatur desiderium eius. Naturale autem desiderium est, quod homo videns effectus inquirat de causa: unde etiam admiratio philosophorum fuit origo philosophiae, quia videntes effectus admirabantur, et quaerebant causam. Istud ergo desiderium non quietabitur, donec perveniat ad primam causam, quae Deus est, scilicet ad ipsam divinam essentiam. Videbitur ergo per essentiam.

Alii plus etiam erraverunt ponentes contrarium: quia dixerunt quod non solum videbimus oculo mentis, sed etiam corporis, essentiam Dei, et quod Christus videt oculo corporali essentiam divinam. Sed hoc non convenit: quod patet primo ex auctoritate quae hic ponitur, quia non diceret *beati mundo corde*; sed, beati qui habent mundos et puros oculos. Ergo dat intelligere, quod non videtur nisi corde, idest intellectu: sic enim accipitur hic cor, sicut et Ephes. I, 18: *illuminatos oculos cordis vestri.* Secundo, quia sensus corporis non potest nisi in suum obiectum; si autem dicatur quod tunc habebit maiorem potentiam, dicendum quod tunc non esset visio corporalis, quia oculus corporalis non videt nisi colores, essentiam autem per accidens, secundum Augustinum Lib. ult. *de Civitate Dei*, c. XIX. Sicut cum video vivens, possumus dicere quod video vitam, inquantum video quaedam indicia quibus indicatur mihi vita sua; ita erit in visione divina, quia tanta erit refulgentia in caelo novo, et terra nova, et corporibus glorificatis, quod per ista dicemur videre Deum quasi oculis corporalibus. Ergo *beati mundo corde* et cetera.

first, he sets out the beatitude which pertains to the vision of God;

second, the beatitude which pertains to the love of neighbor, at *blessed are the peacemakers.*

434. He says then, *blessed are the clean of heart: for they will see God.*

Here there is first a question of literal meaning. For we know that God cannot be seen: *no man has ever seen God* (1 John 4:12). And lest someone say that although no one sees at present, he will see in the future, the Apostle takes this possibility away: *who only has immortality, and inhabits light inaccessible, whom no man has seen, nor can see* (1 Tim 6:16).

But one should know that there are different opinions about this. For some have held that God is never seen in his essence, but in some reflection of his glory; but the Gloss condemns this, commenting on, *man will not see me and live* (Exod 33:20), with two arguments. First, because this opposes the authority of Sacred Scripture, *we will see him as he is* (1 John 3:2). Similarly, *we see now through a glass in a dark manner; but then face to face* (1 Cor 13:12). It is likewise opposed to reason, because the beatitude of man is the last good of man, in which his desire is set to rest. Now, it is a natural desire that a man, seeing an effect, inquires about the cause; hence also the philosophers' wonder was the origin of philosophy, because when they saw effects, they wondered and sought the cause. Therefore, that desire will not be set to rest until it arrives at the first cause, which is God, namely at the divine essence itself. Therefore, he will be seen through his essence.

Others have erred even more, holding the contrary position, for they said that we will see the essence of God not only with the eye of the mind, but with the eye of the body as well, and that Christ sees the divine essence with his bodily eye. But this does not hold together; which is clear, first from the Scriptural text which is mentioned here, because he would not say, *blessed are the clean of heart*, but, 'blessed are they who have clean and pure eyes.' So he gives one to understand that he will not see except with the heart, i.e., the intellect, for heart is taken this way: *the eyes of your heart enlightened* (Eph 1:18). Second, because the sense of a body can only attain to its own object; but if it be said that then it will have a greater power, one should say that then it would not be bodily vision, because the bodily eye sees only colors, and sees the essence *per accidens*, according to Augustine, in the last book of *The City of God* (Ch. 19). Just as when I see something living, we can say that I see life, insofar as I see certain indications by which its life is pointed out to me, so it will be in the divine vision, because the reflection of God in the new heaven and the new earth and the glorified bodies will be so great that by it we will be said to see God as though with the bodily eyes. Therefore, *blessed are the clean of heart.*

Solvit vero illud, *Deum nemo vidit unquam*, tripliciter. Primo quia non visione comprehensiva; secundo oculis corporalibus; tertio in hac vita: quia si alicui datum fuerit quod viderit in hac vita Deum, hoc fuit quia totaliter alienatus est et elevatus supra sensus corporales. Et ideo dicitur **beati mundo corde**: quia sicut oculus videns colorem oportet quod sit depuratus, ita mens videns Deum; Sap. I v. 1: *in simplicitate cordis quaerite illum, quoniam invenitur ab his qui non tentant illum; apparet autem his qui fidem habent in illum*: fide enim purificatur cor; Act. XV, 9: *fide purificans corda eorum*. Et quia visio succedet fidei, ideo dicitur **quoniam ipsi Deum videbunt**.

435. Beati mundo corde, qui scilicet habent munditiam generalem ab alienis cogitationibus, per quam cor eorum templum Dei sanctum est, in quo Deum contemplandum vident: 'templum' enim a 'contemplando' dici videtur. Specialiter vero **beati mundo corde**, idest qui habent munditiam carnis: nihil enim ita impedit spiritualem contemplationem, sicut immunditia carnis. *Pacem sequimini, et sanctimoniam, sine qua nemo videbit Deum*, Hebr. XII, 14.

Et ideo quidam dicunt quod virtutes morales proficiunt ad vitam contemplativam, et praecipue castitas. Et secundum hoc **beati mundo corde**, potest intelligi de visione viae: sancti enim qui habent cor repletum iustitia, vident excellentius quam alii qui vident per effectus corporales: quanto enim effectus sunt propinquiores, tanto Deus magis cognoscitur per illos. Unde sancti qui habent iustitiam, caritatem, et huiusmodi effectus, qui sunt similimi Deo, cognoscunt magis quam alii; Ps. XXXIII, 9: *gustate, et videte quoniam suavis est Dominus*.

436. Beati pacifici, quoniam filii Dei vocabuntur. Hic ponitur septima beatitudo: et, sicut dictum est, virtutes ad optimum disponentes disponunt ad duo, scilicet ad visionem Dei et dilectionem. Et sicut munditia cordis disponit ad visionem Dei, ita pax ad dilectionem Dei disponit, qua filii Dei nominamur et sumus; et sic disponit ad dilectionem proximi, quia, sicut dicitur I Io. IV, v. 20, *qui non diligit fratrem suum quem videt, Deum quem non videt, quomodo potest diligere?*

437. Et notandum quod hic ponuntur duo praemia beatitudinis, videlicet **beati pacifici**, et **beati qui persecutionem patiuntur propter iustitiam**. Et omnia praecedentia reducuntur ad ista duo, et sunt effectus omnium praecedentium. Quid enim agitur per paupertatem spiritus, per luctum, per mansuetudinem, nisi ut mundum cor habeatur? Quid per iustitiam et misericordiam, nisi ut pacem habeamus? Is. XXXII, 17: *fructus iustitiae pax, et cultus iustitiae silentium, et securitas usque in sempiternum*.

He resolves the text, *no man has ever seen God* (1 John 4:12), in three ways. First, that it will not be by a comprehensive vision; second, not with bodily eyes; third, not in this life: because if it were given to someone to see God in this life, this would be because he is entirely estranged and lifted above the bodily senses. And this is why he said, **blessed are the clean of heart**; because just as the eye seeing color must be free from impurities, so it is with the mind seeing God; *think of the Lord in goodness, and seek him in simplicity of heart. For he is found by those who tempt him not: and he shows himself to those who have faith in him* (Wis 1:1), for the heart is purified by faith. *Purifying their hearts by faith* (Acts 15:9). And because vision follows upon faith, therefore it is said, **for they will see God**.

435. Blessed are the clean of heart, namely those who have a general cleanness from unworthy thoughts, by which their heart is a holy temple of God, in which they see God by contemplating; for 'temple' seems to be said from 'contemplating.' But in a particular way, **blessed are the clean of heart**, i.e., those who have cleanness of body; for nothing so impedes spiritual contemplation as uncleanness of body does. *They obtain peace and holiness, without which no one will see God* (Heb 12:14).

And therefore, some say that the moral virtues, especially chastity, advance one toward the contemplative life. And according to this, **blessed are the clean of heart** can be understood as about the vision in this life; for the saints who have a heart filled by justice see more excellently than some who see through bodily effects, for to the degree that effects are closer to God, to that degree God is more known through them. Hence the saints, who have justice, charity, and other such effects, which are most like God, know more than others. *O taste, and see that the Lord is sweet* (Ps 34:8).

436. Blessed are the peacemakers: for they will be called children of God. Here the seventh beatitude is set down; and, as was said, the virtues which dispose one to what is best dispose one to two things, namely to the vision of God and to love. And just as cleanness of heart disposes one to the vision of God, so peace disposes one to the love of God, by which we are called and are sons of God; and thus it disposes one to the love of neighbor, because, *for he who loves not his brother, whom he sees, how can he love God, whom he does not see?* (1 John 4:20).

437. And one should note that two rewards of beatitude are set down here, namely **blessed are the peacemakers** and **blessed are they who suffer persecution for justice's sake**. And all the preceding beatitudes are reduced to these two, and these are the effects of all the preceding. For what is caused by poverty of spirit, by mourning, by meekness, except that one has a clean heart? What by justice and mercy, except that we have peace? *And the work of justice will be peace, and the service of justice quietness, and security for ever* (Isa 32:17).

438. *Beati* ergo *pacifici*. Sed videndum est quid sit pax, et quomodo ad eam possimus pervenire.

Pax est tranquillitas ordinis. Ordo autem est parium dispariumque sua loca cuique tribuens dispositio. Ergo pax est in hoc quod omnes teneant sua loca. Unde debet mens hominis primo Deo subiecta esse. Secundo motus et vires inferiores, quae sunt nobis et brutis communes, subiecta esse homini: per rationem enim homo praeest animalibus; Gen. I, 26: *faciamus hominem ad imaginem et similitudinem nostram, et praesit piscibus maris, et volatilibus caeli, et bestiis universaeque terrae, omnique reptili quod movetur in terra*. Tertio ut homo pacem habeat ad alios, quia sic totaliter erit ordinatus.

Ista autem ordinatio non potest esse nisi in hominibus sanctis; Ps. CXVIII, 165: *pax multa diligentibus nomen tuum*; Is. XLVIII, v. 22: *non est pax impiis*: pacem enim interiorem habere non possunt; Sap. XIV, 22: *in magno viventes inscientiae bello, tot et tam magna mala pacem appellant*. Pacem talem mundus dare non potest; Io. XIV, 27: *non quomodo mundus dat, ego do vobis*. Item non sufficit totum hoc, sed debent inter discordes pacem facere; Prov. XII, 20: *qui ineunt pacis consilia, sequitur eos gaudium*.

Tamen sciendum quod ista pax hic inchoatur, sed non perficitur, quia nullus potest totaliter habere motus brutales rationi subiectos; Rom. VII, 23: *video aliam legem in membris meis repugnantem legi mentis meae, et captivantem me in lege peccati, quae est in membris meis*. Unde vera erit in vita aeterna; Ps. IV, 9: *in pace in idipsum dormiam et requiescam*; Phil. IV, 7: *pax Dei exuperat omnem sensum*.

439. *Quoniam filii Dei vocabuntur*, triplici ratione. Prima est, quia habent officium filii Dei: ad hoc enim Filius dicitur venisse in mundum, ut congregaret dispersos; Ephes. II, 14: *ipse enim est pax nostra*; Col. I, 20: *pacificans in sanguine crucis eius, sive quae in terris, sive quae in caelis*. Secundo, quia per pacem cum caritate pervenitur ad regnum aeternum, in quo omnes filii Dei vocabuntur; Sap. V, 5: *ecce quomodo computati sunt inter filios Dei, et inter sanctos sors illorum est*. Ephes. IV, 3: *solliciti servare unitatem Spiritus in vinculo pacis*. Tertio, quia per hoc homo assimilatur Deo, quia ubi est pax, non est aliqua resistentia; Deo autem nullus resistere potest; Iob IX, 4: *quis restitit ei, et pacem habuit?*

440. Et notandum quod istae beatitudines sibi invicem superaddunt: plus enim est misericordiam consequi quam saturari; quia saturari est impleri eo quod est sibi proportionatum, sed misericordia superabundat. Item non omnes qui misericordiam accipiunt, admittuntur a

438. *Blessed* therefore *are the peacemakers*. But one should see what peace is, and how we can arrive at it.

Peace is the tranquillity of order. Now, order is the arrangement allotting the proper place to equals and unequals. Therefore peace resides in this, that all hold their own places. Hence the mind of man ought first to be subject to God. Second, the motions and inferior powers which are common to us and the brutes should be subject to man, for man has dominion over the animals by reason; *let us make man to our image and likeness: and let him have dominion over the fishes of the sea, and the fowls of the air, and the beasts, and the whole earth, and every creeping creature that moves upon the earth* (Gen 1:26). Third, that a man have peace toward others, because thus he will be entirely ordered.

However, this ordering can only exist in holy men; *much peace have they who love your law* (Ps 119:165); *there is no peace to the wicked* (Isa 48:22), for they cannot have interior peace. *They lived in a great war of ignorance, they call so many and such great evils peace* (Wis 14:22). Such peace the world cannot give; *not as the world gives, do I give unto you* (John 14:27). Similarly, all this is not enough, but they ought to make peace among those who quarrel; *joy follows those who take counsels of peace* (Prov 12:20).

Nevertheless, one should know that this peace is begun here, but not perfected, because no one can have the animal movements entirely subject to reason; *but I see another law in my members, fighting against the law of my mind, and captivating me in the law of sin, that is in my members* (Rom 7:23). Hence true peace will be in eternal life; *in peace in the same I will sleep, and I will rest* (Ps 4:9); *and the peace of God, which surpasses all understanding* (Phil 4:7).

439. *For they will be called children of God*, for three reasons. The first is because they have the duty of a son of God, for the Son is said to have come into the world for this purpose, that he might gather together the scattered; *for he is our peace* (Eph 2:14); *making peace through the blood of his cross, both as to the things that are on earth, and the things that are in heaven* (Col 1:20). Second, because through peace with charity one arrives at the eternal kingdom, in which all will be called sons of God; *behold how they are numbered among the children of God, and their lot is among the saints* (Wis 5:5). *Careful to keep the unity of the Spirit in the bond of peace* (Eph 4:3). Third, because a man is made like God by this, because where there is peace, there is no resistance; but no one can resist God. *Who has resisted him, and has had peace?* (Job 9:4).

440. And one should note that these beatitudes add onto one another. For it is greater to obtain mercy than to have one's fill, because to have one's fill is to complete what is proportioned to oneself, but mercy goes beyond oneself. Similarly, not all who receive mercy are admitted by the

rege ad videndum regem. Item plus est esse filium regis, quam regem videre.

441. Et tamen sciendum, quod per omnia ista unum praemium designatur.

Sed quare ita Dominus per multa voluit significare illud?

Dicendum quod omnia quae in inferioribus divisa sunt, in superioribus congregantur. Et quia in rebus humanis ista inveniuntur dispersa, et nos manuducimur per sensibilia, ideo Dominus per multa significavit illud praemium aeternum.

442. Ista autem septima beatitudo adaptatur dono sapientiae: sapientia enim facit esse filios Dei.

Item notandum, quod in septima beatitudine ponitur pax, sicut in die septima requies, Gen. II, 2.

443. Consequenter ponitur octava beatitudo, quae designat perfectionem omnium praecedentium: tunc enim homo in omnibus illis perfectus est, quando nullam deserit propter tribulationes; Eccli. XXVII, 6: *vasa figuli probat fornax, et homines iustos tentatio tribulationis.* **Beati** ergo **qui persecutionem patiuntur** et cetera.

Sed aliquis forte audiens **beati pacifici**, dicet hos non esse beatos propter persecutionem: quia persecutio pacem turbat, vel totaliter tollit; sed certe non interiorem, sed exteriorem; Ps. CXVIII, 165. *Pax multa diligentibus legem tuam* et cetera.

Ipsa autem persecutio non facit beatum, sed eius causa: unde dicit **propter iustitiam**; I Pet. III, 14: *si quid patimini propter iustitiam, beati.* Chrysostomus: *non dicit 'a Paganis et pro fide,' sed* **propter iustitiam**.

king to see the king. Similarly, it is more to be a son of the king than to see the king.

441. And yet one should know that by all these beatitudes one reward is designated.

But why did the Lord will to signify it through many things this way?

One should say that all things which are divided in lower things are brought together in higher things. And since in human affairs those things are found scattered about, and we are led by the hand through sensible things, for this reason the Lord signified the eternal reward through many things.

442. Now, this seventh beatitude is adapted to the gift of wisdom, for wisdom makes men to be sons of God.

One should note likewise that peace is placed in the seventh beatitude, just as rest in the seventh day (Gen 2:2).

443. Next is set down the eighth beatitude, which indicates the perfection of all the preceding beatitudes; for a man is perfect in all these things when he does not give up at all because of afflictions. *The furnace tries the potter's vessels, and the trial of affliction just men* (Sir 27:6). **Blessed** therefore **are they who suffer persecution**.

But perhaps someone hearing **blessed are the peacemakers** would say that these men are not blessed on account of persecution, because persecution disturbs peace, or takes it away entirely. But certainly not interior peace, but exterior peace; *much peace have they that love your law* (Ps 119:165).

Now, the persecution itself does not make one blessed, but the cause of the persecution; hence he says, *for justice's sake*; but if also you suffer any thing for justice's sake, blessed are you (1 Pet 3:14). Chrysostom: *he does not say, 'from the pagans and for the faith,' but* **for justice's sake**.

Lecture 3

^{5:11} Beati estis cum maledixerint vobis, et persecuti vos fuerint, et dixerint omne malum adversum vos mentientes, propter me: [n. 446]

^{5:12} gaudete et exultate, quoniam merces vestra copiosa est in caelis; sic enim persecuti sunt prophetas qui fuerunt ante vos. [n. 448]

^{5:11} μακάριοί ἐστε ὅταν ὀνειδίσωσιν ὑμᾶς καὶ διώξωσιν καὶ εἴπωσιν πᾶν πονηρὸν καθ᾽ ὑμῶν [ψευδόμενοι] ἕνεκεν ἐμοῦ.

^{5:12} χαίρετε καὶ ἀγαλλιᾶσθε, ὅτι ὁ μισθὸς ὑμῶν πολὺς ἐν τοῖς οὐρανοῖς· οὕτως γὰρ ἐδίωξαν τοὺς προφήτας τοὺς πρὸ ὑμῶν.

^{5:11} Blessed are you when they will revile you, and persecute you, and speak all that is evil against you, untruly, for my sake: [n. 446]

^{5:12} Be glad and rejoice, for your reward is very great in heaven. For so they persecuted the prophets that were before you. [n. 448]

---

444. Prophetae occisi sunt, non quia negaverunt fidem, sed quia veritatem annuntiaverunt; Iohannes Baptista quia veritatem annuntiabat occisus est et martyr fuit.

Et notandum quod haec beatitudo octavo loco ponitur, sicut octavo die circumcisio fiebat in qua quaedam generalis circumcisio martyrum praenuntiatur.

445. Quoniam ipsorum est regnum. Hoc videtur esse idem ex eo quod ponitur in prima beatitudine; unde a Sanctis diversimode exponitur. Quidam enim dicunt quod idem est istud et id quod dicitur **beati pauperes spiritu quoniam ipsum**, et hoc ad designandum perfectionem patientiae, Iac. I, 4; perfectio autem semper designatur per hoc quod revertitur ad sui principium, sicut apparet in circulo. Item ille qui persecutionem patitur propter iustitiam pauper est et debentur sibi omnia alia, quia **mites** et **misericordes**, et sic de omnibus; et ideo non solum primum praemium debetur sibi sed omnia praemia. Alii dicunt quod non est idem; unde dicit Ambrosius quod ponitur regnum caelorum quantum ad gloriam animae et corporis: virtuti enim animae respondet regnum caelorum, sed martyrio respondet beatitudo quae consistit in glorificatione corporum propter supplicia quae passa sunt. Vel aliter: regnum caelorum pauperibus promittitur in spe quia non statim evolant, sed martyribus in re quia statim evolant.

446. Beati estis. Hic tangit dignitatem illorum qui debent docere ipsam doctrinam apostolorum. Et sciendum quod omnes beatitudines ad tria pertinent, quia primae tres sunt ad removendum malum, scilicet **beati pauperes**, **beati mites**, et **beati qui lugent**; aliae quattuor ad operandum bonum; ultima autem pertinet ad patienter sustinendum malum. Debent autem ista tria esse per excellentiam in doctore Sacrae Scripturae, quia in tolerando mala non solum deberet patienter sustinere sed deberet gaudere; item deberet removere mala ab aliis; item deberet tertio illuminare ad bonum. Unde in

444. The prophets were killed, not because they denied the faith, but because they announced the truth; John the Baptist was killed because he announced the truth, and he was a martyr.

And it should be noted that this beatitude is set down in the eighth place, just as circumcision, in which a certain general circumcision of martyrs is foretold, also happened on the eighth day.

445. For theirs is the kingdom (Matt 5:10). This seems to be the same as what is said in the first beatitude, hence it is explained in several ways by the saints. For certain people say that it is the same thing to say **blessed are the poor in spirit for theirs is the kingdom of heaven** (Matt 5:3), and this one is for the sake of indicating the perfection of patience, as in James (Jas 1:4). But perfection is always indicated by the fact that it returns to its own beginning, as appears in a circle. Similarly, someone who suffers persecution for justice's sake is poor and is due all things, for he is **meek** (Matt 5:4) and **merciful** (Matt 5:5), and so on with all of them. And therefore, not only the first reward is owed to him, but all rewards. Others say that it is not the same thing; hence Ambrose says that it refers to the kingdom of heaven as to the glory of the soul and body; for the kingdom of heaven corresponds to the virtue of the soul, but the beatitude corresponds to martyrdom which consists in the glorification of bodies because of the punishments they have suffered. Or it can be another way: the kingdom of heaven is promised to the poor in hope, because they do not immediately carry it off, but to the martyrs in reality, because they do carry it off immediately.

446. Blessed are you. Here he touches on the dignity of those who must teach the very teaching of the apostles. And it should be known that all beatitudes pertain to three things, for the first three are about removing an evil, namely, **blessed are the poor** (Matt 5:3), **blessed are the meek** (Matt 5:4), and **blessed those who mourn** (Matt 5:5); the next four are about the working of good; but the last pertains to patiently enduring evil. But those three should be in the teacher of Sacred Scripture in a most excellent way, for in undergoing evils he should not only patiently endure, but should rejoice; likewise he should remove evils from

istis tribus apostolicam dignitatem commandat per ordinem, et incipit a persecutione quia per hoc designatur perfectio omnium aliarum et significat quod nullus debet assumere officium praedicationis nisi sit perfectus, Prov. XIX, 11: *doctrina viri per patientiam*, Ps. XCI, 15: *bene patientes erunt*.

Circa hoc ergo tria facit:

primo enumerat mala quae passuri erant;

secundo docet modum patiendi: ***gaudete et exultate***;

tertio assignat rationem: ***quoniam merces***.

447. Mala autem vel sunt praesentia vel absentia; item praesentia verbo et facto fiunt: unde totum ponit. Dicit ergo ***beati estis***.

Sed hic movet Augustinus quaestionem, quia primo dicit ***cum vobis maledixerint***, et post ***et dixerint omne malum***, quod idem videtur. Sed sciendum quod maledicunt qui contumeliam visu gerunt, sed omne malum dicunt qui absentibus detrahunt. Maledicunt enim illis quibus multa improperia fiunt, Ier XV, 10: *omnes maledicunt mihi*; I Petri II, 23: *qui cum malediceretur*. ***Beati*** ergo ***cum maledixerint***, id est offenderint verbo et facto. Chrysostomus: *meritum vitae aeternae consistit in duobus: in faciendo bonum et sustinendo malum, et sicut quodcumque factum bonum quantumcumque minimum non caret merito, ita omnis iniuria habet praemium*. ***Et persecuti***, id est expellendo de civitate in civitatem, I Cor. IV, 12: *maledicimur et benedicimus*, et infra XXIII, 34: *ecce ego mitto ad vos prophetas et scribas, et ex illis persequimini de civitate*. ***Et dixerint***, id est confixerint et infamaverint de multis malis; II Cor. VI, 8: *ut seductores*; I Petri IV, 14: *si exprobramini in nomine Christi*. Sed sciendum quod non omnes de quibus dicuntur mala beati sunt, sed requiritur primo ut mendaciter dicatur et secundo quod propter Christum, unde dicit ***mentientes propter me***; et hoc ***propter me*** refertur ad omnia praedicta. Item nota quod idem est quod dicit ***propter me*** et supra ***propter Christum***.

448. ***Gaudete***. Hic docet modum, quomodo scilicet toleranda sunt mala. Supra quando de omnibus loquebatur dixit ***beati qui patiuntur***, id est qui non indignantur; sed in apostolis hoc non sufficit, immo oportet quod exultent; Iac. I, 2: *omne gaudium*; Act. V, 41: *ibant apostoli gaudentes*.

Sed contra, Augustinus: *tolerari ea iubes, non amari*. Dicendum quod non est gaudendum de tribulationibus, sed de spe quam habent propter tolerantiam earum, sicut qui accipit medicinam non gaudet de amaritudine medicinae, sed de spe sanitatis.

others; similarly in the third, he should light the way to the good. Hence in these three things he commissions apostolic dignity in order, and he begins with persecution because by this the perfection of all the others is designated, and it signifies that no one should assume the office of preacher unless he is perfect, *the learning of a man is known by patience* (Prov 19:11), and *they will endure well* (Ps 92:14).

Concerning this he does three things:

first, he enumerates the evils which they were to undergo;

second, he teaches the manner of suffering: ***rejoice and exult***;

third, he assigns a reason: ***for your reward***.

447. But evils are either present or absent; also, they become present in word and in deed: hence he sets forth the whole. Therefore he says, ***blessed are you***.

But Augustine raises this question, for first he says ***when they will revile you***, and afterward, ***and speak all that is evil against you***, which seems to be the same thing. But it should be known that they ***revile*** who inflict abuses on sight, but they ***speak all that is evil*** who detract from those who are absent. For they revile those to whom many taunts are made: *all curse me* (Jer 15:10); or *who when he was reviled, did not return abuse* (I Peter 2:23). Therefore, ***blessed when they revile you***, i.e., when they offend you in word and in deed. Chrysostom: *the meriting of life eternal consists in two things: in doing the good and suffering evil, and just as any good deed, however little, is not lacking in merit, so also every injury has its reward*. ***And persecute you***, i.e., by driving you out of town after town: *we are reviled and we bless* (1 Cor 4:12); and further in this text, ***behold I send to you prophets and scribes and some of them . . . will persecute you from city to city*** (Matt 23:34). ***And*** they will ***speak***, i.e., they will fabricate and accuse you of many evils, *as deceivers* (2 Cor 6:8), *if you be reproached for the name of Christ* (1 Pet 4:14). But it should be known that not everyone about whom evils are said is blessed, but it is required first that it be said falsely, and second for the sake of Christ; hence he says, ***untruly*** and ***for my sake***; and this ***for my sake*** refers to all the things mentioned. Again, observe that it is the same when he says ***for my sake*** and above, ***for the sake of Christ***.

448. ***Rejoice***. Here he teaches the manner, that is, how evils are to be borne. Above, when he was speaking about all things, he said ***blessed are they who suffer*** (Matt 5:10), i.e., who do not resent; but in apostles this does not suffice, but on the contrary, they must exult: *count it all joy* (James 1:2); *the apostles went rejoicing* (Acts 5:41).

But to the contrary, Augustine says *you command these things to be borne, not to be loved*. It must be said that we are not to rejoice in tribulations, but in the hope that we have on account of enduring them, just as the person who receives medicine does not rejoice in the bitterness of the the medicine, but in the hope of health.

449. Et dicit *gaudete et exultate*. Ubi sciendum quod delectari, exultare, gaudere et laetare idem sunt secundum rem, sed differunt ratione. Delectatio enim proprie est ex coniunctione ipsius rei amatae et convenientis; gaudium est non solum in coniunctione sed et in apprehensione; interius laetitia et exultatio sunt effectus consequentes gaudium et delectationem, quia ex hiis primo dilatatur cor: unde laetitia quasi latitia; item non solum cor interius dilatatur, sed quando significatur exterius apparet, et tunc dicitur exultatio, quasi extra apparens.

Gaudendum est autem quia erit ad confusionem infidelium et gaudium fidelium; sic gaudebat beatus Laurentius in craticulam, sicut de eo legitur. Et est duplex causa gaudii: praemium, unde *quoniam merces copiosa in caelo*, scilicet empyreo, unde I Thess. IV, 17: *sic semper cum Domino erimus*. Augustinus: *in hoc quod dicit in caelo nominat obiectum beatitudinis et substantiam quae non in corporalibus erit sed in spiritualibus*, scilicet in fruitione Dei; et ista spiritualia bona designantur per caelos propter soliditatem et firmitatem. Et dicit *copiosa* propter superabundantem mercedem apostolorum; Luce VI, 38: *mensuram bonam*; I Cor. III, 8: *unusquisque accipiet propriam mercedem* Gen. XV, 1: *ego Deus merces tua*. Secunda causa quare gaudendum est exemplum, unde *Sic enim*. Magna enim confortatio est quando assimilantur aliqui magnis et praecedentibus patribus, Act. VII, 52: *quem prophetarum*. Iac. V, 10–11: *exemplum accipite fratres*. Et nota quod in hoc designatur dignitas Christi quia habet prophetas suos patientes pro se sicut in Veteri Testamento, et etiam dignitas apostolorum qui assimilantur prophetis.

449. And he says, *rejoice and exult*. There it should be known that to be delighted, to exult, to rejoice, and to be happy, are the same according to the thing, but differ in account. For delight is properly from the union of the very thing loved and the one coming together with it; joy is not only in this union but also in the apprehension of it; interior happiness and exultation are the effects resulting from joy and delight, for by these things the heart is enlarged: wherefore 'laetitia', happiness, is like 'latitia', largeness. Likewise, not only is the heart enlarged internally, but when it is signified externally, it appears, and then it is called exultation as something appearing without.

But one should rejoice because it will be to the confusion of unbelievers and the joy of believers; in this way blessed Laurence rejoiced on the rack, as it is written of him. And the reason for joy is twofold: first, the reward, hence *for your reward is very great in heaven*, namely, in the fiery one; hence *and so will we be always with the Lord* (I Thess 4:16). Augustine: *in the fact that he says in heaven, he names the object of beatitude and the substance which will not be in bodily things but in spiritual ones*, namely, in the enjoyment of God; and those spiritual goods are denoted by the heavens because of their solidity and firmness. And he says *very great* because of the superabundant reward of the apostles: *a good measure* (Luke 6:38); *every one will receive his own reward* (I Cor 3:8); *I God am . . . your reward* (Gen 15:1). The second reason is that rejoicing is an example, hence *for so they persecuted the prophets*. For it is a great comfort when someone becomes like great men and forefathers: *which of the prophets did your ancestors not persecute?* (Acts 7:52); *take the prophets, my brethren, for an example* (James 5:10). And note that in this the dignity of Christ is indicated, for he has his own prophets suffering for his sake, just as in the Old Testament, and also the dignity of the apostles, which is likened to the prophets.

Lecture 4

5:13 Vos estis sal terrae. Quod si sal evanuerit, in quo salietur? Ad nihilum valet ultra, nisi ut mittatur foras, et conculcetur ab hominibus. [n. 450]

5:14 Vos estis lux mundi. Non potest civitas abscondi supra montem posita. [n. 456]

5:13 Ὑμεῖς ἐστε τὸ ἅλας τῆς γῆς· ἐὰν δὲ τὸ ἅλας μωρανθῇ, ἐν τίνι ἁλισθήσεται; εἰς οὐδὲν ἰσχύει ἔτι εἰ μὴ βληθὲν ἔξω καταπατεῖσθαι ὑπὸ τῶν ἀνθρώπων.

5:14 Ὑμεῖς ἐστε τὸ φῶς τοῦ κόσμου. οὐ δύναται πόλις κρυβῆναι ἐπάνω ὄρους κειμένη·

5:13 You are the salt of the earth. But if the salt lose its savor, wherewith will it be salted? It is good for nothing any more but to be cast out, and to be trodden on by men. [n. 450]

5:14 You are the light of the world. A city set on a mountain cannot be hidden. [n. 456]

---

450. *Vos estis sal*. Supra ostendit Dominus dignitatem apostolorum quantum ad hoc quod in tribulationibus non solum patientes sed etiam gaudentes debebant esse; nunc autem dicit eorum excellentiam quantum ad hoc quod debent alios a malis coercere, et ideo comparat eos sali: *vos estis*.

Et circa hoc duo facit:

primo enim determinat eorum officium quantum ad hoc ut a malis arceant alios;

secundo ostendit quomodo debent se ipsos a malis arcere, ibi *quod si sal evanuerit*.

451. Dicit ergo *vos estis sal*. Comparat eos sali propter quatuor rationes.

Prima, propter salis generationem quae ex aqua est et vento et calore solis: generatio enim spiritualis ex aqua baptismi est et virtute Spiritus Sancti, Ioh. III, 5: *nisi quis renatus fuerit ex aqua et Spiritu Sancto, non potest introire in regnum Dei*, et ex calore solis, id est fervore dilectionis quae est a Spiritu Sancto, Ro. V, 5: *caritas Dei diffusa est in cordibus vestris per Spiritum Sanctum*. Secundo, propter utilitates salis quarum prima est usus quia omnia sale condiuntur: unde significat sapientiam quam debent habere viri apostolici, Eccli. VI, 23: *sapientia enim doctrinae*, Col. IV, 5: *in sapientia ambulate ad eos qui foris sunt*.

Secunda ratio erat Levi. II, 13 quod in omni sacrificio adiungeretur sal, quia doctrina apostolica debet in omni opere nostro relucere.

Tertia ratio est quia consumit superfluitatem humorum et per hoc praeservat a putredine: ita apostoli sua doctrina refrenabant super concupiscentias carnales, I Petri IV, 3: *sufficit praeteritum tempus*; Ro. XIII, 13: *non in comesationibus*.

Quartus effectus est quia reddit terram sterilem: unde dicitur quod aliqui victores extra civitatem quam ceperant superseminabant salem ut scilicet nihil oriretur; ita etiam doctrina evangelica facit terram sterilem, ut scilicet terrena opera in nobis non oriantur, Eph. V, 11: *nolite communicare operibus infructuosis tenebrarum*. Ergo

450. *You are the salt*. Above, the Lord shows the dignity of the apostles by the fact that in tribulations they would not only be suffering, but even rejoicing. But now he speaks of their excellence in the fact that they must deter others from evils, and thus he compares them to salt: *you are*.

And concerning this he does two things:

first, he defines their office as preventing others from evils;

second, he shows how they must protect themselves from evils, at *but if salt loses its savor*.

451. Therefore he says, *you are the salt*. He compares them to salt for four reasons.

First, because of the generation of salt, which is from water and wind and the heat of the sun: for the spiritual generation is from the water of baptism and the power of the Holy Spirit: *unless someone is born again of water and the Holy Spirit, he cannot enter the kingdom of God* (John 3:5); and from the heat of the sun which is the fervor of love that comes from the Holy Spirit, *the love of God has been poured into our hearts by the Holy Spirit who is given to us* (Rom 5:5). Second, because of the uses of salt, the first of which is that all things are seasoned with salt: hence he signifies the wisdom that apostolic men should have, *for the wisdom of doctrine* (Sirach 6:23); *walk in the wisdom of God toward those who are without* (Col 4:5).

The second reason was in Leviticus, for in every sacrifice salt was added (Lev 2:13), for the apostolic teaching should shine out of our every work.

The third reason is that it consumes an excess of humors and by doing so, it preserves from rotting: and in the same way the apostles curbed carnal desires through their teaching: *for the time past is sufficient* (I Pet 4:3); *not in rioting* (Rom 13:13).

The fourth effect is that it renders the earth sterile: hence it is said that some conquerors sowed salt outside the city they had seized so that nothing would grow; so also the evangelical teaching makes the earth sterile, namely so that earthly works do not spring up in us: *have no fellowship with the unfruitful works of darkness* (Eph 5:11). Therefore

apostoli dicuntur *sal* quia habent mordacitatem retrahendo a peccatis; Marci IX, 49: *habete in vobis sal.*

452. Sed posset aliquis dicere: sufficit quod habeam sal. Immo oportet quod virtutes salis preservent te a peccato, et ad hoc inducit quatuor rationes.

453. Prima sumitur ex incorrigibilitate, unde *quod si sal evanuerit.* Illa proprie evanescunt quae amittunt virtutem suam: sicut vinum forte quando amittit virtutem, ita sal quando amittit mordacitatem, Marci IX, 49: *si sal insulsum fuerit, in quo illud condietis?* Unde tunc evanescit aliquis quando in peccato subiacet, Ro. I, 21: *evanuerunt in cogitationibus suis.* Si ergo propter tribulationes vel aliquid aliud a veritate recedis, in quo salieris, id est quo alio sale salietur? Si enim plebs peccat potest corrigi, sed si praelatus, nullus potest emendare, Osee VIII, 5: *usquequo non poterunt emundari.* Et notandum quod Luce XIV, 34 dicitur: *quod si sal infatuatum fuerit*: magna enim fatuitas est dimittere aeterna pro temporali.

454. Secunda ratio sumitur ex utilitate, unde *ad nihilum*, et hoc exponit Lucas XIV, 35: *neque in terra neque in stercore utile est*, quia terram facit sterilem et stercora non fecundat. Ita spirituales quando peccant ad nihilum valent quia non ad saecularia negotia sicut milites et huiusmodi, Ez. XV, 2: *Fili hominis, quid fiet de ligno vitis?* etc., Ps. *omnes declinaverunt.*

455. Tertia ratio sumitur ex periculo imminenti, et habet duos ramos secundum duo pericula. Primum est expulsio, unde *nisi ut mittatur foras*, de Ecclesia scilicet, Apoc. ult. *foris canes.* Item ut auferatur ei dignitas sacerdotalis magisterii, Osee IV, 6: *quia scientiam repulisti*, infra XXI, 43: *auferatur a vobis regnum Dei*, et hoc est *nisi ut mittatur foras.* Secundum periculum est vilificatio, quia qui primo vivunt spiritualiter et deficiunt, contemtibiles fiunt, et hoc est *et conculcetur*, Luce XIV, 30: *hic homo cepit aedificare et non potuit consummare*, Mal. II, 8: *recessistis de via et scandalizastis plurimos in lege.* Et notandum, secundum Augustinum, quod si aliqui sancti homines vilificantur, sicut dicitur supra *et dixerint omne malum* etc., numquam tamen possunt conculcari, quia semper cor habent in caelo, et illi proprie conculcantur qui in terra iacent.

456. *Vos estis lux.* Hic ponitur tertia dignitas apostolorum. Sicut enim debent arcere alios a malis, ita debent et illuminare. Et circa hoc duo facit: primo ostendit eorum dignitatem; secundo removet pusillanimitatem, ibi *non potest civitas.*

Dicit ergo *vos estis lux mundi*, quasi non Iudaeae tantum vel Galileae, sed totius mundi, Act. XIII, 47: *sic enim praecepit Dominus: posui te in lucem gentium.* Et

the apostles are called *salt* because they have the sting of withdrawing from sins: *have salt in you* (Mark 9:49).

452. But someone might say: 'It is enough that I have salt; it is not at all necessary that the virtues of salt preserve you from sin,' and to this four arguments can be made.

453. The first is taken from incorrigibility, hence *but if salt loses its savor.* Those things properly lose their savor which lose their virtue: like strong wine when it loses its virtue, so also salt when it loses its bite: *if salt became bland, wherewith will you season it?* (Mark 9:49). Hence someone loses his salt when he falls into sin: *they became vain in their thoughts* (Rom 1:21). If therefore because of tribulations or something else you fall from the truth, with what will you be salted, i.e., by what other salt will it be salted? For if the masses sin, they can be corrected, but if a prelate does, nothing can repair it: *how long will they be incapable of innocence?* (Hos 8:5). And it should be noted that it says, *but if the salt should grow insipid* (Luke 14:34): for it is a great insipidity to forgo eternal goods for temporal ones.

454. The second reason is taken from usefulness, hence *good for nothing*, and Luke explains this: *neither for the land nor for the dunghill* (Luke 14:35), for it makes the earth sterile and it does not fertilize the dunghill. So are spiritual men good for nothing when they sin, because they are not good for secular affairs, like soldiers and such: *son of man, what will be made of the wood of the vine?* (Ezek 15:2); *all have gone aside* (Ps 53:3).

455. The third reason is taken from imminent danger, and it has two branches according to the two dangers. The first is expulsion, hence *but to be cast out*, of the Church, that is: *without are dogs* (Rev 22:15). Again, that the dignity of priestly magisterium is taken away: *because you have rejected knowledge . . . you shall not do the office of priesthood for me* (Hos 4:6), and below: *the kingdom of God will be taken from you* (Matt 21:43), and here it is *nothing but to be cast out.* The second danger is vilification, because those who live spiritually at first, but then fail, become contemptible, and this is *and to be trodden on*: *this man began to build* (Luke 14:30); *you have departed out of the way, and have caused many to stumble at the law* (Mal 2:8). And according to Augustine it should be noted that if certain holy men are vilified, as is said above, *and they speak all that is evil against you* (Matt 5:11), nevertheless they can never be trampled underfoot, for they always have their hearts in heaven, and only those can be trampled who are lying on the earth.

456. *You are the light.* Here is set forth the third dignity of apostles. For just as they must deter others from evils, so they must also illuminate. And concerning this he does two things: first, he shows their dignity; second, he removes faintheartedness, at *a city . . . cannot be hidden.*

Therefore he says *you are the light of the world*, as though not of Judea alone or of Galilee, but of the whole world: *for thus the Lord commanded: I have set you as a light*

hoc mirabile fuit quod vix in terra sua cognoscebatur, et tamen *in omnem terram exivit*. Sed obicitur quia videtur quod hoc quod dicit **lux** conveniat soli Christo, Ioh. I, 8: *non erat ille lux*, et post *erat lux vera*. Dicendum quod lux essentialiter solus Christus est, sed apostoli dicuntur lux illuminata, scilicet per participationem, sicut oculus est lux illuminans et tamen illuminata.

Et nota quod ista tria, scilicet **beati estis cum vobis maledixerint**, et **vos estis sal** et **vos estis lux**, videntur pertinere ad tres ultimas beatitudines, scilicet ad **beati qui persecutionem patiuntur**, secunda ad **beati pacifici**, quia scilicet pacificant se et alios, tertia ad **beati mundo corde**. Si enim apostoli in his tribus ultimis excellentes fuerunt, multo magis in superioribus.

457. Dixerat Dominus **beati estis cum vobis maledixerint** et **qui persecutionem patiuntur**; possent ergo dicere: nos sustentabimus tot persecutiones, ergo volumus occultare. Et ideo Dominus removet consequenter pusillanimitatem, unde **non potest civitas abscondi**.

Et primo prohibet absconsionem;

secundo ostendit modum quomodo debeant se manifestare, ibi **sic luceat**.

Quod non debeant se abscondere probat duabus rationibus: primo quia non possent etiam si vellent; secundo quia non debent, et hoc est **neque accendunt**.

to the gentiles (Acts 13:47). And this was marvelous because they were scarcely known in their own land, and nevertheless *their sound has gone out to all the earth* (Ps 19:4). But it is objected that it seems that what he calls **light** applies only to Christ: *that man was not the light* and later, *he was the true light* (John 1:8–9). It should be said that light essentially is only Christ, but the apostles are called light illuminated, that is, by participation, as the eye is light illuminating and nevertheless illuminated.

And note that these three, namely, **blessed are you when they revile you** (Matt 5:11), and **you are the salt** and **you are the light**, seem to pertain to the three last beatitudes, namely to **blessed are they who suffer persecution** (Matt 5:10), the second to **blessed are the peacemakers** (Matt 5:9), since namely, they make peace in themselves and others, and the third to **blessed are the clean of heart** (Matt 5:8). For if the apostles were excellent in these three last things, much more would they be in the ones above.

457. The Lord had said **blessed are you when they revile you** (Matt 5:11) and **who suffer persecution** (Matt 5:10); therefore they could say: we will undergo so many persecutions, therefore we want to hide. And thus the Lord removes the resulting faintheartedness, hence **a city . . . cannot be hidden**.

And first, he forbids hiding away;

second, he shows the way that they must make themselves visible, at **so let your light shine** (Matt 5:16).

He proves by two reasons that they must not hide themselves away: first, because they could not even if they wished to; second, because they should not, and this is **neither do men light a lamp** (Matt 5:15).

Lecture 5

5:14 Vos estis lux mundi. Non potest civitas abscondi supra montem posita. [n. 458]

5:15 Neque accendunt lucernam, et ponunt eam sub modio, sed super candelabrum, ut luceat omnibus qui in domo sunt. [n. 459]

5:16 Sic luceat lux vestra coram hominibus, ut videant opera vestra bona, et glorificent Patrem vestrum qui in caelis est. [n. 462]

5:17 Nolite putare quoniam veni solvere legem aut prophetas: non veni solvere, sed adimplere. [n. 463]

5:14 Ὑμεῖς ἐστε τὸ φῶς τοῦ κόσμου. οὐ δύναται πόλις κρυβῆναι ἐπάνω ὄρους κειμένη·

5:15 οὐδὲ καίουσιν λύχνον καὶ τιθέασιν αὐτὸν ὑπὸ τὸν μόδιον ἀλλ᾽ ἐπὶ τὴν λυχνίαν, καὶ λάμπει πᾶσιν τοῖς ἐν τῇ οἰκίᾳ.

5:16 οὕτως λαμψάτω τὸ φῶς ὑμῶν ἔμπροσθεν τῶν ἀνθρώπων, ὅπως ἴδωσιν ὑμῶν τὰ καλὰ ἔργα καὶ δοξάσωσιν τὸν πατέρα ὑμῶν τὸν ἐν τοῖς οὐρανοῖς.

5:17 Μὴ νομίσητε ὅτι ἦλθον καταλῦσαι τὸν νόμον ἢ τοὺς προφήτας· οὐκ ἦλθον καταλῦσαι ἀλλὰ πληρῶσαι.

5:14 You are the light of the world. A city set on a mountain cannot be hidden. [n. 458]

5:15 Neither do men light a lamp and put it under a bushel, but upon a lampstand, that it may shine to all who are in the house. [n. 459]

5:16 So let your light shine before men, that they may see your good works, and glorify your Father who is in heaven. [n. 462]

5:17 Do not think that I am come to destroy the law, or the prophets. I am not come to destroy, but to fulfill. [n. 463]

---

458. Non potest civitas. Civitas congregatio fidelium erat, scilicet ipsa collectio apostolorum, Ps. *gloriosa dicta sunt de te, civitas Dei.* Sita autem erat **in monte**, scilicet Christo, Ys. II: *erit mons domus Domini,* Dan. II, 34: *lapis abscissus est de monte.* Vel **in monte**, id est in perfectione iustitiae, Ps. *iustitia tua sicut montes.* Civitas autem in monte sita non potest se abscondere, ita apostoli. Chrysostomus: *homines in infimo constituti si peccant possunt latere, si constituti in culmine non possunt,* III Reg. I, 20: *in te oculi respiciunt totius Israel.* Hilarius aliter exponit, et quasi idem est sensus: **civitas in monte** Christus est, quia ex parte humanae nature in qua nobiscum communicat civitas est, Ier. I, 18: *dedi te hodie in civitatem;* in monte est, quia in divinitate quae mons est, Ps. *mons Dei, mons pinguis.* Et ideo Christus latere non potuit: et ideo vos, apostoli, non debetis me occultare.

459. Secundum ibi **neque accendunt**, quasi: ponamus quod posset latere, tamen non debetis. Nullus enim beneficium accipiens debet facere contra intentionem dantis. Deus dedit vobis scientiam ad hoc quod communicetis, Petri IV: *unusquisque gratiam quam accepit in alterutrum illam administrantes.* Et hoc est **neque accendunt lucernam**, homines scilicet, vel Pater et Filius et Spiritus Sanctus. Per lucernam potest intelligi primo doctrina evangelica, Ps. *lucerna pedibus:* lucerna enim habet lumen incorporatum; lumen veritatis in Sacra Scriptura positum est, accensa autem est a Patre et Filio et Spiritu Sancto. Vel per lucernam possunt

458. A city . . . cannot be hidden. The city was the congregation of believers, namely, that very gathering of the apostles: *glorious things are said of you, city of God* (Ps 87:3). But it was situated **on a mountain**, namely, in Christ: *the mountain of the house of the Lord* (Isa 2:2); *a stone was cut out of a mountain* (Dan 2:34). Or, **on a mountain**, that is, in the perfection of justice: *your justice like the mountains* (Ps 36:6). But a city situated on a mountain cannot be hidden, and so it is with the apostles. Chrysostom: *if men in the lowest station should sin, they can escape notice, but if those in the highest station do, they cannot escape notice: the eyes of all Israel are upon you* (1 Kgs 1:20). Hilary explains it another way, and the meaning is about the same: **the city on a mountain** is Christ, for on the part of his human nature in which he shares with us, he is the city: *I have made you this day a fortified city* (Jer 1:18); he is on the mountain because he is in divinity which is the mountain: *the mountain of God is a fat mountain* (Ps 68:15). And therefore Christ could not remain hidden: and thus you, apostles, should not hide me.

459. According to that **neither do men light**, as it were: 'let us define what might remain hidden, although you should not hide yourselves.' For no one receiving a benefit should do something against the intention of the one giving it. God gave you knowledge so that you might share it: *as every man has received grace* (1 Pet 4:9–11). And this is **neither do men light a lamp**, men indeed, or the Father, and Son, and Holy Spirit. By **lamp** can be understood first the Gospel teaching: *a lamp to my feet* (Ps 119:105), for a lamp has light as part of it; the light of truth is set down in Sacred Scripture, but it is lit by the Father and the Son and the Holy Spirit. Or by lamp the apostles can be understood,

intelligi apostoli in quantum inditum est eis lumen gratiae, Ioh. V, 35: *ille erat lucerna*, Ps. *paravi lucernam*. Vel per lucernam Christus, quia sicut lucerna lux in testa, ita divinitas in humanitate, II Reg. II, 22: *tu es lucerna mea Domine*.

460. Sic accepta lucerna, per *modium* possumus intelligere tria. Primo, secundum Augustinum, res corporales, propter duas rationes: prima quia modius mensura est, Deut. XXV, 15: *modius aequalis et verus erit tibi*; id autem quod agimus in corpore retribuetur nobis, Cor. *omnes astabimus ante tribunal Christi, ut referat unusquisque propria corporis prout gessit*; vel quia omnia corpora mensurata sunt, divina autem infinita quia extra mensuram. Ponunt ergo lucernam *sub modio* qui doctrinam suam referunt ad commodum temporale, unde pretiosius est illud; contra quod Apostolus I Thess. II, 5: *neque enim fuimus in sermone adulationis*. Secundo modo, secundum Chrysostomum, *modius* dicuntur homines saeculares, quia vacui superius et solidi inferius: superius enim habent insanitatem quia nihil sentiunt de Spiritu Sancto, Cor. II: *animalis homo non percipit ea quae sunt Spiritus Dei*, sed inferius, in saecularibus scilicet negotiis, sapientes sunt, Luce *filii huius saeculi prudenriores filii lucis in generatione sua sunt*; et ista est magis litteralis expositio. Tunc ergo secundum hoc lucerna *sub modio* ponitur quando doctrina occultatur saeculari timore, Ier. *quis tu ut timeas ab homine*, II Tim. III: *laboro usque ad vincula*. Si autem per lucernam intelligatur doctrina evangelica vel Christus, tunc per modium potest intelligi synagoga: non enim propter hoc Christus incarnatus est ut latitaret sub Iudaea, sed ut manifestaret se toti mundo, Ps. *dedi te in lucem gentium*.

461. *Sed super candelabrum*. Hoc tripliciter potest exponi, quia per candelabrum potest significari corpus, per lucernam doctrina evangelica; unde idem est per modium et candelabrum, quasi: non debet doctrina evangelica submitti rebus temporalibus, sed debent omnia ministrare sibi: unde quando tu das res, corpus et etiam vitam ad mortem amore Christi, tunc ponis lucernam super candelabrum. Vel per candelabrum intelligitur Ecclesia, quia illiqui lucerna sunt ponuntur in superiori loco, Eccli. XXV: *lucerna splendens super candelabrum sanctum*. Si autem intelligatur de Christo, tunc per candelabrum crucem, Col. I, 20: *per sanguinem crucis*.

462. *Ut luceat omnibus*. Istud etiam tripliciter exponitur. Per domum Ecclesia potest intelligi, I Tim. IV: *ut scias quomodo oportet conversari in domo Dei quae est Ecclesia*. Vel domus est totus mundus, Hebr. III, 4: *omnis enim domus fabricatur* etc.

Consequenter ponitur modus quomodo debent se manifestare. Et primo ponit modum, quia debent lucere

in the fact that the light of grace is brought in to them: *John . . . was a burning and a shining light* (John 5:35); *I have prepared a lamp for my anointed* (Ps 132:17). Or by lamp can mean Christ, for just as a lamp is a light in a clay jar, so is his divinity in his humanity: *you are my lamp* (2 Sam 22:29).

460. If lamp is taken in this way, we can understand three things by **bushel**. First, according to Augustine, corporeal things, for two reasons: first, because a bushel is a measure, *you will have a just and a true weight* (Deut 25:15)); but what we do in the body will be rendered back to us: *for we must all be manifested before the judgment seat of Christ, that every one may receive the proper things of the body* (2 Cor 5:10). Or because all bodies are subject to measure, but divine things are infinite, since they are outside measure. Therefore, they set the lamp **under a bushel** who suit their teaching to temporal convenience, hence it is costly. Against which the Apostle says, *we never came with words of flattery* (1 Thess 2:5). In the second way, according to Chrysostom, secular men are called a **bushel basket**, for they are empty above and solid below: for above they are frenzied because they perceive nothing from the Holy Spirit: *the sensual man perceives not these things that are of the Spirit of God* (1 Cor 2:14); but below, namely in secular affairs, they are wise: *the children of this world are wiser in their generation than the children of light* (Luke 16:8); and that is the more literal exposition. Therefore according to this a lamp is set **under a bushel** when the teaching is hidden in worldly fear: *who are you that you should fear from a man?* (Isa 51:12); *I labor even unto chains* (2 Tim 2:9). But if by the lamp is understood Gospel teaching or Christ, then the bushel can be understood as the synagogue: for Christ did not become incarnate in order to remain hidden in Judea, but so that he might reveal himself to the whole world, *I have given you to be the light of the Gentiles* (Isa 49:6).

461. *But upon a lampstand*. This is explained in three ways, for by the lampstand can be meant the body, and by the lamp, the Gospel teaching; hence the same thing is meant by the bushel and the lampstand, as it were: the Gospel teaching should not be subjected to temporal things, but they should administer all things to themselves: hence when you give things, your body and even your life up to death for the love of Christ, then you set your lamp upon a lampstand. Or, by the lampstand is understood a church, for those who are lamps are placed in high places, *as the lamp shining upon the holy lampstand* (Sir 26:22). But if lamp is understood to mean Christ, then the lampstand means the cross: *through the blood of his cross* (Col 1:20).

462. *That it may shine to all*. This is also explained in three ways. By the house can be understood the Church: *so that you may know how you ought to behave in the house of God, which is the Church* (1 Tim 3:15). Or the house is the whole world, *for every house is built* (Heb 3:4).

Following is set down how they should make themselves known. And first he sets down the mode, for they

coram hominibus, illuminando eos, Eph. III, 8: *mihi autem omnium sanctorum minimo data est gratia haec: in gentibus evangelizare*; ordinem: ut videant, Iac. II, 18: *ostende mihi ex operibus; finem, quia non propter gloriam propriam*, Cor. II: *non sumus sicut plurimi adulterantes verbum Dei*, et hoc est: *et glorificent*: propter gloriam enim Dei debemus bona operari ut in bona vita glorificetur Deus, Cor. X: *sive manducaveritis* etc.

463. *Nolite putare*. Nota hic quod Dominus quinque modis adimplevit legem: primo quia ea quae erant praefigurata ipse adimplevit, Luce ult. *oportet implere*; secundo legalia observando, Gal. IV, 4: *cum venerit plenitudo*; tertio operando per gratiam, scilicet in sanctificando per Spiritum Sanctum, quod lex facere non poterat, Ro. VIII, 3: *nam quod impossibile erat*; quarto satisfaciendo pro peccatis per quae eramus facti transgressores legis: unde transgressione sublata implevit legem, Ro. III, 25: *quem proposuit Deus propitiationem*; quinto quaedam perfectiones legi apponendo quae vel erant de intellectu legis, vel ad maiorem iustitiae perfectionem. Nota quod lex solvitur tripliciter: negando totaliter, vel eam male exponendo, vel moralia non adimplendo.

must shine ***before men***, enlightening them: *but to me, the least among all the saints is given this grace to preach among the gentiles* (Eph 3:8); and the order, so that men may see: *show me your faith without works and I will show you, by works, my faith* (Jas 2:18); the end, for it is not for the sake of their own glory: *for we are not as many, adulterating the word of God* (2 Cor 2:17), and that is: ***and glorify***: for on account of the glory of God we should do good works so that God might be glorified in a good life: *whether you eat or drink . . . do all for the glory of God* (1 Cor 10:31).

463. *Do not think*. Note here that the Lord has fulfilled the law in five ways: first, because he himself fulfilled those things that were prefigured: *what is written must be fulfilled in me* (Luke 22:37); second, by observing legal things: *when the fullness of time was come, God sent his son* (Gal 4:4); third, by working through grace, namely in sanctifying by the Holy Spirit, which the law was unable to do: *God has done what was impossible to the law* (Rom 8:3); fourth, by satisfying for the sins by which we had been made transgressors of the law: hence having borne the transgression, he fulfilled the law: *whom God proposed to be a propitiation* (Rom 3:25); fifth, by applying certain perfections to the law which either related to the understanding of the law, or to a greater perfection of justice. Note that there are three ways of doing away with the law: either by completely denying it, or by explaining it wrongly, or by not fulfilling its morals.

Lecture 6

5:17 Nolite putare quoniam veni solvere legem aut prophetas: non veni solvere, sed adimplere. [n. 464]

5:18 Amen quippe dico vobis, donec transeat caelum et terra, iota unum aut unus apex non praeteribit a lege, donec omnia fiant. [n. 471]

5:19 Qui ergo solverit unum de mandatis istis minimis, et docuerit sic homines, minimus vocabitur in regno caelorum; qui autem fecerit et docuerit, hic magnus vocabitur in regno caelorum. [n. 471]

5:17 Μὴ νομίσητε ὅτι ἦλθον καταλῦσαι τὸν νόμον ἢ τοὺς προφήτας· οὐκ ἦλθον καταλῦσαι ἀλλὰ πληρῶσαι.

5:18 ἀμὴν γὰρ λέγω ὑμῖν· ἕως ἂν παρέλθῃ ὁ οὐρανὸς καὶ ἡ γῆ, ἰῶτα ἓν ἢ μία κεραία οὐ μὴ παρέλθῃ ἀπὸ τοῦ νόμου, ἕως ἂν πάντα γένηται.

5:19 ὃς ἐὰν οὖν λύσῃ μίαν τῶν ἐντολῶν τούτων τῶν ἐλαχίστων καὶ διδάξῃ οὕτως τοὺς ἀνθρώπους, ἐλάχιστος κληθήσεται ἐν τῇ βασιλείᾳ τῶν οὐρανῶν· ὃς δ᾽ ἂν ποιήσῃ καὶ διδάξῃ, οὗτος μέγας κληθήσεται ἐν τῇ βασιλείᾳ τῶν οὐρανῶν.

5:17 Do not think that I am come to destroy the law, or the prophets. I am not come to destroy, but to fulfill. [n. 464]

5:18 For amen I say unto you, until heaven and earth pass, one jot, or one tittle will not pass of the law, until all be fulfilled. [n. 471]

5:19 He therefore who will break one of these least commandments, and so teach men, will be called the least in the kingdom of heaven. But he who will do and teach, he will be called great in the kingdom of heaven. [n. 471]

---

464. Nolite putare. Posita beatitudine ad quam pertinet doctrina Christi, hic incipit doctrinam suam promulgare. Et primo aperit intentionem suam; secundo proponit regulam et praecepta suae doctrinae, ibi *dico autem vobis*.

Circa primum duo facit:

primo aperit suam intentionem;

secundo ostendit suae adimpletionis rationem, ibi *amen*.

465. Circa primum duo facit:

primo excludit opinatam intentionem;

secundo adstruit veram, ibi *non veni*.

466. Dixerat Dominus apostolis: *beati eritis cum vobis maledixerint* etc.; unde poterant suspicari apostoli quasi tradenda esset doctrina talis propter quam oportebat eos occultari, quasi diceret Christus aliquid contra legem; et ideo Dominus excludit hoc dicens *nolite* etc. Et item quia posset dici quod nullus alius propheta, post Moysen qui dedit, legem solvit, ideo Dominus dicit se amplius facturum, unde *sed adimplere*: nullus enim adimplevit.

Et nota quod istud verbum est multum efficax contra illos qui damnant legem tamquam sit a diabolo, Ioh. iii, *in hoc apparet Filius Dei* etc.; sed ipse confitetur *non veni solvere legem*: ideo non est opus diaboli. Per istud argumentum quidam conversus fuit ad fidem, et fuit frater praedicator. Unde Manichaei abhorrent multum istud capitulum; unde Faustus multipliciter obicit, secundum Augustinum. Et omnes obiectiones reducuntur ad tres. Primo ex auctoritate legis: dicitur enim Deut. iv, 12 *non addetur verbum quod vobis loquor, nec auferetur ex eo*; sed Christus addidit: ergo fecit contra legem. Item, Hebr.

464. Do not think. Having set down the beatitude that the teaching of Christ relates to, here he begins to promulgate his own teaching. And first he makes clear his intention; second, he proposes the rule and commands of his teaching, at *for I say to you* (Matt 5:20).

Concerning the first, he does two things:

first, he makes clear his intention;

second, he shows the reason for its fulfillment, at *amen*.

465. Concerning the first, he does two things:

first, he excludes what might be supposed as his intention;

second, he supplies the true intention, at *I am not come*.

466. The Lord had said to his apostles, *blessed are you when they will revile you* (Matt 5:11); hence the apostles might suspect that such a teaching was to be handed on that they had to hide themselves, as though Christ were saying something against the Law; and thus the Lord excludes this by saying, *do not think*. And again the same thing since it could be said that no other prophet, after Moses who gave it, did away with the Law, therefore the Lord says that he will do it fully, hence *but to fulfill*: for no one had fulfilled it.

And note that this word is most effective against those who condemn the law as though it were from the devil: *for the Son of God appeared for this purpose, to destroy the works of the devil* (1 John 3:8). But he himself acknowledges, *I am not come to destroy the law*: therefore it is not a work of the devil. By this argument a certain man was converted to the faith, and became a fellow preacher. Hence the Manichees abhor greatly this chapter; hence Faustus objects many times against Augustine. And all the objections are reduced to three. The first is from the authority of the law: for it says in Deuteronomy: *let no word be added*

viii, 13 *dicendo novum veteravit prius* etc.; sed Christus dixit se institutorem novae legis, infra xxvi, 28 **hic est sanguis meus**: ergo destruxit vetus. Tertio, Ioh. xiii, 15 *exemplum enim dedi vobis*; omnis ergo Christi actio vera est instructio; si ergo implevit, et nos debemus adimplere: ergo debemus circumcidi et servare omnia legalia. Et ista est communis etiam Nazaraeis et Manichaeis.

467. Dicebat ergo Faustus quod vel ista verba non dixit Iesus, sed dixit Matthaeus qui non interfuit sermoni, sed Iohannes qui interfuit non dixit; vel quod si Christus dixit et Matthaeus scripsit, evangelium aliter exponitur. In Sacra enim Scriptura tripliciter exponitur lex: quia est mosaica, Ro. vii, 6 *soluti sumus a lege mortsi*, in lege Dei; lex naturae, Ro. ii, 14 *cum enim gentes quae legem* etc.; lex veritatis, Ro. viii, 2 *lex Spiritus venit* etc. Ita probatur tripliciter ergo, scilicet: veteris legis, legis naturae quae apud gentiles, Tit. i, 12 *dixit autem quod ex illis priusquam propheta, Cretenses* etc., veritatis, infra xxiii, 34 **ecce ego mitto**. Quod ergo dicit hic **non veni** etc. intelligendum est de lege naturae vel veritatis, quae etiam fit in quibusdam antiquis patribus; et huius signum est quod Dominus, quando loquebatur de praeceptis, quaedam videbatur approbare, quaedam non, scilicet quae sunt propria legis mosaice, scilicet illud *oculum pro oculo* et huiusmodi.

468. Sed contra ista Augustinus sic obicit. Primo quia quicumque negat aliquid de Evangelio, pari ratione poterit negare quodcumque aliud et sic annullare Scripturam; sed homo fidelis quaecumque sunt in Scriptura debet credere. Item quod dicit: loquitur de alia lege et prophetis, falsum est, quia in toto Novo Testamento ubicumque fit mentio de lege intelligitur de lege mosaica, Ro. ix, 4 *quorum est legislatio* etc.; ergo et Dominus de istis loquitur.

469. Unde videndum primo quomodo Christus venit adimplere legem et postea solvemus rationes. Sciendum ergo quod Christus quinque modis adimplevit legem et prophetas.

Primo quia ea que erant praefigurata in lege et prophetis de Christo opere implevit, Luce ult. *oportet implere omnia.*

Secundo ad litteram legalia observando, Gal. iv, 4 *cum venit plenitudo.*

to the word that I speak to you, nor will you take anything away from it (Deut 4:2); but Christ did add to it: therefore he acted against the law. Again, Christ said that he was the institutor of the new law, later in this text: **this is my blood** (Matt 26:28); therefore he has destroyed the old. Third, *for I have given you an example* (John 13:15); therefore every action of Christ is true instruction; thus if he observed the law, we also must observe it. Therefore we must be circumcised and keep all the legal prescriptions. And this is the shared claim of Nazarenes and Manichees.

467. Therefore Faustus said that either Jesus did not say these words, but Matthew, who was not present for this sermon, said this, while John who was present did not say this; or that if Matthew wrote what Christ said, the Gospel is explained some other way. For in Sacred Scripture the law is set forth three ways: because in the law of God there is the Mosaic law: *we are freed from the law of death* (Rom 7:6); there is the law of nature: *for when the gentiles who have not the law do by nature what is of the law* (Rom 2:14); and there is the law of truth, *for the law of the Spirit of life delivered me from the law of sin and death* (Rom 8:2). This is proved in three ways, then, namely: the old law; the law of nature which is among the gentiles, *one of them a prophet of their own, said: the Cretans are always liars* (Tit 1:12); and the law of truth, **Therefore behold I send to you prophets, and wise men, and scribes** (Matt 23:34). Therefore what he says here, **I am not come to destroy**, is to be understood concerning the law of nature or of truth, for it also existed among certain of the ancient fathers; and the sign of this is that the Lord, when he was speaking of the commandments, seemed to approve some of them, and not others, namely, those that are properly of the law of Moses, namely that *eye for an eye* and the ones like it.

468. But Augustine objects against these things in the following way. First, because whoever denies something of the Gospel, by the same reasoning could deny anything else and thus render Scripture void; but the man of faith must believe whatever things are in the Scriptures. Again, because he says he speaks about another law and prophets, it is false, for in the whole New Testament, everywhere law is mentioned, it is understood to be about the law of Moses, *to them belong . . . the giving of the law* (Rom 9:4); therefore also the Lord is speaking of these things.

469. Hence it should be seen first how Christ came to fulfill the law, and afterward we will resolve the arguments. Thus it should be known that Christ fulfilled the law and the prophets in five ways.

First, because those things that were prefigured in the law and the prophets concerning Christ, he fulfilled in his actions: *what is written must be fulfilled in me* (Luke 22:37).

Second, by observing the legal requirements to the letter, *when the fullness of time had come, God sent his son* (Gal 4:4).

Tertio operando per gratiam, quod lex naturae facere non poterat: omnis enim lex ad hoc est quod efficiamur homines iusti; sed hoc fecit Christus per Spiritum Sanctum, Ro. viii *nam quod impossibile erat legi*.

Quarto, secundum Augustinum, satisfaciendo pro peccatis secundum quae eramus facti transgressores legis; unde sublata transgressione dicitur implevisse legem, Ro. iii *quem proposuit Deus propitiationem* etc.

Quinto quaedam perfectiones legi apponendo quae vel erant de intellectu legis vel ad maiorem iustitiae perfectionem, Hebr. vii *neminem ad perfectum*; et ista videtur intentio Christi quia, quando iam fecit mentionem de omnibus legalibus, subiungit *estote ergo perfecti* etc. Solvamus ergo ad rationes Fausti sicut Augustinus solvit.

470. Ad illud *non addetur verbum*, dicendum quod Christus non addidit sed explicavit; illi enim intelligebant de homicidii actu cum dixit *non occides*; Christus exponit quod etiam prohibuit odium et iram. Item ad illud *novum veteravit*, dicendum quod istud novum est idem, quia illud erat figura et istud adimpletio figurarum. Ad illud quod nos debemus observare, dicendum quod aliquid potest significari locutione et figura, et non differt qualitercumque significetur. Christus antequam nasceretur potuit dici: Christus est nasciturus et moriturus, sed modo dicitur: Christus est natus, et huiusmodi, et tamen per hoc configuratur quia diversis verbis pronuntiatur res facta et futura. Unde illud quod figuris significabatur ut futurum, quando iam praeteriit significatur ut praesens per novas figuras, scilicet sacramenta novae legis. Unde Christus licet impleverit, tamen quia iam venit veritas qui cumque impleret faceret iniuriam veritati. Ita ergo intelligitur **non veni soluere**.

471. Amen quippe. Hic ponitur ratio adimpletionis, et videtur triplicem rationem assignare: prima ex immobilitate legis, secunda ex poena solventium, tertia ex praemio adimplentium; secundum ibi **soluerit**, tertium ibi **fecerit et docuerit**. Dicit ergo **amen**. Et sciendum quod in veteri lege praefigurata fuerunt omnia mysteria Christi; sed sicut dicitur Amos iii, 7 *non faciet Dominus verbum nisi*; mysteria ergo Christi durabunt usque in finem ultimum, infra ult. *ecce ego vobiscum*. Unde non omnia prophetarum mysteria in primo Christi adventu impleta sunt, immo implebuntur usque ad finem mundi. Et id quod dixit non potest mutari, Num. xxiii, 19, *dixit Dominus et non faciet?* ergo si lex praedixit ea quae futura sunt, et oportet quod de necessitate fiant. Inde dicit

Third, by working through grace, which the law of nature could not do: for every law is for the sake of making us just men, but Christ did this by the Holy Spirit: *for what the law could not do, God has done by sending his own Son* (Rom 8:3).

Fourth, according to Augustine, by satisfying for the sins by which we were made transgressors of the law; hence having borne the transgression he is said to have fulfilled the law: *whom God proposed to be a propitiation* (Rom 3:29).

Fifth, by applying certain perfections to the law which were either for the understanding of the law or for the greater perfection of justice, *for the law brought nothing to perfection* (Heb 7:19); and these things seem to be the intention of Christ, since, when he made mention of all legal restrictions, he added **be you therefore perfect** (Matt 5:48). Thus we resolve the arguments of Faustus as Augustine resolves them.

470. As for *let no word be added* (Deut 4:2), it should be said that Christ did not add, but expounded; for those men understood the act of homicide when he said, *you shall not kill*. Christ explained that it also forbade hatred and anger. Similarly, regarding *in pronouncing a new he has made the first one old* (Heb 8:13), it should be said that the new one is the same, for the former was a figure and the latter is the fulfillment of figures. As to what we should observe, it should be said that something can be signified by speech and figure, and not be different, however it is signified. Before Christ was born it could have been said: Christ will be born and will die, but now it is said: Christ was born, and that sort of thing, and yet by this is illustrated that future events and completed ones are expressed by different words. Hence what was signified by figures as being in the future, when it has happened is signified in the present by new figures, namely the sacraments of the new law. Hence although Christ observed the law, nevertheless because the truth has come whoever observed it now would do injury to the truth. **Thus I am not come to destroy**, is understood this way.

471. Amen I say to you. Here the reason for the fulfillment is set forth, and it seems a threefold reason is assigned: first from the unmoving character of the law, second from the penalty for those doing away with it, third from the reward for those fulfilling it; the second is at **he therefore who will break one of these least commandments**, the third at **who will break . . . and so teach**. Thus he says **amen**. And it should be known that all the mysteries of Christ were prefigured in the old law; but as is said in Amos: *the Lord will do nothing without revealing his word to his servants* (Amos 3:7), therefore the mysteries of Christ will last until the end times, as is said here, **behold, I am with you**, (Matt 28:20). Hence not all mysteries of the prophets were fulfilled in the first coming of Christ, nor will

amen dico, id est omnia implebuntur successive usque ad finem mundi.

Sciendum quod *amen* hebraeum est, et nullus interpres pro reverentia huius vocabuli, quia Dominus frequenter utebatur eo, ausus fuit mutare. Et sumitur aliquando in vi nominis, unde *amen*: verum; aliquando adverbium est, id est vere, et ita hic sumitur; aliquando pro fiat, unde in Psalmo ubi nos 'fiat' hebraice 'amen': unde dicitur versus: *pro 'vero', 'vere'; pro 'fiat' dicitur 'amen'*. Unde Dominus hic excitat attentionem in audiendo.

472. *Donec transeat*, non secundum substantiam, sed secundum dispositionem, Cor. vii *praeterit figura*, Petri iii *caeli ardentes*. *Donec*: usque ad finem mundi.

Iotha. Iotha apud Graecos est littera quam nos vocamus 'i' parvum; apud Hebraeos autem vocatur ioth; et iotha apud Graecos significat 'y' et est nona littera; omnes enim littera significant aliquem numerum, unde pertinet ad perfectionem decalogi, et forte propter hoc magis posuit *iotha* quam ioth, secundum quod dicunt sancti. *Apex* litteris superponitur tam in hebraeo quam in graeco, sed alia et alia ratione, quia apud Hebraeos alep aliquando sonat 'a' aliquando 'e', et scitur hoc per quaedam puncta et illa vocantur apices; item apud Graecos superponuntur quaedam signa ad distinguendum aspirationes et accentus, et ista etiam vocantur apices apud Graecos. Vult ergo dicere Dominus quod nihil minimum quin etiam oporteat adimpleri.

473. *Qui ergo solverit*. Hic ponitur secunda ratio, et sumitur a poena solventium, quasi: quicumque solverit erit reus poena quasi transgressor divinae observantiae. Sunt autem minima mandata, secundum Chrysostomum, mandata Christi; unde: quicumque *solverit de mandatis istis minimis* quae dicturus sum. Et continuatur sic: quia lex non potest solvi, ergo ex quo ego non solvo, qui cumque solverit erit reus poena. Et dicuntur ea minima primo propter humilitatem, sicut et se vocat parvulum, infra xviii, 3 *nisi efficiamini*; vel dicuntur minima quantum ad transgressionem quia minus peccat qui solvit, sed maiora sunt legi quae praecepit Christus quantum ad observationem, quia lex praecepit *non occides*, Christus non irasci.

474. Aliter Augustinus dicit et Ieronimus: ad litteram loquitur de minimis praeceptis quae sunt in lege quia

they be fulfilled before the end of the world. And what he said cannot be changed: *has the Lord said then and will he not do?* (Num 23:19); therefore if the law predicted these things that are in the future it is also fitting that they happen of necessity. Hence he says *amen I say*, that is, all things will be fulfilled in succession until the end of the world.

It should be known that *amen* is Hebrew, and no translator has dared to change this word out of reverence, for the Lord used it frequently. And it is taken sometimes in force of a noun, hence *amen*: *truth*; sometimes it is an adverb, i.e., *truly*, and so it is taken here; sometimes it stands for *fiat*: 'so be it'; hence in the Psalm where we have 'fiat' for the Hebrew 'amen'. Hence the verse says, *for 'vero', 'truly'; for 'fiat', 'amen' is said*. Hence the Lord here excites the attention of his listeners.

472. *Until heaven and earth pass*, not according to their substance but according to their disposition, *for the fashion of this world is passing away* (1 Cor 7:31), *the day of God when the heavens will burn* (2 Pet 3:12). *Until*: until the end of the world.

Jot. Iota among the Greeks is the letter that we call small 'i'; but among the Hebrews it is called ioth; and iota among the Greeks means 'y' and is the ninth letter; for all letters signify a certain number, hence it belongs to the perfection of the decalogue, and perhaps for this reason he says *jot* rather than ioth, according to what the saints say. *Tittle* is the mark at the top of a letter in Hebrew as well as in Greek, but they mean different things, since among the Hebrews aleph sometimes sounds like 'a' and sometimes like 'e', and this is known by certain points which here are called tittles; while among the Greeks certain marks are written above the letters to distinguish aspirations and accents, and those are what are called tittles among the Greeks. Therefore the Lord means that nothing is so unimportant that it need not be fulfilled.

473. *He therefore who will break*. Here the second argument is set down, and it is taken from the penalty of those who break the law, as it were: whoever breaks the law will be liable to the penalty as a transgressor of divine observance. However there are lesser commandments, according to Chrysostom, commandments of Christ; hence **who will break one of these least commandments** *which I am about to tell you*. And he continues thus: for the law cannot be broken, therefore, by the fact that I do not do away with it, whoever does will be liable to the penalty. And those things are called least first because of humility, as someone might call himself small, as in: *unless you . . . become like children* (Matt 18:3); or they are called least as regards the transgression because he sins less who breaks it, but there are greater things than the law that Christ commands as regards observance, for the law commands: *you shall not kill*, but Christ commands not to grow angry.

474. Augustine says otherwise, as well as Jerome: he speaks literally about the least precepts that are in the law

dixit *iotha* et *apex*; et dicuntur minima, quia principalia sunt: *diliges Dominum Deum tuum et proximum tuum*; unde aliquas observationes dicuntur praecepta minima, sicut multa sunt Levi. xix. Et dicit hoc in suggillationem Pharisaeorum, quia Pharisaei propter suas observantias transgrediebantur multa, infra xv, 6 *irritum fecistis*. Solvitur autem lex tripliciter: primo totaliter eam negando, secundo male interpretando, tertio moralia non implendo.

475. *Et docuerit*. Male facit qui male operatur, sed peius qui docet alios male operari, Apoc. ii, 14 *habes tenentes doctrinam Balaam*; et ideo dicit **qui solverit et docuerit**, scilicet solvere mandata. Et secundum hoc videtur quod qui solvit erit in regno caelorum. Sed sciendum quod, secundum Augustinum, regnum caelorum hic accipitur pro vita aeterna, et voluit Dominus dare intelligere quod nullus erit ibi **qui solverit et docuerit** etc., quia ibi non erit nisi magnus, Ro. ix *quos iustificavit* etc.; unde qui nimis parvus numquam intrabit. Secundo, secundum Rabbanam sic: homines quaerunt famam apud homines quia hoc gloria quaedam est quod homo in regno hominum reputetur magnus; sed **qui solverit minimus reputabitur in regno caelorum**, non existens ibi: parvus enim reputatur ibi qui transgreditur mandata, minimus qui docet transgredi. Et haec satis bona est. Chrysostomus aliter: Scriptura quandoque vocat regnum caelorum finale iudicium, sicut dicit Ps. *Dominus regnavit*; et ibi erunt ordines diversi, sed **minimus** qui docet transgredi mandata, quia ad regnum caelorum, secundum hoc pertinent etiam illi qui sunt in inferno. Gregorius: pro Ecclesia, unde: **minimus vocabitur** in Ecclesia, *quia cuius vita despicitur restat ut eius praedicatio contemnatur*.

Qui fecerit et docuerit. Magnus qui bene facit, se maior qui facit et docet; unde habebit magnam gloriam, infra xvi **qui me confessus fuerit**, Sap. ult. *in omnibus populum tuum magnificasti*.

because he says *jot* and *tittle*; and they are called the least things because the chief things are *love the Lord your God, and your neighbor* (Mark 12:30–31); hence certain observances are called least precepts, like many in Leviticus 19. And he says this to confront the Pharisees, for Pharisees transgressed many things for the sake of their observances, as he says later in this Gospel: **then you have made void the commandment of God for the sake of your tradition** (Matt 15:6). But the law is made void in three ways: first by completely denying it, second by interpreting it badly, and third by not observing its morals.

475. *And so teach*. He does badly who acts badly, but he does worse who teaches others to act badly: *you have there some who hold to the teaching of Balaam* (Rev 2:14); and thus he says, **who will break one of these least commandments and so teach men**, i.e., to break the commandments. And according to this it seems that whoever breaks the commandments will be in the kingdom of heaven. But it should be known that according to Augustine, the kingdom of heaven here is taken for eternal life, and the Lord wanted to convey that no one will be there **who will break one of these least commandments and so teach men**, for none will be there but the great: *whom he justified* (Rom 8:30). Hence whoever is too small will never enter. Second, according to Rabbanus, men seek fame among men because this is a certain glory, that a man be considered great in the kingdom of men; **but who will break . . . will be called the least in the kingdom of heaven**, not existing here: for there a man is considered small for transgressing the commandments, and even smaller for teaching the transgression. And this is good enough. Chrysostom says otherwise: Scripture sometimes calls the final judgment the kingdom of heaven, as it says: *the Lord has reigned* (Ps 99:1); and there there will be different orders, but least will be the one who taught others to transgress the commandments, because to the kingdom of heaven, by this reading, even those who are in hell would belong. Gregory takes it for the Church, hence: **he will be called least** in the Church, *because whose life is despised it remains that his preaching is condemned*.

Who will . . . and so teach. Great is the man who does well, greater still the one who does it and teaches others; hence he will have great glory, **whoever will confess me** (Matt 10:32); *for in all things you have magnified your people* (Wis 19:20).

Lecture 7

5:20 Dico enim vobis, quia nisi abundaverit iustitia vestra plus quam scribarum et Pharisaeorum, non intrabitis in regnum caelorum. [n. 478]

5:21 Audistis quia dictum est antiquis: *non occides*; qui autem occiderit, reus erit iudicio. [n. 482]

5:22 Ego autem dico vobis, quia omnis qui irascitur fratri suo, reus erit iudicio. Qui autem dixerit fratri suo: racha, reus erit concilio. Qui autem dixerit: fatue, reus erit gehennae ignis. [n. 485]

5:23 Si ergo offers munus tuum ad altare, et ibi recordatus fueris quia frater tuus habet aliquid adversum te, [n. 494]

5:24 relinque ibi munus tuum ante altare, et vade prius reconciliari fratri tuo, et tunc veniens offeres munus tuum. [n. 494]

5:25 Esto consentiens adversario tuo cito dum es in via cum eo; ne forte tradat te adversarius iudici, et iudex tradat te ministro, et in carcerem mittaris. [n. 497]

5:26 Amen dico tibi, non exies inde, donec reddas novissimum quadrantem. [n. 501]

5:20 Λέγω γὰρ ὑμῖν ὅτι ἐὰν μὴ περισσεύσῃ ὑμῶν ἡ δικαιοσύνη πλεῖον τῶν γραμματέων καὶ Φαρισαίων, οὐ μὴ εἰσέλθητε εἰς τὴν βασιλείαν τῶν οὐρανῶν.

5:21 Ἠκούσατε ὅτι ἐρρέθη τοῖς ἀρχαίοις· οὐ φονεύσεις· ὃς δ᾽ ἂν φονεύσῃ, ἔνοχος ἔσται τῇ κρίσει.

5:22 ἐγὼ δὲ λέγω ὑμῖν ὅτι πᾶς ὁ ὀργιζόμενος τῷ ἀδελφῷ αὐτοῦ ἔνοχος ἔσται τῇ κρίσει· ὃς δ᾽ ἂν εἴπῃ τῷ ἀδελφῷ αὐτοῦ· ῥακά, ἔνοχος ἔσται τῷ συνεδρίῳ· ὃς δ᾽ ἂν εἴπῃ· μωρέ, ἔνοχος ἔσται εἰς τὴν γέενναν τοῦ πυρός.

5:23 ἐὰν οὖν προσφέρῃς τὸ δῶρόν σου ἐπὶ τὸ θυσιαστήριον κἀκεῖ μνησθῇς ὅτι ὁ ἀδελφός σου ἔχει τι κατὰ σοῦ,

5:24 ἄφες ἐκεῖ τὸ δῶρόν σου ἔμπροσθεν τοῦ θυσιαστηρίου καὶ ὕπαγε πρῶτον διαλλάγηθι τῷ ἀδελφῷ σου, καὶ τότε ἐλθὼν πρόσφερε τὸ δῶρόν σου.

5:25 ἴσθι εὐνοῶν τῷ ἀντιδίκῳ σου ταχύ, ἕως ὅτου εἶ μετ᾽ αὐτοῦ ἐν τῇ ὁδῷ, μήποτέ σε παραδῷ ὁ ἀντίδικος τῷ κριτῇ καὶ ὁ κριτὴς τῷ ὑπηρέτῃ καὶ εἰς φυλακὴν βληθήσῃ·

5:26 ἀμὴν λέγω σοι, οὐ μὴ ἐξέλθῃς ἐκεῖθεν, ἕως ἂν ἀποδῷς τὸν ἔσχατον κοδράντην.

5:20 For I say to you, that unless your justice abound more than that of the scribes and Pharisees, you will not enter into the kingdom of heaven. [n. 478]

5:21 You have heard that it was said to those of old: *you shall not kill*. And whoever will kill, will be liable to the judgment. [n. 482]

5:22 But I say to you, that whoever is angry with his brother, will be liable to the judgment. And whoever will say to his brother: raca, will be liable to the council. And whoever will say: fool, will be liable to hell fire. [n. 485]

5:23 If therefore you offer your gift at the altar, and there you remember that your brother has anything against you; [n. 494]

5:24 Leave there your offering before the altar, and go first to be reconciled to your brother: and then coming you will offer your gift. [n. 494]

5:25 Be in agreement with your adversary quickly, while you are on the way with him: lest perhaps the adversary deliver you to the judge, and the judge deliver you to the officer, and you be cast in prison. [n. 497]

5:26 Amen I say to you, you will not go out from there until you repay the last farthing. [n. 501]

---

476. *Dico autem vobis: nisi abundaverit*. Supra ostendit Dominus quod non erat sua intentio solvere legem sed adimplere; unde hic incipit adimplere. In lege quatuor erant: quaedam scilicet praecepta moralia, quaedam iudicialia, quaedam figuralia et quaedam promissa. Tria istorum Dominus adimplet verbis, scilicet moralia, promissa et iudicialia, id est docet ea adimplere; figuralia autem adimplevit facto in sua passione.

Unde pars ista dividitur in tres:

in prima adimplet legem quantum ad praecepta moralia,

in secunda quantum ad promissa,

in tertia quantum ad iudicialia.

476. *For I say to you, that unless your justice abound*. Above, the Lord shows that it was not his intention to do away with the law, but to fulfill it; wherefore, here he begins to fulfill it. In the law there are four things: namely, moral precepts, judicial ones, figures, and promises. Three of these, namely, the moral precepts, the promises, and the judicial ones, the Lord fulfilled by his words, i.e., he teaches us to fulfill them. But he fulfilled the figures by his deed in his passion.

Hence this part is divided into three:

in the first, he fulfills the law as to the moral precepts,

in the second, as to the promises,

in the third, as to the judicial precepts.

477. Moralia sunt duorum generum: quaedam prohibitiva, quaedam permissiva; primo adimplet prima, secundo secunda, ibi *dictum est super*: '*quicumque dimiserit*'.

Circa primum duo facit:

primo prohibet homicidium;

secundo adulterium, ibi *audistis* etc. '*Non mechaberis.*'

Circa primum duo facit:

primo ponit necessitatem;

secundo adimpletionem, ibi *audistis*.

478. Et dicit ergo *dico autem vobis*. Nota quod iustitia dupliciter sumitur: quandoque enim est quaedam particularis virtus, una de quatuor cardinalibus, et habet materiam determinatam, scilicet bona commutabilia quae veniunt in usum vitae; aliter dicitur virtus generalis quae est communis virtus, quam Philosophus vocat iustitiam legalem, quae est quantum ad impletionem legis: et ita accipitur hic.

Et *plusquam Scribarum*. Et dicit *scribarum et Pharisaeorum*, quia illi erant potiores in iustitia legis quia etiam superaddebant quasdam observantias; ut ergo designet excellentiam Novi Testamenti, ostendit quod etiam illorum iustitiam transcendit. Ideo dicitur qui minor est in regno caelorum, id est Ecclesia maior est illo. Est ergo sensus: *nisi abundauerit*, id est nisi perfectior sit *vestra iustitia quam scribarum et Pharisaeorum, non intrabitis* etc.

479. Et sciendum quod status Evangelii est medium inter statum legis et gloriae, et hoc patet quia Gal. IV, 3: Apostolus comparat puero statum legis et Evangelium perfectae aetati, unde dicit *quamdiu eramus parvuli* etc., et post *lex pedagogus noster fuit in Christo* etc., et Cor. XIII: *cum essem parvulus loquebar ut parvulus* etc.; ergo est medius status. Et hoc naturale est quod nullus potest pervenire ad terminum unum nisi transcendat alium: nullus enim potest pervenire ad senectutem nisi transcendat pueritiam; ita dicit Dominus non posse pervenire ad statum regni caelorum nisi transcendat etc.

Item maiori labori acquiritur melior merces, Cor IX: *qui parce seminat parce et metet*; in lege autem promittebantur temporalia et terrena, Is. I, 19: *si volueritis et audieritis, bona terrae comedetis*; sed hic promittuntur caelestia: ergo iustitia debet in nos abundare quia maior expectatur merces.

480. Sed obicitur contra hoc quod Dominus dicit *nisi abundaverit*, quia iustitia legis consistit in impletione decalogi; sed qui adimplet praecepta decalogi habebit vitam aeternam, infra *si vis ad vitam ingredi, serva mandata*. Et solvitur dupliciter vel tripliciter. Primo quia

477. There are two kinds of moral precepts: some are prohibitive and some permissive; first he fulfills the first kind, then the second kind, at *it has been said: 'whoever will put away'* (Matt 5:31).

Concerning the first, he does two things:

first, he prohibits homicide;

second, adultery, at *you have heard . . . 'do not commit adultery'* (Matt 5:27).

Concerning the first he does two things:

first, he sets down the necessity;

second, the fulfillment, at *you have heard*.

478. Therefore he says *but I say to you*. Note that justice is taken in two ways: for sometimes it is a certain particular virtue, one of the four cardinal virtues, and it has a certain determinate matter, namely, commutable goods useful for life. At other times, it refers to a general virtue that is a common virtue, which the Philosopher calls legal justice, which has to do with the keeping of the law: and it is taken this way here.

More than that of the scribes. And he says *of the scribes and Pharisees*, for they were superior in the justice of the law because they added on certain observances; therefore in order to indicate the excellence of the New Testament, he shows that it transcends even their justice. Therefore it is said whoever is less in the kingdom of heaven, i.e., the Church, is greater than they are. Therefore, this is the sense: *unless your justice abounds*, that is, unless *your justice* is more perfect *than that of the Scribes and Pharisees, you will not enter*.

479. And it should be known that the state of the Gospel is a middle one between the state of the law and that of glory, and this is clear from Galatians: the Apostle compares the state of the law to a child, and the Gospel to advanced age, hence he says, *when we were children* (Gal 4:3), and afterwards, *the law was our pedagogue* (Gal 3:24), and *when I was a child, I spoke as a child* (1 Cor 13:11). Therefore, it is a middle state, and this is natural, for no one can arrive at the end without crossing through something else; for no one can arrive at old age unless he passes through childhood. In this way the Lord says one cannot arrive at the state of the kingdom of heaven unless he climbs through all the rest.

Likewise, a better reward is gained by greater labor: *he who sows sparingly will reap sparingly* (2 Cor 9:6); but in the law, temporal and earthly things are promised: *If you be willing and listen to me, you will eat of the good things of the land* (Isa 1:19). But here heavenly goods are promised, therefore, the justice in us must exceed, for a greater reward is expected.

480. But it is objected against the Lord's saying *unless your justice abounds*, that the justice of the law consists in observing the decalogue; but anyone who fulfills the precepts of the decalogue will have eternal life: *if you wish to enter into life, keep the commandments* (Matt 19:17). And

observatores decalogi nunquam potuerunt intrare nisi in fide et per redemptionem sanguinis Christi, *si enim per legem iustitia ergo Christus gratis mortuus est*. Et ideo dicendum quod illud *si vis ad vitam ingredi* intelligendum est supposita fide; Scribae autem et Pharisei non habebant fidem, Ro. IX, 31: *Israel vero sectans legem iustitiae, in legem iustitiae non pervenit. Quare? Quia non ex fide, sed quasi ex operibus* etc. Et est ista satis bona solutio.

Alia Augustini, qui dicit quod omnes iste impletiones quas Christus facit continentur omnes in veteri lege, quia ibi et ira prohibetur, Levi. XVIII: *ne oderis fratrem tuum in corde tuo*. Ergo quid Dominus superaddit? Dicendum quod addit quantum ad pravum intellectum illorum, Scribarum scilicet et Pharisaeorum, quia credebant quod in illo praecepto *non occides* non prohiberentur nisi ex timore actus, actus homicidii; unde Dominus hoc exposuit, et ideo non simpliciter dicit: nisi abundaverit iustitia super legem, sed *plusquam scribarum et Pharisaeorum*.

481. Alia etiam solutio, cum Augustino: Christus enim dixerat *qui fecerit et docuerit* etc., et *qui solverit* etc.; Pharisaei autem et scribae non faciunt et docent, infra XXIII *dicunt enim et non faciunt* etc.; ergo *nisi abundaverit* etc., id est: quod vos dicitis et faciatis. *Non intrabitis* etc.

Sed remanet alia quaestio, quia Dominus dixit *qui ergo solverit: minimus vocabitur in regno caelorum*, et qui non abundat non intrabit; ergo qui solvit erit. Et solvit Chrysostomus quod aliud est esse in regno et aliud intrare: illi enim propriae intrant qui in dominio regni partem habent, illi sunt qui in quibuscumque morantur; unde etiam illi qui detinentur in carcere dicuntur esse in regno; ita etiam est caelorum, quia addicti paene sunt in regno sed non participant regnum. Augustinus aliter, et dicit quod ex hoc possumus intelligere quod dupliciter dicitur regnum caelorum: quoddam in quod non intrant non habentes iustitiam, et haec est vita aeterna; aliud in quod intrant solventes, et haec est praesens Ecclesia.

482. *Audistis quia dictum est antiquis: 'non occides.'* Hic ponitur adimpletio praecepti. Et circa hoc tria facit: primo ponit praecepta, secundo adimplet, tertio monet ad observantia impletionis; secundum ibi *ego autem dico*, tertium ibi *si ergo offers*. Circa primum duo facit: primo ponit praecepta de prohibitione homicidii, secundo poenam homicidii.

it is solved in two or three ways. First, because observers of the decalogue could never enter except in faith and by the redemption of the blood of Christ, *for if justice comes by the law, then Christ died in vain* (Gal 2:21). And thus it must be said that that passage, *but if you will enter into life* (Matt 19:17), should be understood as assuming faith; but the scribes and Pharisees did not have faith; *but Israel, by following after the law of justice, did not arrive at the law of justice. Why not? Because they sought it not by faith but of works* (Rom 9:31–32). And this is a good enough solution.

Another is that of Augustine, who says that all these observances that Christ makes are each contained in the old law, for there anger is also prohibited: *you shall not hate your brother* (Lev 19:17). Therefore, what did the Lord add to this? It should be said that he adds something with respect to the corrupt understanding of the scribes and Pharisees, for they believed that in that precept *you shall not kill*, they were not forbidden from anything except out of fear of an act, the act of homicide. Hence the Lord explains this and thus he does not simply say: unless your justice is greater than the law, but *greater than that of the scribes and Pharisees*.

481. Still another solution, with Augustine: for Christ had said *but he who will do and teach*, (Matt 5:19), and, *who will break* (Matt 5:19); but Pharisees and scribes do not do and teach, as it says later: *for they say, and do not* (Matt 23:3). Therefore, *unless your justice abounds*, that is, what you say, you must also do, or *you will not enter in*.

But there remains another question, for the Lord said *he therefore who will break . . . will be called the least in the kingdom of heaven* (Matt 5:19), and whoever does not abound will not enter; therefore, whoever breaks the law will enter. And Chrysostom resolves this by saying it is one thing to be in a kingdom and another thing to enter it: for properly speaking, those enter who have a part in the rule of the kingdom, but those are in it who dwell in it somewhere; hence, even those who are kept in prison are said to be in the kingdom. So also it is of heaven, for those who are almost condemned are in the kingdom, but they do not participate in ruling. Augustine says otherwise, that by this we can understand that the kingdom of heaven is said in two ways: one in which no one enters unless he has justice, and this is eternal life; another in which those enter who break the commandments, and this is the present Church.

482. *You have heard that it was said to those of old: 'you shall not kill.'* Here is set forth the fulfillment of the precept. And concerning this he does three things: first he sets forth the precepts, second he fulfills them, third he warns about observing the fulfillment; the second is at *but I say to you*, the third at *if therefore you offer*. Concerning the first, he does two things: first he sets down the precepts about the prohibition of homicide, second, the penalty for homicide.

Dicit ergo *audistis* istud Exo. XX, 13 et Deut. V, 17; et dicit *antiquis* quia, secundum Chrysostomum, sicut si magister alicui suo discipulo: diu est quod elementa docui te, tempus est quod maiora discas, ita Dominus, Hebr. V: *et enim cum deberetis magistri esse propter tempus, rursum indigetis ut vos doceamini quae sint elementa exordii sermonum Dei* etc.

483. Et notandum quod in isto praecepto fit triplex error, quia quidam dixerunt quod non licebat occidere etiam animalia minuta. Sed hoc falsum est quia non est peccatum uti illis quae subdita sunt hominis potestati: est enim naturalis ordo quod plantae sint in nutrimento animalium et quaedam animalia in nutrimentum aliorum; et omnia sunt hominis nutrimentum, Gen. IX, 3: *quasi holera virentia tradidi vobis omnia.* Et Philosophus etiam in *Politicis* dicit quod venatio est sicut iustum bellum.

Secundum, est error quorumdam qui dixerunt: '*non occides*', hominem scilicet; unde dicunt homicidas omnes iudices seculares qui condemnant secundum leges aliquas. Contra quod Augustinus dicit quod Deus non abstulit sibi potestatem occidendi, unde *ego occidam et ego vivere faciam* etc.; ergo licitum est illis quod mandato Dei occidunt, quia tunc Deus facit. Omnis autem lex mandatum Dei est, Prov. VIII, 15: *per me reges regnant,* Ro. XIII, 4: *non enim sine causa gladium portat. Dei enim minister est.* Ergo intelligendum '*non occides*', auctoritate propria.

484. Tertius error est quia aliqui crediderunt '*non occides*' alium, sed licitum est occidere se ipsum, quia invenitur hoc de Samsone, et etiam Catone et de quibusdam virginibus quae iniecerunt se in flammam, secundum quod recitat Augustinus. Sed respondit Augustinus quod qui se occidit hominem occidit, quia alium non debet occidere nisi auctoritate Dei, nec se ipsum nisi a voluntate Dei vel instinctu Spiritus Sancti, et ita excusat Sampsonem.

Qui autem occiderit. Hic ponitur poena: *reus erit iudicio,* id est poena quam lex adiudicabit Exo. XXI, 12.

485. Sequitur *ego autem dico* etc. Posito praecepto veteris legis, hic Dominus adimplet. Et ista adimpletio non evacuat legem, immo facit ad maiorem adimpletionem, quia qui irascitur pronus ad homicidium est, sed quando irascitur non committit homicidium. Ista quodammodo in isto praecepto continetur quia lex ista a Deo data est, et est differentia inter legem hominis et Dei, quia homo est iudex exteriorum actuum, Deus autem interiorum, Reg. XVI: *homines vident ea quae parent, Dominus autem intuetur cor;* unde in hoc '*non occides*' includitur etiam motus ad occidendum. Sed est duplex motus ad nocumentum proximi, scilicet ire et odii; nec est odium idem quod ira inveterata, sed est praedicatio per causam quia ex ira inveterata fit odium.

Therefore he says **you have heard** that '*you shall not kill*' (Exod 20:13; Deut 5:17); and he says **to them of old** because, according to Chrysostom, just as if a teacher says to one of his disciples: for a long time I have taught you these basics, the time has come that you learn greater things; so with the Lord, *since the time is coming when you will be teachers, you need to be taught* (Heb 5:12).

483. And it must be noted that in this precept a threefold error was made, for certain men said that it was not permitted to kill even small animals; but this is false, for it is no sin to use the things that are subjected to the power of man, for it is the natural order that plants be for the nourishment of animals and certain animals be for the nourishment of others; and all things are for the nourishment of man: *every moving thing that lives will be food for you, just as I gave you the green plants* (Gen 9:3). And the Philosopher also says in the *Politics* that hunting is like just war.

Second, there is an error of certain men who said: '*you shall not kill*' means men; hence they call it homicide when secular judges sentence people according to the laws. Against this Augustine says that God did not remove from himself the power of killing, hence *I will kill and I will make live* (Deut 32:39); therefore it is permitted to those who kill by the command of God, for God is the one who does it. But every law is a command from God: *by me kings reign* (Prov 8:15); *he does not bear the sword in vain for he is God's minister* (Rom 13:4). Therefore '*you shall not kill*' is to be understood by proper authority.

484. The third error is that some believed '*you shall not kill*' someone else, but to kill oneself is permitted, for this is found in the story of Samson, and also Cato and certain virgins who threw themselves into a fire, according to Augustine. But Augustine answers that whoever kills himself, kills a man, for one cannot kill another except by God's authority, nor oneself except by the will of God or the inspiration of the Holy Spirit, and in this way he excuses Samson.

But whoever will kill. Here he sets down the punishment: *will be liable to the judgment,* i.e., the punishment that the law adjudicates (Exod 21:12).

485. *But I say to you* follows. Having laid out the precept of the old law, here the Lord fulfills it. And this fulfillment does not make the law void, but to the contrary acts to its greater fulfillment, for someone who gets angry is prone to homicide, but when he gets angry he does not commit homicide. It is somehow contained in this precept because that law was given by God, and there is a difference between the law of men and of God, for a man is judge of external actions, but God of internal ones: *men see the things that appear* (1 Sam 16:7); hence in this '*you shall not kill*' is included also the motive for killing. But there is a twofold motive for hurting one's neighbor, namely, anger and hatred; nor is hatred the same thing as hardened anger, but it is a predication by cause, for hatred happens from

Est ergo differentia quia ira non appetit malum proximo nisi in quantum vult vindictam: unde facta vindicta quiescit; in odio autem ipsum nocumentum est per se volitum et nunquam quiescit appetitus; ergo gravior est motus odii quam irae. Deus autem non solum prohibet motum odii sed ire qui levior est, Ioh.II: *qui odit fratrem suum in tenebris est.*

Ponit autem tres gradus ire: primus gradus est ire latentis in corde, secundus apparentis exterius, tertius prorumpentis in nocumentum. Primus ibi **ego autem dico vobis**, et dicit Augustinus quod lectio debet esse: *sine causa*, quia ille **qui** *sine causa* **irascitur reus erit iudicio**. Ieronimus autem dicit quod *sine causa* non est de textu, quia tunc relinqueretur locus irae; Dominus autem nullum locum irae relinquit.

486. Sed numquid omnis ira contrariatur virtuti? Sciendum quod, sicut Augustinus dicit, circa hoc fuerunt duae opiniones philosophorum: Stoici enim dixerunt quod nulla passio animi cadit in sapientem, immo volebant quod vera virtus; Peripatetici autem dixerunt quod ira cadit in sapientem sed moderata, et est ista verior opinio: quod patet et auctoritate, quia in Evangeliis invenimus istas passiones quodammodo Christo attributas, in quo fuit plenitudo sapientiae; et ratione quia 'si' omnes passiones contrariarentur virtuti, essent aliquae quae deservirent in nocumentum quia non haberent aliquos actus convenientes, et tunc irascibilis et concupiscibilis frustra date fuissent homini. Et ideo dicendum quod ira aliquando est virtus, aliquando non.

Accipitur autem ira tripliciter: primo prout est in solo iudicio rationis absque commotione animi; ista enim non dicitur ira sed iudicium: sic enim Dominus puniens malus iratus apparet, Mich. VII, 9: *iram Domini portabo quonium peccavi ei.*

487. Secundo accipitur prout est passio, et ista est in appetitu sensitivo, et est duplex, quia aliquando ordinatur ratione et continetur sub terminis rationis, quando scilicet irascitur quantum debet, cui debet, et huiusmodi, et tunc est actus virtutis et dicitur ira per zelum. Unde Philosophus etiam dicit quod mansuetudo non est in nullo modo irasci. Et ideo dicit Chrysostomus quod si ira tota tolleretur, tolleretur et disciplina, etc. Ista ergo non est peccatum.

Est tertia ira quae effugit iudicium rationis, et ista semper est peccatum, sed quandoque veniale quandoque mortale, et hoc dicetur ex motu pessimo. Aliquid enim est peccatum mortale vel veniale dupliciter: ex genere vel ex circumstantiis, vel actu et ex consensu; verbi gratia, homicidium enim est actus peccati mortalis ex

hardened anger. Therefore there is a difference, for anger does not seek evil for one's neighbor unless inasmuch as it wants vengeance, hence vengeance accomplished quiets it. But in hatred, the very harming is desired for itself and the appetite is never quieted; therefore hatred is a more serious motive than anger. But God does not only prohibit the motive of hatred but also of anger, which is less grave: *whoever hates his brother is in darkness* (1 John 2:11).

But he sets down three levels of anger: the first level is the anger hiding in one's heart, the second, anger appearing externally, and the third, anger erupting into harm. The first is at **but I say to you**, and Augustine says that the reading should be *without cause*, for the man who gets angry *without cause* **will be liable to the judgment**. Jerome, however, says that *without cause* is not in the text, for then an opening would be given to anger; but the Lord leaves no place for anger.

486. But surely not all anger is contrary to virtue? It should be known, as Augustine says, that concerning this there are two opinions among philosophers: for the Stoics said that no passion of the soul happens in the wise man, for to the contrary, they were the ones desiring true virtue. But the Peripatetics said that anger happens in the wise man, but is moderated, and this is a truer opinion: which is also clear by authority, for in the Gospels we find these passions sometimes attributed to Christ, in whom was the fullness of wisdom; also from reason, for if all passions were contrary to virtue, there would be certain powers of the soul that had no purpose but to harm, for they would not have any suitable act, and then the irascible and concupiscible powers would have been given to man in vain. And therefore it must be said that anger is sometimes a virtue, sometimes not.

But anger is taken in three ways: first, as it is in the judgment of reason alone without any disturbance of the soul; but this is not called anger, but judgment: for so the Lord seems bad and angry when punishing: *I will bear the wrath of the Lord* (Mic 7:9).

487. Second, it can be taken as a passion, and this is in the sensitive appetite, and it is twofold, for sometimes it is ordered by reason and contained within the limits of reason, namely, when one is angry as much as he should be, at what he should be, and so on; and then it is an act of virtue and is called anger from zeal. Hence the Philosopher also says that meekness is not never growing angry. And thus Chrysostom says that if anger were completely taken away, discipline would also be taken away. This kind, therefore, is no sin.

There is a third anger which escapes the judgment of reason, and this is always a sin, but sometimes a venial one and sometimes mortal, and this is determined by the worst impulse. For something is a mortal or venial sin in two ways: either from its genus or circumstances, or by the act and by consent; for example, homicide is an act of mortal

suo genere quia directe contrariatur praecepto divino, et ideo consensus in homicidium est peccatum mortale, quia si actus mortalis, et consensus; similiter si fuerit peccatum veniale, et consensus, et huiusmodi. Aliquando autem peccatum mortale est ex genere, sed tamen motus non est peccatum mortale quia est sine consensu, sicut si ascendit motus concupiscentiae ad fornicandum: si non consentitur non est mortale. Similiter ira est motus ad vindicandum iniuriam illatam; hoc enim est proprie ira; si ergo iste motus, verbi gratia in homicidio, est solum in passione ita quod etiam ratio deducatur, tunc est peccatum mortale; si autem non pervertatur ratio, tunc est veniale. Si autem non sit motus ex genere peccatum mortale, tunc si consensus adhibeatur non est mortale.

488. Quod ergo dicit Dominus *qui irascitur fratri suo reus erit iudicio* intelligendum est de motu tendente in nocumentum, qui motus est peccatum mortale ita quod sit cum consensu, Eccl. ult. *cuncta quae serviunt adducet Deus in iudicium* etc. Et hoc est *ego autem* etc.

Et nota quod nullus propheta loquens de lege Moysi sic locutus est: *ego autem dico* etc., sed tamen inducebant ad observantiam legis Moysi. Ex quo patet quod Dominus ostendit se auctoritatem habere et ostendit se legislatorem quando dicit *ego autem* etc.

489. Consequenter ponitur secundus gradus ire, scilicet quando apparet exterius sine illatione nocumenti.

490. *Racha*, secundum quosdam, non est vox significans aliquem determinatum conceptum, sed est interiectio irascentis. Secundum Augustinum, est sicut 'heu' interiectio dolentis, et significat quemdam affectum unde iam prorumpit ira exterius, non tamen in nocumentum. Secundum Chrysostomum, est interiectio vilipendentis, et sonat in vilipensionem. Utrumque autem istorum prohibitum est, scilicet et ostendere amaritudinem ad fratrem, Apostolus *omnis amaritudo et ira . . . tollatur a vobis*, et despicere eum, Mal. II: *quare despicis?* etc.

Vel *racha*, secundum alios est vox significans determinatum conceptum, et secundum hoc sunt duae opiniones, quia secundum Augustinum idem est quod pannosus a 'rachos', et haec opinio concordat cum illa Crisostomi. Secundum Ieronimum *racha* significat 'vacuum' vel 'inanis': unde *racha*, quasi absque cerebro, et ista est magna iniuria, immo fit iniuria Spiritui Sancto, quando sapientem fratrem plenum Spiritu Sancto, Act. *repleti sunt omnes Spiritu Sancto*, vocat 'vacuum' etc.

491. Sed quaerit Chrysostomus si 'vacuus' est idem quod 'fatuus' quare Dominus dixit postea *qui autem dixit fatue?* Et dixit quod in omnibus idiomatibus sunt verba significantia iniuriam, sed ex usu et consuetudine loquendi fit iniuria: racha enim, licet sit idem quod

sin by its genus because it is directly contrary to the divine precept, and thus consenting to homicide is a mortal sin; for if the act is mortal, consent is as well. Likewise, if it were a venial sin, consenting to it would be as well, and so on. But sometimes a sin is mortal by its genus, but nevertheless the movement is not a mortal sin, because it is without consent, just as when a movement of concupiscence arises toward fornication, if it is not consented to it is not mortal. Similarly, anger is a movement to avenge an inflicted injury; for this is properly anger. But if this movement, for example to homicide, is such that even reason is led astray, then even if the movement is only in the passion, it is a mortal sin; but if reason is not perverted, then it is venial. But if there is no movement with the genus of a mortal sin, then if the consent is given it is not mortal.

488. Therefore, what the Lord says, *whoever is angry with his brother, will be liable to the judgment*, is to be understood about the movement inclining to harm, which movement is a mortal sin if it is consented to: *all things that are done God will bring into judgment* (Eccl 12:14). And this is the *but I say*.

And note that no prophet speaking about the law of Moses spoke in this way: *but I say to you*, but nevertheless they preached observance of the law of Moses. By this it is clear that the Lord shows that he has authority, and he shows that he is the lawgiver when he says, *but I say to you*.

489. Accordingly he sets forth the second level of anger, namely when it appears externally without hastening to harm.

490. *Raca*, according to certain men, is not an expression signifying any definite concept, but an interjection of anger. According to Augustine, it is like 'alas', an interjection of suffering, and it signifies a certain feeling from which anger erupts externally, but not to the point of harm. According to Chrysostom, it is an interjection of spite, and sounds slighting. But either of these is forbidden, whether to show bitterness to one's brother, as the Apostle says: *all bitterness . . . be put away from you* (Eph 4:31), or to despise him, *why does everyone despise his brother?* (Mal 2:10).

Or *raca*, according to others, is an expression signifying a definite concept, and according to this there are two opinions, for according to Augustine it means the same thing as ragged, from 'rachos', and this opinion agrees with that of Chrysostom. According to Jerome, *raca* means 'empty' or 'inane', hence *raca* is, as it were, 'without a brain', and it is a great insult, even an insult to the Holy Spirit, when a wise brother full of the Holy Spirit is called 'empty-headed': *all were filled with the Holy Spirit* (Acts 2:4).

491. But Chrysostom asks if 'empty-headed' is the same as 'foolish', then why did the Lord afterward say *whoever will say: fool*? And he said that in all idioms there are words used to injure, but the injury is done by the use and custom of speaking: *raca* then, can mean the same thing as *fool*, but

fatuus, tamen non in eodem usu, quia racha dicitur familiariter et est peccatum quando dicitur ex ira.

Reus est concilio. Augustinus: plus est Deo reum consilio quam iudicio, quia iudicium, quando adhuc de reo agitur et dubitatur utrum reus sit, Thi. V: *nihil absque iudicio*, sed postquam convincitur de crimine non plus agitur cum reo, sed iudices trahunt se in concilium de pena inferenda. Hilarius: **reus est concilio** sanctorum, quia qui facit iniuriam Spiritui Sancto dignum est quod a sanctis condemnetur. Chrysostomus dicit quod apostoli sic exposuerunt: **reus concilio**, id est ut sit de notitia eorum qui venerunt in concilium contra Christum.

492. Qui autem dixerit: fatue. Hic tertius gradus qui est quando infert nocumentum verbo. Et sicut qui vocat **racha** infert iniuriam Spiritui Sancto, ita qui **fatue** Filio Dei qui *factus est nobis sapientia* Cor.

Reus erit gehennae. Iste est primus locus ubi fit mentio de gehenne, ut aliquis nunquam prius usus sit isto verbo, Dan. X. Spiritus Domini et sicut habetur in testu et caelum. Ier. XIX: circa Ierusalem erat quaedam vallis delectata quae vocatur vallis Tophet sive filiorum Annon; in illa autem valle filii Israel coluerunt idola et Deus comminatus est eis per Ieremiam quo in illa debebant prostrari cadavera eorum, unde Ier. XIX, 6: *et non vocabitur locus iste amplius Thofeth et vallis filii Ennom, sed vallis Occisionis* etc.

493. Gehenna, secundum Hebraeos, idem est quod vallis Ennon. Quia ergo in illa a Nabuchodonosor, quando descendebant de Ierusalem, multi prostrati sunt et occisi, ideo gehennam Dominus vocat locum inferni. Sicut enim promissione terrena quae erat in veteri lege commutavit in bona caelestia et aeterna, ita penas temporales quas infligebat vetus lex commutavit in penas aeternas. Sicut enim et culpe se habent quia plus est ostendere iram exterius quam tenetur interius, et ulterius plus est inferre nocumentum, ita primo est iudicium, secundo concilium, tertio pena determinata; et omnia ista, scilicet iudicium, concilium, gehenna, significant penam inferni. Et dicit multa quia ostendit in hoc diversitatem penarum, quia magis punientur illi qui inferunt nocumentum.

Sed tunc est quaestio. Numquid qui dicunt fratri **fatue** peccat mortaliter? Quidam dicunt quod hyperbolice loquitur ad terrendum. Sed falsum est, quia doctrina Christi est doctrina veritate plena. Unde sciendum quod tertium includit primum et secundum, et secundum includit primum. In primo intelligitur de ira quae est peccatum mortale; et si ex illa prorumpit in verbum vel

not in the same use, for raca is said familiarly and it is a sin when it is said from anger.

Liable to the council. Augustine says: it is more before God to be liable to the council than to judgment, since up until the judgment, culpability is in question and it is uncertain whether someone is liable: *observe these things without prejudice* (1 Tim 5:21); but after someone is convicted of a crime he is no longer dealt with as master of himself, but the judges hand him over to the council for sentencing. Hilary says it means **liable to the council** of the saints, for whoever commits injury to the Holy Spirit deserves to be condemned by the saints. Chrysostom says that the Apostles explained it in this way: **liable to the council**, i.e., he would be considered among those who sat in the council against Christ.

492. But whoever will say: fool. This is the third level, which is when someone inflicts harm through words. And just as someone who says **raca** inflicts injury on the Holy Spirit, so whoever says **fool**, injures the Son of God, who *became wisdom for us* (1 Cor 1:30).

He will be liable to hell fire. This is the first place that mention is made of Gehenna, as no one had ever used this word before (cf. Dan 10). The Spirit of the Lord is held in earthen vessels just as in heaven. Around Jerusalem was a certain favorite valley called the valley of Topheth or of the sons of Annon; but in this valley the sons of Israel worshipped idols and God threatened them through Jeremiah that in that valley their dead bodies would be cast down, hence: *that this place will no more be called Tophet, nor the valley of the sons of Ennom, but the valley of slaughter* (Jer 19:6)

493. Gehenna, according to the Hebrews, is the same as the valley of Ennon. Therefore since in it many were struck down and killed by Nebuchadnezzar when they were coming down from Jerusalem, thus the Lord calls the place of hell Gehenna. For just as he transformed the earthly promises which were in the old law into heavenly and eternal goods, so he also exchanged the temporal punishments that the old law imposed for eternal punishments. But just as the crimes are related to each other, for it is worse to show anger externally than to hold it in, and it is worse still to inflict harm, so also the first is judgment, the second council, and the third a specific punishment. And all these things, i.e., judgment, council, gehenna, signify the punishment of hell. And he says it several times because he shows by this diversity of penalties that those will be punished the most who inflict harm.

But then a question arises. Do those who call a brother **fool** sin mortally? Some people say that he is speaking hyperbolically in order to frighten. But this is false, for the teaching of Christ is a teaching full of truth. Hence it should be known that the third includes the first and the second, and the second includes the first. In the first it is understood that anger is a mortal sin; and if someone erupts from

nocumentum, peccat mortaliter. Ita similiter qui dixit: *fatuae*, est ira quae est peccatum mortale. Sed videtur opus fecisse qui istos, Gal. III: *O insensati Galatae*. Dicendum quod non dicebat ex ira, sed ex necessitate iustitiae, quia secundum hoc etiam flagellum non est peccatum. Et ideo dicit Augustinus quod quando dixit *qui irascitur*, addidit *sine causa*, et in secunda sententia et tertio etiam dicit esse *sine causa*. Tamen secundum eum etiam idem sensus est si non ponatur *sine causa*.

494. Consequenter cum dicit *si ergo offers*, posita adimpletione, ostendit quomodo debeat observari. Et primo ostendit quomodo debeat aliquis se habere ad eum quem laesit; secundo quomodo ad eum qui eum laesit, ibi *esto consentiens*. Circa primum tria facit: primo bonum propositum, secundo usus boni propositi impeditiuum, tertio remedium. Secundum, ibi *et ibi recordatus*; tertium, ibi *relinque*.

Dicit ergo *si offers*, quasi: ergo quia non debes aliquem offendere, si offers. Per hoc honoramus Deum inquantum omnia a Deo recognoscimus esse data nobis, Paral. ult. *tua sunt omnia, et quae de manu tua accepimus, dedimus tibi* etc. Item honoramus Ecclesiam, quia inde pauperes sustententur Ecclesiae. Prov. III, 127: *honora Deum tuum*, non alienum, Is. XLI: *ego Dominus habens*. *Ante altare*, non ioculatoribus, Deut. XII: *cave ne offeras holocausta tua in omni loco quem videris, sed in eo quem elegit Dominus*.

495. Impeditivum est offensio proximi: unde *et ibi recordatus*. Nota quod aliquando tu habes aliquid adversus fratrem tuum, aliquando frater adversum te, quando scilicet vel tu offendis eum, vel ille offendit te. Sed tu debes parcere, Apostolus: *supportantes invicem et donantes vobis ipsis, si quis adversus aliquem habet querelam*. Et quia qui est offensus non dicitur petere veniam ab eo qui offendit, sed e converso, ideo dicit *et ibi recordatus fueris quia frater tuus habet aliquid adversum te* etc., cum secundum Chrysostomum hoc abundatis perfectius est. Ps. *cum his qui oderunt pacem eram pacificus*.

Et dicit *ibi recordatus*, quia forte ante non fuit recordatus: quoniam dat triplex consilium. Primum: *relinque*. Dominus nunquam vult quod bonum dimittatur totaliter propter malum quod offert istud bonum, sed desistere propter malum, Levit. ult. *animal quod immolari potest Domino, si quis noverit, sanctum erit et mutari non poterit, idest nec melius malo, nec peius bono*. Et ideo dicit *relinque*, non *desiste*, id est retine propositum et remove impedimentum. Et hoc est: *et vade prius*.

it into words or violence, he sins mortally. It is likewise with whoever has said: *fool*, for there is anger which is a mortal sin. But the Apostle seems to have acted against these words: *O senseless Galatians* (Gal 3:1). It must be said that he was not speaking out of anger, but out of the necessity of justice, according to which also whipping is not a sin. And therefore Augustine says that when he said **whoever grows angry**, he added *without cause*, and in the second sentence and third he also says *without cause*. Nevertheless, according to him it has the same meaning even if he does not say *without cause*.

494. Afterward when he says **if therefore you offer**, having set down the fulfillment, he shows how it should be observed. And first, he shows how someone should act toward one he has injured; second, how someone should act toward one who has injured him, at **be in agreement**. Concerning the first he does three things: first, he sets down good advice; second, the obstacles to employing that good advice; third, the remedy. The second is at **and there you remember**; the third, at **leave your offering**.

Thus he says **if . . . you offer**, as it were: thus because you should not offend anyone, if you offer. By this we honor God in that we acknowledge that we were given all things by God: *all things are yours, and we have given you what we have received from your hand* (1 Chr 29:14). Similarly we honor the Church, for in this way the poor are supported by the Church: *honor the Lord with your substance* (Prov 3:9), *for I am the Lord . . . I have made you* (Isa 41:13–15). **Before the altar**, not among others joking; *beware lest you offer your holocausts in every place that you will see, but in the place which the Lord will chose* (Deut 12:13–14).

495. The obstacle is offending one's neighbor; hence **and there you remember**. Note that sometimes you have something against your brother, sometimes your brother has something against you, namely when either you offend him or he offends you. But you should forbear, as the Apostle says: *bearing with one another . . . if anyone has a complaint against another* (Col 3:13). And so whoever is offended is not said to seek forgiveness from the one who offended, but vice versa, thus he says, **and there you remember that your brother has anything against you**, although according to Chrysostom it is even more perfect to do more than this: *with those who hated peace I was peaceable* (Psalm 120:7).

And he says **there you remember**, for perhaps beforehand you did not remember: so he gives a threefold counsel. First: **leave your offering**. The Lord never wants a good to be abandoned completely because of an evil that accompanies that good, but to refrain from the evil; *a beast that may be sacrificed to the Lord, if anyone will vow, will be holy, and cannot be exchanged, i.e., neither a better for a worse, nor a worse for a better* (Lev 27:9–10). And thus he says **leave your offering**, not *stop*, i.e., keep your plan and remove the obstacle. And this is **and go first . . . to your brother**.

496. Sed Augustinus hoc obicit quia si Dominus intelligit hoc ad litteram sequitur inconveniens, quia posset esse ille ultra mare. Sed intelligendum quod si non habet oportunitatem inveniendi eum debet ire corde. Intelligatis etiam per *altare* fidem sine qua impossibile est placere Deo. Dicit etiam Augustinus quod si etiam memor esset ante altare peccati mortalis, et vellet offerre, si non haberet oportunitatem confitendi potest offerre cum contritione et proposito confitendi. *Vade* ergo reconciliari, saltem in affectu, et *tunc veniens offeres*, Eccli. XXXIII: *dona impiorum non probat Altissimus.*

Secundum, *offeres munus*: in quo notatur quod per exercitium caritatis in proximum venimus in caritatem Dei, Ioh. *si fratrem tuum quem vides* etc.

497. Esto consentiens. Supra Dominus praemisit unum documentum utile ad observantiam impletionis; nunc ponit aliud, et potest dupliciter continuari cum praecedentibus. Primo sic: Dominus supra determinat quomodo te debeas habere ad eum quem laesisti; nunc docet quomodo te debeas habere ad eum qui te laesit, et hoc est *esto*. Vel aliter, ut adversarius accipiatur large: vel ille qui laesit te, vel quem tu laesisti.

Ita Dominus docet quod reconcilieris fratri tuo. Sed posset aliquis dicere: reconciliabor, et non ita cito. Ideo Dominus dicit *cito*, Eph. IV: *sol non occidat superiracundiam vestram.* Et notandum quod sicut dicit Ieronimus graeco *consentiens* dicit quoddam verbum quod sonat 'benivolum' vel 'clementem'.

498. Sed quaeritur quis sit iste adversarius. Et sciendum quod sunt quinque adversarii quibus consentire debemus, scilicet caro, diabolus, homo, Deus et verbum Dei. De primo, Ier. XVIII: *audi voces adversariorum*; de secundo, Iob XXXVII: *sit ut impius inimicus meus et adversarius meus quasi iniquus*; de tertio, Gal. V: *caro concupiscit adversus spiritus* et Ro. VII: *video aliam legem in membris meis adversantem legi mentis meae*; de quarto, scilicet Deo, qui adversatur peccantibus, et dum punit et dum contraria praecipit, Iob XXX: *mutatus es mihi in crudelem et in duritia manus tuae adversaris mihi*; de quinto, Ps. *eripe de manu peccatoris et de manu contra legem agentis et inqui*, Eccli. VI: *aspera est nimis sapientia indoctis hominibus* etc.

Quare ergo Augustinus de quo horum intelligatur. Non de homine, propter duo. Primo propter id quod sequitur: *ne forte tradat iudici*; quomodo enim hominem traderet Christo qui simul iudicabit utrumque? Secundo quia si moritur numquid non auferetur spes veniae?

496. But Augustine objects that if the Lord understands this literally then something unfitting follows, for one's brother could be overseas. But it must be understood that if one has no opportunity of finding him, he must go there in his heart. You may also understand by *altar* the faith without which it is impossible to please God. Augustine even says that if he has also remembered before the altar a mortal sin, and he wishes to make his offering, if he had no opportunity to confess he can make his offering with contrition and the intention of confessing. Therefore, *go* to be reconciled, at least in one's heart, and *then coming you will offer*; the Almighty does not approve the gifts of the wicked (Sir 34:23).

You will offer your gift: in this it is noted that by the exercise of charity toward one's neighbor we come into the charity of God: *if . . . he who loves not his brother whom he sees* (1 John 4:20).

497. Be in agreement. Above the Lord set forth one useful instruction for the observance of this fulfillment; now he sets down another, and it can be developed in two ways from what went before. First in this way: the Lord taught above how you should treat someone you have hurt; now he teaches how you should deal with someone who has hurt you, and this is *be in agreement*. Or, in another way, so that adversary is taken broadly: either for someone who has hurt you, or someone you have hurt.

Thus the Lord teaches that you should be reconciled with your brother. Yet someone could say 'I will be reconciled, but not right away.' Thus the Lord says, *quickly*: *let not the sun go down upon your anger* (Eph 4:26). And it should be noted that, as Jerome says, in Greek, *in agreement* is a certain word that means 'well-wisher' or 'clement'.

498. But it is asked who this adversary might be. And it should be known that there are five adversaries with whom we should be in agreement, namely man, the devil, the flesh, God, and the word of God. Concerning the first, *hear the voice of adversaries* (Jer 18:19). Concerning the second, *let my enemy be as the ungodly and my adversary as the wicked one* (Job 37:7). Concerning the third, *for the flesh lusts against the spirit* (Gal 5:17), and, *but I see another law in my members, fighting against the law of my mind* (Rom 7:23). And concerning the fourth, namely, God, who is opposed to those sinning, both when he punishes and when he commands the opposite deeds: *you are changed to be cruel toward me and in the hardness of your hand you are against me* (Job 30:21). And concerning the fifth, *deliver me, O my God, out of the hand of the sinner and out of the hand of the transgressor of the law and of the unjust* (Ps 71:4); *how very unpleasant is wisdom to the unlearned* (Sir 6:21).

Therefore Augustine asks which of these should be understood by this verse. It is not about a man who has injured you, because of two things. First, because of what follows: *lest perhaps the adversary deliver you to the judge*, for how would he hand you over to Christ who will judge

Non ergo potest intelligi de homine. Non de diabolo: hoc enim Deus nollet; per hoc quod primus homo ei consentit in miseria devenit. Quamvis quidam, secundum Ieronymum, de eo exponant, qui dicunt quod tunc consentimus diabolo quando observamus pactum quod ferimus cum eo in baptismo, sicut illud *abrenuntio sathan*. Sed haec expositio est extorta.

499. Non de carne, non de Deo, quia dicit **esto consentiens**: licet enim Deus sit cum omni homine, tamen non omnis homo cum Deo. Unde Augustinus dicit quod intelligitur de verbo Dei et lege: quae lex adversatur nobis inquantum peccamus. Tamen Ieronimi et Crisostomi expositio est magis litteralis, qui dicunt **esto consentiens adversario adversario tuo cito dum es in via cum eo**, id est concorda cum homine qui te laesit vel quem tu laesisti, et hoc **cito**, Eccli. V: *ne tardes converti*; **in via**, id est in vita ista.

Consequenter assignat rationem ex inconvenientibus, quae sunt quatuor. Primum: *ne forte tradat te adversarius iudici*: hoc si de verbo Dei intelligatur, plana est littera. Iudex hic accipitur Christus, Io. V: *Pater omne iudicium dedit Filio*, Act. X: *hic est qui constitutus est a Deo iudex vivorum et mortuorum*. Unde sermo Dei tradit nos Christo inquantum accusat nos de peccato quod commisimus contra legem; unde *sermo quem locutus sum ille iudicabit eum in novissimo die* etc. Si autem intelligatur de homine, tunc **tradat** causaliter vel occasionaliter, quia discordia causa est ut iudici tradaris et ex ipso peccato efficeris reus iudici. Et dicit **forte** quia si moritur et tu remanseris in vita ista non auferetur tibi locus penitentiae quia superest Deus propter quem eum debebas diligere; tamen si adversarius esset facilius fit reconciliatio.

500. Sequitur secundum inconveniens **et iudex** etc. Hic minister, secundum Augustinum, est angelus bonus, Ps. *benedicite Domino omnes angeli* etc., *ministri* etc. Nec est dubium quod angeli cum Christo venient ad iudicium et erunt executores eorum quae ibi agentur, infra V: **cum venerit Filius**. Chrysostomus intelligit de angelo malo, quasi ut sit sub potestate diaboli. Sed numquid diabolus dicitur minister Dei? Dicendum quod dupliciter potest aliquis dici minister alicuius: quantum ad factum, id est quia facit voluntatem alterius, vel quantum ad intentionem. Et isto secundo modo non est minister diabolus, quia non servit propter iustitiam Dei, sed propter odium hominum quos punit. Unde primo modo tantum dicitur minister, et simile habetur Ier. XXVII: *omnia regna terrae dedi in manu Nabuchodonosor regis Babylonis serui mei* etc.

both together? Second, because if he dies, will he never have hope of forgiveness? Therefore it cannot be understood about a man. Nor about the devil: for God would not want this; by the fact that the first man agreed with him he fell into misery. Although certain people, according to Jerome, explain it about the devil, saying that we are in agreement with him when we keep the pact that we struck with him in baptism, as we said *I renounce Satan*. But this explanation is forced.

499. It is not about the flesh, nor about God, for he says: **be in agreement**: for although God is with every man, nevertheless, not every man is with God. Hence Augustine says that it is to be understood about God's words and law: which law is opposed to us when we sin. Nevertheless, the explanation of Jerome and Chrysostom is more literal, who say **be in agreement with your adversary**, i.e., agree with the man who has hurt you or whom you have hurt, and do this **quickly**, *delay not to be converted* (Sir 5:8); **on the way**, i.e., in this life.

Afterwards he assigns the reason from the things unfitting to this, which are four. First: **lest perhaps the adversary deliver you to the judge**: if this is understood about the word of God, the literal sense is plain. The judge here is taken for Christ: *the Father . . . has given all judgment to the Son* (John 5:22); and, *to testify that it is he who was appointed by God to be the judge of the living and of the dead* (Acts 10:42). Hence, the words of God hand us over to Christ inasmuch as they accuse us of the sin which we have committed against the law; hence *the word that I have spoken . . . will judge him in the last day* (John 12:48). But if it is understood as being about a man, then he **delivers** you over either for a reason or by chance, for discord is the reason that you would hand someone over to a judge and by this very sin you would become liable to the judge. And he says **perhaps** because if he dies and you remain in this life, the place of repentance will not be taken from you, since God is above all the reason you should love him; but if he were the adversary, reconciliation would happen more easily.

500. The second unfitting thing follows from **and the judge**. This minister, according to Augustine, is a good angel; *bless the Lord, all you his angels . . . ministers* (Ps 102:21). Nor is it doubtful that angels will come with Christ at the judgment and will be the agents of the things that are done there: **when the Son of man will come** (Matt 25:31). Chrysostom understands this as referring to a bad angel, as though it were to be under the power of the devil. But is the devil called a minister of God? It should be said that someone can be called minister of someone else in two ways: as to his deed, i.e., because he does the will of another, or as to his intent. And in this second way the devil is no minister of God, for he does not serve because of the justice of God, but because of his hatred of men whom he punishes. Hence minister is said only in the first way, the same as: *I have given all the kingdoms of the land to Nebuchadnezzar* (Jer 27:6).

Tertium inconveniens: *et in carcerem mittaris*. Hic de carcere inferni intelligitur, de quo Apoc. II: *diabolus missurus est ex vobis in carcerem ut temptemini* etc. Et dicitur carcer per similitudinem, quia illi qui sunt ibi habent libertatem arbitrii ligatam, inquantum sunt obstinati in malo. Tamen si intelligatur de bonis angelis sciendum quod bonus angelus interdum punit. Secundum Dyonisium nunquam tamen punit bonos sed malos sicut qui percussit exercitum Senacherib, IV Reg.

501. Quartum inconveniens: *amen dico tibi, non exies inde, donec reddas novissimum quadrantem*. Quadrans est quidam denarius minutus qui habet duo minuta sub se, et dicebatur quadrans quia erat quarta pars unius denarii magni. Vult ergo dicere Dominus *non exies donec* exsolvas penas et satisfacias pro minimis peccatis, etiam venalibus. Unde accipitur similitudo quadrantis propter parvitatem. Vel, secundum Augustinum, metaphora potest accipi etiam secundum numerum, non tantum secundum quantitatem. Unde potest significare peccata quae committuntur amore terrenorum; et terra est quartum elementum.

502. Sed quare dixit *non exies donec*: ergo contingit exire. Dicendum quod ly *donec* quandoque designat finitum tempus, quandoque infinitum, sicut illud *oportet autem illum regnari donec ponat omnes inimicos sub pedibus eius* etc., Cor. iii . Numquid ergo postea regnare desinet? Absit. Unde ibi ponitur infinite: et sic hic *non exies donec*, id est nunquam exibit quia nunquam reddet novissimum quadrantem. Et quare Hilarius exponit: nullum enim peccatum dimittitur nisi per caritatem, Prov. *universa delicta operit caritas*, ergo qui decedit cum discordia decedit sine caritate, et ita nunquam purgabitur a peccatis. Et nota in hoc quod inferno aeternaliter puniuntur non solum pro peccatis mortalibus sed etiam venalibus, dummodo non sint dimissa prius quando sint in caritate. Et hoc est *non exies inde*.

503. Propter istam difficultatem de ly *donec*, ponuntur aliae expositiones. Unde *in carcere*, id est in carcere praesentis tribulationis, Apoc. II: *ecce diabolus missurus est ex vobis in carcerem, ut temptemini et habebitis tribulationem diebus decem*. Quondam Deus aliquem in praesenti punit pro peccatis non relaxat nisi totaliter purgetur. Chrysostomus cum dicit quod totum potest exponi pro praesenti vita. Unde dicit *esto consentiens*, tam cito quia non solum propter hoc imminet poena aeterna, sed etiam damnum temporale. Unde *ne forte*, ad litteram. Et dicit *forte* quia non semper contingit hoc, quia licet Evangelica promissa sint de bonis aeternis, tamen quandoque Dominus ponit promissa temporalia et poenas aeternas: et hoc est *amen dico tibi* etc.

The third unfitting thing is found at *and you be cast into prison*. Here the prison of hell is understood, about which is written: *the devil will cast some of you into prison, that you may be tried* (Rev 2:10). And it is called a prison by similitude because those who are there have their free will bound, by the fact that they are obstinate in evil. Nevertheless, if it were understood as referring to good angels it should be known that a good angel does punish sometimes. But according to Dionysius it never punishes the good but only the bad, like the one who struck the army of Sennacherib (2 Kgs 18).

501. The fourth unfitting thing is this: *amen I say to you . . . the last farthing*. A farthing is even less than a denarius which has two lesser coins below it, and it was called a 'quadrans' because it was the fourth part of one large denarius. Therefore the Lord means *you will not go out from there until* you pay the price and you satisfy for your least sins, even the venial ones. Hence comparison is made with a farthing because of its smallness. Or, according to Augustine, the metaphor can be taken also according to number, not only quantity. Hence it can signify sins that are committed from love of earthly things; and earth is the fourth element.

502. But why did he say *you will not go out from there until*: therefore, it is possible to get out. It should be said that the *until* sometimes designates a limited time, sometimes an unlimited one, as in, *he must reign until he has put all his enemies under his feet* (1 Cor 15:25). Afterward, then, will he cease to reign? Not at all. Hence what is said there is unlimited: and so also this *you will not go out from there until*, i.e., he will never get out, for he will never repay the last penny. And Hilary explains why: for no one is forgiven of sin except by charity: *charity covers all sins* (Prov 10:12). Therefore, whoever dies with discord dies without charity, and thus he will never be purged from sins. And note in this that they are punished in hell eternally not only for mortal sins but even for venial ones, (provided that they were not forgiven before when they were in charity). And this is *you will not get out from there*.

503. Because of this difficulty about the *until*, other explanations are suggested. Hence *into prison*, that is, the prison of these present tribulations: *behold, the devil will cast some of you into prison, that you may be tried, and you will have tribulation ten days* (Rev 2:10). Once God punishes someone in the present for sins he does not relax until he is totally purged. But Chrysostom says that the whole can be explained as the present life. Hence he says *be in agreement* as quickly as possible, since not only eternal punishment looms, but even temporal damages. Hence, *lest perhaps the adversary deliver you to the judge*, literally. And he says *perhaps* because it does not always happen this way, for although the Gospel promises are about eternal goods, nevertheless sometimes the Lord makes temporal promises and eternal penalties: and this is *amen I say to you*.

Lecture 8

5:27 Audistis quia dictum est antiquis: *non moechaberis*. [n. 504]

5:27 Ἠκούσατε ὅτι ἐρρέθη· οὐ μοιχεύσεις.

5:27 You have heard that it was said to them of old: *do not commit adultery*. [n. 504]

5:28 Ego autem dico vobis, quia omnis qui viderit mulierem ad concupiscendum eam, iam moechatus est eam in corde suo. [n. 506]

5:28 ἐγὼ δὲ λέγω ὑμῖν ὅτι πᾶς ὁ βλέπων γυναῖκα πρὸς τὸ ἐπιθυμῆσαι αὐτὴν ἤδη ἐμοίχευσεν αὐτὴν ἐν τῇ καρδίᾳ αὐτοῦ.

5:28 But I say to you, that whoever will look on a woman to lust after her, has already committed adultery with her in his heart. [n. 506]

5:29 Quod si oculus tuus dexter scandalizat te, erue eum, et proiice abs te; expedit enim tibi ut pereat unum membrorum tuorum, quam totum corpus tuum mittatur in gehennam. [n. 508]

5:29 εἰ δὲ ὁ ὀφθαλμός σου ὁ δεξιὸς σκανδαλίζει σε, ἔξελε αὐτὸν καὶ βάλε ἀπὸ σοῦ· συμφέρει γάρ σοι ἵνα ἀπόληται ἓν τῶν μελῶν σου καὶ μὴ ὅλον τὸ σῶμά σου βληθῇ εἰς γέενναν.

5:29 And if your right eye scandalize you, pluck it out and cast it from you. For it is expedient for you that one of your members would perish, rather than that your whole body would be cast into hell. [n. 508]

5:30 Et si dextera manus tua scandalizat te, abscide eam, et proiice abs te; expedit enim tibi ut pereat unum membrorum tuorum, quam ut totum corpus tuum eat in gehennam. [n. 508]

5:30 καὶ εἰ ἡ δεξιά σου χεὶρ σκανδαλίζει σε, ἔκκοψον αὐτὴν καὶ βάλε ἀπὸ σοῦ· συμφέρει γάρ σοι ἵνα ἀπόληται ἓν τῶν μελῶν σου καὶ μὴ ὅλον τὸ σῶμά σου εἰς γέενναν ἀπέλθῃ.

5:30 And if your right hand scandalize you, cut it off, and cast it from you: for it is expedient for you that one of your members would perish, rather than that your whole body would be cast into hell. [n. 508]

---

504. *Audistis quia dictum est antiquis: 'non moechaberis.'* Supra Dominus adimplevit legem quantum ad praeceptum prohibitivum homicidii; nunc adimplet quantum ad praeceptum prohibitivum adulterii. Et circa hoc tria facit: primo ponit praeceptum; secundo adimpletionem; tertio docet qualiter observari possit. Secundum ibi *ego autem*; tertium ibi *si oculus tuus*. Et convenienter post praeceptum prohibitivum homicidii ponitur praeceptum prohibitivum adulterii, quia adulterium secundum locum tenet post homicidium. Homicidium enim est contra vitam hominis iam existentis; sed adulterium contra vitam hominis generandi: tollit enim certitudinem prolis et per consequens educationem eius.

'Non moechaberis'. 'Mechia' enim est proprie adulterium. Hoc praeceptum est Exo. XXII et Deut. V.

505. Et sciendum quod quia in praeceptis decalogi non prohibetur fornicatio simplex, sed solum adulterium, aliqui crediderunt quod fornicatio simplex non sit peccatum mortale quia non contrariatur legi cum non sit in praeceptis decalogi. Primum dicitur Levit. XIX: *homo si dormierit cum muliere coitu seminis* etc. *Vapulabunt ambo et non morientur* etc., Ergo fornicatio simplex peccatum est veniale; praeterea *omne peccatum iniquitas*; sed qui committit simplicem fornicationem nulli facit iniquitatem: non sibi quia adimplet voluntatem suam, non alteri, non Deo quia non est directe contra eum sicut blasphemia et idolatria et huiusmodi. Ergo non est mortale.

504. *You have heard that it was said: 'do not commit adultery.'* Above the Lord fulfilled the law as to the precept prohibiting homicide; now he fulfills it as to the precept prohibiting adultery. And concerning this he does three things: first, he lays down the precept; second, the fulfillment; third, he teaches how it could be observed. The second is at *but I say to you*, the third at *if your right eye*. And fittingly after the precept prohibiting homicide, the precept prohibiting adultery is discussed, because adultery holds second place after homicide. For homicide is against the life of man already existing; but adultery is against the life of a man to be generated: for it destroys certainty about children and as a result, their education.

'Do not commit adultery.' 'Moechia' is properly adultery. This precept is from Exodus and Deuteronomy (Exod 22; Deut 5).

505. And it should be known that since simple fornication is not prohibited in the precepts of the decalogue, but only adultery, some people believed that simple fornication was not a mortal sin, since it was not against the law if it was not in the precepts of the decalogue. First, it is said in Leviticus: *if a man carnally lie with a woman* (Lev 19:20). Therefore simple fornication is a venial sin; further, *all iniquity is sin* (1 John 5:17). But whoever commits simple fornication does iniquity to no one: not himself, for he fulfills his own will; not another; not God, for it is not directly against him like blasphemy and idolatry and that kind of thing. Therefore, it is not mortal.

506. Dicendum quod certissimum debet esse apud fideles quod omnis simplex fornicatio est peccatum mortale, et breviter omnis usus membrorum genitalium praeter usum matrimonii, Hebr. ult. *fornicatores et adulteros iudicabit Deus* etc.; et dedit seorsum quia sicut adulteros ita et fornicatores *iudicabit*, Thob. IV: *attende tibi ab omni fornicatione* etc., et Deut. XXII: *non est meretrix de filiabus Israel.* Patet ergo per auctoritates Veteris et Novi Testamenti quod est peccatum mortale. Et ratio huius est quia matrimonium est naturale, non solum secundum fidem nostram, sed etiam secundum gentiles, quia naturale est quod homo matrimonialiter coniungatur non cuique indeterminatae sed uni et determinatae. Nec refert quacumque celebritate fiat, quantum ad intentionem nature, quid autem sit de lege naturali pervertitur in hiis quae carent ratione. Coniunctio enim maris et feminae ordinatur ad generationem et educationem. In aliquibus animalibus sola femella sufficit ad educationem, et in talibus pater nunquam intromittit se de educatione filiorum; et ideo non est certitudo prolis, et propterea indifferenter commiscetur cuicumque, sicut patet in canibus. In aliis autem videmus quod in quibuscumque femella non sufficit ad educationem prolis quod ibi commanent mas et femina usque ad prolis educationem. Ergo patet quod cum coniunctio sit propter educationem omnis coniunctio ex qua non sequitur debita educatio est contra naturam. Cum ergo natus indigeat multa cura patris, oportet quod habeat homo determinatam feminam: et hoc est matrimonium. Utrum autem habeat plures, de hoc est alia quaestio. Erit ergo fornicatio sic contra istam educationem: ergo est contra naturam et peccatum mortale. Moyses autem Iudaeis loquebatur sicut magister rudibus auditoribus propositiones manifestissimas: decalogus est initia legis, et ideo non expressit ibi nisi ea quae erant manifesta. Unde aliqui dicunt quod Deus locutus est per se ipsum decalogum, omnia alia reservavit aliis explicanda. Unde in hoc '*non mechaberis*' intelligitur omne peccatum quod est per usum membrorum genitalium praeter matrimonium. Item peccat contra se, Cor. vi: *qui fornicatur in corpus suum peccat* quia actus huiusmodi non debet esse nisi propter generationem alterius. Item in lege quadam peccata non puniebantur per mortem sicut furtum et multa alia: ergo non valet illud quod obicitur de Exo. Patet ergo quod fornicatio est mortale.

Ego autem. Hic Dominus adimplet legem. Pharisaei enim et scribe hoc '*non mechaberis*' intelligebant solum quantum ad actus. Dominus autem prohibet etiam concupiscentiam. Sed obiicit hic Augustinus quod praeceptum decalogi est *uxorem proximi tui non concupisces, non domum, non agrum, non servum, non ancillam* etc.

506. It should be said that it must be absolutely certain among the faithful that every act of simple fornication is a mortal sin, as is basically any use of the genital organs outside of the marital use, *for fornicators and adulterers God will judge* (Heb 13:4); and he gave it separately because he *will judge* fornicators just as adulterers: *take heed to keep yourself . . . from all fornication* (Tob 4:13), and, *there will be no prostitute among the daughters of Israel* (Deut 22:17). Therefore it is clear by the authorities of the Old and New Testaments that it is a mortal sin. And the reason for this is that marriage is a natural thing, not only according to our faith, but even according to the gentiles, for it is natural that a man should be matrimonially joined not to any women indiscriminately, but to one particular woman. Nor does it matter what may be done by any multitude, as far as the intention of nature goes, but what is of natural law is perverted among those who lack reason. For the union of male and female is ordered to generation and education. In other animals the female alone suffices for education, and among such animals the father never involves himself in the education of the children; and thus there is no certainty about the children, and afterward he mingles indiscriminately with any female, as is seen among dogs. But among others we see that wherever the female does not suffice for the education of the children, the male and female remain together throughout the education of the children. Therefore it is clear that since the union is for the sake of the education, every union from which the due education does not follow is against nature. Therefore, since the child born needs much care from the father, it is necessary that a man have a particular woman: and this is marriage. But whether he may have several wives is another question. Fornication therefore will be against that education in the same way: therefore it is against nature and a mortal sin. But Moses spoke the most obvious notions to the Jews as a teacher to a primitive audience: the decalogue is the beginning of a law, and thus it only expresses those things that are most obvious. Hence some say that God himself spoke the decalogue, but he reserved all other things to be explained by others. Hence in this '*do not commit adultery*' is understood every sin that there is by the use of those organs outside marriage. Likewise he sins against himself: *whoever fornicates sins against his own body* (1 Cor 6:18), because such an act should not be except for the generation of another. Likewise, in the law sins such as theft and many others were not punished by death: therefore this objection about Exodus does not hold. Therefore it is clear that fornication is mortal.

I say to you. Here the Lord brings the law to fulfillment. For the Pharisees and scribes understood '*do not commit adultery*' only as to the act. But the Lord prohibits also the desire. But Augustine objects here that a precept of the decalogue is *you shall not covet your neighbor's wife, nor his house, nor his field, nor his manservant, nor his maidservant.*

Ergo Dominus non adimplevit. Et respondet quod intelligit *non concupisces* ad auferendum; unde simul ponit non concupisces uxorem et ancillam .

507. Et nota quod non dicit *qui videt et concupiscit,* sed *qui viderit ad concupiscendum.* Et exponitur dupliciter. Primo sic: *qui viderit ad concupiscendum,* id est ut concupiscat, ut ponatur concomitatem. Et est duplex concupiscentia: una quae est propassio, alia quae est passio. Propassio appellatur quasi imperfecta passio, quando motus sistit in solo appetitu sensibili non ratione consentiente. Passio est quando ratio consentit, et tunc est peccatum mortale. Et ideo dicit **iam mechatus est eam in corde**, quia Deus inspector est cordium, et talis non dimittit actum nisi propter impedimentum.

Vel ly *ad*, secundum Augustinum, importat finem, id est *qui viderit ad concupiscendum*, id est eo fine ut concupiscat. Sed regula est quod quicquid homo facit sub fine peccati mortalis, totum mortale, et quicquid propter finem meritorium, totum meritorium; sicut patet de illo qui vadit ad ecclesiam vel ad furandum: quicquid interim fiat totum est vel meritorium vel peccatum. Est autem duplex consensus: unus in actu, sicut quando ratio praecedit intantum quod vult committere adulterium; alius in delectatione, sicut quando excitat sibi delectationes turpes ut delectetur, quamvis non consentiat. Primo modo est mortale, quando respicit propter hunc finem ut delectetur, et ideo consentit. **Iam mechatus in corde**, quantum ad Deum, Io. XXI: *pepigi fedus cum oculis meis ut ne cogitarem quidem de virgine*, Eccli. IX: *virginem ne respicias ne forte scandalizeris in decore illius.* Chrysostomus etiam dicit quod mulieres quae se parant ad hoc quod concupiscantur peccant mortaliter, Exo. XXI: *si aliquis aperuerit cisternam et foderit et non cooperuerit* etc. Et si nullus concupiscit eam, dicendum quod peccat mortaliter, sicut et ille qui parat venenum, quamvis non sumatur ab illo cui paratur, tamen parans peccat mortaliter quia quantum est in se eum occidit.

508. Quod si oculus. Hic ostendit Dominus quomodo istud praeceptum potest facilius observare, scilicet sic vitando occasiones peccati. Designantur autem per oculum et per manum quatuor. Primo oculus et manus corporalis, et sic intelligendum: **abscinde** corporaliter. Secundum Chrysostomum, hoc non potest stare, quia non est aliquod membrum quod non scandalizet, Ro. VII: *scio quod non habitat in me, hoc est in carne mea,*

Therefore the Lord did not fulfill it. And he answers that he understands *you shall not covet* to the point of carrying off; hence he mentions at the same time you shall not covet the wife or the slave-girl.

507. And note that he does not say *whoever sees and covets,* but **whoever will look on a woman to lust after her**. And it is explained in two ways. The first thus: **whoever will look on a woman to lust after her**, that is, so that he may covet her, as may be considered concomitance. And there are two kinds of concupiscence: one which is a propassion and the other which is a passion. A propassion is called an incomplete passion, as it were, when the movement remains in the sensible appetite alone, without the reason consenting. A passion is when reason consents, and then it is a mortal sin. And thus he says **he has already committed adultery with her in his heart**, for God is the searcher of hearts, and such a person does not refrain from the act except because of some obstacle to it.

Or the **to lust after her**, according to Augustine, conveys purpose, i.e., **whoever will look on a woman to lust**, i.e., for the purpose of lusting after her. But the rule is that whatever a man does for the purpose of mortal sin, is completely mortal, and whatever he does for a meritorious purpose is completely meritorious; as is clear in the case of someone who goes to the church, or who goes to steal: regardless of what is done at the same time, the whole is either meritorious or a sin. But there are two kinds of consent: one consents to the act, as when reason goes first, insomuch that one wills to commit adultery; the other consent is to the pleasure, as when someone excites in himself base sensual pleasures so that he might enjoy them, although he does not consent to the act. The first way is mortal, when someone looks on a woman for the purpose of sensual pleasure, and thus he consents. **He has already committed adultery in his heart**, before God: *I made a covenant with my eyes that I would not . . . think on a virgin* (Job 31:1); *gaze not upon a maiden, lest her beauty be a stumbling block to you* (Sir 9:5). Chrysostom says also that women who adorn themselves in order to be lusted after sin mortally: *if someone opens a pit or digs a pit and does not cover it, and an ox or ass should fall in, the owner of the pit shall pay the price* (Exod 21:33). And if no one lusts after her, it must be said that she sins mortally, like a person who prepares poison, even if it were not consumed by the one it was intended for, still, the person preparing it sins mortally because he did what he could to kill him.

508. And if your right eye. Here the Lord shows how this precept can be more easily observed, namely by avoiding the occasions of sin. But four things are represented by the eyes and by the hands. The first is the physical eye and hand, and it may be understood thus: **cut it off** physically. According to Chrysostom, this reading cannot stand, for there is no member that does not scandalize: *for I know that there does not dwell in me, that is, in my flesh, that which is*

bonum. Unde omnia membra oporteret abscindere: ergo non est hic sensus. Vel aliter. Corpus enim dicitur occidi dupliciter: quantum ad vitam naturae et culpae, Ro. VI: *ut destruatur corpus peccati ut ultra non serviamus peccato,* et sic abscide peccato. Sed tunc sinister non esset innocens: ergo non est hic sensus.

509. Dicendum ergo quod per oculum aliquando intelligitur proximus qui tui est in auxilium: officium enim oculi est ut te in via dirigat. Unde consiliator tuus in rebus mundanis est oculus sinister, in divinis dexter. Officium manus est quod adiuvet te. Unde proximus qui facit negotia in temporalibus, manus sinistra; in spiritualibus dextra, Iob XXIX *oculus fui caeco et pes claudo.* Ergo secundum hunc sensum intelligendo dupliciter oculus vel manus scandalizat, quia si consiliarius aliquis in rebus mundanis vel divinis scandalizat te, **abscide.** Non facit mentionem de sinistro quia si dexter debet, abscidi, multo magis **abscide** etc. Vel aliter. Dominus vult quod non solum in te sed etiam in familiam serves puritatem. Unde si aliquis immunde vivat, **abscide** etc., Ps. *non habitabit in medio domus meae qui facit superbiam.*

Vel possumus oculum vel manum intelligere interioris hominis, Cor. V: *licet is qui foris est noster homo corrumpitur, tamen is qui intus est renovatur de die in diem,* quia sicut exterior ita et interior, Eph. I: *det vobis illuminatos oculos cordis vestri.* Dicitur autem ibi manus vis motiva, oculus intellectiva. Et secundum hoc potest exponi dupliciter. Primo sic: ex hoc quod oculus qui est in parte intellectiva quae habet liberum arbitrium et est in dextra, exterior in sinistra, non dicit Dominus quod abscidas sinistram quia non est in potestate liberi arbitrii quod exteriora membra non moveantur, sed quod interiora non male moveantur et respiciant. Dicit ergo *si oculus tuus scandalizat* ad male cogitandum, remove hunc intellectum; item si mala voluntas, remove eam.

510. Vel aliter, oculus designat bonam intentionem, manus bonam voluntatem. Si ex istis sequatur scandalum vel occasio concupiscentiae, remove etc.; sicut si habet bonam voluntatem visitandi pauperes mulieres, si ex ista sequatur occasio concupiscentiae, **abscide** etc.

Quarto per oculum potest significari vita contemplativa, per manus activa. Ista aliquando scandalizant quia aliquando ex contemplatione nimia incurritur error. Item aliquis quia non est apostolus non implet opus contemplationis, sed degenerat in pigritiam, Tren. I: *viderunt eam hostes et deriserunt sabbata eius:* **abscide** ergo, et vade ad exercitium operis. Vel in vita activa aliquando

good (Rom 7:18). Hence all members would have to be cut off: and therefore this is not the meaning of the verse. Or another reading. For the body is said to be killed in two ways: as to the life of nature and as to the life of guilt: *that the body of sin may be destroyed, to the end that we may serve sin no longer* (Rom 6:6), and so cut away sin. But then the left eye would not be innocent: therefore this is not the meaning.

509. Therefore it should be said that by the eye is sometimes meant a neighbor who has come to help: for the role of the eye is to direct your path. Hence your counselor in ordinary things is your left eye, and in divine things it is your right eye. The role of the hand is to help you. Hence the neighbor who manages temporal affairs is your left hand; the one who manages spiritual matters is your right: *I was an eye to the blind, and a foot to the lame* (Job 29:15). Therefore according to this reading, the eye and hand scandalizing can be understood in two ways, as when a certain counselor in everyday or divine matters scandalizes you. He makes no mention of the left eye because if the right eye must be cut off, the left eye must be even more. Or another way. The Lord wills that not only in you but also in your family you preserve purity. Hence if someone unclean lives with you, **cut** him **off:** *he who works pride will not dwell in the midst of my house* (Ps 101:7).

Or we can understand the eye or the hand of man's inner self: *for which cause we do not faint, but though our outward man is corrupted, yet the inward man is renewed day by day* (2 Cor 4:16), for as the exterior is, so is the interior: *that the eyes of your heart enlightened* (Eph 1:18). But it is said there that a hand is a power of moving, an eye is an intellective power. And according to this it can be explained in two ways. The first like this: by the fact that the eye which is in the intellective part, which has free will, is also in the right, the exterior is in the left, the Lord does not say that you should cut off the left because it is not in the power of free will that the external members do not move themselves, but that the internal members do not move themselves badly and look about wickedly. Therefore he says *if your right eye scandalizes you* by wicked thinking, remove this understanding; likewise, if there is a bad will, remove it.

510. Or another way, the eye represents good intentions, the hand a good will. If scandal or an occasion of lust results from these things, remove them; just as if someone has a good will when visiting poor women, if the occasion of lust follows from it, **pluck it out.**

Fourth, by the eye can be signified the contemplative life, and by the hand, the active life. Sometimes these things scandalize because sometimes error is met with in extreme contemplation. Likewise, someone, because he is not an apostle, may not fill the work of contemplation, but degenerate into laziness: *the enemies have seen her and have mocked at her sabbaths* (Lam 1:7). Therefore, **pluck it out,** and go to the practice of work. Or sometimes in the active

efficiuntur inquieti et incurrunt occasiones peccati: unde transeundum ad alium statum.

511. Primus ergo modus excludendus est; secundus de proximo, tertius de homine interiori, quartus de vita activa et contemplativa faciunt ad expositionem: *expedit enim tibi* etc., et quintus de bono respectu et bona operatione.

life someone becomes restless and falls into occasions of sin: wherefore, he should cross over into the other state.

511. Therefore the first way is to be excluded; the second, about one's neighbor, the third, about the interior man, and the fourth, about the active and contemplative life, make an explanation of *for it is expedient for you that one of your members would perish*; and the fifth concerns good consideration and good action.

Lecture 9

5:31 Dictum est autem: *quicumque dimiserit uxorem suam, det ei libellum repudii.* [n. 512]

5:32 Ego autem dico vobis, quia omnis qui dimiserit uxorem suam, excepta fornicationis causa, facit eam moechari; et qui dimissam duxerit, adulterat. [n. 515]

5:31 Ἐρρέθη δέ· ὃς ἂν ἀπολύσῃ τὴν γυναῖκα αὐτοῦ, δότω αὐτῇ ἀποστάσιον.

5:32 ἐγὼ δὲ λέγω ὑμῖν ὅτι πᾶς ὁ ἀπολύων τὴν γυναῖκα αὐτοῦ παρεκτὸς λόγου πορνείας ποιεῖ αὐτὴν μοιχευθῆναι, καὶ ὃς ἐὰν ἀπολελυμένην γαμήσῃ, μοιχᾶται.

5:31 It has been said: *whoever will put away his wife, let him give her a bill of divorce.* [n. 512]

5:32 But I say to you, that whoever will put away his wife, except for the cause of fornication, makes her commit adultery: and he who will marry her who is put away, commits adultery. [n. 515]

---

512. *Dictum est autem: 'quicumque dimiserit uxorem suam, det illi libellum repudii.'* Postquam Dominus adimplevit praecepta legis prohibitiva, nunc adimplet praecepta legis permissiva.

Et dividitur pars ista in partes duas:

primo adimplet legem quantum ad praecepta permissiva quae pertinent ad Deum;

secundo quantum ad praecepta quae pertinent ad proximum, ibi *audistis quia dictum est: 'oculum pro oculo.'*

Prima in duas: primo adimplet praeceptum permissivum de libello repudii;

secundo de iuramento, ibi *audistis quia dictum est antiquis: 'non periurabis.'*

513. Quantum ad primum duo facit:

primo ponit verba legis;

secunda ipsorum adimpletionem: *ego autem dico vobis quia omnis* etc.

514. Dicitur ergo *dictum est* etc.: Deut. XXIV. Quaestio. Si *'dimiserit uxorem suam det illi libellum repudii':* hoc est praeceptum. Sed dimittere est permissio: Moyses enim permisit, non praecepit. Est autem multiplex permissio, scilicet concessionis, quando licita conceduntur, ut monacho conceditur visitare patrem ab abbate; dispensationis, quando non licita fiunt licita per dispensationem, ut cum aliis dispensative permittitur monachum comedere carnes; indulgentiae, quando permittitur aliquid licitum cuius oppositum melius est, ut permissio Apostoli de secundis nuptiis, et tamen melior est continentia vidualis: et secundum hoc solvas quod hic dicit Glossa, scilicet quod apostoli praeceperunt secundas nuptias, id est indulserunt, vel praeceptum est nisi velis continere: alias non obliget ut praeceptum; sustinentiae, sicut quando Deus permittit mala aliqua fieri, licet ex eis semper aliquod bonum eliciat; tolerantiae, quando aliquod malum toleratur ne peius fiat, sicut hic.

512. *It has been said: 'whoever will put away his wife, let him give her a bill of divorce.'* After the Lord has fulfilled the prohibitive precepts of the law, now he fulfills the permissive precepts of the law.

And this part is divided into two parts:

first, he fulfills the law as to the permissive precepts which pertain to God;

second, as to the precepts that pertain to one's neighbor, at *you have heard that it is said: 'an eye for an eye'* (Matt 5:38).

The first is in two parts: first, he fulfills the permissive precept concerning the bill of divorce;

second, concerning swearing, at *you have heard it said to them of old: 'you shall not forswear yourself'* (Matt 5:33).

513. As to the first he does two things:

first, he sets down the words of the law;

second, their fulfillment: *but I say to you, that whoever will put away his wife.*

514. Therefore he says *it has been said*: (Deut 24:1). A question. If *'whoever will put away his wife, let him give her a bill of divorce'*: this is commanded. But to put away one's wife is a permission: for Moses permitted, he did not command. But there are many kinds of permission, namely: a concession, when permitted things are conceded, as when a monk is allowed to leave the abbey to visit his father; a dispensation, when things that are not permitted become permitted by dispensation, as when it is permitted dispensatively for a monk to eat meat when he is with others; an indulgence, when something permissible, whose opposite is better, is allowed, like the Apostle's permission for second marriages, even though the continence of the widowed is a better thing: and according to this you resolve what the Gloss says here, namely that the apostles commanded second marriages, i.e., they allowed them by way of indulgence, or it was commanded unless you were willing to remain continent: otherwise it would not oblige like a precept. Then there is a forbearance, as when God permits certain evils to happen, although he always draws some good out of them; and a tolerance, when some evil is tolerated lest something worse happen, as here.

'*Quicumque dimiserit uxorem suam*'. Numquid inseparabilitas matrimonii est de lege naturae? Sed numquid per dispensationem est quod in lege Moysi fuit hic '*det illi libellum repudii*' in quo causae repudii scribuntur, secundum Iosephum; vel secundum Augustinum: ideo scribebatur ut mora interveniente et consilio scribarum dissuadente vir a proposito repudiandi desisteret. Secundum Ieronimum super hoc, causa autem permissionis repudiandi uxorem fuit vitatio uxoricidii.

515. Sed numquid repudiatae licebat nubere? *Ego autem dico: facit eam mechari*. Sed est quaestio. Numquid propter fornicationem licet viro uxorem dimittere? Et videtur quia non est malum pro malo reddendum. Dicendum quod Dominus concessit dimittere uxorem propter fornicationem in penam illius qui fidem fregit. Sed numquid tenetur ad hoc ex praecepto? Dicendum quod dimissio uxoris fornicantis introducta est ad corrigendum uxoris crimen. Sed numquid proprio iudicio potest eam dimittere? *Et qui dimissam duxerit adulterat*, quia vir adveniens supra matrimonium.

'*Whoever will put away his wife*'. Is the indissolubility of marriage not from natural law? But it is in the law of Moses by dispensation that here '*let him give her a bill of divorce*' in which the reasons for the divorce are recorded, according to Josephus. Or, according to Augustine: it was written down like this so that there would be an intervening delay, and on the advice of the scribes dissuading him, the man might cease his divorce proceedings. But according to Jerome on this subject, the reason for permitting the divorce of one's wife was to avoid uxoricide.

515. But was the divorced wife allowed to marry? *But I say to you . . . makes her commit adultery*. But it is a question. Was it not permitted for a husband to put away his wife on account of fornication? And it seems that evil should not be rendered for evil. It must be said that the Lord conceded divorcing one's wife for fornication as a penalty to the one who broke faith. But is he bound to this by the precept? It must be said that putting away one's fornicating wife was introduced for the correction of the wife's crime. But can someone put her away by his own judgment? *He who will marry her who is put away, commits adultery*, for the man is intruding on an existing marriage.

Lecture 10

5:33 Iterum audistis quia dictum est antiquis: *non periurabis, reddes autem Domino iuramenta tua.* [n. 516]

5:34 Ego autem dico vobis, non iurare omnino: neque per caelum, quia thronus Dei est; [n. 518]

5:35 neque per terram, quia scabellum est pedum eius; neque per Ierosolymam, quia civitas est magni regis. [n. 520]

5:36 Neque per caput iuraveris, quia non potes unum capillum album facere, aut nigrum. [n. 522]

5:37 Sit autem sermo vester: est, est; non, non; quod autem his abundantius est, a malo est. [n. 523]

5:33 Πάλιν ἠκούσατε ὅτι ἐρρέθη τοῖς ἀρχαίοις· οὐκ ἐπιορκήσεις, ἀποδώσεις δὲ τῷ κυρίῳ τοὺς ὅρκους σου.

5:34 ἐγὼ δὲ λέγω ὑμῖν μὴ ὀμόσαι ὅλως· μήτε ἐν τῷ οὐρανῷ, ὅτι θρόνος ἐστὶν τοῦ θεοῦ,

5:35 μήτε ἐν τῇ γῇ, ὅτι ὑποπόδιόν ἐστιν τῶν ποδῶν αὐτοῦ, μήτε εἰς Ἱεροσόλυμα, ὅτι πόλις ἐστὶν τοῦ μεγάλου βασιλέως,

5:36 μήτε ἐν τῇ κεφαλῇ σου ὀμόσῃς, ὅτι οὐ δύνασαι μίαν τρίχα λευκὴν ποιῆσαι ἢ μέλαιναν.

5:37 ἔστω δὲ ὁ λόγος ὑμῶν ναὶ ναί, οὒ οὔ· τὸ δὲ περισσὸν τούτων ἐκ τοῦ πονηροῦ ἐστιν.

5:33 You have heard it said to them of old: *you shall not forswear yourself: but you shall perform your oaths to the Lord.* [n. 516]

5:34 But I say to you not to swear at all, neither by heaven, for it is the throne of God: [n. 518]

5:35 nor by the earth, for it is his footstool: nor by Jerusalem, for it is the city of the great king: [n. 520]

5:36 neither shall you swear by your head, because you cannot make one hair white or black. [n. 522]

5:37 But let your speech be yes, yes: no, no: and that which is over and above these, is of evil. [n. 523]

---

516. *Audistis quia dictum est antiquis: 'non periurabis.'* Supra Dominus adimplevit unum praeceptum permissivum, scilicet de libello repudii; hic adimplet aliud permissivum, scilicet de iuramento.

Et circa hoc tria facit:
primo enim ponit verba legis;
secundo adimplet;
tertio quaestioni respondet.
Secundum ibi **ego autem**;
tertium ibi **sit sermo**.

517. Est autem considerandum quod in verbis legis duo continebantur, quorum unum erat simpliciter prohibitivum, aliud permissivum. Prohibitivum: periurium, et hoc est **audistis** etc., Levit. XIX, et quasi in eumdem sensum Exo. XXX: *non assumes nomen Domini Dei tui in vanum* etc. Permissivum: **'reddes Domino'**, id est quando contigerit te iurare non per creaturas iurabis sed per Deum, Deut. V: *Dominum Deum tuum timebis et ipsi servies ac per nomen illius iurabit.* Et secundum hoc videtur quod hoc sacramentum, scilicet iurare per Deum, non est peccatum, sed quod permiserit lex hoc quia Iudaei proni erant ad idolatriam, non tamquam liceret, sed ut vitaretur peius, scilicet idolatria.

Sed constat autem quod reverentiam exhibere Deo secundum se bonum est; iurare per Deum est reverentiam exhibere Deo, quia in Glossa dicitur *unusquisque* etc., et Hebr. *homines enim per maiorem sui iurant.* Ergo iurare per Deum secundum se bonum est. Praeterea

---

516. *You have heard it said to them of old: 'you shall not forswear yourself.'* Above the Lord gave the fulfillment of one permissive precept, namely, about the bill of divorce. Here he fulfills another permissive precept, namely, about swearing.

And concerning this he does three things:
first, he sets down the words of the law;
second, he gives their fulfillment;
third, he answers a question.
The second is at **but I say to you**;
the third, at **but let your speech be**.

517. But it must be considered that there are two things contained in the words of the law, one of which was simply prohibitive, the other permissive. The prohibitive one: perjury, and this is **you have heard**, at, *you shall not swear falsely* (Lev 19:12), and almost the same meaning at: *you shall not take the name of the Lord your God in vain* (Exod 20:7). The permissive one: **'perform your oaths to the Lord'**, that is when it happens that you swear, you will swear not by creatures but by God, *you shall fear the Lord your God, and shall serve him only and you shall swear by his name* (Deut 6:13). And according to this it seems that this sacrament, namely, to swear by God, is not a sin, but rather the law permitted it because Jews were prone to idolatry, not as if it were licit, but that the worse thing might be avoided, namely, idolatry.

But it is clear that it is in itself a good thing to show reverence to God; to swear by God is to show reverence to God. And this is clear because in the Gloss it is said *each one*, and, *for men swear by one greater than themselves* (Heb 6:16): therefore, to swear by God is a good thing in

iurare per Deum est testem Deum invocare; sed hoc secundum se bonum est: ergo iurare per se bonum est.

518. Et sciendum quod iurare secundum se non est aliquid ordinatum, immo in se importat inordinationem. Nihil est aliud iurare per Deum quam invocare Deum testem super dicto humano. Hoc autem contingit dupliciter. Aut quia inducitur divinum testimonium ad confirmandum dictum humanum tantum: et hoc non est malum; aut quia expetitur divinum iudicium, quasi: si non ita est, condemnetur a Deo. In factis autem hominum nihil ita est fragile sicut verbum, Iac. III: *si quis in verbo non offendit, hic perfectus est vir.* Unde invocare testem Deum in hoc in quo homo est ita fragilis, hoc est contemnere iudicium Dei, Eccli. XXIII: *vir multum iurans implebitur iniquitate.*

Dominus autem consequenter hic adimplet. Unde **ego autem dico vobis nolite** etc. Ergo iuramentum secundum se est illicitum. Cum ergo iudices compellant homines iurare in causibus suis, videtur quod faciant contra praeceptum; et haec est opinio quorumdam haereticorum dicentium quod nulli iurare licet. Et respondet Ieronimus quod Dominus hic prohibet iurare per creaturas, et hoc propter Iudeos qui proni ad idolatriam: unde non simpliciter prohibet iuramentum. Sed haec non videtur bona expositio quia tunc Dominus nihil adderet verbis legis quae dicit *'reddes Domino iuramenta tua.'* Et ideo dicendum, secundum Augustinum, quod Dominus prohibet iurare per Deum et creaturas.

519. Sed tunc remanet duplex quaestio. Prima, quod Dominus noster destrueret legem quae dicit reddes Domino iuramenta tua; secunda, quia secundum hoc videtur quod iuramentum sit illicitum. Et respondet Augustinus quod sicut libellus repudii non fuit intentus a lege sed permissus propter crudelitatem Iudaeorum, et Dominus adimplevit; quia nullo modo voluit quod daretur similiter hic lex, mandavit quod non periurarent, sed si iurarent non per creaturas sed per Deum. Sed Dominus adimplet cum dicit **nolite** etc. Et sicut qui tacet nullo modo est mendax, ita qui nullo modo iurat magis removetur a periurio.

Ad illud quod dicitur quod iuramentum est illicitum dicendum, secundum Augustinum, quod idem Spiritus Sanctus est qui locutus est in Sacris Scripturis et qui operatus est in sanctis suis. Unde quis sit intellectus Scripturarum patet ex dictis sanctorum. Paulus motus est a Spiritu Sancto, et tamen iuravit dupliciter, quia et iuramento simplicis attestationis, Ro. I: *testis mihi est Deus*; et iuramento execrationis quod est quando quis impignorat salutem suam vel animam suam Deo, 1 Cor. *ego testem Deum invoco in animam meam.* Et si dicatur quod hoc non est iuramentum, hoc ridiculum est quia idem est per Deum et *in animam meam*, Cor.: *cotidie morior per gloriam vestram, frates, quam habeo in Christo Iesu*

itself. Furthermore, to swear by God is to invoke God as witness; but this is good in itself: therefore to swear by God is good in itself.

518. And it should be known that swearing in itself is not something ordered, but on the contrary carries disorder in itself. Swearing by God is nothing other than invoking God as witness to human speech. But this can happen two ways. For either divine testimony is brought in to confirm human speech alone, and this is not evil; or else divine judgment is demanded, as though to say: if it is not so, may he be damned by God. But among the deeds of men, nothing is so fragile as a word, *if any man offend not in word, the same is a perfect man* (Jas 3:2). Hence to invoke God as witness in something in which man is so fragile, is to condemn the judgment of God, *a man who swears much will be filled with iniquity* (Sir 23:12).

But the Lord fulfills this accordingly. Hence **but I say to you not to swear at all**. Therefore swearing in itself is illicit. Therefore since judges compel people to swear in court, it seems that they act against a precept; and this is the opinion of certain heretics who say that swearing is permitted to no one. And Jerome answers that the Lord here prohibits swearing by creatures, and this for the sake of the Jews who were prone to idolatry: hence he does not prohibit swearing simply. But this does not seem a good explanation, for then the Lord would add nothing to the words of the law which says *'perform your oaths to the Lord.'* And therefore it should be said, according to Augustine, that the Lord prohibits swearing by God and by creatures.

519. But then there remains a twofold question. First, that our Lord would have destroyed the law which says render your vows to the Lord; second, because according to this it seems that swearing is illicit. And Augustine answers that just as the bill of divorce was not intended by the law, but permitted on account of the cruelty of the Jews, and the Lord fulfilled it; because in no way did he will that the law be given the same way here, he commanded that they not forswear, but if they swore they should swear not by creatures but by God. But the Lord fulfills it when he says **not to swear**. And just as no one who keeps silence can lie, so also someone who never swears is most removed from perjury.

To the argument that swearing is illicit, it should be said, according to Augustine, that it is the same Holy Spirit who is spoken of in the holy Scriptures and who worked among the holy men. Hence whatever may be the understanding of the Scriptures is clear from the words of the holy men. Paul was moved by the Holy Spirit, and nevertheless he swore twice, for both in an oath of simple testimony: *for God is my witness* (Rom 1:9); and in an oath of imprecation, which is when someone pledges his salvation or his soul to God, *but I call God to witness upon my soul* (1 Cor 1:9). And if it is said that this is not an oath, this is ridiculous, for it is the same thing to swear by God and to swear *upon my soul*: *I die daily, I protest by your glory, brethren* (1 Cor 15:31); and

Domino nostro; et in graeco ly *per* intelligitur *iurante*. Ergo si Paulus iuravit videtur quod Dominus non intendat iuramentum prohibere, sed facilitatem iurandi. Et ostendit quod iuramentum non est secundum se appetendum immo non nisi propter necessitatem iurantis: et ideo dicit Augustinus quod Paulus nunquam iuravit nisi in scribendo quia non debet fieri nisi cum magna cautela et deliberatione et propter necessitatem nisi scilicet exposcit utilitas aliorum.

520. Sed posset dici quod iurare per Deum malum est, sed non per aliquid minus Deo. Et hoc Dominus excludit, unde **neque per caelum** etc. Iurare per creaturas potest esse vel idolatria vel absque idolatria. Si enim attribuatur iudicium rebus illis, scilicet exposcendo iudicium a creaturis, hoc est idolatrare, sicut antiqui qui dicebant caelum esse Deum. Alio modo potest sine peccato et idolatria dupliciter. Primum inquantum creatura impignoratur Deo exposcendo iudicium in ea, sicut quando homines iurant per caput suum. Secundo inquantum in aliqua creatura apparet aliqua evidentia divinae maiestatis, sicut si iuretur per caelum, eius virtus et potentia in caelo manifestatur. Unde hic ponit creaturas excellentes per quas aliquis posset iurare.

Et est ista excellentia in tribus manifesta, scilicet, duo elementa: caelum et terra, sub quibus continentur omnia alia sicut media inter extrema. Et quantum ad hoc dicit **neque per caelum**, Ps. ult. *caelum mihi sedes et terra scabellum pedum meorum* etc. Chrysostomus non dicit **neque per caelum** quia quoddam magnum corpus est, **neque per terram** quae mater est omnium, sed ostendit excellentiam istorum per comparationem ad Deum.

521. Sed numquid Deus habet membra, sicut et situm et huiusmodi? Unde dupliciter exponitur. Primo ad litteram. Illud enim dicitur sedes ubi aliquis requiescit, et ibi requiescit ubi perfecte stat. Quia igitur inter creaturas corporales caelum magis de divina bonitate participat et terra est minus, ideo caelum dicitur sedes, terra scabellum. Item homines consueverunt sedere ad iudicandum. Et quia Dominus per ea quae de caelo veniunt aliquando iudicat, Iob XXVI: *per haec iudicat populos*, scilicet per fulgura et huiusmodi, dicitur **caelum**.

Mystice autem per **caelum** intelliguntur sancti viri, quorum *conversatio est in caelis*, Phil. III, 20. In his Deus iudicat, Cor. II: *spiritualis iudicat omnia*; **terra**, peccatores, propter affectum terrenorum, Phil. III, 20: *qui terrena sapiunt* etc.; et super **scabellum**, quia si legem sub qua sunt non implent punientur.

522. In conversatione hominum ponit civitatem, et inter alias Ierusalem excellit quia ibi colebatur Deus: et

in Greek, the *by* is understood as *may I swear*. Therefore if Paul swore it seems that the Lord did not intend to prohibit swearing, but rather carelessness in swearing. And it shows that swearing is not in itself to be sought, but rather avoided except when necessary: and thus Augustine says that Paul never swore except in writing because it should not be done except with great caution and deliberation and out of necessity unless required for the benefit of others.

520. But it could be said that it is evil to swear by God, but not to swear by something less than God. And the Lord excludes this, hence **neither by heaven**. To swear by creatures can be either with idolatry or without idolatry. For if judgment is attributed to these things, namely by demanding judgment from created things, then that is idolatry, as with the ancients who said the sky was God. In another way it can be without sin or idolatry in two ways. First, inasmuch as a created thing is pledged to God by calling for judgment on it, as when men swear by their heads. Second, inasmuch as in any created thing there appears some evidence of divine majesty, as if it is sworn by the sky, his strength and power are manifest in the sky. Hence here he sets down more excellent created things by which someone could swear.

And this excellence is manifest in three things, namely, the two elements: heaven and earth, under which are contained all other things as middles between extremes. And as to the fact that he says **neither by heaven**: *heaven is my throne and earth my footstool* (Isa 66:1). Chrysostom: he does not say **neither by heaven** because it is some kind of large body, or **nor by the earth** which is mother of all things, but he shows their excellence by their relationship to God.

521. But does God have members and a position and that kind of thing? Hence this is explained in two ways. First, literally. For seat is said of that thing where someone rests, and he rests wherever he perfectly stands. For thus among corporeal created things the heaven participates more greatly in divine goodness and the earth less; thus heaven is called the seat, earth the footstool. Likewise men are accustomed to sitting at judgment. And **heaven** is said because the Lord sometimes judges by those things that come from heaven, *by these he judges people* (Job 36:31), namely by lightning and that sort of thing.

But mystically, by **heaven** holy men are understood, whose conversation is in heaven: *but our conversation is in heaven* (Phil 3:20). Through these God judges: *the spiritual man judges all things* (2 Cor 2:15). **Earth** represents sinners, because of their earthly affections, *who mind earthly things* (Phil 3:19); **footstool**, because if they do not fulfill the law that they are under, they will be punished.

522. For man's way of life, he sets the city, and among the other cities Jerusalem is preeminent because God is

hoc est *neque per Ierosolymam*, Ps. *gloriosa dicta sunt de te civitas Dei*, et *Ierusalem quae aedificatur ut civitas*.

Et in membris corporalibus. Sed quia posset dici quod non debemus iurare per ista maiora sed per minora, ideo dicit *neque per caput*. Quilibet enim potest facere de eo quod suum est quod vult; sed homo non habet potestatem super caput suum quantum ad minima; ergo non debet iurare per illud. Et hoc est *quia non potes capillum album facare aut nigrum*, secundum naturam scilicet, infra, VI, 27: nemo potest *adicere ad staturam suam cubitum unum*.

523. Sed posset dici: quomodo ergo loquemur? Respondet et primo satisfacit quaestioni, secundo ponit rationem. Dicit ergo sit autem sermo. Et potest tripliciter exponi. Primo sic. Si aliquis quaerat: estne hoc, *sit sermo vester*: est vel non. Secundo ut non aliud dicat os et aliud sentiat cor et aliud demonstret opus, Ps. *qui loquuntur pacem cum proximo suo, mala autem sunt in cordibus eorum* etc. Tertio sic, et est magis litteralis. *Sit sermo vester*: *vereque est, est, vereque non est, non est*; quasi dicat: dicatis unum simpliciter. Haec est enim definitio veri: omne quod est, et non esse quod non est. Et ista est Hilarii, II Cor. I, 19: *Christus Iesus non fuit est et non, sed est in illo fuit* etc.

524. *Quod autem* etc. Non dicit *malum est*, sed *a malo est*, non tuo sed ab alio, quia iurare corporis, cum tamen expediret illi credere; et sic Apostolus iuravit. Vel, secundum Chrysostomum, *quod autem his abundantius*, per hoc apparet quod in veteri lege unum iuramentum prohibitivum, scilicet periurare, aliud permisit, scilicet ex necessitate iurare; tertium iuramentum removet, scilicet superstitiosum, quod est quando reverentia exhibetur creaturae quae debetur creatori.

worshipped there; and this is **nor by Jerusalem**: *glorious things are said of you, O city of God* (Ps 87:3), and, *Jerusalem, which is built as a city* (Ps 122:3).

And by members of the body. But because it could be said that we should not swear by the greater members, but by the lesser ones, for this reason he says **nor by your head**. For anyone can do what he wishes with what is his own; but man does not have power over his own head as to every least thing; therefore, he should not swear by it. And this is **for you cannot make one hair white or black**, according to nature, that is: no one can **add to his stature one cubit** (Matt 6:72).

523. But it may be said, how then will we speak? He answers and first satisfies the question, second, gives the reason. Therefore he says **let your speech be**. And this can be explained in three ways. The first in this way. If someone should ask, is this so? **Let your speech be yes, yes; no, no**. It is or it is not. Second, that the mouth not say something and the heart feel something else and the actions show something else again: *who speak peace with their neighbors: but evils are in their hearts* (Ps 28:3). The third is like this, and it is more literal. **Let your speech be yes, yes**: if a thing is, it is; if it is not, it is not; as though he were saying: you shall say one thing simply. For this is the definition of the true: to be what is and not to be what is not. And this is Hilary's explanation, *Christ Jesus . . . was not: it is and it is not. But it is, was in him* (2 Cor 1:19).

524. He does not say *it is evil*, but it **is of evil**, not from your own but from another, since to swear is of the body, although nevertheless it may be expedient that the other might believe; and this is how the Apostle swore. Or, according to Chrysostom, **and that which is over and above these**, by this it is clear that in the old law he prohibited one oath, namely, perjury, but he allowed another, namely, swearing out of necessity. He removes the third oath, namely, a superstitious one, which is when a created thing is shown reverence that is owed to the creator.

Lecture 11

5:38 Audistis quia dictum est: *oculum pro oculo, dentem pro dente*. [n. 525]

5:38 Ἠκούσατε ὅτι ἐρρέθη· ὀφθαλμὸν ἀντὶ ὀφθαλμοῦ καὶ ὀδόντα ἀντὶ ὀδόντος.

5:38 You have heard that it was said: *an eye for an eye, and a tooth for a tooth*. [n. 525]

5:39 Ego autem dico vobis, non resistere malo; sed si quis te percusserit in dexteram maxillam, praebe illi et alteram. [n. 527]

5:39 ἐγὼ δὲ λέγω ὑμῖν μὴ ἀντιστῆναι τῷ πονηρῷ· ἀλλ' ὅστις σε ῥαπίζει εἰς τὴν δεξιὰν σιαγόνα [σου], στρέψον αὐτῷ καὶ τὴν ἄλλην·

5:39 But I say to you not to resist evil: but if one strike you on your right cheek, turn to him also the other. [n. 527]

5:40 Et ei qui vult tecum iudicio contendere, et tunicam tuam tollere, dimitte ei et pallium. [n. 532]

5:40 καὶ τῷ θέλοντί σοι κριθῆναι καὶ τὸν χιτῶνά σου λαβεῖν, ἄφες αὐτῷ καὶ τὸ ἱμάτιον·

5:40 And if a man will contend with you in judgment, and take away your coat, let go your cloak to him also. [n. 532]

5:41 Et quicumque te angariaverit mille passus, vade cum illo et alia duo. [n. 534]

5:41 καὶ ὅστις σε ἀγγαρεύσει μίλιον ἕν, ὕπαγε μετ' αὐτοῦ δύο.

5:41 And whoever will force you one mile, go with him the other two, [n. 534]

5:42 Qui petit a te, da ei; et volenti mutuari a te, ne avertaris. [n. 535]

5:42 τῷ αἰτοῦντί σε δός, καὶ τὸν θέλοντα ἀπὸ σοῦ δανίσασθαι μὴ ἀποστραφῇς.

5:42 give to him who asks of you and from him who would borrow of you turn not away. [n. 535]

---

525. *Audistis quia dictum est: 'oculum pro oculo.'* Supra Dominus adimplevit legem quantum ad praecepta permissiva quae pertinent ad Deum; nunc quantum ad ea quae pertinent ad proximum. Et hoc quantum ad duo: quantum ad actum et quantum ad affectum. Secundum, ibi *diliges proximum.*

Circa primum duo facit:

primo ponit dictum legis,

secundo adimplet.

526. Dicit ergo *audistis* etc *'oculum pro oculo'* debes exigere, Exod. XXI, 24 et Deut. XIX, 21. In istis autem verbis legis alius fuit intellectus legislatoris et Iudaeorum, quia legislatoris intentio fuit statuere modum iudicandi iustitiae quantum ad iudices, ut scilicet poenam determinatam inferrent. Iudaei intelligebant quod unusquisque vindictam acciperet de iniuria sibi illata: quod erat contra legem Lev. XIX, 18: *non quaeras ultionem.*

Adimplet ergo Dominus quantum ad malum intellectum. Unde *ego autem.*

Et circa hoc duo facit. Dupliciter enim adimplet:

primo quantum ad hoc quod non expetatur vindicta;

secundo quantum ad hoc quod bonum faciat inferenti iniuriam, ibi *qui petit a te.*

Circa primum duo facit:

primo adimplet in generali,

secundo in speciali, ibi *sed si quis.*

527. Quantum ad superficiem litterae videtur quod mala lex. Econverso. Sed secundum Augustinum Dominus non destruit, sed implet. Legis enim intentio erat

525. *You have heard that it was said: 'an eye for an eye.'* Above, the Lord fulfilled the law as to the permissive precepts that pertain to God; now, he does it as to those that pertain to our neighbor. And this in two respects: as to the act, and as to the emotion. The second is found at, *'you shall love your neighbor'* (Matt 5:43).

Concerning the first he does two things:

first, he quotes the words of the law,

second, he fulfills it.

526. Therefore he says, *you have heard that it was said*, that you ought to require *'an eye for an eye'* (Ex 21:24: Deut 19:21). But in these words of the law different things were understood by the lawgiver than by the Jews, for the intention of the lawgiver was to establish a mode of judging in justice for the judges, so that they could impose a predetermined penalty. The Jews understood it as each one taking his own retribution for the injuries he had suffered, which was against the law: *seek not revenge* (Lev 19:18).

Therefore the Lord gives the fulfillment as to the wrong understanding. Hence, *but I say to you.*

And concerning this he does two things. For he fulfills it in two ways:

first, as to the fact that retribution is not to be sought;

second, that one should do good to anyone inflicting an injury, at *give to him who asks of you.*

Concerning this he does two things:

first, he gives the fulfillment in general,

second, in the particular, at *but if one strike you.*

527. As to the surface meaning of the letter, it seems to be a bad law. And vice versa. But according to Augustine, the Lord did not destroy, but fulfilled. For the intention

retrahere homines a nimia ultione et immoderata. Dominus autem totaliter prohibet ultionem. Unde si lex dixisset: non quaeras ultionem ultra debitum, et Dominus: nullo modo quaeras, adimplesset dictum legis.

Et considerandi sunt hic secundum Augustinum quinque gradus: unus, illius qui iniuriam intulit et hic est maximus in nequitia; secundus, eius qui iniuriam infert equalem: hic minor est iniquitatis positio; tertius, qui rependit sed minorem quam passus sit; quartus, qui nullam penam rependit; quintus, qui non rependit, sed etiam non impedit quod etiam aliud malum sibi inferatur. Et hoc Dominus docet: unde *ego autem dico vobis non resistere malo* etc. Et intelligitur scilicet de malo non culpae sed penae vel iniuriae, Ro. XII, 19: *non vos defendentes*; et istud satis convenit cum praemisso.

528. Sed posset aliquis dicere: volo vindicare me non ut deiceretur in vindicta, sed ut de cetero non offendar; sed hoc etiam excludit Dominus: *non resistere* etc.

529. Sed videndum est quomodo intelligenda sit ista sententia Domini. Dupliciter enim obicitur, secundum duos errores. Unus gentilium, ut dicit Augustinus in epistola contra Marcellianum, qui ita arguunt quod sine vindicta nulla res publica conservetur. Sic resistitur hostibus et puniuntur fures: quod si non fieret totaliter res publica periret. Ergo lex Evangelica destruit societatem hominum: ergo est abicienda. E converso haeretici dicunt quod sustinent Evangelia, et nolunt detrahere ea quae pertinent ad societatem, auferendo vindictam. Unde dicendum quod isti ex falso intellectu processerunt. Potest enim aliquis resistere malo dupliciter: ex amore publici boni et privati. Deus autem non intendit prohibere quod non resistatur malo pro bono rei publicae, sed quod non exardescat quis in vindictam pro bono privato. Nihil enim magis conservat societatem hominum quam quod homo non habeat potestatem malefaciendi in privato.

Sed item videtur quod Dominus non intendat hoc prohibere; quia naturalis inclinatio est cuiuslibet rei quod resistat malo corrumpenti bonum suum; ergo istud praeceptum non potest servari. Sed dicendum quod naturalis inclinatio est quod quaelibet res repellat proprium nocumentum. Et item naturalis inclinatio quod quaelibet res exponat se ad proprium detrimentum ut vitet detrimentum commune, sicut manus exponit se periculo propter corpus et quaelibet pars pro suo toto. Unde naturale est quod homo sustineat malum pro bono rei publicae, et ad hoc pertinet virtus politica, sicut fortitudo et huiusmodi.

of the law was to draw men away from extreme and unregulated revenge. But God completely prohibits revenge. Hence if the law had said 'do not seek revenge beyond your due,' and the Lord says: 'do not seek it at all,' he would be fulfilling the words of the law.

And here, according to Augustine, five degrees should be considered: one, the man who inflicted an injury, and this is the greatest degree of wickedness; second, the man who retaliates with an equal injury, and this is less of iniquity than the first; the third, someone who strikes back but less than he suffered; fourth, someone who repays no penalty; fifth, someone who not only does not repay, but also does not hinder even if another evil is inflicted on him. And this is what the Lord teaches: hence *but I say to you not to resist evil*. And it is understood to be about an evil, not of guilt, but of penalty or injury: *do not revenge yourselves* (Rom 12:19); and this fits well enough with what has been said.

528. But someone could say: I wish to be vindicated, not in order to delight in revenge, but so that I may not be offended again; but the Lord also excludes this: *do not resist evil*.

529. But it should be seen how these sentences of the Lord may be understood. For two kinds of objections are made, according to two errors. One, as Augustine says in his letter against Marcellinus, is the error of the gentiles, who argued that without retribution no state could be preserved. It is how a stand is made against enemies, and thieves are punished: which measures must be done thoroughly, or the state would perish. Therefore, the Gospel law destroys human society: therefore it should be obliterated. On the other hand, heretics say that the Gospels support revenge and do not wish to take away those things that pertain to society by abolishing it. Hence it should be said that those proceed from a false understanding. For someone can resist evil in two ways: out of love for a public good or for a private one. But the Lord did not intend to prohibit us from resisting evil for the good of the community, but rather that no one should burn with revenge for his own private good. For nothing preserves the society of men more than that a man not have the power of doing evil for his own private ends.

But again it seems that the Lord does not intend to prohibit this; for the natural inclination of anything is to resist evil corrupting its good; therefore this precept cannot be kept. But it should be said that the natural inclination is that everything repel its own harm. And similarly the natural inclination is that everything expose itself to its own detriment so as to avoid damage to the community, as a hand exposes itself to danger for the sake of the body, and any part for the sake of its whole. Hence it is natural that a man endure an evil for the good of the nation, and political virtue, like fortitude and such, pertains to this.

530. Sed Augustinus dicit quod istud *non resistat* etc. Intelligendum est secundum praeparationem animi: quia homo pro utilitate proximi debet esse paratus omnia mala sustinere vel sufferre, et ponit exemplum. Si enim aliquis custodiret freneticum et ille percuteret eum vel huiusmodi, hic si habet benevolentiam ad eum debet esse paratus pro sua salute etiam alia mala sustinere: ita et nos pro utilitate Ecclesiae.

Et notandum quod hoc quod Dominus dicit quodammodo est praeceptum, quodammodo consilium. Praeceptum, si aliquis dimitteret ea ad quae tenetur timore alicuius incommodi temporalis, sicut praelatus qui custodit gregem debet esse paratus in animo sustinere omnia damna antequam dimittat ea ad quae tenetur. Consilium, si non praetermitteret ea ad quae non tenetur, sicut si aliquis propter introitum religionis sustinet plura damna a parentibus, consilium est ut non praetermittat quod melius est.

531. Consequenter quod dixerat Dominus in generali manifestat in speciali: *sed si quis te percusserit*. Triplex damnum potest inferri alicui: in lesione corporis, in ablatione rerum, in coactione operum. Et ponit exemplum de hiis tribus.

Dicit ergo *sed si quis te percusserit in unam maxillam praebe alteram maxillam*; Tren. III, 30. *Dabit percutienti se maxillam*, Is. L, 6: *dedi corpus meum percutientibus et genas meas vellentibus*. Quomodo ista debeant intelligi considerandum est ex gestis sanctorum. Dominus enim qui *cepit facere et docere* hoc non adimplevit: Io. XVIII, 23: *si male locutus sum* etc., et post *cur me caedis*; et Apostolus, Act XXIII, 3: *percutiet te Deus, paries dealbate*. Et ex hoc Augustinus argumentatur quod nos per gesta sanctorum scimus qualiter intelligenda est Scriptura. Unde dicit esse intelligendum in praeparatione animi; et expone hoc sicut supra.

532. Mystice tamen sciendum quod ille in faciem te cedit qui in conspectu tuo tibi contumelias infert, II Cor. XI, 20 *Sustinetis enim si quis in faciem vos cedit*. Maxilla dextera pertinet ad spiritualia, sinistra ad temporalia. Vult ergo dicere quod si sustines iniuriam in spiritualibus, multo magis in temporalibus; quam quod praelati faciunt qui sustinent damna ecclesiarum sed non consanguineorum.

Et qui vult tecum in iudicio contendere. Hoc contingit dupliciter: ad hoc quod aliquis recipiat sua, et tunc non magnum si cedas; sed quod auferat tua, hoc perfectionis si cedas. Et hoc est: *et tunicam tollere*, idest quamcumque rem temporalem, *dans et pallium*, idest quamcumque aliam rem. Et hoc etiam in praeparatione animi; quia si aliquis calumniam tibi facit, caritatem tamen non

530. But Augustine says that *let him not resist* should be understood according to the preparation of the soul: for a man should be prepared to endure or undergo all evils for the benefit of his neighbor, and he gives an example. For if someone were taking care of a deranged man who struck him or did something like that, the first man, if he had good will toward the other, would be prepared to endure even other evils for his welfare: and this you must do for the benefit of the Church.

And it should be noted that what the Lord says is in some cases a precept, and in some cases, a counsel. It is a precept to someone who would abandon what he is bound to by fear of some temporal inconvenience; as a prelate who cares for a flock should be prepared in his soul to endure any losses before he will abandon what he is bound to. It is a counsel, when it does not involve overlooking what one is bound to, as when someone endures many injuries from his parents for the sake of entering religious life, the counsel is that he not let go of what is better.

531. Accordingly, what the Lord said he demonstrates in general and in particular: *but if one strike you*. Three different kinds of harm can be inflicted on someone: by wounding his body, by taking his things, or by forcibly restricting his action. And he gives an example of these three.

Therefore he says, *but if one strike you on your right cheek, turn to him also the other*: he will give his cheek to him who strikes him (Lam 3:30); *I have given my body to the strikers and my cheeks to those who plucked them* (Isa 50:6). How those things should be understood can be seen from the acts of holy men. For the Lord who *began to do and to teach* this did not fulfill it: *if I have spoken evil, give testimony of it; but if not, why do you strike me?* (John 18:23); and the Apostle: *God will strike you, you whited wall* (Acts 23:3). And from this Augustine concludes that we know from the acts of holy men how the Scriptures are to be understood. Hence he says this is to be understood in the preparation of the soul, and explain this as above.

532. Mystically, however, it should be known that the man who strikes you in the face insults you in your sight: *if a man is lifted up, if a man strike you on the face* (2 Cor 11:20). The right cheek has to do with spiritual things, the left one with temporal things. Therefore it means that if you endure an injury in spiritual things, much more should you in temporal matters; against which prelates act who endure the loss of their churches but not of their relatives.

And if a man will contend with you in judgment. This can happen in two ways: someone may contend in order to receive his own things, and then it is no great thing if you yield; but if it is to take away your things, this belongs to perfection if you yield. And this is: *and take away your coat*, that is, any temporal thing, *let go your cloak to him also*, that is, any other thing. And this is also in the preparation

dimittas quam habes ad eum, I Cor. VI, 7: *iam omnino delictum est vobis quod iudicia habetis inter vos.*

533. Istud iudicium vitandum est propter duas rationes. Una est quia si clericus est, se subdendo iudici saeculari renogat dignitati suae. Alia ratio quia quamvis non intendit aliquam calumniam, tamen si videt causam suae contentionis calumniari datur ei occasio similia faciendi; et ideo contendere in iudicio periculosum est.

Item, repetere iudicio contingit, dupliciter: licite et non licite. Illicitum est repetere in iudicio infidelium. Item quod non repetat cum contentione: est enim contentio *impugnatio veritatis cum confidentia clamoris*, Prov. XX, 3: *honor est homini qui separat se a contentionibus.* Licitum immo quasi votivum est dupliciter: quando sunt res pauperum vel ecclesiae; unde si praelatus non repetat peccat. Alia causa est quando ille qui aufert insollentior efficitur et magis procax nisi ei resistatur caritas est, quia tunc anima eius liberatur a morte; quando autem esset res privata et non speraretur correctio, tunc non est contendendum. Omnia ista tamen intelligenda sunt in praeparatione animi.

534. *Si quis te angariaverit*. Angariare proprie est sine iustitia ad aliqua servilia opera mancipare. ***Vade alia duo***, scilicet milia, II Cor. XI: *sustinetis si quis in servitutem redigit.*

Et notandum quod Dominus quodam ordine processit. Primo dixit non esse resistendum malo; postea quod debet homo esse paratus non tantum non resistere, sed penam equalem sustinere, modo plus quia ascendit usque ad duplum.

535. *Qui petit a te*. Hic dicit quod debemus benefacere malefaciendum dupliciter: per modum simplicis dationis et mutui. Quantum ad primum dicit ***qui petit***, Tob. IV, 9: *si multum tibi fuerit, abundanter tribue.* Iob XXI, 16: *si negavi quod volebant pauperibus.* Sed obicitur quia hoc non possunt facere pauperes. Item divites si semper darent nihil eis remaneret. Et solvit dupliciter Augustinus. Primo sic: quod non omnia debes dare quae petit, quia non inhonestum nec iniustum vel irrationabile vel illud quo tu magis indiges; sed quando iuste petit aliquis debes dare: et hoc est praeceptum si teneris, consilium si non teneris. Ieronymus tamen dicit quod intelligitur de bono spirituali quia tale nulli potest esse nocumentum.

536. *Et volenti*: mutuum accipere. Hoc dupliciter: quia quicumque benefacit alteri etiam si simpliciter det aliquid, expectat retributionem, Prov. XIX, 17: *feneratur Domino qui miseretur pauperis, et vicissitudinem suam*

of the soul, for if someone speaks some calumny against you, nevertheless, do not let go of the charity you have for him: *already indeed there is plainly a fault among you, that you have lawsuits with one another* (1 Cor 6:7).

533. This judgment is to be avoided for two reasons. One is that if a cleric is subjected to secular judgment it diminishes his dignity. The other reason is that although he does not intend any calumny, nevertheless if he sees the cause of his contention calumniated, an occasion for doing the same thing will be given to him; and thus it is dangerous to contend in judgment.

Likewise to seek redress in court can happen in two ways: licitly, and illicitly; it is illicit to go to court with unbelievers. Also, one may not go to court contentiously: for contention is *an assault against the truth with the boldness of shouting*; it is an honor for a man to separate himself from quarrels (Prov 20:3). On the other hand, a licit claim can happen two ways: when it is about the affairs of the poor or of the Church; hence if the bishop does not go to court over these, he sins. Another case is when someone who steals becomes even more insolent and more shameless unless he is resisted, charity is that in this case his soul should be delivered from death; but when it is a private matter and no correction is hoped for, then he is not to be condemned. Nevertheless, all these things are to be understood as referring to the preparation of the soul.

534. *And whoever will force you one mile*. Force is properly to enslave someone in some servile work without justice. ***Go . . . the other two***, that is, miles: *you suffer it if anyone brings you into bondage* (2 Cor 11:20).

And it should be noted that the Lord proceeded in a certain order. First he said that evil was not to be resisted; afterward that a man should be prepared not only to not resist, but to endure an equal penalty, but more since he ascends to the double.

535. *Give to him who asks of you*. Here he says that we should do good to evildoers in two ways: by the mode of simple giving and of loaning. As to the first, he says ***who asks***: *if you have much, give abundantly* (Tob 4:9); *if I have denied to the poor what they desired* (Job 31:16). But it is objected that the poor cannot do this. Likewise, if the rich were always giving, nothing would remain to them. And Augustine resolves this two ways. The first, thus, because you should not give everything that someone asks, for not something indecent or unjust or irrational or something that you need more; but when someone asks rightly, you should give: and this is a precept if you are bound, a counsel if you are not bound. Jerome, though, says that it is understood as referring to a spiritual good because that can be harmful to no one.

536. *From him who would*: receive a loan. Here two things: for anyone doing a service to another, even if he simply gives him something, expects retribution: *who has mercy on the poor lends to the Lord, and he will repay him*

reddat ei, Eccl. XI, 1: *mitte panem tuum super transeuntes aquas quia post multa tempora invenies illum.* Vel aliter, **volenti** aliquid accipere ut reddat, **non avertaris**. Et posset videri alicui quod Deus non recompensaret proprium quod speraret ab homine, et ideo posset magis moveri ad dandum quam mutuandum vel reciperet a Deo. Sed Dominus dicit quod etiam a Deo recipiet. Vel dicit **non avertaris**, quia timent aliquando defraudari et ideo non mutuant, Eccli XXX, 12,13: *multi non causa nequitiae non feneraverunt sed fraudai gratis timuerunt* etc., et post, *perdet pecuniam pro fratre et amico.* Et notandum quod hoc potest esse praeceptum et consilium secundum diversas conditiones: quod patet ex dictis.

(Prov 19:17); *cast your bread on running waters, for . . . you will find it again* (Eccl 11:1). Or another way, **who would** receive something that he would return, **turn not away**. And it could seem to someone that God did not recompense the property that he hoped for from a man, and thus he might be moved to give rather than loan, or he would receive it back from God. But the Lord says that he will also receive it back from God. Or he says **turn not away** because sometimes they fear being cheated and so they refuse to make a loan: *many have refused to lend, not out of wickedness, but they were afraid to be defrauded without cause* (Sir 29:10) and further, *lose your money for your brother* (Sir 29:13). And it should be noted that this can be a precept and a counsel according to different situations: which is clear from what has been said.

Lecture 12

5:43 Audistis quia dictum est: *diliges proximum tum, et odio habebis inimicum tuum.* [n. 537]

5:44 Ego autem dico vobis: diligite inimicos vestros, benefacite his qui oderunt vos, et orate pro persequentibus et calumniantibus vos; [n. 540]

5:45 ut sitis filii Patris vestri qui in caelis est, qui solem suum oriri facit super bonos et malos, et pluit super iustos et iniustos. [n. 459]

5:46 Si enim diligitis eos qui vos diligunt, quam mercedem habebitis? Nonne et publicani hoc faciunt? [n. 552]

5:47 Et si salutaveritis fratres vestros tantum, quid amplius facitis? Nonne et ethnici hoc faciunt? [n. 552]

5:48 Estote ergo vos perfecti, sicut Pater vester caelestis perfectus est. [n. 553]

5:43 Ἠκούσατε ὅτι ἐρρέθη· ἀγαπήσεις τὸν πλησίον σου καὶ μισήσεις τὸν ἐχθρόν σου.

5:44 ἐγὼ δὲ λέγω ὑμῖν· ἀγαπᾶτε τοὺς ἐχθροὺς ὑμῶν καὶ προσεύχεσθε ὑπὲρ τῶν διωκόντων ὑμᾶς,

5:45 ὅπως γένησθε υἱοὶ τοῦ πατρὸς ὑμῶν τοῦ ἐν οὐρανοῖς, ὅτι τὸν ἥλιον αὐτοῦ ἀνατέλλει ἐπὶ πονηροὺς καὶ ἀγαθοὺς καὶ βρέχει ἐπὶ δικαίους καὶ ἀδίκους.

5:46 ἐὰν γὰρ ἀγαπήσητε τοὺς ἀγαπῶντας ὑμᾶς, τίνα μισθὸν ἔχετε; οὐχὶ καὶ οἱ τελῶναι τὸ αὐτὸ ποιοῦσιν;

5:47 καὶ ἐὰν ἀσπάσησθε τοὺς ἀδελφοὺς ὑμῶν μόνον, τί περισσὸν ποιεῖτε; οὐχὶ καὶ οἱ ἐθνικοὶ τὸ αὐτὸ ποιοῦσιν;

5:48 ἔσεσθε οὖν ὑμεῖς τέλειοι ὡς ὁ πατὴρ ὑμῶν ὁ οὐράνιος τέλειός ἐστιν.

5:43 You have heard it said: *you shall love your neighbor, and hate your enemy.* [n. 537]

5:44 However, I say to you, love your enemies, do good to those who hate you, pray for those who persecute and calumniate you; [n. 540]

5:45 that you may be the children of your Father who is in heaven, who makes his sun to rise upon the good and the bad and rains upon the just and the unjust. [n. 549]

5:46 For if you love those who love you, what reward will you have? Do not even the publicans do this? [n. 552]

5:47 And if you salute your brethren only, what more do you do? Do not the heathens also do this? [n. 552]

5:48 Be you therefore perfect, as also your heavenly Father is perfect. [n. 553]

---

537. *Audistis quia dictum est: 'diliges proximum tuum.'* Supra Dominus adimplevit legem quantum ad actum permissivum, et hic quantum ad affectum odii, secundum quod videbatur. Et est ultima adimpletio, et sunt satis congrue adimpletionem in dilectione, *plenitudo legis est dilectio* Ro. XIII, 10

Circa hoc ergo duo facit:

primo ponit ea quae sunt legis;

secundo adimplet, ibi *ego autem.*

In istis verbis duo tangit, scilicet *diliges et odio habebis.*

538. Circa primum considerandum quod aliqui intelligebant proximum dici solum familiarem vel consanguineum. Et secundum rei veritatem omnis homo dicitur proximus et etiam angeli: quia dicitur, Luc. X, 36–37, quod ille qui fecit misericordiam semivivo dicitur proximus. Ex quo possumus accipere quod ille dicitur *'proximus'* a quo misericordiam accipimus: sic angeli; vel cui misericordiam debemus: sic homo. Hoc praeceptum est Lev. XIX, 18.

Et voluit Dominus uti isto nomine 'proximus' quia per hoc datur intelligi ratio dilectionis. Omnis enim amicitia super aliquam similitudinem vel propinquitatem fundatur, Eccli. XIII, 19: *omne animal diligit similem*

537. *You have heard it said: 'you shall love your neighbor.'* Above, the Lord gave the fulfillment of the law as to the permissive act, and here as to the emotion of hatred, according to what was seen. And this is the last fulfillment, and fittingly enough he ends the fulfillment with love, for *love is the fullness of the law* (Rom 13:10).

Concerning this he does two things:

first, he sets down those things that are of the law;

second, he gives their fulfillment, at *but I say to you.*

In these words he touches on two things, namely, *love* and *hate.*

538. Concerning the first it should be considered that some people understood the neighbor to be said only of household members and relatives. And according to the truth of the matter every man is called neighbor and even the angels: for it is said in Luke that the one who had mercy on the Samaritan is called his neighbor (Luke 10:36–37). We can take from this that the one is called *'neighbor'* from whom we receive mercy: such as the angels; or to whom we owe mercy: such as a man. This precept is from Leviticus (Lev 19:18).

And the Lord wanted to use this name 'neighbor' because by it he makes us understand the definition of love. For all friendship is based on some likeness or closeness: *every beast loves its like* (Sir 13:19). But there is a certain

sibi. Est autem quaedam similitudo naturalis secundum quam omnes homines conveniunt in specie. Unde sicut naturale est quod omne animal diligat sibi simile, ita naturale quod omnis homo diligat sibi simile. Alia est similitudo politica quia aliquis debet diligere aliquem inquantum est eius civis: et haec politica amicitia. Est etiam similitudo gratiae, et ista est amplior quia se extendit ad omnes qui habent ordinem ad beatitudinem, scilicet angelos et homines: et hoc est praeceptum caritatis quod fundatur super istam unionem. Ergo quod dicit *'diliges proximum'* non intelligendum est tantum in origine sanguinis vel familiaritatis, sed in ordine ad beatitudinem.

539. *'Et odio habebis inimicum tuum.'* Haec verba in nullo loco scripta sunt in lege. Sed accipi possunt ex quibusdam verbis Exod. xxiii, 32, ubi Dominus dixit quod non inirent fedus cum hostibus etc.; et Deut. vii, 2, mandat quod deleant eos usque ad internicionem. Quoniam ex hoc accipiebant quod inimici habendi sunt odio: et propter hunc intellectum dicit *'et odio habebis.'*

Contrarium autem dicunt haeretici. Lex dicit *'odio habebis'* etc.; sed omne odium est peccatum; ergo lex mandat peccatum. Et respondet Augustinus: Iubet diligere inimicos. Hoc arguo quia ipse benefacit bonis et malis; ergo inquantum in hoc Deo assimilamur debemus diligere inimicos. Sed Deus aliquos odio habet, Ro. I, 30: *detractores Deo odibiles.* Et tamen Deus omnia diligit, Sap. XI, 25: *diligis omnia quae sunt.* Unde dicendum quod Deus diligit naturam, sed odit culpam; et similiter lex hoc voluit.

540. Unde Dominus adimplet quantum ad pravum intellectum scribarum et pharisaeorum, qui retorquebant ad odium per se: quod tamen erat contra legem Lev. XIX, 17: *non oderis fratrem tuum.* Sed ipsi intelligebant 'fratrem' de Iudaeis, sunt tamen omnes a Deo creati et ordinati ad unam beatitudinem. Adimplet ergo Dominus: *ego autem* etc. Et circa hos tria facit: ponitur primo adimpletio, secundo ratio probans, tertio concludit principale intentum. Secundum, ibi *ut sitis filii*; tertium, ibi *estote ergo perfecti.* Adimplet autem quantum ad tria, scilicet quantum ad affectum cordis, officium operis in benefaciendo, et oris in orando. Secundum, ibi *benefacite*; tertium, ibi *et orate pro persequentibus.*

Dicit ergo *diligite inimicos.* Sed videtur hoc esse inconveniens. Manifestum est enim quod nulla res potest aufferre motum nature; sed hic est motus naturalis, scilicet odire inimicum. Unde quaelibet res adversatur suo contrario, sicut ovis fugit lupum, etiam in carentibus cognitione, quia ignis persequitur aquam. Ergo quare dicit Dominus *diligite inimicos*?

natural similarity according as all men share in one species. Hence just as it is natural that every animal loves its like, so also it is natural that every man love his like. Another likeness is political, for somone must love another as he is his fellow countryman: and this is political friendship. But there is also the similitude of grace, and this is broader because it is extended to all who are ordered to beatitude, namely, men and angels: and this is the precept of charity that is based on that union. Therefore, his saying *'love your neighbor'* is not to be understood only of those who share the same blood ties or familiarity, but the ordering to beatitude.

539. *'And hate your enemy.'* These words are written nowhere in the law. But they can be taken from certain words of Exodus, where God said that they should not enter into a covenant with their enemies (Exod 23:32); and in Deuteronomy, he commands that they destroy them by complete extermination (Deut 7:2). Certain men have taken from this that enemies should be hated: and because of this understanding he says *'and hate.'*

But heretics say the opposite. The law says *'hate'*; but all hatred is a sin; therefore the law commands sin. Augustine answers: he commands us to love our enemies. I argue this because he himself did good to the good and to the bad; therefore, inasmuch as we should imitate God in this, we should love our enemies. But God does hate some: *detractors, hateful to God* (Rom 1:30). And nevertheless God loves all things: *for you love all things* (Wis 11:25). Hence it should be said that God loves nature, but he hates fault; and likewise, this is what the law wants.

540. Hence the Lord gives the fulfillment as to the wrong understanding of the scribes and Pharisees, who twisted the meaning to hatred simply speaking, which in any case was against the law: *do not hate your brother* (Lev 19:17). But they understood 'brother' to mean the Jews, although all men were created by God and ordered to one beatitude. Therefore the Lord gives this fulfillment: *however, I say to you.* And concerning this he does three things: first, he gives the fulfillment, second, the argument proving it, and third, he concludes with the chief thing intended. The second is at *that you may be the children of your Father*; the third, at *be you therefore perfect.* But he fulfills it as to three things, namely as to the affection of the heart, the duty of deeds of service, and of the mouth in prayer. The second is at *do good*; the third, at *pray for those who persecute* you.

Therefore he says *love your enemies.* But this seems to be unfitting. For it is clear that no thing can take away the inclination of nature; but this is the natural inclination, namely to hate one's enemy. Hence everything is opposed to its contrary, as sheep flee the wolf, also among things lacking thought, for fire pursues water. Why then does the Lord say *love your enemies*?

541. Sed sciendum quod sicut Chrysostomus dicit duplex est amor et duplex odium, scilicet carnis et rationis. Dominus istud praeceptum non dedit carni sed rationi. Quando igitur sentis oriri in te motum odii et ratio compescit illum ad hoc quod non noceas, tunc est odium carnis tantum.

Sed numquid etiam secundum rationem debemus diligere inimicos? Dicendum secundum Augustinum quod sic, quantum ad naturam et non quantum ad culpam. Unde in quo adversarius similis est diligendus est, sicut etiam apparet in rebus naturalibus: quia album adversatur nigro inquantum dissimile est: inquantum enim nigrum et non inquantum color. Unde debemus destruere odium, idest debet nobis displicere hoc quod inimicus est et hoc destruere in eo.

542. Sed iterum quaestio est: numquid tenentur omnes ad hoc? Videtur quod non, quia Augustinus in *Encheridion* dicit quod diligere inimicum perfectionis est; et non est tantae multitudinis quanta creditur exaudiri in oratione cum dicit **dimitte nobis debita nostra, sicut et nos dimisimus** etc. Ergo dimisit Deus debita alicui qui non diligit inimicum. Sed nulli dimittitur debitum nisi in caritate existenti ergo diligere inimicum non est de necessitate salutis.

Sed sciendum, sicut idem dicit Augustinus, quod dupliciter loqui possumus de isto inimico: unomodo antequam veniam petat, aliomodo postquam petit. Postquam autem veniam petit iam non inimicus, sed amicus, reputandus est. Et Dominus non remittit nisi veniam petenti: non ergo praecipit quod dimittas nisi veniam petenti: ergo si non petit remanebit in odio.

543. Dicendum quod diligere inimicum veniam non petentem est quodammodo praeceptum et alio consilium. Omnis enim amicitia fundatur super aliquam unionem. Unio autem quae est inter duos quaedam est communis, quaedam specialis. Specialis est illius a quo multa bona recepi et cum quo familiaritatem habeo semper, et huiusmodi. Generalis, inquantum sumus concives caelestis Ierusalem; et secundum hanc dilectionem non oportet quod in speciali affectu afferar ad quemlibet illius multitudinis, tamen debeo omnes velle esse sicut me ipsum et omnes homines salvos fieri. Et secundum hoc non tenemur diligere inimicum speciali affectu, sed tenemur non excludere eum a communi dilectione. Unde contra praeceptum esset si desiderarem omnes salvos fieri praeter inimicum. Quod autem speciali dilectione ferar in eum, hoc est perfectionis et consilium. Et hoc dicit Augustinus: sufficit non odire, idest ut non excludas generalem dilectionem.

544. Et sciendum quod diligere aliquem est bonum ei velle. Est autem duplex bonum: vitae aeternae et hoc intendit caritas, quia teneor diligere proximum ad vitam

541. But it should be known that as Chrysostom says, both love and hatred are twofold, namely of the flesh and of the reason. The Lord did not give this precept for the flesh, but for the reason. Thus whenever you feel the emotion of hatred arise in you and your reason restrains it so that you do not do any harm, then the hatred is only of the flesh.

But should we also love our enemies according to our reason? It should be said, according to Augustine, that we should, as to nature but not as to fault. Hence your adversary is to be loved in what he shares with you, as also appears among natural things; for white is opposed to black as it is unlike: as black, not as a color. Hence we should destroy hatred, i.e., the fact that he is an enemy should displease us, and we should destroy this in him.

542. But again there is a question: are not all bound to this? It seems not, for Augustine in the *Enchiridion* says that to love an enemy is perfection; and it is not of such a multitude as is believed to be heard in prayer when it says, **and forgive us our debts, as we also forgive our debtors** (Matt 6:12). Therefore God forgave the debts of someone who does not love his enemy. But a debt is forgiven of no one unless he exists in charity; therefore to love an enemy is not of necessity for salvation.

But it should be known, as in the same place Augustine says, that we can speak two ways about this enemy: in one way before he seeks forgiveness, in another way after he seeks it. But after he seeks forgiveness he is no longer an enemy, but is to be considered a friend. And the Lord only forgives those who seek forgiveness: therefore he does not command that you forgive anyone except the one seeking forgiveness: therefore if he does not seek it, he will remain in your hatred.

543. It should be said that to love an enemy who does not seek forgiveness is in one way a precept and in another way a counsel. For all friendship is founded on some union. But there is a certain union between two people that is common and a certain union that is special. The special one is with someone from whom I have received many goods and with whom I always have familiarity and so on. The general one is inasmuch as we are fellow citizens of the heavenly Jerusalem; and according to this love it is not necessary that I bear special affection toward any of this multitude, when I must will all to be like myself and all men to be saved. And according to this we are not bound to love an enemy with special affection, but we are bound to not exclude him from our common love. Hence it would be against this precept if I desired all men to be saved except my enemy. But what I bear him of special love, this is of perfection and counsel. And Augustine says this: it is enough not to hate, i.e., so that you do not exclude general love.

544. And it should be known that to love someone is to will him good. But there are two kinds of good: eternal life, and charity intends this, because I am bound to love

aeternam ut meipsum; aliud temporale, et in hoc non teneor diligere proximum nisi inquantum ista ordinantur ad consequendam vitam eternam. Unde salva caritate possum optare aliquod malum temporale proximo inquantum datur per hoc occasio benefaciendi et perveniendi ad vitam aeternam. Unde dicit Gregorius in *Moralibus* quod signum quod non diligis proximum est quando in eius ruina laetaris; sed possum laetari in ruina temporalium inquantum ordinatur in bonum eiusdem vel aliorum vel multitudinis.

545. Sed quia *probatio dilectionis exhibitio est operis,* et I Io. III, 18 dicitur *non diligamus verbo neque lingua, sed opere et veritate* etc., ideo Dominus subdit **benefacite his** etc. Prov. XXV, 21: *si esurit inimicus tuus ciba illum; si videris asinum odientis te iacere sub onere, non pertransibis sed sublevabis cum eo.* Et hoc in aliquo casu est praeceptum, in aliquo consilium. Praeceptum in casu in quo teneris omni homini etiam inimico, etiam scilicet in extrema necessitate. Consilium autem si dares eleemosynam, non dico communem, quia ab illa non debet excludi inimicus sed si specialem et non excludas inimicum ab ea, hoc consilium et perfectionis.

Orate pro persecutoribus et calumniantibus vos. Posset enim dicere aliquis: Non possumus benefacere quia pauper, ideo dicit **orate pro persecutoribus**. Persecutores dicuntur qui manifeste persecuntur; calumniatores qui per fraudes vel circumventiones nocent, Is. LII, 4: *in Aegyptum descendit populus meus et Assur absque ulla causa calumniarus est eum.* Et habemus exemplum: quia Dominus oravit pro crucissoribus, Luc. XXIII, 24, et Stephanus, Act. VII, 59. Et est hoc praeceptum inquantum non debet' excludi a communi oratione Ecclesiae; consilium autem si aliquam orationem specialem fiunt pro eo, quia hoc facere non teneris etiam pro omnibus animatis .

546. Sed sunt graviores quaestiones, quia invenimus multos prophetas orare contra inimicos. Ps. *fiant filii eius orphani.* Ier. XI, 20: *videam ultionem tuam ex eis,* et multa talia inveniuntur. Et dicendum quod ista verba non dicuntur affectu vindicte, sed spiritu prophetiae, non affectu optantis sed spiritu praedicentis: unde *videam ultionem,* idest videbo; vel dicendum quod *sancti gaudebunt cum viderint vindictam.* Ita sancti qui perfecti sunt in iustitia Dei exoptant divinam iustitiam adimpleri.

547. Alia quaestio est quod I Io. V, 16 dicitur: *si quis scit fratrem suum peccare peccatum non ad mortem, petet,* et post tamen: *est peccatum ad mortem: non pro illo dico ut roget* etc. Ergo in fratribus sunt peccata ad mortem: ergo si non debemus pro illis orare multo minus pro persecutoribus Et solvit Augustinus quod non omne

my neighbor as myself for eternal life; the other is temporal, and in this I am not bound to love my neighbor except insofar as these things lead to eternal life. Hence while preserving charity I can wish some temporal evil on my neighbor to the extent that it would give him the occasion of doing good and attaining eternal life. Hence Gregory says in his *Morals* that the sign that you do not love your neighbor is when you rejoice in his ruin; but I can rejoice in his temporal ruin to the extent that it is ordered to his good or that of others or of the multitude.

545. But because *the proof of love is the showing of deeds,* and it is said, *let us not love in word . . . but in deed* (1 John 3:18), for this reason the Lord supplies **do good to those who hate you**: *if your enemy is hungry, give him to eat* (Prov 25:21); *if you see the donkey of him who hates you lying beneath his burden . . . lift him up with him* (Exod 23:5). And this in certain cases is a precept, in others a counsel. It is a precept in the case in which you are bound to every man, even an enemy, namely, extreme necessity. But it is a counsel if you were giving alms, and I do not mean generally, for you should not exclude your enemy from those, but if you were making a particular donation and you did not exclude your enemy from it, this would be the counsel, and of perfection.

Pray for those who persecute and calumniate you. For someone might say: we cannot do good to others because we are poor; therefore he says, **pray for those who persecute**. They are called persecutors who persecute openly; calumniators are those who harm by deceits and going behind one's back: *my people went down into Egypt . . . and the Assyrian oppressed them with no cause* (Isa 52:4). We have an example, for the Lord prayed for those who crucified him (Luke 23:24), as did Stephen (Acts 7:59). And this is a precept inasmuch as someone should not be excluded from the shared prayers of the Church; but it is a counsel if some particular prayer be offered for him, because one is not bound to do this even when praying for all the living.

546. But there are more serious questions, for we find many prophets praying against their enemies: *may his children be fatherless* (Ps 109:9); *let me see your revenge on them* (Jer 11:20); and many such verses are found. And it should be said that those words are not said with vengeful affection, but in the spirit of prophecy, not the emotion of someone wishing but the spirit of someone foretelling: hence *let me see your revenge,* i.e., I will see; or it should be said that *saints will rejoice when they see the revenge* (Ps 58:10). Thus the saints who are perfect in God's justice wish the divine justice to be fulfilled.

547. Another question is what is said: *if someone knows his brother does a sin that is not to death, let him ask . . . there is a sin unto death. For that I say not that any man ask* (1 John 5:16:). Therefore among our brothers there are sins unto death: therefore if we should not pray for them, even less should we pray for our persecutors. And Augustine

peccatum mortale dicitur ad mortem, sed peccatum in Spiritum sanctum, quod proprie est impaenitentia finalis. Et hoc sufficiat ad praesens, quia de hoc habebitur in 12. Nec est credendum quod sit aliquod peccatum quod non possit veniam consequi, quia nullum ita magnum quod illud Chaym, *maior est iniquitas mea quam ut veniam merear* etc. Sed sicut Deus propter aliqua peccata praecedentia deserit a gratia et propter [hoc] homines cadunt in peccatis, unde et dicuntur indurati vel execati, Ro. I, 24: *tradidit illos Deus in desideria cordis eorum, in immunditiam*, ita propter immanitatem alicuius peccati Deus non dat gratiam ut paeniteat; et istud peccatum est cum homo cognoscit bonum et prosequitur [malum]. Unde non dicitur peccatum ad mortem quin aliqui paeniteant, sed quia quantum est de se non merentur ut apponatur gratia. Unde quia grave est paenitere et cum difficultate ideo dicitur peccatum ad mortem; et quia oratio non fit pro peccatoribus nisi ut convertantur, ideo frustra fit pro talibus. Unde quando Dominus dixit, *Pater, ignosce illis* etc., non oravit pro omnibus persecutoribus, sed pro illis qui praedestinati erant; et ipse sciebat qui erant illi qui converti debebant. Sed quia nos nescimus praedestinatos et qui sint in peccato ad mortem, ideo debemus pro omnibus orare.

Tertia quaestio est, et habetur in Glossa, quia videtur quod non sit conveniens orare pro persecutoribus, quia Apoc XIX, 2 dicitur *vindica sanguinem sanctorum* etc.; ergo possumus petere vindictam et nos. Et solvitur dupliciter ab Augustino. Una solutio, quia cum dicitur *vindica sanguinem*, potest intelligi dupliciter: de hominibus vel de rege iniquo. Dicitur enim aliquis vindicari uno modo, quod destruatur nequitia illius qui per nequitiam te offendit, et ista est optima vindicta; sic Stephanus vindicatus est de Paulo. Uno modo, quod inferatur pena, non quod ipsi vindictam appetant, sed zelo iustitiae. Vel *vindica* non est intelligendum quasi ipsi exoptent vindictam, sed dicuntur clamare inquantum ipsa mors iniusta expetit a Deo ultionem, sicut dicitur Gen. IV, 10 *en sanguis fratris tui Abel clamat ad me* etc.

548. Consequenter Dominus ponit rationes probantes, et sunt duae: una ex exemplo divino, alia ex fine.

549. Quantum ad primum dicit **ut sitis filii Patris vestri**. Sed hoc videtur nihil esse dictum: homo enim fit filius Dei per gratiam; ergo non est ex operibus. Dominus autem videtur innuere quod homo debet bene agere ut gratiam acquirat. Sed sciendum quod ista filiatio non est naturalis, sed similitudinis, Ro. VIII, 29: *quos praescivit et praedestinavit conformes fieri imaginis Filii eius.* Unde quanto aliquis crescit in divina similitudine, tanto in divina filiatione. Inceptio divinae similitudinis est a fide. Nullus autem credit nisi volens: unde ibi operatur

resolves this, because not every mortal sin is said to be 'to death', but only the sin against the Holy Spirit, which is properly final impenitence. And this suffices for now, because it will be dealt with in chapter twelve. Nor should it be believed that there is any sin that cannot be forgiven, for none was so great as that of Cain: *my iniquity is greater than that* (Gen 4:13). But just as God for certain preceding sins withdraws grace, because of which men fall into sin, hence they are also called hard-hearted or blinded: *God gave them up to the desires of their hearts, unto uncleanness* (Rom 1:24); so on account of the savagery of certain sins God does not give the grace of repentance, and this sin is when a man knows the good and pursues evil. Hence it is not called a sin unto death if people do not repent, but because it is so great in itself that they do not deserve that grace be offered. Hence because it is a hard thing to repent of, and it happens with difficulty, thus it is called a sin unto death; and because prayer is not made for sinners except for their conversion, these prayers are thus in vain for such people. Hence when the Lord said, *Father forgive them for they know not what they do* (Luke 23:34), he was not praying for all his persecutors, but for those who were predestined; and he knew who they were who were due to be converted. But because we do not know the predestined or who will be in sin at death, therefore we must pray for all.

The third question, which comes from the Gloss, is that it seems that it is not fitting to pray for persecutors because it is said *he has revenged the blood of his servants* (Rev 19:2); therefore we too must seek revenge. And this is resolved in two ways by Augustine. One solution is that when it is said *revenged the blood*, it is understood two ways: concerning men or concerning the wicked king. For one way someone is said to be vindicated is when the wrongdoing of the one whose wrongdoing offended you is destroyed, and this is the best revenge; and this is how Stephen was vindicated regarding Paul. In another way, when a penalty is inflicted, not because they would seek revenge, but from zeal for justice. Or revenge is not to be understood as though they were desiring revenge, but they are said to cry out in that the unjust death itself seeks retribution from God, as is said: *the blood of your brother Abel cries out to me* (Gen 4:10).

548. Accordingly, the Lord sets down the reasons proving it, and there are two: one from divine example, the other from the end.

549. As to the first he says, **that you may be the children of your Father**. But this seems to be saying nothing: for man becomes a child of God by grace; therefore it is not by works. But the Lord seems to imply that man should act well so that he acquires grace. But it must be known that this sonship is not natural, rather it is a likeness: *for whom he preknew, he also predestined to be conformable to the image of his Son* (Rom 8:29). Hence the more someone grows in divine likeness, the more he grows in divine filiation. The beginning of divine likeness is from faith. But no one

libertas arbitrii, Io. I, 12: *dedit eis potestatem filios Dei fieri, his qui credunt in nomine eius.* Crescit autem similitudo ista ex caritate, amplius crescit per opera, maxime autem quando adipiscetur gloriam, Sap. V: *ecce quomodo computati sunt inter filios Dei* etc, I Io. III, 2: *videbimus eum sicuti est.* **Ut sitis**, ergo, **filii**, per imitationem operum, in spe: in re autem per gloriam in vita aeterna.

550. **Qui est in caelis**, quia praesidet caelum, corporalibus et spiritualibus.

551. **Qui solem.** Hoc potest intelligi de sole et pluvia materiali, ad litteram. Et nota secundum hoc duo: quia si ipse dat bona quae creavit, quare tu non dabis qui dispensas **super bonos**, idest amicos, **et malos**, idest inimicos, Et dicit **super bonos et malos**, quia aliter dat bonis et aliter malis: bonis enim cedit in utilitatem quia nec exaltantur prosperis nec deiciuntur adversis; malis, in detrimentum. Aliud: nota quod bona temporalia non sunt affectanda nec mala temporalia timenda: ex quo bonis aliquando mala et malis multotiens bona dantur.

Vel **qui solem** potest exponi de sole spirituali et pluvia spirituali. Sed obicitur Sap. V, 6: *sol intelligentiae non est ortus nobis,* et Is. V, 6: *nubibus mandabo ne pluant super eam imbrem.* Sed dicendum quod bonis et malis dat ista quantum ad sufficientiam, sed quantum ad efficaciam solis bonis, sicut doctrina Christi bonis est efficax, malis non. Vel per ista duo intelligitur baptismus, et in sole fervor Spiritus sancti, in pluvia aqua.

552. **Si enim.** Hic ponitur secunda ratio. Duo dixerat **diligite inimicos**, etc., et **benefacite** etc., et haec non meritoria sunt nisi ex caritate. Unde **si enim diligitis.** Supple rationem: nulla enim dilectio est meritoria nisi ex caritate quae est qua diligitur aliquis propter Deum; ergo principaliter diligendus est Deus, et omnes homines propter Deum. **Nonne et publicani.** Publicani dicebantur quod preerant publicis tributis, et dicuntur instituti a Publio romano consule, et reputabantur isti sicut modo usurarii propter fraudes quas faciebant, Eccli. XXVI, 28: *difficile exuiit negotians.*

Unde **et si salutaveritis** etc., **nonne ethnici**, qui sunt sine caritate gentiles: *ethnos* enim Graece, 'gens' dicitur Latine.

553. Consequenter Dominus totum quod in hoc capitulo dixerat concludit: **estote ergo vos perfecti sicut et Pater vester**, Gen. XVII, 1: *ambula coram me et esto perfectus,* Hebr. VI, 1: *intermittentes incoationis Christi sermonem, ad perfectionem feramur.* Sed quaestio est

believes unless he wants to: hence that is where our free will operates: *he gave them power to be made the sons of God, to those who believe in his name* (John 1:12). But this likeness grows by charity, growing larger by works, but most of all when someone attains glory: *behold how they are numbered among the children of God* (Wis 5:5); *when he will appear we will be like to him, for we will see him as he is* (1 John 3:2). So **that you may be the children**, therefore, in hope, by imitation in works; but in reality, by glory in eternal life.

550. **Who is in heaven**, because he presides from heaven, over physical things and spiritual ones.

551. **Who makes his sun to rise.** This can be understood literally about the material sun and rain. And note two things according to this: that if he gives the good things that he created, why will you not give, who dispense **upon the good**, i.e., your friends, **and the bad**, i.e., your enemies. And he says **upon the good and the bad**, because sometimes he gives to the good and sometimes to the evil: for he grants things to the benefit of the good because they are neither exalted in prosperity nor dejected in adversity; but it is to the detriment of the evil. Another thing: note that temporal goods are not to be grasped at nor are temporal evils to be feared: from the fact that through good things sometimes evils are given, and through evils, many times goods are given.

Or **who makes his sun** can be explained of the spiritual sun and rain. But it is objected, *the sun of understanding has not risen upon us* (Wis 5:6), and in Isaiah, *I will command the clouds to rain no rain upon it* (Isa 5:6). But it should be said that to the good and the bad he gives these things sufficiently, but efficaciously, only to the good, as the teaching of Christ is efficacious to the good, but not to the wicked. Or by these two things baptism may be understood, and in the sun, the ardor of the Holy Spirit; in the rain, water.

552. **For if you.** Here is set down the second reason. He had said twice **love your enemies**, and **do good**; and these things are not meritorious unless by charity. Hence, **for if you love.** Supply this reason: no love is meritorious except by charity which is the love by which someone is loved on account of God; therefore, God is to be loved chiefly, and all men for the sake of God. **Do not even the publicans**: they were called publicans who were in charge of the public taxes, and they are said to have been instituted by the Roman consul Publius, and they were considered mere usurers because of the cheating they did: *a merchant is hardly free from negligence* (Sir 26:28).

Hence **and if you salute your brethren only . . . do not the heathens also do this**, for the gentiles are without charity; for *heathens* is Greek, and means 'peoples' in Latin.

553. Accordingly the Lord concludes everything he has said in this chapter: **be you therefore perfect as also your heavenly Father is perfect**: *walk before me and be perfect* (Gen 17:1); *leaving the word of the beginning of Christ, let us go on to things more perfect* (Heb 6:1). But the question is

utrum hoc sit praeceptum vel consilium: si praeceptum, ergo omnes tenemur ad perfectionem; si consilium, cum omnes sint filii, omnes debent imitari Patrem.

554. Sed dicendum quod sicut natura distincta est, triplex est perfectio, scilicet simpliciter, secundum naturam et secundum tempus. Prima solus Deus perfectus; secundum naturam quando aliquis habet ea quae natura sua requirit; secundum tempus, sicut puer dicitur perfectus. Loquendo ergo de perfecta dilectione, tunc similiter perfectio Deus diligitur quantum diligendus est; et hoc est in solo Deo: nulla enim creatura potest diligere quantum diligendus est. Diligitur enim ex sua bonitate, quae infinita est: et ideo dicendum quod ly *sicut* importat similitudinem imitationis.

555. Est autem alia perfectio dilectionis possibilis creaturae, ut scilicet Deum diligat secundum totalitatem suam. Et est triplex gradus istius perfectionis; et unus non est possibilis in vita ista; aliae duae possibiles. Ad unum horum omnes tenentur, quia ista totalitas potest referri ad actum, et sic est perfectio patriae. In vita enim ista, propter multas occupationes, non est possibilis ista perfectio.

556. Est etiam totalitas in via quae est intentionis, ut scilicet habeas Deum in omnibus tuis tanquam finem ultimum, nihil cogitato contra eum. Et hoc est praeceptum: omnes enim tenentur se et sua ordinare in Deum.

557. Alia est perfectio media, et ista est religiosorum: quanto enim magis eximitur homo ab actibus mundi, tanto magis cogitat de Deo in actu et plus ascedit ad similitudinem eorum qui sunt in patria. Et propterea apostoli voluerunt esse pauperes, non propter paupertatem, sed ut facilius contemplationi vacarent. Et ideo est virginitas vel continentia de perfectione consilii, quia nuptae cogitant quae mundi sunt, et ideo non ita feruntur in Dei contemplatione.

558. Patet ergo quod alia est dilectio quae est perfectio simpliciter, alia quae possibilis creature, alia media, sicut dictum est.

whether this is a precept or a counsel: if a precept, then all are bound to perfection; if a counsel, since all men are sons, all ought to imitate their Father.

554. But it should be said that just as nature is distinct, perfection is threefold, namely simple perfection, perfection according to nature, and perfection according to time. In the first way, only God is perfect. Perfection according to nature is when someone has those things that his nature requires; according to time, as a child is said to be perfect. Therefore when speaking of perfect love, similarly God is loved perfectly when he is loved as much as he should be loved; and only God can love this way: for no creature can love as much as God should be loved. For he is loved according to his goodness, which is infinite; and so it must be said that the *as also* conveys a likeness by imitation.

555. But there is another perfection of love possible to a creature, namely that it loves God according to its totality. And there are three degrees of this perfection, and one is not possible in this life; but the other two are. To one of these all men are bound, for this totality can be referred to act, and this is the perfection of the heavenly homeland. In this life, because of many occupations, this perfection is not possible.

556. There is another totality in earthly life, which is that of intention, namely so that you hold God as last end in all your doings, thinking nothing contrary to him. And this is the precept: for all are bound to order themselves and their doings to God.

557. The other is the middle perfection, and this is the perfection of religious: for the more a man extracts himself from the acts of the world, the more he may think of God actually and the more he can approach the likeness of those who are in the heavenly homeland. And this is why the apostles wanted to be poor, not because of poverty, but so that they would be more easily free for contemplation. And thus virginity or continence are of the perfection of the counsel, for married people think on the things that are of the world, and thus they are not brought into the contemplation of God.

558. It is clear, then, that the love that is simple perfection is one thing, the love that is possible to a creature is another, and there is another between the two, as was said.

CHAPTER 6

Lecture 1

^{6:1} Attendite ne iustitiam vestram faciatis coram hominibus, ut videamini ab eis; alioquin mercedem non habebitis apud Patrem vestrum qui in caelis est. [n. 559]

^{6:2} Cum ergo facis eleemosynam, noli tuba canere ante te, sicut hypocritae faciunt in synagogis et in vicis, ut honorificentur ab hominibus. Amen dico vobis, receperunt mercedem suam. [n. 562]

^{6:3} Te autem faciente eleemosynam, nesciat sinistra tua quid faciat dextera tua, [n. 565]

^{6:4} ut sit eleemosyna tua in abscondito; et Pater tuus, qui videt in abscondito, reddet tibi. [n. 567]

^{6:1} Προσέχετε [δὲ] τὴν δικαιοσύνην ὑμῶν μὴ ποιεῖν ἔμπροσθεν τῶν ἀνθρώπων πρὸς τὸ θεαθῆναι αὐτοῖς· εἰ δὲ μή γε, μισθὸν οὐκ ἔχετε παρὰ τῷ πατρὶ ὑμῶν τῷ ἐν τοῖς οὐρανοῖς.

^{6:2} Ὅταν οὖν ποιῇς ἐλεημοσύνην, μὴ σαλπίσῃς ἔμπροσθέν σου, ὥσπερ οἱ ὑποκριταὶ ποιοῦσιν ἐν ταῖς συναγωγαῖς καὶ ἐν ταῖς ῥύμαις, ὅπως δοξασθῶσιν ὑπὸ τῶν ἀνθρώπων· ἀμὴν λέγω ὑμῖν, ἀπέχουσιν τὸν μισθὸν αὐτῶν.

^{6:3} σοῦ δὲ ποιοῦντος ἐλεημοσύνην μὴ γνώτω ἡ ἀριστερά σου τί ποιεῖ ἡ δεξιά σου,

^{6:4} ὅπως ᾖ σου ἡ ἐλεημοσύνη ἐν τῷ κρυπτῷ· καὶ ὁ πατήρ σου ὁ βλέπων ἐν τῷ κρυπτῷ ἀποδώσει σοι.

^{6:1} Take heed that you do not your justice before men in order to be seen by them: otherwise you will not have a reward from your Father who is in heaven. [n. 559]

^{6:2} Therefore when you give alms, do not sound a trumpet before you, as the hypocrites do in the synagogues and in the streets, that they may be honored by men. Amen I say to you, they have received their reward. [n. 562]

^{6:3} But when you give alms, do not let your left hand know what your right hand does. [n. 565]

^{6:4} That your alms may be in secret, and your Father who sees in secret will repay you. [n. 567]

---

559. *Attendite ne iustitiam.* Supra Dominus adimplevit legem quantum ad praecepta; nunc incipit adimplere quantum ad promissa. In veteri enim lege promittebantur temporalia, sicut dicit Augustinus, quae erant maxima duo desiderabilia, scilicet gloria mundana et affluentia divitiarum, Deut. XXVIII, 1: *si audieris vocem Domini* etc. Dominus autem docet in hoc capitulo non facere iustitiae opera propter temporalia neque propter gloriam mundi neque propter affluentiam divitiarum.

Dividitur autem hoc capitulum in partes duas. In prima parte docet non esse facienda opera iustitiae propter gloriam mundi; secundo non esse facienda propter divitias, ibi **nolite thesaurizare**.

Circa primum duo facit:
primo ponit doctrinam in generali;
secundo exsequitur per partes, ibi **cum ergo facis**.

Circa primum duo facit:
primo ponit documentum;
secundo documenti rationem assignat, ibi **alioquin**.

560. Dicit ergo **attendite**. Signater dicit **attendite**, propter tres rationes. Primo quia ibi est opus attentione ubi aliquid occulte subintelligitur: ita est de appetitu humanae laudis. Unde Chrysostomus: *occulte intrat et*

559. *Take heed that you do not your justice.* Above the Lord gave the fulfillment of the law as to the precepts; now he begins to give the fulfillment as to the promises. In the old law temporal things were promised, as Augustine says, which were the two most desirable things, namely, worldly glory and abundance of riches: *if you hear the voice of the Lord* (Deut 28:1). But the Lord teaches in this chapter not to do works of justice for the sake of temporal goods nor for worldly glory nor for an abundance of wealth.

However, this chapter is divided into two parts. In the first part he teaches that works of justice are not to be done for the sake of earthly glory; second, they are not to be done for riches, at **do not lay up for yourselves treasures** (Matt 6:19).

Concerning the first he does two things:
first, he sets down the teaching in general;
second, he follows it through its parts, at **therefore when you give alms**.

Concerning the first he does two things:
first, he sets down the instruction;
second, he assigns the reason for the teaching, at **otherwise**.

560. Therefore he says **take heed**. He says **take heed** significantly, for three reasons. First is that attention is important where something hidden might slip in: so it is with the appetite for human praise. Hence Chrysostom says: *it*

omnia quae intus sunt insensibiliter auffert, Ps. *a sagitta volante*. Secundo opus est attentione contra ea quibus difficile resistitur. Augustinus in *Sententiis prosperis*: *quas vires ad nocendum habeat humanae gloriae cupido, non facile noverunt nisi illi qui eis bellum indixerint, quia etsi facile non quaeritur cum negatur difficile tamen quaeritur relinquitur cum offertur*, Io. XII, 39: *propterea credere non poterant*. Tertio quia quam opera sunt maiora tam minus potest homo praecavere. Chrysostumus: *omne malum vexat filios diaboli haec autem filios Dei*, Zach. III, 1: *sathan sedebat a dextris*, idest diabolus insidians bonis operibus.

Et non dixit **attendit**e nisi postquam removit iram animi et concupiscentiam et odium. Animus enim subiectus passionibus non potest attendere quid in corde geratur, Prov. IV, 23,25: *omni custodia serva*, et post, *oculi videant recta*.

Ne iustitiam, idest opus iustitiae. Iustitia quandoque sonat in vitium quando scilicet praesumitur ex propriis viribus, Ro. X, 3: *ignorantes Dei iustitiam* etc; aliquando sonat in virtutem, sicut hic **ne iustitiam**, quae scilicet a vobis exigitur: dixerat enim Dominus **nisi abundaverit** etc. Et determinat quomodo poterat observari. Et si totum referritur ad laudem hominum non valeret, et ideo necessaria est recta intentio. Et hoc est: **ne iustitiam** etc.

561. Sed quaerit Chrysostomus: quid si traham pauperem in partem? Dicendum quod si gloriam habeat in corde et ad gloriam habeat intentionem non valet. Et ideo Gregorius dicit *ita opus fiat in publico ut intentio maneat in occulto*. Et hoc est **ut videamini**.

Sed numquid semper quaerimus gloriam quando volumus videri ab hominibus? Augustinus dicit quod dupliciter aliquid quaeritur: uno modo ut finis ultimus, alio ut necessarium ad finem. Illud autem proprie quaerimus quod volumus ut finem ultimum, aliud autem non proprie quaerimus quod volumus ut necessarium ad finem: sicut aliquis quaerit navem ut vadat in patriam, hic non proprie quaerit navem, sed patriam. Unde si ergo vis videri ab hominibus ut des eis exemplum et propter gloriam Dei, non prohiberis, quia supra dixit **sic luceat lux vestra** etc. Prohibetur autem ne intentio feratur sicut in principalem finem. Et hoc est: **ut videamini ab eis**, tantum, scilicet sic etiam placere hominibus aliquando vituperatur, Gal. I, 10: *si adhuc hominibus placerem*; aliquando laudatur, I Cor. X, 33.

562. Consequenter assignat rationem sui documenti. Unde **alioquin mercedem**. Nullus meretur aliquid apud aliquem cui nihil dat. Unde qui facit aliquid propter

sneaks in and carries off unnoticed everything that is inside; or *from the arrow that flies by day* (Ps 91:6). Second, attention is important against those things that are hard to resist. Augustine says in *The Sentences*: *they do not easily know what powers for harm the desire for human glory may have, except those who have declared war on them, for even if it is easily not sought when it is denied, still it is sought; when it is relinquished nevertheless it is sought; when it is abandoned, then it is bestowed*. And, *therefore they could not believe* (John 12:39). Third, because the greater the works, the less man can guard against it. Chrysostom: *this desire troubles not only the sons of the devil, but also the sons of God*; and, *Satan stood on his right hand to be his adversary* (Zech 3:1), i.e the devil entrapping men through good works.

And he did not say **take heed** until after he had taken away anger of soul and covetousness and hatred. For the soul subject to passions cannot pay attention to what is borne in the heart: *with all care keep your heart* (Prov 4:23), and after *let your eyes look straight ahead* (Prov 4:25).

That you do not do your justice, i.e., works of justice. Justice sometimes represents a vice, namely, when it is presumed upon one's own powers: *they, not knowing the justice of God* (Rom 10:3). Sometimes it represents a virtue, as here, **that you do not your justice**, namely those things that are required of you: for the Lord had said, **unless your justice abound** (Matt 5:20). And he determines how it could be observed. And if it were altogether for the sake of men's praise, it would not have any worth, and thus a right intention is necessary. And this is **that you do not your justice**.

561. But Chrysostom asks: what if I drew a poor man aside? It should be said that if he has glory in his heart and has the intention of glory, it would not have any worth. And thus Gregory says *let the work in public be done so that the intention remains hidden*. And this is **in order to be seen**.

But do we always seek glory when we wish to be seen by men? Augustine says that something can be sought in two ways: in one way as an ultimate end, in another way as something necessary to the end. But we seek something properly which we want as our ultimate end. But what we do not seek properly is what we want as necessary to the end: as someone who seeks a ship so that he may go to his country does not properly seek the ship but the country. Hence if therefore you wish to be seen by men so that you give them an example, and for the glory of God, you are not prohibited, for above he says, **so let your light shine before men** (Matt 5:16). But it is prohibited for your intention to be ordered to it as the principal end. And this is: **in order to be seen by them**, only, that is. In this way also pleasing men is sometimes reproached: *if I yet pleased men, I would not be the servant of Christ* (Gal 1:10); sometimes it is praised: *as I also in all things please all men* (1 Cor 10:33).

562. Next, he assigns the reason for his instruction. Hence **otherwise you will have no reward**. No one merits anything from someone to whom he gives nothing. Hence

homines et non propter Deum dicitur nihil dare. Chrysostomus *quae sapientia eleemosynam dare et mercedem Dei perdere?* De hac mercede loquitur de qua Gen. XV, 1: *ego Dominus, merces,* et supra **merces vestra copiosa est** etc.

Consequenter exequitur per partes cum dicit **cum ergo facis**. Et hoc quantum ad eleemosynam, orationem et ieiunium. Secundum, ibi **cum oratis**; Tertium, **cum ieiunatis**. Et ponit ista tria quia, secundum Chrysostomum, Dominus voluit instruere contra illa quibus fuit temptatus, scilicet de gula, de avaritia et de inani gloria, sicut patet supra IV; et est contra gulam ieiunium, contra avaritiam eleemosyna, contra inanem gloriam oratio: nihil enim eam vincere potest cum etiam de bonis operibus amplietur.

563. Considerantum quod ista tria sunt partes iustitiae dupliciter. Satisfactoriae enim iustitiae est ut qui peccat satisfaciat. Peccatum autem est triplex: vel contra Deum, vel contra seipsum, vel contra proximum. Contra Deum peccatur per superbiam; et huic opponitur humilitas orationis, Eccli. XXXV, 21: *oratio humiliantis se.* Contra proximum per avaritiam, et ideo satisfacit per eleemosynam. Contra se per carnis concupiscentiam, et ideo satisfacit per ieiunium. Ieronymus. *Oratione sanantur pestes cunctae mentis, ieiunio pestis corporis.* Item ista tria sunt partes iustitiae quae est religionis proprius actus: religiosi enim debent offerre sacrificium Deo. Est autem triplex bonum exterius, scilicet res; interius: corpus et anima. Per eleemosynam ergo offerunt exteriora bona, Hebr. ult. *beneficientiae et communionis*; per ieiunium corpora propria, Ro. XII, 1: *exhibeatis corpora vestra hostiam*; per orationem animam: est enim oratio ascensus mentis in Deum, Ps. *dirigatur oratio mea.*

Circa eleemosynam ergo, quae prima est, duo facit: primo excludit modum indebitum, secundo ponit debitum, ibi **te autem**. Circa primum excludit modum indebitum; secundo assignat rationem, ibi **amen dico**. Modum indebitum excludit ex tribus: ex signo, loco et fine.

564. Quantum ad primum dicit **cum ergo facis**, continuatio **attendite ne iustitiam** etc. Unde cum eleemosyna sit pars iustitiae, **cum facis eleemosynam noli** etc. Consuetudo erat apud Iudaeos quod quando faciebant publicas eleemosynas clangebant tubis ad hoc quod pauperes congregarentur. Istud ergo quod ex quadam necessitate inductum fuit malitia hominum pervertit ad gloriam inanem; et ideo Dominus prohibet. Et secundum Chrysostomum idem est quasi tuba clangens quando de quocumque bono appetis apparere etiam si in occulto fiat, Is. XL, 9: *exalta in fortitudine vocem.*

whoever does something for the sake of men and not for God's sake is said to give nothing. Chrysostom says: *what wisdom is it to give alms and lose God's reward?* He speaks of this reward: *I, the Lord am . . . your reward* (Gen 15:1), and above, **for your reward is very great** (Matt 5:12).

Next, he goes through the parts when he says **therefore when you give alms**. And this refers to almsgiving, prayer, and fasting. The second is at **and when you pray** (Matt 6:5); the third, at **when you fast** (Matt 6:16). And he mentions these three things because, according to Chrysostom, the Lord wanted to instruct against those things by which he had been tempted, namely, gluttony, greed, and vainglory, as is clear above; and fasting is against gluttony, almsgiving is against greed, and prayer is against vainglory: for nothing can conquer it since it is even intensified by good works.

563. It should be considered that these three things are parts of justice in two ways. For it is of satisfactory justice that someone who sins makes satisfaction. But sin is threefold: either against God, against oneself, or against one's neighbor. Against God one sins by pride: and to this is opposed the humility of prayer: *the prayer of him humbling himself* (Sir 35:21). We sin against our neighbor by greed, and this is satisfied for by almsgiving. We sin against ourselves by the concupiscence of the flesh, and this is satisfied for by fasting. Jerome says: *by prayer the pestilences of the mind are healed, by fasting the pestilence of the body.* Likewise these three are parts of justice which is the most proper act of religion: for it belongs to religion to offer sacrifice to God. But there are three kinds of goods, namely the external good of belongings, and the interior ones of body and soul. Thus by almsgiving they offer external goods: *do not neglect to do good and to share what you have* (Heb 13:16). By fasting they offer their own body: *present your bodies as a living sacrifice* (Rom 12:1). And by prayer, their souls: for prayer is the raising of the mind to God: *let my prayer be directed* (Ps 141:2).

Concerning almsgiving, which is first, he does two things: first he excludes the improper mode, second, he sets down the due mode, at **but when you give alms**. Concerning the first he excludes the improper mode; second, he assigns the reason, at **amen I say to you**. He excludes the improper mode by three things: sign, place, and end.

564. As to the first, he says **therefore when you give alms**, necessarily **take heed that you do not your justice**. Hence since alms are a part of justice, **therefore when you give alms, do not**. The custom among the Jews was to sound a trumpet when they gave public alms so that the poor would gather around. Thus something that had arisen from a certain necessity was perverted into vainglory by the malice of men. And according to Chrysostom it is the same as sounding a trumpet when you desire to be noticed for a good deed, even if it is done in secret: *lift up your voice with strength* (Isa 40:9).

Sicut hypocritae. Hic primo ponitur de hypocritis. Unde videndum quid est. Hoc nomen 'hypocrita' proprie derivatum est et productum a repraesentatione quae fiebat in ludis theatralibus, ubi inducebant homines habentes facies lamatas ad repraesentandum homines quibus gesta repraesentabant. Unde dicebatur hypocrita ab 'hypo', quod est 'sub', et 'crisyo', quod est 'indicium': alius enim erat et alius videbatur. Et talis est hypocrita qui exterius habet speciem sanctitatis et interius non implet quae ostendit. Gregorius dicit quod non si aliquando cadit propter infirmitatem: illi enim proprie sunt hypocritae qui tantum ut videantur speciem sanctitatis habent.

Consequenter excludit quantum ad locum. Et hoc etiam reprehenditur si simulatoriae fiat, non autem si propter exemplum.

565. *In synagogis*, sicut modo in ecclesia; *et in vicis*, sicut in loco publico, ut videantur. Et hoc est quod supra dixit *coram hominibus; ut honorificentur* etc. Io. V, 44: *quomodo potestis* etc.

Consequenter assignat rationem *amen dico: receperunt mercedem*. Illud est enim merces uniuscuiusque propter quid operatur, Matth. XX, 13: *nonne ex denario convenistis* etc.

Consequenter assignat modum debitum et convenientem; et postea assignat rationem, ibi *ut sit eleemosyna*. Dicit ergo *te autem faciente*. Istud multipliciter exponitur. Chrysostomus enim dicit quod in libro *Canonum apostolorum* sic exponitur quod per sinistram intelligitur populus infidelis, per dexteram fidelis. Unde vult quod nihil fiat coram infidelibus.

566. Contra hoc Augustinus: quia cum facit eleemosynam propter gloriam, et tunc etiam neque a fidelibus debet videri; vel propter utilitatem, et tunc debet fieri coram infidelibus: *hoc proprie utilis est ut videntes* etc.

Alii autem exponunt quod per sinistram intelligit uxorem quae solet impedire aliquando virum ab operibus misericordiae; unde vult quod etiam uxor nesciat. Et similiter intelligendum de quocumque alio. Et similiter obicit contra hoc Augustinus quia hoc praeceptum datur etiam: nullus ergo deberet dicere: *nesciat dextera tua* etc.

567. Unde Augustinus aliter exponit et etiam Chrysostomus, et quasi in idem reducitur. Dicunt quod in Scriptura per sinistram intelliguntur temporalia bona, per dexteram spiritualia, Prov. III, 16: *in dextera illius longitudo* etc. Unde voluit Dominus quod non fieret per gloriam terrenam. Vel aliter et quasi in idem redit: per dexteram aliquando intelliguntur opera virtutis, per sinistram peccata; quasi quando fit opus virtutis non fiat

As the hypocrites. This is the first thing said about hypocrites. Hence we should see what a hypocrite is. This word 'hypocrite' is properly derived and produced from a representation which was done in theatrical plays, where they brought in men having masked faces to represent men whose gestures they imitated. Hence hypocrite was said from 'hypo', which is 'under', and 'crisyo', which is 'sign': for in place of someone, another person was seen. And that is what a hypocrite is, someone who has the appearance of sanctity outwardly and inwardly does not fulfill what he shows. Gregory says that it is not someone who falls through weakness, for those are properly hypocrites who seem to have the appearance of sanctity only so that they may be seen.

Next, he excludes the improper mode as to place. And this also is reproached if it is done by pretense, but not if for the sake of example.

565. *In the synagogues*, just as in the Church of today; *and in the streets*, as in a public place, so that they may be seen. And this is what he said above, *before men; that they may be honored*: *how can you believe?* (John 5:44).

Then he assigns the reason, at *amen I say to you: they have received their reward*. For this is the reward of each person according to his works: *did you not agree with me for a denarius?* (Matt 20:13).

Next, he assigns the due and fitting mode of giving alms; and afterward he assigns the reason at *that your alms may be*. Therefore he says *but when you give alms*. This has many explanations. For Chrysostom says that in the book of the *Canons of the Apostles*, it is explained that by the left hand is understood an unbelieving nation, and by the right a believing one. Hence he wishes that nothing be done in front of unbelievers.

566. Against this Augustine says: for someone gives alms either for the sake of glory, and then it should not be seen even by believers; or else for the sake of benefit, and then it should expressly be done before unbelievers: *that they may see your good works, and glorify your Father* (Matt 5:16).

But others explain that by the left hand is understood a wife who tends to hinder a man from works of mercy; hence he means that even the wife should not know. And the same thing should be understood of anyone else. And Augustine objects similarly against this for this precept is also given to women: therefore no one should say: *do not let your right hand know*.

567. Hence Augustine explains it another way, as well as Chrysostom, and it can be reduced to practically the same. They say that in Scripture temporal goods are meant by the left, and spiritual ones by the right: *length of days is in her right hand* (Prov 3:16). Hence the Lord meant that it should not be done for earthly glory. Or another way and it also amounts to the same: by the right hand is sometimes understood the works of virtue, by the left hand, sins; so that

cum aliquo peccato. Chrysostomus tamen ponit litteralem, et dicit quod Dominus loquitur per excessum, sicut si aliquis dicat: si posset fieri nollet quod hoc sciret pes meus.

Ponitur ratio: *ut sit eleemosyna in abscondito*, et in conscientia tua quae occulta est, I Cor. III: *quae sunt hominis nemo*, et iterum II Cor. I, 12: *gloria vestra haec est testimonium*: sic enim accipitur illud Ro. II, 28: *non enim qui in manifesto Iudaeus* etc.

Et Pater tuus reddet tibi, Hebr. IV, 13: *omnia nuda et aperta* etc. Ier. *pravum est cor hominis*. Augustinus dicit quod in quibusdam exemplaribus invenitur **reddet tibi** palam, quia sicut diabolus conatur aperire et publicare quae in conscientia sunt ut scandalum faciat, ita Deus ad maiorem utilitatem et etiam ad exemplum malorum adducet bona. Unde etiam sancti multi non potuerunt latere, Ps. *adducet quasi lumen iustitiam*, quam scilicet in occulto tenebas. Hoc tamen non videtur esse de textu.

when a work of virtue is done, it should not be done with any sin. Nevertheless, Chrysostom gives a literal reading and says that the Lord speaks by exaggeration, as if someone were to say, 'if it were possible, he would wish that my foot not know this.'

He gives the reason: **that your alms may be in secret**, and in your conscience which is hidden: *the things . . . no man knows* (1 Cor 2:11) and again, *for our glory is this: the testimony of our conscience* (2 Cor 1:12): for in this way is taken what is written: *for it is not that he is a Jew who is so outwardly* (Rom 2:28).

Your Father . . . will repay you: *all things are naked and open to his eyes* (Heb 4:13); *the heart is perverse above all measure* (Jer 17:9). Augustine says that in certain exemplars is found 'he **will repay you** publicly,' for just as the devil tries to open and make public the things that are in the conscience so that he can give scandal, so God for greater benefit and also for the example of evildoers brings forth good things. Hence even many saints could not remain hidden: *he will bring forth your justice as the light* (Ps 37:6), namely, what you were holding in secret. However, this does not seem to be in the text.

Lecture 2

6:5 Et cum oratis, non eritis sicut hypocritae, qui amant in synagogis et in angulis platearum stantes orare, ut videantur ab hominibus. Amen dico vobis, receperunt mercedem suam. [n. 668]

6:5 Καὶ ὅταν προσεύχησθε, οὐκ ἔσεσθε ὡς οἱ ὑποκριταί, ὅτι φιλοῦσιν ἐν ταῖς συναγωγαῖς καὶ ἐν ταῖς γωνίαις τῶν πλατειῶν ἑστῶτες προσεύχεσθαι, ὅπως φανῶσιν τοῖς ἀνθρώποις· ἀμὴν λέγω ὑμῖν, ἀπέχουσιν τὸν μισθὸν αὐτῶν.

6:5 And when you pray, you will not be as the hypocrites, who love to stand and pray in the synagogues and corners of the streets, that they may be seen by men: amen I say to you, they have received their reward. [n. 668]

6:6 Tu autem, cum oraveris, intra in cubiculum tuum, et clauso ostio, ora Patrem tuum in abscondito; et Pater tuus, qui videt in abscondito, reddet tibi. [n. 675]

6:6 σὺ δὲ ὅταν προσεύχῃ, εἴσελθε εἰς τὸ ταμεῖόν σου καὶ κλείσας τὴν θύραν σου πρόσευξαι τῷ πατρί σου τῷ ἐν τῷ κρυπτῷ· καὶ ὁ πατήρ σου ὁ βλέπων ἐν τῷ κρυπτῷ ἀποδώσει σοι.

6:6 But you when you will pray, enter into your chamber, and having shut the door, pray to your Father in secret; and your Father who sees in secret will repay you. [n. 675]

6:7 Orantes autem nolite multum loqui, sicut ethnici; putant enim quod in multiloquio suo exaudiantur. [n. 678]

6:7 Προσευχόμενοι δὲ μὴ βατταλογήσητε ὥσπερ οἱ ἐθνικοί, δοκοῦσιν γὰρ ὅτι ἐν τῇ πολυλογίᾳ αὐτῶν εἰσακουσθήσονται.

6:7 And when you are praying, do not speak much, as the heathens. For they think that in their speaking much they may be heard. [n. 678]

6:8 Nolite ergo assimilari eis. Scit enim Pater vester quid opus sit vobis, antequam petatis eum. [n. 681]

6:8 μὴ οὖν ὁμοιωθῆτε αὐτοῖς· οἶδεν γὰρ ὁ πατὴρ ὑμῶν ὧν χρείαν ἔχετε πρὸ τοῦ ὑμᾶς αἰτῆσαι αὐτόν.

6:8 Be not therefore like to them, for your Father knows what is needful for you, before you ask him. [n. 681]

---

568. *Et cum oratis*. Supra dominus ostendit de opere eleemosynae quod non est faciendum propter humanam gloriam; hic ostendit idem de oratione.

Et circa hoc duo facit:

primo docet modum orandi;

secundo docet quid sit in oratione petendum: *sic ergo orabitis*.

569. Circa primum duo facit:

primo docet vitare in oratione vanitates hypocritarum;

secundo vanitatem gentilium, ibi *orantes*.

570. Circa primum duo facit:

primo excludit modum inconvenientem orandi;

secundo assignat convenientem, ibi *tu autem*.

571. Excludit modum orandi exemplo hypocritarum: unde primo excludit exemplum istud; secundo exponit; tertio rationem assignat. Secundum, ibi *qui amant*; tertium: *amen dico*.

Satis convenienter post eleemosynam agit hic de oratione, quia sicut Eccli. XVIII, 23: *ante orationem* etc. Per bona enim opera, inter quae prima est eleemosyna, anima praeparatur ad orationem, Tren. III, 41: *levemus corda nostra* etc., quod fit quando bona opera consonant.

572. Et notandum quod Dominus non inducit ad orandum, sed docet modum orandi. Et hoc est *cum oraveris non eritis sicut hypocritae qui amant in synagogis et in angulis*. Per *hypocritae* intelliguntur simulatores

568. *And when you pray*. Above the Lord shows what is not to be done regarding almsgiving for the sake of human glory; here he shows the same thing regarding prayer.

And concerning this he does two things:

first, he teaches the way of praying;

second, he teaches what should be in a prayer of petition: *therefore you will pray thus* (Matt 6:9).

569. Concerning the first he does two things:

first, he teaches them to avoid the vanity of hypocrites in prayer;

second, to avoid the vanity of gentiles, at *when you are praying*.

570. Concerning the first he does two things:

first, he excludes an unfitting manner of praying;

second, he designates what is fitting, at *but you*.

571. He excludes the manner of praying by the example of the hypocrites: hence he first excludes this example, second explains, third, assigns the reason. The second is at *who love to stand and pray*; the third, at *amen I say to you*.

Fittingly enough after almsgiving, here he deals with prayer, for as Sirach says: *before prayer, prepare your soul* (Sir 18:23). For by good works, among which almsgiving is first, the soul is prepared for prayer: *let us lift up our hearts with our hands* (Lam 3:41), which happens when good works accord.

572. And it should be noted that the Lord does not compel us to pray, but teaches us the manner of praying. And this is *when you pray, you will not be as the hypocrites, who love to stand and pray in the synagogues and*

qui faciunt totum propter laudem humanam. Et quamvis hoc vitium sit in omni opere vitandum, tamen in oratione specialiter, secundum Chrysostomum, quia oratio est quoddam sacrificium quod offerimus Deo ex intimis cordis, Ps. *dirigatur oratio* etc. Sacrificium non licet offerri nisi Deo; offertur autem hominibus si fiat propter humanam gloriam. Unde tales sunt idolatrae.

Describitur autem hypocrita quantum ad affectum, locum, supra et infra totum. Quantum ad primum dicit *qui amant*. Contingit enim aliquando fieri aliqua titillatio in viris sanctis inanis gloriae, sed non sunt propter hoc in numero hypocritarum nisi ex proposito hoc agant, Ier. II, 24: *in desiderio animae suae*.

573. Et nota duo genera hypocritarum qui manifeste gloriam humanam quaerunt, scilicet qui in locis publicis orant. Unde dicit *in synagogis*, ubi erat congregatio populorum, Ps. *synagoga*; aliqui orant in locis privatis et ex ipsa vitatione gloriae gloriam quaerunt: volunt enim videri quaerere occultum cum tamen ament publicum. Et hoc est *in synagogis et angulis*. Si enim occultum in rei veritate quaererent, non angulum platearum, sed camerae locum quaererent; vel possumus dicere quod quaerunt apertum publicum. Sed duplex est publicum: quoddam deputatum orationi, scilicet synagoga; aliud non deputatum orationi scilicet angulus. Et est proprie angulus ubi duae lineae sese intersecant. Unde *angulis platearum*, enim duae plateae se intersecant, ita quod fit ibi quadrivium; et hoc est valde publicum nec orationi deputatum, Tren. IV, 1: *dispersi sunt lapides*.

Notandum etiam quod unum de rebus facientibus ad orationem est humilitas. Iudith IX, 16: *humilium et mansuetorum*. Ps. CI, 18: *respexisti in orationem*. Sed isti stant quasi superbi.

574. Sed videtur quod in nullo loco sit prohibitum orare ante I Tim. II, 8: *volo omnes viros* etc., Ps. *in ecclesiis benedicite*. Sed dicendum quod non est peccatum nisi sub hac intentione *ut videantur ab hominibus*. Et, sicut dicit Chrysostomus, etsi velle videri ab hominibus noceat in aliis operibus, tamen specialiter in oratione: quia nocet et quantum ad finem et quantum ad substantiam, quia etsi fiat in bona intentione, vix potest homo tenere animum quin evagetur per diversa; multo magis ergo quando fit propter gloriam hominum. Et hoc est *ut videantur*.

Numquid ergo non est orandum in loco publico? Sciendum quod Dominus intendit prohibere modum orandi per quem tollitur inanis gloria, quae numquam quaeritur nisi de aliquo singulari, quia quando sunt multi qui servant unum, ibi non quaeritur gloria ab alio.

street corners. By *hypocrites* is understood pretenders who do everything for human praise. And although this vice is to be avoided in every work, nevertheless it is especially to be avoided in prayer, according to Chrysostom, because prayer is a certain sacrifice that we offer God from our innermost hearts: *let my prayer be directed as incense in thy sight; the lifting up of my hands, as evening sacrifice* (Ps 141:2). A sacrifice is not allowed to be offered except to God; but it is offered to men if it is done for human glory. And such prayers are idolatry.

But the hypocrites are described as to their affection, place, pride, and intention. As to the first, he says *who love*. For sometimes a certain titillation of vainglory happens in holy men, but they are not counted among the hypocrites unless they act for that purpose: *in the desire of his heart* (Jer 2:24).

573. And note there are two kinds of hypocrites who openly seek human glory, that is, who pray in public places. Hence he says, *in synagogues*, where the congregation of the people prays: *congregation* (Ps 82:1). There are others who pray in private places and seek glory by this very avoidance of glory: for they wish to seem to seek privacy, although nevertheless they love what is public. And this is *in the synagogues and street corners*. For if they were truly seeking secrecy, they would not seek the corners of boulevards, but an enclosed place; or rather they would say that they seek a public area. But there are two kinds of public places: certain ones are set aside for prayer, like synagogues; others are not, namely, street corners. And it is properly a corner where two lines intersect. Hence *street corners*, where two streets intersect, so that there is a crossroads; and this is extremely public, and not designated for prayer: *the stones of the sanctuary are scattered* (Lam 4:1).

It should also be noted that one of the things at work in prayer is humility: *the prayer of the humble and meek has always pleased you* (Jdt 9:16). *He has had regard to the prayer* (Ps 102:17). But these people stand as though proud.

574. But it seems that in no place would it be forbidden to pray: *I wish that men pray in every place* (1 Tim 2:8); *in the churches bless* (Ps 68:26). But it should be said that it is not a sin except under the intention *that they may be seen by men*. And, as Chrysostom says, although willing to be seen by men is harmful in other works, nevertheless it is especially so in prayer: for it damages both the end and the constancy, for even if it is done with a good intention, a man can scarcely hold his mind so that it does not wander off into diverse things; much less, then, when this is done for the sake of human glory. And this is *that they may be seen*.

But then should one not pray in a public place? It should be known that the Lord intends to prohibit the manner of praying so that vainglory is removed, which is never sought except by someone on his own, for when there are many who keep one manner of praying, glory is not sought before

Unde Dominus tollit singularem modum orandi ut scilicet nullus oret in loco non deputando orationi, nisi aliquis sit tantae auctoritatis quod etiam aliis ad orandum inducat. Unde secundum Chrysostomum, hoc quod dicit *in angulis* referendum est ad omne illud per quod videris discretus esse ab aliis cum quibus conversaris.

575. *Amen dico.* Hic assignat rationem. Et dicit duo: *merces* et *suam.* Merces uniuscumque est per quam pascitur de opere suo. Unde quando nos facimus aliquid propter gloriam hominum, gloria hominum est merces nostra, cum tamen debemus expectare gloriam Dei veram. Et hoc est *receperunt mercedem suam,* ratione quia usurpaverunt, Gal. ult. *quae seminaverit homo.*

Tu autem. Hic ponit debitum modum. Et primo ponit eum; secundo assignat rationem: *et Pater.* Dicit ergo *tu cum oraveris,* idest orare disponeris, *intra in cubiculum.* Hoc tripliciter exponitur. Intelligitur primo ad litteram de secreto camerae. Sed numquid contrarium faciunt qui ad ecclesiam vadunt? Sed dicendum quod loquitur de oratione privata quae non est facienda nisi in loco privato. Et hoc propter tria. Primo quia concordat fidei, quia tunc confiteris Deum ubicumque esse praesentem, Ps. *Domine ante te omne,* Ier. XXIII, 24: *caelum et terram.* Secundo quia quando cum multis impeditur oratio quae in secreto quieta est, Osee II, 14: *ducam eam in solitudinem.* Tertio quia vitatur inanis gloria, II Reg. XIV: *ingressus est David,* tamen dicendum ut oraret *coram Domino,* solus scilicet *et clauso,* ad litteram, ut etiam excludas possibilitatem adeundi.

576. Secundo per cubiculum potest intelligi interius secretum cordis, Ps. *quae dicitis in cordibus.* **Ostia,** os, Eccli. XXVIII, 28: *ori tuo facito ostia* quasi dicat: *ora silenter.* Et hoc propter tria. Primo quia attestatur fidei, quia tunc confiteris quod Deus cogitationes cordium sciat, I Reg. XVI, 1: *homo videt ea quae parent.* Secundo quia non decet quod alii sciant petitiones tuas, Is. XXIV, 16: *secretum meum mihi.* Tertio, quia si voce loqueris alios impedires, III Reg. VI, 7: *malleus et securis non sunt audita* etc.

Sed quid dicemus de oratione publica? Dicendum quod Dominus loquitur de privata in qua quaeritur utilitas unius, sed etiam in publica quaeritur utilitas multitudinis. Et quia per huiusmodi clamores ad devotionem excitantur aliqui, ideo instituti sunt cantus. Unde Augustinus dicit in libro *de Confessionibus* quod beatus Athanasius, ne nimis delectaretur in cantu, volebat quod omnia legerentur submisse. Sed quia beatus Augustinus

one another. Hence the Lord removes the individual manner of praying, that namely, no one should pray in a place not designated for prayer, except someone with such authority that he may even lead others in prayer. Hence according to Chrysostom, the fact that he says **street corners** is to be referred to everything by which you seem to be set apart from the others with whom you associate.

575. *Amen I say to you.* Here he assigns the reason. And he says two things: *reward* and *their.* The reward of each person is that by which he is fed from his work. Hence when we do anything for the glory of men, the glory of men is our reward, although nevertheless we should wait for the true glory of God. And this is **they have received their reward** because they have usurped it: *what things a man will sow, those also will he reap* (Gal 6:8).

But you. Here he sets down the due manner. And first he sets it down; second, he assigns the reason: *and your Father.* Therefore he says *when you will pray,* i.e., when you are disposed to pray, *enter into your chamber.* This is explained three ways. First, it is understood literally about a separated room. But do not those who go to the church do the opposite? But it should be said that he speaks of private prayer which is only to be done in a private place. And this for three reasons. First, because it agrees with the faith, for then you confess that God is present everywhere: *Lord, all my desire is before you* (Ps 38:9); *do I not fill heaven and earth?* (Jer 23:24). Second, because prayer which in private is quiet, is hindered when with many others: *I will lead her into solitude: and I will speak to her heart* (Hos 2:14). Third, because vainglory is avoided: *and David went in,* so that he could pray *before the Lord* (2 Sam 7:18); alone, that is, *and having shut the door,* literally, so that you exclude also the possibility of anyone coming in.

576. Second, by the chamber can be understood the secret interior of the heart: *the things you say in your hearts* (Ps 4:4). *Door,* mouth: *make doors and bars to your mouth* (Sir 28:28), as though he said: *pray silently.* And this for three reasons. First, because it attests to the faith, for then you confess that God knows the thoughts of your heart: *man sees those things that appear, but the Lord beholds the heart* (1 Sam 16:7). Second, because it is not appropriate that others know your petitions: *my secret to myself* (Isa 24:16). Third, because if you speak aloud, you may impede others' prayer: *neither hammer nor axe . . . was heard* (1 Kgs 6:7).

But what will we say about public prayer? It should be said that the Lord speaks about private prayer in which the benefit of one person is sought, but in public prayer the good of the multitude is also sought. And because some people are excited to devotion by sounds of this kind, chant was instituted. Hence Augustine says in the book of *Confessions,* that blessed Athanasius, lest he become too delighted by the chants, wanted everything to be read quietly.

antequam converteretur multum profuerunt sibi huiusmodi cantus non ausus est contradicere, sed approbat.

577. Sed quaestio: utrum aliquis in loco privato orans debeat dicere verba vel non? Sed distinguendum est hic quia aliquando verba proveniunt ex intentione, aliquando ex impulsione cordis quia, sicut dicitur Iob IV, 2: *conceptum sermonem.* Unde ex ipso impetu spiritus aliqui proferuntur ad aliqua verba dicenda, et hoc est omnis effectus.

Verba autem dupliciter possunt considerari: vel ut debita, et tunc reddenda, sic sunt Horae, Ps. *voce mea ad Dominum;* vel ut utilia ad orandum, et tunc distinguendum de principio et fine quia *melior est finis orationis* etc. Eccl. VII, 9 ecclesiae. Si enim in principio orationis affectus excitatur per verba ad devote orandum, tunc utile est proferre verba; quando autem non excitatur affectus, tunc non sunt proferenda verba et operiendus affectus, quia sicut calidum evaporando diminuitur ita affectus evacuatur per verba, sicut etiam patet de dolore expresso aliis, Ps. *concaluit cor meum intra me,* Ier. XX, 9: *dixi: non loquar in nomine Domini, et factus est ignis* etc. Hoc sic exponit Chrysostomus: sed **clauso ostio.**

578. Tertio modo, sic exponit Augustinus quod per **cubiculum** intelligitur cor, per **ostium** exteriores sensus et etiam 'imaginatio'; quia talis debet intrare cor suum et claudere sensus et imaginationem ut nihil interius intret nisi quod pertinet ad orationem. Et Cyprianus assignat duas rationes: primo quia vituperabile est quod non attendis quae dicis cum loqueris cum rege aliquo; secundo quia Deus quomodo intelliget te si tu te ipsum non intelligis? Hoc est ostium de quo Apoc. III, 20: *ego sto ad hostium et pulso.*

Et Pater tuus. Hic assignat rationem. Nullus enim orat nisi illum quem videt. Deus autem *omnia nuda et aperta* etc. Hebr. IV, 13. **In abscondito,** vel cordis vel loci, **reddet tibi.**

Orantes etc. Hic docet vitare secundum vitium, scilicet multiloquium gentilium. Et circa hoc tria facit: primo docet vitare exemplum gentilium, secundo ponit intentionem, tertio assignat rationem. Secundum, ibi **putant enim;** tertium, ibi **nolite ergo.** Dicit ergo **orantes.** Et nota quod non dicit: *nolite multum orare,* quia hoc est contra illud Ro. XII, 12: *orationi instantes,* et Luc. XXII, 43: *factus in agonia.*

579. Orabat, Luc. VI, 12: *et erat pernoctans in oratione* sed dicit **nolite multum,** Augustinus, in libro *de Orando: non sit multa locutio sed sit multa praecatio si non desit fervens intentio.* Sed multum et paucum, magnum et parvum, relativa sunt. Multum enim potest

But because before he converted blessed Augustine found chants very beneficial, he did not dare to speak against them, but approved them.

577. But a question arises: should someone praying in private say words or not? But here it should be distinguished that sometimes words arise from intention, sometimes from the impulse of the heart, for, as is said: *who can withhold the words he has conceived?* (Job 4:2). Hence by the impulse of the Spirit some people are brought to the point of speaking words, and this is the whole effect.

But words can be considered two ways: either as owed, and then they should be said, like the Hours: *I cried to the Lord with my voice* (Ps 142:1); or as useful for praying, and then a distinction should be made about the beginning and the end, for *better is the end of a prayer than the beginning* (Eccl 7:9). For if in the beginning of a prayer the affections are excited to devout prayer by words, then it is useful to bring in words; but when the affections are not excited by this, then no words should be uttered and the affections should be shut up, for just as heat is diminished by evaporation, so affections are emptied out by words, as is also clear in expressing sorrow to others: *my heart grew hot within me* (Ps 39:3); *then I said: I will not make mention of him nor speak any more in his name* (Jer 20:9). This is how Chrysostom explains, but **having shut the door.**

578. In the third way, as Augustine explains, by **chamber** the heart is meant, by the **door** the external senses as well as the imagination; for such a person should enter his heart and close his senses and imagination so that nothing comes in except what pertains to his prayer. And Cyprian assigns two reasons: first, because it is blameable if you do not attend to what you say when you speak with any king; second, because how will God understand you if you do not understand yourself? This is the door that is spoken of: *I stand at the door and knock* (Rev 3:20).

And your Father. Here he assigns the reason. For no one prays except to someone who sees him. But to God *all things are naked and open* (Heb 4:13). **In secret,** whether of the heart or of place, he **will repay you.**

And when you are praying. Here he teaches us to avoid the second vice, namely, the verbosity of the gentiles. And concerning this he does three things: first, he teaches us to avoid the example of the gentiles, second, he sets down the intention, third, he assigns the reason. The second is at **for they think;** the third, at **be not therefore like to them.** Therefore he says **when you are praying.** And note that he does not say: *do not pray a lot,* for that is against what is said in Romans: *constant in prayer* (Rom 12:12); and in Luke: *in his agony, he prayed the longer* (Luke 22:43).

579. *He passed the whole night in prayer* (Luke 6:12). But he says **do not speak much.** Augustine, in his book *On Prayer: let there not be much speech but much supplication if a fervent intention is not lacking.* But much and little, great and small, are relative. For much can be said two ways in

dici dupliciter in comparatione ad orationem, quae est ascensus ad Deum. Vel multum loquuntur quando verba excedunt orationem, et hoc potest esse dupliciter: si scilicet verba sunt de illicitis, et haec sunt nociva; et quando non adest devotio, tunc magis homo redditur taediosus et orare redditur odiosum. Et ideo dicit Augustinus quod monachi in Aegypto habebant crebras orationes sed breves. Videbant enim quod devotio erat oranti necessaria, quae evacuabatur per multitudinem verborum. Et ideo in Ecclesia statutum est quod diversis horis diversa dicantur, Eccli. V, 1: *ne temere quid loquaris*. Augustinus: *hoc negotium*, scilicet orationis, *plus gemitibus quam verbis* etc.

580. Sicut ethnici. Gentiles colebant daemonia pro diis, Ps. *omnes dii gentium*. In daemonibus scilicet considerandum quod nesciunt futura vel occulta cordium nisi inquantum eis revelantur. Unde necessarium erat gentilibus quod totum diceretur per verba, III Reg. XVIII, 27: *clamate altius* etc.

Item daemones habent affectum mutabilem: unde per verba mutari possunt. Unde dicit Augustinus quod Plato dixit quod verbis mutabantur, Deus autem et omnia scit nec verbis flectitur, Mal. III, 6: *ego Deus et non mutor*, Num. XXIII, 19: *non est Deus ut homo*, Iob XLI, 3: *non parcet ei et verbis potentibis et ad deprecandum compositis*.

581. Putant enim etc. **Nolite ergo** etc. Et quare? **Scit enim** etc. Ps. *Dominus, ante te omne*. Ergo si scit non debemus verbis multiplicare. Sed dicetur: *Deus scit quae nobis sunt necessaria; quare ergo oramus*? Et respondet Ieronimus quod non petimus verbis ut significemus sed ut postulemus.

582. Et item posset dici: *quare proferimus verba*? Respondet Augustinus quod aliter est in oratione quam facimus homini et Deo, quia in homine multum valent verba ad hoc quod flectemus eum; in Deo, ad hoc ut cor nostrum ad eum levemus. Et ideo dicit Augustinus quod cum semper sit habendus affectus ad Deum, tamen oportet aliquando verbis orare ut non deficiat. Et sicut dicit Chrysostomus, ex frequenti oratione provenit quod homo redditur Deo familiaris et Deus ei. Exo. XXXIII, 9: *loquebatur Moyses* etc. Item ex hoc provenit humilitas, quia consideratur altitudo Dei et infirmitas propria, Gen XVIII, 31: *loquar ad Dominum meum*. Item homo ex hoc in actibus suis dirigitur et auxilium a Deo petit, Ps. *levavi oculos meos ad montes* etc., Col. III, 23: *omne quodcumque facit* etc.

relation to prayer, which is a raising up to God. They speak much when the words go outside the prayer, and this can be in two ways: namely, if the words are about something illicit, and these are harmful; and when there is no devotion, then man becomes rather bored and praying becomes hateful. And thus Augustine says that monks in Egypt had frequent but brief prayers. For they saw that devotion was necessary in the one praying, but it was emptied out by a multitude of words. And thus in the Church it was established that different things are said at different hours: *speak not anything rashly* (Eccl 5:1). Augustine: *this matter*, that is, prayer, *is more in groaning than in words*.

580. As the heathens. The gentiles worship demons for their gods: *all the gods of the gentiles are devils* (Ps 96:5). It should be considered in demons that they do not know the future or hidden things of the heart unless they are revealed to them. Hence it was necessary for the gentiles to say everything with words: *Cry louder! Surely he is a god; either he is meditating, or he has wandered away, or he is on a journey, or perhaps he is asleep and must be awakened* (1 Kgs 18:27).

Likewise, demons have changeable affections: hence by words they can be changed. Hence Augustine says that Plato said that they were flattered by words; but God both knows all things and is not persuaded by words: *I, the Lord, do not change* (Mal 3:6); *God is not a man . . . that he should be changed* (Num 23:19); *I will not spare them their words framed in prayer* (Job 41:3).

581. For they think that in their speaking much they may be heard. Be not therefore like to them. And why? **For your Father knows**: *all my desire is before you* (Ps 38:9). Therefore if he knows, we do not need to multiply our words. But it is said: *God knows what we need; why then do we pray?* And Jerome answers that we do not ask in words so that we may show, but so that we may request.

582. And likewise it can be said: *why do we bring forth words?* Augustine answers that we act differently in prayer to God than to a man, for with a man words avail greatly in persuading him; but with God, they avail in raising our heart to him. And thus Augustine says that although we should always have an affection for God, nevertheless, it is fitting to pray with words sometimes so that we do not lose it. And as Chrysostom says, by frequent prayer it comes about that man is made familiar with God and God with him: *the Lord would speak with Moses* (Exod 33:9). Likewise by this, humility comes about, for the highness of God and our own weakness are considered: *I will speak to my Lord* (Gen 18:27). Likewise, by this a man is directed in his actions and seeks help from God: *I have lifted my eyes to the mountains, from whence help will come* (Ps 121:1); *whatever you do, do it from the heart, as for the Lord, not for men* (Col 3:23).

Lecture 3

6:9 Sic ergo vos orabitis: Pater noster qui in caelis es sanctificetur nomen tuum. [n. 583]

6:10 Veniat regnum tuum. Fiat voluntas tua sicut in caelo et in terra. [n.

6:11 Panem nostrum supersubstantialem da nobis hodie.

6:12 Et dimitte nobis debita nostra sicut et nos dimisimus debitoribus nostris;

6:13 et ne inducas nos in temptationem sed libera nos a malo.

6:14 Si enim dimiseritis hominibus peccata eorum dimittet et vobis Pater vester caelestis delicta vestra.

6:15 Si autem non dimiseritis hominibus nec Pater vester dimittet peccata vestra.

6:9 Οὕτως οὖν προσεύχεσθε ὑμεῖς· Πάτερ ἡμῶν ὁ ἐν τοῖς οὐρανοῖς· ἁγιασθήτω τὸ ὄνομά σου·

6:10 ἐλθέτω ἡ βασιλεία σου· γενηθήτω τὸ θέλημά σου, ὡς ἐν οὐρανῷ καὶ ἐπὶ γῆς·

6:11 τὸν ἄρτον ἡμῶν τὸν ἐπιούσιον δὸς ἡμῖν σήμερον·

6:12 καὶ ἄφες ἡμῖν τὰ ὀφειλήματα ἡμῶν, ὡς καὶ ἡμεῖς ἀφήκαμεν τοῖς ὀφειλέταις ἡμῶν·

6:13 καὶ μὴ εἰσενέγκῃς ἡμᾶς εἰς πειρασμόν, ἀλλὰ ῥῦσαι ἡμᾶς ἀπὸ τοῦ πονηροῦ.

6:14 Ἐὰν γὰρ ἀφῆτε τοῖς ἀνθρώποις τὰ παραπτώματα αὐτῶν, ἀφήσει καὶ ὑμῖν ὁ πατὴρ ὑμῶν ὁ οὐράνιος·

6:15 ἐὰν δὲ μὴ ἀφῆτε τοῖς ἀνθρώποις, οὐδὲ ὁ πατὴρ ὑμῶν ἀφήσει τὰ παραπτώματα ὑμῶν.

6:9 Therefore you will pray thus: our Father who art in heaven, hallowed be your name. [n. 583]

6:10 Your kingdom come. Your will be done on earth as it is in heaven.

6:11 Give us this day our supersubstantial bread.

6:12 And forgive us our debts, as we also forgive our debtors.

6:13 And lead us not into temptation. But deliver us from evil. Amen.

6:14 For if you will forgive men their offences, your heavenly Father will forgive you also your offences.

6:15 But if you will not forgive men, neither will your Father forgive you your offences.

---

583. *Sic ergo orabitis.* Supra Dominus docuit modum orandi, scilicet ut vitemus et vanitatem hypocritarum et multiloquium gentilium; hic docet quid debeamus petere in oratione, et circa hoc duo facit: primo ponitur titulus orationis, secundo proponitur oratio. Continuat autem ad praecedentia sic: dixi **orantes nolite multum** etc.; *ergo,* ut paucis loquebaris, *sic orabitis.*

Et nota quod non dicit Dominus: *hoc orabitis,* sed *sic orabitis*: non enim prohibet quin aliis verbis possimus orare, sed docet modum orandi. Et sicut Augustinus in libro *de Oratione* ad Probam: *nullus orat sicut debet nisi petat aliquid eorum quae in oratione Dominica continentur.* Est autem conveniens ut istis verbis oremus quia, sicut dicit Cyprianus in libro *de Oratione Dominicali*: *amica et familiaris est oratio Dominum de suo rogare,* et ponit exemplum quia solet esse apud advocatos qui ponunt verba in ore aliquorum quae dicere debeant in iudicio. Unde oratio ista securissima est, sicut a nostro advocato formata qui sapientissimus est, *in quo sunt omnes thesauri,* Gal. II, 3. Unde dicit Cyprianus: *cum Christum habeamus advocatum apud Patrem pro peccatis nostris, quando pro delictis nostris petimus advocati nostri verba promamus* Ioh. II *advocatum habemus*; ideo dicitur

583. *Therefore you will pray thus.* Above the Lord taught the manner of praying, namely that we avoid both the vanity of the hypocrites and the verbosity of the gentiles. Here he teaches what we should ask in prayer, and concerning this he does two things: first, he gives the title of the prayer, second, he gives the prayer. But he continues to the preceding things in this way: I told you **when you pray, you will not be as the hypocrites** (Matt 6:5); **therefore,** so that you may pray with few words, **you will pray thus.**

And note that the Lord does not say, *pray this,* but **pray thus**: for he does not prohibit us from praying with other words, but he teaches the mode of praying. And just as Augustine in his letter to Probus *On Prayer* says: *no one prays as he should unless he asks something that is contained in the Lord's prayer.* But it is fitting that we pray by those words, for as Cyprian says in his book *On the Lord's Prayer*: *it is a friendly and intimate prayer to ask the Lord with his own words,* and he gives the example that it is the usual way among lawyers who put words into the mouths of those who must speak in court. Hence this prayer is the most sure, as it was formed by our advocate who is the wisest, *in whom are hid all the treasures of wisdom and knowledge* (Col 2:3). Hence Cyprian says: *since we have in Christ an advocate with the Father for our sins, when we ask for our misdeeds, we utter the words of our advocate; and we have*

Hebr. IV, 16: *cum fiducia adeamus* etc., Iac. *postulet autem in fide.*

Et habet tria ista oratio: brevitatem, perfectionem et efficaciam. Brevitatem, propter duo: ut omnes de facili addiscerent, et parvi et magni, quia *ipse est Dominus omnium dives*, Ro. X, 12; secundo ut daret fiduciam de facili impetrandi. Perfecta etiam est, unde Is. X, 23: *verbum abbreviatum*, et, sicut dicit Augustinus, quidquid in aliis orationibus contineri potest totum continetur in ista; unde dicit quod *si convenienter oramus et recte, quaelibet autem verba dicamus, nihil aliud dicimus quam quod in dominica oratione positum est*; Deut. XXXIII, 4: *Dei perfecta sunt opera.* Efficax est, quia oratio, secundum Damascenum, est *petitio decentium a Deo*, Iac. IV, 3: *petitis et non accipitis.* Scire autem quod sit petendum difficillimum est, sicut etiam quod sit desiderandum, Ro. VIII, 26: *nam quod oremus nescimus, ipse autem.* Et quia hanc orationem Deus docuit, ideo efficacissima est, et ideo dicitur Luce IV: *Domine, doce nos.*

584. Dominus autem in ista oratione duo facit: primo ponit orationem; secundo orationis rationem assignat, ibi *si enim dimiseritis.*

Sciendum autem quod in omni oratione, etiam rhetorum, ante petitionem captatur benevolentia. Unde sicut fit in oratione que fit ad homines, similiter debet fieri in oratione quae fit ad Deum, sed alia et alia intentione, quia in homine captatur benevolentia in quantum flectimus animum eius, in Deo in quantum animum nostrum elevemus ad ipsum. Ponit ergo Dominus duo ad captandum benevolentiam quae necessaria sunt oranti: necessarium est enim ut credat eum a quo petit et quod iste velit dare et possit; et ideo ponit **Pater** et **qui es in caelis.** Quod autem dicit Pater ad quinque valet. Primo ad fidei instructionem: fides enim necessaria est oranti.

Tres autem errores fuerunt quibus excludebatur oratio: et duo omnino destruebant orationem, et tertius dabat plus quam debebat. Et illi excluduntur per hoc quod dicit **Pater noster.** Quidam enim dixerunt Deum non habere curam de rebus humanis, Ex. IX, 9: *derelinquit Deus*, unde secundum hoc frustra aliquid petitur a Deo. Alii dixerunt quod Deus habet providentiam, sed providentia illa imponit necessitatem rebus. Tertius error plus dabat, quia dixit quod Deus omnia disponit providentia sua, sed per orationem mutatur dispositio divina.

Isti autem errores excluduntur per hoc quod dicit **Pater noster qui es in caelis**, quia si Pater providentia habet, Sap. XII: *tu autem Pater.* Item secundus error excluditur: 'pater' enim dicitur ad filium et 'dominus' ad servum; ergo in hoc quod dicimus 'Pater,' vocamus nos liberos. Numquam enim fere in Sacra Scriptura invenitur

an advocate with the Father (1 John 2:1). Thus it is said, *let us go with confidence to the throne of grace* (Heb 4:16); and *let him ask in faith* (Jas 1:6).

And this prayer has three things: brevity, perfection, and efficacy. Brevity, for two reasons: that all may easily learn it, both great and small, for *the same is Lord over all, rich unto all who call upon him* (Rom 10:12); second, that he might give the surety of obtaining with ease. It is also perfect, hence: *the consumption abridged* (Isa 10:23), and just as Augustine says, whatever can be contained in other prayers is wholly contained in this; hence he says that *if we pray fittingly and rightly, nevertheless whatever words we use, we say nothing else but what is included in the Lord's prayer: perfect are the works of the Lord* (Deut 33:4). It is efficacious because prayer, according to Damascene, is a *petition of suitable things from God; you ask and you receive not because you ask wrongly* (Jas 4:3). But knowing what to ask for is a difficult thing, just as knowing what to desire: *for we do not know how to pray as we ought, but the Spirit himself asks for us* (Rom 8:26). And because God taught us this prayer, therefore it is the most efficacious, and thus it is said in Luke: *Lord, teach us to pray* (Luke 11:1).

584. But the Lord does two things in this prayer: first, he gives the prayer; second, he assigns the reason for the prayer, at **for if you will forgive men their offences.**

But it should be known that in any speech, even those of rhetoricians, before requests are made, good will is won. Hence as is done in a speech that is made to men, the same must be done in a speech to God, but with different intentions in each, for with men good will is won by persuading the mind; but with God by lifting our mind to him. Therefore the Lord sets down two things to capture good will which are needed for someone praying: for it is necessary that he trust the one he asks and that the other wishes to give and is able to; and thus he says **Father** and **who art in heaven.** But saying Father avails in five ways. The first is for teaching the faith: for faith is needed in the one praying.

But there were three errors by which prayer was excluded: and two completely destroyed prayer, and the third gave more than was due. And those errors are excluded by his saying **our Father.** For some people said God did not have care of human things: *God has abandoned the earth and does not see it* (Ezek 9:9); hence according to this anything asked of God is in vain. Others said that God has providence, but this providence imposes a necessity on things. The third error gave more, for it said that God disposes all things by his providence, but that through prayer the divine disposition is changed.

But these errors are excluded by the fact that he says **our Father who art in heaven**, for if he is a father, he has providence: *but your providence, O Father, governs it* (Wis 14:3). Likewise the second error is excluded: for 'father' is said by a son, and 'lord' by a slave; therefore in the fact that we say 'Father,' we call ourselves free children. For when was it

quod Deus dicatur pater insensibilium creaturarum, licet aliter Iob *quis est pluviae Pater?* Ergo pater dicitur ad filium et per hoc vocamus nos liberos: 'filius' enim habet rationem libertatis; ergo non imponitur nobis necessitas.

Per hoc autem quod dicit **in caelis** excluditur dispositio mutabilis. Valet autem oratio ad hoc ut credamus quod Deus ita disponit omnia secundum quod congruit naturis rerum: ex providentia enim est quod homo per actus suos consequatur finem suum; unde oratio nec mutet providentiam nec est extra providentiam, sed cadit sub ea. Primo ergo valet ad fidei instructionem. Secundo ad sublevationem spei: si enim Pater est vult dare, quia, sicut infra X: **si vos cum sitis mali** etc. Tertio ad caritatem excitandam: naturale enim est quod pater diligat filium et e converso, Eph. V, 1: *estote imitatores*; ideo per hoc provocamur ad imitationem: filius enim debet imitari patrem quantum potest, Ier. III, 19: *Patrem vocabis me.* Quarto provocamur ad humilitatem Mal. *si ego Pater.* Quinto per hoc affectus noster ordinatur ad proximum, Mal. II, 10: *nonne unus est Pater omnium?*

Sed quare non dicimus: *Pater mi?* Duplex est ratio: primo quia hoc sibi voluit Christus reservare quasi sibi proprium, quia est Filius per naturam, nos autem per adoptionem, quod est omnibus commune, Ioh. XX, 17: *ascendo ad Patrem meum* etc.; secundo quia, secundum Chrysostomum, Dominus docet nos non facere singulares orationes sed communiter pro toto populo orare: quae quidem oratio magis est apud Deum accepta. Unde Chrysostomus: *dulcior est ante Deum oratio, non quam transmittit necessitas, sed quam caritas* etc., Iac. *orate pro invicem* etc.

Secundum quod pertinet ad captandum benevolentiam est **qui es in caelis**. Quod dupliciter exponitur. Primo ad litteram, ut intelligamus caelos corporales; non quod sit ibi conclusus, quia Ier. XXIII, 24: *caelum* etc., sed dicitur propter eminentiam ipsius creaturae secundum illud Is. ult. *caelum mihi sedes.* Item per hoc informantur illi qui non possunt elevari supra corporalia, et ideo dicit Augustinus quod ista est ratio quare adoramus in oriente, quia ab oriente surgit caelum; et sicut caelum est supra corpus nostrum, ita Deus supra spiritum; unde datur intelligi quod spiritus noster debet conuerti in ipsum Deum, sicut corpus nostrum convertitur ad ipsum caelum in orando. Dicit autem **qui es in caelis**, ut relevetur intentio tua a terrenis, Petri I: *in hereditatem immarcescibilem.*

Vel per **caelos** intelliguntur sancti, secundum illud Is. I, 2: *audite caeli*, Ps. *tu autem in sancto habitas* etc.;

ever found in Sacred Scripture that God is called father of insensible creatures, with one exception: *who is the Father of the rain?* (Job 38:28). Therefore, father is said for a son, and by this we call ourselves free children: for 'son' includes the notion of freedom; therefore necessity is not imposed upon us.

But by the fact that he says **in heaven** a changeable disposition is excluded. But prayer avails so that we might believe that God disposes all things in a way that befits the natures of things: for it is by providence that man pursues his end through his own actions; hence prayer neither changes providence nor is it outside providence, but falls under it. First, therefore, it avails to the teaching of the faith. Second, for the sustenance of hope: for if he is a Father, he wishes to give, because, it is said below that **if you then, being evil, know how to give good gifts to your children** (Matt 7:11). Third, for exciting charity: for it is natural that a father love his son and vice versa: *be imitators of God, as beloved children* (Eph 5:1). Therefore by this we are provoked to imitation: for a son should imitate his father as much as he can: *you would call me Father* (Jer 3:19). Fourth, we are provoked to humility: *if then I am a Father, where is the honor due me?* (Mal 1:6). Fifth, by this our affections are directed to our neighbor, *is there not one Father of us all?* (Mal 2:10).

But why do we not say *my Father?* For two reasons: first, because Christ wanted to reserve this to himself as his own, for he is Son by nature, but we by adoption, which is shared by all: *I am ascending to my Father and yours* (John 20:17). Second, because according to Chrysostom, the Lord teaches us not to make individual prayers but to pray communally for the whole people: which prayer is indeed more acceptable to God. Hence Chrysostom says: *it is a sweeter prayer before the Lord, not which necessity sends up, but which charity does*; and *pray for one another* (Jas 5:16).

Accordingly, **who art in heaven** belongs to winning the good will of the listener. Which is explained in two ways. First, literally, so that we understand the physical heavens; not that he could be enclosed there, for *do I not fill heaven and earth? Says the Lord* (Jer 23:24). But it is said on account of his eminence over creation according to Isaiah: *heaven is my throne and the earth my footstool* (Isa 66:1). Likewise by these words those who cannot be raised above the level of corporeal things are given a new idea; and thus Augustine says that this is the reason we pray facing east, for from the east the heaven arises; and just as the sky is above our bodies, so is God above our spirit. Hence it is given to be understood that our spirit should be converted to God himself, as our body is turned to heaven in praying. But he says **who art in heaven**, as your intention is raised from earthly things: *into an inheritance that is . . . unfading, kept in heaven for you* (1 Pet 1:4).

Or, by **heaven** is understood the saints, according to Isa 1:2: *hear O heavens*; or: *but you dwell in the holy places*

et dicit hoc ad maiorem fiduciam impetrandi, quia, non longe est a nobis, Ier. VII: *tu in nobis es, Domine*.

585. *Sanctificetur*. Hic ponuntur petitiones, et dicamus eas primo in generali, postea in speciali. In istis petitionibus debemus tria considerare. Petitio enim deservit desiderio: illa enim petimus quae volumus habere; in oratione autem ista continetur totum quidquid desiderare possumus. Secundo continetur ordo quo debemus desiderare. Tertium est quia iste petitiones respondent et donis et beatitudinibus.

Sciendum autem quod naturaliter homo duo desiderat, scilicet consequi bonum et vitare malum. Quatuor autem bona ponuntur hic desideranda. Desiderium autem prius tendit in finem quam in his quae sunt ad finem; finis autem ultimus omnium Deus est; unde primum desiderabile debet esse honor Dei, Cor. *omnia in honorem Dei facite*; et hoc petimus primo hic **sanctificetur nomen tuum**. Inter ea autem quae pertinent ad nos, finis ultimus est vita aeterna; et hoc petimus cum dicimus **adveniat regnum**. Tertium quod debemus petere est de his quae sunt ad finem, scilicet quod habeamus virtutem et merita bona, et hoc ibi **fiat voluntas**; et quid petimus de virtutibus nihil aliud est nisi hoc. Ergo beatitudo nostra ordinatur ad Deum, virtutes ad beatitudinem. Sed necesse est habere subsidium sive temporale sique spirituale, sicut sacramenta Ecclesiae, et hoc petimus ibi **panem nostrum**, exteriorem vel sacramentalem. In istis quatuor omne bonum continetur. Malum autem vitat homo in quantum est impeditivum boni. Primum autem bonum, scilicet honor divinus, non potest impediri, quia si fiat iustitia honoratur Deus, si malum honoratur similiter in quantum illud punit, quamvis non honoretur quantum est in peccante. Peccatum autem impedit beatitudinem, et ideo hoc primo removet cum dicit **et dimitte**. Bono virtutum contrariatur temptatio, et ideo petimus **et ne nos**; defectus quicumque contra necessitatem vitae, et hoc est **sed libera**. Patet ergo quod quidquid desideratur, totum continet dominica oratio.

Et sciendum quod dona Spiritus Sancti possunt istis petitionibus applicari, sed diversimode, quia ascendendo et descendendo: ascendendo, ut prima petitio applicetur timori qui facit paupertatem spiritus et facit quaerere honorem Dei, et ideo dicimus **sanctificetur**; descendendo, ut dicamus quod ultimum donum, scilicet sapientia quae facit filios Dei, applicetur huic petitioni. Sed videndum est de petitione ista **sanctificetur**.

Videtur autem esse incompetens: nomen enim Dei semper sanctum est. Et sciendum quod hoc multipliciter exponitur a sanctis. Primo ab Augustino, et credo quod sit magis litteralis: **sanctificetur**, id est nomen quod semper sanctum, sanctum appareat apud homines; et hoc est honorare Deum: ex hoc enim non accrescit gloria Deo, sed nobis cognitio ipsius, Eccli. XXXVI, 4: *sicut*

(Ps 22:3). And he says this to obtain greater confidence, because it is not far from us: *you are among us, Lord* (Jer 14:9).

585. *Hallowed be*. Here he sets down petitions, and we may say them first in general, then specifically. In these petitions we must consider three things. For a petition is in service of a desire: for we ask for those things that we wish to have; but in this prayer the entirety of what we desire is contained. Second, the order in which we should desire is contained in it. Third is that these petitions correspond to both gifts and beatitudes.

But it should be known that naturally man desires two things, namely, to seek good and avoid evil. But four goods are set forth here as things to be desired. But desire tends toward an end rather than toward those things ordered to the end; but the last end of all things is God; hence the first desirable thing should be to honor God: *do all things for the honor of God* (1 Cor 10:31). And this is what we ask first with **hallowed be your name**. But among things that pertain to us, the last end is eternal life; and this we ask when we say, **your kingdom come**. The third thing we should seek concerns things for the sake of the end, namely, that we have virtue and good merits, and this is at **your will be done**; and what we ask for in virtue is nothing but this. Therefore our beatitude is directed toward God, and our virtues toward that beatitude. But it is necessary to have reinforcement, whether temporal or spiritual, like the sacraments of the Church, and this is what we ask at **our . . . bread**, external or sacramental. In these four things every good is included. But man avoids evil as it is an obstruction to good. But the first good, namely divine honor, cannot be obstructed, because if justice is done God is honored; if evil is done, he is likewise honored in that he punishes it, although he is not honored as much in the one sinning. But sin prevents beatitude, and thus he removes this first by saying **and forgive us our debts**. Temptation is opposed to the good of virtue, and thus we ask **and lead us not into temptation**; or any defect that goes against the necessities of life, at **but deliver us from evil**. Therefore it is clear that whatever is desired, the Lord's prayer contains in its entirety.

And it should be known that the Holy Spirit can be connected with these petitions, but in a different way, by ascending and descending: ascending, as the first petition is related to fear which causes poverty of the spirit and makes us seek the honor of God, and thus we say **hallowed be**; descending, so that we say that the last gift, namely the wisdom making us sons of God, is related to this petition. But we will see about this petition **hallowed be**.

However, it seems to be unfitting: for the name of God is always holy. And it should be said that this has been explained many ways by the saints. First, by Augustine, and I believe that his is the most literal: **hallowed be**, that is the name that is always holy, should be held holy among men; and this is to honor God: for by this God's glory does not increase, but our recognition of it: *so use them to show your*

in conspectu nostro etc. Et satis convenienter post *Pater noster qui es in caelis* dicit *sanctificetur*, quia nihil ita probat filios Dei: bonus enim filius manifestat honorem patris. Secundum Chrysostomum: *sanctificetur*, per nostra opera, quasi: fac nos ita vivere ut ex operibus nostris nomen tuum sanctum appareat, Petri III. Vel secundum Cyprianum: *sanctificetur*, id est sanctifica nos in tuo nomine, Ioh. XVII, 17: *sanctifica eos in nomine*, Is. IV: *et erit vobis*.

Et sciendum quod primo *sanctificetur* intelligitur ut illi qui non sunt sancti fiant sancti: ista enim oratio fit pro toto genere humano; secundo *sanctificetur*, idest in sanctitate perseverant; tertio *sanctificetur*, ut si quid in sanctitate admixtum est removeatur: cotidie enim indigemus sanctificatione propter cotidiana peccata.

586. *Adveniat.* Ista petitio potest respondere vel dono intellectus quod mundat cor, vel pietatis. *Adveniat.* Secundum Chrysostomum et Augustinum, regnum Dei est vita aeterna, et credo quod hoc sit litteralis expositio; petimus ergo *adveniat*, id est fac nos pervenire et participare aeternam beatitudinem, infra XXVI, 34: *venite benedicti*, Luce XXII, 29: *ego dispono vobis*.

Vel aliter, etiam secundum Augustinum: *adveniat*. Christus regnare incepit ex tunc ex quo mundum redemit, Ioh. *data est mihi potestas*; *adveniat* ergo *regnum tuum*, id est consummatio regni tui. Et hoc erit quando inimicos suos ponet sub pedibus suis; unde *adveniat*, id est Domine, venias ad iudicium ut appareat gloria regni tui, Luce *his fieri incipientibus* etc. Et desiderant sancti adventum Christi, quia tunc gloriam perfectam possidebunt, Thi. *non solum autem mihi sed et his*;

sed contrarium dicitur Amos V, 18: *ve desiderantibus diem Domini*, quia tantum, secundum Ieronimum, securae conscientiae est iudicem non timere.

Vel *adveniat*, id est destruatur regnum peccati, et tu Domine regna super nos: quando enim servimus iustitiae tunc Deus regnat, quando autem peccato diabolus, Ro. VI, 12: *non ergo regnat in vestro*, Reg. VIII: *non te repulerunt.*

Et nota quod satis iuste poterant petere *adveniat regnum tuum* qui se filios comprobaverunt dicendo *Pater noster* etc.: filiis enim debetur hereditas; sed regnum istud in caelis est: unde ire non potes nisi caelestis efficiaris. Et ideo consequenter subiungit *fiat voluntas*, id est fac nos esse imitatores caelestium, I Cor. XV, 49: *sicut portavimus.*

glory to us (Sir 36:4). And fittingly enough after *Our Father, who art in heaven*, he says, *hallowed be*, for nothing proves so well the sons of God: for a good son shows honor to his father. According to Chrysostom: *hallowed be*, by our works, as it were: make us so live that by our works your name appears holy (cf. 1 Pet 3:15). Or according to Cyprian: *hallowed be*, i.e., sanctify us in your name: *sanctify them in your name* (John 17:17); *and he will be a sanctification to you* (Isa 8:14).

And it should be known that *hallowed be* is first understood as that those who are not holy might become holy: for this prayer is made for the whole human race. Second, *hallowed be*, i.e., they persevere in holiness; third, *hallowed be*, so that if anything is mixed in with their holiness, it might be removed: for every day we need sanctification because of our daily sins.

586. *Your kingdom come.* This petition can correspond to either the gift of understanding which cleanses the heart, or to piety. *Your kingdom come*: according to Chrysostom and Augustine, the kingdom of God is eternal life, and I believe that this is the literal explanation; therefore we ask *your kingdom come*, i.e., make us attain and share in eternal beatitude, as later: *come, you blessed of my father, receive the kingdom prepared for you* (Matt 25:34); or Luke: *and I confer on you, as my father has conferred on me, a kingdom* (Luke 22:29).

Or, another way, also according to Augustine: *your kingdom come.* Christ began to reign from the time that he redeemed the world: *all power. . . is given to me* (Matt 28:18); therefore *your kingdom come*, i.e., the consummation of your kingdom. And this will be when he puts his enemies under his feet; hence *your kingdom*, i.e.: Lord, may you come to judge so that the glory of your kingdom appears: *when these things begin . . . your redemption is near* (Luke 21:28). And the saints long for the coming of Christ, for then they will possess perfect glory: *and not only for me but for those also who love his coming* (2 Tim 4:8).

But to the contrary it is said: *woe to those who desire the day of the Lord* (Amos 5:18), for according to Jerome, it belongs only to a secure conscience not to fear the judge.

Or *your kingdom come*, i.e., may the reign of sin be destroyed, and you, Lord, reign over us: for when we serve justice then God reigns, but when we serve sin, the devil does: *let no sin reign in your body* (Rom 6:12); *they have not rejected you but me, from reigning over them* (1 Sam 8:7).

And note that they could ask justly enough *your kingdom come* who proved themselves sons by saying *our Father*: for the inheritance is due to sons, but that kingdom is in heaven. Hence you cannot go there unless you are made heavenly. And thus he adds *your will be done*, i.e.: make us imitators of the heavenly ones, *just as we have borne the image of the man of dust, let us also bear the image of the man of heaven* (1 Cor 15:49).

Et nota quod non dicit *fiat voluntas*, quasi Deus faciat voluntatem nostram, sed quasi: voluntas sua impleatur per nos, quae *vult omnes homines salvos fieri*, Thi. IV, Thess., Ps. *doce me facere*. In quo destruitur error Pelagii qui dicebat quod non indigebamus auxilio divino.

587. *Sicut in caelo*. Hoc ab Augustino multipliciter exponitur. Primo sic: *sicut in caelo*, idest sicut angeli in caelo faciunt voluntatem tuam, ita nos in terra voluntatem tuam impleamus; de angelis dicitur Ps. *ministri eius qui facitis* : in quo destruitur error Origenis qui posuit angelum posse peccare.

Vel aliter: *fiat voluntas sicut in caelo et in terra*, idest sicut in Christo ita et in Ecclesia. Caelo enim terra fecundatur: unde et gentiles dicebant deos caelorum masculos, terrae feminas, Ioh. *descendi de caelo*.

Vel per caelos intelliguntur sancti quorum Phil. III, 20: *conversatio in caelis est*; qualis autem est proportio caeli ad terram, talis sanctorum ad peccatores; quasi: Domine, converte peccatores ad faciendum voluntatem tuam.

588. Vel *fiat* etc.: sicut enim caelum comparatur in mundo ad terram, ita spiritus ad carnem in homine; spiritus quantum est de se facit voluntatem Dei, sed caro repugnat, Ro. VII, 23: *video aliam*, Ps. *cor mundum*. Omnes istae petitiones partim hic incoantur, sed in futuro implebuntur.

Chrysostomus autem hoc, scilicet *sicut in caelo*, refert ad omnia praecedentia; unde *adveniat regnum, sicut in caelo et in terra*, et sic de aliis. Item, secundum Chrysostomum, nota quod non dixit: *sanctificemus*, neque: *sanctifices*, sed medio modo; nec dixit: *eamus ad regnum*, sed *adveniat*. Sic in omnibus medium tenuit, et hoc quia ad salutem nostram duo requiruntur: gratia Dei et liberum arbitrium; unde si dixisset: 'sanctifica', nullum locum dedisset libero arbitrio; si: 'faciamus', totum dedisset libero arbitrio, sed medie locutus est et hic: *fiat voluntas* etc.

589. *Panem nostrum*. Postquam docuit petere gloriam Dei, vitam aeternam et operationem virtutum quibus vitam aeternam meremur, hic docet petere omnia quae necessaria sunt ad praesentem vitam. Exponitur autem hoc *panem nostrum* quatuor modis: potest enim exponit de quadruplici pane. Primo de pane qui est Christus, Ioh. VI, 35: *ego sum panis* etc., qui praecipue panis est secundum quod continetur sub sacramento altaris, Ioh. VI, 52: *panis quem ego dabo*, et iterum *caro mea vere est cibus*.

Et dicit *nostrum*, quia non est quorumlibet sed fidelium, Is. IX, 5: *parvulus enim datus est*; ex hoc enim quod aliquis fit membrum Christi in baptismo, potest participare istum panem: et ideo nullo modo debet dari infidelibus non baptizatis.

And note that he does not say *your will be done*, as: may God do our will, but rather: may his will be fulfilled through us, which *wills all men to be saved* (1 Tim 2:4; 1 Thess 4:3); *teach me to do your will* (Ps 143:10). In which is destroyed the error of Pelagius, who said that we did not need divine help.

587. *As it is in heaven*. This is explained in many ways by Augustine. First thus: *as it is in heaven*, i.e., as angels in heaven do your will, so may we fulfill it on earth; it is said of the angels, *his ministers that do his will* (Ps 103:21). In which is destroyed the error of Origen who suggested that an angel could sin.

Or another way: *your will be done on earth as it is in heaven*, i.e., as in Christ, so also in the Church. For from heaven the earth is made fruitful: hence also the gentiles called the gods of heaven male and the gods of the earth female: *I came down from heaven . . . to do the will of him who sent me* (John 6:38).

Or by the heavens are understood the saints of whom it is said: *our citizenship is in heaven* (Phil 3:20). But as the heaven is to the earth, so are the saints to sinners; as though: Lord, convert sinners to doing your will.

588. Or *your will be done*: for as heaven is compared to the earth in the world, so is the spirit to the flesh in man; the spirit, inasmuch as is in it, does the will of God, but the flesh revolts: *I see another law in my members* (Rom 7:23); *create a clean heart in me* (Ps 51:10). All these petitions are partly begun now, but in the future they will be fulfilled.

But Chrysostom refers *as it is in heaven* to all the foregoing things; hence *your kingdom come on earth as it is in heaven*, and so on with the others. Again, according to Chrysostom, note that he did not say, *may we sanctify*, nor *sanctify*, but took a middle way; nor did he say: *let us go to the kingdom* but *your kingdom come*. So in all things he held a middle way, and this because two things are required for our salvation: the grace of God and free will; hence if he had said, 'sanctify', no place would be given to free will; if 'may we do it', all would be given to free will, but he spoke in the mean, and it is: *your will be done*.

589. *Our . . . bread*. After he taught us to seek the glory of God, life eternal, and the working of virtue by which we merit life eternal, here he teaches us to seek all the things that are necessary for the present life. But this, *our bread*, is explained in four ways: for it can be explained by four kinds of bread. First, the bread that is Christ: *I am the bread of life* (John 6:35), which is especially the bread according to which he is contained under the sacrament of the altar: *the bread which I give is my flesh* (John 6:52), and again *my flesh is true food* (John 6:56).

And it says *our*, for it is not for anyone but the faithful: *unto us a child is given* (Isa 9:5). For by becoming a member of Christ in baptism, one can partake of this bread: and thus in no way should it be given to unbaptized unbelievers.

590. *Supersubstantialem.* Ieronimus dicit quod in graeco est 'epiousion', et Symmachus transtulit 'praecipuum' vel 'egregium'; antiqua autem translatio habet **cotidianum**. Quod autem sit **supersubstantialem**, id est super omnes substantias, apparet Eph. I, 20–21 *constituens illum super omnes principatus* etc. **Cotidianum** dicit, quia cotidie debet sumi, sed non ab unoquoque; unde dicitur in libro *de Ecclesiasticis dogmatibus: nec laudo nec vitupero hoc.*

Sed debet cotidie sumi in Ecclesia, vel saltim a fidelibus spiritualiter sumatur cotidie ex fide. In Ecclesia autem orientali non cotidie sumitur in ecclesia, quia non cotidie celebratur missa, immo solum in septimana. Sed quia Ecclesia sustinet, sufficit quod cotidie sumant spiritualiter et non sacramentaliter.

591. *Da nobis.* Si noster, quomodo dicit **da nobis**? Cyprianus: **da nobis**, idest fac nos ita vivere ut istum panem ad utilitatem nostram sumere possimus; unde qui hoc petit, nihil aliud petit nisi perseverantiam in bono, ut scilicet nihil contrarium admisceatur sanctitati, Cor. 9 *qui enim indigne* etc.

592. *Panem nostrum da nobis hodie.* Hic obicit Augustinus quia ista oratio dicitur qualibet hora diei, etiam in Completorio; numquid ergo tunc petimus quod det nobis sumere istum panem? Sed dicendum quod **hodie** dupliciter accipitur: quandoque enim significat determinatum diem, quantoque tota vita praesens; Hebr. III determinatum hodie tangit; unde: da ut in tota praesenti vita possimus istum panem participare.

Et ratione dicit **da nobis hodie**, quia iste sacramentalis panis in hac vita tantum necessarius est: quando enim videbimus eum sicuti est, non indigebimus sacramentis et signis. Unde hic panis singularis et peculiaris tantum necessarius est in praesenti: et nunc cotidie specialiter sumimus, sed tunc continue.

Secundo per panem intelligitur Deus, scilicet ipsa divinitas, Luce XIV, 15: *beatus qui manducabis panem*, Ps. *panem angelorum manducavit.* **Da** ergo **panem supersubstantialem hodie**, ut scilicet secundum modum praesentis vitae possimus eo frui.

Tertio possunt intelligi Dei praecepta, que sunt panis sapientie, Sap. IX: *venite, comedite*; hic enim comedit qui praecepta sapientie custodit, Ioh. VI: *meus cibus est.* Haec divina praecepta nunc sunt panis, quia cum quadam difficultate teruntur considerando et operando, sed postea erunt potus quia sine difficultate reficient.

Quarto intelligitur ad litteram panis corporalis. Dixerat enim Dominus **fiat voluntas**, et voluerat in impletione divinae voluntatis nos esse caelestes; sed memor fragilitatis nostrae, docet petere etiam temporalia quae

590. *Supersubstantial bread.* Jerome says that in Greek this is 'epiousion', and Symmachus translated it 'special' or 'extraordinary'; but the old translation has **daily**. But what would be **supersubstantial**, that is, above all substances, appears in Ephesians: *which he wrought in Christ . . . setting him . . . above all principality* (Eph 1:20–21). He says **daily**, for it should be received every day, but not by everyone; hence it is said in the book *On Church Dogmas: I neither praise nor blame this.*

But it should be received daily in the Church, or at least it may be received spiritually by the faithful in faith. But in the eastern church it is not received daily in church, for the Mass is not celebrated daily, but only once a week. But because the Church allows it, it suffices that they receive spiritually every day, and not sacramentally.

591. *Give us.* If it is ours, how does he say, **give us**? Cyprian: Give us, i.e., make us so live that we can receive this bread to our benefit; hence whoever asks this, asks nothing else but perseverance in good, namely so that nothing contrary will be mixed in with his sanctity: *for whoever eats and drinks unworthily, eats and drinks judgment to himself* (1 Cor 11:29).

592. *Give us this day our supersubstantial bread.* Here Augustine objects that this prayer is said at every hour of the day, even during Compline; do we ask even then that he give us this bread to eat? But it should be said that **this day** is taken in two ways: for sometimes it means a definite day, sometimes all this present life; Hebrews touches the definite today (Heb 3:13), hence: grant that in all this present life we may partake of this bread.

And for this reason he says **give us this day**, because that sacramental bread is only necessary in this life: for when we will see him as he is, we will not need sacraments and signs. Hence this singular and extraordinary bread is only necessary in the present: and now we receive it daily in species, but then we will have it unceasingly.

Second, by bread is understood God, namely, in his divinity: *blessed is he who shall eat bread in the kingdom of God* (Luke 14:15); *mortals ate of the bread of angels* (Ps 78:25). Therefore **give us today our supersubstantial bread**, namely so that we may enjoy it according to the manner of this present life.

Third, the precepts of God can be understood, which are the bread of wisdom: *come, eat of my bread* (Prov 9:5), for he eats who keeps the commands of wisdom: *my food is to do the will of him who sent me* (John 4:34). These divine precepts now are bread, for they are ground with a certain difficulty, by considering and doing, but afterward they will be a drink, for they will refresh without difficulty.

Fourth, it is understood literally as physical bread. For the Lord had said **your will be done**, and he wanted us to be heavenly in fulfillment of the divine will; but mindful of our frailty, he teaches us to ask even for the temporal goods that

necessaria sunt ad sustentationem vitae; unde non docet petere magnifica vel superflua, sed necessaria, I Tim. V: *habentes alimenta*; ita petiit Iacob, Gen. XXVIII, 20: *si dederis mihi panem ad edendum.*

593. Dicit autem **nostrum** propter duo. Ut nemo sibi temporalia appropriet, secundum Chrysostomum primo quia nullus debet comedere panem de rapina, sed de proprio labore; secundo quia bona temporalia quae dantur propter necessitatem ita debemus accipere ut aliis communicemus, Iob XXXI, 17: *si comedi buccellam meam.*

Et dicit Augustinus in libro *de Orando* ad Probam quod ab eo quod excellit et principale est in omnibus particularibus, ad facultatem nostram significat totum: panis enim est magis necessarium homini, Eccli XXVIII: *initium vitae hominis*; et hoc est **supersubstantialem** quia principaliter pertinet ad necessaria.

594. Si autem dicit: **cotidianum**, tunc duplicem habet rationem, secundum Cyprianum. Primo, ut non quaeras temporalia in longinquum tempus, quia alias esses contrarius tibi ipsi: dixisti enim *adveniat regnum tuum*; sed quamdiu *sumus in corpore peregrinamur a Domino*, Cor. V; unde dicendo *adveniat regnum tuum*, et petendo longam vitam, contrarius es tibi ipsi. Vel **cotidianum** dicit contra prodigos qui superflue expendunt et non utuntur pane cotidiano qui sufficit ad unius diei victus.

Sed si noster, quare dicit **da nobis**? Propter duo, secundum Chrysostomum. Primo quia temporalia bona dantur bonis et malis, sed aliter et aliter: quia bonis ad utilitatem, malis ad damnum quia male utuntur; unde malis non datur quia abutuntur, et hoc fit non a Deo sed a diabolo. Et dicit quod simile est sicut si aliquis offerat panem sacerdoti ut sanctificet et postea repetat; posset dicere: da mihi panem quod meus est possessione, de sanctificationi.

595. Hodie dicit quia noluit nos in longinquum tempus petere. Sed movet Augustinus quaestionem quia Dominus in sequentibus docet non habere sollicitudinem de temporalibus: *unde nolite solliciti esse* etc.; ergo videtur quod non debemus orare pro temporalibus. Et respondet quod de omni desiderabili licito possumus orare, quia desiderabilem a Deo expectamus, et quae a Deo expectamus petere possumus; et hoc non tantum in extrema necessitate, sed etiam ad competentem sibi statum. Aliud autem est desiderare, aliud sollicitum esse de aliquo sicut de ultimo fine, quia hoc Dominus prohibet, sicut dicetur infra.

Sed iterum quaeritur de hoc: **da nobis hodie**, quia videtur quod non debemus desiderare nisi ad unum diem; ergo omnes qui aliter desiderant peccant, et tunc peribit vita humana quia nullus congregabit messem in aestate ut comedat in hieme. Et dicendum quod Dominus non intendit prohibere quod aliquis non cogitet de futuris,

are necessary to the support of life; hence he does not teach us to seek splendid or superfluous things, but necessities: *but if we have food . . . we are content* (1 Tim 6:8); thus Jacob asked: *if you will give me bread to eat* (Gen 28:20).

593. But he says **our** for two reasons. So that no one will amass temporal things to himself, according to Chrysostom, first because no one should eat bread from plunder, but from one's own labor; second because we ought to receive temporal goods that are given for necessity so that we may share them with others: *if I have eaten my morsel alone . . . let my shoulder fall from its joint* (Job 31:17–22).

And Augustine says in the book to Probus *On Prayer*, that whatever is chief and most excellent in all particulars, represents the whole to our faculty: for bread is most necessary to man: *the chief thing for man's life is water and bread* (Sir 29:21). And this is **supersubstantial** for it chiefly pertains to necessity.

594. But if he says: **daily**, then there are two reasons, according to Cyprian. First, that you not seek temporal goods for a long time, for otherwise you would act contrary to yourself: for you say, **your kingdom come**, but as long as *we are in the body we are away from the Lord* (2 Cor 5:6). Hence by saying **your kingdom come**, and seeking a long life, you act against yourself. Or he says **daily** against the prodigals who spend excessively and do not use daily bread, which nourishment suffices for one day.

But if it is ours, why does he say **give us**? For two reasons, according to Chrysostom. First, temporal goods are given to good and bad men, but in different ways: for they are to the benefit of the good, but to the blame of the wicked who use them badly; hence to the wicked it is not given because they abuse it, and this is done not by God but by the devil. And he says that it is the same as if someone offered bread to a priest to consecrate and afterward he asked for it back; he could say: give me the bread that is my possession from sanctification.

595. He says **today** because he does not want us to ask for things for a long time. But Augustine raises the question that the Lord afterward teaches us not to have anxiety about temporal things: *Therefore do not worry, saying: what will we eat?* (Matt 6:31). Therefore it seems that we should not pray for temporal things. And he answers that we can pray for every licitly desirable thing, for we expect to receive desirable things from God, and whatever we expect from God we can ask for; and this is not only in extreme necessity, but also what befits our state. But it is one thing to desire, another to worry about something as if it were the last end, for this is what God forbids, as will be said later.

But again it is asked concerning **give us this day**, for it seems that we should not desire beyond one day; therefore all those who desire otherwise sin, and then human life will perish, for no one will harvest in summer so that he may eat in winter. And it should be said that the Lord does not intend to forbid someone from thinking about the future,

sed prohibet quod sollicitudinem non debeat sibi usurpare ante tempus: si nunc enim incumbit sollicitudo hanc debes exequi, sed non illam quae incumbere posset in antea.

596. *Et dimitte*. Hic incipit ponere petitiones quae pertinent ad remotionem mali. Et primo ponit illam per quam removetur malum praecipuum, scilicet culpae; unde ***et dimitte nobis***. Repugnans est quod homo qui vivit de rebus Dei vivat contra Deum. Debita sunt peccata, quia pro peccatis sumus Deo obligati debito: si enim ab alio accepisti aliquid iniuste, teneris ad restitutionem; et quia quando peccas usurpas quod Dei est, quia Dei est quod omnis voluntas reguletur secundum voluntatem Dei, ergo subtrahis quod Dei est et teneris ad restitutionem; solvis autem quando contra voluntatem tuam sustines aliquid secundum voluntatem Dei, infra XVIII, 32: ***omne debitum dimisi***. ***Dimitte*** ergo ***debita***, id est peccata, Ps. *remitte mihi ut refrigerer*.

Ex hoc verbo duo hereses confutantur, scilicet Pelagii et Novationi. Pelagius dixit quod aliqui perfecti homines in vita ista poterant vivere sine peccato et implere illud Eph. V, 27: *ut exhiberet gloriosam Ecclesiam*; sed si hoc, tunc non diceremus **Dimitte**, Prov. XXIV, 16: *septies cadit*, Ioh. *si dixerimus quia peccata*. Novatianus dixit quod homo qui peccat post baptismum mortaliter non potest agere paenitentiam; sed si hoc, tunc frustra diceremus **dimitte**, Ioh. I, 12: *dedit eis potestatem filios Dei fieri*, scilicet per adoptionem gratiae.

597. *Sicut et nos dimittimus debitoribus*. Debitores autem aliqui possunt esse dupliciter: vel quia peccaverunt contra nos, vel quia debent pecuniam; nos autem non monet quod ista secunda debita dimittamus, sed peccata quaecumque, etiam in ablatione bonorum temporalium: indignum enim esset petere veniam a Deo et non dare conservo, Eccli. XXVIII: *homini conservat*, XXIX, 2: *et iterum dimitte proximo* etc.

Sed quid dicendum de illis qui nolunt dimittere et tamen dicunt *Pater noster*? Videtur quod numquam deberent dicere quia mentiuntur; unde dicitur quod quidam subtrahebant istam clausulam ***sicut et nos***. Sed hoc improbatur a Chrysostomo dupliciter: primo quia non servat formam Ecclesiae in orando, secundo quia oratio non est accepta Deo cum id quod Christus dictavit non servat. Unde dicendum quod non peccat dicendo *Pater noster*, quantumcumque sit in rancore et gravi peccato, quia tales deberent facere quidquid boni possent, et eleemosynas et orationes et huiusmodi quae sunt dispositiva ad gratiae recuperationem; nec mentitur, quia ista oratio non funditur in propria persona sed totius Ecclesiae, et constat quod Ecclesia dimittit debita omnibus qui sunt

but he prohibits being seized by anxiety ahead of time: for if now concern presses something upon you, you should do it, but it cannot press upon you what is to come.

596. *And forgive us*. Here he begins to place petitions which belong to the removal of evil. And first he lists the one by which the particular evil is removed, namely, the evil of guilt; hence ***and forgive us***. It is repugnant that a man who lives by God's things would live against God. Debts are sins, for we are obligated to God in debt for our sins: for if you have received anything unjustly from anyone, you are bound to restitution; and because when you sin you usurp what is God's, for it is of God that every will be ruled according to the will of God, therefore you take away what is God's and you are bound to restitution. But you are absolved when you endure something against your will according to God's will, as is said later: ***I forgave you all that debt*** (Matt 18:32). Therefore, ***forgive us our debts***, that is, sins: *forgive me that I may be refreshed* (Ps 39:13).

And with this word two heresies are refuted, that of Pelagius and that of Novation. Pelagius said that some perfect men in this life could live without sin and fulfill Ephesians: *so that he may present to himself a glorious church, having no spot or wrinkle* (Eph 5:27). But if so then we could not say ***forgive us***: *a just man shall fall seven times* (Prov 24:16); *if we say that we have no sin, we deceive ourselves* (1 John 1:8). Novatian said that a man who sins mortally after baptism cannot do penance. But if so, then we would say ***forgive us*** in vain: *he gave to them power to become sons of God* (John 1:12), namely, by adoption in grace.

597. *As we forgive our debtors*. But debtors can be of two kinds: either because they have sinned against us, or because they owe money; but he does not advise us to forgive this second kind of debt, but any sins, even to the loss of our temporal goods: for it is unfitting to ask pardon from God and not to give it to a fellow slave: *A man keeps anger against a man and expects healing from God?* (Sir 28:3); *and pay your neighbor again in due time* (Sir 29:2).

But what is to be said of those who do not wish to forgive and nevertheless say *Our Father*? It seems that they should never say it because they lie; hence it is said that some people omitted that phrase ***as we also forgive***. But this is disproved by Chrysostom in two ways: first, because it does not preserve the Church's form in praying, second, because the prayer is not received by God when what Christ dictated is not preserved. Hence it should be said that he does not sin by saying *Our Father*, however much he may be in rancor and grave sin, for such people should do whatever they can of good, both alms and prayers and such things that dispose one to the recovery of grace. Nor does he lie, for this prayer is not founded on our proper person but on the whole Church, and certainly the Church

in Ecclesia; talis autem amittit fructum quia illi soli consequuntur fructum qui dimittunt.

Sed videtur quod non solum consequuntur fructum illi qui dimittunt offensas. Sed sciendum quod Augustinus sic solvit quantum ad praesens pertinet, quia de dilectione inimicorum dictum est supra quia Deus eo tenore vult nos dimittere offensas quo tenore dimittit ipse nobis culpas: non autem dimittit nisi rognatibus; et ideo quicumque est ita dispositus quod paratus est dare veniam petenti, hic non amittit fructum dummodo in generali non habent odio quemcumque, sicut supra dictum est.

598. *Et ne nos*. Hic aliam petitionem ponit. Alia littera *et ne inferas*, et alia *et ne nos sinas*, et haec est expositio illius: Deus enim neminem temptat quamvis temptari permittat. Et non dicit: Ne nos permittes temptari, quia temptatio utilis est, et temptatur ut sibi et aliis innotescat qui notus est Deo, Eccli. XXXIV, 9: *qui non est temptatus*; sed dicit *et ne nos*, id est non permittas succumbere, sicut si diceret aliquis: volo igne calefieri sed non cremari, Cor. X: *fidelis Deus qui non patietur*.

In ista narratione confutatur error Pelagii quantum ad duo: dixit enim quod homo poterat persistere per liberum arbitrium absque Dei auxilio, quod nihil aliud est nisi temptationi non succumbere; item dixit quod ad Deum non pertinet immutare hominum voluntates. Sed si hoc, non diceret *et ne nos inducas*, quod idem est quod: fac nos non consentire; ergo in potestate sua est mutare voluntatem et non mutare, Phil. II, 13: *Deus est qui operatur in vobis.*

599. *Sed libera*. Haec est ultima petitio. *Libera*, a malo praeterito, praesenti et futuro, culpae et poenae, et ab omni malo. Augustinus: quilibet Christianus in quacumque tribulatione in haec verba lacrimas fundit et gemitus facit, Ps. *eripe me de inimicis*, Ps. LI, 12: *quis tu ut timeas?*

600. *Amen*, idest fiat. Hoc nullus voluit interpretari propter reverentiam, quia Dominus frequenter utebatur eo. In hoc datur securitas impetrandi, dummodo serventur quae dicta sunt.

Sciendum autem quod in hebraeo adduntur tria verba, quae Chrysostomus exponit. Primum est *quoniam tuum est regnum*, postea *et virtus et gloria. Amen*. Et videntur respondere tribus praemissis: *tuum est regnum* ad illud *adveniat regnum tuum*; *virtus* ad *fiat voluntas*; *gloria* ad *Pater noster*, et ad omnia alia quae sunt ad honorem Dei. Vel aliter, quasi: alia ista facere potes quia tu es rex, et ideo nullus potest; tua est virtus, et ideo potes

forgives the sins of all who are in the Church; but such a person loses the fruit of the prayer, for only those who forgive obtain the fruit.

But it seems that not only those who forgive offenses obtain this fruit. But it should be known that Augustine resolves this as it pertains to the present, for it was said above concerning the love of enemies that God wants us to forgive offenses to the extent that he forgives our sins: but he only forgives those asking; and thus whoever is so disposed that he is prepared to give pardon to anyone who asks, he will not lose the fruit of this prayer as long as in general he does not have hatred for anyone, as was said above.

598. *And lead us not*. Here he sets down another petition. Another text has *and do not inflict on us*, and another has *and do not allow us*, and here is the explanation for it: for God tempts no one, although he permits him to be tempted. And he does not say: do not permit us to be tempted, for temptation is a useful thing, and one is tempted so that what is known to God becomes known to him and others: *what does he know, who has not been tried?* (Sir 34:9). But he says, *lead us not*, that is, do not permit us to succumb, as if someone said: I want to be heated in fire but not burned up: *God is faithful, who will not suffer you to be tempted above what you can bear* (1 Cor 10:13).

In this telling the error of Pelagius is refuted in two respects: for he said that a man could persevere by his free will without the help of God, which is nothing but not succumbing to temptation. Likewise he said that God could not change the wills of men. But if so, he would not say *and lead us not into temptation*, which is the same as: make us not consent; therefore it is in his power to change the will or not to change it: *it is God who is at work in you, enabling you both to will and to work* (Phil 2:13).

599. *But deliver us*. This is the last petition. *Deliver us*, from evil past, present, and future, guilt and punishment, and from every evil. Augustine: in these words every Christian in every kind of tribulation pours out his tears and groans: *deliver me from my enemies* (Ps 59:1); *who are you that you fear a mortal man?* (Isa 51:12).

600. *Amen*, that is, let it be done. This no one wanted to translate on account of reverence, for the Lord often used this. In this is given sureness of obtaining our request, as long as those things that were said are preserved.

But it should be known that in Hebrew three phrases are added, which Chrysostom explains. The first is *for yours is the kingdom*, afterward *and the power and the glory. Amen*. And it seems to correspond to three things above: *yours is the kingdom* to *your kingdom come*; *power* to *your will be done*; *glory* to *Our Father*, and to everything else that is for God's honor. Or otherwise, as though to say: you can do those other things because you are the king, and

regnum dare; tua gloria, et ideo Ps. *non nobis, Domine, non nobis* etc.

601. *Si enim dimiseritis.* Dominus in oratione quamdam conditionem adiecerat, scilicet **dimitte**; posset autem ibi ista conditio gravis videri alicui; et ideo Dominus rationem illius ostendit. Et circa hoc duo facit: primo ostendit istam conditionem esse utilem, secundo necessariam. Utilis est quia per eam consequimur remissionem peccatorum, et hoc est **si enim dimiseritis hominibus peccata**, quae contra vos peccaverunt, **dimittet** etc. quae contra eum peccasti, Eccli. XXVIII, 2: *relinque proximo tuo*.

Sed nota quod dicit **si enim dimiseritis hominibus**; homines enim quamdiu innocenter vivunt, dii sunt; quando autem peccant, cadunt in humanam conditionem, Ps. *ego dixi* etc., post *vos autem* etc.: ergo vos qui dii et spirituales estis, **hominibus** peccatoribus dimittetis.

Item nota quod dicit **Pater vester** etc.; offense enim quae secundum homines fiunt propter aliquid terrenum; e contra, homines caelestes qui Patrem habent in caelis nihil discordiae debent habere propter terrenum, Luce VI, 36: *estote misericordes*.

Est etiam ista conditio necessaria, quia sine ea non fit remissio peccatorum, unde **si autem non** etc. Nec mirum, quia numquam aliquod peccatum potest dimitti sine caritate, Prov. VII: *universa delicta*: qui enim habet odium super unum non est in caritate, et ideo non dimittitur ei peccatum, Eccli. XVIII: *homo homini servat*, Iac. II, 13: *iudicium sine misericordia*.

602. Sed posset aliquis credere quod ex quo ita est quod dimittenda est offensa, ergo Ecclesia peccat quando non dimittit. Dicendum quod si ille petat veniam, peccaret si non dimitteret; si autem non petat, tunc non dimittit vel propter odium et sic peccat, vel propter bonum illius vel aliorum, ut scilicet malum non frequentetur, et sic non peccat.

thus no one can; yours is the power, and thus you can give the kingdom; yours is the glory, and thus *not to us Lord but to your name give glory* (Ps 115:1).

601. *For if you forgive.* The Lord attaches a certain condition to the prayer, namely, **forgive**; but this condition here could seem burdensome to someone; and thus the Lord shows the reason for it. And concerning this he does two things: first he shows that this condition is useful; second, necessary. It is useful because by it we obtain the remission of sins, and this is **for if you forgive men their offenses**, which they have sinned against you, **your Father will forgive** what you have sinned against him: *forgive your neighbor* (Sir 28:2).

But note that he says **if you forgive men**; for men, as long as they live innocently, are gods; but when they sin, they fall into the human condition: *I said, you are gods* (Ps 82:6) and after, *but you will die like mortals* (Ps 82:7): therefore, you who are gods and spiritual beings, forgive the sinful **men**.

Again, note that he says **your Father**; for offenses which are according to men are done because of something earthly; on the other hand, celestial men who have a Father in heaven should have no discord for the sake of anything earthly: *be merciful as your Father is merciful* (Luke 6:36).

This condition is also necessary, for without it there can be no remission of sins, hence **but if you do not forgive**. Nor is it surprising for no sin can be forgiven without charity: *charity covers all sins* (Prov 10:12). For whoever hates someone is not in charity, and thus his sins will not be forgiven him: *man keeps anger against man and expects healing from God?* (Sir 28:3); *judgment without mercy to him who has no mercy* (Jas 2:13).

602. But someone might believe from this that this is how sins should be forgiven, and therefore the Church sins when she does not forgive. It should be said that if someone seeks pardon, one would sin if one did not forgive. But if he did not seek it, then one does not forgive either because of hatred, and that is a sin, or because of the sinner's good or that of others, so that, for example, evil may not be repeated, and that is not a sin.

Lecture 4

6:16 Cum autem ieiunatis, nolite fieri sicut hypocritae, tristes; exterminant enim facies suas, ut appareant hominibus ieiunantes. Amen dico vobis, quia receperunt mercedem suam. [n. 603]

6:17 Tu autem, cum ieiunas, unge caput tuum, et faciem tuam lava, [n. 607]

6:18 ne videaris hominibus ieiunans, sed Patri tuo, qui est in abscondito; et Pater tuus qui videt in abscondito, reddet tibi. [n. 609]

6:16 Ὅταν δὲ νηστεύητε, μὴ γίνεσθε ὡς οἱ ὑποκριταὶ σκυθρωποί, ἀφανίζουσιν γὰρ τὰ πρόσωπα αὐτῶν ὅπως φανῶσιν τοῖς ἀνθρώποις νηστεύοντες· ἀμὴν λέγω ὑμῖν, ἀπέχουσιν τὸν μισθὸν αὐτῶν.

6:17 σὺ δὲ νηστεύων ἄλειψαί σου τὴν κεφαλὴν καὶ τὸ πρόσωπόν σου νίψαι,

6:18 ὅπως μὴ φανῇς τοῖς ἀνθρώποις νηστεύων ἀλλὰ τῷ πατρί σου τῷ ἐν τῷ κρυφαίῳ· καὶ ὁ πατήρ σου ὁ βλέπων ἐν τῷ κρυφαίῳ ἀποδώσει σοι.

6:16 And when you fast, be not as the hypocrites, sad. For they disfigure their faces, that they may appear unto men to fast. Amen I say to you, they have received their reward. [n. 603]

6:17 But you, when you fast anoint your head, and wash your face; [n. 607]

6:18 That you appear not to men to fast, but to your Father who is in secret: and your Father who sees in secret, will repay you. [n. 609]

---

603. Cum ieiunatis. Postquam determinavit modum orandi et eleemosynam faciendi, hic determinat modum ieiunandi. Et primo excludit modum inconvenientem; secundo astruit verum ibi **tu autem**.

Circa primum tria facit:

primo docet vitare hypocritarum modi exemplum;

secundo manifestat illud;

tertio rationem sui documenti assignat,

604. Secundum, ibi **exterminant**;

tertium, ibi **amen**.

605. Satis convenienter post orationem de ieiunio tractat, quia gracilis est oratio quam non concomitatur ieiunium. Et non est quia oratio est elevatio mentis in Deum. Quanto autem caro magis roboratur, tanto magis debilitatur . Tob. XII, 8: *bona est oratio cum ieiunio*. Et ubicumque legitur aliqua oratio solemnis facta, ibi fit mentio de ieiunio. Dan. IX, 3, et Ioel. II, 15: *sanctificate*.

Dicit ergo **cum ieiunatis**. Chrysostomus: non dicit: *nolite esse*, quia impossibile est quod ieiunantes non incidant in passiones tristitiae, sicut e converso illi qui ieiunant ex comestione et potatione redduntur laeti. Sed dicit **nolite fieri**, idest non detis operam ut tristes fiamini exterius, sed interius dolendo de peccatis, II Cor. VII, 10: tristitiam *saeculi*, Eccli. XXX, 22: *tristitiam non des animae tuae et ne affligas temetipsum in consilio tuo*.

606. Sicut hypocritae, idest ea intentione. **Hypocritae** dicuntur simulatores, qui simulant personam iusti, sicut supra expositum est. Quando autem fiant tristes, subiungit **exterminant**. Ieronimus: hoc scilicet **exterminant** improprie positum est ut metaphorice, quia exterminare proprie dicitur 'extra terminos ponere': unde sumptum est ab exulibus civitatum. Unde dicitur quod Saul exterminavit magos et ariolos de terra. Hic autem

603. When you fast. After he has defined the manner of praying and giving alms, here he defines the manner of fasting. And first he excludes the unfitting manner; second, he adds the truth at **but you**.

Concerning the first he does three things:

first, he teaches us to avoid the example of the manner of hypocrites;

second, he shows this example;

third, he assigns the reason of his teaching,

604. The second is at **they disfigure**;

the third, at **amen**.

605. Fittingly enough after prayer he treats of fasting, for prayer is thin when not accompanied by fasting. And it is not because prayer is the raising of the mind to God, but the more the flesh is strengthened, the more prayer is weakened: *prayer with fasting is good* (Tob 12:8). And everywhere that it reads that some solemn prayer is done, mention is made of fasting (cf. Dan 9:3); or *sanctify a fast* (Joel 2:15).

Therefore he says **when you fast**. Chrysostom: he does not say, *do not be*, for it is impossible for those fasting not to fall into feelings of sadness, just as on the other hand, those who fast are made happy by eating and drinking. But he says, **do not become**, that is, do not exert yourself to show your sadness externally, but by inward sorrow for sins: *worldly grief produces death* (2 Cor 7:10); *do not give yourself over to sorrow, nor afflict yourself by your own counsel* (Sir 30:21).

606. Like the hypocrites, that is, by this intention. **Hypocrites** are called so from simulators, who simulate the person of a just man, as was explained above. But when they become sad, he adds **they disfigure their faces**. Jerome: this **they disfigure** was improperly set down as metaphorically, for 'exterminare' properly means 'to put outside the boundaries': hence it is taken from those exiled from a nation. Hence it is said that Saul banished magicians and diviners

proprie ponitur quod demoliuntur. Vel dicendum quod *exterminant facies*, ponendo extra modum communem. *Ut videantur*: ista est oratio, Eccli. XIX, 26: *ex visu cognoscitur vir et ab occursu faciei.*

Hic nota, secundum Augustinum, quod non solum gloria quaeritur de pompa vestium sed etiam de vilitate vestium; et secundum eum hoc est magis periculosum quia quod alii fallant de pompa vestium et huiusmodi non potest nocere cum cognoscatur, sed quando quaeritur de squalore corporis potest esse periculum quia si non est spiritualis homo potest de facili inducere in errorem. Dicit tamen Augustinus quod talis potest discerni ex aliis actibus, quia si ex una parte sequitur abiectionem mundi et ex alia acquirit lucra, simulator est. Sed numquid propter hoc quod aliqui hypocritae usurpant sibi vilitatem vestium ad malitiam occultandam, debent dimittere illi qui faciunt propter Deum? Dicendum quod non, quia sicut dicit Glossa non debet dimittere pellem suam ovis quamvis lupus aliquando ea se contegat.

607. Amen. Assignat rationem sui documenti: stultum enim est pro laude hominum amittere praemium aeternum, Gen. XV, 1: *ego Deus, merces tua magna.*

Tu autem. Hic ponitur modus conveniens ieiunandi. Et circa hoc tria facit: primo ponit modum; secundo assignat rationem; tertio utilitatem. Dicit ergo **tu autem**, simile Eccl. IX, 8: *omni tempore sint vestimenta tua candida, et oleum de capite tuo non deficiat.* Et movet hic Augustinus quaestionem quod quamvis consuetudo sit apud multos quod cotidie faciem suam lavent, tamen quod caput ungant ad lasciviam reputatur: numquid ergo hoc Dominus vult? Item dicit Chrysostomus quod ieiunium occulte debet fieri; sed quandocumque videmus aliquem unctum dicemus quod ieiunat.

608. Istis obiectionibus tripliciter respondet Ieronimus. Ita dicit, et credo quod sit magis litteralis, quod consuetudo erat apud Palestinos tempore illo quod homines cotidie ungebant caput oleo et lavabant faciem. Unde illa dixit IV Reg. IV, 2: *non habeo nisi modicum oleo quo ungar.* Unde consuetudo ista inter necessaria computabatur. Vult ergo Dominus dicere quod ille qui ieiunat non debet mutare modum vivendi qui est quod caput ungat et faciem lavet.

Vel aliter, secundum Chrysostomum, Dominus loquitur per excessum sicut etiam supra. **Te autem faciente eleemosynam**; quare, si conveniens esset, deberes facere communia hypocritis. Tertio, secundum Augustinum et etiam Chrysostomum, Dominus loquitur similitudine. Et ista expositio est mystica. Per caput duo intelliguntur. I Cor. XI, 3: *caput viri Christus.* Tunc autem ungis caput quando misericordiam proximo impendis, infra X, 42: *quod uni ex minimis* etc. Vel caput hominis ratio est, vel spiritus, secundum Augustinum, qui est vir, quasi sic debes carnem affligere ut spiritus interius recreatur

from the land. But here it is properly said that they destroy. Or it could be said that **they disfigure their faces**, by placing them beyond the common manner. **So that they may seem**: this is their prayer; *a man is known by his look, and by the encounter of his face* (Sir 19:29).

Note that, according to Augustine, here glory is not only sought in resplendence of clothing, but even in shabbiness of clothing; and according to him this is more dangerous, for the fact that others deceive by splendid clothes and the like, cannot harm since it is recognized, but when it is sought from the squalor of the body it can be a danger because if a man is not spiritual he can easily be led into error. Nevertheless Augustine says that such a man can be detected from his other acts, for if in one area he pursues the abjection of the world and in another he acquires profit, he is a faker. But if some hypocrites make use of shabby clothes to hide their malice, should those who do it for the sake of God abandon it? It should be said no, for as the Gloss says, the sheep should not abandon its fleece although the wolf sometimes disguises himself in it.

607. Amen. He assigns the reason for his teaching: for it is stupid to lose an eternal reward for the sake of men's praise: *I, God . . . am your great reward* (Gen 15:1).

But you. Here he sets down the proper mode of fasting. And concerning this he does three things: first, he sets down the mode; second, he assigns the reason; third, the benefit. Therefore he says **but you**, like in: *let your garments always be white and do not let oil be lacking on your head* (Eccl 9:8). And Augustine here raises the question that although the custom among many is to wash their face every day, nevertheless to anoint one's head is considered lasciviousness: does the Lord then want this? Likewise, Chrysostom says that fasting should be done secretly; but whenever we see someone anointed we say that he is fasting.

608. Jerome responds to these objections three ways. He says, and I believe this is the most literal, that the custom in Palestine at that time was that men anointed their heads and washed their faces every day. Hence it said these things: *I have nothing but a little oil to anoint myself* (2 Kgs 4:2). Hence that custom is considered necessary. Therefore the Lord wishes to say that the man who fasts should not change his mode of living, which is that he anoint his head and wash his face.

Or otherwise, according to Chrysostom, the Lord speaks by way of excess, as he also did above at **but when you give alms**. Because, if it were fitting, you should do all things together with the hypocrites. Third, according to Augustine and also Chrysostom, the Lord speaks by way of likeness. And this is the mystical interpretation. By the head two things are understood: the head of the man is Christ (1 Cor 11:3). But you anoint the head when you show mercy to your neighbor, as below: **whatever you did to one of these little ones, you did to me** (Matt 25:40). Or, according to Augustine, the head of the man is his reason,

per devotionem, II Cor. IV, 16: *licet is qui foris est noster homo corrumpatur, tamen is qui intus est renovatur de die in diem. Noster homo* idest caro *qui foris est*, idest expositus malis, *corrumpitur; is qui intus est*, idest anima munita spe futuri, non accedit humanus furor; *renovatur de die in diem*, idest assidue purior amicus efficitur per ignem tribulationis, *licet is qui foris homo noster.*

609. Dicit autem **faciem tuam lava**, idest conscientiam. Sicut enim homo redditur gratiosus propter faciem honestam hominibus, ita per conscientiam puram Deo, Prov. XX, 11: *qui diligunt cordis munditiam*, Is. LVIII, 5: *nonne hoc est ieiunium quod elegi.* Et dicit **unge caput**, et non *lava*, quia Christus non indiget lotione; sic conscientia nostra.

Ne videaris. Haec est ratio, intelligendum est de ieiunio singulari, non de communi. **Sed patri qui est in abscondito** aeternitatis, Iob XXVIII, 21: *abscondita est ab oculis*. Vel **in abscondito** conscientiae, quia Deus habitat in nobis per fidem.

610. *Reddet* Rom II, 6: *reddet unicuique secundum opera sua*, sic *scrutans corda et renes*. Ps.

or spirit, which is a man, as though, 'You should so afflict your flesh that your inward spirit is renewed through devotion': *though our outward man is corrupted, what is inward is renewed day by day* (2 Cor 4:16). *Our outward man*, that is, the flesh, exposed to evils, *is corrupted; what is inward*, that is the soul, fortified in hope of the future, is not affected by human frenzy; *it is renewed day by day*, i.e., it is a friend made constantly purer by the fire of tribulation.

609. But he says **wash your face**, i.e., your conscience. For as man is made agreeable because of a respectable face for men, so is a pure conscience before God: *Those who love a pure heart . . . will have the king as a friend* (Prov 22:11); *is this the fast that I chose?* (Isa 58:5). And he says, **anoint your head**, and not *wash* it, for Christ does not need cleansing, like our conscience.

Lest you appear. This is the reason, to be understood of individual fasts, not of group fasts. **But your father who is in secret** of eternity: *hidden from the eyes of all* (Job 28:21). Or **in the secret** of your conscience, for God lives in us by faith.

610. **Will repay you**. *He will repay each according to his works* (Rom 2:6), as *he searches the hearts and depths* (Ps 7:9).

Lecture 5

6:19 nolite thesaurizare vobis thesauros in terra ubi erugo et tinea demolitur ubi fures effodiunt et furantur [n. 611]

6:20 thesaurizate autem vobis thesauros in caelo ubi neque aerugo neque tinea demolitur et ubi fures non effodiunt nec furantur [n. 613]

6:21 ubi enim est thesaurus tuus ibi est et cor tuum [n. 614]

6:22 lucerna corporis est oculus si fuerit oculus tuus simplex totum corpus tuum lucidum erit. [n. 614]

6:23 si autem oculus tuus nequam fuerit totum corpus tuum tenebrosum erit si ergo lumen quod in te est tenebrae sunt tenebrae quantae erunt. [n. 614]

6:24 nemo potest duobus dominis servire aut enim unum odio habebit et alterum diliget aut unum sustinebit et alterum contemnet non potestis Deo servire et mamonae [n. 619]

6:25 ideo dico vobis ne solliciti sitis animae vestrae quid manducetis neque corpori vestro quid induamini nonne anima plus est quam esca et corpus plus est quam vestimentum [n. 622]

6:26 respicite volatilia caeli quoniam non serunt neque metunt neque congregant in horrea et Pater vester caelestis pascit illa nonne vos magis pluris estis illis [n. 624]

6:27 quis autem vestrum cogitans potest adicere ad staturam suam cubitum unum [n. 627]

6:28 et de vestimento quid solliciti estis considerate lilia agri quomodo crescunt non laborant nec nent [n. 628]

6:19 Μὴ θησαυρίζετε ὑμῖν θησαυροὺς ἐπὶ τῆς γῆς, ὅπου σὴς καὶ βρῶσις ἀφανίζει καὶ ὅπου κλέπται διορύσσουσιν καὶ κλέπτουσιν·

6:20 θησαυρίζετε δὲ ὑμῖν θησαυροὺς ἐν οὐρανῷ, ὅπου οὔτε σὴς οὔτε βρῶσις ἀφανίζει καὶ ὅπου κλέπται οὐ διορύσσουσιν οὐδὲ κλέπτουσιν·

6:21 ὅπου γάρ ἐστιν ὁ θησαυρός σου, ἐκεῖ ἔσται καὶ ἡ καρδία σου.

6:22 Ὁ λύχνος τοῦ σώματός ἐστιν ὁ ὀφθαλμός. ἐὰν οὖν ᾖ ὁ ὀφθαλμός σου ἁπλοῦς, ὅλον τὸ σῶμά σου φωτεινὸν ἔσται·

6:23 ἐὰν δὲ ὁ ὀφθαλμός σου πονηρὸς ᾖ, ὅλον τὸ σῶμά σου σκοτεινὸν ἔσται. εἰ οὖν τὸ φῶς τὸ ἐν σοὶ σκότος ἐστίν, τὸ σκότος πόσον.

6:24 Οὐδεὶς δύναται δυσὶ κυρίοις δουλεύειν· ἢ γὰρ τὸν ἕνα μισήσει καὶ τὸν ἕτερον ἀγαπήσει, ἢ ἑνὸς ἀνθέξεται καὶ τοῦ ἑτέρου καταφρονήσει. οὐ δύνασθε θεῷ δουλεύειν καὶ μαμωνᾷ.

6:25 Διὰ τοῦτο λέγω ὑμῖν· μὴ μεριμνᾶτε τῇ ψυχῇ ὑμῶν τί φάγητε [ἢ τί πίητε], μηδὲ τῷ σώματι ὑμῶν τί ἐνδύσησθε. οὐχὶ ἡ ψυχὴ πλεῖόν ἐστιν τῆς τροφῆς καὶ τὸ σῶμα τοῦ ἐνδύματος;

6:26 ἐμβλέψατε εἰς τὰ πετεινὰ τοῦ οὐρανοῦ ὅτι οὐ σπείρουσιν οὐδὲ θερίζουσιν οὐδὲ συνάγουσιν εἰς ἀποθήκας, καὶ ὁ πατὴρ ὑμῶν ὁ οὐράνιος τρέφει αὐτά· οὐχ ὑμεῖς μᾶλλον διαφέρετε αὐτῶν;

6:27 τίς δὲ ἐξ ὑμῶν μεριμνῶν δύναται προσθεῖναι ἐπὶ τὴν ἡλικίαν αὐτοῦ πῆχυν ἕνα;

6:28 καὶ περὶ ἐνδύματος τί μεριμνᾶτε; καταμάθετε τὰ κρίνα τοῦ ἀγροῦ πῶς αὐξάνουσιν· οὐ κοπιῶσιν οὐδὲ νήθουσιν·

6:19 Do not lay up for yourselves treasures on earth: where the rust and moth consume, and where thieves break through and steal. [n. 611]

6:20 But lay up to yourselves treasures in heaven: where neither the rust nor moth consumes, and where thieves do not break through, nor steal. [n. 613]

6:21 For where your treasure is, there is your heart also. [n. 614]

6:22 The light of your body is your eye. If your eye be sound, your whole body will be lightsome. [n. 614]

6:23 But if your eye be evil your whole body will be darksome. If then the light that is in you is darkness: the darkness itself, how great will it be. [n. 614]

6:24 No man can serve two masters. For either he will hate the one, and love the other: or he will sustain the one, and despise the other. You cannot serve God and mammon. [n. 619]

6:25 Therefore I say to you, be not solicitous for your soul, what you should eat, nor for your body, what you should put on. Is not the life more than the meat: and the body more than the raiment? [n. 622]

6:26 Behold the birds of the air, for they neither sow, nor do they reap, nor gather into barns: and your heavenly Father feeds them. Are not you of much more value than they? [n. 624]

6:27 And which of you by taking thought, can add to his stature one cubit? [n. 627]

6:28 And for raiment why are you solicitous? Consider the lilies of the field, how they grow: they labor not, neither do they spin. [n. 628]

6:29 dico autem vobis quoniam nec Salomon in omni gloria sua coopertus est sicut unum ex istis [n. 629]

6:30 si autem faenum agri quod hodie est et cras in clibanum mittitur Deus sic vestit quanto magis vos minimae fidei [n. 629]

6:31 nolite ergo solliciti esse dicentes quid manducabimus aut quid bibemus aut quo operiemur [n. 630]

6:32 haec enim omnia gentes inquirunt scit enim Pater vester quia his omnibus indigetis [n. 630]

6:33 quaerite autem primum regnum et iustitiam eius et omnia haec adicientur vobis [n. 630]

6:34 nolite ergo esse solliciti in crastinum crastinus enim dies sollicitus erit sibi ipse sufficit diei malitia sua. [n. 630]

6:29 λέγω δὲ ὑμῖν ὅτι οὐδὲ Σολομὼν ἐν πάσῃ τῇ δόξῃ αὐτοῦ περιεβάλετο ὡς ἓν τούτων.

6:30 εἰ δὲ τὸν χόρτον τοῦ ἀγροῦ σήμερον ὄντα καὶ αὔριον εἰς κλίβανον βαλλόμενον ὁ θεὸς οὕτως ἀμφιέννυσιν, οὐ πολλῷ μᾶλλον ὑμᾶς, ὀλιγόπιστοι;

6:31 μὴ οὖν μεριμνήσητε λέγοντες· τί φάγωμεν; ἤ· τί πίωμεν; ἤ· τί περιβαλώμεθα;

6:32 πάντα γὰρ ταῦτα τὰ ἔθνη ἐπιζητοῦσιν· οἶδεν γὰρ ὁ πατὴρ ὑμῶν ὁ οὐράνιος ὅτι χρῄζετε τούτων ἁπάντων.

6:33 ζητεῖτε δὲ πρῶτον τὴν βασιλείαν [τοῦ θεοῦ] καὶ τὴν δικαιοσύνην αὐτοῦ, καὶ ταῦτα πάντα προστεθήσεται ὑμῖν.

6:34 μὴ οὖν μεριμνήσητε εἰς τὴν αὔριον, ἡ γὰρ αὔριον μεριμνήσει ἑαυτῆς· ἀρκετὸν τῇ ἡμέρᾳ ἡ κακία αὐτῆς.

6:29 But I say to you, that not even Solomon in all his glory was arrayed as one of these. [n. 629]

6:30 And if the grass of the field, which is today, and tomorrow is cast into the oven, God does so clothe: how much more you, O you of little faith? [n. 629]

6:31 Be not solicitous therefore, saying, what will we eat: or what will we drink, or with what will we be clothed? [n. 630]

6:32 For after all these things do the heathens seek. For your Father knows that you have need of all these things. [n. 630]

6:33 Seek you therefore first the kingdom of God, and his justice, and all these things will be added unto you. [n. 630]

6:34 Be not therefore, solicitous for tomorrow; for the morrow will be solicitous for itself. Sufficient for the day is its own evil. [n. 630]

---

611. *Nolite thesaurizare.* Supra Dominus determinavit ne opera propter gloriam faceremus; hic docet quod non debemus in bonis operibus ponere divitiarum finem. Duo enim mala sunt: cupiditas et inanis gloria, quae se invicem consequuntur. Multi enim quaerunt divitias non ad necessitatem sed ad pompam.

Vel potest sic continuari. Dominus supra non docuit nec admonuit ut eleemosynas vel orationes faceremus, sed docuit modum faciendi; nunc vult inducere ad hoc quod ista opera faciamus. Et primo quod eleemosynas; secundo quod orationes, ibi *petite*; tertio quod ieiunium, ibi *arta* est *via*.

612. Vel aliter. Supra docuit quod eleemosynas et ieiunium faceremus et non propter gloriam; hic vult universaliter ostendere quod *nullus*. Sed prima est magis consona litterae et est Chrysostomi.

Secundum igitur hunc sensum, quia omnes quasi idem sint, duo facit: primo docet vitare superfluam curam divitiarum, secundo sollicitudinem necessariorum, ibi *iam dico vobis*. Circa primum duo facit: primo monet non congregare superfluas divitias. Et probat ex ratione instabilitatis; secundo ex damno quod inde provenit, ibi *ubi est thesaurus*. Circa primum duo facit: primo ponit instabilitatem divitiarum terrenarum; secundo ponit

611. *Do not lay up for yourselves treasures.* Above, the Lord prescribed that we not do works for the sake of glory; here he teaches that we should not set riches as our end in good works. For there are two evils: greed and vainglory, which follow upon each other. For many seek riches not for their needs but for ostentation.

Or it can be continued like this. Above, the Lord did not teach or admonish us to do almsgiving or prayers, but rather he taught the manner of doing them; now he wants to induce us to do these works. And first, almsgiving; second, praying, at *ask and you shall receive*; third, fasting, at *the way is narrow*.

612. Or another interpretation. Above, he taught how we should do alms and fasting, and not for glory; here he wants to show completely that *no man can serve two masters*. But the first reading, from Chrysostom, is more consonant with the text.

Therefore according to this sense, for all men are, as it were, the same, he does two things: first, he teaches us to avoid excessive concern for riches, second, anxiety for necessities, at *now I say to you*. Concerning the first he does two things: first, he warns us not to amass excess riches. And he proves it by reason of its instability; second, from the harm that comes from it at *where your treasure is*. Concerning the first he does two things: first, he sets forth the instability of earthly riches; second, he sets down the

stabilitatem divitiarum caelestium quas congregare debemus, ibi *thesaurizate*.

Dicit ergo primo: ita dico quod non debemus facere bona opera propter gloriam terrenam, sed etiam nec divitias congregare. Et hoc est *nolite* etc., *in terra*, idest in quacumque re terrena. Sed secundum hoc videtur quod reges et episcopi faciant contra istud praeceptum. Sed dicendum quod in thesauro duo intelligere, scilicet abundantiam, quae est duplex, scilicet necessaria et superflua. Homini enim privato superfluum est congregare divitias; regi autem non, quia indiget ad regni custodiam et defensionem. Unde hoc prohibetur, scilicet congregare divitias ultra necessitatem personae vel officii. Aliud quod in thesauro intelligitur est fiducia quae habetur in eis; et hoc etiam prohibetur. Et hoc est *nolite thesaurizare*, I Tim. ult.17 *divitibus huius saeculi*, Baruc. III, 18: *argentum thesaurizant et aurum*.

613. Consequenter ostendit instabilitatem. *Ubi ergo*, et ponit tria genera quibus ad litteram divitiae destruuntur. Divitiae enim aut habentur in metallis aut in vestibus aut in lapidibus; et huiusmodi metalla consumuntur rubigine, vestes tinea, fures autem asportant lapides. Vel aliter, alia littera habet *ubi tinea* et comeduntur *comestura exterminant*, et istam exponit Chrysostomus. Temporalia enim tripliciter destruuntur ex parte rerum, quia de vestimento procedit tinea ex luxuria possidentis. Unde dicit *commestura*, ab extraneis. Unde dicit *fures*. Sed posset dici quia hoc non semper contingit. Et dicit Chrysostomus quod si non semper fiat, tamen frequenter contingit, et si non frequenter contingat tamen possibile est fieri. Et hoc Dominus vult argumentari quia docet ponere spem in perpetuis et stabilibus, Ioel. I, 4: *residuum comedet locusta*.

Mystice *erugo* apparet, sed *tinea* latet. Unde per *erugo* possunt intelligi peccata carnalia, per *tinea* spiritualia: quaedam enim peccata committunt in seipsum, et hoc intelligit per eruginem et tineam; quaedam in scandalum alterius, et hoc per *fures*. Vel aliter, rubigo efuscat decora: unde potest intelligi superbia quae bonis operibus insidiatur ut pereant, Eccli. XII, 10: *quasi aeramentum*; tinea corrodit vestimenta quae sunt exteriora opera quae consummuntur per invidiam, Prov. XXV, 20: *sicut vermis ligno* etc. Daemones autem quando non possunt decipere furtive trahunt ad inanem gloriam. Et hoc *ubi fures*. Posita instabilitate terrena, ponit stabilitatem thesauri caelestis. Unde *thesaurizant* idest congregant multitudinem praemiorum in caelestibus.

Et notandum secundum Augustinum quod non est intelligendum de caelo corporeo, quia in nulla re corporali cor nostrum figere debemus nec thesaurum ibi

stability of heavenly riches that we should amass, at *lay up treasures in heaven*.

Therefore he says first: I say thus that you should not do good works for earthly glory, but also do not amass riches. And this is *Do not lay up . . . treasures on earth*, i.e., in any earthly thing. But according to this it seems that kings and bishops act against this precept. But it should be said that two things are understood in treasure, namely abundance, which is twofold, necessary or excess. For it is excessive for a private man to amass riches; but not for a king, who needs it for the care and defense of his kingdom. Hence this is forbidden, namely to amass riches beyond the needs of one's person or office. The other thing that is understood by treasure is the trust that is placed in it; and this is also forbidden. And this is *do not lay up treasure for yourselves*: *charge the rich of the present age not to be highminded . . . but to trust in God* (1 Tim 6:17); *those who laid up silver and gold . . . where is the trace of their works?* (Bar 3:18).

613. Next, he shows the instability. *Where rust*, and he sets down three kinds of things by which riches are literally destroyed. For riches can be had as precious metals, or in clothing, or in precious stones; and thus metals are consumed by rust, clothes by moths, while thieves carry off jewels. Or otherwise, another text has at *where moth* also *feasts are consumed and cleared away*, and Chrysostom explains this. For temporal things are destroyed in three ways: on the part of the thing, for from clothing comes *a moth*; by the extravagance of the owner: hence he says *feasts are consumed*; and from outside causes, hence he says *thieves*. But it could be said that this does not always happen. And Chrysostom says that if it does not always happen, nevertheless it often happens and if not often, nevertheless it is possible. And the Lord wants to argue this, for he teaches us to set our hope on lasting and stable things: *what was left, the locust has eaten* (Joel 1:4).

Mystically, *rust* appears but *moth* is hidden. Hence by *rust* can be understood carnal sins, but by *moth* spiritual ones: for some sins are committed against oneself, and this is understood as *rust* and *moth*; some sins are committed in scandal of another, and this is *thieves*. Or otherwise, tarnish blackens pretty things: hence it can be understood as pride which infiltrates good works so that they perish *like corrosion in copper* (Sir 12:10); the moth corrodes the clothes which are the external works that are consumed by envy: *like a moth in clothing or a worm in wood, sorrow gnaws at the human heart* (Prov 25:20). But demons, when they cannot deceive, stealthily drag someone into vainglory. And this is *where thieves*. Having shown earthly instability, he sets forth the stability of the heavenly treasure. Hence *they store up treasure*, i.e., they amass a multitude of rewards in heaven.

And it should be noted, according to Augustine, that it is not to be understood about the physical heavens, for we should fix our hearts on no physical thing, nor have our

habere. Unde intelligendum in caelo, idest in spiritualibus bonis, idest in ipso Deo, Ps. *caelum caeli Domino*. Ut dicit **thesaurizate** quia si homo carnalis vult magis et magis congregare in terra non debet ei sufficere quod qualemcumque statum habeat in re caelorum, sed quod habeat maiorem mercedem. Et ideo dicit **thesaurizate**, idest abundate praemiis; et dicit **vobis** quia, sicut dicitur Iob XXXV, 7: *porro si iuste egeris.*

614. Quomodo autem thesaurizandum sit ostenditur Luc. XIX, 21: *si vis perfectus esse.* Ergo per eleemosynam thesaurizatur. Et ideo dicit Chrysostomus quod hic inducit ad eleemosynam. Hic thesaurus incorruptibilis est quia nec ex se habet corruptionem, quia nec aerugo ex parte corporis, I Cor. XV, 53: *corruptibile hoc induet*; nec ex parte animae, Is. LX, 21: *populus tuus omnes iusti*; nec ab exterioribus, hoc est ab insidiatoribus, idest daemonibus. Et hoc est **ubi fures**, nec occulte nec manifeste, Is. XI, 9: *non occident nec nocebunt.*

Ubi est thesaurus. Hic vult ostendere quod debemus in caelo et non primum propter nocumentum quod inde provenit. Et est duplex: primum distractio cordis, secundum alienatio a Deo, ibi **nemo potest duobus.** Circa primum duo facit: primo ponit nocumentum distractionis cordis; secundo ostendit huius damni magnitudinem, ibi **lucerna.** Dicit ergo: dixi quod **fures effodiunt** etc.; sed restat aliud inconveniens: Unde **ubi est thesaurus.** Ubi enim est amor ibi oculus, II Cor. IV, 18: *non contemplantibus nobis*; sed isti e converso, Prov. XVII, 24: *oculi stultorum.*

Et quia hoc damnum, scilicet destructio cordis, pauci considerant, ideo Dominus ostendit quantum sit hoc periculum quodam exemplo; unde **lucerna**: per sensibilia instruit de intelligentibus. Ut potest hoc dupliciter legi. Primo ut Dominus proponat similitudinem de caelo corporali, et post adaptet similitudinem ad spiritualia, ibi **si ergo lumen.** Et haec expositio plana est. Et circa hoc tria facit: primo demonstrat officium oculi, secundo utilitatem boni, et tertio damnum mali occulti.

Dicit ergo **lucerna corporis est oculus**, corporalis, qui sicut lucerna dirigit. **Si oculus tuus fuerit simplex**, idest fortis ad videndum, secundum Ieronimum, alias non posset intelligi de oculo corporali; unde **simplex**, id est fortis ad videndum. Homo enim quando habet oculum debile, una res videtur duae. Unde si oculus in uno figere potest propter fortitudinem, totum **corpus tuum lucidum erit**: per lumen enim oculi lux capitur ad dirigenda omnia membra in suis actibus. **Si autem nequam**

treasure there. Hence it is understood about heaven, i.e., in spiritual goods, i.e., in God himself: *the heaven of heaven is the Lord's* (Ps 115:16). And he says **lay up treasure**, for if a fleshly man wishes to amass more and more on earth, it should not be enough for him that he have just any status in heavenly things, but that he have a greater reward. And thus he says **lay up treasure**, i.e., grow rich in rewards: and he says **for yourselves** because as is said: *if you do justice, what more shall you give him?* (Job 35:7).

614. But how treasures are to be laid up is shown: *if you wish to be perfect, go, sell your possessions and give the money to the poor* (Matt 19:21). Therefore treasure is laid up by giving alms. And thus Chrysostom says that here he induces us to give alms. This is the incorruptible treasure, for it can neither have corruption in itself nor rust on the part of its body: *this corruptible body must put on imperishability* (1 Cor 15:53); nor on the part of the soul: *your people shall all be righteous* (Isa 60:21); nor from outward causes, which lie in wait to attack, i.e., demons. And this is **where thieves**, for whether secretly or openly, *they will not kill or harm in all my holy mountain* (Isa 11:9).

Where your treasure is. Here he wants to show what we owe to heaven and not first because of the harm that comes from it. And this is for two reasons: first, the distraction of the heart; second, the alienation from God, at **no one can serve two masters.** Concerning the first he does two things: first, he sets forth the harm of a distracted heart; second, he shows the magnitude of its damage, at **the light of your body.** Therefore he says: I said that **thieves pillage**; but there remains something unfitting: hence **where your treasure is.** For where love is, there the eye is: *we look not at what can be seen but at what cannot be seen, for . . . what cannot be seen is eternal* (2 Cor 4:18); and on the other hand, *the eyes of a fool look to the end of the earth* (Prov 17:24).

And because few consider this loss, namely the destruction of the heart, for this reason the Lord shows how great the danger is by a certain example; hence **the lamp of your body**: by sensible things he instructs us about intellectual things. So that this can be read two ways. First, as though the Lord proposes a likeness to the physical heavens, and afterward he modifies the comparison to spiritual things, at **if the light in you is darkness.** And this explanation is plain. And concerning this he does three things: first, he shows the role of the eye, second, the benefit of the good, and third, the damage in hidden evil.

Therefore he says **the lamp of the body is** physically **the eye**, which directs like a lamp. **If your eye be sound**, i.e., strong at seeing, according to Jerome, otherwise it could not be understood as a physical eye; hence **sound** is strong in seeing. For when a man has a weak eye, one thing seems two. Hence if an eye can be fixed on one thing because of fortitude, the whole **body will be lightsome**: for by the light of the eye, light is caught for directing all the members in their acts. **But if your eye is evil**, i.e., disturbed, namely, by

fuerit, idest turbatus scilicet lippus, etiam *corpus*, idest membra omnia ita agent sicut in tenebris.

615. Consequenter adaptat *si ergo lumen quod in te est*, scilicet lumen rationis, *tenebrae sunt, ipsae tenebrae*. De hoc lumine, Ps. *signatum est super nos*. Vult ergo dicere quod si cor quod est oculus animae obtenebratur applicando se terrenis, alii oculi, qui secundum suam naturam sunt tenebrae, quia non possunt cognoscere nisi corporalia, erunt maximae tenebrae. Unde si ratio que potest in spiritualia dirigitur ad terrena, tunc omnes sensus ad terrena dirigentur. Et hoc est *si ergo* etc. Vel aliter. Dominus vult hic loqui de oculo spirituali; et hoc, *si ergo lumen* etc., inducere ad probandum praemissa per locum a minori et dicuntur sic prius.

Dicit ergo *lucerna corporis tui oculus tuus*. Hic *oculus* potest quatuor modis exponi, scilicet de ratione sicut dictum est, et hoc secundum Chrysostomum et Hilarium. Sicut enim per lucernam illuminantur ad videndum, ita per rationem ad operandum. Prov. XX, 27: *lucerna Domini spiraculum*.

616. *Si oculus tuus fuerit simplex*, idest si ratio tua tota dirigatur in unum, scilicet in Deum, *totum* etc.; et *si nequam*, idest applicatur ad terrena, *totum corpus* etc. Et potest hoc intelligi dupliciter. Erit enim lucidum vel tenebrosum quantum ad praesentia opera. *Lucidum*, si omnia exteriora membra propter Deum operantur. Et hoc fit ratio dirigatur in Deum, quia tunc membra pura conservantur a peccato, cum peccatum non procedat nisi ex consensu mentis. *Tenebrosum autem*, si ratio fuit occupata terrenis, quia tunc membra occupabantur operibus tenebrosis, Ro. XIII, 12: *abiciamus opera tenebrarum*.

Vel aliter, secundum Hilarium, *si oculus*, idest si ratio, simpliciter dirigatur in Deum, *totum corpus tuum lucidum*, quia ex claritate anime redundat claritas ad corpus: ita *fulgebunt iusti*. *Si autem nequem* etc.

617. Aliter secundum Augustinum. Per oculum intelligitur intentio. Sicut enim homo primo respicit distantia ad terminum, postea procedit, ita in operando primo determinat finem et ex fine intentio procedit ad operandum ergo oculus dirigit, Prov. ult. *non extinguetur in nocte lucerna*. Unde si intentio fuerit pura, et opus, sive congeries operum ex illa intentione procedens, erit purum. Et hoc intelligendum est de his quae secundum se bona quia, sicut dicitur Ro. III, 8: *damnatio iusta est* illorum qui dixerunt: *faciamus mala* etc. Si autem intentio fuerit perversa tota operatio redditur tenebrosa. Nec debet videri extraneum si per opera corpus significatur,

infection, also *the body*, i.e., all the members, will act as though in the dark.

615. Accordingly he modifies *therefore if the light that is in you*, namely, the light of reason, *be darkness, how great the darkness itself*. About this light, a Psalm says: *the light of your face is stamped upon us* (Ps 4:6). Therefore he wants to say that if the heart which is the eye of the soul becomes darkened by training itself upon earthly things, the other eyes, which are darkened by their nature, for they cannot recognize any but corporeal things, will be in the greatest darkness. Hence if reason, which is capable of spiritual things, is directed to earthly things, then all the senses are directed to earthly things. And this is *therefore if the light in you*. Or another way. The Lord wants to speak here about the spiritual eye; and he brings up *therefore if the light in you*, to prove what has been said in this passage by a lesser example, and the rest is as before.

Therefore he says *the lamp of your body is your eye*. This eye can be explained in four ways, namely, reason, as was said, and this is the interpretation of Chrysostom and Hilary. For as a lamp illuminates for seeing, so reason illuminates for acting: *the human spirit is the lamp of the Lord, searching the innermost* (Prov 20:27).

616. *If your eye be sound*, i.e., if your reason is completely directed to one thing, namely, God, *your whole body shall be*; and *if worthless*, that is, trained on earthly things, *your whole body shall be darkened*. And this can be understood in two ways. For it will be full of light or darkness as to present works. *Full of light*, if all outward members work for God's sake. And this happens if reason be directed to God, for then the members are preserved pure from sin, since sin does not occur except by the consent of the mind. *But darkness*, if reason was occupied by earthly things, for then the members were occupied by dark works: *lay aside the works of darkness* (Rom 13:12).

Or otherwise, according to Hilary, *if your eye*, i.e., if reason be simply directed to God, *your whole body will be filled with light*, for from the brightness of the soul, brightness overflows to the body: thus *the just will shine like the sun* (Matt 13:43). *But if worthless . . . your whole body will be darkened*.

617. In another way, according to Augustine. By the eye is understood the intention. For as a man first looks at the distance to his destination, and then he sets out, so also in working he first determines the end and from that end his intention proceeds to working. Therefore the eye directs: *her lamp does not go out at night* (Prov 31:18). Hence if the intention were pure, the work or the accumulation of works proceeding from this intention will also be pure. And this is to be understood of those thing that are good in themselves, for as Romans says: *the condemnation is deserved* (Rom 3:8) of those who said: *let us do evil that good may come of it*. But if the intention was perverse, the entire work is rendered dark. Nor should it seem strange if by works the

quia sicut dicitur Col. III, 5: *mortificate membra vestra* etc.

Tertio ponit: *oculus* animae est fides quae dirigit totum opus. Ps. *lucerna pedibus*. **Simplex** est quando non vacillat sed *per dilectionem operatur*; si autem fides fuerit depravata totum corpus, idest opus est **tenebrosum**. Ro. XIV, 23: *omne quod non est ex fide*.

618. Vel aliter. **Oculus**, praelatus qui est in sublimi, secundum IV Reg. XX, 14: *dixerunt viri* etc. *ne extinguas lucernam Israel* etc., Eccli. X, 2: *secundum iudicem populi*. Quod autem dicit **si ergo lumen**, secundum primam expositionem syllogizat ex praecedentibus, sed secundum istas probat praecedens, quasi: tu dicis **si oculus tuus** etc., probatio: **si ergo lumen**, de quo minus providetur, **ipsae tenebrae** etc. Si lumen rationis tenebra et opus. Et quantum ad hoc non mutatur expositio, sed ad alia sic, quia sicut dicit Augustinus, quilibet potest scire ex intentione qualis sit, sed quales effectus habeat opus non potest. Unde lucerna est intentio, sed opus est tenebra, Eph. V: *omne quod manifestatur*. Opus autem non manifestatur.

Vel aliter secundum Chrysostomum. Duplicia sunt opera lucis et tenebrae, Ro. XIII, 12. Opera lucis sunt opera iustitiae. Si ergo opus iustitiae in te sit tenebrosum, idest fiat propter malam intentionem, **ipsae tenebrae**, idest actiones malae **quantae erunt**.

Vel aliter: si fides mala, omnia alia mala quae per fidem dirigantur, et similiter si praelatus malus multo magis subditi.

619. Nemo potest. Supra Dominus posuit unum documentum quod non debemus congregare thesauros in terra quia distrahitur ex hoc cor; nunc ponit aliud, quia scilicet facit alienum a Deo: et hoc est **nemo potest**. Vel aliter potest continuari. Supra monuit quod non debemus thesauros congregare in terra sed in caelo, posset autem aliquis dicere: volo in caelo et in terra congregare; et ideo Dominus hic ostendit esse impossibile, dicens **nemo potest**. Sed prima melior est et est Chrysostomi.

Potest autem haec littera legi dupliciter. Primo, ut hoc **nemo potest** intelligatur conclusivum vel illativae et tunc Dominus, secundum expositionem Chrysostomi et Ieronimi, procedit a communibus opinionibus ad propositum ostendendum. Alio modo potest legi ut Dominus primo proponit quod intendit et postea procedat, et hoc secundum Augustinum. Prosequamur autem utrumque.

620. Secundum ergo primam expositionem duo facit: primo ponit communem hominum opinionem

body is signified, for in the same way it is said: *mortify your earthly members* (Col 3:5).

Third, he sets down: the **eye** of the soul is faith which directs the whole work: *your word is a lamp to my feet* (Ps 119:105). It is **sound** when it does not vacillate, but *works by love* (Gal 5:6). But if faith were corrupted, the whole body, i.e., the work, is **full of darkness**: *all that is not of faith is sin* (Rom 14:23).

618. Or another way. The **eye** is the prelate who is raised on high, according to 2 Samuel: *David's men said to him, you shall go no more into battle with us, lest you put out the lamp of Israel* (2 Sam 21:17) and *as the people's judge is, so are his ministers* (Sir 10:2). But the fact that he says **if then the light that is in you**, by the first interpretation he syllogizes from the things he said before, but according to these what was said before is the proof, as though: 'You say **if your eye**, the proof is: **If then the light that is in you is darkness**, how much less is seen **the darkness itself**. If the light of reason is darkened, so will its work be. And as to this the explanation is not changed, but as to other things it is, for as Augustine says, anyone can know of what kind his intention is, but he cannot know what kind of effects the work will have. Hence the lamp is intention, but the work is darkness: *all that is made manifest by the light becomes visible* (Eph 5:13). But the work is not made manifest.

Or another reading, according to Chrysostom. There are two kinds of works, of light and of darkness (cf. Rom 13:12). The works of light are the works of justice. If then a work of justice in you should be darkened, that is, it is done for a bad intention, **how great will be the darkness itself**, that is, the evil actions.

Or another way: if faith becomes bad, all other things that are directed by faith become bad, and likewise if a prelate is bad how much more those beneath him.

619. No man can serve two masters. Above the Lord gave one teaching that we should not amass treasures on earth, for the heart is distracted by this; now he mentions another thing that explicitly alienates us from God: and this is **no one can serve**. Or it can be continued with another interpretation. Above, he warned that we should not amass treasures on earth but in heaven, but someone could say: 'I want to amass them in heaven and on earth.' And thus the Lord here shows this to be impossible, saying **no man can**. But the first explanation is better, and it is Chrysostom's.

But this text can be read two ways. First, so that **no man can serve** is understood as a conclusion or inference and then the Lord, according to the interpretation of Chrysostom and Jerome, proceeds from common opinions to present his point. It can be read in another way, as the Lord first proposes what he intends and afterwards he proceeds, and this is Augustine's reading. But let us examine both ways.

620. Therefore according to the first explanation, he does two things: first, he sets down the common opinion

et consuetudinem; secundo rationem assignat, ibi *aut enim unum*. Dicit ergo *nemo potest*. Ratio autem huius apparet si accipiamus quid sit proprie servus et quid dominus servi enim ratio consistit in hoc quod est alterius, scilicet domini; unde finis eius est Dominus. Impossibile autem est quod unum feratur in duo tanquam in ultimos fines. Si ergo hoc est esse servi ordinare actus suos in dominum tamquam in ultimum finem, impossibile est quod servat duobus dominis. Is. XXVIII, 20: *angustatum est stratum* etc. Posset tamen servus habere duos quorum unus sit sub alio, sicut finis sub fine est. Vel secundum Glossam. *Nemo potest duobus dominis servire* contrariis, quia si consentiunt sunt unum.

Assignat rationem: *aut unum odio habebit*. Et sciendum quod duplex est dominium. Quidam enim dominantur hoc modo quod a subditis diliguntur, et hoc est dominium regale. Quidam dominantur ut timeantur, et hoc est tyrannorum. Si ergo servus servat dominum amore, et ita oportet quod odiat contrarium; si autem timore servus tunc oportet quod *sustineas*, idest tolleres et alterum. Et hoc est *aut unum* etc. De hoc dominio quod magis sit sustinendum quam diligendum habetur Prov. XXIX, 2: *cum impii sumpserint* fingere etc., idest *sustinebit* patienter tollerando. *Nemo ergo potest duobus*. Sed Deus et diabolus sunt contrarii quia ad contraria inclinant: ergo *non potest* etc. *Mammone*, idest divitiis, persica lingua, secundum Ieronimum.

Sciendum tamen quod aliud est abundare divitiis et servire. Aliqui enim abundant et tamen ad bonum ordinatum, et isti non serviunt divitiis; aliqui habent et tamen ex eis fructum non capiunt nec corporalem nec spiritualem, et isti serviunt, quia se affligunt ut divitias congregent, Eccl. VI, 1: *est et aliud malum* etc. In quacumque enim re homo constituit ultimam finem, illa res est Deus suus, Phil. III, 19: *quorum deus venter est*. Vel per *mammonam* intelligitur diabolus qui praeest divitiis, non quod eas enim dare possit sed quia utitur eis ad decipiendum. Singulis vitiis aliquis spiritus praeest: unde spiritus avaritiae dicitur; per avaritiam homines allicit ad peccandum. Haec est una expositio huius.

621. *Nemo potest*, ut scilicet legatur illative et generaliter. Augustinus autem intelligit specialiter, scilicet de Deo et diabolo qui sunt contrarii, II Cor. VI, 15: *quae conventio Christi ad Belial*. Et quod *non potestis* simul esse participes, III Reg. XVIII, 21: *usquequo claudicat*. *Aut unum* sustinebit, idest diabolum, *et alterum diliget* idest Deum. Et nota quod non dixit e converso sed dixit *aut unum sustinebit*, quia quaelibet creatura naturaliter

and custom of men; second, he gives the reason, at *for he will either hate one*. Therefore he says *no man can serve two masters*. But the reason for this appears if we take what a slave is, properly speaking, and what a slave's master is, for the definition consists in the fact that he is another's, namely, his master's. Hence his end is his master. But it is impossible that one be directed to two things as last ends. Therefore if to be a slave is to order one's acts to one's master as their last end, it is impossible to serve two masters: *for the bed is too narrow to lie upon* (Isa 28:20). But a slave could have two masters of which one is under the other, as one end can be under another. Or according to the Gloss: *No man can serve two masters* who oppose each other, for if they agree, they are one.

He assigns the reason: *for he will hate the one*. And it should be known that there are two kinds of rulership. For some rule so that they are loved by those beneath them, and this is royal rule. Some rule so that they are feared, and this is the rule of tyrants. Therefore if a slave has love for his master, then it must be that he will hate a contrary one; but if the slave holds him in fear then it must be that *you endure*, that is, you tolerate, also the other. And this is *or he will endure the one and despise the other*. About this rule that is more to be endured than to be loved, Proverbs says: *when the wicked* contrive to *assume power, the people groan* (Prov 29:2), that is, they will endure, by patiently tolerating. Therefore no man can serve two. But God and the devil are opposite, for they incline to opposite things: therefore *you cannot serve God and mammon*, which is 'riches' in the Persian tongue, according to Jerome.

However it should be known that to be rich in wealth is not the same as to serve it. For some men are rich and nevertheless ordered to the good, and they are not slaves to riches; others possess riches and nevertheless they do not take physical or spiritual benefit from them, and these are slaves to riches, for they ruin themselves trying to amass riches: *There is another evil that . . . lies heavy upon humankind: God gives riches to some . . . yet allows a stranger to enjoy them* (Eccl 6:1–2). For in whatever thing a man establishes his last end, that thing is his god: *whose god is their belly* (Phil 3:19). Or by *mammon* is understood the devil who controls wealth, not because he could bestow it, but because he uses it to deceive. A certain spirit is in charge of individual vices: hence he is called the spirit of avarice; by avarice he lures men into sin. This is one explanation of this.

621. *No man can serve* may be read as inferred and general. But Augustine understands it specifically, namely, about God and the devil who are opposed to one another: *what concord does Christ have with Belial?* (2 Cor 6:15). And you cannot be partakers of both: *how long will you limp between two sides?* (1 Kgs 18:21). *Or he will* endure *the one*, that is, the devil, and *love the other*, that is, God. And note that he did not say, 'And vice versa' but he said, *or he*

convertitur ad diligendum Deum; sed diabolus quia habet naturam depravatam statim est in horrore, cum nullus diligat malum. Et ideo dixit *aut unum sustinebit*, quia diabolus sustinetur sicut tyrannus opprimens. Sicut aliquis sustineret dominum ancillae cui coniungitur, non quia diligat dominum sed propter ancillam, ita cupidus sustinet diabolum propter cupiditatem quae est ancilla diaboli. Unde quando aliquis vult frui quocumque peccato, ad hoc quod eo fruatur patitur servitutem diaboli. Et hoc est *aut unum sustinebit*. Et inquantum sustinet recedet a mandatis Dei et recedendo contemnit. Et hoc est *et alterum contemnet*.

Sed obicitur hic de hoc quod dicitur quod Deus non habetur odio, quia Ps. dicit *superbia eorum qui te oderunt* etc. Ergo aliquis Deum habet odio propter istam auctoritatem. Augustinus in libro Retractationum retractat quod prius dixerat, quod Deus non habetur odio. Sed tamen utrumque verum est, quia si consideretur id quod est Deus, scilicet ipsa bonitas, non potest haberi odio, quia bonum semper diligitur secundum se. Potest autem haberi odio quantum ad effectum qui est contrarius voluntati. Sic ergo patet quod *non potest duobus dominis servire*, Eccli. II, 14: *vae peccatori terram ingredienti*.

622. Ideo dico vobis. Postquam Dominus ostenderat quod non debemus ponere finem in thesauris terrenis et superfluis, vult etiam ostendere quod in necessariis acquirendis. Et hoc est *ideo dico vobis*. Et circa hoc duo facit: primo prohibet sollicitudinem necessariorum quantum ad praesentia, secundo quantum ad futura, ibi *nolite*. Circa primum duo facit: primo proponit quod intendit; secundo probat propositum, ibi *nonne anima*. Dicit ergo *ideo dico vobis*, quasi: quia non potestis Deo servire et mammone, ideo nullus debet servire divitiis ad hoc quod Deo servatis.

Neque animae. Sed videtur quod anima non indiget cibo. Sed dicendum quod quamvis non indigeat secundum se, tamen indiget inquantum coniuncta corpori, quia aliter ibi esse non posset. Vel vocatur ibi anima animalis vita, Io. XII: *qui amat animam*.

Neque corpori vestro. Nota quod ex hoc verbo sumpserunt exordium haereses. Secundum Augustinum enim fuerunt quidam dicentes non licere homini contemplativo operari; et contra istos fecit Augustinus librum *De opere monachorum*, sed qualiter sit intelligendum hoc quod Dominus dicit, debemus investigare a sanctis. Dicitur autem II Thess III, 10: *qui non vult operari non manducet*, et intelliget de opere manuum, sicut patet per ea quae praemittit. Unde etiam in exemplum ipse Apostolus operatus est manibus.

will endure the one, because every creature naturally tends to loving God; but the devil who has a depraved nature is abhorred at once, since no one loves evil. And thus he said, *or he will endure the one*, for the devil is endured like an oppressive tyrant, as someone would endure the master of the slave girl that he was married to, not that he loved the master, but on account of the slave girl, so someone greedy endures the devil on account of the greed which is the devil's slave girl. Hence when someone wants to prosper in any sin, by the fact that he prospers he suffers the slavery of the devil. And this is *or he will endure the one*. And to the extent that he endures it he will fall away from the commands of God and despise them when falling. And this is *and he will despise the other*.

But it is objected here about the fact that it is said that God is not hated, for the Psalm says *the pride of those who hate you ascends continually* (Ps 74:23). Therefore by this authority someone hates God. Augustine in his *Book of Retractions* retracts what he had previously said, that God is not hated. But nevertheless both are true, for considering what God is, namely, goodness itself, he cannot be hated, for good is always loved in itself. But he can be hated as to his effect which is contrary to the will. Therefore in this way it is clear that *no one can serve two masters*: woe to the sinner going on the earth a double path (Sir 2:12).

622. Therefore I say to you. After the Lord has shown that we must not place our end in earthly and unneeded treasures, he wants to show also that we must not place it in acquiring necessities. And this is *therefore I say to you*. And concerning this he does two things: first, he forbids anxiety for necessities as to the present; second, as to the future, at *do not be solicitous*. Concerning the first he does two things: first, he proposes what he intends; second, he proves his proposition, at *is not your life*. Therefore he says, *therefore I say to you*, as though: 'Because you cannot serve God and mammon, therefore no one should serve riches so that you may serve God.'

Neither for your soul. But it seems that a soul does not require food. But it should be said that although it does not need it in itself, nevertheless it needs it as joined to a body, for it could not be there otherwise. Or the life of an animal is called 'the soul' here: *who loves his life will lose it* (John 12:25).

Nor for your body. Note that by this word heresies have taken root. For according to Augustine there were some who said it was not permitted for a contemplative man to work; and against them Augustine wrote the book *On the Work of Monks*. But how the Lord's words are to be understood we should investigate by the saints. But 2 Thess 3:10 says: *whoever does not wish to work, let him not eat*, and he will realize it from the work of his hands, as is clear by the things said beforehand. Hence even the Apostle himself worked by his hands as an example.

623. Sed numquid omnes tenentur? Si omnes, aut est praeceptum aut consilium, si praeceptum, nullus debet praemittere; si consilium, cui dabatur hoc consilium? Constat quod plebi illi, quia tunc non erant religiosi. Ad consilium autem nullus tenetur nisi ex voto: ergo possent omnes desistere. Dicendum quod hoc est praeceptum et ad hoc omnes tenentur, quia omnibus datur: Apostolus enim toti Ecclesiae loquitur. Sed est aliquid praeceptum dupliciter: per seipsum et propter aliud. Verbi gratia, si accepistis crucem ad eundum ultra mare, praeceptum est quod vadat, et praeceptum per seipsum; sed quod quaeras navem, hoc non propter se sed propter aliud est praeceptum, quia quicumque tenetur ad aliquem finem et ad omnia quae sunt ad finem tenetur. Quilibet autem tenetur ad conservationem vitae suae lege naturae, et ideo tenentur ad omnia alia quibus vita conservatur. Si ergo aliquis habeat unde vivere possit non tenetur laborare manibus, et ideo Apostolus non dicit: *mandamus manibus*, sed *qui non vult operari* etc., quasi: *eo modo tenemini laborare quo manducare*. Qui autem teneantur laborare manibus, hoc ad praesens dimittatur.

Quod autem dicit **solliciti**, sciendum quod sollicitudo pertinet ad providentiam, sed non quaelibet providentia est sollicitudo. Sed sollicitudo proprie nominat providentiam cum studio, quod est vehemens applicatio animi. Unde hic importat sollicitudo vehementem animi applicationem. In ista autem vehementi applicatione, quatuor modis potest esse peccatum. Primo quando est ad temporalia sicut ad ultimum finem; et secundum hoc reprehenditur, Prov. XI, 7: *expectatio sollicita ducet in perditionem*. Secundo quando superflue intendit ad temporalia conquirenda, et sic accipitur Eccl. II, 26: *peccatori autem dedit Deus* etc., et post, *et hoc vanitas est et cassa sollicitudo*. Tertio quando animus nimis se occupabit circa cogitationem temporalium. Unde Ieronimus: *sollicitudo vitanda est sed labor exercendus*, et sic accipitur I Cor. VII, 28: *qui coniunctus est uxori sollicitus est*, quia cor distrahitur ad diversa. Quarto quando sollicitudo est cum quodam timore et desperatione. Videtur enim quibusdam quod numquam tantum acquirere possunt quod possit eis sufficere. Et omnia ista hic prohibentur, sicut patet per sequentia. Et sic isto ultimo modo accipitur. I Reg. IX, 20,3: *ne sis sollicitus, quaere asinas*, idest ne desperes de inventione.

Nonne anima. Supra docuit Dominus ut non essemus solliciti de necessariis, hic inducit huius admonitionis rationem. Et ponit tres rationes: prima sumitur a maiori, secunda a minori, tertia ex opposito. Secundum, ibi **respicite volatilia**; tertium, ibi **nolite**.

623. But are all bound to this? If all, it is either a precept or a counsel; if a precept, no one should omit to do it; if a counsel, to whom was this counsel given? Certainly to the crowd, for at that time there were no religious. But no one is bound to a counsel except by a vow: therefore they could all stop doing it. It should be said that this is a precept and all are bound to it, for it is given to all: for the Apostle speaks to the whole Church. But something is commanded in two ways: for itself and for the sake of something else. For example, if you undertake to go overseas on crusade, it is commanded that you go, and it is commanded in itself; but that you seek a ship, this is not commanded for itself but for the sake of something else, for whoever is bound to a certain end is also bound to all the things that are needed for that end. But whoever is bound to the preservation of his life by the law of nature is therefore also bound to all those things by which life is preserved. Therefore if someone has the means to live, he is not bound to work with his hands, and thus the Apostle does not say: 'we command you to work with your hands,' but *whoever does not wish to work*, as though: 'you are bound to work in whatever way allows you to eat.' But who are bound to work with their hands is a question to set aside at present.

About the fact that he says **solicitous**, it should be known that solicitude pertains to foresight, but not every kind of foresight is solicitude. But solicitude properly means foresight with diligence, which is the vehement application of the soul. Hence here solicitude conveys the vehement application of the soul. But in this vehement application there can be sin in four ways. The first is when there is solicitude for temporal goods as the last end; and this is reproached: *the expectation of the solicitous shall perish* (Prov 11:7). Second, when someone aims for the pursuit of temporal goods excessively, and in this way is taken: *to the sinner God has given vexation, and superfluous care, to heap up and to gather together* (Eccl 2:26), and afterward, *and this is vanity and futile solicitude of the mind*. Third, when the soul occupies itself too much in thinking about temporal things. Hence Jerome says: *solicitude is to be avoided but labor is to be accomplished*, and in this way is taken: *whoever is married is solicitous for his wife* (1 Cor 7:28), for his heart is distracted by different things. Fourth, when there is solicitude with a certain fear and desperation. For it seems to some that they can never acquire as much as could be enough for them. And all these things are forbidden here, as is clear from what follows. And 1 Sam 9:20 is taken according to this last way: *be not solicitous* to seek after the donkeys, that is, do not despair of finding them.

Is not your life. Above the Lord taught us not to be solicitous about necessities; here he gives the reason for this admonition. And he sets down three reasons: the first is taken from the greater, the second from the lesser, and the third from the opposite. The second is at **look at the birds**; the third, at **be not solicitous therefore**.

624. Prima talis: qui dedit maiora dabit minora; sed Dominus dedit animam et corpus; ergo dabit cibum. Et hic est *nonne anima*, idest vita non enim vivimus ut manducemus, sed e converso. Esca enim ordinatur ad vitam et ideo simpliciter vita melior est, sicut finis melior est his quae sunt ad finem. Et similiter vestimentum propter corpus et non e converso. Quod autem Deus deterit animam et corpus, habetur quando primo *formavit Deus* materiam ad corpus, *inspiravit* materiam ad animam. Sed qui dedit conservabit, dando ea quae necessaria sunt. Sap. I, 4: *creavit Deus ut essent.*

Hilarius hoc exponit aliter. Quia enim sollicitudo importat quamdam dubietatem, Dominus vult removere dubietatem futurae resurrectionis animi. *Ne solliciti*, idest non velitis discredere de resurrectione quia ille qui *reformabit corpus* in resurrectione conservabit absque indumento et cibo, sed hoc non est litteralis.

Consequenter ponitur secunda ratio a minori et est talis. Ille qui providit minoribus de quibus minus videtur et maioribus providebit; sed Deus providit plantis et avibus etc. Et circa hanc duo facit: primo deducit rationem quantum ad cibum, secundo quantum ad vestitum, ibi *et de vestimento*. Circa primum duo facit: primo docet abicere sollicitudinem exemplo animalium, secundo propter inefficaciam eius, ibi *quis autem vestrum*. Circa primum quatuor facit: primo inducit ad considerandum bruta animalia; secundo ponit defectum consequentem ea; tertio divinam providentiam; quarto ex hoc argumentatur. Ergo *respicite*, idest considerate, Iob XII: *interroga iumenta*. Ex consideratione enim istorum homo aliquando addiscit, Prov. VI, 6: *vade ad formicam*. *Quoniam non serunt.*

625. Cibus cotidianus panis est; ad eius acquisitionem triplici opere pervenitur: per seminationem, per metitionem et per reconditionem. Unde haec tria excludit ab avibus: *non serunt* etc. Est autem seminatio etiam spiritualis doctrinae, infra XIII, 3 *exiit qui seminat*; bonorum operum, Prov. XI, 18: *seminanti*; elementarum, II Cor. IX, 6: *qui parce seminat parce* etc. Est et mala seminatio: carnalium peccatorum, Gal. ult. *qui seminat in carne*; spiritualium peccatorum, Iob IV, 8: *quin immo vidi eos qui seminant*. Metunt autem sancti praedicatores quando rapiunt aliquos ad fidem. Io. IV, 38: *ego misi vos metere.*

Consequenter ponitur auxilium divinae providentiae: *Et pater* dicit *vester* non *illorum*, quia proprie Deus pater est creaturae rationalis, quae *ad imaginem eius est* Gen. I, 26. Dicit etiam *caelestis*, quia nos habemus aliquid ad caelum attinens, scilicet animam quae pertinet ad similitudinem substantiarum. Unde *pater vester*

624. The first is thus: the one who gave the greater things will give the lesser ones. But the Lord gave the soul and body, therefore he will give food. And this is *is not your soul*, i.e., life, for we do not live so that we may eat but vice versa. For eating is ordered to life and thus life is simply better, as the end is better than those things that are ordered to the end. And likewise clothing is for the sake of the body and not vice versa. But the fact that God gave the soul and the body is found when first *God formed* the matter for the body, *he breathed into* matter for the soul. But the one who gave it will preserve it, by giving those things that are necessary: *God created all things that they might be* (Wis 1:14).

Hilary explains it another way. For because solicitude conveys something of uncertainty, God wants to remove doubt of the future resurrection of the soul. *Be not solicitous*, i.e., do not wish to disbelieve in the resurrection for the one who *will reform your body* in the resurrection will preserve it without clothing or food. But this is not the literal sense.

Then the second reason is set down from the lesser things, and it is like this. The one who provides for lesser things about which less is seen will also provide for greater things. But God provides for plants and birds and such. And concerning this he does two things: first, he deduces the reason as to food; second, as to clothing, at *and about clothing*. Concerning the first he does two things: first, he teaches us to reject solicitude by the animals' example; second, because of its ineffectiveness, at *but which of you by taking thought*. Concerning the first he does four things: first, he has us consider brute animals; second, he points to the lack of worry among them; third, he points to divine providence; fourth, it is argued from these. Therefore, *look*, i.e., consider: *ask the animals and they will teach you* (Job 12:7). For from the consideration of these man learns sometimes: *go to the ant . . . consider her ways and learn wisdom* (Prov 6:6). *For they do not sow.*

625. Food is daily bread; its acquisition requires a threefold work: sowing, reaping, and storing. Hence he excludes these three things from the birds: *they do not sow*. But there is also the sowing of spiritual doctrine, as he says later: *a sower went out to sow* (Matt 13:3); and of good works: *those who sow justice get a true reward* (Prov 11:18); and of elements: *who sows sparingly shall reap sparingly* (2 Cor 9:6). And there is also an evil sowing: of carnal sins: *who sows in his flesh reaps corruption from the flesh* (Gal 6:8), and of spiritual sins: *I have seen those who sow iniquity . . . reap the same* (Job 4:8). But holy preachers reap when they carry people off to the faith.

Next, he mentions the help of divine providence: he says *and your father*, not *their father*, for God is properly the father of rational creatures, who are in his image (Gen 1:26). He also says *heavenly*, for we have something tying us to heaven, namely the soul, which belongs to it by likeness of substance. Hence *your father* feeds those things for which

pascit illa quorum est Deus tantum multo magis nos quorum est pater, Ps. *qui dat iumentis*. Consequenter argumentatur **nonne plus**, idest maioris valoris, ordinatione scilicet, Gen. I, 26: *ut praesit piscibus*. Aliquando enim plus venditur equus quam homo, quia duplex est aestimatio rerum: quantum ad ordinem naturae, et sic homo melior omnium rerum; vel quantum ad aestimationem sive delectationem: et sic aliquando animal plus venditur.

626. Circa istam litteram considerandum quod quidam, et credo quod Origenes, exponunt aliter. Et dicunt quod per **volatilia** intelliguntur sancti angeli qui non exercent labores carnales et tamen Deus pascit eos cibo spirituali: de quo Ps. *panem angelorum*. Sed sicut dicit Ieronimus hoc non potest stare, quia Dominus subiungit **nonne plus**. Hilarius autem per volatilia intelligit daemones itaque aves caeli qui pascuntur, inquantum conservantur in esse naturae, et homines sunt pluris illis, quia Dominus argumentatur: si illi qui sunt praedestinati ad mortem sustentantur a Deo, multo magis nos. Sed secundum Augustinum ista quae Dominus dicit non allegorice accipienda, quia Dominus vult trahere argumentum ab istis sensibilibus ad propositum ostendendum.

Sed sciendum quod hic fuit error quorumdam dicentium non licere spiritualibus viris laborare corporaliter propter similitudinem avium. Contra quos Augustinus, in libro *De operibus monachorum*, dicit quod impossibile est quod homines in omnibus vitam imitantur. Unde aliqui perfecti qui iverunt in desertum et raro ibant ad civitatem: unde oportebat eos multum congregare de victualibus. Apostoli autem, secundum Augustinum, operati sunt manibus. Unde non laborare non pertinet ad perfectionem. Et ponit exemplum Augustinus, quia Deus sperantes in se in tribulatione liberat, sicut patet de Daniele et pueris in fornace. Numquid ergo constitutus in tribulationibus nihil debet agere ad hoc quod liberetur? Immo quod Dominus dixit: **Si vos persecuti fuerint in una civitate, fugite in aliam**. Et ideo dicendum quod Dominus vult quod in omnibus homo faciat quod in se est et sperando in Deum. Deus dabit ei quae viderit expedire. Quod autem aliter faceret temptator esset et stultus. Habet igitur Deus providentiam de factis hominum, ita tamen quod unicuique providet secundum modum suum, quia aliter hominibus et avibus; quia avibus non dedit rationem qua procuret sibi necessaria, sed totum ei inditum est a natura; homini vero dedit rationem qua sibi necessaria procuraret; unde omnia dedit homini dando rationem. Et ideo si fecerimus quod in nobis est et ipse faciet quod in se est.

627. Quis vestrum. Trahit argumentum ex experimento. Manifestum est enim quod sicut Deus animalibus providet in operibus nature, ita hominibus. In homine

he is only God; how much more will he feed us, to whom he is Father: *he gives the animals their food* (Ps 147:9). Accordingly it is argued **are you not more**, that is, of greater value, by ordination, namely: *let him have dominion over the fishes of the sea* (Gen 1:26). For sometimes a horse is sold for more than a man, because the valuation of things is twofold: as to the order of nature, and in this way a man is the best of all things; or as to valuation or enjoyment, and in this way an animal is sometimes sold for more.

626. Concerning this text it should be considered that some people, and Origen, I believe, explain it in another way. And they say that by **birds**, the holy angels are meant, who exert no fleshly labors and nevertheless God feeds them spiritual food: about which the Psalm speaks: *the bread of angels* (Ps 78:25). But as Jerome says, this cannot stand, for the Lord added **are you not worth more than they?** But Hilary understands by birds the demons, and thus the birds of the air who are fed, inasmuch as they are preserved in the being of their nature, and men are more than they, for the Lord argues: if they who are predestined to death are sustained in being by God, how much more are we. But according to Augustine, what the Lord says is not to be taken allegorically, for the Lord wants to draw his argument from these sensible things to display his purpose.

But it should be known that here there was an error of certain people who said that it was not permitted to spiritual men to labor physically, because of the comparison to the birds. Against them, Augustine says in his book *On the Work of Monks* that it is impossible that men imitate this life in everything. Hence there were some perfect men who went into the desert and rarely went into the city: hence it was necessary that they gather much food. But the apostles, according to Augustine, worked with their hands. Hence not working does not belong to perfection. And Augustine gives the example that God delivers those who hope in him in tribulation, as is clear from Daniel and the youths in the furnace. Then should someone experiencing tribulations do nothing so that he might be delivered? The Lord said the contrary: **If you are persecuted in one town, flee to another** (Matt 10:23). And thus it should be said that the Lord wants man to do what he can in all situations, while hoping in God. God will give to him whatever he sees as expedient. For if he did otherwise he would be a tempter and stupid. Therefore God has providence over all deeds of men, so that he provides for each one according to his own manner, differently for birds than for men; for to birds he did not give reason by which to procure their needs; but all their outfitting is from nature. But to man he gave reason by which he may procure his necessities; hence by giving man reason, he gave him all things. And thus if we do what is in us, he will also do what is in him.

627. Which of you. He draws the argument from experience. For it is clear that as God provides for animals in the working of nature, so also for men. For in man there is a

enim est quaedam pars quae subiacet rationi, sicut pars motiva et appetitiva; quaedam quae non, sicut nutritiva et augmentativa. Sed homo secundum ea quae subiacent rationi differt a brutis, et ideo aliter providetur ei, quia sibi per rationem, aliis per naturam. Sed quantum ad ea in quibus cum brutis communicat equaliter providetur omnibus. Omnia enim augentur per opus naturae, et quia augmentum corporis est ex divina providentia, non debemus prae minimia sollicitudine temporalium opera spiritualia dimittere, Sap. VI, 8: *pusillum et magnum*. Et hoc est *quis autem vestrum*.

Hilarius exponit de statu futurae resurrectionis et dicit quod in resurrectione omnes erunt aequales in quantitate et ideo aliquibus addetur de quantitate. Et hoc est *quis autem vestrum*. Sed hoc improbat Augustinus in libro *De civitate Dei*, et credo quod melius dicit. Dicitur enim Phil. III, 21 quod *reformabit corpus nostrae configuratum corpori claritatis*. Ergo ea quae in Christo resurgente apparuerunt et manifestata sunt discipulis, haec debemus sperare in nobis. Sed Christus in eadem quantitate resurrexit in qua prius fuit: ergo nihil ei accrevit; nihil item alicui subtrahitur, quia Dominus dicit *capillus de capite vestro non peribit*. Unde dicendum quod in resurrectione omnes conformabuntur Christo quantum ad aetatem et unusquisque resurget in quantitate in qua habiturus fuisset in illa aetate; quod autem est de defectu naturae, sicut in nanis, tolletur. Unde resurgent in tali quantitate in quali pervenisset si natura non defecisset usque ad talem aetatem, scilicet Christi.

628. *Et de vestimento*. Hic deducit rationem quantum ad vestimentum. Et primo ponit quod intendit: secundo inducit similitudinem; tertio ex illis argumentatur. Secundum, ibi *considerate*; tertium, ibi *si enim fenum*. Convenienter post sollicitudinem cibi et potus de similitudine vestimenti agitur, quia sicut cibus et potus pervenirent ad necessitatem vitae, ita et vestimentum, I Tim. VI, 8: *habentes alimenta*, et Iacob dixit, Gen. XXVIII, 20: *si fuerit mecum Dominus*.

Considerate. Inducit exemplum et proponit duo: comparationem et auxilium divinae promissionis, ibi *dico autem*. Dicit **considerate**. Consideratio autem divinorum operum valet ad hoc quod animus prorumpit in laudem creatoris, *meditabor in omnibus*. **Quomodo crescunt**, I Cor. III, 6: *Deus enim incrementum*. **Non laborant**. Ad vestimentum necessarium est opus viri et mulieris: et hoc est **non laborant neque nent**, vel **non laborant** ad colorandum, **neque nent** ad preparandum. Unde nec propter colorem nec propter substantiam vestimenti laborant.

certain part which is subject to reason, like the motive and appetitive part; and a certain part which is not, like the nutritive and augmentative. But by these parts that are subject to reason man differs from the brutes, and thus he is provided for differently, for he provides for himself by reason, while they do through their nature. But as to those things in which he shares with the brutes, he is equally provided for in all things. For all things are increased by the working of nature, and since the increase of the body is from divine providence, we should not omit spiritual works in our slight solicitude for temporal goods. *He made the little and the great, and he has equally care of all* (Wis 6:8). And this is **which of you**.

Hilary explains the state of future resurrection and says that in the resurrection all are equal in quantity and thus to some, quantity will be added. And this is **which of you by thinking can add to his stature?** But Augustine disproves this in his book *City of God*, and I believe that he speaks better. For it is said: *he will transform the body of our lowness, to conform it to the body of his glory* (Phil 3:21). Therefore those things that appeared in the resurrected Christ and were manifested to his disciples, these we should hope for in ourselves. But Christ rose in the same quantity in which he was before: therefore nothing was added to him and nothing was subtracted from him, for the Lord says *no hair of your head shall perish* (Luke 21:18). Hence it should be said that in the resurrection all will be conformed to Christ as to age and each one will resurrect in the quantity that he would have had at that age; but what is from a defect of nature, as in dwarfs, will be taken away. Hence they will rise in whatever quantity they would have attained if nature had not failed, up to the age of Christ.

628. *And for raiment*. Here he draws out the argument as to clothing. And first he sets down what he intends; second, he draws a comparison: third, he argues from these. The second is at **consider the lilies**; the third, at **for if the grass**. Fittingly, after concern for food and drink, a comparison to clothing is treated, for as food and drink attain to the necessity of life, so also does clothing: *if we have food and clothing, we will be content* (1 Tim 6:8), and Jacob said, *if God will give me bread to eat and clothing to wear . . . then the Lord shall be my God* (Gen 28:20).

Consider the lilies. He brings up an example and proposes two things: a comparison and the help of a divine promise at **But I say to you**. He says **consider**. But the benefit of considering divine works is that the soul breaks forth into praise of the creator: *I will meditate on all your works* (Ps 77:12). **How they grow**: but God gave the growth (1 Cor 3:6). **They neither labor**. For clothing the work of men and women is necessary: and this is **they neither labor nor spin**, or **they neither labor** to dye it, **nor spin** to prepare it. Hence neither for the sake of the dyeing nor for the substance of the clothing do they labor.

629. *Dico autem.* Hic ponitur beneficium divinae promissionis. Ita enim providet quod totum studium humanum non posset ei adaequari, quia quae fiunt secundum artem non possunt adaequari eis quae fiunt secundum naturam. Et hoc est quod *nec Salomon*, qui gloriosior omnibus regibus notis a Iudaeis, II Paral. I, 12. Et dicit *in omni*, quia nec per unum diem habere potuit vestimentum sicut habent flores. Et hoc est expositio Chrysostomi et litteralis. Aliter *nec Salomon* etc., quia ista corporalia habent vestimentum sine sollicitudine; quod non Salomon. Hilarius: anagogice, per lilium sancti angeli, Cant. II, 16: *dilectus meus mihi et ego.* Et vult Dominus amovere sollicitudinem de resurrectione de vestimentis in resurrectione: sicut enim angeli induuntur claritate, ita et corpora nostra induentur.

Si enim faenum. Hic ex exemplo argumentatur. Supra Dominus fecerat mentionem de liliis; hic commutat in faenum, quia intendit argumentari a minori. Unde ponit defectum ex una parte ut ostendat praeeminentiam ex alia. Unde ostendit praeeminentiam quantum ad dignitatem substantiae: quia nos homines, flos faenum, Is. X, L: *exsiccatum est*; durationem quia nos perpetui quantum ad animam, flos quasi momentaneum, *quia hodie est* etc. Et ponit futurum indeterminatum, pro determinato, sicut Gen. XXX, 33: *respondebit mihi cras.* Ps. *fiant sicut fenum tectorum.* Finem: quia homo factus est propter beatitudinem, huiusmodi autem ut in hominis usum veniant, Ps. *qui producit in montibus faenum.* Vel ideo dixit supra *lilia* et postea *faenum*, quia flores ad herbas sicut vestimenta ad homines. Est enim usus vestimentorum scilicet ad protegendum et ornandum: et si Deus minoribus providet ad ornatum multo magis maioribus ad necessitatem, Et hoc est *si faenum* etc. *Modice fidei*, qui nec minora a Deo speratis, infra XIV, 31: *modice fidei, quare.* Hilarius autem non continuat cum praecedenti. Sed sicut per lilia sancti angeli, ita per faenum infideles intelligantur, Is. XL, 7: *vere faenum est populus.* Quia si Deus providet infidelibus praescitis ad poenam, quanto magis nobis praescitis ad vitam aeternam.

630. *Nolite ergo.* Hic argumentatur. Et circa hoc duo facit: primo infert unam conclusionem; secundo ad eandem conclusionem inducit aliam, ibi *haec enim omnia.* Seorsum determinat de sollicitudine cibi et potus et de vestimentis; hic concludit de utroque: unde *nolite.* Et recitanda sunt ea quae supra dicta sunt, quia sollicitudo temporalium prohibetur quantum ad quatuor: ut scilicet non ponamus in eis finem, ut non superflue quaeramus, ut non nimis occupemus mentem in eis, ut non desperemus de providentia Dei. Hic ponuntur quaedam alia,

629. *But I say to you.* Here is set down the benefit of the divine promise. For he so provides that all human diligence could not match it; for those things done by art cannot match those done by nature. And this is what is meant by *not even Solomon*, who was more glorious than all other kings known to the Jews (cf. 2 Chr 1:12). And he says *in all*, for not for one day was he able to have clothing like the flowers have. And this is the explanation of Chrysostom, and the literal sense. Another way, *not even Solomon*, for those corporeal things have clothing without worry, but not Solomon. Hilary says: anagogically, by the lily is meant the holy angels: *my beloved is mine and I am his* (Song 2:16). And the Lord wants to banish concern about the resurrection as to clothing in the resurrection: for as the angels are clothed with brightness, so will our bodies be clothed.

For if the grass. Here he argues from an example. Above the Lord made mention of lilies; here he changes to grass, for he intends to argue from the lesser thing. Hence he points out a defect on the part of one so that he can show the excellence in the other. Hence he shows the excellence as to the dignity of substance: for we are men, a flower is grass: *the grass withers, the flower fades* (Isa 40:7); as to duration, for we are perpetual as to our soul, a flower is almost momentary, for *it is today, and tomorrow is thrown into the oven.* And he uses the indeterminate future for the determinate future, as in Gen 30:33: *my justice will answer for me tomorrow*; or *let them be like the grass on the rooftops* (Ps 129:6). And the excellence of our end: for man was made for beatitude, but things like this come for man's use: *who makes grass grow on the mountains and herbs for the service of men* (Ps 147:8). Or then he said above *lilies* and afterward *grass*, because flowers are to the grass as clothing is to men. For the use of clothing is precisely to protect and ornament: and if God provides for lesser things to be ornamented, much more will he for the needs of greater things. And this is *if the grass of the field. O you of little faith*, who do not hope for lesser things from God, as later: *you of little faith, why did you doubt?* (Matt 14:31). But Hilary does not continue with what has just been said. But as he sees the lilies as the holy angels, so by the grass is understood unbelievers: and indeed *the people are the grass* (Isa 40:7). For if God provides for unbelievers, foreknown for punishment, how much more will he provide for us, foreknown for eternal life.

630. *Be not solicitous therefore.* Here he concludes the argument. And concerning this he does two things: first, he infers one conclusion; second, he reasons to the same conclusion in another way, at *for after all these things the gentiles seek.* He determines separately about the solicitude for food and drink and for clothing; here he concludes about both: at *be not solicitous therefore.* And those things which were said above should be recited, for solicitude of temporal things is forbidden as to four things: namely, that we do not place our end in them; that we do not seek

et ponit unum alium sensum. Unde dicit *nolite ergo* etc., idest quando vivitis in aliqua societate non sitis solliciti habere aliquid speciale in cibis, potibus et vestimentorum, Elli. XXXII, 1: *esto in eis quasi unus*. *Haec enim omnia*, quasi: non debent facere infideles. Unde infideles vituperantur; sed gentiles de hoc vituperantur; ergo etc. Et primo ponit errorem infidelium, secundo improbat, tertio ostendit quid sit faciendum fidelibus. Secundum, ibi *scit*, tertium, ibi *quaerite ergo*. Dicit ergo: dico quod vos non debetis circa hoc esse solliciti quia non debetis *conformari huic saeculo*, Ro. XII, 2.

Haec enim omnia inquirunt. Et hoc propter duo, secundum quod inquirere dupliciter potest sumi: quia potest importare in principio rationem finis, et sic gentes non credunt aeterna, qui ista inquirunt ut finem; vel si non quaerunt ut finem ultimum, tamen quaerunt tota sollicitudine quia non credunt divinam providentiam et per consequens nec Deum, I Thess. IV, 5: *sicut et gentes quae ignorant*.

Consequenter afferat providentiam divinam. Et sciendum quod providentia duo praesupponit: cognitionem et voluntatem, et ideo utrumque ostendit. Nihil est enim aliud providentia nisi ordinatio aliquorum in finem, scilicet praefixo fine eligere vias per quas perveniatur in finem. Unde primo oportet quod cognoscat et velit finem, secundo quod cognoscat ordinem in proportionem eorum quae sunt ad finem, sicut aedificator cognoscit ordinem lapidum ponendorum in domo. Unde oportet ad hoc quod Deus ad hoc quod habeat providentiam de rebus humanis, requiritur quod sciat et cognoscat ea et quod velit dirigere in finem. Et ideo dicit *scit enim*, Eccli. XXIII, 29: *Domino Deo nostro* etc. Hebr. IV, 13: *omnia nuda*; *Pater ergo* vult administrare, Sap. XIV, 3: *tua autem pater gubernat*. Non enim esset pater nisi esset provisor, infra *si vos cum sitis mali*.

Quaerite ergo. Tria hic ponit. Regnum, tanquam finem, quia in regno Dei intelligitur beatitudo aeterna. Tunc enim proprie aliquid regitur quando subditur regulae gubernantis. Sed in vita ista non subduntur totaliter Deo, quia non sumus sine peccatis; et haec erunt in gloria, ubi perfecte faciemus voluntatem divinam; Luc. XIV, 15: *beatus qui manducabit*. Secundo viam rectam: in regnum enim itur per iustitiam. Unde si vis ire ad regnum Dei oportet quod serves iustitiam regni. Et dicit *iustitiam*, non simpliciter, sed *eius*, quia duplex est

them unnecessarily; that we do not occupy our minds too much with them; that we do not despair of the providence of God. Here certain other things are set down, and he sets down one other meaning. Hence he says be not solicitous therefore; that is, when you live in some society, do not be solicitous to have something special as your food, drink, and clothing: *be among them as one of them* (Sir 32:1). *For after all these things the gentiles seek*, as though to say: the unbelievers should not do this. Hence unbelievers are reproached; but the gentiles are reproached with this. And first, he sets down the error of the unbelievers; second, he disproves it; third, he shows what should be done by the faithful. The second is at *your Father knows*; the third, at *ask therefore*. Therefore he says: I say that you should not worry about this, for you should not be *conformed to this age* (Rom 12:2).

For after all these things the gentiles seek. And this is for two reasons, according to which 'seek' can be taken in two ways: for it can convey the notion of the end in the beginning, and in this way the gentiles do not believe in eternal things, who seek after these things as their end; or if they do not seek them as their final end, nevertheless they seek them with all solicitude because they do not believe in divine providence or, as a result, in God: *like the gentiles who do not know God* (1 Thess 4:5).

Accordingly he brings up divine providence. And it should be known that providence presupposes two things: knowledge and will, and thus he shows both. For providence is nothing else than the ordering of things to an end, namely, having fixed on an end, to choose the ways to arrive at that end. Hence first it is necessary to know and will the end; second, to know the end in relation to those things that are for the end, as a builder knows the order of arranging the stones in a house. Hence for God to have providence about human things, it is required that he know and be familiar with them and that he will to direct them to the end. And thus he says *for your father knows*: *all things were known to the Lord our God before they were created* (Sir 23:20); *all are naked and laid bare to the eyes of the one to whom we must render an account* (Heb 4:13). Therefore *your Father* wishes to minister to you: *your providence, O Father, governs* (Wis 14:3). For he would not be father unless he were a provider, as below: *if you who are evil know how to give your children good things* (Matt 7:11).

Seek you therefore. Here he sets down three things. The kingdom, as end, because by the kingdom of God eternal beatitude is meant. For something is properly said to be ruled when it is subject to the rule of a governor. But in life these things are not completely subject to God, for we are not without sins; and these things will be in glory, where we will do the divine will perfectly: *blessed is he who eats bread in the kingdom of God* (Luke 14:15). The second is the right path: for in the kingdom the way is walked by justice. Hence if you want to go to the kingdom of God it is necessary that

iustitia hominis qua suis viribus praesumit posse Dei mandata implere; et *Dei*, quia per auxilium gratiae credit homo se posse salvari, Ro. X, 3: *ignorantes Dei iustitiam*. Tertium est quod ponit *et haec omnia adicientur*. Liberalis venditor post forum aliquid dat et adiicit. Nos convenimus cum Deo *ex denario diurno*, infra XX, 13, qui est vita aeterna. Unde quicquid superaddit totum est quaedam adiectio et non computatio. Et hic est: *et haec omnia adicientur*. Non dicit *dabuntur*, Prov. X, 3: *non affliget*, Prov. XXX, 8: *tantum victui meo*.

Et nota quod *quaerere primo* intelligitur dupliciter: sicut finem aut mercedem. Et sic dicit *quaerite primum regnum Dei*, et non temporalia. Non enim debemus evangelizare ut manducemus, sed e converso. Similiter non primo quaeras regnum Dei: pervertis ordinem.

Et sciendum quod Dominus idem docet in oratione sua, ubi ponuntur septem petitiones. Quia primo debemus quaerere ipsum bonum Dei, scilicet gloriam eius; in aliis autem primo regnum Dei, secundo iustitiam, tertio *fiat voluntas tua*, quarto quae sunt adicienda, *panem nostrum* etc.

Sed contra hoc: *et haec omnia adicientur*, obicit Augustinus quia Apostolus dicit, *in fame et siti* I Cor. IV, 11 et II Cor. XI, 27. Et respondet quod Deus sicut medicus sapiens scit quod expediat. Unde sicut medicus aliquando subtrahit cibum propter salutem corporis, ita Deus propter salutem animae subtrahit temporalia: vel propter bonum suum ut scilicet puniantur peccata praeterita et caveant de futuris, vel propter bonum aliorum ut videndo patientiam proficiant in bonum.

Nolite. Hic prohibet sollicitudinem futurorum. Et primo ponit suam admonitionem; secundo exponit, ibi *crastinus*. Dicit ergo *nolite solliciti*.

631. Et nota quod non intendit Dominus prohibere quod homo non sit aliquid sollicitus quid comedere debeat in crastinum: non enim docet servare maiorem perfectionem quam ipsi apostoli servaverunt. Sed ipse habebat loculos, ut dicitur Io. XII, 6 de Iuda qui portabat pecuniam Domini. Unde non docuit quod non fecit qui *cepit facere et docere*; et iterum apostoli congregaverunt victualia, sicut dicitur Act. XI, IV, 35. Unde hic ponuntur quatuor expositiones, quarum ultima est magis litteralis. Prima Augustini, qui sic dicit: *nolite solliciti in crastinum*, idest de temporalibus. Crastinus enim ponitur pro futuro in Scriptura. Temporalia autem variantur per heri et cras. II Cor. IV, 18: *non cogitantibus nobis, sed*

you keep the justice of the kingdom. And he says *justice*, not simply but *his justice*, for justice is twofold, the justice of a man, by which he presumes by his own powers to be able to fulfill the commands of God; and the justice of God, for by the help of grace a man believes he can be saved: *being ignorant of God's justice* (Rom 10:3). The third is that he states *and all these things will be added unto you*. A generous merchant after the market is over gives something and adds to it. We have agreed with God *on the day's wages*, which is eternal life (Matt 20:13). Hence whatever is superadded to the total is something added and not part of the reckoning. And this is *and all these things will be added unto you*. He does not say 'they will be given': *the Lord does not afflict the just with famine* (Prov 10:3); *give me only the food I need* (Prov 30:8).

And note that to *seek first* is understood two ways: as an end or as a reward. And in this way he says *seek first the kingdom of God*, and not temporal things. For we must not preach the Gospel so that we can eat, but vice versa. Likewise, if you do not first seek the kingdom of God, you pervert the order.

And it should be known that the Lord teaches the same thing in the Lord's prayer, where he lays down seven petitions. For first we should seek God's good itself, namely, his glory; but in other things, first the kingdom of God; second, justice; third, *thy will be done*; fourth, those things that are *added unto you*, *our daily bread*.

But against this, *and all these things will be added unto you*, Augustine objects that the Apostle says he labors *in hunger and thirst* (1 Cor 4:11; 2 Cor 11:27). And he answers that God, like a wise physician knows what is expedient. Hence as a physician sometimes takes away the food for the body's health, so God for the soul's health takes away temporal goods: or for one's own good so that past sins are punished and future ones guarded against, or for the good of others so that they, seeing one's patience, advance in the good.

Be not therefore. Here he forbids solicitude about future things. And first he sets down his own admonition; second, he explains it, at *for tomorrow will bring worries of its own*. Therefore he says *do not worry*.

631. And note that the Lord does not forbid man from being solicitous about what to eat the next day: for he does not teach us to keep a greater perfection than the apostles kept. But he himself had a purse, as is said in John 12:6, about Judas who carried the Lord's money. Hence he did not teach what he did not do, he who *began to do and teach* (Acts 1:1). And again, the apostles gathered provisions, as is said in Acts 11:28–30. And here four interpretations are given, of which the last is the most literal. The first is from Augustine, who says this: *do not worry about tomorrow*, that is, about temporal things. For *tomorrow* is said for the future in Scripture. But temporal things change through yesterday and tomorrow: *we do not think about the things*

ista temporalia quae pertinent ad tempus habent suam sollicitudinem annexam. Et ideo dicit **crastinus enim; sufficit diei**, idest presenti vitae, **malitia**, idest necessitas qua cogimur ad providendum de temporalibus. Et dicitur **malitia** quia ex culpa primi parentis derivatum est.

Chrysostomus: quae congregantur semper congregantur ut sufficiant ad multum tempus. Unde **nolite solliciti in crastinum**, idest ad congregandum superflua. **Crastinus enim**, idest superfluitas rerum temporalium invenit sibi sollicitudinem, quia homines sunt solliciti quomodo eripiant tibi istas divitias. **Sufficit diei**, idest sufficit ut accipias necessaria.

Hilarius: in qualibet actione duo sunt consideranda, scilicet ipsa actio et eventus actionis. Quod enim homo seminet, hoc est actio quaedam, sed quid invenire debeat, hoc eventus quidam est. Vult ergo Dominus quod de his quae non sunt in nobis non debeamus solliciti esse, et hoc est magis litteralis et subtilior.

Quarta etiam est Ieronimi et plana. **Nolite solliciti**, non est intelligendum de tempore futuro, sed vult quod sollicitudo quae debet incumbere in futurum non sit in praesenti; tempore enim messis quaerendi sunt messores et non tempore vindemiarum, et e converso. Et hoc consona litterae: **crastinus**, idest futurum tempus habebit suam sollicitudinem; **sufficit diei malitia**, idest poena, afflictio: sic Eccli. XII, 9: *malitia unius.*

that are seen . . . which are temporal, but the things which are not seen are eternal(2 Cor 4:18). But these temporal things which pertain to time have their own solicitude attached. And therefore he says **for tomorrow will bring worries of its own; sufficent to the day**, i.e., to the present life, **is the evil**, i.e., the necessity by which we are forced to provide about temporal things. And it is called **evil** because it is derived from the fault of our first parents.

Chrysostom: things that are accumulated are always accumulated so that they will be enough for a long time. Hence **do not worry about tomorrow**, i.e., for accumulating unnecessary things. **For tomorrow**, i.e., the excess of temporal things, finds its own worry, for men are worried about how to seize these riches for themselves. **Sufficient to the day**, i.e., it is sufficient to receive necessities.

Hilary: in any action two things are to be considered, namely, the action itself, and the action's result. For that a man sows, this is a certain action, but what he should find, that is a certain result. Therefore the Lord wants us not to worry about those things that are not in our control, and this is the more literal and subtle reading.

The fourth is also from Jerome, and it is straightforward. **Do not worry**, is not to be understood about future time, but he wants the concern that should burden the future not to be in the present; for at the time of the harvest harvesters are sought, and not at the time of grape-gathering, and vice versa. And this is consonant with the text: **tomorrow**, i.e., the future time, will have its own worries; **sufficient to the day** is the evil thereof, i.e., the pain, the affliction, as in Sirach 12:9: *in times of affliction even one's friends disappear.*

CHAPTER 7

Lecture 1

7:1 Nolite iudicare, ut non iudicemini; [n. 632]

7:2 in quo enim iudicio iudicaveritis, iudicabimini: et in qua mensura mensi fueritis, remetietur vobis. [n. 633]

7:3 Quid autem vides festucam in oculo fratris tui, et trabem in oculo tuo non vides? [n. 636]

7:4 Aut quomodo dicis fratri tuo: frater, sine eiiciam festucam de oculo tuo: et ecce trabis est in oculo tuo? [n. 636]

7:5 Hypocrita, eiice primum trabem de oculo tuo, et tunc videbis eiicere festucam de oculo fratris tui. [n. 638]

7:6 Nolite sanctum dare canibus: neque mittatis margaritas vestras ante porcos, ne forte conculcent eas pedibus suis, et canes conversi dirumpant vos. [n. 639]

7:7 Petite, et dabitur vobis; quaerite, et invenietis; pulsate, et aperietur vobis. [n. 640]

7:8 Omnis enim qui petit, accipit, et qui quaerit, invenit, et pulsanti aperietur. [n. 643]

7:9 Aut quis est ex vobis homo, quem si petierit filius suus panem, numquid lapidem porriget ei? [n. 645]

7:10 Aut si piscem petierit, numquid serpentem porriget ei? [n. 646]

7:11 Si ergo vos, cum sitis mali, nostis bona data dare filiis vestris, quanto magis Pater vester, qui in caelis est, dabit bona petentibus se? [n. 647]

7:1 Μὴ κρίνετε, ἵνα μὴ κριθῆτε·

7:2 ἐν ᾧ γὰρ κρίματι κρίνετε κριθήσεσθε, καὶ ἐν ᾧ μέτρῳ μετρεῖτε μετρηθήσεται ὑμῖν.

7:3 τί δὲ βλέπεις τὸ κάρφος τὸ ἐν τῷ ὀφθαλμῷ τοῦ ἀδελφοῦ σου, τὴν δὲ ἐν τῷ σῷ ὀφθαλμῷ δοκὸν οὐ κατανοεῖς;

7:4 ἢ πῶς ἐρεῖς τῷ ἀδελφῷ σου· ἄφες ἐκβάλω τὸ κάρφος ἐκ τοῦ ὀφθαλμοῦ σου, καὶ ἰδοὺ ἡ δοκὸς ἐν τῷ ὀφθαλμῷ σοῦ;

7:5 ὑποκριτά, ἔκβαλε πρῶτον ἐκ τοῦ ὀφθαλμοῦ σοῦ τὴν δοκόν, καὶ τότε διαβλέψεις ἐκβαλεῖν τὸ κάρφος ἐκ τοῦ ὀφθαλμοῦ τοῦ ἀδελφοῦ σου.

7:6 Μὴ δῶτε τὸ ἅγιον τοῖς κυσὶν μηδὲ βάλητε τοὺς μαργαρίτας ὑμῶν ἔμπροσθεν τῶν χοίρων, μήποτε καταπατήσουσιν αὐτοὺς ἐν τοῖς ποσὶν αὐτῶν καὶ στραφέντες ῥήξωσιν ὑμᾶς.

7:7 Αἰτεῖτε καὶ δοθήσεται ὑμῖν, ζητεῖτε καὶ εὑρήσετε, κρούετε καὶ ἀνοιγήσεται ὑμῖν·

7:8 πᾶς γὰρ ὁ αἰτῶν λαμβάνει καὶ ὁ ζητῶν εὑρίσκει καὶ τῷ κρούοντι ἀνοιγήσεται.

7:9 ἢ τίς ἐστιν ἐξ ὑμῶν ἄνθρωπος, ὃν αἰτήσει ὁ υἱὸς αὐτοῦ ἄρτον, μὴ λίθον ἐπιδώσει αὐτῷ;

7:10 ἢ καὶ ἰχθὺν αἰτήσει, μὴ ὄφιν ἐπιδώσει αὐτῷ;

7:11 εἰ οὖν ὑμεῖς πονηροὶ ὄντες οἴδατε δόματα ἀγαθὰ διδόναι τοῖς τέκνοις ὑμῶν, πόσῳ μᾶλλον ὁ πατὴρ ὑμῶν ὁ ἐν τοῖς οὐρανοῖς δώσει ἀγαθὰ τοῖς αἰτοῦσιν αὐτόν.

7:1 Do not judge, and you will not be judged; [n. 632]

7:2 for with what judgment you judge, you will be judged: and with what measure you measure out, it will be measured to you again. [n. 633]

7:3 And why do you see the mote that is in your brother's eye; and do not see the beam that is in your own eye? [n. 636]

7:4 Or how do you say to your brother: let me cast the mote out of your eye; and behold a beam is in your own eye? [n. 636]

7:5 You hypocrite, first cast the beam out of your own eye, and then you will see to cast the mote out of your brother's eye. [n. 638]

7:6 Do not give that which is holy to dogs; neither cast your pearls before swine, lest perhaps they trample them under their feet, and turning upon you, they tear you. [n. 639]

7:7 Ask, and it will be given to you: seek, and you will find: knock, and it will be opened to you. [n. 640]

7:8 For everyone who asks, receives: and he who seeks, finds: and to him who knocks, it will be opened. [n. 643]

7:9 Or what man is there among you, of whom if his son will ask bread, he will give him a stone? [n. 645]

7:10 Or if he will ask him for a fish, will he give him a serpent? [n. 646]

7:11 If you then, being evil, know how to give good gifts to your children: how much more will your Father who is in heaven give good things to those who ask him? [n. 647]

7:12 Omnia ergo quaecumque vultis, ut faciant vobis homines, et vos facite illis. Haec est enim lex, et prophetae. [n. 648]

7:13 Intrate per angustam portam, quia lata porta et spatiosa via est, quae ducit ad perditionem, et multi sunt qui intrant per eam. [n. 649]

7:14 Quam angusta porta et arcta via est, quae ducit ad vitam, et pauci sunt qui inveniunt eam! [n. 652]

7:12 Πάντα οὖν ὅσα ἐὰν θέλητε ἵνα ποιῶσιν ὑμῖν οἱ ἄνθρωποι, οὕτως καὶ ὑμεῖς ποιεῖτε αὐτοῖς· οὗτος γάρ ἐστιν ὁ νόμος καὶ οἱ προφῆται.

7:13 Εἰσέλθατε διὰ τῆς στενῆς πύλης· ὅτι πλατεῖα ἡ πύλη καὶ εὐρύχωρος ἡ ὁδὸς ἡ ἀπάγουσα εἰς τὴν ἀπώλειαν καὶ πολλοί εἰσιν οἱ εἰσερχόμενοι δι᾽ αὐτῆς·

7:14 τί στενὴ ἡ πύλη καὶ τεθλιμμένη ἡ ὁδὸς ἡ ἀπάγουσα εἰς τὴν ζωὴν καὶ ὀλίγοι εἰσὶν οἱ εὑρίσκοντες αὐτήν.

7:12 All things therefore whatsoever that you would have men do to you, do also to them. For this is the law and the prophets. [n. 648]

7:13 Enter in at the narrow gate: for wide is the gate, and broad is the way that leads to destruction, and many there are who go in there. [n. 649]

7:14 How narrow is the gate, and strait is the way that leads to life: and few there are who find it! [n. 652]

---

632. Implevit legem quoad praecepta et quoad promissa, nunc quoad iudicia. Primo ergo ordinat ut non sit temerarium iudicium, et dicit *nolite iudicare* etc., idest ex amaritudine odii; Amos VI, 13: *convertisti iudicium in amaritudinem.* Vel sic. *Nolite*, quantum ad ea quae nostro iudicio non sunt commissa. Domini est iudicium, nobis commisit iudicare de exterioribus, de interioribus vero sibi retinuit. *Nolite* ergo *iudicare* de eis; I Cor. IV, 5: *nolite iudicare ante tempus*; Ier. XVII, 9: *pravum est cor hominis, et quis cognoscet illud?* Nullus enim debet iudicare de aliquo quod sit malus homo: dubia enim in meliorem partem interpretanda sunt. Item iudicium debet esse congruum quantum ad personam iudicantis. Unde si es in eodem peccato, vel maiori, non debes iudicare; ad Rom. II, 1: *in quo enim iudicas alterum, teipsum condemnas.* Item non prohibetur praelatis, sed subditis: unde non debent iudicare nisi subditum.

Sed Chrysostomus: *nolite iudicare* etc., idest nolite iudicare vosmetipsos vindicando. Unde si remittitis, non inde iudicabimini; immo ratione huius misericordiae misericordiam consequemini.

633. Sequitur ratio *in quo enim iudicio iudicaveritis, iudicabimini*; idest, pro quo iudicio iudicaveritis, iudicabimini; Ps. VII, 17: *convertetur dolor eius in caput eius* et cetera. Et infra XXVI, 52: *qui percusserit gladio, gladio peribit.*

Vel sic. Timere debent qui iudicant, ne hoc iudicio Dominus permittat eos puniri, ut in Is. XXXIII, 1: *vae tu qui praedaris, nonne et tu praedaberis?*

634. *In qua mensura* et cetera. Hic ponit rationem sub similitudine iudicii; iudex enim est sicut regula animata: cum enim vis aequare duo, defers ad regulam, et quod superabundat de uno, resecas; sic si aliquis habeat de alieno plusquam debeat habere, id resecat, et reddit

632. He fulfilled the law as regards precepts and as regards promises, and now as regards judgments. First, therefore, he ordains that there be not rash judgment, and he says, *do not judge*, i.e., out of the bitterness of hatred; *you have turned judgment into bitterness* (Amos 6:13). Or in this way: *do not judge* as regards those things which are not entrusted to our judgment. Judgment is the Lord's; he has charged us to judge about exterior things, but he has reserved the interior things for himself. Therefore *do not judge* about these things. *Therefore do not judge before the time* (1 Cor 4:5); *the heart is perverse above all things, and unsearchable, who can know it?* (Jer 17:9–10), for no one should judge about another that he is a bad man; for the doubtful things should be interpreted on the good side. Likewise, judgment should be fitting as regards the person of the one judging. Hence if you are in the same sin, or a greater, you should not judge; *for wherein you judge another, you condemn yourself* (Rom 2:1). Similarly, it is not forbidden to superiors, but to those who are subject; hence they should judge only those subject to them.

But Chrysostom says: *do not judge*, i.e., do not judge by avenging yourselves. Hence if you forgive, you will not be judged for that; rather, by reason of this mercy, you will obtain mercy.

633. There follows *for with what judgment you judge, you will be judged*, i.e., you will be judged for what judgment you judged. *His sorrow will be turned on his own head* (Ps 7:17). And below, *all who take the sword will perish with the sword* (Matt 26:52).

Or in this way: those who judge should fear, lest the Lord permit them to be punished with the same judgment, *woe to you that spoil, will not you yourself also be spoiled?* (Isa 33:1).

634. *With what measure you measure out.* Here he sets down the reason under a likeness of judgment. For the judge is like a living measuring rod: for when you wish to make two things equal, you refer them to a measuring rod, and you cut off from one whatever is in excess; thus if someone were to have more of another's things than he

unicuique quod suum est, idest pro ista mensura remetietur nobis.

635. Sed obiicitur. Aliquis peccat temporaliter, et inde punitur aeternaliter; videtur quod non sit aequum iudicium.

Dico quod in peccato duo sunt consideranda: duratio et offensa; et in offensa duo, scilicet aversio et conversio. Ex parte conversionis culpa finita est; ex parte aversionis, infinita, quia avertitur a Deo qui est infinitus. Cum ergo avertat se ab infinito, infinite puniri debet.

Item ex parte durationis est duo considerare, scilicet actum et maculam. Actus momentaneus est, macula infinita, idest aeterna; ideo infinite, idest aeternaliter, puniri debet. Unde si a daemonibus posset deseri macula, possent liberari a culpa et poena. Similiter a parte poenae est acerbitas, et haec est finita. Item duratio, et haec est infinita.

636. *Quid autem vides festucam in oculo fratris tui, et trabem in oculo tuo non vides?* Hic dicit quod non debet esse iudicium inordinatum: inordinatum enim est quando ab aliquo incipit, non plene examinata causa, aut gravitate delicti. In iudicando enim duo sunt necessaria: cognitio causae et iudicium. De primo Iob XXIX, 16: *causam quam nesciebam, diligentissime investigabam* et cetera. *Quid autem vides festucam*, leve peccatum, *in oculo*, idest in conscientia fratris, *trabem autem*, idest grave peccatum, *in oculo tuo non vides?* Per trabem et festucam docet considerare quantitatem peccatorum: saepe enim qui gravia peccata committunt, reprehendunt eos qui levia, sicut contingit in iudicandis religiosis. Cum aliqui qui gravia faciunt, quae vident levia, in religiosis iudicant gravia; sed absorbentur illa sicut una gutta aquae in multitudine vini.

Item contingit quod aliquis ex infirmitate peccet leviter, et aliquis iudex malus et male affectus, qui vellet punire illum ex odio, considerat festucam in oculo illius, non autem trabem in oculo suo. *Quomodo* ergo, idest qua fronte dicere potes: *frater, sine eiiciam festucam de oculo tuo?* Verecundari debes. Chrysostomus: *quo animo diligit homo magis alium quam se? Si enim corrigis eum animo correctionis, prius corriges te; sed hoc facis odio, vel inani gloria; ideo et cetera.*

637. Sed quaeritur utrum qui in peccato mortali est, possit alium corrigere.

Dico quod aut aliquando fuit in peccato, aut non: si numquam fuit in peccato, debet timere ne cadat, ideo invite debet corrigere; si aliquando in peccato fuit, cum mansuetudine corripere debet. Et ideo forte Dominus

should, the judge would cut it off, and return to each what is his own, i.e., it will be measured out to us according to this measure.

635. But it is objected: someone sins temporally, and hence is punished eternally; it seems that there is not an equal judgment.

I say that there are two things to be considered in a sin: duration and offense. And in offense there are two things to be considered, namely turning away and turning towards. On the part of turning towards a creature, the guilt is finite; on the part of turning away, it is infinite, because one turns away from God who is infinite. Therefore, since one turns himself away from the infinite, he should be punished infinitely.

Likewise, there are two things to be considered on the part of duration, namely the deed and the stain. The act is momentary, the stain infinite, i.e., eternal; therefore it should be punished infinitely, i.e., eternally. Hence if the demons could give up their stain, they could be freed from guilt and punishment. Likewise, on the part of the punishment there is the severity, and this is finite. Likewise the duration, and this is infinite.

636. *And why do you see the mote that is in your brother's eye; and do not see the beam that is in your own eye?* Here he says that there should not be inordinate judgment; for it is inordinate when someone begins when he has not examined fully the case or the gravity of the offense. For two things are necessary in judging: knowledge of the case and judgment. About the first, *the cause which I knew not, I searched out most diligently* (Job 29:16). *And why do you see the mote*, a light sin, *in your brother's eye*, i.e., in his conscience, *and do not see the beam*, i.e., a grave sin, *in your own eye?* By the beam and the mote he teaches us to consider the quantity of sins: for often those who commit grave sins reproach those who commit light sins, as happens in judging the pious, since men who commit grave sins, which they see as light, judge there to be grave sins in the pious; but these sins are swallowed up like one drop of water in a great quantity of wine.

Similarly, it happens that someone sins lightly out of weakness, and a judge, evil and badly disposed, who wishes to punish him out of hatred, attends to the mote in his eye and not to the beam in his own eye. *How* then, i.e., by what audacity can you say, *let me cast the mote out of your eye?* You should be ashamed. Chrysostom: *with what spirit does a man love another more than himself? For if you correct him in the spirit of correction, first correct yourself; but you do this out of hatred, or for vainglory.*

637. But it is asked whether one who is in mortal sin can correct another.

I say that either he was in sin at some time, or not: if he was never in sin, he should fear lest he fall, and therefore he should correct another reluctantly; if he was in sin at some time, he should reproach another with meekness.

permisit Petrum cadere, qui debebat esse pastor Ecclesiae, ut mitius se haberet cum peccatoribus; et de Christo dicit Paulus Hebr. IV, v. 15: *non habemus pontificem qui non possit compati infirmitatibus nostris, tentatum per omnia pro similitudine absque peccato.*

Si autem subiacet peccato, aut est publicum, aut occultum: si occultum, aut ex infirmitate, quia displicet ei quod peccat; et sic corripere potest, quia quod corripit in alio, corripit in seipso; si ex malitia, numquam debet corripere. Si autem publicum, non debet arguere cum severitate, sed mansuete seipsum coniungere illi. Unde contra peccatores non est obiurgandum cum asperitate.

638. Sequitur *hypocrita, eiice primum trabem de oculo tuo*. Incipit Dominus arguendo sicut inferius contra servum nequam et cetera. Augustinus: *ostendit quod intendit reprehendere eum qui assumit auctoritatem quae non est sua.* Ps. XLIX, 16: *peccatori autem dixit Deus: quare tu enarras iustitias meas, et assumis testamentum meum per os tuum? Tu vero odisti disciplinam* et cetera. *Eiice primum*, ieiunando, orando, *trabem de oculo tuo*; et tunc poteris videre festucam in oculo fratris tui.

639. Sequitur *nolite sanctum dare canibus*. In quo ostendit quod iudicium debet esse discretum.

Notandum ergo quid per sanctum, et quid per margaritas. Augustinus: *sancta sunt inviolata et immaculata conservanda; margaritaeque pretiosae non debent contemni.* Per canes, qui lacerant dentibus, haeretici significantur; per porcos, qui conculcant pedibus, immundi. Sancta ergo dare canibus est sancta haereticis ministrare. Item si aliquid spirituale dicatur, et istud contemnitur, porcis datur.

Vel per sancta, ecclesiastica sacramenta; per margaritas, mysteria veritatis. Canis est animal totaliter immundum; porcus partim immundus, partim non. Per canes, infideles; per porcos, mali fideles. *Nolite ergo sanctum dare canibus*, idest sacramenta dare infidelibus. Margaritae, idest sensus spirituales, non debent porcis dari; I Cor. II, 14: *animalis homo non percipit ea quae Dei sunt*, idest, ne forte contemnat; Prov. XXVII, 7: *anima satiata conculcat favum.* Unde *conversi*, ad peccata, *dirumpunt*, quia contemnunt, vel calumniam inferunt.

Sed quare? Nonne Christus multa bona dixit infidelibus, et illi dirumpebant verba sua? Dico, quod hoc fecit propter bonos qui cum malis erant, qui inde proficiebant.

And perhaps the Lord permitted Peter to fall for this reason, he who was to be the pastor of the Church, so that he might bear himself more gently toward sinners. And Paul says about Christ, *for we have not a high priest, who cannot have compassion on our infirmities: but one tempted in all things like as we are, without sin* (Heb 4:15).

Now, if someone is subject to a sin, either it is a public sin, or a hidden one. If a hidden one, it is either out of weakness, since it displeases him that he sins, and thus he can reproach another, because what he reproaches in another, he reproaches in himself; if it is out of malice, he should never reproach another. But if it is a public sin, he should not accuse another with severity, but should meekly unite himself with that man. Hence one should not scold against sinners with harshness.

638. There follows *you hypocrite, first cast the beam out of your own eye*. The Lord begins by accusing, just as he does below against the wicked servant. Augustine: *he shows that he means to blame the one who takes up an authority which is not his own.* As it is written: *but to the sinner God has said: why do you declare my justices, and take my covenant in your mouth? Seeing you have hated discipline* (Ps 49:16–17). *First*, by fasting, praying, *cast the beam out of your own eye*, and then you can see the mote in your brother's eye.

639. There follows *do not give that which is holy to dogs*, in which he shows that judgment should be discerning.

Therefore one should note what is signified by holy things, and what by pearls. Augustine: *the holy things are the inviolate and unstained things to be safe-guarded; and the pearls are precious things which should not be despised.* The dogs, which wound with their teeth, signify heretics; the pigs, which trample with their feet, signify the unclean. So to give holy things to the dogs is to supply holy things to heretics. Likewise, if something spiritual is said and it is despised, it is given to pigs.

Or, holy things signify the ecclesiastical sacraments; pearls, the mysteries of truth. The dog is an animal entirely unclean; the pig is partly unclean, partly not. The dogs signify infidels; the pigs signify those faithful who are evil. *Do not give* therefore *that which is holy to dogs*, i.e., do not give the sacraments to infidels. Pearls, i.e., the spiritual senses, should not be given to pigs; *but the sensual man does not perceive these things that are of the Spirit of God* (1 Cor 2:14), i.e., lest perhaps he should despise them. *A soul that is full will tread upon the honeycomb* (Prov 27:7). Hence *turning* to sin, *they tear you*, because they despise you, or bring in a false accusation.

But why? Did not Christ say many good things to infidels, and they rent asunder his words? I say that he did this for the sake of the good men who were with the evil men, who profited from it.

640. *Petite, et dabitur vobis.* Dedit suam doctrinam, quae est completa et perfecta; hic docet qualiter possit impleri; ad hoc autem est necessaria oratio, et diligens attentio.

Primo ergo docet petere;

secundo dat securitatem ad impetrandum, ibi *aut quis ex vobis* et cetera.

641. Dicit ergo *petite*. Et in hoc vide duas falsas opiniones amoveri. Primam scilicet superborum, qui putant suis viribus praecepta complere. Sed dicit, quod necesse est petere a Deo. *Quod enim habes quod non accepisti?* I Cor. IV, 7.

Item amovet opinionem multorum qui dicunt, quod Deus non curat de orationibus, et quod non impetrarent si peterent; ideo addit *et accipietis*.

642. Item addit *quaerite, et invenietis*. Et hoc exponitur, primo, ut in istis duobus nihil addatur, sed tantum exprimatur modus. Requiritur enim ad petendum sollicita attentio; item fervens devotio: et haec duo innuit, cum dicit *quaerite*, idest orate. Vel *petite*, sicut qui aliquid quaerunt, totam intentionem ibi ponunt. Unde ad illum pertinet quod sponsa dicit in Cant. III, 1: *quaesivi quem dilexit anima mea*. *Et invenietis*; Ps. XXVI, 4: *unam petii a Domino, hanc requiram*. Item *quaerite* ad modum pulsantis: quia qui clamat ad ostium, si non exaudiatur, fortiter pulsat; Cant. VII, 11: *veni, dilecte mi, egrediamur in agrum, commoremur in villis*.

Secundo, exponitur iuxta Augustinum referendo ad ea quae Christus dicit de seipso: *ego sum via, veritas et vita*: si vis per hanc viam ire, pete ab eo, ut vias tuas dirigat, dicens cum Psalmista, XXIV, 4: *vias tuas, Domine demonstra mihi, et semitas tuas edoce me*. Si vis veritatem cognoscere, quaere, et invenies; sed non sufficit viam nosse, et veritatem quaerere, nisi veniamus ad vitam, idest ut in illam ingrediaris, pulsa; unde Ex. XV, 17: *introduces eos, et plantabis in monte haereditatis tuae*. Sed, iuxta eumdem, longe melius, ad instantissimam petitionem omnia ista referuntur.

Item aliter exponitur referendo ad diversos actus, *petite* orando, *quaerite* studendo, *pulsate* operando.

643. *Omnis enim qui petit, accipit* et cetera.

Dicet aliquis, *tu dicis, quod petamus. Credo quod dicitur istud sanctis hominibus, sed non sum de numero istorum*: ideo dicit *omnis qui petit, accipit* et cetera.

Sed videtur falsum esse, quia scribitur Io. c. IX, 31: *scimus, quia peccatores Deus non audit*.

640. *Ask, and it will be given to you.* He gave his teaching, which is complete and perfect; here he teaches how it can be performed. And for this prayer and diligent attention are necessary.

First, then, he teaches us to pray;

second, he gives us an assurance of obtaining, there, *or what man is there among you*.

641. He says then, *ask*. And see that two false opinions are removed by this. The first is that of the proud, who think to fulfill the precepts by their own powers. But he says that it is necessary to ask it from God. *Or what have you that you have not received?* (1 Cor 4:7).

Likewise, he removes the opinion of many who say that God does not attend to prayers, and that they would not obtain if they were to ask; so he adds, *and it will be given to you*.

642. Similarly, he adds, *seek, and you will find*. And this is explained, first, by saying that nothing is added in these two phrases beyond what was said, but only the manner of asking is expressed. For anxious attention is required for asking, and likewise fervent devotion; and he implies these two things when he says, *seek*, i.e., pray. Or *ask*, just as he who seeks something places there his whole concentration. Hence to this pertains what the spouse says, *I sought him whom my soul loves* (Song 3:1). *And you will find*; one thing I have asked of the Lord, this will I seek after (Ps 26:4). Similarly, seek in the manner of one who knocks, because he who shouts at the door, if he is not heard, let him knock boldly. *Come, my beloved, let us go out into the field, let us abide in the villages* (Song 7:11).

Second, it is explained following Augustine, by referring to those things Christ said of himself: *I am the way, and the truth, and the life* (John 14:6): if you wish to travel on this way, ask of him, that he may direct your ways, saying with the Psalmist, *show, O Lord, your ways to me, and teach me your paths* (Ps 24:4). If you wish to know the truth, seek, and you will find; but it is not enough to be familiar with the path, and to seek the truth, unless we come to life, i.e., knock, that you may enter into it; hence, *you will bring them in, and plant them in the mountain of your inheritance* (Exod 15:17). But, according to the same Augustine, by far better, all these things are referred to the most urgent petition.

Likewise, in another way, it is explained by referring to diverse actions, *ask* by praying, *seek* by studying, *knock* by working.

643. *For everyone who asks, receives.*

Someone will say: *you say that we should ask; I believe that this is said to holy men, but I am not of their number.* This is why he says, *everyone who asks, receives*.

But it seems to be false, because it is written, *now we know that God does not hear sinners* (John 9:31).

Et Augustinus solvit id. Si peccatores Deus non audit, quomodo dictum est de publicano quod dicebat: *propitius esto, Domine, mihi peccatori?* Unde addit: peccatores non audit, scilicet volentes remanere in peccatis. Sed sciendum, quod oratio est meritoria et impetratoria; et potest esse meritoria, etiamsi non sit impetratoria.

644. Sed quid est quod dicit quod *omnis qui petit accipit?* Videtur esse falsum, quia non semper accipitur quod petitur.

Dico, quod in quatuor casibus petit homo, et non exauditur. Quia vel petit quod non expedit; infra XX, 22: *nescitis quid petatis;* ideo petenda sunt necessaria ad salutem. Item secundo, quia non bene petit; Iac. IV, 3: *petitis, et non accipitis, eo quod non bene petatis;* ideo petendum est pie, idest cum fide. Item humiliter; unde Lc. I, 48: *respexit humilitatem ancillae suae.* Item pie, idest devote. Item non aliquando auditur, cum pro alio oratur cuius merita contradicunt; Ier. XV, 1: *si steterit Moyses et Samuel coram me, non est anima mea ad populum istum* et cetera. Item non exauditur quia non perseverat; Lc. XVIII, 1: *quia oportet semper orare,* et perseveranter; quia Dominus vult quod crescant vota. Item contingit, quod Dominus exaudit; sed non videtur, quia dat Dominus ad utilitatem, non ad voluntatem, ut accidit Paulo. Augustinus: *bonus Dominus qui saepe non tribuit quod petimus, ut tribuat quod mallemus: et quia nos vocamus eum Patrem, tribuit nobis quod pater filio.*

645. Ideo subdit *quis ex vobis homo quem si petierit filius suus panem, numquid lapidem porriget ei?* Per panem intelligitur Christus; Io. VI, 51: *ego sum panis vivus, qui de caelo descendi* et cetera. Item panis est sacra doctrina; Eccli. XV, 3: *cibabo illum pane vitae et intellectus.* Item caritas; Is. c. XXX, 23: *erit panis terrae uberrimus et pinguis.*

E contrario lapis est diabolus; Iob XLI, 15: *indurabitur cor eius quasi lapis.* Item dicitur obduratio; unde dicitur Ez. XXXVI, 26: *auferam a vobis cor lapideum, et dabo cor carneum.* Item dicitur falsa doctrina; Iob c. XXVIII, 3: *lapidem caliginis, et umbram mortis dividit torrens* et cetera. Unde si quis petit a Deo, ut a Patre, panem, idest Christum, non dabit diabolum.

646. Similiter *si piscem.* Piscis vivit in aquis, et est intelligentia in dogmatibus; Io. IV, 13: *qui biberit ex hac aqua non sitiet amplius.* Et ibid.: *erit fons aquae vivae salientis in vitam aeternam.* Item per aquas tribulationes: unde per pisces, viventes in aquis tribulationis. Vel piscis

And Augustine resolves this. If God does not hear sinners, how is it said of the publican that he said, *O God, be merciful to me a sinner* (Luke 18:13)? Hence he adds: *he does not hear sinners, namely those who wish to remain in sins.* But one should know that prayer is meritorious and impetratory, and it can be meritorious even if it is not impetratory.

644. But why does he say that *everyone who asks, receives*? It seems to be false, because what is asked is not always received.

I say that there are four cases in which a man asks and is not heard. For either he asks what is not expedient; *you do not know what you ask* (Matt 20:22); so one should ask for what is necessary for salvation. Likewise, second, because he does not ask well; *you ask, and receive not; because you ask amiss* (Jas 4:3); so one should ask piously, i.e., with faith. Again, one should ask humbly; hence, *he has regarded the humility of his handmaid* (Luke 1:48). Again, piously, i.e., devoutly. Likewise, sometimes he is not heard when he prays for another whose merits speak against the prayer; *Moses and Samuel will stand before me, my soul is not towards this people* (Jer 15:1). Likewise, he is not heard because he does not persevere; *and he spoke also a parable to them, that we ought always to pray* (Luke 18:1), and perseveringly, because the Lord desires that the desire should grow. Likewise it happens that the Lord hears, but it is not seen, because the Lord gives what is useful, and not what is desired, as happened to Paul. Augustine: *the Lord is good, who often does not give what we ask, that he may give what we would prefer: and because we ourselves call him 'Father,' he gives us what a father would give to a son.*

645. For this reason he adds next, *or what man is there among you, of whom if his son will ask bread, he will give him a stone?* By bread is understood Christ; *I am the living bread which came down from heaven* (John 6:51). Likewise, the bread is sacred doctrine; *with the bread of life and understanding, she will feed him* (Sir 15:3). Likewise, charity; *and the bread of the corn of the land will be most plentiful, and fat* (Isa 30:23).

On the other hand, the stone is the devil; *his heart will be as hard as a stone* (Job 41:15). Similarly, the stone names hardness; hence it is said: *I will take away the stony heart out of your flesh, and will give you a heart of flesh* (Ezek 36:26). It also names false teaching; *the stone also that is in the dark and the shadow of death the flood divides* (Job 28:3). Hence if someone asks God, as a Father, for bread, i.e., Christ, he will not give him the devil.

646. Similarly, *or if he will ask him for a fish.* A fish lives in the water, and is understanding in dogmas; *he that will drink of the water that I will give him, will not thirst for ever* (John 4:13). And in the same passage, *but the water that I will give him, will become in him a fountain of water,*

dicitur fides, quae latet sub aqua, idest custodia spiritus; sed per serpentem falsa doctrina haereticorum.

Dicit ergo *et si petierit piscem, non dabit ei serpentem?* Alius Evangelista ponit tertium, scilicet ovum. Ita quod per panem caritas, per piscem fides, per ovum spes.

647. Infert *ergo si vos, cum sitis mali, nostis bona data dare filiis vestris; quanto magis Pater vester, qui in caelis est, dabit bona petentibus se?*

Sed dicet aliquis: hoc dixit apostolis, qui non erant mali.

Et solvit Chrysostomus: *quia immo ad comparationem bonitatis divinae.* Is. LXIV, v. 6: *omnes iustitiae nostrae quasi pannus menstruatae.* Hieronymus dicit: *et si non omnes mali secundum actum, tamen omnes mali secundum pronitatem ad malum.* Unde habetur Gen. VI, 5: *quia cuncta cogitatio humani cordis intenta est ad malum omni tempore.* Et Ier. XVI, 12: *ecce enim unusquisque ambulat post pravitatem cordis sui.*

Augustinus: *si ergo vos cum sitis mali*: non dicitur, *vos estis mali*, sed *cum sitis mali*, daretis filiis temporalibus temporalia bona quae reputatis bona; multo magis ergo Pater vester qui est summe bonus.

648. Et hoc est quod sequitur *quanto magis Pater vester qui in caelis est, dabit bona petentibus se*, si vultis accipere? *Omnia ergo quaecumque vultis, ut faciant vobis homines, et vos facite illis*; idest, aliis dimittite, si vultis ut dimittatur vobis. Aliqui apposuerunt *omnia bona*; sed non oportet, quia dicit *vultis*. Voluntas autem bonorum, et cupiditas malorum; ideo non est necessarium addere *bona*. Unde quod tibi vis fieri, aliis facias. *Haec est enim lex et prophetae*; et non dicit: tota lex et prophetae, sicut in primis praeceptis: *ab illis enim duobus tota lex pendet et prophetae.*

649. *Intrate per angustam portam.* Ne forte crederet aliquis eo quod dixerat *petite et accipietis*, quod homo totum haberet a Deo sine operibus bonis; ideo docet quod hoc etiam fit per opera bona.

Primo ergo ponit admonitionem;
secundo rationem.
650. Dicit ergo *intrate*, idest conemini ad intrandum.

springing up into life everlasting. Likewise, by water are understood afflictions. Hence by fish are understood those living in the waters of afflictions. Or the fish name the faith, which hides under water, i.e., under the protection of the spirit; but by the serpent is understood the false doctrines of the heretics.

He says then, *or if he will ask him for a fish, will he give him a serpent?* The other Evangelist sets down a third, namely an egg (Luke 11:12). In this way, by bread is understood charity, by fish is understood faith, and by the egg, hope.

647. He brings in, *if you then, being evil, know how to give good gifts to your children: how much more will your Father who is in heaven give good things to them who ask him?*

But someone will say: he said this to the apostles, who were not evil.

And Chrysostom resolves it: *indeed they were, in comparison to the divine goodness.* As it is written: *all our justices as the rag of a menstruous woman* (Isa 64:6). Jerome says: *even if not all are evil according to deed, yet all are evil according to an inclination to evil.* Hence it is said, *and God seeing that the wickedness of men was great on the earth, and that all the thought of their heart was bent upon evil at all times* (Gen 6:5). And, *behold every one of you walks after the perverseness of his evil heart* (Jer 16:12).

Augustine: *if you then, being evil*; he does not say, *you are evil*, but *being evil*, you would give to temporal children the temporal goods which you reckon as good; much more then your Father, who is good in the highest way.

648. And this is what follows, *how much more will your Father who is in heaven give good things to those who ask him* if you wish to receive? *All things therefore whatsoever that you would have men do to you, do also to them*; i.e., give to others, if you wish that something be given to you. Some men set here *all good things*, but it is not necessary, since he says, *you would*. Now, will is of good things, and cupidity of bad; therefore it is not necessary to add *good things*. Hence that which you will to be done for you, do for others. *For this is the law and the prophets*; and he does not say the whole of the law and the prophets, as in the first precept, *on these two commandments depends the whole law and the prophets* (Matt 22:40).

649. *Enter in at the narrow gate.* Lest perhaps someone should think that because he had said, *ask, and it will be given to you*, that a man would get everything from God without good works, he teaches that this also comes about through good works.

First, therefore, he sets down a warning;
second, the reason.
650. He says then, *enter in*, i.e., make an effort at entering in.

Augustinus exponit dupliciter. Christus porta est; Io. X, 9: *ego sum ostium*, quia sine ipso non venitur ad regnum. Haec porta est angusta per humilitatem quia humiliavit se usque ad mortem. Unde: *verbum abbreviatum faciet Dominus super terram*. Unde **intrate per angustam portam**, idest per Christi humilitatem; Lc. ult., 26: *oportuit enim Christum pati, et ita intrare in gloriam suam*: et sic nos oportet. Unde *per multas tribulationes oportet nos intrare in regnum Dei*.

Item, haec porta dicitur caritas; Ps. CXVII, v. 20: *haec porta Domini, iusti intrabunt in eam*. Haec est arctata lege divina; et per hanc debemus intrare servando legem et praecepta.

651. Deinde assignat rationem **quia lata porta et spatiosa via est quae ducit ad perditionem**. Et describit duas portas, unam latam, aliam strictam.

Lata describitur, quia lata diabolus, lata praesumptio superbiae; infra XVI, 18: **portae Inferi non praevalebunt adversus eam**.

Haec porta lata est, quia latum est quod omnes recipit: non enim est quod eam repleat. Item haec porta dicitur iniquitas sive vitium: et haec est lata, quia multipliciter contingit: dicitur enim virtus uno modo, vitium autem multifarie; Osee IV, 2: *maledictum, et mendacium, et homicidium, et furtum, et adulterium inundaverunt, et sanguis sanguinem tetigit* et cetera. Item est via lata: et hoc est opus peccati; Ier. II, 18: *quid tibi vis in via Aegypti?* Item haec via est spatiosa, quia in sui principio videtur esse lata, sed post angustatur, quia exitus eius est ad perditionem, quia *stipendia peccati mors est*.

Et multi sunt qui intrant per eam. Hic tangit numerum, quia ad litteram *stultorum infinitus est numerus*.

652. Angusta est porta, et arcta via quae ducit ad vitam. Haec est contraria praecedenti; et haec est arcta, quia arctata secundum regulam legis, et est via contra viam; Prov. IV, 27: *vias enim quae a dextris sunt, novit Dominus; perversae vero sunt quae sunt a sinistris* et cetera.

Sed potest quaeri, quare via caritatis est arcta, quia videtur quod sit lata; Prov. IV, 11: *ducam te per semitas aequitatis, quas cum ingressus fueris, non arctabuntur gressus tui*. Via autem peccatorum est via stricta; unde Sap. V, 7: *ambulavimus vias difficiles*.

Dicendum quod est via carnis et rationis. Via caritatis in via carnis est stricta via, in via rationis e contra. Et est exemplum de paedagogo: quia quanto plus diligit puerum, magis arctat gressus suos. Unde viae

Augustine explains this in two ways. Christ is the gate; *I am the door* (John 10:9), because without him no one comes to the kingdom. This gate is narrow through humility, because he humbled himself even unto death. Hence, *a short word will the Lord make upon the earth* (Isa 10:23). Hence, **enter in at the narrow gate**, i.e., by the humility of Christ. *Ought not Christ to have suffered these things, and so to enter into his glory?* (Luke 24:26). And so it is necessary for us. Hence, *through many tribulations we must enter into the kingdom of God* (Acts 14:21).

Similarly, this gate is called charity; *this is the gate of the Lord, the just will enter into it* (Ps 117:20). This is the narrow divine law; and through this we should enter by keeping the law and the precepts.

651. Then he gives the reason: **for wide is the gate, and broad is the way that leads to destruction**. And he describes two gates, one wide, another narrow.

It is described as wide because the devil is wide, wide by the presumption of pride; **and the gates of hell will not prevail against it** (Matt 16:18).

This gate is wide, because that which receives all is wide; for there is nothing which would fill it. Likewise, this gate names iniquity or vice; and this is wide, because it happens in many ways. For virtue is said in one way, but vice in many ways; *cursing, and lying, and killing, and theft, and adultery have overflowed, and blood has touched blood* (Hos 4:2). Likewise, there is the wide way, and this is the work of sin; *and now what have you to do in the way of Egypt?* (Jer 2:18). Similarly, this way is the spacious one, because it seems to be wide in its beginning, but afterward it is narrow, because its outlet is into perdition, because *the wages of sin is death* (Rom 6:23).

And many there are who go in there. Here he touches upon the number, because literally, *the number of fools is infinite* (Sir 1:15).

652. How narrow is the gate, and straight is the way that leads to life. This is contrary to what precedes it. And this is narrow, because it is narrowed according to the rule of the law, and it is a way against the other way; *for the Lord knows the ways that are on the right hand: but those are perverse which are on the left hand* (Prov 4:27).

But one might ask why the way of charity is narrow, for it seems that it would be wide; *I will lead you by the paths of equity: which when you will have entered, your steps will not be straitened* (Prov 4:11–12). But the way of sin is a narrow way; hence, *we wearied ourselves in the way of iniquity and destruction, and have walked through hard ways* (Wis 5:7).

One should say that it is the way of the body and of the reason. The way of charity in the way of the flesh is a narrow way, while the way of charity in the way of reason is the other way around. And an example can be found in a teacher,

caritatis in via carnis arctantur, in via rationis e contrario; Ps. CXVIII, 120: *confige timore tuo carnes meas.*

653. *Et pauci sunt qui inveniunt eam*. Hic facit mentionem de difficili et rara inventione in via spiritus: et in via carnis non. Et est ratio: quia via carnis est delectatio, et haec est in promptu; via vero spiritus est occulta; unde Ps. XXX, 20: *quam magna multitudo dulcedinis tuae, Domine, quam abscondisti timentibus te.* Quia enim est in occulto, ideo et *pauci inveniunt eam*. Sed et aliqui inveniunt, et retrocedunt, de quibus dicitur Lucae IX, 62: *nemo mittens manum suam ad aratrum, et aspiciens retro, aptus est regno Dei.*

for the more he loves a child, the more he restricts his steps. Hence the way of charity in the way of the flesh is tightened, while the way of charity in the way of reason is the other way around. *Pierce my flesh with your fear* (Ps 118:120).

653. *And few there are who find it!* Here he mentions that the discovery of the way of the spirit is difficult and rare, but not the discovery of the way of the flesh. And there is a reason: because the way of the flesh is pleasure, and this is ready at hand; but the way of the spirit is hidden. Hence, *O how great is the multitude of your sweetness, O Lord, which you have hidden for those who fear you!* (Ps 30:20). For since it is hidden, *few there are who find it!* But some also find it, and fall back, of whom it is said, *no man putting his hand to the plough, and looking back, is fit for the kingdom of God* (Luke 9:62).

Lecture 2

7:15 Attendite a falsis prophetis, qui veniunt ad vos in vestimentis ovium, intrinsecus autem sunt lupi rapaces. [n. 655]

7:16 A fructibus eorum cognoscetis eos. Numquid colligunt de spinis uvas, aut de tribulis ficus? [n. 658]

7:17 Sic omnis arbor bona bonos fructus facit, mala autem arbor malos fructus facit. [n. 661]

7:18 Non potest arbor bona malos fructus facere, neque arbor mala bonos fructus facere. [n. 661]

7:19 Omnis arbor, quae non facit fructum bonum, exciditur, et in ignem mittetur.[n. 662]

7:20 Igitur ex fructibus eorum cognoscetis eos. [n. 662]

7:21 Non omnis qui dicit mihi, Domine, Domine, intrabit in regnum caelorum; sed qui facit voluntatem Patris mei qui in caelis est, ipse intrabit in regnum caelorum. [n. 663]

7:22 Multi dicent mihi in illa die: Domine, Domine, nonne in nomine tuo prophetavimus, et in nomine tuo daemonia eiecimus, et in nomine tuo virtutes multas fecimus? [n. 666]

7:23 Et tunc confitebor illis, quia numquam novi vos. Discedite a me qui operamini iniquitatem. [n. 667]

7:24 Omnis ergo qui audit verba mea haec, et facit ea, assimilabitur viro sapienti, qui aedificavit domum suam supra petram, [n. 670]

7:25 et descendit pluvia, et venerunt flumina, et flaverunt venti, et irruerunt in domum illam, et non cecidit: fundata enim erat super petram. [n. 672]

7:15 Προσέχετε ἀπὸ τῶν ψευδοπροφητῶν, οἵτινες ἔρχονται πρὸς ὑμᾶς ἐν ἐνδύμασιν προβάτων, ἔσωθεν δέ εἰσιν λύκοι ἅρπαγες.

7:16 ἀπὸ τῶν καρπῶν αὐτῶν ἐπιγνώσεσθε αὐτούς. μήτι συλλέγουσιν ἀπὸ ἀκανθῶν σταφυλὰς ἢ ἀπὸ τριβόλων σῦκα;

7:17 οὕτως πᾶν δένδρον ἀγαθὸν καρποὺς καλοὺς ποιεῖ, τὸ δὲ σαπρὸν δένδρον καρποὺς πονηροὺς ποιεῖ.

7:18 οὐ δύναται δένδρον ἀγαθὸν καρποὺς πονηροὺς ποιεῖν οὐδὲ δένδρον σαπρὸν καρποὺς καλοὺς ποιεῖν.

7:19 πᾶν δένδρον μὴ ποιοῦν καρπὸν καλὸν ἐκκόπτεται καὶ εἰς πῦρ βάλλεται.

7:20 ἄρα γε ἀπὸ τῶν καρπῶν αὐτῶν ἐπιγνώσεσθε αὐτούς.

7:21 Οὐ πᾶς ὁ λέγων μοι· κύριε κύριε, εἰσελεύσεται εἰς τὴν βασιλείαν τῶν οὐρανῶν, ἀλλ᾽ ὁ ποιῶν τὸ θέλημα τοῦ πατρός μου τοῦ ἐν τοῖς οὐρανοῖς.

7:22 πολλοὶ ἐροῦσίν μοι ἐν ἐκείνῃ τῇ ἡμέρᾳ· κύριε κύριε, οὐ τῷ σῷ ὀνόματι ἐπροφητεύσαμεν, καὶ τῷ σῷ ὀνόματι δαιμόνια ἐξεβάλομεν, καὶ τῷ σῷ ὀνόματι δυνάμεις πολλὰς ἐποιήσαμεν;

7:23 καὶ τότε ὁμολογήσω αὐτοῖς ὅτι οὐδέποτε ἔγνων ὑμᾶς· ἀποχωρεῖτε ἀπ᾽ ἐμοῦ οἱ ἐργαζόμενοι τὴν ἀνομίαν.

7:24 Πᾶς οὖν ὅστις ἀκούει μου τοὺς λόγους τούτους καὶ ποιεῖ αὐτούς, ὁμοιωθήσεται ἀνδρὶ φρονίμῳ, ὅστις ᾠκοδόμησεν αὐτοῦ τὴν οἰκίαν ἐπὶ τὴν πέτραν·

7:25 καὶ κατέβη ἡ βροχὴ καὶ ἦλθον οἱ ποταμοὶ καὶ ἔπνευσαν οἱ ἄνεμοι καὶ προσέπεσαν τῇ οἰκίᾳ ἐκείνῃ, καὶ οὐκ ἔπεσεν, τεθεμελίωτο γὰρ ἐπὶ τὴν πέτραν.

7:15 Beware of false prophets, who come to you in the clothing of sheep, but inwardly are ravening wolves. [n. 655]

7:16 By their fruits you will know them. Do men gather grapes from thorns, or figs from thistles? [n. 658]

7:17 Even so every good tree brings forth good fruit, and the evil tree brings forth evil fruit. [n. 661]

7:18 A good tree cannot bring forth evil fruit, neither can an evil tree bring forth good fruit. [n. 661]

7:19 Every tree that does not bring forth good fruit, will be cut down, and will be cast into the fire. [n. 662]

7:20 Wherefore by their fruits you will know them. [n. 662]

7:21 Not everyone who says to me, Lord, Lord, will enter into the kingdom of heaven: but he who does the will of my Father who is in heaven, he will enter into the kingdom of heaven. [n. 663]

7:22 Many will say to me in that day: Lord, Lord, have we not prophesied in your name, and cast out devils in your name, and done many miracles in your name? [n. 666]

7:23 And then will I profess to them, I never knew you: depart from me, you who work iniquity. [n. 667]

7:24 Everyone therefore who hears these my words, and does them, will be likened to a wise man that built his house upon a rock, [n. 670]

7:25 and the rain fell, and the floods came, and the winds blew, and they beat upon that house, and it did not fall, for it was founded on a rock. [n. 672]

7:26 Et omnis qui audit verba mea haec, et non facit ea, similis erit viro stulto qui aedificavit domum suam supra arenam, [n. 673]

7:26 καὶ πᾶς ὁ ἀκούων μου τοὺς λόγους τούτους καὶ μὴ ποιῶν αὐτοὺς ὁμοιωθήσεται ἀνδρὶ μωρῷ, ὅστις ᾠκοδόμησεν αὐτοῦ τὴν οἰκίαν ἐπὶ τὴν ἄμμον·

7:26 And everyone who hears these my words, and does not do them, will be like a foolish man who built his house upon the sand, [n. 673]

7:27 et descendit pluvia, et venerunt flumina, et flaverunt venti, et irruerunt in domum illam, et cecidit, et fuit ruina illius magna. [n. 673]

7:27 καὶ κατέβη ἡ βροχὴ καὶ ἦλθον οἱ ποταμοὶ καὶ ἔπνευσαν οἱ ἄνεμοι καὶ προσέκοψαν τῇ οἰκίᾳ ἐκείνῃ, καὶ ἔπεσεν καὶ ἦν ἡ πτῶσις αὐτῆς μεγάλη.

7:27 and the rain fell, and the floods came, and the winds blew, and they beat upon that house, and it fell, and great was the fall of it. [n. 673]

7:28 Et factum est, cum consummasset Iesus verba haec, admirabantur turbae super doctrinam eius. [n. 677]

7:28 Καὶ ἐγένετο ὅτε ἐτέλεσεν ὁ Ἰησοῦς τοὺς λόγους τούτους, ἐξεπλήσσοντο οἱ ὄχλοι ἐπὶ τῇ διδαχῇ αὐτοῦ·

7:28 And it came to pass when Jesus had fully ended these words, that the people were in admiration at his doctrine. [n. 677]

7:29 Erat enim docens eos sicut potestatem habens: et non sicut scribae eorum et Pharisaei. [n. 678]

7:29 ἦν γὰρ διδάσκων αὐτοὺς ὡς ἐξουσίαν ἔχων καὶ οὐχ ὡς οἱ γραμματεῖς αὐτῶν.

7:29 For he was teaching them as one having power, and not as the scribes and Pharisees. [678]

---

654. Docet cautelas, a quibus cavendum sit. Describitur autem a professione, quia prophetae.

Sed potest quaeri, de quibus prophetis, quia *lex et prophetae usque ad Ioannem*: unde in tempore illo non erant prophetae de Christo, quia in ipso finiuntur.

Ideo dicendum quod prophetae sunt doctores in Ecclesia et praelati.

655. Sed quid est quod dicit *falsi*?

Falsi dicuntur qui non mittuntur. De talibus dicitur Ier. XXIII, 21: *non mittebam eos, et ipsi currebant.* Item falsi dicuntur qui mendacium dicunt; unde Ier. II, 8: *prophetae eius prophetaverunt in Baal.* Sic etiam *multi fuerunt pseudoprophetae in populo*: sicut et in nobis erunt magistri mendaces.

Attendite, idest diligenter cavete, quia occulti sunt, et a laqueis occultis cavendum est. Unde malignitas eorum intrinsecus latet.

656. Dicit ergo *qui veniunt ad vos in vestimentis ovium* et cetera. Oves sunt fideles: *nos autem populus eius, et oves pascuae eius*, Ps. XCIX, 3. Vestimenta autem eorum sunt ieiunium, eleemosynae, quibus se tegunt; II ad Tim. III, 5: *habentes speciem pietatis, virtutem autem eius abnegantes.*

Sed sciendum, quod si lupi se tegant pellibus ovium, non tamen propter hoc ovis perdit pellem suam: sic licet illi mali bonis operibus tegantur, tamen multum boni proficiunt.

657. *Intrinsecus autem sunt lupi rapaces.* Hoc principaliter exponitur de haereticis, ex consequenti de malis praelatis. Unde habetur super illud Io. X, 11: *ego sum pastor bonus*: dicitur quod quidam est pastor, qui gubernat, et regit; quidam lupus, qui perniciem intendit; quidam

654. He teaches caution, whom we should avoid. Moreover, they are described by profession, for they are prophets.

But one can ask of which prophets he speaks, *for all the prophets and the law prophesied until John* (Matt 11:13); hence in that time there were no prophets of Christ, because they are ended in him.

Therefore one should say that the prophets are teachers and superiors in the Church.

655. But why does he mean by *false*?

They are called false who are not sent. About such men it is said, *I did not send prophets, yet they ran* (Jer 23:21). Likewise, they are called false who speak lies; hence, *the prophets prophesied in Baal* (Jer 2:8). Thus *there were also false prophets among the people* (2 Pet 2:1), just as there were many lying teachers among us.

Beware, i.e., be diligently aware, because they are hidden, and one should beware a hidden trap. Hence their malice is hidden within.

656. He says then, *who come to you in the clothing of sheep*. Sheep are the faithful: *we are his people and the sheep of his pasture* (Ps 99:3). And their clothing is fasting and almsgiving, by which they hide themselves. *Having an appearance indeed of godliness, but denying the power thereof* (2 Tim 3:5).

But one should know that if wolves were to hide themselves in sheepskins, still the sheep would not lose its skin on this account; in this way, although these evil ones are hidden by good works, nevertheless they do much good.

657. *But inwardly are ravening wolves.* This is principally explained as about heretics, afterward as about evil leaders. Hence it is found in a commentary on John, *I am the good shepherd* (John 10:11): it is said that one man is a shepherd, who governs and rules; another man a wolf, who

mercenarius qui commodum proprium quaerit. Unde pastor est amandus, lupus fugiendus, mercenarius tolerandus.

Quod ergo dicitur, quod *intrinsecus autem sunt lupi rapaces*, intelligitur de his qui habent intentionem pervertendi plebem, et lupi sunt dicendi. Item mercenarii, scilicet mali Christiani, qui dispergunt malo exemplo, qui vitam habent malam; quantum ad effectum, habent modum lupi; Act. XX, 29: *quoniam intrabunt post discessionem meam lupi rapaces in vos, non parcentes gregi* et cetera. Et dicit *intrinsecus*, quia malam habent intentionem occidendi plebem.

658. *A fructibus eorum cognoscetis eos* et cetera. *A fructibus*, idest operationibus.

Sed videtur contra, quia habent vestes ovium; et vestes sunt opera. Ergo ab eis cognoscentur. Chrysostomus: *fructus est confessio fidei*. Unde si confitetur fidem, non est haereticus. Ad Eph. V, 9: *fructus enim lucis est in omni bonitate, et iustitia, et veritate* et cetera.

Si autem exponatur de simulatoribus, tunc sic exponitur, quod per vestes exteriora opera. Unde ad Gal. V, 22: *fructus autem Spiritus est caritas, gaudium et pax* et cetera.

659. Sed quaeres: qualiter possunt cognosci?

Dicendum quod potest vix aliquis hypocrita esse ita compositus, quin appareat aliquid malitiae vel verbo, vel facto: Prov. XXVII, 19: *quomodo in aquis resplendent vultus prospicientium, sic corda hominum manifesta sunt prudentibus*. Et Seneca: *nemo potest diu fictam ferre personam*.

In duobus autem maxime manifestantur. In his quae subito agenda occurrunt, quia in his quae cum deliberatione quis facit, cavet sibi. Item in tribulationibus; Eccli. VI, 8: *est amicus secundum tempus suum, et non permanebit in die tribulationis*. Item manifestantur quando non possunt quod volunt, vel cum iam consecuti sunt. Unde *principatus virum ostendit*.

660. *Numquid colligunt de spinis uvas?* Per uvas, ex quibus fit vinum, intelligitur spiritualis laetitia: quia *vinum laetificat cor hominis*, Ps. CIII, 15. Per ficus dulcedo ecclesiasticae pacis, quae est caritas. Haec non possunt nasci de tribulis, idest peccatoribus, quia *spinas et tribulos germinabit tibi*, Gen. c. III, 18.

661. Et hoc probat per exemplum *omnis arbor bona bonos fructus facit, mala autem arbor malos fructus facit*. Ex hoc Manichaei assumpserunt duas naturas, scilicet bonam et malam. Sed hoc non est verum: quia videmus de mala creatione bonum fructum, et e converso.

aims at mischief; another man a hired hand, who seeks his own profit. Hence the shepherd is to be loved, the wolf to be fled, the hired man to be tolerated.

Therefore, when he says *inwardly are ravening wolves*, it is understood as about those who have the intention of corrupting the common people, and they should be called wolves. Likewise the hired men, that is, the bad Christians, who spread a bad example, who live a bad life, have the manner of a wolf as regards effect; *I know that, after my departure, ravening wolves will enter in among you, not sparing the flock* (Acts 20:29). And he says, *inwardly*, because they have the evil intention of killing the people.

658. *By their fruits you will know them. By their fruits*, i.e., by their works.

But this seems contrary to what was said before, because they have sheep's clothing, and the clothing is works. Therefore they will not be known by them. Chrysostom: *the fruit is the confession of faith*. Hence if he confesses the faith, he is not a heretic. *For the fruit of the light is in all goodness, and justice, and truth* (Eph 5:9).

And if it is explained as about pretenders, then it is explained in this way, that by clothing is understood exterior works. Hence, *but the fruit of the Spirit is charity, joy, peace, patience, benignity, goodness, longanimity, mildness, faith, modesty, continency, chastity* (Gal 5:22–23).

659. But you ask: how can they be known?

One should say that it is hardly possible for a hypocrite to be so put together that he is not noticed as something evil, either by word or by deed. *As the faces of them that look therein, shine in the water, so the hearts of men are laid open to the wise* (Prov 27:19). And Seneca: *no man can carry a made-up persona for a long time.*

And they are most of all uncovered in two things. In those things which they oppose by acting suddenly, because in those things which someone does with deliberation, he takes caution for himself. Likewise in afflictions; *for there is a friend for his own occasion, and he will not abide in the day of your trouble* (Sir 6:8). Likewise, they are uncovered when they cannot do what they want, or when they have already obtained it. Hence *authority shows the man*, as Bias said.

660. *Do men gather grapes from thorns, or figs from thistles?* By grapes, from which wine is made, is understood spiritual joy; that *wine may cheer the heart of man* (Ps 103:15). By the fig is understood the sweetness of ecclesiastical peace, which is charity. These cannot be born of thistles, i.e., of sinners, because *thorns and thistles will it bring forth to you* (Gen 3:18).

661. And he proves this by an example: *even so every good tree brings forth good fruit, and the evil tree brings forth evil fruit*. From this the Manichees claimed two natures, namely good and evil. But this is not true, because we see good fruit from a bad creation, and vice versa.

Unde ad hoc debes intelligere quod arbor est principium fructus. Sed principium est duplex. Principium naturae, et principium moris. Principium naturae est anima: et quicquid inde procedit naturaliter, totum bonum est. Principium autem moris est voluntas; ideo si voluntas fuerit bona, et opus bonum, cum habeat voluntatem bonam cum intentione bona; quia si vellet furari pro eleemosyna danda, etsi voluntas bona est, non tamen intentio est recta.

662. Sed quid fiet de arbore mala? *Omnis arbor, quae fructum non facit, excidetur*: quia si non facit, vel si omittit facere cum possit, excidetur; unde Io. XV, 6: *si quis in me non manserit, mittetur foras sicut palmes, et arescet, et colligent eum, et in ignem mittent, et ardet.* Unde Lc. XIII, 7 dicitur de ficulnea, quam scilicet praecepit Dominus succidi et tolli: *tollatur impius ne videat gloriam Dei.*

Concludit *ergo a fructibus eorum cognoscetis eos.*

663. *Non omnes qui dicunt mihi, Domine, Domine* et cetera. Posita doctrina, ostendit quod oporteat eam observare, quia nihil aliud sufficit ad salutem.

Et circa mandata, sive doctrinam Dei quatuor sunt necessaria, sive laudabilia: ut ore confiteamur, confirmetur miraculis, et audiatur verbum Dei, et exequatur opere. De primo ad Rom. X, 10: *corde creditur ad iustitiam; ore autem confessio fit ad salutem.* De secundo, Marci ult., 20: *Domino cooperante, et sermonem confirmante sequentibus signis.* Item ut audiatur; Io. VIII, 47: *qui ex Deo est, verba Dei audit.* Item, quarto, requiritur quod faciat; Iac. I, 22: *estote factores verbi, et non auditores tantum.*

Unde vult ostendere quod tria sine quarto non proficiunt; unde dicit **non omnis qui dicit mihi, Domine, Domine** et cetera.

664. Sed videtur hoc esse contrarium Apostolo dicenti *nemo potest dicere Dominus Iesus, nisi in Spiritu Sancto.* Sed qui habet Spiritum Sanctum, intrat in regnum caelorum.

Solvit Augustinus, quod 'dicere' dicitur multipliciter: communiter, et stricte, et proprie. Et stricte non est aliud nisi manifestare affectum et voluntatem; et sic dicitur ab Apostolo: *nemo potest dicere Dominus Iesus, nisi in Spiritu Sancto* et cetera. Et hoc nihil aliud est quam credere Dominum, et obedire. Item communiter, idest ore qualitercumque nuntiare; de quo habetur Ier. XXVI, 13: *populus hic labiis me honorat; cor autem eorum longe est a me.*

Hence you should understand for this passage that the tree is the principle of fruit. But a principle is twofold, a principle of nature, and a principle of custom. The principle of nature is the soul, and whatever proceeds naturally from it is entirely good. But the principle of custom is the will, and therefore if the will is good, the work is also good, when one has a good will with a good intention; for if one wished to steal in order to give alms, even though the will is good, nevertheless the intention is not right.

662. But what happens to the evil tree? *Every tree that does not bring forth good fruit, will be cut down*, because if it does not bring forth, or if it omits to bring forth what it could, it will be cut down. Hence, *if any one abide not in me, he will be cast forth as a branch, and will wither, and they will gather him up, and cast him into the fire, and he burns* (John 15:6). Hence it is said of the fig tree, namely the one which the Lord commanded to be cut down and taken away: *let the wicked one be taken away, lest he see the glory of God* (Luke 13:7).

He concludes, *wherefore by their fruits you will know them*.

663. *Not everyone who says to me, Lord, Lord*. The teaching set down, he shows that it is necessary to obey it, because nothing else is enough for salvation.

And concerning the commands, or God's teaching, four things are necessary or praiseworthy: that we confess with the mouth, that it be confirmed with miracles, that the word of God be heard, and that it be followed by work. About the first, *for, with the heart, we believe unto justice; but, with the mouth, confession is made unto salvation* (Rom 10:10). About the second, *but going forth they preached everywhere: the Lord working withal, and confirming the word with signs that followed* (Mark 16:20). Similarly, that it be heard, *he who is of God, hears the words of God* (John 8:47). Similarly, fourth, it is required that he do it; *but be doers of the word, and not hearers only* (Jas 1:22).

Hence he wished to show that three without the fourth do not profit one; hence he says, **not everyone who says to me, Lord, Lord**.

664. But this seems to be contrary to the Apostle, who says, *and no man can say the Lord Jesus, but by the Holy Spirit* (1 Cor 12:3). But he who has the Holy Spirit will enter into the kingdom of heaven.

Augustine resolves this, by saying that 'to say' is said in many ways: commonly, and strictly, and properly. And strictly it is nothing else but to reveal emotion and will; and in this way the Apostle says, *and no man can say the Lord Jesus, but by the Holy Spirit*. And this is nothing other than to believe in the Lord, and to obey. Likewise commonly, i.e., to announce in any way with the mouth; about which it is said, *this people honors me with their lips: but their heart is far from me* (Isa 29:13).

Vel sic. ***Non omnis qui dicit mihi, Domine, Domine*** et cetera. Ingeminat verbum hoc, ***Domine, Domine***, ad significandum, quod duplex est confessio, scilicet vocis et laudis, quarum neutra sufficit. Ideo Is. XXVI, 13: *populus hic labiis me honorat, cor autem eorum longe est a me.*

665. Quis ergo intrabit? Non qui dicit ***Domine, Domine, sed qui fecerit voluntatem Patris mei*** et cetera. Io. III, 13: *nemo ascendit in caelum, nisi qui descendit de caelo* et cetera. Unde nemo potest ascendere, nisi descendat ut Christus, de quo dicitur Io. VI, 38: *descendi de caelo, non ut faciam voluntatem meam, sed voluntatem eius qui misit me.* Unde oportet facere voluntatem Dei; I Thess. IV, 3: *haec est enim voluntas Dei sanctificatio vestra.* Unde dicebat David Ps. CXLII, 10: *doce me facere voluntatem tuam.* Et etiam sicut Dominus docuit orare, ***fiat voluntas tua.***

Sed notandum, quod per hoc quod dicit ***regnum***, tangitur remuneratio aeterna; unde dicit ***intrabit***. Illud enim regnum in bonis spiritualibus est, non in bonis exterioribus; ideo dicit ***intrabit***. Ideo Cant. I, 4: *introduxit me rex in cellaria sua.* Item dicit ***caelorum***, quia licet aliquis hic divitias habeat, vel honores, hoc totum est propter illud. Unde in sublimibus erit remuneratio.

666. Sed posset aliquis dicere, quod facere miracula sufficit ad salutem. Istud excludit, quia ***multi dicent mihi in illa die: domine, domine, nonne in nomine tuo prophetavimus?*** et cetera.

Et dicit ***multi***, significans eos qui ab unitate recedunt, quia sunt sub multitudine: quia *stultorum infinitus est numerus*, Eccle. I, v. 15. Item introducit hoc ad notitiam eius quod dixerat, quod omnis arbor quae fructum non facit, abscindetur. Et non dixerat a quo; ideo dixit ***mihi***, tamquam iudici constituto; quia *omne iudicium dedit Pater Filio*, Io. V, v. 22.

Item dicit ***in illa die***. Dies terminum nominat, sed non secundum temporis qualitatem, quia dies iudicii aliquando nox dicitur. Aliquando autem dies dicitur, aliquando nox: quia incertum est quando veniet. Unde infra XXV, 6: *media nocte clamor factus est, ecce sponsus venit, exite obviam ei.* Diem dicit Apostolus I ad Cor. IV, 3. Et in Ps. XXXVI, v. 6: *et educet quasi lumen iustitiam meam, et iudicium meum tamquam meridiem.* ***Domine, domine.*** Multiplicat ad significandum maiorem confusionem et timorem; Sap. v. 2: *turbabuntur enim timore horribili.*

667. ***Nonne in nomine tuo daemonia eiecimus?*** Haec est potestas supernaturalis; Iob XLI, 24: *non enim est potestas super terram quae huic*, scilicet potestati diaboli, *valeat comparari.*

Or thus. ***Not everyone who says to me, Lord, Lord***. He doubles this word, ***Lord, Lord***, to signify that confession is twofold, namely of the voice and of praise, of which neither suffices. Therefore, *this people honors me with their lips: but their heart is far from me* (Isa 29:13).

665. Who then will enter? Not he who says, ***Lord, Lord, but he who does the will of my Father***. *And no man has ascended into heaven, except he who descended from heaven* (John 3:13). Hence, no one can ascend unless he descends as Christ did, of whom it is said *because I came down from heaven, not to do my own will, but the will of him who sent me* (John 6:38). Hence it is necessary to do the will of God; *for this is the will of God, your sanctification* (1 Thess 4:3). Hence David said, *teach me to do your will* (Ps 142:10). And also as the Lord taught us to pray, ***your will be done*** (Matt 6:10).

But one should notice that by the fact that he says, ***kingdom***, he touches upon the eternal reward; hence he says, ***will enter***. For that kingdom is in spiritual goods, not in exterior goods; this is why he says, ***will enter***. Therefore, *the king has brought me into his storerooms* (Song 1:3). Likewise, he says, ***of heaven***, because although someone might have riches or honors here, all this is for the sake of that. Hence the reward will be in the most sublime things.

666. But someone could say that to work miracles is enough for salvation. He excludes this, because ***many will say to me in that day: Lord, Lord, have we not prophesied in your name?***

And he says, ***many***, pointing to those who withdraw from unity, because they are in a multitude, because *the number of fools is infinite* (Eccl 1:15). Likewise, he brings this in to draw notice to what he had said, that every tree which does not bear fruit will be cut down. And he did not say by whom, so he said ***to me***, as though to one constituted a judge; because *the Father . . . has given all judgment to the Son* (John 5:22).

Likewise, he says, ***in that day***. The day names a terminus, but not according to the quality of time, because the day of judgment is sometimes called the night. Now, it is sometimes called day, sometimes night, because it is uncertain when he will come. Hence below, *and at midnight there was a cry made: behold the bridegroom comes, go forth to meet him* (Matt 25:6). The Apostle calls it day (1 Cor 4:3). And, *and he will bring forth your justice as the light, and your judgment as the noonday* (Ps 36:6). ***Lord, Lord***: he multiplies it to signify a greater confusion and fear; *these seeing it, will be troubled with terrible fear* (Wis 5:2).

667. ***And cast out devils in your name?*** This is a supernatural power; *there is no power upon earth that can be compared with him who was made to fear no one* (Job 41:24), namely, with the power of the devil.

Sed tunc quaeritur, qualiter qui eiiciunt daemonia, fiunt reprobi.

Respondet Chrysostomus, quod isti mentiuntur. Alia responsio est quod aliquando fuerunt boni, et fecerunt miracula; post facti sunt mali. Sed hoc non potest stare, quia dicit Dominus, **numquam novi vos**.

Alio modo dicendum, quod dicunt **in nomine tuo**, non in nomine Spiritus Sancti. Quidam enim in virtute Spiritus Sancti, quidam non. Ut enim habetur Ier. II, 8, quidam prophetaverunt in nomine Baal. Item quidam per artes magicas.

668. Sed quaeritur qualiter daemones faciunt miracula.

Dico quod non possunt; sed faciunt aliqua quae videntur miracula, non tamen sunt miracula. Illa dicuntur miracula, quando effectus patent, causae latent. Unde potest esse aliquod mirum apud quosdam minus scientes, quod non est apud sapientes, ut patet de eclipsi. Unde cum daemones, veriori modo cognoscant naturalia, possunt facere quae nobis videntur miracula. Aliter secundum Hieronymum. Quia secundum quod dicit, inter dona Spiritus Sancti quaedam sunt quae gratis data sunt: sola caritas est, quae distinguit inter filios Dei et filios diaboli; I Cor. XII, 7: *unicuique datur manifestatio ad utilitatem*, vel ad profectum bonitatis eius, vel Ecclesiae, ut fides quam praedicat manifestetur. Et sic etiam aliquando praelatus male vivens potest miracula facere.

669. Et tunc confitebor illis, quia non novi vos, idest non approbavi, nec etiam cum faciebatis miracula; II Tim. II, 19: *novit Dominus qui sunt eius*. Dicit **non novi vos**, cum dicit **discedite a me**, quia numquam approbati estis.

670. Omnis ergo qui audit et cetera. Ostendit quod sine operibus nihil sufficit, nec etiam auditus verbi Dei; quia auditus ordinatur ad fidem. Rom. X, 17: *fides autem ex auditu*.

Auditus enim non sufficit. Et hoc dupliciter manifestat, quia proponit eventum eius qui audit et facit, et eius qui audit et non facit, sub similitudine. Et primo facit tria. Primo ponit aedificationem; secundo impugnationem, ibi **et descendit pluvia** etc.; tertio immutabilitatem, ibi **et non cecidit** et cetera.

671. Dicit ergo quod non sufficit auditus; auditus enim est necessarius; Io. VIII, v. 47: *quia qui ex Deo est, verba Dei audit*. Sed non sufficit; Rom. II, 13: *non enim auditores verbi sed factores iustificabuntur*. Item bene dicit **verba mea haec**: quia quicquid ad salutem pertinet, ibi continetur. Unde **qui audit verba haec, et**

But then it is asked how those who cast out demons come to be rejected.

Chrysostom responds that they are lying. Another response is that they were good at one time, and worked miracles; afterwards they became evil. But this cannot stand, because the Lord says, **I never knew you**.

In another way, one should say that they say, **in your name**, not in the name of the Holy Spirit. For some work in the power of the Holy Spirit, some not. For it is written that certain men prophesied in the name of Baal (Jer 2:8). Likewise some work through the magical arts.

668. But it is asked how demons work miracles.

I say that they cannot; but they do some things which seem to be miracles, and yet are not miracles. These things are called miracles when the effect is clear, but the causes hidden. Hence something can be marvelous among certain less knowledgeable men, which is not marvelous among the wise, as is clear in the case of eclipses. So since demons know natural things in a truer way, they can do things which seem to us like miracles. In another way, according to Jerome. For as he says, there are certain gifts among the gifts of the Holy Spirit which are freely given; it is only charity which distinguishes between the children of God and the children of the devil. *And the manifestation of the Spirit is given to every man unto profit* (1 Cor 12:7), either for the advance of his goodness, or for the Church, that the faith which he preaches might be made manifest. And thus sometimes even a leader who lives badly can work a miracle.

669. And then will I profess to them, I never knew you, i.e., I have not approved you, not even when you worked miracles; *the Lord knows those who are his* (2 Tim 2:19). He says **I never knew you**, when he says, **depart from me**, because you have never been approved.

670. Everyone therefore who hears these my words. He showed that without works nothing is enough, not even hearing God's word, because hearing is ordered to faith. *Faith then comes by hearing* (Rom 10:17).

For hearing is not enough. And he manifests this in two ways, for he sets forth under a likeness the outcome of the one who hears and does, and of the one who hears and does not. And first, he does three things. First, he sets out the building; second, the attack, at **and the rain fell**; third, the immovability, at **and it did not fall**.

671. He says then that hearing is not enough. For hearing is necessary; *he who is of God, hears the words of God* (John 8:47). But it is not enough; *for the hearers of the law are not just before God, but the doers of the law will be justified* (Rom 2:13). Likewise, he says well, **these my words**, because whatever pertains to salvation is contained there.

facit, assimilabitur viro sapienti. Et non dicit quod sit sapiens, sed *assimilabitur*.

Et potest haec similitudo intelligi de corporali aedificatore: et sic plana est littera. Vel potest intelligi spiritualiter: et sic iste vir est Christus. Eccle. VII, 29: *virum unum de mille repperi*. Domus Christi est Ecclesia: scit enim qualiter oportet aedificare. Unde de ipso Prov. IX, 1: *sapientia aedificavit sibi domum*. Et Prov. XIV, 1: *mulier sapiens aedificat domum suam*. **Supra petram**; I Cor. X, 1: *petra autem erat Christus*. Unde Christus super se aedificat: ipse enim est fundamentum; unde I ad Cor. III, 11: *fundamentum aliud nemo ponere potest praeter id quod positum est, quod est Christus Iesus*. Hoc enim est fundamentum veritatis aeternae. Hoc autem est omnino immobile; Ps. CXXIV, 4: *qui confidunt in Domino sicut mons Sion*.

672. Sequitur impugnatio huius domus *et descendit pluvia*. Pluvia doctrina intelligitur: et est bona, et mala pluvia. Ergo quae irruit, est mala doctrina; Gen. XIX, 24: *Dominus pluit super Sodomam sulphur et ignem*. Item flumina sunt bona, et non bona; Is. XVIII, v. 2: *diripuerunt flumina terram eius*; et per hoc significantur sapientes qui reputant se sapientes esse. Ista flumina ex pluviis generantur. Per ventos daemones. Unde in canonica Iudae, 12: *nubes sine aqua, quae a ventis circumferuntur* et cetera. **Et irruerunt in domum**, idest in Ecclesiam, *et non cecidit*. Non enim dirumpentur funiculi eius in aeternum, Is. c. XXXIII, 20. Et quare? **Fundata erat super petram**, idest Christum.

673. Consequenter ponit similitudinem, ponens eventum illius qui audit et non facit: et circa hoc primo ponit aedificationem; secundo impugnationem, ibi *et descendit pluvia* etc.; tertio ruinam, ibi *et cecidit* et cetera.

Dicit: *et omnis qui audit verba mea haec, et non facit ea, similis erit viro stulto*, qui cecidit a lumine sapientiae. Unde Eccle. IV, v. 13: *melior est servus sapiens, quam senex infatuatus*. Item stultus est diabolus. Domus quam aedificat, est congregatio infidelium; unde Ps. LXXIII, 30: *repletae sunt terrae domibus iniquitatum*.

Et iste *super arenam*. Per arenam infideles qui infructuosi sunt. Item propter numerositatem: *stultorum enim infinitus est numerus*, Eccle. I, 15. Item arena non adhaeret, sic isti semper in iurgio sunt. Fundat ergo super arenam, idest finem, qui est quasi fundamentum, scilicet intentionem suam firmat super bonum temporale.

Hence, *everyone therefore who hears these my words, and does them, will be likened to a wise man*. And he does not say that he is wise, but he **will be likened**.

And this likeness can be understood of a fleshly builder, and in this way the text is clear. Or it can be understood spiritually, and in this way the man is Christ. *One man among a thousand I have found* (Eccl 7:29). Christ's house is the Church, for he knows how it must be built. Hence it is said of him, *wisdom has built herself a house* (Prov 9:1). And, *a wise woman builds her house* (Prov 14:1). **Upon a rock**; and the rock was Christ (1 Cor 10:4). Hence Christ builds upon himself. For he himself is the foundation; hence, *for other foundation no man can lay, but that which is laid; which is Christ Jesus* (1 Cor 3:11). For this is the foundation of eternal truth. Moreover, this is in every way immovable; *those who trust in the Lord will be as Mount Zion: he will not be moved forever who dwells in Jerusalem* (Ps 124:1–2).

672. There follows the attack on this house: **and the rain fell**. By the rain, teaching is understood; and there is good rain and bad rain. So the rain which attacks is bad teaching. *And the Lord rained upon Sodom and Gomorrha brimstone and fire from the Lord out of heaven* (Gen 19:24). Similarly, floods are good, and not good; *whose land the rivers have spoiled* (Isa 18:2); and by this are signified the wise who consider themselves to be wise. These floods are generated by the rains. By the winds are understood demons. Hence in the canonical book of Jude, *clouds without water, which are carried about by winds* (Jude 1:12). **And they beat upon that house**, i.e., on the Church, **and it did not fall**. A tabernacle that cannot be removed: neither will the nails thereof be taken away for ever, neither will any of the cords thereof be broken (Isa 33:20). And why? **It was founded on a rock**, i.e., Christ.

673. Next he sets out a likeness, setting forth the outcome of the one who hears and does not do. And concerning this he first sets out the building process; second, the attack, at **and the rain fell**; third, the destruction, at **and it fell**.

He says: **and everyone who hears these my words, and does not do them, will be like a foolish man**, who fell from the light of wisdom. Hence, *better is a child who is poor and wise, than a king who is old and foolish, who does not know to foresee for hereafter* (Eccl 4:13). Similarly, the fool is the devil. The house which he builds is the congregation of the unfaithful; hence, *those who are the obscure of the earth have been filled with dwellings of iniquity* (Ps 73:20).

Who built his house upon the sand. By sand are understood the infidels, who are unfruitful. Likewise, because of numerousness, for *the number of fools is infinite* (Eccl 1:15). Likewise, sand does not stick together, and in this way those men are always in a quarrel. So it was founded upon sand, i.e., an end, which is like a foundation, that is, he establishes his intention upon a temporal good.

Descendit pluvia, idest bona doctrina, ***venerunt flumina***, idest sacri doctores, ***flaverunt venti***, idest angeli; Ps. CIII, 4: *qui facit angelos suos spiritus*. ***Et irruerunt in domum illam, et cecidit***. Apoc. XIV, 8: *cecidit, cecidit Babylon*, scilicet per praedicationem. ***Et fuit magna eius ruina***.

674. Si velimus adaptare similitudinem, dicendum est sic, quod homo debet aedificare sicut Christus. Et hoc docet Apostolus I Cor. c. III, 10: *unusquisque videat quomodo superaedificet*. Aliquis enim aedificat habitaculum Dei; quidam e contrario, ut infra, et, ut habetur I Cor. III, 12, quidam super stipulam aedificant.

Fundamentum enim est illud super quod ponit aliquis intentionem suam. Quidam enim audiunt ut sciant, et hi aedificant super intellectum: et haec est aedificatio super arenam; unde Iac. I, 23: *qui audit, et non facit, similis est viro consideranti vultum nativitatis suae in speculo*. Unde super mutabile aedificant. Quidam autem audit ut faciat et diligat; et hic aedificat super petram, quia super firmum et stabile; Prov. XXII, 6: *adolescens iuxta viam suam, etiam cum senuerit, non recedet ab illa*. Istud enim fundamentum est super caritatem. Apostolus Rom. VIII, 35: *quis nos separabit a caritate Christi?*

675. Sed hic potest quaeri quare fundamentum quod est in intellectu, instabile, et non firmum est, sed quod in affectu.

Ratio est quia intellectus est universalium: non enim potest scire multa nisi in universali; ideo vagando circa universale non est stabilitas; sed operationes et affectus sunt circa particularia, et circa consuetudinem bonam; ideo si tentatio veniat, adhaeret ei quod consuevit, scilicet operationi bonae: ideo resistit.

676. Sed tunc quaeritur quid intelligat per pluviam.

Ideo dicendum quod diabolus numquam tentat primo in maioribus, sed primo in minoribus, deinde procedit ad maiora. Unde per pluviam cogitatio prava. Tentat ergo in cogitatione prava; et si consentit, tentat postea in maiori, et sic postea augmentatur. Et ex istis fiunt flumina: et post totis viribus irruit, et necessario cadit; Eccli. XIX, 1: *qui spernit modica, paulatim decidit*.

Vel sic. ***Pluvia***, tentatio carnis; ***flumina***, tentatio mundi; ***venti***, tentatio diaboli.

Vel secundum Augustinum pluvia superstitiosa doctrina, cui inhaerens gravissime cadit, et haec facta est ruina magna; sed non magna quando titubat, et non

The rain fell, i.e., good teaching, ***the floods came***, i.e., the sacred teachers, ***the winds blew***, i.e., the angels; *who makes your angels spirits* (Ps 103:4). ***And they beat upon that house, and it fell***. *That great Babylon is fallen, is fallen*, namely by preaching (Rev 14:8). ***And great was the fall thereof***.

674. If we wish to adapt a likeness, one should say thus, that a man ought to build just as Christ did. And the Apostle teaches this: *according to the grace of God that is given to me, as a wise architect, I have laid the foundation; and another builds on it. But let every man take heed how he builds upon it* (1 Cor 3:10). For some build the dwelling place of God; some on the contrary build as below, and some build on straw (1 Cor 3:12).

For the foundation is that upon which someone sets his intention. For some hear that they may know, and these build upon understanding, and this is the building upon sand. Hence, *for if a man be a hearer of the word, and not a doer, he will be compared to a man beholding his own countenance in a glass* (Jas 1:23). Hence, they build upon what is changeable. And some hear that they may do and love, and these men build upon a rock, because they build upon what is firm and stable. *A young man according to his way, even when he is old he will not depart from it* (Prov 22:6). For this foundation is upon charity. The Apostle, *who then will separate us from the love of Christ?* (Rom 8:35).

675. But here it can be asked why the foundation which is in understanding is unstable, and is not firm, while that which is in emotion is.

The reason is that understanding is of universals, for one cannot know many things except in the universal; this is why, wandering around the universal, there is no stability. But operations and emotions concern particulars, and the habitual good; so if temptation comes, one clings to that which is customary, namely to good works, and so one resists.

676. But then it is asked what one may understand by the rain.

So one should say that the devil never tempts first in great things, but first in lesser things, going on from there to the greater. Hence by the rain is understood a bad thought. So he tempts with a bad thought, and if someone consents, he tempts afterward in greater things, and in this way it grows afterward. And from these come the floods. And after this he attacks with his whole force, and the man falls by necessity. *He who contemns small things, will fall by little and little* (Sir 19:1).

Or, in this way: ***rain***, the temptation of the flesh; ***floods***, the temptation of the world; ***winds***, the temptation of the devil.

Or, according to Augustine, the rains are superstitious teachings: those who cling to them fall most gravely, and this is made a great destruction. But it is not great when a

cadit, quia cum accidit tentatio, timet et dolet. Quidam vero totaliter; Ps. CXXXVI, 7: *exinanite, exinanite usque ad fundamentum in ea.* Vel dicitur **ruina magna**, quia impoenitens est cor; Iob XXI, 13: *ducunt in bonis dies suos, et in puncto ad inferna descendunt.*

677. Et factum est cum consummasset Iesus verba haec, mirabantur turbae. Ponitur effectus.

Erat enim triplex modus hominum qui sequebantur Dominum Iesum. Quidam enim mirabantur et scandalizabantur, ut Pharisaei, de quibus inf. XV. Quidam mirabantur, sed non scandalizabantur, ut turbae. Quidam vero, ut perfecti, non mirabantur.

Sed quaerendum de hoc quod dicit **turbae**, quia non erant ibi turbae. Et potest dici quod factus est sermo et turbae, et discipulis; sed in monte sub cacumine montis erat quaedam planities. Discipuli ergo erant in cacumine cum Christo; sed turbae in planitie. Vel potest dici quod primo discipulis, et post turbis. Vel potest dici: secutae sunt eum turbae discipulorum.

678. Sed quae erat ratio admirationis? Quia erat **docens tamquam potestatem habens**. Unde in eo impletur quod dicitur Eccle. c. VIII, 4: *sermo illius potestate plenus est.* Unde quasi **potestatem habens**, quia ut Dominus loquebatur, vel sicut legislator. Vel **sicut potestatem habens**, cum virtute penetrandi cor. Unde dicitur Ps. LXVII, 34: *dabit voci suae vocem virtutis.* Vel cum potestate faciendi miracula: quia quod dicebat miraculis confirmabat.

679. Augustinus dicit, quod omnia quae dicuntur in hoc sermone debent reduci ad septem dona, et ad beatitudines, quia quod primo dicitur **non occides**, hoc pertinet ad donum timoris, et ad beatitudinem paupertatis. Istud autem quo sequitur. **Esto consentiens adversario**, pertinet ad donum pietatis, per quod impletur mansuetudo. Illud autem **non moechaberis** etc. pertinet ad donum scientiae, per quam impletur beatitudo luctus. Istud de sustinendo, ad donum fortitudinis, quo impletur, et ad beatitudinem **beati qui esuriunt et sitiunt iustitiam** et cetera. Illud autem quod dicitur **diligite inimicos vestros**, ad donum consilii, quo impletur beatitudo misericordiae. Per illud vero quod sequitur in VI cap., de non habendo sollicitudinem, usque ad **intrate per angustam portam**, intendit mundare cor: unde pertinet ad donum intelligentiae, et ad beatitudinem quae est munditia cordis; unde **beati mundo corde, quoniam ipsi Deum videbunt**. Quicquid autem sequitur, ad donum sapientiae.

man staggers, and does not fall, for when temptation happens, he fears and sorrows. But some men fall totally; *rase it, rase it, even to the foundation thereof* (Ps 136:7). Or it is called a **great fall** because the heart is impenitent; *they spend their days in wealth, and in a moment they go down to hell* (Job 21:13).

677. And it came to pass when Jesus had fully ended these words, that the people were in admiration at his doctrine. The effect is set down.

For there were three sorts of men who followed the Lord Jesus. For some marveled and were scandalized, like the Pharisees, spooen about below (Matt 15). Some marveled, but were not scandalized, like the crowds. But some, like the perfect, did not marvel.

But one should ask why it says, **the people**, because the crowds were not there. And one can say that the speech was made to the crowds and to the disciples; but there were plateaus on the mountain, under the summit. So the disciples were on the summit with Christ, but the crowds on a plateau. Or one can say that he spoke first to the disciples, and afterwards to the crowds. Or one can say that crowds of disciples followed him.

678. But what was the reason for wonderment? Because he was **teaching them as one having power**. Hence in him is fulfilled what is said, *and his word is full of power* (Eccl 8:4). Hence he spoke as **one having power**, because he spoke as the Lord, or as a law giver. Or, **as one having power**, with the power of penetrating the heart. Hence it is said, *behold he will give to his voice the voice of power* (Ps 67:34). Or with the power of working miracles, because he confirmed what he said with miracles.

679. Augustine says that everything said in this speech should be led back to the seven gifts, and to the beatitudes, because what was said first, **you shall not kill** (Matt 5:21), pertains to the gift of fear, and to the beatitude of poverty. And that which follows, **be in agreement with your adversary quickly, while you are on the way with him** (Matt 5:25), pertains to the gift of piety, through which meekness is fulfilled. And **do not commit adultery** (Matt 5:27), pertains to the gift of knowledge, through which the beatitude of mourning is fulfilled. The one about enduring pertains to the gift of fortitude, by which it is fulfilled, and to the beatitude, **blessed are they who hunger and thirst after justice** (Matt 5:6). And, **love your enemies** (Matt 5:44), pertains to the gift of counsel, by which the beatitude of mercy is fulfilled. But by that which follows in chapter six, about not having anxiety, up to **enter in at the narrow gate** (Matt 7:13), he intends to cleanse the heart. Hence it pertains to the gift of understanding, and to the beatitude which is cleanness of heart; hence **blessed are the clean of heart: for they will see God** (Matt 5:8). And whatever comes after that pertains to the gift of wisdom.

CHAPTER 8

Lecture 1

8:1 Cum autem descendisset Iesus de monte, secutae sunt eum turbae multae. [n. 681]

8:2 Et ecce leprosus veniens adorabat eum, dicens: Domine, si vis, potes me mundare. [n. 682]

8:3 Et extendens Iesus manum, tetigit eum dicens: volo, mundare. Et confestim mundata est lepra eius. [n. 685]

8:4 Et ait illi Iesus: vide, nemini dixeris: sed vade, ostende te sacerdoti, et offer munus tuum quod praecepit Moyses in testimonium illis. [n. 688]

8:1 Καταβάντος δὲ αὐτοῦ ἀπὸ τοῦ ὄρους ἠκολούθησαν αὐτῷ ὄχλοι πολλοί.

8:2 καὶ ἰδοὺ λεπρὸς προσελθὼν προσεκύνει αὐτῷ λέγων· κύριε, ἐὰν θέλῃς δύνασαί με καθαρίσαι.

8:3 καὶ ἐκτείνας τὴν χεῖρα ἥψατο αὐτοῦ λέγων· θέλω, καθαρίσθητι· καὶ εὐθέως ἐκαθαρίσθη αὐτοῦ ἡ λέπρα.

8:4 καὶ λέγει αὐτῷ ὁ Ἰησοῦς· ὅρα μηδενὶ εἴπῃς, ἀλλὰ ὕπαγε σεαυτὸν δεῖξον τῷ ἱερεῖ καὶ προσένεγκον τὸ δῶρον ὃ προσέταξεν Μωϋσῆς, εἰς μαρτύριον αὐτοῖς.

8:1 And when he had come down from the mountain, great multitudes followed him. [n. 681]

8:2 And behold a leper came and adored him, saying: Lord, if you will it, you can make me clean. [n. 682]

8:3 And Jesus stretching forth his hand, touched him, saying: I will it, be made clean. And immediately his leprosy was cleansed. [n. 685]

8:4 And Jesus said to him: see that you tell no man: but go, show yourself to the priest, and offer the gift which Moses commanded for a testimony unto them. [n. 688]

---

680. Posset videri quod ex iactantia loqueretur Dominus; ideo auctoritatem suam signis commendat.

Primo ergo ponuntur signa, quibus liberantur homines a corporalibus periculis;

secundo a spiritualibus, cap. IX.

Circa primum duo facit.

Primo ponit signa quibus homines liberantur a periculis provenientibus ex intrinsecis causis;

secundo ex extrinsecis, ut tempestate, ibi *et ascendente eo in naviculam*.

Commendat auctoritatem, quia statim, quia absens, quia perfecte, quia multos.

Quia statim, in leproso; quia absens, in servo centurionis; quia perfecte, in socru Petri; quia multos, in aliis multis.

Circa primum tria.

Primo testes miraculi introducuntur;

secundo infirmus inducitur, ibi *et ecce leprosus*;

tertio auxilium praebetur, ibi *et extendens Iesus manum, tetigit eum dicens volo, mundare*.

681. Dicit ergo *cum autem descendisset Iesus de monte* et cetera. Mons iste est caelum; Ps. LXVII, 17: *mons in quo beneplacitum est Deo habitare in eo*. Unde postquam descendit de caelo *secutae sunt eum turbae*; Phil. II, v. 7: *exinanivit semetipsum formam servi accipiens, et habitu inventus ut homo* et cetera. Vel per

680. It could seem that the Lord spoke out of boasting; so he commends his authority by signs.

First, then, the signs are set out by which men are freed from bodily dangers;

second, from spiritual (Matt 9).

About the first, he does two things:

first, he sets out the signs by which men are freed from dangers coming from intrinsic causes;

second, from extrinsic, such as a storm, there **and when he entered into the boat** (Matt 8:23).

He commends his authority, because he cures at once, because he cures while absent, because he cures perfectly, and because he cures many.

Because at once, in the leper; because while absent, in the centurion's servant; because perfectly, in the mother of Peter's wife; because many, in many others.

Concerning the first, three things:

first, the witnesses of the miracle are introduced;

second, the sick man is introduced, at **and behold a leper**;

third, help is offered, at **and Jesus stretching forth his hand, touched him, saying: I will it, be made clean.**

681. It says then, **and when he had come down from the mountain**. That mountain is heaven; *a mountain in which God is well pleased to dwell* (Ps 67:17). Hence after he descended from heaven, **great multitudes followed him**; *but emptied himself, taking the form of a servant, being made in the likeness of men, and in habit found as a man* (Phil 2:7).

montem altitudo doctrinae; Ps. XXXV, 7: *iustitia tua sicut montes Dei.* Cum esset in monte, idest cum altam duxit vitam, secuti sunt eum discipuli sui. **Et cum descendisset, secutae sunt eum turbae;** I ad Cor. III, 1: *non potui vobis loqui quasi spiritualibus.*

682. Secundo, persona infirmi introducitur: et ponuntur duo. Primo infirmitas ostenditur; secundo sollicitudo adhibetur.

Infirmitas, quia est **leprosus**: et hoc significat spirituales infirmitates. Quaedam enim infirmitates sunt intra latentes, ut febres: quaedam vero, etsi sunt ab intra, eius tamen effectus patet exterius, ut lepra. Ille ergo leprosus est, cuius mala voluntas manifestatur per malum actum; Is. LIII, 4: *et nos putavimus eum quasi leprosum.*

Sed quaestio est, quia in Luca habetur, quod cum veniret Capharnaum mundavit leprosum.

Dicendum, quod Matthaeus sequitur historiam, quia cum iret in Capharnaum, in via apparuit ei leprosus.

683. Sequitur sollicitudo, quia primo venit; secundo adoravit; unde dicit **ecce leprosus**. Sic peccator per fidem venit, sed adorat per humilitatem; Ps. XXXIII, 19: *humiles spiritu salvabit Deus.* Item confitetur Christi potentiam, cum dicit **Domine, si vis, potes me mundare.** Item vocat Dominum. Si Dominus est, potest salvare. In Ps. XCIX, 3: *scitote, quoniam Dominus ipse est Deus.* Item confidit de Dei misericordia. Misericordem non oportet petere, sed solum indigentiam ei monstrare; sic iste **Domine, si vis, potes me mundare.** Unde Ps. XXXVII, 10: *Domine, ante te omne desiderium meum, et gemitus meus a te non est absconditus.* Item ostendit sapientiam Christi, quia non petit nisi voluntatem suam: quia melius scit, quid opus sit tibi quam ipse. Ideo sapientiae Christi dimisit.

684. Deinde tangit auxilium.

Primo sanat.

Secundo instruit.

Primo tangitur opus;

secundo effectus, ibi **et confestim mundata est lepra eius.**

685. Christus tria facit curando. Extendit manum, quando auxilium impendit; Ps. CXLIII, v. 7: *emitte manum tuam de alto, et eripe me.* Aliquando extendit manum, sed non tangit; Is. LXV, 2: *expandi manus meas tota die ad populum incredulum* et cetera. Aliquando tangit; et hoc est quando immutat, ut in Ps. CXLIII, v. 5: *tange montes,* idest superbos, *et fumigabunt,* per compunctionem.

Sed quare tetigit, cum esset prohibitum in lege?

Or, by the mountain is understood high teaching; *your justice is as the mountains of God* (Ps 35:7). Since he was on the mountain, i.e., since he led a high life, his disciples followed him. **And when he had come down from the mountain, great multitudes followed him.** *And I, brethren, could not speak to you as unto spiritual* (1 Cor 3:1).

682. Second, the sick person is introduced; and two things are set down: first, the sickness is shown; second, the anxiety is introduced.

The sickness, for he is a **leper**; and this signifies spiritual sicknesses. For some sicknesses are hidden within, such as fever; but some, although they are within, yet their effects are exteriorly clear, such as leprousy. So that man is a leper whose evil will is manifested by an evil act. *We have thought him as it were a leper* (Isa 53:4).

But there is a question, because it is said that he cleansed the leper when he came down to Capernaum (Luke 4:31).

One should say that Matthew follows the history, because when he was going into Capernaum, the leper appeared to him in the road.

683. There follows the anxiety, for first he came; second, he adored; hence it says, **behold, a leper**. Thus the sinner comes by faith, but adores through humility; *he will save the humble of spirit* (Ps 33:19). Similarly, he confesses the power of Christ, when he says, **Lord, if you will it, you can make me clean.** Similarly, he calls him Lord. If he is the Lord, he is able to save. *Know that the Lord, he is God* (Ps 99:3). Similarly, he had confidence in God's mercy. It is not necessary to ask for mercy, but only to show him one's need; so this man did, **Lord, if you will it, you can make me clean.** Hence, *Lord, all my desire is before you, and my groaning is not hidden from you* (Ps 37:10). Similarly, he shows the wisdom of Christ, because he asks nothing but his will; because he knows what is beneficial for you better than you yourself do. For this reason, he left it to Christ's wisdom.

684. Then he touches upon the help.

First, he cures.

Second, he instructs.

First, the work is touched upon;

second, the effect, at **and immediately his leprosy was cleansed.**

685. Jesus does three things while curing. He extends his hand, when he lends help; *put forth your hand from on high, take me out, and deliver me* (Ps 143:7). Sometimes he extends his hand but does not touch; *I have spread forth my hands all the day to an unbelieving people* (Isa 65:2). Sometimes, he touches, and this is when he works a change, *Lord, bow down your heavens and descend: touch the mountains,* i.e., the proud, *and they will smoke* through remorse (Ps 143:5).

By why did he touch the leper, since it was forbidden in the law?

Hoc fecit ut monstraret se esse supra legem.Legitur de Eliseo quod non tetigit Naaman, sed misit eum ad Iordanem. Unde iste qui tetigit, videtur solvere legem. Sed secundum veritatem non solvit, quia prohibitum fuit propter contagionem. Quia igitur infici non potuit, tangere potuit. Item tetigit, ut humanitatem monstraret; quia non sufficit peccatori subdi Deo quantum ad divinitatem, sed et quantum ad humanitatem.

686. *Volo, mundare*. Hieronymus dicit, quod quidam male exponunt. Volunt enim quod ly ***mundare*** sit infiniti modi; sed hoc non est verum: immo quia dixerat, ***si vis***, respondit, ***volo***, et ly ***mundare*** est imperativi modi. Unde imperavit qui dixit, et facta sunt.

Item tetigit, ut daret doctrinam de virtute quae est in sacramentis, quia non solum requiritur tactus, sed verba: *quia cum accedit verbum ad elementum, fit sacramentum.*

Et per hoc exclusit tres errores, quando tetigit. Ostendit enim corpus verum contra Manichaeos. Quod dicit ***volo***, dicit contra Apollinarem. Per hoc quod est ***mundare***, ostendit Deum verum contra Photinum.

687. Et sequitur effectus ***et confestim mundata est lepra eius***, et curatus est. Chrysostomus dicit, quod citius quam posset dici hoc verbum, ***mundare***: quia istud in tempore dicitur, illud vero in instanti.

688. *Et ait illi*. Hic instruit eum: parum enim esset sanare nisi instrueret eum; Ps. XXXI, 8: *intellectum tibi dabo, et instruam te.* Primo iniungit ei taciturnitatem ***nemini dixeris***. Chrysostomus: *quia sciebat quod Iudaei calumniabantur de factis suis, ideo dixit* ***nemini dixeris***. Vel aliter. Quia hoc dixit ad exemplum. Quia enim supra docuerat abscondere opera bona; ideo dat exemplum, quod nullus in bonis operibus gloriari debet.

Sequitur ***sed vade, ostende te sacerdotibus***. Et quare hoc dicit? Quia tetigerat leprosum, ne penitus videretur fractor legum. Ad sacerdotes mittitur, ut habetur Lev. XIV, 2. ***Et offer munus tuum*** et cetera. Quare? Quia hoc erat praeceptum legis, quod sanatus a lepra offerret duos pullos turturum.

Sed secundum hoc videtur, quod cum Dominus praeceperit, adhuc sit tenendum. Dicendum quod figurae non debebant cessare, donec penitus veritas manifestaretur. Hoc autem non fuit nisi post resurrectionem.

689. *In testimonium illis*: et hoc exponitur dupliciter. ***Moyses praecepit in testimonium illis***. Et per hoc docet quod praecepta Moysi erant in testimonium Christi, sicut habetur Io. V, 46: *si crederetis Moysi, crederetis*

He did this to show that he is above the law. It is written of Eliseus that he did not touch Naaman, but sent him to the Jordan. Hence this man who touches seems to break the law. But he did not break it in truth, because touching lepers was forbidden on account of infection. So since he could not be infected, he could touch. Similarly, he touched in order to show his humanity, because it is not enough for the sinner to be subject to God with respect to the divinity, but he must be subject also with respect to the humanity.

686. *I will it, be made clean*. Jerome says that certain men explain this badly, for they would have it that *mundare* is in the infinitive mode. But this is not true, but rather because he had said, ***if you will it***, he responded, ***I will it***, and *mundare* is in the imperative mode. Hence he commands what he said, and it was done.

Likewise, he touched that he might give a teaching about the power which is in the sacraments, because there is required not only touch, but words, because as Augustine says in his book *On John*: *when the word approaches the element, the sacrament comes about.*

And by this he excludes three errors, when he touched. For he shows that the body is true, against the Manichees. When he says, ***I will it***, he speaks against Apollinaris. By the words ***be made clean***, he shows himself to be truly God, against Photinus.

687. And there follows the effect: ***and immediately his leprosy was cleansed***, and he was cured. Chrysostom says that it happened faster than one can say the words ***be made clean***, because these are said in time, but that happened in an instant.

688. *And Jesus said to him*. Here he instructs him; for to heal would not be enough unless he also instructed him. *I will give you understanding, and I will instruct you* (Ps 31:8). First, he enjoins him to keep silence: ***see that you tell no man***. Chrysostom: *because he knew that the Jews were misrepresenting his deeds, he said,* ***see that you tell no man***. Or in another way, one can say that he did this as an example. For since he had taught us above to hide our good works, he gives an example, that no one should glory in good works.

There follows ***but go, show yourself to the priest***. And why did he say this? Because he had touched a leper, lest he should seem to be a complete breaker of the law. He is sent to the priest, as is commanded (Lev 14:2). ***And offer the gift***. Why? Because this was a precept of the law, that the one healed of leprosy should offer two young turtle-doves.

But according to this it seems that what the Lord commanded should hold true even now. One should say that the figures were not supposed to cease until the truth was thoroughly manifested. But this did not happen until after the resurrection.

689. *For a testimony unto them*. And this is explained in two ways. ***The gift which Moses commanded for a testimony unto them***. And by this he teaches that the precepts of Moses were in witness to Christ, as it is said, *for if you*

forsitan et mihi. Vel aliter. *In testimonium illis*, idest, contra illos, qui viderunt miracula, et non crediderunt. Vel *in testimonium illis*, scilicet curationis tuae. Quia cum receperint oblationem tuam, non poterunt negare.

690. Item secundum mysticum intellectum tria a Christo iniunguntur. Ut erubescat de peccato; contra illos de quibus dicitur Is. III, 9: *peccatum suum quasi Sodoma praedicaverunt, nec absconderunt.* Unde Eccli. IV, v. 25: *est confusio adducens peccatum, et est confusio adducens gloriam et gratiam.* Item debet ostendere sacerdoti confitendo. Iac. V, v. 16: *confitemini alterutrum peccata vestra.* Et hic videtur Dominus iniungere confessionem. *Et confestim sanatus est*: quia in ipsa contritione quando dolet et proponit confiteri et abstinere, remittitur peccatum, iuxta illud Ps. XXXI, 5: *dixi: confitebor adversum me iniustitiam meam, et tu remisisti iniquitatem peccati mei.* Item iniungitur satisfactio, cum dicit **offer munus tuum.** Item docet observare mandata, cum dicit **sicut praecepit Moyses.**

believed Moses, you would perhaps believe me also; for he wrote of me (John 5:46). Or in another way: **for a testimony unto them**, i.e., against those who saw the miracles and did not believe. Or **for a testimony unto them**, namely to your being cured. Because when they receive your offering, they will not be able to deny it.

690. Likewise, according to a mystical understanding, Christ enjoins three things. That one should be ashamed of sin, against those of whom it is said, *they have proclaimed abroad their sin as Sodom, and they have not hid it* (Isa 3:9). Hence, *for there is a shame that brings sin, and there is a shame that brings glory and grace* (Sir 4:25). Similarly, one ought to show sin to the priest by confessing. *Confess therefore your sins one to another* (Jas 5:16). And here the Lord seems to enjoin confession. **And immediately his leprosy was cleansed**, because in contrition itself, when a man sorrows and intends to confess and to refrain from his sin, the sin is forgiven, *I said I will confess against myself my injustice to the Lord: and you have forgiven the wickedness of my sin* (Ps 31:5). Likewise, satisfaction is enjoined, when he says, **offer the gift**. Likewise, he teaches us to observe the commandments, when he says, **which Moses commanded**.

Lecture 2

8:5 Cum autem introisset Capharnaum, accessit ad eum centurio, rogans eum, [n. 691]

8:6 et dicens: Domine, puer meus iacet in domo paralyticus, et male torquetur. [n. 695]

8:7 Et ait illi Iesus: ego veniam et curabo eum. [n. 696]

8:8 Et respondens centurio ait: Domine, non sum dignus ut intres sub tectum meum, sed tantum dic verbo, et sanabitur puer meus. [n. 697]

8:9 Nam et ego homo sum sub potestate constitutus, habens sub me milites: et dico huic: vade, et vadit; et alii: veni, et venit; et servo meo: fac hoc, et facit. [n. 700]

8:10 Audiens autem Iesus miratus est, et sequentibus se dixit: amen dico vobis, non inveni tantam fidem in Israel. [n. 702]

8:11 Dico autem vobis, quod multi ab oriente et occidente venient, et recumbent cum Abraham, et Isaac, et Iacob in regno caelorum; [n. 704]

8:12 filii autem regni eiicientur in tenebras exteriores: ibi erit fletus et stridor dentium. [n. 705]

8:13 Et dixit Iesus centurioni: vade et sicut credidisti, fiat tibi. Et sanatus est puer in hora illa. [n. 707]

8:5 Εἰσελθόντος δὲ αὐτοῦ εἰς Καφαρναοὺμ προσῆλθεν αὐτῷ ἑκατόνταρχος παρακαλῶν αὐτὸν

8:6 καὶ λέγων· κύριε, ὁ παῖς μου βέβληται ἐν τῇ οἰκίᾳ παραλυτικός, δεινῶς βασανιζόμενος.

8:7 καὶ λέγει αὐτῷ· ἐγὼ ἐλθὼν θεραπεύσω αὐτόν.

8:8 καὶ ἀποκριθεὶς ὁ ἑκατόνταρχος ἔφη· κύριε, οὐκ εἰμὶ ἱκανὸς ἵνα μου ὑπὸ τὴν στέγην εἰσέλθῃς, ἀλλὰ μόνον εἰπὲ λόγῳ, καὶ ἰαθήσεται ὁ παῖς μου.

8:9 καὶ γὰρ ἐγὼ ἄνθρωπός εἰμι ὑπὸ ἐξουσίαν, ἔχων ὑπ᾽ ἐμαυτὸν στρατιώτας, καὶ λέγω τούτῳ· πορεύθητι, καὶ πορεύεται, καὶ ἄλλῳ· ἔρχου, καὶ ἔρχεται, καὶ τῷ δούλῳ μου· ποίησον τοῦτο, καὶ ποιεῖ.

8:10 ἀκούσας δὲ ὁ Ἰησοῦς ἐθαύμασεν καὶ εἶπεν τοῖς ἀκολουθοῦσιν· ἀμὴν λέγω ὑμῖν, παρ᾽ οὐδενὶ τοσαύτην πίστιν ἐν τῷ Ἰσραὴλ εὗρον.

8:11 λέγω δὲ ὑμῖν ὅτι πολλοὶ ἀπὸ ἀνατολῶν καὶ δυσμῶν ἥξουσιν καὶ ἀνακλιθήσονται μετὰ Ἀβραὰμ καὶ Ἰσαὰκ καὶ Ἰακὼβ ἐν τῇ βασιλείᾳ τῶν οὐρανῶν,

8:12 οἱ δὲ υἱοὶ τῆς βασιλείας ἐκβληθήσονται εἰς τὸ σκότος τὸ ἐξώτερον· ἐκεῖ ἔσται ὁ κλαυθμὸς καὶ ὁ βρυγμὸς τῶν ὀδόντων.

8:13 καὶ εἶπεν ὁ Ἰησοῦς τῷ ἑκατοντάρχῃ· ὕπαγε, ὡς ἐπίστευσας γενηθήτω σοι. καὶ ἰάθη ὁ παῖς [αὐτοῦ] ἐν τῇ ὥρᾳ ἐκείνῃ.

8:5 And when he had entered into Capernaum, there came to him a centurion, beseeching him, [n. 691]

8:6 and saying, Lord, my servant lies at home sick of the palsy, and is grieviously tormented. [n. 695]

8:7 And Jesus said to him: I will come and heal him. [n. 696]

8:8 And the centurion making answer, said: Lord, I am not worthy that you should enter under my roof: but only say the word, and my servant will be healed. [n. 697]

8:9 For I also am a man subject to authority, having under me soldiers; and I say to this, go, and he goes, and to another, come, and he comes, and to my servant, do this, and he does it. [n. 700]

8:10 And Jesus hearing this, marvelled; and said to them who followed him: amen I say to you, I have not found such great faith in Israel. [n. 702]

8:11 And I say to you that many will come from the east and the west, and will sit down with Abraham, and Isaac, and Jacob in the kingdom of heaven: [n. 704]

8:12 But the children of the kingdom will be cast out into the exterior darkness: there will be weeping and gnashing of teeth. [n. 705]

8:13 And Jesus said to the centurion: go, and as you have believed, so be it done to you. And the servant was healed at the same hour. [n. 707]

---

691. *Cum autem introisset Capharnaum*. Hic ostenditur virtus Christi ex absentia. Et
     primo designatur pietas centurionis cum fide;
     secundo humilitas, ibi *et respondens centurio* et cetera.
     Circa primum duo, quia designatur
     primo pietas centurionis;
     secundo ostenditur Christi benignitas.
     Et circa primum tria.
     Primo locus ponitur;

691. *And when he had entered into Capernaum*. Here the power of Christ while absent is shown. And
     first, the piety of the centurion with faith is indicated;
     second, the humility, at *and the centurion making answer*.
     Concerning the first, two things:
     first, the centurion's piety is indicated;
     second, Christ's kindness.
     And concerning the first, three things:
     first, the place is set down;

secundo oratio describitur, ibi *Domine, puer meus iacet in domo paralyticus*;

tertio exauditio ponitur, ibi *et ait illi Iesus*.

692. Locus primo *cum introisset Capharnaum*, qui interpretatur 'villa pinguedinis,' scilicet villa gentium, quae pinguedine devotionis defluxit. Ps. LXII, 6: *sicut adipe et pinguedine repleatur anima mea*.

693. Deinde *accessit*.

Sed hic potest quaeri: quia Lucas posuit, quod misit sacerdotes.

Augustinus dicit quod non personaliter venit, sed quod dicitur quod venit, totum refertur ad intentionem: quia ille facit rem cuius auctoritate fit. Chrysostomus aliter, quia dicit quod iste constitutus erat super centum milites, et ideo erat praepositus. Unde Iudaei volentes adulari propter benevolentiam habendam, dixerunt ei: *Domine, nos ibimus, et impetrabimus vobis*. Tunc ut satisfaceret eis, permisit eos abire; sed post ipse secutus est eos.

694. Istud miraculum differt a primo in tribus. Quia primum Iudaeo fuit factum, secundum gentili; per quod datur intelligi, quod non solum pro Iudaeis, sed pro gentibus Christus venit.

Item in primo Iudaeus per se accessit, iste non. Et hoc quia miseretur Dominus aliquorum per propriam devotionem, quorumdam per aliorum intercessionem.

Item iste centurio potest intelligi aliquis angelus praesidens ibi ad salutem gentium, vel primitiae gentium. Item ille fuit leprosus, in quo immunditia quiescit. Paralytici autem sunt qui non possunt membra movere. Leprosi sunt intemperati, et paralytici sunt incontinentes. Et sunt paralytici, qui ex infirmitate peccant; leprosi, qui ex certa malitia. Per centurionem potest intelligi mens. Ad Eph. IV, v. 23: *renovamini spiritu mentis vestrae*.

695. Et iste dicit *Domine, puer meus*, idest servus meus. Et in hoc ostenditur benignitas centurionis, quia ita pro servo orat: unde facit illud quod dicitur in Eccli. XXXIII, v. 31: *si fuerit tibi servus fidelis, sit tibi sicut anima tua*. Et iste servus dicitur inferior pars animae.

Dicit ergo quod *iacet et male torquetur*; et loquitur ex affectu, quia quando aliquis diligit aliquem, reputat parvam aegritudinem valde magnam. Iacet ergo inferior pars animae, quando non potest se erigere, Gal. V, 17: *caro concupiscit adversus spiritum: et torquetur*. Homines lascivi gaudent: *laetantur enim cum male fecerint, et exultant in rebus pessimis*. Sed isti torquentur, quia cum peccent ex infirmitate, cum ceciderint, dolent. Et ita torquentur ex dolore.

second, the petition is described, at *Lord, my servant lies at home sick of the palsy*;

third, the response is set down, at *and Jesus said to him*.

692. First, the place, *when he had entered into Capernaum*, which is interpreted, 'village of fatness,' that is, the village of the gentiles, since it overflowed with the fatness of devotion. *Let my soul be filled as with marrow and fat* (Ps 62:6).

693. *There came to him a centurion.*

But here one can ask a question, because Luke sets down that he sent priests (Luke 7:3).

Augustine says that he did not come personally, but the fact that it says he came is referred to his intention, because he by whose authority a thing comes about does that thing. Chrysostom explains it in another way, for he says that this man had been set up over one hundred men, and so he was in command. Hence the Jews, wishing to flatter him so as to have his good will, said to him, *Lord, we will go, and we will plead for you*. Then, to satisfy them, he permitted them to go; but afterwards he himself followed them.

694. This miracle differs from the first in three ways. For the first was done for a Jew, the second for a gentile; by which one is given to understand that Christ came not only for the Jews, but for the gentiles.

Likewise in the first, the Jew himself approached Christ, but not this man. And this is because the Lord has mercy on some through their own devotion, and on some through the intercession of others.

Likewise, by the centurion can be understood an angel in command there for the salvation of the gentiles, or the firstfruits of the gentiles. Similarly, the man in whom uncleaness rested was a leper; but paralytics are those who cannot move their members. Lepers are intemperate, and paralytics are incontinent. And those who sin out of weakness are paralytics; those who sin out of a fixed malice are lepers. By the centurion can be understood the mind. *And be renewed in the spirit of your mind* (Eph 4:23).

695. And he says, *Lord, my servant*. And the centurion's kindness is shown by the fact that he pleaded in this way for his servant. Hence he does what is said, *if you have a faithful servant, let him be to you as your own soul* (Sir 33:31). And that servant names the lower part of the soul.

He says then that he *lies at home sick of the palsy, and is grieviously tormented*; and he speaks with emotion, because when someone loves someone, he considers a slight sickness very great. Therefore the lower part of the soul lies down when it cannot raise itself; *for the flesh lusts against the spirit* (Gal 5:17). *And is grieviously tormented*. Who are glad when they have done evil, and rejoice in most wicked things (Prov 2:14). But these men are tormented, because since they sin out of weakness, they sorrow when they fall. And in this way they are tormented by sorrow.

696. *Et ait illi Iesus: ego veniam et curabo eum*; idest non loquar. Unde nota quod nullus auderet tantum petere, quantum Dominus dare. Dicit *veniam, et curabo eum*, quia praesentia Christi est causa salutis.

Sed notandum quod ad filium reguli noluit ire, et ad servum ivit; quod esset contra multos qui nolunt visitare nisi magnos, contra illud Eccli. IV, 7: *congregationi pauperum affabilem te facito*.

697. Sequitur *et respondens centurio*. Posita fuit cum fide benignitas centurionis; nunc tangitur humilitas cum fide.

Primo ergo ponitur humilitas et fides;

secundo benignitas Christi, ibi *audiens autem Iesus miratus est*.

Circa primum tria facit.

Primo confitetur suam indignitatem, ibi *sed tantum dic verbo*:

secundo Christi potestatem;

deinde inducit similitudinem, ibi *nam et ego homo sum sub potestate constitutus*.

698. Obtulerat se Dominus benignum. Sed quia iste gentilis erat, reputavit se indignum, dicens *Domine, non sum dignus* et cetera. Sic etiam Petrus dixit, Lc. V, 8: *recede a me, quia homo peccator sum*. Et dicit Augustinus, quod confitendo se indignum, reddidit se dignum. Et sicut iste dicit, sic et nos debemus dicere: non sum dignus ut intres in corpus meum.

699. Deinde tangitur fides centurionis confitentis potestatem Christi: *dic tantum verbo, et sanabitur puer meus*; quia, ut habetur Sap. XVI, 12, *non herba, non malagma sanavit eos, sed sermo tuus, Domine*. Et in Ps. CVI, 20: *misit verbum suum, et sanavit eos*.

700. Deinde inducit similitudinem, et probat a minori. Et describit ordinem primo; secundo potestatem, et dicit *nam et ego homo sum sub potestate constitutus* et cetera.

Et tangitur ordo: quia quidam sunt superiores, ita quod non habent superiorem se; quidam sunt superiores, ita quod habent superiorem se; quidam vero inferiores qui non habent inferiores se; quidam ergo sunt medii; et de istis erat iste, quia erat sub tribuno, sed habebat sub se milites. Habebat enim sub se quosdam quorum erat gubernator; et isti erant milites; unde dicit *et dico uni: vade, et vadit; et alii: veni, et venit*; in quo commendatur nobis obedientia. Ad Hebr. XIII, 17: *obedite praepositis vestris, et subiacete eis*. Item alios habebat servos quibus cibaria ministrabat. Eccli. XXXIII, 25: *cibaria, et virga, et onus asino; panis, et disciplina; et opus servo*. *Et servo meo: fac hoc, et facit*. Unde vult arguere a minori: quia si ego qui sum in potestate constitutus, haec

696. *And Jesus said to him: I will come and heal him*; i.e., I will not speak. Hence notice that no one would dare to ask as much as the Lord gives. He says, *I will come and heal him*, because Christ's presence is the cause of salvation.

But one should notice that he did not wish to go to a ruler's child, but he went to a servant; which would be against many, who will only visit the great, contrary to, *make yourself affable to the congregation of the poor* (Sir 4:7).

697. There follows *and the centurion making answer*. The centurion's kindness with faith had been set down; now his humility with faith is touched upon.

First, then, the humility and faith are set down;

second, Christ's kindness, at *and Jesus hearing this, marvelled*.

Concerning the first, he does three things:

first, he confesses his own unworthiness, at *but only say the word*;

second, Christ's power;

then he brings in a likeness, at *for I also am a man subject to authority*.

698. The Lord shows himself to be kind. But because this man was a gentile, he considered himself unworthy, saying, *Lord, I am not worthy*. So also Peter said, *depart from me, for I am a sinful man, O Lord* (Luke 5:8). And Augustine says that, by confessing himself unworthy, he rendered himself worthy. And just as this man says, so ought we to say: I am not worthy that you should enter into my body.

699. Then he touches upon the faith of the centurion confessing the power of Christ: *but only say the word, and my servant will be healed*. Because, as is had, *for it was neither herb, nor mollifying plaster that healed them, but your word, O Lord* (Wis 16:12). And, *he sent his word, and healed them* (Ps 106:20).

700. Then he brings in a likeness and he argues from the lesser. And he describes first the order; second, the power, and he says, *for I also am a man subject to authority*.

And order is touched upon, because some are superiors such that they have none above them; some are superiors such that they they have one above them; indeed, some are inferiors such that they have none below them. So some are in the middle, and this man was one of those, because he was under the tribune, but had soldiers under himself. For he had certain men under him of whom he was the governor, and these were soldiers. Hence he says, *and I say to this, go, and he goes, and to another, come, and he comes*; in which obedience is commended to us. *Obey your prelates, and be subject to them* (Heb 13:17). Likewise he had other servants to whom he supplied food. *Fodder, and a wand, and a burden are for an ass: bread, and correction, and work for a slave* (Sir 33:25). *And to my servant, do this, and he does it*. Hence he wishes to argue from the lesser, for

possum, quanto magis Dominus dominantium potest et cetera.

701. Sed videndum quod rationales creaturae sunt liberae, et sunt sicut milites; Iob c. XXV, 3: *numquid est numerus militum eius?* Et ideo dicitur Dominus exercituum. Sed creatura irrationalis habet subiectionem servilem, quia non habet liberi arbitrii facultatem. Vult ergo dicere: *quia tibi natura obedit, dic naturae, et obedit tibi, quia sermo tuus iudicio plenus est.*

Videndum est, quod istud duplex dominium invenitur in anima: anima enim praesidet corpori; ratio vero irascibili et concupiscibili. Prima est dominativa potestas, quia ad imperium animae movetur corpus; secunda praeest aliis quadam imperativa potestate, et dominativa, vel regali: unde habent aliquid de motu suo. Et haec sunt quasi milites; Iac. c. IV, 1: *unde bella et lites in vobis? Nonne ex concupiscentiis, quae militant in membris vestris?* I Petr. II, 11: *hortamur vos abstinere a carnalibus desideriis, quae militant adversus animam.*

Debemus ergo dicere huic **vade**, idest malis moribus; **et veni**, scilicet bonis moribus, et **servo** huic, **fac hoc**. Unde corpus debemus operi applicare, ut *sicut exhibuimus membra nostra servire immunditiae et iniquitati ad iniquitatem, ita nunc exhibeamus membra nostra servire iustitiae in sanctificationem*, ut habetur Rom. VI, 19.

702. Audiens autem Iesus miratus est et cetera. Hic tangitur Christi benignitas.

Sed quid est quod dicit **admiratus est**? Quia admiratio non cadit in Deo; quia non fit nisi ex ignorantia causae, quae non potest esse in Deo. Item est apprehensio magnitudinis effectus, quod fit ex imaginatione et phantasia alicuius effectus magni, et sic potest cadere etiam in Christo: unde **admiratus est**, idest magnum reputavit, et hoc turbis sequentibus ostendit.

703. Et commendavit eum, unde sequentibus se dixit: **non inveni tantam fidem in Israel**.

Sed quid est? Nonne in Abraham, Isaac et Iacob fuit maior fides? Dicendum, quod immo; sed quod hic dicitur, intelligitur pro tempore illo.

Sed tunc est quaestio de apostolis, et Martha, et Maria. Et dicendum quod iste maioris fidei erat, quia nullum praeambulum viderat, sicut isti qui miracula viderant. Item Petrus venit ad vocem Andreae, Andreas ad vocem Ioannis. Item in verbo Marthae fuit aliquid dubietatis, quia dixit: *domine, si fuisses hic, frater meus non fuisset mortuus*; quasi absens non posset. Sed in verbo istius nihil fuit dubietatis.

---

if I who am established in power can do these things, how much more can the Lord of lords.

701. But one should see that rational creatures are free, and are like soldiers; *is there any numbering of his soldiers?* (Job 25:3). And therefore he is called the Lord of hosts. But the irrational creature has a servile subjection, because it does not have the faculty of free judgment. Therefore he wishes to say: *because nature obeys you speak to nature; and it obeys you, because your word is full of judgment.*

One should see that these two dominions are found in the soul. For the soul is in command of the body, but reason is in command of the irascible and concupiscible parts. The first is a dominating power, because the body moves at the soul's command; the second stands over the others by a certain imperative power, and dominating, or kingly power: hence they have something of their own motion. And these are, as it were, soldiers; *from whence are wars and contentions among you? Are they not from here, from your concupiscences, which war in your members?* (Jas 4:1). *I beseech you . . . to refrain yourselves from carnal desires which war against the soul* (1 Pet 2:11).

Therefore we should say, **go**, i.e., to evil habits; and **come**, namely to good habits, and **to my servant, do this**. Hence we should devote our bodies to work that *as you have yielded your members to serve uncleanness and iniquity, unto iniquity; so now yield your members to serve justice, unto sanctification* (Rom 6:19).

702. And Jesus hearing this, marveled. Here Christ's kindness is touched upon.

But why does it say that Jesus **marvelled**? For astonishment does not arise in God, since it arises out of an ignorance of the cause, which cannot be in God. There is also the apprehension of the greatness of an effect, which arises from the imagination and phantasm of some great effect, and in this way it can arise even in Christ. Hence **Jesus . . . marvelled**, i.e., considered it great, and he pointed this out to the crowds which followed him.

703. And he commended him, hence he said to those following him, **amen I say to you, I have not found such great faith in Israel**.

But why is this? Was there not greater faith in Abraham, Isaac, and Jacob? Indeed, one should say so; but what he says here is understood as about that time.

But then there is a question about the apostles, and Martha and Mary. And one should say that this man was of greater faith, because he had seen nothing preparatory, as they had who had seen the miracles. And Peter came at the call of Andrew, Andrew at the call of John. And there was something of doubt in the words of Martha, because she said, *Lord, if you had been here, my brother would not have died* (John 11:21); as though he could not work while absent. But there was no doubt in this man's words.

Aliter exponit Chrysostomus. Quia magnum et parvum aliquando dicuntur non absolute, sed in comparatione, sicut dicuntur in domo multi, in theatro pauci. Unde **non inveni tantam fidem in Israel**, scilicet per comparationem illius gentilis. Deut. XXVIII, 43: *advena qui tecum moratur in terra, ascendet super te, eritque sublimior.*

704. Dico autem vobis. Occasione huius agit de comparatione Iudaeorum et gentilium; et primo de vocatione gentilium; secundo de reprobatione Iudaeorum.

Dico quod multi ab oriente et occidente venient et cetera. Et dicitur istud in comparatione, quia *multi sunt vocati, pauci vero electi*; infra XX, 16. **Ab oriente et occidente**, ita quod per hoc totus mundus intelligatur. Vel **ab oriente**, in tempore prosperitatis; **et occidente**, scilicet in tempore adversitatis. Vel **ab oriente**, in tempore iuventutis; **et occidente**, in tempore senectutis. **Et recumbent.** Iste recubitus opulentia est rerum spiritualium, scilicet in contemplatione. Lc. XXII, 29: *ecce dispono vobis regnum, ut edatis et bibatis super mensam meam in regno meo.* Et Is. LXV, v. 13: *ecce servi mei comedent, et vos esurietis; ecce servi mei bibent, et vos sitietis* et cetera.

Sed quare **cum Abraham, Isaac et Iacob**? Quia gentiles per fidem iustificantur, sicut Iudaei, ut habetur Rom. IV, 12 et Gen. XII. Item istis facta est repromissio, quia *in semine tuo benedicentur omnes gentes*, Gen. c. XV, 18. Ideo isti recumbent cum patribus suis.

705. Sequitur ***filii autem regni eiicientur in tenebras exteriores***. Hic ostendit reprobationem Iudaeorum, et describit poenam damni, quia amittent bona, et incurrent mala.

Dicit autem **filii regni**, quia in illis Deus regnabat; Ps. LXXV, 2: *notus in Iudaea Deus, in Israel magnum nomen eius.* Item figuris legis servi erant. Item facta est eis promissio, ut habetur Rom. IV, 13.

706. Eiicientur in tenebras exteriores. Et haec est poena damni. Consequenter enumerat mala quae incurrent, quia qui primo quoad intellectum incurrerunt tenebras interiores, eiicientur postea in tenebras exteriores, quia tunc erunt totaliter alienati a Deo, qui est lux vera. Et hoc est quod dicitur Tob. c. IV, 11: *eleemosyna ab omni peccato et a morte liberat, et non patietur animas ire in tenebras.* Item quantum ad affectum **ibi erit fletus**. Fletus nuntiat dolorem; Is. LXV, 14: *ecce servi mei laetabuntur, et vos confundemini.* Item ostenditur passio in corpore, quia **stridor dentium**: habebunt enim corpora in resurrectione; Prov. XIX, 29: *parata sunt derisoribus iudicia, et mallei, et ferrum*: quae iudicia doloris pertinent ad concupiscibilem, stridor ad irascibilem. Vel secundum Hieronymum, utrumque pertinet ad poenam corporalem, quia resurrectio non erit solum in anima,

Chrysostom explains it in another way. For sometimes great and small are not said absolutely, but in comparison, just as the same number of people are called many in a house, but few in a theatre. Hence, *I have not found such great faith in Israel*, namely by comparison with this gentile. *The stranger who lives with you in the land, will rise up over you* (Deut 28:43).

704. And I say to you. Taking this occasion, he makes a comparison of the Jews and the gentiles; and first, concerning the calling of the gentiles; second, concerning the rejection of the Jews.

I say to you that many will come from the east and the west. And this is said in comparison, because *many are called, but few chosen* (Matt 20:16). *From the east and the west*, such that by this the whole world is understood. Or, *from the east*, in the time of prosperity, *and the west*, in the time of affliction. Or, *from the east*, in the time of youth, and *from the west*, in the time of old age. *And will sit down.* This lying down is a wealth of spiritual things, namely in contemplation. *And I dispose to you . . . a kingdom; that you may eat and drink at my table, in my kingdom* (Luke 22:29). And, *behold my servants will eat, and you will be hungry: behold my servants will drink, and you will be thirsty* (Isa 65:13).

But why *with Abraham, Isaac, and Jacob*? Because the gentiles are justifed by faith, just as the Jews (Rom 4:12; Gen 12). Also because *in your seed will all the nations of the earth be blessed* (Gen 22:18). Therefore these will sit with their fathers.

705. There follows *but the children of the kingdom will be cast out into the exterior darkness.* Here he shows the rejection of the Jews, and describes the punishment of the damned, because they will lose good things, and meet with bad.

And he says, *the children of the kingdom*, because God reigned in them; *in Judea God is known: his name is great in Israel* (Ps 75:2). Also, they had served the figures of the law. Likewise, the promise was made to them (Rom 4:13).

706. Will be cast out into the exterior darkness. And this is the punishment of the damned. Next, he enumerates the evils which they meet with, for first, with respect to the intellect, they meet with interior darkness; afterward they will be thrown into the exterior darkness, because then they will be wholly alienated from God, who is the true light. And this is what is said, *for alms deliver from all sin, and from death, and will not suffer the soul to go into darkness* (Tob 4:11). Likewise, as regards emotion, *there will be weeping*. Weeping announces sorrow; *behold my servants will rejoice, and you will be confounded* (Isa 65:14). Similarly, he indicates suffering in the body, at *gnashing of teeth*, for they will have bodies in the resurrection. *Judgments are prepared for scorners: and striking hammers for the bodies of fools* (Prov 19:29), which judgments of sorrow pertain to the concupiscible part, the gnashing to the irascible part.

sed in corpore: quia erit et multus calor, et multum frigus; Iob XXIV, 19: *transibunt ab aquis nivis ad calorem nimium.*

707. Ostenditur Dei benignitas, cum dicit *et dixit Iesus centurioni: vade, et sicut credidisti fiat tibi.* Sed sequitur effectus *et sanatus est puer*, quia *sermo eius virtute plenus est*, Eccle. VIII, 4.

Or, according to Jerome, both pertain to bodily punishment, because the resurrection will not be only in the soul, but in the body, because there will be much heat, and much coldness. *Let him pass from the snow waters to excessive heat* (Job 24:19).

707. The kindness of God is shown, when it says, *and Jesus said to the centurion: go, and as you have believed, so be it done to you*. But there follows the effect: *and the servant was healed*, because *his word is full of power* (Eccl 8:4).

Lecture 3

8:14 Et cum venisset Iesus in domum Petri, vidit socrum eius iacentem et febricitantem, [n. 708]

8:15 et tetigit manum eius, et dimisit eam febris, et surrexit, et ministrabat eis. [n. 711]

8:16 Vespere autem facto, obtulerunt ei multos daemonia habentes, et eiiciebat spiritus verbo, et omnes male habentes curavit; [n. 713]

8:17 ut adimpleretur quod dictum est per Isaiam prophetam dicentem: *ipse infirmitates nostras accepit, et aegrotationes portavit.* [n. 715]

8:18 Videns autem Iesus turbas multas circum se, iussit ire trans fretum. [n. 716]

8:19 Et accedens unus scriba, ait illi: Magister, sequar te, quocumque ieris. [n. 718]

8:20 Et dicit ei Iesus: vulpes foveas habent, et volucres caeli nidos; Filius autem hominis non habet ubi caput suum reclinet. [n. 719]

8:21 Alius autem de discipulis eius ait illi: Domine, permitte me primum ire, et sepelire patrem meum. [n. 720]

8:22 Iesus autem ait illi: sequere me, et dimitte mortuos sepelire mortuos suos. [n. 721]

8:23 Et ascendente eo in naviculam, secuti sunt eum discipuli eius; [n. 723]

8:24 et ecce motus magnus factus est in mari, ita ut navicula operiretur fluctibus. Ipse vero dormiebat. [n. 725]

8:25 Et accesserunt ad eum discipuli eius, et suscitaverunt eum, dicentes: Domine, salva nos, perimus. [n. 727]

8:14 Καὶ ἐλθὼν ὁ Ἰησοῦς εἰς τὴν οἰκίαν Πέτρου εἶδεν τὴν πενθερὰν αὐτοῦ βεβλημένην καὶ πυρέσσουσαν·

8:15 καὶ ἥψατο τῆς χειρὸς αὐτῆς, καὶ ἀφῆκεν αὐτὴν ὁ πυρετός, καὶ ἠγέρθη καὶ διηκόνει αὐτῷ.

8:16 Ὀψίας δὲ γενομένης προσήνεγκαν αὐτῷ δαιμονιζομένους πολλούς· καὶ ἐξέβαλεν τὰ πνεύματα λόγῳ καὶ πάντας τοὺς κακῶς ἔχοντας ἐθεράπευσεν,

8:17 ὅπως πληρωθῇ τὸ ῥηθὲν διὰ Ἡσαΐου τοῦ προφήτου λέγοντος· αὐτὸς τὰς ἀσθενείας ἡμῶν ἔλαβεν καὶ τὰς νόσους ἐβάστασεν.

8:18 Ἰδὼν δὲ ὁ Ἰησοῦς ὄχλον περὶ αὐτὸν ἐκέλευσεν ἀπελθεῖν εἰς τὸ πέραν.

8:19 καὶ προσελθὼν εἷς γραμματεὺς εἶπεν αὐτῷ· διδάσκαλε, ἀκολουθήσω σοι ὅπου ἐὰν ἀπέρχῃ.

8:20 καὶ λέγει αὐτῷ ὁ Ἰησοῦς· αἱ ἀλώπεκες φωλεοὺς ἔχουσιν καὶ τὰ πετεινὰ τοῦ οὐρανοῦ κατασκηνώσεις, ὁ δὲ υἱὸς τοῦ ἀνθρώπου οὐκ ἔχει ποῦ τὴν κεφαλὴν κλίνῃ.

8:21 ἕτερος δὲ τῶν μαθητῶν [αὐτοῦ] εἶπεν αὐτῷ· κύριε, ἐπίτρεψόν μοι πρῶτον ἀπελθεῖν καὶ θάψαι τὸν πατέρα μου.

8:22 ὁ δὲ Ἰησοῦς λέγει αὐτῷ· ἀκολούθει μοι καὶ ἄφες τοὺς νεκροὺς θάψαι τοὺς ἑαυτῶν νεκρούς.

8:23 Καὶ ἐμβάντι αὐτῷ εἰς τὸ πλοῖον ἠκολούθησαν αὐτῷ οἱ μαθηταὶ αὐτοῦ.

8:24 καὶ ἰδοὺ σεισμὸς μέγας ἐγένετο ἐν τῇ θαλάσσῃ, ὥστε τὸ πλοῖον καλύπτεσθαι ὑπὸ τῶν κυμάτων, αὐτὸς δὲ ἐκάθευδεν.

8:25 καὶ προσελθόντες ἤγειραν αὐτὸν λέγοντες· κύριε, σῶσον, ἀπολλύμεθα.

8:14 And when Jesus had come into Peter's house, he saw his wife's mother lying, and sick of a fever. [n. 708]

8:15 And he touched her hand, and the fever left her, and she arose and ministered to them. [n. 711]

8:16 And when evening had come, they brought to him many who were possessed with devils: and he cast out the spirits with his word: and all who were sick he healed: [n. 713]

8:17 That it might be fulfilled, what was spoken by the prophet Isaiah, saying: *he took our infirmities, and bore our diseases.* [n. 715]

8:18 And Jesus seeing great multitudes about him, gave orders to pass over the water. [n. 716]

8:19 And a certain scribe came and said to him: Master, I will follow you wherever you will go. [n. 718]

8:20 And Jesus said to him: the foxes have holes, and the birds of the air nests: but the Son of man has nowhere to lay his head. [n. 719]

8:21 And another of his disciples said to him: Lord, permit me first to go and bury my father. [n. 720]

8:22 But Jesus said to him: follow me, and let the dead bury their dead. [n. 721]

8:23 And when he entered into the boat, his disciples followed him: [n. 723]

8:24 and behold a great tempest arose in the sea, so that the boat was covered with waves, but he was asleep. [n. 725]

8:25 And they came to him, and awaked him, saying: Lord, save us, we perish. [n. 727]

8:26 Et dicit eis Iesus: quid timidi estis modicae fidei? Tunc surgens imperavit ventis et mari: et facta est tranquillitas magna. [n. 728]

8:26 καὶ λέγει αὐτοῖς· τί δειλοί ἐστε, ὀλιγόπιστοι; τότε ἐγερθεὶς ἐπετίμησεν τοῖς ἀνέμοις καὶ τῇ θαλάσσῃ, καὶ ἐγένετο γαλήνη μεγάλη.

8:26 And Jesus said to them: why are you fearful, O you of little faith? Then rising up he commanded the winds, and the sea, and there came a great calm. [n. 728]

8:27 Porro homines mirati sunt, dicentes: qualis est hic, quia et venti et mare obediunt ei? [n. 729]

8:27 οἱ δὲ ἄνθρωποι ἐθαύμασαν λέγοντες· ποταπός ἐστιν οὗτος ὅτι καὶ οἱ ἄνεμοι καὶ ἡ θάλασσα αὐτῷ ὑπακούουσιν;

8:27 But the men wondered, saying: what manner of man is this, for the winds and the sea obey him? [n. 729]

---

708. Et cum venisset Iesus in domum Simonis Petri et cetera. Commendata est virtus Christi in curatione leprosi, commendata est etiam in curatione festina servi centurionis, hic commendatur in curatione perfecta.

Primo ergo describit curationis locum;
secundo infirmitatis modum;
tertio declarat Christi auxilium;
quarto curationis effectum.

709. Dicit ergo **cum venisset** et cetera. Non tangit Evangelista, quando hoc fuit factum; sed et Lucas, et Marcus transeunt ad alia.

Sed sciendum quod ubi evangelistae ponunt statum, vel aliquid ad ordinem pertinens, signum est, quod ad continuationem historiae pertinet; ubi vero non, signum est, quod ad continuationem memoriae. Unde secundum quod recolebant, scribebant.

Venit **in domum Petri**. Et tria possumus considerare. Honorem quem intulit discipulis suis, quia noluit ire ad domum centurionis; ivit tamen ad domum pauperis piscatoris; unde Ps. CXXXVIII, 17: *nimis honorati sunt amici tui, Deus*. Item informavit in humilitate, quia nihil plus placet Domino. Iac. c. I, 21: *in mansuetudine percipite insitum verbum, quod potest salvare animas vestras* et cetera. Tertio in hoc ostenditur reverentia, quam habuit Dominus ad Petrum, quia se obtulit, licet Petrus non rogaret.

710. Vidit socrum. Vidit oculo scilicet mentis; Ex. III, 7: *vidi afflictionem populi mei in Aegypto*.

Socrum Petri. Per hoc potest intelligi synagoga. *Qui operatus est Petro in apostolatu circumcisionis*, scilicet in Iudaeis, *operatus est et mihi inter gentes* ad Gal. II, 8. Haec febricitabat, scilicet synagoga, febre scilicet invidiae. Vel per istam socrum intelligitur anima aestuans igne concupiscentiae.

711. Et tetigit manum eius. Hic tangit curationem.

Quaerit Chrysostomus, quare curavit servum centurionis solo verbo, istam vero tactu. Et respondet, propter familiaritatem; et in hoc etiam magis ostendebat suam humilitatem: et ideo in tactu auxilium dedit; Ps. LXXII, 23: *tenuisti manum dexteram meam*.

708. And when Jesus had come into Peter's house. The power of Christ was pointed out in the healing of the leper, and also in the rapid healing of the centurion's servant; here it is pointed out in perfect healing.

First, then, he describes the place of the healing;
second, the manner of infirmity;
third, he makes known the help of Christ;
fourth, the effect of the healing.

709. He says then, **and when Jesus had come**. The Evangelist does not touch upon when this was done, but both Luke and Mark go over to other things.

But one should know that where the evangelists place a stop, or something pertaining to order, it is a sign which pertains to the continuation of the history; but where they do not, it is a sign which pertains to the continuation of memory. Hence according as they recalled, they wrote.

He came **into Peter's house**. And we can consider three things. The honor which he brought to his disciples, because he did not wish to go to the house of the centurion, yet went to the house of a poor fisher. Hence, *but to me your friends, O God, are made exceedingly honorable* (Ps 138:17). Similarly, he formed them in humility, because nothing is more pleasing to the Lord. *With meekness receive the ingrafted word* (Jas 1:21). Third, in this is shown the reverence the Lord had toward Peter, because he offered himself, although Peter did not ask.

710. He saw his wife's mother. That is, he saw with the eye of the mind; *I have seen the affliction of my people in Egypt* (Exod 3:7).

His wife's mother. By this is understood the synagogue. *For he who wrought in Peter to the apostleship of the circumcision, wrought in me also among the gentiles* (Gal 2:8). She, namely, the synagogue, was feverish with the fever of envy. Or by this mother-in-law is understood a soul seething in the fire of concupiscence.

711. And he touched her hand. Here he touches upon the healing.

Chrysostom asks why he cured the centurion's servant with only a word, but this woman with a touch. And he responds, on account of familiarity; and in this he shows even more humility. And so he gave help in a touch; *you have held me by my right hand* (Ps 72:24).

712. Sequitur *et surrexit*. Consuetudo est febricitantium, quod quando incipiunt sanari, debiliores sunt quam in infirmitate; sed talis non fuit curatio Domini, immo plenam sanitatem reddidit: quia *Dei perfecta sunt opera*, Deut. XXXII, 4.

Aliter enim curat Dominus, aliter natura. Ideo sequitur *et ministrabat*.

713. *Vespere autem facto*. Hic confirmatur Dei potestas per multitudinem curatorum.

Primo ergo tangit Evangelista multitudinem;

secundo subiungit auctoritatem Scripturae, ibi *ut adimpleretur quod dictum est per Isaiam prophetam*.

714. Dicit ergo quod curavit daemoniacos et male habentes. Et possunt intelligi per daemoniacos peccantes ex malitia: et per male habentes peccantes ex ignorantia.

Unde dicit *vespere autem facto*; quare, nota, hoc non factum fuisse die Sabbati, in quo habebant pro inconvenienti curare; sed in vespere finito Sabbato, *obtulerunt ei multos daemonia habentes*. Vel dicitur vespere, quia Salvator noster vespere venit. *Oritur sol, et occidit*, scilicet Christus, Eccle. I, 5. *Eiiciebat*, sola increpatione: unde ad solam vocem eius fugiebant daemones. Item *male habentes*, ita quod conveniat ei illud quod dicitur in Act. X, 38: *liberavit omnes oppressos a diabolo*.

Unde notandum, quod non omnia miracula Christi posuerunt evangelistae, sed magis vulgata.

715. Et quia videretur mirabile, quod tot curaret; ideo confirmat auctoritate quae habetur Is. LIII, 4: '*infirmitates nostras ipse accepit, et aegrotationes nostras portavit.*'

Et quamvis non ita sit in serie textus, exponamus prout iacet. '*Infirmitates nostras ipse accepit*', idest abstulit: ita quod infirmitates accipiantur pro levibus peccatis. Et '*aegrotationes*', idest maiora peccata, '*portavit*', idest asportavit: vel cum ipse sit Dei virtus et sapientia, '*infirmitates nostras*', scilicet passionis et mortis. Unde passibilitatem accepit ad tollendam infirmitatem et aegrotationem nostram et cetera. I Petr. II, 24: *qui peccata nostra pertulit in corpore suo, ut peccatis nostris mortui, iustitiae vivamus*.

Sed cum Isaias dixerit de peccatis, quaeritur quare hoc de infirmitatibus corporalibus dicatur. Et hoc est, quia plerumque ex peccatis spiritualibus causantur aegritudines corporales.

716. *Videns autem Iesus turbas*. Quia posita sunt miracula contra peccata interiora, hic ponit miracula contra peccata exteriora, scilicet procellam. Et

primo ponit praeambulum ad miraculum, scilicet de introitu navis;

712. There follows *and she arose*. It is usually the case with feverish people that when they begin to be healed, they are weaker than when they were ill; but the Lord's healing was not so, but rather he gave full health, because *the works of God are perfect* (Deut 32:4).

For the Lord heals in one way, nature in another. So there follows *and ministered to them*.

713. *And when evening had come*. Here the power of God is confirmed by the multitude of those healed.

First, then, the Evangelist touches upon the multitude;

second, he adjoins the authority of Scripture, at *that it might be fulfilled, what was spoken by the prophet Isaiah*.

714. It says then that he healed the demon-possessed and those that were sick. And by the demon-possessed can be understood those who sin out of malice, and by the sick can be understood those sinning out of ignorance.

Hence it says, *and when evening had come*. Why? Notice that this was not done on the Sabbath day, on which they thought it unfitting to heal, but in the evening, the Sabbath having been finished. *They brought to him many who were possessed with devils*. Or it says, *evening*, because our Savior comes in the evening. *The sun rises, and goes down, namely Christ* (Eccl 1:5). *He cast out* solely by rebuking; hence the demons flee just at his voice. Likewise, *all who were sick*, such that what it is said in befits him: *healing all that were oppressed by the devil* (Acts 10:38).

Hence one should notice that the evangelists did not set down all the miracles of Christ, but rather the common ones.

715. And because it might seem extraordinary that he should cure so many, he confirms it by the Scriptural text found in Isaiah, '*he took our infirmities, and bore our diseases*' (Isa 53:4).

And although it does not follow the order of the text of the prophecy, let us explain it as it lies. '*He took our infirmities*', i.e., he took them away, so that '*infirmities*' are taken as light sins. And our '*diseases*', i.e., greater sins, he '*bore*', i.e., removed. Or since he himself is the power and wisdom of God, '*our infirmities*', namely suffering and death. Hence he accepted passibility for taking away our infirmity and disease. *Who his own self bore our sins in his body upon the tree: that we, being dead to sins, should live to justice* (1 Pet 2:24).

But since Isaiah spoke about sins, it is asked why this is said of bodily weaknesses. And this is because often bodily diseases are caused by spiritual sins.

716. *And Jesus seeing great multitudes*. Since the miracles against interior sins were set down, here he sets down the miracles against exterior sins, namely the storm. And

first, he sets down something preparatory to the miracle, namely about entering the boat;

deinde miraculum, ibi *tunc surgens imperavit ventis et mari*;

tertio effectum, ibi *et facta est tranquillitas magna*. Circa primum

primo ponit praeceptionem;

secundo mandati adimpletionem.

Circa primum tria.

Primo praecipit ut sequantur;

secundo unum se ingerentem repellit;

tertio alium discipulum arguit.

717. Dicit ergo *videns Iesus turbas* et cetera.

Sed quare intravit navem? Hoc fecit propter duo. Primo, ut ostenderet infirmitatem humanae naturae; secundo, ut placeret discipulis; unde aliquando cum discipulis ascendit in montem, aliquando in desertum, aliquando in navem. Item ut nobis daret exemplum, ne favores hominum quaereremus. Item ad tollendam invidiam Iudaeorum; Is. XLII, v. 3: *linum fumigans non extinguet*.

718. Sequitur repulsio *et accedens unus scriba*: et videtur quod iste valde devote accessit. Et quare repulit? Hieronymus: *quia non habebat bonam fidem*. Et hoc patet: quia solum vocavit eum *Magistrum*; sed veri discipuli vocabant eum *Dominum*. Unde in Io. XIII, 13: *vos vocatis me Magister et Domine*. Item ex mala intentione volebat eum sequi: quia audiebat signum fuisse factum; volebat sequi, ut faceret signa, ut dicitur de Simone mago. Item dicit Chrysostomus, quod in alio peccavit, scilicet in superbia; quia seorsum traxit se. Unde reputabat se digniorem aliis.

Hilarius interrogative legit: *Magister, sequar te?* Culpa istius est, quia quod certum erat, interrogavit, et quod debebat facere, posuit sub dubio.

719. Sequitur *vulpes foveas habent*. Hieronymus exponit ad litteram, quod Deus ad intentionem respondit, ut saepe facit. Volebat sequi; sed intendebat lucrum: et Dominus contra hoc allegat paupertatem; ideo dicit *vulpes foveas habent, et volucres caeli nidos; Filius autem hominis non habet ubi caput suum reclinet*; ut habetur II Cor. VIII, v. 9: *qui egenus factus est cum dives esset* et cetera.

Secundum Augustinum notat eum de triplici vitio. De vitio dolositatis, quia dulcedinem habebat in ore, et venenum in corde, ut habetur Ps. XIII, 3. Item notavit eum de superbia, cum dixit *volucres caeli*, per quos superbia intelligitur. Vel volucres daemones, ut habetur infra XIII, 4, ubi dicitur: *et venerunt volucres, et comederunt ea*. Item de infidelitate, quia non erat in caritate quae habitat in nobis per fidem.

then the miracle, at *then rising up he commanded the winds, and the sea*;

third, the effect, at *and there came a great calm*. Concerning the first,

first, he sets down a precept;

second, the fulfillment of the precept.

Concerning the first, three things:

first, he commands that they follow;

second, he thrusts back one who was pushing himself in;

third, he finds fault with another disciple.

717. It says then *Jesus seeing great multitudes*.

But why did he enter the boat? He did this for two reasons. First, that he might show the weakness of human nature; second, that he might please the disciples. Hence sometimes he went onto a mountain with the disciples, sometimes into the desert, sometimes into a ship. Similarly, that he might give an example, lest we should seek men's applause. Likewise, to take away the envy of the Jews; *smoking flax he will not quench* (Isa 42:3).

718. There follows the thrusting back: *and a certain scribe came*. And it seems that this man approached very devoutly. And why did he thrust him back? Jerome: *because he did not have good faith*. And this is clear, because he only called him *Master*; but the true disciples called him *Lord*. Hence, *you call me Master, and Lord* (John 13:13). Similarly, he wished to follow for a bad reason, for he heard that signs had been done; he wished to follow that he might work signs, as is said of Simon Magus. Likewise, Chrysostom says that he sinned in something, namely in pride, because he drew himself apart from the rest. Hence he considered himself more worthy than the others.

Hilary writes it interrogatively: *Master, will I follow you?* The fault with this is that he asked about what was certain, and placed what he was supposed to do under doubt.

719. There follows *the foxes have holes*. Jerome explains this literally, for God responded to the intention, as he often does. He wished to follow, but he aimed at profit, and the Lord against this admitted poverty. So he says, *the foxes have holes, and the birds of the air nests: but the Son of man has nowhere to lay his head*, as is said, *being rich he became poor, for your sakes* (2 Cor 8:9).

According to Augustine, he censures him for three vices. For the vice of deceitfulness, because he had sweetness in his mouth and poison in his heart (Ps 13:3). Likewise he censured the pride in him, when he said, *the birds of the air*, by which pride is understood. Or, the birds are demons, as where it says, *and while he was sowing some fell by the way side, and the birds of the air came and ate them up* (Matt 13:4). Likewise, for infidelity, because he was not in the charity which dwells in us by faith.

720. Sequitur *alius autem de discipulis eius ait illi*. Primus se ingessit, sed alter se excusavit.

Et ponitur reprobatio excusantis, ibi *Iesus autem ait illi* et cetera.

Domine, permitte me primum ire, et sepelire patrem meum. Et magna est differentia inter istum et praecedentem. Iste vocavit eum *Dominum*, ille vocavit eum *Magistrum*. Item ille dolum allegavit, iste pietatem, quia praeceptum erat de honoratione patris: unde dilationem petiit. Simile habetur III Reg. XIX, 20 de Eliseo.

721. Sequitur istius reprehensio *sequere me*: quia qui vult sequi Christum, non debet dimittere sequi propter aliud negotium temporale; unde Ps. XLIV, 11 dicitur: *obliviscere populum tuum, et domum patris tui*.

Item hoc praecepit ei, quia erant alii qui poterant sepelire. Ideo dixit *dimitte mortuos sepelire mortuos suos*. Item quia accidit, ut saepe, quod qui impeditur aliquo uno negotio, cum unum aliud trahat, cito ruit in aliud; sic si iste ivisset sepelire patrem, haberet fortassis post cogitationes de testamento patris: et ita forte totaliter retraheretur. Is. V, 18: *vae qui trahitis iniquitatem in funiculis vanitatis*. Unde hoc non fuit crudelitatis. Ut si videamus aliquem affectum nimis de morte patris, prohibetur a funere propter periculum, ut habetur Eccli. XXX, 25: *multos occidit tristitia*.

Sed dicit *mortuos* in plurali, quia mortuus erat duplici morte, scilicet morte infidelitatis, et morte corporis. Unde mortuus erat et in corpore et in anima.

722. Unde dat quatuor documenta. Primum scilicet ut qui vocatus est ad statum perfectionis, non cognoscat patrem carnalem per affectionem inordinatam; infra XXIII, 9: *unus est enim Pater vester qui in caelis est*. Secundum est quod inter fideles et infideles retrahitur germanitatis affectus. Unde Lc. XIV, v. 26: *si quis venit ad me, et non odit patrem suum, et matrem, et uxorem, et filios, et fratres, et sorores, adhuc et animam suam, non potest meus esse discipulus*. Et hoc verum est ubi pater et mater retrahunt a Deo. Tertium est, quod infidelium mortuorum non est facienda memoria apud sanctos. Quartum est, quod omnis qui vivit extra Christum, mortuus est, quia ipse est vita, secundum Gregorium.

723. *Et ascendente eo in naviculam*. Positum est praeceptum Domini de transfretatione; hic ponitur executio praecepti. Erant enim manifestata miracula in terra, vult manifestare in aquis, ut ostendat se esse Dominum terrae et maris.

Per istam naviculam intelligitur Ecclesia, vel crux Christi; unde de ista potest dici illud Sap. XIV, 5: *exiguo ligno committunt animas suas*. Discipuli Domini

720. There follows *and another of his disciples said to him*. First, he thrusts himself forward, but then he makes an excuse for himself.

And the rejection of the one excusing himself is set down, at *but Jesus said to him*.

Lord, allow me first to go and bury my father. And there is a great difference between this and what came before. This one called him *Lord*, that one called him *Master*. That one chose deceit, this one piety, because there was a command about honoring one's father. Hence he asked for a delay. A similar thing is found about Eliseus (1 Kgs 19:20).

721. There follows his reproach: *follow me*, because the one who wishes to follow Christ should not give up following for the sake of some temporal activity. Hence, *hearken, O daughter, and see, and incline your ear: and forget your people and your father's house* (Ps 44:11).

Likewise, he commands him this because there were others who could bury his father. So he said, *follow me, and let the dead bury their dead*. Likewise, because it happens often that one who is hindered by some one affair, when he clears it away, suddenly falls into another. Thus if this man had gone to bury his father, afterwards he would probably have had thoughts about his father's will; and in this way he would be wholly drawn back. *Woe to you that draw iniquity with cords of vanity* (Isa 5:18). Hence this was not cruelty. As though we were to see someone greatly affected by the death of his father forbidden from burying him on account of the danger, *for sadness has killed many, and there is no profit in it* (Sir 30:25).

But he says *dead* in the plural, because he was dead with a double death, namely with the death of infidelity and the death of the body. Hence he was dead both in body and in soul.

722. Hence he gives four lessons. The first, namely, that one who is called to the state of perfection should not know his fleshly father through an inordinate affection; *for one is your Father, who is in heaven* (Matt 23:9). The second is that the affinity of affection is taken away between believers and unbelievers. Hence, *if any man come to me, and hate not his father, and mother, and wife, and children, and brethren, and sisters, yea and his own life also, he cannot be my disciple* (Luke 14:26). And this is true where the father and mother draw back from God. The third is that one should not celebrate the memory of the unfaithful dead with the saints. The fourth is that everyone who lives outside of Christ is dead, because he himself is life, according to Gregory.

723. *And when he entered into the boat*. The Lord's command about crossing was set down; here the execution of the command is set down. For the miracles on the earth were shown plainly; he wishes to show that he is the Lord of earth and sea.

By this boat is understood the Church, or the cross of Christ; hence it can be said of it, *men also trust their lives even to a little wood* (Wis 14:5). The Lord's disciples follow

sequuntur eum in Ecclesia per obsequium mandatorum. Item sequuntur eum ascendentem in crucem. Ad Gal. VI, 14: *per quem mihi mundus crucifixus est, et ego mundo.*

724. Deinde subiungitur miraculum. Et

primo ponitur periculum imminens;

secundo discipulorum interpellatio, ibi *et accesserunt*;

tertio eorum exauditio, ibi *et dicit eis Iesus.*

Periculum tangitur ex procella, et Christi dormitione.

725. *Et ecce motus factus est magnus.* Sicut sancti dicunt, non est facta tempestas ex intemperie aeris, sed ex divina ordinatione provenit.

Et hoc factum est multiplici ratione. Primo ut discipuli, qui specialiter dilecti et vocati erant, humilia saperent, et non se extollerent: et hoc significabat futurum periculum, quod imminere debebat tempore passionis. Et post, ut ait Paulus Apostolus II ad Cor. I, 8: *gravati sumus supra virtutem, ita ut nos taederet etiam vivere.* Item alia causa, ut scirent in periculis vivere, et vincere, ut habetur Rom. c. VIII, 37: *in omnibus his superamus propter eum qui dilexit nos.* Item Chrysostomus exponit, quia ipsi erant praedicaturi quae de Christo viderant; ideo ut magis in ipsis experti essent miraculis, et essent certiores, voluit Dominus eos pati. Unde in Ps. LXV, 16: *venite, et narrabo opera Domini.* Citius enim poterant recordari de huiusmodi quae sibi evenerunt.

726. *Ipse vero dormiebat*: et hoc ut ostenderet se verum hominem; sic enim erat in omnibus, ut ubi volebat ostendere divinitatem, semper ostendebat aliquid humanitatis.

Dormiebat, quia habitu inventus est ut homo, Phil. II, 7. Secundum enim divinitatem non dormiebat. Unde Ps. CXX, 4: *non dormitabit, neque dormiet qui custodit Israel.* Item *dormiebat*, ut constituerentur inter timorem et spem. Item ut ostenderet singularitatem, quia in tanta tempestate manebat securus; Prov. VIII, 28: *quando librabat fontes aquarum, quando circumdabat mari terminum suum, et legem ponebat aquis.*

727. Sequitur interpellatio discipulorum *accesserunt discipuli* et cetera. Tantum enim erat ventus, quod oportuit eum evigilare: et totum istud dictum fuit in figura de Iona, quia Ionas in navi dormiebat, et nautae evigilaverunt eum ad interpellationem, isti vero ad salvandum; unde dicunt, *Domine, salva nos, perimus.*

Et primo confitentur potestatem eius dum dicunt, *Domine*; Ps. LXXXVIII, 10: *tu dominaris potestati maris,*

him in the Church by the observance of his commands. Likewise, they follow him by going up onto the cross, *by whom the world is crucified to me, and I to the world* (Gal 6:14).

724. Then the miracle is adjoined. And

first, the imminent danger is set down;

second, the disciples' intercession, at *and they came to him*;

third, their being heard, at *and Jesus said to them.*

Danger is touched upon from the storm, and from Christ's sleep.

725. *And behold a great tempest arose.* As the saints say, a tempest does not arise from the inclemency of the weather, but comes forth from the divine ordination.

And this happened for many reasons. First, so that the disciples, who were specially loved and called, might feel humble, and not exalt themselves; and this signified the future danger which would threaten at the time of the passion. And afterward, as the Apostle Paul says, *we were pressed out of measure above our strength, so that we were weary even of life* (2 Cor 1:8). Likewise another reason, so that they might know to live in danger, and to conquer, as is found, *but in all these things we overcome, because of him who has loved us* (Rom 8:37). Likewise, Chrysostom explains that they were to preach the things of Christ which they had seen. Therefore, that they might be more experienced in these miracles, and might be more certain, the Lord wished them to suffer. Hence, *come and hear, all you who fear God, and I will tell you what great things he has done for my soul* (Ps 65:16). For they could easily remember these sorts of things which happened to them.

726. *But he was asleep.* And this was so that he might show that he was a true man; for so he was in all things, that where he willed to show the divinity, he always showed something of the humanity.

He was asleep, because he was in habit found as a man (Phil 2:7). For he was not asleep in his divinity; hence, *behold he will neither slumber nor sleep, he who keeps Israel* (Ps 120:4). Similarly, *he was asleep*, so that they might be caught between fear and hope. Similarly, so that he might show his uniqueness, since he remained secure in such a tempest; *when we established the sky above, and poised the fountains of waters: when he compassed the sea with its bounds, and set a law to the waters that they should not pass their limits* (Prov 8:28).

727. There follows the disciples' intercession: *and they came to him.* For the wind was so great that it was necessary to wake him. And this had all been said in the figure of Jonas, because Jonas slept in a ship, and the sailors woke him to intercede; indeed, these disciples woke Jesus to save themselves. Hence they say, *Lord, save us, we perish.*

And first, they confess his power, when they say, *Lord*; *you rule the power of the sea: and appease the motion of the*

motum autem fluctuum eius tu mitigas. Item petunt auxilium, quia sciebant ipsum esse Salvatorem; Is. XXXV, 4: *ipse veniet, et salvabit nos.* Item periculum terrenorum exprimunt.

Et hic signatur mors Christi in dormitione, qui et excitatus est per resurrectionem. Vel dicitur dormire in tribulationis et tentationibus sanctorum: et tunc precibus sanctorum evigilat: unde dicitur Ps. XLIII, 23: *exurge, quare obdormis, Domine?* Item dormit in pigris: unde excitandus est, ut admonet Paulus ad Eph. V, 14: *exurge qui dormis, et exurge a mortuis, et illuminabit te Christus.*

728. Sequitur quomodo subvenit **quid timidi estis modicae fidei?** Videtur quod non essent **modicae fidei**, quia dicebant, **salva nos**; sed vere modicae fidei fuerunt, quia non credebant quod etiam dormiens posset salvare. Vel **modicae fidei**, quia si ipsi haberent magnam fidem, ipsi possent imperare mari.

Tunc surrexit et imperavit ventis: tempestas enim oritur ex ventis ut ex causa efficiente, ex aquis ut ex causa materiali: et utrique imperavit; unde Ps. CVI, 25: *dixit, et stetit spiritus procellae.* Et hoc est quod dicitur **et facta est tranquillitas magna**. Sed consuetudo est quod quando fit tempestas, duobus diebus mare non sedatur totaliter. Ideo ut appareat perfectum miraculum, statim **facta est tranquillitas magna**, quia *Dei perfecta sunt opera*, Deut. XXXII, 4.

729. *Porro homines mirati sunt* et cetera. Hic ponitur effectus, scilicet admiratio turbarum.

Quod dicit **homines**, non intelligatis apostolos, quia numquam apostoli sic appellantur; sed per **homines** intellige nautas. Vel, secundum Hieronymum, si etiam intelligas homines, idest apostolos, potest esse quod dubitare potuerunt ut homines, dicentes **qualis est hic?** Hic Chrysostomus addit **homo**; quia enim ipsum viderant dormientem, hominem vocabant; quia signum divinitatis viderant, ideo dubitabant. **Quia venti et mare obediunt ei**: quia omnis creatura suo Creatori obedit; Ps. CXLVIII, 8: *ignis, grando, nix, glacies, spiritus procellarum, quae faciunt verbum eius* et cetera. Non quia animam rationalem habeant, sed quia ad modum obedientis se habent. Ut manus et membra animae obediunt, quia statim moventur ad eius nutum, sic omnia Deo obediunt.

waves thereof (Ps 88:10). Likewise, they beg for help, because they knew that he was the Savior; *God himself will come and will save you* (Isa 35:4). Similarly, they described the danger of the storm.

And the death of Christ is signified here by the sleep, who was also awakened by the resurrection. Or he is said to sleep in the afflictions and temptations of the saints, and then he wakes by the saints' prayers. Hence it is said, *arise, why do you sleep, O Lord?* (Ps 43:23). Similarly, he sleeps in the lazy; hence he should be awakened, as Paul warns, *rise you who sleep, and arise from the dead: and Christ will enlighten you* (Eph 5:14).

728. There follows how he rescued them: **why are you fearful, O you of little faith?** It seems that they were not **of little faith**, because they had said, **save us**; but indeed they were of little faith, because they did not believe that he could save them even while sleeping. Or **of little faith**, because if they had had great faith, they themselves could have commanded the sea.

Then rising up he commanded the winds, for a tempest arises out of winds as out of an efficient cause, and out of water as out of a material cause. And he commanded both; hence, *he said the word, and there arose a storm of wind* (Ps 106:25). And this is what it says, **and there came a great calm**. But usually when there is a storm, the sea does not entirely rest for two days. Therefore, that a perfect miracle might be evident, at once **there came a great calm**, because *the works of God are perfect* (Deut 32:4).

729. But the men wondered. Here the effect is set down, namely the wonderment of the crowd.

Do not take what it says, **men**, as the apostles, because the apostles are never named in this way; but by **men** understand the sailors. Or, according to Jerome, even if you understand the men as the apostles, can it be that they could doubt as the men did, saying, **what manner of man is this?** Here Chrysostom adds, **man**: for since they had seem him sleeping, they called him a man; but because they had seen a sign of the divinity, they doubted. **For the winds and the sea obey him**, because every creature obeys its Creator. *Fire, hail, snow, ice, stormy winds which fulfill his word* (Ps 148:8). Not because they have a rational soul, but because they carry themselves after the manner of one who obeys. As the hand and the members obey the soul, because they move immediately at its nod, so all things obey God.

Lecture 4

8:28 Et cum venisset Iesus trans fretum in regionem Gerasenorum, occurrerunt ei duo habentes daemonia de monumentis exeuntes, saevi nimis, ita ut nemo posset transire per viam illam. [n. 730]

8:29 Et ecce clamaverunt, dicentes: quid nobis et tibi, Iesu, Fili Dei? Venisti huc ante tempus torquere nos? [n. 733]

8:30 Erat autem non longe ab illis grex multorum porcorum pascens. [n. 735]

8:31 Daemones autem rogabant eum dicentes: si eicis nos hinc, mitte nos in gregem porcorum. [n. 736]

8:32 Et ait illis: ite. At illi exeuntes abierunt in porcos. Et ecce magno impetu abiit totus grex per praeceps in mare, et mortui sunt in aquis. [n. 737]

8:33 Pastores autem fugerunt, et venientes in civitatem nuntiaverunt haec omnia, et de his qui daemonia habuerant. [n. 739]

8:34 Et ecce tota civitas exiit obviam Iesu; et viso eo rogabant eum, ut transiret a finibus eorum. [n. 740]

8:28 Καὶ ἐλθόντος αὐτοῦ εἰς τὸ πέραν εἰς τὴν χώραν τῶν Γαδαρηνῶν ὑπήντησαν αὐτῷ δύο δαιμονιζόμενοι ἐκ τῶν μνημείων ἐξερχόμενοι, χαλεποὶ λίαν, ὥστε μὴ ἰσχύειν τινὰ παρελθεῖν διὰ τῆς ὁδοῦ ἐκείνης.

8:29 καὶ ἰδοὺ ἔκραξαν λέγοντες· τί ἡμῖν καὶ σοί, υἱὲ τοῦ θεοῦ; ἦλθες ὧδε πρὸ καιροῦ βασανίσαι ἡμᾶς;

8:30 ἦν δὲ μακρὰν ἀπ᾽ αὐτῶν ἀγέλη χοίρων πολλῶν βοσκομένη.

8:31 οἱ δὲ δαίμονες παρεκάλουν αὐτὸν λέγοντες· εἰ ἐκβάλλεις ἡμᾶς, ἀπόστειλον ἡμᾶς εἰς τὴν ἀγέλην τῶν χοίρων.

8:32 καὶ εἶπεν αὐτοῖς· ὑπάγετε. οἱ δὲ ἐξελθόντες ἀπῆλθον εἰς τοὺς χοίρους· καὶ ἰδοὺ ὥρμησεν πᾶσα ἡ ἀγέλη κατὰ τοῦ κρημνοῦ εἰς τὴν θάλασσαν καὶ ἀπέθανον ἐν τοῖς ὕδασιν.

8:33 οἱ δὲ βόσκοντες ἔφυγον, καὶ ἀπελθόντες εἰς τὴν πόλιν ἀπήγγειλαν πάντα καὶ τὰ τῶν δαιμονιζομένων.

8:34 καὶ ἰδοὺ πᾶσα ἡ πόλις ἐξῆλθεν εἰς ὑπάντησιν τῷ Ἰησοῦ καὶ ἰδόντες αὐτὸν παρεκάλεσαν ὅπως μεταβῇ ἀπὸ τῶν ὁρίων αὐτῶν.

8:28 And when he had come on the other side of the water, into the country of the Gerasens, there met him two who were possessed with devils, coming out of the sepulchres, exceedingly fierce, so that none could pass by that way. [n. 730]

8:29 And behold they cried out, saying: what have we to do with you, Jesus Son of God? Did you come here to torment us before the time? [n. 733]

8:30 And there was, not far from them, a herd of many swine feeding. [n. 735]

8:31 And the devils beseeched him, saying: if you cast us out from here, send us into the herd of swine. [n. 736]

8:32 And he said to them: go. But going out, they went into the swine, and behold the whole herd ran violently down a steep place into the sea: and they perished in the waters. [n. 737]

8:33 And they who kept them fled: and coming into the city, told everything, and concerning those who had been possessed by the devils. [n. 739]

8:34 And behold the whole city went out to meet Jesus, and when they saw him, they beseeched him to depart from their coasts. [n. 740]

---

730. Sequitur *et cum venisset Iesus trans fretum.* Quia posita sunt miracula, quibus dominus liberavit multos a periculis exterioribus; hic ponuntur miracula, quibus fit liberatio a periculis interioribus, sive spiritualibus. Et

primo ponitur miraculum;

secundo effectus, ibi *at illi exeuntes abierunt in porcos.*

Et circa primum

primo ostenditur malitia daemonum quantum ad saevitiam quam in homines exercent;

secundo quantum ad impatientiam, ibi *et ecce clamaverunt* etc.;

730. There follows *and when he had come on the other side of the water.* Since there were set down miracles by which he freed many from exterior dangers, here are set down miracles which bring freedom from interior, or spiritual, dangers. And

first, the miracle is set down;

second, the effect, at *but going out they went into the swine.*

And concerning the first,

first is shown the malice of the demons as regards the ferocity which they practice in men;

second, as regards impatience, at *and behold, they cried out;*

tertio quantum ad nequitiam, quia animalibus brutis nocuerunt, ibi *daemones autem rogabant eum* et cetera.

Circa primum

primo locus describitur;

secundo saevitia daemonum declaratur.

731. Erat quaedam regio quae dicebatur regio Gerasenorum. Gerasa interpretatur 'colonum eiiciens' vel 'advena appropinquans' quia prope gentiles. *Occurrerunt ei duo habentes daemonia.* Ostenditur saevitia, primo quia opprimebant eos; secundo quia homines decipere nitebantur.

Sed quaeritur quare alii evangelistae non faciunt mentionem nisi de uno; iste de duobus. Dicendum quod sine dubio duo fuerunt; sed unus fuit magis famosus.

732. Et erant saevi, quia nocebant non solum corporaliter, sed etiam spiritualiter. Unde in monumentis habitabant, ut inducerent hominibus terrorem. Unde error fuit, quem quidam posuerunt, quod daemones aliquam animam reducerent in corpus mortuum, ut legitur de Simone mago; sed hoc nihil erat, sed fingebant daemones ad homines decipiendum. Unde dicit Porphyrius, quod genus daemonum est fallax. Unde isti magi maxime utuntur corporibus mortuorum: quare habitabant daemones in sepulcris; Is. LXV, 4: *qui habitant in sepulcris, et in delubris idolorum dormiunt.* Erant enim tam saevi, *ut nemo posset transire per viam illam*: quia *in via hac qua ambulabam, absconderunt superbi laqueum mihi,* Ps. CXLI, 4, *superbi,* idest daemones.

733. Sed ostenditur eorum impatientia, quia Christi praesentiam non ferebant; unde dicitur *clamaverunt*: et in hoc ostenditur impatientia; Is. LXV, 14: *clamabitis prae dolore cordis, et prae contritione spiritus ululabitis.* Item fatentur Dei potentiam dicentes *quid nobis et tibi, Iesu Fili Dei?* Vere nihil, quia nulla convenientia Christi ad Belial.

Sed quare hoc dicebant? Quia graviter puniebant homines: et audierant, quia Christus deberet eis potestatem amovere. Unde voluerunt dicere: *et si aliis nocuimus, tibi non nocuimus, quare non debes nos gravare.* Item confitentur Filium Dei. Et in hoc confunduntur Ariani, quia si non sanctis credunt, saltem daemonibus credant.

Sed contra, quia videtur quod non cognoverunt eum: quia I ad Cor. II, 8: *si cognovissent, numquam Regem gloriae crucifixissent* et cetera.

Sed dicendum, quod quando Dominus volebat, humanitatem ostendebat, ita quod se eis occultabat.

734. *Quare venisti ante tempus torquere nos?* Sciunt daemones quod in die iudicii daemones debent suscipere maius tormentum cum dicetur *ite maledicti, in ignem*

third, as regards wickedness, because they harmed the brute animals, at *and the devils beseeched him*.

Concerning the first,

first the place is described;

second, the ferocity of the demons.

731. There was a certain kingdom which was called the kingdom of the Gerasens. Gerasa is interpreted 'casting out the settler', or 'the foreigners drawing near', because it was near the gentiles. *There met him two who were possessed with devils.* The ferocity is shown, first, because they were oppressing them; second, because the men were laboring to trap passers-by.

But it is asked why the other evangelists only mention one, while this Evangelist mentions two. One should say that without doubt there were two, but one was more famous.

732. And they were ferocious, because they harmed the men not only bodily, but even spiritually. Hence they lived in the sepulchres, that they might strike terror into men. Hence there was an error, which certain men held, that the demons would lead a soul back into a dead body, as is written about Simon Magus; but there is nothing to this, but the demons were contriving to deceive men. Hence Porphyry says that the race of demons is deceitful. Hence those magi made great use of the bodies of the dead, which is why the demons were dwelling in the sepulchres. *That dwell in sepulchres, and sleep in the temple of idols* (Isa 65:4). For they were so ferocious that *none could pass by that way*, because *in this way wherein I walked, the proud have hidden a snare for me* (Ps 141:4), *the proud*, i.e., the demons.

733. But their impatience is shown because they did not endure Christ's presence; hence it says, *they cried out*; and by this their impatience is shown. *You will cry for sorrow of heart, and will howl for grief of spirit* (Isa 65:14). And they acknowledged the power of God, saying, *what have we to do with you, Jesus Son of God?* Indeed, nothing, because there is no concord that Christ has with Belial (2 Cor 6:15).

But why did they say this? Because they had heavily punished the men, and they had heard that Christ was destined to take their power away. Hence they wished to say, *even if we have harmed others, we have not harmed you, therefore you should not burden us.* Likewise, they confessed that he was the Son of God, and in this the Arians are confounded, for if they do not believe the saints, they may at least believe the demons.

On the contrary, it seems that they did not know him, because of: *if they had known it, they would never have crucified the Lord of glory* (1 Cor 2:8).

But one should say that when the Lord wished, he showed his humanity such that he hid himself from them.

734. *Did you come here to torment us before the time?* The demons know that on the day of judgment the demons are destined to receive great torment when it is said, *depart*

aeternum. Item credunt aliqui quod daemones usque in diem iudicii non patiuntur poenam sensus, sed poenam damni: et hoc pro isto verbo **quia venisti ante tempus.** Sed contra hoc est quod dicit Damascenus: hoc hominibus mors, quod angelis casus. Sed homines cum moriuntur, statim recipiunt poenam sensus, sic angeli qui ceciderunt. Quidam dicunt quod ignem suum semper secum portant.

Sed quomodo potest hoc fieri, quia iste ignis corporeus est? Dicendum, quod licet hic ignis sit corporalis, habet tamen aliquid spirituale: unde cruciat per modum cuiusdam alligationis; spiritus enim excedit naturam corporis, sed Deus alligat spiritus corporibus; sicut cum alligatur anima corpori, dat corpori ut moveatur secundum voluntatem animae: sicut si datur aliqua praelatura alicui in aliqua ecclesia, ipso non existente in eadem; sic licet iste ignis sit corporeus, ratione spiritualitatis potest agere.

Torquere nos et cetera. Magnum tormentum reputant quod non possint hominibus nocere. Sed si essent in inferno, non possent ita nocere; et ita tormentum eis magnum est intrare in infernum.

735. Erat autem non longe ab eis grex multorum porcorum pascens. Hic tangitur malitia, quia non solum hominibus nocent, sed et brutis. **Grex porcorum**: unde patet quod hoc non erat in Iudaea, quia Iudaei non utuntur porcis.

736. Si eiicis nos, mitte nos in porcos.

Sed quare non petierunt quod mitteret eos in homines? Quia ipsi videbant eum sollicitum circa curam hominum.

Sed quare in greges porcorum? Quia erant magis vicini. Item quia est animal valde immundum. Unde ad designandam immunditiam permisit intrare in porcos: et hoc videtur significari Iob XL, 22: *numquid multiplicabit ad te preces, aut loquetur tibi mollia?*

737. Sequitur Christi concessio **et ait illis: ite** et cetera.

Sed videtur Dominus audisse daemones. Dicendum quod non audivit; sed ex sua sapientia sic fieri permisit, et ordinavit, ut ostendatur malitia daemonum, quia nisi Dominus cohiberet, ita ruerent in homines, sicut ruerunt in porcos. Sed quando Dominus permittit aliquid daemonibus, non totaliter permittit sed imponit eis fraenum, ut in Iob II, 6. Unde ad hoc designandum permisit eos ruere in porcos. Item ad designandum quod nihil possunt nisi ex Dei permissione. Item ut homo suam

from me, you cursed, into everlasting fire (Matt 25:41). And some believe that the demons will not suffer the punishment of the senses until the day of judgment, but the punishment of the damned; and they believe this because of these words, **did you come here to torment us before the time?** But against this is what Damascene says: *this is death for men which was a fall for the angels.* But men, when they die, immediately receive the punishment of the senses; even so the angels who fell. Some say that they always carry their own fire with them.

But how can this be, since this fire is bodily? One should say that, although this fire is bodily, yet it has something spiritual; hence it torments by way of a certain binding. For a spirit exceeds the nature of the body, but God binds spirits to bodies; just as when the soul is bound to a body, it gives movement to the body according to the will of the soul; like if some prelature of a church were given to someone, he himself not being in it. So although that fire is bodily, it can act with the *ratio* of spirituality.

To torment us. They consider it a great torment that they cannot harm men. But if they were in hell, they could not so harm them. And thus it is a great torment for them to enter into hell.

735. And there was, not far from them, a herd of many swine feeding. Here their malice is touched upon, because they not only harm men, but even brutes. **A herd of many swine**: hence it is clear that this was not in Judea, because the Jews do not use pigs.

736. If you cast us out from here, send us into the herd of swine.

And why did they not ask that he send them into men? Because they saw that he was concerned about the cure of men.

But why into the herd of pigs? Because they were more near. Likewise, because the pig is a very unclean animal. Hence to indicate their uncleanness, he permits them to enter into pigs. And this seems to be signified, *will he make many supplications to you, or speak soft words to you?* (Job 40:22).

737. Christ's concession follows, **and he said to them: go.**

But it seems that the Lord listened to demons. One should say that he did not listen, but permitted and ordered it to come about by his own wisdom, that the malice of the demons might be shown, for unless the Lord restrained them, they would wreak havoc in men just as they wreaked havoc in the pigs. But when the Lord permits something to demons, he does not permit it entirely, but puts a bridle on them, *behold he is in your hand, but yet save his life* (Job 2:6). Hence to indicate this, he permitted them to wreak havoc

dignitatem cognosceret, cum ad salutem unius hominis tot millia porcorum permiserit interfici.

738. Sequitur executio mandati *et magno impetu abiit totus grex per praeceps in mare*; in quo denotatur quod nullus a diabolo totaliter potest extingui, nisi porcum se exhibeat, idest totaliter immundum. Unde habetur Apoc. XVIII, 21: *hoc impetu mittetur Babylon civitas illa magna*; II Petri II, 13: *hi velut irrationabilia pecora peribunt, percipientes mercedem iniustitiae* et cetera.

739. Sequitur pastorum admiratio; unde *pastores fugerunt* et nuntiaverunt haec omnia. Unde profecti nuntiaverunt triste et laetum: triste de porcis; sed laetum de daemoniaco curato.

Per istos pastores signantur principes synagogae, qui propter temporalia, quantumcumque possunt, contradicunt Christo.

740. Consequenter sequitur totius populi admiratio *et ecce tota civitas exiit obviam Iesu, et viso eo rogabant eum ut transiret a finibus eorum*. Et quare? Quia multa damna eis fecerat, ideo timebant, quod si plus ibi moraretur quod plura eis faceret damna. Sic aliqui propter detrimentum temporale timent esse cum Christo, ut habetur Is. XXX, 11: *declinate a me semitam: cesset a facie nostra Sanctus Israel*.

Vel aliter. Quia non ex malitia, sed ex devotione, quia indignos se reputabant. Simile dixit Petrus: *recede a me, quia homo peccator sum*.

in the pigs. Also, to indicate that nothing can be except by God's permission. Also, that man might know his own dignity, since he would permit so many thousands of pigs to be killed for the salvation of one man.

738. There follows the execution of the command: *and behold the whole herd ran violently down a steep place into the sea*, in which it is indicated that nothing can be completely destroyed by the devil unless he shows himself to be a pig, i.e., totally unclean. Hence, *with such violence as this will Babylon, that great city, be thrown down* (Rev 18:21). *But these men, as irrational beasts . . . will perish in their corruption, receiving the reward of their injustice* (2 Pet 2:12–13).

739. There follows the swineherds' wonderment; hence, *and they who kept them fled*. Hence having departed, they announced sorrow and joy: sorrow over the pigs, but joy over the demoniac who was healed.

These swineherds signify the chiefs of the synagogue, who speak against Christ as much as they can, for the sake of temporal things.

740. Next, there follows the wonderment of the whole people: *and behold the whole city went out to meet Jesus, and when they saw him, they beseeched him to depart from their coasts*. And why? Because he had brought a great financial loss on them, so they were afraid that if he stayed there longer he would bring more financial losses on them. Thus some fear to be with Christ, because of temporal loss: *take away from me the way, turn away the path from me, let the Holy One of Israel cease from before us* (Isa 30:11).

Or otherwise: not out of malice, but out of devotion, because they considered themselves unworthy. Peter said something similar, *depart from me, for I am a sinful man, O Lord* (Luke 5:8).

Chapter 9

Lecture 1

9:1 Et ascendens Iesus in naviculam transfretavit, et venit in civitatem suam. [n. 742]

9:2 Et ecce offerebant ei paralyticum iacentem in lecto. Videns autem Iesus fidem illorum, dixit paralytico: confide, fili, remittuntur tibi peccata tua. [n. 744]

9:3 Et ecce quidam de scribis dixerunt intra se: hic blasphemat. [n. 747]

9:4 Et cum vidisset Iesus cogitationes eorum, dixit: ut quid cogitatis mala in cordibus vestris? [n. 748]

9:5 Quid est facilius dicere: dimittuntur tibi peccata tua, an dicere: surge, et ambula? [n. 749]

9:6 Ut sciatis autem quoniam Filius hominis habet potestatem in terra dimittendi peccata, tunc ait paralytico: surge, tolle lectum tuum, et vade in domum tuam; [n. 750]

9:7 et surrexit, et abiit in domum suam. [n. 754]

9:8 Videntes autem turbae timuerunt, et glorificaverunt Deum, qui dedit potestatem talem hominibus. [n. 754]

9:1 Καὶ ἐμβὰς εἰς πλοῖον διεπέρασεν καὶ ἦλθεν εἰς τὴν ἰδίαν πόλιν.

9:2 καὶ ἰδοὺ προσέφερον αὐτῷ παραλυτικὸν ἐπὶ κλίνης βεβλημένον. καὶ ἰδὼν ὁ Ἰησοῦς τὴν πίστιν αὐτῶν εἶπεν τῷ παραλυτικῷ· θάρσει, τέκνον, ἀφίενταί σου αἱ ἁμαρτίαι.

9:3 καὶ ἰδού τινες τῶν γραμματέων εἶπαν ἐν ἑαυτοῖς· οὗτος βλασφημεῖ.

9:4 καὶ ἰδὼν ὁ Ἰησοῦς τὰς ἐνθυμήσεις αὐτῶν εἶπεν· ἱνατί ἐνθυμεῖσθε πονηρὰ ἐν ταῖς καρδίαις ὑμῶν;

9:5 τί γάρ ἐστιν εὐκοπώτερον, εἰπεῖν· ἀφίενταί σου αἱ ἁμαρτίαι, ἢ εἰπεῖν· ἔγειρε καὶ περιπάτει;

9:6 ἵνα δὲ εἰδῆτε ὅτι ἐξουσίαν ἔχει ὁ υἱὸς τοῦ ἀνθρώπου ἐπὶ τῆς γῆς ἀφιέναι ἁμαρτίας – τότε λέγει τῷ παραλυτικῷ· ἐγερθεὶς ἆρόν σου τὴν κλίνην καὶ ὕπαγε εἰς τὸν οἶκόν σου.

9:7 καὶ ἐγερθεὶς ἀπῆλθεν εἰς τὸν οἶκον αὐτοῦ.

9:8 ἰδόντες δὲ οἱ ὄχλοι ἐφοβήθησαν καὶ ἐδόξασαν τὸν θεὸν τὸν δόντα ἐξουσίαν τοιαύτην τοῖς ἀνθρώποις.

9:1 And entering into a boat, he passed over the water and came into his own city. [n. 742]

9:2 And behold they brought to him one paralyzed, lying in a bed. And Jesus, seeing their faith, said to the paralyzed man: be of good heart, son, your sins are forgiven you. [n. 744]

9:3 And behold some of the scribes said within themselves: he blasphemes. [n. 747]

9:4 And Jesus seeing their thoughts, said: why do you think evil in your hearts? [n. 748]

9:5 Which is easier, to say, your sins are forgiven you: or to say, arise, and walk? [n. 749]

9:6 But that you may know that the Son of man has power on earth to forgive sins, then said he to the paralyzed man, arise, take up your bed, and go into your house. [n. 750]

9:7 And he arose, and went into his house. [n. 754]

9:8 And seeing it, the multitude feared, and glorified God who gave such power to men. [n. 754]

---

741. Supra posuit miracula contra pericula corporalia; hic ponit miracula contra pericula spiritualia: et secundum hoc duo facit.

Primo ostendit quomodo subvenit sibi occurrentibus;

secundo quomodo inquirit quos salvet, ibi *et circuibat Iesus omnes civitates et castella.*

Circa primum

primo ponit remedium contra peccatum;

secundo contra mortem, ibi *haec illo loquente ad eos* et cetera.

Circa primum

primo ponit remedium contra peccatum remittendo;

741. Above he set forth miracles against bodily dangers; here he sets forth miracles against spiritual dangers. And accordingly, he does two things:

first, he shows how he helps those who come to him;

second, how he seeks out those whom he will save, at *and Jesus went about all the cities, and towns* (Matt 9:35).

Concerning the first,

first he sets forth a remedy against sin;

second, against death, at *as he was speaking these things to them* (Matt 9:18).

Concerning the first,

first, he sets forth a remedy against sin by forgiving it;

secundo peccatores ad se trahendo, ibi *et factum est discumbente eo in domo* et cetera. Et

primo ponit quaedam praeambula ad beneficium;

secundo ponit beneficium ipsum, ibi *ut autem sciatis* et cetera. Et

primo ponitur locus;

secundo devotio offerentium, ibi *et ecce offerebant ei paralyticum*.

742. Dicit ergo *ascendens Iesus in naviculam transfretavit*. Et continuatur haec pars, quia rogabant eum ut ab eis discederet, ideo ascendit navem. Unde dat intelligere quod si dicant aliqui, *recede a nobis, viam mandatorum tuorum nolumus*, Iob XXI, v. 14, statim recedit; unde **ascendit in naviculam**. Haec navicula significat crucem, vel Ecclesiam. *Et venit in civitatem suam*, scilicet in civitatem gentium, quae sibi datae sunt. Unde in Ps. II, 8: *postula a me, et dabo tibi gentes haereditatem tuam*.

743. Sed est quaestio, quare Marcus et Lucas dicunt istud esse factum in Capharnaum; hic vero habetur quod in Nazareth, quae erat civitas sua.

Dicendum quod quaedam erat civitas Christi ratione nativitatis: et haec erat Bethlehem; quaedam ratione educationis; et haec erat Nazareth; quaedam ratione conversationis et operationis miraculorum: et sic Capharnaum. Ideo bene dicitur **in civitatem suam**. Unde dicitur Lc. IV, 23: *quanta audivimus facta in Capharnaum, fac et hic in patria tua*.

Augustinus aliter solvit, quia Capharnaum inter alias civitates Galilaeae erat magis famosa: unde erat quasi metropolis. Et sicut si aliquis esset de aliqua villa iuxta Parisius diceretur quod esset de Parisius propter notitiam loci; sic Dominus, quia erat de finibus Capharnaum, dicebatur inde esse.

Vel aliter, quia praetermittunt aliquid evangelistae, unde aliquid potest addi, quod videlicet transivit per Nazareth, et venit in Capharnaum: et tunc obtulerunt ei.

744. *Ecce offerebant ei paralyticum*. Hic tangitur devotio offerentium: unde in Marco tangitur, quod quia non poterant transire, posuerunt per tegulas.

Iste paralyticus significat peccatorem in peccato iacentem; unde sicut non potest paralyticus se movere, sic nec iste. Illi autem qui portant eum, sunt illi qui suis monitionibus portant eum ad Deum.

second, by drawing sinners to himself, at *and it came to pass as he was reclining at table in the house* (Matt 9:10). And

first, he sets forth certain preambles to the favor;

second, he sets forth the favor itself, at *but that you may know*. And

first, the place is set down;

second, the devotion of those presenting the paralytic, at *and behold they brought to him one paralyzed*.

742. It says then, *and entering into a boat, he passed over the water*. And this part is connected with what went before, because they had asked him to leave them, and so he went up into a boat. Hence he gives one to understand that if some say, *depart from us, we do not desire the knowledge of your ways* (Job 21:14), he immediately withdraws; hence, *and entering into a boat*. This boat signifies the cross, or the Church. *And came into his own city*, namely into the city of the gentiles, who had been given to him. Hence, *ask of me, and I will give you the gentiles for your inheritance* (Ps 2:8).

743. But there is a question, because Mark and Luke say that this was done in Capernaum (Mark 2:31; Luke 5:18), but here it says that it happened in Nazareth, which was his own city.

One should say that one city was Christ's by reason of his birth, and this was Bethlehem; and another one by reason of his education, and this was Nazareth; and another one by reason of familiar association and the working of miracles, and Capernaum was his city in this way. Therefore, well is it said, *into his own city*. Hence it is said, *as great things as we have heard done in Capernaum, do also here in your own country* (Luke 4:23).

Augustine resolves it in another way, for Capernaum was the most famous of the cities of Galilee; hence it was as it were a capital city. And just as if someone were from some village next to Paris he would say that he was from Paris on account of the place's fame, so the Lord, since he was from the region of Capernaum, was said to be from there.

Or in another way, because the evangelists leave something out, hence something can be added, namely that he passed through Nazareth and came into Capernaum, and then they presented the paralytic to him.

744. *And behold they brought to him one paralyzed*. Here the devotion of the ones presenting the paralytic is touched upon. Hence Mark touches upon the fact that, since they could not get through, they let him down through the roof tiles.

This paralytic signifies a sinner lying in sin; hence just as the paralytic cannot move himself, so neither can that sinner. But those who carry him are those who carry him to God by admonition.

745. *Videns autem Iesus fidem illorum* et cetera. Ponit beneficium: ubi possumus tria videre.

Primo quid movit Iesum;

secundo quid sit quod requiritur;

tertio disceptationem contra beneficium.

Curat aliquando Dominus aliquem propter fidem suam, aliquando propter preces suas, et aliorum. *Videns* ergo *fidem illorum dixit*, unde dicitur Mc. XI, 24: *quicquid orantes petitis, credite quia accipietis, et fiet vobis.*

746. *Confide, fili.* Quid ergo requiritur? Fides; Ps. CXXIV, 1: *qui confidunt in Domino sicut Mons Sion; non commovebitur in aeternum qui habitat in Ierusalem.* Et Act. XV, 9: *fide purificans corda eorum.*

Remittuntur tibi peccata tua. Hic tangitur beneficium. Sed quid est quod iste petebat? Sanitatem corporis, et Dominus dat sanitatem animae. Ratio est, quia peccatum erat causa aegritudinis, sicut in Ps. XV, 4: *propter iniquitates eorum multiplicatae sunt infirmitates eorum.* Unde fecit Deus sicut bonus medicus qui causam curat.

747. Deinde ponit disceptationem contra beneficium, ibi *et cum cognovisset Iesus cogitationes eorum* et cetera.

Dicit ergo *ecce quidam de scribis dicebant intra se: hic blasphemat.* Et quare mirabantur? Quia videbant hominem, et non videbant Deum; solius autem Dei est dimittere peccata: ideo dicebant eum blasphemum, iuxta illud Iob XXXIV, 18: *qui dicit regi apostata, qui vocat duces impios* et cetera.

748. *Et cum vidisset Iesus cogitationes eorum, dixit: ut quid cogitatis mala in cordibus vestris?* Hic confutat eos tripliciter: sua cognitione, verbo et facto; cognitione, quia sicut soli Deo pertinet dimittere peccata, sic cognoscere secreta cordis; Ps. VII, 10: *scrutans corda et renes Deus. Cum vidisset,* quia solus scit cogitationes hominum. Et primo reprehendit eorum nequitiam, *ut quid cogitatis mala in cordibus vestris?* Quia blasphemum eum dicebant; Is. I, 16: *auferte mala de cogitationibus vestris.*

749. *Quid est facilius* et cetera. Hic ponit confutationem.

Sed videtur male arguere Dominus, quia arguit a minori affirmando: facilius enim videtur sanare corpus, quam sanare animam.

Sed exponit sic Hieronymus: facilius est dicere quam facere; verum quantum ad factum, fortius est animam quam corpus sanare; sed quantum ad potestatem, eadem est potestas utrobique. Sed si ad dictum referatur, videmus quod mendaces cito mentiuntur, ubi non possunt deprehendi: in his enim quae apparent, deprehendi possunt, sed non in his quae latent. Unde in his audacter

745. *And Jesus, seeing their faith.* He sets forth a favor, where we can see three things:

first, what moved Jesus;

second, what is required;

third, the dispute against the favor.

Sometimes the Lord cures someone on account of his faith, sometimes on account of his prayers, and the prayers of others. *Seeing* then *their faith,* he *said;* hence it is said, *whatever you ask when you pray, believe that you will receive; and they will come unto you* (Mark 11:24).

746. *Be of good heart, son.* What then is required? Faith; *those who trust in the Lord will be as Mount Zion: he will not be moved forever who dwells in Jerusalem* (Ps 124:1–2). And Acts 15:9, *purifying their hearts by faith.*

Your sins are forgiven you. Here it touches upon the favor. But what is it that this man asked for? Health of body, and the Lord gives health of soul. The reason is that sin is a cause of disease, as in, *on account of their sins, their infirmities were multiplied* (Ps 15:4). Hence God acts as the good doctor, who cures the cause.

747. Then he sets forth the dispute against the favor, at *and Jesus seeing their thoughts.*

It says then, *and behold some of the scribes said within themselves: he blasphemes.* And why were they astonished? Because they saw a man, and they did not see God; but only God can forgive sins. And so they called him a blasphemer, in accord with, *who says to the king: you are an apostate: who calls rulers ungodly?* (Job 34:18).

748. *And Jesus seeing their thoughts, said: why do you think evil in your hearts?* Here he silences them in three ways: by his knowledge, his word, and his deed. Knowledge, because just as it pertains only to God to forgive sins, so it pertains only to God to know the secrets of the heart; *the searcher of hearts and reins is God* (Ps 7:10). *And Jesus seeing,* because he alone knows the thoughts of man. And first, he reproaches their wickedness, *why do you think evil in your hearts?* Because they called him a blasphemer; *take away the evil of your devices from my eyes* (Isa 1:16).

749. *Which is easier.* Here he sets forth the refutation.

But the Lord seems to argue badly, because he argues from the lesser by affirming; for it seems easier to heal the body than to heal the soul.

But Jerome explains it this way: it is easier to speak than to do; as regards deeds, to be sure, it is harder to heal the soul than the body, but as regards power, the power to do both is the same. But if Christ's statement is referred to the thing said, we see that liars lie easily where they cannot be found out. For in those things which are evident to all, they can be found out, but not in those things which are hidden.

loquuntur ubi deprehendi non possunt. Facilius est ergo dicere, si non possitis cognoscere.

750. Ideo *ut autem sciatis quia Filius hominis habet potestatem in terra dimittendi peccata*. Ostendit facto. Et primo ponitur finis operationis; secundo modus; tertio efficientia.

Unde dicit. Et propter hoc *ut sciatis quia Filius hominis habet potestatem in terra dimittendi peccata; tunc ait paralytico: surge, tolle lectum tuum, et vade in domum tuam*. Per hoc manifestat se Deum. Supra I, 21. *Ipse enim est qui salvum faciet populum suum a peccatis eorum*.

Dicit *quod Filius hominis*, et dicit *in terra*, et elidit duplicem errorem, scilicet Nestorii et Photini. Dicebat Nestorius quod Filius hominis, et Filius Dei erant duo supposita: nec poterat dici de uno quod dicitur de altero; unde non poterat dici: iste puer creavit stellas. Ideo dicit *hominis*; quia Dei est dimittere peccata.

Item contra Photinum, qui dicebat, quod Christus acceperat initium de Virgine Maria, et merito acquisivit divinitatem: et nitebatur super illud infra XXVIII, 18: *et data est mihi omnis potestas in caelo et in terra*; ideo dicit *in terra*. Unde Baruch III, 38 dicitur: *post haec in terris visus est, et cum hominibus conversatus est*.

751. *Habet potestatem*.

Videtur quod per hoc non ostendatur, quia etiam ipsi apostoli habebant potestatem. Sed dicendum quod ipsi habebant per viam administrationis, non auctoritatis.

752. Hoc autem quod dicitur *ut autem sciatis* etc. dupliciter potest legi: vel ut sint verba Evangelistae, et ita fuit narratoria; vel sint verba Christi dicentis *ut sciatis* etc., et sic oratio est imperfecta, quia ipsi dubitabant. Ideo, ut sciatis quia ego habeo potestatem dimittendi peccata, *ait paralytico: surge* et cetera. Unde verbo curavit, quod proprium est Dei, iuxta illud Ps. XXXII, 9: *dixit, et facta sunt*.

753. Tria habebat infirmus: iacebat in lecto, portabatur ab aliis, ire non poterat. Quia ergo iacebat dixit *surge*; quia portabatur, praecepit ut portaret *tolle lectum tuum*; quia ire non poterat, dixit *et ambula*, *Dei enim perfecta sunt opera*, Deut. XXXII, 4.

Similiter peccatori in peccato iacenti dicitur *surge*, a peccato per contritionem; *tolle lectum*, per satisfactionem; Michaeae VIII, 9: *iram Domini portabo, quia peccavi ei*. *Et vade in domum tuam*, in domum aeternitatis, vel in conscientiam propriam; Sap. VIII, 16: *intrans in domum meam conquiescam in illa*.

Hence in these matters, they boldly speak where they cannot be found out. Therefore it is easier to speak if you cannot know.

750. *But that you may know that the Son of man has power on earth to forgive sins*. He shows it by a deed. And first, the end of the work is set down; second, the mode; third, the efficacy.

Hence he says: and for the sake of this, *that you may know that the Son of man has power on earth to forgive sins, then said he to the paralyzed man arise, take up your bed, and go into your house*. By this he shows that he is God. Above, *for he will save his people from their sins* (Matt 1:21).

He says, *that the Son of man*, and he says *on earth*, and thus he strikes down two errors, namely that of Nestorius and that of Photinus. Nestorius said that the Son of man and the Son of God were two supposita, nor could what is said of one be said of the other; hence one could not say: this boy created the stars. So he says, *of man*, because it belongs to God to forgive sins.

Likewise against Photinus, who said that Christ took beginning from the Virgin Mary, and acquired the divinity by merit. And he depended on that passage below, *all power is given to me in heaven and in earth* (Matt 28:18); so he says, *on earth*. Hence it is said, *afterwards he was seen upon earth, and conversed with men* (Bar 3:38).

751. *Has power*.

It seems that this does not show it, because even the apostles themselves had power. But one should say that they had power by way of administration, not by way of authority.

752. Now, when he says, *but that you may know*, it can be read in two ways: either as the words of the Evangelist, and in this way it has to do with the story; or as the words of Christ, saying *that you may know*. And in this way the sentence is imperfect, because they were doubting. Therefore, that you may know that I have the power of forgiving sins, *then said he to the paralyzed man, arise*. Hence he healed by his word, which is proper to God, *he spoke and they were made* (Ps 32:9).

753. The sick man had three things: he was lying down, he was carried by others, and he could not walk. Therefore, because he was lying, he said, *arise*; because he was carried, he commanded him to carry: *take up your bed*; because he could not walk, he also said, *go into your house*, for *the works of God are perfect* (Deut 32:4).

Similarly, to a sinner lying in sin is said, *arise* from sin by contrition; *take up your bed* by satisfaction; *I will bear the wrath of the Lord, because I have sinned against him* (Mic 7:9). *And go into your house*, into the house of eternity, or into a proper conscience. *When I go into my house, I will repose myself with her* (Wis 8:16).

754. Sequitur executio *surrexit, et abiit. Videntes autem turbae*, non scribae, quia isti dedignabantur, *timuerunt*; Hab. III, 2: *Domine, audivi auditum tuum, et timui.* Sed quo timore? Quia *glorificaverunt Deum*, quia omnia in Deum retulerunt; Ps. CXIII, 1: *non nobis, Domine, non nobis, sed nomini tuo da gloriam. Qui dedit potestatem talem hominibus.* Unde isti non contemnunt, sicut scribae. Sed quia dicitur *hominibus*, ideo Hilarius exponit: *qui dedit talem potestatem hominibus* ut fiant filii Dei, ut in Io. I, 12: *dedit eis potestatem filios Dei fieri.*

754. There follows the execution: ***and he arose, and went into his house. And seeing it the multitude***, not the scribes, because they scornfully refused, ***feared***; *O Lord, I have heard your hearing, and was afraid* (Hab 3:2). But with what fear? Because they ***glorified God***, since they led everything back to God; *not to us, O Lord, not to us; but to your name give glory* (Ps 113:9). ***Who gave such power to men***. Hence these men did not hold Jesus in contempt, as the scribes did. But because it says, ***to men***, Hilary explains it this way: ***that gave such power to men*** that they should become sons of God, *he gave them power to be made the sons of God* (John 1:12).

Lecture 2

9:9 Et cum transiret inde, Iesus vidit hominem sedentem in teloneo, Mattheum nomine, et ait illi: sequere me. Et surgens secutus est eum. [n. 756]

9:10 Et factum est, discumbente eo in domo, ecce multi publicani et peccatores venientes discumbebant cum Iesu et discipulis eius. [n. 758]

9:11 Et videntes Pharisaei dicebant discipulis eius: quare cum publicanis et peccatoribus manducat magister vester? [n. 759]

9:12 At Iesus audiens ait: non est opus valentibus medicus, sed male habentibus. [n. 763]

9:13 Euntes autem discite, quid est: *misericordiam volo, et non sacrificium*. Non enim veni vocare iustos sed peccatores. [n. 764]

9:9 Καὶ παράγων ὁ Ἰησοῦς ἐκεῖθεν εἶδεν ἄνθρωπον καθήμενον ἐπὶ τὸ τελώνιον, Μαθθαῖον λεγόμενον, καὶ λέγει αὐτῷ· ἀκολούθει μοι. καὶ ἀναστὰς ἠκολούθησεν αὐτῷ.

9:10 καὶ ἐγένετο αὐτοῦ ἀνακειμένου ἐν τῇ οἰκίᾳ, καὶ ἰδοὺ πολλοὶ τελῶναι καὶ ἁμαρτωλοὶ ἐλθόντες συνανέκειντο τῷ Ἰησοῦ καὶ τοῖς μαθηταῖς αὐτοῦ.

9:11 καὶ ἰδόντες οἱ Φαρισαῖοι ἔλεγον τοῖς μαθηταῖς αὐτοῦ· διὰ τί μετὰ τῶν τελωνῶν καὶ ἁμαρτωλῶν ἐσθίει ὁ διδάσκαλος ὑμῶν;

9:12 ὁ δὲ ἀκούσας εἶπεν· οὐ χρείαν ἔχουσιν οἱ ἰσχύοντες ἰατροῦ ἀλλ᾽ οἱ κακῶς ἔχοντες.

9:13 πορευθέντες δὲ μάθετε τί ἐστιν· ἔλεος θέλω καὶ οὐ θυσίαν· οὐ γὰρ ἦλθον καλέσαι δικαίους ἀλλὰ ἁμαρτωλούς.

9:9 And when Jesus passed on from there, he saw a man sitting in the custom house, named Matthew; and he said to him: follow me. And he rose up and followed him. [n. 756]

9:10 And it came to pass as he was reclining at table in the house, behold many publicans and sinners came, and sat down with Jesus and his disciples. [n. 758]

9:11 And the Pharisees seeing it, said to his disciples: why does your master eat with publicans and sinners? [n. 759]

9:12 But Jesus hearing it, said: those who are in health do not need a physician, but those who are ill. [n. 763]

9:13 Go then and learn what this means, *I desire mercy and not sacrifice*. For I have not come to call the just, but sinners. [n. 764]

---

755. Hic ponitur, primo, conversio peccatorum;

secundo disceptatio Pharisaeorum, ibi *et videntes Pharisaei dicebant discipulis eius*. Et

primo dicit, qualiter quemdam vocavit ad discipulatum;

secundo quomodo multos ad familiaritatem, ibi *et factum est discumbente eo in domo* et cetera.

756. Dicit ergo *cum transiret inde Iesus*. Quare transivit? Quia insidiabantur ei, ideo nolebat turbas, ut dicitur Eccli. VIII, 13: *non incendas carbones peccatorum*. *Vidit hominem*, vere hominem, quia peccatorem; Ps. LXXXI, 7: *vos autem sicut homines moriemini, et sicut unus de principibus cadetis*. *Sedentem in telonio*, telonio vectigalium. Unde erat locus ubi vectigalia recipiebantur: unde erat in quodam statu ubi vix homo vivere potest sine peccato. *Matthaeum nomine*. Alii appellant eum Levi, ad servandum honorem eius, ut non noscatur ille esse peccator; sed ipse vocat se Matthaeum, quia iustus in principio accusator est sui, dans intelligere quod Dominus non est acceptator personarum. *Et dixit ei: sequere me*. Et hoc magnum est quod moveat Dominus ad sequelam. *Et surgens secutus est eum*. Unde potuit dicere illud Iob XXIII, 11: *vestigia eius secutus est pes meus, viam eius custodivi, et non declinavi ab ea*.

757. Sed obiicitur, quod hoc non potest esse quod ad unum verbum iste secutus est eum.

755. Here is set down, first, the conversion of sinners;

second, the Pharisees' debate, at *and the Pharisees seeing it, said to his disciples*. And

first, it says how he called certain men to discipleship;

second, how he called many to familiarity, at *and it came to pass as he was reclining at table in the house*.

756. It says then, *and when Jesus passed on from there*. Why did he pass on? Because they were plotting against him, so he did not want the crowds, *kindle not the coals of sinners* (Sir 8:13). *He saw a man*, truly a man, because he was a sinner; *but you like men will die: and will fall like one of the princes* (Ps 81:7). *Sitting in the custom house*, the tax office. There was a place where taxes were taken, so he was in a certain position where a man can hardly live without sin. *Named Matthew*. Others call him Levi, to preserve his honor, so that it would not be known that this man was a sinner; but he called himself Matthew, because *the just is first accuser of himself* (Prov 18:17), giving one to understand that the Lord is not an acceptor of persons. *And he said to him: follow me*. And this is a tremendous thing, that the Lord moves him to following. *And he rose up and followed him*. Hence one could say, *my foot has followed his steps, I have kept his way, and have not declined from it* (Job 23:11).

757. But it is objected that this could not be, that he followed him at one word.

Et dicendum quod fama Iesu ita divulgata erat, quod iam beatum se reputabat qui sequebatur eum; ideo ad unum verbum iste secutus est eum. Unde ostenditur obedientia, quia statim secutus est eum.

Sed quare non statim vocavit a principio? Dicendum quod iste sapiens erat sapientia saeculi. Tardavit autem Dominus vocare eum, donec miracula provocarent. Vel dicendum quod istud dictum est per reiterationem, quia iste fuit in praedicatione Domini in monte.

Sed quare ergo sic ponit Matthaeus? Dico ratione humilitatis: quia enim miraculum reputavit vocationem eius, ideo inter miracula recitavit.

Sed quare plus fit mentio de vocatione Petri, et Andreae, et Matthaei, quam aliorum? Dicendum quod inter viliores homines fuerunt piscatores. Item inter peccatores, illi maxime qui vectigal recipiebant. Et ideo specialiter fit mentio, ad cognoscendum quod Deus non est personarum acceptator.

758. Sequitur *et factum est, eo discumbente in domo, ecce multi publicani et peccatores venientes discumbebant cum Iesu et discipulis eius*. Hic tangitur quomodo multos vocavit ad familiaritatem.

Unde dicit *et factum est* et cetera. Alii dicunt quod fecit ei convivium; iste vero tacet. Et verum est quod fecit; unde invitavit multos, ut ad Deum traherentur, quia *cortina cortinam trahit*, Ex. XXXVI. Unde signum est quod aliquis firmiter conversus est ad Dominum, quando alios trahit, quos magis diligit. Unde dicit, quod *multi publicani discumbebant et peccatores cum Iesu*, quia, *si quis aperuerit mihi, intrabo, et caenabo cum eo, et ipse mecum*, Apoc. III, 20.

759. *Et videntes Pharisaei* et cetera. Dictum est qualiter Dominus peccatores invitat ad sequelam, et ad convivium recipit;

hic ponitur disceptatio:

primo de societate;

secundo de convivio, ibi *tunc accesserunt ad eum discipuli Ioannis*.

Circa primum

primo ponitur quaestio;

secundo responsio, ibi *ait Iesus* et cetera.

760. Dicit ergo *et videntes Pharisaei dicebant discipulis eius*.

Notandum quod isti Pharisaei erant malitiosi; unde volebant schisma ponere inter discipulos et Iesum; unde discipulis Iesum accusabant, et discipulos Iesu. Unde volentes erga discipulos accusare Iesum, dicunt *quare cum publicanis et peccatoribus manducat magister*

And one should say that Jesus' fame was so commonly known that already the man who followed him counted himself blessed; therefore this man followed him at one word. Hence obedience is displayed, because he immediately followed him.

But why did not he call him right away, from the beginning? One should say this man was wise with the wisdom of the age, and the Lord delayed calling him until miracles should arouse him. Or one should say that this was said by way of repetition, because this man was at the Lord's sermon on the mount.

But why then does Matthew place it in this way? I say by reason of humility, because he considered his calling a miracle, and so tells of it among the miracles.

But why does he mention the calling of Peter and Andrew and Matthew rather than that of the others? One should say that fishers were among the more worthless men; similarly, those who collected taxes were the greatest among sinners. And therefore he makes special mention of these, that one may know that God is not an acceptor of persons.

758. There follows *and it came to pass as he was reclining at table in the house, behold many publicans and sinners came, and sat down with Jesus and his disciples*. Here he touches upon how many he called to familiarity.

Hence he says, *and it came to pass*. Others say that he threw him a banquet; but this man is silent. And it is true that he gave a banquet; hence he invited many, that they might be drawn to God, because *the curtain draws the curtain* (Exod 36). Now, it is a sign that someone has strongly converted to the Lord, when he draws others whom he loves more. Hence he says that *many publicans and sinners came, and sat down with Jesus and his disciples*, because *if any man will hear my voice, and open to me the door, I will come in to him, and will sup with him, and he with me* (Rev 3:20).

759. *And the Pharisees seeing it*. It having been said how the Lord invites sinners to follow him and receives them at a banquet,

here the debate is set down:

first, about Jesus' society;

second, about the banquet, at *then the disciples of John came to him* (Matt 9:14).

Concerning the first,

first the question is set down;

second, the response, at *but Jesus hearing it, said*.

760. He says then, *and the Pharisees seeing it, said to his disciples*.

One should notice that the Pharisees were malicious; hence they wanted to set up a schism between the disciples and Jesus. So they accused Jesus to the disciples, and accused the disciples to Jesus. Hence, wishing to accuse Jesus to the disciples, they say, *why does your master eat with*

vester? Isti sunt de numero illorum de quibus habetur Prov. VI, 16: *sex sunt quae odit Dominus, et septimum detestatur anima eius*, scilicet *qui seminat inter fratres discordias.*

761. Sed quaeritur quare Lucas dicit istud esse dictum de discipulis.

Et respondet Augustinus, quod eadem est sententia utrobique, licet verba differant, quia totum imputabant doctrinae Magistri: unde Lucas refert ad verba, sed Matthaeus ad sententiam.

762. Sed videtur quod isti recte arguebant, quia sunt vitanda peccatorum consortia.

Sed notandum, quod aliquando sunt vitanda peccatorum consortia propter superbiam et contemptum, ut isti sicut habetur Is. LXV, 5: *non appropinques mihi, quia immundus es.* Alii vero vitant consortia propter peccatorum utilitatem, ut erubescant, et sic convertantur; et sic ut dicit Paulus I ad Cor. VI, 5: *ad verecundiam vestram dico, sic non est inter vos sapiens quisquam.* Item aliquis vitat propter cautelam sui timens ne pervertatur; Eccli. XIII, v. 1: *qui tangit picem, coinquinabitur ab ea.* Et in Ps. XVII, 27: *cum perverso perverteris.* E contrario similiter aliqui commorantur cum peccatoribus ad sui probationem: unde tentatio est sui probatio, ut habetur Eccli. XXVII, 6: et II Petri II, 8: *aspectu enim et auditu iustus erat habitans apud eos.* Et Cant. II, 2: *sicut lilium inter spinas, sic amica mea inter filias.* Et ibi dicit Glossa: *non fuit bonus, qui malos tolerare non potuit.* Item aliqui inter malos commorantur propter conversionem, ut Paulus dicit I Cor. IX, 19: *omnibus omnia factus sum, ut omnes lucrifacerem.*

Sed differentia est, quia peccatoribus perseverantibus et poenitere nolentibus non oportet communicare; de illis vero, de quibus speratur, distinguendum est ex parte illius qui habitat, quia aut est firmus, aut infirmus: si infirmus, habitare cum eis non debet; si firmus, competens est ut cum eis habitet, ut eos ad Deum convertat. Item Iesus medicus erat certus; ideo cum esset cum eis, periculum non timebat; ideo et cetera.

763. Sed sequitur Iesu responsio. Et ponit rationes tres.

Primo ex similitudine dicit *at Iesus audiens dixit: non est opus valentibus medicus.* Et vocat se Dominus medicum: et bene; Ps. CII, 3: *qui sanat omnes infirmitates tuas*, scilicet tam animae, quam corporis; ideo tangit infirmitates et animae, et corporis; unde dicit *non est opus valentibus medicus* et cetera. Valentes dicuntur qui ex superbia reputant se valere, de quibus Apoc. III, 17 dicitur: *dicis: dives sum, et locupletatus, et nullius egeo, et nescis, quia tu es miser, et miserabilis, pauper, caecus, et nudus.* Et talibus non est opus medicus, *sed male*

publicans and sinners? These were of the number of those described, *six things there are, which the Lord hates, and the seventh his soul detests*, namely *him who sows discord among brethren* (Prov 6:16; 19).

761. But it is asked why Luke says that this was said about the disciples (Luke 5:30).

And Augustine responds that there is the same thought in each, although the words are different, because they were accusing the whole of the Master's teaching. Hence Luke refers to the words, but Matthew to the thought.

762. But it seems that these men argued rightly, because one should avoid the company of sinners.

But one should note that sometimes men avoid the company of sinners out of pride and contempt, as these men did, *depart from me, come not near me, because you are unclean* (Isa 65:5). But others avoid such company for the benefit of the sinners, that they might be ashamed, and so be converted. And Paul speaks in this way, *I speak to your shame. Is it so that there is not among you any one wise man?* (1 Cor 6:5). Similarly, someone avoids their company out of care for himself, fearing lest he should be corrupted; *he who touches pitch, will be defiled with it* (Sir 13:1). And, *with the perverse you will be perverted* (2 Sam 22:27). On the other hand, similarly, some linger with sinners to test themselves; hence temptation is their test (Sir 27:6), and: *for in sight and hearing he was just: dwelling among them, who from day to day vexed the just soul with unjust works* (2 Pet 2:8). And, *as the lily among thorns, so is my love among the daughters* (Song 2:2). And the Gloss says there: *he was not good, who could not bear with evil men.* Likewise, some linger among evil men for the sake of conversion, as Paul says, *I became all things to all men, that I might save all* (1 Cor 9:22).

But there is a difference, because it is not necessary to keep company with sinners who persevere in sin and do not wish to repent. But concerning those for whom there is hope, one should distinguish on the part of the one who dwells with them, whether he is firm or weak: if weak, he should not dwell with them; if strong, he is capable of dwelling with them, to convert them to God. And Jesus was the reliable doctor; therefore he did not fear danger when he was with them.

763. There follows Jesus' response. And he sets out three arguments.

First, he speaks from a likeness: *those who are in health do not need a physician.* And the Lord calls himself a doctor, and well does he speak; *who heals all your diseases* (Ps 102:3), namely of both soul and body. So he touches upon infirmities both of soul and body. Hence he says, *those who are in health do not need a physician.* They are called well who consider themselves well out of pride, of whom it is said, *you say, I am rich, and made wealthy, and have need of nothing: and you do not know that you are wretched, and miserable, and poor, and blind, and naked* (Rev 3:17). And a

habentibus, idest peccatum recognoscentibus: sicut dicebat David, Ps. l, v. 5: *iniquitatem meam ego cognosco* et cetera.

764. Secundo inducit auctoritatem dicens *euntes autem discite quid est*; quasi dicat: vos non intelligitis Scripturas, sed ite, et discite quid est, *'misericordiam volo, et non sacrificium.'* Hoc scribitur Osee VI, 6.

Et dupliciter exponitur. Primo ita quod intelligatur unum alii praeferri, quia magis volo misericordiam quam iudicium: unde praefertur sacrificium sacrificio. Sacrificium est agnus, item misericordia: talibus enim hostiis miseretur Deus. Quid ergo istorum melius? Prov. XXI, 3: *facere misericordiam et iudicium magis placet Deo quam victimae.* Vel ita quod unum approbetur, reliquum vero reprobetur; misericordiam volo, sed non sacrificium, quod facitis. Unde Is. I, 15: holocausta nolui, quia *manus vestrae sanguine plenae sunt.*

Vel aliter. *'Misericordiam volo, et non sacrificium.'* Illud enim dicitur aliquis velle, quod vult propter se, et non propter aliud, sicut si medicus diceret: *volo sanitatem*; et sic in operibus quae offerimus Deo, quaedam offerimus propter se, ut diligere Deum et proximum; alia vero propter ista; Michaeae c. VI, 8: *indicabo tibi, homo, quid sit bonum, et quid Dominus requirat a te. Utique facere iudicium, et diligere misericordiam.*

765. Tertio inducit Dominus aliam rationem ex suo officio, ut si aliquis legatus missus esset, et uteretur suo officio, si prohiberetur ab alio, diceret: *stultus es, quia prohibes quod ad me pertinet.* Venerat Dominus ad salvandum peccatores; unde dictum est: *et vocabis nomen eius Iesum: hic enim salvum faciet populum suum a peccatis eorum.* Et ideo dicit **non veni vocare iustos, sed peccatores.** Lucas addit, *ad poenitentiam.* Et iusta est haec additio, quia non venit vocare peccatores, ut remanerent in peccatis, sed ut amoveantur ab eis.

766. Sed potest quaeri de *iustis*, quia nullus iustus, nisi solus Deus, quia omnes sumus peccatores. Item videtur falsum quod dicit, quia Ioannes iustus fuit, Simeon iustus, Zacharias iustus; et tamen eos vocavit.

Dicendum quod distinguendum est de iustitia; quia iustus aliquis dicitur qui peccato non est obnoxius; et sic non est iustus quisquam, quia omnes vel mortali, vel veniali, vel originali sunt obnoxii, saltem quantum ad reatum; et istud penitus delevit, quia, Io. V, v. 40, *ipse venit ut vitam habeant.* Unde non venit vocare iustos, inquantum iustos, sed inquantum peccatores. Item dicitur iustus, qui non est obnoxius peccato mortali: unde *non veni vocare iustos* ad poenitentiam, sed ad maiorem iustitiam. Vel sic. **Non veni vocare iustos**, idest qui de sua

---

doctor is not needed for such, but for **those who are ill**, i.e., who recognize their sin, just as David said, *for I know my iniquity, and my sin is always before me* (Ps 50:5).

764. Second, he brings in a Scriptural authority, saying, **go then and learn what this means**, as though to say: you do not understand the Scriptures, but go, and learn what this means, *'I desire mercy and not sacrifice'* (also Hos 6:6).

And it is explained in two ways. First, in this way: that one is understood to be preferred to the other, because I want mercy more than judgment; hence a sacrifice is preferred to a sacrifice. The lamb is sacrifice, and so is mercy, for God has mercy on such victims. So which of these is better? *To do mercy and judgment, pleases the Lord more than victims* (Prov 21:3). Or in this way, that one is approved, but the remainder rejected; I want mercy, but not the sacrifice you offer. Hence, *and when you stretch forth your hands, I will turn away my eyes from you . . . for your hands are full of blood* (Isa 1:15).

Or, in another way, *'I desire mercy and not sacrifice.'* For one is said to want that which he wants for its own sake, and not for the sake of another; just as if a doctor were to say, *I desire health.* And thus among the works which we offer to God, we offer certain ones for their own sakes, as to love God and neighbor; but others for the sake of these. *I will show you, O man, what is good, and what the Lord requires of you. And certainly to give judgment, and to love mercy are required* (Mic 6:8).

765. Third, the Lord brings in another argument from his office, just as an ambassador, if he were sent and used his office, and were forbidden by another, would say: *you are a fool, because you forbid what pertains to me.* The Lord had come to save sinners; hence it is said, **you will call his name Jesus. For he will save his people from their sins** (Matt 1:21). And so he says, **I have not come to call the just, but sinners.** Luke adds, *to penance* (Luke 5:32). And this addition is just, because he did not come to call sinners that they might remain in sins, but that they might be removed from them.

766. But one can ask about the **just**, because no one is just but God alone, since we are all sinners. Also, what he says seems false, because John was just, Simeon was just, Zachary was just; and yet he called them.

It should be said that one should make a distinction concerning justice. For someone who is not guilty of sin is called just; and in this way there is not anyone just, because all are guilty either of mortal sin, or of venial, or of original, at least with regard to the state of guilt; and he completely blotted this out, because *he came that they might have life* (John 10:10). Hence he did not come to call the just, insofar as they are just, but insofar as they are sinners. Likewise, a man who is not guilty of mortal sin is called just; hence **I have not come to call the just** to penance, but to greater justice. Or in this way: **I have not come to call the just**, i.e.,

iustitia confidunt *sed peccatores*, qui poenitent ignorantes suam iustitiam.

those who are confident of their own justice, **but sinners**, those who repent, not knowing their own justice.

Lecture 3

9:14 Tunc accesserunt ad eum discipuli Ioannis dicentes: quare nos, et Pharisaei ieiunamus frequenter, discipuli autem tui non ieiunant? [n. 767]

9:15 Et ait illis Iesus: numquid possunt filii sponsi lugere quamdiu cum illis est sponsus? Venient autem dies, cum auferetur ab eis sponsus, et tunc ieiunabunt. [n. 768]

9:16 Nemo autem immittit commissuram panni rudis in vestimentum vetus: tollit enim plenitudinem eius a vestimento, et peior scissura fit. [n. 771]

9:17 Neque mittunt vinum novum in utres veteres: alioquin rumpuntur utres, et vinum effunditur, et utres pereunt. Sed vinum novum in utres novos mittunt: et ambo conservantur. [n. 772]

9:14 Τότε προσέρχονται αὐτῷ οἱ μαθηταὶ Ἰωάννου λέγοντες· διὰ τί ἡμεῖς καὶ οἱ Φαρισαῖοι νηστεύομεν [πολλά], οἱ δὲ μαθηταί σου οὐ νηστεύουσιν;

9:15 καὶ εἶπεν αὐτοῖς ὁ Ἰησοῦς· μὴ δύνανται οἱ υἱοὶ τοῦ νυμφῶνος πενθεῖν ἐφ᾽ ὅσον μετ᾽ αὐτῶν ἐστιν ὁ νυμφίος; ἐλεύσονται δὲ ἡμέραι ὅταν ἀπαρθῇ ἀπ᾽ αὐτῶν ὁ νυμφίος, καὶ τότε νηστεύσουσιν.

9:16 οὐδεὶς δὲ ἐπιβάλλει ἐπίβλημα ῥάκους ἀγνάφου ἐπὶ ἱματίῳ παλαιῷ· αἴρει γὰρ τὸ πλήρωμα αὐτοῦ ἀπὸ τοῦ ἱματίου καὶ χεῖρον σχίσμα γίνεται.

9:17 οὐδὲ βάλλουσιν οἶνον νέον εἰς ἀσκοὺς παλαιούς· εἰ δὲ μή γε, ῥήγνυνται οἱ ἀσκοὶ καὶ ὁ οἶνος ἐκχεῖται καὶ οἱ ἀσκοὶ ἀπόλλυνται· ἀλλὰ βάλλουσιν οἶνον νέον εἰς ἀσκοὺς καινούς, καὶ ἀμφότεροι συντηροῦνται.

9:14 Then the disciples of John came to him, saying: why do we and the Pharisees fast often, but your disciples do not fast? [n. 767]

9:15 And Jesus said to them: can the children of the bridegroom mourn, as long as the bridegroom is with them? But the days will come, when the bridegroom will be taken away from them, and then they will fast. [n. 768]

9:16 And nobody puts a piece of raw cloth unto an old garment. For it takes away from the fullness of the garment, and there is made a greater tear. [n. 771]

9:17 Neither do they put new wine into old wineskins. Otherwise the wineskins break, and the wine runs out, and the wineskins perish. But new wine they put into new wineskins: and both are preserved. [n. 772]

---

767. Hic ponitur quaestio de convivio: et sequitur responsio, ibi *et ait Iesus*.

Sed tunc est hic quaestio litteralis, quare Mc. II, 18 et Lc. V, 29 videtur quod ab aliis facta fuerit quaestio: ubi dicitur Mc. II, 18: *quare discipuli Ioannis et Pharisaeorum ieiunant, tui autem discipuli non ieiunant?* Ergo discipuli non dixerunt.

Augustinus solvit. Ita erat quod Pharisaei insidiabantur Christo: unde aliquando secum Herodianos traxerunt, modo vero assumpserunt discipulos Ioannis. Unde potuit et ab aliis, et a discipulis peti.

Sed unde hoc quod ieiunabant? Respondetur hic ex traditionibus suis, vel ex lege, sicut habetur quod in die propitiationis tenebantur ieiunare. Et Zac. VIII, 19: *ieiunium quarti, et ieiunium quinti, et ieiunium septimi, et ieiunium decimi erit domui Iuda in gaudium, et laetitiam, et in solemnitates praeclaras.* Item discipuli Ioannis ieiunabant exemplo magistri sui, qui magnae fuit austeritatis; discipuli vero Christi non ieiunabant.

768. *Et ait illis Iesus.* Hic respondet Iesus, et subtiliter.

Primo assignat causam a parte sua,
deinde a parte discipulorum.

767. Here the question about the banquet is set down; and the response follows, at *and Jesus said*.

But there is a literal question here. Why does it seem in Mark and Luke that the question was asked by others (Mark 2:18; Luke 5:30)? It is said, *why do the disciples of John and of the Pharisees fast; but your disciples do not fast?* (Mark 2:18). So the disciples did not speak.

Augustine resolves it in this way, saying that the Pharisees were plotting against Christ, and hence sometimes they brought Herodians with them; but this time they brought John's disciples. Hence it could be asked both by others and by John's disciples.

But where is this from, that they fasted? It is responded that this was from their own traditions, or from the law, as it is written that they were bound to fast on the day of propitiation. And, *thus said the Lord of hosts: the fast of the fourth month, and the fast of the fifth, and the fast of the seventh, and the fast of the tenth will be to the house of Judah, joy, and gladness, and great solemnities* (Zech 8:19). Similarly, John's disciples fasted by the example of their teacher, who was of great austerity; but Christ's disciples did not fast.

768. *And Jesus said to them.* Here Jesus responds, and subtly.

First, he gives a cause on his part,
then on the part of his disciples.

Circa primum duo facit.

Primo determinat tempus epulandi;

secundo ieiunandi, ibi *venient autem dies cum auferetur ab eis sponsus; et tunc ieiunabunt.*

769. Dicit ergo *numquid possunt filii sponsi lugere quamdiu cum illis est sponsus?* Ubi iste dicit *lugere*, alius dicit *ieiunare*; licet enim ieiunium quamdam habeat laetitiam spiritualem, tamen, ut habetur Hebr. XII, 11, *omnis disciplina in praesenti quidem videtur esse non gaudii, sed moeroris.* Unde est ieiunium spiritualis laetitiae, ut habetur Dan. IX, v. 3: *posui faciem meam ad Dominum Deum meum deprecari, et rogare in ieiunio, sacco et cinere.* Item est luctuosum et afflictionis, ut quando propter dolores.

Respondet dominus de utroque. Sponsus Christus enim est: *qui habet sponsam sponsus est.* Ipse enim est sponsus totalis Ecclesiae, et primordium. Aliud habuit primordium lex vetus, et aliud lex nova; lex enim vetus primordium habuit in timore; lex nova in amore; unde Rom. VIII, 15: *non enim accepistis spiritum servitutis iterum in timore, sed accepistis Spiritum adoptionis filiorum Dei.* Et Hebr. XII, 22: *accessistis ad Montem Sion, et civitatem Dei viventis Ierusalem.* Quia igitur primordium novae legis fuit in amore, ideo discipulos suos nutrire debuit in amore quodam: ideo se *sponsum* nominat, et discipulos *filios*, quia ista sunt nomina amoris. Unde bonum est quod conservem eos; et ideo nolo aliquid grave eis imponere ne abhorreant, et sic retrocedant.

Et ideo qui in religionibus sunt novi, non sunt gravandi. Unde Ambrosius in Lib. *de Simil.* reprehendit eos qui novitios graviter onerant. Et hoc est quod Christus dicit: *numquid possunt filii sponsi lugere?* etc., quasi dicat: non oportet quod ieiunent, sed magis in quadam dulcedine vivere et amore; ut sic legem meam recipiant in amore, ut habetur ad Rom. VI, 4: *quomodo surrexit Christus a mortuis per gloriam Patris, ita et nos in novitate vitae ambulemus.* Unde a Pascha usque ad Pentecosten non fiunt ieiunia, quia tunc recolit Ecclesia novitatem legis.

770. *Venient autem dies* et cetera. Et hoc ad litteram. *Venient dies*, quando scilicet vobis procurantibus *auferetur ab eis sponsus; et tunc ieiunabunt.* Et hoc praedixit eis dicens, Io. XVI, 20: *vos plorabitis, mundus autem gaudebit.* Illi enim qui ante Christum fuerunt, desideraverunt Christi praesentiam, ut Abraham, et Isaias, et alii prophetae. Item post mortem eius desiderata fuit ab apostolis: unde Petrus quasi in continuo dolore erat propter

Concerning the first, he does two things:

first, he determines the time of feasting;

second, the time of fasting, at *but the days will come, when the bridegroom will be taken away from them, and then they will fast.*

769. He says then, *can the children of the bridegroom mourn, as long as the bridegroom is with them?* Where this Gospel says, *mourn*, another says *fast*; for although fasting has a certain joyful spirit, yet, as it is said, *now all chastisement for the present indeed seems not to bring with it joy, but sorrow* (Heb 12:11). Hence there is a fast of spiritual joy, as is found: *and I set my face to the Lord my God, to pray and make supplication with fasting, and sackcloth, and ashes* (Dan 9:3). Likewise, there is also a mournful thing of affliction, and sometimes on account of sorrows.

He responds concerning both. For the bridegroom is Christ: *he who has the bride, is the bridegroom* (John 3:29). For he is the bridegroom and the first beginning of the whole Church. The old law had one first beginning, and the new law another; for the old law had its first beginning in fear, the new law in love. Hence, *for you have not received the spirit of bondage again in fear; but you have received the Spirit of adoption of sons* (Rom 8:15). And, *but you are come to Mount Zion, and to the city of the living God* (Heb 12:22). Since therefore the first beginning of the new law was in love, he had to nourish his disciples in a certain love. For this reason he calls himself a *bridegroom*, and the disciples *children*, because these are names of love. Hence it is good that I should keep them safe; and therefore I do not wish to impose anything heavy on them, lest they shrink from it, and thus draw back.

And therefore those who are new in religion should not be heavily burdened. Hence Ambrose says in the book *On Parables*: he reproached those who burdened novices heavily. And this is what Christ says: *can the children of the bridegroom mourn?* As though to say: it is not necessary that they fast, but rather to live and to love in a certain sweetness, that in this way they may receive my law in love; as is said: *as Christ is risen from the dead by the glory of the Father, so we also may walk in newness of life* (Rom 6:4). Hence there is no fasting from Easter until Pentecost, because at that time the Church recalls the newness of the law.

770. But the days will come. And this literally. *But the days will come, when the bridegroom will be taken away*, namely by your efforts, *and then they will fast.* And he predicted this to them, saying, *you will lament and weep . . . but your sorrow will be turned into joy* (John 16:20). For those who were before Christ desired Christ's presence, as did Abraham, and Isaiah, and the other prophets. Similarly, after his death he was desired by the apostles. Hence Peter

absentiam Christi; et Paulus dicebat, *cupio dissolvi, et esse cum Christo.* Unde tunc erat tempus ieiunandi.

Alia ratio quare in praesentia non tenentur ieiunare, quia ieiunium eligendum est inquantum castigat carnem, ne contra spiritum invalescat; sed cum erat praesens, custodiebat eos ab excessu; ideo non oportebat eos ieiunare; unde in Io. XVII, 12: *pater, cum eram cum eis, conservabam eos.* Sed Ioannes Baptista non habebat hanc virtutem, ideo ieiunare debebant eius discipuli. Sed quando Christus ablatus fuit, eos oportuit ieiunare. Unde Paulus dicit I Cor. IX, 27: *castigo corpus meum et in servitutem redigo* et cetera.

771. *Nemo autem mittit commissuram panni rudis in vestimentum vetus.* Hic ponit aliam rationem a parte discipulorum, et ponit duo exempla.

Unum secundum Augustinum, aliud secundum Hieronymum. Unde secundum Augustinum vult dicere: dictum est quod in praesentia Christi non debebant ieiunare discipuli, nec etiam ex conditione sua, quia imperfectis gravia iniungi non debent. Igitur cum isti sint imperfecti, eis ieiunium iniungi non debet. Ut istud ergo significet, tangit sub metaphora panni et vini.

Quia iustitia consistit in operibus exterioribus, et in novitate affectionis, ideo duo exempla ponit. Dicit ergo *nemo mittit* etc., ut si vellet iungere novum pannum, non ponet *commissuram,* idest depetiaturam, *panni rudis,* idest novi in vestimentum vetus, quia tolleret eius pulchritudinem; sic si aliquis imperfectus habet aliquam consuetudinem vitae suae, si vis imponere ei aliud iugum, recedit ab eo quod consueverat, *et efficitur peior scissura,* ut habetur infra.

772. *Neque mittunt vinum novum in utres veteres.* Ponit hic aliud exemplum de vino; quasi dicat: discipuli mei sunt quasi utres veteres. Vinum novum est lex nova ratione novitatis: unde cum recepissent Spiritum Sanctum, dixerunt eos musto madere, Act. II, v. 13. Unde *neque mittunt vinum novum in utres veteres: alioquin rumpuntur utres.* Unde si homini veteri, qui aliquando habet aliquam consuetudinem, imponis novum vivendi modum, rumpitur cor per intolerantiam. Item *effunditur vinum,* idest non custoditur, *et utres pereunt*: quia conculcaverunt mandata Dei; et ideo pereunt. *Sed vinum novum in utres novos mittunt,* doctrinam spiritualem innovans per affectum, ut dicit Apostolus I Cor. c. II, 13: *spiritualibus spiritualia comparantes.* Prov. II, 10: *si introierit sapientia cor tuum, et scientia animae tuae placuerit, custodiet te, et prudentia servabit te, ut eruaris a via mala, et ab homine qui perversa loquitur* et cetera.

was so to speak in continual sorrow because of Christ's absence; and Paul said, *but I am straitened between two: having a desire to be dissolved and to be with Christ* (Phil 1:23). So then there was a time of fasting.

Another reason why they are not bound to fast in his presence is that one should choose fasting insofar as it chastises the body, lest it become powerful against the spirit; but when he was present, he guarded them from excess, so it was not necessary for them to fast. Hence, *while I was with them, I kept them in your name* (John 17:12). But John the Baptist did not have this power, so his disciples had to fast. But when Christ was taken away, it was necessary for them to fast. Hence Paul says, *but I chastise my body, and bring it into subjection* (1 Cor 9:27).

771. *And nobody puts a piece of raw cloth unto an old garment.* Here he sets forth another argument from the part of the disciples, and he sets out two examples: one according to Augustine, the other according to Jerome.

Hence according to Augustine he wishes to say: it was said that the disciples should not fast in Christ's presence, nor also in their condition, because heavy loads should not be imposed on the imperfect. Therefore, since these men are imperfect, fasting should not be imposed on them. Therefore, to signify this, he touches upon it under the metaphor of cloth and wine.

Since justice consists in exterior works and in the newness of affections, he sets out two examples. He says then, *nobody puts,* just as, if one wished to join together a new cloth, he would not put on *a piece of raw cloth,* i.e., of the new on the old garment, because it would take away its beauty. In this way, if someone imperfect has a customary way of life, and if you wish to impose another yoke on him, he withdraws from that to which he was accustomed, *and there is made a greater tear,* as is said below.

772. *Neither do they put new wine into old wineskins.* Here he sets forth another example, about wine, as though to say: my disciples are like old wineskins. The new wine is the new law, by reason of its newness; hence when they had received the Holy Spirit, the crowds said that they were soaked with new wine (Acts 2:13). Hence, *neither do they put new wine into old wineskins. Otherwise the wineskins break.* Thus, if you impose a new manner of living on an old man, who had for some time a certain custom, his heart is rent by the inability to bear it. Likewise, *the wine runs out,* i.e., he is not guarded, *and the wineskins perish,* because he trampled upon the commands of God; and this is why they perish. *But new wine they put into new wineskins,* renewing spiritual teaching by desire, as the Apostle says, *comparing spiritual things with spiritual* (1 Cor 2:13). *If wisdom will enter into your heart, and knowledge please your soul: counsel will keep you, and prudence will preserve you, that you may be delivered from the evil way, and from the man that speaks perverse things* (Prov 2:10–12).

773. Hieronymus aliter exponit: quia institutum Pharisaeorum vocat vestimentum vetus, novum doctrinam Evangelicam; quasi dicat, non est bonum ut servent documenta vestra, quia sic facerent scissuras veteres, et sic novam doctrinam recipere non possent, sicut videmus quod facilius recipit doctrinam suam, qui non est imbutus contraria doctrina, quam qui est imbutus. Et ideo non est bonum quod vestra imbuantur doctrina.

773. Jerome explains it in another way, for he calls the custom of the Pharisees the old garment, the new, the Gospel teaching; as though to say: it is not good that they keep your doctrines, because thus they rend the old and are unable to receive the new teaching, just as we see that the man who was not steeped in a contrary teaching more easily receives his teaching than one who was steeped. And therefore it is not good that they are steeped in your teaching.

Lecture 4

9:18 Haec illo loquente ad eos, ecce princeps unus accessit, et adorabat eum dicens: Domine, filia mea modo defuncta est, sed veni, inpone manum super eam, et vivet. [n. 775]

9:19 Et surgens Iesus sequebatur eum, et discipuli eius. [n. 779]

9:20 Et ecce mulier quae sanguinis fluxum patiebatur duodecim annis, accessit retro, et tetigit fimbriam vestimenti eius. [n. 780]

9:21 Dicebat enim intra se: si tetigero tantum vestimentum eius, salva ero. [n. 783]

9:22 At Iesus conversus, et videns eam dixit: confide, filia. Fides tua te salvam fecit. Et salva facta est mulier ex illa hora. [n. 784]

9:23 Et cum venisset Iesus in domum principis, et vidisset tibicines, et turbam tumultuantem dicebat: [n. 785]

9:24 recedite, non est enim mortua puella, sed dormit. Et deridebant eum. [n. 787]

9:25 Et cum eiecta esset turba, intravit, et tenuit manum eius, et dixit: puella, surge. Et surrexit. [n. 788]

9:26 Et exiit fama haec in universam terram illam. [n. 789]

9:18 Ταῦτα αὐτοῦ λαλοῦντος αὐτοῖς, ἰδοὺ ἄρχων εἷς ἐλθὼν προσεκύνει αὐτῷ λέγων ὅτι ἡ θυγάτηρ μου ἄρτι ἐτελεύτησεν· ἀλλὰ ἐλθὼν ἐπίθες τὴν χεῖρά σου ἐπ’ αὐτήν, καὶ ζήσεται.

9:19 καὶ ἐγερθεὶς ὁ Ἰησοῦς ἠκολούθησεν αὐτῷ καὶ οἱ μαθηταὶ αὐτοῦ.

9:20 Καὶ ἰδοὺ γυνὴ αἱμορροοῦσα δώδεκα ἔτη προσελθοῦσα ὄπισθεν ἥψατο τοῦ κρασπέδου τοῦ ἱματίου αὐτοῦ·

9:21 ἔλεγεν γὰρ ἐν ἑαυτῇ· ἐὰν μόνον ἅψωμαι τοῦ ἱματίου αὐτοῦ σωθήσομαι.

9:22 ὁ δὲ Ἰησοῦς στραφεὶς καὶ ἰδὼν αὐτὴν εἶπεν· θάρσει, θύγατερ· ἡ πίστις σου σέσωκέν σε. καὶ ἐσώθη ἡ γυνὴ ἀπὸ τῆς ὥρας ἐκείνης.

9:23 Καὶ ἐλθὼν ὁ Ἰησοῦς εἰς τὴν οἰκίαν τοῦ ἄρχοντος καὶ ἰδὼν τοὺς αὐλητὰς καὶ τὸν ὄχλον θορυβούμενον

9:24 ἔλεγεν· ἀναχωρεῖτε, οὐ γὰρ ἀπέθανεν τὸ κοράσιον ἀλλὰ καθεύδει. καὶ κατεγέλων αὐτοῦ.

9:25 ὅτε δὲ ἐξεβλήθη ὁ ὄχλος εἰσελθὼν ἐκράτησεν τῆς χειρὸς αὐτῆς, καὶ ἠγέρθη τὸ κοράσιον.

9:26 καὶ ἐξῆλθεν ἡ φήμη αὕτη εἰς ὅλην τὴν γῆν ἐκείνην.

9:18 As he was speaking these things to them, behold a certain ruler came up, and adored him, saying: Lord, my daughter is even now dead; but come, lay your hand upon her, and she will live. [n. 775]

9:19 And Jesus rising up followed him, with his disciples. [n. 779]

9:20 And behold a woman who had been troubled with an issue of blood for twelve years, came behind him, and touched the hem of his garment. [n. 780]

9:21 For she said within herself: if I will touch only his garment, I will be healed. [n. 783]

9:22 But Jesus turning and seeing her, said: be of good heart, daughter, your faith has made you whole. And the woman was made whole from that hour. [n. 784]

9:23 And when Jesus had come into the house of the ruler, and saw the minstrels and the multitude making a commotion, he said: [n. 785]

9:24 move away, for the girl is not dead, but sleeps. And they laughed him to scorn. [n. 787]

9:25 And when the multitude was driven out, he went in, and took her by the hand, and said: young girl, arise. And she arose. [n. 788]

9:26 And the fame of this went abroad into all that country. [n. 789]

---

774. Posuit miracula quibus adhibentur remedia contra pericula peccati, hic ponit illa quibus adhibentur remedia contra pericula mortis.

Et dividitur in partes duas: quia

primo narrat quo modo vitam restituit;

secundo, quomodo opera vitae, ibi **et transeunte inde Iesu**.

Circa primum

primo ponitur invitatio ad miraculum peragendum;

secundo indicium, ibi **et ecce mulier** etc.;

tertio miraculi praeparatio, ibi **et cum eiecta esset turba**.

Circa primum quatuor facit.

774. He set down the miracles by which remedies are applied against the dangers of sin; here he sets down those by which remedies are applied against the dangers of death.

And it is divided into two parts, because

first, he tells how he restored life;

second, how he restored the works of life, at **and as Jesus passed from there** (Matt 9:27).

Concerning the first,

first the invitation to work the miracle is set down;

second, a sign, at **and behold a woman**;

third, the preparation of the miracle, at **and when the multitude was driven out**.

Concerning the first, he does four things:

Primo describitur tempus invitationis;

secundo persona invitans;

tertio invitatio;

quarto admissio invitationis.

775. Dicit ergo *haec illo loquente*, scilicet in domo Matthaei.

Sed est obiectio: quia Marcus et Lucas alio ordine recitant, scilicet quod iste accessit ad Iesum postquam transfretaverat.

Augustinus solvit quod quando ponitur in evangelistis aliquid ad tempus pertinens, si statim ponitur, repraesentatur tunc ordo historiae; et ideo cum dicitur hic *haec eo loquente*, significatur ordo historiae; sed in Marco et Luca refertur ad ordinem memoriae suae. Vel potest dici quod fuit aliquis locus medius ubi istud accidit. Aliquando enim non dicunt utrum statim, post, vel quando factum quid sit.

776. Sequitur *ecce princeps*. Hic ponitur persona invitans, scilicet princeps synagogae, et dicitur Iairus 'illuminans' vel 'illuminatus'. In Gen. XXIII, 6: *princeps Dei est apud nos*.

777. Sequitur invitatio: et duo facit.

Primo exhibuit reverentiam, quia personaliter *accessit*. Item *adoravit*. Item potestatem confitetur, quia dicit *Domine*. Iste princeps significat antiquos patres, quia isti accesserunt per desiderium, et credentes Christum venturum adoraverunt; Ps. CXXXI, 7: *adorabimus in loco ubi steterunt pedes eius*. Item confitebantur. *Scitote quoniam Dominus ipse est Deus*. Ps. XCIX, 3.

778. Sequitur periculum *filia mea modo defuncta est*.

Contrarium habetur in Luca VIII, 41 et in Marco V, 22 quia ibi dicitur: *filia mea in extremis est*. Et cum essent in via occurrerunt ei famuli, et cetera.

Solvit Augustinus: quia quando iste Iairus recessit, iam erat in extremis, et credebat quod eam non inveniret vivam; ideo magis petebat ut veniret, et resuscitaret eam, quam ut curaret; unde dicit *filia mea modo defuncta est* etc., quasi dicat: credo quod iam mortua sit. Alii igitur dixerunt secundum quod fuit; sed Matthaeus ad intentionem retulit. Ideo Augustinus dat bonum documentum, quod non est necessarium quod eadem verba referantur; sed sufficit quod solum intentio dicatur.

Sed quare dixerunt famuli: *noli vexare magistrum*? Videtur hoc fuisse incredulitatis.

Dicendum quod hoc verum esset, si hoc dicerent ex intentione domini; sed ipsi nesciebant eius intentionem.

first, the time of the invitation is described;

second, the person inviting;

third, the invitation;

fourth, the reception of the invitation.

775. He says then, *as he was speaking these things*, namely in Matthew's house.

But there is an objection, because Mark and Luke tell it in a different order, namely that this man came to Jesus after he had passed over the sea (Mark 5:21; Luke 8:40).

Augustine resolves it by saying that when something is set down in the evangelists which pertains to time, if it is set down at once, then the order of history is represented; and so when it says here, *as he was speaking these things*, the order of history is indicated; but in Mark and Luke it refers to the order of their own memory. Or one can say that there was some middle place where this happened. For sometimes they do not say whether they mean immediately, after, or when something was done.

776. There follows *behold a certain ruler*. Here the person inviting is set down, namely the ruler of the synagogue, and he is called Jairus, 'enlightening' or 'enlightened'. *My Lord, hear us, you are a prince of God among us* (Gen 23:6).

777. There follows the invitation. And he does two things:

first, he showed reverence, because he personally *came up*. Likewise, he *adored*. Similarly, he confessed his power, because he says, *Lord*. This ruler signifies the ancient fathers, because they approached through desire, and, believing that the Christ was to come, they adored; *we will adore in the place where his feet stood* (Ps 131:7). Likewise, they confessed; *know that the Lord, he is God* (Ps 99:3).

778. There follows the danger: *my daughter is even now dead*.

The contrary is said in Luke and in Mark, because there it is said, *my daughter is at the point of death* (Mark 5:23; see also Luke 8:41). And while they were on the way, *some came from the ruler of the synagogue's house, saying: your daughter is dead* (Mark 5:35).

Augustine resolves it, saying that when this man Jairus left, she was already in her last moments, and he believed that he would not find her alive; so he asked rather that Jesus would come and reawaken her than that he would heal her. Hence he says, *my daughter is even now dead*, as though to say: I believe that she is now dead. Therefore, the others spoke according to what happened, but Matthew referred to his meaning. And so Augustine gives a good lesson, that it is not necessary that they be referred to the same words, but it is enough that only the meaning is spoken.

But why did those of the ruler's household say, *why do you trouble the master?* (Mark 5:35; Luke 8:49). This seems to have been unbelief.

One should say that this would be true, if they had said this by their lord's intention, but they did not know his

Chrysostomus sic exponit: *consuetudo est aliquorum quando volunt movere ad pietatem, quod exaggerant malum; ideo ut magis moveret eum, dixit* **defuncta est**.

Ista filia est synagoga, quae filia est principis, scilicet Moysi, quae mortua est per infidelitatem; Luc. XIX, 42: *nunc autem abscondita est ab oculis tuis* et cetera. Sed videtur esse in isto fides infidelitati coniuncta, quia quod credebat quod resuscitaret erat fidei; sed quod credebat quod absens non posset, hoc erat infidelitatis. Unde iste videtur similis Naaman, qui dixit: *putabam quod egrederetur ad me, et stans invocaret nomen Domini Dei sui, et tangeret manu sua locum leprae, et curaret me* et cetera. IV Reg. V, 11.

Sed veni, impone manum tuam super eam, et vivet. Mystice hic significatur appetitus patrum de venturo Christo; unde dicebant: **veni, impone manum tuam**, idest Christum, ut in Ps. CXLIII, 7: *emitte manum tuam de alto.*

779. *Et surgens Iesus secutus est eum.* **Surgens**, scilicet a prandio. Hic habetur documentum misericordiae Christi, quia ad petitionem illius statim ivit, ut habetur Is. XXX, v. 19: *statim ut audierit, respondit tibi dominus.* Item dat exemplum praelatis de sollicitudine, quod statim solliciti sint ad subveniendum peccatis. Item dat documentum obediendi, quia discipulos secum duxit, ut habetur Hebr. XIII, 17: *obedite praepositis vestris.* Sed non duxit Matthaeum, quia adhuc infirmus erat.

780. *Et ecce mulier.* Dat exemplum virtutis: et tria facit.

Primo describitur eius infirmitas;

secundum commendatio mulieris, ibi **dicebat enim intra se** etc.;

tertio benignitas Christi sanantis, ibi **at Iesus conversus** et cetera.

781. Dicit ergo **et ecce mulier**. Ut habetur Lev. XII, mulier quae patiebatur fluxum sanguinis, immunda erat, et non habitabat cum hominibus; ideo non accessit in domo, sed in via.

Et haec significat gentilitatem, quae ingressa est in plenitudinem Iudaeorum, ut habetur ad Rom. XI, 25: *caecitas ex parte contigit in Israel, donec plenitudo gentium intraret.* Haec, scilicet synagoga, habet fluxum sanguinis, scilicet errorem immolatitii sanguinis. Vel potest retorqueri ad peccata carnalia; unde *caro et sanguis regnum Dei non possidebunt*, I Cor. XV, 50.

Haec mulier **patiebatur duodecim annis**, et filia principis erat duodecim annorum; unde haec incepit pati, quando filia principis nata fuit.

intention. Chrysostom explains it in this way: *it is customary among some when they wish to move someone to pity that they exaggerate the evil; for this reason, to move him more, he said,* **my daughter is even now dead**.

This daughter is the synagogue, which is the daughter of the ruler, namely of Moses, which died through infidelity; *but now they are hidden from your eyes* (Luke 19:42). But there seems to be faith joined to infidelity in this man, because the fact that he believed that he would reawaken her was from faith; but the fact that he believed he could not do it while absent was from unbelief. Hence this man seems similar to Naaman, who said, *I thought he would have come out to me, and standing would have invoked the name of the Lord his God, and touched with his hand the place of the leprosy, and healed me* (2 Kgs 5:11).

But come, lay your hand upon her, and she will live. Mystically, this signifies the patriarchs' desire for the coming of Christ; hence they said, **come, lay your hand**, i.e., Christ, *put forth your hand from on high* (Ps 143:7).

779. *And Jesus rising up followed him, with his disciples.* **Rising**, namely from the meal. Here we have an example of Christ's mercy, because he came immediately at his petition, as is found, *at the voice of thy cry, as soon as he will hear, he will answer you* (Isa 30:19). Likewise, he gives an example of concern to leaders, that they might be immediately concerned to rescue those under them from sins. Likewise, he gives an example of obedience, because he brings the disciples with him, as is found, *obey your prelates* (Heb 13:17). But he did not bring Matthew, because he was still weak.

780. *And behold a woman.* He gives an example of virtue; and he does three things:

first, her infirmity is described;

second, the woman's trust, at *for she said within herself*;

third, the kindness of Christ, who heals her, at **but Jesus turning**.

781. He says then, **and behold a woman**. As is said in Leviticus, a woman who suffered from a flow of blood was unclean, and did not dwell with other men (Lev 12); so she did not approach Jesus in the house, but on the road.

And she signifies the gentiles, who have entered into the fullness of the Jews, as is said, *blindness in part has happened in Israel, until the fullness of the gentiles should come in* (Rom 11:25). She, namely the synagogue, has a flow of blood, namely the error of the sacrificial blood. Or it can be referred to sins of the flesh; hence, *flesh and blood cannot possess the kingdom of God* (1 Cor 15:50).

This woman was **troubled . . . for twelve years** and the daughter of the ruler was twelve years old; hence she began to suffer when the daughter of the ruler was born.

782. *Accessit retro et tetigit fimbriam vestimenti eius*. Hic ponitur commendatio ipsius mulieris ex ipsius humilitate, et ex fide quae maxima est ad impetrandum.

Accessit, et tetigit fimbriam a retro. Quare a retro? Quia immunda reputabatur; unde quicquid tangebat, immundum erat secundum legem, ideo timebat ne repudiaret eam. Item non est ausa tangere nisi fimbriam. Praecipiebatur in lege quod in quatuor angulis vestis portarent fimbrias, et ibi habebant tympana ad memoriam mandatorum Dei, et ut sic ab aliis dignoscerentur; et hanc vestem Christus habebat.

Mystice hoc significat gentilitatem, quae accessit per fidem. Sed retro, quia non ipso vivente. Item tetigit vestimentum, scilicet humanitatem, et solum fimbriam, quia per apostolos tantum.

783. *Dicebat enim intra se: si tetigero tantum vestimentum eius, salva ero*. Hilarius dicit: *multa est virtus Christi, quia non solum in anima, sed ex anima in corpus, et ex corpore in vestes redundat*. Et sic omnia quae tetigerunt Christi corpus, habere debemus in reverentiam; Ps. CXXXII, 2: *sicut unguentum in capite quod descendit in barbam, barbam Aaron, quod descendit in oram vestimenti eius* et cetera. *Quod descendit in barbam*, idest divinitas in carnes: *et in oram vestimenti*, idest in apostolos.

Salva ero. Sic si fecerimus, et ei adhaeserimus, salvi erimus. *Omnis enim qui invocaverit nomen Domini, salvus erit*.

784. *At Iesus conversus, et videns eam, dixit: confide, filia*. Hic ponitur Christi benignitas. Et primo ostenditur facto, quia **conversus ad eam**. Et quare? Ne diffideret: quia enim furtive accesserat, non credebat quia converteretur ad eam. Item ut traheretur ad exemplum fides istius. Item ut se Deum ostenderet: unde conversus est conversione misericordiae, et vidit eam oculo pietatis; Zach. I, v. 3: *convertimini ad me, et ego convertar ad vos*.

Item ostenditur eius benignitas verbo, cum dicit **confide**: quia timens accessit, ideo blande eam alloquitur; Is. XXX, 15: *si revertimini, et quiescatis, salvi eritis*. Item vocat eam filiam, ne diffidat; Io. I, 12: *dedit eis potestatem filios Dei fieri*. Item dat spem **fides tua te salvam fecit**. Unde *nostra salus ex fide est*, ut habetur ad Rom. III.

Et sequitur effectus **et salva facta est mulier ex illa hora**; et non ex hora qua Christus dixit, sed ex hora qua tetigit.

782. *Came behind him, and touched the hem of his garment*. Here is set down this woman's trust, out of her humility, and out of faith, which is the greatest thing of all for obtaining what is sought.

She **came behind him, and touched the hem of his garment**. Why from behind? Because she was considered unclean; hence, whatever she touched was unclean according to the law, so she feared lest Christ should reject her. And it is no outrageous deed to touch only the fringe. It was commanded in the law that they should wear fringes on the four corners of their clothing, and they had timbrils there for the memory of God's commandments, and so that they might be distinguished in this way from others; and Christ had this clothing.

Mystically, this signifies the gentiles, who approached by faith. But from behind, because not while he was alive. Likewise, she touched the clothing, namely the humanity, and only the fringe, because only through the apostles.

783. *For she said within herself: if I will touch only his garment, I will be healed*. Hilary says: *the power of Christ is great, because it is not only in the soul, but overflows out of the soul into the body, and out of the body into his clothing*. And thus we ought to hold in reverence everything which has touched the body of Christ; *like the precious ointment on the head, that ran down upon the beard, the beard of Aaron, which ran down to the skirt of his garment* (Ps 132:2). *That ran down upon the beard*, i.e., the divinity into the body; *which ran down to the skirt of his garment*, i.e., into the apostles.

I will be healed. If we act in this way, and if we cling to him, we will be saved. *For every one that will call upon the name of the Lord will be saved* (Joel 2:32).

784. *But Jesus turning and seeing her, said: be of good heart, daughter*. Here Christ's kindness is set down. And first, it is shown by deed: *turning and seeing her*. And why? Lest she should despair, for since she had approached furtively, she did not believe that he would turn to her. Also, so that her faith might be made an example. Likewise, that she might show herself to God; hence the turning was the turning of mercy, and he saw her with the eyes of pity. *Turn to me . . . and I will turn to you* (Zech 1:3).

Similarly, his kindness is shown by word, when he says, **be of good heart**, because she approached fearfully, so he addresses her encouragingly. *If you return and be quiet, you will be saved* (Isa 30:15). Likewise, he calls her **daughter**, lest she despair; *he gave them power to be made the sons of God* (John 1:12). Similarly, he gives hope: **your faith has made you whole**. Hence *our salvation is by faith* (Rom 3).

And there follows the effect: **and the woman was made whole from that hour**; and not from the hour in which Christ spoke, but from the hour in which she touched his garment.

785. *Et cum venisset Iesus in domum principis, et vidisset tibicines* et cetera. Hic ponitur resuscitatio: et quatuor facit.

Primo mortis indicia describuntur;

secundo datur spes, ibi *recedite* etc.;

tertio ponitur resuscitatio;

quarto ponitur effectus;

786. Dicit ergo *cum venisset . . . et vidisset* et cetera. Et quare venerunt tibicines? Turba venit sicut solet fieri etiam de mortuis modo; sed tibicines, quia fuit consuetudo quod veniebant tibicines, et cantabant lugubria, ut alios excitarent ad fletum, ut habetur Ier. IX, 17: *contemplamini, et vocate lamentatrices, et veniant.* Hi tibicines sunt falsi doctores: *lingua enim eorum et adinventiones eorum contra Dominum, ut provocarent oculos maiestatis eius.* Turba autem populus Iudaicus; Ex. XXIII, 2: *non sequeris turbam ad faciendum malum.*

Hanc suscitavit Dominus in domo: tres enim mortuos suscitavit Dominus: puellam in domo, iuvenem in porta, Lazarum in sepulcro.

Quidam enim peccato moriuntur; sed non extra feruntur, et hoc est per consensum in peccatum; sed non exeunt ad extra per opera. Quidam autem extra fertur ad actum; et hic significatur per eum quem suscitat in porta. Quidam vero ex consuetudine iacet in sepulcro, qui significatur per Lazarum.

Haec igitur puella significat peccatorem, qui est in peccato occulto, scilicet in mente. Tibicines sunt qui fovent eum in peccato; Ps. X, v. 3: *laudatur peccator in desideriis animae suae.* Turba est cogitationes: et hanc sanat Dominus.

787. Unde dicit *recedite non est mortua*.

Hic dat spem *non est mortua*, scilicet sibi; *sed dormit*, quia est ita sibi facile resuscitare, sicut alicui aliquem excitare a somno. Simile habetur Io. XI, 11: *Lazarus amicus noster dormit* et cetera.

Non est mortua. Et quare dixit hoc modo? Quia *deridebant eum.* Sed quare voluit derideri? Hoc fuit ut non possent contra miraculum dicere. Unde primo adversarios faciebat confiteri, ut post contradicere non possent.

788. *Et cum eiecta esset turba, intravit.* Et quare eiecta fuit turba? Quia videre non fuit digna. Turba sunt Iudaei qui non convertuntur. Et moraliter ad hoc quod anima suscitetur, oportet quod turba cogitationum expellatur; et tunc intrat Dominus. *Intravit et tenuit manum eius* et cetera. Ps. CXVII, 16: *dextera Domini fecit virtutem.* Tenet manum peccatoris, quando adiutorium ei praebet. *Et surrexit puella*, scilicet ad vitam; sic nos per Dei adiutorium a peccato.

785. *And when Jesus had come into the house of the ruler, and saw the minstrels*. Here the reawakening is set down; and he does four things:

first, the signs of death are described;

second, hope is given, at *move away*;

third, the reawakening is set down;

fourth, the effect is set down.

786. He says then, *and when Jesus had come . . . and saw*. And why did the minstrels come? The crowd came just as it is customary to do even now for a death; but the minstrels came because it was the custom that minstrels came and played sorrowful music, that they might stir others to weeping, as is said, *consider, and call for the mourning women, and let them come* (Jer 9:17). These minstrels are false teachers: *because their tongue, and their devices are against the Lord, to provoke the eyes of his majesty* (Isa 3:8). And crowd is the Jewish people; *you will not follow the multitude to do evil* (Exod 23:2).

The Lord awakened her in the house, for the Lord awakened three dead people: the girl in the house, the young man in the city gates, and Lazarus in the sepulcher.

For some men die by sin, but are not carried outside; and this happens when they consent to sin, but do not go outside by works. Further, some men are carried outside to the act, and they are signified by the one who was awakened in the city gates. But some by forming a habit lie in the sepulcher, and these are signified by Lazarus.

So this girl signifies a sinner who is ensnared in a hidden sin, namely one in the mind. The minstrels are those who encourage her in sin; *for the sinner is praised in the desires of his soul* (Ps 9:24). The crowd is her thoughts, and the Lord heals this.

787. Hence he says, *move away, for the girl is not dead*.

Here he gives hope: *the girl is not dead*, namely to him; *but sleeps*, because it is easy for him to awaken her, just as for someone to arouse someone from sleep. A similar thing is found, *Lazarus our friend sleeps* (John 11:11).

The girl is not dead. And why did he speak this way? Because *they laughed him to scorn*. But why did he wish to be mocked? This was so that they could not speak against the miracle. Hence he first made the adversaries confess, so that afterward they could not contradict the report.

788. *And when the multitude was driven out, he went in*. And why was the crowd thrown out? Because they were not worthy to see. The crowd was Jews who were not converted. And morally: for the soul to be awakened, it is necessary that the crowd of thoughts be expelled; and then the Lord enters. *He went in, and took her by the hand*. The *right hand of the Lord has wrought strength* (Ps 117:16). He takes the hand of the sinner, when he offers him help. *And she arose*, namely to life; in this way, we arise from sin by God's help.

789. Sequitur divulgatio in omnem terram.

789. There follows the spreading abroad of the report into all the land.

Lecture 5

⁹:²⁷ Et transeunte inde Iesu, secuti sunt eum duo caeci clamantes, et dicentes: miserere nostri, Fili David. [n. 791]

⁹:²⁸ Cum autem venisset domum, accesserunt ad eum caeci, et dicit eis Iesus: creditis, quia possum hoc facere vobis? Dicunt ei: utique, Domine. [n. 792]

⁹:²⁹ Tunc tetigit oculos eorum dicens: secundum fidem vestram fiat vobis. [n. 793]

⁹:³⁰ Et aperti sunt oculi eorum. Et comminatus est illis Iesus, dicens: videte ne quis sciat. [n. 793]

⁹:³¹ Illi autem exeuntes diffamaverunt eum in tota terra illa. [n. 794]

⁹:³² Egressis autem illis, ecce obtulerunt ei hominem mutum daemonium habentem; [n. 795]

⁹:³³ et, eiecto daemonio, locutus est mutus, et miratae sunt turbae dicentes: numquam apparuit sic in Israel. [n. 797]

⁹:³⁴ Pharisaei autem dicebant: in principe daemoniorum eiicit daemones. [n. 799]

⁹:²⁷ Καὶ παράγοντι ἐκεῖθεν τῷ Ἰησοῦ ἠκολούθησαν [αὐτῷ] δύο τυφλοὶ κράζοντες καὶ λέγοντες· ἐλέησον ἡμᾶς, υἱὸς Δαυίδ.

⁹:²⁸ ἐλθόντι δὲ εἰς τὴν οἰκίαν προσῆλθον αὐτῷ οἱ τυφλοί, καὶ λέγει αὐτοῖς ὁ Ἰησοῦς· πιστεύετε ὅτι δύναμαι τοῦτο ποιῆσαι; λέγουσιν αὐτῷ· ναὶ κύριε.

⁹:²⁹ τότε ἥψατο τῶν ὀφθαλμῶν αὐτῶν λέγων· κατὰ τὴν πίστιν ὑμῶν γενηθήτω ὑμῖν.

⁹:³⁰ καὶ ἠνεῴχθησαν αὐτῶν οἱ ὀφθαλμοί. καὶ ἐνεβριμήθη αὐτοῖς ὁ Ἰησοῦς λέγων· ὁρᾶτε μηδεὶς γινωσκέτω.

⁹:³¹ οἱ δὲ ἐξελθόντες διεφήμισαν αὐτὸν ἐν ὅλῃ τῇ γῇ ἐκείνῃ.

⁹:³² Αὐτῶν δὲ ἐξερχομένων ἰδοὺ προσήνεγκαν αὐτῷ ἄνθρωπον κωφὸν δαιμονιζόμενον.

⁹:³³ καὶ ἐκβληθέντος τοῦ δαιμονίου ἐλάλησεν ὁ κωφός. καὶ ἐθαύμασαν οἱ ὄχλοι λέγοντες· οὐδέποτε ἐφάνη οὕτως ἐν τῷ Ἰσραήλ.

⁹:³⁴ οἱ δὲ Φαρισαῖοι ἔλεγον· ἐν τῷ ἄρχοντι τῶν δαιμονίων ἐκβάλλει τὰ δαιμόνια.

⁹:²⁷ And as Jesus passed from there, there followed him two blind men crying out and saying, have mercy on us, O Son of David. [n. 791]

⁹:²⁸ And when he had come to the house, the blind men came to him. And Jesus says to them, do you believe that I can do this to you? They say to him, yes, Lord. [n. 792]

⁹:²⁹ Then he touched their eyes, saying: according to your faith, be it done unto you. [n. 793]

⁹:³⁰ And their eyes were opened, and Jesus strictly charged them, saying, see that no man know this. [n. 793]

⁹:³¹ But going out, they spread his fame abroad in all that country. [n. 794]

⁹:³² And when they had gone out, behold they brought him a dumb man, possessed with a devil. [n. 795]

⁹:³³ And after the devil was cast out, the dumb man spoke, and the multitudes wondered, saying, never was the like seen in Israel. [n. 797]

⁹:³⁴ But the Pharisees said, by the prince of devils he casts out devils. [n. 799]

---

790. Supra ostensum est qualiter vitam restituit, hic tangitur quomodo dedit officia vitae. Et

primo tangitur quomodo visum restituit;
secundo quomodo loquelam, ibi *egressis autem illis* et cetera.
Et primo quatuor facit.
Primo ponitur petitio caecorum;
secundo examinatio credentium, ibi *et dicit eis Iesus* etc.;
tertio exauditio, ibi *tunc tetigit oculos eorum*;
quarto instructio illuminatorum, ibi *et comminatus est*.

791. Circa petitionem istorum quinque notare possumus, quae faciunt petitionem exaudibilem. Primo, quia congruum tempus elegerunt ad petendum, quia *transeunte eo*: et in hoc significatur tempus incarnationis, quod est tempus miserendi; unde in Ps. ci, 14: *quia venit tempus miserendi eius*. Et ideo melius exauditi fuerunt,

790. It was shown above how he restored life; here is touched upon how he restored the due functions of life. And

first, how he restored vision is touched upon;
second, how he restored speech, at *but they going out*.

And first, he does four things:
first, the blind men's petition is set down;
second, examination of those who believed, at *and Jesus says to them*;
third, the answer, at *then he touched their eyes*;
fourth, the instruction of those enlightened, at *and Jesus strictly charged them*.

791. Concerning their petition, we can notice five things which make a petition grantable. First, that they chose a fitting time to ask, because it was as he passed by; and in this is signified the time of the incarnation, which is the time of compassion; hence, *it is time to have mercy on it, for the time is come* (Ps 101:14). And therefore they were heeded better,

ut habetur Hebr. V, 7: *exauditus est pro reverentia sua.* Item ad hoc ut impetrarent *secuti sunt eum*: qui enim Deum non sequuntur obediendo, non impetrant. *Duo caeci.* Isti duo caeci sunt duo populi, scilicet Iudaeorum, et gentilium: caeci enim sunt qui fidem non habent; de talibus dicitur Is. LIX, 10: *palpavimus sicut caeci parietem.* Item requiritur fervor devotionis, cum dicitur *clamantes*, ut habetur in Ps. CXIX, v. 1: *ad Dominum cum tribularer clamavi, et exaudivit me.* Item humilitas petentium, cum dicitur *dicentes Fili David, miserere nostri*, ut habetur Dan. IX, 17: *exaudi, Deus noster, orationem servi tui.* Item tangitur fides eorum, quia Filium David nominant, et haec est necessaria, ut habetur Iac. I, 6: *postulet in fide, et nihil haesitans.*

792. Deinde petentes examinat. Primo facto, differendo exauditionem eorum. Tunc enim firma fides ostenditur, quando statim non impetratur; Hab. II, 3: *si moram fecerit, expecta eum, quia veniet.* Unde duxit eos usque ad domum. *Cum autem venisset domum* et cetera. Per domum istam intelligitur Ecclesia, quia ista est domus Dei vel caelum; Ps. CXIII, 16: *caelum caeli Domino.* Item examinavit eos verbo *creditis quia hoc possum facere vobis?* Et hoc non petit quasi ignorans, sed ut meritum eorum augeatur; Rom. X, 10: *corde creditur ad iustitiam, ore autem confessio fit ad salutem.* Item petit ut ostendatur fides aliis, ut sciant quia iuste illuminavit. Item petit ut ad maiora promoveat: magnum enim professi erant, quia Filium David. Sed non sufficiebat, ideo magis ab eis petit. *Creditis, quia possum hoc facere?* Scilicet propria potestate, quod solius Dei est. *Dicunt ei: utique, Domine.* Unde modo *Dominum* vocant, quod est proprium solius Dei.

793. Sequitur exauditio. Et primo ponitur curatio; secundo curationis effectus, ibi *et aperti sunt oculi eorum.*

Ponitur curatio, cum *tetigit oculos eorum, dicens*; unde tetigit, et dixit. Utrumque tamen per se sufficiebat; tamen utrumque fecit, ut significaretur quod caecitas per Verbum incarnatum illuminatur; Io. I, 14: *Verbum caro factum est, et habitavit in nobis, et vidimus gloriam eius.* Unde dicit *secundum fidem vestram fiat vobis*, quia merito fidei illuminantur qui sine fide sunt caeci.

Sequitur effectus *et aperti sunt oculi eorum.* Primo ergo dat lumen; et ita implevit illud: *et vita erat lux hominum.* Is. XXXV, 4: *ipse veniet et salvabit nos.*

794. Sequitur instructio; unde dicit *et comminatus est.*

as is found, *who . . . was heard for his reverence* (Heb 5:7). Similarly, so that they might ask, *they followed him*; for let those who do not follow God by obeying him ask for nothing. *Two blind men.* These two blind men are two peoples, namely the Jews and the gentiles; for the blind are those who do not have faith. About such is said, *we have groped for the wall, and like the blind we have groped as if we had no eyes* (Isa 59:10). Likewise, fervor of devotion is required, when it says, *crying out*, as is had, *in my trouble I cried to the Lord: and he heard me* (Ps 119:1). Likewise, humility in those asking, when it says, *and saying, have mercy on us, O Son of David*, as is found, *now therefore, O our God, hear the supplication of your servant* (Dan 9:17). Likewise, their faith is touched upon, because they call him the Son of David, and this is necessary, as is said, *but let him ask in faith, nothing wavering* (Jas 1:6).

792. Then he examines the ones asking. First, by deed, by delaying their answer. For then their faith is shown to be firm, when what is asked is not immediately obtained; *if it make any delay, wait for it: for it will surely come* (Hab 2:3). Hence he led them all the way to the house. *And when he had come to the house.* By this house is understood the Church, because the Church is the house of God, or heaven; *the heaven of heaven is the Lord's* (Ps 113:24). Similarly, he tested them by word: *do you believe, that I can do this to you?* And he does not ask this as though ignorant, but so that their merit might be increased; *for, with the heart, we believe unto justice; but, with the mouth, confession is made unto salvation* (Rom 10:10). Likewise, he asks so that their faith might be shown to others, that they might know that he enlightens the just. Likewise, he asks so that they might move forward to greater things; for they had professed a great thing, that he was the Son of David. But it was not enough, so he asks more of them. *Do you believe, that I can do this to you?* That is, with my own proper power, which is only God's. *They say to him, yes, Lord.* Hence now they call him *Lord*, which is proper to God alone.

793. There follows the answer. And first, the healing is set down; second the effect of the healing, at *and their eyes were opened.*

The healing is set down, *then he touched their eyes, saying*; hence he touched, and spoke. While either was enough by itself, yet he did both, to signify that blindness is enlightened by the Word incarnate. *And the Word was made flesh, and dwelt among us, and we saw his glory* (John 1:14). Hence he says, *according to your faith, be it done unto you*, because they who without faith are blind are enlightened by the merit of faith.

There follows the effect: *and their eyes were opened.* First, then, he gives light; and thus fulfills: *and the life was the light of men* (John 1:4). *God himself will come and will save you* (Isa 35:4).

794. There follows the instruction; hence it says, *and Jesus strictly charged them.*

Et quare hoc? Alibi enim dicitur: *vade ad tuos, et annuntia* regnum Dei. Chrysostomus: *in bonis nostris duo possumus considerare: quod Dei est, et quod nostri: quod nostri est, debemus latere; quod Dei est, debemus manifestare, ut Paulus Philipp. II. Quaerentes non quae nostra sunt, sed quae Iesu Christi.* Supra V, 16: *ut videant opera vestra bona, et glorificent Patrem vestrum, qui in caelis est.* Unde dicit *videte ne quis sciat*, ut doceat vitare vanam gloriam.

Illi autem, non immemores beneficii accepti exeuntes diffamaverunt eum, ut habetur Is. LXIII, 7: *miserationum Domini recordabor.*

Sed numquid peccaverunt isti, quia contra praeceptum Domini fecerunt? Dico quod non, quia bona fide fecerunt, et ut ostenderent quantum sanctitatis exhibeat Dominus.

795. Egressis illis, ecce obtulerunt ei hominem mutum. Supra Dominus restituit visum caeco; nunc muto restituit loquelam. Et sufficienter iunguntur ista, quia locutio est signum visionis interioris; Is. XXXV, 4: *ipse veniet, et salvabit nos. Et tunc aperientur oculi caecorum, et aures surdorum patebunt.*

Et in hoc tria facit.

Primo describitur infirmus;

secundo tangitur curatio, ibi *et eiecto daemonio, locutus est mutus*;

tertio curationis effectus, ibi *et miratae sunt turbae.*

796. Dicit ergo *egressis autem illis* et cetera. Ab isto non quaeritur fides, sicut a praecedentibus, quia iste erat obsessus a daemonio; ideo non erat compos mentis: et ideo non quaesivit de fide eius.

Et iste significat gentilem populum, qui mutus est ad laudem; Ps. LXXVIII, 6: *effunde iram tuam in gentes, quae te non noverunt.* Item habent daemonium, quia daemonibus immolant; Ps. XCV, 5: *omnes dii gentium daemonia.*

797. Primo ergo ut bonus medicus curavit causam, secundo morbum, quia primo eiecit daemonium, et sic *eiecto daemonio, locutus est mutus.* Sic gentilis dum liberatus est ab idolorum servitute *locutus est mutus*, scilicet laudem Dei; *ut omnis lingua confiteatur, quia Dominus Iesus Christus in gloria est Dei Patris* et cetera. Phil. II, 11.

798. Sequitur effectus *et miratae sunt turbae.* Unde mirabantur super his quae videbant. Et quia mirabantur, ideo dicebant. *Numquam apparuit sic in Israel.*

Verum est quod Moyses fecit miracula, et alii; sed talis non fuerat, scilicet qui tot faceret. Item qui solo tactu. Item qui statim; ita quod ei conveniat: *quis similis tui in fortibus, Domine, quis similis tui?* Ut habetur Ex. XV, 11;

And why was this? For to another he said, *go into your house to your friends, and tell them* the kingdom of God (Mark 5:19). Chrysostom: *we can consider two things in our goods: what is ours, we should hide; what is God's we should manifest, as Paul says, 'seeking not what is ours, but what is Jesus Christ's'* (Phil 2). Above, **that they may see your good works, and glorify your Father who is in heaven** (Matt 5:16). Hence he says, **see that no man know this**, that he might teach them to avoid vainglory.

But they, not forgetful of the benefits received, went out and spread his fame abroad, as is written, *I will remember the tender mercies of the Lord* (Isa 63:7).

But did not these men sin, because they acted against the Lord's command? I say not, because they acted in good faith, and that they might display how great was the holiness the Lord showed them.

795. And when they had gone out, behold they brought him a dumb man. Above, the Lord restored vision to the blind; now he restored speech to the mute. And these things are sufficiently connected, because speech is a sign of interior vision; *God himself will come and will save you. Then will the eyes of the blind be opened, and the ears of the deaf will be unstopped* (Isa 35:4–5).

And in this he does three things:

first, the sick man is described;

second, the healing is touched upon, at **and after the devil was cast out, the dumb man spoke**;

third, the effect of the healing, at **and the multitudes wondered.**

796. He says then, **and when they had gone out.** Faith is not asked of this man, as from the ones before, because this man was possessed by a demon, so he was not in control of his mind. And so he did not ask about his faith.

And this man signifies the gentile people, which was mute with respect to praise; *pour out your wrath upon the nations that have not known you* (Ps 78:6). Likewise, they have demons, because they sacrifice to demons; *for all the gods of the gentiles are devils* (Ps 95:5).

797. First, then, as the good doctor, he cured the cause, and second the disease, because he first cast out the demon, and thus **after the devil was cast out, the dumb man spoke**. In this way the gentile, when he was freed from the servitude of idols, **the dumb man spoke**, namely the praise of God; *that every tongue should confess that the Lord Jesus Christ is in the glory of God the Father* (Phil 2:11).

798. There follows the effect: **and the multitudes wondered.** Hence they marveled over the things which they saw. And since they marveled, they said, **never was the like seen in Israel.**

It is true that Moses worked miracles, and other men; but there was not such a one, namely one who did so many. Likewise, there was never one who worked miracles by touch alone. Nor one who worked immediately, in the way

et Io. X, 25: *opera quae ego facio, testimonium perhibent de me.* Item curat per fidem, quod lex non poterat facere, ut habetur ad Rom. VIII, 2: *lex enim spiritus vitae in Christo Iesu liberavit me a lege peccati et mortis, quod impossibile est legi.*

799. Pharisaei autem dicebant. Pharisaei, idest 'divisi,' quia perverse interpretabantur, ut Eccli. XI, 33: *bona in malum vertent.* Unde dicebant **in principe daemoniorum eiicit daemones.**

Hic dicit Augustinus quod est notandum, quod Christus idem miraculum bis fecit. Et hoc patet, quia diversimode dicunt evangelistae. Unde cum invenimus quasi contraria, possumus referre ad unum, vel ad aliud, dicendo aliud esse miraculum.

which befit him. *Who is like to you, among the strong, O Lord?* (Exod 15:11); and, *the works that I do in the name of my Father, they give testimony of me* (John 10:25). Likewise, he heals through faith, which the law could not do, as is said, *for the law of the spirit of life, in Christ Jesus, has delivered me from the law of sin and of death* (Rom 8:2), which was impossible for the law.

799. But the Pharisees said. The Pharisees, i.e., 'the divided', because they were interpreting his deeds perversely, *for he lies in wait and turns good into evil* (Sir 11:33). Hence they said, **by the prince of devils he casts out devils.**

Here Augustine says that one should note that Christ worked the same miracle twice. And this is clear, because the evangelists speak in different ways. Hence when we find things which are contrary, as it were, we can refer to one or to the other, saying that the miracle was a different one.

Lecture 6

9:35 Et circuibat Iesus omnes civitates et castella, docens in synagogis eorum, et praedicans Evangelium regni, et curans omnem languorem, et omnem infirmitatem. [n. 801]

9:36 Videns autem turbas misertus est eis, quia erant vexati et iacentes, sicut oves non habentes pastorem. [n. 804]

9:37 Tunc dicit discipulis suis: messis quidem multa, operarii autem pauci. [n. 806]

9:38 Rogate ergo Dominum messis, ut mittat operarios in messem suam. [n. 809]

9:35 Καὶ περιῆγεν ὁ Ἰησοῦς τὰς πόλεις πάσας καὶ τὰς κώμας διδάσκων ἐν ταῖς συναγωγαῖς αὐτῶν καὶ κηρύσσων τὸ εὐαγγέλιον τῆς βασιλείας καὶ θεραπεύων πᾶσαν νόσον καὶ πᾶσαν μαλακίαν.

9:36 Ἰδὼν δὲ τοὺς ὄχλους ἐσπλαγχνίσθη περὶ αὐτῶν, ὅτι ἦσαν ἐσκυλμένοι καὶ ἐρριμμένοι ὡσεὶ πρόβατα μὴ ἔχοντα ποιμένα.

9:37 τότε λέγει τοῖς μαθηταῖς αὐτοῦ· ὁ μὲν θερισμὸς πολύς, οἱ δὲ ἐργάται ὀλίγοι·

9:38 δεήθητε οὖν τοῦ κυρίου τοῦ θερισμοῦ ὅπως ἐκβάλῃ ἐργάτας εἰς τὸν θερισμὸν αὐτοῦ.

9:35 And Jesus went about all the cities and towns, teaching in their synagogues, and preaching the Gospel of the kingdom, and healing every disease, and every infirmity. [n. 801]

9:36 And seeing the multitudes, he had compassion on them: because they were distressed, and lying like sheep that have no shepherd. [n. 804]

9:37 Then he says to his disciples, the harvest indeed is great, but the laborers are few. [n. 806]

9:38 Beseech therefore the Lord of the harvest, that he send forth laborers into his harvest. [n. 809]

---

800. Ostensum est qualiter subvenerat occurrentibus, hic tangit quod ad eos ibat: et hic duo tangit.

Primo qualiter impendit quibusdam effectum; secundo quomodo affectum, ibi *videns autem turbas, misertus est eis.*
Et circa primum
primo ostendit ubi impendit auxilium;
secundo quod docuit; tertio quod fecit.

801. Dicit ergo *et circuibat Iesus omnes civitates et castella.* In quo datur praedicatoribus exemplum, quod non sint contenti praedicare in uno loco tantum; Io. XV, v. 16: *posui vos, ut eatis, et fructum afferatis* et cetera.

Omnes civitates et castella. Et bene illud ordinatur cum praecedentibus. Quia dixerant quod in principe daemoniorum eiiciebat daemonia; ideo manifestat se non habere daemonium, ut ei conveniat, Ps. CXIX, 7: *cum his qui oderunt pacem eram pacificus, dum loquebar illis, impugnabant me gratis.*

802. Sequitur quid annuntiabat; duo enim faciebat, quia *in synagogis* erat *docens et praedicans.*

Docens quae ad fidem *praedicans* quae ad mores. Item coram multis, quia in *synagogis*; in Ps. XXXIX, 10: *annuntiavi iustitiam tuam in ecclesia magna*: in quo etiam differt a doctrina haereticorum, quae est in occulto. Secus doctrina Christi; Io. XVIII, 20: *nihil in occulto locutus sum vobis.*

Item tangit quae docet, quia *Evangelium regni*; Io. XVIII, 37: *in hoc natus sum, et ad hoc veni in mundum,*

800. It was shown how he had helped those who approached; here he touches upon the fact that he went to them. And here he touches upon two things:
first, how he imparts an effect to certain ones;
second, how he gives affection, at *and seeing the multitudes, he had compassion on them.*
And concerning the first,
first he shows where he imparts help;
second, what he taught; third, what he did.

801. It says then, *and Jesus went about all the cities and towns.* In which an example is given to preachers that they should not be content to preach in one place only; *I have chosen you; and have appointed you, that you should go, and should bring forth fruit* (John 15:16).

All the cities and towns. And this is well ordered with what came before, because they had said that he cast out demons by the prince of demons; therefore he makes it plain that he does not have a demon, as befits him; *with those who hated peace I was peaceable: when I spoke to them they fought against me without cause* (Ps 119:7).

802. There follows what he announced; for he did two things, since he was *teaching* and *preaching in the synagogues.*

Teaching those things which pertain to faith, *preaching* those things which pertain to morals. Likewise, it was before many people, because he was in the synagogues; *I have declared your justice in a great church* (Ps 39:10), in which it also differs from the teaching of the heretics, which is secret. Not so the teaching of Christ: *in secret I have spoken nothing* (John 18:20).

Likewise, it touches upon what he teaches, *the Gospel of the kingdom*; *for this was I born, and for this came I into the*

ut testimonium perhibeam veritati et cetera. Unde caelestia docebat; Is. XLVIII, 17: *ego Dominus docens te utilia.*

803. Postea ostenditur facto quid fecit **curans omnem languorem et omnem infirmitatem. Languores,** quoad graves infirmitates; **infirmitates,** quoad leves; in Ps. CII, 3: *qui propitiatur omnibus iniquitatibus tuis, qui sanat omnes infirmitates tuas.* Et quare hoc? Ut confirmaret miraculo quod dicebat verbo, ut in Mc. ult., 20: *Domino cooperante, et sermonem confirmante sequentibus signis.* Item ut ostenderet exemplum praedicatoribus ut facerent et docerent; Act. I, 1: *coepit Iesus facere et docere.*

804. Videns autem Iesus turbas, misertus est illis. Hic ostendit qualiter Dominus quibusdam impendit affectum; et hoc contra quosdam; opinio enim fuit quod nullus sufficiebat affectus, sed requirebatur effectus; sed hic dicit **videns Iesus turbas, misertus est illis.**

Et primo tangit quomodo miserebatur; secundo ponit exemplum. Et primo ponit misericordiam Christi; secundo causam.

805. Dicit ergo **videns** etc. scilicet pia consideratione, **misertus est eis,** quia proprium est ei misereri; Ps. CXLIV, 9: *miserationes eius super omnia opera eius.* Istud visum desiderabat David, dicens Ps. XXIV, 16: *respice in me, et miserere mei.* Et quibus misertus est, quia **vexati,** a daemonibus, item **iacentes,** scilicet prostrati ab infirmitatibus. Vel **vexati** erroribus, **iacentes** peccatis, **sicut oves non habentes pastorem.** Unde Prov. XI, 14: *ubi non est gubernator, populus corruet* et cetera. Et Ez. c. XXXIV, 5: *dispersae sunt oves meae, eo quod non esset eis pastor;* et in eodem: *vae pastoribus Israel qui pascebant semetipsos.* Ut Zac. XI, 17: *O pastor et idolum derelinquens gregem.*

806. Tunc dicit discipulis suis. Hic inducit aliquos ad miserendum, et

primo assignat causam;

secundo inducit ad effectum, ibi **rogate ergo Dominum messis ut mittat operarios in messem suam.**

Et ponit duas causas.

Primo multitudinem tendentium ad bonum;

secundo paucitatem doctorum, ibi **operarii autem pauci.**

807. Multi convenerant; ideo dicit **messis quidem multa. Messis** non dicitur quando frumentum florescit, vel cum est in spica, sed tunc quando iam dispositum est ut colligatur; sic homines iam dispositi erant ad credendum per effectum praedicatorum: simile habetur

world; that I should give testimony to the truth (John 18:37). Hence he taught heavenly things; *I am the Lord your God who teaches you profitable things* (Isa 48:17).

803. Next, what he did by deed is shown: **healing every disease, and every infirmity. Disease,** regarding heavy infirmities; **infirmities,** regarding the light; *who forgives all your iniquities: who heals all your diseases* (Ps 102:3). And why is this? That he might confirm by miracle what he taught by word, *the Lord working withal, and confirming the word with signs that followed* (Mark 16:20). Also, that he might show an example to preachers, that they should do and teach; *Jesus began to do and to teach* (Acts 1:1).

804. And seeing the multitudes, he had compassion on them. Here he shows how the Lord gave affection to certain men; and this against the opinion of some, for there has been the opinion that affection suffices for nothing, but rather an effect is required. But here he says, **and seeing the multitudes, he had compassion on them.**

And first, he touches upon how he had compassion; second, he sets forth the example. And first, he sets down Christ's mercy; second, the reason.

805. He says then, **seeing the multitudes,** namely with a pious consideration, **he had compassion on them,** because it is proper to him to be compassionate; *his tender mercies are over all his works* (Ps 144:9). David desired this vision, saying, *look upon me, and have mercy on me* (Ps 24:16). And he had compassion on them, **because they were distressed** by demons, and also **lying,** that is, prostrated by infirmities. Or **distressed** by errors, **lying** in sins, **like sheep that have no shepherd.** Hence, *where there is no governor, the people will fall* (Prov 11:14). And, *and my sheep were scattered, because there was no shepherd* (Ezek 34:5); and in the same place, *woe to the shepherds of Israel, that fed themselves* (Ezek 34:2). As in, *O shepherd, and idol, that forsakes the flock* (Zech 11:17).

806. Then he says to his disciples. Here he leads other men to have compassion, and

first, he gives the reason;

second, he leads them to the effect, at **beseech therefore the Lord of the harvest, that he send forth laborers into his harvest.**

And he sets forth two causes:

first, the multitude of those stretching out toward the good;

second, the scarcity of teachers, at **but the laborers are few.**

807. Many had come together, and so he says, **the harvest indeed is great. The harvest** is not said when the grain flowers, or when it is on the ear, but at the time when it is ready to be collected; thus men were already disposed to believing through the effect of preachers. A similar thing is

Io. IV, 35: *levate oculos vestros, et videte regiones, quoniam albae sunt iam ad messem.*

808. *Et operarii pauci*, scilicet boni; unde Apostolus, I Cor. III, 9: *Dei enim adiutores sumus.* Impendentes ergo quod vestrum est.

809. Et quid? ***Rogate Dominum messis ut mittat operarios in messem suam***. Quando habemus defectum, debemus recurrere ad Deum, cum officium praedicationis non nisi precibus impetretur: qui enim mittit operarios, est Dominus, unde dicitur; *ego misi vos*. Et rogat ut rogetur, ut nobis accumulet meritum, dum pro salute aliorum oramus. Item talem ordinem posuit, ut sanctitas aliorum aliis prosit, ut I Petr. IV, 10: *unusquisque ut accepit gratiam in alterutrum illam administrantes, sicut boni dispensatores multiformis gratiae Dei* et cetera. Unde vult ut quicquid gratiae et sanctitatis receperunt, aliis impendant, et ipse rogatus exaudit. Rogat enim ut ipse rogetur ut eos mittat; Rom. X, 15: *quomodo praedicabunt nisi mittantur?* Acquiritur enim auctoritas; item gratia, unde: *caritas Christi urget nos.*

Item, ***rogate Dominum messis ut mittat operarios***, non quaestuarios qui corrumpunt malo exemplo, ***in messem suam***, scilicet in messem Dei. Quaestuarii enim non mittuntur in messem Dei, sed in messem suam, quia non quaerunt gloriam Dei, sed commodum suum.

found in, *lift up your eyes, and see the countries; for they are white already to harvest* (John 4:35).

808. *But the laborers are few*, namely good men; hence the Apostle: *for we are God's coadjutors* (1 Cor 3:9). Spend therefore what is yours.

809. And what then? ***Beseech therefore the Lord of the harvest, that he send forth laborers into his harvest***. When we have a lack, we should run back to God, since the duty of preaching is only accomplished by prayers: for the one who sent the workers is the Lord, hence he says, *I have sent you* (John 4:38). And he asks that it should be asked, that we might accumulate merit when we pray for the salvation of others. Likewise, he set down such an ordering of things that the sanctity of some might profit others, *as every man has received grace, ministering the same one to another: as good stewards of the manifold grace of God* (1 Pet 4:10). Hence he willed that whatever they received of grace and sanctity, they should expend on others, and he himself hears when he is asked. For he asks that he should be asked to send them. *And how will they preach unless they be sent?* (Rom 10:15). For authority is obtained; likewise grace, hence: *the charity of Christ presses us* (2 Cor 5:14).

Similarly, ***beseech therefore the Lord of the harvest, that he send forth laborers***, not mercenaries who corrupt others by a bad example, ***into his harvest***, namely into God's harvest. For mercenaries are not sent into God's harvest, but into their own harvest, because they do not seek the glory of God, but their own gain.

Chapter 10

Lecture 1

10:1 Et convocatis duodecim discipulis suis, dedit illis potestatem spirituum immundorum, ut eiicerent eos, et curarent omnem languorem, et omnem infirmitatem. [n. 810]

10:2 Duodecim autem discipulorum nomina sunt haec. Primus Simon, qui dicitur Petrus, et Andreas frater eius, Philippus, et Bartholomaeus, [n. 812]

10:3 Iacobus Zebedaei, et Ioannes frater eius, Thomas et Matthaeus publicanus, et Iacobus Alphaei, et Thadaeus, [n. 812]

10:4 Simon Chananaeus, et Iudas Scariotis, qui et tradidit eum. [n. 812]

10:5 Hos duodecim misit Iesus, praecipiens eis, dicens: in viam gentium ne abieritis, et in civitates Samaritanorum ne intraveritis; [n. 813]

10:6 sed potius ite ad oves, quae perierunt domus Israel. [n. 816]

10:7 Euntes autem praedicate dicentes, quia appropinquabit regnum caelorum: [n. 817]

10:8 infirmos curate, mortuos suscitate, leprosos mundate, daemones eiicite: gratis accepistis, gratis date. [n. 818]

10:9 Nolite possidere aurum, neque argentum, neque pecuniam in zonis vestris. [n. 820]

10:10 Non peram in via, neque duas tunicas, neque calceamenta, neque virgam. Dignus est enim operarius cibo suo. [n. 823]

10:1 Καὶ προσκαλεσάμενος τοὺς δώδεκα μαθητὰς αὐτοῦ ἔδωκεν αὐτοῖς ἐξουσίαν πνευμάτων ἀκαθάρτων ὥστε ἐκβάλλειν αὐτὰ καὶ θεραπεύειν πᾶσαν νόσον καὶ πᾶσαν μαλακίαν.

10:2 Τῶν δὲ δώδεκα ἀποστόλων τὰ ὀνόματά ἐστιν ταῦτα· πρῶτος Σίμων ὁ λεγόμενος Πέτρος καὶ Ἀνδρέας ὁ ἀδελφὸς αὐτοῦ, καὶ Ἰάκωβος ὁ τοῦ Ζεβεδαίου καὶ Ἰωάννης ὁ ἀδελφὸς αὐτοῦ,

10:3 Φίλιππος καὶ Βαρθολομαῖος, Θωμᾶς καὶ Μαθθαῖος ὁ τελώνης, Ἰάκωβος ὁ τοῦ Ἀλφαίου καὶ Θαδδαῖος,

10:4 Σίμων ὁ Καναναῖος καὶ Ἰούδας ὁ Ἰσκαριώτης ὁ καὶ παραδοὺς αὐτόν.

10:5 Τούτους τοὺς δώδεκα ἀπέστειλεν ὁ Ἰησοῦς παραγγείλας αὐτοῖς λέγων· εἰς ὁδὸν ἐθνῶν μὴ ἀπέλθητε καὶ εἰς πόλιν Σαμαριτῶν μὴ εἰσέλθητε·

10:6 πορεύεσθε δὲ μᾶλλον πρὸς τὰ πρόβατα τὰ ἀπολωλότα οἴκου Ἰσραήλ.

10:7 πορευόμενοι δὲ κηρύσσετε λέγοντες ὅτι ἤγγικεν ἡ βασιλεία τῶν οὐρανῶν.

10:8 ἀσθενοῦντας θεραπεύετε, νεκροὺς ἐγείρετε, λεπροὺς καθαρίζετε, δαιμόνια ἐκβάλλετε· δωρεὰν ἐλάβετε, δωρεὰν δότε.

10:9 Μὴ κτήσησθε χρυσὸν μηδὲ ἄργυρον μηδὲ χαλκὸν εἰς τὰς ζώνας ὑμῶν,

10:10 μὴ πήραν εἰς ὁδὸν μηδὲ δύο χιτῶνας μηδὲ ὑποδήματα μηδὲ ῥάβδον· ἄξιος γὰρ ὁ ἐργάτης τῆς τροφῆς αὐτοῦ.

10:1 And having called his twelve disciples together, he gave them power over unclean spirits, to cast them out, and to heal all manner of diseases, and all manner of infirmities. [n. 810]

10:2 And the names of the twelve apostles are these: the first, Simon who is called Peter, and Andrew his brother, Philip and Bartholomew, [n. 812]

10:3 James the son of Zebedee, and John his brother, Thomas and Matthew the publican, and James the son of Alpheus, and Thaddeus, [n. 812]

10:4 Simon the Cananean, and Judas Iscariot, who also betrayed him. [n. 812]

10:5 These twelve Jesus sent, commanding them, saying: do not go into the way of the gentiles, and do not enter into the city of the Samaritans. [n. 813]

10:6 But go rather to the lost sheep of the house of Israel. [n. 816]

10:7 And going, preach, saying: the kingdom of heaven is at hand. [n. 817]

10:8 Heal the sick, raise the dead, cleanse the lepers, cast out devils: freely have you received, freely give. [n. 818]

10:9 Do not possess gold, nor silver, nor money in your purses: [n. 820]

10:10 Nor bag for your journey, nor two coats, nor shoes, nor a staff; for the workman is worthy of his hire. [n. 823]

^{10:11} In quamcumque autem civitatem, aut castellum intraveritis, interrogate, quis in ea dignus sit, et ibi manete donec exeatis. [n. 827]

^{10:12} Intrantes autem in domum, salutate eam dicentes: pax huic domui. [n. 830]

^{10:13} Et si quidem fuerit domus illa digna, veniet pax vestra super eam; si autem non fuerit digna, pax vestra revertetur ad vos. [n. 831]

^{10:14} Et quicumque non receperit vos, neque audierit sermones vestros, exeuntes foras de domo vel de civitate excutite pulverem de pedibus vestris. [n. 832]

^{10:15} Amen dico vobis, tolerabilius erit terrae Sodomorum et Gomorrhaeorum in die iudicii, quam illi civitati. [n. 835]

^{10:11} εἰς ἣν δ᾽ ἂν πόλιν ἢ κώμην εἰσέλθητε, ἐξετάσατε τίς ἐν αὐτῇ ἄξιός ἐστιν· κἀκεῖ μείνατε ἕως ἂν ἐξέλθητε.

^{10:12} εἰσερχόμενοι δὲ εἰς τὴν οἰκίαν ἀσπάσασθε αὐτήν [λέγοντες· εἰρήνη τῷ οἴκῳ τούτῳ.]

^{10:13} καὶ ἐὰν μὲν ᾖ ἡ οἰκία ἀξία, ἐλθάτω ἡ εἰρήνη ὑμῶν ἐπ᾽ αὐτήν, ἐὰν δὲ μὴ ᾖ ἀξία, ἡ εἰρήνη ὑμῶν πρὸς ὑμᾶς ἐπιστραφήτω.

^{10:14} καὶ ὃς ἂν μὴ δέξηται ὑμᾶς μηδὲ ἀκούσῃ τοὺς λόγους ὑμῶν, ἐξερχόμενοι ἔξω τῆς οἰκίας ἢ τῆς πόλεως ἐκείνης ἐκτινάξατε τὸν κονιορτὸν τῶν ποδῶν ὑμῶν.

^{10:15} ἀμὴν λέγω ὑμῖν, ἀνεκτότερον ἔσται γῇ Σοδόμων καὶ Γομόρρων ἐν ἡμέρᾳ κρίσεως ἢ τῇ πόλει ἐκείνῃ.

^{10:11} And into whatever city or town you will enter, inquire who in it is worthy, and abide there till you go leave. [n. 827]

^{10:12} And when you come into the house, salute it, saying: peace be to this house. [n. 830]

^{10:13} And if that house is worthy, your peace will come upon it; but if it is not worthy, your peace will return to you. [n. 831]

^{10:14} And whoever will not receive you, nor hear your words: going forth out of that house or city shake off the dust from your feet. [n. 832]

^{10:15} Amen I say to you, it will be more tolerable for the land of Sodom and Gomorrha in the day of judgment, than for that city. [n. 835]

---

810. Supra proposuerat doctrinam suam, hic ministros instituit. Et describuntur numero, potestate et nominum positione.

Numero, unde dicit **convocatis duodecim**. Et quare dicit **duodecim**? Ut ostenderetur conformitas Novi et Veteris Testamenti, quia in Veteri duodecim patriarchae: et isti similiter duodecim. Secunda ratio, ut ostenderetur virtus et effectus futurus per eos: iste enim numerus ex partibus quatuor et tribus in se ductis componitur, ut quater ter, vel ter quater. Per trinarium Trinitas designatur: per quaternarium mundus. Ideo signatur quod in totum mundum debebat eorum praedicatio extendi; unde Dominus Mc. ult., 15: *euntes in mundum universum praedicate Evangelium omni creaturae* et cetera. Item ad signandum perfectionem, quia duodenarius consistit ex duplicitate senarii: senarius enim perfectus est numerus, quia ex omnibus partibus aliquotis: consurgit enim per unum, duo et tria, et istae partes simul iunctae sunt sex. Unde tot vocavit ad signandum perfectionem. Supra, V, 48: **estote perfecti, sicut et Pater vester perfectus est**.

811. Sequitur de potestate eorum: quia **dedit eis potestatem** etc., scilicet ut ipsi faciant, vel facere possint, sicut ipse fecit. Et non solum quae fecit, sed maiora, Io. XIV, 12. Non est enim scriptum quod ad umbram Christi curarentur infirmi, sicut scriptum est quod ad umbram Petri multi curabantur; Act. V, 15. **Immundorum spirituum ut eiicerent eos**. Unde noluit quod ipsi eiicerent, sicut ipse; sed ipse vero proprio, ipsi vero in nomine Christi: unde Mc. ult., 17: *in nomine meo daemonia*

810. Above, he had set forth his teaching; here, he sets up his ministers. And they are described by number, power, and by position of name.

By number, hence it says, **and having called his twelve disciples together**. And why does it say **twelve**? That the conformity of the New and Old Testaments might be shown, because in the Old, there were twelve patriarchs, and these are likewise twelve. A second reason, that the power and effect about to come through them might be shown; for this number is put together out of four parts and three parts led into themselves, as four threes, or three fours. By the three, the Trinity is indicated; by the four, the world. So it is indicated that their preaching should be extended throughout the whole world; hence the Lord says, *go into the whole world, and preach the Gospel to every creature* (Mark 16:15). Likewise to signify perfection, because twelve consists in six doubled; for six is a perfect number, since it arises out of the sum of all the parts. For it arises through one, two, and three, and the parts joined together are also six. Hence he called this many to signify perfection. Above, **be you therefore perfect, as also your heavenly Father is perfect** (Matt 5:48).

811. What follows concerns their power, for **he gave them power**, namely that they themselves might do, or be able to do, as he did. And not only what he did, but greater things (John 14:1). For it is not written that the sick were healed by Christ's shadow, as it is written that many were healed by Peter's shadow (Acts 5:15). **Over unclean spirits**, that they might cast them out. Hence he did not will that they should cast them out as he did; but he cast them out by his own proper name, while they did so in the name of Christ.

eiicient et cetera. Et non solum ut daemonia eiicerent, sed ut **omnem languorem curarent**, ut habetur Mc. ult., 18: *super aegros manus imponent, et bene habebunt.*

Sed si quaeras, quare modo praedicatoribus non datur ista potestas, respondet Augustinus, quia in promptu est maximum miraculum, scilicet quod totus mundus conversus est. Aut ergo facta sunt miracula, et sic habeo propositum; si non, hoc est maximum: quia per duodecim vilissimos homines piscatores totus mundus conversus est.

812. Sequitur nominum positio. Et quare? Ne si veniret aliquis pseudopropheta, qui diceret se esse apostolum, crederetur ei; et propter hoc reprobata est *Epistola fundamenti*, scilicet Manichaei.

Et notandum quod iste semper binos combinat. Et quare? Quia numerus binarius est numerus caritatis. Item ubicumque ponit aliquem qui duobus nominibus vocatur, ponit aliquid per quod notetur differentia.

Item sciendum quod non servat ordinem dignitatis; tamen Petrus semper ponitur primus, qui etiam dicitur **Simon**, idest 'obediens'; unde dicitur Prov. XXI, 28: *vir obediens loquetur victoriam.* **Petrus** a petra dicitur propter eius firmitatem; et Cephas, quod Syrum nomen est, non Hebraeum. **Andreas** 'virile'; unde dicitur Ps. XXVI, 14: *viriliter age, et confortetur cor tuum.* Item **Philippus**, 'os lampadis'; talis debet esse praedicator. Ps. CXVIII, v. 140: *ignitum eloquium tuum vehementer.* **Bartholomaeus**, 'filius suspendentis aquas'; et iste dicitur Christus, de quo Iob XXVI, 8: *qui ligat aquas in nubibus suis.* Item **Iacobus Zebedaei**, qui occisus est ab Herode, qui 'supplantator' dicitur. Et **Ioannes**, qui 'gratia' dicitur; I Cor. XV, 10: *gratia Dei sum id quod sum.* Iste non sequitur ordinem dignitatis, sicut Marcus. Item **Thomas et Matthaeus**. Alii non ponunt **publicanus**; sed iste posuit causa humilitatis. Item alii praeponunt Matthaeum Thomae: iste e contrario. **Thomas** 'abyssus' dicitur, propter profunditatem fidei. **Matthaeus**, 'donatus', ut habetur ad Eph. IV, v. 32: *donantes invicem, sicut et Christus donavit nobis.* **Iacobus Alphaei**, ad differentiam alterius. Iste frater Domini dicitur, quia consobrinus. Et **Thadaeus**, frater Iacobi. Et dicitur Iudas qui scripsit epistolam, et interpretatur 'cor'; Prov. IV, 23: *omni custodia serva cor tuum.* Item **Simon Chananaeus** a Cana villa. Et **Iudas Scariotis**, ad differentiam alterius Iudae; et dicitur vel a

Hence, *in my name they will cast out devils* (Mark 16:17). And not only that they might cast out demons, but **to heal all manner of diseases** as is found, *they will lay their hands upon the sick, and they will recover* (Mark 16:18).

But if you ask why this power is not given to preachers even now, Augustine responds that it is because the greatest miracle is ready at hand, namely that the whole world is converted. Therefore, either miracles were done, and so I have the thing proposed; if not, this is the greatest miracle, because the whole world was converted by twelve of the most lowly men, fishermen.

812. There follows the description by position of name. And why? Lest if some pseudoprophet should come who claimed that he was an apostle, someone should believe him. And because of this the *Fundamental Epistle* namely of the Manichees, is rejected.

And one should notice that this Evangelist always combines pairs of two. And why? Because the number two is the number of charity. Likewise, wherever he sets down someone who is called by two names, he sets down something by which the difference may be noted.

Likewise, one should know that he does not follow the order of dignity; yet Peter is always placed first, who is also called **Simon**, i.e., 'obedient'. Hence it is said, *an obedient man will speak of victory* (Prov 21:28). **Peter** is said from rock, because of his firmness; and Cephas, which is a Syrian name, not Hebrew. **Andrew** means 'manly'; hence it is said, *expect the Lord, do manfully, and let your heart take courage* (Ps 26:14). Likewise **Philip** means 'the mouth of the torch'; the preacher should be such. *Your word is exceedingly refined* (Ps 118:140). **Bartholomew**, 'son of the one upholding the waters'; and this names Christ, of whom it is said, *he binds up the waters in his clouds* (Job 26:8). Similarly, **James the son of Zebedee**, who was killed by Herod, who is called 'one who makes to stumble.' And **John**, who is called 'grace'; *but by the grace of God, I am what I am* (1 Cor 15:10). This Evangelist does not follow the order of dignity, as Mark does. Likewise, **Thomas** and **Matthew**. The other evangelists, Mark and Luke do not put down **the publican** (Mark 3:18: Luke 6:15), but this man sets down the cause of his humility. Also, the others put Matthew before Thomas; this Evangelist, the other way around. **Thomas** means 'the abyss', because of the profundity of his faith. **Matthew** means 'forgiven', as is found: *forgiving one another, even as God hath forgiven you in Christ* (Eph 4:32). **James the son of Alpheus**, to distinguish him from the other. This man is called the 'brother of the Lord', because he was a cousin.

villa, vel a stirpe de tribu Issachar; qui 'mors' dicitur. *Qui tradidit eum.*

And *Thaddeus*, the brother of James. He is also called Judas, the one who wrote the epistle, and he is interpreted 'heart'; *with all watchfulness keep your heart* (Prov 4:23). Likewise, *Simon the Cananean*, from the village of Cana. And *Judas Iscariot*, to distinguish him from the other Judas; and he is named either from a village, or from the stock of the tribe of Issachar; who is interpreted 'death'. *Who also betrayed him.*

Et quare posuit? Ut daret documentum, quod dignitas status non sanctificat hominem. Item est alia ratio, ad notandum quod vix contingit quin in multa congregatione sit aliquis malus; et ideo ita ponitur, ut ostendatur quod boni aliquando non sunt sine malis; Cant. II, 2: *sicut lilium inter spinas, sic amica mea inter filias.* Et Augustinus: *non est domus mea melior quam domus Domini.*

And why did he set this down? To give an example, that dignity of state does not make a man holy. Likewise, there is another reason, to point out that there is hardly ever a large congregation without someone evil; and so he set it down this way to show that good men are sometimes not without evil men. *As the lily among thorns, so is my love among the daughters* (Song 2:2). And Augustine: *my house is not better than the Lord's house.*

813. *Hos duodecim* elegit Deus, et posuit divulgatores Sacrae Scripturae. *Praecipiens eis, et dicens* et cetera. Hic ponit eorum instructionem. Et

primo instruit eos verbo;

secundo exemplo, ibi *et factum est cum consummasset Iesus* et cetera.

Verbo tripliciter.

Primo de officio suo; secundo de sumptibus; tertio de periculis.

Secundo, ibi *nolite possidere aurum neque argentum*; tertio, ibi *ecce ego mitto vos sicut oves in medio luporum.*

Circa officium quatuor mandat.

Primo quo vadant;

secundo quid dicant, ibi *euntes autem praedicate* etc.;

tertio quid faciant, ibi *infirmos curate* etc.;

quarto quo fine, ibi *gratis accepistis, gratis date.* Et

primo dicit quo non vadant;

secundo quo vadant, ibi *sed potius ite ad oves quae perierunt domus Israel.*

814. Et circa primum duo dicit. Primo *in viam gentium ne abieritis et in civitatem Samaritanorum ne intraveritis.* Isti erant medii inter gentiles et Iudaeos, de quibus habetur Lib. IV Reg. XVII, 24 ss., et isti retinuerunt partim ritum Iudaeorum, partim gentilium, et isti multum erant contrarii Iudaeis. Unde prohibet ne vadant ad simpliciter gentiles, nec ad mediocres istos.

815. Sed contrarium videtur quod dixit *ite, docete omnes gentes.* Et Is. XL, 5: *et videbit omnis caro pariter quod os Domini locutum est.* Quid ergo dicit *in viam gentium ne abieritis*?

Dicendum, quod missi sunt ad utrosque: sed ordo debebat observari. Quia primo Iudaeis. Et una ratio est,

813. God chose *these twelve*, and set them up as the spreaders of Holy Scripture. *Commanding them, saying.* Here he sets down their instruction. And

first, he instructs them by word;

second, by example, at *and it came to pass, when Jesus had made an end* (Matt 11:1).

By word, in three ways:

first, concerning their office; second, concerning costs; third, concerning dangers;

the second is at *do not possess gold*; the third is at *behold I send you as sheep among wolves* (Matt 10:16).

Concerning the office, he commands four things:

first, where they should go;

second, what they should say, at *and going, preach*;

third, what they should do, at *heal the sick*;

fourth, by what means, at *freely have you received, freely give.*

And first, he says where they should not go;

second, where they should go, at *but go rather to the lost sheep of the house of Israel.*

814. And concerning the first, he says two things. First, *do not go into the way of the gentiles, and do not enter into the city of the Samaritans.* The Samaritans were intermediate between the Jews and the gentiles (2 Kgs 17:24), and they had retained partly the rite of the Jews, partly the rite of the gentiles, and they were very hostile to the Jews. Hence he forbids them to go to those who were gentiles simply, or to the intermediates.

815. But what he said below, *going therefore, teach all nations* (Matt 28:19), seems contrary to this. And, *and all flesh together will see, that the mouth of the Lord has spoken* (Isa 40:5). So why does he say, *do not go into the way of the gentiles*?

One should say that they were sent to both; but an order should be observed, because first they were sent to the

quia primo fieri debet quod iustitia exigit, quam quod ex misericordia provenit; sed iustitia erat quod primo Iudaeis praedicarent: quia istud ex promissione habebant, ut habetur Rom. XV, 8: *dico autem Christum Iesum ministrum fuisse circumcisionis propter veritatem ad confirmandas promissiones patrum.* Gentibus autem tenebatur ex misericordia; ut enim habetur Rom. XI, 17, gentiles oleastri sunt ab oliva recepti, scilicet a fide antiquorum patrum: unde ibi dicitur, *tu autem cum oleaster esses, insertus es in illis, et socius radicis, et pinguedinis olivae factus es.* Primo ergo oliva nutrienda erat, ut aliquid acciperet ab ea, postmodum oleaster inserendus, Rom. XI, 17. Item volens fideles in fidem patrum introducere, primo voluit Iudaeis praedicari fidem.

Secunda ratio fuit, quia Dominus infundit omnibus id ad quod sunt dispositi; sed multi Iudaeorum erant iam dispositi per fidem. Et sicut ignis primo agit in ea, quae sunt prope, sic Dominus ex caritate primo voluit in his, qui prope erant. Unde dicitur Is. LVII, 19: *venient ut annuntient pacem his qui prope, et pacem his qui longe sunt.*

Item si ad gentiles primo ivisset, Iudaei, qui multum habebant gentiles odio, reprobassent eum ex indignatione; ideo in Act. XIII, v. 46: *vobis primo oportuit praedicari regnum Dei.* Unde dicit **in viam gentium ne abieritis**, idest ne appropinquetis ad viam, quae ducit ad gentes, ut non loquantur de vobis. Sed non dicit *in viam Samaritanorum.*

Et mystice: qui sunt discipuli Dei, non debent ire in viam gentium, nec haereticorum; unde Ier. II, 18: *quid tibi vis in via Aegypti, ut bibas aquam turbidam?*

816. Sed potius ite ad oves quae perierunt domus Israel. Et quare oves? Quia magis perierunt ex culpa Pharisaeorum, quam ex culpa ipsorum. Unde Ps. XCIX, 3: *nos autem populus eius, et oves pascuae eius.* Et I Petr. c. II, 25: *eratis sicut oves errantes; sed conversi estis ad pastorem et episcopum* et cetera.

817. Sed quid facient discurrentes? **Euntes autem praedicate.** Io. XV, 16: *posui vos ut eatis, et fructum afferatis, et fructus vester maneat* et cetera. Et mittit eos, sicut ipse missus est, scilicet ad praedicandum. Unde **agite poenitentiam**, et cetera. Et sicut Iesus inceperat, **agite poenitentiam**, sic praecepit eis. Inceperat, **agite poenitentiam, appropinquabit enim regnum caelorum**; Ps. CXVIII, 155: *longe enim a peccatoribus salus*; sed modo est prope per passionem Christi; Hebr. IX, 12: *per proprium sanguinem introivit semel in sancta, aeterna redemptione inventa.* Unde dicit **appropinquabit**, scilicet

Jews. And one reason is that what justice requires should come about first, before what proceeds from mercy; but it was justice that they should preach first to the Jews, because these had it coming to them from the promise, as is found, *for I say that Christ Jesus was minister of the circumcision for the truth of God, to confirm the promises made unto the fathers* (Rom 15:8). For as is said, the gentiles are wild olives taken in by the olive tree, namely by the faith of the ancient fathers; hence it says there, *you being a wild olive, are ingrafted in them, and are made partakers of the root, and of the fatness of the olive tree* (Rom 11:17). First, therefore, the olive tree was to be nourished, that one might receive something from it, and afterward the wild olive was to be grafted on. Likewise, wishing to lead the faithful into the faith of the fathers, he wished first that the faith should be preached to the Jews.

The second reason was that the Lord pours into all things to which they are disposed; but many of the Jews were already disposed by faith. And just as fire works first on those things which are near, so the Lord out of love wished to work first on these, who were near. Hence it is said, *I created the fruit of the lips, peace, peace to him that is far off, and to him that is near, said the Lord, and I healed him* (Isa 57:19).

Also, if they had gone first to the gentiles, the Jews, who had a great hatred for the gentiles, would have rejected him out of indignation. And so, *to you it behooved us first to speak the word of God* (Acts 13:46). Hence he says, **do not go into the way of the gentiles**, i.e., do not draw near the way which leads to the gentiles, that they may not speak about you. But he does not say, *into the Samaritan's way.*

And mystically: those who are God's disciples should not go into the gentiles' way, nor the heretics'; hence, *and now what have you to do in the way of Egypt, to drink the troubled water?* (Jer 2:18).

816. But go rather to the lost sheep of the house of Israel. And why sheep? Because they were lost more by the Pharisee's fault than by their own fault. Hence, *we are his people and the sheep of his pasture* (Ps 99:3). And, *for you were as sheep going astray; but you are now converted to the shepherd and bishop of your souls* (1 Pet 2:25).

817. But what will they do as they go out? **And going, preach.** *I have chosen you; and have appointed you, that you should go, and should bring forth fruit; and your fruit should remain* (John 15:16). And he sends them just as he was sent, namely to preach. Hence, **do penance.** And just as Jesus had begun, **do penance** (Matt 4:17), so he commands them to begin. He had begun, **do penance, for the kingdom of heaven is at hand** (Matt 4:17). It is written: *salvation is far from sinners* (Ps 118:155), but now it is near through Christ's passion; *by his own blood, entered once into the holies, having obtained eternal redemption* (Heb 9:12). Hence he says, **is**

per passionem meam; unde in eis fundatur per partici-pationem gratiae: *totum enim regnum Dei intra vos est.*

818. Sed possent dicere: *quomodo confirmabimus quae dicemus?* Certe miraculis, sicut ipse fecit. Unde dicit **infirmos curate** et cetera.

Sed si quis diceret: quare non facit modo miracula Ecclesia?

Dicendum, quod miracula facta sunt ad probationem fidei; sed iam fides approbata est. Et ideo sicut qui faceret unam demonstrationem ad probandum aliquam conclusionem, non esset alia probatio necessaria, sic ibi. Unde maximum miraculum est conversio totius mundi: ideo non oportet quod fiant alia; et sicut facta fuerunt alia miracula corporalia, ita fiunt quotidie spiritualia, quia infirmi spiritualiter curantur.

Infirmi enim sunt qui peccato agitantur, qui proni sunt ad peccatum, Rom. XIV, 1: *infirmum autem in fide assumite*: et isti a Domino sanantur. Qui autem consentiunt, mortui sunt, quia separantur a Deo: et isti resuscitantur a Domino, ut Eph. V, 14: *surge qui dormis, et exurge a mortuis.* Item leprosi mundantur; leprosi enim dicuntur qui sunt infectivi aliorum, quia lepra est morbus contagiosus: et isti aliquando curantur. IV Reg. V, 27, dicitur quod lepra Naam adhaesit Giezi. Item daemones eiiciuntur: daemones enim sunt quorum peccatum iam transiit ad effectum, de quibus dicitur Prov. II, 14: *laetantur cum male fecerint, et exultant in rebus pessimis.* Et, ut habetur de Iuda Io. XIII, 27, quod *intravit in eum satanas* et cetera. Et isti aliquando curantur.

819. Et quia possent dicere apostoli: *modo erimus divites; si facimus miracula habebimus multa*, et de hac causa voluit Simon magus facere miracula: hanc causam excludit Dominus dicens *gratis accepistis, gratis date.*

Magnum est facere miracula, sed maius est virtuose vivere. Unde amovet ab eis superbiam, quia potest superbia accidere duobus modis: vel ex cupiditate, vel ex meritis. Una enim est maxima superbia, quando aliquis bonum quod habuit, sibi adscribit. Ideo excludit, quia **accepistis**; I ad Cor. IV, 7: *quid habes quod non accepisti?*

Item, non debetis superbire, quia non ex meritis, sed **gratis.** Qui enim ex meritis, non gratis recipit. Item cupiditatem excludit, **gratis date**, idest non propter aliquod temporale. Pretium enim rei vel maius est, vel aequale. Illum enim quod per pretium tradis, non est ita in corde tuo fixum, sicut pretium quod recipis. Nihil autem est dono Dei aequale, vel maius; Sap. VII, 9: *comparavi illi lapidem pretiosum, quoniam omne aurum in comparatione illius arena est exigua.*

at hand, namely through my passion; hence, it is begun in them by the participation of grace: *for lo, the kingdom of God is within you* (Luke 17:21).

818. But they could say: *how will we confirm what we say?* Certainly by miracles, as he himself worked. Hence he says, **heal the sick**.

But what if someone were to say: why does not the Church work miracles even now?

One should say that the miracles were worked to confirm the faith; but now the faith is confirmed. And therefore, just as he who does one demonstration to prove some conclusion does not need another proof, so here. Hence the greatest miracle is the conversion of the whole world, so it is not necessary that there should be another. And just as bodily miracles were worked, so spiritual miracles are worked daily, since the spiritually sick are healed.

For they are sick who are driven by sin, who are inclined to sin, *now him who is weak in faith, take unto you* (Rom 14:1); and these are healed by the Lord. But they who consent to sin are dead, because they are separated from God; and these are reawakened by the Lord, as it says, *rise you who sleep, and arise from the dead* (Eph 5:14). Likewise, the lepers are cleansed, for they are called lepers who infect others, since leprosy is a contagious disease; and these are sometimes healed. It is said that the leprosy of Naaman clung to Giezi (2 Kgs 5:27). Likewise, demons are cast out, for they are demons whose sins have already taken effect, of whom it is said, *who are glad when they have done evil, and rejoice in most wicked things* (Prov 2:14). And, as is said of Judas, that *satan entered into him* (John 13:27). And these are sometimes cured.

819. And because the apostles could say, *now we will be rich; if we work miracles, we will have many things*, and Simon Magus wished to work miracles for this reason, the Lord excludes this reason, saying, **freely have you received, freely give**.

It is a great thing to work miracles, but it is greater to live virtuously. Hence he removes pride from them, because pride can come about in two ways: either out of greed, or out of merits. For one is the greatest pride of all, when someone has a good which he ascribes to himself. Therefore he excludes this: **have you received**; *for what have you that you have not received?* (1 Cor 4:7).

Similarly, you should not be proud, because you have received not from merits, but **freely**. Likewise, he excludes greed: **freely give**, i.e., not for the sake of something temporal. For the reward for something is either greater than or equal to the thing itself. For that which you hand over as a reward is not so fixed in your heart as the reward which you receive. Now, nothing is equal to or greater than the gift of God; *for all gold in comparison of her, is as a little sand, and silver in respect to her will be counted as clay* (Wis 7:9).

820. *Nolite possidere aurum* et cetera. Quia possent dicere: *unde ergo vivemus?* Ideo de sumptibus instruit illos. Et

    primo prohibet ne sumptus deferant;

    secundo docet a quibus accipiant, ibi *in quamcumque autem civitatem aut castellum intraveritis* et cetera.

821. Dicit ergo *nolite possidere aurum*.

Et notanda sunt verba quae sequuntur, quia dicit iste *nec calceamenta*; Marcus dicit: *calceatos sandaliis*. Item dicit *nec virgam*; Marcus dicit, quod *virgam*: ideo haec verba sunt dubia et difficilia.

Quod enim dicit *nolite* etc. aut est praeceptum, aut est consilium. Sed istud certum est quod est praeceptum, quia ita dicitur *Iesus praecipiens eis* et cetera. Sed apostoli et fuerunt apostoli, et fuerunt fideles. Aut ergo fuit eis praeceptum, inquantum fideles, aut inquantum apostoli. Si inquantum fideles: ergo ad hoc tenentur omnes fideles; et haec fuit quaedam haeresis, ut ait Augustinus, quae dicebat quod nullus posset salvari, nisi hi qui nihil possident. Et haec fuit haeresis Apostolicorum. Item alia haeresis fuit, quod nullus salvaretur, nisi discalceatus pergens et hae fuerunt haereses, non quia malum praeciperent, sed quia non observantibus praecludebant viam salutis.

Si autem praecipitur eis inquantum apostolis, tunc omnes praelati, qui sunt successores apostolorum, ad haec tenentur.

822. Sed esto quod isti non male fecerunt, nonne Paulus male fecit qui portabat, et accipiebat a quibusdam, ut aliis daret? Ideo difficultatem habent haec verba.

Et ideo dicendum, quod fuit una via secundum Hieronymum, exponendo ad litteram, quod praecepit aliquid propter officium apostolatus, et non quod sit de necessitate simpliciter, sed secundum illud tempus. Unde ante passionem praecepit nihil ferre. In passione autem, Lc. XXII, 35: *quando misi vos sine baculo et pera, numquid aliquid defuit vobis?* Et sequitur: *sed nunc qui habet sacculum, emat similiter et peram. Et qui non habet, vendat tunicam, et emat gladium.* Unde ante passionem missi sunt ad Iudaeos; apud Iudaeos autem erat consuetudo, quod suis debebant providere magistris. Ideo nihil ferre praecepit cum mitteret eos ad Iudaeos. Sed ista non erat consuetudo in gentibus; ideo cum missi sunt ad gentes, data est eis licentia portandi sumptus. Portabant igitur quando praedicabant aliis quam Iudaeis.

820. *Do not possess gold.* Because they could say: *on what will we live?* Therefore he instructs them about costs. And

    first, he forbids them to bring expenses;

    second, he teaches that they should accept from certain people, at *and into whatever city or town you will enter.*

821. He says then, *do not possess gold.*

And one should notice the words which follow, because this Gospel says, *nor shoes*; but Mark says: *but to be shod with sandals* (Mark 6:9). Again, he says, *nor a staff*; but Mark says: *but a staff only* (Mark 6:8). So these words seem doubtful and difficult.

For what he says, *do not possess*, is either a command or a counsel. But it is certain that it is a command, because the Gospel speaks in this way: *Jesus sent: commanding them.* But the apostles were both apostles and members of the faithful; therefore, it was a command for them either insofar as they were members of the faithful, or insofar as they were apostles. If insofar as they were members of the faithful, then all the faithful would be bound to this; and this is a particular heresy, as Augustine says, which said that no one could be saved except for those who possess nothing. And this was the heresy of the Apostolici. Similarly, there was another heresy that no one would be saved except the one who traveled without shoes on. And these were heresies, not because they commanded something bad, but because they were closing off the way of salvation to those who did not observe these commands.

But if it is commanded them insofar as they are apostles, then all the Church prelates who were the apostles' successors are bound to this.

822. But let it be that these have not done badly: did Paul do badly, who carried, and accepted things from some to give to others? So these words contain a difficulty.

And so one should say that there was one way of interpreting the passage according to Jerome, explaining literally, saying that he commanded something owing to the office of the apostolate, and that it was not necessary simply, but necessary for that time. Hence before the passion, he commanded them to carry nothing. But in the hour of his passion, *when I sent you without purse, and bag and shoes, did you want anything?* (Luke 22:35). And there follows: *but now he who has a purse, let him take it, and likewise a bag and he who has not, let him sell his coat, and buy a sword.* For before the passion they were sent to the Jews; moreover, it was the custom among the Jews that they should provide for their teachers. Therefore, he commanded them to carry nothing when he sent them to the Jews. But this was not the custom among the gentiles, so when they were sent to the gentiles, permission was given to them to carry expenses. Therefore, they carried things when they preached to those other than the Jews.

Et quia quaedam sunt ad necessitatem, alia quibus emuntur necessaria: et hoc est quod dicitur, quod quaedam sunt divitiae artificiales, ut vestes et calceamenta, ideo utrumque prohibet. Dicit ergo *nolite*, et cetera. Quia omnis pecunia vel est de auro, vel de argento, vel de aere; ideo prohibet ne possideant aurum, nec argentum; unde dicebat Petrus: *argentum et aurum non est mihi; quod autem habeo, hoc tibi do.*

Et quare hoc Deus praecepit? Una ratio est, quia Dominus mittebat pauperes ad praedicandum; ideo posset aliquis credere quod non praedicarent, nisi propter quaestum. Ut igitur ista suspicio amoveatur, ideo praecepit nihil portare. Item ad tollendum sollicitudinem: quia si essent circa hoc nimis solliciti, impediretur verbum Dei. Item prohibet divitias, quae subveniunt in necessitate.

823. Et quia possent dicere: non feremus aurum, non argentum, sed peram possumus, ubi portabimus ova et panem, quae sunt necessaria ad victum? Et istud prohibet *non peram in via*. Et quare hoc prohibuit? Dicit Chrysostomus, ut ostenderet eis virtutem suam: quia sine his poterat eos mittere; unde in Lc. XXII, 35: *quando misi vos sine baculo et pera, numquid aliquid defuit vobis?* Ergo fecit ut ostenderet virtutem suam.

Item quantum ad vestimentum *neque duas tunicas*: non quod non haberent nisi unam tunicam, sed quod non haberent duo paria vestimentorum, ita quod unum reconderent, et aliud induerent. Unde nomine unius tunicae intelligit unum vestimentum; Lc. III, v. 11: *qui habet duas tunicas, det unam non habenti.*

824. *Neque calceamenta.* Et quare prohibuit? Duplex est causa, eadem ratione qua aurum et argentum. Dominus mittebat eos, ut apud omnes, pauperes reputarentur. Unde Apostolus, I Cor. I, 26: *non multum potentes elegit Deus.* Ideo voluit quod abiecti essent: pauperes enim in partibus orientis vadunt discalceati; utuntur tamen quibusdam quae sandalia dicuntur, et fiunt de paleis. Ideo volebat ut irent sicut pauperes illius patriae.

Alia ratio, quia sicut docuit Plato quod homines non multum cooperirent nec pedes, nec caput ut firmaret eos ut magis robusti essent ad sustinendum, praecepit eos ire discalceatos.

Sed *neque virgam.* Et quae est ratio? Aliqui enim equis utuntur, alii vero virga sustinentur: ideo illud minimum etiam prohibuit, ut in ipso totaliter confiderent, secundum illud Ps. XXII, 4: *virga tua, et baculus tuus ipsa me consolata sunt.* Unde quod dicit aliter, quod virgam portent, non fuit praeceptum, nisi pro loco et tempore observandum.

825. Augustinus per aliam viam vadit dicens, quod haec non sunt praecepta, nec consilia, sed sunt

And because certain things are necessary, and there are other things with which the necessary things are bought, and this is what is said, that some things are artificial riches, like clothing and shoes, so he forbids both. He says therefore, ***do not possess***. For all money is made either from gold, or from silver, or from copper; so he forbids them to possess gold or silver; hence Peter said, *silver and gold I have none; but what I have, I give you* (Acts 3:6).

And why did God command this? One reason is that the Lord sent the poor to preach, so someone might believe that they would only preach for gain. Therefore, to remove this suspicion, he commanded them to carry nothing. Likewise, to take away anxiety: for if they were greatly anxious about this, the word of God would have been hindered. Similarly, he forbids riches, which come to the rescue in necessity.

823. And since they could say: we do not carry gold, or silver, but can we carry a bag, where we will carry eggs and bread, which are necessary for living? Then he forbids this: ***nor bag for your journey***. And why did he forbid this? Chrysostom says, to show them his power, since he could send them without these things; hence, *when I sent you without purse, and bag, and shoes, did you want anything?* (Luke 22:35). So he did this to show his power.

Similarly, as regards clothing, ***nor two coats***; not that they should only have one tunic, but that they should not have two equivalent garments, such that they could put one away and wear the other. Hence, one coat has the same meaning as one garment. *He who has two coats, let him give to him who has none* (Luke 3:11).

824. ***Nor shoes***. And why did he forbid this? There are two reasons, the same reasons for which he forbade gold and silver. The Lord sent them to be reputed poor men by all. Hence the Apostle: *the weak things of the world has God chosen* (1 Cor 1:27). So he willed that they should be humbled, for poor men travel unshod in the eastern regions; yet they use certain things which are called sandals, and are made of straw. So he willed that they should travel like the poor men of their homeland.

Another reason: just as Plato taught that men should not cover their feet or head, so that he might strengthen them, that they might be more robust for withstanding hardship, he commanded them to travel unshod.

But ***nor a staff***. And what is the reason? For some men use horses, while others carry walking sticks: so he forbade this least thing, that they might place their trust entirely in him, in accordance with the Psalm, *your rod and your staff, they have comforted me* (Ps 22:4). Hence what he says in another way, that they should carry a walking stick, was not a command, except to be observed at a certain place and time.

825. Augustine goes by another way, saying that these are neither commands nor counsels, but are permissions,

permissiones, ita quod abstinere magis est consilium quam implere. Unde sensus est *nolite* etc., idest, non est negotium, ut alia calceamenta possideatis praeter haec quibus estis calceati. *Neque virgam*, idest nihil, sicut dicitur, *neque festucam*.

Et quare? *Dignus est enim operarius mercede sua* et cetera. Quia vos habetis potestatem accipiendi ab aliis, et ideo non est necessarium, ut portetis. Unde quando aliquid est permissum, si non fiat, non est peccatum; quicquid autem plus fit, supererogationis est. Unde et Paulus, quamvis posset ab aliis recipere, nihil accipiebat, et istud erat supererogatio, ut dicit Augustinus, quia permissis non uti, est supererogationis. Unde Paulus, I ad Cor. IX, v. 15: *melius est mihi mori, quam evacuare gloriam meam*. Et quare? Quia non utebatur isto permisso: *dignus est enim mercenarius* et cetera.

Sed quid est quod aliter dicit, quod ferant virgam? Dicit Augustinus, quod non est inconveniens quod quaedam aliquando dicantur mystice, aliquando ad litteram. Unde quod hic dicit Matthaeus, dicit ad litteram, quod virgam non ferant; quod vero Marcus dicit, mystice intelligitur, quod scilicet non ferant temporalia, sed habeant potestatem accipiendi ab aliis. Unde *dignus est enim operarius cibo suo*. Istud enim non est ibi casuale. Isti operarii sunt de quibus dictum est supra: *rogate Dominum messis, ut mittat operarios in messem suam*.

826. Tertia expositio est *nolite possidere aurum*, idest saecularem sapientiam, *argentum*, eloquentiam saecularem, non *peram*, idest sollicitudinem, *nec duas tunicas*, idest duplicitatem, *nec calceamenta*, idest terrenorum affectionem; fiunt enim calceamenta de pellibus animalium mortuorum.

827. *In quamcumque civitatem aut castellum intraveritis* et cetera. Supra Dominus ordinavit quod apostoli victualia secum non deferrent: et ratione probavit quia *dignus est operarius mercede sua*, nunc determinat modum qualiter accipere debent; et

primo dat modum, quia debent a volentibus dare accipere;

secundo quid fiat volentibus.

Circa primum tria facit.

Primo docet eligere hospitem;

secundo prohibet mutare hospitium;

mandat, tertio, quod hospes salutetur.

828. Dicit ergo: dictum est quod *dignus est operarius cibo suo*, ut sciatis a quo debetis accipere, ne credatis quod domus cuiuslibet vobis sit concessa; ideo *in quamcumque civitatem aut castellum intraveritis, interrogate quis in ea dignus sit*. Et hoc ne propter infamiam hospitis vestra praedicatio contemnatur, ut habetur I ad Tim. III, 7: *oportet autem illum testimonium habere*

in such a way that to refrain is more a counsel than to satisfy oneself. Hence the sense is *do not possess*, i.e., it is not your concern that you should have other shoes than those with which you are shod. *Nor a staff*, i.e., nothing, as is said, *neither a straw*.

And why? *For the workman is worthy of his hire*, because you have the power to receive from others, and so it is not necessary that you should carry things. Hence when something is permitted, if it is not done, it is not a sin; whatever more is done is beyond what is required. Hence also Paul, although he could receive from others, accepted nothing, and this was beyond what was required, as Augustine says, because not to use what is permitted is beyond what is required. Hence Paul, *for it is good for me to die, rather than that any man should make my glory void* (1 Cor 9:15). And why? Because he did not use this permission: *for the workman is worthy of his hire*.

But what is this other thing said, that they should carry a walking stick? Augustine says that it is not unfitting that certain things are sometimes said mystically, sometimes literally. Hence what Matthew says here, he says literally, that they should not carry a walking stick; but what Mark says is understood mystically, namely that they should not carry temporal things, but should have the power of receiving from others. Hence, *the workman is worthy of his hire*. For this is not there by chance. These are the workmen of whom it was said above, *beseech therefore the Lord of the harvest, that he send forth laborers into his harvest*.

826. The third explanation is *do not possess gold*, i.e., the wisdom of the age, *nor silver*, the eloquence of the age, *nor bag*, i.e., anxiety, *nor two coats*, i.e., duplicity, *nor shoes*, i.e., affection for earthly things; for shoes are made from the skins of dead animals.

827. *And into whatever city or town you will enter*. Above, the Lord ordered that the apostles should not carry food with them, and he confirmed it by reason, because *the workman is worthy of his hire*. Now, he determines the way in which they should accept things. And

first, he gives the way, that they should accept from those who wish to give;

second, what would come to those willing.

Concerning the first, he does three things:

first, he teaches them to choose a house of stay;

second, he forbids them to change houses of stay;

third, he commands that the house of stay be greeted.

828. He says then: it was said that *the workman is worthy of his hire*; that you may know from whom you should accept, lest you believe that just anyone's house is granted to you, therefore *into whatever city or town you will enter, inquire who in it is worthy*. And this is lest your preaching should be despised because of the disrepute of the house, as is said, *moreover he must have a good testimony of them who*

bonum ab his qui foris sunt. Secunda ratio, quia si bonus aliquis fuerit, facilius vobis necessaria ministrabit. Et in hoc providet eis. Tertia ratio est, ut excludatur suspicio quaestus: quia cum viderent homines tales pauperes non accipientes nisi a bonis, signum erat eis, quod propter quaestum non praedicabant.

Istas duas expositiones ultimas ponit Chrysostomus; primam Hieronymus. Et hoc dicit Apostolus, I Thess. II, 5: *neque enim aliquando fuimus in sermone adulationis, neque in occasione avaritiae*.

Item dicit **quis in ea sit dignus**, et hoc est, quia magnum ei reputatur, qui tales hospites recipit. Unde Abrahae magnum reputatum est quod hospites recepit, ut habetur ad Hebr. ult., 2: *hospitalitatem nolite oblivisci: per hanc enim quidam placuerunt, angelis hospitio receptis*.

829. Et ibi manete. Hic docet de stabilitate hospitii. **Ibi manete**, idest non transite de hospitio in hospitium. Et quare? Ne sit tristitia hospiti; et si dignus sit, recipiet vos libenter, et ita cum tristitia dimittet; Ier. c. XVIII, 20: *numquid redditur pro bono malum?* Secunda ratio est, ne incurrant notam levitatis, quae non convenit praedicatori. *In populo gravi laudabo te*, Ps. XXXIV, 15. Item ut evadant notam gulae, quia si dimitterent malum hospitium pro bono, imputaretur gulae. Ideo Dominus dicit, quod antequam intrent, petant quis fuerit in ea dignus.

830. Intrantes autem domum salutate eam. Hic notatur salutatio hospitis. Et

primo ponit salutationem;

secundo effectum, ibi **et si quidem fuerit domus illa digna, veniet pax vestra super eam**.

Oportebat enim quod eis qui temporalia ministrabant, spiritualia ministrarent, et non solum spiritualia, sed quae sunt necessaria ad salutem, dicendo **pax huic domui** et cetera. Et iste erat modus salutandi congruus, quia mundus erat in guerra; in Christo autem mundus est reconciliatus: isti enim legati erant Domini, et ad quid? Certe ad pacem; ideo congrua erat haec salutatio.

831. Sequitur effectus quo ad bonos, et quo ad malos. **Et si quidem fuerit domus illa digna** et cetera. Possumus dicere quod domus illa habebit inde quamdam vim benedictionis. Unde apostoli sive episcopi in prima versione ad populum dicunt *pax vobis*. Unde dicitur Num. VI, 27: *invocabunt nomen meum super filios Israel, et ego benedicam eis* et cetera.

Si autem non fuerit digna, pax vestra revertetur ad vos. Sed quid est quod dicit? Nonne dixerat quod primo interrogarent? Ideo ostendit quod in talibus inquisitionibus falluntur homines: *homo enim videt quae patent,*

are without (1 Tim 3:7). A second reason, because if there is some good man, he will more readily supply you with the necessary things. And in this he provides for them. A third reason is to exclude the suspicion of gain, because when men saw such poor men accepting only from the good, it was a sign to them that they were not preaching for the sake of gain.

Chysostom sets out these last two explanations; the first, Jerome. And the Apostle says this, *for neither have we used, at any time, the speech of flattery, as you know; nor taken an occasion of covetousness* (1 Thess 2:5).

Likewise, he says, **who in it is worthy**, and this is because it is considered a great thing to him who receives such guests. Hence it was considered a great thing for Abraham that he received guests, as is found, *and hospitality do not forget; for by this some, being not aware of it, have entertained angels* (Heb 13:2).

829. And abide there. Here he teaches about constancy of the house of stay. **Abide there**, i.e., do not go from house to house. And why? Lest the host be sad; and if he is worthy, he will receive you readily, and thus he will send you away with sorrow; *will evil be rendered for good?* (Jer 18:20). A second reason is lest they bring on themselves a reputation for levity, which does not befit a preacher. *I will praise you in a grave people* (Ps 34:18). Likewise, that they might avoid a reputation of gluttony, because if they were to leave a bad host for a good one, it would be imputed to gluttony. Therefore the Lord says that before they enter, they should ask who in the town is worthy.

830. And when you come into the house, salute it. Here the greeting of the house is recorded. And

first, he sets forth the greeting;

second, the effect, at **and if that house is worthy, your peace will come upon it**.

For it was necessary that they should supply spiritual things to those who supplied temporal things to them; and not only spiritual, but those things which are necessary for salvation, by saying, **peace be to this house**. And this was the fitting manner of greeting, because the world was in strife; but in Christ the world is reconciled; for they were the Lord's ambassadors, and to what end? Certainly for peace; therefore this greeting was fitting.

831. There follows the effect with respect to the good, and with respect to the bad. **And if that house is worthy, your peace will come upon it**. We can say that this house will have a certain force of blessing from there; hence the apostles or bishops say, when they first turn towards the people, *peace be with you*. Hence it is said, *and they will invoke my name upon the children of Israel, and I will bless them* (Num 6:27).

But if it is not worthy, your peace will return to you. But why does he say this? Did he not say that they should ask about their worthiness first? Therefore he shows that men are mistaken in such investigations, *for man sees*

Dominus autem intuetur cor, ut habetur I Reg. XVI, 7. Non enim adhuc ita perfecti erant quod possent cognoscere quis esset dignus.

Pax vestra revertetur ad vos; et hoc est quod aliquis aliquando orat, et laborat pro salute alterius, et tamen effectum non consequitur; et tamen quod facit, non amittit, sed in ipsum redit. Unde **revertetur ad vos**, idest fructus referetur ad vos.

832. **Et quicumque non receperit vos**. Hic agitur de his qui non recipiunt. Et

primo docet eos quid facere debeant;

secundo quid a Deo recipient.

833. Dicit ergo **et quicumque non receperit vos**. Et ponit duas culpas. Unam quod eos non receperant; aliam, quia missi erant ad praedicandum, quia verbum Dei non audiebant.

Ideo **exeuntes foras de domo, vel civitate**, quia aliquando recipiebantur in civitate, sed non in domo; aliquando vero nec in civitate; sicut habetur in Actibus Apostolorum. Quid ergo faciendum? **Excutite pulverem de pedibus vestris**. Et hoc leguntur Paulus et Barnabas fecisse ad litteram, ut habetur Act. c. XIV, 51.

834. Et quare hoc mandat Dominus? Pulvis enim adhaeret pedibus, unde hoc praecepit ad ostendendum quod laborem itineris incassum fecerant. Et hoc erat eis in poenam; quasi dicat: inde estis damnabiles. Tamen dicit Apostolus Phil. II, 16: *non in vacuum laboravi*. Item alia ratio est, quia minimum quod potest haberi, est pulvis; ideo voluit, ut excuterent, in signum quod nihil haberent de eis. Tertia ratio est, quia per pulverem significantur temporalia, per pedes affectus, ad significandum quod in affectibus eorum nihil debet remanere temporale. Quarta causa est mystica. Pedes sunt affectus eorum: quantumcumque enim sunt sancti praedicatores, oportet quod aliquo pulvere affectus eorum moveatur, vel ex aliqua vanagloria etc., ut habetur Io. c. XIII, ubi dicitur quod Dominus lavit pedes discipulorum, et dixit: *qui mundus est, non indiget nisi ut pedes lavet, et est mundus totus*. Unde indigebant lotione quod ad venialia.

Et quare hoc praecepit Dominus? Ad ostendendum quod praedicator committit se periculo. Unde si non credunt ei, hoc in damnationem eorum revertitur.

835. Sed quid est? Nonne habebunt peius? Immo **dico vobis: tolerabilius erit terrae Sodomorum et Gomorrhaeorum in die iudicii quam illi civitati**. Quia, sicut habetur Io. XV, 22: *si non venissem, et locutus non fuissem eis, peccatum non haberent*. Magis enim peccant qui audiunt, et non implent, quam qui numquam audierunt. Ideo forte quod isti Sodomitae non audierunt, ideo

those things that appear, but the Lord beholds the heart (1 Sam 16:7). For they were not yet so perfect that they could know who was worthy.

Your peace will return to you. And this what happens sometimes: someone prays and labors for the salvation of another, and yet does not achieve the effect; and yet he does not lose what he does, but it returns back into him. Hence it **will return to you**, i.e., the fruit will be born back to you.

832. **And whoever will not receive you**. Here he treats of those who do not receive them. And

first, he teaches them what they should do;

second, what they will receive from God.

833. He says then, **and whoever will not receive you**. And he sets forth two faults. One, that they did not receive them; the other, that they did not hear the word of God, since the apostles were sent to preach.

Therefore, **going forth out of that house or city**, because sometimes they were received in a city, but not in a home, but sometimes not in the city either, as is found in the Acts of the Apostles. What then should be done? **Shake off the dust from your feet**. And it is written that Paul and Barnabas did this literally (Acts 13:51).

834. And why did the Lord command this? For dust clings to the feet, hence he commanded this to show that they had undertaken the labor of a journey for nothing. And this was a punishment on them, as though to say: for this you are damnable. Nevertheless, the Apostle says, *I have not run in vain, nor labored in vain* (Phil 2:16). Likewise, another reason is that the least thing which can be had is dust; therefore he willed that they should shake it off as a sign that they would have nothing from them. A third reason is that by dust are signified temporal things, and by feet are signified the affections, to signify that nothing temporal should remain in their affections. A fourth cause is mystical. The feet are their affections: for however much they are holy preachers, it is necessary that their affections be moved by some dust, or out of some vainglory, as is found, where it says that the Lord washed the disciples feet, and said, *he that is washed, needs not but to wash his feet, but is clean wholly* (John 13:10). Hence they needed washing with respect to venial sins.

And why did the Lord command this? To show that the preacher commits himself to danger. Hence if they do not believe him, this turns back unto their damnation.

835. But what is this? Will they not have worse? **Amen I say to you, it will be more tolerable for the land of Sodom and Gomorrha in the day of judgment, than for that city**. Because, as is said, *if I had not come, and spoken to them, they would not have sin* (John 15:22). For they who hear and do not carry out what they hear sin more than they who never heard. Therefore perhaps because the Sodomites did

tolerabilius erit eis. Item isti licet immundi, hospitales tamen erant. Unde quantum ad hoc tolerabilius erit eis.

836. Sed contrarium habetur Gen. XIX, quod peccatum Sodomorum est gravissimum peccatum, ut patet ex poena.

Et dicendum quod in genere peccatorum carnalium illud est gravissimum. Istud autem, quod immediate est contra Deum, sicut idololatria, illo est gravius. Vel dicendum quod non comparat peccatum ad peccatum, sed ad circumstantiam; quia peccabant isti, quibus fuerat praedicatum, illis vero non.

Item redarguit quosdam haereticos qui dicebant quod omnia peccata erant paria, et omnes poenae, et merita omnia, et omnia praemia. Ideo hoc excludit cum dicit *tolerabilius* etc., quia quibusdam peccatoribus erit deterius.

not hear, it will be more tolerable for them. Likewise, although they were unclean, yet they were hospitable. Hence as regards this it will be more tolerable for them.

836. But the contrary is found in Genesis, because the sin of Sodomites is the most grave sin, as is clear from the punishment (Gen 19).

And one should say that this is the gravest sin in the genus of carnal sins. But that which is immediately against God, such as idolatry, is more grave. Or one should say that he does not compare sin with sin, but with circumstance; because these sinned, to whom the word was preached, but it was not preached to those.

Likewise, he refutes certain heretics who said that all sins are equal, and all punishments, and all merits, and all rewards. He excludes this when he says, *more tolerable*, because it will be worse for certain sinners.

Lecture 2

10:16 Ecce ego mitto vos sicut oves in medio luporum. Estote ergo prudentes sicut serpentes, et simplices sicut columbae. [n. 838]

10:17 Cavete autem ab hominibus. Tradent enim vos in conciliis, et in synagogis suis flagellabunt vos; [n. 842]

10:18 et ad praesides, et ad reges ducemini propter me, in testimonium illis, et gentibus. [n. 845]

10:19 Cum autem tradent vos, nolite cogitare quomodo, aut quid loquamini. Dabitur enim vobis in illa hora quid loquamini. [n. 846]

10:20 Non enim vos estis qui loquimini; sed Spiritus Patris vestri qui loquitur in vobis. [n. 849]

10:21 Tradet autem frater fratrem in mortem, et pater filium, et insurgent filii in parentes, et morte eos afficient: [n. 851]

10:22 et eritis odio omnibus hominibus propter nomen meum. Qui autem perseveraverit usque in finem, hic salvus erit. [n. 852]

10:23 Cum autem persequentur vos in civitate ista, fugite in aliam. Amen dico vobis, non consummabitis civitates Israel, donec veniat Filius hominis. [n. 854]

10:24 Non est discipulus super magistrum, nec servus super dominum suum. [n. 858]

10:25 Sufficit discipulo ut sit sicut magister eius, et servus sicut dominus eius. Si patrem familias Beelzebub vocaverunt, quanto magis domesticos eius? [n. 860]

10:26 Ne ergo timueritis eos. Nihil enim est opertum quod non reveletur, et occultum quod non sciatur. [n. 863]

10:16 Ἰδοὺ ἐγὼ ἀποστέλλω ὑμᾶς ὡς πρόβατα ἐν μέσῳ λύκων· γίνεσθε οὖν φρόνιμοι ὡς οἱ ὄφεις καὶ ἀκέραιοι ὡς αἱ περιστεραί.

10:17 Προσέχετε δὲ ἀπὸ τῶν ἀνθρώπων· παραδώσουσιν γὰρ ὑμᾶς εἰς συνέδρια καὶ ἐν ταῖς συναγωγαῖς αὐτῶν μαστιγώσουσιν ὑμᾶς·

10:18 καὶ ἐπὶ ἡγεμόνας δὲ καὶ βασιλεῖς ἀχθήσεσθε ἕνεκεν ἐμοῦ εἰς μαρτύριον αὐτοῖς καὶ τοῖς ἔθνεσιν.

10:19 ὅταν δὲ παραδῶσιν ὑμᾶς, μὴ μεριμνήσητε πῶς ἢ τί λαλήσητε· δοθήσεται γὰρ ὑμῖν ἐν ἐκείνῃ τῇ ὥρᾳ τί λαλήσητε·

10:20 οὐ γὰρ ὑμεῖς ἐστε οἱ λαλοῦντες ἀλλὰ τὸ πνεῦμα τοῦ πατρὸς ὑμῶν τὸ λαλοῦν ἐν ὑμῖν.

10:21 Παραδώσει δὲ ἀδελφὸς ἀδελφὸν εἰς θάνατον καὶ πατὴρ τέκνον, καὶ ἐπαναστήσονται τέκνα ἐπὶ γονεῖς καὶ θανατώσουσιν αὐτούς.

10:22 καὶ ἔσεσθε μισούμενοι ὑπὸ πάντων διὰ τὸ ὄνομά μου· ὁ δὲ ὑπομείνας εἰς τέλος οὗτος σωθήσεται.

10:23 Ὅταν δὲ διώκωσιν ὑμᾶς ἐν τῇ πόλει ταύτῃ, φεύγετε εἰς τὴν ἑτέραν· ἀμὴν γὰρ λέγω ὑμῖν, οὐ μὴ τελέσητε τὰς πόλεις τοῦ Ἰσραὴλ ἕως ἂν ἔλθῃ ὁ υἱὸς τοῦ ἀνθρώπου.

10:24 Οὐκ ἔστιν μαθητὴς ὑπὲρ τὸν διδάσκαλον οὐδὲ δοῦλος ὑπὲρ τὸν κύριον αὐτοῦ.

10:25 ἀρκετὸν τῷ μαθητῇ ἵνα γένηται ὡς ὁ διδάσκαλος αὐτοῦ καὶ ὁ δοῦλος ὡς ὁ κύριος αὐτοῦ. εἰ τὸν οἰκοδεσπότην Βεελζεβοὺλ ἐπεκάλεσαν, πόσῳ μᾶλλον τοὺς οἰκιακοὺς αὐτοῦ.

10:26 Μὴ οὖν φοβηθῆτε αὐτούς· οὐδὲν γάρ ἐστιν κεκαλυμμένον ὃ οὐκ ἀποκαλυφθήσεται καὶ κρυπτὸν ὃ οὐ γνωσθήσεται.

10:16 Behold I send you as sheep among wolves. Therefore be wise as serpents and simple as doves. [n. 838]

10:17 But beware of men. For they will deliver you up in councils, and they will scourge you in their synagogues. [n. 842]

10:18 And you will be brought before governors, and before kings for my sake, for a testimony to them and to the gentiles. [n. 845]

10:19 But when they deliver you up, take no thought how or what to speak: for it will be given you in that hour what to speak. [n. 846]

10:20 For it is not you who speak, but the Spirit of your Father who speaks in you. [n. 849]

10:21 The brother also will deliver up the brother to death, and the father the son: and the children will rise up against their parents, and will put them to death. [n. 851]

10:22 And you will be hated by all men for my name's sake: but he who will persevere to the end, he will be saved. [n. 852]

10:23 And when they persecute you in this city, flee into another. Amen I say to you, you will not finish all the cities of Israel, until the Son of man come. [n. 854]

10:24 The disciple is not above the master, nor the servant above his lord. [n. 858]

10:25 It is enough for the disciple that he should be as his master, and the servant as his lord. If they have called the father of the household Beelzebub, how much more those of his household? [n. 860]

10:26 Therefore, do not fear them. For nothing is covered that will not be revealed: nor hid, that will not be known. [n. 863]

10:27 Quod dico vobis in tenebris, dicite in lumine: et quod in aure auditis, praedicate super tecta. [n. 864]

10:27 ὃ λέγω ὑμῖν ἐν τῇ σκοτίᾳ εἴπατε ἐν τῷ φωτί, καὶ ὃ εἰς τὸ οὖς ἀκούετε κηρύξατε ἐπὶ τῶν δωμάτων.

10:27 That which I tell you in the dark, speak in the light: and that which you hear in the ear, preach upon the housetops. [n. 864]

10:28 Et nolite timere eos, qui occidunt corpus, animam autem non possunt occidere; sed potius eum timete qui potest et animam, et corpus perdere in gehennam. [n. 866]

10:28 καὶ μὴ φοβεῖσθε ἀπὸ τῶν ἀποκτεννόντων τὸ σῶμα, τὴν δὲ ψυχὴν μὴ δυναμένων ἀποκτεῖναι· φοβεῖσθε δὲ μᾶλλον τὸν δυνάμενον καὶ ψυχὴν καὶ σῶμα ἀπολέσαι ἐν γεέννῃ.

10:28 And do not fear those who kill the body, and are not able to kill the soul: but rather fear him who can destroy both soul and body in gehenna. [n. 866]

10:29 Nonne duo passeres asse veneunt, et unus ex illis non cadet super terram sine Patre vestro? [n. 871]

10:29 οὐχὶ δύο στρουθία ἀσσαρίου πωλεῖται; καὶ ἓν ἐξ αὐτῶν οὐ πεσεῖται ἐπὶ τὴν γῆν ἄνευ τοῦ πατρὸς ὑμῶν.

10:29 Are not two sparrows sold for a farthing? And not one of them will fall to the ground without your Father. [n. 871]

10:30 Vestri autem et capilli capitis omnes numerati sunt. [n. 875]

10:30 ὑμῶν δὲ καὶ αἱ τρίχες τῆς κεφαλῆς πᾶσαι ἠριθμημέναι εἰσίν.

10:30 But the very hairs of your head are all numbered. [n. 875]

10:31 Nolite ergo timere; multis passeribus meliores estis vos. [n. 879]

10:31 μὴ οὖν φοβεῖσθε· πολλῶν στρουθίων διαφέρετε ὑμεῖς.

10:31 Therefore fear not: you are better than many sparrows. [n. 879]

10:32 Omnis ergo qui confitebitur me coram hominibus, confitebor et ego eum coram Patre meo qui in caelis est. [n. 880]

10:32 Πᾶς οὖν ὅστις ὁμολογήσει ἐν ἐμοὶ ἔμπροσθεν τῶν ἀνθρώπων, ὁμολογήσω κἀγὼ ἐν αὐτῷ ἔμπροσθεν τοῦ πατρός μου τοῦ ἐν [τοῖς] οὐρανοῖς·

10:32 Everyone therefore who will confess me before men, I will also confess him before my Father who is in heaven. [n. 880]

10:33 Qui autem negaverit me coram hominibus, negabo et ego eum coram Patre meo qui in caelis est. [n. 882]

10:33 ὅστις δ' ἂν ἀρνήσηταί με ἔμπροσθεν τῶν ἀνθρώπων, ἀρνήσομαι κἀγὼ αὐτὸν ἔμπροσθεν τοῦ πατρός μου τοῦ ἐν [τοῖς] οὐρανοῖς.

10:33 But he who will deny me before men, I will also deny him before my Father who is in heaven. [n. 882]

10:34 Nolite arbitrari, quia venerim pacem mittere in terram. Non veni pacem mittere, sed gladium. [n. 883]

10:34 Μὴ νομίσητε ὅτι ἦλθον βαλεῖν εἰρήνην ἐπὶ τὴν γῆν· οὐκ ἦλθον βαλεῖν εἰρήνην ἀλλὰ μάχαιραν.

10:34 Do not think that I came to send peace upon earth: I came not to send peace, but the sword. [n. 883]

10:35 Veni enim separare hominem adversus patrem suum, et filiam adversus matrem suam, et nurum adversus socrum suam: [n. 886]

10:35 ἦλθον γὰρ διχάσαι ἄνθρωπον κατὰ τοῦ πατρὸς αὐτοῦ καὶ θυγατέρα κατὰ τῆς μητρὸς αὐτῆς καὶ νύμφην κατὰ τῆς πενθερᾶς αὐτῆς,

10:35 For I came to set a man at variance against his father, and the daughter against her mother, and the daughter in law against her mother in law. [n. 886]

10:36 et inimici hominis domestici eius. [n. 888]

10:36 καὶ ἐχθροὶ τοῦ ἀνθρώπου οἱ οἰκιακοὶ αὐτοῦ.

10:36 And a man's enemies will be those of his own household. [n. 888]

10:37 Qui amat patrem, aut matrem, plusquam me, non est me dignus. Et qui amat filium, aut filiam super me, non est me dignus. [n. 889]

10:37 Ὁ φιλῶν πατέρα ἢ μητέρα ὑπὲρ ἐμὲ οὐκ ἔστιν μου ἄξιος, καὶ ὁ φιλῶν υἱὸν ἢ θυγατέρα ὑπὲρ ἐμὲ οὐκ ἔστιν μου ἄξιος·

10:37 He who loves father or mother more than me, is not worthy of me; and he who loves son or daughter more than me, is not worthy of me. [n. 889]

10:38 Et qui non accipit crucem suam, et sequitur me, non est me dignus. [n. 892]

10:38 καὶ ὃς οὐ λαμβάνει τὸν σταυρὸν αὐτοῦ καὶ ἀκολουθεῖ ὀπίσω μου, οὐκ ἔστιν μου ἄξιος.

10:38 And he who takes not up his cross, and follows me, is not worthy of me. [n. 892]

10:39 Qui invenit animam suam, perdet illam, et qui perdiderit animam suam propter me, inveniet eam. [n. 894]

10:39 ὁ εὑρὼν τὴν ψυχὴν αὐτοῦ ἀπολέσει αὐτήν, καὶ ὁ ἀπολέσας τὴν ψυχὴν αὐτοῦ ἕνεκεν ἐμοῦ εὑρήσει αὐτήν.

10:39 He who finds his soul, will lose it: and he who will lose his soul for me, will find it. [n. 894]

10:40 Qui recipit vos, me recipit, et qui me recipit, recipit eum qui me misit. [n. 895]

10:40 Ὁ δεχόμενος ὑμᾶς ἐμὲ δέχεται, καὶ ὁ ἐμὲ δεχόμενος δέχεται τὸν ἀποστείλαντά με.

10:40 He who receives you, receives me: and he who receives me, receives him who sent me. [n. 895]

10:41 Qui recipit prophetam in nomine prophetae mercedem prophetae accipiet. Et qui recipit iustum in nomine iusti, mercedem iusti accipiet. [n. 896]

10:41 ὁ δεχόμενος προφήτην εἰς ὄνομα προφήτου μισθὸν προφήτου λήμψεται, καὶ ὁ δεχόμενος δίκαιον εἰς ὄνομα δικαίου μισθὸν δικαίου λήμψεται.

10:41 He who receives a prophet in the name of a prophet, will receive the reward of a prophet: and he who receives a just man in the name of a just man, will receive the reward of a just man. [n. 896]

10:42 Et quicumque potum dederit uni ex minimis istis calicem aquae frigidae tantum in nomine discipuli, amen dico vobis, non perdet mercedem suam. [n. 897]

10:42 καὶ ὃς ἂν ποτίσῃ ἕνα τῶν μικρῶν τούτων ποτήριον ψυχροῦ μόνον εἰς ὄνομα μαθητοῦ, ἀμὴν λέγω ὑμῖν, οὐ μὴ ἀπολέσῃ τὸν μισθὸν αὐτοῦ.

10:42 And whoever will give to drink to one of these little ones a cup of cold water only in the name of a disciple, amen I say to you, he will not lose his reward. [n. 897]

---

837. Supra instruxit Dominus de officio suo, et de necessariis ad victum, modo vero instruit de periculis imminentibus: et circa hoc duo facit.

Primo ponitur instructio in figura;

secundo exponit illam figuram, ibi *cavete autem ab hominibus*.

Circa primum

primo praenuntiat pericula;

secundo quomodo in periculis se habere debent, ibi *estote ergo prudentes sicut serpentes, et simplices sicut columbae.*

838. Dicit ergo *ecce ego mitto vos*. Quia dixerat *in quamcumque civitatem intraveritis* etc., et tunc quod *dignus est operarius cibo suo*: possent credere quod omnes deberent eos recipere, ideo istud excludit; quasi dicat, *non sic erit. Ecce ego mitto vos sicut oves in medio luporum*, unde mitto vos ad pericula. Et hoc dicit propter duo, ne imputaretur eius ignorantiae, vel impotentiae, quod non posset eos tueri. Item dixit eis, ne putarent se deceptos. Et comparat eos ovibus propter mansuetudinem, persecutores vero lupis propter rapacitatem; ipse enim Christus ovis fuit, de quo Is. LIII, 7: *quasi ovis ad occisionem ducetur*. Et discipuli oves; Ps. XCIV, 7: *nos autem populus eius, et oves pascuae eius.*

Sed ut non credatis quod hoc non sit ex mea voluntate *mitto vos in medio luporum*; Io. XX, 21: *sicut misit me Pater, ego mitto vos.*

Et quare voluit sic Deus mittere ad pericula? Hoc fuit ad manifestationem suae virtutis, quia si misisset aliquos armatos, illud imputaretur violentiae eius, non virtuti Dei; ideo pauperes misit. Magnum enim fuit quod per pauperes, et despectos, et inermes, tot fuerint conversi ad Dominum, sicut dicit Apostolus I Cor. I, 26: *non*

837. Above, the Lord instructed them about their office, and about the things necessary for life; but now he instructs them about the approaching dangers. And concerning this, he does two things.

First, the instruction is set forth in a figure;

second, he explains the figure, at *but beware of men.*

Concerning the first,

first he foretells the dangers;

second, how they should carry themselves in dangers, at *therefore be wise as serpents and simple as doves.*

838. He says then, *behold, I send you.* Since he had said, *into whatever city or town you will enter*, and then that *the workman is worthy of his hire* (Matt 10:10), they might believe that all would receive them; therefore he excludes this, as though to say, *it will not be that way. Behold I send you as sheep among wolves*, hence I send you to dangers. And he says this for two reasons: lest it should be attributed to his ignorance or lack of power that he could not protect them. Likewise, he said this to them lest they should consider themselves deceived. And he compares them to sheep because of meekness, but he compares the persecutors to wolves because of rapaciousness; for Christ himself was a sheep, of whom it is said, *he will be led as a sheep to the slaughter* (Isa 53:7). And the disciples are sheep; *we are the people of his pasture and the sheep of his hand* (Ps 94:7).

But so that you do not believe that this is not from my will, *I send you . . . among wolves*; *as the Father has sent me, I also send you* (John 20:21).

And why did God thus will to send them into dangers? This was to manifest his power, because if he had sent armed men, it would be attributed to their violence, not to God's power; so he sent poor men. For it was a great thing that by paupers, and the despised, and the unarmed so many were converted to the Lord, as the Apostle says, *there are not many wise according to the flesh, not many mighty,*

multum potentes elegit et nobiles Deus; sed quae stulta sunt mundi elegit Deus et cetera.

839. ***Estote ergo prudentes sicut serpentes, et simplices sicut columbae***. Hic ostendit quomodo se debeant habere. Et quia duo mala poterant accidere: quia si apostoli consensissent eis, posset eis malum accidere; si contradixissent, posset similiter; ideo ad duo monet eos: ad prudentiam videlicet, et simplicitatem. Ad prudentiam, ut devitent mala illata; ad simplicitatem, ut non inferant mala.

840. Unde, quia mitto vos, ***estote prudentes***. Vult eos habere prudentiam serpentis. Prudentia serpentis in hoc consistit quod semper vult defendere caput. Caput Christus est, quem servare iubet. Unde II ad Tim., c. ult., 7: *bonum certamen certavi, cursum consummavi, fidem servavi*. Item debent servare caput, I Cor. XI, 3, quod est principium totius; Prov. IV, 23: *omni custodia serva cor tuum*. Item alia prudentia est serpentis, quia quando veterascit, transit per foramen arctum, et expoliat vestem, sive pellem; sic nos debemus facere in nostra conversatione. Et dicit Apostolus ad Col. III, 9: *expoliantes veterem hominem cum actibus suis* et cetera. Item debemus habere prudentiam serpentis in praedicatione; quia, sicut habetur Gen. III, 1 ss., propter astutiam serpentis deiectum est genus humanum, quia invasit fragiliorem sexum; item ostendit ei lignum. Sic praedicatores debent peccatores convertere per magis aptos. Item debent suadere de ligno crucis, ut sicut ille profecit in ligno ad malum, ita isti proficiant ad bonum.

841. ***Et simplices sicut columbae***. Comparaverat autem eos ovi, quia non remurmurat, item non nocet; hic comparat columbae, quia non habet iram in corde. Item ***simplices*** contra dolositatem, quae aliud gerit in corde, aliud in ore, iuxta illud Ps. XXVII, 3: *loquuntur pacem cum proximo suo, mala autem in cordibus suis*. Contra tormenta habere patientiam et simplicitatem. Prov. XI, 3: *simplicitas iustorum diriget eos*.

842. Post exponit pericula dicens ***cavete autem ab hominibus*** et cetera. Et primo in generali; secundo in speciali.

Quia isti sunt simplices, possent credere quod mittebat eos ***in medio luporum***, ita quod hoc diceret ad litteram; ideo exponit ***cavete ab hominibus***. Unumquodque enim debet denominari ab eo, quod principalius inest ei. Unde videndum quid principalius movet in homine: si ratio, homo est; si ira, ursus vel leo est; si concupiscentia, tunc non est homo, sed potius porcus, vel canis. Unde licet sint homines per naturam, tamen lupi sunt per affectionem; in Ps. XLVIII, 13: *homo autem cum in honore*

839. ***Therefore be wise as serpents and simple as doves***. Here he shows how they should carry themselves. And because two bad things could happen, since if the apostles agreed with them, something bad could happen to them, while if they spoke against them, something bad could also happen. Therefore he advises them to two things: namely to prudence, and simplicity. To prudence, that they might avoid the bad things inflicted; to simplicity, that they might not inflict bad things.

840. Hence, since I send you, ***therefore be wise***. He wants them to have the prudence of the serpent. The prudence of the serpent consists in this, that it always wants to defend its head. The head is Christ, whom he commands them to protect. Hence, *I have fought the good fight, I have finished the race, I have kept the faith* (2 Tim 4:7). Likewise, they should protect the head, which is the principle of the whole (1 Cor 11:3); *with all watchfulness keep your heart* (Prov 4:23). Also, the serpent has another prudence, because when it grows old, it passes through a narrow opening, and strips off its clothing, or skin; we should do the same in our way of life. And the Apostle says, *stripping yourselves of the old man with his deeds* (Col 3:9). Likewise, we should have the prudence of the serpent when we are preaching, because the human race was cast down due to the cunning of the serpent, because he attacked the weaker sex; likewise, he showed her the tree (Gen 3:1 ff.). Thus preachers should convert sinners through what is more suitable. Similarly, they should persuade men about the tree of the cross, that just as that man advanced toward what is evil by the tree, so those men advance toward what is good.

841. ***And simple as doves***. He had compared them to the sheep, because the sheep does not murmur, and does no harm; here he compares them to the dove, because it has no anger in its heart. Likewise, he says, ***simple***, against the cunning which bears one thing in the heart and another thing in the mouth, in accordance with a Psalm, *who speak peace with their neighbor, but evils are in their hearts* (Ps 27:3). He commands them to have patience and simplicity in the face of torments; *the simplicity of the just will guide them* (Prov 11:3).

842. Afterwards, he explains the dangers, saying, ***but beware of men***. And first in general; second in particular.

Since they are simple men, they might think that he was sending them ***among wolves*** such that he spoke literally; so he explains, ***beware of men***. For each particular thing should be named from that which is more principal in it. Hence one should see what moves more principally in a man: if reason, he is a man; if anger, he is a bear or a lion; if concupiscence, then he is not a man, but rather a pig or a dog. Hence although they are men by nature, nevertheless they are wolves by affection; *and man when he was in honor*

esset, non intellexit; comparatus est iumentis insipientibus, et similis factus est illis et cetera. Et alibi Ps. XXXI, 9: *nolite fieri sicut equus et mulus, in quibus non est intellectus.*

843. *Tradent enim vos* et cetera.

Primo tangit quibus tradentur;

secundo a quibus tradentur, ibi ***tradet autem frater fratrem*** et cetera. Et

primo ostendit quod dictum est;

secundo eos confortat, ibi ***cum autem tradent vos*** et cetera. Et

primo dicit quibus sunt tradendi;

secundo quid sequatur ex ista traditione, ibi ***et in synagogis suis flagellabunt vos.***

844. Circa primum sic. Talis erat mos apud Iudaeos, quod si aliquis primo diceret, vel faceret contra legem, primo vocabatur ad Concilium, et reprehendebatur; sed si secundo, cum reprehensione flagellabatur; sed si tertio, vel occidebatur, cum esset eis potestas, vel occidendus tradebatur ei cui potestas inerat. Et istud factum est, sicut dicitur Act. IV, 1 ss. et V, 16; ibi enim dicitur quod loquentibus apostolis ad populum, comminati sunt eis; et post hoc cum adhuc loquerentur, caesis nuntiaverunt, quod non loquerentur, et tertio lapidaverunt Stephanum, et Iacobum Herodi tradiderunt. Ideo cavete, quia ***tradent vos in Conciliis suis***; Ps. XXV, 4: *non sedi cum Concilio vanitatis, et cum iniqua gerentibus non introibo.*

845. *Et ad praesides et reges ducemini*, ut ad Herodem, et multos alios. Sed magnam debetis habere consolationem, quia ***propter me***, scilicet quem diligitis. Augustinus: *omnia quasi inania et quasi nulla facit amor.* Item ***beati qui persecutionem patiuntur propter iustitiam*** etc. supra V, 10.

Et quid inde sequetur? Hoc erit ***in testimonium illis***, idest contra illos, idest Iudaeos et gentes. Quia enim tradent vos in Conciliis, ideo hoc erit in testimonium contra illos. Item quia ante reges et praesides, hoc similiter erit contra illos. Unde infra XXIII, 34: ***ecce ego mitto ad vos sapientes et Scribas et ex illis occidetis, et flagellabitis in synagogis vestris*** et cetera.

Vel sic: ***in testimonium illis***, scilicet Iudaeis et gentibus, quia mitto vos ad eos, testes fidei meae ad Iudaeos et gentes; unde martyr idem est quod testis; quia per passionem vestram eritis testes passionis meae; Act. I, 8: *et eritis mihi testes in Ierusalem, et in omni Iudaea, et Samaria, et usque ad ultimum terrae* et cetera.

did not understand; he is compared to senseless beasts, and is become like to them (Ps 48:13). And in another place, *do not become like the horse and the mule, who have no understanding* (Ps 31:9).

843. *For they will deliver you up.*

First, he touches upon those to whom they will be handed over;

second, by whom they will be handed over, at ***the brother also will deliver up the brother***.

And first, he shows what was said;

second, he comforts them, at ***but when they will deliver you up***.

And first, he says to whom they will be handed over;

second, what follows from this handing over, at ***they will scourge you in their synagogues***.

844. Concerning the first, he speaks this way. Such was the custom among the Jews, that if someone spoke or acted against the law for the first time, he was first called before the council, and reproached; but if a second time, he was beaten along with the reproach; but if a third time, either he was killed, when it was in their power, or he was handed over to be killed to those who had the power. And this was done, just as is said in Acts (Acts 4:1; 5:16); for there it says that when the apostles were speaking to the people, they were threatened by them; and after this when they were still speaking, having beaten them, they told them that they should not speak; and third, they stoned Stephen, and handed James over to Herod. Therefore beware, because ***they will deliver you up in councils***; *I have not sat with the council of vanity: neither will I go in with the doers of unjust things* (Ps 25:4).

845. *And you will be brought before governors, and before kings*, as to Herod, and many others. But you should have great consolation, because it is ***for my sake***, namely, whom you love. Augustine: *love makes all things as though empty and as though nothing.* Likewise, ***blessed are they who suffer persecution for justice's sake*** (Matt 5:10).

And what will come of this? This will be ***for a testimony to them***, i.e., against them, i.e., the Jews and the gentiles. For since they will hand you over in councils, this will be in witness against them. Likewise, since it will be before kings and governors, this will also be against them. Hence, ***therefore, I say to you, behold I send to you prophets, and wise men, and scribes: and some of them you will put to death and crucify, and some you will scourge in your synagogues*** (Matt 23:34).

Or thus: ***for a testimony to them***, namely to the Jews and the gentiles, because I send you to them as witnesses of my faith to the Jews and gentiles; hence a martyr is the same as a witness, because by your suffering you will be witness to my suffering. *And you will be witnesses unto me in Jerusalem, and in all Judea, and Samaria, and even to the uttermost part of the earth* (Acts 1:8).

846. *Cum autem tradent vos, nolite cogitare quomodo aut quid loquamini* et cetera. Possent dicere apostoli: *nos sumus piscatores insipientes, erimus stupefacti*. Et non est mirum, quia Moyses, qui instructus in lege erat, cum mandaret Dominus quod accederet ad Pharaonem, dixit, *impeditioris linguae sum*. Ex. IV, 10. Ideo ut hoc excludat, dicit *cum autem tradent vos* et cetera.

Et tria facit.
Primo excludit stuporem;
secundo promittit sapientiae donum, ibi *dabitur enim vobis in illa hora quid loquamini*;
tertio auctorem doni, ibi *non enim vos estis qui loquimini, sed spiritus Patris vestri qui loquitur in vobis*.

847. *Nolite* ergo *cogitare* de hoc. Et duo excludit. Et quantum ad id quod dicitur; et quantum ad modum loquendi. Primum pertinet ad sapientiam; secundum ad eloquentiam.

Sed videtur esse contra hoc quod Apostolus Petrus dicit in canonica sua: *parati semper ad satisfactionem omni poscenti vos rationem de ea, quae in vobis est, fide et spe*.

Chrysostomus solvit, quod quando aliquis habet necessitatem respondendi, et habet tempus deliberandi, non debet expectare divinum auxilium; sed apostoli cum erant in tribulatione, non habebant tempus, quare debebant se committere Filio Dei: sic etiam est quod cum aliquis habet facultatem, dèbet facere quod potest; sed certe si non habet tempus, debet se committere Filio Dei, sed non debet tentare Deum si habeat tempus cogitandi. Ideo Dominus non dixit solum *nolite cogitare*, sed dicit *cum tradent vos . . . nolite cogitare* et cetera.

848. Et sequitur ex illa promissione *dabitur enim vobis in illa hora*; quia *in manu Dei sunt omnes sermones nostri*, Sap. c. VII, 16. Et Ex. IV, 12: *ego ero in ore tuo doceboque quid loquaris*. Et Lc. XXI, 15: *ego dabo vobis os et sapientiam*.

849. Et quis est auctor? Certe Spiritus Sanctus. *Non enim vos estis qui loquimini, sed spiritus Patris vestri qui loquitur in vobis*. Simile est quod habetur II Cor. c. XIII, 3: *an experimentum quaeritis eius qui in me loquitur Christus?*

Sed quid est quod videbantur isti arreptitii? Notandum quod omnis actio quae ex duobus causatur, quorum unum est principale agens, secundum vero instrumentale, debet denominari e principaliori. Isti fuerunt agentes instrumentaliter, Spiritus Sanctus principaliter; ideo tota actio debet denominari a Spiritu Sancto.

Sed videndum quod aliquando movet spiritus perturbando rationem, aliquando movet confortando. Unde haec differentia est inter motum diaboli, et Spiritus

846. *But when they will deliver you up, take no thought how or what to speak*. The apostles could say, *we are foolish fishermen, we will be struck dumb*. And it is not a marvel that they would react this way, for Moses, who was instructed in the law, when the Lord commanded that he approach Pharaoh, said, *I have more impediment and slowness of tongue* (Exod 4:10). So, to exclude this, he says, *but when they will deliver you up*.

And he does three things:
first, he excludes stupefaction;
second, he promises the gift of wisdom, at *for it will be given you in that hour what to speak*;
third, the author of the gift, at *for it is not you who speak, but the Spirit of your Father who speaks in you*.

847. Therefore, *take no thought* about this. And he excludes two things, both with respect to what is said, and with respect to the manner of speaking. The first pertains to wisdom, the second to eloquence.

But what the Apostle Peter says in his canonical letter, seems contrary to this: *being ready always to satisfy every one who asks you a reason of that hope which is in you* (1 Pet 3:15).

Chrysostom resolves it, saying that when someone has the need to respond, and has the time to deliberate, he should not expect divine help; but when the apostles were in afflictions, they did not have time, which is why they had to entrust themselves to the Son of God. So also it is that when someone has the ability, he should do what he can; but certainly, if he does not have time, he should entrust himself to the Son of God, but should not tempt God if he has the time to think. For this reason the Lord did not say only, *take no thought*, but he says, *when they will deliver you up, take no thought*.

848. And it follows from this promise: *for it will be given you in that hour*; for *in his hand are both we, and our words* (Wis 7:16). And, *I will be in your mouth: and I will teach you what you should speak* (Exod 4:12). And, *for I will give you a mouth and wisdom* (Luke 21:15).

849. And who is the author? Certainly the Holy Spirit. *For it is not you who speak, but the Spirit of your Father who speaks in you*. Similar is what is said, *do you seek a proof of Christ who speaks in me?* (2 Cor 13:3).

But why is it that they seem to be possessed? One should note that every action which is caused by two things, of which one is the principal agent and the second the instrumental, should be named from the more principal one. These men were agents instrumentally, the Holy Spirit principally, so the whole action should be named from the Holy Spirit.

But one should see that sometimes a spirit moves a man by disturbing his reason, and sometimes it moves a man by strengthening the reason greatly. Hence there is this

Sancti. Homo enim non est dominus, nisi per rationem, per quam est liber; unde quando homo secundum rationem non movetur, tunc est motus arreptitius. Quando cum ratione, tunc dicitur motus a Spiritu Sancto. Motio enim diaboli perturbat rationem. Isti autem, licet a Spiritu Sancto loquerentur, tamen remanebat in eis ratio; et ideo etiam a se loquebantur, non sicut arreptitii. Unde reducit eos ad veritatem propheticam, ut habetur II Petr. I, 19: *et habemus firmiorem propheticum sermonem*.

850. Sed possent dicere apostoli: *quis tradet nos? Non habemus inimicitias.*

Primo ergo ostendit a quibus tradentur;

secundo consolationem adhibet, ibi **qui autem perseveraverit usque in finem, hic salvus erit**.

Aliquis potest male cavere a persecutione sibi praenuntiata in universali tantum; ideo praenuntiat in singulari. Et duo dicit quoad primum.

851. *Tradet autem frater fratrem*. Istud secundum litteram aliquando accidit quod pater tradidit filium, et e converso, et frater fratrem, aut propter timorem, aut propter odium; quia tanta est virtus fidei quod inter homines qui non sunt eiusdem fidei, vix firma sit amicitia. Et hoc est quod dicit **tradet enim frater fratrem** et cetera. Unde dicitur et Ier. IX, 4: *ut unusquisque in fratre suo non habeat fiduciam*. Et ob hoc est necessarium quod caveant, et propter laesionem quam homo patitur, et propter amissionem amicitiae; in Ps. LIV, 13: *si inimicus meus maledixisset mihi, sustinuissem utique*.

852. Item plus, quia non ibitis ad familiares, sed ad extraneos. Et hoc non valebit, quia **eritis odio omnibus hominibus**. Unde in Io. XVI, 2: *venit hora in qua omnis qui occiderit vos, reputabit se obsequium praestare Deo*. Sed numquid fuit hoc verum? Nonne multi fuerunt qui recipiebant eos? Ideo dicebat de hominibus, qui humanitus vivebant. Alii vero, qui Dei erant, eos recipiebant. Sed causa huius assignatur Io. XV, 18: *si de mundo fuissetis, mundus quod suum erat, diligeret; quia vero de mundo non estis, ideo odit vos mundus*.

853. Item promisit Dominus consolationem, quia propter **nomen meum**. Hoc enim vobis dulce debet esse pro nomine meo pati, ut habetur I Petr. IV, 14: *si exprobramini in nomine Christi, beati eritis*.

Item alia ratione confortat eos, quia ad magnum fructum eorum debebat venire tribulatio. Quia enim praevidit multos cadere, ideo monet ad perseverantiam; quia **qui perseveraverit usque in finem, hic salvus erit**. Unde II Tim. ult., 7: *bonum certamen certavi, cursum consummavi, fidem servavi; in reliquo reposita est mihi*

difference between a motion from the devil and one from the Holy Spirit. For man is only a lord by his reason, through which he is free; hence when a man is not moved according to reason, then the one moved is possessed. When a man is moved with reason, then the motion is said to be from the Holy Spirit. For the motion of the devil disturbs reason. But these men, although they spoke by the Holy Spirit, nevertheless reason remained in them; and therefore they spoke also from themselves, not like men possessed. Hence he leads them back to the prophetic truth, as is found, *and we have the more firm prophetical word*. (1 Pet 1:19).

850. But the apostles could say: *who will hand us over? We have no enmities*.

First, he shows by whom they will be handed over;

second, he adds a consolation, at **but he who will persevere to the end, he will be saved**.

Since someone can avoid in a bad way a persecution foretold him only in the universal, he foretells the persecutions in particular. And he says two things regarding the first.

851. *The brother also will deliver up the brother*. This sometimes happened literally, that a father handed over a son, and vice versa, and a brother his brother, either because of fear or because of hatred; because so great is the power of faith that among men who are not of the same faith a firm friendship is hardly possible. And this is what he says, that **the brother also will deliver up the brother**. Hence it is also said, *let every man take heed of his neighbor, and let him not trust in any brother of his* (Jer 9:4). And because of this it is necessary that they beware, both on account of the injury which a man suffers, and on account of the loss of friendship; *for if my enemy had reviled me, I would have borne with it* (Ps 54:13).

852. And more besides, because you will not go to those of your household, but to outsiders. And this will not be well, for **you will be hated by all men**. Hence, *indeed the hour comes, that whoever kills you, will think that he does a service to God* (John 16:2). But was this not true? Were there not many who received them? Therefore he spoke of men who lived in a human way. But the others, who were of God, received them. But the reason for this is given, *if you had been of the world, the world would love its own: but because you are not of the world, but I have chosen you out of the world, therefore the world hates you* (John 15:19).

853. Likewise, the Lord promises consolation, because it will be **for my name's sake**. For it should be sweet for you to suffer for my name, as is found, *if you be reproached for the name of Christ, you will be blessed* (1 Pet 4:14).

Likewise, he comforts them with another reason, because affliction was to come unto a great fruit for them. For since he foresaw that many would fall, he warns them to perseverance, because **he who will persevere to the end, he will be saved**. Hence, *I have fought a good fight, I have finished my course, I have kept the faith* (2 Tim 4:7–8). As to

corona iustitiae, quam reddet mihi Dominus in illa die iustus iudex. Unde in Levitico dicitur quod cauda offerebatur, idest finis.

854. *Cum autem persequentur vos in civitate ista, fugite in aliam.* Supra docuit pericula, in quo exposuit quod dixerat, *ecce ego mitto vos* etc., nunc autem docet quomodo se habere debent.

Et dividitur haec pars: quia

primo docet cavere mala et periculum quoad prudentiam;

secundo docet habere aequanimitatem in periculis, ibi *nolite ergo timere.*

Circa primum

primo docet vitare periculum corporale;

secundo spirituale, ibi *non est discipulus super magistrum.*

Circa primum duo facit.

Primo innuit malum periculorum;

secundo ad tacitam obiectionem respondet, ibi *amen dico vobis* et cetera.

855. Dicit ergo: ita dictum est, quod *qui perseveraverit usque in finem hic salvus erit*, et non propter hoc tentationibus exponatis vos, immo *cum persequentur vos in civitate ista, fugite in aliam*: et hoc infirmis expedit, ne incaute se exponentes deficiant; Prov. XIV, 15: *astutus considerat gressus suos, stultus transibit, et confidit.* Item docet etiam perfectos; et si non propter ipsos, tamen propter aliorum salutem, ut habetur ad Phil. c. I, 24: *manere autem in carne necessarium est propter vos.* Istud autem ostendit Dominus quando propter Herodem fugit in Aegyptum, ut habetur supra II, 14. Item hoc fecerunt discipuli, sicut habetur Act. VIII, 1.

856. Sed contra hoc obiicitur quod habetur Io. X, 12, quod *mercenarius fugit, et dimittit oves.* Ergo videtur quod ad ipsos non pertineat, sed ad mercenarios.

Respondet Augustinus, quod persecutio aut imminet singulari personae: et tunc declinare, et dimittere aliquos debet, per quos fiat salus; si autem toti Ecclesiae, oportet quod vel tota Ecclesia fugiat ad loca tutiora, ut iam factum est; vel quod aliqui fugiant, et aliqui firmi remaneant, aut pastor cum grege remaneat.

857. Sequitur *amen dico vobis, non consummabitis civitates Israel, donec veniat Filius hominis.* Respondet tacitae obiectioni.

Possent dicere: *tu mittis nos ad Iudaeam; si eiiciant, quo ibimus?* Dico, dato quod ab una civitate expellant vos, *fugite in aliam*, et non poteritis peragrare civitates Iudaeae, *donec veniat Filius hominis*, idest donec resurgat a mortuis, et tunc mittet vos ad gentes, ut habetur in. ult., 19: *ite, docete omnes gentes.*

the rest, there is laid up for me a crown of justice, which the Lord, the just judge, will render to me in that day. Hence it says in Leviticus that the tail was offered, i.e., the end.

854. *And when they persecute you in this city, flee into another.* Above he taught about the dangers, in which he explained what he had said, *behold, I send you*; and now he teaches them how they should carry themselves.

And it is divided into parts, because

first he teaches them to beware evils and danger as regards prudence;

second, he teaches them to have equanimity in dangers, at *therefore fear not.*

Concerning the first,

first he teaches them to avoid bodily danger;

second, spiritual danger, at *the disciple is not above the master.*

Concerning the first, he does two things:

first, he refers to the evil of the dangers;

second, he responds to an unmentioned objection, at *amen I say to you.*

855. He says then: it was said thus, that *he who will persevere to the end, he will be saved*, and do not expose yourselves to temptations on this account, but rather *when they will persecute you in this city, flee into another.* And this is expedient for the weak lest, incautiously exposing themselves, they should fail; *a wise man fears and declines from evil: the fool leaps over and is confident* (Prov 14:16). Similarly, he teaches even the perfect to be cautious; even if not for themselves, yet for the sake of the salvation of others, as is found, *but to abide still in the flesh, is needful for you* (Phil 1:24). Moreover, the Lord showed this when he fled into Egypt on account of Herod, as is found above (Matt 2:14). Similarly, the disciples did this (Acts 8:1).

856. But against this is set what is said, that *the hireling flees, and loses the sheep* (John 10:12). So it seems that this does not befit them, but hirelings.

Augustine responds that persecution either threatens a particular person, and then he should avoid it, and leave others through whom safety may be regained; but if it threatens the whole Church, it is necessary either that the whole Church should flee to a safer place, which has already happened, or that some flee and some remain firm, or rather that the pastor should remain with the flock.

857. There follows *amen I say to you, you will not finish all the cities of Israel, till the Son of man come.* He responds to an unmentioned objection.

They could say: *you send us to the Jews; if they should throw us out, where will we go?* I say, given that they throw you out of one city, *flee into another*, and you will not be able to travel over all the cities of Judea *till the Son of Man come*, i.e., until he rises from the dead, and then sends you to the gentiles, *going therefore, teach all nations* (Matt 28:19).

Hilarius aliter exponit. Dicit enim quod loquitur de secunda missione, scilicet cum dicit, **cum persequentur vos**; scilicet de Iudaea fugite ad gentes, sicut habetur Act. XIII, 46: *vobis oportebat primum praedicare regnum Dei: sed quia repellitis illud, et indignos vos iudicatis aeternae vitae, ecce convertimus nos ad gentes.*

Sed possent dicere: *quare vis quod dimittamus nostros?* Quia non poteritis consummare usque in finem, tunc consummabuntur filii Israel.

Mystice sic: cum persequentur vos haeretici cum auctoritatibus suis, eos auctoritatibus repellite; non enim consummabuntur donec manifestetur veritas.

858. Non est enim **discipulus super magistrum**. Hic monet eos ne deficiant: et

primo exemplo;

secundo beneficio, ibi **ne ergo timueritis eos**;

tertio ex divino iudicio, ibi **et nolite timere eos qui occidunt corpus**.

Primo hortatur ne deficiant exemplo; et

primo ponit similitudinem;

secundo applicat ad propositum. Et

primo inducit quod est inconveniens;

secundo quod perfectum est.

859. Dicit ergo **non est discipulus super magistrum**.

Possent enim dicere: *tu dicis quod erimus odio omnibus hominibus; quomodo poterimus tot odia sustinere?* Dederat eis Dominus magnam sapientiam, et magnam potestatem: unde sapientiae debetur honor, potestati reverentia; ideo Dominus ponit se in exemplum quoad utrumque.

Non est discipulus super magistrum, inquantum discipulus; unde si honorem mihi non exhibuerunt qui debetur magistro, nec vobis. Item **nec servus est maior Domino**; et hoc inquantum ad dominium. Unde Io. XIII, 13: *vos vocatis me, Magister, et Domine, et bene dicitis, sum etenim* et cetera.

860. Debet autem esse gloriae unicuique si sit sicut dominus eius vel magister; ideo subdit **sufficit discipulo ut sit sicut magister eius**. Sicut enim est in rebus quod unumquodque perfectum est, quando potest generare sibi simile, sic etiam tunc est perfectus discipulus, cum est persimilis magistro; similiter et de servo. Ideo non debet vobis esse grave si sitis sicut et ego; unde habetur I Petr. II, 21: *Christus passus est pro nobis, vobis relinquens exemplum, ut sequamini vestigia eius.* Et Eccle. II, 12: *quis est qui possit sequi dominum suum?*

861. Deinde vocat eos domesticos: **si patrem familias vocaverunt Beelzebub, quanto magis domesticos eius?**

Hilary explains it in another way. For he says that he is speaking of the second sending, namely when he says, **when they will persecute you**; namely flee from Judea to the gentiles, *to you it behooved us first to speak the word of God: but because you reject it, and judge yourselves unworthy of eternal life, behold we turn to the gentiles* (Acts 13:46).

But they could say: *why do you wish that we lose our own people?* Because you will not be able to bring them to perfection up until the end; then the sons of Israel will be brought to perfection.

Mystically, in this way: when the heretics persecute you with their authority, thrust away their authority; for they will not be brought to perfection until the truth is made plain.

858. The disciple is not above the master. Here he advises them lest they fail. And

first, by example;

second, by benefit, at **therefore do not fear them**;

third, from the divine judgment, at **and do not fear those who kill the body**.

First, he exhorts them by an example, lest they fail; and first, he sets forth the likeness;

second, he applies the likeness to the thing intended. And

first, he brings up what is unfitting;

second, what is perfect.

859. He says then, **the disciple is not above the master**.

For they could say: *you say that we will be hated by all men; how will we be able to endure so much hatred?* The Lord had given them great wisdom, and great power; hence to wisdom honor is due, and to power, reverence. So the Lord put himself forward as an example regarding both.

The disciple is not above the master, insofar as he is a disciple; hence if they did not show the honor which is due to me, the teacher, neither will they show honor to you. Similarly, **nor the servant above his lord**; and this with regard to dominion. Hence, *you call me Master, and Lord; and you say well, for so I am* (John 13:13).

860. But it should be to each one's glory if he is like his lord or teacher; so he adds, **it is enough for the disciple that he should be as his master**. For just as it is in things, that each thing is perfect when it can generate its like, so also the disciple is perfect when he is completely like the teacher; and similarly with regard to the servant. Therefore it should not be a heavy thing for you if you are also like I am; hence, *Christ also suffered for us, leaving you an example that you should follow his steps* (1 Pet 2:21). And, *what is man, said I, that he can follow the king his maker?* (Eccl 2:12).

861. Then he calls them members of the household: **if they have called the father of the household Beelzebub, how much more those of his household?**

Et vocat eos domesticos ad maiorem familiaritatem: unde magnum est donum pati pro Christo, ut habetur Iac. I, 2: *magnum gaudium existimate, fratres, cum in tentationes varias incideritis, scientes quod probatio fidei vestrae patientiam operatur.* Et Act. V, v. 41: *ibant apostoli gaudentes a conspectu Concilii, quoniam digni habiti sunt pro nomine Iesu contumeliam pati.* Unde non est magnum, domesticum pati pro amico. Ad Eph. II, 19: *vos estis cives sanctorum, et domestici Dei.*

862. Unde *si patrem familias vocant Beelzebub*, non est mirum si vobis opprobria dicunt.

Quid autem dicitur *Beelzebub*? Sciendum quod Ninus fuisse dicitur filius Beli: unde imaginem patris fecit honorari, et vocavit 'Bel'. Deinde postmodum translatum est ad aliam linguam, et dictum est Beelzebub. 'Zebub', idest musca: sacrificabatur enim isti cum multo cruore, ubi congregantur multae muscae.

863. *Ne ergo timueritis eos* et cetera. Hic hortatur ne deficiant in tribulationibus ex beneficio. Et primo eos confortat; secundo similitudinem dat; tertio ad propositum applicat.

Dicit ergo: persequentur vos, sed ne timeatis, quia non debetis timere nisi malum; sed magnum bonum est portare quod Dominus portavit. Unde Paulus ad Gal. ult., 17 gloriabatur dicens: *stigmata Domini mei in corpore meo porto.*

Nihil est enim opertum quod non reveletur. Istud potest ad praecedentia referri, vel ad sequentia. Ad praecedentia sic: isti vocabunt vos Beelzebub; sed non est curandum, quia in fine patebit malitia eorum. Ideo non timeatis, quia *nihil opertum quod non reveletur*; ut habetur I Cor. IV, 5: *nolite itaque ante tempus iudicare, quousque veniat Dominus, qui revelabit abscondita tenebrarum, et manifestabit consilia cordium.*

Et occultum. Differt opertum, et occultum: quia *occultum* dicit aliquid non manifestum, sicut est illud quod alius habet in corde, secundum illud supra c. IX, 4: *ut quid cogitatis mala in cordibus vestris?* Opertum autem est etiam aliquid quod, etsi sit manifestum, operitur tamen per aliquid aliud.

Vel potest exponi sic: non timeatis, quia si statim non pateat veritas vestra, tamen postea patebit.

864. Deinde instruit eos Dominus sicut instruitur advocatus: quia primo docetur qualiter debeat allegare antequam proferat ante alios. Sic Dominus discipulos elegerat ad seminandum verbum suum omni populo; ideo primo in occulto volebat eos docere dicens: *quod vobis dico in tenebris, dicite in lumine.* Duo sunt sensus disciplinales: auditus, et visus. Quod *in tenebris* dicitur,

And he calls them members of the household for greater familiarity; hence it is a great gift to suffer for Christ, as is said, *my brethren, count it all joy, when you will fall into diverse temptations; knowing that the trying of your faith works patience* (Jas 1:2–3). And, *and they indeed went from the presence of the council, rejoicing that they were accounted worthy to suffer reproach for the name of Jesus* (Acts 5:41). Hence it is no great thing for a member of the household to suffer for a loved one. *You are fellow citizens with the saints, and the domestics of God* (Eph 2:19).

862. Hence, *if they have called the father of the household Beelzebub*, it is no marvel if they speak reproaches against you.

But what is meant by *Beelzebub*? One should know that Ninus is said to have been the son of Belus; hence he caused the image of his father to be honored, and called it 'Bel'. From there, it was later translated into another language, and was called Beelzebub. 'Zebub', i.e., the fly, for they sacrificed to it with a great deal of blood, where many flies gather.

863. *Therefore do not fear them.* Here he exhorts them by benefit, lest they fail. And first, he comforts them; second, he gives a likeness; third, he applies it to the thing intended.

He says then: they will persecute you, but do not fear, because you should only fear evil; but it is a great good to carry what the Lord carried. Hence Paul gloried, saying, *I bear the marks of the Lord Jesus in my body* (Gal 6:17).

For nothing is covered that will not be revealed. This can be referred either to what came before, or to what follows. To what came before, in this way: they will call you Beelzebub; but it is not to be worried about, because in the end they will suffer their evils. Therefore do not fear, because *nothing is covered that will not be revealed*; as is found, *therefore judge not before the time; until the Lord come, who both will bring to light the hidden things of darkness, and will make manifest the counsels of the hearts* (1 Cor 4:5).

Nor hid. What is covered differs from what is hidden, because he calls *hid* something not manifest, such as that which another man has in his heart, in accordance with, *why do you think evil in your hearts?* (Matt 9:4). But the *covered* is also something which, even if it is manifest, is still covered by something else.

Or it can be explained in this way: do not fear, because if your truth is not well known right away, still it will be well known.

864. Then the Lord instructs them as a witness is instructed, because first one is taught how he should plea before he comes before others. Thus the Lord had chosen the disciples to sow his word in every people; therefore he willed first to teach them secretly, saying, *that which I tell you in the dark, speak in the light.* There are two senses which have to do with learning: hearing and sight. That

occultum est: similiter quod in auribus auditur. ***Quod dico vobis in tenebris, dicite in lumine***, quia in lumine omnia manifestantur. Item occultum est, quod in aure auditur; ideo dicit ***et quod in aure auditis, praedicate super tecta***.

865. Sed contra hoc videtur quod dicitur in Io. XVIII, 20: *in occulto locutus sum nihil*. Sed hoc intelligendum est sic: nihil locutus sum in occulto quod non possit dici in manifesto. Vel sic ***quod dico vobis in tenebris***, idest inter Iudaeos, qui tenebrae sunt. Unde Eph. V, 8: *eratis aliquando tenebrae*. Vel ***quod dico vobis***, qui estis tenebrae, ***dicite in lumine***; I ad Cor. IV, 5: *qui illuminabit abscondita tenebrarum, et manifestabit consilia cordium*.

Et quod in aure auditis, praedicate super tecta. Prov. X, 14: *sapientes abscondunt scientiam*. Et Iob V, 27: *quod auditum est, mente pertracta*. ***Super tecta***, quia in aliquibus regionibus mos est quod tecta sunt plana; ita quod et ibi potest fieri manifestatio omnibus.

Mystice ***super tecta*** praedicat, qui carnem sibi subiiciens aliis praedicat.

866. ***Et nolite timere eos qui occidunt corpus***. Supra ostendit quod non debebant discedere a confessione veritatis, tum propter exemplum, tum propter beneficium, nunc ostendit, quod non debent discedere ex divino iudicio, quia facta subsunt iustitiae divinae.

Vel potest aliter continuari. Docuit qualiter vitandae sunt persecutiones, nunc autem docet quod propter aliquid non desistant ab executione officii. Tria autem poterant impedire: opprobria, timor mortis, affectus carnalis. Docuit ergo quod non desistant propter opprobria; nunc autem quod non propter timorem mortis; deinde quod non propter affectum carnalem, ibi ***nolite arbitrari quia venerim pacem mittere in terram***.

Unde secundum hoc

primo docet quia non timendi sunt qui occidunt corpus, ne praedicatio veritatis dimittatur;

secundo non sunt timendi, quia parum possunt, ibi ***animam autem non possunt occidere***;

tertio ostendit qui sunt timendi, quia qui multum possunt.

867. Primo ergo dicit ***nolite timere eos qui occidunt corpus***. Et quare? Quia corpus in se necessitatem habet moriendi, unde non facit quod non sit aliquando futurum; Rom. c. VIII, 10: *si in vobis est Christus, corpus quidem mortuum est propter peccatum*. Item quia occisio corporis propter gloriam est optabilis; unde Rom. VII, 24: *quis me liberabit de corpore mortis huius?*

which is called ***in the dark*** is hidden, and similarly what is heard in the ears. ***That which I tell you in the dark, speak in the light***, because all things are made manifest in the light. Likewise, what is heard in the ear is hidden, so he says, ***and that which you hear in the ear, preach upon the housetops***.

865. But what is said seems to be against this: *in secret I have spoken nothing* (John 18:20). But this should be understood in this way: I have spoken nothing in secret which could not be said in the open. Or in this way: ***that which I tell you in the dark***, i.e., among the Jews, who are darkness. Hence, *for you were heretofore darkness* (Eph 5:8). Or, ***that which I tell you***, who are darkness, ***speak in the light***; *who both will bring to light the hidden things of darkness, and will make manifest the counsels of the hearts* (1 Cor 4:5).

And that which you hear in the ear, preach upon the housetops. *Wise men lay up knowledge* (Prov 10:14). And, *which you, having heard, consider it thoroughly in your mind* (Job 5:27). ***Upon the housetops***, because in some regions it is the custom that roofs are flat, in such a way that there something can be made manifest to everyone.

Mystically, he preaches ***upon the housetops*** who preaches to others after having subjected his body to himself.

866. ***And do not fear those who kill the body***. Above, he showed that they should not shrink from the confession of the truth, both on account of his example, and on account of the benefit; now he shows that they should not shrink back on account of the divine judgment, because one's deeds are subject to the divine justice.

Or it can be connected in another way. He taught how persecutions are to be avoided, and now he teaches that they should not cease from carrying out their office because of anything. Now, three things can impede one: insults, the fear of death, and carnal affection. So he taught that they should not cease because of insults; and now he teaches that they should not cease because of the fear of death; then, that they should not cease because of fleshly affection, at ***do not think that I came to send peace upon earth***.

Hence according to this

first, he teaches that those who kill the body are not to be feared, lest the preaching of the truth be forsaken;

second, they are not to be feared, because they can do but little, at ***and are not able to kill the soul***;

third, he shows who should be feared, because they can do a great deal.

867. First then he says, ***and do not fear those who kill the body***. And why? Because the body in itself must necessarily die, hence they do not do anything which is not going to happen sometime anyway; *and if Christ be in you, the body indeed is dead, because of sin* (Rom 8:10). Likewise, because the killing of the body is choiceworthy for the sake of glory; hence, *who will deliver me from the body*

Item quia brevis est et momentanea; II ad Cor. IV, 11: *semper enim nos qui vivimus in mortem tradimur.*

Et ideo **nolite timere**. Is. LI, 12: *quis es tu ut timeas ab homine mortali, et a filio hominis, qui quasi foenum arescit?*

868. *Animam autem non possunt occidere*. Hic tangit quod parum possunt, quia animam non possunt occidere; unde spiritus semper vivit; Eccli. XV, 18: *ante hominem vita et mors, bonum et malum: quod placuerit, dabitur ei.* Sicut enim corpus vivit per animam, ita anima per Deum: et ita Deus est vita animae. Non sunt ergo timendi, quia parum possunt.

869. *Nolite* ergo *eos timere; sed potius timete eum qui potest et animam et corpus perdere in gehennam*. Si dicitis quod illi sunt timendi qui corpus occidunt; potius ille timendus est qui potest etiam animam perdere.

Et notandum quod nomen ***gehennae***, ut dicit Hieronymus, non habetur in Scriptura, tamen assumitur a salvatore ab Ier. XIX, 6, ubi dicitur: *ecce dies veniunt, et non vocabitur locus iste amplius vallis filiorum Ennon, sed vallis occisionis.* Unde Ennon vallis est a radice montis Ierusalem, quae erat vallis pinguissima, et vocabatur vallis Ennon. Contigit autem quod locus ille esset consecratus idolo; et ideo quia ad voluptates conversi sunt, comminatus est Dominus quod occiderentur, et quod non vocaretur locus Ennon, sed coriandrum, idest sepulcrum mortuorum; ideo vocat locum istum Gehennam.

Unde dicit: non solum timete eos qui occidunt corpus, ***sed potius timete eum qui potest et animam et corpus perdere in gehennam***, quia Deo non est serviendum propter timorem poenae, sed propter amorem iustitiae, ut habetur Rom. VIII, 15: *non enim accepistis spiritum servitutis in timore; sed accepistis spiritum adoptionis filiorum Dei.*

870. Et notandum quod hic excludit duos errores. Quidam enim dicebant, quod anima, mortuo corpore, perit; et hoc destruit, cum dicit ***qui potest animam . . . mittere in gehennam***. Unde patet quod post corpus remanet.

Item erat positio quorumdam quod non esset resurrectio, sicut habetur I ad Cor. XV, 12. Et hoc excludit, quia si corpus et anima mittitur in Gehennam, constat quod erit resurrectio: et hoc habetur Apoc. XX, 9: *mittentur in resurrectione in stagnum ignis et sulphuris.*

871. *Nonne duo passeres asse veneunt?* Ita dictum est quod isti non sunt timendi, quia non possunt et

of this death? (Rom 7:24). Likewise, because it is short and momentary; *for we who live are always delivered unto death* (2 Cor 4:11).

And therefore, ***do not fear***. Who are you, that you should be afraid of a mortal man, and of the son of man, who will wither away like grass? (Isa 51:12).

868. *And are not able to kill the soul*. Here he touches upon the fact that they can do but little, because they cannot kill the soul; hence the spirit always lives. *Before man is life and death, good and evil, that which he will choose will be given him* (Sir 15:18). For just as the body lives by the soul, so the soul lives by God; and thus God is the life of the soul. Therefore they should not be feared, because they can do but little.

869. Therefore ***do not fear those; but rather fear him who can destroy both soul and body in gehenna***. If you say that those who kill the body should be feared, even more should he be feared who can destroy even the soul.

And one should notice that the name ***gehenna***, as Jerome says, does not appear in the Old Testament Scripture, yet is taken up by the Savior, where it says, *therefore behold the days come, says the Lord, that this place will no more be called Topheth, nor the valley of the son of Ennom, but the valley of slaughter* (Jer 19:6). Hence the valley of Ennom is from the root of the mountain of Jerusalem, which was a most fertile valley, and was called the valley of Ennom. Now, it happened that this place was consecrated to an idol, and so since they had turned to pleasures, the Lord threatened that they would be killed, and that it would not be called the place of Ennom, but the place of the coriander, i.e., the sepulcher of the dead; therefore he calls this place Gehenna.

Hence he says: do not just fear those who kill the body, ***and do not fear those who kill the body . . . but rather fear him who can destroy both soul and body in gehenna***, for one should not serve God because of the fear of punishment, but for the love of justice, as is found, *for you have not received the spirit of bondage again in fear; but you have received the spirit of adoption of sons* (Rom 8:15).

870. And one should notice that he excludes here two errors. For some said that the soul passes away once the body is dead; and he destroys this position, when he says, ***who can destroy both soul and body in gehenna***. Hence it is clear that it remains after the body.

Similarly, some held the position that there is no resurrection (1 Cor 15:12). And he excludes this, because if the body and the soul are sent into Gehenna, it follows that there will be a resurrection. And this is found, *and the devil, who seduced them, was cast into the pool of fire and brimstone in the resurrection* (Rev 20:9).

871. *Are not two sparrows sold for a farthing?* Thus it was said that they are not to be feared, because they cannot

cetera. Item non sunt timendi, quia illud parum quod possunt, non possunt nisi ex divina providentia. Et

primo ponit divinam providentiam circa aves;

secundo circa homines, ibi **vestri autem et capilli capitis omnes numerati sunt**;

tertio indicit eis securitatem **nolite ergo timere** et cetera.

872. Dicit ergo **nonne duo passeres**, per passeres dat intelligere omnes aves parvas, **asse veneunt?** Et in hoc notat vilitatem, quia duo habentur pro asse, quia sicut unitas est minimum in numeris, ita as in ponderibus.

Sed nota, secundum Augustinum, quod aliquid dicitur valere dupliciter: aut secundum dignitatem naturae, et sic unus passer dignior est quam denarius: vel secundum quod ad usum nostrum refertur, et sic dignior est denarius.

Sed obiicitur quod Lucas XII, 6 ponit quinque passeres, et duos asses. Dicendum, quod pauca est differentia: si duo habentur pro asse, et quinque pro duobus, non est magna differentia.

873. Et unus ex illis non cadet super terram sine Patre vestro: sine providentia Patris. Et quare dicit hoc? Quia consonat verbum istud verbo legis, Lev. XIV, quod cum aliquis curabatur a lepra, offerebat duos passeres, et unus immolabatur, alter vero cum ligno cedrino et hyssopo intingebatur in sanguine occisi, et aspergebatur mundandus, et sic vivus dimittebatur. Vult ergo quod duo accipiuntur, et unus non occiditur; et hoc non fit sine providentia Dei.

Hilarius sic exponit: *per duos passeres intelliguntur corpus et anima, et dantur pro asse, idest pro modica delectatione*; Is. l, 1: *ecce in iniquitatibus venumdati estis; et in sceleribus vestris dimisi matrem vestram.* Et istorum unus solus cadit in terram, scilicet corpus; anima autem tendit ad iudicium.

874. Sed obiicitur: non est cura Deo de bobus: ergo nec de passeribus.

Dicendum, quod Deo est cura de omnibus, ut habetur Sap. XII, 13: *non est alius Deus, quam tu, cui cura est de omnibus.*

Sed sciendum quod providet omnibus secundum modum suae naturae. Haec autem est diversitas in rebus creatis, quod quaedam sunt naturaliter liberae, aliae vero non. Illa dicitur creatura libera, in cuius potestate est quod faciat quod vult: non libera, quae hoc non habet. Unde providet rationalibus tamquam liberis, sed providet aliis tamquam servis: sicut paterfamilias aliter providet liberis, aliter servis; liberis providet propter seipsos, sed servis secundum quod sunt in usum dominorum,

do much. Likewise, they are not to be feared because that little which they can do, they can only do with divine providence.

And first, he sets forth the divine providence concerning birds;

second, concerning men, at **but the very hairs of your head are all numbered**;

third, he points out to them their security, **therefore, fear not**.

872. He says then, **are not two sparrows**, by sparrows he gives one to understand all small birds, **sold for a farthing?** And in this he notes their cheapness, since two can be had for a farthing, for just as unity is the least in numbers, so the farthing is the least among weights.

But note, according to Augustine, that something is said to be worth something in two ways: either according to dignity of nature, and in this way one sparrow is worth more than a denarius; or according as it is referred to our use, and in this way the denarius is worth more.

But it is objected that Luke sets down five sparrows and two farthings (Luke 12:6). One should say that the difference is small: if two are had for a farthing, and five for two farthings, there is not a great difference.

873. And not one of them will fall on the ground without your Father: without the Father's providence. And why does he say this? Because these words harmonize with the words of the law, that when someone was cured from leprosy, he offered two sparrows, and one was sacrificed, but the other, along with cedar and a hyssop branch, was dipped in the blood of the one killed, and the man to be cleansed was sprinkled, and so the living one was let go (Lev 14). Therefore he willed that they receive two, and one not be killed; and this comes about only by divine providence.

Hilary explains it this way: *by two sparrows are understood the body and the soul, and they are given for a penny, i.e., for a small pleasure; behold you are sold for your iniquities, and for your wicked deeds have I put your mother away* (Isa 50:1). And only one of these falls to the earth, namely the body; but the soul goes on to judgment.

874. But it is objected: God's care is not about oxen (1 Cor 9:9); therefore neither is it about sparrows.

One should say that God's care is for all, *for there is no other God but you, who have care of all* (Wis 12:13).

But one should know that he provides for each thing according to the mode its own nature. Now, there is this diversity in created things, that certain ones are naturally free, but others not. That creature is called free in whose power it is that he should do what he wills; that creature is not free which does not have this. Hence he provides for the rational creatures as for free men, but provides for the others as for servants, just as the head of a family provides differently for the free men and the servants. He provides

et etiam secundum quod unusquisque magis aptus est ad serviendum. Sic divina misericordia rationalibus distribuit propter seipsos, quia totum fit propter bonum eorum, vel propter malum. Unde eis omnia sunt vel praemia vel poenae meritorum. Quae autem irrationalibus fiunt, vel ad salutem hominum fiunt, vel ad completionem universi, ut habetur III Reg. XIII, quod quidam propheta occisus est a leone, et hoc propter culpam. Mus occiditur a catto ad servandum bonum universi. Hic est enim ordo universi, ut unum animal vivat de alio.

875. Ideo consequenter ostendit aliam curam habere de hominibus et brutis, cum dicit ***vestri autem capilli capitis omnes numerati sunt***. Ostendit quod differentia est providentiae Dei, ex quo diversimode providet. Dixerat enim quod de passeribus non cadit unus in terram sine Patre: hic vero dicit, quod nedum vos non cadetis, sed nec capilli vestri. Et hic notat providentiam circa minimos actus, quia omnia quae in ipsis sunt, ordinantur ad eos, et de his providet Dominus.

876. Sed notandum quod dicit ***numerati sunt***. Sed ratio est, quia consuetum est, quod illud quod vult aliquis sibi retinere, illud numerat; quod vult autem dispensare, alii tradit. Unde haec est differentia inter providentiam rationabilium et aliorum, quia immediate ordinantur ad Deum, quia talis creatura capax Dei est, aliae vero non. Item quae numeramus, nobis conservare volumus; et ideo non dixit superius, quod passeres numerati sunt, quia non in perpetuum durant; sed homines ita sunt ut in perpetuum durent, quia anima perpetua est.

877. Sed hic est quaestio: si capilli numerati sunt, nonne totum in resurrectione reintegrabitur, quod de capillis abscinditur? Et si hoc, indecens erit longitudo.

Dicunt aliqui quod non perit materies; sed quod erit superfluum in una parte, cedet in aliam partem. Sed dato quod nihil fuerit diminutum, quid inde fiet? Ideo intelligendum est quod fuit hic triplex opinio. Quidam dixerunt, quod non resurget nisi quod est de veritate humanae naturae. Alii vero quod non resurget nisi quod decisum est ab Adam, quod sic multiplicatum est in tantam magnitudinem. Alii vero quod non solum quod ab Adam, sed etiam quod decisum est a proximo parente. Unde quicquid additur, quod est de veritate humanae naturae, resurget; sed quod pertinet ad quantitatem partium, non resurget.

for the free for their own sakes, but for the servants according as they are useful to their lords, and also according as each one is more fitted for serving. In this way, the divine mercy distributes gifts to rational creatures for their own sakes, because the whole order of providence is for the sake of their good or for the sake of their evil. Hence to them all things are either a reward or a punishment of merits. But those things which happen to the irrational creatures happen either for the salvation of men, or for the completion of the universe, as is found in Kings (1 Kngs 13), that a certain prophet was killed by a lion, and this because of his guilt. A mouse is killed by a cat to preserve the good of the universe. For this is the order of the universe, that one animal lives off another.

875. This is why he shows next that he has one care over men, and another over the brutes, when he says, ***but the very hairs of your head are all numbered***. He shows what the difference is in God's providence, by which he provides differently for different creatures. For he had said that not one sparrow falls to the ground without the Father; but here he says that, not only will you not fall, but not even your hairs. And here he points out a providence concerning the least actions, because all the things in them are ordered to them, and the Lord provides for these things.

876. But one should note that he says they ***are all numbered***. And the reason is because it is customary that one should number that which he wishes to keep; but what he wishes to distribute, he hands over to others. Hence this is the difference between the providence over the rational creatures and that over the others, because these are ordered directly to God, because such creatures have a capacity for God, while those are not. Likewise, those things which we number, we wish to keep for ourselves; and this is why he did not say above that the sparrows are numbered, because they do not endure everlastingly, but men are such that they endure everlastingly, because the soul is everlasting.

877. But here there is a question: if the hairs are numbered, will not the whole length which was cut off from the hairs be put back together in the resurrection? And if so, the length will be unbecoming.

Some say that the matter will not perish, but what is superfluous in one part will pass into another part. But given that nothing will be lessened, what will come from it? So one should understand that there are three opinions here. Some have said that only that which pertains to the truth of human nature will arise. But others have said that only that will arise which was cut off from Adam, which was thus multiplied into such a great magnitude. But others have said that not only that which was cut off from Adam, but also that which was cut off from the proximate parent. Hence whatever is added, which pertains to the truth of human nature will arise; but that which pertains to the quantity of parts will not arise.

Sed contra hoc videtur, quod calor agens in humidum nutrimentale agit etiam in radicale, et ita homo non consumit unum, quin consumat alterum, cum permisceantur ad invicem.

Ideo aliter dicendum videtur, quod quicquid est de veritate, remanebit solum quantum ad complementum pertinet. Appello autem illud, quod est de veritate humanae naturae, carnem secundum speciem; aliud autem, carnem secundum materiam. Caro autem secundum speciem resurget, non secundum materiam.

878. Sed quid est dictu carnem secundum speciem?

Dicendum quod partes hominis possunt considerari aut quantum ad formam, aut quantum ad materiam. Quantum ad formam semper manent. Si autem consideremus materiam subtractam, aliquid fluit et refluit, ut patet in igne. Si autem igni addantur ligna, ignis secundum speciem manet idem; tamen fluit materia secundum subtractionem lignorum. Unde resurget quod magis perfectum est. Unde non dicit: capilli vestri ponderati sunt, sed *numerati sunt*: unde non resurgent in pondere, sed in forma.

879. *Nolite timere* et cetera. Hic ostendit securitatem ex quo non possunt nisi parum: et illud quod possunt, non possunt sine Dei providentia. *Nolite ergo timere: multis passeribus meliores estis vos*. Omnia enim subiecisti sub pedibus eius, oves et boves universas, insuper et pecora campi; ut habetur in Ps. VIII, 8. Et Gen. I, 26: *faciamus hominem ad imaginem et similitudinem nostram*; et sequitur: *et praesit volatilibus caeli, et piscibus maris, et bestiis, universaeque terrae, omnique reptili quod movetur in terra*.

880. *Omnis ergo qui confitebitur me coram hominibus, confitebor et ego eum coram Patre meo*. Hic tangit utilitatem, quae provenit ex ipsius confessione.

Secundo, damnum quod provenit ex negatione, ibi *qui autem negaverit me coram hominibus, negabo et ego eum coram Patre meo*.

881. Dicit ergo: ita volo quod moriamini et patiamini. Et quare? Certe propter utilitatem vestram. Quia *qui me confitebitur coram hominibus* et cetera. Et elidit errorem cuiusdam, qui dicebat non esse necessarium confiteri fidem, nisi coram Deo in corde, non autem ore coram hominibus; quod hic patet falsum, quia *corde creditur ad iustitiam, ore autem confessio fit ad salutem*, Rom. X, v. 10. *Confitebor illum coram Patre meo*, scilicet cum habebo accessum ad Patrem, quando dicetur *venite, benedicti Patris mei* et cetera.

But against this, it seems that the heat which acts on the nourishing moisture acts also on the original moisture, and thus a man does not consume one without consuming the other, since they are thoroughly mixed together.

Therefore it seems that one should say otherwise, that whatever pertains to the truth will remain only as far as pertains to completion. Now, I call that which pertains to the truth of human nature the body according to species; but the other I call the body according to matter. And the body according to species will arise, not the body according to matter.

878. But what should be called the body according to species?

One should say that the parts of a man can be considered either as regards form, or as regards matter. As regards form, they will always remain. But if we consider the matter subtracted, something flows and flows back, as is evident in fire. But if branches are added to the fire, the fire remains the same according to species, yet was there matter according to subtraction from the branches. Hence that which is more perfect will arise. Wherefore he does not say: your hairs are weighed, but they *are numbered*; hence they will not arise in weight, but in form.

879. *Therefore fear not*. Here he shows the security of the apostles from the fact that their enemies can do but little, and that which they can do, they can only do with God's providence. *Therefore fear not: you are better than many sparrows*. *You have subjected all things under his feet, all sheep and oxen: moreover the beasts also of the fields* (Ps 8:8). And, *let us make man to our image and likeness*, and there follows, *and let him have dominion over the fishes of the sea, and the fowls of the air, and the beasts, and the whole earth, and every creeping creature that moves upon the earth* (Gen 1:26).

880. *Every one therefore who will confess me before men, I will also confess him before my Father*. Here he touches upon the practical gain which comes from confessing him;

second, the curse which comes from denial, at *but he who will deny me before men, I will also deny him before my Father*.

881. He says then: I will that you should die and suffer. And why? Certainly for your advantage. Because the one *who will confess me before men*. And he shatters the error of certain men, who said that it is not necessary to confess the faith, except before God in the heart, but not before men with the mouth; which here lies open as false, because with the heart, *we believe unto justice; but, with the mouth, confession is made unto salvation* (Rom 10:10). *I will also confess him before my Father*, namely when I have access to the Father, when it will be said, *come, you blessed of my Father* (Matt 25:34).

Sed possent dicere: *tu es in terra, hoc potest parum valere*; ideo addit **qui est in caelis**, et ille habet potestatem.

882. Qui autem negaverit verbo, ut Petrus, vel facto, sicut illi de quibus dicitur ad Titum I, 16: *quidam ore confitentur se nosse Deum, factis autem negant.* **Negabo et ego eos**, quando dicet, sicut habetur supra c. VII, 23: **numquam novi vos**, idest numquam approbavi vos.

883. Nolite arbitrari quod venerim pacem mittere in terram et cetera. Supra monuit discipulos, quod non desisterent a praedicatione veritatis, nec propter opprobria, nec propter timorem mortis, nunc autem monet, quod non desistant etiam propter affectum carnalem. Et

primo ostendit quod imminet eis separatio ab affectu carnali;

secundo, quomodo debent se habere, ibi **qui amat patrem aut matrem plus quam me, non est me dignus**.

Circa primum tria facit.

Primo excludit intentionem opinatam;

secundo suum proponit propositum;

tertio exponit.

Secunda ibi **non veni pacem mittere**; tertia ibi **veni enim separare hominem adversus patrem suum** et cetera.

884. Dicit ergo: possent ita opinari: *quid est, Domine, quod tot evenient nobis? In adventu tuo credebamus habere pacem.* Et ideo dicit **nolite arbitrari** et cetera. Sed quid est quod dicit? Nonne habetur Lc. II, 14, quod nato Domino cecinerunt angeli, *gloria in excelsis Deo, et in terra pax hominibus bonae voluntatis?* Et ipse episcopus cum primo vertitur ad populum, dicit: *pax vobis*, et supra nuntiavit Dominus pacem?

Ideo dicendum quod duplex est pax, videlicet bona, et mala. Nomine pacis concordia significatur. Est pax mala, de qua habetur Sap. XIV, 22: *sed in magno viventes inscientiae bello, tot et tam magna mala pacem appellant.* Ista pax est carnalium affectuum. Istam non veni ponere. Unde Apoc. VI, 14: *datum est ei ut sumeret pacem de terra.* Est et pax bona, de qua Eph. II, 14: *ipse est pax nostra qui fecit utraque unum*; et ideo angeli cecinerunt, Lc. II, 14: *et in terra pax hominibus bonae voluntatis.*

885. Ideo, **non veni mittere pacem, sed gladium**. De ratione gladii est dividere. Iste gladius est verbum Dei; Hebr. IV, 12: *vivus est sermo Dei, et efficax, et penetrabilior omni gladio ancipiti.* Unde etiam: *gladium spiritus, quod est verbum Dei*, ad Eph. ult., 17.

Iste gladius missus est in terram. Et quidam crediderunt, quidam non. Et ideo fit bellum, ut habetur ad Gal. IV, 9: *quomodo convertimini iterum ad infirma et egena elementa, quibus denuo servire vultis* et cetera.

But they could say: *you are on earth, this is not very powerful*; therefore he adds, **who is in heaven**: and he has the power.

882. But he who will deny me by word, as Peter, or by deed, as those of whom it is said, *they profess that they know God: but in their works they deny him* (Tit 1:16). **I will also deny him**, when he will say, as is found above, **I never knew you** (Matt 7:23), i.e., I have never approved you.

883. Do not think that I came to send peace upon earth. Above, he warned the disciples that they should not cease to preach the truth, neither on account of insults, nor the fear of death; and now he warns them that they should not cease on account of carnal affection. And

first, he shows that a separation from carnal affection is drawing near to them;

second, how they should carry themselves, at **he that loves father or mother more than me, is not worthy of me**.

Concerning the first, he does three things:

first, he excludes a supposed intention;

second, he sets forth his own intention;

third, he explains.

The second is at **I came not to send peace**; the third, at **for I came to set a man at variance against his father**.

884. It says then, they could be thinking this way: *why is it, Lord, that so much will happen to us? We thought to have peace in your coming.* And so he says, **do not think**. But why does he say this? Is it not found in Luke that the angels sang at the Lord's birth, *glory to God in the highest; and on earth peace to men of good will?* (Luke 2:14). And the bishop himself when he first turns to the people, says, *peace be with you*; and the Lord announced peace above.

Therefore, one should say that peace is twofold, namely good and evil. Harmony is signified by the name of peace. And there is an evil peace, about which it is said, *whereas they lived in a great war of ignorance, they call so many and so great evils peace* (Wis 14:22). This peace is the peace of carnal affection. I have not come to bring this. Hence, *it was given that he should take peace from the earth* (Rev 6:4). And there is a good peace, about which it is said, *for he is our peace, who has made both one, and breaking down the middle wall of partition, the enmities in his flesh* (Eph 2:14). And this is why the angels sang, *and on earth peace to men of good will* (Luke 2:14).

885. Therefore, **I came not to send peace, but the sword.** It is of the notion of a sword to divide. *This sword is the word of God; for the word of God is living and effectual, and more piercing than any two edged sword* (Heb 4:12). Hence also: *the sword of the Spirit, which is the word of God*, (Eph 6:17).

This sword is sent into the earth. And some have believed, some not. And therefore a war is going on, as is found, *how turn you again to the weak and needy elements, which you desire to serve again?* (Gal 4:9). Hence he came to

Unde venit separare istam divisionem. *Venit* ergo ***mittere gladium*** etc. scilicet verbum, sed partim, quia quidem crediderunt, et hoc ex eo fuit; quidam vero non, et hoc ex malitia sua. Hoc tamen causatur etiam ab eo, quia permittit, sicut habetur ad Rom. I, 26: *propterea tradidit illos Deus in passiones ignominiae.*

886. Sed posset aliquis dicere: *venisti separare. Inter quos venisti? Nonne inter diversos et extraneos?* Et ostendit quod non, sed inter coniunctissimos. ***Veni enim***, inquit, ***separare hominem adversus patrem*** et cetera. Duplex est enim maxima coniunctio: quaedam est coniunctio naturalis; quaedam domestica, vel oeconomica; ideo contra utramque mittit gladium. Amicitia naturalis fundatur super actum naturalem, et hic est generatio, vel coniunctio maris et feminae: domestica vel oeconomica super affinitatem. Contra primam ergo ***veni separare hominem adversus patrem***.

Sed est quaestio. Dictum est supra ***non veni solvere legem, sed adimplere***. Sed lex praecipit: *honora patrem tuum* et cetera.

Solutio. Dico quod debes ei obedire ubi non retrahit a Dei amore; sed ubi retrahit, non teneris obedire.

887. ***Et filiam adversus matrem suam***: et hoc quantum ad generationem. ***Et nurum adversus socrum suam***. Et in hoc communicat nova lex veteri, ut habetur Ex. XXXII, ubi dicitur: *si quis est Domini, coniungatur mihi. Congregatique sunt ad eum omnes filii levi, quibus ait: ponat vir gladium super femur suum*. Et sequitur, *et occidat unusquisque fratrem suum, et amicum*. Et illud reputatum est ad laudem Levitarum, ut habetur Deut. XXXIII, 8, ubi dicitur, *levi quoque ait: perfectio tua et doctrina a viro sancto tuo*. Et sequitur, *qui dixit patri suo, et matri suae, nescio vos; et fratribus suis, ignoro vos: et nescierunt filios suos.*

Sed hic est quaestio, quia hic enumerat sex personas; in Luca XII, 53 vero non enumerantur nisi tres.

Et dicendum quod idem est utrobique, quia eadem est mater, et socrus uxoris eius.

888. Item ponit quae ad familiaritatem pertinent, ubi dicit ***et inimici hominis domestici*** et cetera. Et habetur Ier. XX, 10: *et audivi contumelias multorum, et terrorem in circuitu: persequimini, et persequemur eum: ab omnibus viris qui erant pacifici mei*. Et videte quia totum istud habetur Michaeae VII, 6: *filius contumeliam facit patri, et filia consurgit adversus matrem suam, nurus contra socrum suam, et inimici hominis domestici eius.*

create this division. *I came* therefore ***to send . . . the sword***, namely the word. But partially, because some have believed, and this is his doing; but some have not, and this is from their own malice. Yet even this is caused by him, because he permits it, as is found, *for this cause God delivered them up to shameful affections* (Rom 1:26).

886. But someone could say: *you have come to separate. Between whom have you come? Is it not between those who are separated and foreign to one another?* And he shows that it is not, but between the most closely joined. ***For I came***, he says, ***to set a man at variance against his father***. For the two greatest conjoinings are the natural conjoining and the domestic or household conjoining; therefore he sends the sword against both. Natural friendship is founded on the natural act, and this is generation, or the conjoining of husband and wife; the domestic or household is founded on the marriage bond. Against the first, then, ***I have come to set a man against his father***.

But there is a question. It was said above, ***I am not come to destroy, but to fulfill*** (Matt 5:17). But the law commands: *honor your father* (Exod 20:12).

Solution. I say that you should obey him where he does not pull you back from the love of God; but where he pulls you back, you are not bound to obey.

887. ***And the daughter against her mother***: and this as regards generation. ***And the daughter in law against her mother in law***. And the new law has this in common with the old, where it says: *if any man be on the Lord's side let him join with me* (Exod 32:26). All the sons of Levi joined with him, to whom he said: *put every man his sword upon his thigh*. And there follows, *and let every man kill his brother, and friend, and neighbor*. And this was reckoned to the praise of the Levites, where it says, *to Levi also he said: your perfection, and your doctrine be to your holy man* (Deut 33:8). And there follows, *who has said to his father, and to his mother: I do not know you; and to his brethren: I know you not: and their own children they have not known* (Deut 33:9).

But here there is a question, because here six persons are enumerated; but in Luke there are only three enumerated (Luke 12:53).

And one should say that it is the same in both places, but his mother and the mother-in-law of his wife are the same.

888. Similarly, he sets out what pertains to familiarity where he says, ***and a man's enemies will be those of his own household***. And it is said, *for I heard the reproaches of many, and terror on every side: persecute him, and let us persecute him: from all the men who were my familiars* (Jer 20:10). And see that this whole thing is found, *for the son dishonors the father, and the daughter rises up against her mother, the daughter in law against her mother in law: and a man's enemies are they of his own household* (Mic 7:6).

889. *Qui amat patrem aut matrem plusquam me, non est me dignus.* Hic ostendit quomodo in ista divisione se debeant habere. Si vis recipere gladium Domini, oportet quod dividaris ab istis quos dixit. Sed diceret aliquis: *nolo dividi a patre, et huiusmodi*; ideo dicit **qui amat patrem aut matrem plusquam me, non est me dignus.** Hortatur Dominus ut omni amori carnali praeponatur. Et

primo ponit exhortationem;

secundo utilitatem inde sequentem, ibi **qui recipit vos, me recipit.**

890. Et ponit tres gradus. Naturale enim est quod homo diligat patrem, sed magis naturale quod pater filium diligat: item plus naturale quod diligat seipsum.

Quare ergo pater plus diligit filium, quam e converso? Assignant quidam rationem, quia pater habet plus scire de filio, si sit filius, quam filius de patre. Item quanto aliquis diutius adhaeret alicui, tanto magis radicatur in amore eius. Item alia ratio, quia unusquisque magis diligit se quam alium. Sed filius est quaedam pars separata ab eo, pater autem non est pars filii; ideo et cetera. Item naturale est quod unumquodque diligat facturam suam. Sed diversitas est secundum aliquos, quia quoad aliquid filius magis diligit patrem: naturaliter enim fit descensus a patre in filium, tamen naturaliter filius subditus est patri; ideo pater naturaliter diligit filium, etiam pater spiritualis, ut habetur I Cor. IV, v. 14: *non ut confundam vos, hoc scribo, sed ut filios carissimos moneo.* Sed filii naturaliter subiecti sunt patri; ideo naturaliter honorant patrem, et magis irascuntur de iniuria patri illata quam sibi, et magis appetunt gloriam patri quam sibi; Prov. XVII, 6: *gloria filiorum patres eorum.*

Unde **qui amat patrem aut matrem plusquam me, non est me dignus,** quia ipse est Deus. Deus autem prae cunctis est diligendus; Iob XXXII, 21: *non accipiam personam viri, et Deum homini non aequabo.* Deus enim ipsa bonitas est; ideo magis amandus. **Non est** ergo **me dignus qui amat patrem aut matrem plusquam me.**

891. *Et qui amat filium aut filiam* et cetera. Quare diligit filius patrem? Dicendum, quod quicquid habet filius, habet a patre: habet enim a patre nutrimentum et doctrinam. Et hoc non potest filius dare patri; sed quae filius recipit a patre, abundantius recipit a Deo. Ipse enim docet nos, ut habetur Iob c. XXXV, 11: *qui docet nos super iumenta terrae, et super volucres caeli erudit nos* et cetera. Item pascit nos, ut dicitur in Gen. de Iacob. Item conservat nos in perpetuitatem. Et hoc magis habet a Deo homo quam filius a patre. Ideo semper magis est diligendus Deus. *Scio quod Redemptor meus vivit, et in novissimo die de terra surrecturus sum, et rursum*

889. *He who loves father or mother more than me, is not worthy of me.* Here he shows how they should carry themselves amid this division. If you wish to receive the sword of the Lord, it is necessary that you separate yourself from those whom he said. But some may say: *I do not want to be separated from my father, and such*; so he says, **he who loves father or mother more than me, is not worthy of me.** The Lord urges that he be set ahead of every carnal love.

And first, he sets out the exhortation;

second, the practical gain which follows from it, at **he who receives you, receives me.**

890. And he sets out three steps For it is natural that a man should love his father, but more natural that a father should love his son; similarly, it is more natural that he should love himself.

Why then does a father love his son more than the other way around? Some give as a reason that the father has more knowledge about the son, if he is his son, than the son about the father. Similarly, the longer someone clings to someone, the more he is rooted in his love. And another reason, that each man loves himself more than another. But a son is a certain part separated from the father, while the father is not a part of the son. Similarly, it is natural that each man love his own deeds. But according to some there is a diversity of loves, for the son loves the father more in a certain respect: for there is naturally a descent from the father into the son, yet the son is naturally subjected to the father. Therefore the father naturally loves the son, even a spiritual father, as is found, *I write not these things to confound you; but I admonish you as my dearest children* (1 Cor 4:14). But sons are naturally subjected to their father, so they naturally honor the father, and are more angered over an injury to the father than over an injury to themselves, and they desire glory for the father more than for themselves; *the glory of children are their fathers* (Prov 17:6).

Hence, **he who loves father or mother more than me, is not worthy of me,** because he himself is God. Now, God is to be loved before all; *I will not accept the person of man, and I will not level God with man* (Job 32:21). For God is goodness itself; therefore he is to be loved more. Therefore, **he who loves father or mother more than me, is not worthy of me.**

891. *And he who loves son or daughter more than me.* Why does a son love his father? One should say that whatever a son has, he has from his father: for he has nourishment and teaching from his father. And a son cannot give this to his father; but what a son receives from a father, he receives more abundantly from God. For he himself teaches us, as is found, *who teaches us more than the beasts of the earth, and instructs us more than the fowls of the air* (Job 35:11). Likewise, he feeds us, as is said in Genesis about Jacob. Likewise, he keeps us safe for ever. And a man has this more from God than a son from a father. Therefore God should always be loved more. *For I know that my Redeemer lives,*

circumdabor pelle mea, et in carne mea videbo Deum meum, Iob XIX, 25.

892. *Et qui non accipit crucem suam*. Ita dictum est quod qui amat patrem etc. immo dico plus: qui amat seipsum plusquam me, non est me dignus. Quia nihil potest replere totum affectum nisi Deus. Et ideo Deut. VI, 5: *diliges Dominum Deum tuum ex toto corde tuo, et ex tota anima tua, ex tota fortitudine tua.*

Unde dicit **qui non accipit crucem suam et sequitur me, non est me dignus**. Intelligit, quod qui non est paratus etiam mortem pati propter veritatem, et illam maxime mortem, scilicet mortem crucis **non est me dignus**: immo etiam debet gloriari de cruce, sicut habetur ad Gal. ult., 14: *mihi autem absit gloriari nisi in cruce Domini.*

Et in hoc praenuntiat mortem suam, et modum mortis; I Pet. II, 21: *Christus passus est pro nobis, vobis relinquentes exemplum, ut sequamini vestigia eius.*

893. Item aliter exponitur. Quia ille crucem accipit, qui carnem affligit, ut habetur ad Gal. V, 24: *qui Christi sunt, carnem suam crucifixerunt cum vitiis et concupiscentiis suis et cetera.* Item crux fertur in corde, quando contristatur pro peccato, ut dicebat Apostolus, II Cor. XI, 29: *quis scandalizatur, et ego non uror?*

Item non sufficit istud, nisi sequatur Dominum. Unde **et sequitur me**. Si ieiunas, si compateris proximo, non propter me, non es me dignus. Magnum est enim sequi Dominum, ut habetur Eccli. XXIII, 38: *gloria magna est sequi Dominum.*

894. Sed possent dicere, *quid inde habebimus?* Ideo ostendit poenam inobedientium; unde dicit **qui invenit animam suam, perdet eam**. **Anima** sumitur pro *vita*. Aliquis quando est in periculo amittendi denarios, consuevit dicere: amisi denarios; et si liberetur a periculo, dicit se invenisse denarios. Similiter si aliquis est in periculo corporis, et aliqua occasione liberatur, dicit invenisse vitam suam. Qui ergo invenit vitam suam, et in periculo fuerit propter me, et neget me, ut inveniat vitam, non est me dignus. **Et qui perdiderit animam**, idest vitam, idest si exposuerit se morti **propter me, inveniet eam**; Prov. c. VIII, 35: *qui me invenerit, inveniet vitam, et hauriet salutem a Domino.*

895. *Qui recipit vos, me recipit. Hic ponit remedium.* Tu dicis quod ita faciamus. Unde poterimus vivere? Da nobis indulgentiam. Sicut Papa dat legatis potestatem indulgendi, ita dat Dominus mercedem recipientibus eos. Et ponit tria, quorum duo pertinent ad minores. Dicit ergo. **Qui recipit vos, me recipit**: quia Deum habebunt, quia vos estis membra mea, quia membrum de membro. Unde **me recipit**.

and in the last day I will rise out of the earth. And I will be clothed again with my skin, and in my flesh I will see my God (Job 19:25–26).

892. *And he who takes not up his cross*. Thus it was said above that he who loves his father or his mother more than me is not worthy of me. But I say more: he who loves himself more than me is not worthy of me. Because nothing can fill one's whole desire but God. And therefore, *you shall love the Lord your God with your whole heart, and with your whole soul, and with your whole strength* (Deut 6:5).

Hence he says, **and he who takes not up his cross, and follows me, is not worthy of me**. He understands that he who is not prepared even to suffer death for the truth, and that the worst of deaths, namely the death of the cross, **is not worthy of me**: but rather he should even glory in the cross, *as is said, but God forbid that I should glory, save in the cross of our Lord Jesus Christ* (Gal 6:14).

And in this he foretells his own death, and the manner of his death; *for unto this are you called: because Christ also suffered for us, leaving you an example that you should follow his steps* (1 Pet 2:21).

893. Likewise, it is explained in another way. For he takes up the cross who afflicts the body, as is found, *and they that are Christ's, have crucified their flesh, with the vices and concupiscences* (1 Pet 2:21). Similarly, the cross is born in the heart, when one sorrows over sin, as the Apostle says, *who is scandalized, and I am not on fire?* (2 Cor 11:29).

And this is not enough unless he follows the Lord. Hence, **and follows me**. If you fast, if you have compassion on your neighbor, not for my sake, you are not worthy of me. For it is a great thing to follow the Lord, as is said, *it is great glory to follow the Lord* (Sir 23:38).

894. But they could say, *what will we get from this?* So he shows the punishment of disobedience; hence he says, **he who finds his soul, will lose it**. **Soul** is used for life. Often when someone is in danger of losing money, he says: I have lost money; and if he is freed from the danger, says that he has found money. Similarly, if someone is in danger of losing his body, and is freed by some occurance, he says that he has found his life. Therefore, he who finds his life, and is in danger on my account, and denies me to find life, is not worthy of me. **And he who will lose his soul**, i.e., life, i.e., if he exposes himself to death, **for me, will find it**. He who will find me, will find life, and will have salvation from the Lord (Prov 8:35).

895. *He who receives you, receives me*. Here he sets forth the remedy. You say that we should act this way. How will we be able to live? Give us pardon! Just as the Pope gives his legates the power to pardon, so the Lord gives a reward to those who receive them. And he sets forth three things, of which two pertain to subordinates. He says then: **he who receives you, receives me**, because they will have God, since you are my members, since a member comes from a member. Hence, he **receives me**.

Sed possent dicere: *tu es pauper: non est magnum recipere pauperem, sive te.* Immo **qui me recipit, recipit eum qui me misit**, quia, sicut habetur Io. V, 23, *qui honorificat Filium, honorificat et Patrem meum.* Magnum est Deum habere hospitem, sicut Abrahae reputatum est ad laudem, ut habetur Hebr. c. XIII, 2.

896. Item aliud consequetur, scilicet mercedem prophetae. Unde **qui recipit prophetam in nomine prophetae, mercedem prophetae accipiet.** Duo excellentia sunt in propheta. Scilicet prophetia, Ioel II, 28: *effundam de spiritu meo super omnem carnem, et prophetabunt filii vestri, et filiae vestrae,* item donum iustitiae; I ad Cor. I, 30; *ex ipso autem vos estis qui factus est nobis sapientia et iustitia.* **Qui recipit prophetam in nomine prophetae.** Potest sic intelligi: **qui recipit prophetam in nomine prophetae**, idest eo quod propheta est, **mercedem prophetae recipiet.**

Vel aliter. Tu dicis quod recipiamus apostolos: sed venient aliqui pseudoprophetae, vel pseudoapostoli. Ideo dicit: non facio vim de veritate, sed de nomine. Quia qui in nomine prophetae recipit, mercedem habebit. Et quam? Eamdem quam haberes si verum prophetam reciperes. Unde dicit **mercedem prophetae**, idest quam haberet pro propheta.

Item non facit vim quis sit ille, utrum unus vel alter. **Qui** enim **recipit prophetam, recipit mercedem prophetae,** quia propheta inde pronior est ad exercendum opus suum; quia non solum qui faciunt, mercedem recipiunt, sed etiam qui facientibus consentiunt, ut habetur Rom. I in fine. Unde si cooperaris ad bonum, de bono illo recipis mercedem; si ministras subsidia vitae, accipis mercedem; quia aliter non posset officium implere. Et idem est quod sequitur: **qui recipit iustum in nomine iusti, mercedem iusti accipiet.**

897. Sed posset dicere aliquis: *si veniret Petrus, vel Elias, libenter reciperem eum*; ideo subdit **et quicumque potum dederit uni ex minimis,** idest fidelibus, ut habetur inf. c. XXV, 40: **amen dico vobis, quod uni ex his fratribus meis minimis fecistis, mihi fecistis** etc.; quasi dicat: *non curo utrum magni vel parvi sint.*

Posset aliquis dicere: *pauper sum; non habeo quid dare*; ideo addit calicem **aquae frigidae**: non dicit aquae calidae propter inopiam lignorum, ne posset se sic excusare; unde vult dicere: quicquid minimum fecerit, habebit mercedem suam. Et hoc confirmat dicens, **amen dico vobis, non perdet mercedem suam**; Is. XL, 10: *ecce Dominus veniet*; et sequitur: *et merces eius cum illo, et opus illius coram illo.*

But they could say: *you are a poor man; it is no great thing to receive a poor man, or you.* On the contrary, **he who receives me, receives him who sent me**, because, as is found, *he who honors not the Son, honors not the Father* (John 5:23). It is a great thing to have God as a guest, just as it is reckoned to Abraham's praise (Heb 13:2).

896. And another thing follows, namely the prophet's reward. Hence, **he who receives a prophet in the name of a prophet, will receive the reward of a prophet.** There are two excellences in a prophet. Namely prophecy; *I will pour out my spirit upon all flesh: and your sons and your daughters will prophesy* (Joel 2:28); and the gift of justice; *but of him are you in Christ Jesus, who of God is made unto us wisdom, and justice, and sanctification, and redemption* (1 Cor 1:30). **He who receives a prophet in the name of a prophet.** It can be understood in this way: **he who receives a prophet in the name of a prophet**, i.e., because he is a prophet, **will receive the reward of a prophet.**

Or in another way: you say that we will receive the apostles; but there will come pseudoprophets, or pseudoapostles. So he says: I do not put a great weight on the truth, but on the name. Because he who receives in the name of a prophet will have the reward. And what reward? The same which you would have if you were to receive a true prophet. Hence he says, **the reward of a prophet**, i.e., that which one would have for a prophet.

Similarly, he does not place a great weight on who it is, whether it is one prophet or another. For **he who receives a prophet in the name of a prophet, will receive the reward of a prophet**, because by this a prophet is more inclined to carry out his work; for not only those who do receive the reward, but even those who consent to those who do, as is found in the end of Romans (Rom 1:32). Hence if you cooperate toward the good, you receive the reward of that good; if you supply the helps of life, you receive the reward; for otherwise he would not be able to fulfill his office. And what follows is the same: **he who receives a just man in the name of a just man, will receive the reward of a just man.**

897. But someone could say: *if Peter were to come, or Elias, I would freely receive him.* So he adds, **and whoever will give to drink to one of these little ones**, i.e., to the faithful, as is said below, **amen I say to you, as long as you did it to one of these my least brethren, you did it to me** (Matt 25:40), as though to say: *I do not care if they are great or small.*

Someone could say: *I am a poor man; I have nothing to give.* So he adds, **of cold water**; he does not say *of hot,* lest someone could excuse himself because of a lack of firewood. Hence he wants to say: whatever least thing you have done, you will have your reward. And he confirms this, saying, **amen I say to you, he will not lose his reward**; *behold the Lord God will come,* and there follows *behold his reward is with him and his work is before him* (Isa 40:10).

CHAPTER 11

Lecture 1

11:1 Et factum est, cum consummasset Iesus praecipiens duodecim discipulis suis, transiit inde ut doceret et praedicaret in civitatibus eorum. [n. 898]

11:2 Ioannes autem cum audisset in vinculis opera Christi, mittens duos de discipulis suis, [n. 898]

11:3 ait illi: tu es qui venturus es, an alium expectamus? [n. 901]

11:4 Et respondens Iesus ait illis: euntes renuntiate Ioanni quae auditis, et videtis. [n. 904]

11:5 Caeci vident, claudi ambulant, leprosi mundantur, surdi audiunt, mortui resurgunt, pauperes evangelizantur, [n. 905]

11:6 et beatus est qui non fuerit scandalizatus in me. [n. 905]

11:7 Illis autem abeuntibus, coepit Iesus dicere ad turbas de Ioanne: quid existis in desertum videre? Arundinem vento agitatam? [n. 907]

11:8 Sed quid existis videre? Hominem mollibus vestitum? Ecce, qui mollibus vestiuntur, in domibus regum sunt. [n. 909]

11:9 Sed quid existis videre? Prophetam? Etiam dico vobis, et plus quam prophetam. [n. 912]

11:10 Hic enim est de quo scriptum est: *ecce ego mitto angelum meum ante faciem tuam, qui praeparabit viam tuam ante te.* [n. 913]

11:1 Καὶ ἐγένετο ὅτε ἐτέλεσεν ὁ Ἰησοῦς διατάσσων τοῖς δώδεκα μαθηταῖς αὐτοῦ, μετέβη ἐκεῖθεν τοῦ διδάσκειν καὶ κηρύσσειν ἐν ταῖς πόλεσιν αὐτῶν.

11:2 Ὁ δὲ Ἰωάννης ἀκούσας ἐν τῷ δεσμωτηρίῳ τὰ ἔργα τοῦ Χριστοῦ πέμψας διὰ τῶν μαθητῶν αὐτοῦ

11:3 εἶπεν αὐτῷ· σὺ εἶ ὁ ἐρχόμενος ἢ ἕτερον προσδοκῶμεν;

11:4 καὶ ἀποκριθεὶς ὁ Ἰησοῦς εἶπεν αὐτοῖς· πορευθέντες ἀπαγγείλατε Ἰωάννη ἃ ἀκούετε καὶ βλέπετε·

11:5 τυφλοὶ ἀναβλέπουσιν καὶ χωλοὶ περιπατοῦσιν, λεπροὶ καθαρίζονται καὶ κωφοὶ ἀκούουσιν, καὶ νεκροὶ ἐγείρονται καὶ πτωχοὶ εὐαγγελίζονται·

11:6 καὶ μακάριός ἐστιν ὃς ἐὰν μὴ σκανδαλισθῇ ἐν ἐμοί.

11:7 Τούτων δὲ πορευομένων ἤρξατο ὁ Ἰησοῦς λέγειν τοῖς ὄχλοις περὶ Ἰωάννου· τί ἐξήλθατε εἰς τὴν ἔρημον θεάσασθαι; κάλαμον ὑπὸ ἀνέμου σαλευόμενον;

11:8 ἀλλὰ τί ἐξήλθατε ἰδεῖν; ἄνθρωπον ἐν μαλακοῖς ἠμφιεσμένον; ἰδοὺ οἱ τὰ μαλακὰ φοροῦντες ἐν τοῖς οἴκοις τῶν βασιλέων εἰσίν.

11:9 ἀλλὰ τί ἐξήλθατε ἰδεῖν; προφήτην; ναὶ λέγω ὑμῖν, καὶ περισσότερον προφήτου.

11:10 οὗτός ἐστιν περὶ οὗ γέγραπται· ἰδοὺ ἐγὼ ἀποστέλλω τὸν ἄγγελόν μου πρὸ προσώπου σου, ὃς κατασκευάσει τὴν ὁδόν σου ἔμπροσθέν σου.

11:1 And it came to pass, when Jesus had made an end of commanding his twelve disciples, he passed from there, to teach and preach in their cities. [n. 898]

11:2 Now when John had heard in prison the works of Christ: sending two of his disciples he said to him: [n. 898]

11:3 are you he who is to come, or should we look for another? [n. 901]

11:4 And Jesus, responding, said to them: go and relate to John what you have heard and seen. [n. 904]

11:5 The blind see, the lame walk, the lepers are cleansed, the deaf hear, the dead rise again, the poor have the Gospel preached to them. [n. 905]

11:6 And blessed is he who will not be scandalized in me. [n. 905]

11:7 And when they went their way, Jesus began to say to the multitudes concerning John: what did you go out into the desert to see? A reed shaken with the wind? [n. 907]

11:8 But what did you go out to see? A man clothed in soft garments? Behold they who are clothed in soft garments, are in the houses of kings. [n. 909]

11:9 But what did you go out to see? A prophet? Yes I tell you, and more than a prophet. [n. 912]

11:10 For this is he of whom it is written: *behold I send my angel before your face, who will prepare your way before you.* [n. 913]

11:11 Amen dico vobis, non surrexit inter natos mulierum maior Ioanne Baptista. Qui autem minor est in regno caelorum, maior est illo. [n. 915]

11:11 Ἀμὴν λέγω ὑμῖν· οὐκ ἐγήγερται ἐν γεννητοῖς γυναικῶν μείζων Ἰωάννου τοῦ βαπτιστοῦ· ὁ δὲ μικρότερος ἐν τῇ βασιλείᾳ τῶν οὐρανῶν μείζων αὐτοῦ ἐστιν.

11:11 Amen I say to you, there has not risen among those who are born of women anyone greater than John the Baptist: yet he who is the lesser in the kingdom of heaven is greater than he. [n. 915]

11:12 A diebus autem Ioannis Baptistae usque nunc, regnum caelorum vim patitur, et violenti rapiunt illud. [n. 920]

11:12 ἀπὸ δὲ τῶν ἡμερῶν Ἰωάννου τοῦ βαπτιστοῦ ἕως ἄρτι ἡ βασιλεία τῶν οὐρανῶν βιάζεται καὶ βιασταὶ ἁρπάζουσιν αὐτήν.

11:12 And from the days of John the Baptist until now, the kingdom of heaven suffers violence, and the violent bear it away. [n. 920]

11:13 Omnes enim prophetae et lex usque ad Ioannem prophetaverunt, [n. 923]

11:13 πάντες γὰρ οἱ προφῆται καὶ ὁ νόμος ἕως Ἰωάννου ἐπροφήτευσαν·

11:13 For all the prophets and the law prophesied until John: [n. 923]

11:14 et si vultis recipere, ipse est Elias, qui venturus est. [n. 925]

11:14 καὶ εἰ θέλετε δέξασθαι, αὐτός ἐστιν Ἠλίας ὁ μέλλων ἔρχεσθαι.

11:14 and if you will receive it, he is Elias that is to come. [n. 925]

11:15 Qui habet aures audiendi, audiat. [n. 925]

11:15 ὁ ἔχων ὦτα ἀκουέτω.

11:15 He who has ears to hear, let him hear. [n. 925]

---

898. His dictis, *transiit Dominus ut doceret et praedicaret*; et hoc propter tria. Una ratio est, ut quod verbo dixerat, monstraret exemplo; Act. I, 1: *coepit Iesus facere et docere*. Item, ut ostenderet quod etiam impiis est praedicandum. Unde ad Rom. I, v. 14: *sapientibus et insipientibus debitor sum*. Item, ut aliis daret locum praedicandi, ut habetur I Cor. XIV, 30: *quod si aliquid fuerit revelatum sedenti, prior taceat*.

Ioannes autem cum audisset in vinculis opera Christi. Posita est doctrina Christi, et confirmata, et instructi sunt praedicatores; hic confutantur rebelles. Et
    primo confutat discipulos Ioannis;
    secundo scribas, ibi *illis autem abeuntibus* et cetera.
    Circa primum tria facit.
    Primo dubitantes confutat;
    secundo arguit turbas, ibi *cui autem similem aestimabo generationem istam?*
    Tertio persolvit gratias de fide apostolorum, ibi *in illo tempore respondens Iesus dixit* et cetera.
    Circa primum primo ponitur quaestio;
    secundo quaestionis solutio, ibi *et respondens Iesus* et cetera.

899. Dicit ergo *cum audisset in vinculis opera Christi*. Ponitur occasio, quare misit istos. Idem habetur Lc. VII, 18: tamen alio ordine. Dicit ergo quod erat in vinculis, ut Sup. IV. Tunc incepit Iesus miracula facere. Et hoc erat conveniens, ut sol non appareret dum nubes essent. Infra: *lex et prophetae usque ad Ioannem*.

900. *Opera*, idest miracula, *Christi, mittens duos de discipulis suis, ait illi*.

898. Having said these things, the Lord *passed from there, to teach and preach*; and this for three reasons. One reason is so that he might show by example what he had said by word; *Jesus began to do and to teach* (Acts 1:1). Likewise, that he might show that even the impious are to hear preaching. Hence, *to the wise and to the unwise, I am a debtor* (Rom 1:14). Likewise, that he might give place to others for preaching, as is found, *but if any thing be revealed to another sitting, let the first hold his peace* (1 Cor 14:30).

Now when John had heard in prison the works of Christ. Christ's teaching is set forth, and confirmed, and the preachers are instructed; here rebels are silenced. And
    first, he silences John's disciples;
    second, the scribes, at *when they went their way*.
    Concerning the first, he does three things:
    first, he silences the doubters;
    second, he convicts the crowds, at *but to what will I compare this generation?*
    third, he gives thanks for the apostles' faith, at *at that time Jesus answered and said* (Matt 11:25).
    Concerning the first, first the question is set out;
    second, the answer to the question, at *and Jesus responding*.

899. It says then, *now when John had heard in prison the works of Christ*. The occasion for his sending them is set down. The same thing is found in Luke, yet in another order (Luke 7:18). So it says that he was in prison (Matt 4:12); Jesus began to do miracles at that time. And this was fitting, that the sun might not appear as long as there were clouds. Below in this chapter, *for all the prophets and the law prophesied until John*.

900. *The works*, i.e., the miracles, *of Christ, sending two of his disciples he said to him*.

Quidam volunt ex hoc condemnare Ioannem, quia dubitavit an esset Christus, et constat quod dubius in fide est infidelis. Ambrosius super Lucam dicit, quod haec quaestio non fuit infidelitatis, sed pietatis: non enim loquitur de adventu in mundum, sed de adventu ad passionem. Unde miratur si venerat ad patiendum, sicut dixit Petrus: *propitius esto tibi, Domine*.

Sed contra dicit Chrysostomus, quia Ioannes a principio praescivit, cum dixit, *ecce agnus Dei*, Io. I, 29. Constat ergo quod scivit eum fore hostiam immolandam; unde commendatur hic a Domino, quod sit plusquam propheta; sed prophetae noverunt futura.

901. Alia ratio est Gregorii, quod non est quaestio de adventu in mundum, nec ad passionem, sed de descensu ad inferos, quia Ioannes propinquus erat eundo ad Inferos, ideo voluit certificari *tu es qui venturus es* et cetera.

Sed contra hoc obiicit Chrysostomus. Apud illos qui sunt apud Inferos, non est status poenitentiae: unde videtur, quod frustra diceret istud. Sed hoc non est contra Gregorium, quia voluit non ut nuntiaret captivis conversionem, sed iustis ut gauderent.

902. Alia responsio. Legimus quod Dominus multoties interrogaret, non quia dubitaret, sed ut calumniam tolleret, ut in Io. XI, v. 34 interrogavit de Lazaro, *ubi posuistis eum?* Non quia ignoraret, sed ut illi qui ostenderent sepulcrum, non possent negare, nec calumniari: ideo sic fuit de Ioanne. Quia discipuli eius calumniabantur de Christo, ideo ipse misit, non quia ipse dubitaret, sed ne ipsi calumniarentur, sed confiterentur.

Sed quare non ante miserat? Quia ante semper erat cum eis, et ideo certificabat eos; sed cum voluit discedere ab eis, voluit quod ipsi per Christum essent certi.

903. Dicit ergo *tu es qui venturus es, an alium expectamus?* Verum est, quod patres nostri expectaverunt te, ut habetur Exod. IV.

904. *Et respondens ait illis* et cetera. Hinc tangitur Christi responsio. Ioannes habuit multos discipulos, ut habetur Io. IV. Erat ergo inter eos contentio, quia videntes opera Christi praeferebant Christum Ioanni. Item videntes abstinentiam Ioannis, praeferebant Ioannem Christo. Unde

primo quaestionem ponit;

secundo commendat Ioannem.

905. Circa primum respondet secundum adventum ad passionem.

Some wish to condemn John for this, because he doubted whether he was the Christ, and it is agreed that the one who doubts in matters of faith is an infidel. Ambrose says, commenting on Luke, that this question did not arise from infidelity, but from piety; for he is not speaking about the coming into the world, but about the coming to the passion. Hence he wonders whether he had come to suffer, as Peter said: *be merciful to yourself, Lord* (Matt 16:22).

But Chrysostom says against this that John knew from the beginning, since he said, *behold the Lamb of God* (John 1:29). It remains then that he knew that he was going to be the victim sacrificed. Hence he is commended here by the Lord, because he is more than a prophet; but prophets know the future.

901. Another argument is Gregory's, namely that the question here is not about Christ's coming into the world, nor to the passion, but about the descent into hell, because John was very close to going to hell, so he wanted to make certain that *are you he who is is to come*.

But Chrysostom objects against this. Among those who are in hell, there is no state of penance: hence it seems that this would have been said to no purpose. But this is not contrary to Gregory, because he did not want that he should announce conversion to the captives, but to the just, that they might rejoice.

902. Another response. We read that the Lord asked many times, not because he doubted, but to take away false accusation, as in when he asked about Lazarus, *where have you laid him?* (John 11:34), not because he did not know, but so that those who showed him the sepulcher would not be able to deny the miracle or to accuse him falsely. Therefore, so it was with John. Since his disciples were speaking slanderously about Christ, he sent them, not because he himself doubted, but so that they would not speak slanderously, but believe.

But why did not he send them before? Because before he was always with them, and so he assured them; but when he wished to depart from them, he wanted them to be assured by Christ.

903. It says then, *are you he who is to come, or should we look for another?* It is true that our fathers have expected thee (Exod 4).

904. *And Jesus responding said to them*. From this point on Christ's response is touched upon. John had many disciples (John 4). So there was a disagreement among them, since those who saw Christ's works preferred Christ to John. Similarly, those who saw John's fasting preferred John to Christ. Hence

first, he sets forth the question;

second, he commends John.

905. Concerning the first, he responds according to the coming for the passion.

Veniet tempus quo Deus passurus est, et multi scandalizabuntur, quia *Iudaeis scandalum*, I Cor. I, 23. Unde respondet quando hoc erit.

Secundum Chrysostomum ostendere vult quod ille venit, quem prophetae praedixerunt. Unde per prophetas tria erant promissa. Aliquando promittebatur adventus Dei, in aliquibus adventus novi doctoris, in aliquibus adventus sanctificationis et redemptionis. Quomodo ergo cognoscemus quod iste veniet? Et respondet eo modo quo respondetur Is. cap. XXXV, 4: *ecce Deus veniet, et salvabit nos* et cetera. Unde videbitis ista miracula. **Nuntiate** ergo **Ioanni quae audistis**, in doctrinis. **Et vidistis**, in miraculis. Item promittebatur doctor; Ioel II, 22: *filii Sion, exultate*; et sequitur, *quia dedit vobis doctorem iustitiae*. **Caeci vident** et cetera. Et hoc ad litteram. Item, si quaeris quando veniet. Is. LXI, 1: *Spiritus Domini super me, ad annuntiandum mansuetis misit me*, vel ad evangelizandum; et hoc significatur, cum dicitur **pauperes evangelizantur**. Aliquid proprium voluit significare, quasi dicat: *veniet ponere novam doctrinam*. **Pauperes evangelizantur**, idest evangelizatur paupertas; unde Sup. V, 3: **beati pauperes spiritu** etc.; Lc. IV, 18: *Spiritus Domini super me, propter quod unxit me, evangelizare pauperibus misit me*. Item veniet aliquis sanctificatus sanctificans peccatores. Unde Is. VIII, 13: *Dominum exercituum, ipsum sanctificate*. Unde aliquibus promittebatur sanctificatio, quibus sanctificatis alii scandalizabuntur; unde dicitur **et beatus qui non fuerit scandalizatus in me**. Unde ad Hebr. ult., 12: *propter quod et Iesus ut sanctificaret per proprium sanguinem populum, extra portam passus est*. Ideo ostendit signa de adventu.

906. Et si moraliter loquamur, per hoc significatur totus processus sanctificationis hominis. Primo enim peccatori accidit caecitas, quando ratio obtenebratur; Ps. LVII, 9: *supercecidit ignis, et non viderunt solem*; et Is. XLIII, 8: *educ foras populum caecum, et oculos habentem*. Claudus dicitur quando ad diversa mens trahitur, ut dicitur III Reg. cap. XVIII, 21: *ut quid claudicatis in duas partes?* Item fit ulcerosus in insidiis, et leprosus, quia tunc retrahi non potest, et alios inficit. Et post surdus efficitur, quia castigatio non auditur. Ulterius moritur; Ephes. c. V, 14: *surge qui dormis, et exurge a mortuis*. Et omnes istos sanat Dominus. Ultimo fit pauper spiritu, ita quod non est in eo sanitas; Ps. XXXVII, 8: *quoniam lumbi mei impleti sunt illusionibus, et non est sanitas in carne mea* et cetera. Et istos Dominus sanat, et sanati in quamdam soliditatem mentis conscendunt, ubi est vera pax: *pax multa diligentibus legem tuam, et non est illis scandalum*, Ps. CXVIII, 165.

The time will come when God will suffer, and many will be scandalized, for *it will be a stumbling block to the Jews* (1 Cor 1:23). Hence he tells when this will be.

According to Chrysostom, he wishes to show that he has come whom the prophets foretold. Hence three things were promised through the prophets. Sometimes, the coming of God was promised, in some the coming of a new teacher, in some the coming of sanctification and redemption. How then will we know that he will come? And he responds in the same way Isaiah responds, *God himself will come and will save you. Then will the eyes of the blind be opened, and the ears of the deaf will be unstopped* (Isa 35:4–5). Hence you will see these miracles. **Relate** then **to John what you have heard** in teaching **and seen** in miracles. Likewise, a teacher was promised; *O children of Zion, rejoice* (Joel 2:23); and there follows *because he has given you a teacher of justice*. **The blind see**. And this literally. Likewise, if you ask when he will come: *the Spirit of the Lord is upon me, because the Lord has anointed me: he has sent me to preach to the meek* (Isa 61:1); and this is signified when it says, **the poor have the Gospel preached to them**. He wishes to indicate something proper to himself, as though to say: *I will come to set forth a new teaching*. **The poor have the Gospel preached to them**, i.e., poverty has the Gospel preached to it; hence above, **blessed are the poor in spirit** (Matt 5:3). *The Spirit of the Lord is upon me. Wherefore he has anointed me to preach the Gospel to the poor* (Luke 4:18). Likewise, there will come someone holy, who makes sinners holy. Hence, *sanctify the Lord of hosts himself* (Isa 8:13). Hence sanctification was promised to some, by which sanctified ones some will be scandalized; hence he says, **and blessed is he who will not be scandalized in me**. Hence, *wherefore Jesus also, that he might sanctify the people by his own blood, suffered without the gate* (Heb 13:12). Therefore he showed a sign of the coming.

906. And if we speak morally, this signifies the whole process of the sanctification of a man. For first, blindness comes upon a sinner, when the reason is darkened; *fire has fallen on them, and they will not see the sun* (Ps 57:9); and, *bring forth the people who are blind, and have eyes* (Isa 43:8). A man is called wavering when his mind is drawn toward different and opposed opinions, as it is said, *how long do you waver* between two sides? (1 Kgs 18:21). Also, he becomes full of sores in treachery, and leprous, because he cannot draw back, and infects others. And after that he is made deaf, because he does not hear chastisement. Next, he dies; *rise you who sleep, and arise from the dead* (Eph 5:14). And the Lord heals all these things. Finally, he becomes poor in spirit, such that there is no health in him; *for my loins are filled with illusions; and there is no health in my flesh* (Ps 37:8). And the Lord heals these things, and those who are healed arise in a certain solidity of mind, where there is peace: *much peace have they who love your law, and to them there is no stumbling block* (Ps 118:165).

907. *Illis autem abeuntibus* et cetera. Hic satisfacit dubitationi turbarum. Turbae autem audierant testimonium Ioannis de Christo; sed modo videbantur dubitare. Tria enim poterant habere in corde, quia triplici ratione mutat aliquis verbum suum: vel propter animi levitatem, vel propter aliquod commodum, vel quia ex humano spiritu, quando nesciat veritatem, et post cognoscat illam. Ps. XCIII, 11: *scit enim Deus, quoniam cogitationes hominum vanae sunt.* Ideo

primo excludit ab eo levitatem;

secundo appetitum commodi;

tertio ostendit eum propheticam habere veritatem.

908. Dicit ergo *illis abeuntibus* et cetera. Docet nos Dominus magnam curialitatem, quia noluit Ioannem laudare discipulis suis praesentibus, sicut nec aliquem in sua praesentia, sicut habetur Prov. XXVII, 2: *laudet te alienus, et non os tuum: extraneus, et non labia tua.* Quia si bonus est qui laudatur, erubescit; si malus est, adulatur. *Coepit Iesus dicere ad turbas: quid existis in desertum videre?* Numquid existis ad videndum *arundinem?* Non. Sed existis videre hominem firmum. Arundo autem de facili movetur; unde animus cito mutabilis ventus reputatur. Ad Ephes. IV, 14: *ut non simus iam parvuli fluctuantes, et circumferamur omni vento.*

909. Item non est levis pro aliquo commodo. *Sed quid existis videre?* Omnes enim divitiae ad aliquam utilitatem pertinent corporis, et hoc vel in cibo, vel in vestitu: et constat quod in nullo horum facit vim. Non est ergo credendum quod pro aliquo commodo hoc dicat; unde dicit *quid existis videre? Hominem mollibus vestitum?*

Et quare non facit mentionem de cibo? Quia non poterat esse dubium. Vestiebatur autem de pilis camelorum. Unde *qui mollibus vestiuntur*, non sunt in deserto, *sed in domibus regum.*

Aliter exponitur secundum Chrysostomum. Aliqui ex natura leves fiunt, aliqui ex deliciis, ut Os. IV, 11: *fornicatio, et vinum, et ebrietas auferunt cor.* Primum amovet per prius dictum: secundum per hoc quod dicit *mollibus vestitum*; ideo non est inconstans ex deliciis vitae.

910. Sed hic potest fieri quaestio de deliciis vestitus, utrum sit peccatum; quia si non est peccatum, non imputaretur illi diviti, qui quotidie induebatur purpura et bysso, Lc. XVI, 19.

Respondet Augustinus, quod talia non sunt consideranda, sed affectus utentis: quilibet enim debet indui ad modum simul convenientium, ideo magis enucleanda est consuetudo. Nam in aliquibus terris omnes, aut plures induuntur serico. Unde aliqui strictius induunt, aliqui latius, et utroque modo distinguitur: si restrictius, aut

907. *And when they went their way.* Here he satisfies the doubts of the crowds. For the crowds had heard John's testimony about Christ; but now they seemed to doubt. For they could have three things in their heart, because a man changes his mind for three reasons: either due to levity of soul, or for the sake of some profit, or because he acts out of a human spirit, when he does not know the truth, and afterwards knows it. *The Lord knows the thoughts of men, that they are vain* (Ps 93:11). Therefore,

first, he excludes levity from him;

second, the desire of profit;

third, he shows him to have prophetic truth.

908. It says then, *and when they went their way.* The Lord teaches us a great courtesy, because he did not want to praise John with his disciples present, as neither would you want to praise someone in his own presence, as is said, *let another praise you, and not your own mouth: a stranger, and not your own lips* (Prov 27:2). Because if the one praised is good, he blushes; if he is bad, he is flattered. *Jesus began to say to the multitudes concerning John: what did you go out into the desert to see?* Did you go out to see a *reed?* No. Rather you went out to see a steady man. Now, a reed is easily moved; hence a soul quickly changeable is considered the wind. *That henceforth we may no more be children tossed to and fro, and carried about with every wind of doctrine* (Eph 4:14).

909. Likewise, he is not light for the sake of some profit. *But what did you go out to see?* For all riches pertain to some practical gain for the body, and this either in food, or in clothing: and it is agreed that he places weight on none of these. Therefore it should not be thought that he says this for some profit; hence he says, *but what did you go out to see? A man clothed in soft garments?*

And why does he not mention food? Because there could be no doubt. Now, he was clothed with the skins of camels, hence *they who are clothed in soft garments* are not in the desert, but *are in the houses of kings.*

Chrysostom explains this another way. Some men are light by nature, some out of pleasure, as is said, *fornication, and wine, and drunkenness take away the understanding* (Hos 4:11). The first he removes by what was said above; the second, by what he says here, *in soft garments*; therefore he is not unsteady from the delights of life.

910. But a question can arise here about the delights of clothing, whether they are a sin; because if they are not a sin, it would not be counted against those rich men, who are clothed daily in purple and fine linen (Luke 16:19).

Augustine responds that such things should not be considered, but rather the affection of the one using the clothes: for a man should be clothed in a manner like his companions, so one must rather examine the custom. For in some lands, all or many are clothed in silk. Hence some are clothed more narrowly, some more broadly, and either

intentione bona, et hoc est bonum: aut propter vanam gloriam, et hoc malum. Si latius, aut propter superbiam, et hoc malum: aut propter significationem, ut pontifex et sacerdos, et hoc bonum.

911. Mystice per homines qui mollibus vestiuntur, significantur adulatores: ille enim mollibus vestitur, qui verbis blandis molitur, ut in ore homines superbi quaerant gloriam. Et Prov. XXIX, 12: *princeps qui libenter audit verba mendacii, omnes ministros habet impios.*

912. Sed dicerent: non est inconstans, sed humano spiritu loquitur, ideo hoc amovet **sed quid existis videre? Prophetam** et cetera. Unde testimonium perhibet quod non humano spiritu, sed prophetico loquebatur. Unde primo ostendit eum esse prophetam; secundo plusquam prophetam.

Fuit enim propheta, ut habetur Lc. I, 76: *et tu, puer, propheta Altissimi vocaberis* et cetera. Item extollit eum super prophetas dicens **dico vobis: etiam plusquam prophetam**: et hoc quantum ad tria. Primo, quia prophetae est futura praedicere; iste autem non solum futura, sed etiam praesentia ostendit dicens: *ecce Agnus Dei, ecce qui tollit peccatum mundi.* Item non dicitur solum propheta, sed etiam **Baptista**, ut supra cap. III. Item praecursor, ut habetur Lc. I, v. 76: *praeibis enim ante faciem Domini parare vias eius.* Item quantum ad modum: miraculosius enim egit, quam propheta, quia iste ex utero prophetavit, alii non, ut habetur Lc. I, 44: *ecce enim ut facta est vox salutationis tuae in auribus meis, exultavit infans in gaudio in utero meo.*

913. Hic est enim de quo scriptum est. Hic probat Dominus excellentiam Ioannis. Et

primo per auctoritatem;

secundo per specialia eius privilegia, ibi **amen dico vobis** et cetera.

914. Dicit ergo: dixi quod est plusquam propheta, de quo habetur Mal. III, 1: *'ecce ego mitto angelum meum, qui praeparabit viam tuam ante te'* et cetera. In hac auctoritate ponuntur excellentiae Ioannis, quia primo vocat eum angelum: angelus enim est supra prophetam, quia sicut sacerdos est medius inter prophetam et populum, sic propheta inter angelos et sacerdotes. Angelus autem inter Deum et prophetas; unde Zacharias dicit: *angelus qui loquebatur in me*, Zach. I, 9. Angelus est nomen officii, non naturae; unde Ioannes angelus dicitur ex officio. Differentia est enim inter angelum et prophetam, quia angeli manifeste vident, unde habetur inf. XVIII, 10, ubi dicitur: **dico enim vobis, quia angeli eorum semper vident faciem Patris mei qui in caelis est.** Angeli semper vident faciem Dei, prophetae vero non. Unde sicut

way should be divided: if more narrowly, either from a good intention, and this is good, or for the sake of vainglory, and this is bad. If more broadly, either for the sake of pride, and this is bad, or for the sake of signifying something, like a pope or a priest, and this is good.

911. Mystically, the men who are clothed in soft things signify flatterers: for they are clothed with soft things who put together flattering works, that proud men might seek glory in the mouth. And, *a prince who gladly hears lying words, has all his servants wicked* (Prov 29:12).

912. But they say: he is not unsteady, but speaks with a human spirit. So he removes this: **but what did you go out to see? A prophet?** Hence he bears witness that he spoke not by a human spirit, but by a prophetic spirit. Hence first he shows that he is a prophet; second, more than a prophet.

For he was a prophet, as is said, *and you, child, will be called the prophet of the Most High* (Luke 1:76). And he praises him above the prophets, saying, **I tell you, and more than a prophet**: and this as regards three things. First, because it belongs to a prophet to predict the future; but he shows not only the future, but also the present, saying, *behold the Lamb of God, behold him who takes away the sin of the world* (John 1:29). Likewise, he is not called only a prophet, but also **the Baptist**, as above (Matt 3:1). Likewise, he is the forerunner, as is found, *for you will go before the face of the Lord to prepare his ways* (Luke 1:76). Likewise, as regards the mode: for he worked more marvelously than the prophets, because he prophesied from the womb, but not the others, as is found, *for behold as soon as the voice of your salutation sounded in my ears, the infant in my womb leaped for joy* (Luke 1:44).

913. For this is he of whom it is written. Here the Lord proves John's superiority. And

first, by authority;

second, by his special privilege, at **amen, I say to you**.

914. He says then: I said that he is greater than the prophets, of whom it is said, *'behold I send my angel before your face, who will prepare your way before you'* (Mal 3:1). In this Scriptural text are set forth John's excellences, because first it calls him an angel: for an angel is above a prophet, since just as a priest is an intermediate between the prophet and the people, so the prophet is an intermediate between the angels and the priests. Moreover, an angel is between God and the prophets; hence Zacharias says, *the angel that spoke in me* (Zech 1:9). Angel is the name of an office, not of a nature, hence John is called an angel because of his office. For there is this difference between angels and prophets, that angels see clearly, as is found below, **I say to you, that their angels in heaven always see the face of my Father who is in heaven** (Matt 18:10). Angels always behold the face of God, but not the prophets. Hence just as the angels always behold the face of the Father, so John saw

angeli semper vident faciem Patris, sic Ioannes specialiter Christum vidit: et ideo quia specialiter, ideo dicit *'meum.'*

Item dicit *'ante faciem meam.'* Quando rex vadit, praecedunt multi, sed magis familiares praecedunt faciem suam; sic Ioannes honorabilior dicitur, quia missus ante faciem eius: tanto enim honorabilior, quanto propinquior. Item iste praeparabat viam, quia baptizabat; unde dicit *'qui praeparabit viam ante te.'*

915. *Amen dico vobis* et cetera. Supra commendavit Dominus Ioannem per auctoritatem prophetae; nunc intendit eum commendare propriis verbis, et auctoritatem prophetae exponit: et tria facit.

Primo commendat ipsum quantum ad differentiam omnis ordinis et status.

Et primo secundum differentiam caelestium et terrestrium;

secundo quantum ad differentiam legis et Evangelii;

tertio quantum ad differentiam praesentis saeculi et futuri.

Et primo ostendit eum excellentem inter terrestres;

secundo ostendit eum minorem inter caelestes, ibi **qui autem minor est in regno caelorum, maior est illo**.

916. Dicit ergo: dictum est quod Ioannes est angelus, et, ut in summa breviter comprehendam **dico vobis: inter natos mulierum non surrexit maior**. Proprie locutus est cum dixit **surrexit**, quia omnes nascuntur filii irae, ut habetur ad Ephes. II, 3: *eramus natura filii irae, sicut et ceteri*. Quicumque ergo potest ad statum gratiae pervenire, surgit. Unde **inter natos mulierum** et cetera.

Et significanter loquitur, ut ab hac universalitate excludatur Christus, quia mulier corruptionem sonat, sed foemina sexum; unde si alicubi invenitur filius mulieris, ut in Io. XIX, 26: *mulier, ecce filius tuus*, sexum tunc nominat, non corruptionem.

917. Sed quid est quod dicit **inter natos mulierum non surrexit maior**? Estne propter hoc maior omnibus?

Dicit Hieronymus, quod non sequitur: si non surrexit maior, ergo est maior. Chrysostomus autem dicit, quod maior est omnibus.

Secundum ergo primam expositionem dico quod argumentum illud in angelis, ubi est ordo, valorem haberet, quod ille, quo non est alius maior, est maximus; sed inter homines non habet veritatem, quia inter homines non est ordo secundum naturam, sed solum secundum gratiam. Item si dicatur maior omnibus patribus Veteris Testamenti, non est inconveniens: ille enim maior et excellentior est, qui ad maius officium est assumptus:

Christ in a particular way: and so since it was in a particular way, he says *'my.'*

Likewise, he says, *'before your face.'* When a king travels, many go before him, but the more intimate go before his face. Thus John is called more honorable, because he was sent before his face; for one is more honorable the nearer he is. Likewise, he prepared the way, because he baptized; hence he says, *'who will prepare your way before you.'*

915. *Amen, I say to you*. Above, the Lord commended John by the authority of a prophet; now he means to commend him by his own words, and he explains the text of the prophet.

And he does three things: first, he commends him as regards the difference of every order and state.

And first, according to the difference between the heavenly and the earthly;

second, as regards the difference between the law and the Gospel;

third, as regards the difference between the present age and the one to come.

And first, he shows him to be the most excellent among the earthly;

second, he shows him to be the lesser among the heavenly, at *yet he who is the lesser in the kingdom of heaven is greater than he*.

916. He says then: it was said that John is an angel, and, to put it briefly, in summary, *amen I say to you, there has not risen among those who are born of women anyone greater than John the Baptist*. He spoke properly when he said, *risen*, because all are born as children of wrath, as is found, *and were by nature children of wrath, even as the rest* (Eph 2:3). So whoever can arrive at the state of grace rises. Hence, *among those who are born of women*.

And he speaks meaningfully, to exclude the Christ from this generality, because woman denotes corruption, but female only gender; hence if he is found somewhere named as the son of a woman, as in, *woman, behold your son* (John 19:26), he names gender there, not corruption.

917. But why does he say, *there has not risen among those who are born of women anyone greater*? Is it because this man is greater than all?

Jerome says that this does not follow: if there has not arisen a greater, therefore he is greater than all. But Chrysostom says that he is greater than all.

According to the first explanation, I say that this argument has force among the angels, where there is order: that he to whom there is none greater is the greatest; but among men it has no truth, because among men there is no order according to nature but only according to grace. And it is not unfitting if he is called greater than all the Old Testament fathers, for he is greater and more excellent who is taken up for the greater office: for Abraham is greater

Abraham enim maior est inter patres quoad probationem fidei; Moyses vero quoad officium prophetiae, ut habetur Deut. ult., 10: *non surrexit propheta ultra in Israel sicut Moyses.* Omnes isti praecursores Domini fuerunt; nullus autem fuit in tanta excellentia et favore; ideo ad maius officium est assumptus; Lc. I, 15: *erit enim magnus coram Domino.*

918. *Qui autem minor est in regno caelorum, maior est illo.* Occasione istorum verborum quidam locum calumniandi invenerunt: volunt enim omnes patres Veteris Testamenti damnare; si enim maior est aliis, sequitur quod alii non sunt de numero salvandorum, quia per regnum caelorum praesens Ecclesia designatur. Si ergo Ioannes non fuit de praesenti Ecclesia, non fuit de numero electorum, ergo minus alii.

Et haec opinio est erronea, quia constat quod id quod Dominus dicit, in laudem Ioannis introducitur.

919. Potest autem haec locutio exponi tripliciter. Primo, ut per regnum caelorum ordo beatorum intelligatur: et qui inter illos est minor, maior est quolibet viatore. Et ideo praesentem statum appellat Dominus pueritiam. Unde I ad Cor. XIII, 11: *cum autem factus sum vir, evacuavi quae erant parvuli,* unde nominat viatores parvulos. Et hoc verum est intelligendo de maioritate actuali: actu enim maior est qui comprehensor est. Secus de maioritate virtuali, sicut una parva herba maior dicitur virtute, licet alia maior sit quantitate.

Aliter potest exponi, ita quod per regnum caelorum praesens Ecclesia designetur: et hoc est, quod **minor** non dicitur universaliter, sed minor tempore. Supra III et Io. I, v. 15: *qui post me venit, ante me factus est.* Unde ille qui minor est, maior est illo.

Vel aliter potest exponi, quod aliquis dicitur maior dupliciter: vel quantum ad meritum; et sic multi patriarchae sunt maiores aliquibus Novi Testamenti, sicut dicit Augustinus quod caelibatus Ioannis non praefertur coniugio Abrahae: aut comparando statum ad statum, sicut virgines meliores sunt coniugatis; non tamen quaelibet virgo melior quolibet coniugato: unde Ioannes habet istam dignitatem, quod est in quodam confinio, quia maior viatoribus, sed minor comprehensoribus; unde tenet locum medium.

920. *A diebus autem Ioannis usque nunc* et cetera. Hic commendatur quantum ad distinctionem novi et Veteris Testamenti. Et notatur excellentia Ioannis, quia est principium Novi Testamenti, et finis veteris.

921. Ita dixi, quod *qui minor est in regno caelorum, maior est illo*: et hoc pertinet ad hoc, quod ipse est principium Novi Testamenti: sed *a diebus Ioannis Baptistae,*

among the fathers as regards the testing of faith, but Moses is greater as regards the office of prophecy, as is found, *and there arose no more a prophet in Israel like unto Moses* (Deut 34:10). All these were precursors of the Lord, but there was no one in such excellence and favor; therefore he was taken up for the greater office. *For he will be great before the Lord* (Luke 1:15).

918. *Yet he who is the lesser in the kingdom of heaven is greater than he.* Taking the occasion of these words, certain men have found an opportunity for calumny. For they would damn all the fathers of the Old Testament: for if he is greater than the others, it follows that the others are not among the number of the saved, since the present Church is designated by the kingdom of heaven. Therefore, if John was not in the present Church, he was not among the number of the elect; therefore much less the others.

And this opinion is erroneous, because it is agreed that what the Lord says is spoken in praise of John.

919. Now, this speech can be explained in three ways. First, as by the kingdom of heaven is understood the order of the blessed: and the one who is lesser among those is greater than any given wayfarer. And this is why the Lord calls the present state childhood. Hence, *but, when I became a man, I put away the things of a child* (1 Cor 13:11); hence he calls wayfarers children. And this is true, considering actual greatness, for the one greater in act is the one who is a comprehensor. It is otherwise with greatness of power, just as one small herb is called greater on account of power, although another may be greater in size.

It can also be explained in this way, that by the kingdom of heaven the present Church is indicated. And this is because *the lesser* is not said universally, but means the lesser in time. As it says above (Matt 3:11), and *he who will come after me, is preferred before me: because he was before me* (John 1:15). Hence he who is lesser is greater than him.

Or it can be explained in another way, that someone is called greater in two ways: either as regards merit; and thus many patriarchs are greater than some men of New Testament, just as Augustine says that John's celibacy is not preferred to Abraham's wife; or by comparing state to state, as virgins are better than married people; yet not any given virgin is better than any given married person. Hence John has this dignity, which is within a certain limit, because he is greater than the wayfarers, but less than the comprehensors. Hence he holds a middle place.

920. *And from the days of John the Baptist until now.* Here he is commended as regards the distinction between the New and Old Testaments. And John's excellence is pointed out, because he is the beginning of the New Testament, and the end of the Old.

921. I spoke in this way, that *he who is the lesser in the kingdom of heaven is greater than he*; and this pertains to the fact that he is the beginning of the New Testament. But

idest a praedicatione Ioannis, *regnum caelorum vim patitur*.

922. Hoc tripliciter exponitur. Scitis quod in raptu quaedam violentia est, et quidam conatus; unde oportet quod peccator ad hoc quod possit venire ad regnum caelorum, assurgat ad spiritualia, et conetur multum.

Aliter exponitur. Scitis quod rapina est proprie quando alienum praeter voluntatem domini rapitur: praedicatio salutis missa est Iudaeis, et per Christum ubique. Ipse dicit infra XV, 24: *non sum missus nisi ad oves, quae perierunt domus Israel*. Et cum ad eos mitteretur, non receperunt; tamen illi quibus non mittebatur, propter humilitatem rapiebant. Unde supra VII, 12: *multi venient ab oriente et occidente, et recumbent cum Abraham, Isaac et Iacob in regno caelorum; filii autem regni eiicientur in tenebras exteriores* et cetera. Et infra XXI, 43: *auferetur a vobis regnum et dabitur genti facienti fructus eius*. Ideo isti violenter rapiunt. Et haec est expositio Hilarii.

Tertia expositio est. Illud quod rapitur, cum festinatione rapitur, unde Iob: *sicut torrens qui raptim transit in convallibus*, et hoc propter motus velocitatem. Et quia praedicatio ita commoverat corda omnium, videbatur festinus cursus; ideo dicit *vim patitur*, quia per modum cuiusdam festinationis tendunt ad regnum; unde ab ipso incepit Evangelium, et ipse est finis legis.

923. Unde Christus dicit *omnes enim prophetae et lex usque ad Ioannem prophetaverunt*: quia omnes prophetae propter Christum; et inceperunt impleri a praedicatione Ioannis. Unde Lc. ult., 44: *oportet impleri quae scripta sunt de me*. Et hoc *usque ad Ioannem*.

924. Sed quid est? Numquid post Ioannem non fuerunt prophetae? Nonne legimus infra XXIII, 34: *ecce mitto ad vos prophetas, sapientes et Scribas?* et cetera.

Dicendum quod propheta ad duo mittitur: ad confirmandam fidem, et corrigendos mores; Prov. XXIX, 18: *cum prophetia defecerit, dissipabitur populus*. Ad confirmandam fidem, ut habetur I Petr. I, 10: *de qua salute exquisierunt, atque scrutati sunt prophetae, qui de futura in vobis gratia prophetaverunt, scrutantes in quod vel in quale tempus significaret in eis spiritus Christi*. Unde prophetia de istis duobus serviebat; sed iam fides fundata est, quia iam promissa per Christum sunt completa. Sed ad corrigendos mores numquam deficit, nec deficiet prophetia.

Habet ergo excellentiam Ioannes, quia in medio veteris et novae legis; unde missus est ante faciem quasi simul cum Christo.

from the days of John the Baptist, i.e., from the preaching of John, *the kingdom of heaven suffers violence*.

922. This is explained in three ways. You know that in robbery there is a certain violence, and a certain struggle; hence it is necessary that the sinner rise up to spiritual things, and struggle greatly, so that he can arrive at the kingdom of heaven.

It is explained in another way. You know that robbery is when another's property is dragged off against the owner's will: the preaching of salvation was sent to the Jews, and then by Christ was sent everywhere. He himself says below, *I was sent only to the lost sheep of the house of Israel* (Matt 15:24). And when he was sent to them, they did not receive him; yet those to whom he was not sent stole him, because of humility. Hence, *and I say to you that many will come from the east and the west, and will sit down with Abraham, and Isaac, and Jacob in the kingdom of heaven: but the children of the kingdom will be cast out into the exterior darkness* (Matthew 8:11). And below, *the kingdom of God will be taken from you, and will be given to a nation yielding its fruits* (Matt 21:43). Therefore these men violently rob. And this is Hilary's explanation.

There is a third explanation. That which is stolen, is stolen with haste; hence, *as the torrent that passes swiftly in the valleys* (Job 6:15), and this because of the velocity of their motion. And since preaching stirred up the hearts of all in this way, it seemed like a hasty onrush; so he says, *suffers violence*, because they tend toward the kingdom by way of a certain hastiness. Hence the Gospel began from him, and he himself is the end of the law.

923. Hence Christ says, *for all the prophets and the law prophesied until John*, because all the prophets were for the sake of Christ; and their fulfillment began from John's preaching. Hence, *these are the words which I spoke to you, while I was yet with you, that all things must needs be fulfilled* (Luke 24:44). And this is *until John*.

924. But what is this? Were there not prophets after John? Do we not read below, *therefore behold I send to you prophets, and wise men, and scribes?* (Matt 23:34).

One should say that prophets are sent for two purposes: to confirm the faith, and to correct behavior; *when prophecy will fail, the people will be scattered abroad* (Prov 29:18). To confirm the faith, as is found, *of which salvation the prophets have inquired and diligently searched, who prophesied of the grace to come in you. Searching what or what manner of time the spirit of Christ in them did signify* (1 Pet 1:10–11). Hence prophecy served these two purposes; but the faith is already founded, because already the promises have been fulfilled by Christ. But occasions for correcting behavior never come to an end, nor will prophecy come to an end.

Therefore John has this excellence, that he stands in the middle of the old and new law; hence he was sent before the face, as it were, at the same time with Christ.

925. *Et si vultis recipere, ipse est Elias, qui venturus est.* Hic ponit excellentiam Ioannis quoad distinctionem praesentis et futuri. Elias enim fuit praecursor Domini, sicut Ioannes; unde Mal. IV, 5: *ecce ego mittam vobis Eliam prophetam* et cetera. Et Ioannes est Elias.

Sed quid est quod dicit Dominus? Quia interrogatus Ioannes si esset Elias, dixit quod non.

Per hoc autem amovetur quaedam haeresis, quae posuit transmigrationem animae, quod anima videlicet exibat de uno corpore, et intrabat aliud corpus, ideo anima Eliae intraverat Ioannem, ut dicebat. Sed haec opinio falsa est, quia ipse negavit quod esset Elias.

Christus autem dixit, quod Ioannes erat Elias propter triplicem similitudinem. Primo, quia sicut angelus dicitur similis angelo, quia pares in officio, sic Elias et Ioannes pares sunt officio, quia uterque praecursor; Lc. I, v. 76: *ipse praeibit ante faciem Domini parare vias eius* et cetera. Item quantum ad conversationem, quia vitam austeram duxit, ut habetur III Reg. XIX, 6 ss. Item quantum ad persecutionem, quia sicut ille persecutus est a Iezabel, ita iste ab Herode. Unde *si vultis accipere*, secundum quod accipi debet, *ipse est Elias*. Et ut ipsi intelligant quod istud dictum est mystice, subdit *qui habet aures audiendi audiat*, idest, qui habet aures spiritualiter, *audiat*, et intelligat.

925. *And if you will receive it, he is Elias that is to come.* Here he sets forth John's excellence as regards the distinction between the present and the future. For Elias was a precursor of the Lord, just as John was; hence, *behold I will send you Elias the prophet* (Mal 4:5). And John is Elias.

But why does the Lord say this? For when John was asked if he was Elias, he said no.

By this a certain heresy is removed, which posits a transmigration of the soul, namely that the soul went out of one body and entered another body, so the soul of Elias entered John, as was said. But this is a false opinion, because he himself denied that he was Elias.

But Christ said that John was Elias because of a threefold likeness. First, because just as an angel is like an angel, since they are equal in office, so Elias and John are equal in office, because both were precursors; *you will go before the face of the Lord* (Luke 1:76). Likewise, as regards way of life, because he led an austere life (1 Kgs 19:6). Likewise as regards persecution, because just as he was persecuted by Jezabel, so this man was persecuted by Herod. Hence *if you will receive it*, according as it should be received, *he is Elias*. And so that they would understand that this was spoken mystically, he adds, *he who has ears to hear, let him hear*, i.e., he who has spiritual ears, *let him hear*, and understand.

Lecture 2

11:16 Cui autem similem aestimabo generationem istam? Similis est pueris sedentibus in foro, qui clamantes coaequalibus [n. 926]

11:17 dicunt: cecinimus vobis, et non saltastis; lamentavimus, et non planxistis. [n. 933]

11:18 Venit enim Ioannes neque manducans, neque bibens, et dicunt: daemonium habet. [n. 937]

11:19 Venit Filius hominis manducans et bibens, et dicunt: ecce homo vorax, et potator vini, publicanorum et peccatorum amicus. Et iustificata est sapientia a filiis suis. [n. 938]

11:16 Τίνι δὲ ὁμοιώσω τὴν γενεὰν ταύτην; ὁμοία ἐστὶν παιδίοις καθημένοις ἐν ταῖς ἀγοραῖς ἃ προσφωνοῦντα τοῖς ἑτέροις

11:17 λέγουσιν· ηὐλήσαμεν ὑμῖν καὶ οὐκ ὠρχήσασθε, ἐθρηνήσαμεν καὶ οὐκ ἐκόψασθε.

11:18 ἦλθεν γὰρ Ἰωάννης μήτε ἐσθίων μήτε πίνων, καὶ λέγουσιν· δαιμόνιον ἔχει.

11:19 ἦλθεν ὁ υἱὸς τοῦ ἀνθρώπου ἐσθίων καὶ πίνων, καὶ λέγουσιν· ἰδοὺ ἄνθρωπος φάγος καὶ οἰνοπότης, τελωνῶν φίλος καὶ ἁμαρτωλῶν. καὶ ἐδικαιώθη ἡ σοφία ἀπὸ τῶν ἔργων αὐτῆς.

11:16 But to what will I compare this generation? It is like to children sitting in the market place, who, crying to their companions, [n. 926]

11:17 say: we have piped to you, and you have not danced: we have lamented, and you have not mourned. [n. 933]

11:18 For John came neither eating nor drinking; and they say: he has a devil. [n. 937]

11:19 The Son of man came eating and drinking, and they say: behold a man who is a glutton and a wine drinker, a friend of publicans and sinners. And wisdom is justified by her children. [n. 938]

---

926. Cui autem hic prorumpit in increpationem turbarum. Et

    primo ponit quaestionem;

    secundo quamdam similitudinem;

    tertio eam exponit.

927. Procedit ergo sic. Ita comparatur Ioannes Eliae ratione officii, sed cui comparabo hanc generationem?

Et quare dicit hoc hic? Hoc dicit sicut aliquis quando alicui fecit quicquid boni potuit, et ipse est ingratus, nescit cui comparare eum; sic Dominus omnia bona fecerat generationi huic; unde Is. V, 4: *quid ultra debui facere vineae meae, et non feci ei?* Cui ergo potero comparare tantam malitiam?

928. Notandum quod 'generatio' aliquando in Scripturis pro congregatione bonorum accipitur, aliquando malorum, aliquando utrorumque. Pro congregatione bonorum, ut in Ps. CXI, 2: *generatio rectorum benedicetur.* Pro congregatione mala, infra XII, v. 39, ubi dicitur **generatio mala et perversa.** Pro utrisque, Eccle. I, 4, ubi dicitur: *generatio praeterit, generatio ventura est, terra autem in aeternum stat.*

929. Similis est pueris sedentibus in foro et cetera. Hic ponit quamdam similitudinem; et potest exponi secundum planum litterae, vel secundum mysticum sensum.

    Primo ponit similitudinem de pueris;

    secundo adaptat eam, ibi **venit Ioannes neque manducans, neque bibens** et cetera.

926. But to what. Here he breaks forth into a rebuke of the crowds. And

    first, he sets forth a question;

    second, a certain likeness;

    third, he explains it.

927. So he proceeds thus. John is compared to Elias this way by reason of office, but to what will I compare this generation?

And why does he say this here? He says this like a man who, when he did whatever good he could for someone, and the man was ungrateful, does not know to what to compare him; thus the Lord had done all good things for this generation; hence, *what is there that I ought to do more to my vineyard, that I have not done to it?* (Isa 5:4). To what therefore will I be able to compare such malice?

928. One should notice that 'generation' is sometimes taken in Scripture for the congregation of the good, sometimes for the congregation of the bad, sometimes for that of both. For the congregation of the good, as in, *the generation of the righteous will be blessed* (Ps 111:2). For the evil congregation, below, where it says, **an evil and adulterous generation seeks a sign** (Matt 12:39). For both, where it says, *one generation passes away, and another generation comes: but the earth standes forever* (Eccl 1:4).

929. It is like to children sitting in the market place. Here he sets forth a certain likeness; and it can be explained according to the plain letter, or according to a mystical sense.

    First, he sets forth a likeness about children;

    second, he applies it, at **for John came neither eating nor drinking.**

930. Notandum enim quod naturale est homini quaerere delectationes, et semper quaerit illas, et nisi abstrahatur per sollicitudines, statim ruit in malas delectationes, sed pueri non habent sollicitudines, ideo vacant circa illa, quae sibi competunt, hoc est ludere.

931. Item notandum, quod homo naturaliter sociale est, et hoc quia naturaliter unus alio indiget, unde delectatur in convictu; unde Philosophus I *Polit.*: *omnis homo qui solitarius est, aut est melior homine, et est Deus; aut peior homine, et est bestia.* Unde dicitur **sedentibus in foro**, quia nullus per se vult ludere, sed in foro, ubi fit congregatio multorum.

932. Item notandum, quod naturale est homini quod delectatio eius sit in aliqua repraesentatione, unde si videamus aliquid bene sculptum, quod bene repraesentet quod debet, tunc delectamur; ideo pueri qui delectantur in ludis, semper ludos suos faciunt cum aliqua repraesentatione vel belli, vel huiusmodi.

Item notandum, quod ad duas passiones terminantur omnes animi affectus, scilicet vel ad gaudium, vel ad luctum.

933. ***Qui clamantes*** et cetera. Hoc est ita videndum. Ponamus quod sint pueri ex una parte, et alii ex alia, ita quod quidam debeant cantare, alii saltare; unum isti facere, alii eis respondere. Si isti canerent, et illi eis non responderent secundum formam suam, iniuriarentur eisdem, unde dicunt **cecinimus vobis, et vos non saltastis.**

934. Item nihil ita immutat animum, sicut cantus; unde computat Boetius in *Musica* sua de quodam qui coram Pythagora cum alio litigabat, et cantu alii loquebantur. Tunc Pythagoras fecit mutari cantum, et ille quievit; unde omnes exercebantur in musica.

935. Ideo notandum, quod quidam cantus est propter gaudium, sicut habetur Eccli. XL, 20: *vinum et musica laetificant cor*; ideo dicitur **cecinimus**, idest cantum gaudii diximus, **et non saltastis**.

Item consuetudo est, quod sicut aliqui immutantur ad gaudium, ita quidam ad fletum; unde Ier. IX, 17: *vocate lamentatrices, et assumant super nos lamentum* et cetera. Ideo dicunt **lamentavimus**, idest cantus lugubres fecimus, **et vos non planxistis.**

936. Mystice per pueros significatur populus veteris legis, inter quos quidam fuerunt provocatores ad gaudium spirituale, ut David Ps. XXXII, 1: *exultate, iusti, in Domino*, quidam ad luctum, ut Ioel II, 13: *convertimini ad Dominum in toto corde vestro, in ieiunio, fletu et planctu* et cetera. Unde possunt dicere **cecinimus**, idest incitavimus vos ad spiritualem laetitiam, et non suscepistis:

930. For one should notice that it is natural for man to seek pleasures, and he always seeks them, and unless he is drawn away by anxieties, he immediately falls into evil pleasures; but children do not have anxieties, so they are idle concerning those things which pertain to them. This is to play.

931. One should notice also that man is naturally social, and this is because one man naturally needs another, and so delights in intimacy. Hence the Philosopher, in Book I of the *Politics*: *every man who is solitary is either better than a man, and is a god; or worse than a man, and is a beast.* Hence it says, **sitting in the marketplace**, because no one wants to play by himself, but rather in the marketplace, where there is a gathering of many people.

932. One should note that it is natural for man that his delight is in some representation; hence if we see something well sculpted, which represents well what it should, then we are delighted. Therefore the children who delight in games always make their games with some representation, either of war, or of some such thing.

Likewise, one should notice that all the affections of an animal come to a term in two passions, namely either at joy or at sorrow.

933. ***Who crying***. This should be seen in this way. Let us set down that some children are on one side, and others on the other side, such that some play an instrument, and others dance; these do one thing, and the others respond to them. If these played, and those did not respond to them according to their form of game, they would be insulted by them; hence they say, **we have piped to you, and you have not danced.**

934. Now nothing so changes the soul as music; hence Boethius in *On Music* recounts the story of a certain man who was arguing with another man in front of Pythagoras, and others were speaking in song. Then Pythagoras made the music change, and the man quieted; hence all were trained in music.

935. So one should note that there is a certain song on account of joy, as is had, *wine and music rejoice the heart* (Sir 40:20); so it says, **we have piped**, i.e., we spoke with the song of joy, **and you have not danced**.

Likewise, it is usual that just as some are changed toward joy, so some are changed toward weeping; hence, *call for the mourning women, and . . . let them hasten and take up a lamentation for us* (Jer 9:17–18). So they say, **we have lamented**, i.e., we made the sorrowful song, **and you have not mourned**.

936. Mystically, by the children are signified the people of the old law, among whom there were some who called men forth to joy, as David, *rejoice in the Lord, O you just* (Ps 32:1); some who called to sorrow, *be converted to me with all your heart, in fasting, and in weeping, and in mourning* (Joel 2:12). Hence they could say, **we have piped**, i.e., we invited you to spiritual joy, and you did not accept it;

lamentavimus, idest invitavimus ad poenitentiam, et vos non acquievistis.

937. *Venit Ioannes* et cetera. Hic adaptat similitudinem. Et

primo adaptat;

secundo rationes assignat.

938. Dupliciter homines attrahuntur ad bonam vitam: quidam enim per speciem sanctitatis, quidam autem per viam familiaritatis. Dominus et Ioannes diviserunt sibi duas vias. Ioannes, immo Dominus per Ioannem, elegit viam austeritatis; per se elegit viam lenitatis: et tamen per nullum sunt conversi. Unde dicit ***venit Ioannes non manducans, neque bibens***: et hoc ad litteram, quia multum abstinens fuit, ***et dicunt: daemonium habet***, sicut hypocritae bonum in malum convertunt. ***Venit Filius hominis manducans, et bibens***, idest differenter utens cibis, et non valet ei, quia non creditis, immo dicitis ***ecce homo vorax, potator vini, publicanorum amicus***; contra illud Prov. cap. XXIII, 20: *noli esse in conviviis potatorum* et cetera.

939. Hic notandum, quod qui observaret dicta hominum, numquam aliquid bene faceret; Eccle. XI, 4: *qui observat ventos, non seminat, et qui considerat nubes, numquam metet.*

940. Sed hic est quaestio. Quare elegit Dominus per se vitam leniorem, et per Ioannem asperiorem monstravit?

Ista ratio est, quia Dominus confirmabat actus suos miraculis; Ioannes autem non faciebat: ideo si nullam haberet excellentiam, non approbaretur eius testimonium, sicut videmus in sanctis, quia unus habet excellentiam in uno, alius in alio; ut Augustinus habuit excellentiam in doctrina, Martinus in miraculis.

Item alia ratio, quia Ioannes purus homo erat, ideo abstinebat se a carnalibus desideriis; Christus autem Deus erat: ideo si austeritatem duceret, non ostenderetur esse homo; ideo humanam vitam magis assumpsit.

Item Ioannes fuit finis Veteris Testamenti, cui gravia imponebantur; sed Christus fuit initium novae legis, quae procedit per viam mansuetudinis.

941. *Et iustificata est sapientia*. Istud potest dupliciter legi. Uno modo retorquendo ad utrumque quod dictum est de Ioanne et Christo; et tunc est sensus: quando homo facit quod debet, et alius non corrigitur, tunc salvat animam suam, et iustificatur in sermonibus suis. *Iustificata est sapientia*, hoc est Filius Dei, sive Christus, idest iusta apparuit filiis suis, quia exhibuit Iudaeis quod debuit: abstinentiam per Ioannem, mansuetudinem per Christum.

Vel aliter potest dici. Ita dicant filii diaboli, quod ***vorax est et potator vini***; sed filii sapientiae intelligunt quod non est vita in cibo et poto, sed in aequalitate

we have lamented, i.e., we invited you to penance, and you did not agree.

937. *For John came*. Here he applies the likeness. And

first, he applies it;

second, he gives the reasons.

938. Men are drawn to a good life in two ways: for some are drawn by the appearance of holiness, and some by way of intimacy. The Lord and John divided the two ways between them. John, or rather the Lord through John, chose the way of austerity; he chose the way of leniency for himself; and yet they were not converted by either. Hence he says, ***for John came neither eating nor drinking***, and this literally, because he practiced much abstinence, ***and they say: he has a devil***, as hypocrites turn good into evil. ***The Son of man came eating and drinking***, i.e., using food differently, and it did him no good, because you did not believe, but rather you say, ***behold a man who is a glutton and a wine drinker, a friend of publicans and sinners***; contrary to, *be not in the feasts of great drinkers* (Prov 23:20).

939. Here one should notice that one who paid attention to the sayings of men would never do anything good; *he who observes the wind, will not sow: and he who consideres the clouds, will never reap* (Eccl 11:4).

940. But there is a question here. Why did the Lord choose for himself the more lenient way, and showed the severe way through John?

The reason for this is that the Lord confirmed his own actions with miracles, but John did not work miracles. Therefore, if he had had no excellence, his testimony would not have been accepted, as we observe in the saints, because one has excellence in one thing, another in another; as Augustine has excellence in teaching, Martin in miracles.

Likewise another reason, because John was a mere man, so he withheld himself from carnal desires; but Christ was God, so if he had led a life of austerity, he would not have shown himself to be a man. Therefore he took up more the human life.

Likewise, John was the end of the Old Testament, on which heavy burdens were laid; but Christ was the beginning of the new law, which proceeds by way of gentleness.

941. *And wisdom is justified*. This can be read in two ways. One way, by referring back both to what was said about John and about Christ, and then the sense is this: when a man does what he should, and another is not corrected, then he saves his own soul, and is justified in his words. ***Wisdom is justified***, this wisdom is the Son of God, or Christ, i.e., he appears just to his children, because he has shown the Jew what he should have, abstinence through John, gentleness through Christ.

Or it can be read in another way. The devil's children say that he is ***a glutton and a wine drinker***; but wisdom's children understand that life is not in food and drink, but

animi, utendo cibo pro loco et tempore, et abstinendo similiter quando decet, ita quod non excedant in multo, nec deficiant in pauco, ut dicit Apostolus ad Phil. IV, 12: *ubique, et in omnibus institutus sum, et satiari, et esurire, et abundare, et penuriam pati.* Ideo plenam iustitiam non videretur ostendere, si totaliter abstineret, quia crederetur tota iustitia esse in abstinentia; sed in hoc non consistit, sed in animi aequalitate.

Et nota quod dicit *sapientia*, quia uti cibis, vel abstinere secundum moderationem sapientiae est ut abstineat quando debet, et ubi debet.

in evenness of soul, by using food in its place and time, and likewise by abstaining when it is becoming, such that they do not exceed in too much, nor fall short in too little, as the Apostle says, *everywhere, and in all things I am instructed both to be full, and to be hungry; both to abound, and to suffer need* (Phil 4:12). Therefore it does not seem to show full justice if one abstains totally, because he believes that the whole of justice is in abstinence; but it does not consist in this, but in evenness of soul.

And notice that he says, *wisdom*, because to use food or to abstain according to moderation belongs to wisdom, that one may abstain when he should and where he should.

Lecture 3

11:20 Tunc coepit exprobrare civitatibus in quibus factae sunt plurimae virtutes eius, quia non egissent poenitentiam. [n. 943]

11:21 Vae tibi, Corazaim! Vae tibi, Bethsaida! Quia si in Tyro et Sidone factae essent virtutes, quae factae sunt in vobis, olim in cilicio et cinere poenitentiam egissent. [n. 945]

11:22 Verumtamen dico vobis: Tyro et Sidoni remissius erit in die iudicii quam vobis. [n. 949]

11:23 Et tu, Capharnaum, numquid usque in caelum exaltaberis? Usque in infernum descendes. Quia si in Sodomis factae fuissent virtutes quae factae sunt in te, forte mansissent usque in hanc diem. [n. 952]

11:24 Verumtamen dico vobis, quia terrae Sodomorum remissius erit in die iudicii quam tibi. [n. 954]

11:25 In illo tempore respondens Iesus dixit: confiteor tibi, Pater, Domine caeli et terrae, quia abscondisti haec a sapientibus et prudentibus, et revelasti ea parvulis. [n. 955]

11:26 Ita, Pater, quoniam sic fuit placitum ante te. [n. 962]

11:27 Omnia mihi tradita sunt a Patre meo. Et nemo novit Filium nisi Pater: neque Patrem quis novit nisi Filius, et cui voluerit Filius revelare. [n. 963]

11:28 Venite ad me omnes qui laboratis, et onerati estis, et ego reficiam vos. [n. 967]

11:29 Tollite iugum meum super vos, et discite a me, quia mitis sum, et humilis corde, et invenietis requiem animabus vestris: [n. 969]

11:20 Τότε ἤρξατο ὀνειδίζειν τὰς πόλεις ἐν αἷς ἐγένοντο αἱ πλεῖσται δυνάμεις αὐτοῦ, ὅτι οὐ μετενόησαν·

11:21 οὐαί σοι, Χοραζίν, οὐαί σοι, Βηθσαϊδά· ὅτι εἰ ἐν Τύρῳ καὶ Σιδῶνι ἐγένοντο αἱ δυνάμεις αἱ γενόμεναι ἐν ὑμῖν, πάλαι ἂν ἐν σάκκῳ καὶ σποδῷ μετενόησαν.

11:22 πλὴν λέγω ὑμῖν, Τύρῳ καὶ Σιδῶνι ἀνεκτότερον ἔσται ἐν ἡμέρᾳ κρίσεως ἢ ὑμῖν.

11:23 καὶ σύ, Καφαρναούμ, μὴ ἕως οὐρανοῦ ὑψωθήσῃ; ἕως ᾅδου καταβήσῃ· ὅτι εἰ ἐν Σοδόμοις ἐγενήθησαν αἱ δυνάμεις αἱ γενόμεναι ἐν σοί, ἔμεινεν ἂν μέχρι τῆς σήμερον.

11:24 πλὴν λέγω ὑμῖν ὅτι γῇ Σοδόμων ἀνεκτότερον ἔσται ἐν ἡμέρᾳ κρίσεως ἢ σοί.

11:25 Ἐν ἐκείνῳ τῷ καιρῷ ἀποκριθεὶς ὁ Ἰησοῦς εἶπεν· ἐξομολογοῦμαί σοι, πάτερ, κύριε τοῦ οὐρανοῦ καὶ τῆς γῆς, ὅτι ἔκρυψας ταῦτα ἀπὸ σοφῶν καὶ συνετῶν καὶ ἀπεκάλυψας αὐτὰ νηπίοις·

11:26 ναὶ ὁ πατήρ, ὅτι οὕτως εὐδοκία ἐγένετο ἔμπροσθέν σου.

11:27 Πάντα μοι παρεδόθη ὑπὸ τοῦ πατρός μου, καὶ οὐδεὶς ἐπιγινώσκει τὸν υἱὸν εἰ μὴ ὁ πατήρ, οὐδὲ τὸν πατέρα τις ἐπιγινώσκει εἰ μὴ ὁ υἱὸς καὶ ᾧ ἐὰν βούληται ὁ υἱὸς ἀποκαλύψαι.

11:28 Δεῦτε πρός με πάντες οἱ κοπιῶντες καὶ πεφορτισμένοι, κἀγὼ ἀναπαύσω ὑμᾶς.

11:29 ἄρατε τὸν ζυγόν μου ἐφ᾽ ὑμᾶς καὶ μάθετε ἀπ᾽ ἐμοῦ, ὅτι πραΰς εἰμι καὶ ταπεινὸς τῇ καρδίᾳ, καὶ εὑρήσετε ἀνάπαυσιν ταῖς ψυχαῖς ὑμῶν·

11:20 Then he began to upbraid the cities wherein were done most of his miracles, for they had not done penance. [n. 943]

11:21 Woe to you, Corozain, woe to you, Bethsaida: for if in Tyre and Sidon had been wrought the miracles that have been wrought in you, they would have long ago done penance in sackcloth and ashes. [n. 945]

11:22 But I say unto you, it will be more tolerable for Tyre and Sidon in the day of judgment, than for you. [n. 949]

11:23 And you Capernaum, will you be exalted up to heaven? You will go down unto hell. For if in Sodom had been wrought the miracles that have been wrought in you, perhaps it would have remained unto this day. [n. 952]

11:24 But I say unto you, that it will be more tolerable for the land of Sodom in the day of judgment, than for you. [n. 954]

11:25 At that time Jesus answered and said: I confess to you, O Father, Lord of heaven and earth, because you have hidden these things from the wise and prudent, and have revealed them to the little ones. [n. 955]

11:26 Yes, Father; for it has seemed good in your sight. [n. 962]

11:27 All things are delivered to me by my Father. And no one knows the Son, but the Father: neither does any one know the Father, but the Son, and he to whom it has pleased the Son to reveal him. [n. 963]

11:28 Come to me, all you who labor and are burdened, and I will refresh you. [n. 967]

11:29 Take my yoke upon you, and learn from me, because I am meek, and humble of heart: and you will find rest for your souls. [n. 969]

11:30 iugum enim meum suave est, et onus meum leve. [n. 972]

11:30 ὁ γὰρ ζυγός μου χρηστὸς καὶ τὸ φορτίον μου ἐλαφρόν ἐστιν.

11:30 **For my yoke is sweet and my burden light.** [n. 972]

---

942. Supra satisfecit discipulis Ioannis, nunc exprobrat non credentibus: et duo facit.

Primo describitur factum Domini;

secundo verba ipsius, ibi **vae tibi, Corozaim** et cetera.

943. Dicit ergo primo **tunc coepit exprobrare civitatibus** et cetera. Exprobratio est respectu beneficiorum, et respectu datorum. Magnum enim beneficium fecerat Dominus, quia sui praesentia eos illustraverat; unde ingrati erant, et ideo merito exprobrabiles; unde Mich. VI, 3: *popule meus, quid feci tibi, aut quid molestus fui tibi? Quasi dicat, nihil.* Et non exprobravit eos quod peccata egissent, sed quod poenitentiam non fecissent: unde eis conveniebat quod dicitur Iob XXIV, 23: *dedit ei locum poenitentiae, et ipse abutitur eo in superbiam.* Et Rom. cap. II, 4: *an ignoras quod benignitas Dei te ad poenitentiam adducit?*

944. Sed hic est quaestio litteralis, quia Lucas istud alio ordine ponit. Ponit enim in missione discipulorum; iste hic.

Respondet Augustinus. Videtur quod Lucas magis ordinem servet historiae: hic autem seriem memoriae.

Sed tunc obiicitur quod hic dicitur **tunc**; ergo videtur quod hic magis series texatur historiae.

Respondet Augustinus, quod **tunc** tempus indefinitum dicit. Vel aliter potest dici quod bis dixit haec verba, et ideo potuit esse et **tunc** secundum istum, et **tunc** secundum Lucam.

945. **Vae tibi, Corozaim** et cetera. Hic ponuntur verba Domini. Et

primo fit sermo de civitatibus suffragancis,

secundo de metropoli, ibi **et tu, Capharnaum** et cetera. Et

primo comparat culpam ad culpam;

secundo poenam ad poenam, ibi **verumtamen dico vobis** et cetera.

946. Dicit ergo **vae tibi, Corozaim** et cetera. Istae autem sunt civitates sive villae in Galilaea, ubi multa signa Dominus fecerat, et tamen non erant conversae. Ideo dicit **vae tibi** et cetera.

Sed quid est quod facit Dominus? Immo scriptum est Rom. XII, 14: *nolite maledicere* et cetera.

Dicendum quod est maledicere formaliter, et materialiter: formaliter nullus debet maledicere, sed materialiter potest.

Unde notandum quod quaedam coniuncta sunt secundum sensum, quae tamen possunt separari

942. Above he satisfied John's disciples; now he reproaches those who do not believe. And Matthew does two things:

first, the Lord's deeds are described;

second, his words, at **woe to you, Corozain.**

943. It says then first, **then began he to upbraid the cities.** The reproach is with regard to benefits, and with regard to gifts. For the Lord had done them a great benefit, because he had illuminated them with his presence; hence they were ungrateful, and so were deserving of reproach. Hence, *O my people, what have I done to you, or in what have I molested you?* (Mich 6:3), as though to say, *in nothing.* And he did not reproach them because they had committed sins, but because they had not done penance; hence what is said befits them: *God has given him place for penance, and he abuses it unto pride* (Job 24:23). And, *do you not know that the benignity of God leads you to penance?* (Rom 2:4).

944. But here there is a literal question, because Luke 10:13 puts this in a different order. For he puts this in the sending of the disciples; this Evangelist puts it here.

Augustine responds. It seems that Luke preserved more the order of history, but this author the sequence of memory.

But next it is objected that it says here, **then**; therefore it seems that the sequence of history is rather put together here.

Augustine responds that **then** bespeaks an indefinite time. Or otherwise it can be said that he said these words twice, and so there could be both a **then** according to this author, and a **then** according to Luke.

945. **Woe to you, Corozain.** Here the Lord's words are set down. And

first, there is a word about the supporting cities;

second, about the metropolis, there, **and you Capernaum.** And

first, he compares guilt to guilt;

second, punishment to punishment, at **but I say unto you.**

946. He says then, **woe to you, Corozain.** Now, these are cities or villages in Galilee, where the Lord had worked many signs, and yet they were not converted. This is why he said, **woe to you.**

But why does the Lord do this? Rather, it is written, *bless, and curse not* (Rom 12:14).

One should describe what it is to curse formally, and materially: formally, no one should curse, but materially one can.

Hence one should note that certain things are connected in sensation, which nevertheless can be separated in

secundum intellectum, ut in pomo est odor et sapor, quae non possunt separari secundum sensum, licet secundum intellectum. Similiter velle istum non puniri, et velle ordinem iustitiae, non possunt simul esse, nisi secundum intellectum. Unde si maledico isti, quia delector in eius malo, malum est. Si autem non pro malo eius, sed pro ordine iustitiae, sic est bonum. Unde verbum Domini non erat verbum delectantis, sed opus iustitiae nuntiantis.

947. *Vae tibi, Corozaim.* Corozaim interpretatur 'ministerium in eum', Bethsaida 'domus fructuum'. Cui plus committitur, ab eo plus exigitur.

Et quare plus ei exhibuit? Quia ibi suum ministerium implevit: ideo *revelata est ira Dei de caelo super omnem impietatem, et iniustitiam hominum eorum qui veritatem Dei in iustitia retinent*, Rom. I, 18.

Bethsaida 'domus fructuum'. Si igitur multum fructum fecit ibi Dominus, et non faciunt poenitentiam, quid erit eis? Is. V, 4: *expectavi ut faceret uvas, et fecit labruscas.* **Vae tibi . . . quia si in Tyro et Sidone factae essent virtutes, quae factae sunt in vobis, olim in cilicio et cinere poenitentiam egissent. Olim**, idest a longinquis temporibus.

948. Et notate modum poenitentiae, quia **in cinere et cilicio**, quia duo inducunt ad poenitentiam. Unum recordatio delictorum; et hoc significatur in cilicio, quod fit de pilis caprarum: istud enim animal immolabatur pro peccato. Aliud est consideratio mortis et conditio humanae fragilitatis; unde dicitur Gen. III, 19: *pulvis es, et in pulverem reverteris.* Et Iob ult., 6: *ideo reprehendo me, et ago poenitentiam in favilla et cinere.*

949. **Verumtamen dico vobis: Tyro et Sidoni remissius erit in die iudicii quam vobis.** Hic comparat culpam ad culpam: quia si inventi sunt graviores in culpa, deterius erit eis: quia quod audierunt, non fecerunt: ideo gravius erit, secundum quod dicitur Io. cap. XV, 22: *si non venissem, et non eis locutus fuissem, peccatum non haberent.*

950. Notandum quod ex istis verbis tres errores excludit. Quidam dicebant omnia peccata paria, et similiter supplicia; hoc excludit cum dicit, quia istis erit deterius quam Tyro et Sidoni.

Item quidam dixerunt quod non salvabuntur nisi quos praescivit: quia si praedicaretur eis, converterentur; hoc excludit cum dicit quod Tyro et Sidoni male erit, sed tamen deterius istis, quibus nuntiatum est regnum

the understanding, such as smell and flavor are in an apple, which cannot be separated according to sensation, although they can be in the understanding. Similarly, to will that this man not be punished and to will the order of justice cannot both be at the same time, except in understanding. Hence if I curse this man because I delight in his evil, it is bad. But if it is not for his evil, but for the order of justice, in this way it is good. Hence the Lord's word was not the word of one who delights, but the work of one who announces justice.

947. *Woe to you Corozain*. Corazain is interpreted 'service unto him', Bethsaida 'house of fruits'. To whom more is entrusted, of him more is required.

And why did he point to this city more? Because he carried out his own ministry; therefore *the wrath of God is revealed from heaven against all ungodliness and injustice of those men that detain the truth of God in injustice* (Rom 1:18).

Bethsaida, 'house of fruits'. If then the Lord produced much fruit there, and they did not do penance, what will there be for them? *Was it that I looked that it should bring forth grapes, and it has brought forth wild grapes?* (Isa 5:4). **Woe to you . . . for if in Tyre and Sidon had been wrought the miracles that have been wrought in you, they would have long ago done penance in sackcloth and ashes. Long ago**, i.e., in a far distant time.

948. And notice the manner of penance, that is **in sackcloth and ashes**, because two things lead to penance. One is the remembrance of past misdeeds; and this is signified in sackcloth, which is made from the hairs of a she-goat, for this animal was sacrificed for sin. The other is the consideration of death and the condition of human fragility; hence, *you are dust and into dust you will return* (Gen 3:19). And, *therefore I reprehend myself, and do penance in dust and ashes* (Job 42:6).

949. **But I say unto you, it will be more tolerable for Tyre and Sidon in the day of judgment, than for you**. Here he compares guilt to guilt, for if they are found heavier in guilt, it will be worse for them, because they did not do what they had heard. Therefore it will be heavier, in accord with what is said, *if I had not come, and spoken to them, they would not have sin; but now they have no excuse for their sin* (John 15:22).

950. One should note that three errors are excluded by these words. Some men said that all sins are equal, and similarly all punishments; he excludes this when he says that it will be worse for them than for Tyre and Sidon.

Likewise, some had said that only those will be saved whom he foreknew; for if it had been preached to them, they would have converted. He excludes this when he says that it will be bad for Tyre and Sidon, but nevertheless worse for

Dei. Unde Augustinus in libro *Perseverantiae*: *non remunerat Dominus pro his quae fecisset, sed pro his quae facit.*

Item removet tertium errorem, quia dicebant quidam quod Dominus misit prophetas et praedicatores Iudaeis, et non aliis: quia sciebat quod alii non reciperent. Sed hoc excludit, quia si praedicaretur eis, poenitentiam agerent.

951. Sed tunc restat quaestio: quia si Iudaei non credebant, videretur quod Dominus non bene fecisset, cum non misit ad eos, si illi credidissent.

Dicit Gregorius, quod scire secreta Dei non est hominis; tamen secundum quod videtur, quia promissum erat patribus, ideo ad confirmandas promissiones patrum primo praedicavit Iudaeis. Item ut ostenderetur iustior eorum condemnatio, ideo eis praedicavit, et post aliis discipulos misit.

Remigius solvit sic: quia licet ex Tyro et Sidone plures credidissent in maiori multitudine; tamen apud eos erant aliqui perversi, qui nondum erant parati ad credendum; ideo non misit primo ad eos.

Tertiam expositionem ponit Augustinus, quod praescivit Dominus, quia si credidissent, non perseverassent in tempore passionis; et ideo ad eos non misit.

Alia est expositio Augustini, quia praedestinatio est praescientia beneficiorum Dei. Unde quaecumque pertinent ad salutem, sunt effectus praedestinationis in praedestinatis: unde diversimode distribuit Dominus dona sua, quia quibusdam dat cor docile, et pronitatem ad bene agendum; sed hoc non sufficit nisi sit instructor. Item aliquando est instructor, sed cor est durum: et sicut illis non sufficit facilitas ad credendum, sic istis nocet cor durum. Unde quaerere quare istum elegit, non illum, fatuum est quaerere; unde Augustinus: *quare trahat hunc, et non illum, noli iudicare, si non vis errare.*

Unde melius est ut totum torqueatur ad ordinationem Dei, quam ad humana merita.

952. ***Et tu, Capharnaum, numquid usque in caelum exaltaberis?*** In parte ista exprobrat civitati solemniori. Et

primo exprobrat superbiam, et hoc quia magni magis superbiunt;

secundo exprobrat eorum impoenitentiam, ibi ***quia si in Sodomis factae fuissent virtutes*** et cetera.

953. Circa primum primo exprobrat superbiam; secundo minatur poenam.

those to whom the kingdom of God was preached. Hence Augustine says in the book *Perseverance: the Lord does not reward the things a man would have done, but the things which he does.*

Likewise, he removes a third error, for some said that the Lord sent prophets and preachers to the Jews and not to others, because he knew that the others would not receive them. But he excludes this, because if it had been preached to them, they would have done penance.

951. But then a question remains, because if the Jews did not believe, it would seem that the Lord did not work well, when he did not send to those others, if they would have believed.

Gregory says that it does not belong to man to know the secrets of God; yet, following what seems to be true, since the promise was made to the fathers, he first preached to the Jews, to confirm the promises of the fathers. Likewise, that their condemnation might be shown to be more just, he preached to them and afterward sent the disciples to the others.

Remigius resolves it this way: although more would have believed in a greater multitude from Tyre and Sidon, yet there were among them some perverse men, who were not yet prepared to believe; for this reason he did not send to them first.

Augustine sets down a third explanation, that the Lord foreknew that if they had believed, they would not have persevered in the time of the passion; and therefore he did not send to them.

Augustine has another explanation, that predestination is the foreknowledge of God's benefits. Hence whatever things pertain to salvation are effects of predestination in the predestined. Hence the Lord distributes his gifts in different ways, for to some he gives a docile heart, and an inclination to working well; but this is not enough unless there is an instructor. It is similar when there is an instructor, but the heart is hard. And just as a readiness to believe is not enough for these men, so a hard heart injures those. Therefore, to seek why he chose this man and not that one is foolish. Hence Augustine: *why he draws this man and not that one, do not wish to judge, if you do not wish to err.*

Hence it is better that the whole thing be referred to God's ordination than to human merits.

952. ***And you Capernaum, will you be exalted up to heaven?*** In this part he reproaches the more solemn city. And

first, he reproaches pride, and this because the great are more proud;

second, he reproaches their impenitence, at ***for if in Sodom had been wrought the miracles.***

953. Concerning the first, he first reproaches pride; second, a punishment is threatened.

Dicit ergo *et tu, Capharnaum* et cetera. Et est ibi duplex littera. Una interrogative *numquid usque in caelum exaltaberis?* Alia littera: *tu es quae exaltata es usque in caelum*: quia a Domino exaltata est, et praesentia Domini, et multis meritis; Lc. IV, 23: *quanta audivimus facta in Capharnaum, fac et hic in patria tua.* Item a teipsa exaltata es: unde tu numquid exaltaberis per superbiam, vel doctrinam meam?

Quantumcumque exaltata fueris, tamen *ad inferos descendes*: Iob XX, 28: *detrahetur in die furoris domini; haec est pars hominis impii a Deo.* Unde tu quae videris tangere caelum, detraheris ad infernum. Unde propria poena superbi est deiectio; Is. XIV, v. 14 contra illum qui dicebat: *ascendam ad astra caeli*, sequitur, *ad infernum detraheris.*

954. Consequenter arguit de impoenitentia. Et primo comparat quantum ad culpam; secundo quantum ad poenam.

Dicit ergo *quia si in Sodomis* et cetera. Et quare hoc dicit? Ad significandum libertatem arbitrii: quia *ante hominem vita et mors.* Nullus illos monuit: quamvis enim Lot inter illos esset, tamen non fecit miracula. Sed isti viderunt Dominum docentem, et miracula facientem, ideo et cetera. Capharnaum interpretatur 'villa dulcissima,' et per hanc interpretatur Ierusalem.

Verumtamen dico vobis: in die iudicii gravior erit poena tua quam illius terrae, quae subversa est. Vel potest intelligi de habitantibus; Lc. XII, 47: *servus sciens voluntatem domini sui, et non faciens, vapulabit multis.*

955. *In illo tempore respondens Iesus dixit: confiteor tibi, Pater* et cetera. Supra Dominus redarguerat infidelitatem turbarum; nunc gratias agit de fide discipulorum et aliorum credentium. Et

primo reddit gratias Patri tamquam auctori;

secundo ostendit eamdem potestatem se habere, ibi *omnia mihi tradita sunt a Patre meo.*

956. Dicit ergo *in illo tempore*, scilicet quo accidit etc. *respondit*: sed cui respondit? Convenit ei quod dicitur Iob XV, v. 2: *numquid sapiens respondet quasi in ventum loquens?* Non. Unde respondet tacitae obiectioni.

Posset enim dicere aliquis: isti non credunt quibus praedicasti; alii autem credidissent, si praedicatum fuisset illis. Ideo respondet, et responsione redarguit quosdam qui causas electionis inquisierunt, quare videlicet illi elevati sunt in caelum, et isti demersi sunt in profundum; ut Origenes, qui ponebat quod electio ex meritis est. Sed hic reprobat hoc, ostendens quod hoc attribuendum est divinae voluntati.

957. Dicit ergo *confiteor tibi, Pater* et cetera.

He says then, *and you Capernaum*. And there are two ways of reading the text here. One, the interrogative: *will you be exalted up to heaven?* Another way: *it is you who are exalted up to heaven*, because it was exalted by the Lord, and the Lord's presence, and by many merits. *As great things as we have heard done in Capernaum, do also here in your own country* (Luke 4:23). Similarly, you are exalted by yourself; hence will you be exalted by pride or my teaching?

However exalted you have been, yet *you will go down unto hell*. He will be pulled down in the day of God's wrath. *This is the portion of a wicked man from God* (Job 20:28–29). Hence you who have seemed to touch heaven will be dragged down into the depth. Hence the proper punishment of pride is being cast down; against him who says, *I will ascend above the height of the clouds*, there follows *but yet you will be brought down to hell* (Isa 14:14).

954. Next, he accuses the city of impenitence. And first, he makes a comparison with regard to guilt; second, with regard to punishment.

He says then, *for if in Sodom*. And why does he say this? To indicate freedom of judgment, because *before man is life and death* (Sir 15:18). No one warned them, for although Lot was among them, yet he did not work miracles. But these men saw the Lord teaching, and working miracles, therefore. Capernaum is interpreted 'most sweet village', and through this is interpreted as Jerusalem.

But I say unto you: in the day of judgment, your punishment will be heavier than the punishment of that land, which was buried. Or it can be understood as about the inhabitants; *and that servant who knew the will of his lord, and prepared not himself, and did not according to his will, will be beaten with many stripes* (Luke 12:47).

955. *At that time Jesus answered and said: I confess to you, O Father*. Above, the Lord had rebuked the unbelief of the crowds; now he gives thanks for the faith of the disciples and the others who believed. And

first, he gives thanks to the Father as to the author;

second, he shows that he himself has the same power, at *all things are delivered to me by my Father*.

956. *At that time*, i.e., the time in which it happened, *Jesus answered*. But to whom did he answer? What Job says is applicable to him, *will a wise man answer as if he were speaking in the wind?* (Job 15:2). No. Hence he is responding to an unmentioned objection.

For someone might say: those to whom thou didst preach do not believe, while others would have believed, if it had been preached to them. So he responds, and by his response refutes certain men who inquire after the causes of election, namely why these are lifted into heaven, and those are submerged into the deep; such as Origin, who held that election is out of merit. But here he rebukes this, showing that this should be attributed to the divine will.

957. He says then, *I confess to you, O Father*.

Notandum, quod triplex est confessio. Scilicet fidei; unde Rom. X, 10 dicitur: *corde creditur ad iustitiam, ore autem confessio fit ad salutem.* Item confessio peccatorum; Iac. V, 16: *confitemini alterutrum peccata vestra.* Item confessio gratiarum actionis, de qua Ps. CV, 1: *confitemini Domino, quoniam bonus* et cetera. De hoc intelligitur **confiteor tibi, Pater caeli et terrae**.

958. Duae haereses excluduntur, haeresis scilicet Sabellii, qui non distinguit Filium a Patre; unde dicit **confiteor tibi, Pater** et cetera. Sic confitetur auctoritatem Patris et cetera. Item quia eiusdem naturae. Ideo dicit Patrem suum, contra Arium. Et vere Dominus, quia **Pater caeli et terrae**. Et in Ps. XCIX, v. 3: *scitote quoniam Dominus ipse est Deus: ipse fecit nos, et non ipsi nos.* Et dicitur **Pater**, non quia eum creavit, sed quia eum genuit; Ps. LXXXVIII, 27: *ipse invocavit me: Pater meus es tu.*

959. Et quare gratias agit? Agit gratias super quamdam distinctionem, et ponit sic: **quia abscondisti haec a sapientibus et prudentibus, et revelasti ea parvulis**. Unde hic considerare oportet qui sint parvuli, et qui sapientes, et qui prudentes.

Tripliciter autem dicuntur aliqui 'parvuli.' Ad litteram parvuli dicuntur abiecti; unde in Abdia v. 2: *ecce parvulum dedi te, contemptibilis tu es valde.* Item dicitur 'parvulus' humilitate, quia parva de se sentit. Unde Dominus infra XVIII, 3: **nisi conversi fueritis, et efficiamini ut parvuli, non intrabitis in regnum caelorum**. Item simplicitate: unde Apostolus I Cor. XIV, 20: *malitia parvuli estote.*

Unde potest illud intelligi: quia revelasti ea parvulis et abiectis piscatoribus. Et quare? Apostolus reddit rationem dicens, quod *despecta mundi elegit Deus, ut fortia quaeque confundat.* Augustinus exponit: **parvulis**, idest humilibus, non de se praesumentibus: ubi enim humilitas, ibi sapientia. Hilarius exponit de simplicibus. *In simplicitate quaerite illum*, Sap. I, 1.

960. E contrario sapientes et prudentes, quia in carnali sapientia student; Ier. IX, v. 23: *non glorietur sapiens in sapientia sua.* Istis non revelavit, sed rusticis non confidentibus de sapientia sua; Eccle. VII, 24: *dixi: sapiens efficiar, et ipsa longius recessit a me, multo magis quam erat.* Quare Apostolus ad Rom. X, 3: *ignorantes autem Dei iustitiam, et suam quaerentes statuere, iustitiae Dei non sunt subiecti.* Item per sapientes intelligit superbos iactantes se; et talibus non revelavit. Ad Rom. I, 22: *dicentes se esse sapientes, stulti facti sunt.* Item dicit sapientes secundum carnem viventes, quae carnis

One should note that there are three kinds of confession. Namely that of faith; hence, *for, with the heart, we believe unto justice; but, with the mouth, confession is made unto salvation* (Rom 10:10). Likewise, the confession of sins; *confess therefore your sins one to another* (Jas 5:16). Likewise, the confession of favorable actions; about which, *confess to the Lord, for he is good: for his mercy endures for ever* (Ps 105:1). In this sense is understood *I confess to you, O Father, Lord of heaven and earth*.

958. Two heresies are excluded, namely the heresy of Sabellius, who did not distinguish the Son from the Father; hence he says, *I confess to you, Father*. Thus he confesses the authority of the Father. Likewise, that he is of the same nature; for this reason he calls him his own Father, against Arius. And that he is truly the Lord, because *Father, Lord of heaven and earth*. And, *know that the Lord, he is God: he made us, and not we ourselves* (Ps 99:3). And he is called *Father*, not because he created him, but because he begot him; *he will cry out to me: you are my Father* (Ps 88:27).

959. And why does he give thanks? He gives thanks for a certain distinction, and sets it forth in this way: *because you have hidden these things from the wise and prudent, and have revealed them to the little ones*. Hence it is necessary to consider here who are the little ones, and who the wise men, and who the prudent.

Now, someone is called a 'little one' in three ways. Literally, the downcast are called little ones; hence, *behold I have made you small . . . you are exceeding contemptible* (Obad 1:2). Likewise, one is called a 'little one' from humility, because they perceive themselves as little. Hence the Lord says below, *unless you be converted, and become as little children, you will not enter into the kingdom of heaven* (Matt 18:3). Likewise, from simplicity: hence the Apostle says, *in malice be children* (1 Cor 14:20).

Hence this can be understood: because thou hast revealed these things to the little and downcast fishermen. And why? The Apostle gives a reason, saying that *God chose the despised of the world, that he might confound all the strong* (1 Cor 1:27–28). Augustine explains it this way: *to the little ones*, i.e., to the humble, the ones who do not presume from themselves; for where there is humility, there is wisdom. Hilary explains it as about the simple. *Seek him in simplicity of heart* (Wis 1:1).

960. The wise and the prudent are quite the contrary, because they busy themselves in carnal wisdom; *let not the wise man glory in his wisdom* (Jer 9:23). He did not reveal these things to them, but to country people who did not trust in their own wisdom; *I have said: I will be wise: and it departed farther from me, much more than it was* (Eccl 7:24). Which is why the Apostle says, *for they, not knowing the justice of God, and seeking to establish their own, have not submitted themselves to the justice of God* (Rom 10:3). Similarly, by the wise he understands proud men who thrust themselves forward; and he did not reveal these things to

sunt quaerentes, non quae Dei, Phil. II, v. 21. Item *sapientes sunt, ut faciant mala, et bene facere nescierunt*, Ier. IV, 22. *Et revelasti*. Ad Eph. IV, 17: *ut non ambuletis sicut et gentes ambulant in vanitate sensus sui.*

Unde *abscondisti a sapientibus*, revelando parvulis. Sapientiam abscondit a sapientibus, non apponendo gratiam. Unde dicitur ad Rom. I, 28: *tradidit eos in reprobum sensum.*

961. Sed quid est quod gratias reddit, quod abscondit?

Dico quod hoc non facit, ut gaudeat de caecitate eorum, sed de iudicio Dei, qui ita sapienter ordinat. Et quare? Hic non est quaerenda causa: in talibus enim Dei voluntas pro causa est.

962. *Ita, Pater, quia sic placitum est ante te*. Artifex bene potest assignare causam quare lapides quosdam in fundamento, quosdam superius posuit; sed quod hunc posuerit hic, alium ibi, non est alia causa nisi voluntas sua. Sic quod Dominus aliquos salvet, hoc est ad suam misericordiam, quod hos damnet, ad iustitiam. Sed quare circa illum sic misericorditer agit, potius quam circa alium, hoc solum pertinet ad suam voluntatem. Unde ad Rom. IX, 18: *cuius vult miseretur, et quem vult indurat*. Unde sic facit propter beneplacitum. In Ps. CXVIII, v. 108: *beneplacitum fac, domine* et cetera.

963. *Omnia mihi tradita sunt a Patre meo*. Egerat gratias Patri, quia secreta parvulis revelat: posset aliquis credere, quod non posset ipse revelare, unde hoc removens

primo tangit magnitudinem suae potestatis;

secundo invitat ad se quasi dicat: ecce sum potens; *venite* ergo *ad me* et cetera.

Et primo duo facit.

Primo ponit aequalitatem Filii ad Patrem;

secundo spiritualiter applicat ad id de quo agebatur, ibi *et nemo novit Filium nisi Pater.*

964. Dicit ergo: posset dicere aliquis: numquid omnia potest? Respondet *omnia tradita sunt mihi*. Et attende aequalitatem, sed tamen a Patre originem, quod est contra Sabellium.

Sed quid est quod dicit *omnia*? Tripliciter potest exponi. *Omnia*, hoc est: supra omnem creaturam. Infra ult. 18: *data est mihi omnis potestas in caelo et in terra*. Vel *omnia*, idest electi et praedestinati, qui specialiter sunt dati; Io. XVII, 6: *tui erant et eos tradidisti mihi*. Item *omnia*, scilicet intrinseca, idest omnem perfectionem divinitatis; Io. V, v. 26: *sicut Pater habet vitam in semetipso,*

such men. *For professing themselves to be wise, they became fools* (Rom 1:22). Similarly, he calls *wise* those who live according to the flesh, who are seeking after the things which are of the flesh, not the things which are of God (Phil 2:21). Likewise, *they are wise to do evil, but to do good they have no knowledge* (Jer 4:22). **And have revealed**. That henceforward you walk not as also the gentiles walk in the vanity of their mind (Eph 4:17).

Hence, *you have hid these things from the wise* by revealing them to little ones. He hides wisdom from the wise, by not supplying grace. Hence it is said, *God delivered them up to a reprobate sense* (Rom 1:28).

961. But why does he give thanks that he has hidden these things?

I say that he does not do this so as to rejoice over their blindness, but rather over God's judgment, who thus wisely ordered. And why? Here one should not seek a cause, for in such matters the will of God is in place of a cause.

962. *Yes, Father; for so it has seemed good in your sight*. A builder is well able to give a reason why certain stones are in the foundation, while he placed other ones higher; but there is no reason that he should place this one here and the other there but his own will. In this way, that the Lord should save some men is for his mercy; that he should damn these is for justice. But why he acted mercifully with regard to this man rather than with regard to another pertains only to his will. Hence, *therefore he has mercy on whom he will; and whom he will, he hardens* (Rom 9:18). Hence he acts this way on account of his good pleasure. *The free offerings of my mouth make acceptable, O Lord* (Ps 118:108).

963. *All things are delivered to me by my Father*. He had given thanks to the Father, because he revealed secrets to little ones. Someone could think that he himself could not reveal the secrets, hence he excludes this:

first, he touches upon the greatness of his own power;

second, he invites others to himself, as though to say: behold, I have power; *come* then *to me*.

And first, he does two things:

first, he sets out the equality of the Son with the Father;

second, he applies it spiritually to what he was treating, at *and no one knows the Son, but the Father*.

964. It says then: someone could say, can you not do all things? He answers, *all things are delivered to me*. And notice equality, but yet origin from the Father, which is against Sabellius.

But why does he say, *all things*? It can be explained in three ways. *All things*, i.e., above every creature. Below, *all power is given to me in heaven and in earth* (Matt 28:18). Or, *all things*, i.e., the elect and the predestined, who are given in a special way; *yours they were, and to me you gave them* (John 17:6). Likewise, *all things*, i.e., the intrinsic things, i.e., every perfection of the divinity; *for as the Father*

sic Filio dedit vitam habere in semetipso. Et non debemus intelligere carnaliter, quia si dedit, sibi etiam retinuit.

Et haec expositio et Augustini et Hilarii.

Sed posset aliquis dicere: quomodo dedit? Ideo addit modum, cum dicit *a Patre meo*. Unde per generationem hoc recepit.

965. *Et nemo novit Filium nisi Pater*. Modo specialiter ad propositum adaptat, et non solum quantum ad aequalitatem ad Patrem, sed etiam quantum ad consubstantialitatem. Substantia enim Patris superat omnem intelligentiam, cum ipsa essentia Patris dicatur incognoscibilis, sicut substantia Filii. Unde hic notatur aequalitas, et confunditur Arius, qui dicit Patrem invisibilem, Filium autem visibilem.

Et nemo novit Filium nisi Pater. Sed quid est? Nonne sancti noverunt? Dicendum, quod attingendo, vel fide, sed comprehendendo non cognoscunt.

Sed quid est? Nonne Spiritus Sanctus cognoscit? Immo. Sed notandum, quod dictiones exclusivae aliquando adduntur nominibus divinis essentialibus, aliquando personalibus. Et cum adiunguntur personalibus, non excludunt illud quod idem est in natura: unde addita Patri non excludit Filium. Unde ubi dicitur, *regi immortali, invisibili, soli Deo honor et gloria*, I Tim. I, 17, non excluditur alius in natura. Similiter cum dicit hic **nisi Filius**, non excluditur Spiritus Sanctus, qui idem est in natura. Sed cum dicit **nemo novit** etc. intelligitur *nullus homo* **nisi Filius**. Et ita habetur quod novit Filius Patrem. Sed hoc est contra Origenem.

966. Cognoscit enim per comprehensionem. Quia ergo perfecte cognoscit, et est cognoscibilis, ideo habet potestatem revelandi sicut Pater; ideo dicit *et cui voluerit Filius revelare*. Manifestatio enim fit per verbum; Io. XVII, 6: *Pater, manifestavi nomen tuum hominibus* et cetera. Ibid. I, 18: *Deum nemo vidit unquam*. Sed ipse novit: ergo manifestare potuit. Illud ergo quod dixerat de Patre, sibi attribuit. Dixerat enim **abscondisti haec a sapientibus, et revelasti ea parvulis**; sic etiam et Filius potest, ex quo habet eamdem potestatem.

967. *Venite ad me omnes* et cetera. Venite ad mea beneficia. Et primo ponitur invitatio; secundo necessitas invitationis; tertio utilitas.

Dicit ergo **venite ad me**; quod verbum etiam sapientiae est, Eccli. XXIV, 26: *transite ad me omnes qui concupiscitis me et a generationibus meis adimplemini*. Unde appropinquate ad me indocti, quia vult se communicare.

has life in himself, so he has given the Son also to have life in himself (John 5:26). And we should not understand this carnally, because if he gave, he also kept for himself.

And this is the explanation both of Augustine and of Hilary.

But someone could say: how did he give? So he adds the manner, when he says, **by my Father**. Hence he received this through generation.

965. *And no one knows the Son, but the Father*. Now he adapts what he has said in a particular way for his intention, and not only as regards equality with the Father, but also as regards consubstantiality. For the Father's substance is above every understanding, since the Father's very essence is said to be unknowable, just as is the Son's substance. Hence equality is indicated here, and Arius is confounded, who says the Father is invisible, but the Son visible.

Neither does any one know the Father, but the Son. But what is this? Do not the saints know him? One should say that they know him by touch, or by faith, but they do not know him by comprehension.

But what is this? Does not the Holy Spirit know him? Yes indeed. But one should note that exclusive expressions are sometimes added to essential divine names, sometimes to personal. And when they are adjoined to personal names, they do not exclude that which is the same in nature; hence when they are added to the Father, it does not exclude the Son. Hence where it says, *now to the king of ages, immortal, invisible, the only God, be honor and glory for ever and ever* (1 Tim 1:17), another person in the same nature is not excluded. Similarly, when he says here **but the Son**, the Holy Spirit is not excluded, who is the same in nature. But when he says, **neither does any one know**, there is understood *no man* **but the Son**. And so it is stated that the Son knows the Father; but this is against Origen.

966. For he knows by comprehension. Since therefore he knows perfectly, and is knowable, therefore he has the power of revealing just as the Father does; and so he says, **and he to whom it please the Son to reveal him**. For manifestation comes about through a word; *I have manifested your name to all men* (John 17:6). *No man has seen God at any time* (John 1:18). But he knew; therefore he was able to manifest. So he attributes to himself what he had said about the Father. For he had said that **you have hidden these things from the wise and prudent, and have revealed them to the little ones**; so also the Son can, from the fact that he has the same power.

967. *Come to me, all*. Come to my benefits. And first is set down the invitation; second, the necessity for the invitation; third, the usefulness.

He says then, **come to me**; which are also the words of wisdom: *come over to me, all you who desire me, and be filled with my fruits* (Sir 24:26). Hence, *draw near to me, you unlearned* (Sir 51:31), because he wishes to communicate himself.

Sed quae est necessitas? Quia absque me homines laborant nimis; *qui laboratis*. Specialiter hoc potest convenire Iudaeis, quia laborabant in oneribus legum et mandatorum, ut habetur Act. XV, 10: *hoc est onus quod nec nos, nec patres nostri portare potuimus*. Item generaliter quantum ad omnes qui laborant propter humanitatis fragilitatem; Ps. LXXXVII, 16: *pauper sum ego, et in laboribus a iuventute mea*. *Et onerati estis*, onere scilicet peccatorum. Ps. XXXVII, 5: *iniquitates meae sicut onus grave gravatae sunt super me*.

Et quid habebimus si veniamus ad te? *Ego reficiam vos*. Io. VII, 37: *si quis sitit, veniat ad me, et bibat*.

968. Consequenter exponit invitationem.

Et primo exponit;

secundo rationem assignat, ibi *iugum enim meum suave est*.

969. Circa primum sic. Posuerat invitationem, et ad quid; nunc vult ostendere quae sit illa invitatio, dicens *tollite iugum meum super vos*. Sed quid est? Tu dicis, quod vis nos reficere, et a nobis auferre laborem, et statim praecipis ferre iugum? Credebamus esse sine iugo. Dico quod verum est, sine iugo peccati; Is. IX, 4: *iugum enim oneris eius, et virgam humeri eius, et sceptrum exactoris eius superasti*. Non quod sitis sine lege Dei, sed sine iugo peccati; Ps. II, 3: *proiiciamus a nobis iugum ipsorum*. Osee ult., 2: *convertere, Israel, ad Dominum Deum tuum, quoniam corruisti in iniquitate tua* et cetera. Ad Rom. VI, 18: *liberati a peccato, servi facti estis iustitiae*. *Tollite* ergo *iugum meum*, scilicet documenta Evangelica.

Et dicit *iugum*; sicut enim iugum colla boum ad arandum iungit et ligat, sic doctrina Evangelica utrumque populum ligat ad iugum suum.

970. Et quid est illud *discite a me quia mitis sum et humilis corde*? Tota enim lex nova consistit in duobus: in mansuetudine et humilitate. Per mansuetudinem homo ordinatur ad proximum. Unde Ps. CXXXI, v. 1: *memento, Domine, David, et omnis mansuetudinis eius*. Per humilitatem ordinatur ad se, et ad Deum. Is. LXVI, 2: *super quem requiescet spiritus meus nisi super quietum et humilem?* Unde humilitas facit hominem capacem Dei.

971. Item dixerat *et ego reficiam vos*. Quae est ista refectio? *Invenietis requiem animabus vestris*. Corpus enim non reficitur, quamdiu afficitur, et quando ulterius non afficitur, tunc dicitur refectum. Et sicut fames in corpore, sic desiderium in mente: unde impletio desideriorum est refectio; Ps. CII, 5: *qui replet in bonis desiderium tuum*. Et haec requies est requies animae; Eccli. LI, 35: *modicum laboravi, et inveni multam requiem*. Sic in mundo mansueti non quietantur: unde

But why is it necessary? Because without me men labor greatly; *you who labor*. This applies in a special way to the Jews, because they were laboring in the burdens of the law and the commandments; as is said, *this is a yoke upon the necks of the disciples, which neither our fathers nor we have been able to bear* (Acts 15:10). Likewise, it applies in a general way as regards all who labor because of the fragility of humanity; *I am poor, and in labors from my youth* (Ps 87:16). *And are burdened*, namely with the burden of sins. *For my iniquities are gone over me head: and as a heavy burden are become heavy upon me* (Ps 37:5).

And what will we have if we come to thee? *I will refresh you*. If any man thirst, let him come to me, and drink (John 7:37).

968. Next, he explains the invitation.

And first, he explains it;

second, he gives the reason, at *for my yoke is sweet and my burden light*.

969. Concerning the first, thus. He had set out the invitation, and to what; now he wishes to show what the invitation is, saying, *take my yoke upon you*. But why? You say that you want to refresh us, and to take our labor from us, and right away you command us to carry the yoke? We thought to be without a yoke. I say that it is true: without the yoke of sin. *For the yoke of their burden, and the rod of their shoulder, and the sceptre of their oppressor you have overcome* (Isa 9:4). Not that you will be without God's law, but without the yoke of sin; *let us cast away their yoke from us* (Ps 2:3). *Return, O Israel, to the Lord your God: for you have fallen down by your iniquity* (Hos 14:2). *Being then freed from sin, we have been made servants of justice* (Rom 6:18). *Take* therefore *my yoke*, namely the Gospel instruction.

And he says, *yoke*; just as a man joins and binds the necks of the cows for plowing, so the Gospel teaching binds both people to its yoke.

970. And what is this: *learn from me, because I am meek, and humble of heart*? For the whole new law consists in two things: in meekness and humility. By meekness a man is ordered with respect to neighbor. Hence, *O Lord, remember David, and all his meekness* (Ps 131:1). By humility, one is ordered with respect to himself and with respect to God. *But to whom will I have respect, but to him that is poor and little, and of a contrite spirit, and that trembles at my words?* (Isa 66:2). Hence humility makes a man receptive of God.

971. Likewise, he had said, *I will refresh you*. What is this refreshment? *You will find rest for your souls*. For the body is not refreshed for as long as it is affected; and when it is no longer affected, then it is said to be refreshed. And just as hunger is in the body, so desire is in the mind: hence the fulfillment of desires is refreshment. *Who satisfies your desire with good things* (Ps 102:5). And this rest is the rest of the soul; *I have labored a little, and have found much rest to myself* (Sir 51:35). The meek are not set at rest in this way

invenietis requiem sempiternam, scilicet impletionem desideriorum.

972. Sed non miremini si invito vos ad iugum, quia iugum meum non est onus. Quare? *Iugum enim meum suave est*, et delectabile; Ps. CXVIII, 103: *quam dulcia faucibus meis eloquia tua*. **Et onus meum leve**.

Et haec possunt retorqueri ad duo. Iugo tenentur boves, sed onus portatur: unde iugum retorquetur ad praecepta negativa, onus ad affirmativa.

973. Sed videtur hoc esse falsum, quia onus legis novae videtur gravissimum, sicut supra V, 21 dictum est: **audistis quia dictum est antiquis, 'non occides'** . . . **ego autem dico vobis, quia omnis qui irascitur fratri suo, reus erit iudicio**: et sic videtur quod gravius onus sit. Item dictum est supra VII, v. 14: **arcta est via, quae ducit ad vitam**. Item Apostolus II Cor. XI, 23: *in laboribus plurimis*. Unde videtur iugum gravissimum.

Ideo duo sunt consideranda: effectus doctrinae et actus circumstantia; et in omnibus est levis, in effectu doctrina Christi, quia immutat cor, quia facit nos non amare temporalia, sed magis spiritualia: qui enim amat temporalia, modicum amittere est ei magis grave, quam ei qui amat spiritualia, amittere multum. Lex vetus non prohibebat illa temporalia, ideo grave erat eis amittere; sed modo, etsi in principio aliquantulum grave, post tamen parum; Prov. IV, 11: *ducam te per semitas aequitatis, quas cum ingressus fueris, non coarctabuntur gressus tui*. Item quantum ad actum lex onerabat actibus exterioribus. Lex autem nostra est in voluntate solum; unde ad Rom. XIV, 11: *regnum Dei non est esca et potus*. Item lex Christi iucundat; unde Apostolus ad Rom. XIV, 17: *iustitia, et pax, et gaudium in Spiritu Sancto*.

Item quantum ad circumstantiam, quia multae sunt adversitates; unde *qui pie in Christo Iesu volunt vivere, persecutionem patientur* et cetera. II ad Tim. III, 12. Sed istae non sunt graves, quia condiuntur condimento amoris, quia quando aliquis amat aliquem, non gravat eum quicquid patitur pro illo: unde omnia gravia et impossibilia levia facit amor. Unde si quis bene amat Christum, nihil est ei grave, et ideo lex nova non onerat.

in the world; hence you will find an everlasting rest, namely the fulfillment of desires.

972. But do not marvel if I invite you to the yoke, because my yoke is not heavy. Why? Because **my yoke is sweet**, and enjoyable; *how sweet are your words to my palate* (Ps 118:103). **And my burden light**.

And these can be referred back to two things. The yoke holds the cows, but a burden is carried; hence the yoke is referred back to the negative commands, the burden to the affirmative commands.

973. But this seems to be false, because the burden of the new law seems most heavy, as was said above, **you have heard that it was said to those of old: 'you shall not kill'** . . . **But I say to you, that whoever is angry with his brother, will be liable to the judgment** (Matt 5:21–22). And thus it seems that the burden is heavier. Similarly, it was said above, **how narrow is the gate, and straight is the way that leads to life** (Matt 7:14). Likewise the Apostle, *in many more labors* (2 Cor 11:23). Hence the yoke seems most heavy.

For this reason, two things should be considered: the effect of the teaching and the circumstances of actions; and in all things it is light. The teaching of Christ is light in its effect, because it changes the heart. For it makes us not love temporal things, but rather spiritual things: for the one who loves temporal things, to lose only a little is more heavy for him than for the one who loves spiritual things to lose a great deal. The old law did not forbid those temporal things, so it was heavy for them to lose them; but now, although in the beginning a small amount was heavy, yet afterward it was too little; *I will lead you by the paths of equity: which when you will have entered, your steps will not be straitened* (Prov 4:11). Likewise, as regards action, the law burdened one with exterior actions. But our law is only in the will; hence, *for the kingdom of God is not meat and drink* (Rom 14:17). Likewise, the law of Christ renders right actions pleasant; hence the Apostle, *but justice, and peace, and joy in the Holy Spirit* (Rom 14:17).

Similarly, the new law is light as regards circumstance, because there are many adversities. Hence, *and all that will live godly in Christ Jesus, will suffer persecution* (2 Tim 3:12). But these are not heavy, because they are seasoned with the spice of love. For when someone loves something, whatever he suffers for it is not heavy to him: hence love makes all heavy and impossible things light. Hence if someone loves Christ well, nothing is heavy for him, and so the new law does not burden him.

CHAPTER 12

Lecture 1

12:1 In illo tempore abiit Iesus per sata Sabbato, discipuli autem eius esurientes coeperunt vellere spicas, et manducare. [n. 975]

12:2 Pharisaei autem videntes dixerunt ei: Ecce discipuli tui faciunt quod non licet eis facere Sabbatis. [n. 977]

12:3 At ille dixit eis: non legistis quid fecerit David, quando esuriit, et qui cum eo erant: [n. 979]

12:4 quomodo intravit in domum Dei, et panes propositionis comedit, quos non licebat ei edere neque his qui cum eo erant, nisi solis sacerdotibus? [n. 979]

12:5 Aut non legistis in lege quia Sabbatis sacerdotes in templo Sabbatum violant, et sine crimine sunt? [n. 981]

12:6 Dico autem vobis, quia templo maior est hic. [n. 981]

12:7 Si autem sciretis quid est: *misericordiam volo, et non sacrificium*, nunquam condemnassetis innocentes. [n. 982]

12:8 Dominus enim est Filius hominis etiam Sabbati. [n. 982]

12:9 Et cum inde transisset, venit in synagogam eorum. [n. 983]

12:10 Et ecce homo manum habens aridam, et interrogabant eum dicentes: si licet Sabbatis curare? Ut accusarent eum. [n. 985]

12:1 Ἐν ἐκείνῳ τῷ καιρῷ ἐπορεύθη ὁ Ἰησοῦς τοῖς σάββασιν διὰ τῶν σπορίμων· οἱ δὲ μαθηταὶ αὐτοῦ ἐπείνασαν καὶ ἤρξαντο τίλλειν στάχυας καὶ ἐσθίειν.

12:2 οἱ δὲ Φαρισαῖοι ἰδόντες εἶπαν αὐτῷ· ἰδοὺ οἱ μαθηταί σου ποιοῦσιν ὃ οὐκ ἔξεστιν ποιεῖν ἐν σαββάτῳ.

12:3 ὁ δὲ εἶπεν αὐτοῖς· οὐκ ἀνέγνωτε τί ἐποίησεν Δαυὶδ ὅτε ἐπείνασεν καὶ οἱ μετ᾽ αὐτοῦ,

12:4 πῶς εἰσῆλθεν εἰς τὸν οἶκον τοῦ θεοῦ καὶ τοὺς ἄρτους τῆς προθέσεως ἔφαγον, ὃ οὐκ ἐξὸν ἦν αὐτῷ φαγεῖν οὐδὲ τοῖς μετ᾽ αὐτοῦ εἰ μὴ τοῖς ἱερεῦσιν μόνοις;

12:5 ἢ οὐκ ἀνέγνωτε ἐν τῷ νόμῳ ὅτι τοῖς σάββασιν οἱ ἱερεῖς ἐν τῷ ἱερῷ τὸ σάββατον βεβηλοῦσιν καὶ ἀναίτιοί εἰσιν;

12:6 λέγω δὲ ὑμῖν ὅτι τοῦ ἱεροῦ μεῖζόν ἐστιν ὧδε.

12:7 εἰ δὲ ἐγνώκειτε τί ἐστιν· ἔλεος θέλω καὶ οὐ θυσίαν, οὐκ ἂν κατεδικάσατε τοὺς ἀναιτίους.

12:8 κύριος γάρ ἐστιν τοῦ σαββάτου ὁ υἱὸς τοῦ ἀνθρώπου.

12:9 Καὶ μεταβὰς ἐκεῖθεν ἦλθεν εἰς τὴν συναγωγὴν αὐτῶν·

12:10 καὶ ἰδοὺ ἄνθρωπος χεῖρα ἔχων ξηράν. καὶ ἐπηρώτησαν αὐτὸν λέγοντες· εἰ ἔξεστιν τοῖς σάββασιν θεραπεῦσαι; ἵνα κατηγορήσωσιν αὐτοῦ.

12:1 At that time Jesus went through the corn on the Sabbath: and his disciples, being hungry, began to pluck the ears and to eat. [n. 975]

12:2 And the Pharisees seeing them, said to him: behold your disciples do what is not lawful to do on the Sabbath days. [n. 977]

12:3 But he said to them: have you not read what David did when he was hungry, and they who were with him: [n. 979]

12:4 how he entered into the house of God, and ate the loaves of proposition, which were not lawful for him to eat, nor for those who were with him, but for the priests only? [n. 979]

12:5 Or have you not read in the law, that on the Sabbath days the priests in the temple break the Sabbath, and are without blame? [n. 981]

12:6 But I tell you that there is here one greater than the temple. [n. 981]

12:7 And if you knew what this means: *I desire mercy, and not sacrifice*: you would never have condemned the innocent. [n. 982]

12:8 For the Son of man is Lord even of the Sabbath. [n. 982]

12:9 And when he had passed from there, he came into their synagogues. [n. 983]

12:10 And behold there was a man who had a withered hand, and they asked him, saying: is it lawful to heal on the Sabbath days? That they might accuse him. [n. 985]

12:11 Ipse autem dixit illis: quis erit ex vobis homo qui habeat ovem unam, et si ceciderit haec Sabbatis in foveam, nonne tenebit, et levabit eam? [n. 987]

12:12 Quanto magis melior est homo ove? Ita licet Sabbatis benefacere. [n. 989]

12:13 Tunc ait homini: extende manum tuam. Et extendit, et restituta est sanitati, sicut altera. [n. 992]

12:14 Exeuntes autem Pharisaei consilium faciebant adversus eum quomodo perderent eum. [n. 993]

12:15 Iesus autem sciens recessit inde, et secuti sunt eum multi, et curavit eos omnes. [n. 995]

12:16 Et praecepit eis, ne manifestum eum facerent, [n. 995]

12:17 ut adimpleretur quod dictum est per Isaiam prophetam dicentem: [n. 996]

12:18 ecce puer meus quem elegi: dilectus meus in quo bene placuit animae meae. Ponam Spiritum meum super eum, et iudicium gentibus nuntiabit. [n. 996]

12:19 Non contendet, neque clamabit, neque audiet aliquis in plateis vocem eius. [n. 1002]

12:20 Arundinem quassatam non confringet, et linum fumigans non extinguet, donec eiiciat ad victoriam iudicium, [n. 1003]

12:21 et in nomine eius gentes sperabunt. [n. 1005]

12:11 ὁ δὲ εἶπεν αὐτοῖς· τίς ἔσται ἐξ ὑμῶν ἄνθρωπος ὃς ἕξει πρόβατον ἓν καὶ ἐὰν ἐμπέσῃ τοῦτο τοῖς σάββασιν εἰς βόθυνον, οὐχὶ κρατήσει αὐτὸ καὶ ἐγερεῖ;

12:12 πόσῳ οὖν διαφέρει ἄνθρωπος προβάτου. ὥστε ἔξεστιν τοῖς σάββασιν καλῶς ποιεῖν.

12:13 τότε λέγει τῷ ἀνθρώπῳ· ἔκτεινόν σου τὴν χεῖρα. καὶ ἐξέτεινεν καὶ ἀπεκατεστάθη ὑγιὴς ὡς ἡ ἄλλη.

12:14 ἐξελθόντες δὲ οἱ Φαρισαῖοι συμβούλιον ἔλαβον κατ' αὐτοῦ ὅπως αὐτὸν ἀπολέσωσιν.

12:15 Ὁ δὲ Ἰησοῦς γνοὺς ἀνεχώρησεν ἐκεῖθεν. καὶ ἠκολούθησαν αὐτῷ [ὄχλοι] πολλοί, καὶ ἐθεράπευσεν αὐτοὺς πάντας

12:16 καὶ ἐπετίμησεν αὐτοῖς ἵνα μὴ φανερὸν αὐτὸν ποιήσωσιν,

12:17 ἵνα πληρωθῇ τὸ ῥηθὲν διὰ Ἠσαΐου τοῦ προφήτου λέγοντος·

12:18 ἰδοὺ ὁ παῖς μου ὃν ᾑρέτισα, ὁ ἀγαπητός μου εἰς ὃν εὐδόκησεν ἡ ψυχή μου· θήσω τὸ πνεῦμά μου ἐπ' αὐτόν, καὶ κρίσιν τοῖς ἔθνεσιν ἀπαγγελεῖ.

12:19 οὐκ ἐρίσει οὐδὲ κραυγάσει, οὐδὲ ἀκούσει τις ἐν ταῖς πλατείαις τὴν φωνὴν αὐτοῦ.

12:20 κάλαμον συντετριμμένον οὐ κατεάξει καὶ λίνον τυφόμενον οὐ σβέσει, ἕως ἂν ἐκβάλῃ εἰς νῖκος τὴν κρίσιν.

12:21 καὶ τῷ ὀνόματι αὐτοῦ ἔθνη ἐλπιοῦσιν.

12:11 But he said to them: what man will there be among you, who has one sheep: and if it fall into a pit on the Sabbath day, will he not take hold of it and lift it up? [n. 987]

12:12 How much better is a man than a sheep? Therefore it is lawful to do a good deed on the Sabbath days. [n. 989]

12:13 Then he said to the man: stretch forth your hand; and he stretched it forth, and it was restored to health, even as the other. [n. 992]

12:14 And the Pharisees going out made a consultation against him, how they might destroy him. [n. 993]

12:15 But Jesus knowing it, retired from there: and many followed him, and he healed them all. [n. 995]

12:16 And he charged them that they should not make him known, [n. 995]

12:17 that it might be fulfilled what was spoken by Isaiah the prophet, saying: [n. 996]

12:18 behold my child whom I have chosen, my beloved in whom my soul has been well pleased. I will put my Spirit upon him, and he will show judgment to the gentiles. [n. 996]

12:19 He will not contend, nor cry out, neither will any man hear his voice in the streets. [n. 1002]

12:20 The bruised reed he will not break: and smoking flax he will not extinguish, until he send forth judgment unto victory. [n. 1003]

12:21 And in his name the gentiles will hope. [n. 1005]

---

974. Supra audistis quomodo Dominus satisfecit discipulis, et increpavit eos; hic ostendit quomodo Pharisaei reprimuntur.

Et duo facit:

primo ostendit, quomodo redarguit Pharisaeos;
secundo, quomodo commendantur discipuli.

Et primo duo facit:

primo ostendit quomodo confutantur detrahentes discipulis;

974. Above, you heard how the Lord satisfied the disciples, and rebuked them; here he shows how the Pharisees are reprimanded.

And he does two things:

first, he shows how he refuted the Pharisees;
second, how the disciples are commended.

And first, he does two things:

first, he shows how those slandering the disciples are confounded;

secundo, quomodo detrahentes Christo, ibi *et cum inde transisset* et cetera.

Circa primum

primo ponitur occasio reprehensionis;

secundo reprehensio, ibi *Pharisaei autem videntes* etc.;

tertio Christi excusatio, ibi *at ille dixit eis* et cetera.

Ponitur autem duplex occasio;

una ex parte Christi,

secunda ex parte discipulorum, ibi *discipuli autem eius esurientes coeperunt vellere spicas*.

975. Ex parte Christi dicit *in illo tempore abiit Iesus per sata Sabbato*. Sciebat Dominus quod discipuli hoc facturi essent, et tamen elegit Dominus hoc fieri, ut iam inciperet solvere Sabbatum, ut habetur supra c. XI, 13: *lex et prophetae usque ad Ioannem prophetaverunt*.

Sed notandum est quod dicitur *in illo tempore*; quia quod hic ponitur designatio temporis, videtur pertinere ad ordinem historiae; sed Lucas VI, 1 et Marcus II, 23 alio ordine recitant; unde post illud quod respondet Dominus discipulis Ioannis, ponitur istud: unde videntur omnia praecedentia ante mortem Ioannis facta, hic vero post. Et hoc patet per omnia quae dicuntur usque ad XIV cap. quae continuantur, et hic fit mentio mortis Ioannis; ideo intelligendum est quod imminente passione misit Ioannes discipulos, et tunc decollatus est, et tunc haec facta sunt post eius mortem.

Abiit Iesus per sata Sabbato. Per huiusmodi sata intelliguntur sacrae litterae. Sator Christus est; infra XIII, 37: *ipse est qui seminat*. Item populus credentium.

976. *Discipuli autem esurientes coeperunt vellere spicas*. Hic duo consideranda sunt. Primo necessitas, quia esurientes. Et quare? Quia pauperes erant; unde I ad Cor. c. IV, 11: *usque ad hanc horam et esurimus, et sitimus* et cetera. Secunda ratio, quia quotidie impediti erant propter turbas; unde vix habebant locum comedendi, ut habetur Mc. c. VI, 31. Sed quomodo satisfecerunt? Datur nobis exemplum abstinentiae; unde isti non magna fercula quaesierunt, sed spicas, iuxta illud I Tim. VI, 8: *habentes alimenta, et quibus tegamur, his contenti simus*.

Mystice in avulsione spicarum intelligitur multiplicitas intellectus Scripturarum, vel conversio peccatorum.

977. Deinde ponit reprehensionem Pharisaeorum *Pharisaei autem videntes dixerunt ei: ecce discipuli tui faciunt quod non licet eis facere Sabbatis*. Discipuli duo mala faciebant: primo quia spicas alienas vellebant, secundo, quia Sabbatum violabant.

second, how those slandering Christ are confounded, at *and when he had passed from there*.

Concerning the first,

first the occasion of the accusation is set down;

second, the accusation, at *and the Pharisees seeing them*;

third, Christ's defense, at *but he said to them*.

Now, a twofold occasion is set down:

one on the part of Christ,

the second on the part of the disciples, at *and his disciples, being hungry, began to pluck the ears*.

975. On the part of Christ he says, *at that time Jesus went through the corn on the Sabbath*. The Lord knew that the disciples would do this, and yet the Lord chose that this should happen, so that he might begin to unbind the Sabbath, as is found above, *for all the prophets and the law prophesied until John* (Matt 11:13).

But one should notice that it says, *at that time*, because the fact that a designation of time is set down here seems to pertain to the order of history. But Luke and Mark tell it in a different order (Luke 6:1; Mark 2:23); hence this is placed after what the Lord responded to John's disciples. Hence, everything preceding this seems to have been done before John's death, but this after. And this is clear by everything which is said up to chapter fourteen, which is connected to what comes before it, and there John's death is mentioned. So one should understand that John sent the disciples as his death was approaching, and then was beheaded, and then these things happened after his death.

Jesus went through the corn on the Sabbath. By such corn are understood the sacred texts. The sower is Christ; below, *he who sows the good seed, is the Son of man* (Matt 13:37). Also, the people of those who believe.

976. *And his disciples, being hungry, began to pluck the ears*. Here two things should be considered. First, the necessity, for they were hungry. And why? Because they were poor men; and, *even unto this hour we both hunger and thirst* (1 Cor 4:11). A second reason, because they were impeded by the crowds every day; hence they hardly had a place to eat (Mark 6:31). But how did they satisfy their hunger? An example of abstinence is given to us; for these men did not seek a large dish, but ears of corn, in accord with, *but having food, and wherewith to be covered, with these we are content* (1 Tim 6:8).

Mystically, in the pulling off of the ears of corn is understood the multiplicity of understandings of Scripture, or the conversion of sinners.

977. Then he sets down the Pharisees' accusation: *and the Pharisees seeing them, said to him: behold your disciples do what is not lawful to do on the Sabbath days*. The disciples were doing two bad things: first, they were plucking someone else's ears of corn; second, they were violating the Sabbath.

Sed Pharisaei de primo non reprehendebant, quia illud erat permissum in lege, Deut. XXIII; ideo quia permissum erat, non calumniabantur, sed quia in Sabbato, calumniabantur. Et per hoc destruitur haeresis Hebraeorum, qui dicebant legalia debere servari cum Evangelio. Et quia Paulus huic sententiae contrariatur, ideo reprobant Paulum. Contra istos arguit Hieronymus, quia etiam discipuli non servabant.

978. *At ille dicit eis.* Hic ponitur excusatio. Et

primo quibusdam exemplis;
secundo auctoritate, ibi *si autem sciretis.*
Circa primum duo facit.
Primo ponit exemplum in quo aliqui sunt excusati propter necessitatem;
secundo, in quo aliqui propter sanctitatem, ibi *aut non legistis in lege* et cetera.

979. Dicit ergo *at ille dicit* et cetera. Lev. cap. XXIV, 5 legitur quod de pura farinula fiebant duodecim panes, et isti ponebantur in mensa propositionis in Sabbato, et in alio Sabbato amovebantur, et ponebantur alii, et illi primi comedebantur a filiis Aaron. Item habetur I Reg. XXI, 6 quod quando David fugit a Saul, Abimelech divisit illis panes illos: et hoc est quod dicit *nonne legistis quid fecit David quanto esuriit?* Iste enim David erat homo bonus, de quo dicit Dominus quod invenit hominem *iuxta cor suum*, I Reg. XIII, 8.

Sed diceret aliquis: ipse David erat propheta, ideo potuit accipere; ideo addit *et qui cum eo erant.* Panes propositionis dicebantur, qui in Sabbato offerebantur, quibus non licebat uti secundum praeceptum, ut habetur Lev. XXIV, 5.

Sed quid ad propositum? Quia quando hoc fecit, Sabbatum erat. Et hoc patet, quia ibi dicitur: *non habeo panes nisi quos abstuli de mensa Domini*, et hoc non faciebat nisi in Sabbato. Item in die calendarum fiebat festum neomeniae: ideo si in Sabbato accideret, violabatur ex necessitate.

Sed adhuc videtur quod non violavit, quia comedere in Sabbato non est peccatum: unde videtur quod non violavit.

Sed Chrysostomus dicit quod violavit magis Sabbato, quia illos panes accepit quos nemini licebat esse, propter necessitatem. Sabbatum autem invenitur violatum a Machabaeis propter necessitatem.

980. Item notandum, quod dicit Chrysostomus, quod quaedam sunt praecepta, quae praecipiuntur propter se, et haec nulla necessitate frangi possunt; quaedam vero non propter se, sed propter figuram, ideo talia loco et tempore possunt; sicut ieiunium potest modo dimitti in necessitate. Ille autem panis alterius panis erat figura,

But the Pharisees did not accuse them of the first thing, because that was permitted in the law (Deut 23:25). So since it was permitted, they did not find fault with it, but because it happened on the Sabbath, they found fault. And by this is destroyed the heresy of the Hebrews, who said that the laws should be observed with the Gospel. And since Paul was against this opinion, they rejected Paul. Jerome argued against these that even the disciples did not observe the laws.

978. *But he said to them.* Here the defense is set down. And

first, by certain examples;
second, by authority, at *and if you knew.*
Concerning the first, he does two things:
first, he sets forth an example in which some were excused on account of necessity;
second, an example in which some were excused on account of holiness, at *or have you not read in the law.*

979. It says then, *but he said.* It is written that twelve loaves were made from fine flour, and these were set on the table of proposition on the Sabbath, and they were removed on the next Sabbath, and others were set there, and the first ones were eaten by Aaron's sons (Lev 24:5). Similarly, it is said that when David fled from Saul, Achimelech distributed these loaves to them (1 Sam 21:6); and this is what he says, *have you not read what David did when he was hungry?* For this man David was a good man, of whom the Lord says that he found a man *after his own heart* (1 Sam 13:14).

But someone would say: this man David was a prophet, so he could take it; so he adds *and they who were with him.* The loaves which were offered on the Sabbath were called the loaves of proposition, which according to the command it was not lawful to use (Lev 24:5).

But how is this relevant? Because when he did this, it was the Sabbath. And this is clear, because it says there: *I have no loaves, except the ones I have taken from the Lord's table*, and this was only done on the Sabbath. Likewise, on the day of the calendars it was the feast of the new moons; so if it fell on the Sabbath, it was violated by necessity.

But it still seems that he did not violate the Sabbath, because to eat on the Sabbath is not a sin; hence it seems that he did not violate it.

But Chrysostom says that he violated more than the Sabbath, because he took those loaves, which was permitted to no one, on account of necessity. The Sabbath is also found to have been violated by the Machabees on account of necessity.

980. Likewise, one should notice, as Chrysostom says, that there are certain commandments which are commanded for their own sakes, and these cannot be broken by any necessity; but some are commanded not for their own sakes, but for the sake of a figure, and so such commands can be broken at a particular place and time; just as

scilicet panis altaris, qui non solum a sacerdote, sed etiam ab alio populo percipitur; ideo David figurat ibi populum. Unde Apoc. V, 10: *fecisti nos Deo nostro regnum et sacerdotes.*

981. Item ponitur aliud exemplum, quod ponitur propter sanctitatem. Et hoc ibi *nonne legistis in lege quia Sabbatis sacerdotes in templo Sabbatum violant?* In Levitico praeceptum erat, quod oblatio duplicaretur in Sabbato, quae solebat fieri in aliis diebus, et tamen in templo fiebat, et in Sabbato, quia fiebat ad obsequium templi et Dei: unde excusabantur sacerdotes. Unde istud exemplum applicatur, quia apostoli totaliter erant dediti maiori quam templo, scilicet Christo: unde dicit *nonne legistis quia sacerdotes violabant Sabbatum?* Nisi esset propter templum.

Dico autem vobis, quoniam templo maior est hic. Hic ponitur adverbium loci, cuius obsequio ipsi faciunt. Et quod insit aliquid maius templo, patet, quia corpus suum templum est. Item videndum, quod in primo exemplo non ponit, quod sit sine crimine. In secundo ponit quod si aliquis frangit Sabbatum propter necessitatem, non tamen propter hoc omnino caret crimine; sed si propter Deum, penitus excusatur a crimine.

982. Deinde argumentatur ex exemplis. Et primo, quia misericorditer agendum est cum discipulis meis: quia *si sciretis quid est, misericordiam volo, et non sacrificium numquam condemnassetis innocentes,* Os. VI, 6. Et quomodo intelligendum est, dictum est superius. Prov. XXI, 3: *misericordiam facere et iudicium magis placet Domino quam victimae,* et cetera.

Est etiam argumentum aliud quod eos facit innocentes, scilicet obedientia: unde haec possunt, quia praecipio eis, quia *Filius hominis,* ita se consuevit nominare, *est Dominus Sabbati,* et legislator non subiacet legi; Is. XXXIII, 22: *ipse est legifer noster;* ideo habet potestatem, quia habet auctoritatem.

983. *Et cum transisset inde, venit ad synagogam eorum* et cetera.

Supra positum est, quomodo Dominus repulit Pharisaeos derogantes discipulis, hic quomodo repulit se impugnantes. Adversabantur enim primo insidiando; secundo detrahendo; tertio tentando.

Et secundum hoc repulit eos tripliciter.

Secundo, ibi *tunc oblatus est ei homo daemonium habens;*

now fasting can be abandoned in necessity. Now, this bread was a figure of another bread, namely the bread of the altar, which is received not only by the priest, but also by another people; therefore David was a figure of the people there. Hence, *and have made us to our God a kingdom and priests* (Rev 5:10).

981. Likewise, another example is set down, which is set down on account of holiness. And this is at *or have you not read in the law, that on the Sabbath days the priests in the temple break the Sabbath?* It was commanded in Leviticus that the oblation which usually happened on the other days should be doubled on the Sabbath; and yet it happened in the temple, and on the Sabbath, because it was done for the service of the temple and of God. Hence the priests were excused. Hence this example is connected, because the apostles were entirely devoted to one greater than the temple, namely Christ. Hence he says, *or have you not read in the law, that on the Sabbath days the priests in the temple break the Sabbath?* Except it was for the sake of the temple.

But I tell you that there is here one greater than the temple. The word *here* is set down as an adverb of the place whose service these men performed. And that something greater than the temple is present is clear, because his own body is a temple. Likewise, one should notice that in the first example he does not lay down that he was without blame. In the second, he lays down that if someone breaks the Sabbath on account of necessity, he still does not entirely lack fault on this account; but if for God's sake, he is thoroughly excused from blame.

982. Then he argues from the examples. And first, that one should deal mercifully with my disciples, because *if you knew what this means: 'I will have mercy, and not sacrifice'* (Hos 6:6): *you would never have condemned the innocent.* And how this should be understood was said above. *To do mercy and judgment, pleases the Lord more than victims* (Prov 21:3).

There is also another argument which makes them innocent, namely obedience: hence they could do these things because I command them, *for the Son of man,* so he was accustomed to name himself *is Lord even of the Sabbath,* and the legislator is not subject to the law. *The Lord is our lawgiver* (Isa 33:22); therefore he has power, since he has authority.

983. *And when he had passed from there, he came into their synagogues.*

It was set down above how the Lord drove back the Pharisees as they were slandering the disciples; here is set down how he drove them back as they were attacking him. For they were turned against him first by plotting; second, by slandering; third, by tempting.

And in accord with this, he drove them back in three ways.

The second is at *then was offered to him one possessed with a devil* (Matt 12:22);

tertio, ibi *tunc responderunt ei quidam de scribis et Pharisaeis*.

Circa primum duo facit.

Primo ostendit quomodo insidiabantur doctrinae Christi;

secundo quomodo vitae Christi, ibi *exeuntes autem Pharisaei consilium faciebant adversus eum*.

Circa primum duo facit.

Primo ponitur insidiosa interrogatio;

secundo Christi responsio, ibi *ipse autem dixit* et cetera.

Circa primum tria facit.

Primo locus describitur;

secundo occasio;

tertio interrogatio.

984. Dicit ergo *et cum transisset inde, venit in synagogam*. Secundum litteram ita discipuli vellebant spicas, quos excusavit Iesus. Unde cum dicit *et cum transisset*, videtur eodem die inde *transisse*. Sed hoc excluditur Lc. VI, 1 quia in alio Sabbato; propter hoc non est intelligendum, quod statim; unde dicit *venit in synagogam*, ut praedicaret salutem, ut in Io. XVIII, 20: *ego semper docui in templo, et in synagoga, quo omnes Iudaei conveniunt, et in occulto locutus sum nihil*. Et in Ps. XXXIX, 10: *annuntiavi iustitiam tuam in ecclesia magna*.

985. *Et ecce homo manum habens aridam*. Sequitur occasio interrogationis: quia *interrogabant eum* et cetera. Dicitur quod iste fuit caementarius, et habebat manum aridam.

Per istum significatur genus humanum, cuius manus aruit per originale peccatum: vel quilibet peccator, cuius manus et virtus operativa aruit; et quandoque dextera, quia impotentes ad agendum bonum, quamvis potentes ad malum.

986. Tunc ponitur interrogatio; secundo responsio.

Dicit ergo *et interrogabant, si licet Sabbato curare*. Videbant hominem potentem, ideo petierunt si licebat Sabbato curare. Et hoc petebant tentantes, ut habetur Eccli. XIII, v. 14: *ex multa loquela tentabit te*. Non enim animo discendi, sed potius accusandi petebant, ut habetur in Ps. XXVII, 3: *loquebantur pacem cum proximo suo, mala autem in cordibus eorum*.

Sed hic est quaestio, quia Mc. III, 4 habetur quod Dominus interrogavit; hic autem dicitur quod illi interrogaverunt.

Respondet Augustinus, quod utrumque factum est, quia quando ille stetit in medio, et petiit sanari, ipsi interrogaverunt, et Dominus fecit eum surgere, et tunc

---

the third, at *then some of the scribes and Pharisees answered him* (Matt 12:38).

Concerning the first, he does two things:

first, he shows how they were plotting against Christ's teaching;

second, how they were plotting against Christ's life, at *and the Pharisees going out made a consultation against him, how they might destroy him*.

Concerning the first, he does two things:

first, the treacherous questioning is set down;

second, Christ's response, at *but he said to them*.

Concerning the first, he does three things:

first, the place is described;

second, the occasion;

third, the questioning.

984. It says then *and when he had passed from there, he came into their synagogues*. According to the letter, the disciples were plucking grains, whom the Lord defended. Hence when it says, *and when he had passed from there*, it seems that he had *passed from there* on the same day. But this is excluded in Luke because it was on another Sabbath (Luke 6:1, 6:6). For this reason, one should not understand it as happening right away; hence it says, *he came into their synagogues*, that he might preach salvation, as in, *I have always taught in the synagogue, and in the temple, to where all the Jews resort; and in secret I have spoken nothing* (John 18:20). *I have declared your justice in a great church* (Ps 39:10).

985. *And behold there was a man who had a withered hand*. There follows the occasion of the questioning, because *they asked him*. It is said that this man was a stonecutter, and had a withered hand.

By this man is signified the human race, whose hand was withered by original sin; or any sinner whatever, whose hand and operative power has withered; and sometimes the right hand, because they are unable to work good, however much they are capable of evil.

986. Then the questioning is set down; then, the response.

It says then, *and they asked him, saying: is it lawful to heal on the Sabbath days?* They saw a powerful man, so they asked if it were lawful to cure on the Sabbath. And they asked this to tempt him, as is written, *for by much talk he will sift you* (Sir 13:14). For they did not ask with a mind for learning, but rather for accusing, as is had, *who speak peace with their neighbor, but evils are in their hearts* (Ps 27:3).

But there is a question here, because Mark has that the Lord asked (Mark 3:4); but here it says that they asked.

Augustine responds that both were done, because when this man stood in the midst of the assembly and asked to be healed, they asked, and the Lord made him rise up, and

interrogavit. Vel aliter, quia illi observabant eum; unde parabant se ad petitionem, et tunc petiit, quia ipse sciebat, quod petebant ut accusarent eum.

987. *Ipse autem dixit eis*. Hic ponitur responsio. Et

primo respondet verbo;

secundo facto, ibi *tunc ait homini: extende manum tuam*.

In primo tria facit.

Primo allegat consuetudinem;

secundo comparationem, ibi *quanto magis melior est homo ove?*

Tertio inducit conclusionem, ibi *itaque licet Sabbatis benefacere*.

988. Dicit ergo primo *quis erit ex vobis homo qui habeat ovem unam; et si ceciderit haec Sabbatis in foveam, nonne tenebit, et levabit eam?* Consuetudo erat apud eos, quod si ovis caderet in foveam, quod eam die Sabbati sublevabant: intantum enim erant avaritiae dediti, quod praeponebant damnum temporale damno spirituali. Unde conveniebat eis quod dicitur Eccli. X, 9: *avaro nihil est scelestius*. Et sequitur post parum: *animam enim suam venalem habet*, quia scilicet se exponit periculo et damno aeterno pro modico lucro temporali.

989. Secundo ponitur comparatio, *quanto magis melior est homo ove?* Incomparabiliter, quia omnia sunt propter hominem: homini enim est commissum dominium omnium, ut habetur Gen. I, 26: *faciamus hominem ad imaginem et similitudinem nostram*, et sequitur, *ut praesit piscibus maris, et volatilibus caeli, et bestiis terrae*. Et sic quod est ad imaginem, praeest, sicut homo ovi.

990. Ex his concludit *itaque licet benefacere*, scilicet hominibus prodesse; Is. I, v. 16: *quiescite agere perverse, discite benefacere*, quia scriptum est Ex. XX, 10: *opus servile non facietis in eo*. Opus servile est peccatum, ideo licet benefacere.

991. Sed tunc est quaestio. Licetne omnia bona opera facere in Sabbato? Tunc enim liceret arare.

Ideo dicendum, quod opus servile potest intelligi ad litteram, et mystice opus servile est peccatum; Io. VIII, 34: *qui facit peccatum, servus est peccati*. Item servile opus est, in quo magis exercetur corpus quam anima. Anima enim habet dominari corpori. Ideo consiliari non est opus servile. Unde possumus videre quae excusant a Sabbato. Dominus enim excusat discipulos ratione necessitatis, unde necessitas excusat. Item illa, quae ad cultum Dei ordinantur immediate, ut thurificare et cetera. Item illa, quae pertinent ad salutem corporis,

then asked. Or otherwise, that they were watching him; hence they were preparing themselves for the question, and then he asked, because he knew that they were asking that they might accuse him.

987. *But he said to them*. Here the response is set down. And

first, he responds by word;

second, by deed, at **then he said to the man: stretch forth your hand**.

In the first thing, he does three things:

first, he brings forward the normal practice;

second, a comparison, at **how much better is a man than a sheep?**

Third, he brings in the conclusion, at **therefore it is lawful to do a good deed on the Sabbath days**.

988. He says then first, **what man will there be among you, who has one sheep: and if it fall into a pit on the Sabbath day, will he not take hold of it and lift it up?** It was the custom among them that if a sheep fell in a pit, they lifted it up on the Sabbath day; for they were so devoted to greed that they set a temporal curse before a spiritual curse. Hence what is said befits them: *but nothing is more wicked than the covetous man* (Sir 10:9). And there follows after a little, *for such a one sets even his own soul to sale*, namely because he exposes himself to danger and eternal damnation for a little temporal gain.

989. Second, a comparison is set down: **how much better is a man than a sheep?** Incomparably, because all things exist for the sake of man, for dominion over all things was given to man, as is written, *let us make man to our image and likeness* (Gen 1:26), and there follows *and let him have dominion over the fishes of the sea, and the fowls of the air, and the beasts, and the whole earth*. And thus what is made to the image is set before, as a man is set before a sheep.

990. From these things he concludes, **therefore it is lawful to do a good deed**, namely to benefit a man; *cease to do perversely, learn to do well* (Isa 1:16–17), for it is written, *your will do no work on it* (Exod 20:10). Servile work is a sin, therefore it is permitted to do good deeds.

991. But then there is a question. Is it permitted to do all good works on the Sabbath? For then it would be permitted to plow.

Therefore one should say that servile work can be understood literally, and mystically servile work is a sin; *whoever committs sin, is the servant of sin* (John 8:34). Likewise, servile work is work in which the body is used more than the soul. For the soul has dominion over the body. Therefore to take counsel is not servile work. Hence we can see what things make excuses from the Sabbath. For the Lord excuses the disciples by reason of necessity, hence necessity excuses. Also, those things which are ordered immediately to the worship of God, such as burning incense. Also, those things which pertain to the salvation of the body, such as to

ut facere medicinam, emplastra et cetera. Unde isti vituperantur, quia arctant praeceptum legis.

992. *Tunc ait homini: extende manum tuam*. In parte ista respondet facto, et hoc fuit eum curare; non enim curaret nisi licitum esset. Sequitur curatio *et restituta est sanitati sicut altera*.

Mystice homo qui habet manum aridam, idest impotentem ad bene agendum, non potest melius curari quam extendendo manum suam in sublevationem pauperum. Unde Dan. cap. IV, 24: *peccata tua eleemosynis redime*. Et Eccli. III, 33: *ignem ardentem extinguit aqua, eleemosyna resistit peccatis*. Et ibid. IV, 36: *non sit manus tua porrecta ad accipiendum, et collecta ad dandum*.

Et nota quod primo habebat sinistram sanam, *et restituta est sicut altera*, dextra scilicet. Et hoc est, quia primo sunt homines potentes ad malum, ut habetur Is. V, 22: *vae qui potentes estis ad faciendum malum*, sed post sanantur per gratiam, et tunc sunt proni ad bene agendum; Rom. VI, 19: *sicut exhibuistis membra vestra servire immunditiae et iniquitati ad iniquitatem, ita nunc exhibete servire iustitiae in sanctificatione* et cetera.

993. *Exeuntes autem Pharisaei* et cetera. Hic ostendit quomodo insidiabantur ei. Et

primo ponuntur insidiae;

secundo eius declinatio, ibi *Iesus autem sciens recessit inde*;

tertio auctoritas, ibi *ut impleretur quod dictum est per Isaiam prophetam*.

994. Dicit ergo *exeuntes*, scilicet a synagoga, ut impleretur quod habetur in Ps. cap. LIII, 3: *synagoga potentium quaesierunt animam meam*. Exierunt ergo, ut male agerent, sicut Iob I, 12: *egressus est satan a facie Domini*. *Consilium fecerunt*, idest congregationem, *quomodo illum perderent* et occiderent, quia verbis eum vincere non poterant; Ps. I, 1: *beatus vir qui non abiit in consilio impiorum*.

995. *Iesus autem sciens, recessit inde*. Hic ponitur quomodo insidias declinavit. Et primo tangitur declinatio; secundo fructus.

Unde recessit, et quare? Quia nondum erat tempus patiendi. Item recessit, ut suis occasionem daret fugiendi, ut dictum est supra X. Item, ut se hominem monstraret. Item reliquit eos, ut non incitaret eos. Illud enim boni praedicatoris est, cum videt homines motos et incitatos, quod dimittat eos, ut videtur Eccli. VIII, 13: *non incendas carbones peccatorum arguens eos, et ne incendaris flamma ignis peccatorum illorum*.

Et secuti sunt eum multi, unde accessit ad eos qui eum diligebant, qui eum libenter audiebant. Unde

make medicines, plasters, etc. Hence these men are blamed, because they tighten the precept of the law.

992. *Then he said to the man: stretch forth your hand*. In this part he responds by deed, and this was to heal him, for he would not have healed him unless it were permitted. There follows the healing: *and it was restored to health, even as the other*.

Mystically, a man who has a withered hand, i.e., an inability to do good, cannot be cured better than by extending his hand in support of the poor. Hence, *redeem your sins with alms* (Dan 4:24). And, *water quenches a flaming fire, and alms resists sins* (Sir 3:33). And, *do not let your hand be stretched out to receive, and shut when you should give* (Sir 4:36).

And note that first he had a healthy left hand, *and it*, i.e., the right hand, *was restored to health, even as the other*. And this is because men are first capable of evil, as is found: *woe to you who are mighty to do evil* (Isa 5:22); but afterward they are healed by grace, and then are inclined to do good. *For as you have yielded your members to serve uncleanness and iniquity, unto iniquity; so now yield your members to serve justice, unto sanctification* (Rom 6:19).

993. *And the Pharisees going out made a consultation against him*. Here he shows how they plotted against him.

And first, the plot is set down;

second, his avoidance, at *but Jesus knowing it, retired from there*;

third, an authority, at *that it might be fulfilled what was spoken by Isaiah the prophet*.

994. It says then, *the Pharisees going out*, namely from the synagogue, so that it might be fulfilled what is written: *the assembly of the mighty have sought my soul* (Ps 85:14). They went out, therefore, that they might do evil, *and satan went forth from the presence of the Lord* (Job 1:12). *The Pharisees . . . made a consultation*, i.e., a gathering, *how they might destroy* and kill him, since they could not conquer him with words; *blessed is the man who has not walked in the counsel of the ungodly* (Ps 1:1).

995. *But Jesus knowing it, retired from there*. Here is set down how he avoided their plot. And first, the avoidance is touched upon; second, the fruit.

Where did he withdraw from, and why? Because it was not yet the time to suffer. Likewise, he withdrew that he might give to his own the occasion for fleeing, as was said above, commenting on chapter ten. Likewise, that he might show himself to be a man. Likewise, he left them that he might not enrage them. For it belongs to the good preacher, when he sees men moved and excited, that he should leave them, as is seen, *kindle not the coals of sinners by rebuking them, lest you be burnt with the flame of the fire of their sins* (Sir 8:13).

And many followed him; hence he drew near to those who loved him, who heard him gladly. Hence, *my sheep*

Io. X, 3: *oves meae vocem meam audiunt*. **Et curavit eos**. Ponitur curatio; Sap. XVI, 12: *non ergo herba, neque malagma sanavit eos, sed sermo tuus qui sanat omnia*. Et in Ps. CVI, 20: *misit verbum suum, et sanavit eos*. Et quomodo? **Praecepit eis ne manifestum eum facerent**. Et quare? Ut daret nobis exemplum vitandi humanam gloriam, sicut habetur Sup. VI, 1. Item ut parceret Pharisaeis, qui de factis suis calumniabantur.

996. Ut adimpleretur quod dictum est per Isaiam prophetam. Hic introducit auctoritatem, quae habetur Is. XLII, 1.

Et sciendum quod alii apostoli dicunt auctoritates secundum Hebraicam veritatem, alii secundum expositionem Septuaginta, alii sensum solum verbis exprimebant.

Et tria facit.

Primo describit naturam humanam, cum dicit '*ecce puer meus*', quia puer fuit; Lc. II, v. 43: *puer autem Iesus remansit in templo*. Vocatur autem puer, vel a puritate: quia *peccatum non fecit, nec inventus est dolus in ore eius* et cetera. I Petr. II, 22, vel secundum quod puer dicitur servus; unde '*ecce puer*', servus per servilem formam; Phil. II, 7: *exinanivit semetipsum, formam servi accipiens*.

997. Electus '*quem elegi*.' Nota, quod in unoquoque homine sancto sunt tria: divina electio, dilectio et effectus, qui est gratia: et hoc aliter in homine, aliter in Deo. In homine praecedit gratia; secundo diligit; tertio eligit. In Deo vero est e converso. Et hoc est, quia voluntas in homine non est causativa huius effectus, quae est gratia, sed amor et voluntas Dei est causa gratiae; ideo primo eligit quem vult esse bonum; secundo diligit; deinde gratiam adiungit. Unde, secundum hoc, tria ponit.

998. Primo electionem et cetera. In originali non est ly *electus*.

Dicit ergo '*ecce puer meus, quem elegi*' etc., et hoc quantum ad duplicem electionem; quae omnino Christo conveniunt secundum humanam naturam. Ad duo enim est electus. Scilicet ad hoc quod sit Filius Dei, ut habetur Rom. I, 4: *qui praedestinatus est Filius Dei* etc., et Ps. LXIV, 5: *beatus quem elegisti et assumpsisti*. Item est electus ad opus redemptionis humanae, ut Io. III, 16: *sic Deus dilexit mundum, ut Filium suum unigenitum daret* et cetera.

999. Item elegit ut diligat; unde dicitur '*dilectus meus*': si enim aliquos diligit, multo magis unigenitum suum. Unde Io. III, v. 34: *non ad mensuram datus est ei Spiritus*. Et si diligat aliquos, istum tamen speciali dilectione; unde dicit '*in quo complacuit animae meae*', idest voluntati meae: et haec est specialis dilectio, quia voluntas non quiescit nisi ubi invenit placitum. Nihil autem placet, nisi per gratiam, et nihil gratum defuit Christo;

hear my voice (John 10:27). **And he healed them all**. The healing is set down; for it was neither herb, nor mollifying plaster that healed them, but your word, O Lord, which heals all things (Wis 16:12). He sent his word, and healed them (Ps 106:20). And how? **He charged them that they should not make him known**. And why? That he might give us an example of avoiding human glory, as is had above (Matt 6:1). Likewise, that he might be merciful to the Pharisees, who were misrepresenting his deeds.

996. That it might be fulfilled what was spoken by Isaiah the prophet. Here he brings in the authority (Isa 42:1).

And one should know that some apostles quote the Scriptural texts according to the Hebrew truth, others according to the exposition of the Septuagint, and others only express the sense of the words.

And he does three things:

first, he describes the human nature, when he says, '*behold my child*', because he became a child; *the child Jesus remained in Jerusalem* (Luke 2:43). Now, he is called a child either from purity, since he *did no sin, neither was guile found in his mouth* (1 Pet 2:22), or as a slave is called a child. Hence '*behold my child*', a slave through his servile form; he *emptied himself, taking the form of a servant* (Phil 2:7).

997. One chosen, '*whom I have chosen*.' Notice that there are three things in any holy man: divine election, love, and the effect which is grace. And this is in man one way, in God in another. In man, grace comes first; second, he loves; third, he chooses. But in God it is the other way around. And this is because the will in a man is not causative of this effect which is grace, but the love and will of God is the cause of grace; therefore, first he chooses whom he wishes to be good; second, he loves; then he adjoins grace. Hence, according to this, he sets down three things.

998. First, election. In the original there is not this word *chosen*.

It says then, '*behold my servant whom I have chosen*', and this as regards a double election, which belongs to Christ in every way according to his human nature. For he was chosen for two things. Namely, that he should be the Son of God, as is found, *who was predestined the Son of God* (Rom 1:4), and, *blessed is he whom you have chosen and taken to you* (Ps 64:5). Likewise, he was chosen for the work of redeeming mankind, as is said, *God so loved the world, as to give his only begotten Son* (John 3:16).

999. Likewise, he chose that he might love; hence it says, '*my beloved*': for if he loves anyone, much more does he love his own only-begotten, *for God does not give the Spirit by measure* (John 3:34). Hence he says, '*in whom my soul*', that is, my will, '*has been well pleased*.' And this is a special love, for the will does not rest except where it finds something pleasing. But nothing is pleasing except through grace, and nothing pleasing was lacking to Christ; hence,

unde supra III, 17: **hic est Filius meus dilectus, in quo mihi complacui.**

1000. Deinde ponit gratiae collationem: *'ponam Spiritum meum super eum'*, ut habetur Ioel II, 28: *effundam de Spiritu meo super omnem carnem.* Sed in Christo non solum de Spiritu, sed totum Spiritum effudit, ut habetur Io. III, 34: *non ad mensuram datus est ei Spiritus*; et Is. XI, 2: *requiescet super eum Spiritus Domini.* Et hoc inquantum habet formam servi.

1001. Sed quid faciet? Quod officium habebit? *'Iudicium gentibus nuntiabit'*, idest docebit gentes iudicia Dei. Antiquitus gloriabantur Iudaei se esse populum Dei peculiarem; unde dicebant: *non fecit taliter omni nationi, et iudicia sua non manifestavit eis.* Sed illud dictum est gentibus. Unde *'nuntiabit gentibus'*, materialiter, quia potestatem iudicandi accepit super gentes; Act. X, 42: *ipse est qui constitutus est a Deo iudex vivorum et mortuorum.* Et Io. c. V, 22: *Pater omne iudicium dedit Filio.*

1002. Item estne idoneus? Quia in iudicio duo sunt necessaria, clementia et iustitia. Et utrumque ostendit. Et primo quod clementiam habeat. Et quia clementia potest esse in verbis, secundo in factis, quia aliqui etsi non possint aliquid, conqueruntur verbo; ideo haec amovet ab eo.

Unde dicit *'non contendet'*; I Petr. II, 23: *cum malediceretur, non maledicebat.* Et bene congruit ei quod dicitur Prov. XX, 3: *honor est homini qui separat se a contentionibus.* Item aliqui non contendunt, sed murmurant. Sed hoc non faciet iste, quia *'non clamabit.'* Unde Is. LIII, 7: *sicut ovis ad occisionem ducetur, et quasi agnus coram tondente se obmutescet, et non aperiet os suum.* Clamor ex affectione procedit. Et Apostolus praecipit ad Ephes. IV, 31: *omnis indignatio et clamor auferatur a vobis.* Aliqui non clamant, sed conqueruntur: et hoc amovetur *'nec aliquis in plateis audiet vocem eius.'* In plateis vocem emittunt, qui ambulant in viis peccatorum; Thren. IV, 1: *dispersi sunt lapides sanctuarii*; Prov. I, 20: *sapientia dat vocem in plateis.* Tamen iste inter eos non audietur.

Vel aliter: per plateas intelligimus gentiles, quoniam sunt extra sanctuarium. Et licet Christus sustineat praedicari gentibus, tamen in propria persona non praedicavit eis. Unde in plateis non audietur, idest inter gentiles. Ita ergo erat patiens in verbo.

1003. Item in facto, *'arundinem quassatam non confringet.'* Et hoc dupliciter; potest enim legi primo specialiter quantum ad Iudaeos; secundo generaliter quantum ad omnes. Quantum ad Iudaeos duo erant in eis, scilicet regia potestas, et sacerdotalis dignitas.

it says above, **this is my beloved Son, in whom I am well pleased** (Matt 3:17).

1000. Then he sets out the bestowal of grace: *'I will put my Spirit upon him'*, as is found, *I will pour out my Spirit upon all flesh* (Joel 2:28). But in Christ he did not just pour out from the Spirit, but poured out the whole Spirit, as is said, *for God does not give the Spirit by measure* (John 3:34); and, *and the Spirit of the Lord will rest upon him* (Isa 11:2). And this is insofar as he has the form of a slave.

1001. But what will he do? What office will he have? *'He will show judgment to the gentiles'*, i.e., he will teach God's judgment to the gentiles. Formerly, the Jews boasted that they were God's special people; hence they said, *he has not done in like manner to every nation: and his judgments he has not made manifest to them* (Ps 147:9). But it was told to the gentiles. Hence, *'he will show judgment to the gentiles'*, materially, because he received the power of judgment over the nations; *it is he who was appointed by God, to be judge of the living and of the dead* (Acts 10:42). And, *the Father . . . has given all judgment to the Son* (John 5:22).

1002. Likewise, is he not suitable? For in judgment there are two things necessary, mercy and justice. And he points to both. And first that he has mercy. And because mercy can be first in words, second in deeds, because some, even though they cannot do something, they complain by word; so he removes these from him.

Hence it says, *'he will not contend'*; who, when he was reviled, did not revile (1 Pet 2:23). And what is said fits him well: *it is an honor for a man to separate himself from quarrels* (Prov 20:3). Similarly, some do not contend, but they murmur. But this man will not do this, because he will not *'cry out.'* Hence, *he will be led as a sheep to the slaughter, and will be dumb as a lamb before his shearer, and he will not open his mouth* (Isa 53:7). Crying out proceeds from emotion. And the Apostle commanded, *let all . . . indignation, and clamour . . . be put away from you* (Eph 4:31). Some do not cry out, but they complain: and this is removed, *'neither will any man hear his voice in the streets.'* Those raise their voice on the streets who walk in the ways of sinners; *the stones of the sanctuary are scattered in the top of every street* (Lam 4:1). *Wisdom . . . utters her voice in the streets* (Prov 1:20). Yet this man will not be heard among them.

Or in another way: by streets we understand the gentiles, because they are outside the sanctuary. And although Christ endures to be preached to the gentiles, yet in his own person he did not preach to them. Hence he will not be heard in the streets, i.e., among the gentiles. In this way therefore he was patient in word.

1003. Likewise in deed: *'the bruised reed he will not break.'* And this in two ways. For it can be read first with a special regard to the Jews; second, with a general regard to all. As regards the Jews, there were two things in them, namely the kingly power and the priestly dignity.

Regia potestas significatur per arundinem, quae iam quassata erat, quia Romanis erant subditi; ideo facile erat ei ita quassare arundinem. Et bene signatur per arundinem, quia arundo mobilis est, ut habetur supra XI, 7: *quid existis in desertum videre? Arundinem vento agitatam?*

'*Et linum fumigans non extinguit.*' Per linum fumigans sacerdotium significatur: unde sacerdotes lineis vestibus induebantur. Item '*fumigans*': fumus enim extinguitur per ignem. Item fumus fit per debilem ignem, qui plus resolvit quam consummat, et hinc generatur foetor. Hi ergo erant sicut linum fumigans, quia non totaliter fidem amiserant: nec tamen tantum habebant quod cohiberent se a malis. Unde quamvis posset iuste extinguere, tamen '*linum fumigans non extinguet.*'

1004. Item alio modo exponitur quoad omnes, ita quod per arundinem quassatam intelligantur peccatores. Per linum fumigans, quod aliquantulum habet calorem, intelliguntur qui non in peccato sunt, sed tepidi sunt ad opus bonum, et habent aliquid gratiae.

Unde vult dicere: neque peccatoribus praecludit viam salutis. Unde ipse dicit, Ezech. cap. XVIII, 23: *numquid voluntatis meae est mors impii?* Item si aliquis habet gratiam, non extinguet eam. Unde in hoc datur nobis exemplum quod non debemus gratiam alicuius, quam Dominus dedit ei, extinguere, sed potius fovere.

1005. Item non faciet iudicium '*donec eiiciat ad victoriam iudicium.*' Et hoc potest legi specialiter de Iudaeis, scilicet quando omnes vicerit, quia imponebant quod in Beelzebub daemonia eiiciebat; et confutavit eos, tunc imposuit iudicium super eos. Et hoc impletum est per Titum et Vespasianum. Et non solum istud fiet; sed ipsis destructis, '*in nomine eius gentes sperabunt.*' Unde Gen. cap. XLIX, 10: *ipse erit expectatio gentium.*

Vel aliter. Ita sustinet voluntatem, et neminem iudicat; sed cum inimica mors destruetur, tunc omnes gentes adhaerebunt ei, et hoc erit in die iudicii.

The reed signifies the kingly power, which was already bruised, since they were subject to the Romans; so it was easy for him to bruise the reed in this way. And it is well signified by a reed, because a reed is mobile, as is found above, *what did you go out into the desert to see? A reed shaken with the wind?* (Matt 11:7).

'*And smoking flax he will not extinguish.*' The smoking flax signifies the priesthood. Hence the priests were clothed in vestments made of flax. And '*smoking*' because smoke is extinguished by fire. Likewise, smoke arises from a weak fire, which disperses more than it consumes, and this produces a bad smell. Therefore, these men were like smoking flax, because they had not entirely lost the faith, nor yet did they have so much faith that they would restrain themselves from evil. Hence although he could justly extinguish it, yet the '*smoking flax he will not extinguish.*'

1004. Similarly, it is explained in another way with regard to all, such that by the bruised reed are understood sinners. By the smoking flax, which has some quantity of heat, are understood those who are not in sin, but are lukewarm toward good works, and have something of grace.

Hence he wishes to say: neither will he cut the way of salvation off from sinners. Hence he himself says, *is it my will that a sinner should die?* (Ezek 18:23). Similarly, if someone has grace, he will not extinguish it. Hence, in this an example is given to us that we should not extinguish someone's grace, which the Lord gave him, but rather foster it.

1005. Likewise, he will not pass judgment '*until he send forth judgment unto victory.*' And this can be read in a particular way as about the Jews, namely when he has overcome all, because they were accusing him of casting out demons by Beelzebub. And he confounded them, then imposed a judgment on them. And this was carried out by Titus and Vespasian. And not only this will come about, but when these are destroyed, '*in his name the gentiles will hope.*' Hence, *he will be the expectation of nations* (Gen 49:10).

Or in another way: he restrains his will thus, and judges no one; but when hostile death is destroyed, then all the nations will cling to him, and this will be on the day of judgment.

Lecture 2

12:22 Tunc oblatus est ei homo daemonium habens, caecus et mutus, et curavit eum, ita ut loqueretur et videret: [n. 1007]

12:23 et stupebant omnes turbae, et dicebant: numquid hic est Filius David? [n. 1009]

12:24 Pharisaei autem audientes dixerunt: hic non eiicit daemones, nisi in Beelzebub principe daemoniorum. [n. 1009]

12:25 Iesus autem sciens cogitationes eorum, dixit eis: omne regnum divisum contra se desolabitur: et omnis civitas vel domus divisa contra se non stabit. [n. 1010]

12:26 Et si satanas satanam eiicit, adversus se divisus est; quomodo ergo stabit regnum eius? [n. 1012]

12:27 Et si ego in Beelzebub eiicio daemones, filii vestri in quo eiiciunt? Ideo ipsi iudices vestri erunt. [n. 1014]

12:28 Si autem ego in Spiritu Dei eiicio daemones, igitur pervenit in vos regnum Dei. [n. 1016]

12:29 Aut quomodo potest quisquam intrare in domum fortis, et vasa eius diripere, nisi prius alligaverit fortem? Et tunc domum illius diripiet. [n. 1017]

12:30 Qui non est mecum, contra me est: et qui non congregat mecum, spargit. [n. 1020]

12:31 Ideo dico vobis: omne peccatum et blasphemia remittetur hominibus; Spiritus autem blasphemia non remittetur. [n. 1023]

12:32 Et quicumque dixerit verbum contra Filium hominis, remittetur ei; qui autem dixerit contra Spiritum Sanctum verbum, non remittetur ei neque in hoc saeculo, neque in futuro. [n. 1025]

12:22 Τότε προσηνέχθη αὐτῷ δαιμονιζόμενος τυφλὸς καὶ κωφός, καὶ ἐθεράπευσεν αὐτόν, ὥστε τὸν κωφὸν λαλεῖν καὶ βλέπειν.

12:23 καὶ ἐξίσταντο πάντες οἱ ὄχλοι καὶ ἔλεγον· μήτι οὗτός ἐστιν ὁ υἱὸς Δαυίδ;

12:24 οἱ δὲ Φαρισαῖοι ἀκούσαντες εἶπον· οὗτος οὐκ ἐκβάλλει τὰ δαιμόνια εἰ μὴ ἐν τῷ Βεελζεβοὺλ ἄρχοντι τῶν δαιμονίων.

12:25 εἰδὼς δὲ τὰς ἐνθυμήσεις αὐτῶν εἶπεν αὐτοῖς· πᾶσα βασιλεία μερισθεῖσα καθ᾽ ἑαυτῆς ἐρημοῦται καὶ πᾶσα πόλις ἢ οἰκία μερισθεῖσα καθ᾽ ἑαυτῆς οὐ σταθήσεται.

12:26 καὶ εἰ ὁ σατανᾶς τὸν σατανᾶν ἐκβάλλει, ἐφ᾽ ἑαυτὸν ἐμερίσθη· πῶς οὖν σταθήσεται ἡ βασιλεία αὐτοῦ;

12:27 καὶ εἰ ἐγὼ ἐν Βεελζεβοὺλ ἐκβάλλω τὰ δαιμόνια, οἱ υἱοὶ ὑμῶν ἐν τίνι ἐκβάλλουσιν; διὰ τοῦτο αὐτοὶ κριταὶ ἔσονται ὑμῶν.

12:28 εἰ δὲ ἐν πνεύματι θεοῦ ἐγὼ ἐκβάλλω τὰ δαιμόνια, ἄρα ἔφθασεν ἐφ᾽ ὑμᾶς ἡ βασιλεία τοῦ θεοῦ.

12:29 ἢ πῶς δύναταί τις εἰσελθεῖν εἰς τὴν οἰκίαν τοῦ ἰσχυροῦ καὶ τὰ σκεύη αὐτοῦ ἁρπάσαι, ἐὰν μὴ πρῶτον δήσῃ τὸν ἰσχυρόν; καὶ τότε τὴν οἰκίαν αὐτοῦ διαρπάσει.

12:30 ὁ μὴ ὢν μετ᾽ ἐμοῦ κατ᾽ ἐμοῦ ἐστιν, καὶ ὁ μὴ συνάγων μετ᾽ ἐμοῦ σκορπίζει.

12:31 Διὰ τοῦτο λέγω ὑμῖν, πᾶσα ἁμαρτία καὶ βλασφημία ἀφεθήσεται τοῖς ἀνθρώποις, ἡ δὲ τοῦ πνεύματος βλασφημία οὐκ ἀφεθήσεται.

12:32 καὶ ὃς ἐὰν εἴπῃ λόγον κατὰ τοῦ υἱοῦ τοῦ ἀνθρώπου, ἀφεθήσεται αὐτῷ· ὃς δ᾽ ἂν εἴπῃ κατὰ τοῦ πνεύματος τοῦ ἁγίου, οὐκ ἀφεθήσεται αὐτῷ οὔτε ἐν τούτῳ τῷ αἰῶνι οὔτε ἐν τῷ μέλλοντι.

12:22 Then was offered to him one possessed with a devil, blind and dumb: and he healed him, so that he spoke and saw. [n. 1007]

12:23 And all the multitudes were amazed, and said: is not this the Son of David? [n. 1009]

12:24 But the Pharisees hearing it, said: this man does not cast out the devils except by Beelzebub the prince of the devils. [n. 1009]

12:25 And Jesus knowing their thoughts, said to them: every kingdom divided against itself will be made desolate: and every city or house divided against itself will not stand. [n. 1010]

12:26 And if satan cast out satan, he is divided against himself: how then will his kingdom stand? [n. 1012]

12:27 And if I by Beelzebub cast out devils, by whom do your children cast them out? Therefore they will be your judges. [n. 1014]

12:28 But if I by the Spirit of God cast out devils, then is the kingdom of God come upon you. [n. 1016]

12:29 Or how can anyone enter into the house of the strong, and plunder his vessels, unless he first bind the strong? And then he will plunder his house. [n. 1017]

12:30 He who is not with me, is against me: and he who does not gather with me, scatters. [n. 1020]

12:31 Therefore I say to you: every sin and blasphemy will be forgiven men, but the blasphemy of the Spirit will not be forgiven. [n. 1023]

12:32 And whoever will speak a word against the Son of man, it will be forgiven him: but he who will speak against the Holy Spirit, it will not be forgiven him, neither in this world, nor in the world to come. [n. 1025]

12:33 Aut facite arborem bonam, et fructum eius bonum, aut facite arborem malam, et fructum eius malum: siquidem ex fructu arbor agnoscitur. [n. 1034]

12:33 Ἢ ποιήσατε τὸ δένδρον καλὸν καὶ τὸν καρπὸν αὐτοῦ καλόν, ἢ ποιήσατε τὸ δένδρον σαπρὸν καὶ τὸν καρπὸν αὐτοῦ σαπρόν· ἐκ γὰρ τοῦ καρποῦ τὸ δένδρον γινώσκεται.

12:33 Either make the tree good and its fruit good: or make the tree evil, and its fruit evil. For by the fruit the tree is known. [n. 1034]

12:34 Progenies viperarum, quomodo potestis bona loqui, cum sitis mali? Ex abundantia enim cordis os loquitur. [n. 1037]

12:34 γεννήματα ἐχιδνῶν, πῶς δύνασθε ἀγαθὰ λαλεῖν πονηροὶ ὄντες; ἐκ γὰρ τοῦ περισσεύματος τῆς καρδίας τὸ στόμα λαλεῖ.

12:34 O generation of vipers, how can you speak good things, whereas you are evil? For out of the abundance of the heart the mouth speaks. [n. 1037]

12:35 Bonus homo de bono thesauro profert bona, et malus homo de malo thesauro profert mala. [n. 1040]

12:35 ὁ ἀγαθὸς ἄνθρωπος ἐκ τοῦ ἀγαθοῦ θησαυροῦ ἐκβάλλει ἀγαθά, καὶ ὁ πονηρὸς ἄνθρωπος ἐκ τοῦ πονηροῦ θησαυροῦ ἐκβάλλει πονηρά.

12:35 A good man out of a good treasure brings forth good things: and an evil man out of an evil treasure brings forth evil things. [n. 1040]

12:36 Dico autem vobis, quoniam omne verbum otiosum quod locuti fuerint homines, reddent rationem de eo in die iudicii. [n. 1043]

12:36 λέγω δὲ ὑμῖν ὅτι πᾶν ῥῆμα ἀργὸν ὃ λαλήσουσιν οἱ ἄνθρωποι ἀποδώσουσιν περὶ αὐτοῦ λόγον ἐν ἡμέρᾳ κρίσεως·

12:36 But I say unto you, that every idle word that men will speak, they will render an account for it in the day of judgment. [n. 1043]

12:37 Ex verbis enim tuis iustificaberis, et ex verbis tuis condemnaberis. [n. 1045]

12:37 ἐκ γὰρ τῶν λόγων σου δικαιωθήσῃ, καὶ ἐκ τῶν λόγων σου καταδικασθήσῃ.

12:37 For by your words you will be justified, and by your words you will be condemned. [n. 1045]

1006. Supra repulit Dominus eos qui calumniabantur et suae doctrinae, et suae vitae, hic vero repellit eos qui suis miraculis detrahunt. Et

primo ponitur miraculum;

secundo perversitas detrahentium;

tertio confutatio eorum.

Secunda ibi *et stupebant omnes* etc.; tertia ibi *Iesus autem* et cetera.

Circa miraculum duo ponuntur.

Primo ponitur multiplex infirmitas;

secundo perfecta curatio, ibi *et curavit eum, ita ut loqueretur, et videret.*

1007. Dicit ergo *tunc oblatus est ei homo daemonium habens.* De hoc habetur Lc. XI, 14 sub aliis verbis. Sed non est inconveniens; quod recitatur in uno, subticetur in alio. Per istum significatur gentilitas, vel peccator, qui daemonium habet inquantum servus, quia *qui facit peccatum, servus est peccati,* Io. VIII, 34. Iste est caecus privatus lumine gratiae; unde Is. LIX, 10: *palpavimus sicut caeci parietem, et quasi absque oculis attrectavimus* et cetera. Item mutus a confessione fidei. In Ps. XXXVIII, 3: *obmutui, et silui a bonis* et cetera. Et alibi: *quoniam tacui, inveteraverunt ossa mea.*

1008. Sequitur perfecta curatio *et curavit eum,* expellendo mutitatem, *ita ut loqueretur;* expellendo caecitatem, ita ut *videret.* Unde datur perfectio sanitatis; Ps. CII, 3: *qui propitiatur omnibus iniquitatibus tuis, qui sanat omnes infirmitates tuas.* Unde illum non dimisit nec caecum, nec mutum.

1006. Above, the Lord drove back those who were falsely accusing both his teaching and his life; but here he drives back those who slander his miracles. And

first, a miracle is set down;

second, the perversity of those slandering;

third, their refutation.

The second is at *and all the multitudes were amazed.* The third is at *and Jesus knowing their thoughts.*

Concerning the miracle, two things are set down:

first, the manifold infirmity;

second, the perfect healing, at *and he healed him, so that he spoke and saw.*

1007. So it says, *then was offered to him one possessed with a devil, blind and dumb.* This is written about in Luke under different words (Luke 11:14). But it is not unfitting that what is recounted in one be touched upon in another. This man signifies the gentiles, or a sinner, who has a demon insofar as he is a slave, because *he who sins is a slave to sin* (John 8:34). He is blind, deprived of the light of grace; hence, *we have groped for the wall, and like the blind we have groped as if we had no eyes* (Isa 59:10). Likewise, he is mute about the confession of faith. *I was dumb, and was humbled, and kept silence from good things* (Ps 38:3). And in another place: *because I was silent my bones grew old* (Ps 31:3).

1008. There follows the perfect healing: *and he healed him,* by expelling the muteness so that he spoke, and by expelling the blindness so that he saw. Hence perfect health is given; *who forgives all your iniquities: who heals all your diseases* (Ps 102:3). Hence he left him neither blind nor mute.

1009. Sequitur effectus miraculi, scilicet turbarum admiratio, *et stupebant omnes turbae* et cetera. Item eorum confessio; unde *dicebant*, idest confitebantur, *numquid iste est Filius David?* Promissum erat in prophetis, quod Christus de semine David nasceretur; Ier. XXIII, 5: *suscitabo David germen iustum*. Sed videtur impletum, quod supra dictum est cap. XI, 25: *quia abscondisti haec a sapientibus et prudentibus, et revelasti ea parvulis* et cetera. Unde turbae confitebantur. *Pharisaei autem videntes dixerunt: hic non eiicit daemonia, nisi in Beelzebub*, qui est Deus Accaron, ut habetur IV Reg. I, 16, qui dicitur Deus muscarum propter turpissimum ritum sanguinis immolatitii, ratione cuius multae muscae congregabantur. Ideo credebant illum daemonem principem daemoniorum, ideo credebant in potestate illius posse eiici daemonia; Ier. V, 5: *ibo ad optimates, et loquar eis*. Et paulo post, *et ecce magis hi simul confregerunt iugum, ruperunt vincula*.

1010. *Iesus autem sciens cogitationes eorum* et cetera. In parte ista repellit Dominus detrahentes.

Et primo arguit contra dicta;

secundo contra dicentes, ibi *ideo dico vobis*: et cetera.

Dictum redarguit quadruplici argumento.

Secundum ibi *et si satanas satanam* et cetera.

Tertium autem ibi *quomodo ergo* et cetera.

Quartum ibi *qui non est* et cetera.

1011. Primum expressissime ponitur: *omne regnum contra se divisum desolabitur*. Primo ponit maiorem, cum dicit *omne regnum* et cetera.

Triplex est communitas: domus, sive familiae, civitatis, et regni. Domus est communitas consistens ex his, per quos fiunt communes actus; ideo consistit ex triplici coniugatione, ex patre et filio, ex marito et uxore, ex domino et servo. Communitas civitatis omnia continet quae ad vitam hominis sunt necessaria: unde est perfecta communitas quantum ad mere necessaria. Tertia communitas est regni, quae est communitas consummationis. Ubi enim esset timor hostium, non posset per se una civitas subsistere; ideo propter timorem hostium necessaria est communitas civitatum plurium, quae faciunt unum regnum. Unde sicut vita in quolibet homine ita pax in regno; et sicut sanitas nihil est nisi temperantia humorum, sic pax est cum unumquodque retinet ordinem suum. Et sicut, recedente sanitate, tendit homo ad interitum; sic de pace; si a regno discedit, tendit ad interitum. Unde ultimum quod attenditur, est pax. Unde

1009. There follows the effect of the miracle, namely the wonderment of the crowds, *and all the multitudes were amazed*. Likewise, their confession; hence they *said*, i.e., they confessed, *is not this the Son of David?* It had been promised in the prophets that the Christ would be born of the seed of David; *I will raise up to David a just branch* (Jer 23:5). But what was said above seems to be fulfilled, *you have hidden these things from the wise and prudent, and have revealed them to the little ones* (Matt 11:25). Hence the crowds confessed, *but the Pharisees hearing it, said: this man does not cast out the devils except by Beelzebub the prince of the devils*, who is the god of Accaron, as is written, who is called the god of flies because of the most shameful rite of sacrificed blood, on account of which many flies gathered around (2 Kgs 1:16). So they believed that this demon was the prince of demons, and for this reason they believed that one could cast out demons in his power; *I will go therefore to the great men, and I will speak to them* (Jer 5:5). And a little later, *and behold these have together broken the yoke more, and have burst the bonds*.

1010. *And Jesus knowing their thoughts*. In this part, the Lord drives back those who slander.

And first, he argues against what was said;

second, against those who said it, there *therefore I say to you*.

He refutes what was said by four arguments.

The second is at *and if satan cast out satan*;

the third, at *or how can anyone enter into the house of the strong*;

the fourth, at *he who is not with me*.

1011. The first is set down most expressively: *every kingdom divided against itself will be made desolate*. First, he sets down the greater one, when he says, *every kingdom*.

There are three sorts of community: the house or family, the city, and the kingdom. The house is a community formed out of those things which bring about common actions; therefore it is formed out of three conjoinings, out of father and son, out of husband and wife, and out of lord and slave. The community of the city contains all the things which are necessary for the life of man: hence, it is a perfect community as regards the mere necessities. The third community is that of the kingdom, which is the community of completion. For where there is a fear of enemies, one city cannot subsist on its own; therefore, owing to fear of enemies, a community of many cities which makes up one kingdom is necessary. Hence what life is in a man, so is peace in a kingdom; and just as health is nothing but the blending of the humors, so is peace when each one preserves his own order. And just as when health is withdrawn a man tends toward destruction, so it is with peace: if it

Philosophus: *sicut medicus ad sanitatem, sic defensor rei-publicae ad pacem.*

Ideo dicit **omne regnum in se divisum desolabitur**. Osee X, 2: *divisum est cor eorum, nunc interibunt.* Is. III, 5: *tumultuabitur puer contra senem, et ignobilis contra nobilem.*

1012. **Et si satanas satanam eiicit, adversus se divisus est**. Eiectio importat actionem violentam; ideo oportet, quod ubi est contradictio, sit divisio, quia *inter superbos semper sunt iurgia*, Prov. XIII, 10.

Sed posset quis dicere: non est eiectio: quia voluntarie exit. Sed hoc non habet locum, quia talis exitus non est eiectio, sed fit ex obedientia alio imperante; unde hic esset voluntarius exitus. Sed quod involuntarie exeant, apparet per hoc quod dictum est supra, quod inceperunt gemere, et clamare, **quid nobis et tibi, Iesu Fili Dei? Venisti huc ante tempus torquere nos**. Ergo est divisio.

1013. **Quomodo ergo stabit regnum eius?** Quod ad propositum Hieronymus exponit sic: **quomodo stabit regnum eius?** Quasi dicat, regnum diaboli stat in peccatoribus usque ad diem iudicii, quia tunc evacuabitur omnis potestas. Unde si hoc esset, iam esset finis mundi. Rabanus sic **quomodo stabit regnum eius?** Quia si pugnatur contra eum: ergo est in casu; ergo a regno suo debetis cavere. Hilarius. **Quomodo stabit?** Quasi dicat: de potestate mea est, quod ego faciam, quod unus expellat alium. Ergo ego destruo regnum diaboli, et ex hoc debetis mihi adhaerere.

1014. **Si ego in Beelzebub**. Hic ponitur secunda ratio. Si ego eiicio aut hoc facio virtute daemonis, aut virtute Spiritus Sancti: quid autem horum sit, non debetis mihi detrahere. Et

primo prosequitur primam;
secundo secundam, ibi **si autem ego in Spiritu Dei eiicio daemones** et cetera.

1015. Dicit ergo **si ego in Beelzebub eiicio daemones, filii vestri in quo eiiciunt?** Hieronymus exponit dupliciter. Uno modo de exorcistis, de quibus habetur Act. XIX, 13, quod quidam exorcistae eiiciebant daemonia in nomine Iesu Christi. Unde **si ego in Beelzebub eiicio daemones, filii vestri in quo eiiciunt?** Quasi dicat, filii vestri eiiciunt. Si ergo de his non calumniamini, nec de me debetis calumniari. Ideo accipitis personam. Unde **iudices vestri erunt**. Quia ego eiicio in virtute Dei,

withdraws from a kingdom, the kingdom tends toward destruction. Hence the last thing attended to is peace. Hence the Philosopher: *just as a doctor is to health, so the defender of the republic is to peace.*

Therefore he says, **every kingdom divided against itself will be made desolate.** *Their heart is divided: now they will perish* (Hos 10:2). *The child will make it tumult against the ancient, and the base against the honorable* (Isa 3:5).

1012. **And if satan cast out satan, he is divided against himself**. Casting out implies a violent action; therefore it is necessary that where there is contradiction, there is division, because *among the proud there are always contentions* (Prov 13:10).

But someone could say: there is no violence, because he goes out willingly. But this does not have a place, because such going out is not casting out, but arises from obedience to another who commands; hence here would be a voluntary going out. But that they do not go out willingly is clear through what was said above, that they began to groan and to cry out, **what have we to do with you, Jesus Son of God? Did you come here to torment us before the time?** (Matt 8:29). Therefore there is division.

1013. **How then will his kingdom stand?** Which Jerome explains as to the purpose in this way: **how then will his kingdom stand?** As though to say, the devil's kingdom stands in sinners until the day of judgment, because then every power will be made empty. Hence if this were to happen, it would already be the end of the world. Rabanus, thus: **how then will his kingdom stand?** Because if battle is waged against him, then he is in a fall; therefore he should take defensive action for his kingdom. Hilary: **how then will his kingdom stand?** As though to say: it is in my power to cause that one should cast out another. Therefore, I destroy the devil's kingdom, and for this reason you should cling to me.

1014. **And if I by Beelzebub cast out devils**. Here the second reason is set down. If I cast out demons, either I do this by the power of demons, or by the power of the Holy Spirit: but whichever of these is the case, you should not slander me.

And first, the first thing is followed out;
second, the second, at **but if I by the Spirit of God cast out devils**.

1015. He says then, **and if I by Beelzebub cast out devils, by whom do your children cast them out?** Jerome explains this in two ways. One way, as about exorcists, of whom it is written that certain exorcists were casting out demons in the name of Jesus Christ (Acts 19:13). Hence, **if I by Beelzebub cast out devils, by whom do your children cast them out?** As though to say: your children cast out demons. Therefore, if you do not slander these, neither should you slander me. Therefore you accept the person. Hence,

ideo ipsi iudicabunt, sicut infra de regina austri, quod ipsa iudicabit.

Vel potest exponi de apostolis. *Filii vestri*: idest apostoli. Appellat autem eos filios eorum, et non discipulos, ut magis moveantur ad eos. Item ut derogantes eis, seipsos redarguant: quia si isti qui filii vestri sunt, eiiciunt, similiter vos faceretis, si praepararetis vos. Ideo quia isti sunt conscii, quod hoc facio potestate mihi tradita, non in Beelzebub ideo iudices vestri erunt, non solum comparatione, sed auctoritate, sicut habetur infra XIX, 28: *sedebitis et vos super sedes duodecim, iudicantes duodecim tribus Israel*.

1016. *Si autem ego in Spiritu Dei eiicio daemones, igitur pervenit in vos regnum Dei*; quasi dicat: stultus est qui repellit a se quae in bonum suum cedunt; hoc autem, scilicet expellere daemones, redit in bonum vestrum.

Inde ergo potestis colligere quod in Spiritu Sancto, quia digitus Dei est Spiritus Sanctus, sicut Filius manus. Nec tamen est inde aliqua invocatio, sed solum fit istud ex auctoritate. Unde *si in Spiritu Dei eiicio daemones* et cetera.

Sed quare dicitur eiectio daemonum fieri in Spiritu Sancto? Quia ei amor et bonitas appropriatur; ideo repellere diabolum nulli bene ita convenit sicut personae Spiritus Sancti. *Pervenit in vos*; Lc. XVII, 21: *regnum Dei intra vos est*. Et quod fit a Christo potestis cognoscere, et hoc est vestra utilitas, ideo dicit *in vos*.

Vel aliter: *regnum Dei*, idest dominium Dei in hominibus; I ad Cor. XV, 25: *oportet autem illum regnare, donec ponat inimicos sub pedibus eius*. Si ergo daemones iam suppeditari incipiunt, iam pervenit in vos regnum et dominium Dei.

1017. *Aut quomodo potest quisquam intrare in domum fortis?* et cetera. Hic ponitur tertia ratio, per quam Dominus dicta Pharisaeorum confutare intendit, et est argumentum ex his quae accidunt erga homines. Quia cum aliquis est potens in domo sua, non potest inde eiici, nec vasa eius disrumpi, nisi fortior superveniat. Sed Christus spoliat vasa diaboli, expellendo eum ab hominibus, in quibus est ut in vasis propriis. Ergo Christus fortior est eo. Et hanc rationem ponit sub his verbis.

1018. *Fortis*. Iste est diabolus, qui fortis dicitur ex virtute; Iob XLI, 24: *non est potestas, quae huic valeat comparari*. Et fortior efficitur per consensum, quia qui consentit, dat vires supra se; Is. XIX, 2: *pugnabit vir contra fratrem, civitas contra civitatem, et tradam Aegyptum in manu dominorum crudelium*.

they will be your judges. Because I cast out demons in the power of God, so they will judge, just as is said below concerning the queen of the south, that she will judge.

Or it can be explained as about the apostles: *your children*, i.e., the apostles. Now, he calls them their children and not disciples to move them more in their favor. Likewise, so that when they insult them, they might refute themselves, because if these who are your children cast out demons, you would do likewise, if you prepared yourself. Therefore, since these men are aware that I do this by a power handed over to me, not in Beelzebub, therefore they will be your judges, not only by comparison, but by authority, as is said below, *you also will sit on twelve seats judging the twelve tribes of Israel* (Matt 19:28).

1016. *But if I by the Spirit of God cast out devils, then is the kingdom of God come upon you*, as though to say: he is a fool who drives away from himself what falls to his own good. But this, namely to expel demons, falls to your good.

So from that you can gather that he casts out demons in the Holy Spirit, because the finger of God is the Holy Spirit, just as Son is the hand. Nor yet is there some invocation from there, but it comes about solely by authority. Hence, *if I by the Spirit of God cast out devils*.

But why does it say that the casting out of demons is done in the Holy Spirit? Because love and goodness are appropriated to him; therefore to drive out the devil belongs to no one as well as to the person of the Holy Spirit. *Is . . . come upon you*; *for the kingdom of God is in your midst* (Luke 17:21). And that it is done by Christ you are able to know, and this is your practical gain, and for this reason he says, *upon you*.

Or in another way: *the kingdom of God*, i.e., the dominion of God in men; *for he must reign until he has put all his enemies under his feet* (1 Cor 15:25). If then the demons are already beginning to be put under his feet, already the kingdom and dominion of God have come upon you.

1017. *Or how can anyone enter into the house of the strong?* Here the third reason is set down, by which the Lord intends to refute what the Pharisees said, and it is an argument from the things that happen to men. Because when someone is powerful in his house, one cannot cast him out from there, nor plunder his vessels, unless a stronger man comes upon him. But Christ robs the devil's vessels, by expelling him from men, in whom he is as in his own vessels. Therefore Christ is stronger than he is. And he sets out this argument under these words.

1018. *The strong*. This is the devil, who is called strong from his power; *there is no power upon earth that can be compared with him who was made to fear no one* (Job 41:24). And he is made strong by consent, because he who consents gives power over himself; *they will fight brother against brother . . . city against city . . . and I will deliver Egypt into the hand of cruel masters* (Isa 19:2).

Domus ista est mundus, vel congregatio peccatorum, non quia mundum creavit, sed quia ei consentiendo obedivit; unde Io. XII, 31 dicitur *princeps huius mundi*.

Vasa eius sunt homines. Vas dupliciter accipitur. Vas alicuius dicitur quod plenum est illo, ut dicitur vas aquae, quia plenum est aqua, vel vas olei, quia plenum est oleo; sic aliqui vasa diaboli, quia pleni diabolo, et hoc secundum corpus, ut obsessi a diabolo: secundum animam vero illi quorum corda sunt in plenaria voluntate diaboli, ut dicitur de Iuda. Aliquando vasa dicuntur quaelibet instrumenta ad quodcumque officium deputata; unde dicitur vas diaboli qui occasionem peccandi aliis tribuit. Et quocumque modo sumatur, diripit Christus vasa diaboli; ad Col. cap. II, 15: *expolians principatus, et potestates, traduxit confidenter, palam triumphans illos in seipso* et cetera.

1019. Hoc tamen non sufficit, nisi alliget fortem; unde ***nisi prius alligaverit fortem***. Quae est haec alligatio? Quia potestas nocendi, quam habet a seipso, cohibetur a Deo. Unde ex virtute naturae suae potest multa facere, sed ex virtute Dei cohibetur, sicut homo ligatus cohibetur ne impleat quod vult. Unde Ps. CXLIX, 8: *ad alligandos reges eorum in compedibus.* ***Et tunc domum eis diripiet***, quia eo ligato, homines ligati disrumpentur; Is. XLIX, 25: *captivitas a forti tolletur, et quod ablatum fuerit a robusto salvabitur.*

1020. ***Qui non est mecum, contra me est***. Hic ponitur quarta ratio, et hic dat firmitatem omnibus. Posset enim aliquis dicere: si per victoriam auferres, posset procedere ratio; sed non facis per violentiam, sed per passionem, ideo non est signum quod alligaveris. Ideo ponit quartam rationem.

Ratio talis est. Quae conveniunt in uno aliquo, opus simile habent: unde qui opera similia faciunt, non se ad invicem impediunt. Sed ego contraria opera facio eis. Ideo ***qui non est mecum, contra me est***. Primo ponit rationem in generali; secundo exemplificat in speciali.

1021. Dicit ergo ***qui non est mecum*** et cetera. Et diabolus apparet quod non est mecum, quia contrarius est operibus meis; II ad Cor. VI, 15: *quae conventio Christi ad Belial?* Quod autem sit contra eum, habetur Eccli. XXXIII, 15: *contra vitam mors, et contra virum iustum peccator*; sic contra hominem diabolus, qui est pater peccati. Sed in quo contrariatur ei? ***Et qui non congregat mecum, spargit***. Dominus enim congregat, Is. XL, v. 11: *in brachio suo congregabit agnos, et in sinu suo levabit eos; foetas ipse portabit.* Diabolus autem dispergit; unde Io. X, v. 12: *lupus rapit et dispergit oves.*

This house is the world, or the congregation of sinners, not because he created the world, but because it obeys him by consenting. Hence he is called *the prince of this world* (John 12:31).

His ***vessels*** are men. Vessels are taken in two ways. That which is full of something is called a vessel of it, as a vessel of water is so called because it is full of water, or a vessel of oil because it is full of oil. In this way, some men are vessels of the devil because they are full of the devil. And this is according to the body, such as those possessed by the devil; but according to the soul, those whose hearts are fully in the devil's will, as is said of Judas. Sometimes a vessel names any instrument assigned to any office whatever; hence he is called a vessel of the devil who gives others occasion for sinning. And whatever way it be taken, Christ plunders the vessels of the devil; *and despoiling the principalities and powers, he has exposed them confidently in open show, triumphing over them in himself* (Col 2:15).

1019. Yet this is not enough, unless he binds the strong man; hence, ***unless he first bind the strong***. What is this binding? That the power of harming which he has in himself is restrained by God. Hence, by the power of his own nature he can do many things, but he is restrained by the power of God, just as a man bound is restrained from doing what he wishes. Hence, *to bind their kings with fetters* (Ps 149:8). ***And then he will plunder his house***, because with him bound, bound men are plundered; *even the captivity will be taken away from the strong: and that which was taken by the mighty, will be delivered* (Isa 49:25).

1020. ***He who is not with me, is against me***. Here the fourth reason is set down, and this one gives strength to all the reasons. For someone could say: if you bear it away by victory, the argument can work; but you do not work through violence, but through the passion, therefore there is no sign that you bind the devil. For this reason, he sets down the fourth argument.

The argument is like this. Those things which agree in some one thing have similar works; hence, those who do similar works do not obstruct one another. But I do works contrary to them. Therefore, ***he who is not with me, is against me***. First, he sets down the argument in general; second, he illustrates it in a particular.

1021. He says then, ***he who is not with me***. And it is clear that the devil is not with me, because he is opposed to my works; *and what concord has Christ with Belial?* (2 Cor 6:15). And that he is against him is found, *life against death: so also is the sinner against a just man* (Sir 33:15); thus the devil, who is the father of sin, is against man. But in what is he against him? ***And he who does not gather with me, scatters***. For the Lord gathers, *he will gather together the lambs with his arm, and will take them up in his bosom, and he himself will carry those who are with young* (Isa 40:11). But the devil scatters; hence, *the wolf catches, and scatters the sheep* (John 10:12).

1022. Sed Lc. IX, 50 habetur: *qui non est adversus vos, pro vobis est* et cetera. Hic autem dici videtur contrarium.

Chrysostomus dicit quod utrumque particulariter dictum est: unde non intelligitur universaliter, sed in casu, et specialiter, quod qui non habet pactum mecum, contra me est. Unde ibi vocabat discipulos, hic diabolos.

Vel aliter possumus dicere, quod aliter est de Deo, et de homine. Constat, quod Deus naturalis est finis in quem omnia tendunt; ideo qui non est cum Deo, oportet quod sit separatus ab eo; unde III Reg. XVIII, 21: *ut quid claudicatis in duas partes? Si Dominus est Deus, sequimini eum.* Sed de homine ad hominem non est ita, quia qui non est pro me, non propter hoc contra me est.

1023. *Ideo dico vobis, omne peccatum et blasphemia remittetur hominibus* et cetera. Postquam confutavit dictum ipsorum, hic invehitur contra eos.

Primo ex gravitate peccati;

secundo ex mala intentione;

tertio ex futuro iudicio.

Secunda ibi *aut facite arborem bonam* et cetera. Tertia ibi *dico autem vobis* et cetera.

Circa primum facit duo.

Primo praemittit quasdam sententias generales;

secundo explicat, ibi *et quicumque dixerit verbum contra Filium hominis* et cetera.

1024. Dicit ergo: ita factum est sicut dicitis *ideo dico vobis* et cetera. Et ponit duas sententias.

Primo de remissione generaliter peccati: dico: *omne peccatum*, scilicet facti, *et blasphemia*, scilicet dicti, *remittetur hominibus*, scilicet si poeniteant. Unde in Ps. CII, 3: *qui propitiatur omnibus iniquitatibus tuis, qui sanat omnes infirmitates tuas.* Et alibi, Ps. XXXI, 1: *beati quorum remissae sunt iniquitates, et quorum tecta sunt peccata.* Et in hoc destruitur opinio Novatii, qui dicebat quod non omnia peccata sint remissibilia: hic autem dicitur, quod omne peccatum est remissibile.

Secundo ponit speciale, quod non remittitur, dicens *Spiritus autem blasphemiae non remittetur*, idest voluntas blasphemandi, scilicet quando ex certa malitia blasphemat. Et haec dicta sunt generaliter.

1025. Deinde accedit ad speciem, et exponit. Et primo, primum dictum exponit. Ita dictum est, quod *omne peccatum* et cetera. Et quod hoc sit verum, ostendo de isto, quia blasphemia quae est contra Filium, remissibilis est. Unde *quicumque dixerit verbum contra Filium hominis, remittetur ei*, scilicet si poeniteat. *Qui autem dixerit contra Spiritum Sanctum*, verbum, *non remittetur ei neque in hoc saeculo, neque in futuro.* Et, ut dicit Augustinus, haec verba ita sunt difficilia, quod non sunt fortiora verba in Evangelio.

1022. But it says, *he who is not against you, is for you* (Luke 9:50). But here it seems to say the contrary.

Chrysostom says that both were said particularly: hence it is not understood universally, but in a certain case, and in a particular way, that he who does not have an agreement with me is against me. Hence there he spoke of the disciples, here of devils.

Or we can say otherwise that it is one way with God, and another with man. It is agreed that God is the natural end to which all things tend; therefore he who is not with God is necessarily separated from him. Hence, *how long do you halt between two sides? If the Lord is God, follow him* (1 Kgs 18:21). But it is not this way as regards a man to a man, because he who is not for me is not for that reason against me.

1023. *Therefore I say to you: every sin and blasphemy will be forgiven men.* After he has refuted what they said, here an argument is brought in against them:

first, from the gravity of sin;

second, from evil intention;

third, from the future judgment.

The second is at *either make the tree good*. The third, at *but I say unto you*.

Concerning the first, he does two things:

first, he prefaces a certain general statement;

second, he explains it, at *and whoever will speak a word against the Son of man*.

1024. He says then: it was done just as you say, *therefore I say to you*. And he sets out two statements.

The first is about the forgiveness of sins generally: *every sin*, namely of deed, *and blasphemy*, namely of word, *will be forgiven men*, namely if they repent. Hence, *who forgives all your iniquities: who heals all your diseases* (Ps 102:3). And in another place, *blessed are they whose iniquities are forgiven, and whose sins are covered* (Ps 31:1). And in this is destroyed the opinion of Novatian, who said that not all sins are forgivable; but here it says that every sin is forgivable.

Second, he sets down a particular which is not forgiven, saying, *but the blasphemy of the Spirit will not be forgiven*, i.e., the will to blaspheme, namely when one blasphemes out of certain malice. And these things are said generally.

1025. Then he approaches the species, and explains. And first, he explains the first thing he said. It was said thus, that *every sin*. And that this is truth, I show by the fact that the blasphemy against the Son is forgivable. Hence, *and whoever will speak a word against the Son of man, it will be forgiven him*, namely if he repents. *But he who will speak against the Holy Spirit, it will not be forgiven him, neither in this world, nor in the world to come.* And as Augustine says, these words are so difficult that there are no stronger words in the Gospel.

1026. Dicendum ergo, quod triplex est modus exponendi. Quidam exponunt ad litteram, quia ipsi videbant ipsum miracula facientem, et opera Spiritus Sancti, et dicebant eum habere spiritum immundum; ideo blasphemabant contra Spiritum Sanctum.

Et in hoc diversa est expositio. Quidam dicunt quod utrumque debet referri ad personam Filii. Sed in Filio duplex est natura, divina et humana; et secundum divinam et spiritus est et sanctus est. Unde Filius dicitur Spiritus Sanctus, non secundum quod sumitur in ratione unius vocabuli, et sic exponit Hilarius. Et est sententia. *Quicumque dixerit verbum contra Filium*, et contra humanam naturam motus ex infirmitate, habet excusationem; sed quicumque dixerit contra divinam, hic non habet rationem veniae.

Alii exponunt de Spiritu Sancto, secundum quod est tertia in Trinitate persona. Unde *quicumque dixerit contra Filium hominis*, idest humanam naturam, *remittetur ei*; sed qui contra Spiritum Sanctum operantem, hic non habet veniam. Haec videtur plena expositio, et hanc videtur dicere textus.

1027. Sed Augustinus obiicit sic. Constat quod omnes Pagani blasphemant, quia non credunt Spiritum Sanctum esse in Ecclesia. Item multi sunt haeretici, et tamen istis non praecluditur via veniae. Item multi Iudaei et cetera. Sed posset aliquis dicere: intelligendum est post acceptam fidem. Sed ad hoc: si hoc sic est, est ne neganda ei poenitentia, si poeniteat? Item non dicit, *quicumque Christianus*, sed generaliter, *quicumque*. Quomodo ergo solverit?

Augustinus solvit dupliciter. Una est expositio in *Sermone Domini in monte*, et illam retractat. Aliam vero ponit in libro *de Verbis Domini*.

1028. Unde intelligere debetis, quod peccatum in Spiritum Sanctum non dicitur blasphemia Spiritus Sancti, sed accipitur ex modo peccandi.

Spiritui sancto attribuitur bonitas, caritas et amor; bonitati malitia respondet, caritati invidia. Si quis ergo cognoscens veritatem, ex malitia deroget veritati, peccat in Spiritum Sanctum. Item si aliquis videat opera sanctitatis in aliquo, et ex invidia deroget: invidia enim sanctitatis, non personae, peccatum irremissibile est; non quia impossibile sit quod remittatur, sed quia tanta labes est peccati, quod ex divina iustitia fit quod non poeniteat. Unde illi qui dicebant, quod in Beelzebub daemonia eiiciebat, non peccabant in Spiritum Sanctum, ut ait Augustinus, quia ad profundam malitiam non venerant et cetera. Sed hoc incepit dicere, non quia hoc facerent, sed ut ipsi qui inceperant, caveret ne ad hunc statum venirent.

1026. One should say then that there are three ways of explaining them. Some explain them literally, for these fellows saw him working miracles, and the works of the Holy Spirit, and they said that he had an unclean spirit. Therefore they blasphemed against the Holy Spirit.

And within this there are different explanations. Some say that both should be referred to the person of the Son. There are two natures in the Son, the divine and the human; and according to the divine he is both spirit and holy. Hence the Son is called the Holy Spirit, not according as it is taken as one name, and Hilary explains it this way. And it is an opinion. *Whoever will speak a word against the Son of man* and against the human nature, moved by infirmity, has an excuse. But whoever speaks against the divine, this man has no reason for pardon.

Others explain it as about the Holy Spirit, according as he is the third in the Trinity of persons. Hence, *whoever will speak a word against the Son of man*, i.e., the human nature, *it will be forgiven him*; but he who speaks against the Holy Spirit working, this man has no pardon. This seems to be a full explanation, and the text seems to say this.

1027. But Augustine objects thus. It is agreed that all the pagans blaspheme, because they do not believe that the Holy Spirit is in the Church. Likewise, there are many heretics, and yet the way of life is not cut off to these. Likewise there are many Jews. But someone could say: one should understand it as after the faith was accepted. But to this he replies: if this is so, is penance denied to them if they repent? Likewise, he does not say, *any Christian whatever*, but generally, *whoever*. How then did he resolve it?

Augustine resolves it in two ways. One is the exposition in *The Sermon of the Lord on the Mount*, and that one he retracts. But he sets out another in the book *On the Words of the Lord*.

1028. Hence you should understand that the sin against the Holy Spirit is not called blasphemy of the Holy Spirit, but is taken from the manner of sinning.

To the Holy Spirit are attributed goodness, charity, and love; goodness responds to evil, charity to envy. Therefore if someone, knowing the truth, insults the truth out of malice, he sins against the Holy Spirit. Similarly, if someone should see works of holiness in someone and slander him out of envy; for envy of holiness, not of a person, is an unforgivable sin, not because it is impossible that it be forgiven, but because it is such a great disaster of sin that out of divine justice it comes about that he does not repent. Hence those who said that he cast out demons in Beelzebub did not sin against the Holy Spirit, as Augustine says, because they had not arrived at profound malice. But he begins to say this, not because they did this, but that those who began might beware lest they arrive at this state.

Hunc sensum reprobat, et retractat Augustinus, quia sic esset aliquis status, pro quo non esset orandum, quod non est verum in via.

1029. Ideo aliter exponit in libro *de Verbis Domini,* et est talis.

Notate quod non dixit, **quicumque dixit verbum blasphemiae,** sed, **verbum** infinite. Sed tale quod infinite ponitur, non universaliter tenetur, sed aliquando particulariter, ut Io. XV, 22: *si non venissem, et locutus non fuissem eis, peccatum non haberent*; non simpliciter, sive universaliter, sed non haberent peccatum infidelitatis: ita similiter qui dixit verbum; non quodcumque verbum, sed tale verbum est, quod si dicatur, irremissibile est.

Quod autem sit illud, dicit Augustinus. Spiritus Sanctus caritas est, per quam membra Ecclesiae Capiti Christo uniuntur, et omne peccatum remittitur per Spiritum Sanctum. Quod etsi remittit tota Trinitas, tamen Spiritui Sancto appropriatur propter amorem. Ille ergo qui habet cor impoenitens, loquitur contra Spiritum Sanctum. Unde ipsa impoenitentia opponitur caritati Spiritus Sancti. Unde non quicumque quodcumque verbum dixerit, sed istud verbum, scilicet verbum impoenitentiae, istud irremissibile est.

Et dicit **verbum,** non *verba,* quia consuetudo est in Scriptura, multa verba unum verbum dicere; unde in Isaia Dominus saepe dicit, *dices verbum meum,* licet multa verba ei diceret. Unde non contradicit ei quod dictum est supra, ibi **dico vobis, omne peccatum et blasphemia** etc., quia qui contra Spiritum Sanctum dixerit verbum, blasphemat. Unde quidam magister interrogatus, quid esset peccatum in Spiritum Sanctum, dixit: *impoenitentia thesaurizat sibi iram.*

1030. Sed quid est quod **non remittitur neque in hoc saeculo, neque in futuro**? Numquid aliqua peccata remittentur in futuro?

Augustinus dicit quod non. Ergo non dicitur quod aliqua in praesenti et alia in futuro remittantur; sed ideo quod sic hic remittitur peccatum, ut valeat in futuro.

Vel aliter. Quia quaedam peccata, scilicet mortalia, in praesenti remittuntur, sed alia, scilicet venialia, in futuro; sicut si aliquis moritur in aliquo veniali, constat quod remittatur. Unde aliqua misericordia erit in futuro, quia tunc adhuc erit viator.

1031. Chrysostomus valde plane exponit, et dicit, quod hic loquitur de duplici blasphemia: contra Filium hominis, et Spiritum Sanctum. Isti blasphemabant Filium hominis, quia dicebant quod potator erat vini. Item alia eorum blasphemia erat contra Spiritum Sanctum, quia dicebant quod in spiritu daemoniaco eiiciebat daemones. De prima habebant excusationem, quia non sciebant; sed de hoc quod contra Spiritum Sanctum

Augustine rejects and retracts this sense, because in this way there would be some state for which one should not pray, which is not true in this life.

1029. Therefore he explains it another way in the book *On the Words of the Lord* and the explanation is of this sort.

Notice that he did not say, **whoever will speak a word of blasphemy,** but rather **a word,** indefinitely. But such a thing as is set down indefinitely is not taken universally, but sometimes particularly, as in, *if I had not come, and spoken to them, they would not have sin* (John 15:22), not simply or universally, but they would not have the sin of infidelity. So likewise he who spoke a word; not any word whatever, but such a word that, if it is said, cannot be forgiven.

Which is this, says Augustine. The Holy Spirit is charity, through whom the members of the Church are united to Christ the Head, and every sin is forgiven through the Holy Spirit. For even if the whole Trinity forgives, still it is appropriated to the Holy Spirit on account of love. Therefore, the man who has an impenitent heart speaks against the Holy Spirit. Hence this very impenitence is opposed to the love of the Holy Spirit. Hence not any word whatever he may have said, but this word, namely the word of impenitence, this is unforgivable.

And he says, **a word,** not *words,* because it is the custom in Scripture to call many words one word; hence in Isaiah, the Lord always says, *you will speak my word,* although he spoke many words to him. Hence what was said above at **therefore I say to you: every sin and blasphemy will be forgiven,** does not contradict him, because he who speaks a word against the Holy Spirit blasphemes. Hence a certain teacher, being asked what is the sin against the Holy Spirit, said: *impenitence stores up wrath for itself.*

1030. But why is it that **it will not be forgiven him, neither in this world, nor in the world to come**? Will some sins be forgiven in the future?

Augustine says not. So it is not said because some are forgiven in the present and some in the future, but because sin is forgiven here that one may do well in the future.

Or in another way: because some sins, namely mortal sins, are forgiven in the present, while others, namely venial, are forgiven in the future; as when someone dies in some venial sin, it is agreed that the sin is forgiven. Hence there will be some mercy in the future, because then one will still be a wayfarer.

1031. Chrysostom explains it very plainly, and says that he speaks here of two blasphemies: against the Son of man, and against the Holy Spirit. These men blasphemed the Son of man because they said that he was a wine drinker. And their other blasphemy was against the Holy Spirit, because they said that he cast out demons in a demoniacal spirit. They had an excuse for the first, because they did not know; but they did not have an excuse for what they said against

dicebant, non habebant excusationem, quia sciebant per Scripturas, et ideo non remittetur.

1032. Sed quid est quod dicit *neque in hoc saeculo, neque in futuro*? Dicitur hoc quia aliquod peccatum punitur in hoc saeculo, aliquod in alio, aliquod hic et ibi. Quoddam in hoc saeculo tantum, ut patet in poenitentibus. Quoddam in futuro tantum, ut illi de quibus dicitur Iob XXI, 13: *ducunt in bonis dies suos, et in puncto ad inferna descendunt.* Quod vero hic et in futuro, est peccatum in Spiritum Sanctum: unde *non remittetur neque in hoc saeculo, neque in futuro*, non quia fiat remissio in futuro, sed quia poena erit in futuro. Unde sensus est quod non remittetur, quin poenam patiatur in hoc saeculo, et in futuro. Sic loquuntur sancti de peccato isto.

1033. Notandum autem quod Magister in *Sententiis*, dist. XLIII, Lib. 2, ponit distinctionem, et assignat sex species peccati in Spiritum Sanctum: desperationem, praesumptionem, impoenitentiam, obstinationem, impugnationem veritatis agnitae, et invidiam fraternae gratiae. Unde dicuntur in Spiritum Sanctum peccare, qui contra appropriata Spiritui Sancto peccant. Patri appropriatur potentia, Filio sapientia, Spiritui Sancto bonitas. Ille ergo in Patrem dicitur peccare, qui ex infirmitate peccat: ille in Filium qui ex ignorantia: ille in Spiritum Sanctum qui ex malitia.

Sed sciendum, quod peccare ex malitia est quando quis voluntarie peccat, quod est ex certa malitia, et hoc dupliciter: vel quia habet inclinationem ad peccatum, vel quia non habet. Quando enim aliquis homo peccata committit multa, ex hoc relinquitur in eo habitus peccandi, et sic peccat ex electione. Item aliquis peccat, quia removetur id per quod retrahebatur a peccato. Retrahitur autem a peccato per spem vitae aeternae: unde qui non sperat in vitam aeternam, peccat ex certa malitia. Ad Ephes. IV, v. 19: *qui desperantes semetipsos tradiderunt impudicitiae.* Unde qui peccat ex inclinatione, peccat in Spiritum Sanctum, scilicet ex hoc quod recedit ab eo quod retrahit a peccato.

Hoc autem fit sex modis. In Deo enim sunt misericordia et iustitia. Ex contemptu misericordiae fit desperatio; ex contemptu iustitiae praesumptio. Item ex parte aversionis, quia convertit se ad bonum fragile, sic fit obstinatio. Item ex parte aversionis, quia non proponit ad Deum reverti, fit impoenitentia. Item ex parte remedii, scilicet spei et caritatis, fit impugnatio veritatis agnitae, et invidentia fraternae dilectionis. Haec sunt peccata in Spiritum Sanctum.

the Holy Spirit, because they knew through the Scriptures, and therefore it will not be forgiven.

1032. But why does he say, *neither in this world, nor in the world to come*? This is said because some sin is punished in this age, some in the other, some both here and there. Certain ones in this age only, as is clear in penitents. Certain ones in the future only, as those of whom it is said, *they spend their days in wealth, and in a moment they go down to hell* (Job 21:13). But what is punished both here and in the future is the sin against the Holy Spirit. Hence *it will not be forgiven him, neither in this world, nor in the world to come*, not because there will be forgiveness in the future, but because there will be punishment in the future. Hence the sense is that it will not be forgiven, but rather punishment is suffered in this age and in the age to come. Thus speak the saints about this sin.

1033. One should notice that the Teacher places a distinction in the *Sentences* (dist. 43, book 2), and assigns six species of sin against the Holy Spirit: despair, presumption, impenitence, obstinacy, fighting against recognized truth, and envy of a brother's grace. Hence they are said to sin against the Holy Spirit who sin against the things appropriated to the Holy Spirit. To the Father is appropriated power, to the Son wisdom, to the Holy Spirit goodness. Therefore that man is said to sin against the Father who sins out of weakness; that man is said to sin against the Son who sins out of ignorance; that man is said to sin against the Holy Spirit who sins out of malice.

But one should know that to sin out of malice is when someone sins voluntarily, which is from certain malice, and this in two ways: either because he has an inclination to the sin, or because he does not have an inclination. For when a man commits many sins, there remains in him from this a habit of sinning, and thus he sins by choice. Similarly, someone may sin because that by which he was restrained from sin is removed. Now, one is withheld from sin by the hope of eternal life. Hence he who does not hope for eternal life sins out of certain malice. *Who despairing, have given themselves up to lasciviousness* (Eph 4:19). Hence he who sins from an inclination sins against the Holy Spirit, namely from the fact that he withdraws from that which restrains him from sin.

Now, this comes about in six ways. For in God there are mercy and justice. From contempt of mercy there comes despair; from contempt of justice, presumption. Likewise on the part of aversion, because one turns himself toward some impermanent good, and from this there comes obstinacy. Likewise on the part of aversion, because one does not intend to be turned back to God, there comes impenitence. Likewise on the part of the remedy, namely on the part of hope and love, there comes about fighting against a recognized truth and envy of a brother's love. These are the sins against the Holy Spirit.

Si ergo sit impoenitentia actualis, sic non remittitur; non quia non remittatur omnino, sed quia non facile remittitur, quia non habet aliquam rationem remittendi, sed ex sola gratia Dei, ut si aliquis habeat febrem, utpote tertianam, habet unde sanari potest; sed si habet 'emitriteum', non habet unde sanari possit de se, quia non sanatur nisi ex divino adiutorio.

1034. Sequitur *aut facite arborem bonam, et fructum eius bonum, aut facite arborem malam, et fructum eius malum*. Supra Dominus confutavit Pharisaeorum ritum, prout erant contra ipsius opera loquentes, ostendens gravitatem peccati, nunc contra ipsos dicentes pravam eius esse doctrinam. Et

primo ponit similitudinem;

secundo adaptat;

tertio rationem assignat.

Secunda ibi *progenies viperarum* etc.; tertia ibi *ex abundantia cordis os loquitur*.

Circa primum duo facit.

Primo ponit similitudinem;

secundo inducit probationem, ibi *siquidem ex fructu arbor cognoscitur*.

1035. Dicit ergo *aut facite arborem bonam et fructum eius bonum* et cetera. Istud dupliciter exponitur. Una expositio secundum Chrysostomum et Hieronymum; alia secundum Augustinum.

Secundum Ioannem Chrysostomum sic exponitur. Vult ostendere vituperationem eorum esse irrationabilem; unde comparat actus ad vitam, sicut fructus ad arborem. Si aliquis videt fructum bonum, iudicat arborem esse bonam; similiter, e converso, si malum. Isti videbant actus Christi, puta expellere daemones, et hoc erat bonum; ideo valde irrationabile est quod dicitis. Et optime procedit ab effectu in causam, ut dicit Apostolus ad Rom. I, 20: *invisibilia enim ipsius a creatura mundi per ea quae facta sunt, intellecta conspiciuntur* et cetera. Unde vult dicere: aut vos, scilicet Pharisaei, facite, idest concedatis, quia si fructus bonus est, quod arbor bona est: aut facite, idest dicite quod fructus malus est, et ita arbor mala. Et hoc non potestis dicere.

Augustinus autem refert ad intentionem. Isti dicebant, quod in Beelzebub daemonia eiiciebat. Vult ergo ostendere ex qua radice hoc processerit, quia ex malitia cordis: ideo dicit *aut facite*. Hic ponuntur duo, unum meritorium, ut fiat, *facite* etc., et date operam et studium ut sitis arbor bona, quod non potest homo sine praeparatione. Unde facite ut sitis arbor bona, et tunc erit fructus bonus, et verba bona. Quod autem sequitur, est ut caveant, scilicet *aut facite arborem malam, et fructum eius malum*: aut studebitis malitiae, et sic eritis arbor mala, et fructus malus; Ier. II, 21: *ego plantavi te vineam*

If therefore there is actual impenitence, in this way it is not forgiven; not because it is in no way forgiven, but because it is not easily forgiven, because it has no reason to be forgiven except by the sole grace of God. As when someone has a fever, such as a three day fever, he has something by which he can be healed; but if he has an 'emitriteus', he has nothing by which he can be healed, because he is not healed except by divine help.

1034. There follows *either make the tree good and its fruit good: or make the tree evil, and its fruit evil*. Above, the Lord refuted the ceremony of the Pharisees, according as they were speaking against his works, showing the gravity of the sin; now he speaks against those saying his teaching was corrupt. And

first, he sets out a likeness;

second, he applies it;

third, he gives a reason.

The second is at *O generation of vipers*; the third, at *out of the abundance of the heart the mouth speaks*.

Concerning the first, he does two things:

first, he sets out a likeness;

second, he brings in a proof, at *for by the fruit the tree is known*.

1035. He says then, *either make the tree good and its fruit good*. This is explained in two ways: one explanation according to Chrysostom and Jerome, another according to Augustine.

According to John Chrysostom, it is explained in this way. He wishes to show that their fault-finding is irrational, so he matches action to life, as fruit to a tree. If someone sees good fruit, he judges that the tree is good; similarly, the other way around if the fruit is bad. These men saw Christ's action, namely expelling demons, and this was good. Therefore what you say is very irrational. And he proceeds from effect to cause in the best way, as the Apostle says, *for the invisible things of him, from the creation of the world, are clearly seen, being understood by the things that are made* (Rom 1:20). Hence he wishes to say: either you, namely the Pharisees, make, i.e., concede, that if the fruit is good, the tree is good; or make, i.e., say, that the fruit is evil and so the tree evil. And this you cannot say.

But Augustine refers it to the intention. They said that he cast out demons in Beelzebub. Therefore, he wishes to show from what root this would have proceeded, that it would have proceeded from malice of heart. So he says: *either make*. Here two things are set down. One meritorious, that one *make the tree good*, and work and study that you may be a good tree, which a man cannot do without preparation. Hence strive that you may be a good tree, and then there will be good fruit, and good words. And what follows is said that they may beware, namely *or make the tree evil, and its fruit evil*: or you will be eager for evil, and thus you will be an evil tree, and the fruit evil. *Yet I planted you a*

meam electam, quomodo conversa es mihi in pravum, vi-nea aliena?

1036. Secundum autem utramque lecturam convenit probatio quae sequitur *siquidem ex fructu arbor cognoscitur* etc., quia per fructum bonum bona, per fructum malum mala.

1037. *Progenies viperarum* et cetera. Et hoc diversimode subditur praemissis secundum diversas expositiones.

Secundum Augustinum est quaedam applicatio ad propositum sic. Dictum est *aut facite* et cetera. Et vos facitis malum. Vos estis arbor mala, et quia arbor mala, mala facitis, quia non potestis bona loqui.

Secundum expositionem aliorum ostendit ex quo procedat haec malitia, et vocat Pharisaeos *progenies viperarum*, quia qui a pueritia malitiam habent, firmius tenent; ideo malitia viperae dicitur malitia eorum; Prov. cap. XXII, 6: *adolescens iuxta viam suam, cum senuerit, non recedet ab ea.* Ideo pluries qui parentes habent malos, promptiores sunt ad malum; Ier. XIV, 20: *cognovimus iniquitates patrum nostrorum.* Unde bonum est, quod homo a consuetudine subdat se bono operi. Item natura serpentum est, quod cum lingua venenum eiiciunt, sic mali faciunt; Iob XX, 16: *occidit eum lingua viperae.* Et in Ps. CXXXIX, 4: *acuerunt linguas suas sicut serpentes.*

Ideo dicit *quomodo potestis bona loqui?* Non dicit *bona facere*, sed *loqui*, quia filii estis viperae, quae nocet lingua; ideo cum sitis imitatores patrum sceleris, *quomodo potestis bona loqui?* Quasi dicat, *non potestis.*

1038. Et assignat rationem: et
primo in generali;
secundo in speciali, ibi *bonus homo de bono thesauro profert bona* et cetera.

1039. Dicit ergo: ita non potestis loqui. Unde? Quia mali estis. Quare? *Quia ex abundantia cordis os loquitur*, quia vox est signum intellectus.

Dicit *ex abundantia cordis*, quia, secundum Chrysostomum, cum aliquis ex malitia loquitur, signum est quod maior malitia sit in corde, quia de hoc quod intus retinet, nullum timet. Dum ergo aliquid ex malitia profert, signum est quod magis sit intus, quod proferre non audet. Ideo dicit *ex abundantia cordis os loquitur.* Et ex abundantia malitiae interius os loquitur, et hoc est in bono, et in malo. Unde Ier. XX, 9: *factus est sermo Domini in me quasi ignis* et cetera. Item in malo similiter, quia aliqui ex malitia concipiunt aliquid quod non possunt

chosen vineyard, all true seed: how then are you turned unto me into that which is good for nothing, O strange vineyard? (Jer 2:21).

1036. But according to either reading, the proof which follows fits in: *for by the fruit the tree is known*, because by good fruit a good tree is known, by evil fruit an evil tree.

1037. *O generation of vipers.* And this is connected to what came before in different ways, according to the different explanations.

According to Augustine, there is a certain application to the thing intended in this way. It was said, *either make the tree good . . . or make the tree evil.* And you make it evil. You are the evil tree, and because you are an evil tree, you do evil, because you cannot speak good.

According to the others' explanation, he shows what this malice proceeds from, and calls the Pharisees a *generation of vipers*, because those who have malice from boyhood hold it more firmly. For this reason their malice is called the malice of a viper; *a young man according to his way, even when he is old he will not depart from it* (Prov 22:6). For this reason oftentimes those who have evil parents are more prompt to do evil; *we acknowledge, O Lord, our wickedness, the iniquities of our fathers* (Jer 14:20). Hence, it is good that a man should apply himself to good works out of custom. Likewise, it is the nature of serpents that they spit out venom with the tongue; thus do evil men. *The viper's tongue will kill him* (Job 20:16). And, *they have sharpened their tongues like a serpent: the venom of asps is under their lips* (Ps 139:4).

So he says, *how can you speak good things?* He does not say *do good things*, but *speak*, because you are the sons of vipers, which harm with the tongue. So since you are imitators of your father's wicked deeds, *how can you speak good things?* As though to say, *you cannot.*

1038. And he gives the reason. And
first, in general;
second, in particular, at *a good man out of a good treasure.*

1039. He says then: you cannot speak good things. For what reason? Because you are evil. Why? *For out of the abundance of the heart the mouth speaks*, because the voice is a sign of the intellect.

He says, *out of the abundance of the heart*, because, according to Chrysostom, when someone speaks out of malice, it is a sign that there is a greater malice in the heart, because he has nothing to fear from what he keeps within. Therefore, when something is brought forth out of malice, it is a sign that there is more inside, which he does not dare bring forth. This is why he says, *out of the abundance of the heart the mouth speaks.* And out of an abundance of malice, the interior mouth speaks, and this is in the good and in the evil. Hence, *the word of the Lord came in my*

retinere; Iob XXXII, 18: *coarctat me spiritus uteri mei et cetera.*

1040. *Bonus homo de bono thesauro profert bona.* Quod dixerat *ex abundantia cordis os loquitur*, exponit in particulari. Verbum quod egreditur de cogitatione, est sicut donum quod egreditur de thesauro. Unde si cogitatio est bona, verbum est bonum, et e contrario. Bonus thesaurus est scientia veritatis et timor Domini; Is. XXXIII, v. 6: *divitiae salutis sapientia et scientia, timor Domini ipse thesaurus est.* Item malus thesaurus est mala cogitatio; et de hoc non procedit nisi malum; Prov. X, 2: *nil proderunt thesauri impietatis.*

Videte: quod de verbis ibi dicitur, istud etiam intelligitur de operibus. Sicut enim cogitatio est radix sermonis, ita intentio operationis; ideo si intentio est bona, opus est bonum. Unde ibi Glossa, *tantum facis quantum intendis.*

1041. In bono videtur habere instantiam. Ponatur quod aliquis velit furari ut det eleemosynam, actus est malus et intentio bona: ergo et cetera.

Dico. Intentio et voluntas quandoque distinguuntur, quando scilicet in uno et eodem aliud est voluntas et intentio. Voluntas est de obiecto volito, intentio de fine: voluntas est sicut si volo ire ad fenestram ut videam transeuntes, haec est intentio, quasi extra tentio: unde oportet quod voluntas et intentio unum sint. Unde possumus large considerare intentionem, et voluntatem, et sic in isto. Si voluntas est mala, actus est malus. Tamen si excludatur, et sumatur proprie, non est verum.

1042. Sed, posito quod intentio et actus voluntatis unum sint, quid inde?

Est dicendum, quod principalitas meriti consistit circa caritatem, ex consequenti circa meritum aliarum virtutum. Meritum enim respicit praemium essentiale, penes quod consideratur caritas. Sic unumquodque opus, quod in maiori fit caritate, magis habet de merito. Sola caritas habet Deum pro obiecto et fine. Unde meritum caritatis respondet praemio substantiali, meritum aliarum virtutum praemio accidentali. Quia igitur caritas informat intentionem, quanto aliquis ex maiori caritate aliquid intendit, tantum facit; sed quantum ad praemium accidentale non.

1043. *Dico autem vobis* et cetera. Dominus istos reprehendit propter gravitatem peccati, et propter malitiam eorum; nunc propter futurum iudicium, quod fide tenemus: dicitur enim Iob XIX, 29: *fugite a facie gladii, quoniam ultor iniquitatum gladius est: et scitote esse iudicium*; Eccle. XII, 14: *cuncta quae fiunt, adducet Dominus in iudicium pro omni errato, sive bonum sive malum sit.*

heart as a burning fire shut up in my bones (Jer 20:9). And similarly in the evil, because some conceive something out of malice which they cannot keep within; *for I am full of matter to speak of, and the spirit of my bowels constrains me* (Job 32:18).

1040. *A good man out of a good treasure brings forth good things.* He explains in the particular what he had said, *out of the abundance of the heart the mouth speaks.* A word which is brought forth from thought is like a gift which is brought forth from a treasure. Hence if the thought is good, the word is good, and vice versa. The good treasure is the knowledge of truth and the fear of the Lord; *riches of salvation, wisdom and knowledge: the fear of the Lord is his treasure* (Isa 33:6). Likewise the evil treasure is an evil thought, and nothing comes from this but evil; *treasures of wickedness will profit nothing* (Prov 10:2).

See: what is said there about words is also understood with regard to works. For just as thought is the root of words, so intention is the root of works. Therefore, if the intention is good, the work is good. Hence the Gloss there: *as much as you intend, that much you do.*

1041. In the good there seems to be an objection. Let it be supposed that someone wills to steal in order to give alms: the act is evil and the intention good. Therefore.

I say: intention and will are sometimes distinguished, namely when the will and the intention are different in one and the same. The will is of the object willed, the intention is of the end. The will is as when I go to the window to see those passing by, this is intention, as it were beyond the holding. Hence it is necessary that the will and the intention be the same. Hence we can consider intention and will broadly, and so it is in this case. If the will is evil, the act is evil. Yet if the wide sense is excluded, and it is taken properly, it is not true.

1042. But, if it is set down that the intention and the act of the will are one, what then?

One should say that the principle of merit consists in charity, and by consequence in the merit of the other virtues. For merit regards the essential reward, according as charity is considered. Thus whatever work is done in greater charity has more merit. Only charity has God for its object and end. Hence the merit of charity corresponds to the substantial reward, and the merit of the other virtues to the accidental rewards. Since therefore charity shapes the intention, as much as someone intends something from a greater charity, that much he does; but not as regards the accidental reward.

1043. *But I say unto you.* The Lord reproached them because of the gravity of their sin, and because of their malice; now, because of the future judgment, which we hold by faith. For it is said, *flee then from the face of the sword, for the sword is the revenger of iniquities: and know you that there is judgment* (Job 19:29). *And all things that are done, God will bring into judgment for every error, whether it be good or evil*

Item II ad Cor. V, 10: *omnes enim nos oportet manifestari ante tribunal Christi, ut referat unusquisque propria corporis, prout gessit, sive bonum sive malum.* Unde ibi erit examinatio, quia reddet unusquisque rationem de factis suis. Ideo addit etiam de verbis, dicens **dico autem vobis, quoniam omne verbum otiosum quod locuti fuerint homines, reddent rationem de eo in die iudicii.** Et hoc dicitur Sap. I, 8: *qui loquitur iniqua, non poterit latere.* Et subditur, quod *sermo obscurus in vacuum non ibit.*

1044. Sed quid est quod dicit **de verbo otioso**? Verbum otiosum dupliciter dicitur. Uno modo omne verbum malum dicitur otiosum; quia illud dicitur otiosum quod non consequitur finem, sicut si aliquis quaerit hominem, et non invenit, dicitur otiose quaesiisse. Verbum autem datur ad instructionem. Quando ergo proficit, non est otiosum: ad Ephes. IV, 29: *omnis sermo malus ex ore vestro non procedat; sed si quis bonum ad aedificationem fidei, ut det gratiam audientibus* et cetera. Et secundum Chrysostomum, respicit ad propositum, quia dixerant quod **in Beelzebub** et cetera. Istud verbum erat perniciosum, ideo etiam otiosum, secundum Hieronymum. Differt quidem perniciosum, et otiosum, quia perniciosum est quod nocumentum infert, otiosum vero quod non affert utilitatem. Gregorius dicit, quod otiosum dicitur, quod caret pia utilitate, vel necessitate. Unde quodlibet verbum quod profertur leviter, dicitur otiosum, nisi habeat piam utilitatem, vel piam necessitatem.

Sed constat quod isti dixerant verbum perniciosum: quare ergo non facit mentionem nisi de otioso? Quia vult arguere a minori: quia si de otioso oportet reddere rationem, multo magis de pernicioso.

1045. Deinde ostendit rationem **ex verbis enim tuis iustificaberis** et cetera. In iudicio mundi aliquando innocentes puniuntur, et mali liberantur, quia iudicium fit secundum dicta testium; in iudicio Dei ex homine ipso seipsum accusante, scilicet ex sui confessione. Unde ut non credas, quod iudiceris per ea quae alii dicent de te, sed per ea quae tu dices de te, ideo dicit **ex verbis enim tuis iustificaberis, et ex verbis tuis condemnaberis.** Sicut Lc. XIX, 22: *ex ore tuo te iudico, serve nequam.*

(Eccl 12:14). Likewise, *for we must all be manifested before the judgment seat of Christ, that everyone may receive the proper things of the body, according as he has done, whether it be good or evil* (2 Cor 5:10). Hence there will be an examination there, for each one will give a reason for his deeds. For this reason, he also adds something about words, saying, **but I say unto you, that every idle word that men will speak, they will render an account for it in the day of judgment.** And this is said, *he who speaks unjust things cannot be hid* (Wis 1:8). And it is added further down that *an obscure speech will not go for naught* (Wis 1:11).

1044. But what is it that he says about an **idle word**? An idle word is said two ways. In one way, every evil word is called idle, because that is called idle which does not obtain its end, as when someone seeks a man and does not find him, he is said to have sought him idly. But a word is given for instruction. Therefore when it profits the hearer, it is not idle; *let no evil speech proceed from your mouth; but that which is good, to the edification of faith, that it may administer grace to the hearers* (Eph 4:29). And according to Chrysostom, he looks to the matter at hand, for they had said that **by Beelzebub.** That word was most pernicious, and therefore also idle. According to Jerome, the pernicious and the idle differ, for the pernicious is that which brings harm, but the idle is that which bears no usefulness. Gregory says that what lacks a pious usefulness or necessity is called idle. Hence any word which is brought forth lightly is called idle, unless it has a pious usefulness, or a pious necessity.

But it is known that these men had spoken a pernicious word: why then does he only mention the idle word? Because he wishes to argue from the lesser, for if a reason must be given for an idle word, much more for a pernicious one.

1045. Then he shows the reason: **for by your words you will be justified.** In the judgment of the world, the innocent are sometimes punished, and the evil set free, because judgment is made according to spoken testimony; in God's judgment, judgment is made by the man himself accusing himself, namely by his own confession. Hence that you may not believe that you will be judged by the things which others say about you, but by the things which you say about yourself, for this reason he says, **for by your words you will be justified, and by your words you will be condemned.** As in, *out of your own mouth I judge you, you wicked servant* (Luke 19:22).

Lecture 3

12:38 Tunc responderunt ei quidam de scribis et Pharisaeis dicentes: Magister, volumus a te signum videre. [n. 1047]

12:39 Qui respondens ait illis: generatio mala et adultera signum quaerit, et signum non dabitur ei nisi signum Ionae prophetae. [n. 1048]

12:40 Sicut enim fuit Ionas in ventre ceti tribus diebus et tribus noctibus, sic erit Filius hominis in corde terrae tribus diebus et tribus noctibus. [n. 1051]

12:41 Viri Ninevitae surgent in iudicio cum generatione ista, et condemnabunt eam, quia poenitentiam egerunt in praedicatione Ionae. Et ecce plusquam Iona hic. [n. 1053]

12:42 Regina austri surget in iudicio cum generatione ista, et condemnabit eam, quia venit a finibus terrae audire sapientiam Salomonis. Et ecce plusquam Salomon hic. [n. 1058]

12:43 Cum autem immundus spiritus exierit ab homine, ambulat per loca arida, quaerens requiem, et non invenit. [n. 1059]

12:44 Tunc dicit: revertar in domum meam unde exivi. Et veniens invenit vacantem, scopis mundatam et ornatam. [n. 1063]

12:45 Tunc vadit, et assumit septem alios spiritus secum nequiores se, et intrantes habitant ibi, et fiunt novissima hominis illius peiora prioribus. Sic erit generationi huic pessimae. [n. 1065]

12:38 Τότε ἀπεκρίθησαν αὐτῷ τινες τῶν γραμματέων καὶ Φαρισαίων λέγοντες· διδάσκαλε, θέλομεν ἀπὸ σοῦ σημεῖον ἰδεῖν.

12:39 ὁ δὲ ἀποκριθεὶς εἶπεν αὐτοῖς· γενεὰ πονηρὰ καὶ μοιχαλὶς σημεῖον ἐπιζητεῖ, καὶ σημεῖον οὐ δοθήσεται αὐτῇ εἰ μὴ τὸ σημεῖον Ἰωνᾶ τοῦ προφήτου.

12:40 ὥσπερ γὰρ ἦν Ἰωνᾶς ἐν τῇ κοιλίᾳ τοῦ κήτους τρεῖς ἡμέρας καὶ τρεῖς νύκτας, οὕτως ἔσται ὁ υἱὸς τοῦ ἀνθρώπου ἐν τῇ καρδίᾳ τῆς γῆς τρεῖς ἡμέρας καὶ τρεῖς νύκτας.

12:41 ἄνδρες Νινευῖται ἀναστήσονται ἐν τῇ κρίσει μετὰ τῆς γενεᾶς ταύτης καὶ κατακρινοῦσιν αὐτήν, ὅτι μετενόησαν εἰς τὸ κήρυγμα Ἰωνᾶ, καὶ ἰδοὺ πλεῖον Ἰωνᾶ ὧδε.

12:42 βασίλισσα νότου ἐγερθήσεται ἐν τῇ κρίσει μετὰ τῆς γενεᾶς ταύτης καὶ κατακρινεῖ αὐτήν, ὅτι ἦλθεν ἐκ τῶν περάτων τῆς γῆς ἀκοῦσαι τὴν σοφίαν Σολομῶνος, καὶ ἰδοὺ πλεῖον Σολομῶνος ὧδε.

12:43 Ὅταν δὲ τὸ ἀκάθαρτον πνεῦμα ἐξέλθῃ ἀπὸ τοῦ ἀνθρώπου, διέρχεται δι᾽ ἀνύδρων τόπων ζητοῦν ἀνάπαυσιν καὶ οὐχ εὑρίσκει.

12:44 τότε λέγει· εἰς τὸν οἶκόν μου ἐπιστρέψω ὅθεν ἐξῆλθον· καὶ ἐλθὸν εὑρίσκει σχολάζοντα σεσαρωμένον καὶ κεκοσμημένον.

12:45 τότε πορεύεται καὶ παραλαμβάνει μεθ᾽ ἑαυτοῦ ἑπτὰ ἕτερα πνεύματα πονηρότερα ἑαυτοῦ καὶ εἰσελθόντα κατοικεῖ ἐκεῖ· καὶ γίνεται τὰ ἔσχατα τοῦ ἀνθρώπου ἐκείνου χείρονα τῶν πρώτων. οὕτως ἔσται καὶ τῇ γενεᾷ ταύτῃ τῇ πονηρᾷ.

12:38 Then some of the scribes and Pharisees answered him, saying: Master we want to see a sign from you. [n. 1047]

12:39 Answering he said to them: an evil and adulterous generation seeks a sign: and a sign will not be given to it, except the sign of Jonas the prophet. [n. 1048]

12:40 For as Jonas was in the whale's belly for three days and three nights: so will the Son of man be in the heart of the earth for three days and three nights. [n. 1051]

12:41 The men of Niniveh will rise in judgment with this generation, and will condemn it: because they did penance at the preaching of Jonas. And behold one greater than Jonas is here. [n. 1053]

12:42 The queen of the south will rise in judgment with this generation, and will condemn it: because she came from the ends of the earth to hear the wisdom of Solomon, and behold one greater than Solomon is here. [n. 1058]

12:43 And when an unclean spirit has gone out of a man he walks through dry places seeking rest, and finds none. [n. 1059]

12:44 Then he says: I will return into my house from which I came out. And coming he finds it empty, swept, and garnished. [n. 1063]

12:45 Then he goes, and takes with him seven other spirits more wicked than himself, and they enter in and dwell there: and the last state of that man in made worse than the first. So will it be also to this wicked generation. [n. 1065]

1046. Supra Dominus confutavit detrahentes suis miraculis, et doctrinae, hic arguit tentantes; et hic duo facit.

    Primo ponitur interrogatio tentativa;
    secundo reprobatio, ibi **respondens ait illis**.

1046. Above, the Lord refuted those who slandered his miracles and teaching; here he convicts those who were testing him. And he does two things:

    first, the questioning to test him is set down;
    second, the refutation, at **answering he said to them**.

1047. Dicitur ergo *tunc responderunt*; hoc est postquam multa miracula viderant, et postquam multa verba sapientiae audierant, ita quod impletum est in eo quod dicitur Eccli. XXII, 9: *cum dormiente loquitur qui narrat stulto sapientiam*. *Magister, volumus a te signum videre*.

Magister dicunt tentando; Ps. XXVII, 3: *loquuntur pacem in ore suo, mala autem in cordibus eorum*. *Volumus a te signum videre*. Nonne multa signa viderant? Ita; sed alius evangelista sic exponit dicens, Lc. XI, v. 16: *volumus signum de caelo videre*, sicut legitur Lib. I Reg. XII, 18 quod Samuel fecit tonitruum: et Elias qui fecit ignem descendere, IV Reg. I, 10. Proprium enim Iudaeorum est signum petere, ut habetur I ad Cor. I, 22: *Iudaei signum petunt*. Sed cum signa dedisset terrena, non credebant; etiam si daret caelestia, non crederent; Io. III, 12: *si terrena dixi vobis, et non creditis, quomodo si dixero caelestia, credetis?*

1048. *Qui respondens ait illis* et cetera. Consequenter repellit eos: et duo facit.

Primo petitionem negat;

secundo indignitatem ostendit, ibi *viri Ninivitae* et cetera.

Primo designat quod quaerebant;

secundo denegat.

1049. Dicitur ergo *qui respondens ait illis: generatio mala et adultera signum quaerit*. *Malos* enim dicit, quia insidiatores erant. Dicitur quis malus, quia nocet proximo. Generatio ergo mala, et iniqui filii. Dicitur *adultera generatio*, Is. LVII, 3: *vos autem accedite huc filii auguratricis, semen adulteri, et fornicariae*.

1050. Ita ergo ista generatio iniquitati subiecta *signum quaerit, sed non dabitur ei nisi signum Ionae prophetae*. Is. VII, 11: *pete tibi signum a Domino Deo tuo in profundum inferni, sive in excelsum supra* et cetera.

Petebat ergo signum de caelestibus, sed non erant digni videre. Hoc enim dedit apostolis suis, qui viderunt eum ascendentem, qui gloriam Dei viderunt in monte. Sed istis non dabitur nisi signum in inferno, quantum ad animam, et de terra, quantum ad corpus. Unde *non dabitur ei nisi signum Ionae prophetae*. Unde signatur mors Christi, et ostenditur caritas Dei, sicut dicit Apostolus ad Rom. V, 8: *cum adhuc peccatores essemus, secundum tempus Christus pro nobis mortuus est* et cetera. Item, ostenditur potestas resuscitantis ut habetur I ad Cor. XV, 20 ss. Et haec sunt signa eorum, quae in nobis esse debent.

Per mortem Christi significatur nobis quod nos mori debemus peccato; per resurrectionem vero, quod nos debemus a peccato resurgere.

1047. It says then, ***then some of the scribes and Pharisees answered him***, and this after they had seen many miracles, and they had heard many words of wisdom, so that it was fulfilled in them, *he speaks with one who is asleep, who utters wisdom to a fool* (Sir 22:9). ***Master we want to see a sign from you***.

They say, ***Master***, testing; *who speak peace with their neighbor, but evils are in their hearts* (Ps 27:3). ***We want to see a sign from you***. Had they not seen many signs? Yes, but the other evangelists explain it in this way, saying, *and others tempting, asked of him a sign from heaven* (Luke 11:16), as it is written, that Samuel made thunder, and that Elias made fire come down (1 Sam 12:18; 2 Kgs 1:10). For it belongs to the Jews to ask for a sign, as is said, *the Jews require signs* (1 Cor 1:22). But when he had given earthly signs, they did not believe; even if he were to give heavenly signs, they would not believe; *if I have spoken to you earthly things, and you believe not; how will you believe, if I were to speak to you heavenly things?* (John 3:12).

1048. ***Answering he said to them***. Next, he drives them back; and he does two things:

first, he denies their request;

second, he shows their shamelessness, at ***the men of Niniveh***.

First, he points out what they were seeking;

second, he refuses.

1049. It says then, ***answering he said to them: an evil and adulterous generation seeks a sign***. He says, ***evil***, because they were treacherous plotters. Someone is called evil who harms his neighbor. An evil generation, then, and wicked children. It is called an ***adulterous generation***; *but draw near here, you sons of the sorceress, the seed of the adulterer, and of the harlot* (Isa 57:3).

1050. So then, this generation subjected to iniquity ***seeks a sign: and a sign will not be given to it, except the sign of Jonas the prophet***. *Ask a sign of the Lord your God either unto the depth of hell, or unto the height above* (Isa 7:11).

So they were seeking a sign from heaven, but they were not worthy to see. For he gave this to the apostles, who saw him ascend, and who saw God's glory on the mount. But none is given to these but a sign in hell, as regards the soul, and from the earth, as regards the body. Hence, ***a sign will not be given it, except the sign of Jonas the prophet***. Hence the death of Christ is indicated, and God's charity is shown, as the Apostle says, *when as yet we were sinners, according to the time, Christ died for us* (Rom 5:8–9). Likewise is shown the power of rising from the dead (1 Cor 15:20). And these are signs for them, which signs should be in us.

The death of Christ indicates to us that we should die to sin; but the resurrection of Christ, that we should rise from sin.

1051. *Et sicut Ionas fuit in ventre ceti tribus diebus et tribus noctibus*, scilicet secundum veritatem, *sic Filius hominis erit in corde terrae*. Et in hoc confunditur error Manichaei dicentis, quod non in veritate mortuus est.

Et dicit *in corde terrae*, quia sicut cor hominis est in profundo, ita Christus in profundo terrae. Vel *in corde terrae*, idest in corde terrenorum et discipulorum, qui desperabant de eo, ut habetur Lc. ult., 21: *nos autem sperabamus, quod ipse esset redempturus Israel*.

1052. *Tribus diebus et tribus noctibus*. Sed hic est quaestio litteralis. Videtur hoc esse falsum, quia hora nona expiravit, et sepultus est in vespere, resurrexit autem in mane tertiae diei.

Dicit Augustinus, quod aliqui volunt dicere, quod computanda est hora qua positus fuit in cruce. Unde primam noctem dicunt illam tenebrositatem quae apparuit, secunda fuit nox diei veneris, tertia diei Sabbati.

Sed secundum Augustinum non valet: posset tamen nobis suppetere, si tota die Dominica fuisset in sepulcro. Ideo aliter dicendum, quod dies naturalis pro die et nocte, sumitur pro spatio viginti quatuor horarum. Sed, sicut dicit Augustinus, in Scriptura aliquando sumitur pars pro toto. Sic ergo dicendum, quod Christus per synecdochen fuit tribus diebus et tribus noctibus in sepulcro, quia sexta feria pro tota die et etiam pro praecedenti nocte sumitur: de die vero secunda non est dubium; tertia vero nox pro nocte et die sequenti.

Tamen si secundum veritatem inspicimus, fuit duabus noctibus et uno die integro, ad signandum quod suum simplum destruxit nostrum duplum. In nobis erat poena et culpa, in eo poena solum, ideo et cetera.

1053. *Viri Ninivitae surgent in iudicio cum generatione ista*. Hic ponit indignitatem.

Hic est quaestio litteralis. Nonne multa miracula fecit? Nonne Lazarum resuscitavit, et multa alia? Quid est ergo *non dabitur ei nisi signum Ionae prophetae*?

Respondeo. Non dabitur tale signum quale petebant: vel non dabitur signum ad utilitatem eorum; sciebat enim quod non reverterentur, quia indurati erant. Sed signa fecit propter fideles et electos, quales post multi fuerunt.

1054. *Viri Ninivitae* et cetera. Haec est indignitas. Et

primo praeferuntur gentiles;

secundo ponitur ratio, ibi *cum autem immundus spiritus exierit ab homine* et cetera.

1051. *For as Jonas was in the whale's belly for three days and three nights*, that is, according to the truth, *so will the Son of man be in the heart of the earth three days and three nights*. And in this the error of Manichees is refuted, who said that he was not truly dead.

And he says, *in the heart of the earth*, because just as the heart of a man is in the deep part of him, so Christ was in the deep parts of the earth. Or, *in the heart of the earth*, i.e., in the heart of the earthly, and of the disciples, who despaired about him, as is found, *but we hoped, that it was he that should have redeemed Israel* (Luke 24:21).

1052. *Three days and three nights*. But there is a literal question here. It seems that this is false, because on the ninth hour he expired, and he was buried in the evening, and arose on the morning of the third day.

Augustine says that some want to say that the hours during which he was suspended on the cross should be included in the reckoning. Hence they call the first night that darkness which appeared; the second was the night of the holy day; the third was the night of the Sabbath day.

But according to Augustine, this does no good: yet it could have been enough for us if the Lord had been in the sepulcher the whole of the Lord's day. Therefore one should say otherwise, that the natural day for day and night is taken instead of the space of twenty-four hours. But, as Augustine says, sometimes in Scripture the part is taken for the whole. So one should speak in this way, that Christ was in the sepulchre three days and three nights by a synecdoche, because the sixth day is taken for the whole day and even for the preceding night; about the second day there is no doubt; but the third night is taken for the night and day following.

Yet if we examine it according to truth, two nights and one complete day passed, to signify that his own simple sum destroyed our double. Punishment and guilt were in us, and in him only punishment, therefore.

1053. *The men of Niniveh will rise in judgment with this generation*. Here he sets down the shamelessness.

There is a literal question here. Did he not do many miracles? Did he not raise Lazarus, and many others? Why then does he say, *a sign will not be given it, except the sign of Jonas the prophet*?

I respond. Such a sign as they were seeking will not be given; or no sign will be given for their benefit, for he knew that they would not be converted, because they were hardened. But he did signs for the sake of the faithful and the elect, of the same sort as many which happened later.

1054. *The men of Niniveh*. This is the shamelessness. And

first, the gentiles are given preference;

second, the reason is set out, at *and when an unclean spirit has gone out of a man*.

Videte. Aliquis est bonus vel quia non peccat, vel quia poenitet.

Primo ergo praefert eos qui poenituerunt, scilicet gentiles;

secundo qui peccatum non fecerunt, ibi *regina austri* et cetera.

1055. Comparaverat Dominus resurrectionem suam Ionae; ideo possent credere quod istis accideret sicut Ninivitis qui liberati sunt; sed isti non solum non fuerunt liberati, sed fuerunt etiam dispersi. Unde *viri Ninivitae surgent*.

In verbis istis excluditur unus error Iudaeorum, quod resurrectio erit ante iudicium, et quod in medio reaedificabitur Ierusalem. Et adducunt pro se quod dicitur Is. XXV, 6: *faciet Dominus in monte hoc convivium pinguium*.

Alii dixerunt quod iusti et martyres resurgent ante alios per mille annos, et adducunt pro ipsis quod dicitur Apoc. XX, 1: *vidi angelum descendentem de caelo habentem clavem abyssi et catenam magnam in manu sua; et* sequitur, *et apprehendit draconem serpentem antiquum, qui vocatur diabolus, et ligavit eum ut non amplius gentes decipiat, donec consummentur mille anni*. Utrumque excluditur cum dicit *surgent cum generatione ista*, simul boni et non boni.

1056. *Et condemnabunt*, comparatione, non auctoritate, quia inter condemnandos resurgent; Ez. V, 5: *ista est Ierusalem, in medio gentium posui eam et in circuitu eius terras: contempsit iudicia mea ut plus esset impia quam gentes, et praecepta mea ultra quam terrae quae in circuitu eius sunt*.

1057. Et in quo condemnabunt? *Quia poenitentiam egerunt*; isti vero noluerunt facere poenitentiam. Dominus incepit praedicationem suam a poenitentia: Ioannes similiter, et non audierunt; Ier. VIII, 6: *nullus est qui agat poenitentiam super peccato suo*. Item illi fecerunt poenitentiam in una praedicatione Ionae; Iesus autem multas praedicationes eis fecerat, et tamen non sunt conversi; Io. XV, 24: *si opera non fecissem quae nullus alius fecit, peccatum non haberent*. Item conversi sunt in praedicatione unius prophetae; sed isti non solum habuerunt prophetam, sed Filium Dei. Unde habetur ad Hebr. c. I, 1: *multifarie, multisque modis, olim Deus loquens patribus in prophetis, novissime diebus istis, locutus est nobis in Filio, quem constituit haeredem universorum, per quem fecit et saecula* et cetera.

Et sequitur *ecce plusquam Ionas hic*, ut habetur ad Hebr. III, 3: *amplioris gloriae enim iste prae Moyse dignus est*. Ergo Ninivitae praeferuntur, quia poenitentiam egerunt.

Attend. Someone is good either because he does not sin, or because he repents:

first then he gives preference to those who repent, namely the gentiles;

second, those who did not sin, at *the queen of the south*.

1055. The Lord compared his resurrection to Jonas, so they could believe that it would happen to them as to the Ninivites, who were freed. But they were not only not freed, but were also dispersed. Hence, *the men of Niniveh will rise*.

In these words one error of the Jews is excluded, that the resurrection will be before the judgment, and that Jerusalem will be rebuilt inbetween. And they bring in on their behalf what it says, *and the Lord of hosts will make . . . a feast of fat things* (Isa 25:6).

Others said that the just and the martyrs will arise before the others for a thousand years, and they bring in on their behalf what it says, *and I saw an angel coming down from heaven, having the key of the bottomless pit, and a great chain in his hand. And he laid hold on the dragon the old serpent, which is the devil and satan, and bound him for a thousand years . . . that he should no more seduce the nations, till the thousand years be finished* (Rev 20:1–3). Both are excluded when he says, *will rise in judgment with this generation*, the good and the not good at the same time.

1056. *And will condemn it*, by comparison, not by authority, because they will rise among those to be condemned; *this is Jerusalem, I have set her in the midst of the nations, and the countries round about her. And she has despised my judgments, so as to be more wicked than the gentiles; and my commandments, more than the countries that are round about her* (Ezek 5:5–6).

1057. And in what will they condemn them? *Because they did penance*, but these would not do penance. The Lord began his preaching from penance, and John similarly, and they did not listen; *there is none that does penance for his sin* (Jer 8:6). Likewise, those had done penance at Jonas' one preaching; and Jesus had preached to them many times, and yet they were not converted; *if I had not done among them the works that no other man has done, they would not have sin* (John 15:24). Likewise, they were converted at the preaching of one prophet; but these not only had a prophet, but the Son of God. Hence it is said, *God, who, at sundry times and in diverse manners, spoke in times past to the fathers by the prophets, last of all, in these days has spoken to us by his Son, whom he has appointed heir of all things, by whom also he made the world* (Heb 1:1).

And there follows *behold one greater than Jonas here*, as is found, *for this man was counted worthy of greater glory than Moses* (Heb 3:3). Therefore the Ninivites are preferred, because they did penance.

1058. *Regina austri surget in iudicio cum generatione ista, et condemnabit eam*, scilicet in sapientia, quam isti noluerunt recipere. De ista habetur III Reg. X, 24, quod venit audire sapientiam Salomonis. Per istam signatur Ecclesia ex fidelibus; Ps. XLIV, 10: *astitit regina a dextris tuis in vestitu deaurato, circumdata varietate et cetera*. *Regina* dicitur, quia regere se debet; Prov. XX, 8: *rex qui sedet in solio iudicii, dissipat omne malum intuitu suo et cetera*. Et dicitur *austri* ratione Spiritus Sancti; Cant. IV, 16: *surge, aquilo, et veni, auster, perfla hortum meum et cetera*. Ista regina *surget in iudicio cum generatione ista*.

Nota quod non dicitur quod non peccaverit, sed non fuit rebellis. Quare? *Quia venit a finibus terrae audire sapientiam Salomonis*, sicut habetur III Reg. X, 24: *et non oportuit quod vos veniretis a finibus terrae, quia hic est*. Unde: *ecce plusquam Salomon hic*, quia ille rex temporalis erat et peccator, iste vero innocens et aeternus; Dan. VII, 14: *potestas eius potestas aeterna, quae non auferetur, et regnum aeternum, quod non corrumpetur*.

1059. *Cum autem immundus spiritus exierit ab homine* et cetera. Ostendit supra gentiles esse potiores Iudaeis, hic vult confirmare exemplo: et

primo ponit exemplum;

secundo adaptat, ibi *sic erit generationi huic pessimae*.

Exemplum ponit de spiritu immundo.

Notare debetis quod aliquando ponitur exemplum ex re gesta, aliquando ex parabola. Et quando ponitur ex re gesta, oportet quod unumquodque seorsum exponatur ita quod utrumque indiget expositione sua, sicut hic positum est exemplum de Iona. Aliquando ponitur exemplum de parabola, ut cum dicitur, *simile est regnum caelorum* et cetera. Hic non oportet ponere quid sit in regno caelorum. Possumus ergo dicere secundum Hieronymum, quod sit similitudo et parabola, et sic est unus sensus. Vel ex re gesta secundum Augustinum, et sic est duplex sensus.

Immundus spiritus exit ab homine dupliciter, quia hominem aliquando torquet corporaliter, aliquando spiritualiter. Unde videndum quomodo impleatur homo spiritu immundo; quomodo corporaliter et quomodo spiritualiter; tertio quomodo pertineat ad propositum.

Quatuor ergo dicuntur.

Primo liberatio a spiritu immundo;

secundo iterata vexatio;

tertio gravitas;

quarto secundae vexationis occasio.

1060. Dicit ergo *si spiritus immundus exierit ab homine*. Omnis res quae commiscetur viliori rei, immunda dicitur; quae puriori, purior; ut si argentum plumbo

1058. *The queen of the south will rise in judgment with this generation, and will condemn it*, namely in wisdom, which these men did not wish to receive. It says about this woman that she came to hear the wisdom of Solomon (1 Kgs 10:24). She signifies the Church of the faithful; *the queen stood on your right hand, in gilded clothing; surrounded with variety* (Ps 44:10). She is called **queen** because she should rule herself; *the king, that sits on the throne of judgment, scatters away all evil with his look* (Prov 10:8). And she is called *of the south* by reason of the Holy Spirit; *arise, O north wind, and come, O south wind, blow through my garden, and let the aromatical spices of it flow* (Song 4:16). This queen *will rise in judgment with this generation*.

Note that it does not say she did not sin, but that she did not become rebellious. Why? *Because she came from the ends of the earth to hear the wisdom of Solomon*, as is said, *and it is not necessary that you should come from the ends of the earth, because he is here* (1 Kgs 10:1). Hence, **behold one greater than Solomon is here**, because that man was a temporal king and a sinner, but this man is innocent and eternal; *his power is an everlasting power that will not be taken away: and his kingdom that will not be destroyed* (Dan 7:14).

1059. *And when an unclean spirit has gone out of a man.* He showed above that the gentiles are more powerful than the Jews; here he wishes to confirm it by example. And

first, he sets out an example;

second, he applies it, at *so will it be also to this wicked generation*.

He sets out an example concerning an unclean spirit.

You should notice that sometimes an example from history is set out, sometimes from a parable. And when it is set out from history, one must explain each one separately in the way each one needs its explanation, just as the example of Jonas was set out here. Sometimes, an example from a parable is set out, as when it says, *the kingdom of God is like*. In this case it is not necessary to set down what there is in the kingdom of heaven. So we can say according to Jerome that this is a likeness and a parable, and thus there is one sense. Or it is from history, according to Augustine, and thus there is a twofold sense.

An unclean spirit goes out from a man in two ways, because sometimes it tortures a man bodily, sometimes spiritually. Hence one should see how a man is filled with an unclean spirit; how bodily, and how spiritually; third, how it pertains to the thing set forth.

So four things are said:

first, the liberation from the unclean spirit;

second, the repeated disturbance;

third, the gravity;

fourth, the second occasion of disturbance.

1060. He says then, **and when an unclean spirit has gone out of a man**. Anything which is mixed with a baser thing is called unclean; that which is mixed with a purer

iungatur, fit vilius: sic spiritus creatus, si adhaereat inferiori se, dicitur spiritus immundus. Et iste exit aliquando ab homine quem corporaliter vexat, aliquando quem spiritualiter, ut in baptismo.

1061. Consequenter ponitur iterata vexatio, et occasio. Et primo ex parte daemonis; secundo ex parte eorum qui vexantur.

Ex parte daemonis primo quantum ad illos alios; secundo quantum ad istos: haec enim est consuetudo daemonis, quod non potest quiescere nisi noceat, quia ab initio peccatum dilexit. Unde cum ab aliquo expellitur, quaerit ubi vexet.

1062. Unde dicit **ambulat per loca arida, quaerens requiem, et non invenit**. Unde aliquando requiem non invenit. In quibus autem inveniat, dicitur Iob XL, 16: *sub umbra dormit, in secreto calami, in locis humentibus*. Loca humentia sunt corda voluptatibus dedita; loca arida sunt qui contemnunt voluptates, qui a prosperitatibus declinant. Et de hoc Ezech. XXXVII, 11: *aruerunt ossa nostra, et periit spes nostra*. Dicit **ambulat**, et explorat quemcumque hominem quem decipiat. Unde pro hoc quod dicitur **ambulat**, sollicitudinem ostendit; I Petr. V, vers. 8: *sobrii estote et vigilate, quia adversarius vester diabolus tamquam leo rugiens circuit quaerens quem devoret*. **Quaerens requiem, et non invenit**, nisi in locis humentibus. Ita fuit de Iudaeis, quod exiens a Iudaeis ivit ad gentiles, qui aridi sunt ab humore gratiae divinae; sed non invenit requiem, quia expulsus est, quia verbum Dei receperunt.

1063. *Tunc dicit: revertar in domum meam unde exivi.* Ex verbo isto potestis colligere quod si diabolus aliquando expellitur ab aliquo, quia agit poenitentiam, non tamen totaliter dimittit eum: sicut de Christo legitur Lc. IV, 13, quod dimisit ad tempus. Hoc ergo est intelligendum, ut semper solliciti sint homines ne revertatur. Et hoc est quod dicit **revertar** et cetera.

1064. *Et veniens invenit eam vacantem*. Hic ponitur occasio ex parte eius qui secundo affligitur. Si volumus ad Iudaeos retorquere, planum est quod cum expelleretur a gentibus, rediit ad Iudaeos.

Unde triplex ponitur occasio. Scilicet otiositas; unde dicit **vacantem**; Eccli. XXXIII, 29: *multam malitiam docuit otiositas*. Ideo Hieronymus: semper aliquid boni facito ut te diabolus inveniat occupatum. Unde **vacantem**, idest otiosum; Thren. I, 7: *viderunt eam hostes, et deriserunt Sabbata sua*. **Scopis mundatam**, quia quod mundatur scopis non mundatur, nisi quia leviter adhaeret. Unde idem est scopare, quod leviter mundare, et inde scopatio imperfecta mundatio. Item **ornatam** et hoc est superficialis ornatus. Mundatio perfecta debet

---

thing is called more pure; as when silver is joined to lead, it becomes base. Thus a created spirit, if it clings to one inferior to itself, is called an unclean spirit. And this spirit sometimes goes out from a man whom he troubles bodily, sometimes one whom he troubles spiritually, as in baptism.

1061. Next, the repeated disturbance is set down, and the occasion. And first, on the part of the demon; second, on the part of those who are troubled.

On the part of the demons, first as regards those others; second as regards these. For this is the custom with a demon, that he cannot rest unless he is harming, because he has loved sin from the beginning. Hence, when he is expelled from someone, he seeks where he may trouble someone else.

1062. Hence, he says, **he walks through dry places seeking rest, and finds none**. Hence, sometimes he does not find rest. Now it says what things he may find rest in: *he sleeps under the shadow, in the covert of the reed, and in moist places* (Job 40:16). The moist places are in the hearts of those given over to pleasure; the dry places are those who despise pleasures, who turn aside from successes. And about this it is said, *our bones are dried up, and our hope is lost, and we are cut off* (Ezek 37:11). He says, **he walks**, and seeks which man he may deceive. Hence when it says, **he walks**, he shows solicitude; *be sober and watch: because your adversary the devil, as a roaring lion, goes about seeking whom he may devour* (1 Pet 5:8). **Seeking rest, and finds none**, except in the moist places. So it happened with the Jews, that going out from the Jews he came to the gentiles, who were dry of the moisture of divine grace; but he did not find rest, because he was driven out, since they received the word of God.

1063. *Then he says: I will return into my house from which I came out*. From these words you can gather that if the devil is sometimes expelled from someone because he does penance, yet he does not leave him entirely; as is written about Christ, that the devil departed from him for a time (Luke 4:13). So this should be understood, so that men may be always anxious lest he return. And this is what he says, *I will return*.

1064. *And coming he finds it empty*. Here is set down the occasion on the part of him who is afflicted a second time. If we wish to refer it to the Jews, it is clear that when he was driven out of the gentiles, he returned to the Jews.

Hence three occasions are set out. Namely idleness; hence he says, **empty**; *for idleness has taught much evil* (Sir 33:29). Therefore Jerome says, *always be doing something good, so that the devil may find you occupied*. Hence, **empty**, i.e., idle; *the enemies have seen her, and have mocked at her Sabbaths* (Lam 1:7). **Swept**, because what is cleaned with a broom is not cleaned, unless because the dirt clung lightly. Hence to sweep and to clean lightly is the same thing, and hence sweeping is an imperfect cleaning. Likewise, **garnished**, and this is decorated on the surface.

cum igne fieri, sicut habetur in lege, quod vasa igne debebant mundari. Item illud quod ornatur, aliam habet ex se pulchritudinem, aliam ex ornatu tantum, de qua in Ps. CXLIII, 12: *filiae eorum compositae, circumornatae ut similitudo templi* et cetera. Sed qui volunt esse securi, debent habere pulchritudinem interiorem; Ps. XLIV, v. 14: *omnis gloria eius filiae regis ab intus, in fimbriis aureis, circumamicta varietatibus* et cetera. Sed quando fit ornatus solum in exterioribus, non relinquitur a daemonibus. Ita est de Iudaeis, quia ipsi servabant Sabbata, in quibus magis vacabant a bonis quam a malis. Item totam curam ponebant in minimis legis.

1065. *Tunc vadit, et assumit septem alios spiritus nequiores se*. Hic ponitur de secunda vexatione graviori, et ostenditur gravior primo quantum ad numerum; secundo quantum ad durationem; tertio quantum ad effectum.

Quantum ad numerum, quia ***assumit septem***. Secundum Chrysostomum exponitur ad litteram, quia cum aliquis cadit, et non cavet, tunc deterius accidit ei; Io. V, 14: *ecce sanus factus es; iam noli peccare, ne deterius aliquid tibi contingat*. Secundum Augustinum ***assumit septem***, et hoc dupliciter. Aliquando enim poenitens agit poenitentiam, sed negligenter se habet, et tunc fit proclivior; ad Rom. I, 28: *propter quod tradidit illos dominus in reprobum sensum*.

Et per hoc quod dicit ***septem***, universitas vitiorum signatur. Aliter secundum beatum Augustinum: aliqui peccant aliquo peccato, et in statu poenitentiae addunt simulationem. Et sicut septem sunt dona Spiritus Sancti, sic septem simulationes. Unde primo erant vitia simplicia, tunc adduntur simulationes vitiorum, quae sunt deteriores: et dicuntur ***septem***, vel propter universitatem vitiorum, vel propter Sabbatum.

Et qui hoc modo peccant, fient perseverantiores in malo, unde dicit ***et intrantes habitant ibi***, quia inde recedere nolunt; Ier. VIII, v. 5: *populus in Ierusalem aversus est aversione contentiosa, apprehenderunt mendacium, et noluerunt reverti*. Si exponatur de Iudaeis, patet, quod habitat in eis, et discedere ab eis non vult.

Et fiunt novissima illius hominis peiora prioribus. Hic ponitur aggravatio quantum ad effectum. Ad litteram, qui magis punitur, magis aggravatur. Unde II Petr. II, 21: *melius erat viam veritatis non cognoscere, quam post agnitionem retrorsum reverti*. Item quantum ad Iudaeos, quia peius egerunt blasphemando Christum, quam colendo idola.

Perfect cleaning should be done with fire, as is it written in the law that a vessel should be cleaned with fire. Similarly, that which is decorated has one beauty from itself, another from decoration only, about which it is said, *their daughters decked out, adorned round about after the similitude of a temple* (Ps 143:12). But those who wish to be secure should have interior beauty; *all the glory of the king's daughter is within golden borders* (Ps 44:14). But when the decoration is only in exterior things, it is not abandoned by demons. Thus it is with the Jews, because they kept the Sabbath, on which they rested more from good than from evil. Likewise, they put all their interest in the least things of the law.

1065. *Then he goes, and takes with him seven other spirits more wicked than himself*. Here the second, heavier disturbance is set down, and it is shown to be heavier, first as regards number; second, as regards duration; third, as regards effect.

As regards number, because he ***takes with him seven***. According to Chrysostom, this is explained literally, because when someone falls, and does not take heed, then something worse happens to him; *behold you are made whole: sin no more, lest some worse thing happen to you* (John 5:14). According to Augustine, he ***takes with him seven***, and this in two ways. For sometimes the penitent one does penance, but carries himself negligently, and then becomes more prone to vice; *and as they liked not to have God in their knowledge, God delivered them up to a reprobate sense* (Rom 1:28).

And by what he says, ***seven***, the universality of vices is signified. In another way, according to blessed Augustine: some men sin by a sin, and in the state of penance they add simulation. And just as there are seven gifts of the Holy Spirit, so there are seven simulations. Hence, first there were simple vices, then there are added simulations of the vices, which are worse: and they are called ***seven*** either on account of the universality of vices, or on account of the Sabbath.

And those who sin in this way become more persistent in evil, hence he says, ***they enter in and dwell there***, because they do not wish to leave; *why then is this people in Jerusalem turned away with a stubborn revolting? They have laid hold on lying, and have refused to return* (Jer 8:5). If it is explained as about the Jews, it is clear that he dwells in them, and does not wish to withdraw from them.

And the last state of that man in made worse than the first. Here the being made heavier is set down as regards effect. Literally, he who is punished more is made heavier. Hence, *for it had been better for them not to have known the way of justice, than after they have known it, to turn back* (2 Pet 2:21). Likewise, as regards the Jews, because they did worse by blaspheming Christ than by worshipping idols.

1066. Ideo sequitur *sic erit generationi huic pessimae*, quia deterius erit eis quam unquam fuerit eis in Aegypto.

1066. So there follows *so will it be also to this wicked generation*, because it will be worse for them than it ever was for those in Egypt.

Lecture 4

^{12:46} Adhuc eo loquente ad turbas, ecce mater eius, et fratres stabant foris, quaerentes loqui ei. [n. 1068]

^{12:46}Ἔτι αὐτοῦ λαλοῦντος τοῖς ὄχλοις ἰδοὺ ἡ μήτηρ καὶ οἱ ἀδελφοὶ αὐτοῦ εἱστήκεισαν ἔξω ζητοῦντες αὐτῷ λαλῆσαι.

^{12:46} As he was yet speaking to the multitudes, behold his mother and his brethren stood outside, seeking to speak to him. [n. 1068]

^{12:47} Dixit autem ei quidam: ecce mater tua, et fratres tui foris stant quaerentes te. [n. 1070]

^{12:47} [εἶπεν δέ τις αὐτῷ· ἰδοὺ ἡ μήτηρ σου καὶ οἱ ἀδελφοί σου ἔξω ἑστήκασιν ζητοῦντές σοι λαλῆσαι.]

^{12:47} And one said unto him: behold your mother and your brethren stand outside, seeking you. [n. 1070]

^{12:48} At ipse respondens dicenti sibi, ait: quae est mater mea, et qui sunt fratres mei? [n. 1071]

^{12:48} ὁ δὲ ἀποκριθεὶς εἶπεν τῷ λέγοντι αὐτῷ· τίς ἐστιν ἡ μήτηρ μου καὶ τίνες εἰσὶν οἱ ἀδελφοί μου;

^{12:48} But answering the one who told him, he said: who is my mother, and who are my brethren? [n. 1071]

^{12:49} Et extendens manum in discipulos suos, dixit: ecce mater mea, et fratres mei. [n. 1075]

^{12:49} καὶ ἐκτείνας τὴν χεῖρα αὐτοῦ ἐπὶ τοὺς μαθητὰς αὐτοῦ εἶπεν· ἰδοὺ ἡ μήτηρ μου καὶ οἱ ἀδελφοί μου.

^{12:49} And stretching forth his hand towards his disciples, he said: behold my mother and my brethren. [n. 1075]

^{12:50} Quicumque enim fecerit voluntatem Patris mei, qui in caelis est, ipse meus frater, soror, et mater est. [n. 1075]

^{12:50} ὅστις γὰρ ἂν ποιήσῃ τὸ θέλημα τοῦ πατρός μου τοῦ ἐν οὐρανοῖς αὐτός μου ἀδελφὸς καὶ ἀδελφὴ καὶ μήτηρ ἐστίν.

^{12:50} For whoever will do the will of my Father, who is in heaven, he is my brother, and sister, and mother. [n. 1075]

1067. In parte praecedente Dominus confutavit adversarios; nunc commendat discipulos credentes etc. praesentia assumpta matris et fratrum.

Primo ponitur praesentia;

secundo denuntiatio;

tertio discipulorum commendatio.

1068. Dicit ergo *adhuc eo loquente.*

Sed hic est quaestio litteralis, quare Lc. c. VIII, 19, ubi ponuntur eadem verba quae dicta sunt, non ponuntur verba quae sequuntur, sed subditur: *factum est autem cum loqueretur, extollens vocem quaedam mulier* et cetera. Et ita videtur esse contrarietas.

Solvit Augustinus: quod absque dubio ita dictum est, ut Matthaeus narrat, quod *adhuc eo loquente*, idest dum esset in narratione et cetera. Sed potest esse quod contigerit quod Lucas dicit, et quod iste: et potest esse, quod Lucas praeoccupet, vel ad ordinem suae memoriae referat.

1069. *Ecce mater eius, et fratres stabant foris* et cetera. De matre nulla dubitatio quin sit illa, de qua dictum est I cap.; de fratribus autem potest esse quaestio.

Et quia fit mentio de fratribus, ideo est occasio haeresis, quod cum Virgo genuisset Iesum, Ioseph cognovit Mariam et genuit inde filios; quod haereticum est, quia post partum virgo inviolata permansit. Fuit etiam opinio, quod isti essent filii Ioseph de alia uxore. Sed hoc nihil est, quia credimus, quod sicut mater Iesu fuit virgo,

1067. In the preceding part, the Lord refuted his adversaries; now he commends the disciples who believe, using the presence of his mother and brothers.

First, their presence is set down;

second, the announcement;

third, the commendation of the disciples.

1068. It says then, *as he was yet speaking.*

But here there is a literal question: why is that in Luke where the same words which were said are set down, the words which follow are not set down, but this is added next, *and it came to pass, as he spoke these things, a certain woman from the crowd, lifting up her voice, said to him: blessed is the womb that bore you* (Luke 11:27). And so there seems to be a contrariety.

Augustine resolves it, saying that without doubt it was said as Matthew describes, that *as he was yet speaking,* i.e., while he was telling the story. But it could be that it happened as Luke says, and as this Evangelist says. And it could be that Luke anticipated, or referred to the order of his own memory.

1069. *Behold his mother and his brethren stood outside.* About the mother, there can be no doubt but that it was she who was spoken of in chapter one; but there can be a question about the brothers.

And because mention is made of the brothers, it is an occasion of the heresy that when the Virgin had begotten Jesus, Joseph knew Mary and begot sons of her; which is a heresy, because she remained a virgin inviolate after the birth. There has also been the opinion that these were Joseph's sons by another wife. But this amounts to nothing,

sic Ioseph, quia virgini virginem commendavit: et sicut in fine, sic etiam et in principio.

Qui sunt ergo isti fratres? Hieronymus dixit quod fratres dicuntur multis modis. Aliqui enim fratres natura, sicut supra I: *Iacob genuit Iudam et fratres eius*. Aliquando fratres qui sunt unius gentis: Deut. XVII, 15: *non poteris constituere regem, qui non sit frater tuus*. Aliquando religione, ut omnes Christiani, ut infra XXIII, 8. Et in hoc inolevit consuetudo quod homines eiusdem religionis dicuntur fratres. Aliquando homines de una parentela, ut Iosue II, 12, *detisque mihi signum ut salvetis patrem meum, et matrem, et fratres*. Aliquando omnes homines, qui ab uno Patre, scilicet Deo; Mal. II, 10: *numquid non est Pater unus omnium? Numquid non Deus unus creavit nos? Quare ergo unusquisque despicit fratrem suum?*

Nullo istorum modorum dicuntur hic fratres Domini; ideo uno modo dicuntur fratres, quia consanguinei. Unde Gen. XIII, 8 dixit Abraham ad Lot, *fratres enim sumus*, quamvis Lot nepos esset Abraham. Sic isti fratres erant, quia consobrini erant.

1070. Consequenter ponitur denuntiatio poenitentiae eorum *dixit autem ei quidam: ecce mater tua et fratres tui foris stant quaerentes te*. Quare hoc dixerit, et qua necessitate, exponitur in Luca VIII, 19 quia tanta erat multitudo, quod non poterant intrare.

Mystice per matrem significatur synagoga; unde Cant. III, 11: *egredimini, et videte Regem Salomonem in diademate quo coronavit illum mater sua*. *Et fratres*, idest Iudaei, qui foris stant derelinquentes Christum; Iob VI, v. 15: *fratres mei dereliquerunt me*. Quaerunt, sed non inveniunt, ut habetur ad Rom. c. IX, 31: *Israel sectando legem iustitiae, in legem iustitiae non pervenit*.

1071. *At ille respondens* et cetera. Ponitur responsio Christi: et duo facit.

Primo confutat interrogantem;

secundo commendat discipulos, ibi *et extendens manum* et cetera.

1072. Dicit autem ipse *quae est mater mea et qui sunt fratres mei?* Ex isto loco quidam negaverunt Christum sumpsisse carnem vere, sed phantastice. Unde exponebant: non est haec mater mea, neque hi fratres mei. Quod est contra Apostolum ad Gal. IV, 4: *misit Deus Filium suum factum ex muliere* et cetera. Item ad Rom. I, 3: *qui factus est ex semine David secundum carnem*. Item Dominus eam recognovit in cruce: *mulier, ecce filius tuus*, ut habetur Io. XIX, 26.

1073. Chrysostomus. Quare inquit Dominus: *quae est mater mea, et qui sunt fratres mei?* Et dicit duo; quorum unum est sanum, aliud non. Dicit enim quod mater et fratres aliquid humanum passi sunt, quia videntes

because we believe that just as the mother of Jesus was a virgin, so was Joseph, because he entrusted a virgin to a virgin; and as it was in the end, so also in the beginning.

So who are these brothers? Jerome said that men are called brothers in many ways. For some are brothers by nature, as above, *and Jacob begot Judas and his brethren* (Matt 1:2). Sometimes brothers are those who are of one race: *you will set him whom the Lord your God will choose out of the number of your brethren* (Deut 17:15). Sometimes by religion, as all Christians, as below (Matt 23:8). And in this way the custom grew up that men of the same religion are called brothers. Sometimes, men of one kinship, as in, *that you will save my father and mother, my brethren and sisters* (Jos 2:13). Sometimes all men, who are from one Father, namely God; *have we not all one Father? Has not one God created us? Why then does every one of us despise his brother, violating the covenant of our fathers?* (Mal 2:10).

These men are not called the Lord's brothers in any of those ways; therefore they are called brothers in one way, because they are related by blood. Hence Abraham said to Lot, *we are brethren* (Gen 13:8), although Lot was Abraham's nephew. These men were brothers in this way, because they were children of his mother's sister.

1070. Next, the announcement of their presence: *and one said unto him: behold your mother and your brethren stand outside, seeking you*. Why he said this, and why it was necessary, is explained in Luke, because the multitude was so great that they could not enter (Luke 8:19).

Mystically, the mother signifies the synagogue; hence, *go forth, daughters of Zion, and see King Solomon in the diadem, with which his mother crowned him* (Song 3:11). *And your brethren*, i.e., the Jews, who stand outside abandoning the Christ; *my brethren have passed by me* (Job 6:15). They seek, but they do not find, as it says, *but Israel, by following after the law of justice, is not come unto the law of justice* (Rom 9:31).

1071. *But answering the one who told him*. Christ's response is set down; and he does two things:

first, he refutes the one questioning;

second, he commends the disciples, at *and stretching forth his hand*.

1072. Now, he himself says, *who is my mother, and who are my brethren?* From this passage, some have denied that Christ assumed true flesh, but said that he assumed phantastical flesh. Hence they explained it: this is not my mother, nor are these my brothers. Which is contrary to the Apostle: *God sent his Son, made of a woman* (Gal 4:4). Likewise, *who was made to him of the seed of David, according to the flesh* (Rom 1:3). Likewise, the Lord acknowledged her on the cross: *woman, behold your son* (John 19:26).

1073. Chrysostom. Why did the Lord say, *who is my mother, and who are my brethren?* And he says two things, of which one is sound, the other not. For he says that the mother and brothers suffered something human, because

Christum praedicantem, et turbam sequentem, elationem habuerunt; ideo volebant quasi quamdam gloriam habere; ideo Dominus voluit ostendere, quod illud quod faciebat, non habebat ex eo quod assumpserat ex matre, sed ex Patre.

Haec positio partim sana est: nam quantum ad fratres sana est, quia sic habetur Io. c. VII, 5: *neque enim fratres eius credebant in eum*. Sed de matre Domini non sana est, quia creditur quod numquam peccavit, nec mortaliter, nec venialiter: de ea namque dicitur Cant. IV, 7: *tota pulchra es, amica mea, et macula non est in te*. Et Augustinus: *cum de peccato agitur, nullam prorsus volo de ea fieri mentionem.*

1074. Solvit ergo aliter Hieronymus, quod iste qui denuntiavit, insidiose denuntiaverat: volebat enim explorare, an ita intenderet spiritualibus, quod non curaret de temporalibus. Ideo affectui respondet. Unde nec matrem plus dilexisset, nisi plus spiritualitatis habuisset. Unde dicit **quae est mater mea?** Non eam matrem esse negat, sed intendit prohibere inordinatum affectum. Unde supra X, 37: **qui amat patrem aut matrem plusquam me non est me dignus.**

1075. Consequenter ponitur commendatio discipulorum. Et primo commendat discipulos; secundo universaliter omnes credentes.

Dicit ergo **et extendens manum in discipulos dicit: ecce mater mea**; quasi dicat: *plus diligo istos quam affectus matris meae vel fratres; praeponendus enim est affectus Spiritus Sancti.*

Et non solum extendit ad istos, sed ad omnes. Unde dicitur **quicumque fecerit voluntatem Patris mei qui in caelis est, ipse meus frater, soror et mater est.** Habebat enim generationem caelestem et temporalem: unde praeponit caelestem temporali. Illi enim qui faciunt voluntatem Patris mei, illi attinent ei secundum generationem caelestem; unde Io. VIII, 39: *si filii Abrahae estis, opera Abrahae facite*. Ipse enim venit ut faceret voluntatem eius, ut habetur Io. IV, 34: V, 30 et VI, 38.

Frater dicit quantum ad firmiores, et **soror** quantum ad debiliores.

1076. Sed quid est quod dicit **et mater est**? Dicendum quod quilibet fidelis, qui facit voluntatem Patris, scilicet qui simpliciter obedit, ille frater est, quia similis est ei, qui voluntatem Patris implevit. Qui autem non solum facit, sed alios convertit, generat Christum in aliis, et sic fit mater. Sicut e contra occidit Christum in aliis, qui provocat eos ad malum. Apostolus ad Gal. IV, v. 19: *filioli mei, quos iterum parturio, donec formetur Christus in vobis.*

when they saw Christ preaching, and the crowd following, they had a feeling of exaltation. So they wanted, as it were, to have a certain glory. So the Lord wanted to show that he did not derive what he was doing from what he had taken from his mother, but from the Father.

This position is partly sound, for as regards the brothers it is sound, for so it is said, *for neither did his brethren believe in him* (John 7:5). But it is not sound as regards the Lord's mother, because it is believed that she never sinned, neither mortally, nor venially; for of her it is said, *you are all fair, O my love, and there is not a spot in you* (Song 4:7). And Augustine: *when we treat of sin, I wish to make absolutely no mention of her.*

1074. So Jerome resolves it another way, saying that the one who announced their presence had announced it treacherously, for he wished to test whether he would so strive after spiritual things that he would not take care of temporal things. So he responds to the disposition. Hence, he would not have loved his mother more unless she had had more spirituality. Hence, he says, **who is my mother?** He does not deny that she is his mother, but means to forbid inordinate affection. Hence above, **he who loves father or mother more than me, is not worthy of me** (Matt 10:37).

1075. Next, the commendation of the disciples is set down. And first, he commends the disciples; second, all believers universally.

It says then, **and stretching forth his hand towards his disciples, he said: behold my mother**, as though to say, *I love these more than the affection of my mother or brothers; for the affection of the Holy Spirit is to be preferred.*

And he did not only extend his hand to those men, but to all. Hence it says, **for whoever will do the will of my Father, who is in heaven, he is my brother, and sister, and mother.** For he had a heavenly generation and a temporal one; hence he set the heavenly one before the temporal. For those who do the will of my Father, they will hold fast to him according to a heavenly generation. Hence, *if you are the children of Abraham, do the works of Abraham* (John 8:39). For he himself came that he might do his will (John 4:34, 5:30, 6:38).

He says **brother** as regards the stronger, and **sister** as regards the weaker.

1076. But why does he say, **and mother**? One should say that any one of the faithful who does the Father's will, namely the one who simply obeys, that one is a brother, because he is similar to him who fulfilled the Father's will. But he who not only does the Father's will, but converts others, begets Christ in others, and so becomes a mother. Just as vice versa, he who incites others to evil kills Christ in others. The Apostle: *my little children, of whom I am in labor again, until Christ is formed in you* (Gal 4:19).